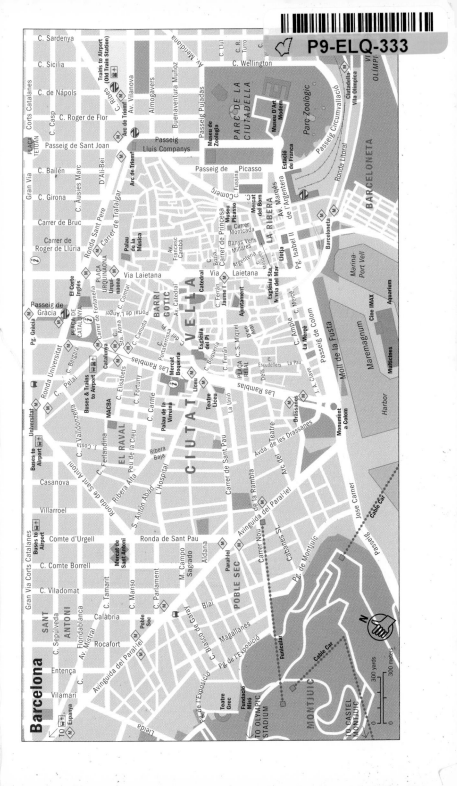

Madrid Metro

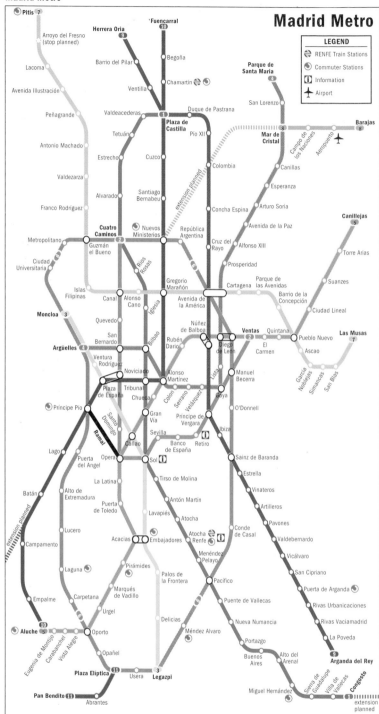

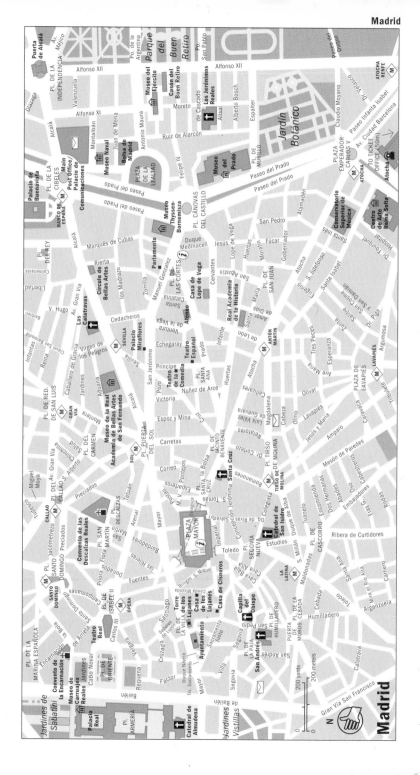

Madrid

Barcelona Metro

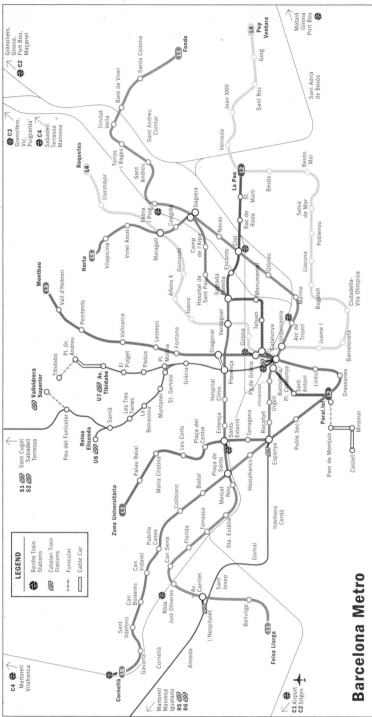

Barcelona Metro

 Let's Go writers travel on your budget.

"Guides that penetrate the veneer of the holiday brochures and mine the grit of real life."
—*The Economist*

"The writers seem to have experienced every rooster-packed bus and lunar-surfaced mattress about which they write."
—*The New York Times*

"All the dirt, dirt cheap."
—*People*

Great for independent travelers.

"The guides are aimed not only at young budget travelers but at the independent traveler; a sort of streetwise cookbook for traveling alone."
—*The New York Times*

"Flush with candor and irreverence, chock full of budget travel advice."
—*The Des Moines Register*

"An indispensible resource, *Let's Go*'s practical information can be used by every traveler."
—*The Chattanooga Free Press*

Let's Go is completely revised each year.

"Only *Let's Go* has the zeal to annually update every title on its list."
—*The Boston Globe*

"Unbeatable: good sightseeing advice; up-to-date info on restaurants, hotels, and inns; a commitment to money-saving travel; and a wry style that brightens nearly every page."
—*The Washington Post*

All the important information you need.

"*Let's Go* authors provide a comedic element while still providing concise information and thorough coverage of the country. Anything you need to know about budget traveling is detailed in this book."
—*The Chicago Sun-Times*

"Value-packed, unbeatable, accurate, and comprehensive."
—*Los Angeles Times*

Let's Go Publications

Let's Go: Alaska & the Pacific Northwest 2000
Let's Go: Australia 2000
Let's Go: Austria & Switzerland 2000
Let's Go: Britain & Ireland 2000
Let's Go: California 2000
Let's Go: Central America 2000
Let's Go: China 2000 **New Title!**
Let's Go: Eastern Europe 2000
Let's Go: Europe 2000
Let's Go: France 2000
Let's Go: Germany 2000
Let's Go: Greece 2000
Let's Go: India & Nepal 2000
Let's Go: Ireland 2000
Let's Go: Israel 2000 **New Title!**
Let's Go: Italy 2000
Let's Go: Mexico 2000
Let's Go: Middle East 2000 **New Title!**
Let's Go: New York City 2000
Let's Go: New Zealand 2000
Let's Go: Paris 2000
Let's Go: Perú & Ecuador 2000 **New Title!**
Let's Go: Rome 2000
Let's Go: South Africa 2000
Let's Go: Southeast Asia 2000
Let's Go: Spain & Portugal 2000
Let's Go: Turkey 2000
Let's Go: USA 2000
Let's Go: Washington, D.C. 2000

Let's Go *Map Guides*

Amsterdam	New Orleans
Berlin	New York City
Boston	Paris
Chicago	Prague
Florence	Rome
London	San Francisco
Los Angeles	Seattle
Madrid	Washington, D.C.

Coming Soon: Sydney and Hong Kong

Let's Go

2000

SPAIN & PORTUGAL
INCLUDING MOROCCO

Olivia Lorillard Cowley
Editor

Benjamin Arthur Railton
Associate Editor

Aarup Kubal
Associate Editor

Researcher-Writers:

Katharine Douglas	**Claire Lewis**
Holly E. Fling	**Rochelle Kristen Mackey**
Benjamin Forkner	**James T. Platts**
Brooke M. Lampley	**Tim Plerhoples**

St. Martin's Press ⚓ New York

HELPING LET'S GO If you want to share your discoveries, suggestions, or corrections, please drop us a line. We read every piece of correspondence, whether a postcard, a 10-page email, or a coconut. Please note that mail received after May 2000 may be too late for the 2001 book, but will be kept for future editions. **Address mail to:**

> **Let's Go: Spain & Portugal**
> **67 Mount Auburn Street**
> **Cambridge, MA 02138**
> **USA**

Visit Let's Go at **http://www.letsgo.com,** or send email to:

> **feedback@letsgo.com**
> **Subject: "Let's Go: Spain & Portugal"**

In addition to the invaluable travel advice our readers share with us, many are kind enough to offer their services as researchers or editors. Unfortunately, our charter enables us to employ only currently enrolled Harvard students.

HOW TO USE THIS BOOK

Welcome to *Let's Go Spain, Portugal, and Morocco*. You have just bought yourself a travel companion. Our job is not to hold your hand, but simply to assist you along the way. Before you go, make sure to read the **Essentials** section. This is where you can find valuable information on everything from how to get a Hostelling International card to what you should pack.

At the start of each of the chapters on Spain, Portugal, and Morocco, there is a section entitled **Life and Times,** which talks about the history, art, festivals and entertainment, and food of each of these countries. Life and Times is followed by Essentials sections for each of the individual countries. This is country-specific information that is meant to help you during your travels.

From there, coverage of Spain begins with **Madrid,** and moves from there into the provinces that make up **Central Spain,** then down to **Andalucía,** beginning an outward spiral which eventually ends in **Northwestern Spain.** From there it is on to **Spain's Islands, Portugal,** and finally **Morocco.** Each chapter begins with a regional intro; each town and city is broken down into several sections: **Orientation and Practical Information, Accommodations, Food, Sights,** and **Entertainment.** For smaller towns, categories occasionally get thrown together. This organization is intended to make our book reader-friendly; we hope it works for you.

And so we give you **SPAM** (**S**pain, **P**ortugal, **A**ndorra, and **M**orocco). Unlike our namesake—the famed mystery meat—we want you to know exactly what you're ingesting. So without further ado, here are some of the guide's special features:

CHAPTER 1: DISCOVER. This is where and how we convince you to "discover" Spain, Portugal, and Morocco. There's also a list of **suggested itineraries,** designed to highlight the best each county has to offer (factoring in time constraints,). They are by no means mandatory itineraries; they're just to get you thinking.

⊫ GETTING THERE

At the start of each city, just after the introduction, we list the best ways to get there, including the most convenient transit hubs and the form of transportation that makes the most sense.

◪ We think these thumbs are a great idea. Whenever you see one, it means whatever you're reading about—hostel, restaurant, bar, or sight—is one of our favorites.

SIGHTS. In most cities, sights are listed individually in a paragraph like this and ranked from best to worst. The only exceptions are those that appear in walking tour format; in this case they are listed geographically. *(Practical information pertaining to these sights—address, directions, phone number, hours, and prices—is italicized, like this, at the end of the listings.)*

So go. Have fun. We hope you'll love these countries as much as we do.

CONTENTS

DISCOVER SPAIN, PORTUGAL, AND MOROCCO **1**

Things to Do 2
Suggested Itineraries 3

ESSENTIALS **7**

When to Go 7
Documents and Formalities 8
Customs 13
Money 14
Safety and Security 18
Health 20
Insurance 23
Packing 24
Accommodations 25
Camping and the Outdoors 26
Keeping in Touch 28
Getting There and Around 30
Specific Concerns 39
Alternatives to Tourism 43
Other Resources 46

SPAIN **48**

Life and Times 48
Essentials 64

MADRID **71**

COMUNIDAD DE MADRID 114
Alcalá de Henares 114
San Lorenzo del Escorial 115
Sierra de Guadarrama 118
Aranjuez 120

CENTRAL SPAIN **122**

CASTILLA LA MANCHA 122
Toledo 122
Almagro 129
Cuenca 130
Sigüenza 134
CASTILLA Y LEÓN 136
Segovia 136
Ávila 142
Salamanca 146
Daytrips from Salamanca 153
Zamora 155
León 156
Valladolid 161
Palencia 163
Burgos 165
Soria 170
Daytrips from Soria 172
EXTREMADURA 173
Cáceres 174
Daytrips from Cáceres 177
Mérida 179
Badajoz 183

ANDALUCÍA **186**

SEVILLA 186
Daytrips from Sevilla 204
Huelva 206
Córdoba 207

Jerez de la Frontera 215
Sanlúcar de Barrameda 219
Chipiona 220
Arcos de la Frontera 221
Cádiz 223
Vejer de la Frontera 228
Tarifa 230
Algeciras 231
Gibraltar 233
COSTA DEL SOL 236
Málaga 237
Daytrips from Málaga 241
Marbella 242
Nerja 244
Almuñécar 245
Almería 247
Mojácar 248
Ronda 249
Antequera 252
Granada 255
Daytrips from Granada 265
La Alpujarra 266
Jaén 268
Baeza 269
Úbeda 270
Cazorla 271

EAST COAST **273**

VALENCIA 273
Valencia 274
Daytrips from Valencia 280
Morella 282
Játiva (Xàtiva) 282
Gandía 283
Alicante (Alacant) 285
Costa Blanca 289
MURCIA 292
Murcia 293
La Manga del Mar Menor 294

BARCELONA **296**

NEAR BARCELONA 328
Montserrat 328
Sitges 330

NORTHEASTERN SPAIN **333**

CATALUÑA (CATALUNYA) 333
COSTA DORADA 334
Tarragona 334
COSTA BRAVA 337
Tossa de Mar 337
Palafrugell 340
Daytrips from Palafrugell 342
Girona 345
Figueres (Figueras) 350
Portbou 354
CATALÁN PYRENEES 355
Ripoll 355
Núria 357
Puigcerdà 357
Parc Nacional d'Aigüestortes 359

Val d'Aran 360
ANDORRA 362
Andorra la Vella 363
Around Andorra 365
Outdoor Activities 366
ARAGÓN 367
Zaragoza 368
Daytrips from Zaragoza 374
Tarazona 375
Teruel 376
ARAGONESE PYRENEES 378
Jaca 378
Valle de Hecho 380
Valle de Ansó 381
Parque Nacional de Ordesa 382
Valle de Benasque 384
LA RIOJA AND NAVARRA 385
Logroño 386
Haro 388
Pamplona (Iruña) 391
Olite 398
Tudela 399
Estella 400
NAVARRESE PYRENEES 402
Sangüesa 402
Roncesvalles and Auritz-Burguete 404
Valle de Salazar: Ochagavía 405
Valle de Roncal 406
PAÍS VASCO (EUSKADI) 407
San Sebastián (Donostia) 408
Daytrips from San Sebastián 416
Bilbao (Bilbo) 417
Guernica (Gernika) 423
Vitoria-Gasteiz 425

NORTHWESTERN SPAIN 429
ASTURIAS AND CANTABRIA 429
ASTURIAS 430
Oviedo 430
PICOS DE EUROPA 433
Cangas de Onís 434
Arenas de Cabrales 437
Potes 438
ASTURIAN COAST 439
Llanes 439
CANTABRIA 441
Santander 441
Santillana del Mar 445
Comillas 446
San Vicente de La Barquera 447
GALICIA (GALIZA) 448
Santiago de Compostela 448
RÍAS BAJAS (RÍAS BAIXAS) 456
Vigo 456
Daytrips from Vigo 457
Pontevedra 459
Daytrips from Pontevedra 461
Ría de Muros y Noya 462
SOUTH RÍAS ALTAS 463
Cabo Finisterre (Cabo Fisterra) 463
La Coruña (A Coruña) 464
NORTH RÍAS ALTAS 467
Rías de Cedeira and Vivero 468
Ría de Ribadeo 470

BALEARIC ISLANDS 471
MALLORCA 473
Palma 473
Western Mallorca 479
Northern Mallorca 481
Southeast Mallorca 482
MENORCA 482
Mahón (Maó) 482
Ciutadella (Ciudadela) 486
Daytrips Around Menorca 488
Ibiza 489
Eivissa (Ibiza City) 490
FORMENTERA 495

CANARY ISLANDS 497
GRAN CANARIA 500
Las Palmas 500
TENERIFE 506
Santa Cruz de Tenerife 506
Los Cristianos and Playa de las Américas 508
Puerto de la Cruz 509
FUERTEVENTURA 512
Puerto del Rosario 512
Corralejo 513
Morro Jable 515
LANZAROTE 516
Arrecife 516
GOMERA 520
San Sebastián de Gomera 520
EL HIERRO 523
LA PALMA 523

PORTUGAL 524
Life and Times 524
Essentials 535

LISBON (LISBOA) 540
DAYTRIPS FROM LISBON 559
Queluz 559
Estoril 559
Cascais 560
Sintra 561
Ericeira 565
Setúbal 566

ALGARVE 569
Lagos 569
Daytrips from Lagos 574
Albufeira 576
Faro 577
Olhão 580
Tavira 581

CENTRAL PORTUGAL 584
ALENTEJO 584
Évora 584
Elvas 588
Beja 590
RIBATEJO AND ESTREMADURA 592
Santarém 592
Caldas da Rainha 594
Óbidos 596
Peniche 597
Nazaré 600
Daytrips from Nazaré 602
Leiria 603

Batalha 605
Fátima 606
Tomar 608
THE THREE BEIRAS 611
Coimbra 611
Figueira da Foz 617
Aveiro 619

NORTHERN PORTUGAL 623
DOURO AND MINHO 623
Porto (Oporto) 623
Braga 630
Guimarães 634
Caldas de Gerês 636
Viana do Castelo 637
Alto Minho 640
TRÁS-OS-MONTES 642
Bragança 642
Vila Real 644

MOROCCO 647
Life and Times 647
Essentials 657
EXPLORING MOROCCO 663
THE MEDITERRANEAN COAST 663
Tangier 663
Ceuta 670
Chefchaouen (Chaouen) 671

THE MIDDLE ATLAS 672
Meknes 672
Daytrips from Meknes 677
Fez 679
THE ATLANTIC COAST 687
Asilah 687
Larache 689
Rabat 690
Casablanca 696
El-Jadida 700
Essaouira 702
Agadir 705
THE HIGH ATLAS 706
Marrakesh 707
The Ourika Valley 713
High Atlas Mountains 714
Taroudannt 716
THE SOUTHERN DESERTS 717
Ouarzazate 717
The Drâa Valley 719
The Dadès Valley 721
The Ziz Valley 723

APPENDIX 726
Language 726
Glossary 729

INDEX 733

MAPS

Spain and Portugal
Transportation............... xii-xiii
Chapter Divisions.......... xiv-xv
Suggested Itineraries 4-5
Spain........................... 50-51
Madrid........................ 72-73
Central Madrid 74-75
Comunidad de Madrid 115
Castilla La Mancha 123
Toledo 125
Cuenca 131
Castilla y León 137
Segovia 139
Ávila 143
Salamanca 147
León 157
Burgos............................ 165
Extremadura 173
Andalucía 187
Sevilla 188-189
Córdoba 209
Jerez.............................. 217
Cádiz 225
Gibraltar 235
Málaga 239
Granada 257
The Alhambra................. 261

Valencia and Murcia 273
Valencia 275
Alicante.......................... 287
Barcelona............... 298-299
Central Barcelona 300-301
Cataluña........................ 335
Girona 347
Andorra 363
Aragón 367
Zaragoza........................ 369
La Rioja & Navarra......... 385
Pamplona 393
País Vasco..................... 407
Donostia-San Sebastián.. 409
Bilbao 419
Vitoria-Gasteiz............... 425
Asturias & Cantabria...... 429
Picos de Europa 435
Santander 440-441
Galicia........................... 449
Santiago de Compostela. 451
La Coruña...................... 465
Islas Baleares 471
Palma............................ 475
Mahón........................... 483
Eivissa (Ibiza) 491
Islas Canarias................ 499

Las Palmas.................... 501
Portugal 525
Lisbon 542-543
Lisbon Metro 545
Sintra 563
Algarve 570-571
Lagos 573
Évora 585
Coimbra 613
Porto 625
Braga 631
Morocco 648-649
Tangier 665
Meknes 673
Volubilis Ruins............... 678
Féz el-Jdid
and Ville Nouvelle........... 681
Fez el-Bali 683
Rabat............................. 691
Casablanca 697
Marrakesh 709

COLOR INSERTS
Barcelona............color insert
Barcelona Metro ...color insert
Madrid Metro........color insert

RESEARCHER-WRITERS

Katharine Douglas   *Madrid, Extremadura, the Canary Islands*
All hail hard-core Kate, Queen of Madrid and the Canary Islands. Handed an incredible itinerary, Kate refused to let even Las Palmas get her down. Along the way, she revolutionized Madrid's sights, doubled coverage of the Canaries, and even dodged some flying foam (but not too strenuously). Her insightful, detailed marginalia kept us informed and testified to her true dedication to the guide.

Holly E. Fling   *Northeastern Spain, Castilla La Mancha, and Eastern Andalucía*
Holly attacked Northeastern Spain without ever looking back. Winner of the longest itinerary award, she tackled the Pyrenees, *San Fermines*, and the heat and tourists of Toledo, then jetted to Andalucía—just for kicks. We thank her for always being able to take on "just one more town," for her constant professionalism and attention to detail, and for her comical love of the camera.

Benjamin Forkner   *Northwestern Spain, Castilla y León, Northern Portugal and Granada*
Has there ever been a funnier researcher? We think not. Ben wrote about "off-the-beaten-path" Spain and Portugal with wit and skill, and handled a camera like the future Hollywood producer that he is. In the meantime, he managed to churn out more high-quality drawings than Picasso in the Blue Period. We just want to say that we knew him when.

Brooke M. Lampley   *Northern Andalucía*
A veteran traveler, Brooke breezed through Córdoba and Sevilla with such ease that we swore she was born to research. Her understanding of art and architecture were trumped only by her contributions to Sevilla's nightlife sections. Our only regret is that we couldn't have worked with her longer.

Claire Lewis   *Costa del Sol*
A former researcher for *Let's Go: London*, Claire hopped down to Costa del Sol on a moment's notice. Who knew we would love her even more than the Málaga tourist office did? We thank her for her sophisticated, humorous prose, and for helping us out when we needed it most.

Rochelle Kristen Mackey   *Barcelona, the Balearic Islands, and the Eastern Coast*
Rochelle had an itinerary that most RWs only dream about. She hopped from island to island and beach to beach, with a little bit of Gaudí in between. Irregular transportation and unfriendly hostel owners were no match for this resourceful traveler, who braved Eivissa nightlife, windsurfing lessons, and Spain's most popular city to produce a vastly improved Barcelona—and an equally good tan.

James T. Platts   *Portugal and Western Andalucía*
Jamie knows Portugal and Portugal knows Jamie. Unfazed by deadlines, and armed with his sturdy cargo shorts and a Portuguese cellphone, Jamie conquered the country, leaving no laundromat, bus company, or internet cafe unchecked. In his wake he left a more consistently-researched and thorough version of Spain's not-so-little sibling.

Tim Pierhoples   *Morocco and the Southern Andalucía*
Meet Tim, handyman extraordinaire. He did a heavy-duty fix-er-up-er on Morocco, making the chapter more comprehensive, readable, and generally attractive. Whether dodging the hustlers in Tangier, hiking the Toukbal Trek, bargaining for camels, or mastering geology from a speeding (un-air-conditioned) rental car, Tim produced great new coverage and strengthened the old.

ACKNOWLEDGMENTS

SPAM THANKS: Our fabulous RWs who went above and beyond the call of duty. Adam, our savior, for being so thorough. Brendan for shite, and Hard GI. Elena for teaching us consistency. Matt and Melissa for pretty charts. Jonathan, Valerie, Sarah, Julie, Sonesh, Brendan, and Ben for making pod-life fun. Production for fixing things. Dan and Jon for maps. Anup for late night help. Jess, Kate, Alex, Kathy, Kate U., Melissa, Matt, Rich, Esti and others for proofing. Anne, Ben W, and Ben H for holding it all together.

OLIVIA THANKS: Ben for sanity and efficiency, Aarup for unlimited dedication, and to both of you for being so much fun. Adam for genuinely caring. Elena for chats. Jonathan, Valerie, Sarah, and Ben for early mornings. Alice, Pete, Melissa, and Jay for home-life. Kate and Melissa for craziness. Sonesh for advice. Esti for the opportunity. Dina and Emily for life outside LG. Meg, Lacy, Reyhan, Emma, Sarah, Adama, Emily, Rommy, Steph, Dimple, Leigh, and Nevine for understanding. Kelsey and the Doubs for taking care of me. Savannah for being my best friend. Mom and Dad for being so unconditional.

BEN THANKS: Olivia for knowing just when to be an editor, just when to be a crazy woman with an equally crazy sense of humor, and just when not to play Belle and Sebastian. Aarup for giving us his all even though he was only paid for half, and for just caring so much about it all. Adam for making me a firm believer in the chain of command. Steve and Norris for being just as good friends long-distance. The two Mark Rs. for being such good teachers and relatives, respectively, all summer. Mom, Dad, and Annie, 'cause you're just so awesome. Grammy, for continually showing me what life and love are all about. And of course Con, who's managed to be both the guide and the destination on the most wonderful journey of them all.

AARUP THANKS: Olivia for her remarkable dedication and sense of humor. Ben for his incredible efficiency—I'm not sure if Olivia and I would have made it if you weren't there to balance us out. Marshall, Waka, and the rest of team Italy for being so funny and so fun to work with. Adam for being the best ME—I was lucky to get to work with you on both books. The Romance room for late night candy, early morning breakfasts, and everything in between. And of course, thanks to Mom, Dad, Amit, and Anup.

Editor
Olivia Lorillard Cowley
Associate Editors
Benjamin Arthur Railton, Aarup Kubal
Managing Editor
Adam Stein

Publishing Director
Benjamin Wilkinson
Editor-in-Chief
Bentsion Harder
Production Manager
Christian Lorentzen
Cartography Manager
Daniel J. Luskin
Design Managers
Matthew Daniels, Melissa Rudolph
Editorial Managers
Brendan Gibbon, Benjamin Paloff, Kaya Stone, Taya Weiss
Financial Manager
Kathy Lu
Personnel Manager
Adam Stein
Publicity & Marketing Managers
Sonesh Chainani, Alexandra Leichtman
New Media Manager
Maryanthe Malliaris
Map Editors
Kurt Mueller, Jon Stein
Production Associates
Steven Aponte, John Fiore
Office Coordinators
Elena Schneider, Vanessa Bertozzi, Monica Henderson

Director of Advertising Sales
Marta Szabo
Associate Sales Executives
Tamas Eisenberger, Li Ran

President
Noble M. Hansen III
General Managers
Blair Brown, Robert B. Rombauer
Assistant General Manager
Anne E. Chisholm

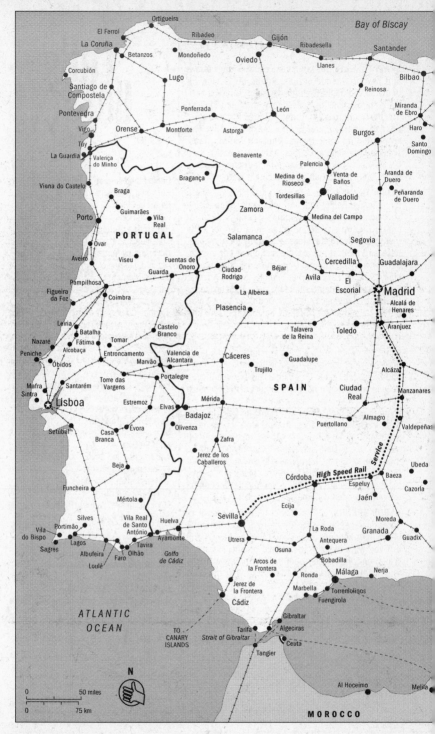

Bay of Biscay

ATLANTIC
OCEAN

PORTUGAL

SPAIN

MOROCCO

N

0   50 miles

0   75 km

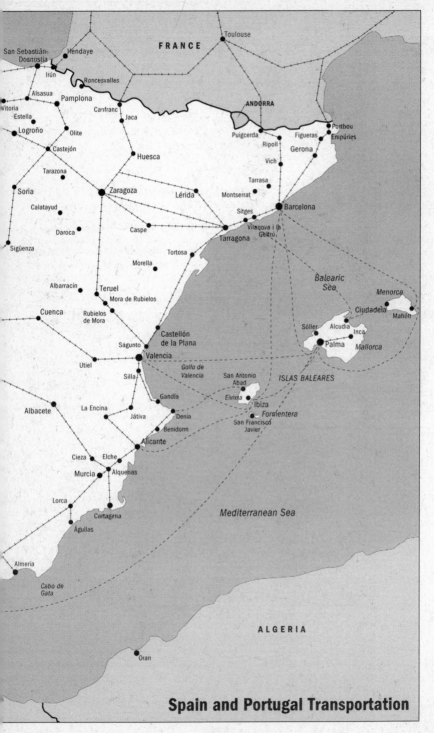

Spain and Portugal Transportation

ASTURIAS AND CANTABRIA
pp. 429–447

Oviedo
ASTURIAS   Santander
CANTABRIA

Santiago de
Compostela

GALICIA
pp. 448–470

León

Burgos

Valladolid

Viana do
Castelo   Bragança

DOURO AND MINHO   TRÁS-OS-MONTES
pp. 623–641   pp. 642–646

CASTILLA Y LEÓN
pp. 136–172

Porto

THE THREE BEIRAS
pp. 611–622

Aveiro

Salamanca

Coimbra

PORTUGAL

MADRID
pp. 71–121
Madrid

RIBATEJO AND
ESTREMADURA
pp. 592–610

Castelo Branco

Toledo

LISBON
pp. 540–568

EXTREMADURA
pp. 173–185

CASTILLA-
LA MANCHA
pp. 122–135

Lisbon
Setúbal

ALENTEJO
pp. 584–591

Mérida

Badajoz

Évora

Beja

Córdoba

ANDALUCÍA
pp. 186–272

Sevilla

Granada

Lagos   Faro

ALGARVE
pp. 569–583

ATLANTIC
OCEAN

Málaga

Gibraltar

Algeciras

ISLAS CANARIAS
pp. 497–523
↓

Tangier

MOROCCO
pp 647–725

Chapter Divisions

TO
RABAT
↓

FRANCE

IS VASCO
407–428

Vitoria

NAVARRA

● Pamplona

ANDORRA
pp. 362–366

LA RIOJA
AND
NAVARRA
pp. 385–406

Logroño

RIOJA

CATALUÑA
pp. 333–361

● Girona

Zaragoza

ARAGÓN
pp. 367–384

● BARCELONA
pp. 296–332

S P A I N

N

Teruel

0   50 miles

0   75 kilometers

TO
MENORCA

Cuenca ●

Mallorca
● Palma

Valencia ●

VALENCIA

BALEARIC ISLANDS
pp. 471–496

Ibiza

● Eivissa/Ibiza

Formentera

Menorca

Ciudadela ● ● Mahón

Alicante

EAST COAST
pp. 273–295

Murcia ●

MURCIA

M E D I T E R R A N E A N   S E A

ALGERIA

LET'S GO PICKS

BEST VIEWS: Arcos de la Frontera (Spain), from the Balcón de Coño (p. 223). **Granada (S),** the glowing Alhambra at night (p. 261). **Montserrat (S),** learn why it's called "the mountain of a hundred peaks" (p. 328). **Sagres (Portugal),** once considered the end of the world (p. 574). **Meknes (Morocco),** people-watch from the roof of the Madrassa Bou Inania (p. 677).

BEST BEACHES: Cádiz (S), blue flags everywhere (p. 227). **Praia da Rocha (P),** the best the Algarve has to offer (p. 575). **San Sebastián (S),** not too hot, not too cold (p. 415). **Essaouira (M),** if it's good enough for Jimi...(p. 705). **Menorca (S),** caves, ruins, and secluded coves (p. 488). **Tossa de Mar (S),** fall in love with "Blue Paradise" (p. 337).

BEST NIGHTLIFE: Ibiza (S), need you ask? (p. 493). **Barcelona (S),** where everything is creative (p. 323). **Salamanca (S),** just what happens when you put a bunch of students together (p. 153). **Marrakesh (M),** no booze, but you'll feel like you've had too much (p. 710). **Lagos (P),** with the most bars per square meter (p. 573).

BEST FESTIVALS: San Fermines (S), hands down (p. 396). **Las Fallas (S),** a pyromaniac's paradise (p. 279). **La Rapa das Bestas (S),** who's gonna shear your wild horses? (p. 469). **Carnaval (S),** Mardi Gras, only better (p. 227). **Festa da Sardinha (P),** booze and fish, booze and fish (p. 599). **International Art Festival (M),** where talent from the world over descends on beautiful Asilah (p. 688).

MOST ROMANTIC: Tossa de Mar (S), just ask Ava Gardner (p. 337). **Essaouira (M),** love in a purple haze (p. 702). **Menorca (S),** to get away from it all (p. 482). **Mojácar (S),** Spain's most romantic plazas (p. 248). **Guimarães (P),** serenity is achieved in the garden outside the castle (p. 634).

BEST HIKING: Parque Nacional de Ordesa (S), idyllic and magnificent (p. 382). **Picos de Europa (S),** for amazing paragliding and spelunking (p. 433). **Toubkal Massif (M),** trekking up North Africa's highest peak (p. 715). **Garajonay National Park (S),** the world's last laurasilva forest (see p. 521). **Parque Nacional da Peneda-Gerâs (P),** Romans ruins, megalithic graves, and no trail markers—or tourists (p. 636).

MOST BIZARRE: Ibiza (S), where everyone lets loose (p. 493). **Pamplona (S),** Europe's biggest summer fiesta (p. 396). **Figueres (S),** Dali's theater/museum/ego trip (p. 352). **Fez (M),** chaotic medina confusion (p. 684). **Évora (P),** Capella dos Ossos, a chapel made entirely of human bones (p. 587).

BEST FOOD/DRINK: Valencia (S), home to *paella* (p. 278). **Porto (P),** port wine from the source (p. 627). **Jerez de la Frontera (S),** center of the sherry triangle (p. 217). **Haro (S),** 17 *bodegas* making La Rioja's finest (p. 389). **Marrakesh (M),** delicious o.j. at the world's wildest market (p. 710). **San Sebastián (S),** *pintxos*—little bites of heaven (p. 413). **Belém (P),** home of the famed *pastiche de Belém* (p. 549).

BEST ARCHITECTURE: Toledo (S), whose cathedral is ostentatious—and rightfully so (p. 126). **León (S),** cathedral is the pride of the lions (p. 159). **Lisbon (P),** the futuristic Park of Nations (p. 555). **Barcelona (S),** Gaudí's the name, Modnernisme's the game (p. 314). **Casablanca (M),** 'cause the Hassan II Mosque is just so big (p. 699).

BEST SUICIDAL NAP SPOT: Llanes (S), on the edge of the Po. San Pedro (p. 440).

BEST MOVIE SET: Merzouga (M), the set of every desert movie, ever (p. 725).

BEST HITCHCOCK IMPERSONATION: Ilhas Berlengas (P), and its thousands of feathered friends (p. 599).

DISCOVER SPAIN, PORTUGAL, AND MOROCCO

FACTS AND FIGURES		
■ **SPAIN**	■ **PORTUGAL**	■ **MOROCCO**
■ **Population:** 39,371,000	■ **Population:** 9,964,000	■ **Population:** 27,225,463
■ **Size:** 504,784 sq. km	■ **Size:** 92,389 sq. km	■ **Size:** 458,730 sq. km
■ **Capital:** Madrid	■ **Capital:** Lisbon	■ **Capital:** Rabat
■ **Currency:** peseta (ptas)	■ **Currency:** escudo ($)	■ **Currency:** dirham (dh)

SPAIN

Spain is a budget traveler's dream. It is an inexpensive, politically stable, country where art and architecture, beaches, and nightlife vie for supremacy. The landscape is a microcosm of all that Europe has to offer. You can ski or surf, enjoy Picasso or cave paintings, dance until dawn or just chat in a plaza cafe. It is the perfect destination for first-time travelers, for seasoned adventurers, for families with young children, or for college students in search of that "craziest summer ever." You can do Spain in one week, one month, or one year. But you must do it at least once.

Madrid, Barcelona, and Sevilla—Spain's three great cities—offer unique blends of art, architecture, and cosmopolitan life. The northeast has become a mecca for art lovers; it encompasses not only Barcelona, but also the Costa Brava, which inspired the likes of Chagall and Dalí and is still home to many of Dalí's works. Farther north are the natural havens of the Pyrenees and Picos de Europa where adventure tourism reigns. Though less of a tourist draw, the Baroque cathedrals of Burgos and León draw church enthusiasts; but no religious monument in Spain can compete with the crowds at the cathedral in Santiago de Compostela, which marks the end of the Camino de Santiago. For partiers, Spain offers some of the world's wildest festivals and its most hopping nightlife. And then there is Andalucía, Spain's southernmost region and the breeding ground for those passionate cultural expressions (flamenco, bullfighting, *tapas*) that set Spain significantly apart from the rest of Europe.

PORTUGAL

Sandwiched between Spain and the Atlantic Ocean, Portugal is the forgotten country of Western Europe. What most people do know of Portugal is superficial; it colonized Brazil, invented sugary-sweet port wine, and hosted Expo '98 (which was, incidentally, a disaster). But there is much more to discover in Portugal. It shares the beaches, nightlife, and strong architectural tradition of its larger neighbor to the east, yet culturally and geographically it is quite distinct. Much of the land is more undeveloped than Spain's, and some of its regions—particularly Trás-os-Montes in the north—are more pristine than any in Europe. Its small towns have a similarly untouched feel, with medieval castles overlooking rushing rivers and peaceful praças. Portugal's greatest strength, like Spain's, is its diversity. Lisbon, the capital and largest city, is a fascinating and growing metropolis. To the south, the Algarve, Portugal's most touristed region, offers the country's wildest nightlife and its most spectacular beaches. To the north are the thriving university town of Coimbra, the vibrant regional capital of Porto, and the unrivaled wilderness and charming towns of Portugal's hinterland.

MOROCCO

For anyone who has never ventured to the developing world, Morocco is an experience. It is not a land of hustlers, drugs, and prostitutes, nor is it a land of snake charmers and carpet sellers. Morocco is, however, a land of extremes, characterized by the snow-capped peaks of the Atlas mountains and the hot sun on golden sand dunes, by industrialized coastal cities and isolated desert towns, by the sheer insanity of Marrakesh's Djemâa el-Fna and the peaceful seclusion of Essaouira's beaches. European backpackers come to Morocco to "see Africa," but they stay for the medinas (large outdoor markets where you can buy everything from a camel to a toothbrush to fresh orange juice), the excursions (treks on foot, four-wheel-drive, and camel into the Sahara or up North Africa's highest peak), and the history (towering mosques, crumbling kasbahs, and Roman ruins).

THINGS TO DO

CULTURAL HIGHLIGHTS

Spain, Portugal, and Morocco are *alive.* Two millennia of invading cultures have come and gone from this southwestern-most corner of Europe, and the result is a vibrant, if confused, *alegría.* The region bursts at the seams. You can see it every Sunday in Madrid's Rastro (p. 113), in the happy chaos of Fez's medina (p. 684), in the sidewalk cafes of Lisbon's Baixa (p. 551), and in Spain's spectacular festivals. During *Carnaval* in Cádiz (p. 227), Valencia's *Las Fallas* (p. 280), Sevilla's *Feria de Abril* (p. 201), and Pamplona's infamous *San Fermines* (p. 396), there is no denying the region's overwhelming cultural exuberance.

Still, like all passions, it is not entirely manic. Iberia's poignant expressions of heartbreak are often as blood-quickening as its celebrations. The ritually tragic expressions inherent in *flamenco* and *fado* bring tears to the eyes of even the most macho of bullfighters, who in turn create tragedies of life-and-death on the bloody sand. Actual tragedy on a larger scale has scarred Spain for a good part of this century—Picasso's powerfully cryptic *Guernica* (p. 104) and the propagandistic Valley of the Fallen (p. 118) give travelers a taste of the pain of Fascism. All of this inherited emotional activity demands a break now and then. The thin-aired reverence of Montserrat (p. 328) and the urban calm to be found in a rowboat in the Retiro (p. 100) or on a surreal bench in Parc Güell (p. 319) inspire contemplative relaxation; more untouched than the rest of Europe is touched, Portugal's Trás-os-Montes (p. 642) will make even the most devout of urbanites kiss the ground.

ARCHITECTURE

From the traditionally conservative to the unconventionally decadent, the buildings and monuments of Iberia form a collage of architectural styles. The remains of ancient civilizations are everywhere—from the Celtiberian tower of O Castro de Baroña (p. 462) and the ruins of the Roman Augusta Emerita at Mérida (p. 179) to the Torre D'en Gaumés Talayotic settlement in Menorca (p. 489). Despite the Reconquest's attempt to desecrate everything Muslim, the Catholic monarchs somehow managed to preserve the essence of Moorish form. The results are spectacular: the Alhambra in Granada (p. 261); the Mezquita in Córdoba (p. 218); the

Castelo dos Mouros in Sintra (p. 564). This combination of styles has dominated the history of Iberian construction. Both decidedly Catholic countries, Spain and Portugal have thrown money and artistic talent into the construction of some of the world's most ornate religious complexes, ranging from the pastiche of the Convento de Cristo (p. 610) to the imposing El Escorial (p. 116), from which the Inquisition was conducted. Spain's magnificent cathedrals can be Gothic (p. 140 and p. 159), Plateresque (p. 152), built on top of mosques (p. 207), or just plain bizarre, as in Gaudí's magnificent, still-unfinished Sagrada Familia in Barcelona (p. 317)—a brilliant climax of the Modernista style. Colorfully modern, the movement dominated Spanish architecture for much of the 20th century. The quest for truly modern architecture will continue into the next millennium, and has manifested itself most recently in Lisbon's expansive Park of Nations (p. 555) and Bilbao's Guggenheim Museum (p. 421). Iberia's next masterpiece, the aquarium-theater Ciudad de las Artes and Las Ciencias in Valencia (p. 278), opens its doors this year.

THE GREAT OUTDOORS

Iberia's best-kept secret is perhaps its seemingly unlimited selection of national parks and mountain ranges. Hidden amid cathedrals and museums are some diverse natural wonders. In Iberia, nature can be the mist that surrounds hikers as they head down into the valleys of the Pyrenee's Parque Nacional de Ordesa (p. 382). Sometimes it is the parched, dusty plains of Castilla La Mancha, which served as Cervantes's greatest inspiration (p. 122). Nature can be the rocky coves on Mallorca, where dirt roads wind down through wild olive groves to the pebble-strewn shores below (p. 473). In Picos de Europa, nature often means rocky mountainsides where nothing lives save the occasional moss or mountain goat (p. 433). Visitors to the south witness the power of nature in the cavernous gorges that define the small white town of Arcos de la Frontera (p. 221). And in the Canary Islands, nature comes in the form of the wildflower-covered volcanic craters of Parque Nacional de las Cañadas del Teide (p. 511) and the serene and spectacular laurasilva forest on Gomera (p. 521).

SUGGESTED ITINERARIES

THE BEST OF SPAIN AND PORTUGAL (4 WEEKS) Start off in **Madrid** (2 days, 4 nights, p. 71), with daytrips to the austere palace of **El Escorial** (1 day, p. 116) and the medieval streets of **Toledo** (1 day, p. 122). From here, visit the university town of **Salamanca** (1 day, p. 146) and cross the border into **Portugal,** heading up to the unpretentious **Porto** (2 days, p. 623). Swallow your port and continue down the coast to the beach resort of **Figueira da Foz** (2 days, p. 617). After a few days in the sun, hit the sights, sounds, and cafes of **Lisbon** (2 days, 3 nights, p. 540) with a daytrip to the town of **Sintra** (1 day, p. 561). From Lisbon, head south to the Algarve, stopping in **Lagos** (2 days, p. 569) where hordes of visitors dance the night away. Sleep off your hangover on the 7hr. express bus from Lagos to **Sevilla** (2 days, p. 186) and prepare yourself for a romantic stroll along the Guadalquivir River. Once you've taken in the

sights of this historic port and modern metropolis, delve deeper into Arab-influenced Andalucía—don't miss the Mezquita in **Córdoba** (2 days, p. 207) and the world-famous Alhambra in **Granada** (2 days, p. 255). From Granada head up the Mediterranean Coast to **Valencia** (1 day, p. 274), where the food—*paella* and oranges—rivals the new planetarium as Valencia's top attraction. From Valencia it's on to **Barcelona** (3 days, p. 296), one of Europe's most vibrant cities. After a tour of bizarre Modernista architecture and raging nightlife, take a daytrip to the beaches in **Tossa de Mar** (1 day, p. 337), the monastery in nearby **Montserrat** (1 day, p. 328), or the Dalí museum in **Figueres** (1 day, p. 350). From Barcelona continue on to **San Sebastián** (2 days, p. 408) and **Bilbao** (1 day, p. 417), home of the new Guggenheim Museum, before concluding your tour back in Madrid.

Bay of Biscay

Northern Spain
in three weeks

La Coruña
Oviedo
Picos de Europa
Santander
Bilbao

Santiago de
Compostela

Pontevedra
León
Burgos

Vigo
Valladolid

Viana do Castelo
Bragança
Braga
Zamora

PORTUGAL
Porto
Salamanca
Segovia

**Best of Spain
and Portugal** in
four weeks
Ávila
El
Escorial
Madrid

Coimbra

Figueira
da Foz
Toledo

Tomar

Cáceres

Sintra
Portalegre

SPAIN

Lisbon
Mérida
Elvas
Badajoz

Sétubal
Evora

Córdoba

ANDALUCÍA

Vila Real
de Santo
António
Huelva
Sevilla
Granada

Sagres
Lagos
Utrera

*Golfo
de Cádiz*
Best of Spain
in three weeks
Ronda
Nerja

Arcos de
la Frontera
Málaga

ATLANTIC
OCEAN
Cádiz
Marbella

Gibraltar
Algeciras

Strait of Gibraltar
Ceuta

Tangier

Melilla

N

0   50 miles

0   75 km

MOROCCO

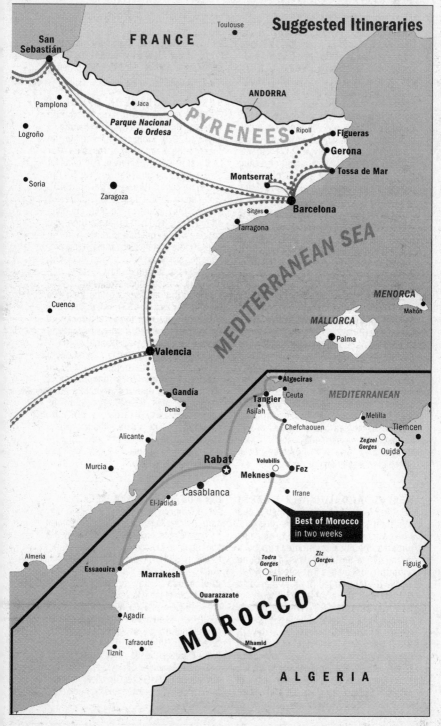

Suggested Itineraries

FRANCE

Toulouse

San Sebastián

Pamplona

Jaca

ANDORRA

Logroño

Parque Nacional
de Ordesa

PYRENEES

Ripoll

Figueras

Gerona

Soria

Zaragoza

Montserrat

Tossa de Mar

Cuenca

Sitges

Barcelona

Tarragona

MEDITERRANEAN SEA

MENORCA

Mahón

MALLORCA

Palma

Valencia

Gandía

Algeciras

MEDITERRANEAN

Denia

Tangier

Ceuta

Asilah

Alicante

Chefchaouen

Melilla

Tlemcen

Zegzel
Gorges

Oujda

Murcia

Rabat

Volubilis

Fez

Meknes

Casablanca

Ifrane

El-Jadida

Best of Morocco
in two weeks

Almeria

Essaouira

Marrakesh

Todra
Gorges

Ziz
Gorges

Tinerhir

Figuig

Ouarazazate

Agadir

MOROCCO

Tafraoute

Tiznit

Mhamid

ALGERIA

BEST OF SPAIN (3 WEEKS) Begin in **Madrid** (2 days, 4 nights, p. 71), with daytrips to **El Escorial** (1 day, p. 116) and **Toledo** (1 day, p. 122). Then take the high-speed train to **Córdoba** (2 days, p. 207), and on to **Sevilla** (2 days, p. 186), two of Spain's most beautiful and intriguing cities. From there catch the bus to the peaceful *pueblo blanco* (white town) of **Arcos de la Frontera** (1 day, p. 221) before heading south to the tanning fields of Spain's Costa del Sol. **Marbella** (1 day, p. 242) warrants a quick stopover, if for nothing else than the celebrity-watching and nightlife. For more peaceful beaches and a laid-back environment, **Nerja** (1 day, p. 244) is a much better choice. After a few days of serious sun, head inland to experience the cobblestone streets and world-renowned Alhambra in **Granada** (2 days, p. 255). From there it's an 8 hr bus ride along the coast to **Valencia** (1 day, p. 274). If you're looking to escape the city, indulge your athletic side with watersports on the beaches in nearby **Gandía** (1 day, p. 283). After that, head up the coast to Spain's jewel, **Barcelona** (2 days, p. 296), a pleasure for art and nightlife lovers alike. Worthwhile daytrips in Cataluña are as easy to find as its beauty: partake of **Tossa de Mar's** beaches (1 day, p. 337), breathtaking mountain views from **Montserrat** (1 day, p. 328), or saying Hello Dalí in **Figueres** (1 day, p. 350). From Barcelona, it is a 7-hour bus ride to the beaches and *tapas* of **San Sebastián** (2 days, p. 408). Finally, it's on to **Bilbao** (1 day, p. 417), home of the incredible Guggenheim museum.

BEST OF ANDALUCÍA (2 WEEKS)
Start in Madrid and take the high-speed AVE train to **Córdoba** (2 days, p. 207), where you can tour the Mezquita mosque-turned-cathedral. From there, hop back on the AVE to **Sevilla** (2 days, p. 186) for a couple days of sight-seeing. From Sevilla it's a quick trip down to the Costa del Luz and the soft-sand beaches of **Cádiz** (2 days, p. 223). Next, it's on to the real Andalucía and the classic *pueblo blanco* **Arcos de la Frontera** (1 day, p. 221). Party with the beautiful people in the Costa del Sol resort town of **Marbella** (1 day, p. 242); when that gets to be too expensive, take off to the more peaceful beaches of **Nerja** (2 days, p. 244). Then continue inland to **Granada** (2 days, p.

255), where the Alhambra and Albacín are sights for sore eyes. Get away from it all with a daytrip to the small mountain towns of the **Alpujarras** (1 day, p. 266). From there, take a train back to Madrid.

BEST OF NORTHERN SPAIN (3 WEEKS) Any northern itinerary should start with the colorful city of **Barcelona** (3 days, p. 296). From there, head up the coast to the resort town of **Tossa de Mar** (2 days, p. 337), where you can relax for a few days before continuing to the intriguing city of **Girona** (1 day, p. 345). While there, take a daytrip to **Figueres** (1 day, p. 350), home to the museum-monument of Salvador Dalí. From there, go north to **San Sebastián** (2 days, p. 408), where there's plenty of *tapas*, bars, and beaches for everyone. It's an easy trip from there to **Bilbao** (1 day, p. 417), site of the new Guggenheim museum. Then, it's on to the mountains of the **Picos de Europa** (2 days, p. 433), where beautiful nature reigns. From the Picos, duck into Galicia, exploring the small towns and superb, undiscovered beaches of the **Rías Altas** (2 days, p. 456). Come out of hiding and walk the famous Camino de Santiago to **Santiago de Compostela** (2 days, p. 448), one of the world's great pilgrimage sites. Near Santiago are the gorgeous **Islas Cíes** (1 day, p. 457). No trip to Spain is complete without a visit to **Madrid** (2 days, 4 nights, p. 71), with daytrips to **El Escorial** (1 day, p. 116) and **Toledo** (1 day, p. 122).

BEST OF MOROCCO (2 WEEKS) To get to Morocco from Spain, hop on a ferry from Spanish **Algeciras** to **Tangier.** Though it's not the most enjoyable of cities, any visit from Spain to Morocco must include Tangier (1 day, p. 663). The trick? Get in and out as quickly as possible, and continue on to **Chefchaoun** (1 day, p. 671). Relaxed? Head down to the enchanting imperial cities of **Fez** (2 days, p. 679), **Meknes** (2 days, p. 672), and **Marrakesh** (2 days, p. 679). Next it's down to the southern desert town of **Ouarzazate** (1 day, p. 717) for a camel trek. From Ouarzazate, go back through Marrakesh to **Essaouira** (2 days, p. 702). Then travel up the coast, stopping briefly in **Rabat** (1 day, p. 690) before heading back north to Tangier.

ESSENTIALS

WHEN TO GO

Summer is **high season** (*temporada alta*) for coastal and interior regions in Spain, Portugal and Morocco; winter is high season for ski resorts and the Canary Islands. In many parts of Spain and Portugal, high season extends back to **Semana Santa** (Holy Week; Mar. 29-Apr. 4) and includes festival days (see **Festivals and Holidays,** see p. 62, p. 534, and p. 656). Tourism reaches its height in August; the coastal regions overflow while inland cities empty out, leaving closed offices, restaurants, and lodgings.

Traveling in the **off-season** (*temporada baja*) has many advantages, most noticeably lighter crowds and lower prices. Many hostels cut their prices by 50% or more, and reservations are seldom necessary. But while major cities and university towns may burst with vitality, many smaller seaside towns virtually shut down. Tourist offices and sights cut their hours nearly everywhere. During Morocco's momentous religious event, Ramadan, there is little activity outside the sacred realm.

CLIMATE

The following information is drawn from the International Association for Medical Assistance to Travelers *World Climate Charts*. In each monthly listing, the first two numbers represent the average daily maximum and minimum temperatures in degrees **Celsius.** The remaining number indicates the average number of days with a measurable amount of **rain.**

SPAIN

Avg. Temp (low/high)	January		April		July		October	
	Temp	Rain	Temp	Rain	Temp	Rain	Temp	Rain
Barcelona	6-13	5	11-18	9	21-28	4	15-21	9
Cádiz	9-15	9	13-20	6	20-27	0	17-23	7
Granada	2-12	7	7-20	10	17-34	1	10-23	7
Madrid	2-9	8	7-18	9	17-31	2	10-19	8
Málaga	8-17	7	13-21	6	21-29	0	16-23	6
Palma	6-14	8	10-19	6	20-29	1	10-18	9
Santander	7-12	16	10-15	13	16-22	11	12-18	14
Santiago de C.	5-10	21	8-18/	7	13-24	1	11-21	10
Sevilla	6-15	8	11-24	7	20-36	0	14-26	6
Valencia	6-15	5	10-20	7	20-29	2	13-23	7
Zaragoza	2-10	6	8-19	8	18-31	3	6-14	6

PORTUGAL

Avg. Temp (low/high)	January		April		July		October	
	Temp	Rain	Temp	Rain	Temp	Rain	Temp	Rain
Bragança	0-8	15	5-16	10	13-28	3	7-18	10
Évora	6-12	14	10-19	10	16-30	1	13-22	9
Faro	9-15	9	13-20	6	20-28	0	16-22	6
Lisbon	8-14	15	12-20	10	17-27	2	14-22	9
Porto	5-13	18	9-18	13	15-25	5	11-21	15

MOROCCO

Avg. Temp (low/high)	January		April		July		October	
	Temp	Rain	Temp	Rain	Temp	Rain	Temp	Rain
Essaouira	11-17	6	14-19	5	17-22	0	16-22	3
Fez	4-16	8	9-23	9	18-36	1	13-26	7
Marrakesh	4-18	7	11-26	6	19-38	1	14-28	4
Rabat	8-17	9	11-22	7	17-28	0	14-25	6
Tangier	8-16	10	11-18	8	18-27	0	15-22	8

To convert from °C to °F, multiply by 1.8 and add 32.
To convert from °F to °C, subtract 32 and multiply by 0.55.

°CELSIUS	-5	0	5	10	15	20	25	30	35	40
°FARENHEIT	23	32	41	50	59	68	77	86	95	104

DOCUMENTS AND FORMALITIES

ENTRANCE REQUIREMENTS.
Passport (p. 11). Required for citizens of Great Britain, Canada, New Zealand, and the United States.
Visa (p. 12). Required only for citizens of Australia and South Africa.
Work Permit (p. 12). Required for all foreigners planning to work in Spain, Portugal, and Morocco.
Driving Permit (p. 36). Required for all those planning to drive.

EMBASSIES AND CONSULATES

Questions concerning visas and passports go to consulates, not embassies (which handle weightier matters).

SPANISH

Australia: Embassy: 15 Arkana St., **Yarralumla,** ACT 2600. Mailing address: P.O. Box 9076, Deakin, ACT 2600. (tel. (02) 62 73 35 55; fax 62 73 39 18). **Consulates:** Level 24, St. Martins Tower, 31 Market St., **Sydney,** NSW 2000 (tel. (02) 92 61 24 33 or 92 61 24 43; fax 92 83 16 95); 540 Elizabeth St., 4th fl., **Melbourne,** VIC 3000 (tel. (03) 9347 19 66 or 93 47 19 97; fax 93 47 73 30).

Canada: Embassy: 74 Stanley Ave., **Ottawa,** ON K1M 1P4 (tel. (613) 747-2252; fax 744-1224). **Consulates:** 1 Westmount Sq., Suite 1456, **Montreal,** PQ H3Z 2P9 (tel. (514) 935-5235; fax 935-4655); Simtoe Place, 200 Front St., Suite 2401, P.O. Box 15, **Toronto,** ON M5V 3K2 (tel. (416) 977-1661; fax 593-4949).

Ireland: Consulate: 17A Merlyn Park, Ballsbridge, **Dublin** 4 (tel. (035) 269 1640; fax 269 1854).

New Zealand: Embassy: Refer to Embassy in Australia.

South Africa: Embassy: 169 Pine St., Arcadia, P.O. Box 1633, **Pretoria** 0083 (tel. (012) 344 3875; fax 343 4891). **Consulate:** 37 Shortmarket St., **Cape Town** 8001 (tel. (012) 222 415; fax 222 328.

U.K.: Embassy: 39 Chesham Pl., **London** SW1X 8SB (tel. (020) 72 35 55 55; fax 72 59 53 92). **Consulates:** 20 Draycott Pl., **London** SW3 2RZ (tel. (020) 75 89 89 89; fax 75 81 78 88); Suite 1A, Brook House, 70, Spring Gardens, **Manchester** M2 2BQ (tel. (0161) 236 1233; fax 228 7467); 63 N. Castle St., **Edinburgh** EH2 3LJ (tel. (0131) 220 1843, 220 1439, or 220 1442; fax 226 4568).

U.S.: Embassy: 2375 Pennsylvania Ave. NW, **Washington, D.C.** 20037 (tel. (202) 728-2332; fax 728-2308). **Consulates:** 150 E. 58th St., 30th fl., **New York,** NY 10155 (tel. (212) 355-4080; fax 644-3751); **others** in Boston, Chicago, Houston, Los Angeles, Miami, New Orleans, Puerto Rico, San Francisco, and Washington, D.C.

PORTUGUESE

Australia: Embassy: 23 Culgoa Circuit, **O'Malley,** ACT 2606. Mailing address P.O. Box 9092, Deakin, ACT 2600 (tel. (02) 62 90 17 33; fax 62 90 19 06). **Consulate:** 132 Ocean St., **Edgecliff,** NSW 2027; mailing address P.O. Box 568, **Sydney,** NSW 2001. (tel. (02) 93 26 18 44; fax 93 27 16 07).

Canada: Embassy: 645 Island Park Dr., **Ottawa,** ON K1Y OB8 (tel. (613) 729 0883; fax 729-4236). **Consulates:** 2020 University, Suite 1725, **Montréal,** QU H3A 2A5 (tel. (514) 499-0621 or 499-0359; fax 499-0366); 438 University Ave., Suite 1400, **Toronto,** ON M5G 2K8 (tel. (416) 217-0966 or 217-0971; fax 217-0973); 700 W. Pender St., Suite 904, **Vancouver,** BC V6C 1G8 (tel. (604) 688-6514; fax 685-7042).

New Zealand: Embassy: Refer to Embassy in Australia. **Consulates:** 55 Ford St., **Auckland** 5 (tel. (09) 309 1454; fax 308 9061); Deleite touche Tohmatsu, **Wellington** 1 (tel. (04) 472 1677; fax 472 8023).

South Africa: Embassy: 599 Leyds St., Mucklenuk, **Pretoria** (tel. (012) 341 2340; fax 341 3975). **Consulates:** 201 Barclays Sq., 296 Walker St., Sunnyside, **Pretoria,** (tel. (012) 341 5522; fax 341 5690); Diamond Corner Building, 68 Eloff St., 3rd fl., **Johannesburg** (tel. (011) 293 8206; fax 333 9009); 320 W. St., 16th fl., P.O. Box 315, **Durban** (tel. (031) 305 7511; fax 304 6036).

U.K.: Embassy: 11 Belgrave Sq., **London** SW1X 8PP (tel. (020) 72 35 53 31; fax 72 45 12 87). **Consulate:** Silver City House, 62 Brompton Rd., **London** SW3 1BJ (tel. (020) 7581 8722; fax 7581 3085).

U.S.: Embassy: 2125 Kalorama Rd. NW, **Washington, D.C.** 20008 (tel. (202) 328-8610; fax 462-3726). **Consulates:** 630 5th Ave., 3rd fl., Suite 310, **New York,** NY 10111 (tel. (212) 246-4580 or 246-4582; fax 459-0190); **others** in Boston, Chicago, Coral Gables (FL), Dominican Republic, Houston, Honolulu, Los Angeles, Newark, New Bedford (MA), New Orleans, Philadelphia, Providence, San Francisco, San Juan (PR), Waterbury (CT), and Washington, D.C.

MOROCCAN

Australia: Embassy: 11 West St., North **Sydney,** NSW 2060 (tel. (02) 99 22 49 99; fax 99 23 10 53; email maroc@magna.com.au). **Consulate:** same.

Canada: Embassy: 38 Range Rd., **Ottawa,** ON K1N 8J4 (tel. (613) 236-7391 or 236-7392; fax 236-6164). **Consulate:** 1010 Sherbrooke West St., Suite 1510, **Montreal,** QU H3A 2R7 (tel. (514) 288-8750; fax 288-4859).

South Africa: Embassy: Pretoria (tel. (012) 343 0230; fax 343 0613).

U.K.: Embassy: 40 Queens Gate Gardens, **London** SW7 5NE (tel. (020) 7581 5001; fax 7225 3862).

U.S.: Embassy: 1601 21st St. NW, **Washington, D.C.** 20009 (tel. (202) 462-7979; fax 265-0161). **Consulates:** 10 East 40th. St., 23rd fl., **New York,** NY 10016 (tel. (212) 213-9644; fax 758-2625); 1821 Jefferson Place NW, **Washington, D.C.** 20036 (tel. (202) 462-7979; fax 452-0106).

EMBASSIES IN SPAIN, PORTUGAL, AND MOROCCO

Foreign embassies and consulates are listed in the individual **Essentials** sections for **Spain** (p. 69), **Portugal** (p. 539), and **Morocco** (p. 662). Consulates give legal advice and medical referrals and can readily contact relatives back home. In extreme cases, they may offer emergency financial assistance.

ESSENTIALS

PASSPORTS

REQUIREMENTS. Citizens of Australia, Canada, Ireland, New Zealand, South Africa, the U.K., and the U.S. need valid passports to enter Spain, Portugal, and Morocco, and to re-enter their own countries. Spain, Portugal, and Morocco do not allow entrance if the holder's passport expires in under six months; returning home with an expired passport is illegal, and may result in a fine.

PHOTOCOPIES. It is a good idea to photocopy the page of your passport with your photograph, passport number, and other identifying information, along with other important documents such as visas, travel insurance policies, airplane tickets, and traveler's check serial numbers, in case you lose anything. Carry one set of copies in a safe place and apart from the originals and leave another set at home. Consulates recommend that you carry an expired passport or official copy of your birth certificate in a part of your baggage separate from other documents.

LOST PASSPORTS. If you lose your passport, immediately notify the local police and the nearest embassy or consulate of your home government. To expedite its replacement, you will need to know all information previously recorded and show identification and proof of citizenship. Although new passports can be ready in as little as an hour, in some cases a replacement may take weeks to process, and it may be valid only for a limited time. Any visas stamped in your old passport will be irretrievably lost. In an emergency or if it is after business hours, ask for temporary traveling papers that will permit you to reenter your home country.

NEW PASSPORTS. All applications for new passports or renewals should be filed several weeks or months in advance of your planned departure date. Most passport offices do offer emergency passport services for an extra charge. Citizens residing abroad who need a passport or renewal should contact their nearest embassy or consulate.

Australia: Citizens must apply for a passport in person at a post office, a passport office (located in most major cities), or an Australian diplomatic mission overseas. For more info, call toll-free (in Australia) 13 12 32, or visit www.dfat.gov.au/passports.

Canada: Application forms are available at all passport offices, Canadian missions, many travel agencies, and Northern Stores in northern communities. For additional info, contact the Canadian Passport Office, Department of Foreign Affairs and International Trade, Ottawa, ON, K1A 0G3 (tel. (613) 994-3500; www.dfait-maeci.gc.ca/passport). Travelers may also call (800) 567-6868 (24hr.)

Ireland: Citizens can apply for a passport by mail to either the Department of Foreign Affairs, Passport Office, Setanta Centre, Molesworth St., Dublin 2 (tel. (01) 671 1633; fax 671 1092; www.irlgov.ie/iveagh), or the Passport Office, Irish Life Building, 1A South Mall, Cork (tel. (021) 272 525). Obtain an application at a local Garda station or post office, or request one from a passport office.

New Zealand: Application forms for passports are available from most travel agents. Applications may be forwarded to the Passport Office, P.O. Box 10526, Wellington, New Zealand (tel. 0800 225 050; www.govt.nz/agency_info/forms.shtml). Children can no longer be endorsed on a parent's passport—they must apply for their own.

South Africa: Passports are issued only in Pretoria. However, all applications must still be submitted or forwarded to the applicable office of a South African consulate. The completion of an application normally takes 3 months or more. Contact the nearest Department of Home Affairs Office (www.southafrica-newyork.net/passport.htm).

United Kingdom: Application forms are available at passport offices, main post offices, and many travel agents. Apply by mail or in person to one of the passport offices, located in London, Liverpool, Newport, Peterborough, Glasgow, or Belfast. The process takes about four weeks, but the London office offers a 5-day, walk-in rush service; arrive early. The U.K. Passport Agency can be reached by phone at (0870) 521 0410, and more information is available at www.open.gov.uk/ukpass/ukpass.htm.

United States: Citizens may apply for a passport at any federal or state courthouse or post office authorized to accept passport applications, or at a U.S. Passport Agency, located in most major cities. Refer to the "U.S. Government, State Department" section of the telephone directory or the local post office for addresses. Passports may be renewed by mail or in person for US$40. Processing takes 3-4 weeks. For more info, contact the U.S. Passport Information's 24-hour recorded message (tel. (202) 647-0518) or check travel.state.gov/passport_services.html.

VISAS AND WORK PERMITS

Citizens of Australia and South Africa need a **visa** to enter Spain, Portugal, or Morocco; citizens of Great Britain, Canada, New Zealand, and the United States do not need visas.

Admission as a visitor does not include the right to **work,** which is authorized only by a work permit; entering Spain, Portugal, or Morocco to study requires a special visa. For more info, see **Alternatives to Tourism,** page 43.

IDENTIFICATION

When you travel, always carry two or more forms of identification on your person, including at least one photo ID. A passport combined with a driver's license or birth certificate usually serves as adequate proof of your identity and citizenship. Many establishments, especially banks, require several IDs before cashing traveler's checks. Never carry all your forms of ID together, however; you risk being left entirely without ID or funds in case of theft or loss. It is useful to carry extra passport-size photos to affix to the various IDs or railpasses you may acquire.

STUDENT AND TEACHER IDENTIFICATION. The **International Student Identity Card (ISIC)** is the most widely accepted form of student identification. Flashing this card can procure you discounts for sights, theaters, museums, accommodations, meals, train, ferry, bus, and airplane transportation, and other services. Present the card wherever you go, and ask about discounts even when none is advertised. The international identification cards are preferable to institution-specific cards because the tourism personnel in Spain, Portugal, and Morocco are taught to recognize the former. For U.S. cardholders traveling abroad, the ISIC also provides insurance benefits (see **Insurance,** p. 23). In addition, cardholders have access to a toll-free 24-hour ISIC helpline whose multilingual staff can provide assistance in medical, legal, and financial emergencies overseas (tel. (800) 626-2427 in the US and Canada; elsewhere call collect 44 (020) 86 66 90 25).

Many student agencies issue ISICs, including STA Travel in Australia and New Zealand; Travel CUTS in Canada; USIT in Ireland and Northern Ireland; SASTS in South Africa; Campus Travel and STA Travel in the U.K.; Council Travel, STA Travel, and via the web (www.counciltravel.com/idcards/index.htm) in the U.S.; and any other travel agency with a student focus. When you apply for the card, request a copy of the International Student Identity Card Handbook, which lists some of the available discounts by country. The card is valid from September of one year to December of the following year and costs AUS$15, CDN$15, or US$20. Applicants must be at least 12 years old and degree-seeking students of a secondary or post-secondary school. Because of the proliferation of phony ISICs, many airlines and some other services require additional proof of student identity, such as a signed letter from the registrar attesting to your student status that is stamped with the school seal or your school ID card. The **International Teacher Identity Card (ITIC)** offers the same insurance coverage, and similar but limited discounts The fee is AUS$13, UK£5, or US$20. For more information on these cards, contact the **International Student Travel Confederation (ISTC),** Herengracht 479, 1017 BS Amsterdam, Netherlands (from abroad tel. 31 20 421 28 00; fax 421 28 10; email istcinfo@istc.org; www.istc.org).

YOUTH IDENTIFICATION. The International Student Travel Confederation also issues a discount card to travelers who are 25 years old or younger but not students. Known as the **International Youth Travel Card (IYTC)** (formerly the **GO25 Card**), this one-year card offers many of the same benefits as the ISIC, and most organizations that sell the ISIC also sell the IYTC. A brochure that lists discounts is free when you purchase the card. To apply, you will need either a passport, valid driver's license, or copy of a birth certificate, as well as a passport-sized photo with your name printed on the back. The fee is US$20.

CUSTOMS

Upon entering Spain, Portugal, and Morocco, you must declare certain items from abroad and pay a duty on the value of those articles that exceed the allowance established by customs. Keeping receipts for purchases made abroad will help establish values when you return. It is wise to make a list, including serial numbers, of any valuables that you carry with you from home; if you register this list with customs before your departure and have an official stamp it, you will avoid import duty charges and ensure an easy passage upon your return. Be especially careful to document items manufactured abroad.

Upon returning home, you must declare all articles acquired abroad and pay a **duty** on the value of articles that exceed the allowance established by your country's customs service. Goods and gifts purchased at **duty-free** shops abroad are not exempt from duty or sales tax at your point of return; you must declare these items as well. "Duty-free" merely means that you need not pay a tax in the country of purchase. For more specific information on customs requirements, contact the following information centers:

Australia: Customs National Information Line (1 300 363; www.customs.gov.au.)

Canada: Canadian Customs, 2265 St. Laurent Blvd., Ottawa, ON K1G 4K3 (tel. (613) 993-0534; 24hr. automated tel. (800)-461-9999; www.revcan.ca).

Ireland: The Collector of Customs and Excise, Custom House, Dublin 1 (tel. (01) 679 2777; fax 671 2021; email taxes@revenue.iol.ie; www.revenue.ie/customs.htm).

New Zealand: New Zealand Customhouse, 17-21 Whitmore St., Box 2218, Wellington (tel. (04) 473 6099; fax 473 7370; www.customs.govt.nz).

South Africa: Commissioner for Customs and Excise, Private Bag X47, Pretoria 0001 (tel. (012) 314 9911; fax 328 6478).

United Kingdom: Her Majesty's Customs and Excise, Custom House, Nettleton Road, Heathrow Airport, Hounslow, Middlesex TW6 2LA (tel. (020) 8910 3602/3566; fax 8910 3765; www.hmce.gov.uk).

United States: U.S. Customs Service, Box 7407, Washington D.C. 20044 (tel. (202) 927-6724; www.customs.ustreas.gov).

MONEY

If you stay in hostels, eat out at low-priced establishments, and see a few sights, expect to spend around US$40 a day in **Spain,** US$35 a day in **Portugal,** and US$15 in **Morocco.** If you stay in big cities or take long bus/train rides, plan on spending more. For more specific information on exchange rates and banking hours, see each country's **Essentials** section.

THE EURO. On January 1, 1999, Spain and Portugal accepted the **euro** as their common currency of the future. The euro will first enter circulation on January 1, 2002, but national currencies will continue to be accepted until July 1, 2002. All prices in this year's guide remain in the respective national currencies. Updated info on the euro can be found on the EU's website at www.europa.eu.int.

CURRENCY AND EXCHANGE

As a general rule, it's cheaper to convert money after arriving. It's good to bring enough foreign currency to last for the first 24 to 72 hours of a trip to avoid being penniless after banking hours or on a holiday. Travelers living in the U.S. can get foreign currency from the comfort of their home; **Capital Foreign Exchange** (tel. (888)-842-0880) or **International Currency Express** (tel. (888)-278-6628) will deliver foreign currency (for over 120 countries) or traveler's checks overnight (US$15) or 2nd-day (US$12) at competitive exchange rates.

Watch out for commission rates and check newspapers for the standard rate of exchange. Banks generally have the best rates. A good rule of thumb is only to go to banks or *Casas de Cambio* that have at most a 5% margin between their buy and sell prices. **Exchange offices** often lie near transportation hubs and tend to have longer hours than banks. **Hotels** also often have longer hours but usually charge higher commissions, particularly when cashing traveler's checks. Since you lose money with each transaction, convert in large sums (unless the currency is depreciating rapidly). Also, using an ATM card or a credit card (see p. 17) will often get you the best possible rates, although such transactions often charge hefty fees.

In Spain, Portugal, and Morocco, Western currency is often preferred to local, but avoid using Western money when you can. Throwing dollars around for preferential treatment may be offensive, and it can attract thieves. It also marks you as a foreigner and invites locals to jack up prices.

TRAVELER'S CHECKS

Traveler's checks are one of the safest and easiest means of carrying funds, because they can be refunded if stolen. Several agencies and banks sell them, usually for face value plus a small percentage (1-4%) commission. Members of the American Automobile Association, and some banks and credit unions, can get American Express checks commission-free; see **Driving Permits and Insurance,** page 36. **American Express** and **Visa** are the most widely recognized. If you're ordering checks, do so well in advance, especially if you are requesting large sums.

Each agency provides refunds if your checks are lost or stolen, and many provide additional services, such as toll-free refund hotlines in the countries you're visiting, emergency message services, and stolen credit card assistance. In order to collect a **refund for lost or stolen checks,** keep your check receipts separate from your checks and store them in a safe place or with a traveling companion. Record check numbers when you cash them, leave a list of check numbers with someone at home, and ask for a list of refund centers when you buy your checks. Always bring your passport with you when you plan to use the checks.

American Express: Call 800 251 902 in Australia; in New Zealand 0800 441 068; in the U.K. (0800) 52 13 13; in the U.S. and Canada (800)-221-7282. Elsewhere, call U.S. collect 1-(801)-964-6665; www.aexp.com. Checks can be purchased for a small fee (1-4%) at American Express Travel Service Offices, banks, and American Automobile Association offices. AAA members (see p. 36) can buy the checks commission-free. American Express offices cash their checks commission-free (except where prohibited by national governments), but often at slightly worse rates than banks. *Cheques for Two* can be signed by either of two people traveling together. The booklet *Traveler's Companion* lists travel office addresses and stolen check hotlines for each European country.

Citicorp: Call (800)-645-6556 in the U.S. and Canada; in Europe, the Middle East, or Africa, call the London office at 44 (020) 75 08 70 07; from elsewhere, call U.S. collect 1-(813)-623-1709. Traveler's checks in 7 currencies. Commission 1-2%. Guaranteed hand-delivery of traveler's checks when a refund location is not convenient. Call 24hr.

Thomas Cook MasterCard: From the U.S., Canada, or Caribbean call 800-223-7373; from the U.K. call (0800) 622 101; elsewhere, call 44 (1733) 318 950 collect. Checks available in 13 currencies. Commission 2%. Offices cash checks commission-free.

ESSENTIALS

Visa: Call (800)-227-6811 in the U.S.; in the U.K. 0800 895 078; from elsewhere, call 44 (1733) 318 949 and reverse the charges.

CREDIT CARDS

In Spain and Portugal, credit cards are often accepted at local establishments, including budget lodgings, restaurants, and supermarkets; they are accepted almost everywhere in big cities. Chain stores, fancy restaurants and upmarket accommodations almost always accept credit cards. In Morocco, count on credit cards only for plane tickets, major hotels, and international organizations. Major credit cards—usually **MasterCard** and **Visa**—can be used to extract cash advances in local currency from associated banks and teller machines throughout Spain, Portugal, and Morocco. Credit card companies get the wholesale exchange rate, which is generally 5% better than the retail rate used by banks and other currency exchange establishments. **American Express** cards also work in some ATMs, as well as at AmEx offices and major airports. All such machines require a **Personal Identification Number (PIN).** You must ask your credit card company for a PIN before you leave; without it, you will be unable to withdraw cash with your credit card outside your home country. If you already have a PIN, check with the company to make sure it will work abroad.

CASH CARDS

Cash cards—popularly called ATM cards—are widespread in Spain, Portugal, and, to a lesser extent, Morocco. Depending on the system that your home bank uses, you can probably access your own personal bank account whenever you need money. ATMs get the same wholesale exchange rate as credit cards. Despite these perks, do some research before relying too heavily on automation. There is often a limit on the amount of money you can withdraw per day (usually about US$500, depending on the type of card and account), and computer networks sometimes fail. If you're traveling from the U.S. or Canada, memorize your PIN code in numeral form since machines elsewhere often don't have letters on their keys. Also, if your PIN is longer than four digits, ask your bank whether the first four digits will work, or whether you need a new number, as most foreign machines won't accept PIN numbers of more than 4 digits.

GETTING MONEY FROM HOME

AMERICAN EXPRESS. Cardholders can withdraw cash from their checking accounts at any of AmEx's major offices and many of its representatives' offices, up to US$1000 every 21 days (no service charge, no interest). AmEx also offers Express Cash at any of their ATMs. Express Cash withdrawals are automatically debited from the Cardmember's checking account or line of credit. Green card holders may withdraw up to US$1000 in a seven day period. There is a 2% transaction fee for each cash withdrawal, with a US$2.50 minimum/$20 maximum. To enroll in Express Cash, Cardmembers may call (800)-CASH-NOW (227-4669) in the U.S.; outside the U.S. call collect 1-(336)-668-5041. The AmEx national number in Spain is 1-322-5300, in Portugal it is 1-72-00027.

WESTERN UNION. Travelers from the U.S., Canada, and the U.K. can wire money abroad through Western Union's international money transfer services. In the U.S., call 800-325-6000; in the U.K., call (0800) 833 833; in Canada, call (800)-235-0000. To cable money within the U.S. using a credit card (Visa, MasterCard, Discover), call (800)-CALL-CASH (225-5227). The rates for sending cash are generally US$10-11 cheaper than with a credit card, and the money is usually available at the place you're sending it to within an hour.

U.S. STATE DEPARTMENT (U.S. CITIZENS ONLY). In emergencies, U.S. citizens can have money sent via the State Department. For US$15, they will forward money within hours to the nearest consular office, which will disburse it according to instructions. The office serves only Americans in the direst of straits abroad; non-American travelers should contact their embassies for information on wiring cash. Check with the State Department or the nearest U.S. embassy or consulate for the quickest way to have the money sent. Contact the Overseas Citizens Service, American Citizens Services, Consular Affairs, Room 4811, U.S. Department of State, Washington, D.C. 20520 (tel. (202) 647-5225; nights, Sundays, and holidays 647-4000; fax (on demand only) 647-3000; travel.state.gov).

SAFETY AND SECURITY

Spain and Portugal are both politically stable and safe countries; travelers should follow the general tips given here to avoid tourist-related crimes, but need not be overly concerned. Morocco has a higher crime rate and visitors should be especially careful while exploring. See the **Essentials** sections for **Spain** (p. 67), **Portugal** p. 536), and **Morocco** (p. 660) for more specific information.

The following government offices provide travel information and advisories by telephone or on their websites:

Australian Department of Foreign Affairs and Trade. Tel. (02) 6261 1111; www.dfat.gov.au.

Canadian Department of Foreign Affairs and International Trade (DFAIT). Tel. (800)-267-8376 or (613) 944-4000 from Ottawa; www.dfait-maeci.gc.ca. Call for their free booklet, *Bon Voyage...But.*

U.K. Foreign and Commonwealth Office. Tel. (0171) 238 4503; www.fco.gov.uk.

U.S. Department of State. Tel. (202) 647-5225; travel.state.gov. For their publication *A Safe Trip Abroad,* call (202) 512-1800.

GENERAL SAFETY TIPS

To avoid unwanted attention, try to blend in as much as possible. Respecting local customs (which in more rural areas of Spain and Portugal and all of Morocco means dressing conservatively) may placate would-be hecklers. The gawking camera-toter is a more obvious target than the low-profile traveler. Familiarize yourself with your surroundings before setting out; if you must check a map on the street, duck into a cafe or shop. If you are traveling alone, be sure that someone at home knows your itinerary and **never admit that you're traveling alone.**

PROTECTING YOUR VALUABLES. To prevent easy theft, don't keep all your valuables in one place. **Photocopy** important documents to allow you to recover them if they are lost or filched. Carry one copy separate from the documents and leave another copy at home. Label every piece of luggage both inside and out. **Don't put a wallet with money in your back pocket**. If you carry a purse, buy a sturdy one with a secure clasp, and carry it crosswise on the side, away from the street with the clasp against you. Secure packs with small combination padlocks that slip through the two zippers. A **money belt** is the best way to carry cash; you can buy one at most camping supply stores. A nylon, zippered pouch with a belt that sits inside the waist of your pants or skirt combines convenience and security. Avoid keeping anything precious in a **fanny-pack** (even if it's worn on your stomach): your valuables will be highly visible and easy to steal.

CON ARTISTS AND PICKPOCKETS. Con artists and hustlers often work in groups, and unfortunately children are among the most effective. They possess an innumerable range of ruses. Be aware of certain classics: sob stories that require money, rolls of bills "found" on the street, mustard spilled (or saliva spit) onto your shoulder distracting you for enough time to snatch your bag.

In city crowds and especially on public transportation, **pickpockets** are amazingly deft at their craft. Rush hour is no excuse for strangers to press up against you on the metro. Also, be alert in public telephone booths. If you must say your calling card number, do so very quietly; if you punch it in, make sure no one can look over your shoulder.

ACCOMMODATIONS AND TRANSPORTATION. Never leave your belongings unattended; crime can occur in even the most demure-looking hostel or hotel. If you feel unsafe, look for places with either a curfew or a night attendant. *Let's Go* lists locker availability in hostels and train stations, but you'll need your own **padlock.** Lockers are useful if you plan on sleeping outdoors or don't want to lug everything with you, but don't store valuables in them.

Be particularly careful on city **buses,** carry your backpack in front of you where you can see it, don't check baggage on trains, and don't trust anyone to "watch your bag for a second." Thieves thrive on **trains;** professionals wait for tourists to fall asleep and then carry off everything they can. Use good judgement in selecting a train compartment: never stay in an empty one, and use a lock to secure your pack to the luggage rack. Keep important documents and other valuables on your person and try to sleep on top bunks with your luggage stored above you.

GETTING AROUND. If you are using a **car,** learn local driving signals and wear a seatbelt. Study route maps before you hit the road; some roads have poor (or non-existent) shoulders, few gas stations, and roaming animals. In many regions, road conditions necessitate driving more slowly and more cautiously than you would at home. If you plan on spending a lot of time on the road, you may want to bring spare parts. For long drives in desolate areas invest in a cellular phone (from

US$35 in Spain and Portugal) and a roadside assistance program (see p. 36). If your car breaks down, wait for the police to assist you. *Let's Go* does not recommend **hitchhiking** under any circumstances, particularly for women—see **Getting Around,** page 38, for more information.

SELF-DEFENSE. There is no sure-fire set of precautions that will protect you from all of the situations you might encounter when you travel. A good self-defense course will give you more concrete ways to react to different types of aggression. **Impact, Prepare, and Model Mugging** can refer you to local self-defense courses in the United States (tel. (800)-345-5425) and Vancouver, Canada (tel. (604) 878-3838). Workshop (2-3 hours) start at US$50 and full courses run US$350-500. Both women and men are welcome.

DRUGS

Laws vary from country to country, but, needless to say, **illegal drugs** are best avoided altogether; the average sentence for drug possession in Spain is about seven years. You are subject to the laws of the country in which you travel, not to those of your home country, and it is your responsibility to familiarize yourself with these laws before leaving. In Spain, Portugal, and Morocco all recreational drugs—including marijuana—are illegal (for more information on Morocco, see page 660). Buying or selling *any* type of drug may lead to a hefty prison sentence. A meek "I didn't know it was illegal" will not suffice. If you carry **prescription drugs** while you travel, it is vital to have a copy of the prescriptions themselves readily accessible at country borders.

HEALTH

On the whole, Spain and Portugal conform to most Western standards of health. **Morocco**—although better than most of Africa—presents more potential health-care hassles; for more specific health information about Morocco, see page 660). *Let's Go* lists information on how to access **24-hour pharmacies** in every major town or city.

Common sense is the simplest prescription for good health while you travel. Travelers complain most often about their feet and their gut, so take precautionary measures: drink lots of fluids to prevent dehydration and constipation, wear sturdy, broken-in shoes and clean socks, and use talcum powder to keep your feet dry. To minimize the effects of jet lag, "reset" your body's clock by adopting the time of your destination as soon as you board the plane.

If your regular **insurance** policy does not cover travel abroad, you may wish to purchase additional coverage, particularly for traveling in Morocco. With the exception of Medicare, most health insurance plans cover members' medical emergencies during trips abroad; check with your insurance carrier to be sure. For more information on insurance, see p. 23.

BEFORE YOU GO

PACKING. For minor health problems, bring a compact **first-aid kit.** In your **passport,** write the names of any people you wish to be contacted in case of a medical emergency, and also list any **allergies** or medical conditions you would want doctors to be aware of. Allergy sufferers might want to obtain a full supply of any necessary medication before the trip. Carry up-to-date, legible prescriptions or a statement from your doctor stating the medication's trade name, manufacturer, chemical name, and dosage. While traveling, be sure to keep all medication with you in your carry-on luggage.

IMMUNIZATIONS. Take a look at your immunization records before you go. Travelers over two years old should be sure that the following vaccines are up to date: **MMR** (for measles, mumps, and rubella); **DTaP** or **Td** (for diptheria, tetanus, and pertussis); **OPV** (for polio); **HbCV** (for haemophilus influenza B); and **HBV** (for hepatitus B). Adults traveling to **Morocco** should consider an additional dose of **Polio** vaccine if they have not already had one during their adult years. **Hepatitis A** vaccine and/or **immune globulin** (IG) is also recommended for travelers to Morocco. If you will be spending more than four weeks in Morocco, you should consider being vaccinated for typhoid.

MEDICAL CONDITIONS. Those with medical conditions (e.g., diabetes, allergies to antibiotics, epilepsy, heart conditions) may want to obtain a stainless steel **Medic Alert** identification tag (US$35 1st year, $15 annually thereafter), which identifies the condition and gives a 24-hour collect-call information number. Contact the Medic Alert Foundation, 2323 Colorado Ave., Turlock, CA 95382 (tel. (800)-825-3785; www.medicalert.org). Diabetics can contact the **American Diabetes Association**, 1660 Duke St., Alexandria, VA 22314 (tel. (800)-232-3472), to receive copies of the article "Travel and Diabetes" and a diabetic ID card, which carries messages in 18 languages explaining the carrier's diabetic status.

If you are **HIV** positive, you may want to contact the Bureau of Consular Affairs, #4811, Department of State, Washington, D.C. 20520 (tel. (202) 647-1488; auto-faxback (202) 647-3000; travel.state.gov). Anyone seeking residence, work and student permits in Spain must take a medical exam (which may include an AIDS test).

EMERGENCY MEDICAL ASSISTANCE. If you are concerned about being able to access medical support while traveling, contact one of two services: **Global Emergency Medical Services (GEMS)** has products called *MedPass* that provide 24-hour international medical assistance and support coordinated through registered nurses who have online access to your medical information, your primary physician, and a worldwide network of screened, English-speaking doctors and hospitals. Subscribers also receive a personal medical record that contains vital information in case of emergencies, and GEMS will pay for medical evacuation if necessary. Prices start at about US$35 for a 30-day trip and run up to about $100 for annual services. For more info, contact them at 2001 Westside Dr. #120, Alpharetta, GA 30004 (tel. 800-860-1111; fax (770) 475-0058; www.globalems.com).

The **International Association for Medical Assistance to Travelers (IAMAT)** has free membership and offers a directory of English-speaking doctors around the world who treat members for a set fee, as well as detailed charts on immunization requirements, diseases, climate, and sanitation. Chapters include: **U.S.,** 417 Center St., Lewiston, NY 14092 (tel. (716) 754-4883, 8am-4pm; fax (519) 836-3412; email iamat@sentex.net; www.sentex.net/~iamat); **Canada,** 40 Regal Rd., Guelph, ON N1K 1B5 (tel. (519) 836-0102) or 1287 St. Clair Avenue West, Toronto, ON M6E 1B8 (tel. (416) 652-0137; fax (519) 836-3412); **New Zealand,** P.O. Box 5049, Christchurch 5 (fax (03) 352 4630; email iamat@chch.planet.org.nz).

GENERAL HEALTH TIPS

For more specific information on **disease,** especially if you will be traveling to **Morocco** for significant periods of time, consult the U.S. **Centers for Disease Control and Prevention (CDC)** (tel. (888)-232-3299; www.cdc.gov). It is an excellent source of information for travelers around the world and maintains an international fax information service for travelers. The CDC also publishes the booklet "Health Information for International Travelers" (US$20), an annual global rundown of disease, immunization, and general health advice. Orders can be made by phone (tel. (202) 512-1800) with a major credit card (Visa, MC, or Discover).

The **United States State Department** (travel.state.gov) compiles Consular Information Sheets on health, entry requirements, and other issues for all countries of the world. For quick information on travel warnings, call the **Overseas Citizens' Ser-**

vices (tel. (202) 647-5225; after-hours 647-4000). To receive the same Consular Information Sheets by fax, dial (202) 647-3000 directly from a fax machine and follow the recorded instructions.

EVERYDAY HAZARDS. Heat exhaustion, characterized by dehydration and salt deficiency, can lead to fatigue, headaches, and wooziness. Avoid heat exhaustion by drinking plenty of clear fluids and eating salty foods, like crackers. Alcoholic beverages are dehydrating, as are coffee, strong tea, and caffeinated sodas. Wear a hat, sunglasses, and a lightweight long-sleeve shirt in hot sun, and take time to acclimate to a hot destination before seriously exerting yourself. Heat stress can eventually lead to **heatstroke,** characterized by rising body temperature, severe headache, and cessation of sweating. Heatstroke is rare but serious, and victims must be cooled off with wet towels and taken to a doctor as soon as possible.

If you're prone to **sunburn,** bring sunscreen with you and apply it liberally and often. Protect your eyes with good sunglasses, since ultraviolet rays can damage the retina of the eye after too much exposure. If you get sunburned, drink more fluids than usual and apply Calamine or an aloe-based lotion

INSECTS. Many diseases are transmitted by insects—mainly mosquitoes, fleas, ticks, and lice. Be aware of insects in wet or forested areas, while hiking, and especially while camping. **Mosquitoes** are most active from dusk to dawn. Use insect repellents, wear long pants and long sleeves (fabric need not be thick or warm; tropic-weight cottons can keep you comfortable in the heat), and buy a mosquito net. Wear shoes and socks, and tuck long pants into socks. Soak or spray your gear with permethrin, which is licensed in the U.S. for use on clothing. Natural repellents can be useful supplements: taking vitamin B-12 pills regularly can eventually make you smelly to insects, as can garlic pills. Calamine lotion or topical cortisones (like Cortaid) may stop insect bites from itching, as can a bath with a half-cup of baking soda or oatmeal. **Ticks**—responsible for Lyme and other diseases—can be particularly dangerous in rural and forested regions.

FOOD AND WATER. Prevention is the best cure: be sure that everything you eat is cooked properly and that the water you drink is clean, especially in Morocco, where the risk of contracting traveler's diarrhea or other diseases is higher than in Spain and Portugal. While it is probably okay to drink the water in most of the major cities, in less-developed areas you should never drink unbottled water which you have not treated yourself. In risk areas, don't brush your teeth with tap water or rinse your toothbrush under the faucet, and keep your mouth closed in the shower. Ice cubes are just as dangerous as impure water in liquid form. Salads and uncooked vegetables (including lettuce and coleslaw) are full of untreated water. Other culprits are raw shellfish, unpasteurized milk, and sauces containing raw eggs. Peel all fruits and vegetables yourself, and beware of watermelon, which is often injected with impure water. Watch out for food from markets or vendors that may have been washed in dirty water or fried in rancid cooking oil, such as juices and peeled fruits. Always wash your hands before eating, or bring a quick-drying liquid hand cleaner like Purrell.

Traveler's diarrhea results from drinking untreated water or eating uncooked foods. It can last three to seven days. If the nasties hit you, have quick-energy, non-sugary foods with protein and carbohydrates to keep your strength up. Over-the-counter remedies (such as Pepto-Bismol or Imodium) may counteract the problems, but they can complicate serious infections. The most dangerous side effect of diarrhea is dehydration; the simplest and most effective anti-dehydration formula is 8 oz. of (clean) water with a ½ tsp. of sugar or honey and a pinch of salt. Soft drinks without caffeine or salted crackers are also good. If you develop a fever or your symptoms don't go away after four or five days, consult a doctor. You may have dysentery (see below). If children develop traveler's diarrhea, consult a doctor, since treatment is different.

Parasites such as microbes and tapeworms also hide in unsafe water and food. **Giardia,** for example, is acquired by drinking untreated water from streams or lakes all over the world. Symptoms of parasitic infections in general include swollen glands or lymph nodes, fever, rashes or itchiness, digestive problems, eye problems, and anemia. Boil your water, wear shoes, avoid bugs, and eat only cooked food.

WOMEN'S HEALTH

Women traveling in unsanitary conditions are vulnerable to **urinary tract** and **bladder infections,** common and severely uncomfortable bacterial diseases that cause a burning sensation and painful, frequent urination. Women are also susceptible to **vaginal yeast infections.** Wearing loose trousers or a skirt and cotton underwear will help. Yeast infections can be treated with an over-the-counter remedy like Monostat or Gynelotrimin. Bring supplies from home, as they may be difficult to find on the road. Some travelers opt for a natural alternative such as plain yogurt and lemon juice douche if other remedies are unavailable.

Tampons and **pads** are sometimes hard to find when traveling, and your preferred brands may not be available, so it may be advisable to take supplies along. **Reliable contraceptive devices** may also be difficult to find. Women on the pill should bring enough to allow for possible loss or extended stays. Bring a prescription, since forms of the pill vary a good deal.

Women who need an **abortion** while abroad should contact the **International Planned Parenthood Federation,** European Regional Office, Regent's College Inner Circle, Regent's Park, London NW1 4NS (tel. (171) 487 7900; fax 487 7950), for more information.

INSURANCE

Travel insurance generally covers four basic areas: medical/health problems, property loss, trip cancellation/interruption, and emergency evacuation. Although your regular insurance policies may well extend to travel-related accidents, you may consider purchasing travel insurance if the cost of potential trip cancellation/interruption or emergency medical evacuation is greater than you can absorb.

Medical insurance (especially university policies) often covers costs incurred abroad; check with your provider. **Medicare does not cover foreign travel.** Canadians are protected by their home province's health insurance plan for up to 90 days after leaving the country; check with the provincial Ministry of Health or Health Plan Headquarters for details. **Homeowners' insurance** (or your family's coverage) often covers theft during travel and loss of travel documents (passport, plane ticket, railpass, etc.) up to US$500.

ISIC and **ITIC** provide basic insurance benefits, including US$100 per day of in-hospital sickness for a maximum of 60 days, US$3000 of accident-related medical reimbursement, and US$25,000 for emergency medical transport (see **Identification,** p. 12). Cardholders have access to a toll-free 24-hour helpline whose multilingual staff can provide assistance in medical, legal, and financial emergencies overseas (tel. 800-626-2427 in the U.S. and Canada; elsewhere call the U.S. collect 713-267-2525. **American Express** (tel. 800-528-4800) grants most cardholders automatic car rental insurance (collision and theft, but not liability) and ground travel accident coverage of US$100,000 on flight purchases made with the card.

Prices for travel insurance purchased separately generally run about US$50 per week for full coverage, while trip cancellation/interruption may be purchased separately at a rate of about US$5.50 per US$100 of coverage.

INSURANCE PROVIDERS. Council and **STA** (see p. 31) offer a range of plans that can supplement your basic coverage. Other private providers in the **U.S. and Canada** include: **Access America** (tel. 800-284-8300; fax (804) 673-1491); **Berkely Group/**

Carefree Travel Insurance (tel. 800-323-3149 or (516) 294-0220; fax (516) 294-1095; info@berkely.com; www.berkely.com); **Globalcare Travel Insurance** (tel. 800-821-2488; fax (781) 592-7720; www.globalcare-cocco.com); and **Travel Assistance International** (tel. 800-821-2828 or (202) 828-5894; fax (202) 828-5896; email wassist@aol.com; www.worldwide-assistance.com). Providers in the **U.K.** include **Campus Travel** (tel. (01865) 258 000; fax 792 378) and **Columbus Travel Insurance** (tel. (0171) 375 0011; fax 375 0022). In **Australia** try **CIC Insurance** (tel. (02) 9202 8000).

PACKING

Pack according to the extremes of climate you may experience and the type of travel you'll be doing. **Pack light:** a good rule is to lay out only what you absolutely need, then take half the clothes and twice the money. The less you have, the less you have to lose (or store, or carry on your back). Don't forget the obvious things: no matter when you're traveling, it's always a good idea to bring a rain jacket, a warm jacket or wool sweater, and sturdy shoes and thick socks. You may also want to add one outfit beyond the jeans and t-shirt uniform, and maybe a nicer pair of shoes if you have the room. Remember that wool will keep you warm even when soaked through, whereas wet cotton is colder than wearing nothing at all.

In Spain and Portugal, **shorts,** deemed unfashionable except on beaches, are relatively uncommon. In Morocco, especially for women, they are virtually unacceptable. Beyond this fact, standard Western wear works everywhere in Iberia. Morocco has different, slightly stricter standards. Dressing conservatively is the best bet for safety and sanity. Avoid short skirts, sleeveless tops, and shorts. For more details, see **Women Travelers**.

If you plan on hitting the nightlife, jeans and a t-shirt just won't cut it. The Spanish and Portuguese like to party, and they party in style. Women will probably want to wear a skirt or dress pants and a nice top. Spanish and Portuguese men generally wear jeans and a nice shirt, with a belt and leather shoes. Everyone should avoid flip-flops, tevas, birkenstocks, or sneakers when going out. Oh, and leave that baseball hat at home.

LUGGAGE. If you plan to cover most of your itinerary by foot, a sturdy **frame backpack** is unbeatable. **Internal-frame packs** mold better to your back, keep a lower center of gravity, and can flex adequately on difficult hikes that require a lot of bending and maneuvering. **External-frame packs** are more comfortable for long hikes over even terrain—like city streets—since they keep the weight higher and distribute it more evenly. Look for a pack with a strong, padded hip belt to transfer weight from your shoulders to your hips. Good packs cost anywhere from US$150 to US$500. Before you leave, pack your bag, strap it on, and imagine yourself walking uphill on hot asphalt for three hours; this should give you a sense of how important it is to pack lightly. Organizations that sell packs through mail-order are listed on page 26.

Toting a **suitcase** or **trunk** is fine if you plan to live in one or two cities and explore from there, but a very bad idea if you're going to be moving around a lot. Make sure suitcases have wheels and consider how much they weigh even when empty. Hard-sided luggage is more durable but more weighty and cumbersome. Soft-sided luggage should have a PVC frame, a strong lining to resist bad weather and rough handling, and its seams should be triple-stitched for durability.

In addition to your main vessel, a small backpack, rucksack, or courier bag may be useful as a **daypack** for sight-seeing expeditions; it doubles as an airplane **carry-on.** An empty, lightweight **duffel bag** packed inside your luggage may also be useful. Once abroad you can fill your luggage with purchases and keep your dirty clothes in the duffel.

ELECTRIC CURRENT. In Spain, Portugal, and Morocco, electricity is 220 volts AC, enough to fry any 110V North American appliance. 220V appliances don't like

110V current, either. Visit a hardware store for an adapter (which changes the shape of the plug) and a converter (changes the voltage). Don't make the mistake of using only an adapter (unless appliance instructions explicitly state otherwise).

CONTACT LENSES. Machines which heat-disinfect lenses will require a small converter (about US$20) to 220V. Consider switching temporarily to chemical disinfection, but check with your lens dispenser to see if it's safe to switch; some lenses may be damaged by a chemical system. Supplies may be expensive and difficult to find; bring enough saline and cleaner for your entire vacation.

FILM. Film in Spain, Portugal, and Morocco is generally rather expensive. Thus, it makes sense to bring film from home and, if you will be seriously upset if the pictures are ruined, develop it at home as well. If you're not a serious photographer, you might want to consider bringing a **disposable camera** or two rather than an expensive permanent one.

OTHER USEFUL ITEMS. No matter how you're traveling, it's always a good idea to carry a first-aid kit including sunscreen, insect repellent, and vitamins (see **Health**, p. 20). Other useful items include: an umbrella; sealable plastic bags (for damp clothes, soap, food, shampoo, and other spillables); alarm clock; waterproof matches; sun hat; needle and thread; safety pins; sunglasses; pocketknife; plastic water bottle; compass; string (makeshift clothesline and lashing material); towel; padlock; whistle; rubber bands; flashlight; cold-water soap; earplugs; electrical tape (for patching tears); tweezers; garbage bags; a small calculator for currency conversion; a pair of flip-flops for the shower; a money-belt for carrying valuables; deodorant; razors; tampons; and condoms.

ACCOMMODATIONS

For more specific information on accommodations, see the **Essentials** section of **Spain** (p. 67), **Portugal** (p. 537), and **Morocco** (p. 661).

HOSTELS

> **A HOSTELER'S BILL OF RIGHTS.** There are certain standard features that we do not include in our hostel listings. Unless we state otherwise, you can expect that every hostel has: no lockout, no curfew, free hot showers, secure luggage and valuables storage, and no key deposit.

Hostels are generally dorm-style accommodations, often in single-sex large rooms with bunk beds, although some hostels do offer private rooms for families and couples. They sometimes have kitchens and utensils for your use, bike or moped rentals, storage areas, and laundry facilities. There can be drawbacks: some hostels close during certain daytime "lock-out" hours, have a curfew, don't accept reservations, impose a maximum stay, or, less frequently, require that you do chores.

For their various services and lower rates at member hostels, hosteling associations, especially **Hostelling International (HI),** can definitely be worth joining. HI hostels are scattered throughout Spain, Portugal, and Morocco, and many accept reservations via the International Booking Network (Australia tel. (02) 2261 1111, Canada tel. 800-663-5777, U.K. tel. (01629) 581 418, Ireland tel. (01) 301 766, New Zealand tel. (09) 379 4224, U.S. tel. 800-909-4776; www.hiayh.org/ushostel/reserva/ibn3.htm) for a nominal fee. HI's web page lists the web addresses and phone numbers of all national associations and can be a great place to begin researching hosteling in a specific region (www.iyhf.org). Other comprehensive hosteling websites include www.hostels.com and www.eurotrip.com/accommodation.To join HI, contact one of the following organizations in your home country:

Australian Youth Hostels Association, 422 Kent St., Sydney NSW 2000 (tel. (02) 9261 1111; fax 9261 1969; email yha@yhansw.org.au; www.yha.org.au). 1-yr. membership AUS$44, under 18 AUS$13.50.

Hostelling International-Canada, 400-205 Catherine St., Ottawa, ON K2P 1C3 (tel. 800-663-5777 or (613) 237-7884; fax 237-7868; email info@hostellingintl.ca; www.hostellingintl.ca). 1-yr. membership CDN$25, under 18 CDN$12; 2-yr. CDN$35.

An Óige (Irish Youth Hostel Association), 61 Mountjoy St., Dublin 7 (tel. (01) 830 4555; fax 830 5808; email anoige@iol.ie; www.irelandyha.org). 1-yr. membership IR£10, under 18 IR£4, families IR£20.

Youth Hostels Association of New Zealand, P.O. Box 436, 173 Cashel St., Christchurch 1 (tel. (03) 379 9970; fax 365 4476; email info@yha.org.nz; www.yha.org.nz). 1-yr. membership NZ$24, ages 15-17 NZ$12, under 15 free.

Hostelling International South Africa, P.O. Box 4402, Cape Town 8000 (tel. (021) 24 2511; fax 24 4119; email info@hisa.org.za; www.hisa.org.za). 1-yr. membership SAR50, under 18 SAR25, lifetime SAR250.

Scottish Youth Hostels Association, 7 Glebe Crescent, Stirling FK8 2JA (tel. (01786) 891 400; fax 891 333; email info@syha.org.uk; www.syha.org.uk). Membership UK£6, under 18 UK£2.50.

Youth Hostels Association of England and Wales, 8 St. Stephen's Hill, St. Albans, Hertfordshire AL1 2DY, England (tel. (01727) 855 215 or 845 047; fax 844 126; email yhacustomerservices@compuserve.com; www.yha.org.uk). 1-yr. membership UK£11, under 18 UK£5.50, families UK£22.

Hostelling International Northern Ireland, 22-32 Donegall Rd., Belfast BT12 5JN, Northern Ireland (tel. (01232) 324 733 or 315 435; fax 439 699; email info@hini.org.uk; www.hini.org.uk). 1-yr. membership UK£7, under 18 UK£3, families UK£14.

Hostelling International-American Youth Hostels, 733 15th St. NW, Suite 840, Washington, D.C. 20005 (tel. (202) 783-6161; fax 783-6171; email hiayhserv@hiayh.org; www.hiayh.org). 1-yr. membership US$25, over 54 US$15, under 18 free.

CAMPING AND THE OUTDOORS

For more specific information on camping, see the **Essentials** sections of **Spain** (p. 68), **Portugal** (p. 538), and **Morocco** (p. 661).

CAMPING AND HIKING EQUIPMENT

SLEEPING BAG. Most sleeping bags are rated by "season," or the lowest outdoor temperature at which they will keep you warm ("summer" means 30-40°F at night and "four-season" or "winter" often means below 0°F). Sleeping bags are made either of down (warmer and lighter, but more expensive and miserable when wet) or of synthetic material (heavier, more durable, and warmer when wet). Prices vary, but might range from US$80-210 for a summer synthetic to US$250-300 for a good down winter bag. **Sleeping bag pads,** including foam pads (US$10-20) and air mattresses (US$15-50) cushion your back and neck and insulate you from the ground. **Therm-A-Rest** brand self-inflating sleeping pads are part foam and part airmattress and partially inflate when you unroll them, but are costly at US$45-80. Bring a **"stuff sack"** or plastic bag to store your sleeping bag and keep it dry.

TENT. The best tents are free-standing, with their own frames and suspension systems; they set up quickly and only require staking in high winds. Low-profile dome tents are the best all-around. When pitched their internal space is almost entirely usable, which means little unnecessary bulk. Tent sizes can be somewhat misleading: two people can fit in a two-person tent, but will find life more pleasant in a four-person. If you're traveling by car, go for the bigger tent, but if you're hiking, stick with a smaller tent that weighs no more than 5-6lbs (2-3kg). Good two-person tents start at US$90, four-person tents at US$300. Seal the seams of your tent with waterproofer, and make sure it has a rain fly. Other tent accessories include a **battery-operated lantern,** a **plastic groundcloth,** and a **nylon tarp.**

BACKPACK. If you intend to do a lot of hiking, you should have a frame backpack. **Internal-frame packs** mold better to your back, keep a lower center of gravity, and can flex adequately to allow you to hike difficult trails that require a lot of bending and maneuvering. **External-frame packs** are more comfortable for long hikes over even terrain since they keep the weight higher and distribute it more evenly. Whichever you choose, make sure your pack has a strong, padded hip belt, which transfers the weight from the shoulders to the legs. Any serious backpacking requires a pack of at least 65 liters. Sturdy backpacks cost anywhere from US$125-420. This is one area where it doesn't pay to economize—cheaper packs may be less comfortable, and the straps are more likely to fray or rip. Before you buy any pack, try it on and imagine carrying it, full, a few miles up a rocky incline. Better yet, insist on filling it with something heavy and walking around the store to get a sense of how it distributes weight before committing to buy it. A **waterproof backpack cover** will prove invaluable. Otherwise, plan to store all of your belongings in plastic bags inside your backpack.

BOOTS. Be sure to wear hiking boots with good **ankle support** which are appropriate for the terrain you plan to hike. Your boots should fit snugly and comfortably over one or two wool socks and a thin liner sock. Breaking in boots properly before setting out requires wearing them for several weeks; doing so will spare you from painful and debilitating blisters.

OTHER NECESSITIES. **Raingear** in two pieces, a top and pants, is far superior to a poncho. **Synthetics,** like polypropylene tops, socks, and long underwear, along with a pile jacket, will keep you warm even when wet. When camping in autumn, winter, or spring, bring along a **"space blanket,"** which helps you to retain your body heat and doubles as a groundcloth (US$5-15). Plastic **canteens** or water bottles keep water cooler than metal ones do, and are virtually shatter- and leakproof. Large, collapsible **water sacks** will significantly improve your lot in primitive campgrounds and weigh practically nothing when empty, though they are bulky and heavy when full. Bring **water-purification tablets** for when you can't boil water, unless you are willing to shell out money for a portable water-purification system. Though most campgrounds provide campfire sites, you may want to bring a small **metal grate** or **grill** of your own. For those places that forbid fires or the gathering of firewood, you'll need a **camp stove.** The classic Coleman stove starts at about US$40. You will need to purchase a **fuel bottle** and fill it with propane to operate it. A **first aid kit, swiss army knife, insect repellent, calamine lotion,** and **waterproof matches** or a **lighter** are other essential camping items.

BUYING EQUIPMENT. The mail-order/online companies listed below offer lower prices than many retail stores, but a visit to a local camping or outdoors store will give you a good sense of items' look and weight.

Campmor, P.O. Box 700, Saddle River, NJ 07458 (U.S. tel. 888-226-7667, elsewhere tel. 1-201-825-8300; email customer-service@campmor.com; www.campmor.com).

Discount Camping, 880 Main North Rd., Pooraka, South Australia 5095, Australia (tel. (08) 8262 3399; fax 8260 6240; www.discountcamping.com.au).

Eastern Mountain Sports, 327 Jaffrey Rd., Peterborough, NH 03458 (tel. 888-463-6367 or (603) 924-7231; www.emsonline.com; email emsmail@emsonline.com).

L.L. Bean, Freeport, ME 04033-0001 (U.S./Canada tel. 800-441-5713; U.K. tel. (0800) 962 954; elsewhere tel. 1-207-552-6878; www.llbean.com). If your purchase doesn't meet your expectations, they'll replace or refund it.

Mountain Designs, P.O. Box 1472, Fortitude Valley, Queensland 4006, Australia (tel. (07) 3252 8894; fax 3252 4569; www.mountaindesign.com.au).

Recreational Equipment, Inc. (REI), Sumner, WA 98352 (tel. 800-426-4840 or (253) 891-2500; www.rei.com).

YHA Adventure Shop, 14 Southampton St., London, WC2E 7HA, U.K. (tel. (01718) 368 541). The main branch of one of Britain's largest outdoor equipment suppliers.

WILDERNESS SAFETY

Stay warm, stay dry, and stay hydrated. The vast majority of life-threatening wilderness situations result from a breach of this simple dictum. On any hike, however brief, you should pack enough equipment to keep you alive should disaster befall. This includes **raingear, hat** and **mittens,** a **first-aid kit,** a **reflector,** a **whistle, high energy food,** and extra **water.** Dress in warm layers of **synthetic materials** designed for the outdoors, or **wool.** Pile fleece jackets and Gore-Tex raingear are excellent choices. Never rely on **cotton** for warmth. This "death cloth" will be absolutely useless should it get wet. Make sure to check all equipment for any defects before setting out, and see **Camping and Hiking Equipment,** above, for more information.

Check **weather forecasts** and pay attention to the skies when hiking. Whenever possible, let someone know when and where you are going hiking, either a friend, your hostel, a park ranger, or a local hiking organization. See **Health,** page 20 for information about outdoor ailments such as heatstroke, hypothermia, giardia, rabies, and insects, as well as basic medical concerns and first-aid.

For more information, consult *How to Stay Alive in the Woods,* by Bradford Angier (Macmillan, US$8.)

KEEPING IN TOUCH

MAIL

For information on sending mail from abroad, see the **Essentials** sections of **Spain** (p. 68), **Portugal** (p. 538), or **Morocco** (p. 661).

Sending airmail to Spain from the U.S. requires between 4 and 7 days. To Portugal, allow 7 to 10 days. Airmail to Morocco usually requires around two weeks, but it could either go more quickly or much more slowly. Mailing from European locations to any of these countries is a few days faster; from Australia, New Zealand, or South Africa, a couple of days slower. Mail sent to smaller towns will take longer. Envelopes should be marked "air mail" or "par avion." There are several ways to arrange pick-up of letters sent to you while you are abroad.

General Delivery: Mail can be sent internationally through Lista de Correos in Spain, Posta Restante in Portugal, or Poste Restante in Morocco. The mail will go to a special desk in the central post office, unless you specify a post office by street address or postal code. As a rule, it is best to use the largest post office in the area, and mail may be sent there regardless of what is written on the envelope. It is usually safer and quicker to send mail express or registered. When picking up your mail, bring a form of photo ID, preferably a passport. There is generally no surcharge; if there is a charge, it should not exceed the cost of domestic postage. If the clerks insist that there is nothing for you, have them check under your first name as well. Mark the envelope "HOLD" and address it with the last name capitalized and underlined, as follows:

Spain: Mail should be addressed as follows: TSAO, Connie; Lista de Correos; City Name; Postal Code; SPAIN; AIR MAIL.

Portugal: Mail should be addressed as follows: RAILTON, Annie; Posta Restante; Post Office Street Address; City Name; Postal Code; PORTUGAL; AIR MAIL.

Morocco: It is best to send mail to a major hotel or AmEx office instead. If you want to try, mail should be addressed as follows: <u>DOUB</u>, Kelsey; Poste Restante; Post Office Address; City Name; MOROCCO; AIR MAIL.

American Express: AmEx's travel offices throughout Iberia and Morocco will act as a mail service for cardholders if you contact them in advance. Under this free **Client Letter Service,** they will hold mail for up to 30 days and forward upon request. Address the letter in the same way shown above. Some offices will offer these services to non-cardholders (especially those who have purchased AmEx Travelers Cheques), but you must call ahead to make sure. *Let's Go* lists AmEx office locations for most large cities. A complete list is available free from AmEx (tel. 800-528-4800).

If regular airmail is too slow, **Federal Express** (U.S. tel. for international operator 800-247-4747; Spain 900-100-871; Portugal 91-3299900; Morocco 212-2-54-21-33) can get a letter from New York to Madrid in two days for a whopping US$50; rates among non-U.S. locations are similarly expensive (London to Madrid, for example, costs upwards of US$45). For a cheaper alternative, try **DHL** (U.S. tel for international operator 800-225-5345; Spain 902-12-24-24; Portugal 1-810-0080; Morocco 2-972020), which can get a document from New York to Madrid in one to two days for US$38.10. By **U.S. Express Mail,** a letter from New York would arrive within four days and would cost US$19.

Surface mail is by far the cheapest and slowest way to send mail. It takes one to three months to cross the Atlantic and two to four to cross the Pacific—appropriate for sending large quantities of items you won't need to see for a while. When ordering books and materials from abroad, always include one or two **international Reply Coupons (IRCs)**—a way of providing the postage to cover delivery. IRCs should be available from your local post office and those abroad (US$1.05).

TELEPHONES

CALLING SPAIN, PORTUGAL, AND MOROCCO FROM HOME

Let's Go lists the city **telephone code** under **Practical Information** in Portugal and Morocco. The bracketed 0 for Portugal and Morocco codes is necessary **only if you are calling from a different area code within the same country.** If you are calling from another country, you will not need to dial the parenthesized number. For example, we have listed the telephone code for Lisbon as (0)1. To reach Lisbon from elsewhere in Portugal, dial 01, then the number. To reach Lisbon from another country, dial 1, then the number. Spain no longer has city or area codes.

To place a direct international call, dial:

1. The international access code of your home country. **International access codes** include: Australia 0011; Ireland 00; New Zealand 00; South Africa 09; U.K. 00; U.S. 011. Country and city codes are sometimes listed with a zero in front (e.g., 033), but after dialing the international access code, drop successive zeros (e.g., with an access code of 011, dial 011 33).
2. The **country code:** Spain 034, Portugal 351, Morocco 212.
3. For Portugal or Morocco, the phone code (see the city's **Practical Information** section).
4. The local number.

CALLING FROM SPAIN, PORTUGAL, OR MOROCCO

For information about telephones abroad, see the **Essentials** sections of **Spain** (p. 68), **Portugal** (p. 538), or **Morocco** (p. 661). Most useful communication information (including **international access codes, calling card numbers, country codes, operator** and **directory assistance,** and **emergency numbers**) is also listed on the inside back cover of this book.

Wherever possible, use a **calling card** (see below) for international phone calls, as the long-distance rates for national phone services are often exorbitant. You can usually make direct international calls from pay phones, but if you aren't using a calling card you may need to drop your coins as quickly as your words. Where available, prepaid phone cards and occasionally major credit cards can be used for direct international calls, but they are still less cost-efficient. Look for pay phones in public areas, especially train stations, as private pay phones are often more expensive. Although incredibly convenient, in-room hotel calls invariably include an arbitrary and sky-high surcharge (as much as US$10).

If you do **dial direct,** you must first insert the appropriate amount of money or a prepaid card, then dial the international access code (Spain 07, Portugal and Morocco 00), then the country code and number. **Country codes** include: Australia 61; Ireland 353; New Zealand 64; South Africa 27; U.K. 44; U.S. and Canada 1.

The expensive alternative to dialing direct or using a calling card is using an international operator to place a **collect call.** An English-speaking operator from your home nation can be reached by dialing the appropriate service provider listed above; they will typically place a collect call even if you don't have one of their phone cards.

CALLING CARDS

Setting up a calling card account is probably your best and cheapest bet for making calls from overseas. Calls are billed either collect or to your account. **MCI WorldPhone** also provides access to MCI's Traveler's Assist, which gives legal and medical advice, exchange rate information, and translation services. Other phone companies provide similar services to travelers. **To obtain a calling card** from your national telecommunications service before you leave home, contact the appropriate company below.

USA: AT&T (tel. 888-288-4685); **Sprint** (tel. 800-877-4646); or **MCI** (tel. 800-444-4141; from abroad dial each company's access number for the country).

Canada: Bell Canada **Canada Direct** (tel. 800–565-4708).

U.K.: British Telecom **BT Direct** (tel. (0800) 34 51 44).

Ireland: Telecom Éireann **Ireland Direct** (tel. 800 250 250).

Australia: Telstra **Australia Direct** (tel. 13 22 00).

New Zealand: Telecom New Zealand (tel. (0800) 000 000).

South Africa: Telkom South Africa (tel. 09 03).

EMAIL AND INTERNET

Email is an attractive communication option and increasingly easy to access in Spain, Portugal, and Morocco. Those with a student account through their university or an AOL account may not be able to access it from overseas. Instead, try setting up an account through a free, web-based email provider like **Hotmail** (www.hotmail.com), **RocketMail** (www.rocketmail.com), or **Yahoo! Mail** (www.yahoo.com). Many free providers are funded by advertising and some may require subscribers to fill out a questionnaire. Almost every internet search engine has an affiliated free email service.

GETTING THERE AND AROUND

For country-specific information on traveling, traveling organizations, and travel discounts, see the **Getting There and Around** sections for **Spain** (p. 64), **Portugal** (p. 535), and **Morocco** (p. 657). Much of the following general information refers to planning your trip to and from these countries and for general European travel.

Fares on all modes of transportation are either "single" (one-way) or "return" (roundtrip). "Period returns" require you to return within a specific number of days; "day return" means you must return on the same day. Unless stated otherwise *Let's Go* always lists single fares. Round-trip fares on trains and buses are generally 75% above the one-way fares.

BY PLANE

When it comes to airfare, a little effort can save you a bundle. If your plans are flexible enough to deal with the restrictions, courier fares are the cheapest. Tickets bought from consolidators and standby seating are also good deals, but last-minute specials, airfare wars, and charter flights often beat these fares. The key is to hunt around, to be flexible, and to persistently ask about discounts. Students, seniors, and those under 26 should never pay full price for a ticket.

Airfares to Spain, Portugal, and Morocco peak between mid-June and early September, and holidays are also expensive periods in which to travel. Midweek (M-Th morning) round-trip flights run US$40-50 cheaper than weekend flights, but the latter are generally less crowded and more likely to permit frequent-flier upgrades. Return-date flexibility is usually not an option for the budget traveler; traveling with an "open return" ticket can be pricier than fixing a return date when buying the ticket and paying later to change it.

Round-trip flights are by far the cheapest; "open-jaw" (arriving in and departing from different cities) and round-the-world, or RTW, flights are pricier but reasonable alternatives. Patching one-way flights together is the least economical way to travel. Flights between capital cities or regional hubs will offer the most competitive fares.

BUDGET AND STUDENT TRAVEL AGENCIES

A knowledgeable agent specializing in flights to the region can make your life easy and help you save, too, but agents may not spend the time to find you the lowest possible fare—they get paid on commission. Students and under-26ers holding **ISIC and IYTC cards** (see **Identification,** p. 12), respectively, qualify for big discounts from student travel agencies. Most flights from budget agencies are on major airlines, but in peak season some may sell seats on less reliable chartered aircraft.

Campus/usit Youth and Student Travel, 52 Grosvenor Gardens, **London** SW1W 0AG (tel. (0870) 240 1010); www.usitcampus.co.uk). Other offices include: 19-21 Aston Quay, O'Connell Bridge, **Dublin** 2 (tel. (01) 677 8117; fax 679 8833); New York Student Center, 895 Amsterdam Ave., **New York,** NY, 10025 (tel. (212) 663-5435; email usitny@aol.com).

Council Travel (www.counciltravel.com). U.S. offices include: Emory Village, 1561 N. Decatur Rd., **Atlanta,** GA 30307 (tel. (404) 377-9997); 273 Newbury St., **Boston,** MA 02116 (tel. (617) 266-1926); 1160 N. State St., **Chicago,** IL 60610 (tel. (312) 951-0585); 10904 Lindbrook Dr., **Los Angeles,** CA 90024 (tel. (310) 208-3551); 205 E. 42nd St., **New York,** NY 10017 (tel. (212) 822-2700); 530 Bush St., **San Francisco,** CA 94108 (tel. (415) 421-3473); 1314 NE 43rd St. #210, **Seattle,** WA 98105 (tel. (206) 632-2448); 3300 M St. NW, **Washington, D.C.** 20007 (tel. (202) 337-6464). **For U.S. cities not listed,** call 800-2-COUNCIL (226-8624). Also 28A Poland St., **London,** W1V 3DB (tel. (0171) 287 3337), **Paris** (tel. (01) 44 41 89 89), and **Munich** (tel. (089) 39 50 22).

CTS Travel, 44 Goodge St., **London** W1 (tel. (0171) 636 0031; fax 637 5328; email ctsinfo@ctstravel.com.uk).

STA Travel, 6560 Scottsdale Rd. #F100, Scottsdale, AZ 85253 (tel. 800-777-0112 fax (602) 922-0793; www.sta-travel.com). A student and youth travel organization with over 150 offices worldwide. U.S. offices include: 297 Newbury Street, **Boston,** MA 02115 (tel. (617) 266-6014); 429 S. Dearborn St., **Chicago,** IL 60605 (tel. (312) 786-9050); 7202 Melrose Ave., **Los Angeles,** CA 90046 (tel. (323) 934-8722); 10 Downing St., **New York,** NY 10014 (tel. (212) 627-3111); 4341 University Way NE, **Seattle,** WA 98105 (tel. (206) 633-5000); 2401 Pennsylvania Ave., Ste. G, **Washington, D.C.** 20037 (tel. (202) 887-0912); 51 Grant Ave., **San Francisco,** CA 94108 (tel. (415) 391-8407). In the U.K., 6 Wrights Ln., **London** W8 6TA (tel. (0171) 938 4711). In New Zealand, 10 High St., **Auckland** (tel. (09) 309 0458). In Australia, 222 Faraday St., **Melbourne** VIC 3053 (tel. (03) 9349 2411).

ESSENTIALS

Travel CUTS (Canadian Universities Travel Services Limited), 187 College St., Toronto, Ont. M5T 1P7 (tel. (416) 979-2406; fax 979-8167; www.travelcuts.com). 40 offices across Canada. Also in the U.K., 295-A Regent St., **London** W1R 7YA (tel. (0171) 255 1944).

Wasteels, Victoria Station, London, U.K. SW1V 1JT (tel. (0171) 834 7066; fax 630 7628; www.wasteels.dk/uk). A huge chain in Europe, with 203 locations. Sells Wasteels BIJ tickets, which are discounted (30-45% off regular fare) 2nd-class international train tickets with unlimited stopovers (must be under 26); sold only in Europe.

Other organizations that specialize in finding cheap fares include:

Cheap Tickets (tel. 800–377-1000) flies worldwide to and from the U.S.

Travel Avenue (tel. 800–333–3335) rebates commercial fares to or from the U.S. and offers low fares for flights anywhere in the world. They also offer package deals, which include car rental and hotel reservations, to many destinations.

COMMERCIAL AIRLINES

The commercial airlines' lowest regular offer is the **APEX** (Advance Purchase Excursion) fare, which provides confirmed reservations and allows "open-jaw" tickets. Generally, reservations must be made 7 to 21 days in advance, with 7- to 14-day minimum and up to 90-day maximum-stay limits, and hefty cancellation and change penalties (fees rise in summer). Book peak-season APEX fares early, since by May you will have a hard time getting the departure date you want. Although APEX fares are probably not the cheapest possible fares, they will give you a sense of the average commercial price, from which to measure other bargains. Specials advertised in newspapers may be cheaper but have more restrictions and fewer available seats.

OTHER CHEAP ALTERNATIVES

AIR COURIER FLIGHTS. Couriers help transport cargo on international flights by guaranteeing delivery of the baggage claim slips from the company to a representative overseas. Generally, couriers must travel light (carry-ons only) and deal with complex restrictions on their flight. Most flights are round-trip only with short fixed-length stays (usually one week) and a limit of a single ticket per issue. Most of these flights also operate only out of the biggest cities, like New York. Generally, you must be over 21 (in some cases 18), have a valid passport, and procure your own visa, if necessary. Groups such as the **Air Courier Association** (tel. 800-282-1202; www.aircourier.org) and the **International Association of Air Travel Couriers,** 220 South Dixie Hwy., P.O. Box 1349, Lake Worth, FL 33460 (tel. (561) 582-8320; email iaatc@courier.org; www.courier.org) provide their members with lists of opportunities and courier brokers worldwide for an annual fee. For more information, consult *Air Courier Bargains* by Kelly Monaghan (The Intrepid Traveler, US$15) or the *Courier Air Travel Handbook* by Mark Field (Perpetual Press, US$10).

CHARTER FLIGHTS. Charters are flights a tour operator contracts with an airline to fly extra loads of passengers during peak season. Charters can sometimes be cheaper than flights on scheduled airlines, some operate nonstop, and restrictions on minimum advance-purchase and minimum stay are more lenient. However, charters fly less frequently than major airlines, make refunds particularly difficult, and are almost always fully booked. Schedules and itineraries may also change or be cancelled at the last moment (as late as 48 hours before the trip, and without a full refund), and check-in, boarding, and baggage claim are often much slower. As always, pay with a credit card if you can, and consider traveler's insurance against trip interruption. **Discount clubs** and **fare brokers** offer members savings on last-minute charter and tour deals. Study the contracts closely; you don't want to end up with an unwanted layover. **Travelers Advantage,** Stamford, CT (tel. 800-548-1116; www.travelersadvantage.com; US$60 annual fee includes discounts, newsletters, and flight directories), specializes in European travel and tour packages.

STANDBY FLIGHTS. To travel standby, you will need considerable flexibility in the dates and cities of your arrival and departure. Companies that specialize in standby flights don't sell tickets but rather the promise that you will get to your destination (or near your destination) within a certain window of time (anywhere from 1-5 days). You may only receive a monetary refund if all available flights which depart within your date-range from the specified region are full, but future travel credit is always available. Carefully read agreements with any company offering standby flights, as tricky fine print can leave you in the lurch. To check on a company's service record, call the Better Business Bureau of New York City (tel. (212) 533-6200). It is difficult to receive refunds, and clients' vouchers will not be honored when an airline fails to receive payment in time.

TICKET CONSOLIDATORS. **Ticket consolidators,** or **"bucket shops,"** buy unsold tickets in bulk from airlines and sell them at discounted rates. The best place to look is the Sunday travel section of any major newspaper, where many shops place tiny ads. Call quickly, as availability is typically extremely limited. Not all bucket shops are reliable establishments; insist on a receipt with full details of restrictions, refunds, and tickets, and pay by credit card. For more info, check the website **Consolidators FAQ** (www.travel-library.com/air-travel/consolidators.html) or the book *Consolidators: Air Travel's Bargain Basement,* by Kelly Monaghan (Intrepid Traveler, US$8).

FLYING AROUND EUROPE

Flying across Europe on regularly scheduled flights can devour your budget. U.S. citizens can also purchase **Eurair** passes (US$99 each, airport taxes not included, reservations recommended) to travel between 50 European cities; for information call 888-387-2479 (fax (512) 404-1291; www.eurair.com). Student travel agencies sell cheap tickets, and budget fares are frequently available in the spring and summer on high-traffic routes between northern Europe and resort areas in Spain. Consult budget travel agents and local newspapers. The **Air Travel Advisory Bureau** in London (tel. (0171) 636 5000; www.atab.co.uk) can also point the way to discount flights. See individual country **Getting Around** sections for more information.

FURTHER READING

Worldwide Guide to Cheap Airfare, Michael McColl. (Insider Pub., US$15).

Discount Airfares: The Insider's Guide, George Hobart. (Priceless Pub., US$14).

The Official Airline Guide, an expensive tome available at many libraries, has flight schedules, fares, and reservation numbers.

Travelocity (www.travelocity.com). A searchable online database of published airfares. Online reservations.

TravelHUB (www.travelhub.com). A directory of travel agents that includes a searchable database of fares from over 500 consolidators.

BY TRAIN

Spanish and Portuguese trains are generally comfortable, convenient, and reasonably swift. Second-class travel is pleasant, and compartments, which seat two to six, are excellent places to meet fellow travelers. Trains, however, are not always safe; lock your compartment door and keep your valuables on your person. For long trips make sure you are on the correct car, as trains sometimes split at crossroads. Towns listed in parentheses about European train schedules require a train switch at the town listed immediately before the parenthesis.

Even with a railpass, you are not guaranteed a seat on a train unless you make a reservation (US$3-10); they are advisable during the busier holiday seasons, and often required on major lines. Also, while many high-speed or quality trains (such as InterCity) are included in a railpass, a supplement (US$10-25) is required to ride certain other trains, such as Spain's AVE and Talgo 200.

For overnight travel, a tight, open bunk called a **couchette** is an affordable luxury (about US$20). Both seat and couchette reservations can be made by your local travel agent or in person at the train station (reserve at least a few hours in advance for seats; at least a few days for couchettes).

> **JUST SAY NO.** If you are planning on traveling in just Spain and Portugal, do not buy a Eurailpass or Europass. Train travel in these countries is less expensive than the rest of Europe, where passes can save you from paying for expensive train fares. A Eurailpass/Europass only makes sense for those planning on traveling in other European countries as well.

RAILPASSES. Railpasses allow you to jump on any train in the specified zone, go wherever you want whenever you want, and change your plans at will for a set length of time. With your railpass you will receive a timetable for major routes and a map with details on possible ferry, steamer, bus, car rental, and hotel discounts. In practice, it's not so simple. You still must stand in line to pay for supplements, seat reservations, and couchette reservations, as well as to have your pass validated when you first use it. More importantly, railpasses don't always pay off. For ballpark estimates, consult the **DERTravel** or **RailEurope** railpass brochure for prices of point-to-point tickets. Add them up and compare with railpass prices. If you're under age 26, look into BIJ tickets (see **Rail tickets,** p. 35).

A **Eurailpass** remains perhaps the best option for non-EU travelers who plan on hitting major cities in several countries. Eurailpasses are valid in most of Western Europe (except for Britain), including Austria, Belgium, Denmark, Finland, France, Germany, Greece, Hungary, Italy, Luxembourg, Netherlands, Norway, Portugal, Republic of Ireland, Spain, Sweden, and Switzerland. These passes must be sold at uniform prices determined by the EU, so no particular travel agent is better than another as far as the pass itself is concerned. However, some agents tack on a $10 handling fee.

EURAIL PASSES	15 days	21 days	1 month	2 months	3 months
1st class Eurailpass	US$554	US$718	US$890	US$1260	US$1558
Eurail Saverpass	US$470	US$610	US$756	US$1072	US$1324
Eurail Youthpass: ages 12-25	US$388	US$499	US$623	US$882	US$1089

Eurail Saverpass: Unlimited first-class travel for those traveling in a group of 2-5.

Eurail Flexipasses: Limited first-class travel within a two-month period: 10 days (US$654), 15 days (US$862). These prices drop to $556 and $732, respectively, when you travel in a group of 2-5.

Youth Flexipasses: Second-class travel for those under 26: 10 days (US$458), 15 days (US$599). Children 4-11 pay half price, and children under 4 travel free.

Europasses: Combines France, Germany, Italy, Spain, and Switzerland in one plan. With a Europass you can travel in any of these five countries from 5-15 days within a window of 2 months. First-class adult prices begin at US$348 and increase by about US$42 for each extra day of travel. With purchase of a first-class ticket you can buy an identical ticket for your traveling partner for 40% off. Second-class youth tickets begin at US$233 and increase incrementally by about US$29 for each extra day of travel. Children between the ages of 4-11 travel for half the price of a first-class ticket. For a fee, you can add associate countries (Portugal, Austria/Hungary, Belgium/Luxembourg/Netherlands, Greece Plus (Greece and ADN/HML ferry between Italy and Greece)): $60 for 1 associated country; $100 for 2. For those traveling in groups of 2-5 individuals, the new

Saverpass offers first-class travel starting at US$296 per person. The Europass introduces planning complications; you must plan your routes so that they only make use of countries you've "purchased." If you cut through a country you haven't purchased you will receive a fine. You should plan your itinerary before buying a Europass. It will save you money if your travels are confined to between three and five adjacent Western European countries, or if you know that you want to go only to large cities. Europasses are not appropriate if you like to take lots of side trips—you'll waste rail days. If you're tempted to add lots of rail days and associate countries, consider the Eurailpass.

BUYING RAILPASSES. If you choose to buy a Eurorail pass or Europass, it is best to buy it before leaving. Only a few places in major European cities sell these passes (at a marked-up price). Eurailpasses are not refundable once validated; if your pass is completely unused and invalidated and you have the original purchase documents, you can get an 85% refund from the place of purchase. You can get a replacement for a lost pass only if you have purchased insurance on it under the Pass Protection Plan (US$10). All Eurailpasses can be purchased from a travel agent, or from **Rail Europe Group,** 500 Mamaroneck Ave., Harrison, NY 10528 (in the U.S. tel. 888-382-7245; fax 800-432-1329; in Canada tel. 800-361-7245; fax 905-602-4198; www.raileurope.com), which also sells point-to-point tickets. They offer special rates for groups of ten or more travelling together.

INTERRAIL PASSES. For EU citizens, there are **InterRail Passes;** six months' residence in Europe makes you eligible. The **Under 26 InterRail Card** (UK£159-259) allows either 14 days or one month of unlimited travel within one, two, three or all of the seven zones into which InterRail divides Europe; the cost is determined by the number of zones the pass covers. If you are from a European country and you buy a ticket including your zone, you only have to pay 50% fare for the tickets inside your own country. For information and ticket sales in Europe, contact **Student Travel Center,** 1st Fl. 24 Rupert St., London, W1V7FN (tel. (020) 74 37 81 01; fax 77 34 38 36; www.student-travel-centre.com). Tickets are also available from travel agents or main train stations throughout Europe.

In addition to simple railpasses, many countries (and Europass and Eurail) offer **rail-and-drive passes,** which combine car rental with rail travel—a good option for travelers who wish both to visit cities accessible by rail and make side trips into the surrounding areas. Several national and regional passes offer companion fares, allowing two adults traveling together to save about 50% on the second of two passes. Some of these passes can be bought only in Europe, some only outside of Europe, and for some it doesn't matter; check with a railpass agent or with national tourist offices. See the respective national **Getting There and Around** sections for more details.

DISCOUNTED RAIL TICKETS. For travelers under 26, **BIJ** tickets (Billets Internationals de Jeunesse) are a great alternative to railpasses. Available for international trips within Europe as well as most ferry services, they knock 20-40% off regular second-class fares. Tickets are good for 60 days after purchase and allow a number of stopovers along the normal direct route of the train journey and must be bought in Europe. Tickets are sold under the names **Route 26, Eurotrain,** and **Wasteels.** They are available from European travel agents, at Wasteels or Eurotrain offices (usually in or near train stations), or directly at the ticket counter in some nations. Contact Wasteels in Victoria Station, adjacent to Platform 2, London SW1V 1 JT (tel. (020) 78 34 70 66; fax 630 76 28).

FURTHER READING
European Railway Server: mercurio.iet.unipi.it/home.html

On the Rails Around Europe, Melissa Shales. Passport Books (US$19).

Traveling Europe's Trains, Jay Brunhouse. Pelican Publishing (US$16).

Europe By Eurail 1999, Laverne Ferguson. Globe Pequot (US$16).

Eurail and Train Travel Guide to Europe, Houghton Mifflin (US$15).

BY BUS

Though European trains and railpasses are extremely popular, the bus network of Portugal is more extensive, efficient, and often more comfortable. In Spain, the bus and train systems are on generally on par, with the exception of the northwest, where buses are definitely the best alternative.

Eurolines, 4 Cardiff Rd., Luton, bedfordshire L41 1pp (U.K. tel. (0990) 14 32 19; fax (01582) 40 06 94; 54 Grosvenor Gardens, London SWIV 1BS (tel. 020) 79 50 16 61; fax 79 50 16 62; email welcome@eurolines.uk.com; www.eurolines.co.uk), is Europe's largest operator of Europe-wide coach services. A Eurolines Pass offers unlimited 30-day (under 26 and over 60 UK£199; 26-60 UK £229) or 60-day (under 26 and over 60 UK£249, 26-60 UK£279) travel between 30 major tourist destinations. In the low season (Oct. to mid-June) prices are UK£30-50 less. Eurolines also offers **Euro Explorers,** seven complete travel loops throughout Europe with set fares and itineraries.

BY CAR

Cars offer speed, freedom, access to the countryside, and an escape from the town-to-town mentality of trains. Unfortunately, they also insulate you from the *esprit de corps* of rail traveling. Although a single traveler won't save by renting a car, four usually will. If you can't decide between train and car travel, you may benefit from a combination of the two; Rail Europe and other railpass vendors offer rail-and-drive packages for both individual countries and all of Europe.

Before setting off, know the laws of the countries in which you'll be driving. The **Association for Safe International Road Travel (ASIRT)** can provide more specific information about road conditions. It is located at 5413 West Cedar Lane #103C, Bethesda, MD 20814 (tel. (301) 983-5252; fax 983-3663; email asirt@erols.com; www.asirt.org). Western Europeans use unleaded gas almost exclusively.

INTERNATIONAL DRIVING PERMIT (IDP). If you plan to drive a car while in the region, you should have an International Driving Permit (IDP), though Spain, Portugal, and Morocco allow travelers to drive with a valid American or Canadian license for a few months. It may be a good idea to get an IDP anyway, in case you're in a situation (e.g. an accident or being stranded in a smaller town) where the police do not speak English; information on the IDP is printed in ten languages, including Spanish, French, Portuguese, and Arabic.

Your IDP, valid for one year, must be issued in your own country before you depart; AAA affiliates cannot issue IDPs valid in their own country. To get an IDP you must be at least 18 years old, have a valid driver's license, two passport pictures, and another form of identification. When on the road you will always be asked to present your driver's license with the IDP.

Australia: Contact your local Royal Automobile Club (RAC) or the National Royal Motorist Association (NRMA) if in NSW or the ACT (tel. (08) 9421 4298; www.rac.com.au/travel). Permits AUS$15.

Canada: Contact any Canadian Automobile Association (CAA) branch office in Canada, or write to CAA, 1145 Hunt Club Rd., Suite 200, K1V 0Y3 Canada. (tel. 613-247-0117; fax 247-0118; www.caa.ca/CAAInternet/travelservices/internationaldocumentation/idptravel.htm). Permits CDN$10.

Ireland: Contact the nearest Automobile Association (AA) office or write to the U.K. address given below. Permits IR£4. The Irish Automobile Association (tel. (01) 677 94 81) is on 23 Suffolk St., Rockhill, Blackrock, Co. Dublin. Also honors foreign automobile memberships (24hr. breakdown service tel. (800) 66 77 88; toll-free in Ireland).

New Zealand: Contact your local Automobile Association (AA) or their main office at Auckland Central, 99 Albert St. (tel. (9) 377 4660; fax 302 2037; www.nzaa.co.nz.). Permits NZ$8.

South Africa: Contact your local Automobile Association of South Africa office or the head office at P.O. Box 596, 2000 Johannesburg (tel. (11) 799 10 00; fax 799 10 10). Permits SAR28.50.

U.K.: Visit your local A.A. Shop, contact the **A.A. Headquarters** (tel. (0990) 448866), or write to: The Automobile Association, International Documents, Fanum House, Erskine, Renfrewshire PA8 6BW. To find the location nearest you that issues the IDP, call (0990) 50 06 00. More info available at www.theaa.co.uk/motoring/idp.asp. Permits £4.

U.S.: Visit any American Automobile Association (AAA) office or write to AAA Florida, Travel Related Services, 1000 AAA Drive (mail stop 100), Heathrow, FL 32746 (tel. (407)-444-7000; fax 444-7380). Sells the International Driving Permit (IDP). You do not have to be a member of AAA to receive an (IDP/IADP). Permits US$10.

CAR INSURANCE. Most gold or platinum credit cards cover standard insurance. If you rent, lease, or borrow a car, you will need a **green card,** or **International Insurance Certificate,** to prove that you have liability insurance. Obtain it through the car rental agency; most include coverage in their prices. If you lease a car, you can obtain a green card from the dealer. Some travel agents offer the card; it may also be available at border crossings. Verify whether your auto insurance applies abroad; even if it does, you will still need a green card to certify this to foreign officials. If you have a collision abroad, the accident will show up on your domestic records if you report it to your insurance company. Rental agencies may require you to purchase theft insurance in countries that they consider to have a high risk of auto theft. Ask your rental agency about Spain, Portugal, or Morocco.

RENTALS. You can **rent** a car from a U.S.-based firm (Alamo, Avis, Budget, or Hertz) with European offices, from a European-based company with local representatives (Europcar), or from a tour operator (Auto Europe, Europe By Car, and Kemwel Holiday Autos) which will arrange a rental for you from a European company at its own rates. Multinationals offer greater flexibility, but tour operators often strike better deals. Rentals vary by company, season, and pick-up point. Most available cars will have standard transmission—cars with automatic transmission are difficult to find and much more expensive. Reserve well before leaving for the region and pay in advance if at all possible. It is always significantly less expensive to reserve a car from the U.S. than from Spain, Portugal, or Morocco. Always check if prices quoted include tax, unlimited mileage, and collision insurance; some credit card companies will cover this automatically. Ask about discounts and check the terms of insurance, particularly the size of the deductible. Non-Europeans should check with their national motoring organization (like AAA or CAA) for international coverage. Ask your airline about special fly-and-drive packages; you may get up to a week of free or discounted rental. Minimum age in Spain and Portugal is usually 25 with the larger agencies (Hertz, Avis) and 21 at smaller, local businesses. Minimum age in Morocco is almost always 21. At most agencies, all that's needed to rent a car is a U.S. license and proof that you've had it for a year, although in Spain, you may need an international driver's license.

BY BICYCLE

Today, biking is one of the key elements of the classic budget Eurovoyage. With the proliferation of mountain bikes, you can do some serious natural sightseeing.

If you are nervous about striking out on your own, **Blue Marble Travel** (in Canada tel. (519) 624-2494; in Paris tel. (01) 42 36 02 34; in U.S. tel. 800-258-8689 or (973) 326-9533; www.bluemarble.org) offers bike tours designed for adults aged 20 to 50. Pedal with or without your 10 to 15 companions through Portugal and Spain. Full-time graduate and professional students may get discounts, and "stand-by" fares may be obtained in Europe through the Paris office.

Many airlines will count your bike as your second piece of luggage, and a few charge extra. The additional fee runs about US$60-110 each way. Bikes must be packed in a cardboard box with the pedals and front wheel detached; airlines sell bike boxes at the airport (US$10). Most ferries let you take your bike for free or for a nominal fee. You can always ship your bike on trains, though the cost varies.

Riding a bike with a frame pack strapped on it or your back is about as safe as pedaling blindfolded over a sheet of ice; panniers are essential. The first thing to buy, however, is a suitable **bike helmet** (US$25-50). U-shaped **Citadel** or **Kryptonite locks** are expensive (starting at US$30), but the companies insure their locks against theft of your bike for one to two years. For mail order equipment, **Bike Nashbar**, 4111 Simon Rd., Youngstown, OH 44512 (tel. 800-627-4227; www.nashbar.com), beats all competitors' offers and ships anywhere in the U.S. or Canada.

Renting a bike beats bringing your own if your touring will be confined to one or two regions. *Let's Go* lists bike rental shops for most larger cities and towns. Some youth hostels rent bicycles for low prices. Some train stations rent bikes and often allow you to drop them off elsewhere; check train stations throughout the region for similar deals.

BY MOPED AND MOTORCYCLE

Motorized bikes don't use much gas, can be put on trains and ferries, and are a good compromise between the high cost of car travel and the limited range of bicycles. However, they're uncomfortable for long distances, dangerous in the rain, and unpredictable on rough roads and gravel. Always wear a helmet, and never ride with a backpack. If you've never been on a moped, the windy roads of the Pyrenees and the congested streets of Madrid are not the place to start.

Before renting, ask if the quoted price includes tax and insurance, or you may be hit with an unexpected additional fee. Avoid handing your passport over as a deposit; if you have an accident or mechanical failure you may not get it back until you cover all repairs. Pay ahead of time instead.

BY THUMB

 HITCHHIKERS BEWARE. *Let's Go* strongly urges you to consider seriously the risks before you choose to hitch. We do not recommend hitching as a safe means of transportation, and none of the information presented here is intended to do so. Women traveling alone should not hitch.

No one should hitch without careful consideration of the risks involved. Not everyone can be an airplane pilot, but any bozo can drive a car. Hitching means entrusting your life to a random person who happens to stop beside you on the road and risking theft, assault, sexual harassment, and unsafe driving. In spite of this, there are gains to hitching. Favorable hitching experiences allow you to meet local people and get where you're going, especially in areas where public transportation is sparse or unreliable. The choice, however, remains yours.

Where one stands is vital. Experienced hitchers pick a spot outside of built-up areas, where drivers can stop, return to the road without causing an accident, and have time to look over potential passengers as they approach. Hitching (or even standing) on super-highways is usually illegal: one may only thumb at rest stops or at the entrance ramps to highways. Finally, success will depend on what one looks like. Successful hitchers travel light and stack their belongings in a compact but visible cluster. Most Europeans signal with an open hand, rather than a thumb; many write their destination on a sign in large, bold letters and draw a smiley-face under it. Drivers prefer hitchers who are neat and wholesome. No one stops for anyone wearing sunglasses.

Safety issues are always imperative, even for those who are not hitching alone. Safety-minded hitchers avoid getting in the back of a two-door car and never let go of their backpacks. They will not get into a car that they can't get out of again in a hurry. If they ever feel threatened, they insist on being let off, regardless of where they are. Acting as if they are going to open the car door or vomit on the upholstery will usually get a driver to stop. Hitchhiking at night can be particularly dangerous; experienced hitchers stand in well-lit places, and expect drivers to be leery of nocturnal thumbers (or open-handers).

SPECIFIC CONCERNS

WOMEN TRAVELERS

Women exploring on their own inevitably face some additional safety concerns, but it's easy to be adventurous without taking undue risks. In **Spain** men may be freer with unwanted comments and gestures than you are accustomed to. In **Portugal,** women travelers are treated with respect (blondes, an anomaly among Portuguese, may be the occasional exception).

If you are concerned, you might consider staying in hostels which offer single rooms that lock from the inside or in religious organizations that offer rooms for women only. Communal showers in some hostels are safer than others; check them before settling in. Stick to centrally located accommodations and avoid solitary late-night treks or metro rides.

The less you look like a tourist, the better off you'll be. Dress conservatively, especially in rural areas. Shorts and t-shirts, even if unrevealing by Western standards, may identify you as a foreigner and should be avoided. Trying to fit in can be effective, but dressing to the style of an obviously different culture may cause you to be ill at ease and a conspicuous target. Wearing a conspicuous **wedding band** may help prevent unwanted overtures. Some travelers report that carrying pictures of a "husband" or "children" is extremely useful to help document marriage status. Even a mention of a husband waiting back at the hotel may be enough in some places to discount your potentially vulnerable, unattached appearance.

In cities, you may be harassed no matter how you're dressed. Your best answer to verbal harassment is no answer at all; feigned deafness, sitting motionless and staring straight ahead at nothing in particular will do a world of good that reactions usually don't achieve. The extremely persistent can sometimes be dissuaded by a firm, loud, and very public "Go away!"

Don't hesitate to seek out a police officer or a passerby if you are being harassed. *Let's Go: Spain & Portugal* lists emergency numbers (including rape crisis lines) in the Practical Information listings of most cities. Memorize the emergency numbers in the places you visit. Carry a **whistle** or an airhorn on your keychain, and don't hesitate to use it in an emergency. An **IMPACT Model Mugging** self-defense course will not only prepare you for a potential attack, but will also raise your level of awareness of your surroundings as well as your confidence (see **Self Defense,** p. 20). Women also face some specific health concerns when traveling (see **Women's Health,** p. 23).

Although all the above holds, **Morocco** is a special case. Women are often veiled and even secluded in their own homes. Women travelling alone should be especially cautious. Visitors will feel safer and more comfortable (and will avoid offending local sensibilities) by not wearing short skirts, sleeveless tops, and shorts; moreover, females should always wear bras. Women—particularly non-Moroccans—may be gawked at, commented upon, approached by hustlers, followed, and, while in a crowd, have their butts and breasts squeezed. Moroccan women may hiss at "indecently" clad female travelers. Again, the best response may be silence. Yelling "shuma"—meaning shame—will frequently embarrass harassers, especially in the presence of onlookers. If maltreatment persists, protest loudly and often, and look out for a policeman or other respectable figure. Strolling arm in arm with another woman, common in Europe and North Africa, can lessen the risk of harassment or violence; so can wearing a head scarf. Women should not enter local Moroccan **bars**; other women there are most likely prostitutes. Women in Morocco may also be refused a **room** at vacant hotels and hostels.

FURTHER READING

A Journey of One's Own: Uncommon Advice for the Independent Woman Traveler, Thalia Zepatos. Eighth Mountain Press (US$17).

Adventures in Good Company: The Complete Guide to Women's Tours and Outdoor Trips, Thalia Zepatos. Eighth Mountain Press (US$7).

Active Women Vacation Guide, Evelyn Kaye. Blue Panda Publications (US$18).

Travelers' Tales: Gutsy Women, Travel Tips and Wisdom for the Road, Marybeth Bond. Traveler's Tales (US$8).

TRAVELING ALONE

There are many benefits to traveling alone, among them greater independence and challenge. As a lone traveler, you have greater opportunity to interact with the residents of the region you're visiting. Without distraction, you can write a great travel log in the grand tradition of Mark Twain, John Steinbeck, and Charles Kuralt. Traveling alone can also be a great way to meet people. On the other hand, any solo traveler is a more vulnerable target of harassment and street theft. Lone travelers need to be well-organized and look confident at all times. Try not to stand out as a tourist, and be especially careful in deserted or very crowded areas. If questioned, never admit that you are traveling alone. Maintain regular contact with someone at home who knows your itinerary.

Connecting: Solo Traveler Network, P.O. Box 29088, 1996 W. Broadway, Vancouver, BC V6J 5C2, Canada (tel. (604) 737-7791; email info@cstn.org; www.cstn.org). Bi-monthly newsletter features going solo tips, single-friendly tips and travel companion ads. Annual directory lists holiday suppliers that avoid single supplement charges. Advice and lodging exchanges facilitated between members. Membership US$25-35.

Travel Companion Exchange, P.O. Box 833, Amityville, NY 11701 (tel. (516) 454-0880 or 800-392-1256; www.travelalone.com). Publishes the pamphlet *Foiling Pickpockets & Bag Snatchers* (US$4) and *Travel Companions,* a bi-monthly newsletter for single travelers seeking a travel partner (subscription US$48).

FURTHER READING

Traveling Solo, Eleanor Berman. Globe Pequot (US$17).

The Single Traveler Newsletter, P.O. Box 682, Ross, CA 94957 (tel. (415) 389-0227). 6 issues US$29.

OLDER TRAVELERS

Senior citizens are eligible for a wide range of discounts on transportation, museums, movies, theaters, concerts, restaurants, and accommodations. If you don't see a senior citizen price listed, ask, and you may be delightfully surprised. Agencies for senior group travel are growing in popularity. These are only a few:

ElderTreks, 597 Markham St., Toronto, ON, Canada, M6G 2L7 (tel. (800)-741-7956 or (416) 588-5000; fax 588-9839; email passages@inforamp.net; www.eldertreks.com).

Elderhostel, 75 Federal St., Boston, MA 02110-1941 (tel. (617) 426-7788 or (877) 426-8056; email registration@elderhostel.org; www.elderhostel.org). Programs at colleges, universities, and other learning centers in Spain, Portugal, and Morocco on varied subjects lasting 1-4 weeks. Must be 55 or over (spouse can be of any age).

The Mature Traveler, P.O. Box 50400, Reno, NV 89513 (tel. (775) 786-7419 or (800)-460-6676). Has soft-adventure tours for seniors. Subscription$30.

Walking the World, P.O. Box 1186, Fort Collins, CO 80522 (tel. (970) 498-0500; fax 498-9100; email walktworld@aol.com; www.walkingtheworld.com). Trips to Portugal.

FURTHER READING

No Problem! Worldwise Tips for Mature Adventurers, Janice Kenyon. Orca Book Publishers (US$16).

A Senior's Guide to Healthy Travel, Donald L. Sullivan. Career Press (US$15).

Unbelievably Good Deals and Great Adventures That You Absolutely Can't Get Unless You're Over 50, Joan Rattner Heilman. Contemporary Books (US$13).

BISEXUAL, GAY, AND LESBIAN TRAVELERS

Some consider the gay scene in **Spain** the most open in Europe; in the major cities (like Madrid, Barcelona, and Eivissa), people are characteristically tolerant. Other party cities such as Sitges have vibrant gay communities as well. Scour bookstores, bars, and kiosks for the bi-monthly magazine *Entiendes...?,* with articles in Spanish about gay issues and a comprehensive list of gay services, groups, activities, and, yes, personal ads. **Portugal** is more conservative. Gays and lesbians are generally accepted in Lisbon and, increasingly, in Porto, but are invisible elsewhere in the country. No law promotes anti-gay discrimination, but social traditionalism—particularly strident Catholicism—may foster prejudice. Nonetheless, Lisbon staged its first gay rights parade in 1995, manifesting a burgeoning collective gay identity. In **Morocco,** civil and Islamic law prohibit homosexuality.

Gay's the Word, 66 Marchmont St., London WC1N 1AB (tel. (0171) 278 7654; email gays.theword@virgin.net; www.gaystheword.co.uk). The largest gay and lesbian bookshop in the U.K. Mail-order service available. No catalogue of listings, but they will provide a list of titles on a given subject.

Giovanni's Room, 345 S. 12th St., Philadelphia, PA 19107 (tel. (215) 923-2960; fax 923-0813; email giophilp@netaxs.com). An international feminist, lesbian, and gay bookstore with mail-order service which carries the publications listed here.

International Gay and Lesbian Travel Association, 4331 N. Federal Hwy., Suite 304, Fort Lauderdale, FL 33308 (tel. (954) 776-2626 or (800)-448-8550; fax (954) 776-3303; email IGLTA@aol.com; www.iglta.com). An organization of over 1350 companies serving gay and lesbian travelers worldwide. Call for lists of travel agents, accommodations, and events.

International Lesbian and Gay Association (ILGA), 81 rue Marché-au-Charbon, B-1000 Brussels, Belgium (tel./fax 32 2502 24 71; email ilga@ilga.org; www.ilga.org). Not a travel service. Provides political info, such as homosexuality laws of countries.

FURTHER READING

Spartacus International Gay Guide. Bruno Gmunder Verlag (US$33).

Damron Men's Guide, Damron's Accommodations, and *The Women's Traveller.* Damron Travel Guides (US$14-19). For more information, call (415) 255-0404 or (800)-462-6654 or check their website (www.damron.com).

Ferrari Guides' Gay Travel A to Z, Ferrari Guides' Men's Travel in Your Pocket, Ferrari Guides' Women's Travel in Your Pocket, and *Ferrari Guides' Inn Places.* Ferrari Guides (US$14-16). For more information, call (602) 863-2408 or (800)-962-2912 or check their website (www.q-net.com).

The Gay Vacation Guide: The Best Trips and How to Plan Them, Mark Chesnut. Citadel Press (US$15).

TRAVELERS WITH DISABILITIES

Wheelchair accessibility varies widely in Iberia but is generally inferior to that in the United States. Access in Morocco is minimal. In Spain and Portugal, handicapped access is common in modern and big city museums. Check out www.geocities.com/Paris/1502 for general information on traveling for the disabled.

Rail is probably the most convenient form of travel for disabled travelers in Europe. Guide dog owners should inquire as to the specific quarantine policies of each destination country. At the very least, they will need to provide a certificate of immunization against rabies. Hertz, Avis, and National car rental agencies have hand-controlled vehicles at some locations.

The following organizations provide information that might be of assistance:

Mobility International USA (MIUSA), P.O. Box 10767, Eugene, OR 97440 (tel. (541) 343-1284 voice and TDD; fax 343-6812; email info@miusa.org; www.miusa.org). Sells *A World of Options: A Guide to International Educational Exchange, Community Service, and Travel for Persons with Disabilities* (US$35).

Moss Rehab Hospital Travel Information Service (tel. (215) 456-9600; www.mossresourcenet.org). A telephone and internet information resource center on international travel accessibility and other travel-related concerns for those with disabilities.

Society for the Advancement of Travel for the Handicapped (SATH), 347 Fifth Ave., #610, New York, NY 10016 (tel. (212) 447-1928; fax 725-8253; email sathtravel@aol.com; www.sath.org). Advocacy group publishing a quarterly color travel magazine *OPEN WORLD* (free for members or US$13 for nonmembers). Also publishes a wide range of information sheets on disability travel facilitation and accessible destinations. Annual membership US$45, students and seniors US$30.

The following organizations arrange tours or trips for disabled travelers:

Directions Unlimited, 720 N. Bedford Rd., Bedford Hills, NY 10507 (tel. (800)-533-5343; in NY (914) 241-1700; fax 241-0243; email cruisesusa@aol.com). Specializes in arranging individual and group vacations, tours, and cruises for the physically disabled. Group tours for blind travelers.

The Guided Tour Inc., 7900 Old York Rd., Suite 114B, Elkins Park, PA 19027-2339 (tel. (800)-783-5841 or (215) 782-1370; email gtour400@aol.com; www.guidedtour.com). Organizes travel programs for persons with developmental and physical challenges.

FURTHER READING

Resource Directory for the Disabled, Richard Neil Shrout. Facts on file (US$45).

Wheelchair Through Europe, Annie Mackin. Graphic Language Press ((760) 944-9594; email niteowl@cts.com) (US$13).

Global Access (www.geocities.com/Paris/1502/disabilitylinks.html) has links for disabled travelers in Spain and Portugal.

MINORITY TRAVELERS

Spanish people suffer from little interaction with other races. It shows in some expressions, like "Don't be a Moor," meaning mind your manners. Infrequent incidents are rarely violent or threatening, just a little awkward. They occur out of naiveté or ignorance. Don't be struck by a Spaniard's unabashed eagerness when meeting a foreigner who is not Caucasian. This reaction is not ethnic insensitivity but rather curiosity, as odd as it may seem. **Portugal** is comfortably anti-racist. Its ethnic composition reflects its rich colonial history (in Africa and the Americas), complementing a healthy indigenous mix. People of various ethnicities have little to fear, since post-Salazar Portugal is eager to liberalize. In **Morocco,** nationality invites harassment more than ethnicity. Asian and blond travelers, and those who flaunt their wealth or national identity, are common targets.

TRAVELERS WITH CHILDREN

Family vacations often require that you slow your pace, and always require that you plan ahead. When deciding where to stay, remember the special needs of young children; if you pick a hostel or *pensión*, call ahead and make sure it's child-friendly. Restaurants often have children's menus and discounts. Virtually all museums and tourist attractions also have a children's rate. Children under two generally fly for 10% of the adult airfare on international flights (this does not necessarily include a seat). International fares are usually discounted 25% for children from two to 11. Finding a private place for **breast feeding** is often a problem while traveling, so pack accordingly.

FURTHER READING

Backpacking with Babies and Small Children, Goldie Silverman. Wilderness Press (US$10).

Take Your Kids to Europe, Cynthia W. Harriman. Globe Pequot (US$17).

How to take Great Trips with Your Kids, Sanford and Jane Portnoy. Harvard Common Press (US $10).

Have Kid, Will Travel: 101 Survival Strategies for Vacationing With Babies and Young Children, Claire and Lucille Tristram. Andrews and McMeel (US$9).

Adventuring with Children: An Inspirational Guide to World Travel and the Outdoors, Nan Jeffrey. Avalon House Publishing ($15).

Trouble Free Travel with Children, Vicki Lansky. Book Peddlers (US$9).

DIETARY CONCERNS

Vegetarians may find cooking their new pastime after trekking through Spain, Portugal, and Morocco. Fresh and inexpensive produce is available at the many local markets; *Let's Go* lists locations and hours in nearly every town. At restaurants it is often quite difficult to get a vegetarian meal of any variety. Asking for two first courses (*primer platos*) may work; the main dish (*segundo plato*) invariably contains meat. When in doubt, order a cheese sandwich (*sandwich de queso*), french fries (*papas fritas*), or rice (*arroz*). *Let's Go* lists some exceptions, especially vegetarian-inclined restaurants in larger cities and tourist resorts.

If it's **kosher,** chances are it's difficult to find in Spain, Portugal, and Morocco. Nevertheless, travelers who wish to keep kosher should contact synagogues and other Jewish institutions in or near their destination for options. If you are strict in your observance, you may have to prepare your own food on the road. **The Jewish Travel Guide** lists synagogues, kosher restaurants, and Jewish institutions in over 80 countries. It is available from Vallentine-Mitchell Publishers, Newbury House 890-900, Eastern Ave., Newbury Park, Ilford, Essex, U.K. IG2 7HH (tel. (0181) 599 88 66; fax 599 09 84). It is available in the U.S. ($16) from ISBS, 5804 NE Hassallo St., Portland, OR 97213-3644 (tel. (800)-944-6190).

For a description of typical cuisine in Spain, Portugal, and Morocco, refer to the **Food** section in each country's introduction. Health-related concerns, such as **diabetes,** are dealt with in **Health**, page 21.

ALTERNATIVES TO TOURISM

STUDY

Spain is one of the most popular destinations in the world for study-abroad students. To find out more, contact U.S. university programs and youth organizations that set students up at Spanish universities and language centers for foreign students. Ask for the names of recent participants in the programs, and get in touch with them. Many of the programs cluster around Madrid and Sevilla. If you are fluent, enroll directly in a Spanish college (non-Spanish students have practically taken over Salamanca, for example). While Portugal is not as common a destination for study abroad, most universities in **Portugal** open their gates to foreign students, and foreigners can enter language and cultural studies programs at most of them. Study abroad is rare in **Morocco**, though it is somewhat common in Rabat.

Studying in **Spain** or **Portugal** requires a good deal of regulatory paperwork. Any student planning to stay longer than three months must obtain a visa from their national consulate. Those students studying only for the summer (i.e., for less than three months) need only a passport. Individual universities and programs have their own requirements, most of which involve a basic knowledge of Spanish and a minimum grade point average.

UNIVERSITIES

Most American undergraduates enroll in programs sponsored by U.S. universities. However, if your Spanish or Portuguese is already good, local universities can be much cheaper than an American university program, though it can be hard to receive academic credit. Schools that offer study abroad programs to foreigners are listed below.

American Institute for Foreign Study, College Division, 102 Greenwich Ave., Greenwich, CT 06830 (tel. (800)-727-2437 ext. 6084; www.aifs.com). Organizes programs for high school and college study in universities in Spain and Portugal. Summer, fall, spring, and year-long programs available. Scholarships available. Contact Dana Maggio with questions at dmaggio@aifs.com.

Central College Abroad, Office of International Education, 812 University, Pella, IA 50219 (tel. (800)-831-3629 or (515) 628-5284; fax 628-5316; email Study-Abroad@Central.edu; studyabroad.com/central/). Offers semester- and year-long study abroad programs in Spain and Portugal. US$25 application fee. Scholarships available. Applicants must be at least 18, have completed their freshman year of college, and have a minimum 2.5 GPA.

School for International Training, College Semester Abroad, Admissions, Kipling Rd., P.O. Box 676, Brattleboro, VT 05302 (tel. (800)-336-1616 or (802) 258-3267; fax 258-3500; www.worldlearning.org). Runs semester- and year-long programs in Spain and Portugal. Programs cost US$8200-10,300, all expenses included. Financial aid available and U.S. financial aid is transferable. Also runs the **Experiment in International Living,** Summer Programs (tel. (800)-345-2929; fax (802) 258-3428; email eil@worldlearning.org). Founded in 1932, it offers cross-cultural, educational homestays, community service, ecological adventure, and language training in Spain and Portugal. Programs are 3-5weeks long and run from US$1800-$5000. Positions as group leaders are available world-wide for college graduates with strong, experienced language skills for the host country and experience working with high school students.

Council on International Educational Exchange (CIEE), 205 East 42nd St., New York, NY 10017 (tel. (888)-COUNCIL (268-6245); fax (212) 822-2699; www.ciee.org) sponsors work, volunteer, academic, internship, and professional study abroad programs in Spain and Portugal.

International Association for the Exchange of Students for Technical Experience (IAESTE), 10400 Little Patuxent Pkwy. #250, Columbia, MD 21044-3510 (tel. (410) 997-3068; fax 997-5186; email iaste@aipt.org; www.aipt.org). Operates 8- to 12-week programs in Spain and Portugal for college students who have completed 2 years of study in a technical field. Non-refundable US$50 application fee; apply by Dec. 16 for summer placement.

LANGUAGE SCHOOLS

Programs are run by foreign universities, independent international or local organizations, and divisions of local universities. Programs generally cost anywhere from US$1000 a month.

Eurocentres, 101 N. Union St. #300, Alexandria, VA 22314 (tel. (800)-648-4809, (703) 684-1494 for consumer representative; fax 684-1495; www.eurocentres.com) or Eurocentres, Head Office, Seestrasse 247, CH-8038 Zurich, Switzerland (from abroad tel. 41 1 485 50 40; fax 481 61 24). Language programs and homestays in Spain and Portugal for approximately US$1132 a month. Programs run 2 weeks to a full academic year for beginners to advanced.

Language Immersion Institute, 75 South Manheim Blvd., The College at New Paltz, New Paltz, NY 12561 (tel. (914) 257-3500; fax 257-3569; email lii@newpaltz.edu; www.newpaltz.edu/lii). Provides language instruction at all levels in Arabic, French, Portuguese, and Spanish. Weekend courses offered at New Paltz and in New York City. They also conduct two-week summer courses and some overseas courses in Spain. Program fees are about US$275 for a weekend or US$650 per 2 weeks.

World Exchange, Ltd., White Birch Rd., Putnam Valley, NY 10579 (tel. (800)-444-3924 or (914) 526-2299; fax 528-9187; email info@worldexchange.org; www.worldex-change.org), is a reciprocal language learning program for those 20 years of age and over. 1-to 4-week language-based homestay programs are offered in Spain (up to 14 days, US$850; 15-28 days, US$1,150). Includes room and board, teaching materials, processing fees and organizational assistance. Opportunities to host visitors from same countries in some parts of the USA.

WORK

Obtaining a work permit in Spain is a complicated process. EU citizens, if they intend to stay for more than three months, must apply for a residence card (*tarjeta de residencia*) within 30 days of arrival. Application can be made at a regional police headquarters or a Foreigner's Registration Office, and you will need a contract of employment, three photos, and a passport. Non-EU citizens must first obtain a *visado especial* from the Spanish embassy in their country of residence, which requires a copy of the employment contract and a medical certificate. Portugal's regulations are similar, although both EU and non-EU citizens can obtain a work permit with a residence visa.

The most commonly available jobs continue to be in the areas of teaching (particularly English) and child care (especially *au pair* services, but also as private tutors). While jobs in those areas are generally available year-round (with September the best time to look for a teaching job), other, more tourist-specific jobs will often open up in the early summer. One favorite of seasoned work-travelers is "touting," which involves enticing tourists to enter a certain restaurant or club.

In **Spain,** the national employment service (*Oficinas de Empleo*) has a monopoly on the job-finding market, and is probably the best place to begin a search. Many seasoned travelers, however, go straight to a particular town's Yellow Pages (*Las Paginas Amarillas*) or even go door-to-door in the town in which they are staying. In **Portugal,** the English-language weekly newspaper *Anglo-Portuguese News* carries job advertisements. In **Morocco,** your best bet is to contact your national consulate for a list of schools with openings.

AU PAIR
Accord Cultural Exchange, 750 La Playa, San Francisco, CA 94121 (tel. (415) 386-6203); fax 386-0240; email leftbank@hotmail.com; www.cognitext.com/accord), offers Au pair jobs to people aged 18-29 in Spain. Au pairs work 5-6 hours a day, 30 hours a week, plus 2 evenings of babysitting. Light housekeeping and childcare in exchange for room and board plus US$250-400 per month salary. Program fees US$750 for the summer, US$1200 for the academic year. US$40 application fee.

interExchange, 161 Sixth Ave., New York, NY 10013 (tel. (212) 924-0446; fax 924-0575; email interex@earthlink.net) provides information on international work, au pair programs, and *au pair* positions in Spain and Portugal.

TEACHING ENGLISH
International Schools Services, Educational Staffing Program, P.O. Box 5910, Princeton, NJ 08543 (tel. (609) 452-0990; fax 452-2690; email edustaffing@iss.edu; www.iss.edu). Recruits teachers and administrators for American and English schools in Spain and Portugal. All instruction in English. Applicants must have a bachelor's degree and two years of relevant experience. Nonrefundable US$100 application fee. Publishes *The ISS Directory of Overseas Schools* (US$35).

Office of Overseas Schools, A/OS Room 245, SA-29, Dept. of State, Washington, D.C. 20522-2902 (tel. (703) 875-7800; fax 875-7979; email overseas.school@state.gov; state.gov/www/about_state/schools/). Keeps a list of schools abroad and agencies that arrange placement for Americans to teach abroad.

VOLUNTEER

Volunteer jobs are readily available almost everywhere. You may receive room and board in exchange for your labor. You can sometimes avoid the high application fees charged by the organizations that arrange placement by contacting the individual workcamps directly; check with the organizations.

Peace Corps, 1111 20th St. NW, Washington, D.C. 20526 (tel. (800)-424-8580; www.peacecorps.gov). Write for their "blue" brochure, which details application requirements. Opportunities in a variety of fields in developing nations including Morocco. Volunteers must be U.S. citizens, age 18 and over, and willing to make a 2-year commitment. A bachelor's degree is usually required.

Service Civil International Voluntary Service (SCI-VS), 814 NE 40th St., Seattle, WA 98105 (tel./fax (206) 545-6585; email sciivsusa@igc.apc.org). Arranges placement in workcamps in Spain and Portugal for those age 18 and over. Local organizations sponsor groups for physical or social work. Registration fees US$50-250, depending on the camp location.

Volunteers for Peace, 1034 Tiffany Rd., Belmont, VT 05730 (tel. (802) 259-2759; fax 259-2922; email vfp@vfp.org; www.vfp.org). A nonprofit organization that arranges speedy placement in 2-3 week workcamps in Morocco comprising 10-15 people. Most complete and up-to-date listings provided in the annual *International Workcamp Directory* (US$15). Registration fee US$195. Free newsletter.

OTHER RESOURCES

USEFUL PUBLICATIONS

Andalucía Magazine, published quarterly. Provides info on the history, culture, politics, and current events of Spain's southernmost province. Web edition www.andalucía.com/magazine.

The Broadsheet, monthly magazine aimed at English speakers in Madrid. Features current cultural and social events, as well as news. Web edition www.thebroadsheet.com.

Canarian Weekly, the first weekly news magazine of the Canary Islands. Free at over 500 locations. Web edition www.canarianweekly.com.

Focus Magazine, monthly online magazine about the Mediterranean world. Includes information on Morocco. www.focusmm.com.au/~focus.

Cities of Spain, David Gilmour. Concise and useful guide to Spain's major urban centers. Ivan R Dee., Inc. (US$23).

Contemporary Spain: A Handbook, Christopher Ross. Broad and informative discussion of Spanish politics, culture, society, and travel. Edward Arnold (US$19).

Eating and Drinking in Spanish: Reading Menus in Spanish-Speaking Countries, Andy Herbach and Michael Dillon. Extremely useful for anyone planning to eat a meal in Spain. Capra (US$7).

Simple Etiquette in Spain, Victoria McGuinness. Beginner's guide to Spanish customs and manners. Paul Norbury (US$7).

Morocco: the Traveller's Companion, Margaret and Robin Bidwell. Excellent introduction to travel in Morocco. I.B. Taurius & Co. (US$20).

Morocco: Sahara to the Sea, Mary Cross. Overview of Moroccan culture and history, as well as current events and travel information. Abbeville Press (US$20).

TRAVEL BOOK PUBLISHERS

Hunter Publishing, 130 Campus Drive, Edison, NJ 08818-7816 (tel. (800)-255-0343; email kimba@mediasoft.net; www.hunterpublishing.com). Has an extensive catalogue of travel books, guides, language learning tapes, and quality maps, the *Charming Small Hotel Guide to Spain* (US$15), and the *Nelles Guides* to Spain and the Canary Islands (each US$16).

John Muir Publications, P.O. Box 613, Sante Fe, NM 87504 (tel. (800)-888-7504; fax (505) 988-1680). In addition to many travel guides, publishes an excellent series of books by veteran traveler Rick Steves, including *Mona Winks: Self-Guided Tours of Europe's Top Museums* (US$19).

Rand McNally, 150 S. Wacker Dr., Chicago, IL 60606 (tel. (800)-234-0679 or (312) 332-2009; fax 443-9540; email storekeeper@randmcnally.com; www.randmc-nally.com), publishes a number of comprehensive road atlases (each US$10).

THE WORLD WIDE WEB

The Web has come to **Spain** and **Portugal.** There are numerous general websites about both countries, and many of them address tourists directly. Moreover, many businesses in both countries have their own websites as well. **Morocco's** presence on the internet is much less substantial, although new sites are springing up every day, especially in the major cities. **Tourism on Morocco,** listed below, is the best place to start.

All About Spain (www.red2000.com/spain/index.html) has an excellent photo tour of Spain, traveler's yellow pages, and information on major regions and cities.

Arab Net (www.arab.net/morocco/morocco_contents.html) has good historical, cultural, and tourist information on Morocco, including a list of links.

CyberSpain (www.cyberspain.com) has a wide variety of tourist and cultural info as well as links to other good sites inside and outside of Spain.

MadridMan (www.madridman.com) is a site devoted entirely to the city of Madrid, with tons of useful info for visitors as well as history, culture, and current events sections.

Morocco Today (www.morocco-today.com/indexnm) is a comprehensive source of information on Moroccan current events, government, and society.

Sí, Spain (www.SiSpain.org), run by the Spanish Ministry of Foreign affairs, offers cultural and historical info, tourist info, and another great set of links.

Tourism in Morocco (www.tourism-in-Morocco.com) has helpful information on all aspects of traveling to and within Morocco, plus city-specific info.

Turespaña (www.tourspain.es) is the official Spanish tourism site. It offers reams of national and city-specific info, an information request service, helpful links on all aspects of travel, and a nifty festival locator.

Welcome to Portugal (www.portugal.org) has general info on Portugal plus information of specific interest to the traveler.

WWWSpain (www.clark.net/pub/jumpsam/wwwspain.htm) is a thorough list of links.

Xacobeo 99 (www.xacobeo.es) is the Camino de Santiago's official website.

Microsoft Expedia (expedia.msn.com) has everything you'd ever need to make travel plans on the web: compare flight fares, look at maps, make reservations. FareTracker, a free service, sends you monthly mailings about the cheapest fares to any destination.

The CIA World Factbook (www.odci.gov/cia/publications/factbook/index.html) has tons of vital statistics on Spain, Portugal, and Morocco. Check it out for an overview of each country's economy, and an explanation of its system of government.

Shoestring Travel (www.stratpub.com), an alternative to Microsoft's monolithic site, is budget travel e-zine that features listings of home exchanges, links, and accommodations information.

Foreign Language for Travelers (www.travlang.com) can help you brush up on your Arabic, French, Portuguese, or Spanish.

Let's Go (www.letsgo.com) is where you can find our newsletter, information about our books, up-to-the-minute links, and more.

SPAIN

LIFE AND TIMES

SPAIN

With a history that spans over 50 constitutions, an endless array of amorphous kingdoms controlled by indigenous Iberians, Celts, Romans, Visigoths, Arabs, and French, and an empire that spread to the Americas, Spain can only be described, imprecisely, as a *mestizo* (mixed) culture.

HISTORY AND POLITICS

Spain was colonized and came to be characterized by a succession of civilizations—**Basque** (considered indigenous), **Tartesian, Iberian, Celtic, Greek, Phoenician,** and **Carthaginian**—before the **Romans** dropped in with a vengeance in the 3rd century BC. Over nearly seven centuries, the Romans drastically altered the face and character of Spain, introducing Rome's language, architecture, roads, irrigation techniques, and use of grapes, olives, and wheat. A slew of Germanic tribes, including Swabians and Vandals, swept over Iberia in the early 400s AD, but the **Visigoths,** newly converted Christians, emerged above the rest. The Visigoths established their court at Barcelona in 415 and effectively ruled Spain for the next 300 years, although more as a collection of politically disorganized, fragmented tribes than as a unified whole.

THE MOORISH OCCUPATION (711-1492 AD). Following Muslim unification and a victory tour through the Middle East and North Africa, a small force of Arabs, Berbers, and Syrians invaded Spain in 711. Practically welcomed by the divided Visigoths, the Moors encountered little resistance, and the peninsula soon fell under the dominion of the caliphate of Damascus. These events precipitated the infusion of Muslim influence (although Catholics and Jews were tolerated for the most part), which peaked in the 10th century. The Moors set up their Iberian capital in Córdoba. During Abderramán III's rule (936-76), some considered Spain the wealthiest and most cultivated country in the world. Abderramán's successor, however, the dictator Al Mansur (976-1013), snuffed out all opposition within his extravagant court and undertook a series of military campaigns that climaxed with the destruction of Santiago de Compostela, a Christian holy city, in 997.

Tension between Moors and Christians was never continuous; most of the time, in fact, they lived in peace. The turning point in Muslim-Christian relations came when Al Mansur died, leaving a power vacuum in Córdoba. At this point, caliphate holdings shattered into petty states called *taifas*. With power less centralized, Christians were able to gain the upper hand. The Christian policy was official (although not always de facto) toleration of Muslims and Jews, which fostered a syncretic culture and even a style of art, **Mudéjar.** Later, though, countless Moorish structures were ruined in the Reconquest, and numerous mosques were replaced by churches (like Córdoba's Mezquita; see p. 212). In this game of life-and-death and convert-or-get-out, relations were not cordial.

THE CATHOLIC MONARCHS (1469-1516). In 1469, the marriage of **Fernando de Aragón** and **Isabel de Castilla** joined Iberia's two mightiest Christian kingdoms. By 1492, the dynamic duo had captured Granada (the last Moorish stronghold) and shuttled off Columbus to explore the New World. By the 16th century, the pair's strong leadership made Spain's empire the world's most powerful. The Catholic Monarchs introduced the **Inquisition** in 1478, executing and then burning heretics, principally Jews (even those who had earlier converted). The Spanish Inquisition had dual aims: to strengthen the authority of the Church and to unify Spain more cohesively. In approximately 50 years of rule, the Catholic Monarchs greatly heightened Spain's position as a world economic, political, and cultural power—made all the more enduring by conquests in the Americas. Spain proved braver than neighboring countries in financing such risky endeavors and—over the next 300 years—would reap the rewards.

THE HABSBURG DYNASTY (1516-1713). The daughter of Fernando and Isabel, **Juana la Loca** (the Mad), married **Felipe el Hermoso** (the Fair) of the powerful Habsburg dynasty. Mr. Handsome (who died playing *cesta punta*, or jai alai) and Mrs. Crazy (who refused to believe he had died and dragged his corpse through the streets) produced **Carlos I** (Charles V, 1516-56), who reigned over an immense empire (as the last official Holy Roman Emperor) comprising modern-day Netherlands, Belgium, Austria, Spain, parts of Germany and Italy, and the American colonies. Fortunately, he spent more time in Spain than in any other country, but the task of maintaining political stability was monumental. Carlos did his part: as a good Catholic, he embroiled Spain in a war with Protestant France; as an art patron of superb taste, he nabbed Titian as his court painter; as a fashion plate, he introduced Spain to the Habsburg fashion of wearing only black.

But trouble was brewing in the Protestant Netherlands (then called the Low Countries and Flanders). After Carlos I died, his son **Felipe II** (1556-98) was left holding the bag full of rebellious territories. More conservative than his father, he still would not stand pat, annexing Portugal after its ailing King Henrique died in 1580. One year later the Dutch declared their independence from Spain, and Felipe began warring with the Protestants, spurring an embroilment with England. The war with the British ground to a halt when **Sir Francis Drake** and bad weather buffeted the **Invincible Armada** in 1588. His enthusiasm (and much of his European empire) sapped, Felipe retreated to his grim, newly built palace, **El Escorial** (see p. 116) and remained there through the last decade of his reign.

Felipe III (1598-1621), preoccupied with both religion and the finer aspects of life, allowed his favorite adviser, the **Duque de Lerma,** to pull the governmental strings. In 1609, Felipe III and the Duke expelled nearly 300,000 of Spain's remaining Moors. Mustached **Felipe IV** (1621-65) painstakingly held the country together through his long, tumultuous reign. In the beginning of his rule, the impressionable young king was manipulated by the **Conde Duque de Olivares,** but Felipe wisened up as he settled in and dismissed Olivares in 1643. Emulating his great-grandfather Carlos I, Felipe IV discerningly patronized the arts (painter Diego Velázquez and playwrights Lope de Vega and Calderón de la Barca were in his court) and architecture (the Buen Retiro in Madrid; see p. 100), and donned extravagant black garb. Then the **Thirty Years' War** (1618-48) broke out over Europe, and defending Catholicism drained Spain's resources; the war ended with the marriage of Felipe IV's daughter, María Teresa, and Louis XIV of France. Felipe's successor **Carlos II** (1665-1700), the *"hechizado"* (bewitched), was epileptic and impotent, the product of generations of inbreeding. From then on, little went right: Carlos II died, Spain fell into a depression, and cultural bankruptcy ensued.

BOURBONS, CONSTITUTIONS, AND LIBERALS (1713-1930). The 1713 Treaty of Utrecht seated **Felipe V** (1713-46), a Bourbon grandson of Louis XIV, on the Spanish throne. The king built huge, showy palaces (to mimic Versailles in France) and cultivated a flamboyant, debauched court. Despite his undisciplined example, the Bourbons who followed Felipe ably administered the Empire, at last beginning to regain control of Spanish-American trade previously lost to northern Europeans. They also constructed scores of new canals and roads, organized settlements, and instituted agricultural reform and industrial expansion. **Carlos III** (1759-88) was probably Madrid's finest "mayor," founding academies of science and art and generally beautifying the capital. Spain's global standing recovered enough for it to team with France to help the American colonies gain independence from Britain, as evidenced by Captain Gálvez's heroic victories in the American South.

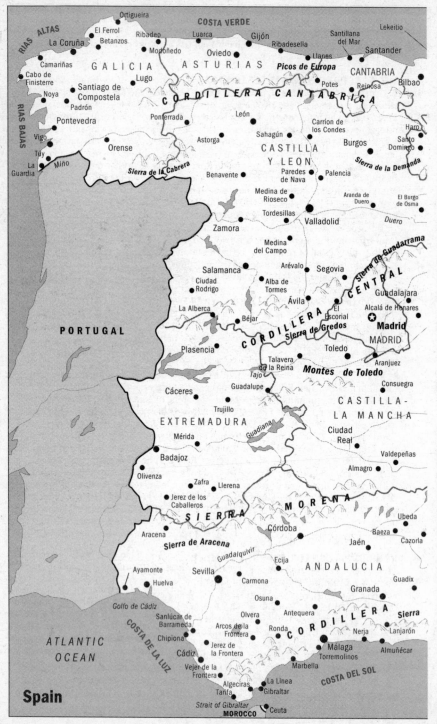

Spain

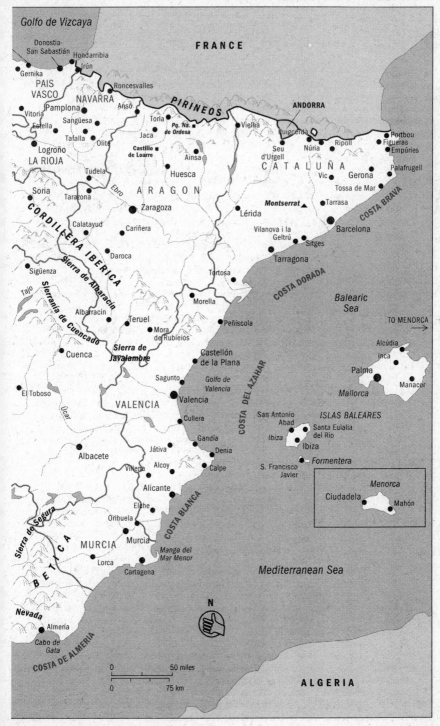

JEWS IN SPAIN For centuries, Jews were peacefully settled throughout Iberia. A 15th-century rabbi noted that the Jews in Castilla were "the most distinguished in all the realms of the dispersion: in lineage, in wealth, in virtues, in science." Yet in 1369, **Enrique de Trastámara** defeated his half-brother **Pedro the Cruel** (a legendary Richard III-type) at Montiel, inaugurating the Trastámara dynasty that was to produce **Isabel la Católica.** Always a bit precarious, tolerance in Castilla was replaced by Christian rigidity akin to the scene in 14th-century France. The 1391 pogroms started soon after, as thousands of Jews were massacred and many more forcibly converted. Even those who did convert, called *conversos,* were persecuted and tortured. Paradoxically, *conversos* could rise to the high ranks of political, ecclesiastical, and intellectual institutions and become connected with Christian aristocratic and merchant classes. Catholic saint and author **Teresa of Ávila** (1515-1582), for example, was the child of a *converso,* as was **Luís de Santángel,** the secretary of Isabel and a principal supporter of Columbus. The mass conversion led to a complex situation as a "tainted" upper class desperately disavowed its Semitic heritage by devising false genealogies, among other tactics. As a result, *converso* culture became neither entirely Jewish nor Christian.

Napoleon then invaded Spain (1808-14) on his quest for world domination. The invasion's battles were particularly bloody; painter **Francisco de Goya** captured the brutality in two brilliant works (see **Painting,** p. 54). The French occupation ended, ironically enough, when the Protestant Brits defeated the Corsican's troops at Waterloo (1814). This victory led to the restoration of arch-reactionary **Fernando VII** (1814-33), who sought to revoke the progressive Constitución de Cádiz of 1812. Galvanized by Fernando's ineptitude and inspired by liberal ideas in the new constitution, most of Spain's Latin American empire soon threw off its yoke. Domestically, parliamentary liberalism was restored in 1833 upon Fernando VII's death and survived the conservative challenge of the **Carlist Wars** (1833-40); it would predominate Spanish politics until **Primo de Rivera's** mild dictatorship in the 1920s. Rapid industrialization and prosperity marked 19th-century Spain. It was during this period that the wealth produced by Cataluña's industrial-inspired Renaixença (Renaissance) financed the **Modernista** movement in architecture and design, a movement which produced lengthy construction projects for Barcelona's bourgeoisie. But Spain's loss to the U.S. in the 1898 **Spanish-American War** cost the Spanish the Philippines, Puerto Rico, Cuba, and their lingering dreams of empire. Meanwhile, much of Spain remained indigent and agricultural.

THE SECOND REPUBLIC AND THE CIVIL WAR (1931-1939). In April 1931, **King Alfonso XIII** (1902-31), disgraced by his support for Rivera's dictatorship, shamefully fled Spain, thus giving rise to the **Second Republic** (1931-36). Republican Liberals and Socialists established safeguards for farmers and industrial workers, granted women's suffrage, assured religious tolerance, and chipped away at traditional military dominance. National euphoria, however, faded fast. The 1933 elections split the Republican-Socialist coalition, in the process increasing the power of right-wing and Catholic parties in the parliamentary *Cortes.* Military dissatisfaction led to a heightened profile for the Fascist *Falange* (founded by Rivera's son José), which further polarized national politics. By 1936, radicals, anarchists, Socialists, and Republicans had formed a loosely federated alliance to win the next elections. But the victory was short-lived. Once **Generalísimo Francisco Franco** snatched control of the Spanish army, militarist uprisings ensued, and the nation plunged into war. The three-year **Civil War** (1936-39) ignited worldwide ideological passions. Germany and Italy dropped troops, supplies, and munitions into Franco's lap, while the stubbornly isolationist U.S. and liberal European states were slow to aid the Republicans. Although Franco enjoyed popular support in Andalucía, Galicia, Navarra, and parts of Castilla, the Republicans controlled the population and industrial centers. The Soviet Union, somewhat indirectly, called for a **Popular Front** of Communists, Socialists, and other leftist sympathizers to battle Franco's fascism. Soon, however, the West abandoned the coalition, and aid from the Soviet Union waned as Stalin began to see the benefits of an alliance with Hitler. Without international aid, Republican forces found themselves cut off from necessary food and supplies, and began to surrender to the Nationalists. All told, bombings, executions, combat, starvation, and disease took nearly 600,000 lives, and in 1939 Franco's forces marched into Madrid and ended the war.

FRANCO AND THE TRANSITION TO DEMOCRACY (1939-1999).

Brain-drain (as leading scientists, artists, and intellectuals emigrated or were assassinated en masse), worker dissatisfaction, student unrest, regional discontent, and international isolation characterized the first few decades of Franco's dictatorship. Several anarchist and nationalist groups, notably the Basque **ETA (Euskal Herritarrok),** resisted the dictatorship throughout Franco's reign, often via terrorist acts. In his old age, Franco tried to smooth international relations by joining NATO and encouraging tourism, but the "national tragedy" (as it was later called) did not officially end until Franco's death in 1975. **King Juan Carlos I** (1975-), grandson of Alfonso XIII and nominally a Franco protégé, carefully set out to undo Franco's damage. In 1978, under centrist premier Adolfo Suárez, Spain adopted a new constitution in a national referendum that led to the restoration of parliamentary government and regional autonomy. The post-Franco years have been marked by progressive social change. Divorce was legalized in 1981; women now vote more than men and comprise over 50% of universities' ranks. Problems may still plague Spain, but violent regionalists remain in the minority. Most, in fact, seem satisfied with the degree of regional autonomy. By the early 1980s, many regions controlled everything but foreign relations.

Charismatic **Felipe González** led the **PSOE (Spanish Socialist Worker's Party)** to victory in the 1982 elections. González opened the Spanish economy and championed consensus policies, overseeing Spain's integration into the European Community (EC; now the EU) in 1986. Despite his support for continued membership in NATO (he had originally promised to withdraw if he won) and unpopular economic stands, González was reelected in 1986 and continued a program of massive public investment. The years 1986 to 1990 were outstanding for Spain's economy, as the nation enjoyed an average annual growth rate of 3.8%. By the end of 1993, however, recession had set in. In 1993, González and the PSOE only barely maintained a majority in Parliament over the increasingly popular conservative **Partido Popular (PP).** Revelations of large-scale corruption led to a resounding Socialist defeat at the hands of the PP in the 1994 European parliamentary elections. Negative attention triggered losses in regional elections in the President's homeland, Andalucía, a traditional Socialist stronghold. A second cascade of high-profile scandals in late 1994 further destabilized the PSOE government; the most damaging was the arrest of four interior ministry officials charged with organizing an illegal undercover organization, GAL (Anti-terrorist Liberation Groups), to combat Basque separatists in the 1980s; González himself was eventually pestered into admitting his complicity in GAL "death squads."

José María Aznar led the PP into power after González's support eroded and has managed to maintain his delicately balanced coalition while leading the Spanish economy to its best performance in years. Fears of a rightist reversion have faded and most Spaniards seem pleased with the process of parliamentary democracy, if not always with its results and policies. Despite notable exceptions, most regional movements have been more cooperative than subversive to the central government in Madrid.

CURRENT EVENTS.

The last year has seen important progress in one of Spain's most pressing areas of concern, Basque nationalism and terrorism. On September 12, 1998, the federal government issued the **Lizarra Declaration,** which called for an open dialogue between all parties (including the militant ETA) and was endorsed by the **Basque National Party (PNV).** Six days later, ETA publicly declared a truce with the national government. Moreover, the newest Basque president, **Juan José Ibarretxe,** has the support of the PNV, the political wing of ETA, and the federal government, and has pledged to maintain and strengthen the peace. Although isolated bombings have continued to occur (including one at Franco's tomb in May 1999), ETA has denied responsibility and vowed to continue the ceasefire. On the national front, the conservative Partido Popular and José María Aznar have to date sustained their majority, but not without a strong challenge from the resurgent Socialist Worker's Party (PSOE) and its leader **José Borrell.** The PSOE needs to gain only six seats in the European Parliament and 15 in the national Congreso to become the majority party, and some predict such a victory in the next elections.

Spain's economy continues to improve. January 1, 1999 marked the inauguration of the **European Monetary Union** (with its new, transnational currency, the **euro**), which the Spanish government and citizens fully supported. The union has not hindered Spain's economic progress. Spain's inflation, while still the highest in Western Europe, has declined, and the economy has demonstrated impressive growth overall. Culturally and spiritually, the nation is in great shape. The truce with ETA has made Bilbao, already a huge tourist attraction with its new **Guggenheim Museum** (see p. 421), safer and more appealing than ever, and tourism nationwide is at an all-time high. As Spain prepares to enter the next millennium, its prospects for peace and prosperity have never been better.

LANGUAGE(S)

Spain's four regional languages and their various dialects differ more than cosmetically, although some spelling variations are merely superficial. **Castilian** *(castellano)*, known around the world as *español* (Spanish), is spoken almost everywhere and is Spain's official language. **Catalán** *(catalá)* is spoken in Cataluña and has given rise through permutations to **Valencian** *(valenciá)*, the regional tongue of Valencia in the east, and **Mallorquín,** the principal dialect of the Balearic Islands. The once-Celtic northwest corner of Iberia gabs in **Galician** *(gallego)*, which is closely related to Portuguese. Although more prevalent in the countryside than in cities, Galician is now spreading among the young, as is **Basque** *(euskera)*, spoken in País Vasco and northern Navarra. All of these languages have standardized grammar rules and ancient literary traditions, both oral and written. Regional television broadcasts, native film industries, strong political associations, and extensive schooling have helped save them from extinction.

City and provincial names in this text are usually listed in Castilian first, followed by the regional language in parentheses where appropriate. We find it most useful, however, to adhere to common usage, and if a town is almost exclusively referred to according to its regional name, then we have written it as such. Info within cities (i.e., street names or plaza names) is always listed in the regional language. Generally, when traveling throughout Spain, Castilian names will suffice and are universally understood. However, it is wise within the specific regions to exercise politeness and respect toward the native language.

Let's Go provides a **phrasebook, glossary,** and **pronunciation guide** in the back of the book for all terms used recurrently throughout the text (see p. 726).

THE ARTS

PAINTING

Residents of the Iberian peninsula were creating art as early as 13,000 BC, the birthdate of the fabulous cave paintings at **Altamira** (see p. 446). Over this long stretch, Spanish painting has seen a series of luminaries separated by several lulls. Although Flemish, French, and Italian influences have all played important roles, such heavy hitters as El Greco, Diego Velázquez, Francisco Goya, and Pablo Picasso have forged a dazzling, distinctive, and hugely influential body of work.

In the 11th and 12th centuries, fresco painters and manuscript illuminators decorated churches and their libraries along the Camino de Santiago and in León and Toledo. **Pedro Berruguete's** (1450-1504) use of traditional gold backgrounds in his religious paintings exemplifies the Italian-influenced style of early Renaissance works. Berruguete's style is especially evident in his masterpiece, the altarpiece of San Tomás in Ávila (1499-1503; see p. 146). Not until after Spain's imperial ascendance in the 16th century did painting reach its **Golden Age** (roughly 1492-1650). Felipe II imported foreign art and artists in order to jump-start native production and embellish his palace, El Escorial. Although he came to Spain seeking a royal commission, Cretan-born Doménikos Theotokópoulos, known as **El Greco** (1541-1614), was rejected by Felipe II for his shocking and intensely personal style. Confounding his contemporaries, El Greco received newfound appreciation in the 20th century for his haunting, elongated figures and dramatic use of light and color. Setting up camp in Toledo, El Greco graced the Church of Santo Tomé with his masterpiece, *The Burial of Count Orgaz* (1586-1588; see p. 122).

Felipe IV's foremost court painter, **Diego Velázquez** (1599-1660), is generally considered one of the world's greatest artists. Whether representing Felipe IV's family or lowly court jesters and dwarves, Velázquez painted with the same naturalistic precision. Working slowly and meticulously, he captured light with a virtually photographic quality. Nearly half of this Sevillian artist's works reside in the Prado, notably his famous *Las Meninas* (1656; see **Museo del Prado,** p. 103). Other Golden Age painters of note include **José de Ribera** (1591-1652), **Francisco de Zurbarán** (1598-1664), and **Bartolomé Esteban Murillo** (1618-1682). Each treated religious subjects with a distinctive vision: Italian-born Ribera took a realistic and even crude approach, Sevillian Zurbarán painted for monastic orders in a fittingly austere style, and Murillo depicted Catholic scenes with idealism and sentimentality.

During the era of Spain's waning power, **Francisco de Goya** (1746-1828) ushered European painting into the modern age. Hailing from provincial Aragón, Goya rose to the position of official court painter under the degenerate Carlos IV. Not bothering with flattery, Goya's depictions of the royal family come closer to caricature, as Queen María Luisa's haughty, cruel jawline in the famous *The Family of Charles IV* (1800) can attest. After an earlier Neoclassical period during which Goya stuck to smiling scenes of upper class gaiety, his later paintings graphically protest the lunacy of warfare. His series of etchings *The Disasters of War* (1810-1814), which includes the landmark *El dos de mayo* and *El tres de mayo*, records the horrific Napoleonic invasion of 1808. Deaf and despondent in his later years, Goya painted nightmarish and wildly fantastic visions, inspiring Expressionist and Surrealist artists of the next century. The Prado museum houses an entire room of his chilling *Black Paintings* (1820-1823; see p. 103).

It is hard to imagine an artist who has had as profound an effect upon 20th-century painting as Andalucian-born **Pablo Picasso** (1881-1973). A child prodigy, Picasso headed for Barcelona, which was a breeding ground of Modernist architecture and political activism. Bouncing back and forth between Barcelona and Paris, Picasso in 1900 began his Blue Period, characterized by somber depictions of society's outcasts. His permanent move to Paris in 1904 initiated his Rose Period, during which he probed into the curiously engrossing lives of clowns and acrobats. With his French colleague Georges Braque, he founded **Cubism,** a method of painting objects simultaneously from multiple perspectives. His gigantic 1937 mural *Guernica* portrays the bombing of that Basque city by Nazi planes during the Spanish Civil War (see p. 423). A vehement protest against violence and fascism, *Guernica* resides in the Centro de Arte Reina Sofía in Madrid (see p. 104).

Catalán painter and sculptor **Joan Miró** (1893-1983) created simplistic, almost child-like shapes in bright, primary colors. His haphazard, undefined squiggles became a statement against the authoritarian society of Fascist Spain. By contrast, fellow Catalán **Salvador Dalí** (1904-89) scandalized both high society and leftist intellectuals in France and Spain by supporting the Fascists. Dalí's name is virtually synonymous with **Surrealism.** The wildly mustached painter tapped into

SPAIN

dreams and the unconscious for images like the melting clocks in *The Persistence of Memory* (1931). His haunting *Premonition of the Civil War* (1936), subtitled *Soft Construction with Boiled Beans*, envisioned war as a distorted monster of putrefying flesh. A shameless self-promoter (he often spoke of himself only in the third person), Dalí founded the Teatre-Museo Dalí in Figueres, which defines Surrealism in its collection, its construction, and its very existence (see p. 352).

Since Franco's death in 1975, a new generation of artists has thrived. With new museums in Madrid, Barcelona, Valencia, Sevilla, and Bilbao, Spanish painters and sculptors once again have a national forum for their work. Catalán **Antonio Tapiès** constructs collages out of unusual and unorthodox materials and is a founding member of the self-proclaimed "Abstract Generation," while **Antonio López García** has distinguished himself for his hyperrealist paintings. Upstarts include abstract artist **José María Sicilia**, sculptor **Susana Solano**, and **Miguel Barceló**, whose portraits resemble swarms of black flies.

ARCHITECTURE

Spanish architecture is as impressive and wildly diverse as the various civilizations that have called the Iberian peninsula home. Continental trends tended to arrive here late, only to be transformed into distinctively Spanish styles.

Scattered **Roman ruins** testify to six centuries of colonization. Highlights include some of the finest remains in existence: the aqueduct in Segovia (see p. 140), the theater in Mérida (see p. 181), and the town of Tarragona (see p. 334). Other vestiges of the Roman past lie at the ruined towns of Itálica (near Sevilla; see p. 204), Sagunto (near Valencia; see p. 280), and Empúries (near Palafrugell; see p. 344).

After the invasion of 711, the **Moors** constructed mosques and palaces throughout southern Spain. Because the Koran forbade representations of humans and animals, architects lavished buildings with stylized geometric designs, red-and-white horseshoe arches, ornate tiles, courtyards, pools, and fountains. The spectacular 14th-century **Alhambra** in Granada (see p. 261) and the **Mezquita** in Córdoba, one-time capital of the Muslim empire (see p. 212), epitomize the Moorish style.

The combination of Islam and Christianity created two architectural movements unique to Spain: **Mozarabic** and **Mudéjar**. The former describes Christians under Muslim rule (Mozarabs) who adopted Arab devices like the horseshoe-shaped arch and the ribbed dome. The more common Mudéjar architecture was created by Moors in the years between Christian resurgence (11th century) and the Reconquest (1492). Extensive use of brick and elaborately carved wooden ceilings typify Mudéjar style, which reached its height in the 14th century with **alcázars** (palaces) in Sevilla and Segovia and **synagogues** in Toledo and Córdoba.

The first Gothic cathedral in Spain was built in Burgos (1221; see p. 168), followed closely by Toledo and León. The **Spanish Gothic** style, like that elsewhere in Europe, brought pointed arches, flying buttresses, slender walls, airy spaces, and stained-glass windows. There were variations, though: the Catalán style, for example, employed internal wall supports rather than external buttresses. Other Spanish alterations of the French original include centrally placed *coros* (choirs) and oversized *retablos* (brightly colored carved pieces placed above the high altar).

New World riches inspired the **Plateresque** ("in the manner of a silversmith") style, a flashy embellishment of Gothic that transformed wealthier parts of Spain. Intricate stonework and extravagant use of gold and silver splashed 15th- and 16th-century buildings, most notably in Salamanca, where the university practically drips with ornamentation. In the late 16th century, **Italian Renaissance** innovations in perspective and symmetry arrived in Spain to sober up the Plateresque style. **El Escorial** (1563-84), Felipe II's grand palace, was designed by Juan de Herrera, one of Spain's most prominent architects, and best exemplifies the unadorned Renaissance style (see p. 116).

Opulence seized center stage once again in 17th- and 18th-century **Baroque** Spain. The Churriguera brothers pioneered this style—called, appropriately, **Churrigueresque**—which is equal parts ostentatious, ornamental, and difficult to pronounce. Wildly elaborate works with extensive sculptural detail and twisted columns, like the altar of the Toledo cathedral (see p. 126), help set this period in Spanish architecture apart.

In the late 19th and early 20th centuries, Catalán's **Modernistas** burst onto the scene in Barcelona, led by the eccentric genius of **Antoni Gaudí, Luis Domènech i Montaner,** and **José Puig i Caldafach.** Modernista structures defy previous standards with their voluptuous curves and abnormal textures. The new style was inspired partly by Mudéjar relics, but far more so by organic forms and unbridled imagination. Spain's outstanding architectural tradition continues to this day with such trendsetters as **Josep María Sert, Ricardo Bofill,** and **Rafael Moneo.**

LITERATURE

Spain's literary tradition first blossomed in the late Middle Ages (1000-1500). The 12th-century *Cantar de Mío Cid* (Song of My Cid), an epic poem and Spain's oldest surviving work, chronicles national hero El Cid's life and military triumphs, from his exile from Castilla to his return to grace in the king's court. Fernando de Rojas's *La Celestina* (1499), a tragicomic dialogue most noted for its folkloric witch character, helped pave the way for picaresque novels like *Lazarillo de Tormes* (1554) and *Guzmán de Alfarache* (1599), rags-to-riches stories about mischievous boys *(pícaros)* with good hearts. This literary form surfaced during Spain's **Golden Age** (1492-1681). Poetry particularly thrived in this era. Some consider the sonnets and romances of **Garcilaso de la Vega** the most perfect ever written in Castilian. Along with his friend **Joan Boscán,** Garcilaso introduced the "Italian" (or Petrarchan) sonnet to Iberia. **Francisco de Quevedo** also contributed to the rebirth of sonnets, treating erotic themes with a sardonic twist. The reverent **Santa Teresa de Ávila** and **San Juan de la Cruz** blessed Spain with mystical autobiographical writings. This period also bred outstanding dramas, including works from **Calderón de la Barca** and **Lope de Vega,** who wrote nearly 2000 plays. Both espoused the Neoplatonic view of love, claiming that love always changes one's life dramatically and eternally. **Miguel de Cervantes'** two-part *Don Quixote de la Mancha* (1605-15)—often considered the world's first novel—is the most famous work of Spanish literature. Cervantes relates the satiric parable of the hapless, slightly askew Don and his sidekick, Sancho Panza, who think themselves bold *caballeros* (knights) out to save the world.

The 19th century bred a multiplicity of styles, from the biting journalistic prose of **Mariano José de Larra** to **José Zorrilla's** romantic poem *Don Juan Tenorio* (1844) to the naturalistic novels of **Leopoldo Alas ("Clarín").** The modern literary era began with the **Generación del '98,** a group led by essayist **Miguel de Unamuno** and cultural critic **José Ortega y Gasset.** Reacting to Spain's embarrassing defeat in the Spanish-American War (1898), these nationalistic authors argued, through essays and novels, that each individual must spiritually and ideologically attain internal peace before society can do the same. These authors heavily influenced the **Generación del 1927,** a clique of experimental lyric poets who used Surrealist and vanguard poetry to express profound humanism. This group included **Jorge Guillén, Federico García Lorca** (assassinated at the start of the Civil War), **Rafael Alberti,** and **Luis Cernuda.** In the 20th century, the Nobel Committee has honored playwright and essayist **Jacinto Benavente y Martínez** (1922), poet **Vicente Aleixandre** (1977), and novelist **Camilo José Cela** (1989), author of *La Familia de Pascal Duarte* (1942). Female writers, like **Mercè Rodoreda** and **Carmen Martín Gaite,** have likewise earned critical acclaim. Since the fall of the Fascist regime in 1975, Spanish artists have again flocked to Madrid, just as they did in the early part of the century. In the 1980s, an avant-garde spirit—known as *La Movida* (see p. 106)—was reborn in the capital. **Ana Rossetti** and **Juana Castro** led a new generation of erotic poets into the 80s. With this newest group of poets, women are at the forefront of Spanish literature for the first time.

SPAIN

FLAMENCO FRILLS AND DRILLS Few things are more exciting than a free-wheeling *sevillana*, the reason the feisty flamenco dancer is Spain's beloved cultural icon. The woman's *bata de cola*—a colorful 19th-century style dress with trains, frills, ribbons, and polka dots—immediately catches the eye. But flamenco is not limited to *sevillanas;* numerous variations form the core of any master's repertoire. Other traditional flamenco dances include:

Soleares (Soléas): One of the oldest and most dignified flamenco forms, it reduces even stoic onlookers to tears. **Bulerías:** Near the end of a performance, the rhythm picks up and the entire company gets down in this—the *bulería*. **Alegrías:** The brisk pace and liveliness of *alegrías* (joy) make them crowd-pleasers. **Fandango:** The *fandango* dance may have originated in Huelva, but nearly every town in Andalucía has added a twist. **Farruca:** Boundless strength and refined beauty generally make strange bed-fellows, but not in the *farruca*.

MUSIC

Flamenco, the combination of *cante jondo* (melodramatic song), guitar, and dancing, originated among Andalucian gypsies and remains extremely popular today (see **Flamenco Frills and Drills,** below). **Paco de Lucía,** an internationally renowned guitarist who experiments with a jazz-flamenco combination, rattles flamenco purists. The guitar was also the instrument of choice for one of Spain's greatest musicians, **Andrés Segovia,** while equally talented **Pablo Casals** performed on the cello. Singer **Camarón de la Isla,** who died young in 1992, maintains a devoted following throughout the peninsula. Singer-songwriters voiced underground discontent during the Franco years and became outwardly famous for it afterwards. **Joan-Manuel Serrat** is perhaps the biggest name; other singers of note are **Albert Pla, María del Mar Bonet, Lluís Llach,** and **Ana Belén.** American pop music is everywhere in Spain, but Spanish pop sometimes gives it a run for its money. **Mecano** hypnotizes audiences around the world, and Barcelona band **El Último de la Fila** and big-forum **Héroes del Silencio** are well worth a listen. Other popular groups and soloists are **Presuntos Implicados, Los Rodríguez,** and **Manolo Tena.** Barcelona-born **José Carrera** and **Plácido Domingo,** of "Three Tenors" fame, are recognized as two of the world's finest opera singers. And no one can forget **Julio Iglesias,** beloved the world over.

FILM

Spain's first film, *Ría en un Cafe* (directed by Fructuos Gelabert), dates from 1897, and director **Segundo de Chomón** is recognized world-wide as a pioneer of early cinema. The Surrealist **Luis Buñuel,** close friends with **Salvador Dalí,** produced several early classics, most notably *Un Chien Andalou* (1929). Later, and in exile from Francoist Spain, he produced a number of brilliantly sardonic films including *Belle du Jour* (1967).

One of the greatest influences on Spanish film was not a filmmaker, but a politician. Franco's regime (1939-75) defined Spanish film both during and after his rule. Censorship stifled most creative tendencies and left the public with nothing to watch but cheap westerns *(chonzos)* and bland spy flicks. As government supervision slacked in the early 1970s, Spanish cinema showed signs of life, led by **Carlos Saura's** dark and subversive hits such as *El Jardin de las Delicias* (1970) and *Cría Cuervos* (1975).

In 1977, in the wake of Franco's death, domestic censorship laws were revoked, bringing artistic freedom along with financial hardship for Spanish filmmakers, who found their films shunned domestically in favor of newly permitted foreign films. Internationally, however, depictions of the exuberant excesses of liberated Spain found increasing attention. **Pedro Almodovar's** *Law of Desire* (1986), featuring **Antonio Banderas** as a homosexual, perhaps best captures the risqué themes of transgression and sexuality most often treated by contemporary Spanish cinema. His *Women on the Verge of a Nervous Breakdown* (1988) expresses post-Franco disillusion in an unrefined, fashion-conscious Madrid. Other directors to look for in Spain include **Bigas Luna,** director of the controversial *Jamón Jamón* (1992), **Fernando Trueba, Vicente Aranda, Victor Érice,** and **Pilar Micó.** Trueba's *Belle Epoque* won an Oscar in 1994, a testament to growing international respect for Spanish cinema. Hopefully, such international recognition and popularity will help relieve some of the economic woes plaguing the Spanish film industry.

BULLFIGHTING

A visit to Spain is not complete without the experience of a bullfight. The national spectacle that is bullfighting dates, in its modern form, back to the early 1700s. With bullfighting growing in popularity, Roman amphitheaters like those in Sevilla and Córdoba were rebuilt and embellished, and bulls were bred to possess aggressive instincts. The techniques of the modern bullfighter (matador) were developed around 1914 by Juan Belmonte, considered one of the greatest matadors of all time (others include Joselito, Manolete, and Cristina, the first female matador). Belmonte's techniques made bullfighting both more exciting and more dangerous, as he emphasized proximity to the bull's horns and intricate capework rather than just the simple kill.

A bullfight is divided into three principal stages: in the first, *picadors* (lancers on horseback) pierce the bull's neck; next, assistants on foot thrust *banderillas* (decorated darts) into the back; and finally, the matador performs the kill. If a matador has shown special skill and daring, the audience waves white handkerchiefs to implore the bullfight's president to reward the coveted ears (and, very rarely, the tail) to the matador. Although bullfighting has always had its critics—the Catholic church in the 17th century felt that the risks made it equivalent to suicide—the late 20th century has seen an especially strong attack from animal rights' activists. Whatever its faults, however, bullfighting is an essential element of the Spanish national consciousness and will almost certainly continue to be one. For an American take on the myth, meaning, and *machismo* of the bullfight, check out Ernest Hemingway's *Death in the Afternoon* (1932) and *The Sun Also Rises* (1926).

FOOD AND DRINK

In their cuisine, the Spanish prize fresh ingredients, light sauces, and pig products. Each region has its own repertoire of dishes based on indigenous produce, meats, and fish. While the best-known Spanish dishes—*paella, gazpacho,* and *tortilla española*—are from Valencia, Andalucía, and Castilla, respectively, País Vasco, Navarra, Cataluña, and Galicia traditionally cook up many of Spain's most intriguing dishes.

TYPICAL FARE

The wilds of the sea are tamed deliciously and distinctively throughout Spain. **País Vasco** masters *bacalao* (cod), *chipirones en su tinta* (squid in its own ink), *sopa de pescado* (fish soup), mouth watering *angulas a la bilbaína* (baby eels in garlic), earthy *pimientos del piquillo* (roasted red peppers), and sumptuous *rellenos* (stuffed peppers). **Galicians** savor *empanadas* (pastry) with particularly tasty *bonito* (tuna), *pulpo* (octopus), *mejillones* (mussels), and *santiaguiños* (spider crabs). **Catalunya,** renowned for its cuisine, has blessed the world with *zarzuela,* a seafood and tomato bouillabaisse, and its own brand of *langosta* (lobster). A common favorite are *torradas,* hearty toast spread with crushed tomato and often topped with *butifarra* (sausage) or ham. **Menorca** miraculously whips mayonnaise (named for its capital Mahón) into every dish, while **Mallorca's** *ensaimada,* angel hair pastry smothered in powdered sugar, sweetens breakfasts. Chefs in the **Balearic Islands** also stir up various fish stews, while **Andalucíans** have famously—and lightly—mastered the art of frying fish and sautéing *rabo de toro* (bull's tail).

Valencia glories in countless uses of rice; its *paella*, a saffron-seasoned dish made with meat, fish, poultry, vegetables, or snails, is world-famous (there are over 200 varieties alone throughout the region). In the north, **Asturias** warms to *fabada* (bean stew), complemented by *queso cabrales* (blue cheese). **Castilla** churns out a dense *cocido* (stew) of meats, sausage, and chick-peas, as well as *chorizo*, a seasoned savory sausage. For pork lovers, oh-so-tender *cochinillo asado al horno* (roast suckling pig) is a glutton's delight. Adventurers shouldn't miss **Navarra's** quirky *perdiz con chocolate* (partridge in chocolate).

Spaniards love ham; you will be hard-pressed to find a non-vegetarian restaurant in any region that does not offer it. *Jamón serrano* or *jamón del país* (the best of which comes from pigs fed only acorns) is cured and zestier than regular ham, itself known as *jamón york* or *jamón dulce*. **Vegetarians beware**—not only is ham everywhere, but Spanish chefs often take a "vegetarian" request to mean "with tuna" and will substitute this canned catch for other kinds of meat. Alternatively, you may enjoy sinking your teeth into *queso* (cheese). The best known are *queso de Burgos*, a soft, mild cheese thought to heal the sick, and *queso manchego*, a fairly sharp cheese made from sheep's milk.

Consumed in bars and *tascas* (*tapas* bars), *tapas* tantalize taste buds all around Spain. *Tapas* are bite-size servings, while *raciones* are bigger portions (sometimes equal in size to entrees). These munchables come in countless varieties, which are often region-specific as well. *Tabernas* serve *tapas* from a counter, while *mesones* bring them to the table. *Tortilla de patata* (potato and egg omelette) and *tortilla francesa* (plain omelette) are abundant, as are *bocadillos* (thick baguette sandwiches) and *sandwiches* (flimsy sandwiches on white bread, often grilled). The **Glossary of Food and Restaurant Terms** (see p. 729) lists helpful food terms and translations.

MEALS AND DINING HOURS

Spaniards start their day with a continental breakfast of coffee or thick, liquid chocolate and *bollos* (rolls), *churros* (lightly fried fritters), or other pastries. As in most of Europe, Spaniards devour their biggest meal, the *comida*, at midday (around 2-3pm). This traditionally consists of several courses: an *entremesa* (appetizer) of soup or salad; a main course of meat, fish, or *paella;* and a dessert of fruit, *queso* (cheese), or some sweets. Supper at home is light, usually a sandwich or tortilla, consumed near 8pm. Eating out time is after 9pm, and in some restaurants as late as midnight. A rendezvous at one or more *tascas*—featuring *tapas* and drinks—is a common substitute for the evening meal. Dessert lovers will enjoy the famed *turrón* (almond nougat), marzipan, and other candied fruits and cakes, as well as the smooth, custard-like *flan*.

RESTAURANTS

While some restaurants are open from 8am to 1 or 2am, most serve meals from 1 or 2 to 4pm and in the evening from 8pm until midnight. Eating at the bar is often cheaper than at tables. The bill won't be brought to your table unless you request it. In big cities, the tourist office rates nearby *restaurantes* on a fork system, five forks meaning gourmet. Full *restaurante* meal prices range from about 800ptas to perhaps 1800ptas in a four-forker. *Cafeterías* are ranked by cups, one to three. Also, many *bar-restaurantes* (and some *hostales*) have cozy *comedors* (dining rooms) on the premises. Diners will repeatedly come across three options. **Platos combinados** (combination platters) include a main course and side dishes on a single plate, plus bread and sometimes a drink. The **menú del día**—two or three dishes, bread, wine/beer/mineral water, and dessert—is Spaniards' common choice for the *comida*, and a good deal at roughly 800-1500ptas. Generally, you'll have several options, although advertised items are periodically not available. Those dining **á la carte** choose from individual entrees. A full meal ordered this way typically runs twice as much, if not more, than the *menú*.

DRINKS

Spanish **wine** is uniformly good. When in doubt, the *vino de la casa* (house wine) is an economical, often delectable choice. Also good is *vino tinto* (red wine), *vino blanco* (white wine), or *vino rosado* (rosé). For a taste, get a *chato* (small glass). Mild, fragrant reds are Spain's best vintages, but the corps of fine wines is vast. La Mancha's **Valdepeñas** are light, dry reds and whites, drunk without long aging. Catalunya's whites and **cavas** (champagnes) and Aragón's Cariñena wines pack bold punches. **Sidra** (alcoholic cider) from Asturias and País Vasco, and **sangría** (a red-wine punch with sliced peaches and oranges, seltzer, sugar, and a dash of brandy) are delicious alcoholic options. A popular light drink is *tinto de verano*, a cool mix of red wine and carbonated mineral water.

Jerez (sherry), Spain's most famous wine, hails from Jerez de la Frontera in Andalucía (see p. 215). Try the dry *fino* and *amontillado* as aperitifs, or finish off a rich supper with the sweet *oloroso* or *dulce*. The *manzanilla* produced in Sanlúcar (near Cádiz) has a salty aftertaste, ascribed to the region's salt-filled soil.

Wash down your *tapas* with a *caña (de cerveza)*, a normal-sized draft-beer. A *tubo* is a little bigger than a *caña*, and small beers go by different names—*corto* in Castilla, *zurito* in Basque. **Mixed drinks** are referred to as *copas*, and small shots of hard liquor as *chupitos*. Beer and Schweppes is a **clara**. **Calimocho,** popular with young crowds, mixes Coca Cola and red wine. Older drinkers prefer **sol y sombra** (literally sun and shade—brandy and anise).

Spain whips up numerous non-alcoholic quenchers as well, most notably **horchata de chufa** (made by pressing almonds and ice together) and the flavored crushed-ice **granizados.** Shun the machine-made versions of either drink—they don't do the drinks justice. Coffee and milk *do* mix. *Café solo* means black coffee; add a touch of milk for a *nube;* a little more and it's a *café cortado;* all's fair with *café con leche*—half coffee, half milk—often imbibed at breakfast; savor steamed milk with a dash of coffee, a *leche manchada;* and top it off with a *blanco y negro*, an ice-cream-and-coffee float.

THE MEDIA

NEWSPAPERS AND MAGAZINES

ABC, palpably conservative and pro-monarchist, is the oldest national daily paper. It jostles with the more liberal *El País* for Spain's largest readership. *El Mundo* is a younger left-wing daily renowned for its investigative reporting. Barcelona's *La Vanguardia* maintains a substantial Catalán audience, while *La Voz de Galicia* dominates the northwest. *Diario 16*, the more moderate counterpart to *El Mundo*, publishes the popular newsweekly *Cambio 16*, whose main competition is *Tiempo*. *Hola*, the original *revista del corazón* (magazine of the heart), caters to Spain's love affair with aristocratic titles, Julio Iglesias, and "beautiful" people. The nosier, less tasteful tabloid *Semana* has gossip galore and readers aplenty.

TELEVISION

Channel surf to the state-run TVE1 and La2 or private stations Tele5 and Antena3. Each region has its own network, broadcast in the local vernacular. In Madrid, the local channel is TeleMadrid (TM3). Canal Plus is Spain's top-notch HBO equivalent. It appears scrambled during movies but features free sitcoms and music videos on Sunday mornings. Tune in to news at 3pm and 8:30pm on most stations. Programming includes well-dubbed American movies, sports, steamy Latin American *telenovelas* (soaps), game shows (such as the popular and dangerous *Juego de la Oca*, or *Game of the Goose*), jazzed-up documentaries, and cheesy three-hour variety extravaganzas. View fab American series like *Baywatch* and *Seinfeld* and their Spanish equivalents. If all else fails, *fútbol* games and bullfights are guaranteed to hold your attention. Check newspapers for listings.

SPORTS

¡Viva España! Spanish athletes have made important contributions to most of the world's sports. Miguel Indurain, a Basque hero and Spain's most decorated athlete, may not have been able to win a sixth straight *Tour de France* title before his retirement, but he is remembered fondly by his fanatical fans. Spaniards, whether old favorites like Aranxta Sanchez-Vicario and Conchita Martínez or up-and-comers like Carlos Moya and Alex Corretja, star in tennis. Golfer José-María Olazabal is one of the world's best, with two Green Jackets in his closet to prove it. As with cuisine, regional specialties spice up the sports scene, including *cesta punta* (known internationally as jai alai) from Basque country, wind surfing along the south coast, and skiing in the Sierra Nevadas and Pyrenees. The most popular sport is of course *fútbol*, which unites Spaniards who agree to disagree, vehemently, on local teams' fates. Their professional teams rank with the finest in Europe, featuring clubs such as F.C. Barcelona and Real Madrid, whose rosters read like a world all-star roll. On top of that, the entire country lives and dies by the fortunes of the national team. Despite having one of their best squads in years, the Spanish team was knocked out of World Cup '98 in the first round. Only Real Madrid fans had any solace, with their team's surprising European Champions Cup win. If an entire city seems desolate on Saturday afternoon, don't fret—go to a bar and prepare for the emotional eruptions as the game unfolds.

FESTIVALS AND HOLIDAYS

Festivals and holidays are a large part of Spanish culture. They can transform the quietest towns into huge parties overnight; they also result in closed establishments, higher prices, and scarce accommodations. The list here is for major festivals only; practically every village in Spain has its own local festivals. The dates of listed below are valid for the year 2000 only; some dates will change in 2001.

DATE	FESTIVAL	LOCATION
January 1	New Year's Day	National
January 6	Epiphany	National
March 2-12	*Carnaval*	National, but especially in Cádiz (p. 227) and Cataluña
March 12-19	*Las Fallas*	Valencia (p. 280)
April 10-16	Festival of Religious Music	Cuenca (p. 134)
April 17-23	*Semana Santa* (Holy Week)	National
April 20	Maundy Thursday	National (except Valencia and Cataluña)
April 21	Good Friday	National
April 23	Easter	National
April 23	*Festa di Sant Jordi* (St. George's Day)	Barcelona (p. 328)
late April to early May	*Feria de Abril* (April Fair)	Sevilla (p. 203)
May	International Music and Dance Festival	Granada (p. 265)
May 1	May Day/*Fiesta del Trabajo* (Labor Day)	National
first week in May	*Feria del Caballo* (Horse Fair)	Jerez de la Frontera (p. 218)
early to mid-May	*Concurso de Patios Cordoboses* (Patio Festival)	Córdoba (p. 214)
3rd week of May	San Isidro Festival	Madrid (p. 112)
June	International Jazz Festival	Sitges (p. 331)
June or July	International Guitar Festival	Córdoba (p. 214)
June 11	*Romería del Rocío* (Rocio Pilgrimage)	El Rocío and Sevilla (p. 204)
June 22	Corpus Christi	National, with special celebrations in Toledo, La Laguna (near Tenerife), and Granada (p. 265)
June 20-29	*Festival de San Juan* (Festival of St. John)	Alicante (p. 289)

DATE	FESTIVAL	LOCATION
June 23	*Dia de Sant Joan*	Barcelona (p. 328)
June 29	*Batalla del Vino*	Haro (p. 390)
July	*Festival Cueva de Nerja*	Nerja (p. 245)
July to August	*Festival de Música d'Estiu*	Ciutadella (p. 488)
July to August	*Festival de Jazz de la Costa Brava*	Callela (p. 342)
July to August	*Festival de Teatro Clásico*	Mérida (p. 179)
July to September	*Festival Internacional de la Porta Ferrada*	Sant Feliu (p. 343)
July 6-14	*San Fermines* (Running of the Bulls)	Pamplona (Iruña) (p. 396)
mid- to late July	*Festival de Jazz*	San Sebastián (p. 415)
July 25	*Día de Santiago Apóstal* (Feast of St. James the Apostle)	National, but especially in Santiago de Campostela
late July	*Festival International de Cine* (International Film Festival)	San Sebastián (p. 415)
August 15	*La Asunción* (Feast of the Assumption)	National
mid August	*Moros y Cristianos*	Across Valencia province
August 19-27	*Semana Grande*	Spain's northern coast
September to November	*Festivales de Otoños*	Madrid (p. 112)
September 11	*Fiesta Nacional de Catalunya*	Barcelona (p. 328)
October 12	*Fiesta Nacional de España* (Spain's National Day)	National
mid-October	*Festival Internacional de Cine Fantástico de Stiges* (International Film Festival of Fantastic Cinema)	Sitges (p. 331)
November 1	All Saints' Day	National
December 6	*Día de la Constitución* (Constitution Day)	National
December 8	*La Inmaculada Concepción* (Feast of the Immaculate Conception)	National
December 25	*Navidad* (Christmas)	National
December 31	New Year's Eve	National

RECOMMENDED READING

TRAVEL LITERATURE. English scribes have penned several top-notch Spanish travel narratives. Richard Ford's witty 19th-century account, *Handbook for Travellers in Spain and Readers at Home*, remains a favorite. Most time-honored classics are region-specific, including Washington Irving's *Tales of the Alhambra*, Bloomsbury Circle-expatriate Gerald Brenan's *South from Granada*, Robert Graves' *Mallorcan Stories*, and Laurie Lee's *As I Walked Out One Midsummer Morning*. For native flavor, read Nobel prize-winning Camilo José Cela's *Journey to the Alcarria*, based on rural Castilla.

FICTION, BOTH SPANISH AND FOREIGN. Start with *Poema del Mio Cid* and Cervantes' *Don Quixote*. Among the popular modern novelists are the moving Carmen Laforet *(Nada)*, post-modern Juan José Millás *(El desorden de tu nombre)*, lyrical Esther Tusquet *(El mismo mar de todos los veranos)*, and amusing Manuel Vázquez Montalbán *(Murder in the Central Committee)*. Spain has also inspired a number of prominent American and British authors. Ernest Hemingway immortalized bullfighting, *machismo*, and *San Fermines* in *The Sun Also Rises* and inspired liberal humanists everywhere with *For Whom the Bell Tolls*, which dealt with the Spanish Civil War. Graham Greene takes a walk (with a priest, all around Spain) on the lighter side in the humorous *Monsignor Quixote*.

ART AND ARCHITECTURE. The definitive work on Spanish art history is Bradley Smith's *Spain: A History in Art*. For late twentieth century art, check out William Dyckes' *Contemporary Spanish Art*. The standard text on Spanish architecture is Bernard Bevan's *History of Spanish Architecture*. For the latest (1980-present) scoop, peruse Anatzu Zabalbeascoa's *The New Spanish Architecture*. Fred Licht's collection of essays, *Goya*, is a must-read for fans of the artist, and books on Picasso, Dalí, and Gaudí can be found with minimal fuss.

HISTORY AND CULTURE. Written in 1968, James Michener's best-seller *Iberia* continues to captivate audiences for its thoroughness, insight, and style. *Barcelona*, by Robert Hughes, delves deep into the culture of Catalunya. George Orwell's *Homage to Catalonia*, a personal account of the Civil War, rivals *Iberia* and *Barcelona* in quality and fame. A handful of other historians and works stand out—Richard Fletcher's comprehensive *Moorish Spain*, J.H. Elliot's masterful *Imperial Spain 1469-1716*, and Raymond Carr (*Spain 1808-1975*) and Stanley Payne (*The Franco Regime 1936-1975*) on the modern era. For a Spaniard's take on Spanish history, try Juan Lalaguna's *A Traveller's History of Spain* (part of the international Traveller's History series).

ESSENTIALS

The information in this section is mostly designed to help travelers get their bearings once they are in Spain. For information about general **travel preparations** (including passports and permits, money, health, packing, international transportation, and more), consult the **Essentials** section at the beginning of this book. Essentials also has important information about alternatives to tourism (**work** and **study** programs in Spain; see p. 43) and for those with specific concerns: **women travelers** (p. 39); **solo travelers** (p. 40); **older travelers** (p. 40); **bisexual, gay, and lesbian travelers** (p. 41); **travelers with disabilities** (p. 41); **minority travelers** (p. 42); **travelers with children** (p. 42); and travelers with **dietary needs** (p. 43).

GETTING THERE AND GETTING AROUND

Transportation to and within Spain is quite good. The easiest, quickest, and often cheapest method of entering Spain is by plane, although Barcelona is well-connected to the European rail system. Despite a romanticized view of European train travel, buses offer the most extensive coverage and are the best option for short trips. Trains are better for longer journeys within Spain, as domestic flights can be somewhat pricey. Spain's islands are accessible by both plane and ferry. For general information on traveling within Europe, see **Getting There and Around**, page 30.

BY PLANE

All major international airlines offer service to Madrid and Barcelona, most serve the Balearic and Canary Islands, and many serve Spain's smaller cities. **Iberia** (in U.S. and Canada tel. (800) 772-4642; in U.K. tel. (171) 8 30 00 11; in Spain tel. 902 400 500; in South Africa tel. (11) 884 92 55; in Ireland tel. (1) 407 30 17; www.iberia.com) serves all domestic locations and all major international cities, including the U.S. **Aviaco**, a subsidiary of Iberia, covers only domestic routes. Ask about youth and other discounts—Iberia usually offers a range of ticket types with different restrictions and prices. Some fares purchased in the U.S. require a 21-day minimum advance purchase, and children under 12 may be eligible for 25% off fares with a 21-day advance purchase.

Iberia's two less-established domestic competitors often offer cheaper fares and are worth looking into. **Air Europa** (in U.S. tel. (888) 238-7672 or (718) 244-6016; in Spain tel. 902 30 06 00; email easyspain@g-air-europa.es; www.g-aireuropa.es) flies out of New York City and most European cities to Madrid, Málaga, Tenerife, and Santiago de Compostela. Discounts available for youth under 22. **SpanAir** (in U.S. tel. (888) 545-5757; in Spain tel. 902 13 14 15; fax 971 49 25 53; www.spanair.com) also offers international and domestic flights.

SpanAir Spain Pass: good for flying to any airport within Spain, including Mallorca and Menorca. No minimum stay; maximum stay 3 months. Reservations must be made before arriving in Spain. Valid for 1 year. Under 12 65% discount. 3 tickets US$195, 4 tickets US$240, 5 tickets US$295. Additional tickets US$50. **SpanAir Spain Pass B** is the same as Spain Pass A, but also includes Lanzarote, Gran Canaria, or Tenerife. 3 tickets US$245, 4 tickets US$290, 5 tickets US$345. Additional tickets US$50.

Iberia Spain Airpass: good for all mainland airports and the Balearic Islands. Reservations must be made in conjunction with the transatlantic ticket. Maximum stay 60 days. The Canaries can be added for US$50. Oct.-June 14 US$240; June 15-Sept. US$260.

BY TRAIN

Spanish trains are clean, relatively punctual, and reasonably priced, but tend to bypass many small towns. Spain's national railway is **RENFE** (www.renfe.es). Avoid *tranvía*, *semidirecto*, or *correo* trains—they are very slow.

AVE (Alta Velocidad Española): High-speed trains dart between Madrid and Sevilla (hitting Ciudad Real and Córdoba). AVE trains soar above others in comfort and price, not just speed. The 10am and noon trains are cheapest.

Talgo: Sleek trains zip passengers in air-conditioned compartments from Madrid to Málaga, Cádiz/Huelva, or Algeciras. It's more comfortable, possibly faster, and twice as pricey as *Cercanías-Regionales* trains.

Talgo 200: *Talgo* trains on AVE tracks. These currently service only Madrid-Málaga and Madrid-Cádiz/Huelva. Changing a Talgo 200 ticket carries a 20% fine.

Intercity: Cheaper than Talgo, but fewer stops. A/C and comfy. 5 lines: Madrid-Valencia, Madrid-Zaragoza-Barcelona, Madrid-Alicante, Madrid-Zaragoza-Logroño-Pamplona, and Madrid-Murcia-Cartegena.

Estrella: A pretty slow night train that has *literas* (bunks).

Cercanías: Commuter trains from large cities to suburbs and towns, with frequent stops.

Regional: Like *cercanías* but older; multi-stop, cheap rides to small towns and cities.

There is absolutely no reason to buy a Eurail pass if you are planning on traveling just within Spain and Portugal. Trains are cheap, so a pass saves little money. For the most part buses are an easier and more efficient means of traveling around Spain. There are several passes that cover travel within Spain. Ages 4-11 cost half-price; children under 4 are free. You must purchase railpasses before departure.

Spain Flexipass offers 3 days of unlimited travel in a 2-month period. 1st-class US$196, 2nd-class US$154. Up to 7 additional rail-days US$40 (1st-class), US$32 (2nd-class).

Iberic Railpass is good for 3 days of unlimited 1st-class travel in Spain and Portugal for US$204. Up to 7 additional rail-days US$44.

Spain Rail 'n' Drive Pass is good for 3 days of unlimited 1st-class train travel and 2 days of travel in a rental car. Prices from US$239-389, depending on how many people are traveling and the type of car.

Tarjeta Joven, available with a valid ISIC, allows for unlimited travel within Spain for 7 consecutive days (19,000ptas), 15 consecutive days (23,000ptas), or 30 consecutive days (30,000ptas).

BY BUS

Bus routes, far more comprehensive than the rail network, provide the only public transportation to many isolated areas and almost always cost less than trains. Comfort standards tend to be high, especially for longer journeys, although leg room may be slightly limited. For those traveling primarily within one region, buses are probably the best method of transport.

Spain has numerous private companies; the lack of a centralized bus company may make itinerary planning an ordeal. Companies' routes rarely overlap; it's unlikely that more than one will serve your intended destination. We list the major national companies, along with the phone number of the Madrid or Barcelona office below; you will likely use other companies for travel within a region.

ALSA (tel. 91 528 28 03). Serves Madrid, Galicia, Asturias, and Castilla y León. Also to Portugal, Morocco, France, Italy, and Poland.

Auto-Res/Cunisa, S.A. (tel. 91 551 72 00). From Madrid to Castilla y León, Extremadura, Galicia, and Valencia.

Julia Via Internacional (tel. 91 490 40 00). Runs throughout Iberia and Western Europe, and to Morocco.

Linebús (tel. 93 265 07 00). Runs to France, the U.K., Netherlands, Italy, and Morocco.

SAIA (International Autocares) (tel. 91 530 76 00). Runs to Belgium, Germany, France, Netherlands, and Andorra.

Samar, S.A. (tel. 91 468 48 39). To Aragón, Toulouse (in France), Andorra, and Portugal.

BY CAR

For more info on renting and driving a car in Spain, see page 36. Spain's highway system connects major cities by four-lane *autopistas* with plenty of service stations. Fast may be in vogue, but **speeders beware:** police can "photograph" the speed and license plate of your car, and issue a ticket without pulling you over. Purchase **gas** in super (97-octane), normal (92-octane), diesel, and unleaded. Prices are astronomical by North American standards: about 125ptas per liter. **Renting** a car in Spain is considerably cheaper than in many other European countries. You may want to check with **Atesa,** Spain's largest national rental agency. The Spanish automobile association is **Real Automóbil Club de España (RACE),** C. Jose Abascal, 10, Madrid (tel. 91 447 32 00; fax 91 447 79 48).

BY THUMB

In Spain, hitchers report that Castilla and Andalucía offer little more than a long, hot wait, and that hitchhiking out of Madrid is virtually impossible. The Mediterranean Coast and the islands are much more promising. Approaching people for rides at gas stations near highways and rest stops purportedly gets results.

MONEY

Banking hours in Spain from June through September are generally Monday through Friday 9am to 2pm; from October to May, banks are also open Saturday 9am to 1pm. Some banks are open in the afternoon as well. **Banco Central Hispano** often provides good rates, especially on traveler's checks. The following rates are from August 1999. For more information on money, see p. 14.

US $1 = 158.57 PESETAS (PTAS)	**100PTAS = US $0.63**
CDN $1 = 105.93 PTAS	**100PTAS = CDN $0.94**
UK £1 = 253.18 PTAS	**100PTAS = UK £0.40**
IR £1 = 211.27 PTAS	**100PTAS = IR £0.47**
AUS $1 = 100.95 PTAS	**100PTAS = AUS $0.99**
NZ $1 = 83.62PTAS	**100PTAS = NZ $1.20**
SAR 1 = 26.01 PTAS	**100PTAS = SAR 3.84**
POR 1$ = 0.8299 PTAS	**100PTAS = POR 120.49$**
MOR 1DH = 16.17 PTAS	**100PTAS = MOR 6.18DH**
EURO = 166.39 PTAS	**100PTAS = EURO 0.60**

TIPPING. Tipping is not very common in Spain and certainly not expected. In restaurants, all prices include service charge; tipping is optional. Satisfied customers occasionally toss in some spare change—usually no more than 5%. Train, airport, and hotel porters get 100-150ptas per bag, while taxi drivers sometimes get 5-10%.

IVA (TAX). Spain has a 7% **Value Added Tax,** known as IVA, on all restaurant and accommodations. The prices listed in *Let's Go* include IVA unless otherwise mentioned. Retail goods bear a much higher 16% IVA, although listed prices are usually inclusive. Non-EU citizens who have stayed in the EU fewer than 180 days can claim back the tax paid on purchases at the airport. Ask the shop where you have made the purchase to supply you with a tax return form.

SAFETY AND HEALTH

EMERGENCY TEL. **Local police:** 091. **National police:** 092. **Medical:** 061.

Spain has a low crime rate, but visitors can always fall victim to tourist-related crimes. For general safety tips, see page 18. Tourists should take particular care in Madrid, especially in the Centro, and in Barcelona around Las Ramblas.

Terrorism has not been a problem in Spain since the Basque separatist movement, Euskal Herritarrok (ETA), called a ceasefire in September of 1998. They have continued to observe it. Their terrorist activities, which occurred mainly in País Vasco (Basque Country), were primarily targeted at local politicians.

For general **health** information, see page 20.

ACCOMMODATIONS

YOUTH HOSTELS

Red Española de Albergues Juveniles (REAJ), C. Jose Ortega y Gasset, 71, Madrid 28006 (tel. 91 347 77 00; fax 91 401 81 60), the Spanish Hostelling International (HI) affiliate, runs 165 youth hostels year-round. Prices depend on location (typically some distance away from town center) and services offered, but are generally between 1500-2500ptas for guests under 26 and higher for those 26 and over. Breakfast is usually included; lunch and dinner are occasionally offered at an additional charge. Hostels usually lockout around 11:30am, and have curfews between midnight and 3am. As a rule, don't expect much privacy—rooms typically have from 4 to 20 beds in them. To reserve a bed in high season (July-Aug. and during *fiestas*), call well in advance. A national **Youth Hostel Card** is usually required (see **Hostels,** p. 25). HI cards are also available from Spain's main youth travel company, **TIVE.** Occasionally, guests can stay in a hostel without one and pay extra, or pay 300ptas extra per night for six nights to become a member.

PENSIONES AND HOSTALES

! **COULD** *LET'S GO* **BE WRONG?** The prices quoted in *Let's Go* were gathered during the summer of 1999; there is a good chance that they will increase by up to 500ptas by the end of 2000. Don't refuse to pay the owner's price simply because it is more than that quoted in the book. *Let's Go* may update annually, but unfortunately prices update annually as well. On the other hand, if the price is substantially more (over 1000ptas), ask other guests what they are paying to make sure you are getting charged the proper amount.

Spanish accommodations have many aliases, distinguished by the different grades of rooms. The cheapest and barest options are **casas de huéspedes** and **hospedajes,** while **pensiones** and **fondas** tend to be a bit nicer. All are basically just boarding

SPAIN

houses. Higher up the ladder, **hostales** generally have sinks in bedrooms and provide sheets and lockers, while **hostal-residencias** are similar to hotels in overall quality. The government rates *hostales* on a two-star system; even establishments receiving one star are typically quite comfortable. The system also fixes each *hostal*'s prices, posted in the lounge or main entrance. *Hostal* owners invariably dip below the official rates, especially in the off season (Sept.-May). In most cases, the owner lives in the same building.

The highest-priced accommodations are **hoteles,** which have a bathroom in each room but are usually too expensive for the budget traveler. The cream of the crop are the beautiful **Paradores Nacionales**—castles, palaces, convents, and historical buildings that have been converted into luxurious hotels that often are interesting sights in their own right. For a *parador,* 12,000ptas per night is a bargain.

Frequently owners will ask to copy your passport number when you check in, and in some cases they will keep it until you pay your bill. Always ask to see a room and verify the price before paying. Haggling for prices, especially in small inns, is common practice. Single rooms in cities are hard to come by, so solo travelers may have to pay for a double.

If you have any troubles (with rates or service), ask for the **libro de reclamaciones** (complaint book), which by law must be produced on demand. The argument will usually end immediately, since all complaints must be forwarded to the authorities within 48 hours. Report any problems to tourist offices who may help resolve disputes for you. In our listings, **full bath** or **bath** refers to a shower and toilet, while **shower** means just a shower stall in the room. Most rooms that we list have winter heating, as Spanish winters (particularly in the north and the mountains) can be quite chilly; when a listing says "heat in winter" it is to differentiate it from the other accommodations in the area, which are probably unheated. Air-conditioning (A/C) is mentioned when it is available.

In less-touristed areas, **casas particulares** (private residences) may sometimes be the only option. **Casas rurales** (rural cottages) and **casas rústicas** (farmhouses), officially referred to as *agroturismo*, have overnight rates from 1000 to 3500ptas. Both are common in northern Asturias and Castilla y León. In the Pyrenees and Picos de Europa, there are several **Refugios,** rustic mountain huts for hikers.

CAMPING

In Spain, **campgrounds** are generally the cheapest choice for two or more people. Most charge separate fees per person, per tent, and per car; others charge for a *parcela*—a small plot of land—plus possible per-person fees. Although it may seem like an inexpensive option, prices can get high for lone travelers, and even for pairs. Campgrounds are categorized on a three-class system, with rating and prices based on amenity quality. Like hostels, they must post fees within view of the entrance. They must also provide sinks, showers, and toilets. Ritzier ones may have playgrounds, grocery stores, cafes, restaurants, post offices, bike or moped rentals, or pools. Most tourist offices provide info on official areas, including the hefty *Guía de campings.* Reservations are usually necessary in the summer.

KEEPING IN TOUCH

Some useful **communication information** (including international access codes, calling card numbers, country codes, operator and directory assistance, and emergency numbers) is listed on the **inside back cover.**

PHONES. The central Spanish phone company is **Telefónica.** Spain has a great pay-phone network. **Phone booths** are marked by signs that say *Teléfono público* or *Locutorio;* most bars have pay phones, though they are often only coin-operated. Local calls cost 20ptas. The best way to make local calls is with a **phone card,** issued in denominations of 1000 and 2000ptas and available at tobacconists (*estancos* or *tabacos;* identified by brown signs with yellow lettering and tobacco leaf icons) and most post offices. American Express and Diner's Club cards now work as phone card substitutes in most pay phones. International calls can be made using phone cards, but are very expensive; the best way to call home is with an international calling card issued by your phone company. Numbers for major international calling cards (AT&T, MCI, Canada Direct, BT Direct, Ireland Direct, Telestra Australia, Optus Australia, Telecom New Zealand, and Telkom South Africa) are listed below, as well as on the inside back cover.

FAX. Most Spanish post offices have **fax services.** Some photocopy shops and telephone offices *(Telefónica)* also offer fax service, but they tend to charge more than post offices (whose rates are standardized by the government), and faxes can only be sent, not received. For a fax to North America, expect to spend around 1800ptas for the first page and 600ptas for each additional page, plus 16% IVA.

MAIL. Air mail *(por avión)* takes five to eight business days to reach the U.S. or Canada; service is faster to the U.K. and Ireland and slower to Australia and New Zealand. Standard postage is 87-120ptas, depending on the destination. **Surface mail** *(por barco)*, while considerably less expensive than air mail, can take over a month, and packages will take two to three months. **Registered** or **express mail** *(registrado* or *certificado)*, is the most reliable way to send a letter or parcel home, and takes four to seven business days (letter postage 237ptas). Spain's **overnight mail** is not worth the added expense, since it is not exactly "overnight." For better service, try private companies such as DHL, UPS, or the Spanish company SEUR; look under *mensajerías* in the yellow pages. Their reliability does, however, come at a high cost. **Stamps** are sold at post offices and tobacconists *(estancos* or *tabacos)*. Mail letters and postcards from the yellow mailboxes scattered throughout most cities, or from the post office in small towns.

EMAIL. Email is easily accessible within Spain and much quicker and more reliable than the regular mail system. Cybercafes are listed in most towns and all cities. In small towns, if internet access is not listed, your best bet is to check the library or the tourist office (where occasionally travelers may get access for a small fee). You will usually pay between 500 and 1200ptas per hour in Spain. To set up a free email account, see **Email and the Internet,** page 30.

EMBASSIES AND CONSULATES

Embassies and consulates are usually open Monday through Friday, mornings and evenings, with *siestas* in between—call for specific hours.

Australian Embassy: Santa Engracia, 120, **Madrid** 28003 (tel. 91 441 93 00; fax 91 442 53 62; email information@embaustralia.es; www.embaustralia.es). **Consulates:** Gran Vía Carlos III, 98, 3rd fl., **Barcelona** 08028 (tel. 93 330 94 96; fax 93 411 09 04); Federico Rubio, 14, **Sevilla** 41004 (tel. 95 422 09 71; fax 95 421 11 45).

British Embassy: C. Fernando el Santo, 16, **Madrid** 28010 (tel. 91 700 82 00; fax 91 700 83 11). **Consulate-General:** Edificio Torre, Av. Diagonal, 477, 13th fl., **Barcelona** 08036 (tel. 93 419 90 44; fax 93 405 24 11; email brconbcn@alba.mssl.es). **Consulates:** Centro Colón, Marqués de la Ensenada, 16, 2nd fl., **Madrid** 28004 (tel. 91 308 52 01; fax 91 308 08 82); Pl. Nueva, 8B, **Sevilla** 41001 (tel. 95 422 88 75; fax 95 421 03 23); Alameda de Urquijo, 2, 8th fl., **Bilbao** 48008 (tel. 94 415 76 00; fax 94 416 76 32); Pl. Mayor, 3D, **Palma de Mallorca** 07002 (tel. 971 71 24 45; fax 971 71 75 20); Av. Isidor Macabich, 45, 1st. fl., Apartavo 307, **Ibiza** 07800 (tel. 971 30 18 18; fax 971 30 19 72); Pl. Calvo Sotelo, 1/2, **Alicante** 03001 (tel. 96 521 60 22; fax 96 514 05 28); Po. Pereda, 27, **Santander** 39004 (tel. 942 22 00 00; fax 942 22 29 41); Edificio Duquesa, Duquesa de Parcent, 8, **Málaga** 28001 (tel. 95 221 75 71; fax 95 222 11 30); Edificio Cataluña, C. Luis Morote, 6, 3rd fl., **Las Palmas** 35080 (tel. 928 26 25 08; fax 928 26 77 74).

Canadian Embassy: C. Núñez de Balboa, 35, **Madrid** 28001 (tel. 91 431 43 00; fax 91 431 23 67; info.ic.gc.ca/Tourism). **Consulates:** Pg. Gràcia, 77, 3rd fl., **Barcelona** 08008 (tel. 93 215 07 04; fax 93 487 91 17); Edificio Horizonte, Pl. Malagueta, 3, 1st fl., **Málaga** 29016 (tel. 95 222 33 46; fax 95 222 40 23; email concon@microcad.es).

Irish Embassy: Po. Castellana, 46, 4th fl., **Madrid** 28046 (tel. 91 576 35 00; 91 435 16 77; email irlmad@ibm.net). **Consulate:** Gran Via Carlos III, 94, **Barcelona** 08028 (tel. 93 451 90 21; fax 93 411 29 21).

New Zealand Embassy: Pl. Lealtad, 2, 3rd fl., **Madrid** 28014 (tel. 91 523 02 26; fax 91 523 01 71). **Consulate:** Travesera de Gracia, 64, 4th fl., **Barcelona** 08006 (tel. 93 209 03 99; fax 93 202 08 90).

South African Embassy: Claudio Coello, 91, 6th fl., **Madrid** 28006 (tel. 91 435 66 88; fax 91 577 74 14; email sudafrica@arrakkis.es). **Consulates:** Teodora Lamadrid, 7-11, **Barcelona** 08022 (tel. 93 418 64 45; fax 93 418 05 38; email sudafrica@ceisei.es); Las Mercedes, 31, Las Arenas, **Bilbao** 48930 (tel./fax 94 464 11 24); Franchy y Roca, 5, 6th fl., **Las Palmas de Gran Canaria** 35007 (tel. 928 22 60 04; fax 928 22 60 15).

U.S. Embassy: C. Serrano, 75, **Madrid** 28006 (tel. 91 587 22 00; fax 91 587 23 03). **Consulate General:** Pg. Reina Elisenda, 23, **Barcelona** 08034 (tel. 93 280 22 27; fax 93 205 52 06). **Consulates:** Po. Delicias, 7, **Sevilla** 41012 (tel. 95 423 18 85; fax 95 423 20 40); Edificio Arca, C. Los Martínez Escobar, 3, Oficina 7, **Las Palmas** 35007 (tel. 928 27 12 59; fax 928 22 58 63); Centro Comercial "Las Rampas," Fase 2, Planta 1, Locales 12G7 & 12G8, **Fuengirola (Málaga)** 29640 (tel. 95 247 48 91; fax 95 246 51 89); C. Paz, 6, Local 5, **Valencia** 46003 (tel. 96 351 69 73; fax 96 352 95 65); Cantón Grande, 6-8 E, **La Coruña** 15003 (tel. 981 21 32 33; fax 981 22 88 08); Av. Jaume III, 26, **Palma de Mallorca** 07012 (tel. 971 72 50 51; fax 971 71 87 55).

MADRID

There are a few minutes, in the orange light of Madrid's early morning, when the city finally seems to sleep. Just moments later, steel shutters blink open and the streets once again fill with an unending stream of traffic. While tourists inundate the city, spending their days absorbing its "Old World" monuments, world-renowned museums, and raging nightlife, Madrid's largely transplanted population of 4,500,000 roams the labyrinthine streets and neighborhoods, living life with a simple and energetic joy.

Madrid's history does not read like that of rival European capitals. Although the city witnessed the coronation of Fernando and Isabel, Madrid did not gain importance until Habsburg King Felipe II moved the court here in 1561. At that time the city, which was far from vital ports and rivers, seemed an unlikely choice for a capital. Nevertheless, it immediately became a seat of wealth, culture, and imperial glory, serving as the center of Spain's 16th- and 17th-century Golden Age of literature, art, and architecture. In the 18th century, Madrid witnessed a Neoclassical rebirth—King Carlos III embellished the city by building wide, tree-lined boulevards and scores of imposing buildings. In the 19th century, however, Madrid was scarred by the Peninsular Wars against Napoleon, the bloody inspiration for Francisco de Goya's most famous canvases.

In 1939, Madrid was the last city, save Valencia, to fall in the Spanish Civil War. Though it was hostile to Franco's nationalism, the city was forced to serve as the center of his government. This time, its location—smack in the center of the country—was considered its greatest strength. With Franco's death nearly 40 years later came an explosion known as *la Movida* ("Shift" or "Movement"). After decades of totalitarian repression, Madrid burst out laughing and crying, and life poured into the city. A 200,000-strong student population took to the streets and stayed there, shedding the decorous reserve of their predecessors. In their frenetic, whirlwind-like state, post-Franco youth seemed neither cognizant of their city's history nor preoccupied with its future.

Today the city continues to serve as the country's political, intellectual, and cultural center. It has become a city of immigrants—families hoping to find relief from Spain's high unemployment, students seeking higher education at Madrid's universities, and yet-to-be-discovered artists all flood the growing city. Despite contrasting ages, histories, and customs, the residents of Madrid share a common belief in the city's grandeur.

HIGHLIGHTS OF MADRID

■ The **Palacio Real's** Baroque elegance and beautiful gardens (see p. 97).
■ Felipe IV's magnificent park, **Retiro** (see p. 100)
■ Three of the world's great museums: the **Museo del Prado** (see p. 103), the **Centro de Arte Reina Sofía** (see p. 104), and the **Museo Thyssen-Bornemisza** (see p. 105).
■ The **cafes** along Po. Prado by day (see p. 101); the **bars** in Pl. Santa Ana by night; the throbbing **clubs** in El Centro, Malasaña, and Chueca by morning (see p. 107).
■ The somber and majestic **El Escorial** (see p. 116).

■ GETTING THERE AND AWAY

BY PLANE

All flights land at **Aeropuerto Internacional de Barajas,** 30 minutes northeast of Madrid. A branch of the **regional tourist office** (tel. 91 305 86 56), in the international arrivals area, has maps and info (open M-F 8am-8pm, Sa 8am-1pm). Branches of the **Brújula** accommodations service, located in the airport and at the Bus-Aeropuerto stop, can help visitors find places to stay (see **Accommodations,** p. 83).

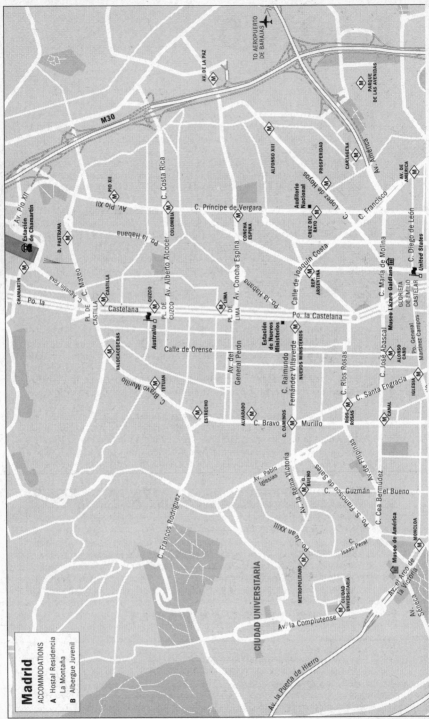

Madrid

ACCOMMODATIONS

A Hostal Residencia
La Montaña

B Albergue Juvenil

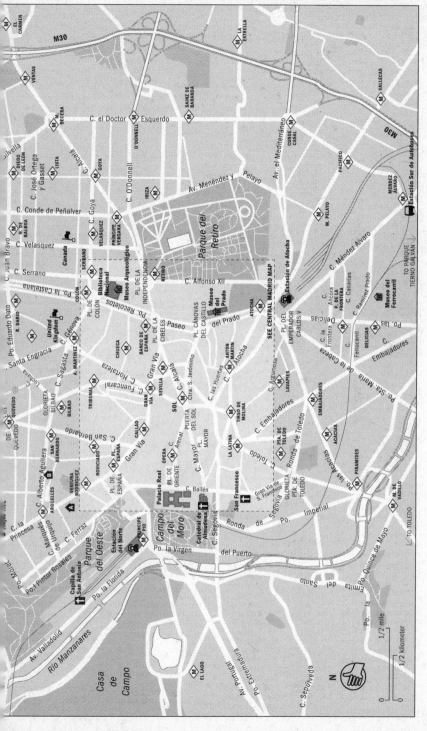

Central Madrid

ACCOMMODATIONS

(H.=Hostal; H.-R.=
Hostal-Residencia)
A A. Juvenil (HI)
B H.-R. Rios
C H. Nebrija
D H.-R. Lamalonga
E H. Lauria
F H.-R. Maria
G H.-R. Josefina/
 H.-R. Alibel
H H.-R. Portugal/
 H. Paz
I H.-R. Miño

J H.-R. Monte Iguelo/
 H.-R. Rober
K H.-R. Luz
L H. Madrid
M H. Esparteros
N H.-R. Encarnita/
 H.-R. Maria del Mar
O H. Cruz-Sol/
 H. Santa Cruz
P H.-R. Domínguez
Q H. Abril
R H. Medieval
S H. Margarita

T H. Palacios/
 H. Ribadavia
U H. Mónaco
V H. Lorenzo
W H.-R. Mondragón/
 H. Aguilar
X H.-R. Lido
Y H. Carreras,
 H. Villar, and
 H.-R. Regional
Z H. Abulense/
 H. Leones
a H. Rodríguez
b H. Armesto
c H. Gonzalo
d H.-R. Sud-Americana

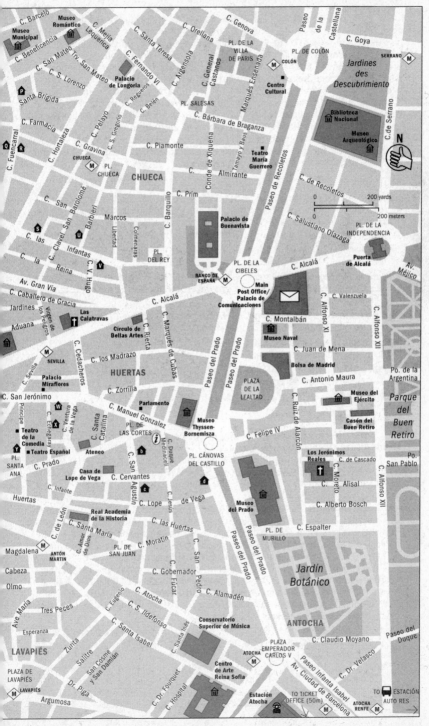

The **Barajas metro line,** inaugurated in June 1999, connects the airport to all of Madrid (130ptas). From the airport, follow signs to the metro. Take line 8 to Mar de Cristal, and switch to line 4. Changing to line 2 at the Goya stop will bring you to Sol, smack in the middle of Madrid's best accommodations and sights. Another option is the green **Bus-Aeropuerto** (look for "EMT" signs just outside the doors), which leaves from the national and international terminals and runs to the city center (4:45am-6:17am, every 25min.; 6:17am-10pm, every 15min.; 10pm-1:45am, every hr.; 385ptas). The bus stops underground beneath the Jardines del Descubrimiento in **Plaza de Colón** (M: Colón). After surfacing in Pl. Colón, walk toward the neo-Gothic statue that overlooks the **Paseo de Recoletos** on the opposite side of the gardens. The Colón metro station (brown line, L4) is across the street. Fleets of **taxis** swarm the airport. Taxi fare to central Madrid should cost around 3000ptas, including the 350pta airport surcharge.

AIRLINES

Iberia: Santa Cruz de Marcenado, 2 (tel. 91 587 81 56). M: San Bernardo. Open M-F 9:30am-2pm and 4-7pm. Reservations and info (tel. 902 40 05 00) open 24hr. **Aviaco,** C. Maude, 51 (tel. 91 554 36 00), is a domestic affiliate. International affiliates **Tap Air Portugal** (tel. 91 542 06 02) and **Portugalia** (tel. 902 100 145) fly to Portugal.

Air France: Pl. España, 18, 5th fl. (tel. 91 330 04 02; reservations tel. 91 330 04 40). M: Pl. España. Open M-F 9am-5pm.

American Airlines: C. Pedro Texeira, 8, 5th fl. (tel. 91 597 25 85). M: Santiago Bernabeu. Open M-F 9am-5:30pm. Reservations (tel. 91 597 20 68) open M-F 9am-6:30pm, Sa 9am-2pm.

British Airways: C. Serrano, 60 (tel. 91 577 69 59). M: Serrano. Open M-F 9am-5pm. Reservations (tel. 91 376 96 66) open M-F 9am-7pm.

Continental: C. Leganitos, 47, 9th fl. (tel. 91 559 27 10). M: Pl. España. Open M-F 9am-6pm. Reservations open M-F 9am-7pm.

Lufthansa: Cardenal Marcelo Española, 2 (tel. 91 302 94 26; reservations tel. 902 22 01 01), located outside city limits.

USAir: Santa Cruz de Marcenado, 31 (tel. 91 541 55 58). M: San Bernardo.

BY TRAIN

Two *Largo Recorrido* (long distance) **RENFE** stations, **Madrid-Chamartín** and **Madrid-Atocha,** connect Madrid to the rest of the world. Call RENFE (tel. 91 328 90 20) for reservations and info. **RENFE Main Office,** C. Alcalá, 44, at Gran Vía (M: Banco de España) sells tickets. Schedules and **AVE** (tel. 91 534 05 05) and **Talgo** tickets are also available. Open M-F 9:30am-8pm.

Estación Chamartín: (24hr. tel. 91 328 90 20; Spanish only), Agustín de Foxá. M: Chamartín. Bus #5 runs to and from Sol (45min.); the stop is just beyond the lockers. Ticket windows open 6:45am-10:30pm. Chamartín services both international and domestic destinations. Most *cercanías* (local) trains leave from Chamartín. To: **Barcelona** (7hr., 10 per day, 7am-12:50am, 4900-6400ptas); **Lisbon** (10hr., 1 per day, 8:10am or 12:30am, 7000-10,000ptas); **Paris** (13hr., 3 per day, 10am-10:45pm, 7000-10,000ptas); **Nice** (22hr., 3 per day, 10am-10:45pm, 14,000ptas). Chamartín is a mini-mall of useful services, including a **tourist office** (tel. 91 315 99 76; open M-F 8am-8pm, Sa 9am-1pm), currency exchange, accommodations service, post office, car rental, police, and **lockers** (400-600ptas).

Estación Atocha: (tel. 91 328 90 20). M: Atocha. Ticket windows open 6:30am-11:30pm. No international service. Trains to: Andalucía, Castilla-La Mancha, Extremadura, Valencia, Castilla y León, and El Escorial. **AVE** service (tel. 91 534 05 05) to **Córdoba** (1¾hr., 15 per day, 5:30am-10pm, 6000ptas) and **Sevilla** (2½hr., 18 per day, 5:30am-10pm, 8200ptas). The cast-iron atrium of the original station has been turned into a simulated rainforest. Art galleries, boutiques, restaurants, and cafes are additional diversions. **Luggage storage** (400-600ptas) is by the rainforest.

BY BUS

Numerous private companies, each with its own station and set of destinations, serve Madrid, but most buses pass through the **Estación Sur de Autobuses,** C. Méndez Alvaro, s/n (tel. 91 468 42 00 or 91 468 45 11). M: Méndez Álvaro. Info booth open daily 7am-11pm. (For more general information, see **By Bus,** p. 65.)

> **Estación Auto Res:** Pl. Conde de Casal, 6 (tel. 91 551 72 00). M: Conde de Casal. To **Cuenca** (2½hr., 7am-10pm, 1315ptas; express 2hr., 1600ptas); **Salamanca** (3¼hr., 4 per day, 7am-9:30pm, 1460ptas; express 2½hr., 2210ptas); **Valencia** (4hr., 13 per day, 7am-1am, 2865ptas).

> **Estación Empresa Alacuber:** (tel. 91 376 01 04), on Po. Moret. M: Moncloa. To **El Pardo** (20min., every 13min., 8am-7pm, 135ptas).

> **Estación Empresa Continental Auto:** C. Avenida de América, 34 (tel. 91 356 23 07). M: Cartagena. To: **Alcalá de Henares** (40min., every 15min., 7am-midnight, 250ptas); **Guadalajara** (1hr., every hr., 7am-midnight, 475ptas); **Toledo** (1½hr., every 30min., 7am-8:50pm, 570ptas).

> **Estación Empresa Larrea:** Po. Florida, 11 (tel. 91 530 48 00). M: Príncipe Pío (via extension from M: Ópera). To **Ávila** (2hr., 4 per day, 7:15am-8pm, 910ptas).

> **Estación Herranz:** (tel. 91 890 41 00), on C. Princesa, in the Intercambio de Moncloa. M: Moncloa. To **El Escorial** (1hr., every hr., 7:15am-10:45pm, 450ptas) and **Valle de los Caídos** (20min., El Escorial 3:15pm, returns 5:30pm, 420ptas), via El Escorial.

> **Estación La Sepulvedana:** Po. Florida, 11 (tel. 91 530 48 00). M: Príncipe Pío (via extension from M: Ópera). To **Segovia** (1½hr., every hr., 6:30am-10:45pm, 775ptas) and **Ávila** (2hr., 3 per day, 7:15am-8pm, 925ptas).

BY THUMB AND RIDESHARE

Hitchhiking is legal only on minor routes (though always a risk). The Guardia Civil de Tráfico picks up highway hitchhikers and deposits them at nearby towns or on a bus. No official organization arranges shared journeys; hitchers often try the message boards listed on page 81 for rideshare offers.

▄ GETTING AROUND MADRID

MAPS

The *Plano de Madrid* (street map) and the *Plano y Guía de Transportes* (public transportation map), free at city tourist offices, are fantastic. **El Corte Inglés** (see p. 81) also offers convenient one-page maps of Madrid. For a comprehensive map with street index, purchase the *Almax* map (650ptas) at any newsstand.

METRO

Madrid has a clean and relatively safe metro that puts almost every other major city's subway system to shame. Trains run frequently; only on Sundays and late at night is the wait more than five minutes. Green timers hanging above most platforms show the amount of time since the last train departed. The free *Plano del Metro* (available at any ticket booth) and the wall maps of the metro and surrounding neighborhoods (posted in every station) are clear and helpful. All stations also have signs with schedules and fare info.

Ten lines connect Madrid's 164 stations; over 40 are brand new this year. Lines are distinguished by color and number. An individual metro ticket costs 130ptas, but savvy riders opt for the **bonotransporte** (ticket of 10 rides for either the metro or bus system) at 680ptas. Buy both at machines in any metro stop and at *estancos* (tobacco shops) and newsstands. For more details, call **Metro info** (tel. 91 580 19 80) or ask at any ticket booth. Remember to hold on to your ticket or pass until you leave the metro—riding without one incurs an outrageous fine.

Trains run every day from 6am to 1:30am. Violent crime in the metro stations is almost unheard of, and women usually feel safe traveling alone. Do watch out for pickpockets in crowded cars. If you feel uncomfortable, avoid empty cars and ride in the first car near the conductor. At nighttime avoid the stations to the north, which are less frequented than most others. Metro stations Chueca, Gran Vía, Sol, Tirso de Molina, La Latina, and Plaza de España surface in areas that can be intimidating after midnight. Still, the metro is generally clean, efficient, and safe.

BUS

Unlike the metro, buses provide a view of Madrid and are a great way to see the city. Like the metro, the bus system is exceptional. Most stops are clearly marked. For extra guidance in finding routes and stops, try the handy *Plano de los Transportes*, available at newsstands (200ptas), or the free *Madrid en Autobús*, available at bus kiosks.

The fare is 130ptas and a 10-ride *bonotransporte* pass, sold at newsstands and *estancos* (tobacco shops), costs 680ptas. Buses run from 6am to 11:30pm. From 11:30pm until 3am, night buses travel from Pl. Cibeles to the outskirts every 30 minutes; from 3-6am, they run every hour. Night buses (N1-N20), the cheapest form of transportation for late-night revelers, are listed in a special section of the *Plano*. Buses stop all along the marked routes, not just in Pl. Cibeles. For more info, call **Empresa Municipal de Transportes** (tel. 91 406 88 10; Spanish only).

TAXI

Madrid is filled with taxis around the clock. If one does not appear when you need it, or if you want to summon one to your door, call 91 445 90 08 or 91 447 32 32. A green *libre* sign in the window or a lit green light indicates availability. The base fare is 170ptas, plus 50-75ptas per km. Common fare supplements include: airport (350ptas); bus and train stations (150ptas); luggage charge (50ptas per bag); Sundays and holidays (6am-11pm, 150ptas); nighttime (11pm-6am, 150ptas). The fare from the city center to the airport is about 3000ptas.

If you have a complaint or think you've been overcharged, demand a *recibo oficial* (official receipt) and *hoja de reclamaciones* (complaint form), which the driver is required to supply. Take down the license number, route taken, and fare charged. Drop off the forms and info at the **Ayuntamiento (City Hall)**, Pl. Villa, 4 (tel. 91 447 07 15 or 447 07 14), to request a refund.

To request **taxi service for the disabled**, call 91 547 82 00, 91 547 85 00, or 91 547 86 00. Rates are identical to those of other taxis. If you leave possessions in a taxi, visit or call the **Negociado de Objetos Perdidos**, Pl. Legazpi, 7 (tel. 91 588 43 46). Open M-F 9am and 2pm. Drivers are obligated to turn in any items within 48 hours.

CAR RENTAL

There is no reason to rent a car in Madrid. If congested traffic and nightmarish parking don't unnerve you, aggressive drivers and annoying mopeds will. Don't drive unless you're planning to zoom out of the city, and even then bus and train fares will be cheaper. Per kilometer surcharges apply to rentals of less than a week. Tobacco shops sell parking permits. If driving to destinations outside of Spain, a larger car rental chain is your best bet. The tourist office has a complete list of car rental companies, including **Avis** (tel. 91 305 42 73 or 91 547 20 48) and **Hertz** (tel. 91 393 60 00). For more information, see **Car Rental,** page 36.

Autos Bravo: C. Toledo, 136 (tel. 91 474 80 75). M: Puerta de Toledo. Medium car 12,000ptas per day, 75,000ptas per week. Unlimited mileage, insurance included. Open M-F 9am-2pm and 4:30-8pm, Sa 9am-1:30pm.

Autos Viaducto: C. Martín de los Héroes, 23 (tel. 91 541 55 41), and Av. Mediterráneo, 4 (tel. 91 433 12 33 or 91 552 10 44). Cheapest rate 5468ptas per day, including insurance. 100km free, 18ptas for every km over 100km. 16% IVA not included. Open M-F 9am-1:30pm and 4-7:30pm.

MOPED RENTAL

Popular with Madrid's residents, mopeds are swift and easy to park. A lock and helmet are necessary. Rent from **Motocicletas Antonio Castro**, C. Conde Duque, 13 (tel. 91 542 06 57). M: San Bernardo. A Honda costs 4500ptas per day (8am-8pm) or 19,500ptas per week, including unlimited mileage and insurance. Deposit of 40,000ptas required. 16% IVA not included. Renters must be at least 18 and have an International Driver's Permit and photo ID. (Open M-F 8am-1:30pm and 5-8pm.)

⚓ ORIENTATION

The "Kilometro 0" sign in front of the police station in **Puerta del Sol** marks the intersection of eight of Madrid's most celebrated streets, and the starting point of the country's major highways. To make Madrid's infinite plazas and serpentine streets more navigable, the city is broken down into five major neighborhoods: **Centro, Huertas, Malasaña and Chueca, Bilboa,** and **Argüelles**.

Most of Madrid's prominent sights, including the **Ópera** and **Plaza Mayor**, radiate from Sol in the Centro. Just west of Sol off C. Mayor, Plaza Mayor is the hub of activity for tourists and *madrileños* alike; the plaza houses both contemporary cafes and the churches and the historical buildings of **Habsburg Madrid**, also known as **Madrid de los Asturias**. Farther west of Sol, via C. Arenal, lies the reigning monument of **Bourbon Madrid**, the Palacio Real. This section of Madrid, also known as **Ópera**, hosts fantastic gardens and churches.

To the east of Sol lies **Huertas**, once the literary district and now the center of cafe and theater life. Huertas is bordered by C. Alcalá to the north, Po. Prado to the east, Sol to the west, and C. Atocha to the south. Centered around **Plaza Santa Ana**, Huertas is crowded with some of the best budget accommodations in the city, as well as some of the best *tapas* bars. It is also the ideal starting point for exploring the city's three great museums (see **Museums**, p. 103) or the lush **Parque del Buen Retiro** (p. 100).

Also south of Sol and west of Huertas is the area around metro stops **La Latina** and **Tirso de Molina**, which has less prestige and fewer tourists than the rest of Old Madrid. **El Rastro**, a gargantuan ancient flea market, is staged here every Sunday morning. Farther south lies **Lavapiés**, a working-class neighborhood.

North of Sol, the grand avenue **Gran Vía** is the comercial center of Madrid, scarring the horizon with skyscrapers and fast-food joints. Linked to C. de Fuencarral, it acts as the southern border of **Malasaña** and **Chueca**, full of über-cool restaurants and shops. Beyond Gran Vía and east of Malasaña and Chueca lies modern Madrid. Running the length of Madrid from **Atocha** in the south to **Plaza de Castilla** in the north, **Paseo del Prado, Paseo de Recoletos,** and **Paseo de la Castellana** pass the Prado, the fountains at the **Plazas Cibeles** and **Colón,** and the elaborate skyscrapers beyond Pl. Colón, including the twin towers of the **Puerta de Europa**.

> **READ THIS** The **Guía del Ocio**, available behind the counter of any news kiosk, should be your first purchase in Madrid (125ptas). It has concert, theater, sports, cinema, and TV schedules. It also lists exhibits, restaurants, bars, and clubs. Although it is in Spanish, the alphabetical listings of clubs and restaurants are invaluable even to non-speakers. The *Guía* comes out on Thursday or Friday, so be sure that you are buying an up-to-date copy instead of last week's issue. For an English magazine with articles on new finds in and around the city, pick up *In Madrid,* distributed free at tourist offices and many restaurants. Live Music and Nightlife sections are basically an English translation of the *Guía. The Broadsheet,* free at bookstores, is a no-frills listing of English classifieds. This self-proclaimed "lifesaver for English speakers in Madrid" is geared toward long-term residents. The weekly *Segundamano*, on sale at kiosks, is essential for apartment or roommate seekers.

The area northwest of Sol holds the **Plaza de España** and the tall **Torre de Madrid,** the pride of 1950s Spain. Still farther northwest of Sol lie **Argüelles** and **Bilboa,** energetic neighborhoods spilling over from **Moncloa.** Both are student districts, filled with cheap eateries and neon nightclubs.

Madrid is much safer than other major European cities, but Sol, Pl. España, Pl. Chueca, and Malasaña's Pl. Dos de Mayo are still intimidating late at night. As a general rule, avoid the parks and quiet residential streets after dark. Watch out for thieves and pickpockets in crowds, and be wary of opportunists who target tourists with their clever scams; con artists are a tradition here.

⁊ PRACTICAL INFORMATION

TOURIST AND FINANCIAL SERVICES

Tourist Offices: English is spoken at all tourist offices. Those planning trips outside the Comunidad de Madrid can visit region-specific offices within Madrid; ask the tourist offices below for their addresses. **Municipal,** Pl. Mayor, 3 (tel. 91 366 54 77 or 91 588 16 36; fax 91 366 54 77). M: Sol. Hands out indispensable city and transportation maps and a complete guide to accommodations, as well as *En Madrid* and *In Madrid,* monthly activities and information guides. Open M-F 10am-8pm, Sa 10am-2pm. **Oficinas de Información,** C. Princesa, 1 (tel. 91 541 23 25), off Pl. España. M: Pl. España. Has the same fabulous maps as the municipal office. **Regional/Provincial Office of the Comunidad de Madrid,** Mercado Pta. de Toledo, Ronda de Toledo 1, stand #3134 (tel. 91 364 1876). M: Pta. de Toledo. In a gallery with large banners on a plaza across from the metro station. Brochures, transport info, and maps for towns in the Comunidad. Open M-F 9am-7pm, Sa 9:30am-1:30pm. Other offices at Estación Chamartín (see **By Train,** p. 76) and the airport (see **By Plane,** p. 71). **El Corte Inglés** has **free maps** and info (see p. 81).

▧ General Info Line: Dial 010. 20ptas. per min. Run by the Ayuntamiento. They'll tell you anything about Madrid, from the nearest police station's address to zoo hours. Ask for *ingles* and they will transfer you to an English speaking operator.

Tours: Read the fine print before signing on. The following are given in English. **Pullmantur,** Pl. Oriente, 8 (tel. 91 541 18 05 or 91 541 18 06). M: Ópera. Tours of Madrid, averaging around 4000ptas; also excursions to outlying areas. **Trapsatur,** San Bernardo, 23 (tel. 91 542 63 20). M: Santo Domingo. **Juliá Tours,** Gran Vía, 68 (tel. 91 559 96 05). M: Pl. de España. Offers tours of Andalucía, Portugal, and Morocco.

Budget Travel: Viajes TIVE, C. Fernando el Católico, 88 (tel. 91 543 74 12; fax 91 544 00 62). M: Moncloa. Exit the metro at C. Isaac Peral, walk straight down C. Arcipreste de Hita, and turn left on C. Fernando el Católico; it is on your left. ISIC 700ptas, HI cards 1800ptas. Organizes group excursions and language classes. Lodgings and student residence info. English spoken. Arrive early to avoid long lines. Open M-F 9am-2pm, Sa 9am-noon. **Comunidad de Madrid, Dirección General de Juventud,** C. Alcalá, 30 and 32 (tel. 91 580 40 00 or 580 42 42). M: Banco de España. Offers many of the same services as TIVE, but does not sell tickets. **Viva,** Pl. Callao, 3 (tel. 902 32 52 75; fax 91 531 76 95). Arranges trips, car rentals, and documentation. **Viajes Lanzani,** Gran Vía, 88 (tel. 91 541 47 32). M: Gran Vía. Info on discount and student airfare, bus and train tickets, discounted tours, excursion packages, and accommodations.

Currency Exchange: Banco Central Hispano charges no commission on cash or traveler's checks and offers the best rates on AmEx traveler's checks. **Main branch,** C. de Alcalá, 49 (tel. 91 558 41 00). M: Banco de España. Open Jun-Aug. M-F 8:30am-2:30pm; in Sept.-May M-Th 8:30am-2:30pm, F-Sa 8:30am-1pm. Banks usually charge 1-2% commission (min. charge 500ptas). Booths in Sol and Gran Vía, open as late as 2am and on weekends, have poor rates and are not a good deal for cashing traveler's checks, despite their charging commission. On the other hand, for small-denomination bills they may be the best option. **ATMs** are everywhere in Madrid. **Servi Red, Servi Caixa,** and **Telebanco** machines accept bank cards with one or more of the Cirrus, PLUS, EuroCard, and NYCE logos. For more info, see **Cash Cards,** p. 17.

American Express: Pl. Cortés, 2 (tel. 91 322 55 00; info tel. 91 572 03 03). M: Sevilla. From the metro stop, go down C. Seducers and turn left on C. San Jerónimo; office is on the left. The office has *Agencia de Viajes* written in big letters on the windows. In addition to currency exchange (1% cash and 2% traveler's check commission; no commission on AmEx traveler's checks), they'll hold mail for 30 days and help send and receive wired money. In an emergency, AmEx cashes personal checks up to US$1000 for cardholders. Open M-F 9am-5:30pm, Sa 9am-noon. Express Cash machine outside (24hr.). To report or cancel lost traveler's checks, call toll free 900 99 44 26. To report other problems, call toll free tel. 900 94 14 13. Both lines available 24hr.

LOCAL SERVICES

Message Boards: At **Librería Turner** and **Booksellers** (see **Shopping: Books,** p. 113); **TIVE** travel agency (see above), with tons of cheap travel tickets and rideshare offers; and **Albergue Juvenil Santa Cruz (HI),** with mostly rideshares (see **Accommodations,** p.14). Also check the classifieds in *En Madrid*.

Luggage Storage: **Estaciones Chamartín.** Self-serve, automatic lockers in the *consigna* area by the bus stop. Lockers 400-600ptas per day. Open daily 6:30am-12:30am. **Estación Atocha.** Same services, prices, and hours. Exit the *largo recorrido* area and the lockers are to the left. **Estación Sur de Autobuses.** Bags checked (800ptas).

El Corte Inglés: C. Preciados, 3 (tel. 91 379 80 00). M: Sol. **C. Goya, 76** (tel. 91 432 93 00). M: Goya. **C. Princesa, 56** (tel. 91 454 60 00). M: Argüelles. **C. Raimundo Fernández Villaverde, 79** (tel. 91 556 23 00). M: Nuevos Ministerios. Giant chain of department stores. Their motto is: "A place to shop. A place to dream." Good maps, haircutting, cafeteria-restaurant, supermarket, telephones, tapes and CDs, books in English, electronics, and fawning salespeople. Currency exchange with no commission but mediocre rates. Open M-Sa 10am-9pm, Su 10am-2pm.

English-Language Periodicals: International edition dailies and weeklies available at kiosks everywhere, especially on the Gran Vía, Paseos del Prado, Recoletos, and Castellana and around Pta. Sol. If you're dying for the *New York Times* (425ptas), try one of the **VIPS** restaurants (see **Red-Eye Establishments,** p. 16).

Language Service: **Forocio** (*Foreign Ocio*), C. Mayor, 6, 4th fl. (tel. 91 522 56 77). An organization dedicated to bringing foreigners and natives together to share languages and good times. Sponsors weekly international parties and organizes group trips to other parts of Spain. Open daily 10am-8pm.

Libraries: **Bibliotecas Populares** (info tel. 91 445 98 45). A large branch is at M: Puerta de Toledo (tel. 91 366 54 07). English-language periodicals. Open M-F 8:30am-8:45pm. **Biblioteca Nacional** (tel. 91 580 78 23), on C. Serrano next to the Museo Arqueológico. M: Serrano. Limited to scholars doing doctorate and post-doctorate research. To use the facilities, bring letters of recommendation and a project proposal, and overinflate your importance. Open M-F 9am-9pm, Sa 9am-1pm. **Washington Irving Center,** C. Marqués Villamagna, 8 (tel. 91 587 22 00). M: Serrano or Colón. From the station, walk up C. Serrano and turn left on C. Marqués de Villamagna. Good selection of American magazines and books. Anyone over 16 can check books out for 2 weeks by filling out a form. Allow about 1 week for processing. Open M-F 2-6pm.

Religious Services: **Our Lady of Mercy English-Speaking Parish,** C. Alfonso XIII, 165 (morning tel. 91 533 20 32; afternoon tel. 91 554 28 60), on the corner of Pl. Habana. Sunday mass in English 11am. **Immanuel Baptist Church,** C. Hernández de Tejada, 4 (tel. 91 407 43 47). English services Su 11am and 7pm. **Community Church of Madrid,** C. Bravo Murillo, 85. M: Cuatro Caminos. At the Colegio El Porvenir. Multi-denominational Protestant services in English Su 10am. **British Embassy Church of St. George,** C. Núñez de Balboa, 43 (tel. 91 576 51 09). M: Velázquez. Services Su 8:30, 10, and 11:15am. **Sinagoga Beth Yaacov,** C. Balmes, 3 (tel. 91 445 98 43 or 445 98 35), near Pl. Sorolla. M: Iglesia. Services F 8pm, Sa 9:15am. Kosher restaurant can be reserved. Passport sometimes required. Spanish only. **Centro Islámico,** C. Alonso Cano, 3 (tel. 91 448 05 54). M: Iglesia. Services and language classes. Open M-F 9am-2pm and 5-8pm.

MADRID

Women's Services: Librería de Mujeres, C. San Cristóbal, 17 (tel. 91 521 70 43), near Pl. Mayor. M: Sol. Walk down C. Mayor and make a left on C. Esparteros, take the first right on C. Postas, and then the first left onto C. San Cristóbal. The shop's motto: *"Los libros no muerden, el feminismo tampoco."* ("Books don't bite, neither does feminism.") Books and gifts, but more of a resource for Spanish speakers. Helpful with finding local support and discussion groups. Open M-F 10am-2pm and 5-8pm. **Women's Issues** (tel. 900 19 10 10 or 91 347 80 00).

Gay and Lesbian Services: Colectivo de Gais y Lesbianas de Madrid (COGAM), C. Fuencarral, 37 (tel./fax 91 523 00 70), directly across from the Ministry of Justice. M: Gran Vía. Provides a wide range of services and activities of interest to gays, lesbians, and bisexuals. English usually spoken. Free screenings of gay-interest movies, COGAM youth group (25 and under), and HIV-positive support group (tel. 91 522 45 17; M-F 6-10pm). Reception daily M-F 5-9pm. Free counseling M-Th 7-9pm. Library open daily 7-9pm. COGAM also publishes the semi-monthly *Entiendes...?,* a magazine in Spanish about gay issues, as well as the *Pink and Black Pages* listing gay services, groups, activities, and personals (magazine available at many kiosks and bookstores). **Berkana Librería Gai y Lesbiana** has good guides, contact information, and listings (see **Books,** p. 113). **Most entertainment guides list gay and lesbian clubs. GAI-INFORM,** a gay info line (tel. 91 523 00 70), provides info in Spanish (and sometimes French and English) about gay associations, leisure activities, and health issues. The same number has info on sports, workshops in French and English, dinners, and on **Brujulai,** COGAM's weekend excursion group. Open daily 5-9pm.

Laundromat: Lavandería Donoso Cortés, C. Donoso Cortés, 17 (tel. 91 446 96 90). M: Quevedo. From the metro, walk down C. Bravo Murillo to C. Donoso Cortés. Self-service wash 600ptas, detergent 60ptas. Open M-F 9am-2pm and 3:30-8pm, Sa 9am-2pm. **Lavandería Automática SIDEC,** C. Don Felipe, 4. M: Tribunal. Wash 600ptas, detergent 25ptas. Open M-F 10am-9pm. **Maryland,** C. Meléndez Valdés, 52 (tel. 91 543 30 41). M: Argüelles. Go up C. Princesa and turn right on C. Hilarión, which intersects C. Meléndez Valdés. Wash and detergent 800ptas. Open M-F 10:30am-8pm, Sa 10am-2pm.

EMERGENCY AND COMMUNICATIONS

Emergency: tel. 091 (national police) or 092 (local police).

Police: C. Luna, 17 (tel. 91 521 12 36). M: Callao. From Gran Vía, walk down C. Arenal. This station has forms in English. To report crimes committed in the **metro,** go to the office in the Sol station (tel. 91 521 09 11). Open daily 8am-11pm. **Guardia Civil** (tel. 062 or 91 534 02 00). **Protección Civil** (tel. 91 537 31 00).

Crisis Lines: Poison Control (24hr. tel. 91 562 04 20). **Rape Hotline** (tel. 91 574 01 10). Open M-F 10am-2pm and 4-7pm (other times machine-recorded instructions).

Help Lines: AIDS Info Hotline (tel. 900 11 10 00) M-F 9am-2pm. **Detox** (tel. 900 16 15 15). English spoken. Daily 9am-9pm. **Alcoholics Anonymous,** C. Juan Bravo, 40-bis, 2nd fl. (English tel. 91 309 19 47; crisis line in Spanish tel. 91 341 82 82). M: Núñez de Balboa. 20pta min. charge. **English-Language Helpline** (tel. 91 559 13 93) offers confidential help from trained volunteers. Open daily 7-11pm. 20pta min. charge.

Late-Night Pharmacy: (info tel. 098). Check *Farmacias de Guardia* listings in local papers to find pharmacies open after 8pm. One located at **C. Mayor, 59** (tel. 91 548 00 14), near the M: Sol. Listings of the nearest on-duty pharmacy are also posted in all pharmacy windows.

Hospitals: Prompt appointments are hard to obtain, but public hospitals don't require advance payment. Emergency rooms are the best option for immediate attention. **Anglo-American Medical Unit,** Conde de Aranda, 1, 1st fl. (tel. 91 435 18 23). M: Serrano or Retiro. Doctors, dentists, and optometrists. Run partly by British and Americans. Regular personnel on duty 9am-8pm. Not an emergency clinic. 8000ptas for initial visit. Credit cards accepted. Embassies and consulates also keep lists of English-speaking doctors in private practice. **Hospital Clínico San Carlos** (tel. 91 330 30 00), on Pl. Cristo Rey. M: Moncloa. Open 24hr.

Emergency Clinics: In a **medical emergency,** dial 061. **Equipo Quirúrgico Municipal No. 1,** C. Montesa, 22 (tel. 91 588 51 00). M: Manuel Becerra. **Hospital Ramón y Cajal,** Ctra. Colmenar Viejo (tel. 91 336 80 00). Bus #135 from Pl. Castilla.

Post Office: Palacio de Comunicaciones, Pl. Cibeles (tel. 902 19 71 97). M: Banco de España. Enormous, ornate palace on the far side of the plaza from the metro. Info (main vestibule) open M-F 8am-10pm or call the useful info line (tel. 91 537 64 94). Open for stamp purchase and certified mail (main door) M-F 8:30am-10pm, Sa 8:30am-8pm, Su 9:30am-1:30pm. Lista de Correos (window 80) open M-F 8:30am-9:30pm, Sa 8:30am-8pm. Send packages (door N) M-F 8:30am-9pm, Sa 8:30am-1:30pm. Telex and **fax** service (door H, right of main entrance) open M-F 8am-midnight, Sa-Su 8am-10pm. Windows may change. English and French spoken at info desk. **Postal Code:** 28080.

Internet Access: New internet centers are popping up in Madrid almost as fast as you can say "yahoo." The following listings are spread out among major neighborhoods.

   ▨ **La Casa de Internet,** C. Luchana, 20 (tel. 91 446 55 41). M: Bilboa. 800ptas per hr.; 600ptas with student ID. Open 10am-10pm.

   Sol.Com, Pta. Sol, 6. M: Sol. 750ptas per hr. Open daily 9am-11pm.

   Aroba 25, Gran Vía, 80 (tel. 91 559 84 79). M: Gran Vía. 600ptas per hr. Open 10am-10:30pm.

   Cestein, C. Leganitos, 9 y 11 (tel. 91 548 27 75). M. Pl. de España. 400ptas per 30min.

   Net Café, C. San Bernardo, 81 (tel. 91 594 09 99). M: San Bernardo. Buy a drink and get an hour of free use. Open M-Th 6pm-2am, F-Su 4pm-3am.

Telephones: Telephone Info: tel. 1003. No English spoken. 10ptas per min. (For more info, see **Keeping in Touch,** p. 29.)

▛ ACCOMMODATIONS

The demand for rooms is always high and increases dramatically in summer. Never fear—Madrid is inundated with hostels. Prices average about 2400ptas per person for a basic hostel room, a bit more for a two-star *hostal*, and slightly less for a bed in a *pensión*. Accommodation prices may decrease significantly in the off-season (Oct.-Apr.) Try bargaining down the price if you plan on staying a while.

   Viajes Brújula: Torre de Madrid, 14, 6th fl. (tel. 91 559 97 04 or 91 559 97 05; fax 91 548 46 24). M: Plaza España. Located in a huge building with signs for Alitalia on the ground floor. For 300ptas, they make reservations for any participating locale in Spain. You must go in person. You pay a deposit of one-third of the room price, which is then subtracted from the price of the accommodation. Not every establishment is signed up with Brújula (no HI youth hostels); nevertheless, it's a good deal and a safe bet if you are tired and need a bed. English spoken. Open M-F 9am-7pm. Branch offices at **Estación Atocha** (tel. 91 539 11 73), at the AVE terminal (open daily 8am-10pm); **Estación Chamartín** (tel. 91 315 78 94; open daily 7am-11:30pm); and the **airport bus terminal** (tel. 91 575 96 80) in Pl. Colón (open daily 8am-10pm).

HOSTALES AND PENSIONES

In Madrid, the difference between a one-star *hostal* and a *pensión* is often minimal. A room in a one- or two-star *hostal* has at least the basics: bed, closet space, desk with chair, sink and towel, window, light fixture, fake flowers, a lock on the door, and the occasional religious icon. Winter heating is standard, air-conditioning is not. Unless otherwise noted, communal bathrooms (toilet and shower) are the norm. Most places accept reservations, but none require them. Reservations are, however, recommended in summer and on weekends year-round, especially in the Puerta del Sol area and at the first place *Let's Go* lists in each district. Hostels in Madrid are generally well-kept and comfortable. Owners are usually accustomed to opening the doors, albeit groggily, at all hours or providing keys for guests, but ask before club-hopping into the wee hours; late-night lockouts or confrontations with irate owners are never fun.

Pensiones are like boarding houses: they sometimes have curfews and often host guests staying for longer periods of time *(estables)*. Towels and sheets are provided but not always changed daily. The same goes for *casas de huéspedes* or simply *casas*. The best deals are found outside central locations, and Madrid's stellar public transportation makes virtually any locale central.

EL CENTRO: SOL, ÓPERA, AND PLAZA MAYOR

Puerta del Sol is the center of the city in the center of the country. All roads converge here (it's Spain's km 0) and most visitors ramble through at least once. Signs indicating *hostales* and *pensiones* stick out from flower-potted balconies and decaying facades on narrow, sloping streets. For better deals in quieter spots, stray several blocks from Sol. Don't be afraid to climb that extra flight of stairs; prices drop the higher up you go. The following listings fall in the area between the Sol and Ópera metro stops. Price and location in the Centro are as good as it gets, especially if you are planning to brave the nightlife. Buses #3, 25, 39, and 500 serve Ópera; buses #3, 5 (from Atocha), 15, 20, 50, 51, 52, 53, and 150 serve Sol.

⬛ Hostal Paz, C. Flora, 4, 1st and 4th fl. (tel. 91 547 30 47). M: Ópera. Do not be deterred by the dark street, parallel to C. Arenal, off C. Donados or C. Hileras. Peace abounds in all the rooms, especially those overlooking the courtyard. Satellite TV, A/C, and spotless, spacious bathrooms. Reservations encouraged. Laundry 1100ptas. Singles 2500ptas; doubles 3800ptas, with shower 4300ptas; triples with shower 5700ptas. Visa, MC.

Hostal-Residencia Luz, C. Fuentes, 10, 3rd fl. (tel. 91 542 07 59), off C. Arenal. M: Ópera. 12 sunny, newly redecorated rooms with hardwood floors. Bathrooms so clean you won't mind sharing. Satellite TV, fax service, and public phone. Laundry 1000ptas. Singles 2500ptas; doubles 3600ptas; triples 5500ptas. Discounts for stays of 15 days or more. 7% IVA not included.

Hostal Esparteros, C. Esparteros, 12, 4th fl. (tel. 91 522 59 76). Cheap, small, but comfortable rooms with either balcony or large windows. So high up it's almost quiet. Friendly, English-speaking owner provides loads of info on Madrid's history and sights. Laundry 1000ptas. Singles 1800ptas, with shower 2200ptas; doubles with bath 3200; triples with shower 4400ptas.

Hostal Madrid, C. Esparteros, 6, 2nd fl. (tel. 91 522 00 60; fax 91 532 35 10). M: Sol. Off C. Mayor. The backpacker's equivalent of a 5-star hotel. Spacious rooms with shiny wood floors and large windows. All have TVs, telephones, enormous closets, telephones, A/C and new bathrooms. Reservations recommended. Singles 5000ptas; doubles 8500ptas; triple with balcony 10,000ptas. Visa.

Hostal-Residencia María del Mar, C. Marqués Viudo de Pontejos, 7, 2nd and 3rd fl. (tel. 91 531 90 64). M: Sol. Off C. Correo from Pta. Sol. Rooms have high ceilings, shiny floors, and shapely furniture—just don't get stuck in one of the 2 windowless singles. Lounge with TV. No smoking in common areas. 2am curfew. Hot showers 200ptas; cold showers 100ptas. Singles with sink 1800ptas; doubles 3000ptas, with bath 4500-5000ptas; triples with bath 6500ptas.

Hostal-Residencia Cruz-Sol, Pl. Santa Cruz, 6, 3rd fl. (tel. 91 532 71 97). M: Sol. Ample rooms with parquet floors and cavernous ceilings, many overlooking the plaza. Appreciate the creative wallpaper. No winter heating. Singles 2000ptas, with bath 4000ptas; doubles 3500ptas, with bath 4500ptas; triples 3500ptas, with bath 5000ptas.

Hostal-Residencia Santa Cruz, Pl. Santa Cruz, 6, 2nd fl. (tel./fax 91 522 24 41). M: Sol. Palatial lounge gives way to closet-like rooms. Reservations accepted by fax. Tiny, sinkless singles 2800ptas, with shower 3500ptas; doubles 4000ptas, with bath 5000ptas; triples 5000ptas, with bath 6000ptas.

Hostal-Residencia Rober, C. Arenal, 26, 5th fl. (tel. 91 541 91 75). M: Ópera. Spotless and spartan, barren walls and tight bed corners give it that hospital feel. Smoking is strictly prohibited. All 14 pristine rooms have their own tiny TVs. A/C. Singles with shower 3000ptas, with bath 3400ptas; doubles with bath 5300ptas; triples with bath 6500ptas. Prices don't include 7% IVA. Visa, MC, AmEx.

Hostal-Residencia Miño, C. Arenal, 16, 2nd fl. (tel. 91 531 50 79). M: Ópera. Don't be deterred by the deer's head by the entrance. Diverse rooms range from large with hardwood floors and balconies to small with vinyl underfoot. Avoid the rooms overlooking C. Arenal, where closed windows shut off air circulation. Singles 2800ptas, with shower 2900ptas; doubles with shower 3900 ptas, with bath 4500ptas; triples 5400ptas.

Hostal Portugal, C. Flora, 4, ground fl. (tel. 91 559 40 14). M: Ópera. Great location and cheap prices make up for cramped, stuffy quarters. Like its namesake, the hostel is quickly becoming a favorite with Americans. English spoken. 2000ptas per person.

Monte Iguelo, C. Arenal, 26, 4th fl. (tel. 91 548 05 31). Children's drawings on the walls give it the feel of a kindergarden classroom. Inexpensive rooms provide a taste of home. Small rooms with TVs and refrigerators. Singles 2200 ptas; doubles 4500ptas with bath; luxurious triples 4800ptas. Visa, MC.

Hostal-Residencia Encarnita, C. Marqués Viudo de Pontejo, 7, 4th fl. (tel. 91 531 90 55). M: Sol. Above the María del Mar. Typical hostel charm: dim rooms, soft beds, cheap nature posters. Hot showers 200ptas, cold showers 100ptas. Singles 1500ptas; doubles 2600ptas, with bath 2900ptas; triples 3900ptas.

HUERTAS

Although *madrileños* have never settled on a nickname for this neighborhood, the area between C. San Jeronimo and C. de las Huertas is generally referred to as Huertas. It is also Madrid's theater district. Nighttime is a concert of post-theater chatter and pre-bar naughtiness. Though quieter than Centro, Malasaña and Chueca, Pl. Santa Ana offers some of the best bars in Madrid. It's centrally located—Sol, Pl. Mayor, el triángulo del arte, and the Atocha train station are all within walking distance. Sol-bound buses stop near accommodations on C. Príncipe, C. Nuñez de Arce, and C. San Jerónimo; buses #14, 27, 37 and 45 run along Po. del Prado. The metro stops are Sol and Antón Martín.

Hostal Gonzalo, C. Cervantes, 34, 3rd fl. (tel. 91 429 27 14, fax. 91 420 20 07). M: Antón Martín. Off C. León, which is off C. Atocha. A budget traveler's dream: newly renovated rooms have sparkling baths, firm beds, TV, and fans in summer. Singles 4500ptas; doubles 5500ptas; triples 7000ptas. Ask about discounts.

Hostal Villar, C. Príncipe, 18, 1st-4th fl. (tel. 91 531 66 00; fax 91 521 50 73; email hvillar@arrakis.es). M: Sol. From the metro, walk down C. San Jerónimo and turn right on C. Príncipe. The 1970s stormed through this building, leaving in their wake 46 brown rooms. Comfortable rooms have TVs, telephones, slanted floors, and A/C. Singles 2350ptas, with bath 3000ptas; doubles 3400ptas, with bath 4400ptas; triples 5500ptas, with bath 5900ptas; quads 6000ptas, with bath 7600ptas. Visa, MC.

Hostal Aguilar, C. San Jerónimo, 32, 2nd fl. (tel. 91 429 59 26 or 91 429 36 61; fax 91 429 26 61). M: Sol. More than 50 clean, modern rooms with vast bathrooms, telephones, A/C, and coin-operated TVs. Elegantly sparse lounge with deep couches. Singles 3500ptas; doubles 5800ptas; triples 7500ptas. 1500ptas per extra person. Visa, MC.

Hostal R. Rodríguez, C. Nuñez de Arce, 9, 3rd fl. (tel. 91 522 44 31), off Pl. Santa Ana. M: Sol. Reception decor makes even the cheapest of travelers feel like royalty. Just watch out for cramped triples and sagging mattresses. Shared baths only. Reception 24hr. English spoken. Spacious singles 3000ptas; doubles 4000ptas; triples 6000ptas.

Hostal-Residencia Sud-Americana, Po. Prado, 12, 6th fl. (tel. 91 429 25 64). M: Antón Martín or Atocha. Across from the Prado. 8 rooms, all with faux-leather armchairs, some with balconies. Rooms facing the Prado have excellent views. Singles 2500ptas; doubles 4800ptas; 1 triple 6000ptas.

Hostal Armesto, C. San Agustín, 6, 1st fl. (tel. 91 429 90 31). M: Antón Martín. In front of Pl. Cortés. Tastefully decorated with carnation-pink bedspreads, this small hostel offers a quiet night's sleep. Some rooms have a garden view; all have private baths and TVs. Singles 5000ptas; doubles 6000ptas; triples 7500ptas.

MADRID

Hostal-Residencia Carreras, C. Príncipe, 18, 3rd fl. (tel. 91 522 00 36). M: Antón Martín, Sol, or Sevilla. Off C. San Jerónimo, between Pl. Santa Ana and Canalejas. Cheap and spacious rooms lit by fluorescent bulbs. Rooms in the annex next door have modern baths. House rules are strictly enforced, including no noise after midnight. Singles 2000ptas, with shower 3200ptas, with bath 3500ptas; doubles 3500ptas, with shower 4000ptas, with bath 4500ptas; triples 4500ptas, with shower 4800ptas, with bath 6000ptas. Advance payment required.

Hostal-Residencia Regional, C. Príncipe, 18, 4th fl. (tel. 91 522 33 73). M: Antón Martín, Sol, or Sevilla. In the same building as Carreras. Go for the showers–they are monstrous and actually have water pressure. Singles 2500ptas, with shower 3000ptas; doubles 3400ptas, with shower 4400ptas; triples 4400ptas, with shower 5500ptas.

Hostal Leones, C. Nuñez de Arce, 14, 2nd fl. (tel. 91 531 08 89). A classic hostel with narrow hallways and spartan rooms. Show the proprietor your *Let's Go* and get a 10% discount. Singles 2100ptas; doubles 3600ptas, with bath 4200ptas.

Hostal Abulense, C. Nuñez de Arce, 15, 3rd fl. (tel. 91 522 81 44). M: Sol. A friendly proprietress runs this simple and slightly cramped hostel with very cheap rates. The doorbell, which chimes "Jingle Bells" and Beethoven's Fifth, provides entertainment. Communal bathroom. Showers 150ptas. Small singles 1400ptas; fair-sized doubles 2400ptas; triples 3300ptas. Discounts on longer stays.

Hostal-Residencia Mondragón, C. San Jerónimo, 32, 4th fl. (tel. 91 429 68 16). M: Sol. In the same building as the Aguilar and several other hostels. Spain's first motion picture was filmed in this building in 1898 (see p. 58). Ask for a room off the gardenia-filled terrace. Hot water runs only in communal bathrooms. Singles 2000ptas; doubles 2800ptas, with shower 3000ptas; triples 3900ptas.

Hostal-Residencia Lido, C. Echegaray, 5, 2nd fl. (tel. 91 429 62 07). M: Sol. Off C. San Jerónimo near Pl. Canalejas. The rickety steps don't seem to keep guests away. A diverse selection of rooms, some with large balconies. Avoid the windowless single. Long-term guests preferred. Ask nicely for kitchen access. Breakfast 350ptas. Singles 2000ptas; doubles 3500ptas. Monthly: singles 35,000ptas; doubles 65,000ptas.

GRAN VÍA

The neon lights of Broadway and the Champs-Élysées have met their match in Gran Vía. It glows and pulsates with the sharp lights of sex shops, McDonald's, and five star-hotels, in a 24-hour parade of flashing cars, swishing skirts, and stack-heeled shoes. *Hostal* signs scatter the horizon, but accommodations tend to be overpriced and less comfortable. This is not a street you want to be returning to late at night; Centro and Huertas provide safer bargains. Buses #1, 2, 44, 46, 74, 75, 133, 146, 147, and 148 reach Callao; buses #1, 2, 3, 40, 46, 74, 146, and 149 service both Pl. España and Callao. The closest metro stops are Gran Vía and Callao.

Hostal Margarita, Gran Vía, 50, 5th fl. (tel. 91 541 91 82; fax 91 541 91 88). M: Callao. Stucco walls, light wood shutters, and baby-blue beds make for an airy feel. Rooms are tastefully sparse, with big windows, pretty bathrooms, TVs, and telephones. Laundry service 1200ptas. Singles 3200 ptas, with shower 4000ptas; doubles 5100ptas; triples 6600ptas. 20% discount on stays over 1 week. Visa, MC.

Hostal A. Nebrija, Gran Vía, 67, 8th fl., elevator A (tel. 91 547 73 19). M: Pl. España. Pleasant and spacious rooms in a very tidy building, heavily furnished in medieval style; huge windows reveal great views. The guard on the 1st floor protects patrons from the vices of Gran Vía. Singles 3100ptas; doubles 4100ptas; triples 6100ptas. Visa, AmEx.

Hostal-Residencia Alibel, Gran Vía, 44, 8th fl. (tel. 91 521 00 51). M: Callao. Well-lit rooms with great views. French spoken. Laundry service available. Singles 3000ptas; doubles with shower 4500ptas; triples with shower 6000ptas. Visa, MC.

Hostal Lauria, Gran Vía, 50, 4th fl. (tel./fax 91 547 35 49). M: Callao. Ultra-comfortable rooms with abnormally large beds and showers. Homey salon with stereo and TV. Use of kitchen and refrigerator. English spoken. Laundry 1200ptas. Reservations recommended a week in advance. Singles 4280ptas; doubles 5900ptas; triples 6500ptas. Visa, MC.

Hostal-Residencia María, Miguel Moya, 4, 2nd fl. (tel. 91 522 44 77). M: Callao. Located just off Pl. Callao. Airy, spacious rooms, away from the noise and hustle of Gran Vía. All with TVs and private baths, some with fans. Singles 3100ptas; doubles 4500ptas; triples 6000ptas. 7% IVA not included. Visa, MC.

Hostal-Residencia Lamalonga, Gran Vía, 56, 2nd fl. (tel. 91 547 26 31 or 91 547 68 94). M: Santo Domingo. Chandeliers and fake flowers abound. The large bathrooms and front hall compete for the sparkle award. All rooms have TVs and baths. Singles 4100ptas; doubles 6000ptas; triples 8000ptas. 10% discount for stays over 5 days. Visa, MC.

Hostal Josefina, Gran Vía, 44, 7th fl. (tel. 91 521 81 31). M: Callao. Heavy gray drapes, peeling paint, and dramatic decor give hallways a Gothic ambience. The rooms, however, have a slightly lighter feel. Singles 2700ptas, with shower 3000ptas; doubles with shower 4000ptas; triples with shower 6000ptas.

MALASAÑA AND CHUECA

Split down the middle by C. Fuencarral, Malasaña and Chueca are both hard-core party pits for Madrid's youth. Hostels and *pensiones* are almost as abundant as the clubs, although they are more affordable. But unless techno helps you sleep, make sure your room has sound-proof windows. Chueca is hip and fun but can be dangerous, especially for solo travelers. Buses #3, 40, and 149 run along C. Fuencarral and Hortaleza. Metro stops Chueca, Gran Vía, and Tribunal serve the area.

Hotel Mónaco, C. Barbieri, 5 (tel. 91 552 46 30; fax 91 521 16 01). M: Chueca or Gran Vía. Once a brothel catering to Madrid's high society (Alfonso XIII, the king's grandfather, is rumored to have been a frequent visitor), the hotel still encourages naughtiness. Frescoes of Eve-like temptresses prod and pry the imagination while hundreds of mirrors and *Palacio*-sized beds allow the reality. Each room is a different adventure. All rooms with bath. Lively bar area and cafeteria. Simple singles 7490ptas; doubles 10,700ptas; triples 13,500ptas; quads 15,000ptas. All major credit cards accepted.

Hostal Palacios and **Hostal Ribadavia,** C. Fuencarral, 25, 1st-3rd fl. (tel. 91 531 10 58 or 91 531 48 47). M: Gran Vía. Both hostels are run by the same cheerful family. Palacio (1st and 2nd fl.) offers larger rooms with TVs; Ribadavia (3rd fl.) is older, but still full of comfortable rooms. Singles 2500ptas, with bath 3500ptas; doubles with shower 3800ptas, with bath 4800ptas; triples 5500ptas, with bath 6600ptas; quads with bath 7500ptas. Visa, MC, AmEx.

Hostal Lorenzo, C. las Infantas, 26, 3rd fl. (tel. 91 521 30 57; fax 91 532 79 78). M: Gran Vía. Tastefully decorated rooms with all the amenities–TVs, telephones, A/C, music, and chandeliers. Sound-proof windows muffle the daytime traffic and the nighttime revelry below. Bored? Turning the knob by the bed produces music through ceiling speakers. All rooms with bath. Breakfast 300ptas. Reservations recommended. Singles 4500ptas; doubles 6300ptas; triples 9000ptas. Credit cards accepted.

Hostal Abril, C. Fuencarral, 39, 4th fl. (tel. 91 531 53 38). M: Tribunal or Gran Vía. Standard and comfortable. Though Abril was renovated in 1994, they seem to have forgotten the lighting. Singles 1900ptas, with shower 2200ptas, with bath 2500ptas; doubles 2200-3200ptas, with bath 3400ptas; triples 4500ptas, with bath 4600ptas.

Hostal-Residencia Domínguez, C. Santa Brígida, 1 (tel. 91 532 15 47). M: Tribunal. Go down C. Fuencarral toward Gran Vía, turn left on C. Santa Brígida, and climb up one flight of dark steps. Modern bathrooms are almost as big as the rooms, which are bare except for TVs. Hospitable owner ready with tips on local nightlife. Reservations recommended. Singles 1900ptas, with bath 2500ptas; doubles with bath 4000ptas.

Hostal Medieval, C. Fuencarral, 46, 2nd fl. (tel. 91 522 25 49). M: Tribunal. On the corner of C. Augusto Figueroa. No medieval decor here, just peach walls and geraniums. The lounge honors the royal couple and Real Madrid. Singles with shower 3000ptas; doubles with shower 4300ptas, with bath 5500ptas; triples with shower 6200ptas.

ELSEWHERE

Near the **Chamartín** train station budget lodgings are rare, as they are in nearly all the residential districts located away from the city center. Near the **Madrid-Atocha** train station are a handful of hostels, the closest of which are down Po. Santa María de la Cabeza. The tourist office in Pl. Mayor has a full list of lodgings.

Albergue Juvenil Santa Cruz de Marcenado (HI), C. Santa Cruz de Marcenado, 28 (tel. 91 547 45 32; fax 91 548 11 96). M: Argüelles. From the metro, walk 1 block down C. Alberto Aguilera away from C. Princesa, turn right on C. Serrano Jóve, then left on C. Santa Cruz de Marcenado. Modern, recently renovated facilities near the student district mostly house traveling college students. The 72 beds fill quickly, even in winter. Message board and lounge for late-night card playing. English spoken. Rooms have cubbies; recommended lockers are outside the rooms (200ptas extra). Breakfast included. Sheets, but no towels, provided. 3-day max. stay. 1:30am curfew is strictly enforced. Silence after midnight. Reception daily 9am-1:30pm. Reserve a space (by mail, fax, or in person only) in advance, or arrive early and pray. Closed Christmas and New Year's. An HI card is required and can be purchased for 1800ptas. Dorms 950ptas, over 26 1300ptas.

Hostal-Residencia Rios, C. Juan Álvarez Mendizábal, 44, 4th fl. (tel. 91 559 51 56). M: Ventura Rodríguez, From the metro, face the green shrubbery, walk 3 blocks up C. Princesa (to your left) to C. Rey Francisco, go 3 blocks to J. A. Mendizábal, and turn left again. Nothing fancy; just clean, cheap, comfortable rooms. Singles 1600ptas; doubles with shower 3200ptas.

CAMPING

Tourist offices can provide info about the 13 campsites within 50km of Madrid. Similar info is in the *Guía Oficial de Campings* (official camping guide), a big book which they gladly let you look through but don't give away (most bookstores carry it). The *Mapa de Campings* shows the location of every official campsite in Spain. Also ask for the brochure *Hoteles, Campings, Apartamentos*, which lists hotels, campsites, and apartments in and around Madrid. For further camping info, contact the *Consejería de Educación de Juventud* (tel. 91 522 29 41).

Camping Osuna (tel. 91 741 05 10; fax 91 320 63 65), on Av. Logroño. M: Canillejas. From the metro cross the pedestrian overpass, walk through the parking lot, and turn right along the freeway. Pass under two bridges (the first a freeway and the second an arch) and look for campground signs on the right. Everything you need in a campsite. 660ptas per person, per tent, and per car. 7% IVA not included.

Camping Alpha (tel. 91 695 80 69), on a shady site 12.4km down the Ctra. de Andalucía in Getafe. M: Legazpi. From the metro station take bus #447, which stops next to the Nissan dealership (10min., every 30min. until 10pm). Ask the driver to let you off at the pedestrian overpass near the Amper building. Cross the bridge and walk 1.5km back toward Madrid along a busy highway. Alpha has a pool and just about every other amenity. 590ptas per person and car, 640ptas per tent. IVA not included.

FOOD

In Madrid, it's not hard to fork it down without forking over too much. You can't walk a block without tripping over at least five *cafeterías*, where a sandwich, coffee, and dessert sell for around 600ptas. Vegetarians should check out the *Guia del Ocio*, which has a complete listing of Madrid's vegetarian havens under the section "Otras Cocinas."

For a full meal at a *restaurante*, one step up from the typical *cafetería*, expect to spend at least 1100ptas. Keep in mind the following essential buzz words for quicker, cheaper *madrileño* fare: *bocadillo* (a sandwich on hard role, 350-400ptas); *sandwich* (a sandwich on sliced bread, ask for it *a la plancha* if you want it grilled, 300ptas); *croissant* (with ham and cheese, 250ptas); *ración* (a large *tapa*, served with bread 300-600ptas); and *empanada* (a puff pastry with meat fillings, 200-300ptas). See the **Glossary of Food Terms**, p. 729, for additional useful translations.

In general, *restaurantes* are open from 1 to 4pm and 8pm to midnight; in the following listings, this is the case unless otherwise noted. More casual establishments such as *mesones*, *cafeterías*, *bares*, *cafés*, *terrazas*, and *tabernas* serve drinks and foodstuffs all day until midnight, though some are closed on Sundays.

Groceries: %Dia and **Simago** are the cheapest city-wide supermarket chains. More expensive are **Mantequerías Leonesas, Expreso,** and **Jumbo.** Every **El Corte Inglés** has a huge food market with an excellent selection (it shows in the price), located either on the basement or top floor.

Markets: Mercado de San Miguel, a covered market on Pl. San Miguel, off the northwest corner of Pl. Mayor, sells the finest seafood and produce in the city at high prices. Open M-Th 9:30am-2pm and 5:30-8:30pm, F-Sa 9am-2:30pm and 5:30-9pm. **Mercado de la Cebada,** at the intersection of C. Toledo and C. San Francisco, is less expensive. Open M-Sa 8am-2pm and 5:30-8pm.

Specialty Shops: Pastry shops are everywhere. The sublime **Horno La Santiaguesa,** C. Mayor, 73, sells everything from *roscones de reyes* (sweet bread for the Feast of the Epiphany) to *empanadas* and pastries doused in rich chocolate. Open M-Sa 8am-9pm, Su 8am-8pm. **Horno San Onofre,** C. San Onofre, 4, off C. Fuencarral, serves sumptuous fruit tarts and *suspiros de modistilla* (seamstress's sighs), a *madrileño* specialty. Open M-Sa 9am-9pm, Su 9am-8pm. **El Gourmet de Cuchilleros,** C. del Maestros Ville, just through Pl. Mayor's Arco de Cuchilleros, is a gourmet store stocking regional specialties, including Spanish jams, honey, nuts, and vintage wines. Open daily 10am-2pm and 5-9pm. Homesick Americans will love **Taste of America,** Po. Castellana, 28 (tel./fax 91 435 70 39), an American grocery store complete with brownie mix and macaroni and cheese. Open M-Sa 10am-9pm, Su 10:30am-9pm.

Red-Eye Establishments: *Guía del Ocio* lists late-night eateries under *Cenar a última hora.* The chain **VIPS,** at Gran Vía, 43 (tel. 91 542 15 78; M: Callao), Serrano, 41 (M: Serrano), Calle Princesa, 5 (M: Ventura Rodríguez), and other scattered locations is a standard late-night option. A diner with cushioned booths, average service, and overpriced burgers with cheese fries. VIPS also carries English books and magazines, records, and canned food. Open daily 9am-3am. **7-Eleven** stores are scattered about in Ópera, Alonso Martinez (C. Mejía Lequerida), and Av. America. **Hot & Cool,** C. Gaztambide in Moncloa-Argüelles, serves fresh *bocadillos* until 3am on weekends.

EL CENTRO: SOL, ÓPERA, AND PLAZA MAYOR

Tourists overrun this area. Typical fare abounds, and prices run high. Streets off M: Ópera teem with crowded cafes, markets, and restaurants. Restaurants with menus in several different languages are tourist traps. Cruise to nearby Pl. Santa Ana for better deals, but don't miss the Museo del Jamón. The surrounding streets, especially those through the **Arco de los Cuchilleros** in the southwest corner of Pl. Mayor, house old specialty shops and renowned *mesones*. Head here for garlicky *tapas* and pitchers of *sangría* served in a festive, albeit touristy, atmosphere.

Museo del Jamón, C. San Jerónimo, 6 (tel. 91 521 03 46). M: Sol. Five other much-loved locations throughout the city, including one on Gran Vía. If for some reason the pork perfume and in-your-face slabs of *jamón serrano* are rattling your nerves, head upstairs to the dining room (opens at 1pm) for a sampling of the chef's specialties (600-1160ptas). Succulent Iberian ham is served up in every form you could possibly desire. Entrees 350-1150ptas. Open M-Sa 9am-12:30am, Su 10am-12:30am. Visa, AmEx.

Casa Lhardy, C. San Jerónimo, 8 (tel. 91 521 33 85), at C. Victoria. M: Sol. 1839-style dining at 2039-style prices in one of Madrid's oldest restaurants. House specialty *cocido* (3600ptas) is guarded by uniformed men. Former Prime Minister Felipe González comes here on occasion. Budget hounds congregate on the ground floor for cognac, sherry, *consomé* (200ptas each) and Madrid's best hors d'oeuvres. Gourmet foodstuffs for sale. Open M-Sa 1-3:30pm and 9-11:30pm, Su 1-3:30pm. Visa, MC, AmEx.

Can Punyetes, C. Señores de Luzón, 5 (tel. 91 542 09 21), off C. Mayor. M: Ópera. The old wrought iron tables and fireplace beautify this neighborhood secret. Best known for its *tostadas* (495-775ptas). A/C. Entrees laden with fresh vegetables 465-1030ptas. *Menú* 1350ptas. Open M-Sa 1-5pm and 8pm-12:30am.

Taquería La Calaca, C. Fuentes, 3 (tel. 91 541 74 23), off C. Arenal. M: Ópera. Save yourself a flight to Mexico and instead imagine your way there after a monstrous margarita (600ptas). Entrees 1150ptas. Open Su-Th 1-4:30pm and 8pm-1am, F-Sa 1-4:30pm and 8pm-2:30am.

Bar-Restaurante Sabatini, C. Bailén, 15 (tel. 91 547 92 40). M: Ópera. Opposite the Sabatini Gardens, which are next to the Palacio Real. Come at sunset and bring a date—tables face some of Madrid's most famous and romantic sights. Open daily 8am-11pm.

Restaurante Rodriguez, C. San Cristobal, 15 (tel. 91 531 11 36). M: Sol. Locals will tell you that a cheap meal exists in this area, but you have to search. Well, here it is. *Menu de casa* 1000ptas, entrees from 500ptas. Open 1-4pm, 8-11:30pm.

HUERTAS

Pl. Santa Ana is a favorite spot to kill a couple hours with a beverage and a snack. It is a green, shady, and generally happy place. Unlike in Pta. del Sol, you might actually sit next to a real Spanish person. **Calles Echegaray, Ventura de la Vega,** and **Manuel Fernández González** are the best food streets; quality is high and prices low.

■ **Casa Alberto,** C. Huertas, 18 (tel. 91 429 93 56). M: Antón Martín. Patrons spill out into the night air to wait for a spot at the bar. The interior is decorated in the old world style. The *tapas* are all original house recipes. Try the *gambas al ajillo* (shrimp in garlic and hot peppers, 1250ptas) or the filled *canapes* (275-350ptas). Visa, MC.

Restaurante Integral Artemisa, C. Ventura de la Vega, 4 (tel. 91 429 50 92), off C. San Jerónimo. M: Sol. Elegant veggie food served in a new-age environment. All proceeds from Wednesday dinners go to humanitarian organizations. A/C. Entrees 1175-2595ptas. Non-vegetarian entrees 1200-1600ptas. *Menú* 1200ptas. Open daily 1:30-4pm and 9pm-midnight. Visa, MC, AmEx.

Gula Gula, C. Infantes, 5 (tel. 91 522 87 64), off C. Echegaray near C. Huertas. M: Antón Martín. So exotic that waiters and waitresses often wear bikinis. All you can eat salad bar 1500ptas. Make reservations on weekends. Open for lunch and dinner.

Taberna D'a Queimada, C. Echegaray, 17 (tel. 91 429 32 63 or 429 58 81), 1 block down from C. San Jerónimo. M: Sol. Wine sacks, *sangría* jugs, and a lone bagpipe hang from the cluttered ceiling. Entrees 975-2800ptas. *Menú* 2000ptas. Separate *tapas* menu (475-1400ptas). Across the street is the identical **Taberna D'a Queimada II,** under the same management. A/C. Both open daily noon-5pm and 7:30pm-midnight.

Mesón La Caserola, C. Echegaray, 3 (tel. 91 429 39 63), off C. San Jerónimo. M: Sol. Despite its proximity to Sol, La Caserola's prices and atmosphere remain more local than tourist. Also serves breakfast, *tapas* (400-900ptas), and hefty *bocadillo*-and-beer combos named after relatives (the *suegra,* or mother-in-law, is pork loin and lettuce). A/C. Many entrees around 900ptas. Two hearty *menús* (1000-1500ptas.) Open M noon-1:30am, Tu-Su 7:30-1:30am. Visa, MC, DC.

LAVAPIÉS-LA LATINA-ATOCHA

The neighborhoods south of Sol, bounded by C. Atocha and C. Toledo, are residential and working class. No caviar or champagne here, but plenty of *menús* for around 1000ptas. Still, eating a la carte is often a better bargain. *Bocadillo* (sandwich) joints along **Calle Santa Isabel,** by Madrid-Atocha and the Reina Sofía, slap together greasy sandwiches and garlic-laden *tapas* at reasonable prices.

■ **El Estragón,** Pl. de la Paja, 10 (tel. 91 365 89 82). M: La Latina. Uphill off C. Segovia, facing La Capilla del Obispo. Vegetarian food that might make even die-hard meat-eaters reconsider. Though quite big, multiple levels ensure an intimate dining experience.

Delicious and creative *menú* (1900ptas) without the pitfalls of sketchy meat dishes. Open daily 1-5pm and 8:30pm-midnight.

El Granero de Lavapiés, C. Argumosa, 10 (tel. 91 467 76 11), off the plaza. M: Lavapiés. For 16 years, frescoes, inventive vegetarian specials, and fresh bread have kept this hideaway packed with locals. Vegetarian *menú* 1200ptas. Open daily 1-4pm.

La Farfalla, C. Santa María, 17 (tel. 91 369 46 91). M: Antón Martín. One block from the metro along C. Huertas; look for the butterfly above the entrance. La Farfalla's specialty is Argentine-style grilled meat (1100-1750ptas), but don't miss their thin-crust pizza (700ptas). Open for dinner Su-Th until 3am, F-Sa until 4am. Visa.

La Biotika, C. Amor de Diós, 3 (tel. 91 429 07 90), at C. Santa María. An intimate haven for the tofu-deprived. Also sells herbal remedies and foodstuffs *a llevar* (to go). *Menú* 1100ptas. Open M-F 1-4pm and 8-11:30pm, Sa-Su 1:30-4pm and 8-11:30pm.

GRAN VÍA

If you came to Spain to escape fast-food chains, stay clear of Gran Vía. Luckily, **Calle Fuencarral** is lined with cheap eateries.

Costa Del Sol (tel. 91 522 02 82 or 91 531 01 79). M: Gran Vía. Opposite C. Valverde. Unlike its namesake, this place is virtually tourist-free. The worn front hides a ship-shape restaurant with inexpensive and gargantuan meals. Entrees 400-875ptas. Lunchtime *menú* 1000ptas. Open daily 1-4pm and 7pm-midnight.

Museo Chicote, C. Gran Vía, 12 (tel. 91 532 97 80). M: Gran Vía. Lose yourself in the leather booths amidst pictures of Spanish celebs. Don't miss the museum of rare liquor bottles. The best deals are for breakfast, with coffee and fresh pastries (240-400ptas).

MALASAÑA AND CHUECA

Malasaña and Chueca, both above Gran Vía, are divided in atmosphere along C. Hortaleza. Closer to the Ópera, Malasaña's restaurants often feature new and adventurous menus, filled with veggie options. Watch the colorful characters who fill the maze of tiny streets; watch them more closely after dark. Malasaña's understated settings, however, are no match for the glam of Chueca, a fantastically gay district with lots of good places to wine and dine before a night of debauchery.

MALASAÑA

El Tazumal, C. Madera, 36 (tel. 91 522 79 82). M: Tribunal. From the station, walk down to C. Espirítú Santo, turn right, then turn left on C. Madera. Tasty and unique cuisine from El Salvador in a down-home setting. Try the national favorite, *pupusas* (loosely described as small, thick tortillas) with cheese or meat (275ptas). Entrees 275-1300ptas. Open W-M 1:30-4:30pm and 8pm-midnight.

La Gata Flora, C. 2 de Mayo, 1, and across the street at C. San Vicente Ferrer, 33 (tel. 91 521 20 20 or 91 521 27 92). M: Noviciado or Tribunal. You can't miss the pink exterior. Once named one of the best price/quality joints in town. Menu 1075ptas. Pizzas and pastas 825-1125ptas. Luscious salads 550-700ptas. *Sangría* 600-900ptas. Open Su-Th 2-4pm and 8:30pm-midnight, F-Sa 2-4pm and 8:30pm-1am. Visa, MC.

La Granja Restaurante Vegetariano, C. San Andrés, 11 (tel. 91 532 87 93), off Pl. 2 de Mayo. M: Tribunal. A warm atmosphere with plants, tiles, and pottery produces a pleasant dining experience. Ask the generous owner about smoking the hookah after your meal. Entrees 600-750ptas, salads 650ptas. Lunchtime *menú* 975ptas. Open W-M 1:30-4:30pm and 9pm-midnight. Visa.

CHUECA

El 26 de Libertad, C. Libertad, 26 (tel. 91 522 25 22), off C. las Infantas. M: Chueca. Once voted one of Madrid's 100 best menus (it was 95th, but who's counting?). Innovative and exotic Spanish cuisine. Lunchtime *menú* (1250ptas) is fantastic. Dinner is served in a yellow room whose cheeriness helps you swallow the price (2500ptas). Open M-F 1-4pm and 8pm-midnight, Sa 1-4pm and 9pm-1am.

MADRID

La Carreta, C. Barbieri, 10 (tel. 91 532 70 42 or 91 521 60 97), off C. las Infantas. M: Gran Vía or Chueca. Specializes in Argentinian, Uruguayan, and Chilean meals. Lunch *menú* 1500ptas. Entrees around 900ptas. If your budget allows, try the delicious Martín Fierro dessert (890ptas), named after the Argentinian national novel, or skip dessert and **tango.** Classes offered M-Tu 7pm. Performances Sa-Su 8:30pm-5am. Reservations recommended. Open daily 1:30-5pm and 9pm-5am. Visa, MC, AmEx.

La Gastroteca, Pl. de Chueca 8. (tel.91 532 25 64) M: Chueca. Another of Madrid's new imaginative kitchens, and they know it; enter only after ringing the bell. If you are craving meat and are willing to splurge, treat yourself here. Excellent *menú* 1600ptas. Entrees 2400-2980ptas. Open M-F.

Nabucco, C. Hortaleza, 108 (tel. 91 310 06 11), a few blocks off Pl. Santa Bárbara. M: Alonso Martínez or Chueca. With a burnt-orange backdrop inspired by the dirt of Sevilla's Plaza de Toros, this Italian restaurant is an upscale setting for cheap, hearty meals. Pizzas 730-935ptas. Pasta 865-975ptas. Salads 590-875ptas. Open M-F 1:30-4pm and 8:45pm-midnight, Sa-Su 8:45pm-1am. Visa, MC, AmEx.

Restaurante Zara, C. las Infantas, 5 (tel. 91 532 20 74), off C. Hortaleza. M: Gran Vía. Young and beautiful locals swarm this island of colorful Cuban cuisine. Daily "tropical" specials 1400ptas. Meat entrees 700-1100ptas. Open M-F. Visa, MC, AmEx.

Chez Pomme, C. Pelayo, 4 (tel. 91 532 16 46), off C. Augusto Figueroa. M: Chueca. Vegetarian food with a starchy entree *menú* (700-800ptas) and creative salads (750-930ptas). Lighter *menú* 1000ptas. Open M-Sa 1:30-4pm and 8:30-11:30pm.

Taberna Carmencita, C. San Marcos, 36 (tel. 91 531 66 12), at C. Libertad. M: Chueca. Popular with tourists, this classic restaurant, founded in 1850, evokes pre-Civil War Madrid. Lunch *menú* 1070ptas, dinner *menú* 1400ptas. Entrees 900-2600ptas. Open M-F 1-4pm and 9pm-midnight, Sa 9pm-midnight. Visa, MC, AmEx.

Tienda de Vinos, C. Augusto Figueroa, 35 (tel. 91 521 70 12), off C. Hortaleza. M: Chueca. Look for the red doors. Once a major leftist hangout and now crumbling romantically. Classic, cheap Spanish standards. Entrees 500-900ptas.

BILBAO

The area north of Glorieta de Bilbao, in the "V" formed by C. Fuencarral and C. Luchana and including Pl. Olavide, is overflowing with bars, clubs, cafes, and restaurants. Most bars and restaurants serve splendid, cheap *tapas* to the youthful crowd which swarms the area at night. Lunch gets pricier farther north in a more gentrified area. The metro stop is Bilbao.

Collage, C. Olid, 6. (tel. 91 448 45 62), off C. Fuencarral. M: Bilbao. Madrid's latest installment of interpretive food. Don't let the understated decor fool you; the meals here explode with flavors, as traditional dishes are spiced-up and loaded with vegetables. Only the hip need enter. Entrees 650-2850ptas. Open M-Sa. Visa, MC, AmEx.

La Tarterie, C. Cardenal Cisneros, 24 (tel. 91 593 85 27), right off C. Luchana, which is off Glorieta de Bilbao. M: Bilbao. Tasty food for starving artists. This restaurant/art gallery pulls off the dual role with temporary exhibits of local experimental art. Great quiches (675ptas), salads (650ptas), and pizzas (775-1050ptas).

Pizza Buona, C. Hartzenbusch, 19 (tel. 91 445 78 68), off C. Cardenal Cisneros, which is just off C. Luchana. M: Bilbao. An Italian restaurant decked out in patriotic green, red, and white on a German-named street in the heart of Spain. A/C. Tasty and greasy pizzas 575-895ptas. Open daily 1-5pm and 8pm-1am. Credit cards accepted.

Bar Samara, C. Cardenal Cisneros, 13 (tel. 91 448 80 56). M: Bilbao. Bills itself as Egyptian, but offers Middle Eastern staples. Narrow bar fills with college students after dark. A/C. Hummus, *baba ghanoush,* and *tajine* salads 400-550ptas. Kebabs and other entrees from 1175ptas. Open Su and Tu-Th until midnight, F-Sa until 1am.

ARGÜELLES

Argüelles is a middle-class neighborhood near the Ciudad Universitaria. It's geared toward locals instead of tourists, and is therefore full of inexpensive markets, moderately priced restaurants, and informal neighborhood bars. Check out the quiet *terrazas* on C. Pintor Rosales, overlooking the park.

Cáscaras, C. Ventura Rodríguez, 7 (tel. 91 542 83 36). M: Ventura Rodríguez. The sleek interior enhances the dining experience. Popular for *tapas, pinchos,* and ice-cold Mahou beer in the early afternoon and evening. A/C. Vegetarian dishes 675-975ptas. Tortillas 745-955ptas. Salads 675-935ptas. Non-vegetarian fare as well. Open M-F 7am-1am, Sa-Su 10am-2am. Visa, MC, AmEx.

La Vaca Argentina, Po. Pintor Rosales, 52 (tel. 91 559 66 05). M: Moncloa or Argüelles. Near the Rosaleda. Famous for its regional steak specialties and infamous for its cowhide wallpaper. Scrumptious and tender fillets 1100-4500ptas. Salads 450-750ptas. Open daily 1-4:30pm and 9pm-12:30am. Visa, MC, AmEx.

La Crêperie, Po. Pintor Rosales, 28 (tel. 91 548 23 58). M: Ventura Rodríguez. The cherub decorations are almost as sweet as their dessert crepes (370-645ptas). Enjoy affordable lunch and dinner crepes (535-805ptas) on the chic Po. Rosales *terraza*. Open for lunch daily 1:30-4:15pm, for dinner Su-Th 8pm-1am.

Ristorante Capriccio, C. Rodriguez San Pedro, 66 (tel. 91 549 91 16). M: Argüelles. Exit at C. Alberto Aguilera. Simple but hearty menu, with heaping plates of fresh pasta (900-1300ptas) and homemade rolls. A/C. Delivery. Gourmet pizzas 700-950ptas. Open M-F 1-4pm and 9pm-1am, Sa-Su 1-4pm and 9pm-late. Visa, MC, AmEx.

TAPAS

Not so long ago, bartenders in Madrid used to cover *(tapar)* drinks with saucers to keep the flies out. Later, servers began putting little sandwiches on top of the saucers, and there you have it: *tapas.* Hopping from bar to bar gobbling *tapas* is an active alternative to a full sit-down meal and a fun way to sample food you might never dream of even trying. Most *tapas* bars (a.k.a. *tascas* or *tabernas*) are open noon to 4pm and 8pm to midnight or later. Some, like **Museo del Jamón,** double as restaurants, and many cluster around **Plaza Mayor** (beware the tourist traps!) and **Plaza Santa Ana,** which is very hip on Sundays.

La Toscana, C. Manuel Fernández González, 10-17 (tel. 91 429 60 31), at C. Ventura de la Vega. M: Sol. Despite the antique lettering and wrought iron, the *tapas* are anything but medieval. Jam-packed on weekends. Try the *morcilla* (250ptas), but don't ask what you're eating until you're done. Open Th-Tu noon-4pm and 8pm-midnight.

TAPAS So finally you've found a hostel, only been lost twice, and are ready to experience some of Madrid's infamous lifestyle. Clearly, it's time for some drinks and *tapas.* The only problem is, what the hell are you going to order? To the untrained reader, *tapas* menus are often cryptic and undecipherable—if the bar has even bothered to print any. To make sure you don't end up eating the stewed parts of the oxen you rode in on, just keep the following words in mind. Servings come in three sizes: *pincho* (normally eaten with toothpicks between sips of beer), *tapa* (small plate), or *racion* (sizable, meal portion). *Aceitunas* (olives), *albondigas* (meatballs), *anchoas* (anchovies), *callos* (tripe), *chorizo* (sausage), *croqetas* (breaded and fried combinations), *gambas* (shrimp), *jamon* (ham), *patatas alioli y bravas* (potatoes with sauces), *pimentoes* (peppers), *pulpo* (octopus), and *tortillla* (omelette) comprise any basic menu. More adventurous travelers should try *morcilla* or *sesos;* just don't ask what they are. Bartenders will often offer tastes of tapas with your drink and strike up a conversation in the spirit of Madrid's generosity and charm. To ensure full treatment and local respect, the house *cerveza* is always a good choice. *Sangría,* a mixture of wine and fruit juices, seems innocent but is very sharp—natives drink it by the jar and box in the sweltering summers.

La Trucha, C. Nuñez de Arce, 6 (tel. 91 429 58 33). M: Sol. Cramped but cheap. Their fresh vegetables and daily specials are popular with locals. Impressive selection of seasonal veggies (800-1500ptas), but don't skip the stewed bull's tail. Entrees 200-2500ptas. Open M-Sa 12:30-4pm and 7:30pm-midnight. Visa, MC, AmEx.

La Princesita, C. Princesa, 80 (tel. 91 543 30 47). M: Argüelles. From open to closing, students crowd the bar to enjoy regional specialties, including *queso de Cabrales* (goat cheese, 100ptas) and *empanada asturiana* (250ptas). Open M-Sa 10am-11:30pm.

Los Caracoles, Pl. de Cascorro, 18 (tel. 91 365 94 39). M: La Latina. Snails and more. Dine in the company the owner and his jovial friends. Open daily 10:30am-4pm and 7-11:30pm.

Cafetería-Restaurante El Encinar del Bierzo, C. Toledo, 82 (tel. 91 366 23 89). M: La Latina. A neighborhood landmark. House specialties *conejo al ajillo* (rabbit with garlic, 2000ptas) and *gambas a la plancha* (fried shrimp, 1100ptas). *Menú* 1300ptas. Open daily 1-4:30pm and 9pm-midnight.

CLASSIC CAFES

Coffee in Madrid's cafes may be expensive (200-450ptas), but included in the price are atmosphere, history, and image. It's customary to linger for an hour or two in these historic cafes, an economical way to soak up a little of Madrid's culture and finally write those postcards you bought a few days ago.

■ Café Gijón, Po. Recoletos, 21 (tel. 91 521 54 25). M: Colón. On its 100th anniversary in 1988, Gijón was designated a historic site for its intellectual significance. It has long since been a favorite of the literati. Check out how smart you look in the mirrors and forget how much that cup of coffee costs. Open daily 9am-1:30am.

Café Círculo de Bellas Artes, C. Alcalá, 42 (tel. 91 360 54 00). M: Banco de España. Tourists rest weary museum feet outside and enjoy a reasonably priced snack (beer 350-500ptas, sandwiches 400-600ptas). For a 100pta cover, lounge on leather couches beneath high frescoed ceilings and fabulous crystal lights. Expensive drinks deter starving artist types. Coffee or tea 200ptas. Open M-F 9am-1am, Sa-Su 9am-3am. Credit cards accepted.

Café de Oriente, Pl. Oriente, 2 (tel. 91 547 15 64). M: Ópera. A beautiful, old-fashioned cafe catering to a ritzy, older crowd. Spectacular view of the Palacio Real from the *terraza*, especially at night when a spotlight illuminates the palace. Prices are significantly cheaper inside. Specialty coffees 540-840ptas. Open daily 8:30am-1:30am.

Nuevo Café Barbieri, C. Av. María, 45 (tel. 91 527 36 58). M: Lavapiés. Intellectuals lurk in this crumbling cafe, amid curling paint and dusty red drapes. Art films some nights in the back room—pick up a schedule. Cocktails 700ptas.

Café Comercial, Glorieta de Bilbao, 7 (tel. 91 531 34 52). M: Bilbao. Traditional cafe with high ceilings, cushioned chairs, and huge mirrors perfect for people-watching. Frequented by artists and Republican aviators alike. The first anti-Franco protests appeared here. Sandwiches from 350ptas. Beer 335ptas. The upstairs **Cybercafe Comercial** reflects its move to the 21st century with Coin-operated computers 100ptas for 8min., 500ptas per hr. A/C. Open Su-Th 7am-1am, F-Sa 7am-3am.

☎ SIGHTS

You need good shoes to walk around in.

— A shoemaker

Madrid, large as it may seem, is a walker's city. Its fantastic public transportation system should be used as little as possible. Although the word *paseo* refers to a major avenue—such as *Paseo de la Castellana* or *Paseo del Prado*—it literally means "a stroll." Do just that from Sol to Cibeles and from the Plaza Mayor to the Palacio Real—sights will kindly introduce themselves. The city's art and architecture and its culture and atmosphere convince wide-eyed walkers that it was once the capital of the world's greatest empire. While Madrid is perfect for walking, it also offers some of the world's best places to stop strolling. Whether soothing tired feet after perusing the Triángulo de Arte or suffering from a hangover after a night in Chueca, there's nothing better than a shady sidewalk cafe.

For hard-core sightseers with a checklist of destinations, the municipal tourist office's *Plano de Transportes* map, which marks monuments as well as bus and metro lines, is indispensable. In the following pages, sights are arranged by neighborhood, offering opportunities for extensive walking tours in each district. Each section has a designated center from which all directions are given. If you are trying to design a walking tour of the entire city, it is best to begin in Centro, the self-evident nucleus of Madrid. The neighborhoods naturally fall in geographical order from there; a good day of sightseeing might move from historic Madrid, to the cafes of Huertas, to the celebrated *paseos*, to a stroll through the Retiro. El Pardo falls last, as it is a separate trip—buses to its palace and pastures leave from Moncloa. Remember that to truly experience the monuments, you should also try to enjoy Madrid's unhurried pace—in between sights, stop, relax, and people-watch from one of Madrid's many cafes.

CENTRO

The area known as El Centro, spreading out from the Puerta del Sol ("Gate of Sun"), is the gateway to the history and spirit of Madrid. Although several rulers carved the winding streets, the Habsburg and Bourbon families left the Centro's most celebrated monuments. As a result, the Centro is divided into two major sections: Madrid de los Hapsburgs and Madrid de los Borbones. All directions are given from the Puerta del Sol. For convenience, the metro stop closest to each sight (often not M: Sol) is also listed.

PUERTA DEL SOL. Kilómetro 0—the origin of six national highways fanning out to the rest of Spain—marks the country's physical and psychological center in the most chaotic of Madrid's numerous plazas, Puerta del Sol. Sol blazes all day and night with the lights of taxis, bars, street performers, and newsstands. A web of pedestrian-only tributaries originating at the Gran Vía leads a rush of consumers down a gallery of stores, funneling them into Sol.

It was not until the late 19th century that Sol became the true nucleus of Madrid. In the 16th century, an eastward-facing gate, known as the Gateway to the Sun, stood in Puerta del Sol. Today, government buildings dominate the plaza, where citizens and tourists alike converge upon *El oso y el madroño*, a bronze statue of a bear and a strawberry tree, now a symbol of Madrid. On New Year's Eve, citizens congregate in Sol to gobble up one grape per chime as the clock strikes midnight.

HABSBURG MADRID

"Old Madrid," the city's central neighborhood, is the most densely packed with both monuments and tourists. In the 16th century, the Habsburgs built **Plaza Mayor** and the **Catedral de San Isidro** from scratch. Many of Old Madrid's buildings, however, date from much earlier, some as far back as the Moorish empire. When Felipe II moved the seat of Castilla from Toledo to Madrid (then only a town of 20,000) in 1561, he and his descendants commissioned the court architects (including Juan de Herrera) to update many of Madrid's buildings to the latest styles. After only a century of development and expansion, Madrid more than doubled in population. Today, central Madrid, from the celebrated street of Alcalá to the iron verandas of Plaza Mayor, still reflects the power of the Hapsburgs and the architecture of Juan de Herrera.

PLAZA MAYOR. In 1620, Pl. Mayor was completed for Felipe III; his statue, installed in 1847, still graces the plaza's center. Though designed by Juan de Herrera, the architect of the austere El Escorial, Pl. Mayor is much softer in style. Its elegant arcades, spindly towers, and pleasant verandas are defining elements of the "Madrid style" of architecture, which inspired architects across the city and throughout the country. With lances of exaggerated length, 17th-century nobles on horseback spent Sunday afternoons chasing bulls in the plaza. The nobility had such a jolly time that eventually everyone joined in the fun. Citizens, on foot and armed with sticks, also began running hither and thither after those pesky bulls. The tradition came to be known as a *corrida*, from the verb *correr* (to run).

Toward evening, Pl. Mayor awakens as *madrileños* resurface, tourists multiply, and cafe tables fill with lively patrons. On Sunday mornings, the plaza holds a rare coin and stamp sale, marking the starting point of **El Rastro** (see p. 113). During the annual **Fiesta de San Isidro** (May 15-22), the plaza explodes. *(From Pta. Sol, walk down C. Mayor. The plaza is on the left. M: Sol.)*

CATEDRAL DE SAN ISIDRO. This cathedral, which commemorates San Isidro, protector of crops and patron saint of Madrid, has had a turbulent history. It was designed in the Jesuit Baroque style at the beginning of the 17th century, and in 1769 San Isidro's remains were brought here. During the Civil War rioting workers burned the exterior and damaged much of the cathedral—only the primary nave and a few Baroque decorations remain from the original. San Isidro, which has since been restored, reigned as *the* cathedral of Madrid from the late 19th century until the Catedral de la Almudena (see p. 97) was consecrated in 1993. *(From the Pta. Sol, take C. Mayor to Pl. Mayor, cross the plaza, and exit onto C. Toledo. The cathedral is located at the intersection of C. Toledo and C. Sacramento. M: Latina. Open for mass only.)*

IGLESIA DE SAN FRANCISCO EL GRANDE. Dedicated to St. Francis of Assisi, this church features an outstanding facade, a Bourbon addition to the original 12th-century structure. In the 13th century, Saint Francis himself allegedly built a convent next door, where the **Capilla de Cristo de los Dolores** now stands. When King Carlos III transformed Madrid in the 18th century, he had Francisco Sabatini remodel the church in the Neoclassical style. Inside, Goya's *Saint Bernard of Siena Preaching* hangs alongside Velázquez's *Aparition of the Virgin before Saint Anthony*. *(From Pta. Sol, go down C. Mayor and turn left at the end on C. de Bailen, which leads directly to the church. M: Puerta de Toledo or Latina. Open in summer Tu-Sa 11am-1pm and 5-8pm. Free.)*

PLAZA DE LA VILLA. When Felipe II made Madrid the capital of his empire in 1561, most of the town huddled between Pl. Mayor and the Palacio Real, stretching north to today's Ópera and south to Pl. Puerta de Moros; Pl. Villa marks the heart of what was once old Madrid. Though only a handful of medieval buildings remain, the plaza still features a stunning courtyard (surrounding the statue of Don Alvara de Bazón), beautiful tile-work, and eclectic architecture. The horseshoe-shaped door on C. Codo is one of the few examples of Gothic-Mudéjar left in Madrid, and the 15th-century **Torre de los Lujanes** (on the left when looking from C. Mayor) is the sole remnant of the once lavish residence of the Lujanes family. Across the plaza is the 17th-century **Ayuntamiento (Casa de la Villa),** designed in 1640 by Juan Gomez de Mora as both the mayor's home and the city jail. Inside is Goya's *Allegory of the City of Madrid* (1819). The neighboring **Casa de Cisneros,** a 16th-century Plateresque house, also served as a government building when Habsburg officials annexed it for the city's growing bureaucracy. *(From Pta. Sol, go down C. Mayor, past Pl. Mayor. The plaza is on the left. M: Sol.)*

RIO MANZANARES. Past the Pta. Toledo, the Río Manzanares, Madrid's notoriously puny river, snakes its way around the city. The broad Baroque **Puente de Toledo** (a triumphal arch commissioned by Joseph Bonaparte to celebrate his brother Napoleon) makes up for the river's inadequacies. Sandstone carvings on both sides of the bridge depict San Isidro and his family. The austere **Puente de Segovia,** which fords the river along C. Segovia, was conceived by Juan de Herrera. Both bridges afford gorgeous views and are popular with young couples. *(To reach Puente de Toledo from Pta. Sol, go down C. Mayor, through the Pl. Mayor, and onto C. Toledo; follow Toledo to the bridge. For the Puente de Segovia, take C. Mayor from Pta. Sol, turn left on C. de Bailen, and right on C. Segovia, which crosses the river. M: Sol.)*

OTHER SIGHTS. As the legend goes, the **Iglesia de San Andrés** began as a Mudéjar mosque. A 17th-century overhaul, commissioned by Felipe IV, infused the original structure with Baroque intricacies and brought the sarcophagus of San Isidro to the **Capilla de San Isidro.** *(From Pta. Sol, go down C. Mayor, through the Pl. Mayor onto C. Toledo, and right on C. Duque de Alba. Open for mass only.)* The **Parque de las Vistillas,** named for the tremendous *vistillas* (views) of Palacio Real, Nuestra Señora de la Almudena, and the surrounding countryside, provides a stunning photo-op. It can be dangerous at night. *(Located in the Pl. Gabriel Miró. From Pta. Sol, go down C. Mayor, turn left on C. Bailen, and then right on C. Morería into the plaza.)*

BOURBON MADRID

Weakened by plagues and political losses, the Habsburg era in Spain ended with the death of Carlos II in 1700. Felipe V, the first of Spain's Bourbon monarchs, ascended the throne in 1714 after the 12-year War of Spanish Succession. Bankruptcy, industrial stagnation, and widespread moral disillusionment compelled Felipe V to embark on a crusade of urban renewal. His successors, Fernando VI and Carlos III, fervently pursued the same ends, with wonderful results. Today, the lavish palaces, churches, and parks that remain are the most touristed in Madrid; a walk around them will require planning and patience.

PALACIO REAL. The impossibly luxurious **Palacio Real** lounges at the western tip of central Madrid, overlooking the Río Manzanares. Felipe V commissioned Giovanni Sachetti to replace the Alcázar, which had burned down in 1734, with a palace that would dwarf all others; he succeeded. When Sachetti died, Filippo Juvara took over the project, basing his new facade on Bernini's rejected designs for the Louvre. The shell took 40 years to build, and the decoration of its 2000 rooms (with a vast collection of porcelain, tapestries, furniture, armor, and art) dragged on for over a century. When Alfonso XIII abdicated in 1931, the Second Republic abandoned the costly construction. Today, the unfinished palace is only used by King Juan Carlos and Queen Sofía on special occasions. Although only a fragment is complete, the palace stands as one of Europe's most grandiose residences.

The palace's most impressive rooms are decorated in the Rococo style. The **Salón de Gasparini,** site of the king's ceremonial dressing before the court, houses Goya's portrait of Carlos IV and a Mengs ceiling fresco. The **Salón del Trono (Throne Room)** also contains a ceiling fresco, painted by Tiepolo, outlining the qualities of the quintessential ruler. The **Real Oficina de Farmacía (Royal Pharmacy)** features crystal and china receptacles used to hold royal medicines, and the **Biblioteca** shelves first editions of *Don Quijote.* Also open to the public is the **Real Armería (Armory),** which displays the swords of El Cid, the armor of Carlos V and Felipe II, and other medieval weapons and instruments of torture. Look for the hundreds of ornate timepieces, collected mainly by Carlos IV, strewn about the palace. *(From Pta. Sol, take C. Mayor, and turn right on C. Bailen. M: Sol. Open Apr.-Sept. M-Sa 9am-6pm, Su 9am-3pm; Oct.-Mar. M-Sa 9:30am-5pm, Su 9am-2pm. 850ptas, with tour 950ptas; students 350ptas, with tour 850ptas. EU citizens free Wednesday. Arrive early to avoid lines.)*

CATHEDRAL DE LA ALMUDENA. Begun in 1879 and finished a century later, the cathedral—especially its interior—is a stark contrast to the gilded Palacio Real. After a 30-year hibernation, the cathedral received a controversial face-lift. The reasons for the controversy are immediately apparent, as the cathedral's frescoes and stained glass windows contain a discordant mix of traditional and abstract styles. The simplicity of the gray stone walls clashes with the ceiling's brilliant colors and sharp geometric shapes. *(From Pta. Sol, go down C. Mayo and turn right on C. Bailen; the cathedral is just before the Palacio Real. Open M-F 10am-1:30pm and 6-8:45pm, Su 10am-2pm and 6-8:45pm. Closed during mass.)*

PLAZA DE ORIENTE. A minor architectural miscalculation was responsible for this sculpture park. Most of the statues in the plaza were designed for the palace roof, but because they were too heavy, they were instead placed in this shady plaza. An equestrian statue of Felipe IV, sculpted by Pietro Tacca, dominates the

MADRID

plaza; other notable structures include the Teatro Real, inaugurated by Isabel II. Elegant *terrazas* encompass the plaza, offering an opportunity to treat yourself to an overpriced coffee. *(From Pta. Sol, take C. Arenal to the plaza.)*

OTHER SIGHTS. The **Jardines de Sabatini,** to the right if you are facing the palace, is the romantic's park of choice. On the other hand, the view from **Campo de Moro,** opened to the public just 13 years ago, is straight out of a fairy-tale.

HUERTAS

The area east of Sol is a wedge bounded by C. de Alcalá to the north, C. Atocha to the south, and Po. Prado to the east. From the wedge's western apex at Sol, a myriad of streets slope downward, outward, and eastward toward various points along Po. Prado. Carrera de San Jerónimo splits the wedge a bit north of center, running directly from Sol down to Pl. Cánovas de Castillo. Huertas's sights, from authors' houses to famous cafes, are reflections of its artistic focus. Home to Cervantes, Góngora, Quevedo, Calderón, and Moratín at its heyday during the "Siglo de Oro" (see **Literature,** p. 57), Huertas enjoyed a fleeting return to literary prominence when Hemingway frequented the neighborhood in the 1920s. **Plaza Santa Ana** and its *terrazas* are the center of this old literary haunt; all directions in this section start from there.

CASA DE LOPE DE VEGA. Although Golden Age writers Lope de Vega and Miguel de Cervantes were bitter rivals, Vega's 17th-century house is ironically located on C. Cervantes. (Odder still, Cervantes is buried on C. Lope de Vega.) A prolific playwright and poet, Lope de Vega spent the last 25 years of his life, and wrote over two thirds of his plays, in this house. The highlights include the simple garden described in his works and the library filled with crumbling books. Among the more interesting tidbits revealed on the mandatory tour are the little tokens of affection Vega would leave for his daughters. *(C. Cervantes, 11. With your back to Pl. Santa Ana, turn left on C. Prado, right on C. León, and left on C. Cervantes. Tel. 91 429 92 16. Open Tu-F 9:30am-2pm, Sa 10am-1:30pm. 200ptas, students 100ptas. Wednesday free.)*

CIRCULO DE BELLAS ARTES. Designed by Antonio Palacios, this building encloses two stages and several studios for lectures and workshops run by prominent artists. Many facilities are for *socios* (members) only, but exhibition galleries for all media are open to the public. If you have a few hours to spare and some spiffy threads stashed away, your few (100) extra *pesetas* will buy you a cup of coffee and reward you with a sublime taste of a decadent lifestyle. *(C. Alcalá, 42. From Pl. Santa Ana, go up C. del Principe, cross C. San Jeronimo, and continue towards C. Alcalá. Turn right on C. Alcalá; the building is on the right. Hours and admission vary with exhibitions. For information on the cafe, see p. 94.)*

OTHER SIGHTS. Juan de Villanueva's simple **Real Academia de la Historia** houses a magnificent old library, another example of Madrid-style architecture. *(At the intersection of C. León and C. Huertas. From Pl. Santa Ana, take C. Principe and turn left on C. Huertas.)* Also impressive are the **Palacio Miraflores** and the **Palacio del Marqués de Ugena** designed by the premier 18th-century architect, Pedro de Ribera. *(Palacio Miraflores C. San Jerónimo, 15. Palacio de Marqés de Ugena Pl. Canalejas, 3.)*

GRAN VÍA

Urban planners paved the Gran Vía in 1910 to link C. Princesa with Pl. Cibeles. After Madrid gained wealth as a neutral supplier during World War I, the city funneled much of its earnings into making the Gran Vía into one of the world's great thoroughfares. Today, movie theaters and fast-food joints produce the most Americanized street in Madrid. Still, Gran Vía is a sight in itself—be sure to stroll (quickly) among the shops and skyscrapers.

At Gran Vía's highest elevation in **Plaza de Callao** (M: Callao), C. Postigo San Martín splits off southward, where you'll find the famed **Monasterio de las Descalzas Reales** (see p. 106). Westward from Pl. Callao (left when facing the conspicuous sex shop), the Gran Vía makes its descent toward **Plaza de España** (M: Pl. España). Next to Pl. España are two of Madrid's tallest skyscrapers, the **Telefónica building** (1929) and the **Edificio de España** (1953). Louis S. Weeks of the Chicago School designed the Telefónica building, the tallest concrete building in existence at the time (81m), and Franco designed the Edificio de España. Tucked between the two skyscrapers on C. San Leonardo is the small **Iglesia de San Marcos,** a Neoclassical church composed of five intersecting ellipses—a Euclidean dream, the church doesn't have a single straight line. **Museo de Cerralbo** lingers nearby (see p. 106).

MALASANA AND CHUECA

By night, these districts bristle with Madrid's alternative scene. The area between **Calle de Fuencarral** and **Calle de San Bernardo** is home to some of Madrid's most avant-garde architecture and current art exhibitions. Though not packed with historic monuments, the labyrinthine streets provide many spontaneous undocumented "sights," from platform-shoe stores to street performers.

IGLESIA DE LAS SALESAS REALES. Bourbon King Fernando VI commissioned this church in 1758 at the request of his wife, Doña Bárbara. The Baroque-Neoclassical domed church is clad in granite, with facade sculptures by Alfonso Vergaza and a dome painting by the brothers González Velázquez. The church's ostentatious facade and interior prompted critics to pun on the queen's name: "Barbaric queen, barbaric tastes, barbaric building, barbarous expense," they said, giving rise to the expression *"¡qué bárbaro!"* Today, the expression refers to absurdity, extravagance, or just plain craziness. For nightlife in surrounding streets that defines ¡qué bárbaro!, see p. 109. *(M: Chueca. From the metro stop, turn right on C. de Gravina and left on Conde de Xiquena.)*

ARGÜELLES

The 19th century witnessed the growth of several neighborhoods around the core of the city, north and northwest of the Palacio Real. Today, the area known as Argüelles and the zone surrounding **Calle San Bernardo** form a cluttered mixture of elegant middle-class houses, student apartments, and bohemian hangouts, all brimming with cultural activity. Heavily bombarded during the Civil War, Argüelles inspired Chilean poet Pablo Neruda, then a resident, to write *España en el corazón.* Directions in this section are given from the Argüelles metro stop.

TEMPLE DE DEBOD. Built by Pharaoh Zakheramon in the 4th century BC, it's the only Egyptian temple in Spain. In appreciation of Spanish archaeologists who helped rescue monuments from the floods of the Aswan dam, the Egyptian government shipped the temple stone by stone to Spain. The temple and two of its three original gateways stand in a peaceful haven in the **Parque de la Montaña**. *(M: Argüelles. From the metro, walk down C. Princesa and turn right on C. Ventura Rodriguez into the Parque de la Montaña; the temple is on the left. Tel. 91 409 61 65. Open in summer Tu-F 10am-2pm and 6-8pm, Sa-Su 10am-2pm; off-season Tu-F 10am-2pm and 4-6pm, Sa-Su 10am-2pm. 300ptas, students 150ptas. Wednesday free.)*

ERMITA DE SAN ANTONIO DE LA FLORIDA. Although out of the way, the Ermita is worth the trouble. It contains Goya's pantheon—a frescoed dome arches above his buried corpse. Curiously enough, Goya's skull, apparently stolen by a phrenologist, was missing when the corpse arrived from France. *(M: Principe Pio. From the metro, go left on C. de Buen Altamirano, walk through the park, and turn left on Po. Florida; the Ermita is at the end of this street. Tel. 91 542 07 22. Open Tu-Su 10am-2pm. Free.)*

CASA DEL CAMPO. Shaded by pines, oaks, and cypresses, families and joggers roam the city's largest park by day. Early morning reveals evidence of questionable nighttime activities, so stay away at night. Inside the amusement park **Parque de Atracciones,** you too can ride the roller coaster. *(M: Argüelles. Walk up C. Princesa and through the park. Tel. 91 463 29 00. Open Su-F noon-11pm, Sa noon-midnight.)* The **Zoo/Aquarium** is five minutes away. *(Tel. 91 512 37 70. M-F 10:30am-9pm, Sa-Su 10:30am-9:30pm. 1615ptas, children under 8 1300ptas.)*

OTHER SIGHTS. Parque del Oeste is a large, sloping park known for the **Rosaleda** (rose garden) at its bottom. A yearly competition determines which award-winning rose will be added to the permanent collection. *(M: Moncloa. From the metro, take C. Princesa. Open daily 10am-8pm.)* A prime example of Fascist Neoclassicism, the arcaded **Cuartel General del Aire (Ejército del Aire)** commands the view on the other side of Arco de la Victoria (by the Moncloa metro station). The complex was to form part of the "Fachada del Manzanares" urban axis linking Moncloa, the Palacio de Oriente, San Isidro, and the Iglesia de San Francisco. The building looks suspiciously like El Escorial. **Museo de América** (see p. 105) is a bit farther down the avenue, past the **Arco de Moncloa.** The **Faro de Moncloa** is a 92m high metal tower near the museum that offers views of the city. From the tower, you can see El Escorial on a clear day. *(200ptas to ascend the Faro de Moncloa.)*

RETIRO

Felipe IV intended the 300-acre Parque del Buen Retiro, once a hunting ground, to be a "buen retiro" (nice retreat). Today it's full of palm-readers, soccer players, and sunbathers. The northeast corner of the park swells with medieval monastic ruins and waterfalls. On weekends, the promenades fill with musicians, families, and young lovers. On summer nights (when only the north gate remains open), the lively bars and cafes fill with teenagers, families, and couples. It is easily accessible from the Retiro metro stop, and all directions are given from there. Avoid venturing alone into the park after dark. *(M: Retiro)*

ESTANQUE GRANDE. A rectangular lake in the middle of the park, the Estanque Grande is popular among rowers (often shirtless). The lake has been the social center of the Retiro ever since aspiring caricaturists, fortune-tellers, sunflower-seed vendors, and drug pushers first parked their goods along its marble shores. *(M: Retiro. With your back to the metro stop, turn right on C. Alcalá and walk until you reach Pta. Alcalá; enter the park on Av. Mejico which leads to the lake. Boat rentals daily 9:30am-8:30pm. Paddle boats 560ptas for 4 people, motorboats 155ptas per person.)*

PALACIO DE CRISTAL. Built by Ricardo Velázquez to exhibit Philippine flowers, this exquisite steel-and-glass structure hosts a variety of art shows, with subjects ranging from Bugs Bunny to Spanish portraiture. A popular sight for fashion photographers, the Palacio de Cristal may provide a backdrop for models feeding the swans. *(Open Tu-Sa 11am-2pm and 5-8pm, Su 10am-2pm. Admission varies, but often free.)*

PALACIO DE VELÁZQUEZ. Where all artists should dream of having their art displayed, this Velázquez creation has billowing ceilings, marble floors, and ideal lighting. The Palacio de Velázquez exhibits works in conjunction with the Museo de Arte Reina Sofía (see p. 104). *(From the metro, turn right on C. Alcalá, walk through Pta. Alcalá, pass the Estanque, and turn left on Paseo del Venezuela. Tel. 91 575 62 45. Open M-Sa 11am-8pm, Su 11am-6pm. Free.)*

OTHER SIGHTS. Bullets from the 1921 assassination of prime minister Eduardo Dato permanently scarred the eastern face of **Puerta de Alcalá** (1778), outside the Retiro's Puerta de la Independencia. To the south, the **Casón del Buen Retiro** faces the park (see p. 104); behind it sits the **Museo del Ejército** (see p. 106). The two buildings are remnants of Felipe IV's palace, which burned down in 1764.

THE PASEOS: A WALKING TOUR

The most striking feature on any map of Madrid is the one grand avenue that splits the city in two, running from Madrid-Atocha in the south to Madrid-Chamartín in the north. Madrid's great thoroughfare is really three fused segments (from south to north: Po. Prado, Po. Recoletos, and Po. Castellana) that represent three eras of urban expansion. Carlos III, the city's urban visionary, laid the Po. Prado from 1775 to 1782. The road connects Atocha to Pl. Cibeles, passing the Museo del Prado, the Thyssen-Bornemisza, and the Ritz Hotel along the way. Along Po. Recoletos, extending from Pl. Cibeles to Pl. Colón, the newest members of the *clase*

PAGAN LOVIN' The Plaza de Cibeles, with its infamous marble fountain, has been Madrid's physical and spiritual axis since its construction in 1781. Depicting the fertility goddess's triumph over the emblematic Castilian lions, the fountain's image of Cybele has long captivated citizens. Legend has it that the fleet-footed Atalanta, one of Cybele's maids, would take as her lover only the man who could outrun her. No man was up to the challenge until one cunning suitor instructed his cohorts to scatter golden apples (as distractions) in Atalanta's path. The goddess Cybele, watching the prank, was overcome with wrath at men's evil ways. So, after punishing the plotters by turning them into lions, she hitched them up to her own carriage. This assertion of power and sexuality charmed Madrid, resulting in the proverb *"mas popular qué Cibeles"* (more popular than Cybele).

alta (upper class) congregate at luxuriously shaded *terrazas*. Contemporary Madrid stretches further north along Po. Castellana (lined with bank buildings from the 1970s and 80s) to Pl. Castilla's twin towers (Puerta de Europa). In the summer, a late afternoon stroll along the *paseos* should include a stop at one of the fabulous chic cafes of the Po. Castellana. Unlike Madrid's other sights sections, this one is designed as a walking tour. Strolls along Po. Prado and Po. Recoletos combine well with a tour of Huertas or the Retiro; even a walk to the post office in Pl. Cibeles can incorporate the majority of the sights along the *paseos*.

PASEO DEL PRADO. Modeled after the Piazza Navona in Rome, Paseo Prado marks the center of Madrid's art district. Virtually every major museum is in the vicinity of this "museum mile," known as the Triángulo de Arte. Directly across from iron-framed **Estación de Atocha,** the **Centro de Arte Reina Sofía** (p. 104), home to Picasso's *Guernica,* vogues with its glass elevators in Pl. Emperador Carlos V.

Walking up Po. Prado, you'll pass the **Jardín Botánico** on the right. Opened during Carlos III's reign, the garden showcases over 30,000 species of plants, ranging from traditional roses to medicinal herbs. Just about anyone will appreciate the garden's vast collection of imported trees, bushes, and flowers. *(Open daily in summer 10am-9pm; in winter 10am-6pm; in spring and fall 10am-7pm. 200ptas, students 100ptas.)* Next to the Jardín Botánico is the world-renowned **Museo del Prado** (see p. 103) and behind it, on C. Ruiz de Alarcón, stands the **Iglesia de San Jerónimo,** Madrid's royal church. Built by Hieronymite monks and re-endowed by the Catholic Monarchs, the church has witnessed a few joyous milestones, including the coronation of Fernando and Isabel and the marriage of King Alfonso XIII. These days, only the highest of high-society weddings grace the church. *(Open daily 8am-1:30pm and 5-8:30pm.)* Back on Po. Prado, to the north in Pl. Lealtad, stands the **Obelisco a los Mártires del 2 de Mayo,** filled with the ashes of those who died in the 1808 uprising against Napoleon. Its four statues represent Constancy, Virtue, Valor, and Patriotism, and the flame burns continuously in honor of the patriots. Behind the memorial sits the colonnaded Greco-Roman-style **Bolsa de Madrid (Stock Exchange),** designed by Repullés. Ventura Rodríguez's **Fuente de Neptuno,** in Pl. Cánovas de Castillo, is one of three aquatic masterpieces along the avenue.

The arts of the Po. Prado transform into the Po. Recoletos at the tulip-encircled **Plaza de Cibeles.** Madrid residents successfully protected this emblem of their city (best viewed at dusk) during Franco's bomb raids by covering it with a pyramid of sandbags. To the right are the **Museo Naval** and the eye-popping **Palacio de Comunicaciones,** where you can mail your letters in true style. Antonio Palacios and Julián Otamendi of Otto Wagner's Vienna School designed the neo-Baroque structure in 1920. On the northeastern corner of the intersection (behind black gates) is the former **Palacio de Linares,** a 19th-century townhouse built for Madrid nobility. Long abandoned by its former residents and proven by a team of "scientists" to be inhabited by ghosts, it was transformed into the **Casa de América,** with a library and lecture halls for the study of Latin American culture and politics. It sponsors art exhibitions, tours of the palace, and guest lectures.

PASEO DE RECOLETOS. Continuing north toward the brown **Torres de Colón (Columbus Towers),** you'll pass the **Biblioteca Nacional,** where the sleek **Museo del Libro** displays treasures from the monarchy's collection, including a first-edition copy of *Don Quijote. (Entrance at #20. Open Tu-Sa 10am-9pm, Su 10am-2pm. Free.)* Behind the library lies the huge **Museo Arqueológico Nacional** (see p. 106). The museum entrance is on C. Serrano, a thoroughfare lined with expensive boutiques and set in the posh **Barrio de Salamanca.**

The museum and library huddle just beyond the modern **Plaza Colón** (M: Colón) and the adjoining **Jardines del Descubrimiento (Gardens of Discovery).** At one side loom huge clay boulders, inscribed with odd trivia about the New World, including Seneca's prediction of the discovery, the names of all the mariners on board the caravels, and citations from Columbus's diary. From a thundering fountain in the center of the plaza rises a neo-Gothic spire to Columbus. The fountain's spray can be refreshing in Madrid's dry summer heat. Concerts, lectures, ballets, and plays are performed in the **Centro Cultural de la Villa,** the underground municipal art center located beneath the statue and the waterfall. *(Tel. 91 575 60 80.)*

PASEO DE LA CASTELLANA. Nineteenth and early 20th-century aristocrats dislodged themselves from Old Madrid to settle along **Paseo de la Castellana.** During the Civil War, Republican forces used the mansions as barracks. Most of them were torn down in the 60s when banks and insurance companies commissioned new and innovative structures. Competition begot architectural excellence, offering the lowly pedestrian a rich man's spectacle of architecture and fashion. Some notables include Moneo's **Bankinter,** #29, the first to integrate rather than demolish a townhouse; **Banco Urquijo,** known as "the coffeepot"; the Sevillian-tiled **Edificio ABC,** #34, the former office of the conservative, monarchical newspaper; the pink **Edificio Bankunion,** #46; **Banca Catalana Occidente,** #50 (on Glorieta de Emilio Castelar near the American Embassy), which looks like a delicate ice cube on a cracker; and the famous **Edificio La Caixa,** #61.

Just south of the American Embassy, between Pl. Colón and Glorieta de Emilio Castelar and under the C. Juan Bravo overpass, is an **Open-air Sculpture Museum** displaying works by Miró, González, and Chillida. Look up—the works are hanging from the bridge as well.

A number of intimate private museums, including the **Museo Lázaro Galdiano** (see p. 106), are located just off Po. Castellana. At **Plaza de Lima** (M: Lima) is the 110,000-seat **Estadio Santiago Bernabéu,** home to the beloved **Real Madrid,** champions of the 1998 *Copa de Europa* (for more info, see **Fútbol,** p. 112). Farther north, the **Puerta de Europa,** consisting of two 27-story leaning towers connected by a tunnel, dominates Pl. Castilla (M: Pl. Castilla). They were designed by American John Bergee as a doorway to the city.

EL PARDO

Built as a hunting lodge for Carlos I in 1547, El Pardo was enlarged by generations of Habsburgs and Bourbons. Though Spain's growing capital eventually engulfed El Pardo, it still stands as one of Spain's greatest country palaces. El Pardo gained attention in 1940 when Franco decided to make it his home; he resided here until his death in 1975. Although politics have changed, the palace is still the official reception site for distinguished foreign visitors who wine, dine, and decide the fate of millions among gorgeous Renaissance and Neoclassical furniture and chandeliers. Renowned for its collection of tapestries—several of which were designed by Goya—the palace also holds a Velázquez painting and Ribera's *Techo de los hombres ilustres (Ceiling of the Illustrious Men).* During his stay, Franco fitted the palace with modern amenities including TV and air conditioning—to prevent them from clashing with the elegant decor, he had them cunningly camouflaged. You can also see the bedroom cabinet in which Franco kept Santa Teresa's silver-encrusted hand. Entrance to the palace's **capilla** and the nearby **Casita del Príncipe,** created by Juan de Villanueva (of Museo del Prado fame), is free. *(Take bus #601 from the stop in front of the Ejército del Aire building above M: Moncloa*

(15min., 150ptas). Palace open Apr.-Sept. M-F 9:30am-6pm, Su 9:25am-1:40pm; Oct.-Mar. M-F 10:30am-5pm, Su 9:55am-1:40pm. Compulsory 45min. guided tour in Spanish. 650ptas, students 250ptas. Wednesday free for EU citizens.)

🏛 MUSEUMS

Madrid's great museums need no introduction. If you plan on visiting the three famous ones, your best bet is the **Paseo del Arte** ticket (1275ptas) that grants admission to the Museo del Prado, Museo Thyssen-Bornemisza, and Centro de Arte Reina Sofía. The pass is on sale at all three museums.

MUSEO DEL PRADO

Po. Prado at Pl. Cánovas del Castillo. M: Banco de España. Tel. 91 420 37 68. Open Tu-Sa 9am-7pm, Su 9am-2pm. 500ptas, students 250ptas, Sa after 2:30 and Su free.

The Prado is Spain's pride and joy, as well as one of Europe's finest museums. In 1785, architect Juan de Villanueva began construction of the Neoclassical building, following Carlos III's order for a museum of natural history and sciences. In 1819 Fernando VII transformed it into the royal painting archive; the museum's 7000 pieces are the result of hundreds of years of Bourbon art collecting. The walls are filled with Spanish and foreign masterpieces, including a comprehensive selection from the Flemish and Venetian schools.

The museum is well organized: each room is numbered and described in the museum's free guide. The sheer quantity of paintings means you'll have to be selective—walk past the rooms of imitation Rubens and Rococo cherubs and into the groves of the masters. The museum's guidebooks help you sift through the floors and offer extensive art history and criticism (100-3000ptas).

DIEGO VELÁZQUEZ

The second floor houses Spanish and Italian works from the 16th and 17th centuries. The most notable of these are an unparalleled collection of works by Diego Velázquez (1599-1660), court painter and interior decorator for Felipe IV (portraits of the foppish monarch abound). Because of their unforgiving realism and use of light, Velázquez's works resonate even in the 20th century. Several of his most famous paintings are here, including *Las hilanderas (The Tapestry Weavers)*, *Los borrachos (The Drunkards)*, and *La fragua de Vulcano (Vulcan's Forge)*. With *Las lanzas (The Spears* or *The Surrender of Breda)*, Velázquez began to experiment with spatial perspective, developing the technique to imply continuous movement in the canvas. Smoke from a recent battle clears in the background as an anxious horse dominates the foreground. Velazquez's technique, called illusionism, climaxed in his magnum opus *Las meninas (The Maids of Honor)*, since dubbed an "encounter" rather than a painting,. The "snapshot quality" of the figures transformed painting in the 17th century—the style was duplicated only by the Impressionists 200 years later.

FRANCISCO GOYA

In 1785, Francisco de Goya y Lucientes (1746-1828) became the court portraitist. Perhaps the most interesting aspect of his works is that he managed to depict the royal family so unflatteringly and satirically without being expelled from court. Some suggest that he manipulated light and shadow to focus the viewer's gaze on the figure of the queen (rather than the centrally located king) in *La familia de Carlos IV*—a discreet way of supporting contemporary popular opinion about the true power behind the monarchy. The stark *Dos de Mayo* and *Fusilamientas de Tres de Mayo*, which depict the terrors of the Revolution of 1808, may be Goya's most recognized works. Also notable is the expressionless woman in *La maja vestida* and *La maja desnuda*. Perhaps the most evocative pieces in the Goya collection are the *Pinturas Negras (Black Paintings)*. These paintings were aptly named for the darkness of both the colors and the subject matter—Goya painted them in the house where he lived at the end of his life, deaf and alone. *Sat-*

urno devorando a su hijo (Saturn Devouring His Son) stands out among the *Pinturas Negras*, a reminder from an ailing artist that time eventually destroys its creations. Goya violently captures the moment when Saturn eats his children, upon hearing a prophesy that one of them would overthrow him.

ITALIAN, FLEMISH, AND OTHER SPANISH ARTISTS

The Prado also displays many of **El Greco's** (Doménikos Theotokópoulos, 1541-1614) religious paintings. *La Trinidad (The Trinity)* and *La adoración de los pastores (The Adoration of the Shepherds)* are characterized by El Greco's luminous colors, elongated figures, and mystical subjects. On the second floor are other works by Spanish artists, including **Murillo's** *Familia con pájaro pequeño (Family with Small Bird)*, **Ribera's** *El martirio de San Bartholomeo (Martyrdom of Saint Bartholomew)*, and **Zurbarán's** *La inmaculada*.

The Prado has a formidable collection of **Italian** works, including **Titian's** portraits of Carlos I and Felipe II and **Raphael's** *El cardenal desconocido (The Unknown Cardinal)*. **Tintoretto's** rendition of the homicidal seductress Judith and her hapless victim Holofernes, as well as his *Washing of the Feet* are here as well. Some minor **Botticellis** and a slew of his imitators are also on display. Among the works by **Rubens,** *The Three Graces* and *The Adoration of the Magi* best reflect his voluptuous style.

As a result of the Spanish Habsburgs' control of the Netherlands, the **Flemish** holdings are also top-notch. **Van Dyck's** *Marquesa de Legunes* is here, as well as works by **Albrecht Durer.** Especially harrowing is **Peter Breughel the Elder's** *The Triumph of Death*, in which death drives a carriage of skulls on a decaying horse. **Hieronymus Bosch's** moralistic *The Garden of Earthly Delights* is a favorite, with detailed depictions of hedonism and the destiny that awaits its practitioners.

CASÓN DEL BUEN RETIRO

Three minutes from the Prado sits the Casón del Buen Retiro. Once part of Felipe IV's Palacio del Buen Retiro, the Casón was destroyed in the Napoleonic wars. The rebuilt version normally houses the Prado's 19th- and 20th-century works, currently on loan to the Reina Sofia. *(C. Alfonso XXII, 28. Tel. 91 330 28 60. Closed for renovations until at least 2002.)*

MUSEO NACIONAL CENTRO DE ARTE REINA SOFÍA

C. Santa Isabel, 52, opposite Estación Atocha at the south end of Po. Prado. M: Atocha. Tel. 91 467 50 62. Open M and W-F 10am-9pm, Su 10am-2:30pm. 500ptas, students 250ptas. Sa after 2:30pm and Su free.

Since Juan Carlos I decreed this renovated hospital the national museum in 1988, the Reina Sofía's collection of **20th-century art** has grown steadily. The second and fourth floors are a maze of permanent exhibits charting the Spanish avant-garde and contemporary movements. Rooms dedicated to Juan Gris, Juan Miró, and Salvador Dalí, which include Miró's *Man with a Pipe* and some of Dalí's early works, illustrate Spain's vital contributions to the Surrealist movement.

Picasso's masterwork *Guernica* is the centerpiece of the Reina Sofía's permanent collection. It depicts the Basque town bombed by the Germans at Franco's request during the Spanish Civil War. Picasso denounced the bloodshed in a huge, colorless work of contorted, agonized figures. The screaming horse in the center represents war, and the twisted bull—an unmistakable national symbol—symbolizes Spain. When asked by Nazi officials whether he was responsible for this work, Picasso answered, "No, you are." He gave the canvas to New York's Museum of Modern Art on the condition that they return it to Spain when democracy was restored. In 1981, five years after Franco's death, *Guernica* was delivered to Madrid's Casón del Buen Retiro. The subsequent move to the Reina Sofía sparked an international controversy—Picasso's other stipulation had been that the painting hang only in the Prado, to affirm his equivalent status with artists like Titian and Velázquez. The museum surrounds *Guernica* with its preliminary sketches and many other Picasso paintings and sculptures, testimony to his breadth of talent. Two other works of note are *Woman in Blue* and *Painter with Model*.

▨MUSEO THYSSEN-BORNEMISZA

On the corner of Po. Prado and C. San Jerónimo. M: Banco de España. Bus #6, 14, 27, 37, or 45. Tel. 91 369 01 51. Open Tu-Su 10am-7pm. No one admitted after 6:30pm. 700ptas, seniors and students with ISIC 400ptas, under 12 free.

Unlike the Prado and the Reina Sofía, the Thyssen-Bornemisza covers a wide range of periods and media, with exhibits ranging from 14th-century canvases to 20th-century sculptures. The museum is housed in the 18th-century Palacio de Villahermosa and contains the former collection of Baron Heinrich Thyssen-Bornemisza. The baron donated his collection in 1993, and today the museum, with over 775 pieces, is the world's most extensive private showcase. To view the collection in chronological order and observe the evolution of styles and themes, begin on the top floor and work your way down.

The top floor is dedicated to the **Old Masters** collection, which includes such notables as Hans Holbein's austere *Portrait of Henry VIII* and El Greco's *Annunciation*. The organization of the Thyssen-Bornemisza provokes natural comparisons across centuries—note how the representation of the body evolves from Lucas Cranach's *The Nymph of the Spring* to Titian's *Saint Jerome in the Desert* to Anthony van Dyck's *Portrait of Jacques Le Roy*. In both variety and quality, the Thyssen-Bornemisza's **Baroque** collection, including pieces by Caravaggio, José de Ribera, and Claude Lorraine, overshadows that of the Prado.

The movement from the dark canvases of the top floor to the vibrant ones below reflects the revolutionary command of light and the arbitrary use of color that became popular in the 17th century. In the 17th-century Dutch works, such as Frans Hals's *Family Group in a Landscape*, artists began to master the use of natural light to illuminate subjects. The **Impressionist** and **Post-Impressionist** collections explode with texture and color—look for works by Renoir, Manet, Pisarro, Degas, Monet, van Gogh, Toulouse-Lautrec, Cézanne, and Matisse. Though less well-known, the **Expressionist** artists are also well-represented, with noteworthy works by Nolde, Marc, and Beckmann.

The highlight of the tour is the museum's **20th-century** collection. The modern artists represented include Picasso, Léger, Mondrian, Miró, Kandinsky, Gorky, Pollack, Rothko, Dalí, Hopper, Chagall, Ernst, Klee, and O'Keefe, to name a few.

OTHER MUSEUMS

▨**MUSEO DE LA REAL ACADEMIA DE BELLAS ARTES DE SAN FERNANDO.** A beautiful museum with a collection of Old Masters surpassed only by the Prado. Goya's *La Tirana* and Velázquez's portrait of Felipe IV are masterpieces; the Raphael and Titian collections are also excellent. Other attractions include a room dedicated to Goya (a former academy director) and 17th-century canvases by Ribera, Murillo, Zurbarán, and Rubens. The **Calcografía Real (Royal Print and Drawing Collection)**, in the same building, houses Goya's studio and organizes temporary exhibitions. *(Alcalá, 13. Tel. 91 522 00 46. M: Sol or Sevilla. Open Tu-F 9am-7:30pm, Sa-M and holidays 9:30am-2:30pm. 400ptas, students 200ptas. Sa and Su free.)*

▨**MUSEO DE AMÉRICA.** This under-appreciated museum recently reopened after painstaking renovations; it is now a can't-miss. It documents the cultures of America's pre-Columbian civilizations and the effects of the Spanish conquest. Artifacts include solid gold Columbian ornaments and Mayan treasures. The renovations added state-of-the-art multimedia exhibits. *(Av. Reyes Católicos, 6, near Av. Puerta de Hierro and next to the Faro de Moncloa. Tel. 91 549 26 41. M: Moncloa. Open Tu-Sa 10am-3pm, Su 10am-2:30pm. 500ptas, students 200ptas. Sunday free.)*

CONVENTO DE LA ENCARNACIÓN. Designed by Juan de Herrera's disciple Juan de Gómez (the architect of Pl. Mayor), the convent houses about 1500 relics of saints, including a vial of San Pantaleón's blood, believed to liquefy every year on July 27. According to the legend, if the blood does not liquefy, disaster will strike Madrid. The permanent collection contains pieces by José de Ribera and Goya's brother-in-law, Francisco Bayeu. *(Pl. Encarnación, off C. Bailén just east of Palacio Real. Tel. 91 542 00 59. M: Ópera. Open Tu-Th and Sa 10:30am-12:45pm and 4-5:45pm, Su 11am-1:45pm. 425ptas, students 225ptas. EU citizens free Wednesday.)*

MADRID

LA MOVIDA After 40 years of Franco-imposed repression, Madrid was a cultural explosion waiting to happen. Franco's death in 1975 served as a catalyst for change: not a day had passed before every newspaper had printed a pornographic photo on its front page. *El Destapeo* ("the uncorking" or "uncovering" which followed Franco's regime) and *la Movida* ("the Movement," which took place a few years later) both exploded in Madrid, inspiring political diversity, apolitical revelry, and eccentricity of all kinds. Filmmaker Pedro Almodóvar became a reflection of the movement and its most famous member, creating farcical films about loony grandmothers, outgoing young women, unapologetic homosexuals, and eclectic students. Gradually, *la Movida* became too much for the city. Artists and club-rats were forced to give up their favorite pastimes for practical jobs—no one could afford to keep up the careless and eccentric lifestyle that *la Movida* represented. Remnants of *la Movida* are still visible, however, in today's outrageous clubs, ambitious bars, and in the excitement of young *madrileños* planning to *ir de marcha* ("to party," literally "to go marching").

MUSEO ARQUEOLÓGICO NACIONAL. The history of the Western world is on display in this huge museum. Amid other astounding items from Spain's past is the country's most famous archaeological find, *Dama de Elche*, a 4th-century funerary urn. Outside stands a replica of the Altamira caves and their Paleolithic paintings. The museum also houses Moorish ivories from Andalucía and golden Visigoth crowns. *(C. Serrano 13, behind the Biblioteca Nacional. Tel. 91 577 79 12. M: Serrano. Open Tu-Sa 9:30am-8:30pm, Su 9:30am-2:30pm. 500ptas, students 250ptas. Saturday free after 2:30pm.)*

MONASTERIO DE LAS DESCALZAS REALES. In 1559 Juana of Austria, Felipe II's sister, converted the former royal palace into a convent; today it is home to 26 Franciscan nuns who watch over Juana's tomb. The **Salón de Tapices** contains 10 renowned tapestries based on cartoons by Rubens, as well as Santa Ursula's jewel-encrusted bones and *El viaje de Santa Ursula y las once mil vírgenes (The Journey of Santa Ursula and the Eleven Thousand Virgins)*. *(Pl. Descalzas, between Pl. Callao and Pta. de Sol. Tel. 91 559 74 04. M: Callao or Sol. Open Tu-Th and Sa 10:30am-12:45pm and 4-6pm, F 10:30am-12:45pm, Su 11am-1:45pm. 650ptas, students 250ptas. EU citizens free on Wednesday.)*

MUSEO DEL EJÉRCITO. In this stately fragment of the Palacio del Buen Retiro is a vast collection of military paraphernalia. Each room of the museum is dedicated to a different period or conquest; the most famous contains a fragment of the sword Columbus plunged into the ground when he discovered the New World. *(C. Méndez Núñez, 1, just north of Casón del Buen Retiro. Tel. 91 522 89 77. M: Retiro or Banco de España. Open Tu-Su 10am-2pm. 100ptas, students 50ptas, under 18 free. Saturday free.)*

MUSEO CERRALBO. This palatial residence-turned-museum displays an eclectic collection of period furniture and ornamentation. The music room has a Louis XVI-style French piano, and the chapel houses El Greco's *The Ecstasy of Saint Francis*. *(C. Ventura Rodríguez, 17. Tel. 91 547 36 46. M: Ventura Rodríguez. Open Tu-Sa 9:30am-2:30pm, Su 10am-2pm. 400ptas, students 200ptas. Wednesday and Sunday free.)*

MUSEO LÁZARO GALDIANO. Among the riches of this private collection are an overwhelming display of Italian Renaissance bronzes and Celtic and Visigoth-brasses. The array of paintings includes Leonardo da Vinci's *The Savior* and Hieronymous Bosch's *Ecce Homo*. *(C. Serrano, 122. Turn right off Po. Castellana onto C. María de Molina. Tel. 91 561 60 84. M: Rubén Dario. Open Sept.-July Tu-Su 10am-2pm. 300ptas. Sunday free.)*

MUSEO ROMÁNTICO. Housed in a 19th-century mansion built by a disciple of Ventura Rodríguez, this museum is an exquisite time capsule of the Romantic period's decorative arts. *(C. San Mateo, 13. Tel. 91 448 10 71. M: Alonso Martínez. Open Sept.-July Tu-Sa 9am-3pm, Su 10am-2pm. 400ptas, students 200ptas. Sunday free.)*

♫ NIGHTLIFE

Simply put, *madrileños* like to party. Whether on a *terraza* in the summer or in a *barrio* bar in the winter, the night hours are characterized by a steady stream of pedestrian traffic as revelers meander from place to place. Proud of their nocturnal offerings—they'll tell you with a straight face that they were bored in Paris or New York—*madrileños* insist that no one goes to bed until they've "killed the night" and, in some cases, a good part of the following morning.

An average night includes several neighborhoods and countless venues, perhaps starting in the *tapas* bars of Huertas, moving to a first-session disco in Malasaña, and then to the wild parties of Chueca. Some clubs don't even bother opening until 4 or 5am; the only (relatively) quiet nights of the week are Sunday and Monday.

For clubs and discos, life begins around 2am. Many discos have "afternoon" sessions for teens (7pm-midnight; cover 250-1000ptas), but the "night" sessions (lasting until dawn) are when people really let their hair down. The *entrada* (cover) often includes a drink and can be as high as 2000ptas; men may be charged up to 500ptas more than women, if women are charged at all. Keep an eye out for *invitaciones* and *oferta* cards—in stores, restaurants, tourist publications, tourist offices, and in the streets—that offer discounts or free admission.

For current info on what's going on, scan Madrid's entertainment guides (see **Read This**, p. 79). The *Guía del Ocio* is an indispensable tool, featuring the latest hotspots and information about virtually all of Madrid's nighttime establishments.

CENTRO

In the middle of Madrid and at the heart of the action are the grandiose and flamboyant clubs of El Centro. With multiple floors, swinging lights, cages, and discoballs, they fulfill even the wildest club-rat's expectations. The mainstream clubs found among these streets are often tourist hotspots; as a result, a night of fun here is the most expensive in the city. El Centro covers more territory than Madrid's other neighborhoods, so make a plan and bring a map.

Joy Eslava, C. Arenal, 11 (tel. 91 366 37 33). M: Sol or Ópera. A 3-tiered disco featuring 3 bars, laser lights, and live entertainment. Because of its prominent location, Joy Eslava is packed with international tourists grooving to disco, techno, R&B, and salsa. Watch out for the rising stage—you might end up a superstar. Cover 1500-2000ptas, includes 1 drink. Open M-Th 11:30pm-dawn, F-Sa 7-10:15pm and 11:30pm-5:30am.

Refugio, C. Dr. Cortezo, 1. M: Tirso de Molina. Don't miss the club—it's the first door on the left from the metro stop. Steel doors covered in steel vines lead to a jungle of racy *fiestas de espuma* (foam parties). Friday and Saturday nights bring "shows" like the *concurso de pollas* (penis competition). An outrageous gay scene, but fun for all. Cover 1000ptas, includes 1 drink. Open Tu-Su midnight-dawn.

Mad Cafe Club, Virgen del los Peligros, 4 (tel. 91 532 62 28), off C. de Alcalá. M: Sevilla. The metallic decor reflects the light of hundreds of candles. Chic artists come here to lounge on pillows and dance to jazz and techno. Open 12:30am-dawn.

Heaven, C. Veneras, 2 (tel. 91 548 20 22). M: Santo Domingo. Heavenly drag performances and underwordly parties for a primarily gay crowd. Special "groove Sundays." Drinks 650-900ptas. Cover 500-1500ptas, includes 1 drink. Open 1:30am-dawn.

El Barbu, C. Santiago, 3 (tel. 91 542 56 98), across C. Mayor from the Ayuntamiento. M: Sol or Ópera. Chill to techno spun by a former Studio 54 DJ. Art exhibitions draw a glam, black-clad crowd. Open Tu-Su 8am-3am.

Kathmandú, C. Señores de Luzón, 3 (tel. 91 541 52 53), off C. Mayor, facing the Ayuntamiento, close to El Barbu. M: Sol. Jammed with locals dancing to high-energy techno and acid jazz. Cover 800ptas, includes 1 drink. Open Th 11pm-5am, F-Sa 11pm-6am.

Azúcar, Po. Reina Cristina, 7 (tel. 91 501 61 07). M: Atocha. Sweet, sweet salsa. No sneakers allowed. Salsa classes daily 9:30-11pm. Cover 1200ptas, Sa 1500ptas, includes 2 drinks. Open M-Th 11:30pm-5am, F-Sa 11pm-6:30am, Su 9pm-dawn.

▨HUERTAS

Within Huertas lies **Plaza Santa Ana,** brimming with *terrazas*, bars, and live street music. Many bars convert to clubs as the night unfolds, spinning house and techno on intimate dance floors. Be sure to check out the larger *discotecas* on **Calle Atocha.** Most locals begin their evenings in Huertas and emerge from Malasaña and Chueca (see p. 109) in the morning.

DISCOTECAS

Kapital, C. Atocha, 125 (tel. 91 420 29 06), a block off Po. Prado. M: Atocha. Take the metro—it's the safest way here. One of the most extreme results of *la Movida,* this *macro-discoteca* tries harder to impress than its glittered clientele. Two dance floors, a sky-light lounge, and several bars contribute to 7 floors of over-stimulation. Packed with 20-somethings who can afford the 1200pta cover (includes 1 drink). Drinks 800-1000ptas. Open Th 12:30-6am, F-Su 6-11pm and 12:30-6am.

Angels of Xenon, C. Atocha, 38 (tel. 91 369 38 81). M: Antón Martín. Black walls and 2 disco balls provide ambience for a mostly gay crowd. Don't worry about feeling under-dressed; when the bubble machine comes out, you'll be pretty happy you left your best at home. Cover 1500ptas, includes 1 drink. Open F-Sa midnight-7am.

No Se Lo Digas a Nadie, C. Ventura de la Vega, 7, next to Pl. Santa Ana. M: Sevilla. Don't be thrown off by the art exhibition sign; head through the garage doors and see what's on display. Oops, the secret's out. Drinks 500-800ptas. Live music starts around 12:15am.

BAR-MUSICALES

▨ **Cardamomo,** C. Echegaray, 15 (tel. 91 369 07 57). M: Sevilla. Where Madrid's beauti-ful people come to watch flamenco. You're beautiful too—join them. Open 7pm-4am.

Kasbah, C. Santa Maria, 17. M: Antón Martín. The place to wear those big-ass shoes. Enjoy the wild decor while listening to the DJs spin some of the best jungle and techno in Madrid. Beer 350ptas. Open daily 11pm-dawn.

La Comedia, C. Príncipe, 16 (tel. 91 521 51 64). M: Sevilla. Clubbers often spill out into the street to cool off from the R&B inside. Cover 1000ptas, includes 1 drink. Open Su-Th 3pm-4am and 5-9am, F-Sa 3pm-9am.

La Boca del Lobo, C. Echegaray, 11 (tel. 91 429 70 13). M: Sevilla. The wolf on the sign won't eat you, but waterfall mirrors in the bathrooms may drench you. Understated inte-rior complements the stylish crowd. Open 11pm-dawn.

Café Central, Pl. Angel, 10 (tel. 91 369 41 43), off Pl. Santa Ana. M: Antón Martín or Sol. Art Deco meets old-world cafe. An older audience enjoys high-class jazz. Beer 300-500ptas. Cover 700-1500ptas. Open 1:30pm-3:30am.

Café Jazz Populart, C. Huertas, 22 (tel. 91 429 84 07). With walls covered in old trum-pets and clarinets, this bar tries to discover Madrid's jazz talent. Even if they fail, they still have an extensive bar. Live jazz, blues, reggae, and flamenco. Shows Su-W 11pm, F-Sa 11pm and 12:30am. Open Su-Th 6pm-12:30am, F-Sa 6pm-3am.

BARS

Mauna Loa, Pl. Santa Ana, 13 (tel. 91 429 70 62). M: Sevilla or Sol. Feels like Hawaii—birds fly freely between low chairs and the scantily clad dance to upbeat tunes. *"Fuerte* volcano" drinks 825-1650ptas. Open Su-Th 7pm-2am, F-Sa 7pm-3am.

Naturbier, Pl. Santa Ana, 9 (tel. 91 429 39 18). M: Sol or Sevilla. Locals pour in for the excellent locally brewed *bier,* inspired by their motto: "beer is important to human nutri-tion." Superior lager 350-675ptas. Open Su-Th 11:30am-1am, F-Sa 11am-3am.

Viva Madrid, C. Manuel Fernández González, 7 (tel. 91 429 36 40), next to Pl. Santa Ana. M: Sol or Sevilla. *"Lo mejor del mundo"* (the best of the world) is their humble motto. Lovely *terraza* is packed with plants, tiled walls, and classy clientele. Beer 400ptas, cocktails 1000ptas. Open daily 1pm-7am.

Punto y Coma, Pl. Santa Ana, at the corner of C. Prado. M: Sol or Sevilla. The "pearl of the plaza." Casual college crowd. Beer 300ptas. Open nightly until 1am.

El Café de Sheherezade, C. Santa María, 18, a block from C. Huertas. M: Antón Martín. Recline on opulent pillows while sipping exotic infusions in the dark, mellow, bohemian atmosphere. Decor inspires hedonistic thoughts. Thursday features Middle Eastern music. Offers *pira* (pipe 600-1000ptas). Open daily 7pm-5am.

La Fontana de Oro, C. Victoria, 2. M: Sol. One of many new bars with a pub theme. It houses a statue of a saint, but the selection of liqueurs (450-650ptas) encourages less-than-saintly behavior. Open M-Th 11am-3am, F-Sa 11am-5am.

GRAN VÍA

Even the side streets of Gran Vía never sleep, pulsating in the early morning to the bass of landmark clubs. As the flashy and boisterous clubs demonstrate, subtlety never was a strong point for the area. Lost? Just follow the people and music.

Soul Kitchen, Mesonero Romanos, 13 (tel. 91 532 15 24). M: Gran Vía or Callao. Where *"la música es funky."* Those in the know arrive around 4am. A revived hotspot and the only real hip-hop club in town. Cover 1000ptas, 2000ptas after 2am, includes 1 drink. Open W-Sa midnight-5:30am.

Tierra, Cabarello de Gracia, 20 (tel. 91 532 72 71), off C. Montero (to be safe, walk over one block to C. Peligios). M: Gran Vía. Black interior with psychedelic glow-in-the-dark design plays host to damn good house. So dark you won't know who just did that. Beer 500ptas. Open Th-Sa midnight-4:30am.

Goa After Club, C. Mesonero Romanos, 13 (tel. 91 531 48 27). M: Callao or Gran Vía. After-hours party features high-energy techno and even higher-energy clubbers. The intoxicated, sleep-deprived crowd dances so hard, you won't believe your eyes. Drinks 700-1000ptas. Cover 1000ptas, includes 1 drink. Open Sa-Su 6-10am.

MALASAÑA & CHUECA

The dark cafes and darker clubs of Malasaña and Chueca filter jazz, techno, and foam into the night and early morning. Known for their bohemian crowds, Malasaña's hotspots radiate from **Plaza 2 de Mayo** and **Calle San Vincente Ferrer.** People are high on life, drugs, and booze; be wary at night. **Calle de Pelayo** is the main drag in flamboyant and gay Chueca. The safest walking route at night is up C. Fuencarral from Gran Vía and right on C. Augusto Figueroa.

Café la Palma, C. La Palma, 62 (tel. 91 522 50 31). M: San Bernardo or Noviciado. Eclectic and friendly crowd. Lounge in the comfy pillow room. Open daily 4pm-morning.

Midday, C. Amaniel, 13 (tel. 91 547 25 25). M: Noviciado. The after-hours club for Madrid's beautiful people. Techno and house. Open Su 9am-3pm.

Black & White, C. Libertad, 34 (tel. 91 531 11 41). M: Chueca. A lively disco/bar with room to chat, mingle, and groove on the packed dance floors. 2 floors of fun for a mostly gay and lesbian crowd. Wednesday is international exchange night. Beer 500ptas, mixed drinks 800ptas. Open daily 9pm-4am, F-Sa 9pm-5am.

Morocco, C. Marques de Leganes, 7 (tel. 91 531 31 77). M: Santo Domingo. Moves at an inhuman pace to techno under some crazy lighting. Cover 900ptas, includes 1 drink. Open Th 12am-5am. F-Sa 9pm-5:30am.

Vía Láctea, C. Velarde, 18 (tel. 91 466 75 81). M: Tribunal. This famous club is always packed. The loudspeakers might leave you deaf. Open daily 7:30pm-3am.

La Tetera de la Abuela, C. Espíritu Santo, 19. M: Noviciado. "Granny's Teapot." Granny's brewing some wicked tea. Open Su-Th 7:30pm-1am, F-Sa 7:30pm-2am.

Davai, C. Flor Baja, 1 (tel. 91 547 57 11). M: Pl. España or Callao. 2 packed floors of dancers swinging to jungle, house, and tight jazz. Open daily 12:30-6am.

Rick's, C. Clavel, 8. M: Chueca. Mostly gay men lounge in Chueca's hottest bar. A confused but comfortable setting—have cocktails at the bar or play a heated game of foosball. Look good, be happy. Beer 600-900ptas. Open daily 11pm-morning.

Café Figueroa, C. Augusto Figueroa, 17 (tel. 91 521 16 73), on the corner of C. Hortaleza. M: Chueca. Smoke-filled, dimly lit cafe is otherworldly. Mostly gay clientele. Beer 300-425ptas. Coffee 250-450ptas. Open Su-Th 3pm-1am, F-Sa 3pm-2:30am.

Star's Cafe, C. Marques de Valdeiglesias, 5 (tel. 91 522 27 12). M: Chueca. A stylish cafe during the week, a vivacious dance club on the weekends. Come well-dressed and don't forget your cell phone. Open Su-Th 10am-2pm, F-Sa 10am-4am.

Acuarela, C. Gravina, 8, off C. Hortaleza. M: Chueca. A welcome alternative to the club scene. Spend hours just chilling. Beer 400ptas. Open Su-Th 4pm-2am, F-Sa 4pm-4am.

El Truco, C. Gravina, 10 (tel. 91 532 89 21). M: Chueca. Classy bar featuring local artists' works. Lesbian-friendly. Open Su-Th 8pm-2am, F-Sa 9pm-4am. Same owners run **Escape,** a club down the street. Both are strong enough for a man, but designed particularly for a woman. Open F-Sa midnight-7am.

Bolero Terraza, Po. Castellana, 33 (tel. 91 554 91 51). M: Rubén Darío. An ultra-fashionable *terraza.* Claw your way to the bar. Drinks 1000ptas. Open daily 7:30pm-3am.

BILBAO

In the student-filled streets radiating from **Glorieta de Bilbao,** it's easy to find a cheap drink and even easier to find someone to drink it with. Although discos are plentiful, *terrazas* are packed with boisterous customers late into the night, sipping icy Mahou on Pl. Olavide, C. Fuencarral, and C. Luchana.

Vaivén, Travesía de San Mateo, 1. M: Tribunal. The most exclusive salsa club in the city. Crawling with well-dressed people looking to meet the man/woman of their dreams. Mid-week concerts. Beer 600ptas, mixed drinks 900ptas. Open daily 9pm-4am.

Clamores Jazz Club, C. Albuquerque, 14 (tel. 91 445 79 38), off C. Cardenal Cisneros. M: Bilbao. Swanky, pink neon setting and some of Madrid's more interesting jazz. The cover (300-1500ptas) gets slipped into the bill. Live jazz every night but Monday. Open July-Aug. M-Th 7pm-3am, F-Sa 7pm-4am; Sept.-June Su-Th 7pm-3am, F-Sa 7pm-4am.

Archy, C. Marqués de Riscal, 11 (tel. 91 308 31 62), off C. Almagro from Pl. Alonso Martínez. M: Ruben Darío. Known as a *puerta rigurosa.* Translation: "tight door"—dress your best unless you like standing in line all night. Open Th-Sa 11pm-morning.

Barnon, C. Santa Engracia, 17 (tel. 91 447 38 37). M: Alonso Martínez or Tribunal. Real Madrid's stud *fútbol* forward owns this hip-hop bar, packing it with VIPs. You can be a VIP too if you sport the proper uniform—wear something tight, short, and revealing. Open Su-Th 10pm-3am, F-Sa 10pm-4am.

Big Bamboo, C. Barquillo, 42 (tel. 91 562 88 38) M: Alonso Martínez. Walk 3 blocks east of C. Pelayo on C. Gravina, and turn left on C. Barquillo. A friendly, international club that jams to smooth reggae. Open Tu-Th 10pm-6am, F-Sa 10pm-7am.

MONCLOA

Students inundate the streets, sporting their favorite tight jeans, halter tops, denim jackets, and little black bags. The area clears out weekdays in June (when exams hit) and everyday in August (during family vacations).

Galileo Galilei, C. Galileo, 100 (tel. 91 534 75 57 or 91 534 75 58), off C. Alberto Aguilera. M: Moncloa or Quevedo. A relatively diverse crowd dances to some of Madrid's most lively pop bands. 80s decor. Beware of young couples doing their own exploring in dark corners. Cover free-1500ptas. Open Su-Th 6pm-3am, F-Sa 6pm-5am.

Patato Bar, C. Hilavion Eslava, at C. Fernando El Católico. M: Moncloa. Loud, welcoming bar. A great place to start the night. Fiesty *sangría* 500ptas. Open daily until 1am.

Chapandaz, C. Fernando Católico, 1 block from Arcipreste de Hita. M: Moncloa. The street is lined with bars and clubs, but only Chapandaz has stalactites and the mysterious *leche de pantera* (panther's milk). Mixed drinks 500ptas. Open daily until 2am.

♫ ENTERTAINMENT

MUSIC

In summer, the city sponsors free concerts, ranging from classical and jazz to bolero and salsa, at Pl. Mayor, Lavapiés, Oriente, and Villa de París. See **Read This,** page 79, for informative publications. Call ahead for prices.

The **Auditorio Nacional,** C. Príncipe de Vergara, 146 (tel. 91 337 01 00; M: Cruz del Rayo), home to the National Orchestra, features Madrid's best classical performances (800-4200ptas). The **Fundación Juan March,** C. Castelló, 77 (tel. 91 435 42 40; M: Núñez de Balboa), sponsors free weekly concerts (F-Su) and hosts a university lecture series (Tu-W 7:30pm). **Teatro Monumental,** C. Atocha, 65 (tel. 91 429 81 19; M: Antón Martín), is home to Madrid's Symphonic Orchestra. Reinforced concrete—a Spanish invention—was first used in its construction in the 1920s, so prepare for unusual acoustics. For opera and *zarzuela* (Spanish light opera), head for the ornate **Teatro de la Zarzuela,** C. Jovellanos, 4 (tel. 91 524 54 00; M: Banco de España), modeled on Milan's La Scala. The grand 19th-century granite **Teatro de la Ópera** (tel. 91 559 35 51), on Pl. Ópera, is the city's principal venue for classical ballet. Most theaters shut down in July and August.

Flamenco in Madrid is tourist-oriented and expensive. A few nightlife spots are authentic (see **Cardamomo,** p. 108), but they, too, are pricey. **Café de Chinitas,** C. Torija, 7 (tel. 91 547 15 01 or 91 547 15 02; M: Santo Domingo), is as overstated as they come. Shows start at 10:30pm and midnight, but the memories last forever (they'd better—the cover starts at 4000ptas). At **Corral de la Morería,** C. Morería, 17 (tel. 91 365 84 46 or 91 365 11 37; M: La Latina), by the Viaducto on C. Bailén, shows start at 10:45pm and last until 2am. The 4000pta cover includes one drink. **Teatro Albéniz,** C. Paz, 11 (tel. 91 521 99 98; M: Sol), hosts an annual *Certamen de Coreografía de Danza Española y Flamenco* that features original dance and music, including extraordinary flamenco (tickets 700-2000ptas).

FILM

In summer, the city sponsors free movies and plays, all listed in the *Guía del Ocio* and the entertainment supplements of Friday's newspapers. In July, look out for the **Fescinal,** a film festival at the Parque de la Florida. In summer, the **Parque del Retiro** occasionally shows free movies at 11pm.

Most cinemas show three films per day, at around 4:30pm, 7:30pm, and 10:30pm. Tickets cost 600-700ptas. Some cinemas offer weekday-only matinee student discounts for 550ptas. Wednesday is *día del espectador,* when tickets cost around 500ptas—show up early. Check the *versión original (V.O. subtitulada)* listings in *Guia del Ocio* for English movies subtitled in Spanish. Three excellent movie theaters are centered near M: Ventura Rodríguez, between Pl. España and Argüelles. **Princesa,** C. Princesa, 3 (tel. 91 541 41 00), shows mainstream Spanish films and subtitled foreign films. The theater/bar **Alphaville,** C. Martín de los Heros, 14 (tel. 91 559 38 36), behind Princesa and underneath the large patio, shows both current alternative and mainstream Spanish titles. **Renoir,** C. Raimundo Fernández Villaverde, 10 (tel. 91 541 41 00), a few doors down by the popcorn vendor, shows highly acclaimed recent films, many foreign and subtitled. The state-subsidized *filmoteca española* in the Art Deco **Ciné Doré,** C. Santa Isabel, 3 (tel. 91 369 11 25; M: Antón Martín), is Madrid's finest repertory cinema (tickets 200-400ptas).

THEATER

Huertas, east of Sol, is the theater district. In July and August, Pl. Mayor, Lavapiés, and Villa de París frequently host plays as theaters move outdoors. For a complete listing of theaters and shows, consult the *Guía del Ocio.* Seeing a play in Madrid is an entertaining way to participate in traditional culture and to practice your Spanish. Theatergoers should consult the well-illustrated magazines published by state-sponsored theaters, such as *Teatro Español, Teatro de la Comedia,* and the superb *Teatro María Guerrero.* Tickets can be purchased at theater box offices or at ticket agencies (**FNAC** tel. 91 595 62 00; **Librería Crisol** tel. 91 322 47 00; **TelEntrada** tel. 902 38 33 33).

MADRID

ATHLETICS

FÚTBOL. Spaniards obsess over *fútbol* (soccer). If either **Real Madrid** or **Atlético de Madrid** wins a match, count on streets clogged with honking cars. Every Sunday and some Saturdays between September and June, one of these two teams plays at home. Real Madrid plays at **Estadio Santiago Bernebéu,** Po. Castellana, 104 (tel. 91 457 11 12; M: Lima). Atlético de Madrid plays at **Estadio Vicente Calderón,** C. Virgen del Puerto, 67 (tel. 91 366 47 07; M: Pirámides or Marqués de Vadillos). Tickets cost 3000-7000ptas. If tickets are sold out, shifty scalpers lurk around the stadium a few days before the game. For the big games—Atlético vs. Real, either team vs. F.C. Barcelona *(La Barça)*, key tournament matches in April and May, or the summer *Copa del Rey* and *Copa de Europa* games—scalpers are really the only option.

RECREATION. For **cycling** info and bicycle repair, spin over to **Ciclos Muñoz** (tel. 91 475 02 19), on C. Pablo Ortíz (M: Usera; open M-F 9am-2pm and 5-8pm, Sa 9am-2pm). **Swimmers** splash in the outdoor pools at: **Casa de Campo** (tel. 91 463 00 50), on Av. Angel (M: Lago); the indoor **Municipal de La Latina,** Pl. Cebada, 2 (M: La Latina); **Aluche** (tel. 91 706 28 28) on Av. General Fenjul (bus #17, 34, or 139); and **Peñuelas,** (tel. 91 474 28 08), on C. Arganda (M: Delicias or bus #18). (All pools open daily 10:30am-8pm; 500ptas, ages 4-13 225ptas.) Gallop over to the **Hipódromo de Madrid,** Ctra. de La Coruña, km 7800 (tel. 91 357 16 82), for **horse-racing.** Call the **Oficina de Información Deportiva** (sports information; tel. 91 463 55 63) for more info. The tourist office's *Plano de las Instalacions Deportivos Muncipales* lists areas open to the public.

THE BULLFIGHT

Bullfighters are either loved or loathed. So too are the bullfights themselves. Nevertheless, the bullfight is a Spanish tradition, and locals joke that the bullfights are the only things in Spain ever to start on time.

Corridas (bullfights) are held during the Festival of San Isidro and every Sunday in summer from March to October; they occur less frequently during the rest of the year. Look for posters in bars and cafes (especially on C. Victoria, off C. San Jerónimo). **Plaza de las Ventas,** C. Alcalá, 237 (tel. 91 356 22 00; M: Ventas), east of central Madrid, is the biggest ring in Spain. A seat runs 450-15,200ptas, depending on whether it's in the sun *(sol)* or shade *(sombra)*; shade is more expensive. Tickets are usually available the Friday and Saturday before and the Sunday of the bullfight. If you're intrigued by the lore but not the gore, head to the **Museo Taurino,** C. Alcalá, 237 (tel. 91 725 18 57), at Pl. Monumental de Las Ventas. The museum displays a remarkable collection of capes, bullfighters' outfits, and posters of famous *corridas.* (Open Tu-F 9:30am-2:30pm, on fight days 10am-1pm. Free.) The bullfighting school (tel. 91 470 19 90; M: Batán) often has its own *corridas* for free.

From May 15 to 22, the **Fiestas de San Isidro** provide a bullfight every day with the top *matadors* and fiercest bulls. The festival is nationally televised; those without tickets can crowd into bars.

FESTIVALS

The brochure *Las Fiestas de España*, available at tourist offices and the bigger hotels, contains historical background and general information on Spain's festivals. Madrid's **Carnival** (March 2-12 in 2000) was inaugurated in the Middle Ages and prohibited during Franco's dictatorship. Now the city bursts with street fiestas, dancing, and processions. In late April, the city bubbles with the high quality **International Theater Festival.** Around May 15, the **Fiesta de San Isidro,** in honor of Madrid's patron saint, bring concerts, parades, and Spain's best bullfights. Throughout the summer, the city sponsors the **Veranos de la Villa,** an outstanding and varied set of cultural activities, including free classical music concerts, movies in open-air settings, plays, art exhibits, an international film festival, opera, *zarzuela* (Spanish operetta), ballet, and sports. The **Festivales de Otoño** (Autumn Festivals), from September to November, also bring an impressive array of music, theater, and film. On November

1, **Todos los Santos** (All Saints' Day), an International Jazz Festival, brings great musicians to Madrid. The **Día de la Constitución** (Day of the Constitution, or National Day) on December 6 heralds the arrival of the National Company of Spanish Classical Ballet in Madrid. Tourist offices have all the information.

■ SHOPPING

It may not be Paris or London, but Madrid is the trendiest city in Spain. Most shops open from 10am-2pm and 5-8pm. Some have begun to stay open on Saturday afternoon and during lunch. By law, *grandes almecenes* (department stores) may open only the first Sunday of every month, a law that reflects the state's Roman Catholic heritage. Many small boutiques close in August, when practically everyone flees to the coast. **Inal** publishes a yearly *Guía Esencial para vivir en Madrid*, which includes descriptions of most stores.

MALLS

La Vaguada (M: Barrio del Pilar; bus #132 from Moncloa), in the northern neighborhood **Madrid-2,** is Madrid's first experiment in super-malls. It offers everything the homesick could want: 350 shops, including the Body Shop, Burberry's, a food court with Colonel Sanders and Ronald McDonald, multicinemas and a bowling alley (open daily 10am-10pm).

By far the poshest shopping mall is the **Galería del Prado,** Pl. Cortes (M: Banco de España), located beneath the Hotel Palace and across the Castellana from the Ritz (open M-Sa 10am-9pm). Of course, don't forget **El Corte Inglés** (see p. 81).

EL RASTRO (FLEA MARKET)

For hundreds of years, El Rastro has been a Sunday morning tradition in Madrid. From Pl. Mayor and its Sunday stamp and coin market, walk down C. Toledo to Pl. Cascorro (M: La Latina), where the market begins, and follow the crowds to the end, at the bottom of C. Ribera de Curtidores. In El Rastro you can find anything from pots to jeans to antique tools. Although the main street is a labyrinth of cheap jewelry, incense, and sunglasses, each side street has its own concert of venders and wares. Antique-sellers contribute their peculiar mustiness to C. del Prado. *Tapas* bars and small restaurants line the streets and provide an air-conditioned respite. The flea market is a paradise for pickpockets, so leave your camera in the room and turn that backpack into a frontpack. Police are everywhere if you have any problems. El Rastro is open Sundays and holidays from 9am to 2pm.

BOOKS

FNAC, C. Preciados, 28 (tel. 91 595 62 00). M: Callao. The best music and book selection in town. Books in English. Open M-Sa 10am-9:30pm, Su noon-9:30pm.

Librería Crisol, C. Juan Bravo, 38 (tel. 91 322 48 00). M: Diego de León. A high-powered place with futuristic interior design; service and prices to match. Open M-Sa 10:30am-10:30pm, Su 11am-3pm and 5-9pm. Many other locations around Madrid.

Booksellers, C. José Abascal, 48 (tel. 91 442 79 59 or 91 442 81 04). M: Gregorio Marañón. A vast array of new books in English, plus American and English magazines. Open M-F 9:30am-2pm and 5-8pm, Sa 10am-2pm.

Librería de Mujeres, C. San Cristóbal, 17 (tel. 91 521 70 43), near Pl. Mayor. International bookstore. English spoken. (See **Women's Services,** p. 82.)

Berkana Librería Gai y Lesbiana, C. Gravina, 11 (tel./fax 91 532 13 93). M: Chueca. Gay and lesbian bookstore with loads of contact info for foreigners and a free map of gay Madrid. Open M-F 10:30am-2pm and 5-8:30pm, Sa noon-2pm and 5-8:30pm.

English Editions, Pl. San Amaro, 5 (tel. 91 571 03 21), off C. General Perón. M: Estrecho. Used novels bought and sold. Excellent selection. Also a mini-mart featuring English and American food specialties. Call for hours.

Altair, C. Gaztambide, 31. M: Argüelles. Travel bookstore. Open M-Sa 10am-2pm and 4:30-8pm.

COMUNIDAD DE MADRID

The Comunidad de Madrid is an autonomous administrative region, shaped like an arrowhead and pointing right at the heart of Castilla y León (ouch). Historically, this area, along with Madrid and Castilla La Mancha, was known as Castilla La Nueva (New Castile). Comunidad de Madrid's small towns make interesting and refreshing daytrips from the city.

ALCALÁ DE HENARES

Residents of Alcalá (pop. 165,000) pride themselves on their town's distinguished offspring—Miguel de Cervantes—as well as their university's famed alumni, among them Golden Age authors Francisco de Quevedo and Lope de Vega, as well as exceptional Renaissance architecture. The combination of the three draw many a daytripper from nearby Madrid.

⊉ ORIENTATION AND PRACTICAL INFORMATION. Plaza de Cervantes is the main square. To get there from the train station, turn left as you exit and then bear right onto Po. Estación. After Vía Complutense (about 5 blocks down), take the first right onto C. Libreros and the plaza will be on your left.

The **train station** (tel. 91 563 02 02) is located on Po. Estación. Cercanías trains run from Madrid's Estación Atocha and back about every 15 minutes (45min., round-trip 650ptas). The **Continental-Auto bus station**, Av. Guadalajara, 5 (tel. 91 888 16 22), runs buses every 15 minutes between Alcalá and Madrid (45min., 290ptas). To reach the city center from the bus station, turn right on Av. Guadalajara and continue as it turns into C. Libreros. The helpful **tourist office**, Callejón de Santa María, 1 (tel. 91 889 26 94), at Pl. Cervantes, has a list of tourist sites and a detailed map of Alcalá (open daily June and Aug. 10am-2pm and 5-7:30pm; Mar.-May 10am-2pm and 4-6:30pm; July and Sept. Tu-Su 10am-2pm and 5-7:30pm). **Banco Central Hispano**, Pl. Cervantes, 4, has an **ATM. Emergency:** tel. 091 or 092; **ambulance** tel. 061; **Red Cross**, Pl. Cervantes, 12 (tel. 91 883 60 63 or 91 881 40 83; 24-hour emergency tel. 91 522 22 22); **police** tel. 91 881 92 63. **Post office** (tel. 91 219 71 97), Pl. Cervantes, 5, inside Banco Argentina (open M-F 8:30am-7pm, Sa 9:30am-1pm); **postal code:** 28801 to 28807.

⌐◻ ACCOMMODATIONS AND FOOD. Some of the least expensive rooms lie within **Hostal Jacinto**, Po. Estación, 2, 2nd staircase, 1-D (tel. 91 889 14 32), three blocks from the train station. Firm beds, floral bedspreads, TVs, and an unusual selection of art grace this hostel. (Singles with shower 2600ptas; doubles with shower 4500ptas, with bath 5000ptas; triples 6000ptas.) For food, Alcalá's famed *almendras garrapiñadas* (honey and sugar-coated almonds) beg to be tried. More sustenance awaits at **Mesón Las Cuadras de Rocinante**, C. Carmen Calzado, 1 (tel. 91 880 08 88), off C. Mayor. If it's good enough for Don Quijote's horse, it's good enough for you (huge, delicious, and cheap entrees 400-2300ptas; open 11am-midnight). **Restaurante Topeca '75** (tel. 91 888 45 25), on C. Mayor half a block from Pl. Cervantes, is a mirrored bar done in shades of green with a classy dining room upstairs (menú 1700ptas; open 1-4pm).

◙ SIGHTS. The huge **Plaza de Cervantes,** blessed with a statue of its namesake and filled with cafes and rose bushes, bursts with color each summer. At the end of the plaza opposite C. Libreros lie the **Ruinas de Santa María,** the remains of a 16th century church destroyed during the Civil War. In the surviving Capilla del Oidor, white Gothic plaster works surround the fountain where Cervantes was christened. (Open T-Su noon-2pm and 6-9pm. Free.) Just east of Pl. Cervantes in Pl. San Diego sits the **Colegio Mayor de San Ildefonso** (tel. 91 889 04 00), center of the once illustrious humanist university. Founded by Cardinal Cisneros in 1499, it opened for classes in 1508. In the **Parafino,** where doctorates were once awarded,

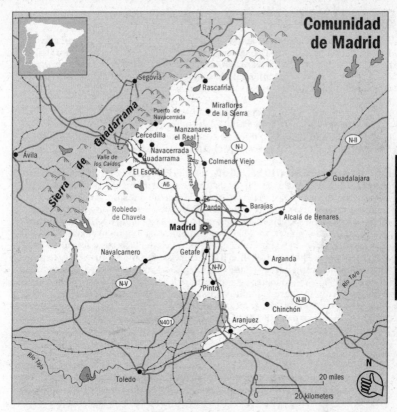

Comunidad de Madrid

the king now presents the "Premio Cervantes," Spain's most prestigious literary award. The Parafino and **Capilla de San Ildefonso** both have spectacular Mudéjar ceilings. (Required tour M-F 11:30am, 12:30, 1:30, 5, and 6pm; Sa-Su at 11, 11:45am, 12:30, 1:15, 2, 5, 5:45, 6:30, 7:15, and 8pm. 300ptas.) The town's **Catedral Magistral,** at the intersection of C. Mayor and C. de Escritorios, is one of the few in the world with this title; to be so named every priest must be a university magistrate. Undergoing restoration, it will not be reopened until the end of 1999.

Down C. Mayor from Pl. Cervantes is **Casa de Cervantes** (tel. 91 889 96 54), the reconstruction in situ of the house where the author was born. Currently under expansion, the house displays a variety of period furniture and editions of Don Quijote in languages Cervantes never knew. (Open Tu-F 10:15am-2pm and 4-6:45pm, Sa-Su 10:15am-2pm and 4-6:30pm. Free.) The **Convento de San Bernardo,** at Pl. Palacio a block north of the cathedral, hides a gorgeous 17th-century elliptical interior behind a simple facade. (Required tour M-F 6pm, Sa 12:30, 1:30, 5, 6, and 7pm, Su 5, 6, and 7pm. 350ptas.)

SAN LORENZO DEL ESCORIAL

They called it the eighth wonder of the world and they were right. In the shadow of Felipe II's somber colossus, El Escorial—half monastery and half mausoleum— the town of San Lorenzo is the most popular daytrip from Madrid. Although Felipe II constructed El Escorial for himself and for God, today, the complex, with its magnificent library, palaces, frescoes, and art treasures, seems as though it were made for tourists. Whatever you do, **do not come on Monday,** when the whole complex and most of the town is closed.

⚡ ORIENTATION AND PRACTICAL INFORMATION. Autocares Herranz buses, the easiest way to travel, leave from **Madrid's** Moncloa Metro station (1hr., 1 per hr., 7:15am-10:45pm, 450ptas) and whisk travelers to El Escorial's Plaza Virgen de Gracia, the center of town. The **Autocares Herranz** office, C. Reina Victoria, 3 (tel. 91 890 41 00, 91 890 41 22, or 91 890 41 25), and C. Rey, 27, sell tickets to Madrid. From the bus stop, exit left and turn right up C. Florida Blanca to get to the **tourist office,** C. Florida Blanca, 10 (tel. 91 890 15 54; open M-Sa 10am-6pm). El Escorial's **train station** (tel. 91 890 07 14; RENFE info tel. 91 328 90 20), on Ctra. Estación, is 2km from town. Trains run to **Madrid-Atocha** and **Madrid-Chamartín** (1hr., every 20min., 5:57am-10:17pm, round-trip 790ptas). To get to the tourist office from the train station, take the shuttle to Pl. Virgen de Gracia, and go right on C. Florida Blanca. **Emergency:** tel. 091 or 092; **police,** C. Gobernador, 2 (tel. 91 890 52 23).

🏠🍴🎉 ACCOMMODATIONS, FOOD, AND FIESTAS. Since rooms fill up quickly in July and August and the situation gets dire during the festivals (Aug. 10-20), it's best to visit El Escorial as a daytrip. From the bus stop to **Hostal Vasco,** Pl. Santiago, 11 (tel. 91 890 16 19), walk up C. Rey two blocks and turn right. The hostel has a terrace on the plaza, and some rooms have balconies overlooking the bustle below. In the evenings, the shadows of the monastery provide amazing views. (Breakfast 425ptas. 4300ptas per person.) To reach the **Residencia Juvenil "El Escorial" (HI),** C. Residencia, 14 (tel. 91 890 59 24; fax 91 890 06 20), from C. Rey near Pl. Virgen Gracia, turn right at C. San Pedro Regalado, and go up the steps with the stone balls. When the road forks, take the middle path (C. San Milán), then follow C. Residencia to the hostel (15min.). (Breakfast included; lunch and dinner available. HI card required. Reservations accepted. 2000ptas per person, over 26 2600ptas.) To sleep under the stars, go to **Camping Caravaning El Escorial** (tel. 91 890 24 12), 7km away on Ctra. de Guadarrama, km 14.8. (650ptas per person, per tent, and per car). The center's many cafes are busy throughout the day. Purchase bread, cheese, and wine at the **Mercado Público,** C. Rey, 7, two blocks off C. Floridablanca (open M-Sa 9am-2pm and 6-9pm). During the **Festivals of San Lorenzo** (Aug. 10-20), parades of giant figures line the streets and fireworks fill the sky. Folk dancing contests and horse-drawn cart parades in the forest of Herría mark **Romería a la Ermita de la Virgen de Gracia,** the second Sunday in September.

EL ESCORIAL

Tel. 91 890 59 03, 91 890 59 04, or 91 866 02 38. Complex open Apr.-Sept. Tu-Su 10am-7pm; Oct.-Mar. Tu-Su 10am-6pm. Last admission to palaces, pantheons, and museums is 1hr. before closing. Monastery 850ptas, students 350ptas, guided tour 950ptas. EU citizens free Wednesdays. Casitas 325ptas.

THE MONASTERY

The **Monasterio de San Lorenzo del Escorial** was a gift from Felipe II to God, his people, and himself. Built to commemorate his victory over the French at the battle of San Quintín in 1557, Felipe squelched frivolity in the design of what was to be his royal monastery and mausoleum. Juan Bautista de Toledo was commissioned to design the complex in 1561; when he died in 1567, Juan de Herrera inherited the job. Except for the Panteón Real and minor additional work, the monastery was finished in just 21 years. According to tradition, Felipe oversaw much of the work from a chair-shaped rock, **Silla de Felipe II** (Felipe's Chair), 7km from the site. The king, however, was a part of all building decisions—Herrera had to have every detail approved.

Considering the resources that Felipe II—whose father Carlos I had ruled the most powerful empire in the world—commanded, the building is noteworthy for its austerity, symmetry, and simplicity; in Felipe's words, "majesty without ostentation." Fulfilling the *desornamentado* style, the monastery is pieced together with granite hewn from the surrounding quarries. The entire structure is built around a gridiron pattern. Four massive towers pin the corners, and a great dome surmounts the towers of the central basilica, giving the ensemble a pyramidal

THE DEAD KING'S CLUB The **Panteón Real** was another brainchild of Felipe II. Although he didn't live to see its completion, the king is buried here along with his father Carlos I and most of their royal descendants. Servants dumped bygone nobles in the adjoining rooms so that the bodies could dry before being stuffed into tombs; drying time varied based on the climate and the body's fat content (about 15-20 years).

The stairway and the crypt are elegantly adorned with black and red marble and jasper—a colorful combination that, along with the gold cherubs and high ceilings, make the crypt look like a *discoteca*. Of the 26 marble sarcophagi, 23 contain the remains of Spanish monarchs, and three are still empty. All of the late Spanish kings, with the exception of Felipe V and Fernando VI, are buried here—only those whose sons become monarchs can join the macabre club.

shape. At Felipe II's behest, steep slate roofs—the first of their kind in Spain—were introduced from Flanders. Slate spires lend grace to the grim structure, further mellowed by the glowing *piedra de Colmenar* stone. Variations of this Habsburg style (or *estilo herrerense*) of unadorned granite and red brick, slate roofs, and corner towers, appear throughout Spain—particularly in Madrid and Toledo.

To avoid the worst of the crowds, enter El Escorial by the traditional gateway on the west side (C. Floridablanca), where you'll encounter a collection of Flemish tapestries and paintings. The collection exudes much of the same severity as the monastery, with dark paintings like El Greco's *Martirio de San Mauricio y la Legión* and Roger van der Weyden's glowing-ember *Calvary*. The adjacent **Museo de Arquitectura and Pintura** has an outstanding exhibition on the construction of El Escorial, comparing it to other related structures; there is also a display of wooden models of 16th-century machinery. Though masterpieces by Bosch, Dures, El Greco, Titian, Tintoretto, Velázquez, Zurbarán, Van Dyck, and others hang from the walls, the majority of the collection now lies in Madrid's Prado Museum.

The **Palacio Real,** lined with *azulejos* (tiles) from Toledo, includes the **Salón del Trono (Throne Room)** and two dwellings: Felipe II's spartan 16th-century apartments and the more luxurious 18th-century rooms of Carlos III and Carlos IV. Copies of tapestries by Goya, El Greco, and Rubens blanket the walls in the Bourbon half of the palace. Pastoral images cover the **Puertas de Marguetería,** German doors made from 18 different types of trees—some from as far as North America.

The long **Sala de Batallas (Battle Room)** links the two parts of the palace with commanding frescoes by Italian artists Grabelo and Castello. Castile and Spain's greatest victories—including Juan II's 1431 triumph over the Muslims at Higueruela, Felipe's II's two successful expeditions in the Azores, and the Battle of San Quintín—are detailed on the walls and ceiling. Downstairs, in the royal chambers, Felipe II's miniscule bed attests to his (relative) asceticism.

The **Biblioteca** (library) on the second floor holds numerous priceless books and manuscripts (though several fires have reduced the collection). Alfonso X's *Cantigas de Santa María*, the Book of Hours of the Catholic monarchs, Saint Teresa's manuscripts and diary, the gold-scrolled *Aureus Codex* (by German Emperor Conrad III, 1039), and an 11th-century *Commentary on the Apocalypse* by Beato de Liébana are just a small selection of the manuscripts.

The lower main cloister segues into the cool and magnificent **basílica.** Marble steps lead to an altar adorned by two groups of elegant sculptures. The figures on the left represent assorted relatives of Felipe II, including parents Carlos I and Isabel, daughter María, and sisters María (Queen of Hungary) and Leonor (Queen of France). Those on the right depict Felipe II with his three wives and his son Carlos. The **Coro Alto** (High Choir) has a magnificent ceiling fresco of an angel-filled heaven. The **cloister** shines under Titian's fresco of the martyrdom of St. Lawrence.

The nearby **Panteón Real** (see **The Dead King's Club**, page 117) filled with tombs of past monarchs, glistens with intricate gold and marble designs completed in 1654. Felipe II ordered that its design allow for mass to be conducted over his father's tomb. The connecting **Pudreria,** where bodies would dry before being buried, is thankfully out of commission. Two centuries later, the **Panteón de los Infantes** was constructed for the same purpose, and has space for over 50 babies. Rumors run that many of the royalty's illegitimate children, including a son of Charles V, lie within the crypts.

THE CASITAS

Commissioned by the Prince of Asturias, who later became Carlos IV, the **Casita del Príncipe** has a splendid collection of ornaments, including chandeliers, lamps, rugs, furniture, clocks, tapestries, china, and engraved oranges. The French roughed up the *casita* during the Napoleonic invasions, but many rooms were redecorated by Fernando VII in the then-popular Empire style. To get to the *casita*, follow the right side of the Ctra. Estación to the corner of the monastic complex, turn the corner, and fork left (15min.). Three kilometers toward Ávila sits the simpler **Casita del Infante**, commissioned by Gabriel de Borbón, Carlos's brother, in the mid-16th century.

NEAR EL ESCORIAL: EL VALLE DE LOS CAÍDOS

In a once untouched valley of the Sierra de Guadarrama, 8km north of El Escorial, Franco forced prisoners to build the overpowering monument of Santa Cruz del Valle de los Caídos (Valley of the Fallen) as a memorial to those who gave their lives in the Civil War. Although ostensibly a monument to both sides, the massive granite cross (150m tall and 46m wide) implicitly honors only those who died "serving Dios and España," (i.e. the fascist Nationalists); many of the Republican prisoners-of-war died under the grueling conditions of its construction. Apocalyptic tapestries line the cave-like **basilica,** which is also decorated with death-angels carrying swords and angry light fixtures. Behind the chapel walls lie a multitude (nine levels) of dead. The high altar, located directly underneath the mammoth cross with its mammoth statues, is testimony to modern Spain's view of Franco—although Franco lies buried underneath, there is no mention of his tomb in tourist literature. El Valle de los Caídos is accessible only via El Escorial. (Mass daily 11am. Open daily June-Aug. 9:30am-7pm; Sept.-May 10am-6pm. 650ptas, seniors and students 250ptas. EU citizens free Wednesdays. Funicular to the cross 350ptas.) **Autocares Herranz** runs one bus to the monument (15min., leaves El Escorial Tu-Su 3:15pm and returns 5:30pm, round-trip plus admission 870ptas, funicular not included).

SIERRA DE GUADARRAMA

The Sierra de Guadarrama is a pine-covered mountain range halfway between Madrid and Segovia. Its dark geological shapes dominate the local economy and local imaginations, providing the major mountains with interesting names: *La Mujer Muerta* (The Dead Woman) stands to the west, the *Sierra de la Maliciosa* (Mountain of the Evil Woman) to the east, and, between the two, the less-imaginatively-named *Siete Picos* (Seven Peaks). The ominous names do nothing to deter the influx of summer and winter visitors who come to hike and ski, basing themselves in the Sierras' canopied hamlets.

CERCEDILLA

Cercedilla is the ideal base for venturing into the Sierras. Set in a picturesque chalet town full of budget accommodations, and blessed with great weather, Cercedilla draws many a vacationer. In the summer, cooler temperatures and a relaxed pace lure hot and tired city-dwellers; in the winter, skiers revel in the nearby resorts. For those weary of Madrid's sights, the Sierra has no monuments, churches, or museums, and the most exciting event in the town's history is its mention in Quevedo's 17th century novel, *El buscón*.

MADRID

⚑ ORIENTATION AND PRACTICAL INFORMATION. Cercedilla makes an easy daytrip from Madrid or Segovia. The **train station** (tel. 91 852 00 57), at the base of the hill on C. Emilio Serrano, sends trains to: **Puerto de Navacerrada** (30min., every hr., 9:35am-7:35pm, 130ptas); **Segovia** (45min., 9 per day, 7:30am-12:22am, 300ptas); **Los Cotos** (45min., every hr., 9:35am-7:35pm, 475ptas); **El Escorial** (1hr., 9 per day, 7:30am-12:22am, 155ptas); **Madrid** (1½hr., over 30 per day, 11:37am-9:37pm, 485ptas). To get to town from the station, go uphill, fork right at the top, and continue straight at the train tracks (15-20min.). The **bus station**, Av. José Antonio, 2 (tel. 91 852 02 39), is across the street from the Ayuntamiento. **Bike rental** is available opposite the train station. **Emergency:** tel. 091 or 092; **police:** tel. 91 852 02 00; **medical assistance: Centro Médico** (tel. 91 852 04 97).

⚑⚑ ACCOMMODATIONS AND FOOD. On Ctra. Las Dehesas, two youth hostels afford views of the Sierras. The **Villa Castora (HI)** (tel. 91 852 03 34) is closest to the train station, about 1½km up Ctra. Las Dehesas on the left (20min.). Rooms have baths and the first floor has a terrace. The pool is open in summer. (Breakfast included. Reception daily 8am-10pm. Reservations recommended 15 days in advance. Doubles 2550ptas, over 26 3450ptas; quads 3800ptas, over 26 5200ptas.) **Las Dehesas (HI)** (tel. 91 852 01 35), closer to the trails and tucked back among the trees just beyond the Agencia del Medio Ambiente on Ctra. las Dehesas (30min.), has rooms that are more peaceful and idyllic. HI cards, required at both, are available on the spot for 1800ptas. **Hostal Longinos** (tel. 91 852 15 11), near the train station, is a more expensive option. A restaurant and fountained courtyard accompany decadent accommodations. (All rooms with bath. Singles 4800ptas; doubles 6000ptas.) **Camping,** which is strictly controlled throughout the Sierra de Guadarrama, is no longer allowed within Cercedilla's town limits. A list of campsites is available at the **Conserjería de Medio Ambiente** (see **Hiking,** below). Supermarket **Maxcoop,** C. Doctor Cañados, 2 (tel. 91 852 00 13), is in the town center off Av. Generalísimo (open M-Sa 9:30am-2pm and 5:30-9pm, Su 9:30am-2pm). Tons of restaurants peddle inexpensive *bocadillos* and *raciones* in the town itself.

⚑ HIKING. The **Consejería de Medio Ambiente,** Ctra. las Dehesas (tel. 852 22 13), a wooden chalet 2km up the road (30min. from the train station), functions as a tourist office and offers hiking info. The free leaflet *Sendas* (self-guided trails) is especially good. From July to October, free guided tours of the valley depart at 10am from the shelter across the road from the chalet (open daily 10am-6pm). Most of the hiking begins up the **Carretera las Dehesas,** uphill from the train station. The **Calzada Romana,** atop the Carretera, offers hiking along an ancient Roman road that once connected Madrid to Segovia.

PUERTO DE NAVACERRADA AND LOS COTOS

A magnet for outdoorsy types year-round, **Puerto de Navacerrada** (tel. 91 262 10 10) offers bland **skiing** in the winter (Dec.-Apr.) and beautiful **hiking** in the summer. While Cercedilla has excellent day hikes, backpackers set out from Navacerrada on more strenuous overnight trails. For hiking, exit the train station, turn left at the highway, and turn left again (off the road) at the large intersection marking the pass. The dirt path leads uphill to several trail heads leading through the pine forests (25min.). A little **train** leaves for Navacerrada from the Cercedilla station. The **Cercanías** line that travels between Madrid and Cercedilla also passes through Navacerrada a few stops later (1¾hr., 445ptas).

   Los Cotos is another popular winter resort. Nearby **Rascafría** has two well-regarded ski stations: **Valdesqui** (tel. 91 515 59 39) and **Valcotos** (tel. 91 435 15 48). Both are open in winter, daily 10am to 5pm. For more info on winter sports, consult the tourist office in Madrid or call the resorts. **Cercanías trains** run from Madrid to Los Cotos (2hr., 7:30am-9:30pm, 485ptas), via Cercedilla and Navacerrada.

MADRID

STRAWBERRIES AND STEAM Spain's second locomotive, which first ran from Madrid to Aranjuez on February 9, 1851, was dubbed the **strawberry train**. Built during the reign of Isabel II, it became all the rage, carting Aranjuez strawberries to Madrid during the week and *madrileños* to Aranjuez on weekends. For the past 10 years, tourists have relived those bygone days in an exact replica of that first steam train, complete with officious costumed porters. (Info tel. 902 22 88 22. Train runs Apr. 18-Oct. 18 Sa-Su and holidays only. Leaves from Madrid-Atocha at 10am, arrives in Aranjuez an hour later. Returns at 7:15pm. Round-trip fare, including admission to all sights and plenty of strawberries, 3250ptas, children 2000ptas.)

ARANJUEZ

Two rivers converge at the heart of green Aranjuez (pop. 40,000). Once a getaway for generations of Habsburg and Bourbon royalty, today it is common folk who stroll through the city's wondrous gardens and dazzling palaces. Famed for its strawberries and asparagus, Aranjuez is pleasurable to the eyes and stomach alike.

⛏ PRACTICAL INFORMATION. From the **train station** (tel. 91 891 02 02), it's a 10-minute walk to the town center. With your back to the station, turn right, walk to the end of the street, then turn left onto tree-lined Ctra Toledo. Follow the road to the right (when you can see the palace), left at the fork, and go under an arch. The tourist office is diagonally on the left. Municipal bus L2 stops outside the station and on C. Stuart (M-F every 30min., Sa-Su every hr., 110ptas). **Trains** go to: **Toledo** (30min., 10 per day, 7:48am-9:12pm, 325ptas); **Madrid** (45min.; *cercanías* to Atocha every 15min., 5:40am-11:30pm; *regionales* to Chamartín, 11 per day, 5:56am-9:50pm; 380-480ptas); **Cuenca** (2hr., 5 per day, 6:10am-9:36pm, 1000ptas). **AISA** runs from the **bus station,** C. Infantas, 8 (tel. 91 891 01 83), to **Madrid's Estación Sur de Autobuses** (45min.; M-F 20-30 per day, 6am-1pm; Sa 6 per day, 7:45am-10:15am; Su 5 per day, 8am-2:15pm; 405ptas). For **taxis,** call 91 891 11 39. The **tourist office** (tel. 91 891 04 27), in Pl. San Antonio, supplies maps and brochures (open Tu-Su 10am-2pm and 4-6pm). **Emergency:** tel. 091 or 092; **police,** C. Infantas, 36 (tel. 91 891 00 22). **Post office,** C. Peña Redonda, 3 (tel. 91 891 11 32), is off C. Capitán Gómez (open M-F 8:30am-2:30pm, Sa 9:30am-1pm); **postal code:** 28300.

🍴 ACCOMMODATIONS AND FOOD. Accommodations in Aranjuez tend to be both costly and luxurious. **Hostal Infantes,** Av. Infantas, 4-6 (tel. 91 891 13 41; fax 91 891 66 43), features a hotel-like entrance with hotel-like rooms. Rooms with bath also have TV and A/C. (Singles 1900-1950ptas, with shower 2800-3000ptas; doubles 3400-3500ptas, with shower 5400-5800ptas, with bath 5800-6200ptas; triples with shower 7000-7500ptas, with bath 7500-8000ptas. Visa, MC.) **Camping Soto del Castillo** (tel. 91 891 13 95), across Río Tajo and off the highway to the right (2km from palace—watch for the signs), is a first-class site amid lush fields (electricity 500ptas; 600ptas per person, 500ptas per car, 525-650ptas per tent).

The town's **strawberries** and **asparagus** have been famous for centuries. Nowadays, many of Aranjuez's strawberries are actually grown in other areas of Spain and sold to unsuspecting tourists as *fresón con nata* (strawberries with cream; 350-450ptas) at kiosks and cafes throughout town. These imitations are huge—real Aranjuez strawberries are on the smaller side. Aranjuez's restaurants are plentiful and expensive. **Brigantino,** Po. Puarteles, 14 (tel. 91 801 17 51). From the end of C. Infantos, turn right on C. Foso and make the first left. Excellent Italian dishes await on tiled tables under a frescoed ceiling. (Pastas 900-1150ptas, pizzas 750-1075ptas. Open W-Su noon-4:30pm and 8pm-12:30am, Tu 8pm-12:30am.)

🕓 SIGHTS. The Tajo and its tributary, the Jarama, water the palace's beautiful **gardens.** River walkways run from the **Jardín de la Isla,** which sprouts banana trees and a mythological statue garden, to the huge **Jardín del Príncipe,** originally created for the amusement of Carlos IV. (Both open daily June-Sept. 8am-8:30pm; Oct.-May 8am-6:30pm. Free.) Inside the park, the **Casa del Labrador** (tel. 91 891 03 05), a mock laborer's cottage, is a treasure trove of Neoclassical decorative arts. It also houses the queen's private quarters, overflowing with such knick-knacks as Roman mosaics from Mérida and sketches of Madrid embroidered in silk. The **Casa de Marinos,** once the quarters of the Tajo's sailing squad, stores royal gondolas. (Both open June-Aug. Tu-Su 10am-6:15pm; Sept.-May Tu-Su 10am-5:15pm. Casa del Labrador 500ptas, students 225ptas. Casa de Marinos 325ptas, students 225ptas.)

The stately **Palacio Real,** splendid in white brick, was originally designed by Juan de Herrera—chief architect of El Escorial—under the direction of Felipe II. In the years to come, both Felipe VI and Carlos III had the palace enlarged and embellished to suit their own tastes. Now, room after opulent room displays Vatican marble mosaics, crystal chandeliers, and mirrors from La Granja. Flemish tapestries and ornate French clocks are everywhere. The Oriental **porcelain room,** with three-dimensioned wallpaper and Rococo ceramic work, and the Mozarabic **smoking room,** which bears a striking resemblance to the Alhambra, are particularly remarkable. Keep an eye out for the velvet-covered baby's toilet and dumbbells at the end of the tour. (Open Apr.-Sept. Tu-Sa 10am-6:15pm; Oct.-Mar. Tu-Sa 10am-5:15pm. Compulsory 30min. tour in Spanish. 650ptas, students 250ptas. EU citizens free Wednesday.)

MADRID

CENTRAL SPAIN

CASTILLA LA MANCHA

Cervantes chose to set Don Quijote's adventures in La Mancha (*manxa* means parched earth in Arabic) in an effort to evoke a cultural and material backwater. While Castilla La Mancha is indeed one of Spain's least developed regions, no fantasy of the Knight of the Sad Countenance is needed to transform the austere beauty of this battered, windswept plateau. Its tumultuous history, gloomy medieval fortresses, and awesome crags provide enough food for the imagination.

Long ago, this region was at the center of conflicts between Christians and Muslims. When Christian forces pranced into Muslim Spain, La Mancha became the domain of the military orders Santiago, Calatrava, Montesa, and San Juan. These were modeled after such crusading institutions as the Knights Templar, a society of powerful warrior-monks. In the 14th and 15th centuries, the region saw fearsome struggles between the kingdoms of Castilla and Aragón. All this warring left La Mancha in a state of utter destruction.

The region is Spain's largest wine-producing area (Valdepeñas and Manzanares are popular table wines), and its abundant olive groves and excellent hunting influence many local recipes. Stews, roast meats, and game are all *manchego* staples. *Gazpacho manchego* (a hearty stew of rabbit, lamb, chicken, and pork) and *queso manchego* (Castile's beloved cheese) are both indigenous specialties.

> **HIGHLIGHTS OF CASTILLA LA MANCHA**
>
> ■ **Toledo,** glorious former capital of the Holy Roman, Visigothic, and Muslim empires, especially its **cathedral,** one of Spain's best (see below).
> ■ **Cuenca's** famed **casas colgadas** (hanging houses; see p. 130).

TOLEDO

For Cervantes, Toledo was a "rocky gravity, glory of Spain and light of her cities." Cossío called it "the most brilliant and evocative summary of Spain's history." To the architecture-loving tourist, Toledo is paradise. Toledo has been successively a Roman settlement, capital of the Visigoth kingdom, stronghold of the Emirate of Córdoba, and imperial city under Carlos V. To the military historian, Toledo is equally interesting, as it produced swords for most of medieval Europe and conquistadors such as Francisco Pizarro. Modern-day Toledo (pop. 65,000) may be marred by armies of tourists and caravans of kitsch, but it remains a treasure trove of Spanish culture. The city's numerous churches, synagogues, and mosques share twisting alleyways, emblematic of a time when Spain's three religions peacefully coexisted. Visitors pay monetary homage to Toledo's Damascene swords and knives, colorful pottery, and almond-paste marzipan.

▮ GETTING THERE

The easiest way to get to Toledo is by **train** from: **Aranjuez** (30min., 10 per day, 7:48am-9:12pm, 325ptas) or **Madrid** (1¼hr., 10 per day, 8:32am-8:26pm, 750ptas).

▮ ORIENTATION AND PRACTICAL INFORMATION

Toledo is an almost unconquerable maze of narrow streets where pedestrians and cars battle for sovereignty. To get to **Plaza de Zocodóver** in the town center, take bus #5 or 6 (115ptas) from the stop on the right after you exit the **train station** or

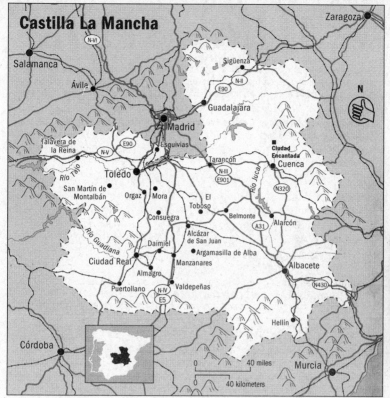

Castilla La Mancha

from the stop directly outside the **bus station.** Alternatively, it's not a bad walk from either station, albeit completely unshaded and mostly uphill (20-30min.). From the bus station, exit from the restaurant, head straight toward the traffic circle, and take the first right along the steep highway that surrounds the city. From the train station, *do not* take the big bridge across the Tajo. Instead, turn right after leaving the station and follow the left fork uphill to a smaller bridge, Puente de Alcántara. Cross the bridge to the stone staircase (through a set of arches); after climbing the stairs, turn left and continue upward, veering right at C. Cervantes to Pl. Zocodóver. Despite the well-labeled streets, you will probably get lost in Toledo. Enjoy it—it's the best way to discover the town's beauty.

Trains: Po. Rosa, 2 (tel. 925 22 30 99), in an exquisite neo-Mudéjar building opposite the Puente de Azarquiel. One line only runs to **Madrid's Atocha** (1½hr., 10-20 per day, M-F 6:30am-9:42pm, Sa-Su 8:30am-9:42pm, 640ptas), sometimes via **Aranjuez** (35min., 9 per day, 6:30am-8:56pm, 365ptas).

Buses: (tel. 925 21 58 50), 5min. from the city gate. From Pl. Zocodóver, take C. Armas. Serviced by various companies. To **Madrid** (1½hr., every 30min., M-Sa 5:30am-10pm, Su 8:30am-11:30pm, 590ptas). **SAMAR** (tel. 925 22 39 15 or 925 22 12 17) buses go to **Valencia** (M-F 1 per day, 3pm, 2400ptas).

Public Transportation: Buses #5 and 6 stop to the right of the train station and directly outside the bus station; both head to Pl. Zocodóver (115ptas).

Taxis: tel. 925 25 50 50.

Car Rental: Avis (tel. 925 21 45 35 or 925 21 57 94), on C. Venancio González, and **Hertz** (tel. 925 25 38 90), on Po. Rosa near the train station.

CENTRAL SPAIN

Tourist Office: (tel. 925 22 08 43; fax 925 25 26 48), just outside the Puerta Nueva de Bisagra, on the north side of town. From Pl. Zocodóver, take C. Armas, the main street (which changes names several times), downhill and through the gates (Puertas de Bisagra); the office is across the intersection (15min.). From the train station, turn right and take the busy right-hand fork across the bridge (Puente de Azarquiel); follow the city walls until you reach the plaza. The office is across the road, outside the walls. There is a **second office** in Pl. Ayuntamiento (tel. 925 25 40 30), opposite the cathedral. English spoken. Both open M-F 9am-6pm, Sa 9am-7pm, Su 9am-3pm.

Currency Exchange: Banco Central Hispano, C. Comercio, 47 (tel. 925 22 98 00). Open M-F 8:30am-2:30pm.

Luggage Storage: At the bus station (100-200ptas) and train station (400ptas). Both open daily 7am-9:30pm.

Emergency: tel. 091 or 092. **Police:** (tel. 925 21 34 00), Av. Portugal.

Pharmacy: (tel. 925 22 17 68), Pl. Zocodóver. List of late-night pharmacies posted.

Hospital: Hospital Virgen de la Salud (tel. 925 26 92 00), Av. Barber.

Post Office: C. Plata, 1 (tel. 925 22 36 11), off Pl. Zocodóver via C. Comercio. Lista de Correos. Open M-F 8:30am-8:30pm, Sa 9am-2pm. **Postal Code:** 45070.

Internet Access: Scorpions (tel. 925 21 25 56), C. Pintor Matías Moreno. 100ptas for 6min. Open daily noon-midnight. Visa, MC, AmEx.

■ ACCOMMODATIONS AND CAMPING

Toledo is chock-full of accommodations, but finding a bed during the summer can be a hassle, especially on weekends. If you run into trouble, try the tourist office.

Residencia Juvenil San Servando (HI) (tel. 925 22 45 54), Castillo San Servando, uphill from the train station (10min.). Cross the street from the station, turn left and then immediately right up Callejón del Hospital. When the steps reach a road, turn right and then right again, following the signs to Hospital Provincial. The steep walk uphill just past the hospital leads to a 14th-century castle—that's not for you; you're going to the annex. If alone at night, take a cab. 48 rooms, each with 4 bunk beds, some with views. Laundry 500ptas. Pool in summer, TV room. Reception open 7-9:40am, 10am-7:40pm, 8-11:50pm. Curfew 12:30am. No reservations. Dorms 1125ptas, over 26 1325ptas. Closed various times throughout the year—call ahead.

Pensión Nuncio Viejo, C. Nuncio Viejo, 19, 3rd fl. (tel. 925 22 81 78), the street leading off the cathedral. The 6 rooms may be cramped and dim, but the motherly owner is a great cook. Meals 850ptas. Singles 1800ptas; doubles 3500ptas, with bath 3800ptas.

Pensión Castilla, C. Recoletos, 6 (tel. 925 25 63 18). From Pl. Zocodóver, head up C. Sillería, go diagonally left through Pl. San Agustín, and turn right. Comfortable and spacious rooms. Singles 2200ptas; doubles with bath 3900ptas.

Pensión Segovia, C. Recoletos, 4 (tel. 925 21 11 24), next to Pensión Castilla. Friendly owner and dog welcome visitors with clean and comfortable rooms. Singles 2200ptas; doubles 3000ptas; triples 4500ptas.

Pensión Descalzos, C. Descalzos, 30 (tel. 925 22 28 88), down the steps off Po. San Cristóbal. Great views. Rooms with bath have TVs and A/C. Breakfast 225-800ptas. Singles 2500ptas, with bath 3690ptas; doubles 3500-4000ptas, with bath or shower 5000-5900ptas; triples with bath 7000-7500ptas. Visa, MC. Closed Feb.

Camping: Camping El Greco (tel. 925 22 00 90), 1.5km from town on the road away from Madrid (C-502). Bus #7 (from Pl. Zocodóver) stops at the entrance. Wooded and shady 1st-class site between the Tajo and an olive grove. 595ptas per person (children 495ptas), 620ptas per tent, 550ptas per car. 7% IVA not included. **Circo Romano,** Av. Carlos III, 19 (tel. 925 22 04 42). 2nd-class site. Closer but noisier. 595ptas per person (children 495ptas), 620ptas per tent, 550ptas per car.

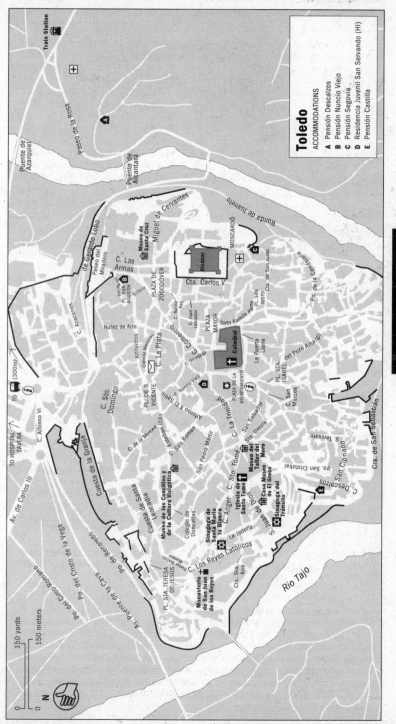

FOOD

Toledo grinds almonds into marzipan of every shape and size, from colorful fruity nuggets to half-moon cookies; *pastelerías* beckon on every corner. If your pocket allows, dining out in Toledo can be a pleasurable culinary experience (*menús* 1400-1600ptas). Alternatively, buy fresh fruit and the basics at **Frutería-Pan,** C. Real Arrabal, opposite the tourist office (open daily 9am-10pm). The **mercado** is in Pl. Mayor, behind the cathedral (open July-Sept. 9am-2pm and 5-8pm; Oct.-June M-Sa 8:30am-2pm). **Udaco** is a mini-market on Pl. San Justo, down C. Sixto R. Parro from Puerta Llana (open M-F 8am-2:45pm and 5-9pm, Sa 8am-3:30pm).

Pastucci, C. Sinagoga, 10 (tel. 925 21 48 66). From Pl. Zocodóver take C. Comercio; keep to the right and turn right through the underpass. Colorful and popular. Pastas 850-975ptas, salads 625-975ptas. Open daily 12:15pm-midnight. Visa, MC.

Restaurante El Zoco, C. Barrio Rey, 7 (tel. 925 22 20 51), off Pl. Zocodóver. Attractive and reasonably priced, and consequently filled with English-speaking patrons. A/C. *Menús* 800-1500ptas, entrees 950-1100ptas. Open daily 1:30-4pm and 8-10:30pm.

Restaurante-Mesón Palacios, C. Alfonso X El Sabio, 3 (tel. 925 21 59 72), off C. Nuncio Viejo. Three *menús* tempt weary sight-seers (900, 1500, or 2500ptas). Entrees 650-1900ptas. Open M-Sa 1-4pm and 7-11pm, Su 1-4pm. Visa, MC, AmEx.

SIGHTS

Toledo has an excellent collection of museums, churches, synagogues, and mosques, making the city almost impossible to see in just one day. Within its fortified walls, which are attributed to 7th-century King Wamba, Toledo's major attractions form a belt around its middle. An east-west tour, beginning in Pl. Zocodóver, is mostly downhill. Most sights are closed on Mondays.

CATHEDRAL. Built between 1226 and 1498, Toledo's grandiose cathedral boasts five naves, delicate stained glass, and unapologetic ostentation; it is also the seat of the Primate of Spain. Noteworthy pieces include the 14th-century Gothic *Virgen Blanca* by the entrance, El Greco's *El Espolio*, and Narciso Tomés's *Transparente*, a Spanish-Baroque whirlpool of architecture, sculpture, and painting. In the **Capilla Mayor,** the enormous Gothic altarpiece stretches to the ceiling. The tomb of Cardinal Mendoza, founder of the Spanish Inquisition, lies to the left. Beneath the dome is the **Capilla Mozárabe,** the only venue where the ancient Visigoth mass (in Mozarabic) is still held. The **treasury** flaunts ornamentations, including a replica of one of Columbus's ships and a 400-pound, 16th-century gold monstrosity lugged through the streets during the annual Corpus Christi procession. The **Sacristy** is home to 18 El Grecos and 2 Van Dycks, along with the portraits of every archbishop of Toledo. The red hats hanging from the ceiling mark the Cardinals' tombs. (*At Arco de Palacioz, southwest of Pl. Zocodóver. Tel. 925 22 22 41. Open July-Aug. M-Sa 10:30am-1:30pm and 3:30-7pm, Su 10:30am-1:30pm and 4-6pm; Sept.-June M-Sa 10:30am-1:30pm and 3:30-6pm, Su 10:30am-1:30pm and 4-6pm. 500ptas. Tickets sold at the store opposite the entrance, open daily 8am-8pm. Respectable dress required.*)

ALCÁZAR. Toledo's most formidable landmark, the Alcázar has been a stronghold for Romans, Visigoths, Moors, and Spaniards. Each of these groups has rebuilt the structure according to their own necessities and architectural tastes. Much of the building was reduced to rubble during the Civil War, when Fascist troops besieged by Republicans used the Alcázar as their refuge. Don't miss the room that details Colonel Moscardó's refusal to surrender the Alcázar, even at the cost of his son's life. You can also visit the dark, windowless basement refuge where over 500 civilians hid during the siege. The rooms above ground have been turned into a national military museum complete with armor, swords, guns, knives, and…dried plants. (*Cuesta Carlos V, 2, uphill from Pl. Zocodóver. Tel. 925 22 30 38. Open Tu-Su 9:30am-2:30pm. 200ptas. EU citizens free Wednesday.*)

EL GRECO'S THREE MISTAKES

Upon a visit to the sacristy room of Toledo's cathedral, the eye is quickly drawn to the large El Greco painting at the end of the room. El Greco painted *El Espolio*—his first painting—specifically for the cathedral, although neither party had thought to negotiate costs before the completion of the work. The cathedral's clergy were unhappy with the painting due to three mistakes El Greco had inadvertently made. The first mistake is an anachronism: the scene depicts the point in the Bible at which the Roman soldiers are about to remove Jesus' gown, but the soldier standing to his left is wearing distinctly 16th-century armor. El Greco's second mistake was painting three women in the bottom left corner; according to the New Testament, no women was present at that moment. The clergy's final complaint was that the artist painted men's heads above the head of Jesus; even in art, Christ is more holy than mere humans. The two parties went to court over the matter, eventually working out a compromise. In the end, El Greco won something more valuable than money—the court battle threw him into the spotlight, earning him a slew of new commissions and spreading his reputation.

EL GRECO. Greek painter Doménikos Theotokópoulos (more commonly known as El Greco) spent most of his life in Toledo. Many of his works are displayed throughout town, but the majority of his masterpieces have long since been carted off to the Prado and other big-name museums. On the west side of town, the **Iglesia de Santo Tomé** houses El Greco's famous *El entierro del Conde de Orgaz (The Burial of Count Orgaz)*. The stark figure staring out from the back is El Greco himself, and the boy is his son, Jorge Manuel, who built Toledo's city hall. *(Pl. Conde. Tel. 925 25 60 98. Open daily June-Aug. 10am-7pm; Sept.-May 10am-6:45pm. 200ptas.)* Downhill and to the left lies the **Casa Museo de El Greco.** This oddly arranged museum has 19 works by El Greco, including a copy of the *Vista y plano de Toledo (Landscape of Toledo)*, a detailed painting of the city. *(C. Samuel Levi, 3. Tel. 925 22 40 46. Open Tu-Sa 10am-2pm and 4-6pm, Su 10am-2pm. 200ptas; students, under 18, and over 65 free. Sa and Su afternoon free.)* Outside handsome Puerta Nueva de Bisagra on the way to Madrid, 16th-century **Hospital Tavera** displays five El Grecos as well as several works by his mentor, Titian. *(Cardenal Tavera, 2. Tel. 925 22 04 51. Open daily 10:30am-1:30pm and 3:30-6pm. 500ptas.)*

THE OLD JEWISH QUARTER. Samuel Ha-Leví, diplomat and treasurer to Pedro el Cruel, built the **Sinagoga del Tránsito** (1366). Its simple exterior hides an extraordinarily ornate sanctuary with Mudéjar plasterwork and an *artesonado* (intricately designed wood) ceiling. The walls are crawling with Hebrew inscriptions, mostly taken from psalms. Inside, the **Museo Sefardí** is packed with artifacts, including a Torah (parts of which are over 400 years old) and a beautiful set of Sephardic wedding costumes. *(C. Samuel Levi. Tel. 925 22 36 65. Open Tu-Sa 10am-2pm and 4-6pm, Su 10am-2pm. 400ptas, students and under 18 200ptas. Free Sa after 4pm and Su.)* **Sinagoga de Santa María la Blanca** (1180), down the street to the right, was originally built to be a mosque, but was then purchased by Jews and used as the city's principal synagogue; in 1492 it was converted into a church. Now secular, the Moorish arches and a tranquil garden make for a pleasant retreat. *(Open daily June-Aug. 10am-2pm and 3:30-7pm; Sept.-May 10am-2pm and 3:30-6pm. 200ptas.)*

MONASTERIO DE SAN JUAN DE LOS REYES. At the far western bulge of the city, with views of the surrounding hills and Río Tajo, stands the Franciscan Monasterio de San Juan de los Reyes, commissioned by Isabel and Fernando to commemorate their victory over the Portuguese in the Battle of Toro (1476). The light-filled cloister, covered with the initial of the *Reyes Católicos*, mixes Gothic and Mudéjar architecture. This eclectic style contrasts with the very Gothic Plateresque church interior. The Catholic monarchs had planned to use the church as their burial place but changed their minds after their victory over Granada. *(Tel. 925 22 38 02. Open daily June-Aug. 10am-2pm and 3:30-6pm; Sept.-May until 5pm. 150ptas.)*

REMEMBERING SEPHARAD When Toledo fell to Alfonso VI in 1085, Jewish culture blossomed under his tolerant reign. Jewish poets (including Yehuda Ha-Leví), doctors, translators, and bankers rose to prominence, occasionally intermarrying with noble Christian families and serving in royal courts. This period of *toledancia*—a pun on Toledo and tolerance—did not last. Mounting nationalism and anti-Semitism during the 1492 Inquisition led to persecution, forced conversion, expulsion, and, at times, even holocaust. Today, only two of eight synagogues remain in what was once Spain's largest Jewish community (Sepharad). Jews of *toledano* descent, some of whom still speak *Ladino*, a variation on 15th-century Spanish, have recently reappeared: a Jewish-American woman made headlines when she entered a Toledo home with the same key her ancestors had used 500 years before.

OTHER SIGHTS. Toledo was the seat of Visigoth rule and culture for three centuries prior to the 711 Muslim invasion. The **Museo del Taller del Moro,** on C. Bulas near Iglesia de Santo Tomé, features outstanding woodwork, plasterwork, and tiles. (*Taller de Moro, 200. Tel. 925 22 45 00. Open Tu-Sa 10am-2pm and 4-6:30pm, Su 10am-2pm. 100ptas.*) The exhibits at the **Museo de los Concilios y de la Cultura Visigótica** pale in comparison to their beautiful setting in a 13th-century Mudéjar church. (*C. San Clemente, 4. Tel. 925 22 18 72. Open Tu-Sa 10am-2pm and 4-6:30pm, Su 10am-2pm. 100ptas, students 50ptas.*) The impressive and untouristed **Museo de Santa Cruz** (1504) exhibits a handful of El Grecos in its eclectic art collection. Oddly enough, it also holds the remains from archaeological digs throughout the province. (*C. Cervantes, 3, off Pl. Zocodóver. Tel. 925 22 10 36. Open M 10am-2pm and 4-6:30pm, Tu-Sa 10am-6:30pm, Su 10am-2pm. 200ptas, students 100ptas.*)

ENTERTAINMENT

The best area for the city's trademark souvenirs is C. San Juan de Dios, by the Iglesia de Santo Tomé. The shop owners are aggressive but willing to haggle. The town goes crazy for **Corpus Christi,** celebrated the eighth Sunday after Easter—citizens parade through the streets with the cathedral's gold monstrance.

For nightlife, try C. Santa Fe, east of Pl. Zocodóver, through the arch. It's filled to the brim with beer and local youth. Look for **Bar Black and Blue** (tel. 925 22 21 11), a busy blues bar on small Pl. Santiago Caballeros off C. Cervantes, which offers live blues performances Thursdays at 10:30pm (beer 300ptas; no cover; open until 3am). C. Sillería and C. Alfileritos, west of Pl. Zocodóver, are home to more upscale bars and clubs, including **Bar La Abadía,** Nuñez de Arce, 5 (tel. 925 25 11 40), whose cavernous basement makes for a great game of hide-and-seek (open M-Th 8am-midnight, F-Su noon-midnight). **Zaida,** in the Centro Comercial Miradero, downhill on C. Armas, is a perennial hot spot for dancing. Fully primped 20- and 30-somethings pour in around midnight. (No cover. Open 9pm-5am.)

DAYTRIPS FROM TOLEDO

A hop, skip, and a jump south of Toledo lands you at the small **San Martín de Montalbán,** home to an amazing castle poised on an enormous pile of gray granite rocks and leaning out over an abysmal gorge of the River Torión. The castle was first Visigothic, then an Arab fortress, and later an enclave of the cabalistic Knights Templar. Legend has it that a buried treasure is hidden inside the walls.

Cervantes freaks come to La Mancha to follow in the footsteps of the writer and his characters. Cervantes met and married Catalina de Palacios in the main church in **Esquivias** in 1584. He supposedly began writing his masterpiece while imprisoned in the **Cueva del Medrano,** in the town of **Argamasilla de Alba.** It was in **El Toboso,** 100km southeast of Toledo, that Quijote fell nobly in love with Dulcinea. El Toboso is home to the **Casa Cervantes,** which has a fine collection of Cervantes memorabilia, including translations of *Don Quijote* in 30 different languages. (Pl. Cervantes. Tel. 925 52 20 16. Open Sa 10am-1:30pm. 100ptas.)

Of all Manchegan villages, tiny **Consuegra** provides perhaps the most raw material for an evocation of Quijote's world. The **castle,** called *Crestería Manchega* by locals, was Roman, then Arab, then a Castilian fortress. It keeps erratic hours, but the view of the surrounding plains justifies a climb any time. El Cid's only son, Diego, died in the stable; you can visit a lavish monument in his honor near the Ayuntamiento. Though small, Consuegra is home to a palace, a Franciscan convent, and a Carmelite monastery. Learn more at the **Museo de Consuegra** (tel. 925 47 37 31), next to the Ayuntamiento (hours not fixed; 100ptas). Plan around inconvenient bus departure times so you don't have to spend the night. **Samar buses** (tel. 925 22 39 15) depart from the Toledo bus station (10 per day, 535ptas). Buses return to Toledo from C. Castilla de la Mancha (7 per day). Purchase tickets from the driver when returning from Consuegra; when coming from Toledo, purchase them at the ticket office. For greater flexibility, rent a car and use Toledo as a base for excursions into this region.

ALMAGRO

Theater buffs and city slickers seeking solace will find sleepy Almagro (pop. 9000) appealing. A famed classical theater festival in July and August attracts hundreds of visitors to the cobblestone streets, whitewashed houses, and 16th-century theatrical monuments, which go largely unnoticed for the rest of the year. Although Almagro only comes alive in the summer months, the town's complete lack of self-consciousness contributes to its authenticity and charm.

🗹 ORIENTATION & PRACTICAL INFORMATION. The **train station** (tel. 926 86 02 76) is outside the city center, at the end of the tree-lined Po. Estación. To get from the station to the **Plaza Mayor,** walk down Po. Estación and turn left onto C. Rondo de Calatrava (a sign points to the **Centro Urbano**); turn right onto C. Madre de Dios (another Centro Urbano sign), which becomes C. Fería and leads to the plaza (10min.). Trains run to: **Ciudad Real** (15min., 4 per day, 290ptas); **Aranjuez** (2hr., 3 per day, 1580ptas); **Madrid-Atocha** (2¾hr., 4 per day, 1790ptas). Change at Ciudad Real for connections to Córdoba, Sevilla, Granada, Valencia, and other major cities. **Buses** (tel. 926 86 02 50), which are cheaper and more convenient, stop at a modest brick building at the far end of Ejido de Calatrava, on the left side of the Hospedería Municipal de Almagro. To get to Pl. Mayor from the bus station, turn left on C. Madre de Dios (follow the sign to the Centro Urbano) and take the road straight to the plaza (10min.). **Aisa** buses leave for **Ciudad Real,** the connection point for most other major cities (20min., M-Sa 7 per day, 8am-6:15pm, 230ptas) and **Madrid** (2¼hr., M-Sa 3 per day, 7am-4pm, 1600ptas). The bus station is closed on Sundays. The schedule is not well-documented, so it is advisable to always check the transportation listings and plan in advance.

The **tourist office,** C. Bernardas, 2 (tel. 926 86 07 17), is inside the Palacio del Conde de Valdeparaíso. From Pl. Mayor, take a right on C. Mayor de Carnicerías and another right on C. Bernardas. No one speaks English, but they do have brochures for the entire region of Castilla la Mancha and the only contemporary map of Almagro in existence. (Open Apr.-June and Sept. Tu-F 10am-2pm and 5-8pm, Sa 10am-2pm and 5-7pm, Su 11am-2pm; July-Aug. Tu-F 10am-2pm and 6-9pm, Sa 10am-2pm and 6-8pm, Su 11am-2pm; Oct.-Mar. Tu-F 10am-2pm and 5-7pm, Sa 10am-2pm and 5-6pm, Su and holidays 11am-2pm.) A **Banco Central Hispano** (tel. 926 86 00 04) sits alongside Pl. Mayor (open May-Sept. M-F 8:30am-2:30pm; Oct.-Apr. M-F 8:30am-2:30pm, Sa 8:30am-1pm). **Emergency:** tel. 863 00; **police** (tel. 609 01 41 36), at the Mercado Encomienda Tercia, adjacent to Pl. Mayor; **Centro de Salud (health clinic),** C. Mayor de Carnicerías, 11 (tel. 926 86 10 26 or 926 88 20 16). **Post office** (tel. 926 86 00 52), on C. Mayor de Carnicerías (open M-F 8:30am-2:30pm, Sa 9am-1pm); **postal code:** 13270.

▐▐ ACCOMMODATIONS & FOOD. The dark hallways and ancient furnishings of **Hospedería Municipal de Almagro,** Ejido de Calatrava, s/n (tel. 926 88 20 87; fax 926 88 21 22), testify to the majestic building's 500-year history. Firm beds, telephones, and TVs provide for a comfortable stay. Reservations can be made as late as the day of arrival (most of the year) or as early as years in advance for the months of July and August, during the theater festival. (Singles with bath 3000ptas; doubles with bath July-Aug. 4800ptas, Sept.-June 4000ptas; doubles with shower July-Aug. 4000ptas, Sept.-June 3200ptas. Visa, MC.) Pl. Mayor is also filled with restaurants such as **Restaurante Airén** (tel. 926 88 26 56), which offers entrees ranging from pizzas and pastas to salads and sandwiches (entrees 700-1800ptas).

▣ ▐ SIGHTS & ENTERTAINMENT. Every July, prestigious theater companies and players from around the world descend on Almagro for the ■**Festival Internacional de Teatro Clásico de Almagro.** Daily performances of Spanish and international classics take place in the Corral de Comedias, Hospital de San Juan de Dios, Teatro Municipal, Claustro de los Domínicos, Teatro Infantil, Teatro en la Calle, and Seminarios. The **box office** is in the Palacio de los Medrano, C. San Agustín, 7. (Tel. 902 10 12 12. Open May-June Th 11am-1:30pm, July daily 11:30am-2pm and 7-10:30pm. Shows in July, daily 10:45pm. Tickets 1700-2300ptas, Tuesday half-price. Tickets should be purchased before the festival. Visa, MC accepted by phone.) The festival also has an office in Madrid at C. Principe, 14 (tel. 91 521 07 20).

The navigational center of Almagro, the **Plaza Mayor,** is also the cultural hub. There you can find the **Corral de Comedias,** an open-air multilevel theater resembling Shakespeare's Globe. This theater is the only one left intact from the "Golden Age" of Spanish drama. Here, performers act out the works of such literary masters as Cervantes and Lope de Vega. (Tel. 926 88 24 58. Open Tu-F 10am-2pm and 5-8pm, Sa 10am-2pm and 5-7pm, Su 11am-2pm and 5-7pm. Admission 1200ptas.) Directly across the plaza from the *corral* and through some arches, the new **Museo Nacional del Teatro** displays the history of Spanish drama. (Tel./fax 926 88 22 44. Open Tu-F 10am-2pm and 4-7pm, Sa 10am-2pm and 4-6pm, Su 11am-2pm. 400ptas, students 200ptas, seniors and under 18 free. Sa and Su afternoon free.) The final stop on the theater tour is the **Teatro Municipal,** C. San Agustín, 20. Follow C. San Agustín out of Pl. Mayor and look for a crimson building on the right. Inside is a renovated theater as well as a collection of elaborate costumes. (Open Tu-F 10am-2pm and 5-8pm, Sa 10am-2pm and 5-7pm, Su and holidays 11am-2pm. Museo Nacional ticket allows entrance to all three sights.)

The Pl. Mayor's long balconies and green window frames are characteristic of Fugger-style architecture. The Fuggers were a 16th-century family of German bankers who lent money to the monks of Calatrava and Emperor Carlos V. The **Fugger house,** C. Arzobispo Canizares, 6, also the site of the Universidad Popular, is open to the public. From Pl. Mayor, take C. Fería and make a left onto C. Arzobispo. Almagro's other hometown hero is Diego de Almagro, hailed by locals as the conquistador of Chile; unfortunately other accounts reveal that he was executed for conspiracy against fellow conquistador Francisco Pizarro.

CUENCA

Cuenca (pop. 43,500) owes its fame to its location. Perched atop a hill, the vertical city is surrounded by two rivers and the stunning rock formations they have created. These natural boundaries have served the city well; Muslims and then Christians settled in Cuenca because it was nearly impenetrable. Yet Cuenca strains against its borders, forcing much of the city's modern commercial life to spill down the hill into New Cuenca. The enchanting old city, however, safeguards most of Cuenca's unique charm, including the famed *casas colgadas* (hanging houses) that dangle high above the Río Huécar.

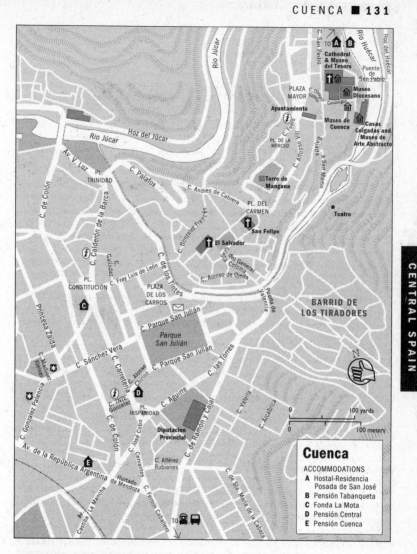

Cuenca

ACCOMMODATIONS
A Hostal-Residencia
   Posada de San José
B Pensión Tabanqueta
C Fonda La Mota
D Pensión Central
E Pensión Cuenca

CENTRAL SPAIN

GETTING THERE

Trains run to Cuenca from **Aranjuez** (2hr., 5 per day, 6:10am-9:36pm, 1000ptas) and **Valencia** (3½hr., 4 per day, 8:12am-6:12pm, 1515ptas). **Buses** go from **Madrid** (2½hr., 7am-10pm, 1315ptas; express 2hr., 1600ptas).

ORIENTATION AND PRACTICAL INFORMATION

When you exit the train station, the back of the bus station is right in front of you; head up the steps to C. Fermín Caballero and turn right. To get to **Plaza Mayor** in the old city from either station, go left until you hit the first bus shelter and catch bus #1 or 2; the old city's the last stop (every 30min.; #1 on the ½hr., 7am-10pm; #2 on the ¼hr., 7:15am-9:45pm; 85ptas). To reach Pl. Mayor by foot, take a left from the bus station along C. Fermín Caballero, which becomes C. Cervantes, then C.

José Cobo, and finally (after passing through Pl. Hispanidad) **Calle Carretería,** the town's main drag. From here, turn right on C. Fray Luis de León and head upward; it's a grueling walk to Pl. Mayor and the old city (20-25min.).

Trains: (tel. 969 22 07 20), Po. Ferrocarril, in the new city. To: **Aranjuez** (2hr., 6 per day, 7:05am-6:55pm, 1000ptas); **Madrid** (2½-3hr., 6 per day, 7:40am-6:40pm, 1375ptas); **Valencia** (3-4hr., 4 per day, 7:40am-6:40pm, 1515ptas).

Buses: (tel. 969 22 70 87; call **Auto Res** at tel. 969 22 11 84 for prices), C. Fermín Caballero. To **Madrid** (2½hr.; 7 per day; M-Sa 7:30am-8pm, Su 7:30am-10pm; 1315-1615ptas). To **Toledo,** buy a ticket on the AISA (3hr., M-F 1 per day, 5:30am, 1620ptas). **SIAL** to **Barcelona** (3½hr., M-Sa 1 per day, 9:30am, 4320ptas).

Taxis: Radio-Taxi (tel. 969 23 33 43). Train station to Pl. Mayor 500-600ptas.

Tourist Office: C. González Palencia, 2 (tel. 969 17 88 00), in the new city near C. Carretería. No English. Supposedly open daily 9am-2pm. You'll do better at the **Municipal Tourist Office** (tel. 969 23 21 19), Pl. Mayor, opposite the Ayuntamiento. Brochures, maps, a video, hiking and excursion routes, an interactive computer, and lots of info about the goings on about town. English spoken. Open daily 9am-9pm.

Currency Exchange: Banco Central Hispano, C. Carretería, 23 (tel. 969 211 726). **ATM.** Open May-Sept. M-F 8:30am-2:30pm; Oct.-Apr. M-F 8:30am-2:30pm, Sa 8:30am-1pm.

Luggage Storage: Train station (400ptas per day; open daily 7am-9:30pm) or bus station (200ptas per day; open daily 7am-9pm).

Emergency: tel. 091 or 092. **Police:** C. Martínez Kleyser, 4 (tel. 969 22 48 59).

Pharmacy: Farmacia Castellanos, C. Cervantes, 20 (tel. 969 21 23 37), at the corner of C. Alferez Rubianes. List of late-night pharmacies in the window.

Post Office: Parque de San Julián, 16 (tel. 969 22 90 16). Open M-F 8:30am-8:30pm, Sa 9:30am-2pm. Smaller **branch** with fewer services right next to RENFE station. Open M-F 8:30am-2:30pm, Sa 9:30am-1pm. **Postal Code:** for the large post office, 16004.

Internet Access: La Repro, C. Jorge Torner, 20 (tel. 969 24 01 36), 1st left off C. Julio from C. Fermín Caballero. 300ptas for 20min., 500ptas for 40min., 600ptas per hr. Open M-F 10:30am-2pm and 5:30-8:30pm, Sa 10:30am-2pm.

ACCOMMODATIONS

The lack of cheap accommodations in the old city is made up for by the abundance in the new city. Rooms on the hill tempt with spectacular views of the old town for a bit more. Both tourist offices have a complete list of places to stay.

Pensión Tabanqueta, C. Trabuco, 13 (tel. 969 21 12 90). Head up C. San Pedro from the cathedral; it turns into C. Trabuco after Pl. Trabuco. Most rooms have a fabulous view, all have a fabulous price. The bar below has a terrace and seats for admiring the sights. Singles 2000ptas; doubles 4000ptas; triples 6000ptas.

Hostal-Residencia Posada de San José, C. Julián Romero, 4 (tel. 969 21 13 00; fax 969 23 03 65), near the cathedral. Cash in that extra traveler's check for cushy beds, historic echoes (it's a 17th-century convent), and gorgeous views. Then let loose with *sangría* (750-800ptas) on the terrace. Reserve 2-3 weeks in advance. Singles 2500-2800ptas, with shower 4100-4700ptas; doubles 4100-4700ptas, with bath 8200-9100ptas; triples 5800-6200ptas, with bath 11,000-14,000ptas. Visa, MC, AmEx.

Pensión Cuenca, Av. República Argentina, 8, 2nd fl. (tel. 969 21 25 74), in the new city. Take C. Fermín Caballero from the bus station to the busy intersection; the street to the left is C. Hurtado de Mendoza, which becomes Av. República Argentina. Shiny new furniture and amiable owners almost as great as the TV lounge. Singles 1800ptas, with shower 2100ptas; doubles 2700ptas, with shower 3800ptas.

Pensión Central, C. Alonso Chirino, 7, 2nd fl. (tel. 969 21 15 11), off C. Carretería. Clean rooms with huge beds and high ceilings. Breakfast 200ptas; lunch or dinner 900ptas. Singles 1500-1700ptas; doubles 2500-2800ptas; triples 3450-3900ptas.

Fonda La Mota, Pl. Constitución, 7, 1st fl. (tel. 969 22 55 67), at the end of C. Carretería. Rooms have sparkling new bathrooms and TVs. Breakfast 250ptas. Showers 200ptas. Singles 2300-2700ptas; doubles 4000ptas, with bath 5300ptas.

☐ FOOD

Restaurants around Pl. Mayor are expensive and mediocre. Budget eateries line C. Cervantes and C. República Argentina, but the cafes off C. Fray Luis de León are even cheaper. *Resoli*, a liqueur of coffee, sugar, orange peel, and eau-de-vie, and *alajú*, a nougat of honey, almonds, and figs, will give you something to smile about. The **market** is on C. Fray Luis de León (open daily 8:30am-2pm). Groceries are available at supermarket **%Día,** Av. Castilla La Mancha at Av. República Argentina (open M-Th 9:30am-2pm and 5:30-8:30pm, F-Sa 9am-2:30pm and 5:30-9pm).

Posada de San José, C. Julián Romero, 4 (tel. 969 21 13 00). The cafe at this former convent boasts spectacular views and delicious regional *tapas*. Great salad for two (850ptas). Wonderful *pisto* (stew made of tomatoes, peppers, and onions; 575ptas). *Raciones* 750ptas. Open Tu-Su 8am-11am and 6-11:30pm.

Restaurante Italiano Piccolo, Av. República Argentina, 14 (tel. 969 23 20 35). Ask your server for the stories behind the pictures on the wall—Pica's got the real scoop. Vegetarian starters 775-1350ptas. Great pizzas 700-975ptas. Pastas 750-975ptas. *Menú* 1350ptas (M-F, lunch only). Visa, MC, AmEx.

Mesón Casas Colgadas (tel. 969 22 35 09), C. Canónigos, to the left of the Museo de Arte Abstracto, in a 14th-century *casa colgada* (hanging house). Bypass the expensive restaurant for the bar; it's the same fabulous view with cheaper fare. *Raciones* 200-1000ptas, *bocadillos* 350-1100ptas. Bar open M-Sa 1-4pm and 7-11pm, Su 1pm-11pm. Restaurant open M 1:30-4pm, Tu-Su 1:30-4 and 9-11pm. Visa, MC, AmEx.

☐ SIGHTS

▨CASAS COLGADAS. Cuenca draws its fame from the gravity-defying *casas colgadas* (see **Living on the Edge,** above). They dangle over the riverbanks as precariously today as they did six centuries ago. In his memoirs, Surrealist filmmaker Luis Buñuel recalls a pre-war visit to one of the *casas*, in which he spied birds flying beneath the toilet seat. Walk carefully across the Puente de San Pablo bridge (not for anyone suffering from vertigo) to get a spectacular view of the *casas* and the surrounding cliffs. Even better, do it at sunset. Two hiking trails along the **Hoz del Júcar** and **Hoz del Huécar,** across the bridge, present fantastic views of the old city and the gorges that isolate it. Maps are available from the municipal tourist office. *(Down C. Obispo Valero from Pl. Mayor.)*

LIVING ON THE EDGE Very little is known about Cuenca's unique 14th-century *casas colgadas*. They were supposedly built to house kings; one is even named Casa del Rey. Casa de la Sirena, the only other remaining original hanging house, got its name from the siren-like screams emitted by a Cuenca *señorita* when she flung herself out of the window after her son was killed by her lover. Despite their striking appearance, the *casas* did not become famous until recently. Indeed, the *casas* were completely run down when the city of Cuenca decided to rehabilitate them early in this century, transforming them into magnificent museums. Now one of Central Spain's greatest tourist attractions, they draw thousands of visitors each year.

MUSEO DE ARTE ABSTRACTO ESPAÑOL. Inside one of the *casas*, the award-winning Museo de Arte Abstracto Español displays important works by the wacky and internationally-renowned "Abstract Generation" of Spanish painters. All pieces were chosen by artist Fernando Zóbel, one of the school's major figures. The well-designed museum exhibits works by Canogar, Tápies, Chillida, and Zóbel himself. Don't miss the "White Room" upstairs. Striking views of the gorge are an added benefit. *(Pl. Ciudad de Ronda. Tel. 969 21 29 83. Open Tu-F and holidays 11am-2pm and 4-6pm, Sa 11am-2pm and 4-8pm, Su 11am-2:30pm. 500ptas, students 250ptas.)*

CATHEDRAL. The cathedral, constructed under Alfonso VIII six years after he conquered Castile, dominates Pl. Mayor. A perfect square, 25m on each side, it is the only Anglo-Norman Gothic cathedral in Spain. A Spanish Renaissance facade and tower were added in the 16th and 17th centuries, only to be torn down when deemed aesthetically inappropriate. A 1724 fire prevented a subsequent attempt to build a front, leaving the current exterior incomplete and strangely reminiscent of a Hollywood set. Wonderfully colorful stained-glass windows illuminate the entrance like a sunset. Inside, the **Museo del Tesoro** houses some late medieval Psalters and a great deal of gold jewelry. More impressive is the **Sala Capitular** and its delightful ceiling. *(Cathedral open June-Aug. 11am-2pm and 4-6pm; Sept.-May 10:30am-2pm and 4-6pm. Mass 9:20am. Free. Museum open daily 11am-2pm and 4-6pm. 200ptas.)*

OTHER SIGHTS. Down C. Obispo Valero, the **Museo de Cuenca** is a treasure trove of archeological finds, including Roman mosaics, ceramics, coins, and excellent Visigoth jewelry. *(Tel. 969 21 30 69. Open Tu-Sa 10am-2pm and 4-6pm, Su 10am-2pm. 200ptas, students 100ptas.)* Perhaps the most beautiful of the museums along this short street is the **Museo Diocesano.** Exhibits are imaginatively displayed and include Juan de Borgoña's altarpiece from local Convento de San Pablo, many colossal Flemish tapestries, splendid rugs, and two El Grecos—*Oración del huerto* and *Cristo con la cruz. (Tel. 969 22 42 10. Open Tu-F 11am-2pm and 4-6pm, Sa 11am-2pm and 4-8pm, Su 11am-2pm. 200ptas.)*

🎵 ENTERTAINMENT

New Cuenca's nighttime bar scene extends into the wee hours of the morning. Several bars with loud music and young, snazzily dressed crowds line small C. Galíndez, off C. Fray Luis de León, a long, dark, and sweet walk down the hill from Old Cuenca; a taxi will cost about 500ptas. Check out the bar under **Pensión Tabanqueta** on C. Trabuco. For more bars and nightclubs, take the winding street/staircase just off Pl. Mayor across from the cathedral toward the Río Júcar, where you'll encounter an army of empty bottles. Cuenca rings with song during the **Festival of Religious Music.** This famous international celebration occurs the week before Holy Week.

SIGÜENZA

The sleepy town of Sigüenza (pop. 5000) perches on a hill in what seems to be the middle of nowhere—halfway between Madrid and Zaragoza. Pinkish stone buildings and red-roofed houses cluster around a storybook Gothic cathedral and castle. During the Civil War, the Republicans seized the cathedral and the Nationalists the castle, making for one hell of a shoot-out. Despite heavy damages, Sigüenza's medieval architecture has been painstakingly restored, and peace has returned to this tranquil town.

◪ PRACTICAL INFORMATION. The **train station** (tel. 949 39 14 94 or 608 62 38 85) is at the end of Av. Alfonso VI. Trains run to: **Soria** (30min., 5 per day, 9:51am-8:38pm, 800ptas); **Madrid** (1½-2hr., 11 per day, 5:19am-9:04pm, 1700ptas); **Zaragoza** (2hr., 3 per day, 10am-4pm, 2200ptas). Call a **taxi** at 949 39 14 11. To get to the **tourist office** (tel. 949 34 70 07), follow Av. Alfonso VI past Parque de la Alameda to the first intersection. The office is on the left in the restored Ermita del Humilladero and offers a list of accommodations. (Open Tu-F 10am-2pm and 4:30-7pm, Sa-Su 9am-2:30pm and 4:30-7pm.) Across the intersection sits **Banco Hispano Central,** Av. Calvo Siteco, 9 (open M-F 8:30am-2:30pm). **Luggage storage** is available at the train station until midnight (300ptas). **Emergency:** tel. 949 30 00 19; **Red Cross** (tel. 949 39 13 33), on Cra. Madrid; **police** (tel. 949 39 01 95), Carretera de Atienzo. **Post office,** C. Villaviciosa, 10 (tel. 949 39 08 44), off Pl. Hilario Yabén (open M-F 8:30am-2:30pm, Sa 9:30am-1pm); **postal code:** 19250.

▚▟ ACCOMMODATIONS AND FOOD. Although you can "do" Sigüenza in a couple of hours, it's a fun place to spend the night. **Pensión Venancio,** C. San Roque, 3 (tel. 949 39 03 47), is charming. From the station, follow Av. Alfonso VI, turn left at the first intersection onto Av. Pio XII, then take the first right. For those backpackers who just couldn't leave the make-up at home, the airy rooms sport mirrors (singles 2000ptas; doubles 3800ptas; triples 5000ptas). Cheap places to eat are everywhere. **Restaurante El Mesón,** Roman Pascual, 14 (tel. 949 39 06 49), has entrees for 400-1700ptas (open 11:30am-3:30pm; Visa). **Canfran Muela,** C. Cardenal Mendoza, 2, sells groceries (open M-Sa 9am-2pm and 5-8pm).

◉ SIGHTS. From the bottom of the hill, two buildings jut out from Sigüenza's low skyline: the cathedral and the fortified **castillo,** a 12th-century castle-turned-*parador* (luxury hotel). Restored in the 1970s, the castle merits an uphill stroll through the cobblestone streets, if just to peek in at the luxuriously decorated *parador*. To get to the magnificent **◨cathedral,** follow Av. Alfonso VI uphill (it changes to C. Humilladero), then take a left onto C. Cardenal Mendoza. Work on the cathedral began in the mid-12th century and continued until the 16th century; it combines Romanesque, Mudéjar, Plateresque, and Gothic styles. One of the structure's most renowned features is the 15th-century **Tumba del Doncel,** commissioned by Isabel in memory of a favorite page who died fighting the Muslims in Granada. The **sacristry's** elaborate Renaissance ceiling boasts 304 stone portraits carved by Alanso de Covarrubias. The faces belong to Christians and Moors, monks and countesses, dandies and dames. The adjoining chapel houses an El Greco *Anunciación* and a ceiling so magnificent that the church thoughtfully provides a mirror on the floor to help you view it. (Tel. 619 36 27 15. Open May-Nov. M-F 11am-1:30pm and 4:30-6:30pm, Sa-Su 10:30am-1:30pm and 5:30-6:30pm. Tours in Spanish 11am, noon, 12:45pm, 4:30pm, and 5:45pm. Free. No entry during services unless you wish to participate.) Opposite the cathedral, the small **Museo de Arte Antiguo (Museo Diocesano)** exhibits medieval and early modern religious works, including a Ribera and a Zurbarán. (Tel. 949 39 10 23. Open Apr.-Sept. Tu-F noon-2pm and 4-5pm, Sa-Su 11am-2pm and 5-7pm. 200ptas.)

CASTILLA Y LEÓN

Castilla y León's cities emerge like islands from a sea of burnt sienna. Reigning strong in the region, these urban personages survey their surroundings from splendid cathedrals and sumptuous palaces. The monuments—the majestic Gothic cathedrals of Burgos and León, the slender Romanesque belfries along León's Camino de Santiago, the intricate sandstone of Salamanca, and the proud city walls of Ávila—have emblazoned themselves as regional and national images.

Well before Castilla's famous 1469 confederation with Aragón, when Fernando of Aragón and Isabel of Castilla were united in world-shaking matrimony, it was clear that Castilla had its act together. In the High Middle Ages, the region emerged from obscurity to lead the Christian charge against Islam. Castilian nobles, sanguine from the spoils of combat, introduced the concept of a unified Spain (under Castilian command, of course), and *castellano* ("Spanish") became the dominant language throughout the nation. Imperious León, Castilla's comrade in arms, though chagrined to be lumped with Castilla in a 1970s provincial reorganization, has much in common with its co-province. Neither has been as economically successful as their more high-tech northeastern neighbors.

Castilian gastronomy favors red meats and vegetables such as potatoes (which can be grown in relatively cold climates). One favorite is *cocido castellano*, a stew of beef, ham, potatoes, sausage, carrots, and garlic. Castilians also tend to get hyperbolically excited about their lamb dishes.

HIGHLIGHTS OF CASTILLA Y LEÓN

- Segovia's impressive **Alcázar** (palace) and hulking **aqueduct** (see below).
- The spectacular manicured **gardens** at **La Granja** (see p. 142).
- **Ávila,** the best preserved medieval walled city in Europe (see p. 142).
- The lovely Plateresque architecture of the **University of Salamanca** (see p. 151).
- **Burgos's** imposing **Gothic cathedral,** Spain's biggest and best (see p. 168).

SEGOVIA

Legend has it that the devil built Segovia's famed aqueduct in one night, in an effort to win the soul of a Segovian water-seller named Juanilla. When the shocked Juanilla woke up to find the aqueduct almost completed, she prayed to the Virgin Mary, who made the sun rise a bit earlier in order to foil the Devil's scheme. Segovia's aqueduct may not have won Juanilla's soul, but it has intrigued visitors ever since Roman times. During its period of greatest prosperity, in the 12th and 13th centuries, Segovia had the most Romanesque monuments in Europe. The remaining cathedrals and castles represent Castilla at its finest, a labyrinthine town (pop. 55,000) of twisted alleys, fruit stands, and paseos. As always, pleasure has its price: prices for food and accommodations are much higher than in Madrid. On the far side of the Sierra de Guadarrama, 88km northwest of Madrid, Segovia is close enough to the capital to be a daytrip but definitely warrants a longer stay.

▐ GETTING THERE

Trains run to Segovia from **Ávila** (1hr., 16 per day, 980ptas) and **Madrid** (2hr., 9 per day, 6:17am-8:17pm, 775ptas). **Buses** go from: **Ávila** (1hr., M-F 7 per day, Sa-Su 2 per day, 555ptas); **Madrid** (1½hr., every hr., 6:30am-10:45pm, 775ptas); **Salamanca** (3hr., 1-3 per day, 8:30am-5:30pm, 1260ptas).

▐ ORIENTATION AND PRACTICAL INFORMATION

To get to **Plaza Mayor,** the city's historic center and site of the **tourist office,** take any bus from the train station (100ptas). On weekdays, some buses go only as far as Po. del Salón, in which case go left up the steps of **Puerta del Sol,** turn right on C.

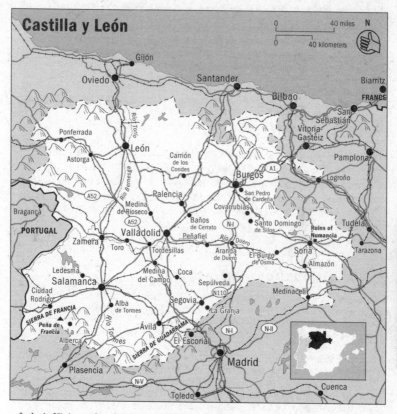

Castilla y León

0   40 miles   N

0   40 kilometers

Gijón

Oviedo

Santander

Biarritz

Bilbao

FRANCE

San Sebastián

Vitoria-Gasteiz

Ponferrada

Río Torío

León

Carrión de los Condes

Pamplona

Astorga

Río Esla

A1

Logroño

Palencia

Burgos

A52

Bragança

Medina de Ríoseco

San Pedro de Cardeña

A52

Baños de Cerrato

Covarrubias

N-I

Santo Domingo de Silos

Tudela

PORTUGAL

Zamora

Valladolid

Peñafiel

Río Duero

Ruins of Numancia

Toro

Tordesillas

Aranda de Duero

El Burgo de Osma

Soria

Tarazona

Ledesma

Salamanca

Medina del Campo

Coca

Sepúlveda

Almazón

Ciudad Rodrigo

Alba de Tormes

N110

Medinaceli

SIERRA DE FRANCIA

Segovia

Peña de Francia

Río Tormes

Ávila

La Granja

N-I

La Alberca

SIERRA DE GUADARRAMA

El Escorial

N-II

Plasencia

N-V

Madrid

Toledo

Cuenca

Juderia Vieja, and make the first left onto C. Isabel La Católica up to the plaza. For the fastest route from the **bus station** to Pl. Mayor, make a left from the station onto C. Ezekiel González and walk until you get to the first round intersection with a statue. Turn right onto C. Puente de Sancti Spiritus, and take the stairs up to the park. Cross the park and go up the steps of Pta. Sol. Turn right on C. Juderia Vieja, and make the first left onto C. Isabel La Catolica up to the plaza (15min.).

The city is impossible to navigate without a map. Locals describe it as the "Stone Ship." The Alcázar is the bow, the aqueduct the stern, and the cathedral towers the mainmast. Both Pl. Mayor (10min.) and the Alcázar (20min.) are uphill from Pl. de Azoguejo, next to the **aqueduct.** Running between Pl. Mayor and Pl. Azoguejo is **Calle Isabel la Católica-Calle Juan Bravo-Calle Cervantes,** a pedestrian thoroughfare.

Trains: (tel. 921 42 07 74), Po. Obispo Quesada. Only one line: the Segovia-Madrid regional. To **Madrid** (2hr., 9 per day, 775ptas) and **Villalba** (1hr., 500ptas, halfway along the same line, transfer point for El Escorial, Ávila, León, and Salamanca). The bus is often a better bet unless you're coming directly from the Madrid airport.

Buses: Estacionamiento Municipal de Autobuses, Po. Ezequiel González, 12 (tel. 921 42 77 25), at the corner of Av. Fernández Ladreda. To: **La Granja** (20min., 10-14 per day, round-trip 200ptas)**; Ávila** (1hr., M-F 8 per day, Sa-Su 1 per day, 555ptas); **Madrid** (1¾hr., every hr., 765ptas); **Valladolid** (2hr., M-F 11 per day, Sa-Su 7-9 per day, 855ptas); **Salamanca** (3hr., 3 per day, 1245ptas).

Public Transportation: Transportes Urbanos de Segovia, Pl. Mayor, 8 (tel. 921 46 03 29). Buses 90-100ptas.

Taxis: Taxis pull up by the train and bus stations. **Radio Taxi:** tel. 921 44 50 00.

Car Rental: Avis, C. José Zorrilla, 123 (tel. 921 42 25 84).

Tourist Office: Municipal Office, Pl. Mayor, 10 (tel. 921 46 03 34), in front of the bus stop on the corner opposite the cathedral. Complete info on accommodations, bus and train schedules, and sights posted in the windows. Indispensable map pinpoints sights and up-scale hostels. Some English and French spoken. Open daily 10am-2pm and 5-8pm. **Regional Tourist Office,** Pl. Azoguejo, 1 (tel. 921 44 03 02), at the foot of the steps leading to the top of the aqueduct. Less crowded; also acts as the Oficina de Juventud. Piles of glossy brochures in multiple languages. Open daily 10am-8pm.

Currency Exchange: Banks line Av. Fernandez Ladreda and **ATMs** surround Pl. Azoguejo and Pl. Mayor.

Luggage Storage: Lockers at the train station (400ptas). Open daily 5:45am-10pm.

Emergency: Municipal Police, C. Guadarrama, 26 (tel. 921 43 12 12).

Medical Services: Hospital Policlínico, C. San Agustín, 13 (tel. 921 41 90 65).

Post Office: Pl. Dr. Laguna, 5 (tel. 921 43 16 11), up C. Cronista Lecea from Pl. Mayor. Lista de Correos. Open M-F 8:30am-8:30pm, Sa 9:30am-2pm. **Postal Code:** 40001.

Internet Access: Kitius, Av. Fernandez Ladreda, 28 (tel. 608 10 69 69). A heavenly, air-conditioned salon. 900ptas per hr. Open M-Sa, 9am-2pm and 5-8:30pm. **Ludos,** C. José Zorilla, 26 (tel 921 44 44 69). A noisy cafe. 600ptas per hr. Open daily 1pm-3am.

ACCOMMODATIONS AND CAMPING

Segovia graces almost every tour's itinerary, so finding a hostel during the summer can be a nightmare. The regional tourist office's list of accommodations is valuable, but be prepared to pay 2500ptas or more for a single. The *pensiones* are significantly cheaper, but often offer little more than windowless, sinkless closets.

Hostal Juan Bravo, C. Juan Bravo, 12, 2nd fl. (tel. 921 46 34 13), on the main thoroughfare in the old town, near Iglesia de San Martín. According to the owner, Segovia and his hostel both qualify as paradise. With bright, newly renovated rooms and built in closets, he might be right. Singles 2500ptas, with bath 3500ptas; doubles 3800ptas, with bath 4800ptas; triples 5000ptas, with bath 6500ptas. Visa, MC.

Residencia Juvenil "Emperador Teodosio" (HI) (tel. 921 44 11 11 or 44 10 47), on Av. Conde de Sepúlveda. From the train station, go right, cross the street, and walk along Po. Obispo Quesada, which soon becomes Av. Conde de Sepúlveda (10min.). The hostel is on the left. From the bus station, go right on C. Ezequiel González, which becomes Av. Conde de Sepúlveda (10min.). The hostel is on the right. Look for its huge red fire escape. Modern amenities and hotel-like doubles and triples, all with private baths, make it nearly impossible to get a room. 3-night max. stay. Dorms 1000ptas, with full meals 2200ptas; over 26 1450ptas, with full meals 3000ptas. Open July-Aug.

Hostal Don Jaime, Ochoa Ondategui, 8 (tel. 921 44 47 87). With your back to the bottom of the aqueduct stairs, the first street on the left. Simple rooms off the elegant salon, which is a great place to meet other travelers. Great breakfasts (375ptas). Singles 3000ptas; doubles 3800ptas, with bath 5500ptas; triples with bath 6800ptas.

Pensión Ferri, C. Escuderos, 10 (tel. 921 46 09 57), off Pl. Mayor. Could not be more central. Clean, small rooms. Showers 300ptas. Singles 1450ptas; doubles 2300ptas.

Camping: Camping Acueducto, Ctra. Nacional, 601, km 112 (tel. 921 42 50 00), 2km toward La Granja. Take the AutoBus Urbano from Pl. Azoguejo to Nueva Segovia (100ptas). 2nd-class campsite. Hot water. 500ptas per person and per tent.

FOOD

Steer clear of Pl. Mayor, Pl. Azoguejo, and all signs on worn "medieval" parchment. *Sopa Castellana* (soup with bread, eggs, and garlic), *cochinillo asado* (roast suckling pig), lamb, and *croquetas* are regional specialities. The many

CENTRAL SPAIN

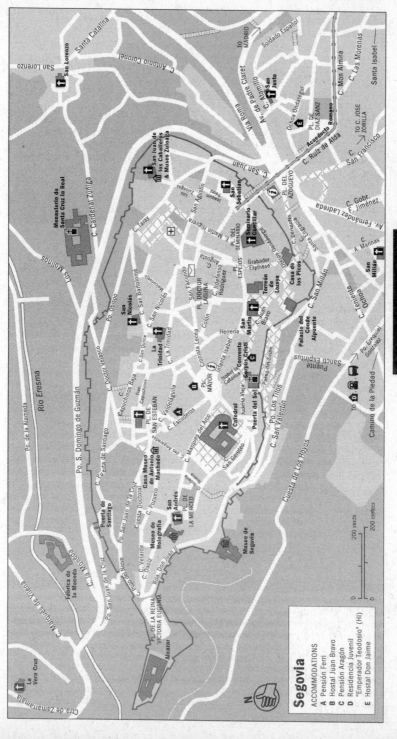

Segovia

ACCOMMODATIONS

A Pensión Ferri
B Hostal Juan Bravo
C Pensión Aragón
D Residencia Juvenil "Emperador Teodosio" (HI)
E Hostal Don Jaime

sights and steps of Segovia offer the perfect opportunity for a picnic. Fruit and vegetable stands crowd C. Juan Bravo and its neighboring streets. **%Día**, C. Fernández Jimenez, 3, off C. Fernández Ladreda, is a discount supermarket (open M-Th 9:30am-2pm and 5:30-8:30pm, F-Sa 9am-2:30pm and 5:30-9pm).

Bar-Mesón Cueva de San Esteban, C. Valdeláguila, 15 (tel. 921 46 09 82), off Pl. San Esteban and C. Escuderos. Swords, shields, and meat hang from the ceiling. Entrees 675ptas and up. *Menú* 900ptas. Open daily 10am-midnight.

Restaurante La Almuzara, C. Marqués del Arco, 3 (tel. 921 46 06 22), past the cathedral toward the Alcázar. Excellent vegetarian restaurant with greenery-inspired frescoes. Big salads 400-900ptas, entrees 700-1300ptas. Open Tu-Su, dinner only.

Pomares Restaurante, C. San Agustin, 24 (tel. 921 43 54 21), on the right after the post office. Quiet location and hearty, cheap menu (1200ptas) make it a magnet for locals. *Raciones* 550-1100ptas. Open daily 1-4pm and 8:30-11pm.

La Concepción, Pl. Mayor, 15 (tel. 921 46 09 30). The cheapest spot on Pl. Mayor. Tempts with fresh sandwiches (450-625ptas) and tarts (525ptas). Excellent for people-watching at night when the plaza really gets going. Open daily 9am-2am. Visa, AmEx.

◉ SIGHTS

Segovia rewards the wanderer. Whether palace, church, house, or sidewalk, almost everything deserves close observation. Look for *esgrafía*, lacy patterns on the facades of buildings. Also be sure to explore the northern parts of town, outside the walls and away from the Alcázar. For a long walk, tour the less frequented monasteries and churches along the Rio Eresma.

◪AQUEDUCT. The serpent-like aqueduct, built by the Romans around 50 BC to pipe in water for thirsty legions from the Río Frío 18km away, commands the entrance to the old city. Supported by 128 pillars that span 813m, the two tiers of 163 arches were constructed out of some 20,000 blocks of granite—without any mortar to hold them together. This spectacular feat of engineering, restored by the monarchy in the 15th century, can transport 30 liters of water per second and was in use until the late 1940s. Construction to restore the aqueduct's function has begun again. Though the grand structure reaches its maximum height of 28.9m beside Pl. Azoguejo, there is no reason to limit your viewing to that particular spot. *(From the Pl. Mayor, go down C. Infanta Isabel, right on C. Herreria, and follow C. Canalejas to the Pl. del Seminario. In the plaza, go right on C. Conde de Gazola, left on C. Obispo Gandasegui and down the stone stairs.)*

◪CATHEDRAL. In 1525, Charles V commissioned the construction of a cathedral to replace the 12th-century one destroyed in the "Revolt of the Comunidades." This new one, he hoped, would tower over the Pl. Mayor. When it was finished 200 years later, with 23 chapels and a silver and gold *tesoro*, the cathedral earned its nickname as "The Lady of all Cathedrals." The *Sala Capitular*, hung with well-preserved 17th-century tapestries, displays a silver and gold chariot and an incredible number of crucifixes, chalices, and candelabras. Many of the most stunning architectural aspects are vestiges of the old cathedral, including the main facade and a cloister designed by Juan Guas. Don't miss the intricate sculptures on the altarpiece, crafted by the Baroque master Sabatini. The museum holds an excellent collection, including Coello's 16th-century painting *La Duda de Santo Tomás (The Doubt of Saint Thomas)*. *(Faces the Pl. Mayor. Tel. 921 46 22 05. Open daily Apr.-Oct. 9:15am-6:45pm; Nov.-Mar. 9:30am-5:45pm. 250ptas.)*

ALCÁZAR. The Alcázar, a classic late-medieval castle, dominates the far northern end of the old quarter. The surrounding countryside and Queen Eugenia's gardens make for a Kodak moment. Due to its strategic position at the convergence of the Ríos Clamores and Ermesa, fortifications have occupied the site since the time of the Celts. Alfonso X, who allegedly believed he was God, took the original 11th-

LA MUJER MUERTA According to local folklore, the picturesque mountain silhouette south of Segovia known as **La Mujer Muerta (The Dead Woman)** commemorates a bloody but moving turn of events. *La mujer*, the wife of a chief, was widowed when her twin sons were but young boys. As only one of the two could inherit his father's rule, the mother grew fearful of impending fratricide once the children came of age. She offered her life to God as a sacrifice, hoping this act would save both her sons. Unfortunately it settled nothing. On a summer's day years later, as the two young men prepared to fight each other for supremacy, it suddenly began to snow. By the time the storm dissipated, a snow-capped mountain had materialized upon the scene of the proposed battleground. As all soon acknowledged, it was the resting body of the twins' mother. *Segovianos* insist that two small clouds float closer to the mountain at dusk—the two sons kissing their mother good night.

century fortress and further beautified it. Successive monarchs added to the Alcázar's grandeur, the culmination coming with the 1474 coronation of Isabel I as Queen of Castilla.

Trappings from its illustrious past fill the castle: tapestries, armor, thrones, sculptures, and paintings. The walls of the *Sala de Reyes* (royal room) are adorned with wood- and gold-inlaid friezes of monarchs. In the *Sala de Solio* (throne room), the inscription above the throne reads: "tanto monta, monta tanto" (she mounts, as does he). Contrary to popular belief, this saying does not mean anything dirty. Instead it says that Fernando and Isabel had equal authority as sovereigns. The *Sala de Armas* holds an arsenal of medieval weaponry. If you feel strong, climb the 140 steps up a nausea-inducing spiral staircase to the top of the *Torre de Juan II* (80m high), where you will be rewarded with a marvelous view of Segovia and the surrounding amber plains. *(From the Pl. Mayor, follow C. Marques del Arco and its continuation and walk through the park. Tel. 921 46 07 59. Open daily Apr.-Sept. 10am-7pm; Oct.-Mar. 10am-6pm. 400ptas, seniors 250ptas.)*

OTHER SIGHTS. 14th- and 15th-century palaces adorn historic Segovia. **Torreón de Lozoya** has lovely Renaissance courtyards and hosts art exhibitions. *(Pl. San Martín, off C. Juan Bravo. Open M-F 7-9:30pm, Sa noon-2pm and 7-9:30pm. Free.)* The **Palacio del Conde Alpuente** epitomizes Segovian *esgrafía*. *(Up C. Juan Bravo in an alley to the left.)* Though significantly more humble than a *palacio*, the **Casa-Museo de Antonio Machado** holds its own among Segovia's historic treasures. The poet's 13-year residence (1919-1932) has been left untouched. *(C. Desamparados, 5. From the Pl. Mayor, go down C. Marques del Arco and right on C. Desamparados. Open daily 4-7pm. Free.)* **Iglesia de San Millán** is the city's finest example of Romanesque architecture. Its frescoes were discovered under a layer of paint only 30 years ago. *(C. Fernández Ladreda, near the bus station. Open daily during mass only, 8pm.)*

OUTSIDE THE WALLS. A walk away from the city past the meandering Eresma River offers a welcome change of pace, and there are several sights of interest. However, such pleasure comes at a cost—be prepared for a grueling uphill trek back to the city. Be sure to see **Iglesia de la Vera Cruz**, a mysterious 12-sided basilica built by the cabalistic Knights Templar in 1208. Beneath its lofty vaults are two hidden chambers where clergymen guarded their lives and their valuables from robbers and highwaymen. The Knights Templar gathered to perform initiation ceremonies in these same rooms. *(Follow C. Pozo de la Nieve, on the left with your back to the Alcázar, and head down the 2nd stone staircase; you'll be on Po. San Juan de la Cruz. From there it is a 20-min. walk. Tel. 921 43 14 75. Open Apr.-Sept. Tu-Su 10:30am-1:30pm and 3:30-7pm; Oct.-Mar. Tu-Su 10:30am-1:30pm and 3:30-6pm. 200ptas.)*

🎵 ENTERTAINMENT

Packed with bars and cafes, Pl. Mayor is the center of Segovian nightlife. Pl. Azoguejo and C. Carmen, near the aqueduct, are filled with bars as well, though they are mostly frequented by the high school set. Club headquarters are at C. Ruiz de Alda, off Pl. Azoguejo. **Sabbat,** Po. del Salón, fills the paseo with long lines and techno. For decent jazz, locals head to **El Saxo Bar,** C. del Seminario, 2.

From June 24-29, Segovia celebrates a **fiesta** in honor of San Juan and San Pedro. According to local lore, the sun reflects the general joy and intoxication by rising in circles. During the festival there are free open-air concerts on Pl. Azoguejo, and dances and a fireworks display on June 29.

Three kilometers northwest of Segovia, **Zamarramala** hosts the Fiestas de Santa Agueda on Feb. 5. Women take over the town's administration for a day, dress up in beautiful, old-fashioned costumes, and parade through the streets. They parody men to commemorate an abortive sneak attack on the Alcázar in which the women of Zamarramala tried to distract the castle guards with wine and song. After three days, they torch the "Pelele," a doll symbolic of local men.

NEAR SEGOVIA: LA GRANJA DE SAN ILDEFONSO

The easiest way to get to La Granja is by **bus** from Segovia (20min., 10-14 per day, 200ptas round-trip). From the bus stop, walk up the hill and through the ornate gates. Signs from there will guide you to the palace and gardens.

The royal palace of La Granja, 9km southeast of Segovia, is the most extravagant of the four royal summer retreats (the others are El Pardo, El Escorial, and Aranjuez). Felipe V, the first Bourbon King of Spain and grandson of Louis XIV, detested the Habsburgs' austere El Escorial. Nostalgic for Versailles, he commissioned La Granja in the early 18th century, choosing the sight based on its hunting and gardening potential. After centuries of the royalty's summer "sojourns" at the palace, a fire destroyed the living quarters of the royals and their servants in 1918. The rubble was rebuilt in 1932 to house one of the world's finest collections of Flemish tapestries. The most notable is the series entitled *The Honours* by Pierre van Aelst, which consists of nine elaborate tapestries; it was said to be an allegory of Emperor Charles' moral development. Red marble interior, gilded woodwork, frescoed ceilings, and golden urns make for a visual extravaganza. (Tel. 921 47 00 19. Open daily June-Sept. Tu-Su 10am-6pm; Oct.-Mar. Tu-Sa 10am-1:30pm and 3-5pm, Su 10am-2pm; Apr.-May Tu-F 10am-1:30pm and 3-5pm, Sa-Su 10am-6pm. 650ptas, students 250ptas. EU citizens free on Wednesdays.)

Outside are the ■manicured **gardens,** designed by Frenchman Rene Carlier. The cool pathways and rich flowerbeds, while impressive, are no match for the decadent *Cascadas Nuevas.* This ensemble of illuminated fountains, pools, and pavilions represents the continents and four seasons. Neptune, Apollo, Minerva, and a group of dragons frolic in the spray. (Gardens free except W, Sa-Su after 3pm; 325ptas, students 200ptas. Fountains turned on W, Sa-Su at 5:30pm.) At the **Real Fabrica de Cristales,** also outside the palace, visitors can follow the evolution of the wine bottle and visit the amazing collection of contemporary glass art. (Tel. 921 47 17 12; fax 921 47 15 72. Open daily Apr.-Sept. 11am-8pm; Oct.-Mar. 11am-7pm. 400ptas, seniors and students 200ptas.)

ÁVILA

Oh, if walls had ears, what stories Ávila's medieval *murallas* could tell. One of Castilla's most important provincial capitals, Ávila (pop. 50,000) is renowned for the 2.5km of magnificently preserved 12th-century stone walls that encircle its old city. Santa Teresa de Jesús and San Juan de la Cruz, famed 16th-century mystics, writers, and religious reformers, lived out their spiritual days here, penning tracts and founding monastic communities. But though Ávila is crazy for Santa Teresa, poor San Juan got a bit lost in the shuffle. Museums and monuments depict Santa Teresa's divine visitations and ecstatic visions in exhaustive detail, and Ávila's inhabitants have taken the heroine as their patron saint, naming everything from pastries to driving schools after her. Santa Teresa would have been pleased at the peace of Ávila life. Today, the inner walls are a time warp, untouched by pollution, advertisements, or the blare of tourist traffic. Just west of Segovia and northwest of Madrid, Ávila is a reasonable daytrip from either.

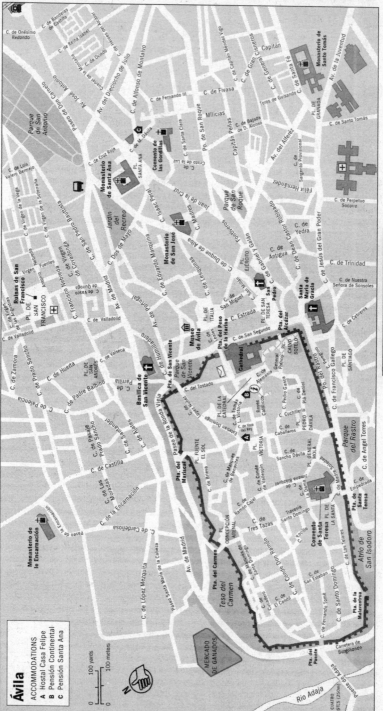

Ávila

ACCOMMODATIONS
A Hostal Casa Felipe
B Pensión Continental
C Pensión Santa Ana

0 _____ 100 yards
0 _____ 100 meters

Parque de San Antonio

C. de Onésimo Redondo
C. de Banderas de Castilla
C. de Reina Isabel
C. de Oviedo
C. de José Antonio
Av. de Don Carmelo
Po. de Don Antonio
C. de Luis Valero Bermejo
C. de Virgen de la Vega
C. de Virgen de la Soterraña
C. de Virgen de las Angustias
C. de Virgen de la Soterraña
Antonio Fuentes
C. de Santa Rosa
C. de Covaleda
C. de Francisco Nebreda
C. de Vasco
C. de Quiroga
C. de Valladolid
C. de Zamora
C. de Prado Sancho
C. de Huerta
C. de Padre Balbino
C. de Palencia
C. de Valencia
C. de Pasaje Prado Sancho
C. de Alates
C. de Sanchidrián
C. de Castilla
C. de Las Moradas
C. de la Encarnación
C. de Cardeñosa
Paseo de la Estación
C. de López Mezquita
Paseo Santa María la Cabeza
Av. de Madrid

Monasterio de la Encarnación

Ruinas de San Francisco
PL. DE SAN FRANCISCO

Av. de Dieciocho de Julio
Av. de Alfonso de Montalvo
C. de Fernando III
C. de Fivasa
C. de Capitán Méndez Vigo
Capitán
C. de Gran Cisneros
C. de Santa Fé
Milicias
Po. de San Roque
Capitán Peñas
C. de Bajada de D. Alonso
PL. DE GRANADA
C. de Santo Tomás
Av. de la Juventud
Monasterio de Santo Tomás
Toros de Guisando
Av. del Alférez
C. de Sargento Provincial
C. de Cristo de la Luz
C. de Perpetuo Socorro
Félix Hernández
Frontineros
Parque de San Roque
C. de Yedra
C. de Antigua
C. de Dean Castro Robledo
C. de Jesús del Gran Poder
C. de Trinidad
C. de Nuestra Señora de Sonsoles
C. de Cebreros

Convento de las Gordillas
C. de Santa Clara
PL. SANTA ANA
C. de Santa Ana
Monasterio de Santa Ana
Jardín del Recreo
C. de Isaac Peral
C. de Madres
Juan de la Cruz
Monasterio de San José
C. de Eduardo Marquina
C. de Leocadio
C. de Dos de Mayo
Av. de Madrid
C. de Portugal
Av. de la Inmaculada
C. de Humilladero

Ejército y Galán
Gabriel y Galán
San Pedro
PL. DE SAN PEDRO
Santa María de Gracia
PL. DE ITALIA
C. de San Segundo
Santa de Gracia
PL. DE SANTIAGO
PL. DE SANTIAGO
C. de Francisco Gallego

Museo de Ávila
C. de Caños
C. de la Harina
Pta. del Peso de la Harina
Pta. de San Vicente
Basílica de San Vicente
Parque de San Vicente
Paseo de la Ronda Vieja
C. del Tostado
C. de San Miguel
C. de Estrada

Catedral
General Franco
CALVO SOTELO
Po. del Rastro
PL. DE LA CATEDRAL
C. L. Victoria
Reyes Católicos
C. de Pedro Gasca
C. de Vista del Rey
PL. DE VISTA DEL REY
C. de Caballeros
C. de Pedro Dávila
PEDRO DÁVILA
C. Cuchillería
Sancho Dávila
C. GENERAL MOLA
C. de Reyes
C. de Santo Tomás
C. de Tomás Luis de Victoria
PL. VICTORIA
C. del Conde de Viñasola
C. de Jiménez Blanco
Zancabria
C. de Madre Soledad
C. de la Dama
PL. de Tres Tazas
Travesía Santo Domingo

Pta. del Carmen
Teso del Carmen
MERCADO DE GANADOS

Convento de Santa Teresa
PL. DE LA SANTA
Pta. de Santa Teresa
Atrio de San Isodoro
C. de Empedrada
Pta. de la Malaventura
Carretera de Burgohondo
C. de Santo Domingo
C. de Los Teatos

PL. FUENTE EL SOL
Pta. del Mariscal
C. de Marqués de Benavites
C. de Buena
PL. CONCEPCIÓN ARENAL
C. de Ramón Cajal
C. de Conde Don Ramón
C. de San Esteban
C. de Cuadro
C. El Candil
C. de Fernando Tomé
Pta. del Puente
Río Adaja

TO CUATRO POSTES (250m)

N

■ GETTING THERE

Trains run to Ávila from **Valladolid** (1hr., 7 per day, 7:11am-8:41pm, 1065ptas) and **Madrid** (2hr., 12 per day, 6am-8:47pm, 980ptas). **Buses** go from **Salamanca** (1-2hr., 2-7 per day, 8am-10pm, 750ptas) and **Madrid** (2hr., 4 per day, 7am-8pm, 910ptas).

■ ORIENTATION AND PRACTICAL INFORMATION

The tangled city has two main squares: **Plaza de la Victoria** (known to locals as Pl. del Mercado Chico) inside the city walls, and **Plaza de Santa Teresa** just outside. Pl. Santa Teresa is the social center and the best place to find a meal. In general, stick to the labeled streets; twisting alleys will suddenly lead you outside of town. To get to Pl. Santa Teresa from the **train station**, head straight on Av. Jose Antonio as you exit the station, turn right on Av. del Dieciocho, left on Av. Madrid, and left on C. Duque de Alba, which will lead you into the plaza (15min.). From the **bus station**, cross the intersection across from the station to get on C. Duque de Albe, which feeds right into Pl. Santa Teresa (10min.). Municipal bus #1 (75ptas) runs to Pl. Victoria from the stop near the train station, one block toward town.

Trains: (tel. 920 25 02 02), on Av. José Antonio. To: **El Escorial** (1hr., 7 per day, 500ptas)**; Villalba,** for transfer to **Segovia** (1hr., 16 per day, 980ptas); **Valladolid** (1½hr., 7 per day, 965-1500ptas); **Madrid** (1½-2hr., 20-25 per day, fewer on weekends, 835-1500ptas); **Salamanca** (1¾hr, 3 per day, 835ptas).

Buses: Av. Madrid, 2 (tel. 920 22 01 54), at Av. Portugal on the northeast side of town. To: **Segovia** (1hr., M-F 7 per day, Sa-Su 2 per day, 555ptas); **Madrid** (1½hr., 5-8 per day, 910ptas); **Salamanca** (1½ hr., M-Sa 4 per day, Su 2 per day, 700ptas).

Taxis: Pl. Santa Teresa (tel. 920 21 19 59) and at the train station (tel. 920 22 01 49). From train station to Pl. Santa Teresa 350ptas, plus 25ptas per piece of luggage.

Tourist Office: Pl. Catedral, 4 (tel. 920 21 13 87), opposite the cathedral entrance. From Pl. Santa Teresa, go through the main gate and turn right on C. Alemania. Friendly, bilingual staff. Map has routes for city tours. Open daily 10am-2pm and 4-7pm.

Police: Av. Inmaculada, 11 (tel. 920 21 11 88).

Medical Services: Hospital Provincial, Jesús del Gran Poder, 42 (tel. 920 35 72 00). **Ambulance:** tel. 920 22 14 00.

Post Office: Pl. Catedral, 2 (tel. 920 21 13 54), to the left when facing the cathedral entrance. Open M-F 8:30am-8:30pm, Sa 9:30am-2pm. **Postal Code:** 05001.

Internet Access, C. Estrada, 12 (tel. 920 257 475), down the stairs. 700ptas per hr. Open M-F 10am-2pm and 5-9pm, Sa 11am-2pm.

■ ACCOMMODATIONS

Ávila's walls are brimming with comfortable and reasonable accommodations. Those near the cathedral and Pl. Santa Teresa fill up in the summer, so call a day in advance. Ávila's only *albergue*, **Residencia Juvenil "Duperier" (HI),** has limited space and sits far from the city center.

Pensión Continental, Pl. Catedral, 6 (tel. 920 21 15 02; fax 920 25 16 91), next to the tourist office. Winding wooden staircase leads to spacious tiled rooms, all with phone. Singles 2200ptas; doubles 3700ptas, with bath 4500ptas; triples 5500ptas, with bath 6700ptas; 6 room suite 11,500ptas. 7% IVA not included. Visa, MC, AmEx.

Hostal Casa Felipe, Pl. Victoria, 12 (tel. 920 21 39 24), near the cathedral. Rooms with TVs and sinks; many have balconies overlooking the plaza. Singles 2200ptas; doubles with shower 4000ptas; triples 4500. Prices decrease Oct.-June.

Pensión Santa Ana, C. Alfonso Montalvo, 2, 2nd fl. (tel. 920 22 00 63). From the train station, down Av. José Antonio and off Pl. Santa Ana. Spacious rooms with new TVs and clean bathrooms. Singles 2500ptas; doubles 4200ptas; triples 4700ptas.

◑ FOOD

Budget sandwich shops cluster around Pl. Victoria. The most affordable restaurant row is C. San Segundo, off Pl. Santa Teresa, although the *terrazas* on the plaza are perfect for people-watching and an after dinner *cafe con leche*. The city has won fame for its *ternera de Ávila* (veal) and *mollejas* (sweetbread). The *yemas de Santa Teresa* or *yemas de Ávila*, local confections made of egg yolk and honey, are delectable. Every Friday, the **mercado** in Pl. Victoria sells cheap produce (open 10am-2pm). **El Arbol**, C. Alfonso de Montalvo, 1 (tel. 920 21 16 32), off Pl. Santa Ana, is a decent supermarket (open June-Aug. M-Sa 9:30am-2pm and 5:30-8:30pm; Sept.-May M-Sa 9:30am-2pm and 5-8pm).

Restaurante El Grande, Pl. Santa Teresa, 8 (tel. 920 22 30 83). A festive and busy family-style restaurant with extensive outdoor seating. *Raciones* 375-800ptas, *menú* 765ptas. Open daily noon-4pm and 8pm-midnight.

Gran Muralla, C. San Segundo, 18. Flashy Chinese restaurant with hanging lanterns and a 3-D mountain. Cheap, plentiful, and downright tasty servings. Lunchtime *menú* 765ptas, entrees 490-940ptas. Open daily 11:30am-4:30pm and 7:30pm-12:30am.

Casa Patas, C. San Millán, 4 (tel. 920 21 31 94), off Pl. Santa Teresa. Finding a table at this small, colorful restaurant can be tough. *Menú* 1200ptas, entrees 400-2000ptas. Open daily 9:30am-11:30pm. Visa.

Bocatti, C. San Segundo, 26 (tel. 920 25 10 80). A 50s-inspired sub shop with checkered tiles, Americana on the walls, and Elvis on the jukebox. Cold and hot sandwiches on freshly baked bread 295-490ptas. Open daily noon-midnight.

◉ SIGHTS

THE CITY WALLS (LAS MURALLAS). Ávila's inner city is surrounded by Spain's oldest and best-preserved medieval walls. Construction of the *murallas medievales* (as they are called) began in 1090, though most were completed in the next century. It was this concentrated burst of activity that gave the walls their unusual uniformity; in all, 2500 battlements, 88 towers, and 6 gates guard the historic inner city. The most imposing of the towers, **Cimorro,** is also the cathedral's bold apse. On the inside, in the corner to the right of the cathedral, are the outlines of two windows and two balconies—all that remains of a former Alcázar. If you wish to walk on the walls (200m are open to the public) start from the Puenta del Alcázar. *(With your back to Pl. Santa Teresa, the puenta is directly in front of you. Open June-Aug. Tu-Su 11am-1:30pm and 5-7:30pm; Sept.-May Tu-Su 10:30am-3:30pm. 200ptas.)*

The best view of the walls and of Ávila itself is from the **Cuatro Postes,** a four-pillared structure past the Río Adaja on the highway to Salamanca, 1.5km northwest of the city. It was at this spot that Santa Teresa was caught by her uncle while she and her brother were trying to flee to the Islamic south. *(From Pl. Santa Teresa, walk through the inner city and out the Puenta del Puente; follow the road to your right for 25min.)*

INSIDE THE WALLS

CATHEDRAL. Some believe that the profile of the huge cathedral looming over the watchtowers inspired Santa Teresa's famous metaphor of the soul as a diamond castle. Begun in the second half of the 12th century, it is the oldest Spanish cathedral in the transitional style between Romanesque and Gothic. The cathedral on its own is a worthy sight, covered with ornate details, from the golden ceiling fixture to the carved floors. View the **Altar de La Virgen de la Caridad,** where 12-year-old Santa Teresa prostrated herself after the death of her mother. Behind the main altar is the alabaster **tomb** of Cardinal Alonso de Madrigal, an Ávilan bishop and prolific writer whose dark complexion won him the title "El Tostado" (the Toasted). The nickname spread, and during the Golden Age it actually became popular to call any literary windbag *un tostado.* The **trascora** in the center is a cherubic rendition of the *Adoracion de los Magos.* The cathedral **museum** displays enormous *libros de* *canti* (hymnals) and Juan de Arfe's silver, six-leveled **Custodia del Corpus,** complete with swiveling bells. *(From Pl. Santa Teresa, walk through the puerta and take the first right onto C. Cruz Vieja, which leadings to the cathedral. Tel. 920 21 16 41. Open daily Apr.-Oct. 10am-1pm and 3:30-6pm; Nov.-Mar. 10am-1:30pm and 3:30-5:30pm. 250ptas.)*

OTHER SIGHTS. Santa Teresa's admirers built the 17th-century **Convento de Santa Teresa** on the site of her birthplace and childhood home. Gregorio Fernandez's work adorns the walls. *(From Pl. Santa Teresa, go left on C. San Segundo, right on Po. Rastro, and right through Pta. Santa Teresa. Open daily May-Sept. 9:30am-1:30pm and 3:30-9pm; Oct.-Apr. 9:30am-1:30pm and 3:30-8:30pm.)* The **Sala de Reliquias,** a small building near the convent, holds some great Santa Teresa relics, including her right ring finger, the sole of her sandal, and the cord with which she flagellated herself. *(Open daily 9:30am-1:30pm and 3:30-7:30pm. Free.)*

OUTSIDE THE WALLS

MONASTERIO DE LA ENCARNACIÓN. A short distance outside the city walls is the Monasterio de la Encarnación, where Santa Teresa lived for 30 years. The mandatory guided tour visits Santa Teresa's tiny cell and the small rooms where nuns peered at their guests through little barred windows. On the main staircase, Santa Teresa had her mystical encounter with the child Jesus. Ask for the brochure for a dramatic re-creation of the scene and a transcript of their dialogue. Upstairs from the cloister, a museum features a collection of furnishings, letters, and other personal effects given to the convent by wealthier nuns as bribes to procure entrance. Currently, 27 barefoot Carmelite nuns shuffle quietly through the halls of the monastery. *(Po. Encarnación, northwest of the city. Open daily June-Aug. 10am-1pm and 4-7pm, Sept.-May 10am-1pm and 3:30-6pm. 150ptas. Tour in Spanish, 10-15min.)*

MONASTERIO DE SANTO TOMÁS. The Monasterio de Santo Tomás was built some distance from the city walls as the summer refuge of Fernando and Isabel and a seat of the Inquisition. Inside the church and in front of the *retablo* (altarpiece) is the tomb of Prince Don Juan, Fernando and Isabel's only son, who died in 1497 at the age of 19. To the right (when facing the altar) is the **Capilla del Santo Cristo,** where Santa Teresa came to pray and confess. Also here are three contrasting cloisters: the Tuscan **Cloister of the Noviciate,** the Gothic **Cloister of Silence,** and the Renaissance-Transition **Cloister of the Kings.** *(Pl. Granada, 1. At the end of C. Jesús del Gran Poder (or Av. Alferéz Provisional). Church open daily 8am-1pm and 4-8pm. Museum open daily 11am-12:45pm and 4-7pm. Cloisters 100ptas, museum 200ptas, church free.)*

FESTIVALS. Fairs and parades of *gigantes y cabezudos* (giant effigies) pass through when the city gets a little crazy honoring Santa Teresa (Oct. 7-15). In the second or third week of July, the **Fiestas de Verano** bring exhibits, folk-singing, dancing, pop groups, fireworks, and a bullfight.

SALAMANCA

At first glance, Salamanca appears to consist of a multitude of golden arches. They are made of the burning sandstone that forms the walls, medallions, and bell towers of everything from the 13th-century university to Alberto Churriguera's Plaza Mayor. While Salamanca boasts features of a great medieval city—ancient Gothic convents and towering cathedrals—it is the university that has brought the city fame and the students who bring it character. During medieval times, Salamanca's university was grouped with those of Bologna, Paris, and Oxford as one of "the four leading lights of the world." Countless eminent Spanish intellectuals, including Antonio de Nebrija, Fernando de Rojas, and Miguel de Unamuno, have trod its hallowed halls. These days, though it lacks the prestige of years past, Salamanca's university is still filled with students, and its many study-abroad programs insure an international clientele.

CENTRAL SPAIN

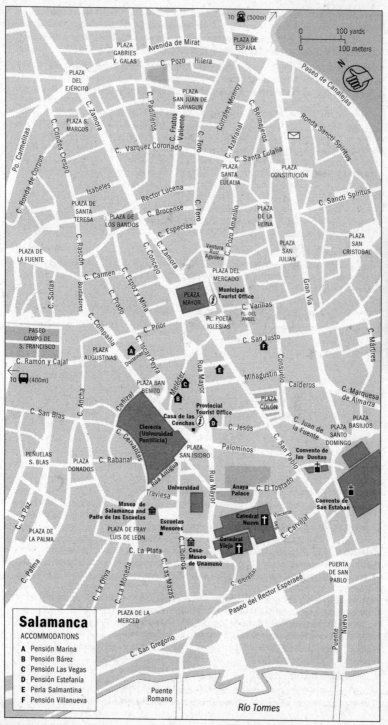

TO � (500m)

PLAZA GABRIES V. GALAS
Avenida de Mirat
PLAZA DE ESPAÑA
0 100 yards
0 100 meters
N

PLAZA DEL EJÉRCITO
C. Pozo Hilera
Paseo de Canalejas

C. Padilleros
PLAZA SAN JUAN DE SAHAGUN
Corrales Monroy
C. Bermejeros
Ronda Sancti Spíritus
✉

PLAZA S. MARCOS
C. Zamora
C. Frutos Valiente
C. Toro
C. Azafranal
C. Santa Eulalia

Po. Carmelitas
C. Ronda de Corpus
C. Condes Crespo
C. Vazquez Coronado
PLAZA SANTA EULALIA
PLAZA CONSTITUCIÓN
C. Sancti Spíritus

Isabeles
Rector Lucena
C. Toro
PLAZA DE LA REINA
PLAZA SAN CRISTOBAL

PLAZA DE SANTA TERESA
PLAZA DE LOS BANDOS
C. Brocense
C. Especias
C. Pozo Amarillo
PLAZA SAN JULIAN

PLAZA DE LA FUENTE
C. Rascón
C. Carmen
C. Concejo
C. Zamora
Ventura Ruiz Aguiera

C. Sorias
Bordadores
C. Espoz y Mina
C. Prado
PLAZA DEL MERCADO
Municipal Tourist Office

PASEO CAMPO DE S. FRANCISCO
C. Compañia
C. Prior
PLAZA MAYOR
C. Varillas
Gran Via
C. Mártires

C. Ramón y Cajal
TO 🚌 (400m)
PLAZA AUGUSTINAS
A
Desamino
C. Isar Pevia
Rua Mayor
PL. POETA IGLESIAS
PL. DEL ANGEL
Consuelo

C. San Justo
F
E
Miñagustin
Calderos
C. Marquesa de Almarza

C. Ancha
C. San Blas
C. Cañizal
Meléndez
C
B
PLAZA SAN BENITO
Provincial Tourist Office
PLAZA COLÓN

Casa de las Conchas
i
D
C. Jesús
C. Juan de la Fuente
PLAZA BASILIOS
PLAZA SANTO DOMINGO

PEÑUELAS S. BLAS
PLAZA DONADOS
C. Cervantes
C. Rabanal
Clerecía (Universidad Pontificia)
PLAZA SAN ISIDRO
Palominos
C. San Pablo
Convento de las Dueñas
✝

C. La Paz
Rua Antigua
Traviesa
Universidad
Rua Mayor
Anaya Palace
C. El Tostado
Convento de San Esteban
✝

PLAZA DE LA PALMA
C. Palma
Museo de Salamanca and Patio de las Escuelas
Escuelas Menores
Vincente
Catedral Nuevo
C. Carvajal

PLAZA DE FRAY LUIS DE LEON
C. La Plata
C. Libreros
Casa-Museo de Unamuno
Catedral Vieja
PUERTA DE SAN PABLO

C. La Oliva
C. La Moneda
C. Las Mazas
C. Gibraltar
Puente Nuevo

PLAZA DE LA MERCED
Paseo del Rector Esperaeé

C. San Gregorio
Puente Romano
Río Tormes

Salamanca

ACCOMMODATIONS

A Pensión Marina
B Pensión Bárez
C Pensión Las Vegas
D Pensión Estefanía
E Perla Salmantina
F Pensión Villanueva

⌐ GETTING THERE

Trains run to Salamanca from **Valladolid** (1¾hr., 5 per day, 7am-8:45pm, 1400ptas) and **Madrid** (2½hr., 4 per day, 8:45am-7:30pm, 2090ptas). **Buses** go from **Madrid** (3¼hr., 4 per day, 7am-9pm, 1460ptas) and **Cáceres** (4hr., 3-6 per day, 1696ptas).

⤢ ORIENTATION AND PRACTICAL INFORMATION

Picture-perfect **Plaza Mayor** is both the social and the geographic center of town. Most sights and budget hostels lie south of the plaza around R. Mayor; areas to the north tend to be newer and more expensive. Farther north, beyond **Plaza de España,** are working-class districts. The **universidad** is south of Pl. Mayor, near **Plaza de Anaya.** From the **train station,** either catch bus #1 (75 ptas) to Gran Vía, which is a block from Pl. Mercado (next to Pl. Mayor), or, with your back to the station, turn left down Po. Estación to Pl. España and walk down C. Azafranal (or C. Toro) to Pl. Mayor (30min.). From the **bus station,** either catch bus #4 to Gran Vía or walk down C. Filiberto Villalobos, cross busy Av. Alemania/Po. San Vincente, and go down C. Ramón y Cajal. Keep the park on your left; at the end (just after the Iglesia de la Purís), head left and go up C. Prior, which runs to Pl. Mayor (20min.).

TRANSPORTATION

Trains: (tel. 923 12 02 02), Po. Estación Ferrocarril, northeast of town. **RENFE Office,** Pl. Libertad, 10 (tel. 923 21 24 54). Open M-F 9am-2pm and 5-8pm. 2 regional lines. To: **Ávila** (2hr., 3 per day, 6:40am-10:15pm, 1100ptas); **Palencia** (2hr., 2 per day, 6:30am and 8pm, 1800ptas); **Valladolid** (2hr., 10 per day, 3:30am-10:05pm, 1500ptas); **Burgos** (3hr., 5 per day, 2:25am-7:50pm, 2400ptas); **Madrid** (3½hr., 4 per day, 6:40am-10pm, 2500ptas); **Lisbon** (6hr., 1 per day, 4am, 4600ptas); **Barcelona** (11½hr., 2 per day, 6100ptas).

Buses: Av. Filiberto Villalobos, 71-85 (tel. 923 23 67 17). Info open M-F 8am-8:30pm, Sa 9am-2:30pm and 4:30-6:30pm, Su 10am-2pm and 4-7pm. To: **Ciudad Rodrigo** (1hr.; M-F 11 per day, 6:45am-7:30pm; Sa 5 per day, 8:30am-5:45pm; 720ptas); **Zamora** (1hr.; M-F 20 per day, 6:40am-10:35pm; Sa 10 per day, 7:45am-8:30pm; 525ptas); **Ávila** (1-2hr., 2-7 per day, 8am-10pm, 750ptas); **Valladolid** (2hr., 6 per day, 8am-10pm, 930ptas); **Segovia** (3hr., 1-3 per day, 8:30am-5:30pm, 1260ptas); **Madrid** (regular 3hr.; M-Sa 14 per day, 7am-11pm; Su 3 per day, 7am-11pm; 2230ptas; express 2½hr., 12-15 per day, 2690ptas); **León** (3hr., 3 per day, 11am-6:30pm, 1675ptas); **Cáceres** (4hr., 3-8 per day, 1700ptas); **Barcelona** (11½hr., 3 per day, 8:10am-11pm, 6475ptas). Also to: La Alberca, Bilbao, Burgos, Cuenca, Valencia, Sevilla, Mérida, Trujillo, Badajoz, Zafra, and Santander.

Taxis: Tele-taxi (24hr. tel. 923 25 00 09) and **Radio Taxi** (24hr. tel. 923 27 11 11).

Car Rental: Avis, Po. Canalejos, 49 (tel. 923 26 97 53). Open M-F 9:30am-1:30pm and 4-7pm, Sa 9am-1:30pm. **Europcar,** Po. Canalejos, 123 (tel. 923 26 90 41). Open M-F 9:30am-1:15pm and 4:30-7:30pm, Sa 9:30am-1:15pm.

TOURIST, FINANCIAL, AND LOCAL SERVICES

Tourist Office: Municipal, Pl. Mayor, 14 (tel. 923 21 83 42). Large, helpful office. Open M-Sa 9:30am-2pm and 4:30-6:30pm, Su 10am-2pm and 4:30-6:30pm. **Provincial** (tel. 923 26 85 71), R. Mayor, at the Casa de las Conchas. Open M-F 10am-2pm and 5-7pm, Sa-Su 10am-7pm. **Info booths** open occasionally July-Sept. Students distribute maps, info, and hostel listings from booths in Pl. Anaya, the train station, and the bus station. **Café Alcaraván,** C. Compañía, 12, and **Restaurante El Bardo** (see **Food,** p. 150) have message boards offering rideshares, language trades, and rooms to rent.

Budget Travel: TIVE, Po. Carmelitas (also known as Av. Alemania), 83 (tel. 923 26 77 31). Student services, but no ticket sales. Long lines—go early. Open M-F 9am-2pm. **Juventus Travel,** Pl. Libertad, 4 (tel. 923 21 74 07; fax 923 21 74 08). Ticket sales. Open M-F 9:45am-1:45pm and 4:30-8pm, Sa 10am-1:30pm.

Currency Exchange: ATMs on C. Torro. **Banco Central Hispano** is on R. Mayor.

Luggage Storage: At the train station (300ptas) and bus station (75ptas per item).

English Bookstore: Cervantes (tel. 923 21 86 02; fax 923 26 18 95), on Pl. Santa Eulalia. Exit Pl. Mayor on C. Torro, follow C. Torro to C. Azafranal, and take C. Azafranal to Pl. Santa Eulalia; Cervantes is on your right. Enormous bookstore with a variety of volumes to choose from. Open M-F 9:45am-1:30pm and 4:30-8:30pm, Sa 9:45am-1:45pm.

Gay and Lesbian Services: Colectivo de Gais y Lesbianas de Salamanca has a telephone line (tel. 923 24 64 71) staffed M 7-9pm.

EMERGENCY AND COMMUNICATIONS

Emergency: tel. 091 or 092. **Police:** (tel. 923 27 91 38), in the Ayuntamiento, Pl. Mayor, or at Ronda de Sancti-Spiritus, 8 (tel. 923 26 53 11).

Hospital: Hospital Clínico Universitario, Paseo San Vicente, 108 (tel. 923 29 11 00).

Post Office: Gran Vía, 25-29 (tel. 923 27 04 11). Lista de Correos. Open M-F 8:30am-8:30pm and Sa 9:30am-2pm. **Postal Code:** 37001.

Internet Access: Informática Abaco Bar, C. Zamora, 7 (tel. 923 26 15 89), near Pl. Mayor. 150ptas per 30min. Open M-F 9:30am-1am, Sa 12:30pm-1am, Su 4pm-1am. **Campus Cibermático,** Pl. Mayor, 10, 1st fl. (tel. 923 27 11 31), down from the tourist office. 250ptas per 30min. Open M-F 11am-1:30pm and 5-7pm.

ACCOMMODATIONS AND CAMPING

Thanks to floods of student visitors, reasonably priced *hostales* and *pensiones* pepper the streets of Salamanca (especially off Pl. Mayor and C. Meléndez). The local tourist office has a full listing of accommodations. Try to make reservations in advance, especially during July and August.

Pensión Estefanía, C. Jesús, 3-5 (tel. 923 21 73 72 or 923 24 87 48), off Pl. Mayor. Experience the glory of Estefanía. Prime location and nice, clean rooms. The smell of the owner's cooking will entice you—but you can't have any! Showers 150ptas. Singles without sink or shower 2000ptas; doubles with shower 3500ptas; triples 4600ptas.

Hostal La Perla Salamantina, C. Sánchez Barbero, 7 (tel. 923 21 76 56). Exit Pl. Mayor via Pl. Poeta Iglesias, cross the street, and take the first right. Plenty of spacious rooms and a comfortable TV lounge. Singles 2000ptas, with shower 2500ptas; doubles with shower 3800ptas, with bath 4800ptas.

Pensión Marina, C. Doctrinos, 4, 3rd fl. (tel. 923 21 65 69), between C. Compañía and C. Prado. If you're traveling in a group of 2 and don't mind the 3-floor hike, this place is perfect. Comfortable beds and an elegant lounge that seems too nice for backpackers. Showers 200ptas. Doubles with bath 3000ptas.

Pensión Las Vegas, C. Meléndez, 13, 1st fl. (tel. 923 21 87 49), down C. Corrillo. Unlike those in the other Las Vegas, these beds don't rent by the hr. Instead you'll find cushy mattresses and TVs at a reasonable price. Hot showers 150ptas. Singles 1500ptas; doubles 3000ptas, with bath 3500ptas; triples 4000ptas, with bath 4500ptas.

Pensión Bárez, C. Meléndez, 19 (tel. 923 21 74 95). Romantic windows in several large, simple rooms. Generous owners provide TV lounge. Try to avoid the closet-sized room in the back. Showers 150ptas. Singles 1500ptas; doubles 3500ptas; triples 4500ptas.

Pensión Villanueva, C. San Justo, 8, 1st fl. (tel. 923 26 88 33). Exit Pl. Mayor via Pl. Poeta Iglesias, cross the street, and take the first left. Soft beds and spacious rooms. Singles 1500ptas, with shower 2000ptas; doubles 3000ptas, with shower 3200ptas; triples 4500ptas. Prices can change depending on the day of the week and the month.

Camping: Regio (tel. 923 13 88 88), on Ctra. Salamanca, 4km toward Madrid. Albertur buses leave from the Gran Vía every 30min. A 1st-class site with all the amenities: nature, hot showers, nearby public transportation. Pool, tennis courts, restaurants, and currency exchange in a luxury tourist complex next door. 425ptas per person, per tent, and per car; 375ptas for a 1-person tent. Visa, MC. **Don Quijote** (tel. 989 18 92 73), on Ctra. Salamanca, 4km toward Aldealengua. Minivans leave from the Gran Vía. A small, 2nd-class campsite. 375ptas per person and per tent, 350ptas per car.

◢ FOOD

Cafes and restaurants surrounding Pl. Mayor provide cuisine as varied and unique as their patrons. Be wary, however, of inflated prices in the major cafes in Pl. Mayor and R. Mayor. Instead, seek out back-alley spots where a full meal costs about 1000ptas. **Simago,** C. Torro, 82, has a downstairs **supermarket** with a large selection of fresh produce (open M-Sa 9:30am-8:30pm).

Restaurante El Bardo, C. Compañía, 8 (tel. 923 21 90 89), between the Casa de Conchas and the Clerecía. Tasty traditional Spanish food, reasonable prices, and a lively downstairs bar make El Bardo appealing to tourists and locals alike. Meat dishes 1000-1800ptas, salads 600-850ptas, vegetarian *menú* 1000ptas. Open daily 10am-5pm and 7pm-1am. Visa, MC.

Cervecería del Comercio, C. Pozo Amarillo, 23. Exit Pl. Mayor on C. Torro, take the first right, continue to the end of the street, and take a left. Eat a quiet meal in this uncrowded spot amidst a collection of photos documenting the history of Pl. Mayor and the university. Meat dishes 1200-1900ptas, salads 600ptas. Open daily 10am-1am.

La Parrilla de la Calleja, C. Ventura Ruiz Aguilera, 7. Exit Pl. Mayor on C. Torro and take the first right. Enjoy your meal in the greenhouse courtyard or the rustic brick interior decorated with bottles of wine and hanging pig legs. You'll have to dig deeper into your money belt, but it's worth it. Meat dishes 1300ptas, salads 1000ptas. Open daily 10am-1am.

La Luna Latina, C. Libreros, 4. Colorful paintings, fun waitstaff, and music that makes you regret not taking those salsa lessons. Vegetarian *platos combinados* 875-975ptas, meat dishes 975-1800ptas, salads 900ptas, *menú* 1100ptas. Open daily 10am-1am.

La Enominación, R. Mayor, 16. Prime outdoor seating for people-watching. Meat dishes 1000-2000ptas, salads 600ptas. Open 10am-1am. Visa, MC.

◉ SIGHTS

▓ PLAZA MAYOR. Salamanca's Plaza Mayor has been called one of the most beautiful squares in Spain. The grandeur of the architecture, designed by Alberto Churriguera (see **Architecture,** p. 56), is an illustration of Salamanca's rich history. The archway medallions portray past monarchs and Spanish heroes from the 19th century, when the square hosted bullfights. Locals might advocate the release of a few bulls into the plaza during the peak summer months, when the plaza floods with wide-eyed tourists and buzzing camcorders.

CASA DE LAS CONCHAS. From Pl. Mayor, exit onto R. Mayor (though the archway opposite the clock). Follow this street until you reach a second plaza with a water fountain. Take a right and note the face of the building on your right. Yup, those are shells. The 15th-century Casa de las Conchas (House of Shells), with over 300 sandstone scallop halves, is one of Salamanca's most famous landmarks. Pilgrims who journeyed to Santiago de Compostela (see p. 448) traditionally wore shells to commemorate their visit to the tomb of St. James the Apostle (in Spanish, Santiago). The owner of the *casa*, a knight of the Order of Santiago, created this monument to honor the renowned pilgrimage. The building now serves as a public library and houses the Provincial Tourist Office. *(Tel. 923 26 93 17. Open M-F 9am-9pm, Sa 10am-2pm and 5-8pm, Su 10am-2pm and 5-8pm. Free.)*

CLERECÍA. Directly across from the Conchas is the Clerecía (Royal College of the Holy Spirit). The narrow street prevents one from truly appreciating the wonderful, Baroque facade. The college, founded in 1611 by Queen Margarita de Austria (Felipe III's wife), has a unique U-shaped groundplan, allowing visitors to peer over the Cloister of Studies into the lower gallery and courtyard. *(Tel. 923 26 46 60. Open for mass M-Sa 1:15pm and 7:30pm, Su 12:30pm. Free.)*

RIBBIT FOR HER PLEASURE. Within the 16th-century facade of the university's entryway lies a hidden frog with an ambiguous (or should we say amphibious?) significance. Some believe the frog, said to be Salamanca's "gray eminence," represents the dankness of prison life, while others say it refers to the earthly pleasures of the flesh and the conflict between desire and virtue. Whatever its purpose may be, legend promises that those who can spot the frog without assistance will be blessed with good luck and even marriage.

For those who think this is all a bunch of bull(frog), here's a hint. Look to the far right of Fernando and Isabel and up a tad(pole). There's the frog—as for the spouse, however, you're on your own.

◪THE UNIVERSITY

Tel. 923 29 44 00. Museum tel. 923 29 12 25. From Pl. Mayor follow R. Mayor, veer right onto R. Antigua, then left onto C. Libreros; the university is on the left. University and museum open M-F 9:30am-1:30pm and 4-7:30pm, Sa 9:30am-1:30pm and 4-7pm, Su 10am-2pm. Admission 300ptas, students and seniors 150ptas. Tickets sold until 30min. before closing.

The focal point of Salamanca, the great university, established in 1218, is best entered from the **Patio de las Escuelas,** left off C. Libreros. The statue here portrays Fray Luis de León, a university professor and one of the most respected literati of the Golden Age. A Hebrew scholar and classical Spanish stylist, Fray Luis was arrested by the Inquisition for translating Solomon's *Song of Songs* into Castilian and for preferring the Hebrew version of the Bible to the Latin one. After five years of imprisonment, he returned to the university and began his first lecture, *"Decíamos ayer…"* ("As we were saying yesterday…"). The university's entryway is one of the best examples of Spanish Plateresque, a style named after the work of *plateros* (silversmiths). The central medallion represents Fernando and Isabel.

The old lecture halls inside are open to the public. **Aula Fray Luis de León** has been left in more or less its original state. Students in medieval times considered the hard benches luxurious, as most students then sat on the floor. A plaque bears Unamuno's famous love poem to the students of Salamanca. The **Paraninfo** (auditorium) contains Baroque tapestries and a portrait of Carlos IV attributed to Goya. Fray Luis is buried in the 18th-century **chapel.** The **Antigua Biblioteca** (old library) is the most spectacular room of all, located atop a magnificent Plateresque staircase displaying statues and historic books. Salamancan souvenir shops often reproduce the sign in the library that threatens excommunication for those who steal or damage books. (Oh, and don't miss the room of fossilized turtles, apparently the second most important such collection in the world.)

On the exterior patio are the **Escuelas Menores,** with a smaller version of the main entryway's Plateresque facade. There the **University Museum** preserves the **Cielo de Salamanca,** the library's famous 15th-century fresco of the zodiac, painted on the ceiling by the celebrated Gallego brothers, Francisco and Fernando. Take a peek at the intricate strongbox with its many locks.

◪CASA MUSEO DE UNAMUNO.

To the right of the university's main entrance is the absorbing Casa-Museo de Unamuno. Miguel de Unamuno, Rector of the University at the beginning of this century, is revered as one of the founding figures of the Spanish literary movement known as the "Generation of '98." Unamuno passionately opposed dictatorship and encouraged his students to do so as well. His stand against General Primo de Rivera's 1923 *coup d'état* led to his dismissal from the rector's post; he was triumphantly reinstated some years later. Unamuno's intricate origami and thoughts on his birth create some of the more charming exhibits. *(Tel. 923 29 44 00, ext. 1196. Open July-Sept. Tu-F 9:30am-1:30pm, Sa-Su 10am-noon; Oct.-June Tu-F 9:30am-1:30pm and 4-6pm, Sa-Su 10am-2pm. Research room open M-F 8:30am-2:30pm. Mandatory tour in Spanish every 30min., 300ptas. Ring bell if house appears closed.)*

MUSEO DE SALAMANCA. The Museo occupies a beautiful 15th-century building that was once home to Álvarez Albarca, physician to Fernando and Isabel. Along with the *Casa de las Conchas*, this structure is among Spain's most important examples of 15th-century architecture; to a certain extent, the building upstages the art inside. The museum does have an intriguing collection of painting and sculpture as well as some temporary exhibits in archaeology and ethnology. Its most important canvases are Juan de Flandes's portrait of Saint Andrew and Luis de Morales's *Llanto por Cristo muerto*, both from the 16th century, and Vaccaro's *Inmaculada*. *(Tel. 923 21 22 35. Open Tu-F 9:45am-1:45pm and 4:45-7:15pm, Sa 10:15am-1:15pm and 4:45-7:45pm, Su 10:15am-1:45pm. 200ptas.)*

NEW CATHEDRAL. Rome wasn't built in a day, and neither was this. In fact, it took 220 years (1513-1733) to construct this striking Gothic Spanish cathedral. While several subsequent architects decided to retain the original late-Gothic style, they could not resist adding touches from later periods, most notably its Baroque tower. Restorers from the 20th century succumbed to the same temptation, adding an astronaut, a bull, and even a demon eating ice cream to the side entrance's facade. *(From Pl. Mayor, walk down R. Mayor into Pl. Anaya; the New Cathedral is in front of you. Open daily Apr.-Sept. 9am-2pm and 4-8pm; Oct.-Mar. 9am-1pm and 4-6pm. Free.)*

CATEDRAL VIEJA. The smaller Catedral Vieja (1140) was built in the Romanesque style. Apocalyptic angels separate the sinners from the saved inside the arresting cupola. The oldest original part of the cathedral is the **Capilla de San Martín,** with brilliantly colored frescoes dating from 1242. The **Capilla de Santa Bárbara,** also called the Capilla del Título, was what students used to face as they took their final exams. The **cathedral museum** features a paneled ceiling by Fernando Gallego and houses the Mudéjar Salinas organ (one of the oldest in Europe). Be sure to check out the famed **Patio Chico,** behind the cathedral, to get a splendid view of both cathedrals. *(Museum tel. 923 21 74 76. Cathedral open daily Apr.-Sept. 9am-2pm and 4-8pm; Oct.-Mar. 9am-1pm and 4-6pm. Cathedral, cloister, and museum 300ptas.)*

CONVENTO DE SAN ESTEBAN. While on a fundraising endeavor, Columbus spent time in one of Salamanca's most dramatic monasteries, the Convento de San Esteban. During the afternoon, its facade becomes a solid mass of light depicting the stoning of St. Stephen and the crucifixion of Christ. The beautiful **Claustro de los Reyes (Kings's Cloister)** displays a medley of Gothic and Plateresque. Churriguera's central altarpiece (1693) in the church is a masterpiece of Spanish Baroque. *(Downhill from the cathedrals. Tel. 923 21 50 00. Open daily Apr.-Sept. 9am-1pm and 4-8pm; Oct.-Mar. 9am-1pm and 5-6:30pm. 200ptas.)*

CONVENTO DE LAS DUEÑAS. Convento de las Dueñas, formerly the palace of a court official, has one of the most elegant cloisters in Salamanca. Medallions adorning the walls depict famous Salamancans, while exuberantly gargoyled columns line the 2nd floor. A shop selling holy candies made by the nuns is on the 1st floor. *(Near Convento de San Esteban. Tel. 923 21 54 42. Open daily Apr.-Sept. 10:30am-2pm and 4:30-7pm; Oct.-Mar. 10:30am-1pm and 4:30-5:30pm. 200ptas, students 100ptas.)*

PUENTE ROMANO. Take a stroll to the Puente Romano, a 2000-year-old Roman bridge spanning the scenic Río Tormes. The bridge was part of an ancient Roman road called the *Camino de la Plata* (Silver Way) that ran from Mérida in Extremadura to Astorga. The *Camino* was very important during the Roman occupation of Spain and some say that even Hannibal and his elephants once crossed it. Nowadays you are more likely to find students (and an occasional horse) basking in the sun by the river. The bridge is guarded at its near end by a headless, granite bull, called the **Toro Ibérico.** Though it dates back to pre-Roman times, the bull gained fame in the 16th century. It was then that it appeared in *Lazarillo de Tormes*, the prototype of the picaresque novel and a predecessor of *Don Quijote*. In one episode the novel's short hero gets his head slammed into the bull's stone ear after he cheats his employer. *(Pl. Mayor.)*

♫ ENTERTAINMENT

The **Plaza Mayor** is the town's social center. It is filled day and night with locals, students, and tourists who come to lounge in its cafes or to take a stroll. At night, members of various local college or graduate-school **tunas** (medieval-style student troubadour groups) often finish their rounds here. Dressed in traditional black capes, they strut around the plaza with guitars, mandolins, *bandurrias*, and tambourines, serenading women. When the show is over, the musicians make excellent drinking partners. Student nightlife is also concentrated on the Gran Vía, C. Bordadores, and side streets. Bars, which sometimes don't open until 3am, blast music so loud, it's a wonder that the beats don't have the same effects as the Lisbon earthquake of 1755 (which damaged Salamanca's Cathedral Vieja). C. Prior and C. Rua Mayor are full of bars; locals gather in the charming *terrazas* on Pl. de la Fuente, off Av. Alemania. More intense partying occurs off C. Varillas.

Camelot, C. Bordadores, 3 (tel. 923 21 21 82). Medieval chic. Go to Camelot to drink a lot. This monastery-turned-club is one of the stops on the **Gatsby** and **Cum Laude** (C. Prior) club-hopping routes. Beer 330ptas, mixed drinks 550 ptas.

Café Moderno, Gran Vía, 75 (tel. 923 26 01 47). This popular bar attracts much of the post-theater crowd. Participate in one of the frequent games (like Wheel of Fortune) while dancing to American top-40. Beer 300ptas, mixed drinks 500ptas.

Submarino, C. San Justo, 27, off Gran Vía. Built in an old submarine. Mainly gay clientele grooves to techno beats under black lights. Beer 350ptas, mixed drinks 550ptas.

Birdland, C. Azafranal, 57 (tel. 923 26 13 57), by Pl. España. Drink to modern funk jazz. Small tables by large windows overlooking the square make Birdland a good nest for couples. Beer 300ptas, mixed drinks 500ptas. Open nightly 5pm-4:30am.

Pub Rojo y Negro, C. Espoz y Mina, 22. Scrumptious coffee, liqueur, and ice cream in an old-fashioned setting catering to couples. Ice cream 200-1100ptas. Beer 370ptas, mixed drinks 575ptas. Open M-F noon-2:30am, Sa-Su noon-4:30am.

Café Novelty, on Pl. Mayor. The oldest cafe in town and a meeting place for students and professors. Even Miguel de Unamuno was a regular. Beer 175ptas, mixed drinks 300ptas. Open until 2am.

El Corrillo Café, C. Meléndez, 14-18 (tel. 923 27 19 17). Live jazz (or hip hop on the radio) for the ultra-hip in a chill setting with abstract art. Make friends with the bald bartender with 4 hula-hoop earrings. Performances 1000ptas.

Lugares, a free, slim pamphlet distributed at the tourist office and at some bars, lists everything from movies and special events to bus schedules. Posters at the **Colegio Mayor** (Palacio de Anaya) advertise university events, free films, and student theater. During the summer, Salamanca sponsors the **Verano Cultural de Salamanca,** with silent movies, contemporary Spanish cinema, pop singers, and theater groups. On June 12, in honor of San Juan de Sahagún, there is a **corrida de toros** charity event. From September 8 to 21, Salamanca indulges in festivals and exhibitions, most with bull themes. This is also a fun place to be during *Semana Santa*.

DAYTRIPS FROM SALAMANCA

CIUDAD RODRIGO

The honey-colored stonework of Ciudad Rodrigo, a medieval town just 27km from Portugal, can be seen glistening from the surrounding plains. The old city's flower-covered walls enclose intricate 18th-century defenses and other masonry treasures. These stone features and a quirky cathedral make it a perfect daytrip from Salamanca (1¼hr. by bus).

⚄ PRACTICAL INFORMATION. Ciudad Rodrigo is easily accessible by bus from Salamanca; trains are infrequent and the station is 35 minutes from the old city. The **bus station** (tel. 923 46 10 09) is on C. Campo de Toledo, and buses go to **Salamanca** (1¼hr., M-F 8 per day, Sa 5 per day, Su 3 per day, 720ptas). From the bus station's main entrance, take a left (with the station behind you) and then the second right (uphill), and pass through the stone arch; the **tourist office,** Pl. Amayuelas, 5 (tel. 923 46 05 61), is immediately on your left, across the street and before the cathedral (open M-Sa 10am-2pm and 5-8pm). Municipal **police** are at Pl. Mayor, 27 (tel. 923 46 04 68). **Post office,** C. Dámaso Ledesma, 12 (tel. 923 46 01 17), in Pl. Mayor, in a bizarre 16th-century building also known as **Casa de los Vásquez** (open M-F 8:30am-2:30pm, Sa 9am-1pm).

⚄⚄ ACCOMMODATIONS AND FOOD. Pensión Madrid, C. Madrid, 20 (tel. 923 46 24 67), off Pl. Mayor on the side perpendicular to the Ayuntamiento, has well-ventilated rooms. (Doubles 3000ptas; super triple with bath and kitchenette 6000ptas.) For good, cheap food and wall-to-wall pictures of the baddest bulls and the matadors who love them, check out **El Sanatorio,** Pl. Mayor, 12 (tel. 923 46 00 24), which serves meat dishes (350-850ptas) and salads (500ptas). Cafes on Pl. Mayor serve inexpensive *platos combinados* (450-575ptas).

⚄ SIGHTS. The **cathedral** is the town's masterpiece. Originally a Romanesque church commissioned by Fernando II of León, it was later modified in the 16th-century Gothic style. The **coro** (chorus) was the master work of Rodrigo Alemán, who worked on it from 1498 to 1504. Look for the sculptor's signature—a carving of his head hidden among the rest of the carvings. The two 16th-century organs star in a series of concerts every August. The cathedral's **claustro** alone merits a trip to Ciudad Rodrigo. The columns are covered with figures doing everything from making love to playing peek-a-boo, even flirting with cannibalism. The cathedral's **museum** is filled with strange but interesting pieces, including an ancient clavichord, the cathedral's "ballot box," richly embroidered robes and slippers worn by bishops and priors, and Velázquez's *Llanto de Adam y Eva por Ariel muerto.* (Cathedral open daily 9:30am-1pm and 4-8pm. Free. Cloister and museum open daily 10am-1pm and 4-6pm. 200ptas. Great tours in Spanish.)

Also of note is the 14th- and 15th-century **Castillo de Enrique de Trastámara,** by Gonzalo Arias de Genizaro, with a view that spans the surrounding countryside and the Agueda River. It has gone from being the home of noble families to a resort for modern-day nobility, as it is now a *parador de turismo* (luxury hotel).

ALBA DE TORMES

Santa Teresa left her heart in Alba de Tormes. In fact, it's in a big urn, along with her body, in the lovely **Convento de la Anunciación,** which she founded in 1571. In her autobiography, she writes that her heart was pierced by an angel of the Lord with a fiery dart and after repeated stabbings, she was left "on fire with the great love of God." Her heart and the convent lie in Plazuela de Santa Teresa, two blocks from peaceful Pl. Mayor. If you'd like a tour, ask a guide at the **Museo Teresiano** across the street. The museum holds other parts of Santa Teresa and bits of San Juan de la Cruz. (Open daily 10am-1:30pm and 4-7:30pm. Donation requested.) A few blocks down from Pl. Mayor is the **Castillo de los Duques de Alba,** remnants of a 15th- to 16th-century structure which was excavated from 1991-3. The castle displays Renaissance frescoes and an archaeological exhibit of the uncovered remains. Long wires hooked to the castle's top appear to provide a clothesline for locals. (Open July-Aug. Sa-Su; Sept.-June tourist office staff can let you in.) Though small, Alba de Tormes also boasts seven churches, monasteries, and convents, plus a neo-Gothic basilica. Alba de Tormes makes an easy daytrip by **bus** from Salamanca (30min., 8-12 per day, 175ptas). The **tourist office,** C. Lepanto, 4 (tel. 923 30 08 98), aids visitors when it's open (hours not fixed, but open daily June-Aug. about 11am-1pm and 4:30-6:30pm; Sept.-May 10:30am-2pm and 4-6:30pm).

LA ALBERCA AND PEÑA DE FRANCIA

Three mountain ranges to the south conceal some delightful small towns on the plains of Castilla y León and Extremadura. **La Alberca,** a charming, rustic village, was the first rural town in the country to be named an official National Historic-Artistic Monument (1940). Above La Alberca in the Sierra de Francia rises the province's highest peak, **Peña de Francia** (1723m). Determined souls can scale the mountain from La Alberca. **Empresa V. Cosme** (tel. 923 30 02 71) runs **buses** from Salamanca to La Alberca (1½hr.; M-F 2 per day; Sa 1 per day, 12:30pm; Su 1 per day, 9:30am; 625ptas). For more info about La Alberca or Peña de Francia, contact the **tourist office** (tel. 923 41 52 91, ext. 15; open June-Sept. M-F 10am-1pm and 5-7pm, Sa 10am-1pm and 4-6pm, Su 10am-1pm).

ZAMORA

Provincial Zamora (pop. 65,000) has not seen much action since the 12th century, when Sancho II died here during his attempt to subdue his rebellious sister Doña Urraca and consolidate his hold on the House of Castilla. Although she had been passed over in her father's will in favor of Sancho, Urraca managed to steal away her brother's inheritance by threatening to sleep with every man in the House of Castilla if the kingdom was not passed to her. Vestiges of this illustrious and shocking past attract some history buffs—but not too many of them.

⚐ ORIENTATION AND PRACTICAL INFORMATION. The train and bus stations are both a 20-minute walk from Pl. Mayor. Upon exiting the train station, go straight through the rotary onto C. Alfonso Peña (which becomes Av. Tres Cruces). Continue to Pl. Alemania and turn left onto C. Alfonso IX. Walk two blocks and turn right on **Calle de Santa Clara,** a major pedestrian street that leads to Pl. Mayor. From the entrance of the bus station, turn left and then left again along the side of the station. Make yet another left onto C. Alfonso Peña and follow the directions from the train station.

Trains leave from the station (tel. 980 52 19 56; 24hr. tel. 980 52 11 10) at the end of C. Alfonso Peña. Though prices and times are known to fluctuate, trains go to: **Valladolid** (1½hr., 2 per day, 8:34am and 7:20pm, 1000ptas); **Madrid** (4hr., 4 per day, 2:35am-6:20pm, 3200ptas); **La Coruña** (7hr., 2 per day, 1:40am and 5pm, 4400ptas); and **Barcelona** (12hr., 1 per day, 7:40pm, 5900ptas). **Buses** depart from C. Alfonso Peña, 3 (tel. 980 52 12 81 or 980 52 12 82), to: **Valladolid** (1½hr.; M-F 7 per day, 8:30am-8:15pm; Sa 5 per day, 8:30am-6pm; Su 3 per day, 8:30am-8pm; 800ptas); **León** (2hr., 7 per day, 7am-7:30pm, 1160ptas); **Madrid** (3½hr.; M-Sa 6 per day, 7am-8pm; Su 6 per day, 10:30am-9pm; 1600ptas); **La Coruña** (7hr., 3 per day, 6:55am-2:35pm, 3125ptas); **Barcelona** (12hr., 3 per day, 8:30am-midnight, 6675ptas); **Bragança, Portugal** (2hr., 3 per week, M 2:45pm, W 4pm, F 12:15am, 2000ptas).

The **tourist office,** C. Santa Clara, 20 (tel. 980 53 18 45; fax 980 53 38 13), hands out multilingual brochures, maps, and a hostel guide (open M-F 9am-2pm and 5-7pm, Sa 10am-2pm and 5-10pm); **luggage storage** is available in the bus station (90ptas per bag; open daily 7am-midnight) and train station (300ptas per bag; open 24hr.). **Municipal police** tel. 980 54 87 26. **Post office,** C. Santa Clara, 15 (tel. 980 51 33 71 or 980 51 07 67; fax 980 53 03 35), past C. Benquente, offers Lista de Correos and **fax** service (open M-F 8:30am-8:30pm, Sa 9am-2pm); **postal code:** 49014.

⚐⌂ ACCOMMODATIONS AND FOOD. For simple rooms at reasonable prices, try the streets off C. Alfonso Peña by the train station or off C. Santa Clara near Pl. Mayor. Call ahead during the fiestas the last week of June, and try negotiating prices in the off-season. If you want to stay close to the train and bus stations, check out **Pensión Fernando III,** Pl. Fernando III, 2 (tel. 980 52 36 88). From the bus station entrance, take the first two lefts and then the first right uphill off C. Alfonso Peña onto C. Brahones. The large, sunlit rooms are a bargain. All rooms have sinks; bathrooms are down the hall. (Curfew 1am. Singles 1000-1300ptas;

doubles 2000-2500ptas; triples 2900ptas.) If you'd rather be near Pl. Mayor, try **Pensión Balborraz** (tel. 980 51 55 19), on C. Balborraz. From the tourist office, walk down C. Santa Clara toward Pl. Mayor. Balborraz is the street on the left just before the plaza. Spacious, old, dim rooms. (Singles 1500ptas; doubles 2400ptas.)

Dining in Zamora tends to be expensive. Restaurants cluster near C. Santa Clara and around Pl. Mayor, particularly on C. Herreros. Roast meats, especially *preses de ternera* (veal) and *bacalao a la tranca* (cod), are regional specialties. The **Mercado de Abastos,** in a domed building just to the left off C. Santa Clara after the tourist office, provides all the basics (open M-F 7am-2pm). Steer a shopping cart at **Champion** on C. Victor Gallego. When traveling down Av. Tres Cruces (with the train and bus stations behind you), take a right U-turn onto C. Victor Gallego just before reaching a small plaza. (Open M-Sa 9:15am-9:15pm.)

🔂 **SIGHTS.** Zamora's foremost monument is its mostly Romanesque **cathedral** (1135), a stocky building topped with a Byzantine dome. Take a moment to observe the detail and complexity of the main altar, made of marble, gold and silver. Don't miss the golden angels on the baby blue background above. Inside the cloister, the **Museo de la Catedral** features the priceless 15th-century **Black Tapestries.** These gruesome tapestries tell the story of the Trojan War, depicting, among other things, numerous warriors and princesses right before they were decapitated. (Cathedral open daily 10am-1pm and 5-8pm. Free. Museum open Apr.-Sept. Tu-Sa 11am-2pm and 5-8pm, Su 11am-2pm; Oct.-Mar. Tu-Sa 11am-2pm and 4-6pm, Su 11am-2pm. 300ptas.) **Roman walls** uphill from the cathedral command a fine view of the mighty Río Duero. Look back toward the city center at the **Iglesia de San Isidoro;** gargoyle-like white storks often perch there.

Eight handsome **Romanesque churches** remain within the walls of the old city, each gleaming in the wake of recent restoration. If you suspect they all look the same, drop by the intricately carved porch of **La Magdalena.** The luminescent marble-veined windows in **Iglesia San Juan** and the bright green-and-orange organ in **Iglesia San Ildefonso** are also worth a look. (All open July-Oct. Tu-Sa 10am-1pm and 5-8pm; Nov.-June only during mass. Free.) The **Museo de Semana Santa,** in sleepy Pl. Santa María la Nueva, is a rare find. Hooded mannequins stand guard over elaborately sculpted floats from the turn of the century. To reach the museum from Pl. Mayor, take C. Sacramento and turn right on C. Barandales. (Open M-Sa 10am-2pm and 5-8pm, Su 10am-2pm. 300ptas.)

Entertainment in Zamora consists of the periodical festivals that take over the plaza and a decent nightlife found in the bars on C. Herreros. **Mesón Los Abuelos,** C. Herreros, 30, is the local hangout. You would be hard-pressed to find any real *abuelos* (grandfathers) in this youth-filled dance club. (Open daily noon-3am.)

LEÓN

Images of lions are everywhere in León and residents of the city refer to themselves as *leones* ("lions"). Strangely, the city's name has nothing to do with lions—rather it stems from *legio* (Latin for legion), a name that the 7th Roman Legion gave the town in AD 68. Formerly the seat of the Asturia-León kingdom and the center of Christian Spain, today León is a bustling provincial capital and university town. Its financial success comes from its fertile agricultural hinterland and the deposits of iron and cobalt surrounding the city. The city itself is best known for its cathedral, whose spectacular blue stained-glass windows have earned the city the nickname *La Ciudad Azul* (The Blue City). Proud *leoneses* boast that their cathedral is the finest in of all Spain; they may very well be right.

📧 **GETTING THERE**

Trains run to León from: **Valladolid** (1½hr., 7 per day, 7:30am-9pm, 1400ptas); **Burgos** (2hr., 8 per day, 2000ptas); **Oviedo** (2½hr., 8 per day, 7:30am-11pm, 925-1600ptas). **Buses** go from **Valladolid** (2hr., 9 per day, 12:45am-9:45pm, 1070ptas).

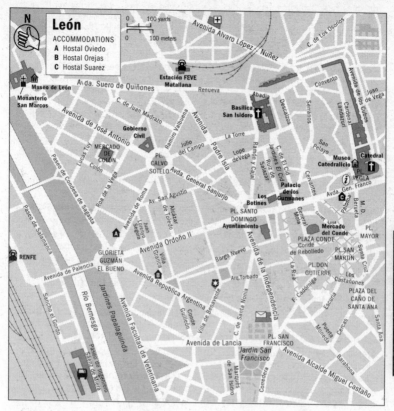

▶ ORIENTATION AND PRACTICAL INFORMATION

Most of León, including the old city and modern commercial district, lies on the east side of the **Río Bernesga.** The bus and train stations are across the river in the west end. Av. Palencia (a left out of the bus station or right out of the train station) leads across the river to **Plaza Guzmán el Bueno,** where, after the Glorieta Guzmán Bueno rotary, it becomes **Avenida de Ordoño II** and leads to León's cathedral. Av. Ordoño II then bisects the new city and at Pl. Santo Domingo becomes **Avenida del Generalísimo Franco,** which splits the old town in two.

TRANSPORTATION

Trains: RENFE, Av. Astorga, 2 (info. tel. 987 27 02 02; station tel. 987 22 37 04). With Pl. Guzmán el Bueno behind you, cross the river and continue on Av. Astorga until the station is on the left. Open 6am-10pm. To: **Astorga** (45min., 12 per day, 1:50am-8:29pm, 600ptas); **Palencia** (1½hr., 17 per day, 12:15am-9:42pm, 1065ptas); **Valladolid** (2½hr., 12 per day, 12:25am-8:32pm, 1240ptas); **Oviedo** (2½hr., 8 per day, 4:55am-8:05pm, 925-1500ptas); **Madrid** (4½-5½hr., 9 per day, 1:08am-7:05pm, 3315 ptas); **La Coruña** (7hr., 5 per day, 4:05am-5:08pm, 3200-4400ptas). **FEVE,** Av. Padre Isla, 48 (tel. 987 22 59 19), north of Pl. Santo Domingo. Trains to local destinations. A full train and bus schedule is printed daily in *Diario de León* (110ptas).

Buses: Estación de Autobuses (tel. 987 21 00 00), Po. Ingeniero Saenz de Miera. Info open M-Sa 7:30am-9pm. To: **Astorga** (45min.; M-F 16 per day, 6:30am-9:30pm; Sa 7 per day, 9:30am-8:30pm; Su 6 per day, 9:30am-8:30pm; 405ptas); **Valladolid** (2hr., 8 per day, 2:30am-10:30pm, 1070ptas); **Zamora** (2½hr.; M-F 5 per day, 8am-6pm; Sa

4 per day, 8am-5pm; Su 4 per day, 10:15am-7pm; 1170ptas); **Madrid** (4½hr.; M-F 12 per day, 2:30am-10:30pm; Sa-Su 8 per day, 2:30am-7:30pm; regular 2610ptas, express 4200ptas); **Santander** (5hr., F 3:30pm and Su 7:30pm, 2680ptas).

Taxis: Radio Taxi (tel. 987 24 24 51).

Car Rental: Hertz, C. Sampiro, 20 (tel. 987 23 19 99). Must be at least 25 and have had a license for at least 1 year. Open M-F 9am-2pm and 4-7pm, Sa 9am-1pm.

TOURIST, FINANCIAL, AND LOCAL SERVICES

Tourist Office: Pl. Regla, 4 (tel. 987 23 70 82; fax 987 27 33 91), in front of the cathedral. Free city maps, regional brochures, and accommodations guide. English spoken. Open M-F 10am-2pm and 5-7:30pm, Sa 10am-2pm and 4:30-8:30pm, Su 10am-2pm.

Budget Travel: TIVE, C. Arquitecto Torbado, 4 (tel. 987 20 09 51), just off Pl. Cortes. ISIC 500ptas. HI cards 1800ptas. Open M-F 9am-2pm.

Currency Exchange: Banco Central Hispano, Pl. Santo Domingo. Follow Av. Ordoño II into the plaza. Open M-F 8:30am-2:30pm.

Luggage Storage: At the **train station,** lockers 400ptas. Open 24hr. At the **bus station,** 25ptas per bag. Open M-F 9am-2pm and 6-8pm, Sa 9am-2pm.

English Bookstore: Pastor, Pl. Santo Domingo, 4 (tel. 987 22 58 56). Follow Av. Ordoño II into the plaza. Open M-F 10am-12:30pm and 4:30-8pm, Sa 10am-1:45pm.

EMERGENCY AND COMMUNICATIONS

Emergency: call 091 or 092. **Police:** C. Villa Benavente, 6 (tel. 987 20 73 12).

Medical Services: Hospital Virgen Blanca (tel. 987 23 74 00).

Post Office: (tel. 987 23 40 79; fax 987 23 47 01), Jardín San Francisco. From Pl. Santo Domingo, go down Av. Independencia; the post office is opposite Parque San Francisco on the left. Lista de Correos and **faxes.** Open 8am-8pm. **Postal Code:** 24071.

Internet Access: Locutorio La Rúa, C. La Rúa, 8 (tel. 987 23 01 06). Take C. Ancha from Pl. Santo Domingo and turn right on C. La Rúa. 500ptas per hr. Open M-F 9:30am-2:30pm and 4:30-11pm, Sa 9:30am-2:30pm. **Pub Sherwood** (tel. 987 22 28 20), C. Juan Lorenzo Seguro. From Av. Ordoño II, with your back to the river, take a left onto C. Juan Lorenzo Seguro. 500ptas per hr. Open daily 7am-4am.

■ ACCOMMODATIONS

Budget beds are not scarce in León, but hostels and *pensiones* often fill during the June fiestas. Look on Av. de Roma, Av. Ordoño II, and Av. República Argentina, which lead into the new town from Pl. Guzmán el Bueno. *Pensiones* are also scattered on the streets by the train and bus stations. These establishments are less centrally located and are surrounded by empty streets that can be a bit intimidating at night. Check the tourist office map for more locations.

Hostal Oviedo, Av. Roma, 26, 2nd fl. (tel. 987 22 22 36), off Pl. Guzmán el Bueno. Friendly and accommodating proprietors offer huge, well-maintained rooms, many with sinks and terraces. Expect to see lots of Americans. Heated in winter. Public telephone. Singles 2000ptas; doubles 3300ptas; triples 5000ptas.

Hostel Suárez, Av. Generalísimo Franco, 7 (tel. 987 25 42 88). Prime location, seconds away from the cathedral. Large windows make for great people-watching. Kitchen. No heat. Singles 1800ptas; doubles with bath 3000ptas.

Hostel Orejas, Av. República Argentina, 28 (tel. 987 25 29 09), off Pl. Guzmán el Bueno. Large windows illuminate each brand-new room, complete with bath, shower, and all the amenities. Wheelchair accessible. Singles 5000ptas; doubles 6000ptas.

Consejo de Europa (HI), Po. Parque, 2 (tel. 987 20 02 06). With the river on the right, walk along Av. Facultad de Veterinaria. When you reach Pl. Toros, walk behind the stadium to Po. Parque. A basic but recently renovated hostel. Reservations recommended. Open late June-Aug. Breakfast 300ptas. Dorms 950ptas, over 26 1100ptas.

🍴 FOOD

Inexpensive eateries cluster near the cathedral and on the small streets off Av. Generalísimo Franco; also check Pl. San Martín, near Pl. Mayor. Meat-lovers will rejoice as many variations of pork top the local menus. In June, 3500km of trout-fishable streams invite the **International Trout Festival.** Fresh produce in all shapes and sizes is available at the **Mercado Municipal del Conde,** Pl. Conde, off C. General Mola (open M-Sa 9am-3:30pm). For groceries, try **Día Auto Servicion** in Pl. Picara Justina, on Av. República Argentina (open M-Sa 9:30am-2:15pm and 5-8:15pm).

Calle Ancha (tel. 987 21 01 83), C. Generalísimo Franco, between C. General Mola and C. Conde Luna. A 2min. walk from the cathedral. Fill your belly with fresh veggies, quiche, or fish in a modern, hip setting. Both the gourmet vegetarian *menú* (900ptas) and the non-vegetarian *menú económica* (950ptas) are great deals—they come with a bottle of wine. Open daily 1-4pm and 9:15pm-midnight. Visa, MC.

Cafetería-Restaurante Catedral, C. Mariano Domínguez Berrueta, 17 (tel. 987 21 59 18), to the right when facing the cathedral. Monumental portions make the 1300pta *menú* a great bargain. Salads 600ptas. Sandwiches 500-700ptas. Open M and Th-Sa 1-4 and 8-11pm, Tu-W 8-11pm. Visa, MC.

Zalacain, C. la Rúa, 24 (tel. 987 21 08 21). Walk down Av. Generalísimo Franco when facing the cathedral and take a right on C. la Rúa. Classic vegetarian specialities and pleasant outdoor seating. Salads 700ptas. Meat dishes 925-1800ptas. Visa, MC.

Lleras 38, C. Burgos Nuevo, 48 (tel. 987 20 51 63), less than a block from the intersection with Av. República Argentina. A funky restaurant offering everything from spaghetti and trout to melon and tongue. *Menú* 1100ptas. Open daily 8am-1am.

👁 SIGHTS

📷CATHEDRAL. The 13th-century Gothic cathedral, *La Pulchra Leonina*, is arguably the most beautiful cathedral in Spain. It is also one of Spain's best examples of Gothic architecture. The exceptional facade depicts smiling saints amidst bug-eyed monsters munching on the damned. But the real attractions are the glorious rose windows (with their spirals of saints), the vivid stained-glass interior, and the glass gardens (with tiny faces and luminous petals). The cathedral's museum includes gruesome wonders, including a skeleton, a "Statue of Death," and a sculpture depicting the skinning of a saint. *(Tel. 987 87 57 70. Cathedral open daily 8:30am-1:30pm and 4-8pm, until 7pm in winter. Free. Museum open M-F 9:30am-1:30pm and 4-7pm, Sa 9:30am-1:30pm. 500ptas. You must be accompanied by a guide to see much of the exhibit.)*

BASÍLICA SAN ISIDORO. The Basílica San Isidoro was dedicated in the 11th century to San Isidoro de Sevilla. After his death his remains were brought from Muslim-dominated Andalucía to the Christian stronghold of León. The corpses of countless royals rest in the impressive Panteón Real, where the ceilings are covered by vibrant 12th-century frescoes. The unusual Annunciation and medieval agricultural calendar are particularly noteworthy. Admission to the pantheon includes entrance to the library, which houses a 10th-century handwritten Bible, and to the treasury, home of Doña Urraca's famous agate chalices. *(Open July-Aug. M-Sa 9am-8pm, Su 9am-2pm; Sept.-June M-Sa 9am-1:30pm and 4-7pm, Su 9am-2pm. 400ptas.)*

OTHER SIGHTS. The **Museo de León** displays an extensive archaeological collection with pieces dating from the Paleolithic era. *(Pl. San Marcos. Tel. 987 24 50 61. Open Tu-Su Oct.-April 10am-2pm and 4:30-8pm, May-Sept. 10am-2pm and 5-8:30pm. Closed Sunday afternoon. 200ptas.)* Next door to the museum lies the Plateresque **Monasterio San Marcos.** Once a rest stop for pilgrims en route to Santiago, the monastery now caters to a different class of travelers as León's only five-star hotel. **Los Botines,** in Pl. Santo Domingo, is one of the few buildings outside of Catalunya designed by Antoni Gaudí. The relatively restrained structure still contains hints of the style that would emerge later in his life (see **Barcelona,** p. 296). While visiting the cathedral and San Isidoro, keep an eye out for some of the city's **Roman walls.**

♪ ENTERTAINMENT

For bars, discos, and techno music, head to the *barrio húmedo* (drinker's neighborhood) around **Plaza de San Martín**. To get to the *barrio*, walk up Av. Generalísimo Franco towards the cathedral and take a right on Legión Condor (which becomes Platerias Candiles). Take a right where the street ends, and head left. **El Bacanal** (tel. 987 21 38 51) attracts crowds to its Caravaggio-covered walls (beers 150ptas, drinks 600ptas). Mellower music, pastel walls, and actual breathing space characterize **El Robote** (across the square). After 2am, the crowds weave to **Calle Lancia** and **Calle Conde de Guillén,** both heavily populated with discos and bars.

Plenty of hip cafes line Av. Generalísimo Franco. **El Gran Café** (tel. 987 27 23 01), on C. Cervantes one block off Av. Generalísimo Franco, delivers live jazz nightly to its chic clientele. The red velvet seating area and saloon upstairs both overlook the street below. (Beers 300ptas, mixed drinks 500ptas.) **La Gargola** has cushy yellow-striped sofas and tall, translucent orange shades. For more romantic, secluded spots, explore C. La Paloma and other narrow streets around the cathedral.

Fiestas commemorating St. John and St. Peter occur from June 21-30. Highlights include a *corrida de torros* (bullfight) and the feast days of San Juan (John) on June 25 and San Pedro (Peter) on June 30. King Juan Carlos I and his wife Sofía attend the fiestas and the cathedral's **International Organ Festival** every year.

NEAR LEÓN: ASTORGA

Upon approaching Astorga, visitors might imagine themselves facing a giant version of a child's drip-castle. And so appears the fanciful ■**Palacio Episcopal (Bishop's Palace),** designed by Antoni Gaudí in the late 19th century. Gaudí created these converging arches, elaborate stained glass, and jutting turrets after the old palace burned down in 1886. As the construction dragged on for 20 years after the bishop's death, the expense proved enormous for the poor parish. Even upon completion no bishop dared occupy the fairy-tale home. Today the palace houses the fascinating and eclectic **Museo de los Caminos** (tel. 987 61 88 82), which illustrates the various *caminos* (paths) that have passed through 2000 year-old Astorga. The second floor houses Gaudí's dazzling stained-glass windows—have a look at those in the dining room and the gorgeous chapel. From the top floor, try squeaking open a window to get a stork's-eye-view of the land. (Open daily June-Sept. 10am-2pm and 4-8pm; Oct.-May 11am-2pm and 3:30-6:30pm. 250ptas; 400ptas with entrance to the cathedral museum.)

The **cathedral,** opposite Gaudí's palace, is definitely worth a quick visit, though it'll be a bit of a let-down for those coming from León. Pay special attention to the detailed 18th-century facade and the beautiful choir loft. The cathedral's **museum** has ten rooms filled with religious relics. (Cathedral open daily June-Sept. 9:30-10:30am and 5-6:30pm; Oct.-May 9:30-10:30am and 4:30-6pm. Free. Museum open daily June-Sept. 10am-2pm and 4-8pm; Oct.-May 11am-2pm and 3:30-6:30pm. 250ptas, 400ptas for a joint ticket to the Museo de los Caminos.)

To get to the town center from the RENFE **train station** (tel. 987 84 21 22), Pl. Estación, follow C. Pedro de Castro across Puerta de Rey. A large building (Casa Granell) is on the right. Pass the wall, turn right onto Los Sitios, and walk to the palace. Trains make the trip to **León** (45min., 8 per day, 400ptas). The **bus station** (tel. 987 61 91 00), on Av. Ponferrada across from the Palacio Episcopal, is close to the town's sights. Buses also run to **León** (45min., 16 per day, 425ptas). To get to the **tourist office,** stand with your back to the palace gate and face the plaza (with the cathedral on the right). The grey tourist office is right in front of you, just beyond the plaza. (Open M-Sa 10am-1:30pm and 4-8pm.) **Luggage storage** at the train station (400ptas). **Police** (tel. 987 61 60 80), at Pl. San Miguel; **ambulance** (tel. 987 61 85 85). **Post office,** on C. Alfereces.

Rooms in Astorga tend to be expensive. One option is **Pensión García**, C. Bajada de Postigo, 6 (tel. 987 61 60 46). Take the main street that runs past the cathedral and Gaudí's palace until you reach the fourth plaza, Pl. Mayor (Pl. España). Then take C. Bañeza (to the right as you face the Ayuntamiento), which becomes C. Bajada de Postigo just down the hill. The small *pensión* offers clean, sunny rooms, all with bath. (Singles 2500ptas; doubles 3800ptas.) **Restaurants** abound around the cathedral and on Av. Murallas near the bus station. Try **Restaurante Triton,** Gabriel Franco, 12 (tel. 987 61 87 49) for good food and great outdoor seating (entrees 475-1300ptas, salads 425ptas, *menú del día* 1100ptas; Visa, MC).

VALLADOLID

When Fernando and Isabel were married here in 1469, Valladolid stood at the forefront of Spanish politics, finance, and culture. Close to a century later, shady dealings by minister Conde Duque de Lerma brought the glory days to an end. In return for a whopping bribe, Lerma took Valladolid (then capital of Castilla) out of the running for capital of Spain. Madrid won, Valladolid lost, and history moved on. Yet today, the city makes up for its lack of national status with an impressive sculpture museum and endearing quirks. Fountains are lit in day-glo pink and green, architecture from the 70s challenges graceful Renaissance forms, and on certain summer days, Supermarket Simago blasts American music up and down the main pedestrian thoroughfare while the locals hum along.

⬛ GETTING THERE

Trains run to Valladolid from: **Salamanca** (2hr., 10 per day, 3:30am-10pm, 1500ptas); **León** (2½hr., 12 per day, 12:25am-8:30pm, 1240ptas); **Madrid** (2½hr., 9 per day, 8:30am-8:30pm, 1895ptas). **Buses** go from **Salamanca** (2hr., 6 per day, 8am-10pm, 930ptas) and **Burgos** (2hr.; 3 per day; 10:15, 10:45am, and 7:30pm; 1060ptas).

⬛ ORIENTATION AND PRACTICAL INFORMATION

The **bus** and **train stations** sit on the southern edge of town. To get from the bus station to the **tourist office,** turn right on C. San José and take the first left onto C. Ladrillo. Angle right onto C. Arco de Ladrillo, which cuts through the wooded park Campo Grande and ends at Pl. Zorrilla; the tourist office is straight across on C. Santiago. From there, walk down C. Santiago to get to **Plaza Mayor.** The **cathedral** is a ten-minute walk from Pl. Mayor (on the right as you face the Ayuntamiento).

TRANSPORTATION

Flights: Villanubla Airport, León Highway (N-601), km 13 (tel. 983 41 54 00). Taxi to airport 1800ptas. Daily trips to Barcelona, Madrid, and Paris. Service to Islas Baleares in summer. Info open daily 12:30-7:30pm. **Iberia,** C. Gamazo, 17 (tel. 983 30 06 66 or 983 30 26 39). Open M-F 9:30am-1:30pm and 4-7pm, Sa 9:30am-1:30pm.

Trains: Estación del Norte (tel. 983 30 35 18 or 983 30 75 78), C. Recondo, at the end of Campo Grande. Info (tel. 983 20 02 02) open daily 7am-11pm. To: **Zamora** (1½hr., 1 per day, 4:50pm, 1000ptas); **Burgos** (1½hr., 6 per day, 7am-8pm, 1060ptas); **León** (1½hr., 7 per day, 7:30am-9:01pm, 1400ptas); **Salamanca** (1¾hr., 5 per day, 7:15am-8:45pm, 1400ptas); **Madrid** (4hr., 10 per day, 7:11am-9:05pm, 1900ptas); **Santander** (4¾hr., 5 per day, 7:15am-6:40pm, 2000ptas).

Buses: Puente Colgante, 2 (tel. 983 23 63 08). Info open daily 8:30am-8:30pm. From the train station, turn left and follow C. Recondo, which becomes C. Puente Colgante (5min.). To: **Zamora** (1½hr., 7 per day, 8:30am-8:15pm, 795ptas); **Burgos** (2hr., 4-6 per day, 1:35-7:15pm, 1600ptas); **León** (2hr., 9 per day, 12:45am-9:45pm, 1070ptas); **Madrid** (2½hr., 19 per day, 12:30am-9:30pm, 1560ptas); **Oviedo** (4hr., 4 per day, 11am-2:15am, 2145ptas); **San Sebastián** (5hr., 1 per day, 12:15pm, 2785ptas); **Barcelona** (9hr.; 3 per day; 9:45am, 12:15 and 9:45pm; 5975ptas).

Taxis: Radio Taxi (tel. 983 29 14 11) is on call 24hr.

CENTRAL SPAIN

TOURIST AND LOCAL SERVICES

Tourist Office: C. Santiago, 19 (tel. 983 34 40 13). Maps, museum info, and a useful hotel info booklet. English spoken. Open daily 10am-2pm and 5-7pm.

Budget Travel: TIVE, Edifício Administrativo de Uso Múltiple, 3rd fl. (tel. 983 35 45 63). From Pl. Zorilla, take C. María de Molina to C. Doctrinos. Follow it across Puente Isabel la Católica and past the parking lot. Open M-F 9am-2pm.

Currency Exchange: At the bus station and **Banco Central Hispano,** corner of Av. Acera Recoletos and C. Perú. No commission. Open M-F 8:30am-2:30pm.

Luggage Storage: Estación del Norte has lockers (300ptas). Check bags at the bus station. 50ptas per bag. Open M-Sa 8am-10pm.

El Corte Inglés: (tel. 983 27 23 04 or 983 47 83 00), C. Constitución, a left off C. Santiago. Maps and guidebooks in English. Currency exchange. Open M-Sa 10am-9pm.

EMERGENCY AND COMMUNICATIONS

Emergency: tel. 091 or 092.

Medical Services: Hospital Pío del Río Hortega (nighttime tel. 983 42 04 00), C. Santa Teresa. Some doctors speak English.

Post Office: (tel. 983 33 06 60; fax 983 39 19 87), Pl. Rinconada. From Pl. Mayor, take C. Jesús. **Faxes** and Lista de Correos. Open M-F 8:30am-8:30pm, Sa 8:30am-2pm. **Postal Code:** 47001.

Internet Access: Intermática Perú, C. Peru, 14 (tel. 983 21 71 28). 300ptas for 30min., 500ptas per hr.

▌ ACCOMMODATIONS

Cheap lodgings, all with winter heating, are abundant. Though a little dark and scary, the streets off Av. Acera Recoletos as you leave the train station are packed with hostels, as are the street near the cathedral and behind Pl. Mayor at Pl. Val.

Pensión Dos Rosas, C. Perú, 11, 2nd fl. (tel. 983 20 74 39). From the train station, walk up Av. Acera Recoletos and turn right on C. Perú. Perfumed singles sport shiny crimson bedsheets; doubles are spacious and sunny. Bathrooms down the hall. Portable heaters in winter. Singles 1650ptas; doubles 2900ptas; triples 4100ptas.

Pensión Dani, C. Perú, 11, 1st fl. (tel. 983 30 02 49), below Dos Rosas. Clean rooms with TVs. Baths down the hall. Singles 1450ptas; doubles 2600ptas; triples 4100ptas.

Fonda Vianesa, C. Montero Calvo, 1 (tel. 983 30 58 92). Walk down C. Santiago with the fountain at your back. Dark halls, clean rooms, and great location. Shared baths. Singles 1500ptas; doubles 2500ptas.

▐ FOOD

Competition keeps prices down, making even the most elegant of restaurants accessible to budget diners. Eateries abound between Pl. Mayor and Pl. Val; explore the area near the cathedral for *tapas*. The **Mercado del Val,** on C. Sandoval in Pl. Val, has fresh foods (open M-Sa 6am-3pm). **Supermarket Simago,** on the corner of C. Santiago and C. Montero Calvo, has groceries (open M-Sa 9:30am-9pm).

Casa San Pedro Regalad, Pl. Ochavo, 1 (tel. 983 34 45 06), on the corner of C. Platerías, 2 blocks from Pl. Mayor. Roasted meats and veggies. *Menú* M-F 1100ptas, Sa-Su 1250ptas. Open daily 1:30-3:30pm and 8-11pm. Visa, MC, AmEx.

Restaurante Covadonga, C. Zapico, 1 (tel. 983 33 07 98), off Pl. Val. As elegant as a restaurant can be and still have "Polly," the talking stuffed parrot. *Menú* 995ptas. Entrees 350-1275ptas. Open Aug.-June M-Sa 1-4pm and 9-11:30pm, Su 1-4pm.

Restaurante Chino Gran Muralla, C. Santa María, 1 (tel. 983 34 23 07), off C. Santiago, north of Pl. Zorrilla. Look for the hanging dragons. Warm greetings at the door, good Chinese eats inside. *Menú* 685-1000ptas. Open daily 11:30am-5pm and 7pm-12:30am.

👁 SIGHTS

🖼MUSEO NACIONAL DE ESCULTURA. The Museo Nacional de Escultura in the **Colegio de San Gregorio** offers the thrill of 20 churches in one convenient location. The more than 20 rooms chart the region's religious art history through transplanted segments of now-destroyed monasteries and churches, including figurines, tableaux, sculpted choirs, and intricate ceilings. *(Open Tu-Sa 10am-2pm and 4-6pm, Su 10am-2pm. 400ptas, students 200ptas. Saturday afternoon and Sunday free.)*

CATHEDRAL. The cathedral was designed by Juan de Herrera, the creator of El Escorial. Its interior is imposing and severe, with light gray stone and large, colorless windows. Only the gold of the *retablo* interrupts the stolidly monochromatic atmosphere. The extensive **Museo Diocesano,** inside, is worth a visit for its original model of the basilica, its many statues of Jesus, Mary, and the saints, and its gruesome Jesus with real matted hair. *(Pl. Universidad. Cathedral open Tu-F 10am-1:30pm and 4:30-7pm, Sa-Su 10am-2pm. Free. Museum tel. 983 30 43 62. 250ptas.)*

CASA DE CERVANTES. From the looks of Casa de Cervantes, one might conclude that the writer died of boredom. There is an amusing collection of old books and furniture, but the medieval bed-warmer is the real highlight. *(Off C. Castro. Open Tu-Sa 10am-3:30pm, Su 10am-3pm. 400ptas, students 200ptas. Sunday free.)*

🎵 ENTERTAINMENT

Valladolid's cafes and bars are lively, though nothing to write home about. A student crowd fills the countless bars on C. Paraiso and head to pubs in Pl. San Miguel later on. Cafes on C. Vincente Meliner, near Pl. Dorado, draw an older crowd. **Tiutiu,** on Pl. Marti Monsó (to the left of Pl. Mayor when facing Ayuntamiento), deserves its title as most popular bar in Valladolid. Discotecas **Charlot,** on C. Espirito Santo off Rio Pisuerga, and **La Rosaleda,** across the Rio Pisuerga off Av. Salamanca, have thumping beats (both open 8pm-8am).

With over 12 cinemas and theaters, Valladolid satisfies any movie/drama buff. If you can, catch **International Cinema Week** (Oct. 21-31). Look for schedules for movies and for Valladolid's first-division soccer team, **Real Valladolid,** in *El Monde de Valladolid* or *El Norte de Castilla.* The week of September 21 marks the **Fiesta Mayor** celebrations, which feature bullfights, carnivals, and parades.

PALENCIA

Palencia's (pop. 82,000) charm is rooted in its lovely streets and public gardens, combined with a historical origin shrouded in the myths spun by 11th-century monks, Pilgrims en route to Santiago, and eager local politicians. Though low on pizzazz, Palencia will please any traveler craving a healthy dose of Romanesque and Visigothic architecture.

🛈 PRACTICAL INFORMATION. The **train** and **bus stations,** next to the park Los Jardinillos, lie just above **Calle Mayor,** the main pedestrian artery and shopping zone. **Trains** (tel. 979 74 30 19) steam from Los Jardinillos to: **Valladolid** (45min., 22 per day, 6:40am-11pm, 480ptas); **Burgos** (1hr., 11 per day, 800ptas); **León** (1¼hr., 15 per day, 890-1025ptas); **Madrid** (4hr., 16 per day, 6:40am-8pm, 2400ptas). The **bus station** (tel. 979 74 32 22) is just to the right of the train station (info booth open daily 9:30am-8pm). To: **Carrión** (30min., 3 per day, 315ptas); **Valladolid** (45min., 7 per day, 385ptas); **Burgos** (1½hr., 3 per day, 720ptas); **Madrid** (3½hr., 7 per day, 1885ptas). The bus station has **luggage storage** (100ptas per day; open M-F 9:30am-7pm, Sa 9:30am-2pm), as does the train station (300ptas per day; 24hr.) The **tourist**

office, C. Mayor, 105 (tel. 979 74 00 68; fax 979 70 08 22), distributes free maps (open M-Sa 10am-2pm and 5-7pm). Change currency at **Banco Central Hispano,** C. Mayor, 37 (open M-F 8:30am-2:30pm). **Emergency:** tel. 091 or 092. Two **post offices:** the one at Pl. León, 1 (tel. 979 74 21 80; fax 979 74 22 60), sends and receives **faxes;** the second office (tel. 979 74 21 77), next to the train station, provides Lista de Correos (both open M-F 8:30am-8:30pm, Sa 9:30am-2pm); **postal code:** 34001.

⌐⌐ ACCOMMODATIONS AND FOOD. Plenty of reasonably priced hostels with clean, plain rooms line side streets off C. Mayor. The youth hostel, **Victorio Macho (HI),** C. Dr. Fleming, s/n (tel. 979 72 04 62), is only open July to August 15. Call ahead, as groups often take over. Bus B from Los Jardinillos (every 12min., 45ptas) saves trekkers a hike. (HI members only. 1000ptas, over 26 1450ptas). **Pensión Gredos,** C. Valentin Calderon, 18 (tel. 979 70 28 33), three blocks down and a left off C. Mayor from Pl. León, has comfy beds and a patio (breakfast 350ptas; singles 1800ptas; doubles 3500ptas). Numerous restaurants and *tapas* bars line the streets just off C. Mayor. At **█Bar-Restaurante El Coso,** C. Eduardo Dato, 8 (tel. 979 74 67 58), off Pl. León, posters of matadors and bloody bulls line the walls and a stuffed bull's head watches diners eat (*bocadillos* 500ptas).

█ SIGHTS. Palencia's biggest attraction is its 14th-century Gothic cathedral, **Santa Iglesia de San Antolín,** where 14 year-old Catherine of Lancaster married 10 year-old Enrique III in 1388. During the tour, guides illuminate the various altars and then lead visitors down a stone staircase to the spooky **Cripta de San Antolín,** a 7th-century sepulchre. The cathedral's **museum** houses El Greco's famed *San Sebastián* and some spectacular 16th-century Flemish tapestries—not to mention a tiny caricature of Carlos V. (Cathedral tel. 979 70 13 47. open M-Sa 10:30am-1:30pm and 4-6:30pm, Su 9:30am-1:30pm. Free. Tours in Spanish 100ptas. Museum open M-Sa 10:30am-1pm and 4-6pm. 300ptas.) Of the other churches in town, the favorite of El Cid fans is **Iglesia de San Miguel,** on C. General Mola, which runs parallel to the river. According to legend, it was here that El Campeador wed Doña Jimena. (Tel. 979 74 07 69. Open daily 9:30am-1:30pm, 6-8pm.)

NEAR PALENCIA: CARRIÓN DE LOS CONDES

Forty kilometers north of Palencia on the Camino de Santiago, the tiny riverside town of Carrión (pop. 1000) hides some incredible sights. On the south side of 12th-century **Iglesia de Santa María** is a depiction of the legendary tribute of four Carrión maidens to Moorish conquerors. Supposedly, Santa María foiled the transaction by sending four menacing bulls to gore the Moors. (Tel. 979 88 00 72. Open daily 9am-2pm and 4:30-6:30pm. Mass daily at 8:30am, holidays 10:30am and noon.) On the far side of the Río Carrión looms the secularized **Monasterio de San Zoilo.** Faces of saints and popes stare down from the ornate arches of its Renaissance cloister, now partially open to the public. Situated near the exit are the tombs of the notorious Infantes de Carrión. In the *Cantar del Mío Cid,* they married, deflowered, beat, and then abandoned El Cid's daughters in the middle of the forest. (Tel. 979 88 00 49 or 979 88 01 35. Open Tu-Su 10:30am-2pm and 4-6pm. 200ptas.) Carrión's hidden treasure is the **Convento de Santa Clara,** also known as **Las Clarisas.** To see the **museo,** ring the bell and ask Señor Antonio to let you in. The one-room collection includes shepherds' nutcrackers, a statue of baby Jesus with a toothache, and numerous baby-doll clothes made especially for the infant Christ (Tel. 979 88 01 34. Open Tu-Su 10:30am-1pm and 4:30-7pm. 200ptas.)

Buses (tel. 979 74 32 22) carry day-trippers to Carrión from **Palencia** (30min.; M-Sa 4 per day, 8am, 1:30pm, 6:30pm, and 8:30pm; Su 2 per day, 8am and 7:15pm; 315ptas). Carrión's **tourist office** is in a wood-frame hut across the street from Café-Bar España, where the bus drops you off (not a government office, so hours vary). If you'd like to spend the night, **Hostal La Corte,** C. Santa María, 34 (tel. 979 88 01 38), provides luxurious, spotless rooms, and an elegant restaurant (singles 2000-2500ptas; doubles 4000-4500ptas). Or stay with the nuns at **Convento Santa Clara** (singles 1000ptas, free for pilgrims). **El Edén Camping** hugs the river two blocks from the central Café-Bar España (300ptas per person, 300-400ptas per tent).

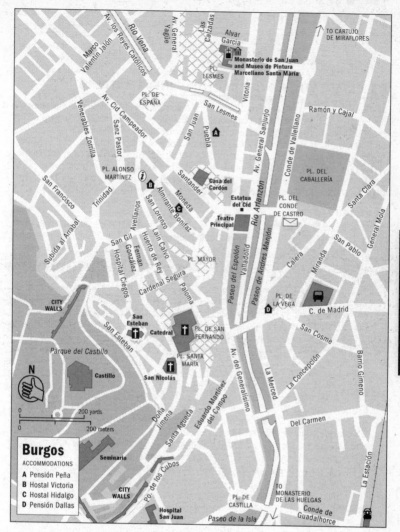

Burgos

ACCOMMODATIONS

A Pensión Peña
B Hostal Victoria
C Hostal Hidalgo
D Pensión Dallas

CENTRAL SPAIN

BURGOS

Burgos lives in the shadow of its overwhelming history and its Gothic cathedral. During its 500 years as the capital of Castile, Burgos witnessed the birth of both the extraordinary cathedral and Rodrigo Díaz de Vivar, better known as El Cid Campeador, the national hero of Spain (actually born in the nearby town of Vivar). Nine centuries after El Cid's banishment from town, General Franco stationed his headquarters here in a revival of nationalist politics. Today's Burgos is significantly more relaxed. During the day natives share the galeria-lined streets and duck-filled riverbanks with history-seeking tourists and international pilgrims backpacking along the Camino de Santiago. At night, folks hit *mesóns* for Burgos's Black Pudding and Ribera de Duero wines, then welcome sunrise from alley pubs and neon-flushed *discotecas*.

⌐ GETTING THERE

Trains run to Burgos from **Valladolid** (1½hr., 6 per day, 7am-8pm, 1060ptas) and **Madrid** (4hr.; 3 per day; 8:30am, 1:30pm and 5:30pm; 3000ptas). **Buses** go from **Bilbao** (2hr., 4 per day, 8:30am-7pm, 1435ptas).

ⓘ ORIENTATION AND PRACTICAL INFORMATION

The Río Arlanzón splits Burgos into north and south sides. The **train** and **bus stations** are on the south side, while the **cathedral** and all other sights of interest are located to the north. From the train station, follow Av. Conde de Guadalhorce across the river and take the first right onto Av. Generalísimo Franco, which turns into Po. Espolón farther down. From the bus station, follow C. Madrid through Pl. Vega and across the river, then turn right on P. Espolón; the cathedral stands several hundred meters north. Upstream, along the *paseo* at C. Santander, stands a large statue of El Cid. The **Plaza José Antonio** (or **Plaza Mayor**) is between the cathedral and the tourist office.

TRANSPORTATION

Trains: (tel. 947 20 35 60), at the end of Av. Conde de Guadalhorce across the river from Pl. Castilla. A 10min. walk southwest of the city center, or a 300-500pta taxi ride. Info open daily 7am-10pm. **RENFE,** C. Moneda, 21 (tel. 947 20 35 60). Open M-F 9am-1pm and 4-7pm, Sa 9am-1pm. To: **Palencia** (1hr., 11 per day, 500-1200ptas); **Valladolid** (1½hr.; M-F 6 per day, 8:50am-8:20pm; Sat 3 per day; Sun 4 per day, 3pm-8:20pm; 925-1700ptas); **Logroño** (2hr., 4 per day, 1800ptas); **León** (2hr., 8 per day, 2000ptas); **Madrid** (3½hr., 10 per day, 3000ptas); **San Sebastián** (4hr., 8 per day, 2400ptas); **Bilbao** (4hr., 5 per day, 1800ptas); **Santiago** (8hr., 3 per day, 4500ptas); **Barcelona** (8hr., 12 per day, 5000ptas).

Buses: C. Miranda, 4 (tel. 947 28 88 55), just off Pl. Vega, on the south side of the river. To: **Vitoria-Gasteiz** (1½hr.; M-Sa 8 per day, 3:15am-10pm; Su 1 per day, 9pm; 940ptas); **Valladolid** (2hr.; M-Sa 3 per day; 10:15am and 10:45am, 7:30pm; 1060ptas); **Santander** (2¾hr., 4 per day, 3:15am-10pm, 1350ptas); **Bilbao** (2-3hr., 8 per day, 6:15am-9:30pm, 1420ptas); **Madrid** (3hr., 12-15 per day, 1:45am-9:45pm, 1920ptas); **León** (3½hr., M-Sa 1 per day, 10:45am, 1700ptas); **San Sebastián** (3½hr.; 7 per day; M-Sa 3:15am-10pm, Su 3:15am-midnight; 1825ptas); **Pamplona** (3½hr., 5 per day, 7:15am-6:30pm, 1900ptas); **Barcelona** (7½hr., 3-4 per day, 11:30am-3:00pm, 4960ptas).

Taxis: Abutaxi (tel. 947 27 77 77) and **Radio Taxi** (tel. 947 48 10 10). 24hr. service. Taxis gather by stations and in Pl. Santo Domingo de Guzmán.

Car Rental: Hertz, C. General Mola, 5 (tel. 947 20 16 75), on the block parallel to C. Miranda near Pl. Vega. Must be at least 25. Small cars with unlimited mileage 11,000ptas for 1 day, cheaper for longer rentals. All major credit cards. Open M-F 9am-2pm and 4-7pm, Sa 9am-1pm. **Avis,** C. Maestro Justa del Río, 2-4 (tel. 947 20 06 06). Must be at least 23. Special weekend rate of 21,425ptas for 3 days. Open M-F 8:30am-1:30pm and 4-7pm, Sa 9am-1pm.

TOURIST, FINANCIAL, AND LOCAL SERVICES

Tourist Office: Pl. Alonso Martínez, 7 (tel. 947 20 31 25). English spoken. Open M-F 9am-2pm and 5-7pm, Sa-Su and holidays 10am-2pm and 5-8pm.

Budget Travel: Viajes TIVE, C. General Yagüe, 20 (tel. 947 20 98 81), off Pl. España. English spoken. Student IDs 700ptas. Open M-F 9am-2pm.

Currency Exchange: Banco Central Hispano, C. Vitoria, 6, near the bus station, next to El Cid statue and Pl. Vega. Open May-Sept. M-F 8:30am-2:30pm, Oct.-Apr. M-F 8:30am-2:30pm, Sa 8:30am-1pm. For **ATMs,** hunt down Telebanco or SirviRed signs.

Luggage Storage: Lockers at the train station (400ptas). 24hr. Check bags at the bus station. 100-150ptas per bag. Open M-F 9am-8pm, Sa 9am-6pm.

EMERGENCY AND COMMUNICATIONS

Emergency: tel. 091 or 092. **Police:** tel. 947 20 55 00.

Medical Services: Ambulance tel. 947 28 18 28.

Post Office: Pl. Conde de Castro, 1 (tel. 947 26 27 50; info tel. 947 20 41 20). El Cid points the way across the river from Pl. Primo de Rivera; the post office is the big building at the first intersection. Lista de Correos. Open M-F 8:30am-8:30pm, Sa 9:30am-2pm. **Postal Code:** 09070.

Internet Access: Cafe Cabaret Ciber-Cafe, C. Puebla, 21 (tel. 947 20 27 22; www.render.es/cabaret). 500ptas for 30min., 300ptas for each additional 30min. Printing 10ptas per page. Open Su-Th 5pm-2am, F-Sa 4pm-4am.

Telephones: Locutorio Telefónico (tel. 947 26 42 28; fax 947 27 93 59), Pl. Alonso Martínez, near the tourist office. **Fax** service. Open daily 10am-3pm and 4-11pm.

▐ ACCOMMODATIONS AND CAMPING

For cheap hostels, scout the streets near Pl. Alonso Martínez on the north side of the river. The C. San Juan area is also dotted with reasonably priced hostels. Reservations are crucial for the festivals in June and July and are advisable in August.

Pensión Peña, C. Puebla, 18, 2nd fl. (tel. 947 20 63 23). From Pl. España, take C. San Lesmes; C. Puebla is the 3rd right. Small, elegant rooms with big windows. Family-run for nearly 50 years. Laundry service and storage of luggage and bicycles. Singles 1600ptas, with sink 1700ptas; doubles 2800ptas, with sink 2900ptas.

Pension Dallas, Pl. Vega, 1-6 (tel. 947 20 54 57). From the bus station, walk toward the cathedral and look right before crossing C. Valladolid. Clean, comfy bedrooms and communal baths. Winter heating. Showers 300ptas. Singles 2000ptas, doubles 4000ptas.

Hostal Victoria, C. San Juan, 3, 2nd fl. (tel. 947 20 15 42). From El Cid's statue, walk up C. Santander past Pl. Calvobotelo and turn right onto C. San Juan. Simple, attractive rooms with sinks. English and French spoken. Public telephone and luggage storage. Singles 2500ptas; doubles 4500ptas; triples 6000ptas; quads 8000ptas.

Hostal Hidalgo, C. Almirante Bonifaz, 14 (tel. 947 20 34 81), off C. San Juan, one block from Pl. Alonso Martínez. High ceilings and hardwood floors. Singles 2100ptas; doubles 3000-3900ptas; triples 5100ptas; 2nd fl. quads 7000ptas. Open July-Sept.

Camping Fuentes Blancas. The "Fuentes Blancas" bus leaves from Pl. España (July-Sept. 15 9:30am, 12:30, 4:15, and 7:15pm; 75ptas). 575ptas per person, per tent, and per car; plus 7% IVA. Open Apr.-Sept.

▐ FOOD

Burgos natives take pride in the delicious *queso de Burgos* (cheese) and *morcilla*, a sausage concocted from blood and rice. The area around Pl. Alonso Martínez teems with restaurants serving these staples. C. San Lorenzo is *tapas* heaven. **Mercado de Abastos (Norte),** near Pl. España, and the smaller **Mercado de Abastos (Sur),** on C. Miranda next to the bus station, sell fresh meat and bread for sandwiches. (Both open M-Sa 7am-3pm; Mercado Norte reopens F 5:30-8pm.) **Spar Supermercado,** on C. Concepción, midway between C. Hospital Militar and C. San Cosme, prepares you for picnics (open M-F 9am-2pm and 5-8pm, Sa 9am-2pm).

La Riojana, C. Avellanos, 10 (tel. 947 20 61 32). Perfect for famished diners willing to ignore health concerns and just shove tasty grub down the hatch. The 900pta *menú* will fill the emptiest of stomachs. *Bocadillos* 200-300ptas. Open daily noon-1am.

Gaia Comedor Vegetariano, C. San Francisco, 31 (tel. 947 23 76 45). Gazpacho, salads, asparagus crepes, and creamy vegetable *pasteles* make for a light, flavorful *menú* (1000ptas). Also posts info on tai chi, yoga, and the world's ills. Open M-Sa 1:30-4pm.

La Posada (tel. 947 20 85 13), Pl. Santa Domingo de Guzmán, behind El Cid statue. A shrine to Spain's most valiant matadors. Try the vegetable plate of the day. Entrees 600-1600ptas. *Menú* 1800ptas. Open daily 1-4pm and 9-11pm. Visa, MC.

Mesón la Amarilla, C. San Lorenzo, 26, (tel. 947 20 59 36), between Pl. Mayor and Pl. Alonso Martínez. Try the mild and sweet *queso de Burgos con miel* (400ptas). *Raciones* 500-750ptas. Entrees 1100-1600ptas. Open daily 9am-4pm and 7pm-2am.

EL CID CAMPEADOR Although Rodrigo Díaz de Vivar (a.k.a. El Cid), Spain's real-life epic hero, was not born in Burgos itself, some of the most celebrated incidents of his life took place here. After the cathedral, the **Estatua del Cid** in Pl. General Primo de Rivera is Burgos's most revered landmark. Díaz de Vivar ("Cid" comes from the Arabic for lord) won his fame through bold exploits at home and in battle against Moors and Christians. Despite the statue's inscription and the legends behind him, El Cid was no traditional Christian hero. A particularly successful mercenary, he spent much of his life exiled from a number of Christian states whose nobles he had outraged; he was even known to ally himself with Muslims. All the same, El Cid is thought to be the most famous Castilian of all time, and the medieval epic poem celebrating his life, *Cantar de Mío Cid* (c. 1140), is considered the first great work of Castilian literature. Tradition compels Burgos's boys to climb the statue and fondle the testicles of El Cid's horse, ensuring their own strength, courage, and fame.

SIGHTS

CATHEDRAL. The spires of Burgos's magnificent Gothic cathedral rise high above the city. Though the first stone was set in the 13th century by Reconquest hero Fernando III (El Santo), the cathedral gained additions during the following three centuries. As a result, the 13th-century Gothic north facade appears stark when compared to the intricate 15th-century towers and the beautiful 16th-century stained-glass dome of the **Capilla Mayor.** Here, parts of El Cid's body lie with the body of his wife Doña Jimena; his coffin hangs several meters overhead in the 18th-century Baroque sacristy. Another curious inhabitant of the cathedral is the eerily lifelike **papamoscas** (fly-catcher), high up near the main door in the central aisle. As it tolls the hours, the strange creature opens its mouth and gulps, much to the joy of onlookers below. *(Tel. 947 20 47 12. Open daily 9:30am-1pm and 4-7pm. Admission to sacristy, museum, and Capilla Mayor 400ptas, students 200ptas.)*

MUSEO-MONASTERIO DE LAS HUELGAS REALES. The Museo-Monasterio de las Huelgas Reales, built by King Alfonso VIII in 1188, is not centrally located but worth the trek. Once a summer palace for Castilian kings and later an elite convent for Cistercian nuns, the monastery has been closely associated with Spanish royalty since the Middle Ages; the abbess of Las Huelgas has traditionally served as a personal advisor to the king. Inside the monastery, the **Museo de Telas (Textile Museum)** houses the burial wardrobe of Fernando de Cerda (1225-1275) and family. After Napoleon's troops snatched the entombed corpses' jewelry, Spaniards later stripped the bodies to put their stunning gold-silk smocks and beaded hats on display. *(Take the "Barrio del Pilar" bus from Pl. España to the Museo stop (65ptas). Tel. 947 20 16 30. Open Apr.-Sept. Tu-Sa 10:30am-1:15pm and 4-5:45pm, Su 10:30am-2:15pm; Oct.-Mar. Tu-F 11am-1:15pm and 4-5:45pm, Sa 11am-1:15pm and 4-5:45pm, Su 10:30am-2:15pm. 650ptas, students and under 14 250ptas, under 5 free.)*

CASTLE. The ruins of a medieval castle preside over Burgos from a hill high above the cathedral. Napoleonic troops demolished sections of the walls and building, which are still undergoing reconstruction. The bleached castle rocks offers an astounding view of the red roofs of Burgos and the surrounding countryside. *(From Museo del Retablo, climb the 200 steps.)*

MUSEO DE PINTURA MARCELIANO SANTA MARÍA. This renovated museum among the ruins of the **Monasterio de San Juan** stands chock full of Burgalese paintings. One of the galleries is devoted to the work of the Romantic painter who gives the museum its name, while the other displays contemporary exhibits. *(Follow C. Vitoria away from El Cid's statue and take the 2nd left. Tel. 947 20 56 87. Open Tu-Sa 10am-1:50pm and 5-7:50pm, Su 10am-1:50pm. 25ptas.)*

CASA DEL CORDÓN. The restored Casa del Cordón was built by Castilian constables in the 15th century and later reincarnated as the Savings Bank of Burgos. Here

Columbus met with Fernando and Isabel after his second trip to America. Felipe el Hermoso (the Handsome) died here after an exhausting game of *pelota* (jai-alai). Upon his death, his wife Juana dragged his corpse through the streets, thus inspiring her nickname, Juana la Loca (the Mad). *(On C. Santander, on the other side of the statue of El Cid, on the right.)*

CHURCHES. Across from the cathedral stands the **Iglesia de San Nicolás,** with 15th- and 16th-century Hispano-Flemish paintings and altars. *(Pl. Santa Maria. Open July-Sept. M 9am-8pm, Tu-Su 9am-2pm and 4-8pm; Oct.-June Tu-F 6:30-7:30pm, Sa 9:30am-2pm and 5-7pm. Free.)* Altarpiece fans should head to the **Iglesia de San Esteban/ Museo del Retablo.** Eighteen 16th- to 18th-century altars depict the life of Christ and various saints. *(C. Pozo Seco. Open Tu-Sa 10:30am-2pm and 4:30-7pm, Su 10:30am-2pm. 200ptas, students 100ptas, under 11 free.)*

🎵 ENTERTAINMENT

Party-seekers inundate Burgos after dark. By midnight C. Avellanos (across from Pl. Alonso Martínez, near the tourist office) boils with night owls. As C. Avellanos simmers down, crowds snake into nearby C. Huerto del Rey. If you have to hit the sack early on a Saturday night, that's okay; wake up Sunday and join the crowds still dancing at *discotecas* along C. San Juan. Nightlife switches into overdrive the last week in June, when Burgos honors patron saints Peter and Paul with concerts, parades, fireworks, bullfights, and dances. The day after **Corpus Christi,** citizens parade through town with the *Pendón de las Navas*, a banner captured from the Moors in 1212.

La Flor, C. Avellanos, 9. Though a bit bright, it draws the largest crowd. Beer 200ptas, mixed drinks 500ptas. Open M-Sa 7pm-4am, Sun 7pm-midnight.

Twenty, Pl. Huerto del Rey, 20 (tel. 947 26 46 72). Sweat to the latest hits under red wood and blue neon. Beer 200ptas, mixed drinks 600ptas. Open 7pm-whenever.

Pub Tastos, Pl. Huerto del Rey, 7. Packs booty-shakers in after 1am. Beer 250ptas, mixed drinks 450ptas. Open daily 7pm-5am.

Cerviceria Flandes, Pl. Huerto del Rey, 21 (tel. 947 26 59 60). "All the world in imported beers." Beer 200ptas, mixed drinks 500ptas. Open M-Th 6pm-1am, F-Su 6pm-5am.

Okra, C. Francisco, 7. Burgos's gay hotspot. Offers a simple bar and dance floor. Beer 225ptas, mixed drinks 600ptas. Open Su-W 6pm-2:30am, Th-Sa 6pm-4am.

Besame Mucho, off Pl. Lesmes. Offers 200pta beer, 400pta mixed drinks, and no memory the next morning whatsoever. Arrive after 2am.

NEAR BURGOS: SANTO DOMINGO DE SILOS

Remember that Gregorian chant album that reached #1 on global charts? Since 1993, the Benedictine monks of Santo Domingo de Silos (pop. 380) have sold 5 million recordings. In the **Abadía de Santo Domingo de Silos,** listeners are transported back in time as the black-cloaked monks chant along with the organ and the soothing echoes of their own voices. You can sit in at morning song at 7:30am, high mass at 9am, *sexta* at 1:45pm, vespers at 7pm, and *completas* at 9:30pm. (Tel. 947 39 00 68. Open Tu-Sa 10am-1pm and 4:30-6pm. 200ptas, under 14 free.) Perhaps more interesting than the church itself is the Romanesque **cloister** next door, whose highlights include an ancient pharmacy of 300-year-old chemicals, skulls, and preserved animal parts. Beyond the monastery, the sole option for entertainment is hiking in the hills. Ask for directions to **La Yecla** (2.5km from Silos) where a precarious walkway leads through a narrow gorge above a small waterfall. Rooms are easy to find in this friendly (though pricey) little town, a good thing since visitors without cars are almost obligated to stay the night. **Hostal Cruces** (tel. 947 39 00 64) offers rooms, with baths, practically within earshot of the monks (singles 3000ptas; doubles 4500ptas). Near the bus station, **Hostal Santo Domingo** (tel. 947 39 00 53) offers comfortable rooms (singles with bath, shower, telephone and TV 3500ptas). A **bus** runs to Santo Domingo from **Burgos** (1½hr.; departs Burgos M-Th 5:30pm, F 6:30pm, Sa 2pm; departs Santo Domingo M-Th and Sa 8:30am; 630ptas).

CENTRAL SPAIN

SORIA

Though modern development has encroached upon provincial Soria (pop. 33,000), the city retains a leisurely pace. Black-bereted men tote bundles of local bread past Romanesque churches, and Soria's inhabitants still religiously observe the evening *paseo*, strolling and chatting with friends and neighbors every evening before dinner. Although the city proper is best used as a base for exploring surrounding towns, two intriguing architectural anomalies, the Monasterio de San Juan de Duero and the Ermita San Saturio, await on the outskirts of Soria.

▐ GETTING THERE

Trains run to Soria from **Madrid** (3hr., 3 per day, 8:20am-7pm, 1790ptas). **Buses** go from **Logroño** (1½hr., 5 per day, M-Sa 6:45am-7pm, Su 9:30am-10pm, 825ptas) and **Zaragoza** (2½hr.; M-Sa 5 per day, 7:30am-4:30pm; Su 1 per day, 9am; 1100ptas).

▐ ORIENTATION AND PRACTICAL INFORMATION

To get to the city center from the **bus station,** take either the shuttle bus (see **Buses,** below) or walk for 15 minutes. From the traffic circle outside the station, signs on Av. Valladolid point the way downhill to the *centro ciudad*. Keep walking for about five blocks, then bear right at the fork, after the traffic light, onto Po. Espolón, which borders the Parque Alameda. When the park ends you'll see central **Plaza Mariano Granados** directly in front of you. To get to the center from the **train station,** either take the shuttle (see **Trains,** below) or turn left onto C. Madrid and follow the signs to *centro ciudad*. Continue on C. Almazán as it bears left and becomes Av. Mariano Vicen; follow for about six blocks (veering left on C. Alfonso VIII at the next fork) until you reach Pl. Mariano Granados (20min.). From the side of the plaza opposite the park, C. Marqués de Vadillo leads to pedestrian **Calle El Collado,** the main shopping street that cuts through the old quarter to **Plaza Mayor.**

TRANSPORTATION

Trains: Estación El Cañuelo (tel. 975 23 02 02), Carretera de Madrid. Shuttle buses run from Pl. Mariano Granados to the train station 20min. before train departure times (50ptas). To **Alcalá de Henares** (2¾hr., 7 per day, 7:40am-7:35pm, 1490ptas) and **Madrid** (3hr., 7 per day, 7:40am-7:35pm, 1790ptas).

Buses: (tel. 975 22 51 60), Av. Valladolid, at Av. Gaya Nuño. Shuttle bus from Pl. Mariano Granados (every hr. on the ½hr., 9:30am-2:30pm, 30ptas). Info open 9am-7pm and 8-10pm. Most tickets available 30min. before departure, except on holidays when seats may be reserved days before. **Therpasa** (tel. 975 22 20 60) goes to: **Tarazona** (1hr., 5 per day, 7:30am-5:30pm, 545ptas) and **Zaragoza** (2¼hr.; M-Sa 5 per day, 7:30am-8pm; Su 2 per day, 6pm and 9pm; 1075ptas). **La Serrana** (tel. 975 24 09 13) to **Burgos** (2½hr., 3 per day, 7am-6:30pm, 1250ptas). **Linecar** (tel. 975 23 00 33) goes to: **Zaragoza** (2½hr.; 2-5 per day; M-F 9:45am-9:30pm, Sa 1:10-9:30pm, Su 1-9:30pm; 1100ptas) and **Valladolid** (3hr.; 2-3 per day; M-Sa 9:40am-7pm, Su 11am-7pm; 1460ptas). **Continental Auto** (tel. 975 22 44 01) to: **Logroño** (1½hr.; 7-8 per day; M-Th and Sa 11am-9:45pm, F and Su 11am-12:15am; 825ptas); **Pamplona** (2hr.; 6 per day; M-Th and Sa 10:45am-9:45pm, F and Su 10:45am-12:15am; 1485ptas); **Madrid** (2½hr.; 6-8 per day; M-Th and Sa 8:15am-8:45pm, F 8:15am-11:45pm, Su 9:15am-11:45pm; 1780-2900ptas). **RENFE-Iñigo** (tel. 975 22 89 89) to **Salamanca** (5hr., 2 per day, 3:45pm and 1:50am, 2590ptas) and **Barcelona** (6hr., 2-3 per day, 12:20-5:20pm, 3890ptas).

Taxis: (tel. 975 21 30 34 or 975 22 17 18). Stands at Pl. Mariano Granados and bus station. To ruins of Numancia 1000ptas (negotiable).

Car Rental: Europcar, C. Angel Terrel, 5 (tel. 975 22 05 05), off C. Sagunto. 6270ptas per day, plus IVA; 47,000ptas per wk. Open M-F 9:30am-1:30pm and 4:30-8pm.

TOURIST, FINANCIAL, AND LOCAL SERVICES

Tourist Office: (tel./fax 975 21 20 52), Pl. Ramón y Cajal, on the side of Pl. Mariano Granados opposite the park. It's the glass hut set back from the street. Ask for the *Ruta de los poetas* map. Open M-F 9am-2pm and 5-7pm, Sa-Su 10am-2pm and 5-8pm.

Currency Exchange: Banco Hispano Central, C. Collado, 56, off Pl. Ramon Bento Aceño. Open May-Sept. M-F 8:30am-2:30pm; Oct.-Apr. M-F 8:30am-2:30pm, Sa 8:30am-1pm.

Luggage Storage: Bags checked at the bus station (1st day 75ptas, 25ptas each additional day). Open daily 9am-7pm and 8-10pm.

EMERGENCY AND COMMUNICATIONS

Emergency: tel. 091 or 092. **Municipal Police:** tel. 975 21 18 62.

Medical Services: Hospital General (tel. 975 22 15 50), Po. Santa Barbara.

Post Office: Po. Espolón, 6 (tel. 975 22 20 00), off Pl. Mariano Granados. Open M-F 8:30am-8:30pm, Sa 9:30am-2pm. **Postal Code:** 42071.

Internet Access: Ofimatica de Marco, C. Condes de Gomara, 8 (tel. 975 21 23 79). 1 computer at 300ptas per 30min. Open M-F 9am-2pm and 5-8pm, Sa 10am-2pm.

▐ ACCOMMODATIONS AND CAMPING

Affordable hostels are sprinkled in the streets around Pl. Olivo and Pl. Salvador, both near Pl. Mariano Granados. Reservations, necessary during the *fiestas* in the last week of June, are also wise mid-July through mid-September.

Residencia Juvenil Antonio Machado (HI), Pl. José Antonio, 1 (tel. 975 22 00 89). From Pl. Mariano Granados, take C. Nicolás Rabal until you reach Pl. José Antonio, or turn right at the stoplight coming from the bus station. A seasonal hostel and your cheapest bet, if, of course, you can snag a bed. 3-night max. stay. Curfew 11:30pm. Reservations not accepted. Members only. Dorms 950ptas, over 26 1350ptas. July-Aug. 15.

Pension Ersogo, C. Alberca, 4 (tel. 975 21 35 08). Facing Pl. Mariano Granados, with your back to the park, head diagonally through Pl. Ramon y Cajal and take the 1st right on C. Alberca. Ring the bell on the right-hand door on the 2nd floor. Friendly owners and well-lit rooms. Singles 2000-2100ptas; doubles 3200ptas; triples 4500ptas.

Casa Diocesana Pío XII, C. San Juan, 5 (tel. 975 21 21 76). From Pl. Marciano Granados, head up C. El Collado and turn right on C. San Juan. Nice rooms with baths and crucifix. July-Aug. singles 2800ptas; doubles 3850ptas; Sept.-June singles 2380ptas; doubles 3370ptas.

Camping: Camping Fuente la Teja (tel. 975 22 29 67), 2km from town on Cra. Madrid (km 233). Swimming pool. 425ptas per person and per car, 475ptas per tent; plus IVA. Open *Semana Santa* to Sept.

◖ FOOD

Soria's specialties include *chorizo* and *migas* (fried bread crumbs), and the region's butter is celebrated throughout Spain. C. M. Vincente Tutor is peppered with bars and inexpensive restaurants. Buy fresh produce, meat, and fish at the **market** in Pl. Bernardo Robles on C. Estudios, left off C. Collado (open M-Sa 9am-1pm). Cruise the **supermarket** aisles at **%Dia-Autoservicio Descuento,** Av. Mariano Vicen, 15, 3½ blocks from Pl. Mariano Granados toward the train station (open M-Sa 9am-2pm and 5-8pm).

Nueva York, C. Collado, 14 (tel. 975 21 27 84), 1 block past Pl. San Esteban. Not quite the Big Apple, but tasty nonetheless. Get here in time for breakfast (served until 12:30pm). Open daily June-Aug. 8am-10pm; Sept.-May 8am-9:30pm. Visa.

Bar Restaurante Regio, Pl. Ramón y Cajal, 7 (tel. 975 21 30 76). A fine selection of *bocadillos* (275-650ptas), *raciones* (350-1600ptas), and *menús* (1500ptas). The *tortilla de patata* is a steal at 300ptas. Open daily 1-4:30pm and 8:30pm-midnight.

◖ SIGHTS

The great 20th-century poet Antonio Machado once likened the **Río Duero** to a drawn bow which forms an arc around Soria. To find the river from Pl. Mariano Granados, walk past the sign for restaurant Nueva York and straight down C. Zapatería. Halfway down the hill, C. Zapatería changes to C. Real. Follow this road to Pl. San Pedro; the bridge lies straight ahead.

CENTRAL SPAIN

ERMITA DE SAN SATURIO. Soria's biggest draw is actually across the river; it's well worth the trek. The 17th-century Ermita de San Saturio, built into the side of a cliff, is a heavenly retreat where light seeps into the caves through stained-glass windows. Note the window from which a 6-year-old child fell in 1772, landing on his knees unharmed; he was supposedly saved by San Saturio. *(1.5km downstream. Turn right with the road after crossing the bridge. Open May-Sept. Tu-Su 10:30am-2pm and 4:30-8pm; Oct.-Apr. Tu-Su 10:30-6:30pm. Free.)*

MONASTERIO SAN JUAN DE DUERO. The Monasterio San Juan de Duero sits tranquilly by the river, amid cottonwoods and green, green grass. The church itself, dating from the 12th century, is quite simple. The remarkable and graceful arches, combining Romanesque and Islamic styles, are all that remain of the 13th-century cloister. Inside, a small museum displays medieval artifacts. *(Turn left after crossing the bridge. Open June-Aug. Tu-Sa 10am-2pm and 5-9pm, Su 10am-2pm; Sept.-Oct. and Apr.-May Tu-Sa 10am-2pm and 4-8pm, Su 10am-2pm; Nov.-Mar. Tu-Sa 10am-2pm and 3:30-6pm, Su 10am-2pm. 100ptas; under 18, over 65, and students free. Sa and Su free.)*

MUSEO NUMANTINO. The Museo Numantino shows off the impressive Celto-Iberian and Roman artifacts excavated from nearby Numancia. *(Po. Espolón, 8. Tel. 975 22 13 97. Open June-Sept. Tu-Sa 9am-2pm and 5-9pm, Su 9am-2pm; Oct.-May Tu-Sa 9am-8:30pm, Su 9am-2pm. 200ptas; under 18, over 65, and students free. Sa and Su free.)*

🎵 ENTERTAINMENT

Early evening finds revelers in Pl. Ramón Benito Aceña and Pl. San Clemente, both off C. Collado. Late-night festivities center at the disco-bars grouped around the intersection of Rota de Calatañazer and C. Cardenal Frías, near Pl. Toros. Many Spanish fiestas involve watching bulls and eating, but Soria ingeniously combines the two. During the **Fiesta de San Juan** (beginning the first Wednesday after June 24th), each day starts with a running of the bulls and ends with eating them.

DAYTRIPS FROM SORIA

RUINS OF NUMANCIA

Archeology fans will enjoy the ruins of Numancia, a hilltop settlement 7km north of Soria that dates back more than 4000 years. The Celto-Iberians had settled here by the 3rd century BC, and tenaciously resisted Roman conquest. It took 10 years of the Numantian Wars and the direction of Scipio Africanus to dislodge them. Scipio erected a system of walls 9km long, 3m tall, and 2.5m thick to encircle the town and starve its residents. After his victory, he kept 50 survivors as trophies, sold the rest into slavery, burned the city, and divided its lands among his allies. Numancia, however, lived on as a metaphor for patriotic heroism in Golden Age and Neoclassical tragedies. The ruins, though battered, are still worth a visit. Check out the foundations of the Roman houses and the underground wells. All excavated artifacts now hang at the Museo Numantino in Soria. *(Tel. 975 18 07 12. Open June-Aug. Tu-Sa 10am-2pm and 5-9pm, Su 10am-2pm; Sept.-Oct. and Apr.-May Tu-Sa 10am-2pm and 4-8pm, Su 10am-2pm; Nov.-Mar. Tu-Sa 10am-2pm and 3:30-6pm, Su 10am-2pm. 100 ptas; under 18, over 65, and students free. Sa-Su free.)* Getting to Numancia without a car can be a problem. There is a **bus** to **Garray**, 1km from the ruins (15min., M-F 5:45pm, 90ptas), but buses don't pass by again until 2:15pm the next day. If you need to spend the night, try **Pensión Goyo**, C. Ramon Benito Aceña, 5 (tel. 975 25 20 07; singles 1700ptas, doubles 2500ptas).

EL BURGO DE OSMA

El Burgo de Osma (pop. 5100) is worth the trip for travelers with a car. Those who venture past the town's gritty exterior and explore the streets around the cathedral will be rewarded. Two of the more attractive buildings are the **Hospital de San Agustín** and **Casa Consistorial** in Pl. Mayor. Monk Don Pedro de Osma erected the magnificent 13th-century Gothic **cathedral** on the site of an earlier church. The cathedral's two **museums** have an important collection of codices, including an illuminated Beato de Liébana commentary on the Apocalypse and a 12th-century charter, one of the earliest written examples of Castilian vernacular. (Tel. 975 34 03 22. Open Tu-Su 10am-1pm and 4-7pm. Free; tour of museums 350ptas.) **Gonzalo Ruiz** (tel. 975 22 20 60) sends **buses** from **Soria** (50min.; M-Sa 2 per day, 1:30pm and 6:30pm; Su 1 per day, 10:30am; 460ptas).

Extremadura

0 | 20 miles
0 | 20 kilometers

TO SALAMANCA
TO ÁVILA
TO MADRID
TO SEVILLA
TO CORDOBA

Río Tajo
Alcántara
Coria
Plasencia
Aldeanueva de la Vera
Jarandilla de la Vera
Cuacos
Villanueva de la Vera
Navalmoral de la Mata
Valencia de Alcántara
Arroyo de la Luz
Cáceres
Trujillo
Guadalupe
NV E90
Alburquerque

PORTUGAL
Elvas
Montijo
Mérida
Villanueva de la Serena
Badajoz
NV E90
Olivenza
Castuera
Villafranca de los Barros
Zafra
Jerez de los Caballeros
Llerena
Río Guadiana

N

CENTRAL SPAIN

EXTREMADURA

The aptly named Extremadura is a land of harsh beauty and cruel extremes. Arid plains bake under the intense summer sun, relieved by scattered patches of glowing sunflowers. Yet the traveler who braves the Extremaduran plains is rewarded with stunning ruins and intimate, peaceful towns. Compared to the hectic pace of nearby Madrid, life in Extremadura is slower and less modern, as if the region's rich history dominates its character in the present as well.

These were the lands that hardened New World conquistadors such as Hernán Cortés and Francisco Pizarro, but the conquering heroes never returned to share their spoils with their native land. Today, *extremeños* continue to struggle in one of the more economically depressed regions of Spain. Extremadura has never had a healthy tourist industry; the Roman ruins of Mérida attract most of the region's visitors. But in recent years, brochures and street maps have begun to spring up in tourist offices throughout the region, a sure sign of its growing popularity.

Extremadura has more to offer than history and ruins. Traditional Extremaduran cuisine is particularly appealing. Tempting specialties include rabbit, partridge, lizard with green sauce, wild pigeon with herbs, and *faisán a la Alcántara* (pheasant with a truffle and port wine sauce). *Extremeño* soups are also delicious. *Cocido* (chick pea stew) warms *extremeños* in winter, while the many varieties of gazpacho (including an unusual white one) cool in the summer.

HIGHLIGHTS OF EXTREMADURA

■ The spectacular remains of a **10th-century Arab castle** in Trujillo (see p. 178).
■ The awesome **Teatro Romano** and other Roman ruins at **Mérida** (see p. 179).
■ The whitewashed walls of **Zafra**, best of the tranquil *pueblos blancos* (see p. 182).

CÁCERES

Founded by Romans in 34 BC, the thriving provincial capital and university town of Cáceres (pop. 80,000) is the closest Extremadura comes to a big city. Between the 14th and 16th centuries, rival noble families vied for social and political control, each building a miniature palace to demonstrate their power and wealth. As a result, the old city is a wonderful maze of palaces, museums, and churches. Although Cáceres's newer areas are less interesting, the *Parque del Príncipe* and a healthy nightlife provide ample amusement for a short stay. If the days get too long, you can also use the city as a base for exploring the rest of Extremadura. From Cáceres it is possible to enter Portugal by bus or train through Badajoz, or by train via Valença de Alcántara.

▐ GETTING THERE

Trains run to Cáceres from **Madrid** (4hr., 5 per day, 9am-10:30pm, 2340-4000ptas). **Buses** go from **Badajoz** (1½hr., 2 per day, 1000ptas) and **Sevilla** (4hr., 3 per day, 6:30am-9pm).

▐ ORIENTATION AND PRACTICAL INFORMATION

Both Cáceres's old and new cities lead out from the **Plaza Mayor** (a.k.a. Plaza General Mola), flanked by the **Ciudad Monumental** (old city) and the commercial street of **Avenida de España.** The plaza is 3km from the **bus** and **train stations,** which face each other across the intersection of Av. Hispanidad and Av. Alemania. To get to the center of town from either station, take bus #1 at the intersection to the last stop, Pl. Obispo Galarza (80ptas). Go right upon exiting the bus (in front of the green gas station) and take the first left, first right, and first left down the steps to Pl. Mayor. Bus #2 stops on Av. Hispanidad, around the corner to the right as you emerge from the bus station, and runs to **Plaza de América,** hub of the new downtown area (80ptas). From there, "Ciudad Monumental" signs point up the tree-lined Av. España (Po. Canovas) toward Pl. Mayor. When the *avenida* ends, follow C. San Pedro to the right. When this runs into the Plaza de San Juan, take C. Pintores to the Pl. Mayor.

TRANSPORTATION

Trains: (tel. 927 23 50 61), on Av. Alemania, 3km from the old city across the highway from the bus station. To: **Mérida** (1hr., 4 per day, 500ptas); **Badajoz** (2hr., 3 per day, 980-1800ptas); **Madrid** (4½hr., 5 per day, 2300-3925ptas); **Lisbon** (6hr., 1 per day, 4475ptas); **Sevilla** (4hr., 1 per day, 2300ptas).

Buses: (tel. 927 23 25 50), on Ctra. Sevilla, across from the train station, 3km from the old city. Info window open M-F 7:30am-11:30pm, Sa-Su 8:30am-11:30pm. Fewer buses on weekends. To: **Madrid** (4-5hr., 8 per day, 2390ptas); **Sevilla** (4hr., 5-7 per day, 2250ptas); **Salamanca** (4hr., 3-6 per day, 1695ptas); **Badajoz** (1½hr., 9 per day, 825-1085ptas); **Mérida** (1hr., 2-3 per day, 675ptas); **Trujillo** (45min., 7-10 per day, 385ptas); **Valencia de Alcántara** (2½hr., 2 per day, 940ptas); **Valladolid** (5½hr., 3-4 per day, 2670ptas).

Taxis: Stands at Pl. Mayor and bus and train stations. **Radio Taxi** (tel. 927 23 23 23).

Car Rental: Hertz, Av. Virgen de Guadalupe, 3 (tel. 927 22 43 45). With your back to the bus and train stations, walk up Av. Alemania. At the Pl. de América, take a left on C. Gil Cordero; Av. Virgen de Guadalupe is at the end of this street. Minimum age 25.

TOURIST, FINANCIAL, AND LOCAL SERVICES

Tourist Office: Pl. Mayor, 10 (tel. 927 24 63 47). No English spoken. Open M-F 9am-2pm and 4-6:30pm, Sa-Su 9:15am-2pm; in summer M-F 9:30am-2pm and 5-8pm, Sa-Su 9:15am-2pm. The **Patronato de Tourismo,** C. Ancha, 6 (tel. 927 25 55 97), within the old city, has good maps of the monuments. From Pl. Mayor, take C. Estrella (at the

Arco de la Estrella entrance) into the old city, make a left on C. Condes, and then a right on C. Ancha. Same hours as the tourist office.

Currency Exchange: Banks line Av. España and the streets leading to Pl. Mayor.

Luggage Storage: At the train station (400ptas per day) and bus station (75ptas per item per day).

EMERGENCY AND COMMUNICATIONS

Emergency: tel. 091 or 092. **Police: Municipal** (tel. 927 24 84 24), C. General Margallo.

Late-Night Pharmacy: Four lie in Pl. Mayor, all with the *farmacias de guardia* (late-night pharmacies) list posted in the window.

Hospital: Hospital Provincial (tel. 927 25 68 00), on Av. España, off Pl. Mayor.

Post Office: (tel. 927 22 50 71) on C. Miguel Primo de Rivera, off Av. España on the left from Pl. de América. Open for stamps and Lista de Correos M-F 8:30am-8:30pm, Sa 9:30am-2pm. **Postal Code:** 10071.

Internet Access: Internet, Plaza de Bruselas, 4 (tel. 927 62 60 93). From Pl. de América, take Av. España and make a left onto C. Primo de Rivera. Cross the intersection onto C. Dr. Fleming. Take the first left into the Pl. de Bruselas. Open M-Sa 10am-2pm and 6-10:30pm. 400ptas for 30 min., 600ptas per hr. Students receive 10% discount.

▌ ACCOMMODATIONS

Hostales and *pensiones* line Pl. Mayor and are scattered throughout the new city. Prices are somewhat higher than in larger cities. Make reservations in advance for summer weekends.

Pensión Marquez, Gabriel y Galán, 2 (tel. 927 24 99 60), off Pl. Mayor, opposite the town hall. Cheap and central, Marquez has colorful bedspreads and slanted walls. Doubles 3000ptas; triples 4500ptas. Shower included. No winter heating.

Pensión Carretero, Pl. Mayor, 22 (tel. 927 24 74 82), opposite the tourist office. High ceilings and low beds. TV lounge. Singles 2000ptas, with sink 2500ptas; doubles 3000ptas; triples 4500ptas; quads 6000ptas. No winter heating. Visa, MC.

Hostal Residencia Almonte, C. Gil Cordero, 6 (tel. 927 24 09 25). Head away from Pl. Mayor on Av. España; C. Gil Cordero is right off Pl. de América. A 90-room monster with luxuries in every room: full bath, TV, phone, fluffy towel, and firm bed. Parking garage for three lucky cars 500ptas. Singles 2890ptas; doubles 4494ptas; triples 5620ptas.

Camping: Ciudad de Cáceres, Ctra. Nacional, 630, km 549.6 (tel. 927 23 04 03 or 23 01 30). First-class site just outside of Cáceres, east toward Salamanca. 450ptas per person, per tent, and per car. Children 425ptas.

▯ FOOD

Like every Pl. Mayor, the one in Cáceres is full of restaurants and cafes serving up cheap *bocadillos* (400-600ptas), *raciones* (300-600ptas), and *menús* (900-1200ptas). Explore the side streets off Pl. Mayor for less-touristed local bars and *confiterias*. For groceries, there's always **Super Spar**, C. Parras, 4, at the junction of C. San Antón and C. San Pedro (open M-F 9:30am-2pm and 6-8:30pm, Sa 9:30am-2pm).

El Toro, C. General Ezponda, 2 (tel. 927 22 90 34), just off Pl. Mayor. Yuppified Spanish cuisine in an attractive terra-cotta setting, complete with marble floors. Salads 500ptas. Entrees 700-2500ptas. *Menú* 1200 or 1800ptas. Open Tu-Su.

Pizza Queen, Pl. Mayor, 6 (tel. 927 24 85 31), near the tourist office. Escape the touristy cafes and dig into some cheap and satisfying pizza. Pizza slices from 280ptas. Pasta 280-450ptas. Open Su-Th 1-4pm and 7pm-1am, F-Sa 1-4pm and 7pm-4am.

SIGHTS AND ENTERTAINMENT

The golden, stork-filled **barrio antiguo** is home to one of the most varied architectural ensembles in Europe. Roman, Arabic, Gothic, Renaissance, and even Incan influences (via the conquistadors) have left their mark. The main attraction is the neighborhood as a whole; since most buildings don't open their doors to tourists, the best way to experience the *barrio antigua* is to allow yourself to wander among the curving walls and bird-nests. The neighborhood's manageable size and a handy map from the tourist office will help.

From Pl. Mayor, take the stairs on the left of the tourist office to the **Arco de la Estrella,** the entrance into the walled old city. In front of Arco de la Estrella, **Plaza de Santa María** lies between stone buildings.

CATEDRAL DE SANTA MARÍA. A statue of San Pedro de Alcántara, one of Extremadura's two patron saints, eyes the plaza from a corner pedestal of the Catedral de Santa María. His shiny toes are a result of the myth that anyone who rubs them will have good luck. The cathedral itself, built between 1229 and 1547, is Romanesque and Gothic, with a Renaissance ceiling. The *retablo mayor* (altarpiece) is in Plateresque style, constructed with pine and cedarwood. Cáceres's nobility are buried beneath their family crests on the cathedral floor; you can see some of the same crests on the palaces nearby. *(Open daily for mass. Free.)*

CASA Y TORRE DE LAS CIGÜEÑAS. Historically, Cáceres's aristocracy resolved their disputes through violence, and the monarchs removed all battlements and spires from local lords' houses as punishment. Due to Don Golfín's loyalty to the ruling family, his Casa y Torre de las Cigüeñas (House and Tower of the Storks) was the only one allowed to keep its battlements. Storks nest on its spires every spring. *(From the Arco, turn right onto C. Estrella, left onto C. Condes, and continue to Pl. de San Mateo. Continue down C. Condes to the Plaza de las Veletas, where you can see Casa y Torre de las Cigüeñas on your left.)*

MUSEO DE CÁCERES. Inside the Casa de las Veletas (House of Weathervanes), Museo de Cáceres (Museo Arqueológico Provincial) exhibits Celtiberian stone animals, Roman and Visigothic tombstones, an El Greco, and crafts. The main attraction is the 11th-century Arab *aljibe* (cistern), which supplied Cáceres with water until 1935 and is now a wishing well. *(Across from the Casa y Torre de las Cigüeñas. Tel. 927 24 72 34. Open Tu-Sa 9am-2:30pm, Su 10:15am-2:30pm. 200ptas, students free.)* Nearby **Convento de San Pablo** is late Gothic eye-candy for architecture buffs. *(To the left of Casa y Torre de las Cigüeñas.)*

CASA DEL SOL. Many mansions branch off from the Arco de la Estralla, each emblazoned with a different family crest. The most famous is the 16th-century Casa del Sol, the residence of the Solis family, whose crest has become something of an emblem for the city. *(In the Plaza de San Mateo, next to the Iglesia de San Mateo.)*

OTHER SIGHTS. The Casa de Toledo-Moctezuma was built by the grandson of the Aztec princess Isabel Moctezuma (Tecuixpo Istlaxochitl) to represent a unification of the old and new worlds. *(To the left as you enter the Arco de la Estrella.)* In another Golfín-owned palace, the Palacio de los Golfines de Arriba, Francisco Franco was proclaimed head of the Spanish state and Generalissimo of its armies on October 26, 1936. *(Near C. Olmos and C. Adarros de Santa Ana.)*

ENTERTAINMENT. At night, revelers crowd the **Plaza Mayor** and its environs or stroll along **Avenida de España** or C. Pizarro, which is dotted with live-music bars. Later at night, the party moves to the area called **La Madrala,** near Pl. Albatros in the new city. From the Pl. Mayor, take Av. España, make a right on Primo de Rivera, cross the intersection onto C. Dr. Fleming, and take a right into La Madrala.

AT&T
direct
service

Exploring the corners of the earth? We're with you. With the world's most powerful network, **AT&T Direct®** Service gives you fast, clear connections from more countries than anyone,* and the option of an English-speaking operator. All it takes is your AT&T Calling Card. And the planet is yours.

For a list of AT&T Access Numbers, take the attached wallet guide.

AT&T

*Comparison to major U.S.-based carriers.

AT&T Direct® Service

AT&T Access Numbers

Austria ●	0800-200-288	Egypt ● (Cairo)	510-0200
Albania ●	00-800-0010	(Outside Cairo)	02-510-0200
Armenia ● ▲	8◆10111	Estonia	800-800-1001
Bahrain	800-000	Finland ●	9800-100-10
Belgium ●	0-800-100-10	France	0-800-99-0011
Bulgaria ▲	00-800-0010	Germany	0800-2255-288
Croatia	0800-220111	Greece ●	00-800-1311
Czech Rep. ▲	00-42-000-101	Hungary ●	00-800-01111
Cyprus ●	080-90010	Ireland ✓	1-800-550-000
Denmark	8001-0010	Israel	1-800-94-94-949

Italy ●	172-1011	Russia ● ▲	
Luxembourg †	0-800-0111	(Moscow) ▶	755-5042
Macedonia, F.Y.R. of ○		(St. Petersburg) ▶	325-5042
	99-800-4288	Saudi Arabia ○	1-800-10
Malta	0800-890-110	South Africa	0-800-99-0123
Monaco ●	800-90-288	Spain	900-99-00-11
Morocco	002-11-0011	Sweden	020-799-111
Netherlands ●	0800-022-9111	Switzerland ●	0-800-89-0011
Norway	800-190-11	Turkey ●	00-800-12277
Poland ● ▲	00-800-111-1111	U.K. ▲ ✤	0800-89-0011
Portugal ▲	0800-800-128	U.K. ▲ ✤	0500-89-0011
Romania ●	01-800-4288	U.A. Emirates ●	800-121

FOR EASY CALLING WORLDWIDE

1. Just dial the AT&T Access Number for the country you are calling from.
2. Dial the phone number you're calling. *3.* Dial your card number.

For access numbers not listed ask any operator for **AT&T Direct®** Service. In the U.S. call 1-800-331-1140 for a wallet guide listing all worldwide AT&T Access Numbers.
Visit our Web site at: www.att.com/traveler
Bold-faced countries permit country-to-country calling outside the U.S.

- ● Public phones require coin or card deposit.
- ▲ May not be available from every phone/payphone.
- ▶ Additional charges apply outside the city.
- ○ Calling available to most countries.
- ◆ Await second dial tone.
- ✓ Use U.K. access number in N. Ireland.
- ✤ If call does not complete, use 0800-013-0011.
- † Collect calling from public phones.
- ○ Public phones require local coin payment through the call duration.

When placing an international call *from* the U.S., dial 1 800 CALL ATT.

© 1999 AT&T

DAYTRIPS FROM CÁCERES

TRUJILLO

Perched on a steep granite hill, Trujillo (pop. 10,000) is known as the "Cradle of Conquistadors." Over 600 explorers and plunderers of the New World, including Peru's conqueror Francisco Pizarro and the Amazon's first explorer, Francisco de Orellana, hailed from here. Scattered with medieval palaces, Roman ruins, and Arabic fortresses, Trujillo is a hodgepodge of histories and cultures. However, the most impressive monument is the 10th-century Moorish castle, commanding the top of the hill and a resplendent panorama of Extremadura. Twentieth-century residents take pride in the well-preserved beauty of their churches, palace, and castle, adorning them with lovely gardens and flowering vines.

⃞ ORIENTATION AND PRACTICAL INFORMATION. The **bus** station (tel. 927 32 12 02) is on the road to Badajoz at the foot of the hill (look for the **AutoRes** sign). Buses offer access to many nearby cities and towns, including **Cáceres** (45min., 6-10 per day, 385ptas) and Madrid. To get to the **Plaza Mayor** (15min.), turn right as you exit the station (up Av. de Miajadas). Turn right on C. de la Encarnación, following signs to the tourist office, then left on C. Chica; turn left on C. Guia and right on C. Burgos, continuing onto the Plaza. The **tourist office** (tel. 927 32 26 77) is across the plaza and posts info in its windows when closed. (Open M-F 9:30am-2pm and 4-6:30pm; in summer M-F 9:30am-2pm and 5-7:30pm, Sa-Su 9:45am-2pm.) **Currency exchange** available at **Banco Central Hispano**, Pl. Mayor, 25 (tel. 927 24 24 24). **Medical emergency** tel. 927 32 20 16; **police**, C. Carniceria, 2 (tel. 927 32 01 04 or 927 32 10 16), just off Pl. Mayor. **Post office**, Po. Ruiz de Mendoza, 28 (tel. 927 32 05 33), on the way from the station to Pl. Mayor (open M-F 9am-2:30pm, Sa 9:30am-1pm); **postal code**: 10200. **Telephone code**: 927.

⃞ ACCOMMODATIONS AND FOOD. Enjoy the luxuries of a real hotel at the spotless **Hostal Trujillo**, C. de Francisco Pizarro, 4-6 (tel. 927 32 26 61). From the train station, turn left on the Av. de Miajadas, right on C. de la Encarnacion, and right onto C. de Francisco Pizarro. All rooms with full bath and TV. (Singles 2670ptas; doubles 4500ptas; triples 6000ptas.) Or try **Pensión Boni**, C. Mingo de Ramos, 7 (tel. 927 32 16 04), off Pl. Mayor to the right of the church. Airy patio rooms with floor-to-ceiling windows; the claustrophobic, however, should avoid the showers. (Singles 2500ptas; doubles 3000ptas, with bath 3500ptas; luxury triple with full bath and A/C 5500ptas.)

For a delicious meal, head to **Mesón-Restaurante La Troya**, Pl. Mayor, 8-12 (tel. 927 32 13 64), decorated in the style of a typical Spanish house with local *artesania* (crafts). The three-course *menú* is 1990ptas. (Open daily 1-4:30 and 9-11:30pm.) **Nuria's**, Pl. Mayor, 27 (tel. 972 32 09 07), across the plaza, is less expensive, with *bocadillos* for 325-650ptas or a traditional Extremaduran *menú* with regional wine for 1550ptas. (Open daily 1-4pm and 8pm-2am. Visa, MC.)

⃞ SIGHTS. Unlike those in Cáceres and Badajoz, Trujillo's monuments successfully blend with the Plaza Mayor and new city. The **Plaza Mayor** was the inspiration for the Plaza de Armas in Cuzco, Perú, which was constructed after Francisco Pizarro defeated the Incas. Palaces, arched corridors, and sprawling cafes surround the central fountain and the **Estatua de Pizarro.** The gift of an American admirer of Pizarro, the bronze statue was erected in 1927 and, like the plaza, has a twin in Perú.

Festooned with stork nests, **Iglesia de San Martín** dominates the northeastern corner of the plaza, while a baroque organ fills the church's interior. The church has several historic tombs, but contrary to local lore, Francisco de Orellana does not rest here. (Evening and Sunday mass not open to the public.) Across the street, the seven chimneys of the **Palacio de los Duques de San Carlos** reputedly symbolize the religions conquered by Spaniards in the New World. (Open daily 10am-1pm and 4:30-6:30pm. 100pta donation requested.)

To get to the **Casa-Museo de Pizarro,** walk uphill on the stone road to the right of the Iglesia de San Martín. The bottom floor of the house is a reproduction of the living quarters of a 15th-century *hidalgo* (nobleman), and the top floor is dedicated to the life and times of Francisco Pizarro. (Open daily 11am-2pm and 4-8pm. 250ptas, seniors and students 100ptas.) The Gothic **Iglesia de Santa María** is located even farther up the hill from the Casa-Museo, through the Puerta de Santiago. According to legend, the giant soldier Diego García de Paredes (known as the "Extremaduran Samson") picked up the fountain at age 11 and carried it to his mother; the giant was buried here after he twisted his ankle and fell to his death. The church's 27-panel Gothic *retablo* at the high altar was painted by master Fernando Gallego. (Open daily 10:30am-2pm and 5-8pm; Su mass 11am. 50ptas.) To the left of the church is the restored **Museo de la Coria,** which explores the relationship between Extremadura and Latin America, both in the past and future. (Open Sa-Su 11:30am-2pm. Free.)

At the top of the hill are the spectacular ruins of a ▨**10th-century Arab castle.** Battlements and ramparts offer a view of the unspoiled landscape, with Trujillo on one side and fields scarred with ancient walls on the other. Inside the castle's intact walls lie remnants of its *aljibe* (cistern) and the entrance to the lower-level (and very dark) dungeons. (Open daily dawn to dusk. Free.)

GUADALUPE

Two hours east of Trujillo and a four-hour bus ride southwest of Madrid, Guadalupe rests on a mountainside in the Sierra de Guadalupe. For pilgrims and backpackers, the **Real Monasterio de Santa María de Guadalupe,** with its eclectic history and decadent architecture, is a worthy daytrip. The fairy tale Monastery has even been nicknamed "the Spanish Sistine Chapel."

In 1340 at the Battle of Salado, Alfonso XI, supposedly aided by the Virgin Mary, defeated a much superior Muslim army. As a token of his gratitude, he commissioned the lavish Real Monasterio. Years later it became customary to grant licenses for foreign expeditions on the premises. Columbus finalized his contract with Fernando and Isabel here. To pay homage to the city, he named one of the islands he discovered Guadalupe (now known as Turugueira). The hour-long tour allows visitors to admire the **museum** containing embroidered ecclesiastical finery, the Gothic and Mudejar **cloisters,** and the towering **basilica** (whose *retablo* was designed by El Greco's son). The most prominent object in the basilica is the **icon of the Virgin,** which is made of wood, blackened with age, and cloaked in gold and silver robes. Also of note is the **sacristy,** with its ornately decorated walls and Francisco de Zurburban's portraits of monks. (Monastery open daily 3:30-6:30pm; in summer 9:30am-1pm and 3:30-6:30pm. 300ptas.)

Transportation to and from Guadalupe can be somewhat tricky; most visitors arrive on tour buses or in their own cars. **Buses** run to **Cáceres** (somewhat irregular; call Empresa Mirat, tel. 927 23 25 50), **Madrid** (4hr., 1 per day, 2500ptas), and **Trujillo** (2hr., 1 per day). Bus schedules virtually force an overnight stay in Guadalupe, but they provide for a pleasant calm before returning to a larger city. The **tourist office** in **Plaza Mayor** posts info on the door (open Tu-Su 10am-2pm and 5-7pm); follow signs from the bus station. Travelers looking for food or beds should head to Pl. Mayor. At dreamy **Hostal Cerezo,** Gregorio López, 12 (tel. 927 36 73 79), the airy rooms all have tidy baths. (Singles 2800ptas; doubles 4300ptas; triples 5400ptas. 7% IVA not included. Visa.) If you have some extra time, be sure to sample local cuisine and liqueurs; the monks had strict rules about the quality of cooking, and their devotion to food is reflected in today's cuisine. **Mesón Típico Isabel,** Pl. Santa María Guadalupe, 13 (tel. 927 36 71 26), off the Pl. Mayor, offers modern rooms, private baths, and a popular bar (singles 3000ptas; doubles 4000ptas; bar open daily 8:30am-4pm and 11pm-1am).

CENTRAL SPAIN

MÉRIDA

If you like Roman ruins, then you'll love Mérida (pop. 60,000). This town, which is known for having the most ruins in Spain, warrants at least a day's visit. As a reward for services rendered to the Roman Empire, in 26 BC, Augustus Caesar gave a heroic group of veteran legionnaires a new city in Lusitania, a province comprised of Portugal and part of Spain. The veterans chose a lovely spot surrounded by several hills on the banks of the Río Guadiana and founded their new home, which they named "Augusta Emerita." Not content to rest on their laurels and itching to gossip with fellow patricians in Sevilla and Salamanca, soldiers proceeded to build the largest bridge in Lusitania, now the Puente Romano. The nostalgic crew adorned their "little Rome" with baths, aqueducts, temples, a hippodrome, an arena, and a famous amphitheater. Today, Mérida's ruins are part of the city and are complemented by walkways, small plazas, and the world-class Museo Romano. In July and August, the spectacular *Festival de Teatro Clásico* presents some of Europe's finest classical and modern theater and dance, performed among the ruins.

▐ GETTING THERE

Trains run to Mérida from: **Cáceres** (1hr., 4 per day, 500ptas); **Sevilla** (4½hr., 1 per day, 4:30pm, 1790ptas); **Madrid** (5½hr., 3 per day, 9am-2:40pm, 3000ptas). **Buses** go from **Badajoz** (1½hr., 7 per day, 610ptas).

▐ ORIENTATION AND PRACTICAL INFORMATION

Plaza de España, the town center, is two blocks up from the Puente Romano and easily accessible from the **Teatro Romano.** The cafes and shops around the plaza quickly transform into quiet residential neighborhoods, and streets often lose their signs. From the **bus station** to Pl. España, cross the suspension bridge (**Puente de Lusitania**) in front of the station and turn right on Av. de Roma. Walk along the river until you reach the Puente Romano, then turn left on C. Puente, which leads straight into Pl. España (20min.). To get to Pl. España from the **train station,** take C. Cardero (on your left as you exit the station) and its continuation, C. Camilo José Cela. Bear right onto C. Felix Valverde Lillo, and follow it to Pl. España (5-10min.).

TRANSPORTATION

Trains: (tel. 924 31 81 09), C. Cardero. Buses generally run more frequently. Info window open daily 7am-11pm. To: **Cáceres** (1hr., 4 per day, 500-1200ptas); **Badajoz** (1hr., 7 per day, 400-1100ptas); **Zafra** (1hr., 2 per day, 400ptas); **Madrid** (4hr., 5 per day, 2800-4100ptas); **Sevilla** (4½hr., 1 per day, 1650ptas). For trains to **Lisbon,** transfer in Cáceres (2 per day, 2900ptas).

Buses: (tel. 924 37 14 04), Av. Libertad, in the "Polígono Nueva Ciudad." To: **Cáceres** (1hr., 2 per day, 675ptas); **Badajoz** (1hr., 10 per day, 610ptas); **Zafra** (1¼hr., 8 per day, 600ptas); **Sevilla** (3hr., 14 per day, 1600ptas); **Salamanca** (5hr., 4 per day, 2185ptas); **Madrid** (5½hr., 8 per day, 2760-3790ptas); **Valladolid** (6hr., 3 per day, 3350ptas); **Burgos** (9hr., 1 per day, 4200ptas); **Barcelona** (12hr., 1 per day, 6425ptas); **San Sebastián** (13hr., 1 per day, 5885ptas).

Taxis: Teletaxi (24hr. tel. 924 31 57 56).

Car Rental: Avis (tel. 924 37 33 11 or 909 26 32 32), at the bus station. Mid-sized car 9685ptas per day, 51,565ptas per week. IVA and insurance included. Open M-F 9am-1pm and 5-8pm, Sa 9am-1pm. Must be 25 to rent.

TOURIST, FINANCIAL, AND LOCAL SERVICES

Tourist Office: (tel. 924 26 32 32), on C. P.M. Plano, across the street from the Museo Romano and to the left as you exit the Teatro. From Pl. España, the town center, head up C. Santa Eulalia, which becomes a pedestrian shopping street, then bear right on C. J. Ramon Melida at the little circle with the statue. The tourist office is at the end of the street to the right (10-15min.). Friendly, multilingual staff doles out small maps, theater schedules, and lists of accommodations. Open M-F 9am-1:45pm and 4-6pm, Sa-Su 9:15am-1:45pm; in summer M-F 9am-1:45pm and 5-7:15pm, Sa-Su 9:15am-1:45pm. Get theater tickets at the **Caja Rural de Extremadura,** C. Felix Valerde Lillo, 17 (tel. 924 31 68 98; email festivalmerida@cajarural.com), or at the theater. Tickets 700-3500ptas.

Luggage Storage: Available at the bus station (100ptas per day) and train station (400ptas per day).

EMERGENCY AND COMMUNICATIONS

Emergency: tel. 091 or 092. **Police:** (tel. 924 31 24 58) on C. Vespiano. From Pl. España, turn left on C. Trajano, go through Pl. Constitución, turn right on C. Almendralejo, and left on C. Vespiano.

Medical Services: Residencia Sanitaria de la Seguridad Social Centralita (tel. 924 38 10 00). From Pl. España, follow the C. John Lennon, curving right onto C. Graciano. Follow this through its multiple name changes; the hospital is on your right after Pl. de Toros. **Emergency:** tel. 924 38 10 18.

Post Office: (tel. 924 31 24 58), Pl. Constitución. Follow signs to the *parador;* the office is directly opposite. From Pl. España, turn left on C. Trajano and follow it to the plaza. Open for Lista de Correos M-F 8:30am-8:30pm, Sa 9:30am-1pm. **Postal Code:** 06800.

Internet Access: Cafe Internet, C. Banos, 25 (tel. 924 38 86 58). Worthwhile even if you don't use the computers, this cafe is a sign of Mérida's urbanization. Turn right on C. Z. Vincente from Pl. España, left on C. Sagasta, and right on C. Banos — it's on the left. 350ptas for 30min., 500ptas for 1hr., 900ptas for 2hr. Prices include a beer.

▌ ACCOMMODATIONS

Even during *siesta*, the streets of Mérida are crowded with visor-sporting tourists. Thankfully, there are a number of centrally located budget accommodations. The Romans didn't use plastic and neither will you; expect to pay in cash.

Pensión El Arco, C. Cervantes, 16 (tel. 924 31 83 21 or 30 32 70). Follow C. Santa Eulalia up from Pl. España; C. Cervantes is on the left. The gregarious owner of this *pensión* collects mementos from guests; the reception area doubles as a gallery of signed photos of kings and queens. Spacious rooms complete with patterned headboards. No sinks or baths in rooms. Singles 1800ptas; doubles 3000ptas.

Hostal Nueva España, Av. Extremadura, 6 (tel. 924 31 33 56 or 924 31 32 11). From the train station turn left off C. Cardero onto Av. Extremadura. Closets are huge; you may have to hide in there to escape the sound of avenue traffic. However, all rooms have spotless private baths. Singles 2800ptas; doubles 4800ptas; triples 6800ptas. Parking garage 900ptas per car.

Hostal-Residencia Senero, C. Holguín, 12 (tel. 924 31 72 07), off the winding street to the left of Hotel Emperatriz (on Pl. España). Clean and comfortable with space-saving baths and quieter rooms than the Pl. España allows. Rooms overlooking the patio can get a bit hot and stuffy. Singles 2400ptas; doubles 4000ptas; triples 5100ptas. Cheaper in the off season.

▌ FOOD

Plaza de España is filled with outdoor cafes; however, the budget traveler won't find many deals here. For the cheapest option, markets provide ample supplies, and the ruins are the ideal picnic setting. The **market** is on C. San Francisco, in between C. Lillo and Sta. Eulalia; take C. Trajano from Pl. España (open M-Sa 8am-2pm). For **groceries,** try **EcoStop,** (tel. 924 31 11 51) on C. Cabo Verde. With your back to the theater entrance, turn right and then left to get to C. Cabo Verde. (Open M-F 9:30am-2:30pm and 5:30-9pm, Sa 9:30am-3pm. Visa, MC.)

Casa Benito, C. San Francisco, 3 (tel. 924 31 55 00), to the left as you face the market. Relax and sip a beer (100ptas) under the ivy canopy. *Tapas* 100-500ptas, *bocadillos* 400-800ptas. Kitchen open daily 1-4pm and 9pm-midnight; bar open daily and nightly.

Bar-Restaurante Briz, C. Félix Valverde Lillo, 5 (tel. 924 31 93 07). Large bar and lots of locals. Entrees 750-1400ptas. Hefty *menú* (1350ptas). Open 1-4pm and 9pm-midnight. Visa, MC.

Cafeteria Lusi (tel. 924 31 31 11). Facing the Hotel Emperatriz in the Pl. España, take the first walkway to left. The inside is structured around a circular and social bar. The little plaza outside is ideal for people-watching and *tapas*-consuming. Take advantage of the fresh fruit options (175-225ptas).

👁 SIGHTS

MUSEO NACIONAL DE ARTE ROMANO. This elegant museum includes all the Roman memorabilia you could ask for: statues, dioramas, coins, remains of wall paintings, and an excavated street. There is even a Roman road which passes under and through the museum. To catch a glimpse of what Augusta Emerita once was, take a tour of the **cripta.** *(To get to the museo, follow C. Santa Eulalia from Pl. España and bear right down C. Juan Ramón Melida. Tel. 924 31 16 90. Open Tu-Sa 10am-2pm and 4-6pm, Su and holidays 10am-2pm; in summer Tu-Sa 10am-2pm and 5-7pm, Su and holidays 10am-2pm. 400ptas, students 200ptas. Saturday afternoons and Sundays free.)*

🏛 ROMAN RUINS

*The **combined ticket** to visit the Teatro Romano, the Anfiteatro Romano, the Casa del Mitreo, the Casa del Anfiteatro, and Alcazaba is the cheapest way to see all the monuments. Combined ticket 8000ptas, EU students 400ptas, Saturday afternoons and Sunday mornings free. All open daily in summer 9:30am-1:45pm and 5pm-7:15pm; the rest of the year schedules subject to change.*

Roman edifices crumble slowly and beautifully, and the remains of ancient monuments are strewn throughout Mérida. Over the wide, shallow Río Guadiana, the **Puente Romano,** one of the Romans' largest bridges, is still the main entrance into town.

🏛 **TEATRO ROMANO.** The spectacular *teatro* was a gift from Agrippa, a Roman administrator, to the city in 16 BC. The 6000 seats face a *scaenaefrons*, an incredible marble colonnade built upstage. **Teatro Clásico** performances take place here. *(Located in a park across the street from the Museo Nacional. Tel. 924 31 25 30. Staffed daily noon-2pm and 7:30-11:30pm. Performances July-Aug., 10:45pm. Tickets 700-3500ptas.)*

ANFITEATRO ROMANO. The most popular entertainment at the time was found in the 16,000-seat *anfiteatro*. Inaugurated in 8 BC, the *anfiteatro* was used for man-to-man gladiator combat, combat between animals, and even contests between men and wild animals. *(Separate admission 600ptas.)*

CIRCO ROMANO. Near the theater complex is the Circo Romano, or hippodrome. The most famous Lusitanian racer, Diocles, got his start here and ended his career in Rome with a whopping 1462 victories. Once filled with cheering spectators, the

BULLBOARDS Staring glassy-eyed out the window of your preferred mode of transportation, you may notice rather unusual monuments along the highway: massive, black paper cut-outs of solitary bulls. Once upon a time (in the 1980s) these cut-outs were advertisements for *Soberano Coñac* (cognac). In the early 1990s, however, billboards were prohibited on national roads. A plan was drafted to take the bulls down, but Spaniards protested, as the lone bull towering along the roadside had become an important national symbol. After considerable clamoring and hoofing, the bulls were painted black and left to loom proudly against the horizon. The familiar shape now decorates t-shirts and pins in souvenir shops, but the real thing is still impressive. Keep your eyes peeled as you whiz through the countryside.

CENTRAL SPAIN

arena (capacity 30,000) is now a quiet public park. *(From outside the ruins, follow the curve of the road to the right, turn left on C. Cabo Verde over the train tracks, and turn right on Av. Juan Carlos.)*

CASA DEL MITREO AND CASA DEL ANFITEATRO. These ruins of Roman homes house some of the world's finest Roman mosaics. Take special note of the Casa del Mitreo's **Mosaico Cosmólogico,** which depicts the ancient Romans' conception of the world and the forces of nature. *(For Casa del Mitreo, walk down Po. Alvarez with Teatro Romano on your left and take a right on Vía Ensarele; Casa del Anfiteatro is to the left of the anfiteatro with your back to the entrance.)*

OTHER RUINS. Also of note is the **Alcazaba,** a Moorish fortress built with materials discarded by the Visigoths to guard the Roman bridge. Go for the view of the river and Puente Romano—despite a cistern filled with river water, not much else remains. *(Down the banks of the Guadiana and near Pl. España.)* At the end of C. Rambla Mártir Santa Eulalia stand the **museo, basílica,** and **iglesia,** all commemorating a martyred child, Santa Eulalia. During the course of repairs to the church in 1990 (it was originally constructed in the 6th century, turned over to the Arabs in 875, and rebuilt in 1230 during the Reconquest), layers of ruins were uncovered. These newly discovered ruins include Roman houses dating from the 3rd to 1st centuries BC, a 4th-century necropolis, and a basilica dedicated to Santa Eulalia. *(From Pl. España, take C. Santa Eulalia and bear left onto the rambla. Museum and basilica open daily 4-5:45pm, in summer daily 10am-1:45pm and 5-7:15pm. They are part of the combined ticket to the Roman ruins; see above. Church open daily during services at 8:30am and 8pm. Free.)*

NEAR MÉRIDA: LOS PUEBLOS BLANCOS

Named for their glowing whitewashed walls, the *pueblos blancos,* a series of tranquil towns in southern Extremadura, merit a visit from Mérida or Badajoz.

■**ZAFRA.** Known as "little Sevilla" for its gaiety and resemblance to the Andalucian city, **Zafra** is full of lovely white buildings with iron balconies and delicate tilework. It is home to stunning 17th- and 18th-century mansions (such as the **Casa de los Marqueses de Solanda,** a Renaissance Alcázar and now a *parador de turismo*), and charming plazas. Also noteworthy is the courtyard of **Hernan Cortes Parador,** designed by El Escorial's architect, Juan de Herrera. Exiting the bus station, walk down the dusty road straight ahead to get to the town center. Call 924 55 39 07 to confirm bus schedules to Sevilla and Cáceres. Zafra has a **train station** (tel. 924 55 02 15), but it's a hike from town.

LLERENA. Picturesque **Llerena** was an important seat of the Inquisition, the center of the military Orden de Santiago, and a 14th-century frontier town. Now home to a beautiful palm-treed Pl. Mayor, Llerena is a textbook example of Mudéjar architecture. The church of **Nuestra Senora de la Granada** is a blend of Mudéjar and Baroque elements. Buses run from Zafra (1¼hr., 4 per day, 510ptas) and Mérida (1½hr., 5 per day, 1200ptas) during the week.

JEREZ DE LOS CABALLEROS. The area around **Jerez de los Caballeros** is a mysterious prehistoric settlement, with vestiges of the Megalithic culture. Roman inscriptions, funerary monuments, and mosaics remain from later eras, as does the decorated brick and painted stucco of the 13th-century Knights Templar's **Castilla Fortaleza.** In 1312, the knights were put to death in the tower of their own church; since then it has been dubbed the **Torre Sangrienta** (bloody tower). Buses run to and from Zafra (4 per day, 400ptas) and Mérida (1 per day, 1200ptas).

OLIVENZA. Olivenza was founded by the Portuguese Knights Templar. Its **Santa Maria Magdalena** is rich in the Portuguese Manueline style. The **Santa Casa de Misericordia** is also worth a visit. Buses run from Badajoz (7 per day, 235ptas).

BADAJOZ

Badajoz (pop. 120,000) is often not much more than a necessary stop en route to or from Portugal. While the Moorish ruins and 13th-century cathedral provide for a distracting afternoon, the neglected new city offers little but industrial pollution. Its proximity to Portugal has rendered it the site of countless border disputes; the border is 7km to the west, and Elvas, Portugal, lies 11km beyond. However, settlement since prehistoric times has certainly developed Badajoz's nightlife. Street parties erupt in the evening in the Plaza de España, and jealous Portuguese revelers often cross the border to partake.

█ GETTING THERE

Trains run to Badajoz from **Elvas, Portugal** (15min., 3 per day, 12:30-4:30pm, 460$). **Buses** go from **Cáceres** (1½hr., 9 per day, 825-1085ptas) and **Sevilla** (3½hr., 6 per day, 1690ptas).

▮ ORIENTATION AND PRACTICAL INFORMATION

Plaza de España is the heart of Badajoz, bridging the narrow streets of the old town and the more commercial neighborhoods near **Plaza Libertad.** From Pl. España, C. Juan de Ribera leads to Pl. Libertad (5min.) and the tourist office. Between Pl. de España and Pl. Libertad is **Plaza San Francisco** (also right off C. Juan Ribera), where the post office, supermarket, and restaurants surround a small park. Pl. de España is across the unsightly Río Guadiana from the **train station.** To get from the train station to the center of town, follow Av. Carolina Coronado straight to the Puente de Palmas, cross the bridge, and go straight on C. Prim and its continuation. Turn left on C. Juan de Ribera to get to Pl. de España, right to get to Pl. Libertad (35min.). The #1 bus takes you from the train station to Pl. Libertad, stopping directly across from the **tourist office.** To Pl. de España from the **bus station,** turn left, take a quick right, and then turn left on C. Damión Tellez Lafuente. It becomes C. Fernando Cazadilla, passes through Pl. Constitución, becoming first Av. Europa and then C. Pedro de Valdivia, and runs uphill to the plaza (20min.).

Flights: Aeropuerto de Badajoz (tel. 924 21 04 00), Carretera Madrid-Lisboa, 10km east of the city. Small national airport services Palma, Mallorca, and Tenerife, with **AirEuropa** and **Futuro** terminals. From Pl. España, walk down C. Zurbaran; turn left on Av. Ronda del Pillar and cross the bridge out of the city. It makes more sense to take a cab (2000ptas.).

Trains: (tel. 924 27 11 70), Av. Carolina Coronado. It's probably easier to take a bus. To get from the train station to Pl. Libertad, take bus #1. Info booth open daily 6am-9pm. To: **Mérida** (1½hr., 7 per day, 400-1200ptas); **Zafra** (2 per day via Mérida, 925ptas); **Cáceres** (2½hr., 4 per day, 850-1900ptas); **Madrid** (5hr., 2 per day, 4000-4500ptas); **Lisbon** (5½hr., 1per day, 2635ptas); **Barcelona** (2 per day, 6800-8300ptas).

Buses: C. José Rebollo López, 2 (tel. 924 25 86 61). Buses #3, 6a, 6b, and 9 run between the bus station and Pl. Libertad. Info window open daily 7:45am-9pm. To: **Zafra** (1hr., 5-9 per day, 745ptas); **Mérida** (1½hr., 7 per day, 610ptas); **Cáceres** (1½hr., 2 per day, 1000ptas); **Madrid** (4hr., 8 per day, 3200ptas); **Sevilla** (4½hr., 5 per day, 1670ptas); **Salamanca** (5hr., 4 per day, 2900ptas); **Lisbon** (6hr., 3-6 per day, 3000ptas).

Taxis: At bus and train stations and Pl. de España. **Radio-Taxi** (24hr. tel. 924 24 31 01).

Tourist Office: Pl. Libertad, 3 (tel. 924 22 27 63). City maps and glossy brochures in multiple languages, but staff does not speak English. Open M-F 9:30am-2pm and 5-7:30pm, Sa-Su 9:45am-2pm. For tips on nightlife, visit the **Oficina de Informacion Juvenil,** Pasaje de San Juan, 2P (tel. 924 21 00 88). On the right as you walk up C. San Juan from Pl. de España.

Luggage Storage: In the bus station (50ptas per item) and train station (400ptas).

Emergency: tel. 091 or 092. **Police:** (tel. 924 23 02 53) on Av. Ramón y Cajal. From Pl. Libertad, take Av. Ramón y Cajal. Located at the far corner of the avenida and C. Dosmos.

Hospital: Hospital Provincial, Pl. Minayo, 2 (tel. 924 22 47 43). From Pl. de España, walk toward Pl. San Francisco on C. Juan de Ribera; it's on your left before you reach the plaza.

Post Office: Pl. San Francisco, 4 (tel. 924 22 02 04). Main entrance on Pl. San Francisco. Open for stamps and Lista de Correos M-F 8:30am-8:30pm, Sa 9am-2pm. **Postal Code:** 06001.

ACCOMMODATIONS

Most hostels are near Pl. España; they are scarce, however, so keep an eye out.

Hostal Niza II, C. Arco-Agüero, 45 (tel. 924 22 38 81). From Pl. de España go down C. Ramón Albarran, and turn left on C. Arco-Agüero. Large rooms, lofty ceilings, and an owner eager to provide maps, brochures, and history. In the heart of Badajoz; on weekends, try an interior room and/or pillow over the head to block out the sounds of revelry. Singles 1700ptas; doubles 3200ptas; triples 4800ptas. Visa, MC.

Hostal Victoria, C. Luís de Camoes, 3 (tel. 924 27 16 62), a 2min. walk down the boulevard from the train station, on a quiet street to your left. Ideal location if just passing through by train. Small, modern rooms with phones and occasional A/C. TV lounge. Singles 2000ptas, with shower 2500ptas; doubles with bath and TV 4280ptas.

Pension Pintor, C. Arco-Agüero, 26 (tel. 924 22 42 28). From Pl. de España go down C. Ramón Albarran, and turn left on C. Arco-Agüero. Spartan but spacious rooms. A very tiny dog with a very loud bark guards the clean, tiled bathroom. Singles 2000ptas; doubles 3000ptas; triples 4500ptas.

FOOD

For cafes and restaurants, check around **Plazas España, Libertad,** and especially **San Francisco.** For **groceries,** try **Simago,** next to the post office on Pl. San Francisco (open M-Sa 9:15am-9:15pm; Visa, MC). **El Tronco,** C. Muñoz Torrero, 16 (tel. 924 22 20 76), right off Pl. España (with your back to the cathedral) serves typical Extremaduran fare. With yellow stucco on the outside and antlers and tile floors inside, the decor is as eclectic as its crowd. Young and old mingle at the bar for drinks and *tapas.* (*Menú* 1250ptas. Open Tu-Sa 9am-4pm and 8pm-2am.) **Café Bar La Ría,** Pl. de España, 7 (tel. 924 22 20 05), is a popular hangout and cafeteria for locals. Best on the go for cheap meals and ice cream. (Large, tasty entrees 800-2100ptas. *Menú* 980ptas. A/C. Open W-M 8am-1am.)

SIGHTS AND ENTERTAINMENT

In 1995, Badajoz inaugurated its ■**Museo Extremeño e Iberoamericano de Arte Contemporáneo** (tel. 924 26 03 84). Its five floors exhibit recent works from Spain, Portugal, and Latin America, contrasting the distinct cultures of these regions. The permanent collection includes a few controversial creations like Marta María Pérez Bravo's photograph of a woman's breasts as a communion offering. From Pl. de España, head down C. Juan Ribera, continuing as it turns into Av. Europa. The museum is on your left after Pl. Constitución. (Open Tu-Sa 10:30am-1:30pm and 5-8pm, Sun 10:30am-1:30pm; in summer Tu-Sa 10:30am-1:30pm and 6-9pm, Sun 10:30am-1:30pm. Free.)

While the newer parts of Badajoz are stuffed with banks and ice cream stands, the old city around **Plaza de España** and **Plaza San Francisco** is rich with history. Visit the 13th-century **cathedral,** a converted mosque, in Pl. de España. The tower celebrates the town's varied eras, with three windows—one Romanesque, one Gothic, and one Plateresque. Nearby Pl. San Francisco is a delightful and romantic spot. However, the neighborhood gets progressively more run-down as you walk farther uphill from the two plazas.

CENTRAL SPAIN

The ruins of the **Alcazaba,** a Moorish citadel, stand at the top of the hill. For a tour of the old city and the ruins, take C. San Juan up the hill from Pl. de España, and veer left on C. M. Zancudo to enter **Plaza Alta.** Continue through the plaza and across the C. S. de Figueroa to reach the top. (Open Tu-Su 10am-3pm. 200ptas; EU citizens, students, and under 21 free.) Nearby is the **Torre del Apéndiz,** nicknamed Torre de Espantaperros ("to shoo away Christian dogs"), which served as the Alcazaba's watchtower and has become the city's emblem. Just below the ruins sits the simple and informative **Museo Arqueológico Provincial** (tel. 924 22 23 14); note the prehistoric collection and Visigoth artistry.

Nightlife in Badajoz spills out from the bars and fills several blocks of the *centro;* partiers come from neighboring towns, and sometimes even Portugal, to partake. The best revelry takes place out in the streets, not in clubs. **Calle de San Blas,** off Pl. de España, is wriggling with teens passing around *minis* (large glasses) of *cerveza* or cider (325ptas). **Calle de Zurbarán,** also off Pl. de España, is filled with 20-somethings. Later in the evening, around 2am, the party shifts to the pubs of **Plaza Conquistadores,** where revelry continues into the morning. To get there from Pl. Libertad, head away from the tourist office on Av. de Huelva.

ANDALUCÍA

Andalucía derives its spirit from an intoxicating amalgam of cultures. The ancient kingdom of Tartessus—the same Tarshish mentioned in the Bible for their fabulous troves of silver—grew wealthy off the Sierra Nevada's rich ore deposits. The Greeks and Phoenicians established colonies and traded up and down the coast, and the Romans later cultivated wheat, olive oil, and wine from the fertile soil watered by the Guadalquivir. In the 5th century AD, the Vandals flitted through the region on their way to North Africa leaving little more than a name—Vandalusia (House of the Vandals). The Moors provided a more enduring influence. Arriving in AD 711 and establishing a yet unbroken link to Africa and the Muslim world, they bequeathed the region with far more than the flamenco music and gypsy ballads proverbially associated with southern Spain.

Under Moorish rule, which lasted until 1492, Sevilla and Granada reached the pinnacle of Islamic arts, and Córdoba matured into the most culturally influential Islamic city. The Moors preserved, perfected, and blended Roman architectural techniques with their own, creating a style that became distinctively and uniquely Andalucian. Intriguing patios, garden oases with fountains and fish ponds, and alternating red brick and white stone were its hallmarks. Two descendant peoples, the Mozarabs, or "Muslim-like" Christians, and later the Mudéjares, Moors conquered by Christians, made further architectural impacts, the former with horseshoe arches and the latter with intricate wooden ceilings. More importantly, the mingling of Roman and Moorish influences helped spark the European Renaissance, merging Classical wisdom and science with that of the Arab world.

However rich in history and culture, Andalucía has been one of the poorest regions of Spain, and many residents have chosen to flee rather than face a future of indigence. In the 1960s severe droughts and stagnant industrialization forced fourteen percent of the region's population to emigrate, resulting in one of the largest peacetime emigrations Europe has seen this century. Despite Spain's recent economic boom, residents still complain that even with a university education, finding a good job here is as probable as winning ONCE, the national lottery. At the same time, Andalucians still retain an unshakable faith in the good life. The *festivales*, *ferias*, and *carnavales* of Andalucía—no matter how sober the religious theme—are world famous. Catholicism has never been this much fun.

HIGHLIGHTS OF ANDALUCÍA

- **Sevilla's** beautiful streets, historic cathedral, and amazing nightlife (see below).
- **Córdoba's** unique and bizarre **Mezquita,** with its brilliant red-and-white horseshoe-arch colonnade and its tranquil Patio de los Naranjos (see p. 212).
- **Baeza,** a taste of quintessential Spain (p. 269).
- Granada's legendary **Alhambra** and gorgeous and fascinating **Albaícin** (see p. 261).
- Desolate and beautiful **Cabo de Gata** (p. 248).

SEVILLA

Sevilla's charm is infectious. Site of a small Roman acropolis founded by Julius Caesar, capital of the Moorish empire, focal point of the Spanish Renaissance, and guardian angel of traditional Andalucian culture, this city has yet to disappoint its visitors. Jean Cocteau included it with Venice and Peking in his trio of magical cities; Santa Teresa denounced it as the work of the devil. *Carmen, Don Giovanni,* and *The Barber of Seville* are only a few of the artistic works inspired by this metropolis. The 16th-century maxim *"Qui non ha visto Sevilla non ha visto maravilla"* ("he who has not seen Sevilla has not seen a marvel") remains true

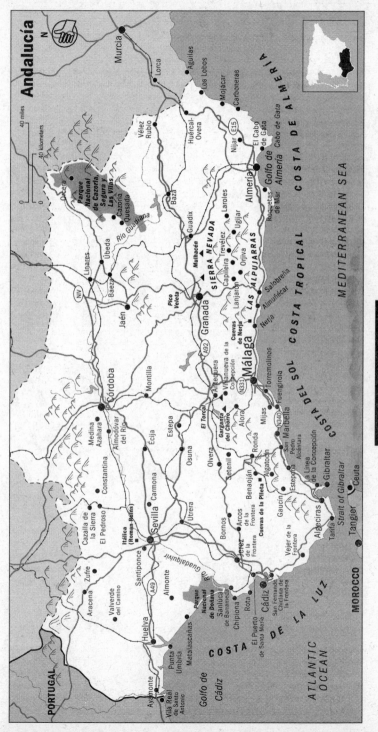

Andalucía

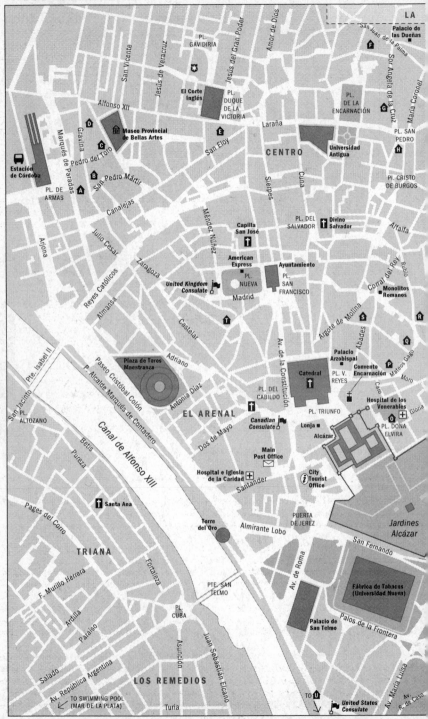

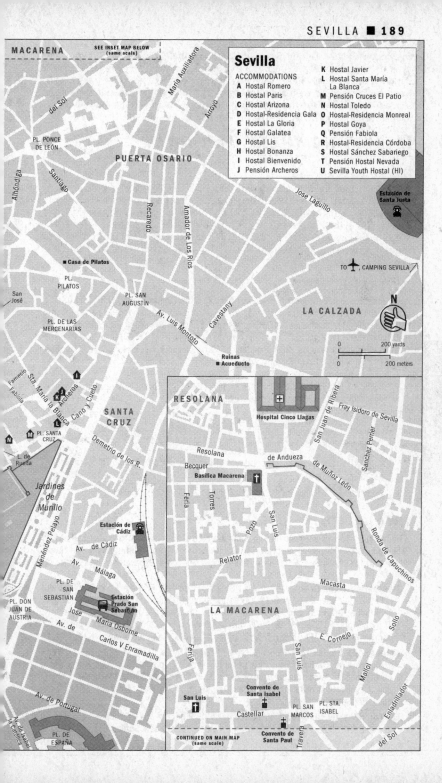

MACARENA

SEE INSET MAP BELOW
(same scale)

Sevilla

ACCOMMODATIONS
A Hostal Romero
B Hostal Paris
C Hostal Arizona
D Hostal-Residencia Gala
E Hostal La Gloria
F Hostal Galatea
G Hostal Lis
H Hostal Bonanza
I Hostal Bienvenido
J Pensión Archeros

K Hostal Javier
L Hostal Santa María
  La Blanca
M Pensión Cruces El Patio
N Hostal Toledo
O Hostal-Residencia Monreal
P Hostal Goya
Q Pensión Fabiola
R Hostal-Residencia Córdoba
S Hostal Sánchez Sabariego
T Pensión Hostal Nevada
U Sevilla Youth Hostal (HI)

PUERTA OSARIO

del Sol

PL. PONCE
DE LEÓN

Santiago

Recaredo

Amador de los Ríos

María Auxiliadora

Arroyo

Jose Laguillo

Estación de
Santa Justa

Alhóndiga

■ Casa de Pilatos

PL.
PILATOS

San
José

PL. DE LAS
MERCENARIAS

PL. SAN
AUGUSTÍN

Av. Luis Montoto

Cavestany

TO ✈ CAMPING SEVILLA

LA CALZADA

N

0   200 yards

0   200 meters

Ruinas
■ Acueducto

Famesio

Sta. María la Blanca

Fabiola

Archeros

Cano y Cueto

SANTA
CRUZ

Demetrio de los R.

N

M

PL. SANTA
CRUZ

L. de
Rueda

Jardines
de
Murillo

Menéndez Pelayo

Estación de
Cádiz

Av. de Cádiz

Av.
Málaga

PL. DE
SAN
SEBASTIAN

Estación
Prado San
Sebastián

PL. DON
JUAN DE
AUSTRIA

Jose
María Osborne

Av. de

Carlos V Enramadilla

Av. de Portugal

PL. DE
ESPAÑA

RESOLANA

Hospital Cinco Llagas

San Juan de Ribera

Fray Isidoro de Sevilla

Sánchez Perrier

Resolana

Becquer

Basílica Macarena

de Andueza

de Muñoz León

Feria

Torres

Pozo

San Luis

Ronda de Capuchinos

Relator

Macasta

LA MACARENA

E. Cornejo

San Luis

Sollio

Mallol

Enladrillador

Ferija

Convento de
Santa Isabel

San Luis

Castellar

PL. SAN
MARCOS

PL. STA.
ISABEL

CONTINUED ON MAIN MAP
(same scale)

Convento de
Santa Paul

Travería

del Sol

five centuries later. During *Semana Santa* and the *Feria de Abril*, two of the most extravagant festivals in Europe, Sevilla's jasmined balconies and exotic parks spring to life. Matadors, flamenco dancers, and virgins lead the town in endless revelry. Sevilla's reputation for gaiety is rivaled only by its notoriety as *la sartenilla de España* (the frying pan of Spain)—not even the mellow Guadalquivir River can quell the blistering summer heat.

⌂ GETTING THERE AND AWAY

BY PLANE

All flights depart and land at **Aeropuerto San Pablo** (tel. 954 44 90 00), 12km out of town on Ctra. Madrid. A taxi ride between the airport and the town center costs about 2000ptas. **Los Amarillos** (tel. 954 41 52 01) runs a bus from outside the Hotel Alfonso XIII in the Pta. Jerez (every hr., 750ptas). **Iberia**, C. Almirante Lobo, 2 (tel. 954 22 89 01; nationwide tel. 902 400 500), has an office in front of the Torre de Oro (open daily 9am-1:30pm and 4:30-7:30pm). They book flights to **Madrid** (45min., 3-4 per day) and **Barcelona** (55min., 2-3 per day), as well as international destinations.

BY TRAIN

All train service is centralized in the modern **Estación Santa Justa** (tel. 954 54 02 02), on Av. Kansas City. Services include an info booth, luggage storage, a telephone office, a cafeteria, and an ATM. Buses C1 and C2 link Santa Justa and the Prado de San Sebastián bus station. They stop on Av. Kansas City, to the left as you exit the train station. In town, the **RENFE office**, C. Zaragoza, 29 (tel. 954 22 26 93), is near Pl. Nueva (open M-F 9am-1:15pm and 4-7pm).

AVE trains run to **Córdoba** (45min., 17 per day, 7:50am-7:50pm, 2300ptas) and **Madrid** (2½hr., 20 per day, 6:30am-11pm, 8200ptas).

Talgo trains run to: **Huelva** (1½hr., 4 per day, 8:50am-8:20pm, 980ptas); **Córdoba** (1½hr., 6 per day, 7:50am-7:50pm, 2300ptas); **Antequera** (2hr., 4 per day, 7:40am-5:40pm, 1570ptas); **Cádiz** (2hr., 12 per day, 6:35am-9:27pm, 1600ptas); **Jaén** (2hr., 1 per day, 6:46pm, 2210ptas); **Málaga** (2½hr., 5 per day, 7:40am-8:10pm, 2090ptas); **Granada** (3½hr., 5 per day, 7:40am-5:40pm, 2610ptas); **Cáceres** (5½hr., 1 per day, 7:40pm, 2200ptas); **Almería** (5½hr., 3 per day, 7:40am-5:40pm, 4175ptas); **Valencia** (8½hr., 4 per day, 8:11am-9:50pm, 5300ptas); **Barcelona** (12hr., 6 per day, 8:11am-9:50pm, 6400ptas).

BY BUS

The old bus station at **Prado de San Sebastián,** C. Manuel Vazquez Sagastizabal, s/n (tel. 954 41 71 11), mainly serves Andalucía. Buses C1 and C2 link Estación Santa Justa and Prado de San Sebastián. As is usual, service decreases on Sundays.

Transportes Alsina Graells (tel. 954 41 88 11). Open daily 6:30am-11pm. To: **Córdoba** (2hr., 10 per day, 8am-9pm, 1200ptas); **Málaga** (2½hr., 10 per day, 7am-midnight, 1850ptas); **Granada** (3hr., 9 per day, 8am-11pm, 2400ptas); **Jaén** (4hr., 4 per day, 7:30am-6pm, 2120ptas); **Nerja** (4½hr., 1 per day, 6pm, 2300ptas); **Almería** (7hr., 1 per day, 3:30pm, 3780ptas); **Murcia** (8hr., 2 per day, 8am and 11am, 4630ptas).

Transportes Comes (tel. 954 41 68 58). Open M-Sa 6:30am-9pm, Su 7:15am-10:30pm. To: **Cádiz** (1½hr., 12 per day, 7am-9:30pm, 1300ptas); **Jerez de la Frontera** (2hr., 8 per day, 3-8pm, 875ptas); **El Puerto de Santa María** (2hr., 2 per day, 1050ptas); **Tarifa** (3hr., 4 per day, 9am-8pm, 2020ptas); **Algeciras** (3½hr., 4 per day, 9am-8pm, 2100ptas).

Los Amarillos (tel. 954 41 52 01). Open daily 7:30am-2pm and 2:30-8pm. To: **Arcos de la Frontera** (2hr., 2 per day, 8am and 4:30pm, 905ptas); **Sanlucar** and **Chipiona** (2hr., 9 per day, 7am-9pm, 970ptas); **Ronda** (2½hr., 6 per day, 7am-5pm, 1235ptas);

Marbella (3hr., 3 per day, 8am-4pm, 1820ptas); **Fuengirola** (3½hr., 3 per day, 8am-4pm, 2060ptas); **Barcelona** (16hr., 1 per day, 8820ptas).

Enatcar-Bacoma (tel. 954 41 46 60). Open daily 9:30am-9pm. To **Valencia** (10hr., 2 per day, 6080ptas) and **Barcelona** (16hr., 1 per day, 8820ptas).

The newer bus station at **Plaza de Armas** (tel. 954 90 80 40 or 954 90 77 37), on the river bank, serves destinations beyond Andalucía, including Portugal and other European countries (open daily 5:30am-11:30pm). Services include an ATM, a cafeteria, photocopies, and luggage storage. Buses C1, C2, C3, and C4 stop nearby.

Socibus (tel. 954 90 11 60 or 902 22 92 92; fax 954 90 16 92). Open daily 8:30am-12:45am. To: **Madrid** (6hr., 15 per day, 2715ptas) and **Portugal** (1 per day, various destinations including Lagos, from 2745ptas).

Damas (tel. 954 90 80 40). Open M-F 8am-1:30pm and 4:30-10:45pm, Sa-Su 10:30am-1:30pm and 8-10:45pm. To: **Huelva** (1¼hr., 26 per day, 875ptas); **Badajoz** (3½hr., 6 per day, 1690ptas); **Lisbon** (9hr., 2 per day, 4500ptas).

Alsa Internacional (tel. 954 90 78 00 or 902 42 22 42). July-Sept. 1000ptas more. Th and Sa, 1 per day to: **Toulouse** (21hr., 12,600ptas); **Lyon** (28hr., 18,800ptas); **Geneva** (30hr., 18,000ptas); **Zurich** (31hr., 20,500ptas). In Spain, to: **Cáceres** (4hr., 3 per day, 6:30am-9pm); **Salamanca** (9½hr., 5 per day); **León** (13hr., 3 per day).

▐ GETTING AROUND

To reach El Centro from the train station, catch bus #27 to **Plaza de la Encarnación,** several blocks north of the cathedral. To get directly to Barrio Santa Cruz and the cathedral from either the train station or the bus station at **Prado de San Sebastián,** take bus C1 or C2. From Pr. San Sebastián it is easiest to walk. Go straight out of the station to the main road, cross, and walk to the right for about two blocks; C. Santa María La Blanca will be on the left. From **Barrio Santa Cruz** it is a 10-minute walk along C. Ximénez de Enciso and C. Rodrigo Caro to the cathedral.

Buses C1, C2, C3, and C4 connect the newer bus station **Plaza de Armas** to Pr. San Sebastián and the center. To walk to El Centro from Pl. Armas (10min.), walk upstream (right when facing the river) three blocks and make a right onto C. Alfonso XII. To get to the cathedral (20min.), exit right onto Po. Cristobal Colón along the river and take the first left onto C. Adriano. This street leads to C. García Vinuesa, which ends at the cathedral.

Public Transportation: (tel. 954 41 11 52). The city bus network is extensive and useful. Most lines run every 10 min. (6am-11:15pm) and converge on Pl. Nueva, Pl. Encarnación, or in front of the cathedral on Av. Constitución. Limited **night service** departs from Pl. Nueva (every hr., midnight-2am). City **bus guides** are available at any tourist office and at most tobacco shops *(estancos)* and kiosks. Fare 125ptas, *bonobús* (10 rides) 560-650ptas. Particularly useful are buses C3 and C4, which circle the center, and #34, which hits the youth hostel, university, cathedral, and Pl. Nueva.

Taxis: Tele Taxi (tel. 954 62 22 22). **Radio Taxi** (tel. 954 58 00 00). Base rate 350ptas, 25% surcharge Sunday.

Car Rental: Hertz, Av. República Argentina, 3 (tel. 954 27 88 87), and at the airport (tel. 954 51 47 20). Min. age 25. From 10,000ptas a day. Open M-F 9am-1:30pm and 4-7pm, Sa 9am-1pm. **Triana Rent A Car,** C. Almirante Lobo, 7 (tel. 954 56 44 39 or 954 33 68 97). Min. age 21. From 5100ptas a day.

Moped Rental: Alkimoto, C. Fernando Tiraolo, 5 (tel. 954 58 49 27), near Est. Santa Justa. 4700ptas per day.

Bike Rental: El Ciclismo, Po. Catalina de Ribera, 2 (tel. 954 41 19 59), in Pta. Carne, at the north end of Jardines de Murillo. 1500ptas per day. Open M-F 10am-1:30pm and 6-8pm, Sa 10am-1pm.

✦ ORIENTATION

Over the centuries, Sevilla has incorporated a number of neighboring villages, now colorful neighborhoods. The **Río Guadalquivir** flows roughly north to south through the city. Most of Sevilla, including the alleyways of the old **Barrio de Santa Cruz,** is on the east bank. The historic and proud **Barrio de Triana** and modern, middle-class **Barrio de los Remedios** occupy the west bank. The **cathedral,** next to Barrio de Santa Cruz, is Sevilla's centerpiece. If you're disoriented, look for its conspicuous *giralda* (the minaret-turned-bell tower). **Avenida de la Constitución,** home of the tourist office, runs alongside the cathedral. **El Centro,** a busy commercial pedestrian zone, lies north of the cathedral, starting where Av. Constitución hits **Plaza Nueva,** site of the Ayuntamiento. **Calle Sierpes,** a popular street for shopping, takes off from Pl. Nueva and runs northward through El Centro.

⁊ PRACTICAL INFORMATION

TOURIST AND FINANCIAL SERVICES

Tourist Offices: Junta de Andalucía, Av. Constitución, 21B (tel. 954 22 14 04; fax 954 22 97 53), 1 block from the cathedral. A good first stop. Excellent regional and city info. Superb city map (100ptas). English spoken. Perpetually swamped, but most crowded before and after *siesta*. Open M-F 9am-7pm, Sa 10am-2pm and 3-7pm, Su 10am-2pm. **Info booths** in Est. Santa Justa and Pl. Nueva stock maps and bus guides.

Currency Exchange: Banco Central Hispano, C. Sierpes, 55 (tel. 954 56 26 84). Open M-F 8:30am-2:30pm.

American Express: Pl. Nueva, 7 (tel. 954 21 16 17). Changes cash and traveler's cheques without commission, holds mail, and offers emergency services for cardholders. Open M-F 9:30am-1:30pm and 4:30-7:30pm, Sa 10am-1pm.

LOCAL SERVICES

Luggage Storage: At Pr. San Sebastián bus station (250ptas; open 6:30am-10pm), Pl. Armas bus station (30ptas for 1st day, 85ptas for each additional day; lockers 300ptas), and Santa Justa train station (300-500ptas).

El Corte Inglés: Pl. Duque de la Victoria, 7 (tel. 954 22 09 31 or 954 58 17 00), and 6 other locations. Excellent map (49ptas), currency exchange, guidebooks in English, supermarket, telephones, and clean public bathrooms. Open M-Sa 10am-9:30pm.

English Bookstore: Vertice, C. San Fernando, 33 (tel. 954 21 16 54; fax 954 22 56 54), near Pta. Jerez. Large and diverse collection of English-language texts. Open M-F 9:30am-2pm and 5-8:30pm, Sa 10am-1:30pm. July closed Sa. **Librería Beta,** a chain with stores all over Sevilla, has an English-language section.

VIPS: C. República Argentina, 25 (tel. 954 27 93 97), 3 blocks from Pl. Cuba. International newspapers, non-perishable groceries, restaurant. Open Su-Th 8am-2am, F 8am-3am, Sa 9am-3am.

Women's Center: C. Alfonso XII, 52 (tel. 954 90 47 76 or 954 90 61 12). Info on feminist and lesbian organizations, plus legal and psychological services for rape victims. Employment listings for women. Open daily 9am-2pm.

Gay and Lesbian Services: COLEGA (Colectiva de Lesbianas y Gays de Andalucía), Cuesta del Rosario, 8 (tel. 954 56 33 66). Open Tu and Th 6-9pm.

Laundromat: Lavandería Robledo, C. F. Sánchez Bedoya, 18, 1 block from the cathedral. Wash and dry 950ptas for 5kg. Open M-F 10am-2pm and 5-8pm.

Swimming Pool: Mar de Plata (tel. 954 45 40 85), C. Pablo I, in Triana. From Pl. Cuba, take Av. República Argentina past Pl. República Dominicana and make the next right (or take bus C1 or C2 to Pl. República Dominicana). 450ptas, under 12 200ptas. Open Tu-F 2:30-4:30pm, Sa-Su 11am-8pm.

EMERGENCY AND COMMUNICATIONS

Emergency: tel. 091 or 092. **Police:** Po. Delicias, 15 (tel. 954 61 54 50).

24-Hour. Pharmacy: Check list posted at any pharmacy for those open 24hr.

Medical Assistance: Ambulatorio Esperanza Macarena (tel. 954 42 01 05). **Hospital Universitario Virgen Macarena** (tel. 954 24 81 81), Av. Dr. Fedriani. English spoken.

Post Office: Av. Constitución, 32 (tel. 954 21 64 76), opposite the cathedral. Lista de Correos and **faxes.** Open M-F 10am-8:30pm, Sa 9:30am-2pm. **Postal Code:** 41080.

Internet Access: Cibercenter, C. Julio Cesar, 8 (tel. 954 22 88 99), off C. Reyes Católicos. 250ptas per 15min. Open daily 9am-9pm. **Alfalfa 10,** Pl. Alfalfa, 10 (tel. 954 21 38 41). 600ptas per hr. Open noon-10pm. **TOR'NET Cybercafe,** C. Torneo, 35 (tel. 954 90 07 81). 6 computers. 300ptas for 15min., 400ptas for 30min., 700ptas per hr. Open Tu-Sa 10am-2pm and 5pm-dawn, Su 5pm-dawn.

▐ ACCOMMODATIONS AND CAMPING

During *Semana Santa* and *Feria de Abril*, rooms vanish and prices soar. Make reservations months ahead. At other times, call a day or two before arriving. The tourist office has lists of *casas particulares* that open on special occasions. Accommodations prices are often negotiable.

BARRIO DE SANTA CRUZ AND EL ARENAL

The narrow streets east of the cathedral around C. Santa María la Blanca are full of cheap hostels with virtually identical rooms. The neighborhood is overwhelmingly touristed, but its narrow streets and fragrant, shady plazas are all within a few minutes' walk of the cathedral, river, Alcázar, and El Centro.

Hostal-Residencia Córdoba, C. Farnesio, 12 (tel. 954 22 74 98), off C. Fabiola. Immaculate, family-run joint with spacious rooms and a beautiful indoor patio. A/C. Singles with toilet 3200-5000ptas, with shower 4500-7000ptas; doubles with toilet 4700-7500ptas, with shower 6500-9000ptas.

Hostal Santa María la Blanca, C. Santa María la Blanca, 28 (tel. 954 42 11 74). Great bargain for the district. Hallways decorated with paintings of bullfights and women. Fans available upon request. Singles 1500ptas, with bath 2000ptas; doubles 3000ptas, with bath 4000ptas; triples 4500ptas, with bath 6000ptas.

Hostal Sánchez Sabariego, C. Corral del Rey, 23 (tel. 954 21 44 70), on the continuation of C. Argote de Molina. Follow signs to Hostel Sierpes. Friendly hostel with antique furniture and painstakingly decorated rooms. A/C and heat upstairs for 500ptas more. You get your own key. Public telephone available. Singles 2500-3000ptas; doubles with bath 4500-6000ptas.

Hostal-Residencia Monreal, C. Rodrigo Caro, 8 (tel. 954 21 41 66). From the cathedral, walk uphill on C. Mateos Gago and take the 1st right. Rooms have A/C and little sinks; some have balconies. Ask for a spacious 3rd fl. room. Singles 2500ptas; doubles 5000ptas, with bath 7000ptas; triples 5600ptas, with shower 9300ptas. Visa, MC.

Hostal Toledo, C. Santa Teresa, 15 (tel. 954 21 53 35), off C. Ximénez de Enciso. Quiet, comfortable hostel, with clean private baths. Singles with shower 3500-6000ptas, with bath 4000-8000ptas; doubles 6000-12,000ptas.

Pensión Fabiola, C. Fabiola, 16 (tel. 954 21 83 46). Basic rooms with fans surround a plant-filled patio. Up to 4 in a room. Singles 2000-4500ptas; doubles 4000-8500ptas, with bath 5000-9000ptas; triples 5000-10,000ptas, with bath 7000-12,000ptas.

Hostal Goya, C. Mateos Gago, 31 (tel. 954 21 11 70; fax 954 56 29 88), near the cathedral. Ample but dark rooms cooled by fans. Lounge area. Doubles with shower 6200ptas, with bath 6995ptas; triples with shower 8690ptas, with bath 9735ptas.

Hostal Javier, C. Archeros, 16 (tel. 954 41 23 25). Well-furnished, comfortable rooms with fans. Singles 2500-4000ptas, with bath 3500-6000ptas; doubles 4000-7000ptas, with bath 5000-8000ptas; triples 7500-11,000ptas. Visa, MC.

Pensión Hostal Nevada, C. Gamazo, 28 (tel. 954 22 53 40), in El Arenal. From Pl. Nueva, take C. Barcelona and turn right on C. Gamazo. Cool courtyard. Dim, tapestry-laden rooms, some with free A/C. Parking 2000ptas per day. Singles 2200-2500ptas, with bath 3000-3500ptas; doubles 4000-4500ptas, with bath 5000-8500ptas.

Hostal-Residencia Capitol, C. Zaragoza, 66 (tel. 954 21 24 41), near Pensión Hostal Nevada. Spacious rooms. Lounge with phone and TV. A/C. Singles 2750-4000ptas; doubles with shower 4750-7500ptas, with bath 5500-10,000ptas. Visa, MC, AmEx.

Hostal Bienvenido, C. Archeros, 14 (tel. 954 41 36 55). Small singles with big windows; spacious doubles with balconies. 3rd floor is oven-like in July-Aug. All rooms have bidet and sink. 2000ptas per person.

Pensión Archeros, C. Archeros, 23 (tel. 954 41 84 65). Relaxed, friendly owner oversees decent rooms facing a fern-laden patio. Singles 2000ptas; doubles 3500ptas, with shower 4500ptas.

Pensión Cruces El Patio, C. Cruces, 10 (tel. 954 22 96 33 or 954 22 60 41). Dim interior rooms, mostly dorms. Fans on request. Up to 5 people in a room (1500ptas per person). Singles 2000ptas; doubles 3000-3500ptas, with bath 4000-4500ptas.

EL CENTRO

El Centro, a mess of narrow streets radiating from Pl. Encarnación, is as charming as it is disorienting. Hostels here are few and far between, however.

■ **Hostal Lis,** C. Escarpín, 10 (tel. 954 21 30 88), on an alley near Pl. Encarnación. Each room decorated with its own unique Sevillian tiles. Large rooms with showers (soon to be baths) and fans. Singles 2000-3000ptas; doubles 3500-3900ptas; triples 5000-6000ptas. Discounts for large student groups.

Hostal La Gloria, C. San Eloy, 58, 2nd fl. (tel. 954 22 26 73), at the end of a lively shopping street. Tiled floors and a lounge with TV and phone. Singles 2000ptas; doubles 3500ptas, with bath 4500ptas; triples 6000ptas.

Hostal-Residencia Zahira, C. San Eloy, 43 (tel. 954 22 10 61; fax 954 21 30 48). Hotel-sized lobby masks smaller rooms. All rooms have bath and A/C. Lounge with TV. Singles 3500-4000ptas; doubles 6000-7000ptas. Visa, MC, AmEx.

Hostal Generalife, C. Fernan Caballero, 4 (tel. 954 22 16 73), off C. San Eloy. Small, family-run hostel. All rooms with fans. Communal baths. Singles 2000-4000ptas; doubles 3500-7000ptas. Visa, MC.

NEAR ESTACIÓN PLAZA DE ARMAS

Most hostels around the Pl. Armas bus station are on C. Gravina, parallel to C. Marqués de las Paradas and two blocks from the station. These are generally the nicest, cheapest, and quietest accommodations in the city.

■ **Hostal Paris,** C. San Pedro Mártir, 14 (tel. 954 22 98 61 or 954 21 96 45; fax 954 21 96 45), off C. Gravina. Brand-new, clean, and classy—the best value in town. All rooms with bath, A/C, phone, and TV. Singles 3500ptas; doubles 5000-6000ptas. Student discounts. Visa, MC, AmEx.

Hostal Arizona, C. Pedro del Toro, 14 (tel. 954 21 60 42), off C. Gravina. Clean, attractive rooms with fans and tiled floors; some have balconies. Singles 2000ptas; doubles 3000ptas, with bath 4000ptas; triples 4500ptas.

Hostal Residencia Gala, C. Gravina, 52 (tel. 954 21 45 03). Friendly owner. Clean, simple rooms and baths. Some rooms are windowless, and there is no A/C. Laundry 1500ptas per load. Singles 2000ptas, with bath 2500ptas; doubles 4000ptas, with bath 4500ptas; triples 5500ptas.

Hotel Paraiso, C. Gravina, 27 (tel. 954 21 79 19). Hotel virtues—cleanliness, spaciousness, and convenience—at reasonable prices. All rooms have full bath, TV, A/C, and phone. Singles 5000ptas; doubles 6000ptas; triples 7500ptas. Visa, MC.

ANDALUCÍA

ELSEWHERE AND CAMPING

Sevilla Youth Hostel (HI), C. Isaac Peral, 2 (tel. 954 61 31 50; fax 954 61 31 58). Take bus #34 from Pr. San Sebastían; it stops behind the hostel just after Po. Delicias. A bit out of the way. Bright, white, and disinfected. Up to 4 per room. Many private baths. Wheelchair accessible. Dorms 1300ptas, over 26 1800ptas. Non-members can pay an additional 300ptas a night for 6 nights to become members.

Camping Sevilla, Ctra. Madrid-Cádiz, km 534 (tel. 954 51 43 79), near the airport. From Pr. San Sebastián, take bus #70, which stops 800m away at Parque Alcosa. A happy medium between city and country. Grassy sites, hot showers, supermarket, and pool. 460ptas per person, per car, and per tent; children 375ptas.

Club de Campo, Av. Libertad, 13, Ctra. Sevilla-Dos Hermanas (tel. 954 72 02 50), 8km out of town. Los Amarillos buses leave from C. Infante Carlos de Borbón, at the back of Pr. San Sebastián, to Dos Hermanas (every 45min., 140ptas). Lots of grass and a pool. 485ptas per person and per car, 475ptas per tent; children 395ptas.

⬛ FOOD

Sevillians offset the merciless midday sun by keeping their cuisine light. The city claims to be the birthplace of *tapas;* locals prepare and devour them with a vengeance. Other favorites include *caracoles* (snails) and *cocido andaluz* (a thick soup of chick peas). Defying the need for hydration, locals imbibe Sevilla's Cruzcampo beer, a light, smooth pilsner. **Mercado del Arenal,** near the bullring on C. Pastor y Leandro, between C. Almansa and C. Arenal, has fresh meat and produce and screaming vendors (open M-Sa 9am-2pm). For a **supermarket,** try **%Día,** C. San Juan de Ávila, near El Corte Inglés (open M-F 9:30am-2pm and 6:30-9pm, Sa 9am-1pm).

BARRIO DE SANTA CRUZ AND EL ARENAL

Restaurants near the cathedral cater almost exclusively to tourists. Beware the unexceptional, omnipresent *menús* featuring *gazpacho* and *paella* for 1000ptas. Food and prices improve in the backstreet establishments between the cathedral and the river in El Arenal, and along sidestreets in the Barrio Santa Cruz.

Restaurante-Bar El Baratillo/Casa Chari, C. Pavia, 12 (tel. 954 22 96 51), on a tiny street off C. Dos de Mayo. Call or ask in advance for the tour-de-force: homemade *paella* with a jar of wine, beer, or *sangría* (2500ptas for 2). *Menú* 500ptas. Open M-F 8am-10pm, Sa noon-5pm.

Pizzería San Marco, C. Mesón de Moro, 6 and 10 (tel. 954 21 43 90 or 954 56 43 90), off C. Mateos Gago. In a huge, atmospheric, 12th-century Moorish bathhouse. Reliable and comprehensive Italian menu. Packed with tourists and locals. Thin-crust pizzas drowned in chunky toppings 675-995ptas, pastas 675-795ptas. Open Tu-Su 1:15-3:30pm and 8:15pm-12:30am, F-Sa until 1am. Visa, MC.

Bodega Santa Cruz, C. Rodrigo Caro, 1 (tel. 954 21 32 46). Take C. Mateos Gago from the fountain in front of the cathedral; it's on the 1st corner on the right. Casual and crowded at all hours. A variety of tasty *tapas* (175-200ptas). Open daily 8am-midnight.

Casa Diego, Pl. Curtidores, 7 (tel. 954 41 58 83), 1 block from C. Santa María la Blanca. Traditional Sevillian food and exceptional *gazpacho*. *Menú* 1000ptas, entrees 450-1200ptas. Open M-F 1-4pm and 8:30-11:30pm, Sa 1-4pm. Visa, MC.

Bar Cáceres, C. San José, 24. The closest thing to a buffet-style breakfast in Sevilla. An impressive spread of cheeses, jams, and countless other condiments. *Desayuno de la Casa* (orange juice, coffee, ham, eggs, toast) 600ptas. Open daily 7:30am-8pm.

Texas Lone Star Saloon, C. Placentines, 25 (tel. 954 56 04 91). A collection of American beers and American tourists. The Tex-Mex cuisine is surprisingly delicious. Entrees 825-1200ptas. Beer 150-500ptas, jar of margarita 1750ptas. Open daily 1pm-2am.

EL CENTRO

This area belongs to professionals and shoppers by day and young people at night.

Habanita, C. Golfo, 3 (tel. 606 71 64 56), off C. Pérez Gaídos. Cuban food served Spanish style (as *tapas* and *raciones*) on a tropical outdoor patio. Vegetarian options. Black beans and rice 225-1000ptas. Open Tu-Su 12:30-4:30pm and 8:30pm-12:30am.

El Rinconcillo, C. Gerona, 40 or C. Alhóndiga, 2 (tel. 954 22 31 83). This *bodega*, founded in 1670, is a popular pit-stop with quite a history. Drink on top of wine barrels. *Tapas* 185-300ptas, *raciones* 225-1850ptas. Visa, MC.

Jalea Real, Sor Ángela de la Cruz, 37 (tel. 954 21 61 03). From Pl. Encarnación, walk 150m on C. Laraña, then turn left at Iglesia de San Pedro. Fabulous vegetarian cuisine. Interesting salads 475-800ptas, *menú* 1250ptas. Open July-Aug. M-F 1:30-5pm and 8:30-11:30pm, Sa 8:30-11:30pm; Sept.-June M-Sa 2-5pm and 8:30-11:30pm.

Bar El Rincón San Eloy, C. San Eloy, 24 (tel. 954 21 80 79). Airy courtyard, wine barrels, massive beer taps, and bullfight posters. *Tapas* 175-250ptas, *raciones* 600-1300ptas, *menú* 900ptas, entrees 400-1200ptas. Open M-Sa 10am-11:30pm.

Bodegón Alfonso XII, C. Alfonso XII, 33 (tel. 954 21 12 51), near the Museo de Bellas Artes. A/C and American video games make this a popular hangout. Breakfast with coffee 175-400ptas. *Menú* 800ptas. Open daily 7am-11:30pm.

TRIANA AND BARRIO DE LOS REMEDIOS

This old maritime neighborhood, on the far side of the river, was once a separate village. Avoid overpriced C. Betis and plunge down less expensive sidestreets.

La Ortiga, C. Procurador, 19 (tel. 954 33 74 18), off C. Castilla. An ecological organization operates this pleasant health food *tapas* bar where all ingredients are organically grown. Scheduled poetry readings; art often exhibited on the walls. Open M-Sa June-Aug. 8pm-12:30am; Sept.-May 5pm-12:30am.

Casa Cuesta/Cervecería Ruiz, C. Castilla, 3-5 (tel. 954 33 33 37), 1 block from the Puente Isabel II. Walk to the beautiful dining room in the back of the bar. Expensive, but worth it. *Raciones* 600-1500ptas, entrees 550-1700ptas. Restaurant open W-M 8:30am-12:30am; bar open 1:30-4:30pm and 9pm-midnight. Visa, AmEx.

Café-Bar Jerusalem, C. Salado, 6, at C. Virgen de las Huertas. Bar with an international crowd and creative *tapas*. Chicken, lamb, or pork and cheese *shoarmas* called a *bocadillo hebreo*—it's not kosher, but sure is tasty (400-625ptas). Open daily 8pm-3am.

Freiduría Santana, C. Pureza, 61 (tel. 954 33 20 40), parallel to C. Betis, 1 block from the river. Both the fresh fried fish and the restaurant itself are local institutions. Free samples ease the wait. Seafood served by the kg. Open Sept.-July Tu-Su 7pm-midnight.

Casa Manolo, C. San Jorge, 16 (tel. 954 33 47 92 or 954 33 32 08), 2 blocks from Puente Isabel II. A Spanish diner. Seafood *tapas* 200ptas, *menú* 1600ptas, entrees 750-1500ptas. Open daily June-Aug. noon-midnight; Sept.-May 9am-midnight.

🔘 SIGHTS

Sevilla is filled with sights, from the famous Alcázar and cathedral to the churches, monuments, and winding streets of the *casco viejo* and Barrio de Santa Cruz.

BARRIO DE SANTA CRUZ

🔲THE CATHEDRAL

Tel. 954 21 49 71. Open M-Sa 10:30am-6pm, Su 2-7pm. Tickets sold until 1hr. before closing. 700ptas, seniors and students 200ptas, under 12 free. Sunday free.

In 1401, Christians destroyed the 12th-century Almohad mosque to clear space for a massive cathedral. The *reconquistadores* demonstrated their religious fervor by constructing a church so great, they said, that "those who come after us will take us for madmen." It took more than a century to build but today stands as the world's third-largest cathedral and the biggest Gothic edifice ever constructed.

All that remains of the former mosque is the famed minaret **La Giralda**, built in 1198. The tower and its twins in Marrakesh and Rabat are the oldest and largest surviving Almohad minarets, with the lower walls standing 2.5m thick. When the cathedral was built, the bronze spheres at the top of the tower were replaced by cymbals. Further alterations to the belfry were made throughout the 16th century, including the addition of 25 bells.

The inside of the structure is disorienting; the points of interest listed here are in counter-clockwise order. In the middle of the cathedral, the **main chapel** and its altar stand opposite the dark wooden **choir** made of recycled mahogany from a 19th-century Austrian railway. The **retablo mayor** (altarpiece), one of the largest in the world, is a golden wall of intricately wrought figurines depicting 36 biblical scenes. The floor mirror reflects distorted versions of visitors and an accurate image of the ornate dome above. Encircling the choir leads to the **Sepulcro de Cristóbal Colón** (Columbus's tomb). The black and gold coffin-bearers represent the eternally grateful kings of Castilla, León, Aragón, and Navarra. There is considerable mystery surrounding the actual whereabouts of Columbus's remains; chances are they don't lie inside the cathedral.

Farther on and to the right stands the cathedral's precious museum, the **Sacristía Mayor,** which holds works by Ribera and Murillo and a glittering Corpus Christi icon, **La Custodia Processional.** A small, disembodied head of John the Baptist eyes visitors who enter the gift shop and overlooks two keys presented to the city of Sevilla by Jewish leaders after King Fernando III ousted the Muslims in 1248. The neighboring **Sacristía de los Cálices** (or **de los Pintores**) maintains a collection of minor canvases by Zurbarán and Goya. In the corner of the cathedral are the impressive **Sala de Las Columnas** and the perfectly oval **cabildo** (chapter house). Outside the cathedral proper, on the north end, the elegant **Patio de Los Naranjos** (Orange Trees) evokes the bygone days of the Arab Caliphate.

ALCÁZAR. The imposing 9th-century walls of the Alcázar sit next to Pl. Triunfo and face the cathedral. The walls and several interior spaces, including the **Patio del Yeso** and the exquisitely carved **Patio de las Muñecas,** remain from the Moorish era. The latter patio displays a bed where Queen Isabel once slept. Of the Christian additions, the most notable is the **Patio de las Doncellas (Maids' Court).** Court life in the Alcázar revolved around this colonnaded quadrangle, encircled by archways adorned with glistening tilework. The theme of kaleidoscopic detail carries over into the adjacent chambers. The astonishing golden-domed **Salón de los Embajadores** is allegedly the site where Fernando and Isabel welcomed Columbus back from America. Nearby, the **Corte de las Muñecas** contains the palace's private quarters, decorated with the building's most exquisite carvings. Verdant gardens stretch from the residential quarters in all directions. (*Pl. Triunfo, 7. Tel. 954 50 23 23. Open Tu-Sa 9:30am-7pm, Su 9:30am-5pm. 700ptas; students, disabled, over 65, and under 16 free. Audio guides, available in several languages, give anecdotes, historical info, and a clearly marked route through the buildings and gardens; 400ptas.*)

CASA LONJA. Between the cathedral and the Alcázar stands the 16th-century Casa Lonja, built by Felipe II as a *Casa de Contratación* (commercial exchange) for trade with the Americas. In 1785, Carlos III converted the building into the **Archivo General de las Indias (Archive of the Indies).** Today it contains a collection of over 44,000 documents relating to the discovery and conquest of the New World. Among its books is Juan Bautista Muñoz's "definitive" history of the conquest, commissioned by Carlos III. Other highlights of the collection include Juan de la Costa's wildly inaccurate *Mapa Mundi* and letters from Columbus to Fernando and Isabel, as well as a 1590 letter from Cervantes (pre-*Don Quijote*) requesting employment in America. (*Tel. 954 21 12 34. Exhibits open M-F 10am-1pm. Free. Full access to documents is restricted to scholars.*)

ANDALUCÍA

WALKING TOUR: BARRIO DE SANTA CRUZ

The tourist office has a detailed map of the winding alleys, wrought-iron gates, and courtyards of the Barrio de Santa Cruz. King Fernando III forced Jews in flight from Toledo to live in this former ghetto. Haloed with geraniums, jasmine, and ivy, every street corner in the neighborhood echoes with a legend. On **Calle Susona**, a glazed skull above a door recalls the beautiful Susona, a Jew who fell in love with a Christian knight. When Susona learned that her father and friends planned to kill several inquisitors, including her knight, she warned her lover. A bloody reprisal was unleashed on the Jewish ghetto, during which Susona's entire family was slaughtered. She requested that her skull be placed above the doorway in atonement for her betrayal, and the actual skull supposedly remained until the 18th century. C. Susona leads to **Plaza Doña Elvira**, where Sevillian Lope de Rueda's works, precursors to the dramas of Spain's Golden Age, were staged. A turn down C. Gloria leads to Pl. Venerables, site of the 17th-century **Hospital de los Venerables**, a hospital-church adorned with art from the Sevillian school, including Leal and Montañés. *(Tel. 954 56 26 96. Open daily for guided visits 10am-2pm and 4-8pm. 600ptas, students and seniors 300ptas. Visa, MC.)*

  Calle Lope de Rueda, off C. Ximénez de Enciso, is graced with two noble mansions, beyond which lies the charming and fragrant **Plaza de Santa Cruz**. South of the plaza are the **Jardines de Murillo**, a shady expanse of shrubbery and benches. **Convento de San José** cherishes a cloak and portrait of Santa Teresa of Ávila. *(C. Santa Teresa, off Pl. Santa Cruz. Open daily 9-11am.)* The church in Pl. Santa Cruz houses the grave of the artist Murillo, who died in what is now known as the **Casa Murillo** after falling from a scaffold while painting frescoes in Cádiz's Iglesia de los Capuchinos. The house has information on Murillo's life and work. *(C. Santa Teresa, 8. Tel. 954 22 12 72. Open M-F 8am-3pm and 4-8pm. Free.)* **Iglesia de Santa María la Blanca** was built in 1391 on the foundation of a synagogue. It features red marble columns, Baroque plasterwork, and Murillo's *Last Supper*. *(C. Santa María la Blanca. Open M-Sa 10-11am and 6:30-8pm, Su 9:30am-2pm and 6:30-8pm.)*

  The Barrio de Santa Cruz is also home to several excellent **art galleries.** Pl. Alianza, the small square at the end of C. Rodrigo Caro, houses the **Estudio de John Fulton.** Fulton is an accomplished artist and the first American bullfighter ever to fight in Mexico City's ring. Some of his works are reputedly painted in bull's blood. *(Open M-Sa 11am-2pm and 4:30-7:30pm, Su 11am-2pm.)*

SIERPES AND THE ARISTOCRATIC QUARTER

Originating from the plaza, **Calle de Sierpes** cuts through the Aristocratic Quarter. At the beginning of this pedestrian street lined with shoe stores, fan shops, and chic boutiques, a plaque marks the spot where the royal prison once loomed. Some scholars believe Cervantes began writing *Don Quijote* there.

AYUNTAMIENTO. The Ayuntamiento has 16th-century Gothic and Renaissance interior halls, a richly decorated domed ceiling, and a Plateresque facade. It often displays art exhibitions; check with the tourist office for information. *(Pl. San Francisco. Tel. 954 59 01 45. Open Tu-Th 5:30-7:30pm, Sa 11am-1pm.)*

IGLESIA DEL SALVADOR. Iglesia del Salvador, fronted by a Montañés sculpture, is a 17th-century church built on the foundations of what was once the city's main mosque. The courtyard and the belfry's base are remnants of the old mosque. As grandiose as a cathedral, it is adorned with outstanding baroque *retablos* (altarpieces), sculptures, and paintings, including Montañés's *Jesús de la pasión*. *(Pl. Salvador, 1 block from C. Sierpes. Open daily 6:30-9pm.)*

OTHER SIGHTS. A few blocks southeast of Pl. Salvador stand the excavated ruins of an old **Roman temple.** The remaining columns rise 15m from below street level and offer a glimpse of the literal depth of Sevilla's history. *(C. Mármoles.)* A few blocks east of Pl. Salvador, the **Casa de Pilatos** houses Roman antiquities, Renaissance and baroque paintings, several courtyards, and a pond. Use the bell if the gate is closed during visiting hours. *(Pl. Pilatos. Tel. 954 22 52 98. Open daily 9am-7pm.*

500ptas for each floor.) The interesting **Iglesia de la Anunciación** features a pantheon honoring illustrious *sevillanos*, including poet Gustavo Adolfo Bécquer. *(Pl. Encarnación; enter on C. Laraña. Open daily 9am-1pm.)*

EL ARENAL AND TRIANA

Immortalized by Siglo de Oro writers Lope de Vega, Quevedo, and Cervantes, El Arenal and Triana (across the river) were Sevilla's chaotic 16th- and 17th-century mariners' neighborhoods.

▧MUSEO PROVINCIAL DE BELLAS ARTES. This museum contains Spain's finest collection of works by painters of the Sevilla school, most notably Murillo, Valdés Leal, and Zurbarán, as well as El Greco and Dutch master Jan Breughel. The building itself is a work of art—take time to sit in its shady gardens. *(Pl. Museo, 9, off C. Alfonso XII. Tel. 954 22 07 90. Open Tu 3-8pm, W-Sa 9am-8pm, Su 9am-3pm. 250ptas, EU citizens and students free.)*

TORRE DEL ORO. The 12-sided Torre del Oro (Gold Tower), built by the Almohads in 1200, overlooks the river from Po. Cristóbal Colón. While a glaze of golden tile once sheathed its squat frame, today a tiny yellow dome is the only reminder of its original splendor. Inside is the **Museo Náutico,** with engravings and drawings of Sevilla's port in its heyday. *(Tel. 954 22 24 19. Open Sept.-July Tu-F 10am-2pm, Sa-Su 11am-2pm. 100ptas. Tuesday free.)*

TORRE DE LA PLATA. On the far bank of the river, the Torre del Oro was connected to the Torre de la Plata (Silver Tower) by underwater chains meant to protect the city from river-borne trespassers. The river was later diverted to its present course, exposing El Arenal (the former sandbank). The Torre de la Plata has been absorbed by a bank building, but one side still lies near the corner of C. Santander and C. Temprado.

PASEO DE MARQUÉS DE CONTADERO

The inviting riverside esplanade Po. Marqués de Contadero stretches along the banks of the Guadalquivir from the base of the Torre del Oro. Bridge-heavy boat tours of Sevilla leave from in front of the tower (1hr., 700ptas).

PLAZA DE TOROS DE LA REAL MAESTRANZA. The tiled boardwalk leads to Pl. Toros de la Real Maestranza, a veritable temple of bullfighting. Home to one of the two great bullfighting schools (the other is in Ronda), the plaza fills to capacity for the 13 *corridas* of the *Feria de Abril* as well as weekly fights. *(Tel. 954 22 45 77. Open on non-bullfight days 10:30am-2pm and 4-6pm, on bullfight days 10am-3pm. Tours every 30min., 400ptas. See **La Corrida,** p. 203, for tickets and other info.)*

HOSPITAL DE LA CARIDAD. A 17th-century complex of arcaded courtyards, the hospital was founded by Don Miguel de Marañe, who is believed to be the model for legendary Sevillian Don Juan. This playboy allegedly converted to a life of piety and charity after stumbling out of an orgy into a funeral cortège that he was told was his own. His body rests inside the crypt of the **Iglesia de San Jorge,** part of the hospital. The church's walls display paintings and frescoes by Valdés Leal and Murillo. Murillo supposedly couldn't refrain from holding his nose when he saw Leal's morbid *Finis Gloria Mundi,* which depicts corpses of a peasant, a bishop, and a king beneath a stylized rendition of Justice and the Seven Deadly Sins. *(Behind the Teatro de la Maestranza on C. Temprado. Tel. 954 22 32 32. Open M-Sa 9am-1:30pm and 3:30-6:30pm, Su 9am-1pm. 400ptas.)*

OTHER SIGHTS. Just before the Puente de Isabel II lies Eduardo Chillida's sculpture entitled **Monumento a la Tolerancia** (Monument to Tolerance). The abstract figure has its back turned to the ruins of the **Castillo de la Inquisición (Castle of the Inquisition).** Across the river lies the wealthy neighborhood of **Triana,** once home to Sevilla's potters, tile-makers, and gypsies. **Pottery** studios and stores line both C. Alfarería (Ceramics Street) and C. Antillano Campos; C. Antillano Campos, 6, contains Sevilla's oldest kilns. Off C. Correa, two blocks inland from the river and midway between Puente de Isabel II and Puente de San Telmo, stands the **Iglesia de Santa Ana,** Sevilla's oldest church and the focal point of the exuberant fiestas that take over the area in July. *(Open M and W 7:30-8:30pm.)* The terraced riverside promenade **Calle Betis** is an ideal spot from which to view Sevilla's skyline.

▧ LA MACARENA

When most people hear "Macarena," they think of the song and dance popular in the mid-1990s. But to Sevillians, La Macarena is the Virgin of Sevilla, after whom an enchanting chuch and neighborhood are named. The quarter, northwest of El Centro, is traversed by the *ruta de los conventos* (route of convents).

CONVENTS. The founder of **Convento de Santa Inés,** as legend has it, was pursued so insistently by King Pedro the Cruel that she disfigured her face with boiling oil so he would leave her alone. Cooking liquids are used more positively today—the cloistered nuns sell patented puff pastries and coffee cakes through the courtyard's revolving window. *(C. María Coronel.)* **Convento de Santa Paula** includes a church with Gothic, Mudéjar, and Renaissance elements, a magnificent ceiling, and sculptures by Montañés. *(Pl. Santa Paula, s/n. Tel. 954 53 63 30. Open Tu-Su 10am-1pm and 4:30-6:30pm.)* The **museum** next door has Ribera's *St. Jerome.* Nuns here peddle scrumptious homemade marmalades and angel-hair pastry. *(Pl. Santa Paula, 11. Open Tu-Su 10am-12:30pm and 4:30-6:30pm.)*

CHURCHES. Opposite the belfry of the Iglesia de San Marcos rises **Iglesia de Santa Isabel,** featuring an altarpiece by Montañés. Nearby stands the exuberantly Baroque **Iglesia de San Luis,** crowned by octagonal glazed-tile domes. The site of the church was the endpoint of a 12-step prayer route based on the ascent to Golgotha. More recently, it has been immortalized by the Cruzcampo beer logo. *(C. San Luís. Open W-Th 9am-2pm, F-Sa 9am-2pm and 5-8pm.)* A stretch of **murallas,** created in the 12th century, runs between the Pta. Macarena and Pta. Córdoba on the Ronda de Capuchinos road. Flanking the west end of the walls, the **Basílica Macarena** houses the venerated image of *La virgen de la macarena,* which is hauled around town during *Semana Santa* processions. A **treasury** glitters with the virgin's jewels and other finery. *(Pl. San Gil. Tel. 954 37 01 95. Basilica open daily 9:30am-1pm and 5-8pm. Free. Treasury open daily 9:15am-1pm and 5-8pm. 300ptas.)* Toward the river is **Iglesia de San Lorenzo y Jesús del Gran Poder,** with Montañés's remarkably lifelike sculpture *El cristo del gran poder.* Worshipers kiss Jesus' ankle through an opening in the bulletproof glass for luck. *Semana Santa* culminates in a procession honoring his statue. *(Pl. San Lorenzo. Tel. 954 38 45 58. Open Sa-Th 8am-1:30pm and 6-9pm, F 7:30-10pm. Free.)*

OTHER SIGHTS. A large garden beyond the *murallas* and the basilica leads to the **Hospital de las Cinco Llagas,** a spectacular Renaissance building recently renovated to host the Andalucian parliament. Toward the river is the **Alameda de Hércules,** a leafy promenade patrolled by prostitutes and other shady types at night and site of the tremendous Sunday morning *Rastro* (flea market).

ELSEWHERE

▧ **PARQUE DE MARÍA LUISA.** In 1929, Sevilla made elaborate plans for an Ibero-American world fair. Though plans for the fair were interrupted by the stock market crash, the event bequeathed the lovely landscapes of the Parque de María Luisa, framed by Av. Borbolla and the river. Innumerable courtyards, turquoise-tiled benches, and tailored tropical gardens send many visitors off to *siesta*-land. On the park's northeast edge, the twin spires of **Plaza de España** poke above the city skyline. The plaza is the perfect setting for a Sunday afternoon outing, evoking images of horse-drawn carriages, top hats, puffy dresses, bottles of wine beside the fountain, and **boat rides** along the narrow moat. Mosaics depicting every provincial capital in Spain line the decaying colonnade. The balconies above offer a beautiful view. *(Park open daily 8am-10pm. Boat rides 300ptas for 1hr.)*

MUSEO ARQUEOLÓGICO. Sevilla's Museo Arqueológico shows off a small collection of pre-Roman and Roman artifacts excavated in the surrounding provinces. *(Pl. América, in the park. Tel. 954 23 24 01. Open Tu 3-8pm, W-Sa 9am-8pm, Su 9am-2:30pm. 250ptas, EU citizens free.)*

MUSEO DE ARTE CONTEMPORÁNEO. Across the river and north of Triana lies the Museo de Arte Contemporáneo. The complex holds the collection of the former Modern Art Museum and includes paintings by 20th-century painters like Joan Miró. *(C. Américo Vespucio, 2. Tel. 954 48 06 11. Open Tu-Sa 10am-10pm, Su 10am-3pm. 300ptas, EU citizens free. Tuesday free. Guided tours at 11am, noon, 6pm, and 7pm.)*

OTHER SIGHTS. On C. San Fernando stands the 18th-century **Antigua Fábrica de Tabacos (Old Tobacco Factory),** setting of Bizet's *Carmen* and now part of the university. Near the river on Palos de la Frontera is the 17th-century **Palacio de San Telmo,** built as a sailor training school. Saint Telmo, patron saint of sailors, hovers over the door amid a maelstrom of marine monsters. Nearby, one can also visit the old grounds of **EXPO '92,** now mostly used as dance floors.

🎵 ENTERTAINMENT

The tourist office and stores distribute *El Giraldillo*, a free monthly magazine with complete listings on music, art exhibits, theater, dance, fairs, and film.

NIGHTLIFE

Sevilla's reputation for gaiety is tried and true. A typical Sevillian sampling of *marcha* (partying) begins with visits to several bars for *tapas* and *copas*, continues with dancing at nightclubs, and culminates in an early morning breakfast of *churros con chocolate*. Most clubs don't get going until well after midnight; the real fun often starts after 3am. Popular bars cluster around Pl. Alfalfa in El Centro, C. Mateos Gago near the cathedral, C. Adriano by the bullring, and C. Betis across the river in Triana. In the summer, crowds sweep towards the river in hopes of a breeze—even on "slow" nights, *terrazas* will stay open until 4am.

🎵 **La Carbonería,** C. Levies, 18 (tel. 954 21 44 60), off C. Santa María La Blanca. Each night at this funky hotspot brings free live music, from flamenco to rock to jazz, in an intimate, cave-like space. Established 30 years ago to support artists and musicians censored during Franco's dictatorship. Includes a huge outdoor patio and bar (also with live music) hidden beyond the door at the far side of the cave. Pick a drink while staring at the astounding bottle collection and complement it with their delicious *tapas*. Beer 200-275ptas. Open M-Sa 8pm-3:30am, Su 8pm-2:30am.

🎵 **Cervecería El Tremendo,** C. San Felipe, 15. A modest-looking bar without tables or chairs serving only local beer. So popular, locals crowd not only the bar, but the entire vicinity. Beer 100-150ptas. Open Th-Tu noon-4:30pm and 8pm-12:30am.

El Tamboril, Pl. Santa Cruz, s/n (tel. 954 56 15 90). Put on your best and come see *sevillanas* and *rumbas* with well-to-do Spaniards. Performances start at midnight. Delicious *sangría* 300ptas a glass. Visa, MC.

Garlochí, C. Boteros, 26 (tel. 954 22 78 75), near Pl. Salvador. A Baroque den of cherubs, chandeliers, and brass-framed mirrors. Try the *sangre de Garlochí* (pomegranate liqueur, champagne, and whiskey; 600ptas). Beer 250-300ptas. Open daily 9pm-3am.

Catedral, Cuesta del Rosario, 12. Underground space intensified by metal, stone, and wood decor. Free entrance for women and those who arrive with coupons (available in stores, restaurants, and hostels). Cover for men 1000ptas, includes 1 drink or 2 beers. Open Th-Tu midnight-8am, W midnight-6am.

Abades, C. Abades, 13 (tel. 954 22 56 22; www.sol.com/Abades). This 18th-century palace is now a charming bar. Sip *agua de Sevilla* (500ptas) or non-alcoholic *Saufco* (700ptas) to the sounds of the gurgling fountain. Open daily 4pm-dawn. Visa, MC.

Isbillya, Po. Colón, 2 (tel. 954 21 04 60). A popular gay bar in an Interesting, theater-like space. Beer 250-450ptas, mixed drinks 200-2000ptas. Open daily 8pm-5am.

Lo Nuestro, C. Betis, 31A. A local hangout in an area plagued by touristy bars. Images of bulls and matadors plaster the rust-colored walls. *Sevillanas* are spontaneous and frequent. Mixed drinks 300-900ptas. Open daily 10pm-dawn.

Haca, C. Amor de Dios, 25. The most popular gay disco in town. Modest entrance; be sure to knock. Open Su-Th 10:30pm-5am, F-Sa 10:30pm-8am.

Bar To-Ca-Me, C. Reyes Católicos, 25, just around the corner from Isbillya. Popular gay bar. Famous for their *to-ca-me* (vodka, coconut, grenadine, cream). Mixed drinks 200ptas. Open June-Aug. Su-Th 6pm-3am, F-Sa 7pm-5am; Sept.-May daily 5pm-2am.

Antigüedades, C. Argote de Molina, 40, just north of the cathedral. Themed decor changes every few weeks. Outdoor tables host a crowd of mixed ages and nationalities. Beer 200ptas, mixed drinks 600ptas. Open Su-Th 8pm-3am, F-Sa 9pm-4am.

THEATERS

MOVIES. Cine Avenida (C. Marqués de las Paradas, 15; tel. 954 22 15 48), **Cine Cristina** (Pta. Jerez, 1; tel. 954 22 66 80), and **Cines Warner Lusomundo** (Co. Comercial, Pl. Legión, s/n; tel. 902 23 33 43) all show predominantly American films dubbed in Spanish. **Corona Center** screens subtitled films, often in English. (Pagés del Corro y Paraíso, s/n, in the mall between C. Salado and C. Paraíso in Barrio de Triana. Tel. 954 27 80 64. Around 600-700ptas, W half price, Th two for one. Morning matinees W, Sa, and Su. For more info check under "Cinema" in *El Giraldillo*.)

PERFORMING ARTS. The venerable **Teatro Lope de Vega** has long been the city's leading stage. Ask about scheduled events at the tourist office or check the bulletin board in the university lobby on C. San Fernando. (Near Parque María Luisa. Tel. 954 23 45 46.) If you can't see a show, at least stop by for a drink at **Casino,** the popular *terraza* outside. **Sala La Herrería** and **Sala La Imperdible** put on avant-garde productions. (Pl. San Antonio de Padua. Both at tel. 954 38 82 19.) **Teatro de la Maestranza** is a splendid concert hall accommodating both orchestral performances and opera. (On the river next to Pl. Toros. Tel. 954 22 33 44. Box office open daily 10am-2pm and 6-9pm.) On spring and summer evenings, neighborhood fairs are often accompanied by free **open-air concerts** in Barrios de Santa Cruz and Triana.

FLAMENCO

The lightning-quick stomping and footwork of Andalucía's flamenco dancers dazzle the eyes, while the wailing *cantaores* delight the ears. Three tourist-ridden venues feature comparably flashy shows. **Los Gallos,** Pl. Santa Cruz, 11 (tel. 954 21 69 81; fax 954 22 85 22; www.infor.es/gallos), is small and intimate. Buy tickets in advance (at hostels or stores in Barrio Santa Cruz) and arrive early. (Shows nightly 9pm and 11:30pm. Cover 3500ptas, includes one drink.) **El Arenal** is similarly sized, but is a *tablao-restaurante*, so you're expected to eat. (Shows nightly 9:30-11:15pm and 11:30pm-1:15am.) **El Palacio Andaluz,** Avda. María Auxiliadora, 18B (tel. 954 53 47 20 or 954 42 56 02), distinguishes itself by using an immense theater for performances. (Book ahead with hostels. Shows nightly 10pm)

FÚTBOL

Sevilla has two wildly popular pro teams within its city limits. The pride of the Guadalquivir is **Betis,** which plays in Estadio Benito Villamarín (tel. 954 61 03 40), downstream on Av. Palmera. Team **Sevilla** has suffered from coaching changes and recently was demoted to second division, leaving followers humiliated. Sevilla plays in the Estadio Sámche Pizjuán (tel. 954 53 53 53), east of Av. Menéndez Pelayo on Av. Eduardo Dato. Tickets can be purchased at the respective stadiums; price and availability depend on the quality of the match-up. Even if you can't make it, you'll know who's won by the colors worn by the crowds in the streets (Betis wears green and white, Sevilla white and red). Sevilla's fans are so dedicated that all international battles fought on Spanish turf are held here.

SEVILLANAS When in Sevilla, do as the *Sevillanos* do. *Sevillana* is the widely popular folk form of flamenco. While elegant flamenco dancers must study technique for years, just about anyone can perform *sevillanas*. In little bars in Sevilla, yuppie couples, chic young women, and toothless old men take the dance floor side-by-side when the guitar begins to play its mournful song. A partnered dance, the *sevillana* consists of four segments that together act out a courting ritual. The basic step is easy to pick up; ask sweetly for an impromptu lesson, and before long you'll be twisting your wrists like a native. During the *Feria de Abril* the whole world takes to the streets, stomping their feet, flipping their skirts, and holding their heads high as they turn and sashay. If you can't catch the dancing live, Carlos Saura's movie *Sevillanas* showcases variations on the dance.

BULLFIGHTS

The cheapest place to buy bullfight tickets is at the ring on Po. Marqués de Contadero. However, when there's a good *cartel* (line-up), the booths on C. Sierpes, C. Velázquez, and Pl. Toros might be the only source of advance tickets. **Ticket prices,** depending on the quality of both seat and *matador*, can run from 3000ptas for a *grada de sol* (nosebleed seat in the sun) to 13,000ptas for a *barrera de sombra* (front-row seat in the shade). Buying a ticket from a scalper usually adds 20% to the ticket price. *Corridas de toros* (bullfights) or *novilladas* (cut-rate fights with young bulls and novice bullfighters) are held on the 13 days around the *Feria de Abril* and into May, every Sunday in June, more often during Corpus Christi in June and early July, and again during the *Feria de San Miguel* near the end of September. During July and August, they occur on occasional Thursdays. It's obvious when a top-notch *matador* is scheduled to fight: hours before the big event, the ring is surrounded by throngs of young female fans who don their most seductive dresses and alluring lipstick in hopes of catching the eye of their hero. Some of the most popular Sevillian bullfighters include the aging Curro Romero and Emilio Muñoz, known as "El Espártaco" (Spartacus). (For current info and **ticket sales,** call 954 22 35 06. For more info on **Bullfighting,** see p. 59.)

FESTIVALS

Sevilla swells with tourists during the *fiestas*, and with good reason—they are insanely fun. If you're in Spain during any of the major festivals, head straight to Sevilla. You won't regret it (if you can remember it, that is).

■**SEMANA SANTA.** Sevilla's world-famous *Semana Santa* lasts from Palm Sunday to Good Friday (April 21). Penitents in hooded cassocks guide floats lit by hundreds of candles through the streets. Americans may think they've gone back in time to the 1950s Deep South, as hundreds of people parade by in KKK-esque attire. Don't fret—this ceremony, which dates back to centuries before America was even discovered, has nothing to do with racism. Book a room well in advance, and expect to pay triple the ordinary price. The tourist office has a helpful booklet with advice on how and where to eat and sleep during the week's festivities.

■**FERIA DE ABRIL.** Two or three weeks after *Semana Santa*, the city rewards itself for its Lenten piety with the six-day *Feria de Abril*. Begun as part of a 19th-century revolt against foreign influence, today circuses, bullfights, and flamenco shows roar into the night in a showcase of local customs. The fairgrounds are on the southern end of Barrio Los Remedios. A spectacular array of flowers and lanterns decorates over 1000 kiosks, tents, and pavilions. Unfortunately, these are privately owned by families and businesses. The only way to get in is by making friends with the locals. However, people-watching from the sidelines can be almost as exciting: costumed girls dance *sevillanas* and men parade on horseback through the streets of Sevilla.

ANDALUCÍA

ROMERÍA DEL ROCÍO. The *Romería del Rocío* (June 11) takes place 50 days after Easter on Pentecost and involves the veneration of the *Blanca Paloma* (white dove) by candlelight parades and traditional dances. The festival culminates with a pilgrimage from Sevilla to the nearby village of Rocío, 80km away. Hundreds of Sevillians participate in the two-day trek, living off food from strangers and camping by the road at night. In the best Spanish fashion, the Romería is half penitence, half party. Singing and dancing break out around campfires and *sevillanas* ring until sunrise.

DAYTRIPS FROM SEVILLA

OSUNA

Julius Caesar founded Osuna (pop. 17,500), naming it after the *osos* (bears) that once lumbered about the land. The peaceful stone mansions are a testimony to Osuna's more recent days as a cushy ducal seat. The **Colegiata de Santa María de la Asunción** (tel. 954 81 04 44), from Pl. Mayor uphill along C. Farfana Boya, past the intersection and to the right of the bus station, was commissioned by the Dukes of Osuna in the Renaissance style and now houses the **Museo de Arte Sacro Panteón Ducal**. Goya's portrait of the Osuna family now hangs in the Museo del Prado in Madrid, but the Colegiata contains an impressive array of paintings, including religious artifacts and five Riberas. (Knock to enter. Open May-Sept. 10am-1:30pm and 4-7pm; Oct.-April Tu-Su 10am-1:30pm and 3:30-6:30pm. 300ptas.) On the right side of the church sits the university and ◪**Monasterio de la Encarnación** (tel. 954 81 11 21), a Baroque church founded by the Duke of Osuna in the 17th century and lavishly decorated in the 18th. A resident nun will show you room upon room of polychromed wooden sculptures, silver crucifixes, painted tiles, and handmade Christ-doll clothes. Make sure to knock and wait until the previous tour group finishes. (Open Tu-Su 10am-1:30pm and 3:30-6:30pm. 250ptas.)

Trains stop at the small station on Av. Estación (tel./fax 954 81 03 08), a 15-minute walk from the town center (open 6am-10pm). To reach Pl. Mayor from the train station, walk up Av. Estación, curving right on C. Mancilla. At Pl. Salitre, turn left on C. Carmen and then right on C. Sevilla, which leads into the plaza. Trains run to: **Antequera** (50min., 3 per day, 8:37am-7:01pm, 820ptas); **Sevilla** (1hr., 6 per day, 6:30am-7:53pm, 985ptas); **Málaga** (1½hr., 3 per day, 8:37am-6:02pm, 1175ptas); **Granada** (2½hr., 3 per day, 8:37am-7:01pm, 1740ptas); **Almería** (4½hr., 2 per day, 8:37am-6:02pm, 3310ptas). The **bus** station (tel. 954 81 01 46), on Av. Constitución, is a 10-minute walk from the center. To get to Pl. Mayor from the bus station, walk downhill on C. Santa Ana past tiny Pl. Santa Rita; continue on Av. Arjona until you hit the plaza. **Empresa Dipasa/Linesur** (tel. 954 98 82 22) runs buses to **Sevilla** (1½hr., 11 per day, 6:15am-7:40pm, 830ptas). **Alsina Graells** (tel. 954 81 01 46) connects to: **Antequera** (1hr., 5 per day, 750ptas); **Málaga** (2½hr., 2 per day, 1525ptas); **Granada** (3½hr., 3 per day, 1905ptas). Pick up a map at the **Oficina de Turismo** (tel. 955 82 14 00), in the Pl. Mayor (open daily 9:30am-2:30pm and 5-7:30pm; closed Su morning). **emergency**, tel. 091 or 092; **municipal police** (tel. 954 81 00 50), in Pl. Mayor; **Hospital Nuestra Señora de la Merced** (tel. 954 81 09 00). **Postal code:** 41640.

Hostal Caballo Blanco, C. Granada, 1 (tel. 954 81 01 84), furnishes comfy rooms with bath and A/C. (Breakfast 350ptas; lunch and dinner 1800ptas each. Parking 400ptas per day. Singles with bath 3000-3500ptas; doubles with shower or bath 5300-5800ptas.) **Casa Curro,** Plazuela Salitre, 5 (tel. 955 82 07 58), has a fantastic beer and *tapas* deal (135ptas)—two will fill you up. From Pl. Mayor take C. Sevilla for two blocks and turn left on C. Carmen. (Entrees 350-1400ptas. Visa, MC.) A **Pardillo supermarket** is at C. Carrera, 75 (open M-Sa 9am-2pm and 5:30-9:20pm).

ITÁLICA

Just 9km northwest of Sevilla, the village of Santiponce (pop. 6200) shelters the ruins of Itálica, the first important Roman settlement in Iberia. Itálica, constructed in 206 BC, was the birthplace of emperors Trajan (AD 53) and Hadrian (AD 76). The city walls and Nova Urbs were constructed between AD 300 and 400, otherwise known as the *apogeo* (apex). In the following centuries, Itálica's power declined, and by the 5th century Sevilla had become the regional seat of power. Archaeological excavations began in the 18th century and continue today. The **anfiteatro,** among Spain's largest, seats 25,000. It used to stage fights between gladiators and lions; today it hosts more mellow classical music performances. (Tel. 955 99 73 76. Open June-Aug. Tu-Sa 9am-8pm, Su 9am-3pm; Sept-May Tu-Sa 9am-5:30pm, Su 10am-4pm. 250ptas, EU citizens free.) Some buildings and streets have preserved mosaic floors. For schedules and info on the annual **Festival Internacional de Itálica,** which brings dance, classical music, and theater to Itálica in July and August, check Sevilla's *El Giraldillo.* To get there, take Empresa Casal's **bus** (tel. 954 41 06 58) toward Santiponce from C. Marqués de las Paradas, 33, across from the Pl. Armas bus station. Tell the driver you're going to Itálica, and get off at the last stop (30min., every 30min., 100ptas).

CARMONA

Thirty-three kilometers east of Sevilla, ancient Carmona (pop. 25,000) dominates a tall hill overlooking the gold and green countryside. Once a thriving Arab stronghold, it was later the favorite 14th-century retreat of Pedro the Cruel. Moorish palaces mingle with Christian Renaissance mansions in a network of streets partially enclosed by fortified walls. The **Puerta de Sevilla,** a horseshoe-shaped passageway with both Roman and Arab elements, and the Baroque **Puerta de Córdoba,** on the opposite end of town, once linked Carmona to the east and west. From the bus stop, walk directly away from the back end of the bus onto C. San Pedro. Cross the roundabout and walk through the Puerta de Sevilla. Enter the **Alcázar de la Puerta Sevilla** (tel. 954 19 09 55) though the tourist office on your right. The Alcázar originally served (unsuccessfully) as a Carthaginian fortification against Roman attack. During the reign of Augustus, the structure was expanded to its current size. (Open M-Sa 10am-6pm, Su 10am-3pm. 200ptas, students 150ptas, seniors and children under 12 100ptas. Tours M-Sa 11am, noon, 1, 4, and 5pm.) From the Alcázar, take C. Prim and then C. Martin to find Pl. Marqués de las Torres, where the late-Gothic **Iglesia de Santa María** (tel. 954 14 13 30) was built over an old mosque. The splendid **Patio de los Naranjos** remains from Moorish days. An even older Visigothic liturgical calendar graces one of the columns. (Open Tu-Sa 11am-2pm and 5-7pm. Mass Tu-Sa 9-11am and 7-9pm, Su 9am-12:30pm and 7-9pm.) The **Alcázar del Rey Don Pedro,** an old Almohad fortress and now a ritzy hotel, guards the eastern edge of town.

In the opposite direction from the bus stop, straight along C. Enmedio, lie the ruins of the **Necrópolis Romana,** Avda. de Jorge Bonsor, 9 (tel. 954 14 08 11; fax 954 19 14 76). Highlights include the **Tumba de Servilia** and **Tumba del Elefante,** where depictions of Mother Nature and Eastern divinities are overshadowed by the presence of a giant stone elephant. The **Museo Arqueológico** displays remains from over a thousand tombs that were unearthed at the necropolis. (Both open June-Aug. Tu-F 8:30am-2pm, Sa 10am-2pm; Sept.-May Tu-F 10am-2pm and 4-6pm, Sa-Su 10am-2pm. 250ptas, EU citizens free.)

Carmona is a convenient **bus** ride from Sevilla (1hr., M-F 21 per day, Sa 10 per day, Su 7 per day, 7am-10pm, 295ptas). In Sevilla, buses depart from Prado de San Sebastián, platforms 25 and 26. In Carmona, buses return to Sevilla from the main square, along Av. Jorge Bonsor (23 per day, 6:15am-9pm). The **tourist office,** Arco de la Puerta de Sevilla, s/n (tel. 954 19 09 55; fax 954 19 00 80), is located at the Puerta de Sevilla, down C. San Pedro from the bus stop (open M-Sa 10am-6pm, Su 10am-3pm). **Police** (tel. 954 14 00 08), Pl. San Fernando; **medical assistance** (tel. 954 14 09 97), C. Paseo de La Feria. **Post office,** C. Prim, 29 (tel. 954 14 10 24; open M-F 8:30am-2:30pm, Sa 9:30am-1pm); **postal code:** 41410.

Carmona's few accommodations are generally cheaper than Sevilla's. **Casa Carmelo,** C. San Pedro, 15 (tel. 954 14 05 72), a vintage 19th-century casino turned *pensión,* is toward the Alcázar from the bus stop. Don't miss the doorway surrounded by all of the shop windows. (Singles with toilet 1750-2000ptas; doubles 3000-4000ptas, with bath 4000-5000ptas. Su-Th curfew 1:30-2am.) **Restaurante San Fernando,** C. Sacremento, 3 (tel. 954 14 35 56), is a refreshingly cool and classy hideaway (open Tu-Sa 1:30-4pm and 9pm-midnight, Su 1:30-4pm).

HUELVA

Conveniently located near the Spain-Portugal border, Huelva can be more than just a stopover. In a city marked by industrialization, it's easy to overlook the benefits of nearby beaches, great bars, and a remarkably friendly atmosphere. Huelva is not worth going out of the way for, but those heading to or from Portugal should not shy away; an evening spent on the Av. Pablo Rada can be quite enchanting.

⊓ ORIENTATION & PRACTICAL INFORMATION. The central axis of the city is **Avenida Martín Alonso Pinzón** (a.k.a. Gran Vía). From the train station, go out the front door, cross the street, and go straight down the street directly in front of you (C. Alonso XII). At the third intersection turn either right or left. From the bus station, go out and cross Av. Alemania. Take C. Gravina, turn left onto C. M. Nuñez, then right onto C. Concepción and go straight for a couple of blocks. This street now runs parallel to Av. Martin Alonso Pinzón, so turn left and cross over. **Trains** leave from the station (tel. 959 24 56 14) on Av. Italia to: **Sevilla** (1½hr., 3 per day, 8:50am-8:20pm, 890ptas); **Córdoba** (2¼hr., 1 per day, 12:12pm, 2700ptas); **Madrid** (4¼hr., 1 per day, 4:55pm, 8200ptas). **Buses** depart from Av. Dr. Rubio (tel. 959 25 69 00) to: **Sevilla** (DAMAS: 1hr., 22 per day, 7am-8:30pm, 890ptas); **Faro, Portugal** (DAMAS: 2½hr., 2 per day, 9am-6pm, 700ptas; ALCOTAN: 2½hr., 1 per day, 9:40am or 5:10pm, 1080ptas); **Cádiz** (DAMAS: 5hr., 1 per day, 10am, 2235ptas); **Madrid** (SOCIBUS: 6hr., 3 per day, 9:45am-10:45pm, 3255ptas); **Lisbon** (AGOBE: 6½hr., M,W, and F 1 per day, 1:10pm, 3700ptas). There is a **tourist office** at Av. de Alemania, 12 (tel. 959 25 74 03), right across the street from the bus station (open M-F 9am-7pm, Sa 10am-2pm). **Police,** Av. Tomás Dominguez de Ortiz, 2 (tel. 959 24 93 50). **Post office,** Av. Tomás Dominguez de Ortiz, 1 (tel. 959 24 91 84); **internet access** on C. Ginés Martin, 14 (tel. 959 25 14 11; open daily 9am-1:30pm and 4:30-8:30pm; 300ptas for 30min., 500ptas per hr.).

⊓⊓⊔ ACCOMMODATIONS, FOOD, & ENTERTAINMENT. Most of the accommodations in Huelva cluster between the train station and Av. Martin Alonso Pinzón. A decent option is **Hostal Virgen del Rocio,** C. Tendaleras, 18 (tel. 959 28 17 16), a charmless but perfectly functional hostel with ample bedroom space and a public lounge with TV (2am curfew on weeknights, none on weekends; singles with sink 2500ptas, doubles with bath 4500ptas; Visa, MC, AmEx). Another choice is **Hostal Residencia Calvo,** C. Rascón, 31 (tel. 959 24 90 16). Don't be dissuaded by the dingy exterior of this building—inside you will find a strangely spacious, small-scale hotel. Lounge offers leather sofas, TV, and fan. All rooms have sinks but bathrooms are in the hall. (Singles 1100-1200ptas, doubles 2200-2400ptas, triples 3300-3600ptas; prices may go up in summer.)

For fresh meats and veggies, try the **Mercado de Carmen,** the town's biggest market, at the intersection of C. Barcelona, C. Carmen, and C. Duque de la Victoria. **Restaurante Trattoria Camilo e Pepone,** Isaac Peral, 3 (tel. 959 24 13 63), is *the* place to go for big portions at reasonable prices. Locals say it's the best pizzeria in town. (Pizzas 550-850ptas; salads 600-850ptas. Open daily 12:30-5pm and 8:30pm-midnight.) For drinks, check out **Bar La Prensa,** Gran Vía, 15 (tel. 959 24 02 11), which vaguely resembles a Parisian hangout. High wooden chairs and incredible air-conditioning keep you comfortable while sipping drinks (500ptas) and eating pastries. **Helados La Ibense,** C. Concepción, 10 (tel. 959 24 96 47), is the best *heladería* in Huelva (cones 90-340ptas, drinks 100-125ptas, *granizados* 135-275ptas). At night locals gather at the bars and cafes around Av. Pablo Rada.

CÓRDOBA

"Sevilla is a young girl, gay, laughing, provoking—but Córdoba...Córdoba is a dear old lady."

Nowhere else are the remnants of Spain's Islamic, Jewish, and Catholic heritages so visibly intermixed as in Córdoba (pop. 315,000). This Andalucian historical and cultural melange has left Córdoba a unique artistic and architectural legacy. Roman mosaics in the Alcázar are reminiscent of the playwright and philosopher Seneca, who settled here during the Roman occupation. The famous mosque testifies to Córdoba's political and intellectual reemergence under Islamic rule (711-1263) and the influence of the beloved Jewish philosopher Maimonides, who spearheaded the return to centrality which helped make Córdoba the seat of the Western caliphate. Even the Palacio del Marqués de Viana (14th century) anticipates Spain's Golden Age (16th-17th centuries), a time when literary luminaries such as poet Luís de Góngora resided here. Córdoba, though a small city, is not overwhelmed by its incredible history. Springtime festivals, flower-ridden patios, and a busy nightlife make it one of Spain's most beloved cities. Both delicate and wise, Córdoba may be a "a dear old lady," but she is far from tired.

▐ GETTING THERE

Córdoba is easily accessible by **AVE** trains from **Madrid** (1¾hr., 15 per day, 5:30am-10pm, 6000ptas) and **Sevilla** (45min., 15 per day, 7:50am-7:50pm, 2300ptas). It can only be reached by bus from **Granada** (3hr., 9 per day, 7:30am-8pm, 1515ptas).

▐ ORIENTATION AND PRACTICAL INFORMATION

Córdoba is split into two parts: the old city and the new city. The modern and commercial northern half extends from the train station on Av. América down to **Plaza de las Tendillas,** the center of the city. The old part in the south is a medieval maze known as the **Judería** (Jewish quarter). This tangle of beautiful and disorienting streets extends from Pl. Tendillas to the banks of the Río Guadalquivir, winding past the **Mezquita** and **Alcázar.**

TRANSPORTATION

Planes: Córdoba Airport (tel. 957 21 41 00), Av. del Aeropuerto.

Trains: (tel. 957 40 02 02), Av. América. To: **Sevilla** (AVE 45min., 15 per day, 2300-2700ptas; regular 1¼hr., 12 per day, 1065-2200ptas); **Antequera** (1½hr., 3 per day, 1500ptas); **Madrid** (AVE 2hr., 16 per day, 6000-7100ptas; regular 2-6hr., 13 per day, 3700-6000ptas); **Málaga** (AVE 2¼hr., 5 per day, 2000-2200ptas; regular 3hr., 15 per day, 1650-3000ptas); **Cádiz** (AVE 2½hr., 2 per day, 3700ptas; regular 3-4hr., 5 per day, 2370-3700ptas); **Granada** (4½hr., 3 per day, 2130-2785ptas); **Algeciras** (5½hr., 2 per day, 2800-3300ptas); **Barcelona** (10-11hr., 5 per day, 6100-8400ptas). For international tickets, contact **RENFE,** Ronda de los Tejares, 10 (tel. 957 49 02 02).

Buses: There are two bus stations. One is on Av. de América, across from the train station. The other is at C. Diego Serrano, 14, 1 block from Av. Medina Azahara. To reach the town center from C. Diego Serrano, exit left, make an immediate left, then go right onto Av. Medina Azahara. When you reach the park, Av. República Argentina will be directly in front of you. From there, cross the park and walk into Pl. A Grilo, down C. Concepción and straight into Pl. Tendillas. **Alsina Graells Sur** (info tel. 957 40 40 40; tickets tel. 957 27 81 00) covers most of Andalucía. To: **Sevilla** (2hr., 10-14 per day, 1200ptas); **Antequera** (2½hr., 3 per day, 1075ptas); **Granada** (3hr., 8 per day, 1515-1635ptas); **Málaga** (3-3½hr., 5 per day, 1540ptas); **Marbella** (4hr., 2 per day, 2085ptas); **Cádiz** via Los Amarillos or Comes Sur (4-5hr., 5 per day, 2120ptas); **Algeciras** (5hr., 2 per day, 2805ptas); **Almería** (5hr., 1 per day, 2995ptas). **Bacoma** (tel. 957 45 65 14) to: Baeza, Ubeda, Valencia, and **Barcelona** (10hr., 1 per day, 7625ptas). **Socibus** (tel. 902 22 92 92) provides exceptionally cheap service to

Madrid (4½hr., 7 per day, 1540ptas), departing from Camino de los Sastres in front of Hotel Melia. **Transportes Ureña** (tel. 957 40 45 58) runs to **Jaén** (2hr., 7 per day). **Eurobus** (tel. 902 11 96 99) to: **Sevilla** (2hr., 3 per day); **Bilbao** (11½hr., 3 per day); **San Sebastián** (12hr., 3 per day). Intra-provincial buses depart from Av. República and Po. Victoria: **Autocares Priego** (tel. 957 29 01 58) runs anywhere in the Sierra Cordobesa; **Empresa Carrera** (tel. 957 23 14 01) functions in the Campiña Cordobesa; **Empresa Ramírez** (tel. 957 41 01 00) runs buses to nearby towns and camping sites.

Taxis: There are taxi stands throughout the city in most busy areas, and you can call them at tel. 957 45 00 00. **Radio Taxi** (tel. 957 47 02 91) charges a minimum of 385ptas.

Car Rental: Hertz (tel. 957 40 20 60), in the train station. Cheapest car 7800ptas per day. Min. age 25. Open M-F 8:30am-9pm, Sa 9am-1pm and 3:30-7pm, Su 9am-1pm.

TOURIST, FINANCIAL, AND LOCAL SERVICES

Tourist Offices: Provincial Tourist Office, C. Torrijos, 10 (tel. 957 47 12 35; fax 957 49 17 78), in the Junta de Andalucía, near the Mezquita. From the train station, take bus #3 (bus stops on Av. América between the train and bus stations) along the river until the stone arch is on the right. Office is 1 block up C. Torrijos. Abundant info on Andalucía. English-speaking staff with good free map of the monument section. Open M-Sa June-Sept. 9:30am-8pm; Oct.-May 9:30am-6pm. The less-crowded **Oficina Municipal de Turismo y Congresos** (tel./fax 957 20 05 22), Pl. Judá Leví, next to the youth hostel, gives out maps and can answer all Córdoba-specific questions. Open M-Sa June-Sept. 8:30am-2:30pm; Oct.-May 9am-2pm and 4:30-6:30pm.

Currency Exchange: Banco Central Hispano (tel. 957 47 42 67), Pl. Tendillas, charges no commission. Open June-Aug. M-F 8:30am-2:30pm; Sept.-May M-F 8:30am-2:30pm, Sa 9am-1pm. Banks and **ATMs** dot Pl. Tendillas.

Luggage Storage: Lockers at the train and main bus stations (300-600ptas). Open 24hr.

El Corte Inglés: Av. Ronda de los Tejares, 30 (tel. 957 47 02 62), on the corner of Av. Gran Capitán. Supermarket (5th fl.) and a thorough map with traffic directions (575ptas). Open M-Sa 10am-9:30pm.

English Bookstore: Librería Luque, C. Cruz Conde, 19, off Pl. Tendillas. Actually a Spanish bookstore, but it carries English books.

EMERGENCY AND COMMUNICATIONS

Emergency: tel. 091 or 092. **Police:** (tel. 957 47 75 00), Av. Medina Azahar.

Medical Assistance: Red Cross Hospital (tel. 957 42 06 66; emergency tel. 957 22 22 22), Po. Victoria. English spoken. **Ambulance:** tel. 29 55 70.

24-Hour Pharmacy: On a rotating basis. Refer to the list posted outside the pharmacy in Pl. Tendillas or the local newspaper.

Post Office: C. Cruz Conde, 15 (tel. 957 47 81 02), near Pl. Tendillas. Lista de Correos. Open M-F 8:30am-8:30pm, Sa 9:30am-2pm. **Postal Code:** 14070.

Internet Access: El Navegante Café Internet, C. Llanos del Pretorio, 1 (tel. 957 49 75 36), off Av. América near the train station. A bar with a nautical theme. 250ptas for 15min., 350ptas for 30min., 600ptas per hr. Open daily 8am-3:30pm and 8pm-3am.

Telephone: Information tel. 1003.

▌ ACCOMMODATIONS

Hostels in Córdoba are on the whole quite impressive: charming, well-maintained, and affordable. Prices are generally higher in summer. Córdoba is especially crowded during *Semana Santa* and from May through September, so you may have to call two to three months in advance to make reservations.

IN AND AROUND THE JUDERÍA

The Judería's whitewashed walls, narrow, twisting streets, and proximity to major sights make it the nicest and most convenient area in which to stay. During the day, souvenir booths and cafes keep the streets lively; at night the area seems desolate and spooky and is probably not the best place to walk alone.

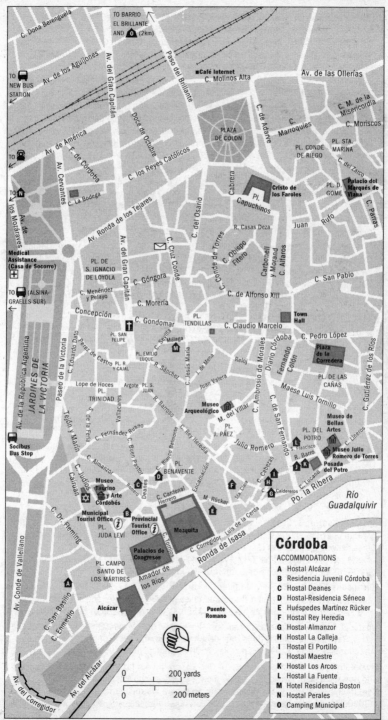

ANDALUCÍA

Córdoba

ACCOMMODATIONS

A Hostal Alcázar
B Residencia Juvenil Córdoba
C Hostal Deanes
D Hostal-Residencia Séneca
E Huéspedes Martínez Rücker
F Hostal Rey Heredia
G Hostal Almanzor
H Hostal La Calleja
I Hostal El Portillo
J Hostal Maestre
K Hostal Los Arcos
L Hostal La Fuente
M Hotel Residencia Boston
N Hostal Perales
O Camping Municipal

▓ **Residencia Juvenil Córdoba (HI)** (tel. 957 29 01 66; fax 957 29 05 00), Pl. Juda Leví, next to the municipal tourist office and a 2min. walk from the Mezquita. Convenient and a bargain, this is definitely *the* place to stay in Córdoba. Huge, modern, and antiseptic, all rooms are doubles with private baths or quads with shared bath. Wheelchair accessible. A/C. Public telephones. Reservations recommended. Breakfast 195ptas, lunch and dinner 650ptas each. 1300ptas per person, ages 26 and up 1800ptas. 300ptas extra per day for nonmembers for 6-night stay to gain membership.

▓ **Hostal Deanes,** C. Deanes, 6 (tel. 957 29 37 44). From the top left corner of the Mezquita take C. Cardenal, then turn right onto C. Romero which becomes C. Deanes. The hostel will be on the left. Perfectly situated and wonderfully designed. Despite the lack of some modern conveniences, visitors will enjoy bare white walls, high ceilings, and an enormous patio. No reservations. Doubles 4000ptas, with bath 5000ptas.

Hostal-Residencia Séneca, C. Conde y Luque, 7 (tel./fax 957 47 32 34), 2 blocks from the Mezquita; follow C. Céspedes. Impeccably maintained by an energetic English- and French-speaking owner. All rooms have fans. Common room with TV and public phone. Reserve a week ahead. 1000ptas extra for A/C. Singles with sink 2250-2500ptas, with bath 4100-4500ptas; doubles with sink 4200-4600ptas, with bath 5200-5700ptas; triples with exterior bathroom 6000-6450ptas. Breakfast and tax included.

Hostal Alcázar, C. San Basilio, 2 (tel. 957 20 25 61), on a tiny alley off the Jardines Santo Mártires, 2 blocks uphill from the Alcázar. Dainty furnishings and floral motif reminiscent of a charmless motel. Fans. Breakfast (500ptas) is included in the price, so let them know if you don't want it. Reservations recommended. Singles 2000-2500ptas; doubles with sink 2800-3300ptas, with bath 3800-4300ptas. Visa, MC, AmEx.

BETWEEN THE MEZQUITA AND CALLE DE SAN FERNANDO

This quieter, more residential area of Córdoba is still near the sights but a step away from the tourists. Some hostels are so nice you might want to stay a while.

▓ **Hostal La Fuente,** C. San Fernando, 51 (tel. 957 48 78 27 or 957 48 14 78; fax 957 48 78 27), off C. Corregidor Luis de la Cerda. Spanish authenticity meets modern comforts. Relax with the friendly owners in the traditional bar or beautiful courtyard. All rooms with bath, some with TV. Breakfast 275ptas. Parking 700ptas. Half of the building has A/C (at no extra charge); soon all rooms will. Singles 3000ptas; doubles 4000-5000ptas; 1800ptas per person for large groups. Visa, MC, AmEx.

Hostal Maestre, C. Romero Barros, 4-5 (tel. 957 47 24 10). From the Mezquita, follow the river towards Pl. Potro (away from the Alcázar), walk uphill and take a right (10min.). All rooms have private bathrooms, some have TVs (no extra charge); for 750ptas you can make that fan an A/C. 10% discount for *Let's Go* readers and special discounts available for large groups. English-speakers on staff. Parking 850ptas per day. Singles 2000-2750ptas; doubles 4000-4750ptas; triples 6000-6500ptas.

Hostal Almanzor, C. Cardenal González, 10 (tel./fax 957 48 54 00), 3 blocks from the Mezquita at the end of C. Rey Heredía closest to the river. Spotless rooms with balconies, flowing drapes, and TVs; some have A/C and heat (at no charge). All singles have king-sized beds. Reception 24hr. Parking included. Singles 1500-2500ptas, with bath 2000-3000ptas; doubles with bath 3000-4000ptas. Visa, MC, AmEx.

Huéspedes Martínez Rücker, Martínez Rücker, 14 (tel. 957 47 25 62). Take a right off the right side of the Mezquita. The owner takes pride in his hostel and it shows. Rooms are sparse and clean, and all have fans. 1500ptas per person; up to 5 in a room.

Hostal El Portillo, C. Cabezas, 2 (tel. 957 47 20 91), off C. Caldereros, the continuation of C. Rey Heredía. Quaint patio, friendly owners, and affordable prices. Fans. Common bathrooms. Single 2000ptas; doubles 2500-3000ptas; triples 3500-4000ptas.

Hostal los Arcos, C. Romero Barros, 14 (tel. 957 48 56 43; fax 957 48 60 11), next door to Hostal Maestre. Fans and TVs in all rooms, as well as public telephone and laundry drying facilities. Parking 1000ptas a day. Reservations recommended. Singles 1500-2000ptas; doubles 3500-4500ptas; triples 5000-6500ptas. Visa, MC, AmEx.

Hostal Rey Heredia, C. Rey Heredia, 26 (tel./fax 957 47 41 82), on the long, narrow street parallel to the Mezquita. Tiled rooms with fans and high ceilings. Clean and modern common bathrooms. Singles 1500ptas; doubles 3000ptas; triples 4000ptas.

AROUND PLAZA DE LAS TENDILLAS AND BEYOND

Just five minutes from the Judería, rooms in this busy area offer a glimpse of bustling, modern Córdoba. From the RENFE station, take bus #3 to Pl. Tendillas; from the main bus station, take bus #7. Those with an early morning train or bus to catch are best off staying on the far side of Av. República Argentina, near the train station and away from the center of the city.

Hotel Residencia Boston, C. Málaga, 2 (tel. 957 47 41 76; fax 957 47 85 23), on the corner of Pl. Tendillas. Good value for modern comforts: A/C, TV, phones, and baths. Breakfast 400ptas. Parking nearby. Singles with small bath 3200-3800ptas; doubles with bath 5300-6300ptas; triples 6300-7300ptas. Visa, MC, AmEx.

Hostal Perales, Av. Mozárabes, 15 (tel. 957 23 03 25), a half block from the train station and around the corner from both bus stations. Look for the yellow sign. Small rooms on a loud street. Stay here if proximity to transport is a priority. 1500-2000ptas per person.

CAMPING

Camping Municipal, Av. Brillante, 50 (tel. 957 28 21 65). From the train station, turn left on Av. América, left on Av. Brillante, and walk uphill for about 20min. Or take bus #10 or 11 from Av. Cervantes near the station. Pool, currency exchange, supermarket, restaurant, free hot showers, laundry service. Camping equipment for rent. Wheelchair accessible. Individual tent 400 ptas, family tent 560ptas; tax not included.

◖ FOOD

The Mezquita area attracts nearly as many high-priced eateries as tourists to eat in them, but a five-minute walk in any direction yields local specialties at reasonable prices. C. Dr. Fleming, past the Alcázar, is sprinkled with small restaurants serving moderately priced dishes. Even cheaper eateries cluster farther away from the Judería in **Barrio Cruz Conde,** around Av. Menéndez Pidal and Pl. Tendillas. Regional specialties include *salmorejo* (a gazpacho-like cream soup topped with hard-boiled eggs and pieces of ham) and *rabo de toro* (bull's tail simmered in tomato sauce). **Supermarket Simago,** C. Jesús María, lies half a block from Pl. Tendillas (open M-Sa 9am-9pm).

El Pincantón, C. F. Ruano, 19. From the top right corner of the Mezquita, walk up Romero and turn left. Take ordinary *tapas,* pour on a *salsa picante,* stick it in a roll, and *voilà,* you've got lunch (150-300ptas). Nothing else as cheap or as filling. No seats. No English spoken. Open daily 10am-2pm and 8pm-midnight.

Mesón San Basilio, C. San Basilio, 19 (tel. 957 29 70 07), to the left of the Alcázar, past Campo Santo de los Martires. The locals love it, and so will you. The two-tiered dining room makes for a special and breezy atmosphere. *Menú del día* 1000ptas, *raciones* 400-1500ptas, meat and fish dishes 800-1750ptas. There is also a full bar with wine (75-225ptas) and beer (110-175ptas). Open daily June-Aug. 12:30-4pm and 8pm-midnight; Sept.-May noon-4pm and 7-11:30pm.

El Churrasco, C. Romero, 16. Straight from the top left corner of the Mezquita. Although primarily a meat-lover's paradise, even vegetarians will think they are in Eden. A little pricey, but a nice treat. Entrees 600-2800ptas. Glass of wine 375 ptas. Open daily 1-4pm and 8pm-midnight. Visa, MC, Amex.

Sociedad de Plateros, C. San Francisco, 6 (tel. 957 47 00 42), between C. San Fernando and Pl. Potro. A Córdoba mainstay since 1872. *Tapas* 200-300ptas, *raciones* and *media raciones* 400-700ptas. Bar open Tu-Su 8am-4pm and 8pm-2:30am, meals served 1-4pm and 8pm-midnight. Open M-Sa in summer. Visa, MC.

Meson de la Luna, Calleja de la Luna, s/n (tel. 957 29 77 17), near Pl. Campo Santo de Los Martires. It may look like every other cafe in Córdoba, but the food sets it apart. Meat and fish dishes 1900-2200ptas, salads 1000ptas. The 7 set menus range in price 1600-2100ptas. Open daily 11am-1am; bar open until 5am. Visa, MC, Amex.

O Mamma Mia, C. Reyes Católicos, 5 (tel. 957 47 00 52), off Av. Gran Capitán. Sick of traditional Spanish food? Pretend you're in Italy. Every pizza is a work of art. Pizzas 635-950ptas. Pastas 595-895ptas. Open Su-Th 1:30-4pm and 8:30pm-midnight, F-Sa 1:30-4pm and 8:30pm-1am. Visa, MC.

Taberna Casa Salinas, Puerto Almodovar, s/n (tel. 957 29 08 46). A few blocks from the synagogue, up C. Judíos and to the left. Pepe Salinas has been running this place for over 40 years. Stroll through the bar to the outdoor patio to sample *raciones* (500-800ptas) and fine wines (100ptas). Open Sept.-July Th-Tu 11:30am-5pm and 8:30pm-12:30am.

Cafetín Halal, C. Rey Heredia, 28 (tel. 957 48 32 35). Relax in the cushioned den or on the peaceful patio and try a *batido* (shake) with fruit or nuts (275-300ptas). No alcohol served; there's a mosque upstairs. Tea 225-700ptas. Coffee 100-250ptas. Open June-Aug. Tu-Su 4-11pm; Sept.-May Tu-F 5-10pm, Sa-Su 4-10pm.

Taberna San Miguel, Pl. San Miguel, 1 (tel. 957 47 83 28 or 957 47 01 66), 1 block from Pl. Tendillas. A classic *tapas* spot with bullfighting decor. *Raciones* 800-2200ptas. Wine 100-250ptas, beer 175ptas. Open Sept.-July M-Sa noon-4pm and 6pm-midnight.

Taberna Santa Clara, C. Osio, 2 (tel. 957 47 50 36). From the right side of the Mezquita, take C. Martinez Rucker and turn left. Two pages of meat-free dishes. Hot entrees 350-1150ptas, cold entrees 650-1850ptas, salads 650-750ptas. Visa, MC.

👁 SIGHTS

🕌 LA MEZQUITA

Tel. 957 47 05 12. Open June-Aug. M-Sa 10am-7pm, Su 9am–11am and 1:30pm-sunset; Sept.-May M-Sa 10am-5:30pm, Su 2-5:30pm. 750ptas, ages 8-11 375 ptas. Same ticket valid for Museo Diocesano de Bellas Artes. Last ticket sold 30min. before closing. Mass M-Sa 9:30am; Su 11am, noon, and 1pm.

Built in 784 on the site of a Visigoth basilica, Córdoba's Mezquita was intended to be the world's grandest mosque. Over the next two centuries, this architectural masterpiece was enlarged to cover an area of several city blocks, making it the largest mosque in the Islamic world at the time. The 14th-century Mudéjar door, **La Puerta del Perdón,** opens to the left. Visitors enter through the **Patio de los Naranjos,** an arcaded courtyard featuring carefully spaced orange trees, palm trees, and fountains. Inside, 850 pink and blue marble, alabaster, and stone columns—no two the same height—support hundreds of red-and-white striped two-tiered arches. At the far end of the Mezquita lies the **Capilla Villaviciosa,** where Caliphal vaulting, greatly influential in later Spanish architecture, appeared for the first time. In the center, the **Mihrab** is the naturally lit central dome where the Muslims guarded the Qur'an. Its prayer arch faces Mecca. The intricate gold, pink, and blue marble Byzantine mosaics shimmering across its arches were given by the Emperor Constantine VII to the *cordobés* caliphs. His gift is estimated to weigh close to 35 tons.

When the Christians conquered Córdoba in 1236 they converted the Mezquita into a church. The **Capilla Mayor (High Chapel)** was enlarged in 1384. In 1523, Bishop Alonso Manrique, an ally of Carlos V, proposed to build a Renaissance cathedral in the center of the mosque. The town rallied violently against the idea, promising a swift, painful death for any worker who helped tear down the Mezquita. Nevertheless, the Christians soon erected the towering **Crucero** (transept) and **Coro** (choir dome), combining the Renaissance style of the epoch with elements of a mosque. The townspeople were far from pleased. Even Carlos V lamented the changes to the Mezquita, griping, "You have destroyed something unique to create something commonplace." Fortunately what remains is far from commonplace.

enclosed garden and almond grove. After moving from Granada, Azahara missed the Sierra Nevada. To appease her, Abderramán planted the white-blossoming almond groves as a substitute for her beloved snow. The **Salón de Abd al-Rahman III,** also known as the *salón rico,* on the lower terraces, is being restored to its original intricate and geometrical beauty. A complete tour of the ruins takes between 20 and 45 minutes, depending on your level of interest. (Tel. 957 32 91 30. Open May-Sept. Tu-Su 10am-2pm and 6-8:30pm; Oct.-Apr. Tu-Sa 10am-2pm and 4-6:30pm, Su 10am-2pm. 250ptas, EU citizens free.)

Madinat al-Zahra is difficult to reach without an organized tour group. The **0-1 bus** (tel. 957 25 57 00, or see the list in the tourist office) leaves from Av. República Argentina in Córdoba for Cruce Medina Azahara, stopping 3km from the site (every hr., 115ptas). From the bus stop, it's about a 45-minute walk (mostly uphill). On the way back, the bus stop is along the highway at the cross, on the opposite side of the street from the gas station. A **taxi** costs about 1600ptas. **Córdoba Visión** (tel. 957 23 17 34; fax 957 23 73 94) offers transportation and a two-hour guided visit to the sight in English, Spanish, or French. (Tours May-Sept. Tu-Sa 10:30am-6pm, Su 10:30am; Oct.-Apr. Tu-Sa 10:30am-4pm, Su 10:30am. 2500ptas. Meets at Triunfo de San Rafael near the mosque.)

JEREZ DE LA FRONTERA

Though unremarkable in appearance, Jerez de la Frontera (pop. 200,000) is the cradle of three staples of Andalucian culture: flamenco, Carthusian horses, and, of course, *jerez* (sherry). It is the sheer quantity and quality of this third staple that draws in the tourists. The city also makes a good departure point for several popular tourist itineraries: the *ruta de los pueblos blancos* (route of the white villages), the *ruta del toro* (bulls), the *ruta de la atlántico* (coast), and, of course, the *ruta del vino* (wine).

▐▀ GETTING THERE

The easiest way to get to Jerez is by train from: **Cádiz** (40min., 20-35 per day, 6:40am-10:10pm, 400ptas); **Sevilla** (1hr., 20 per day, 6:35am-9:27pm, 900-1400ptas); **Madrid** (4¼hr., 2 per day, 10:05am and 4:03pm, 7800-9000ptas).

▐ ORIENTATION AND PRACTICAL INFORMATION

The labyrinthine streets of Jerez are difficult to navigate without a map. Get one free from the tourist office or buy one from any bookstore or newsstand (around 500ptas). To reach the town center from the **bus station,** exit left onto C. Cartuja, which becomes C. Medina, which leads into **Plaza Romero Martínez** (the city's commercial center). From here, walk left on C. Cerrón, which leads to C. Santa María and C. Lencería, heading into **Plaza del Arenal.** From the **train station,** exit to the right and take C. Cartuja to the bus station, then follow the directions above.

TRANSPORTATION

Flights: Airport (tel. 956 15 00 00), 7km from town on Ctra. Jerez-Sevilla. Taxi to the airport 1500-2000ptas. **Iberia** (tel. 956 18 43 94) and **British Airways** (tel. 956 15 00 93) both have their offices at the terminal. Flights operate regularly to and from Madrid and Barcelona, as well as other major European cities.

Trains: (tel. 956 34 23 19), Pl. Estación, at the end of C. Medina after it becomes C. Cartuja. **RENFE,** C. Larga, 34 (tel. 956 33 48 13). To: **Cádiz** (45min., 12 per day, 7:45am-10:30pm, 375ptas); **Sevilla** (1¼hr., 12 per day, 6:30am-8:30pm, 895ptas); **Madrid** (4½hr., 2 per day, 8:36am and 4:59pm, 7800-9000ptas); **Barcelona** (12hr., 2 per day, 8:36am and 7:36pm, 6600-9100ptas).

Buses: (tel. 956 34 52 07), on C. Cartuja, at the corner of C. Madre de Dios, 2 blocks from the train station. **Transportes Generales Comes** (tel. 956 34 21 74) to: **Puerto**

Santa María (30min., 4-6 per day, 7am-8:30pm, 180ptas); **Cádiz** (1hr., 19 per day, 7am-9pm, 350ptas); **Vejer** (2hr., 1 per day, 6:45pm, 800ptas); **Ronda** (2¾hr., 4 per day, 7:45am-3:30pm, 1270ptas). **Los Amarillos** (tel. 956 32 93 47) to **Arcos** (45min., every hr., 7:15am-8:15pm, 225ptas) and **Córdoba** (4hr., 1 per day, 1925ptas). **Linesur** (tel. 956 34 10 63) to: **Sanlúcar** (30min., every hr., 7am-9pm, 210ptas); **Chipiona** (1hr., 12 per day, 7am-9pm, 295ptas); **Sevilla** (1½hr., 12 per day, 6:30am-11pm, 870ptas); **Algeciras** (2hr., 8 per day, 7:15am-10pm, 1425ptas). **Secorbus** (tel. 902 22 92 92) to **Madrid** (7hr., 6 per day, 8:50am-11:50pm, 2945ptas).

City buses: Each of the 12 lines runs every 15min., most passing through Pl. Arenal and by the bus station. One ride 110ptas. Info office (tel. 956 34 34 46) in Pl. Arenal.

Car Rental: Niza, C.N. IV Madrid-Cádiz, KM, 637, and a branch on Av. Alvaro Domecq (tel. 956 30 28 60, fax 956 18 12 87). Starts at 7500ptas per day. Min. age 21. Open daily 8:30am-1pm and 4:30-8pm.

Tourist Office: C. Larga, 39 (tel. 956 33 11 50; fax 956 33 17 31). From Pl. Arenal, take C. Lencería to C. Larga. Friendly, English-speaking staff doles out highly technical info on sherry production and *bodegas* tours. Free maps. Open June-Aug. M-F 9am-2pm and 5-8pm, Sa 10am-2pm and 5-7pm; Sept.-May M-Sa 8am-2pm and 4-7pm.

Emergency: tel. 091 or 092. **Police:** tel. 956 33 03 46.

Medical Assistance: Ambulatorio de la Seguridad Social (tel. 956 34 84 68), C. José Luis Díaz.

Post Office: Main Office, C. Cerón, 2 (tel. 956 34 22 95), off Pl. Romero Martínez. Lista de Correos. Open M-F 8:30am-8:30pm, Sa 10am-2pm. **Postal Code:** 11480.

Internet Access: RJP Informática, C. Larga, 2nd fl. of the Centro Comercial (tel. 32 12 53). 400ptas for 30min., 700ptas per hr. Open M-F 9:30am-1:30pm and 5:30-9pm, Sa 10:30am-1:30pm. **Cybersur,** C. Divina Pastora, 48 (tel 956 32 87 90). 275ptas for 15min., 450ptas for 30min., 700ptas per hr. Open M-F 10am-1:30pm and 5:30-8:30pm, Sa 10:30am-2pm.

ACCOMMODATIONS

In Jerez, finding a place to crash is as easy as finding a cork to sniff. Look along C. Medina, near the bus station, and C. Arcos, which intersects C. Medina at Pl. Romero Martínez. The area may not be interesting to look at, but it's close to the fountains and *terrazas* of C. Larga. Prices increase during Jerez's festivals.

Albergue Juvenil (HI), Av. Carrero Blanco, 30 (tel. 956 14 39 01; fax 956 14 32 63), in an ugly suburb, a 25min. walk or 10min. bus ride from downtown (bus L-8 from the bus station, bus L-1 from Pl. Arenal). Clean and modern, with spacious doubles, a pool (open July-Aug.), tennis and basketball courts, mini-soccer field, library, TV and video room, and a rooftop terrace. Laundry service available. Check-out 10am. Call ahead. Dorms 800-1300ptas, over 26 1100-1800ptas.

Hostal San Andrés, C. Morenos, 12 (tel. 956 34 09 83; fax 956 34 31 96). Take C. Fontana (off C. Medina) for 1 block, then turn left; C. Morenos is the 1st right. Friendly, family-run place has two beautiful patios, one with stained glass, the other with hanging grapes. Singles 1600-2500ptas; doubles 2500-4500ptas.

Hostal Sanvi, C. Morenos, 10 (tel. 956 34 56 24). Follow directions for Hostal San Andrés. Friendly management gives it that family-run feel. Generic hotel rooms at hostel prices. Singles 1800-2000ptas; doubles with bath 3500ptas.

FOOD

Tapas-hoppers bounce around Pl. Arenal, C. Larga and northeast on Av. Alcalde Álvaro Domecq around Pl. Caballo. Supermarket **Cobreros** sells the basics on the second floor of the Centro Comercial, on C. Larga, next door to McDonald's (open daily 9am-2pm and 5:30-9:30pm).

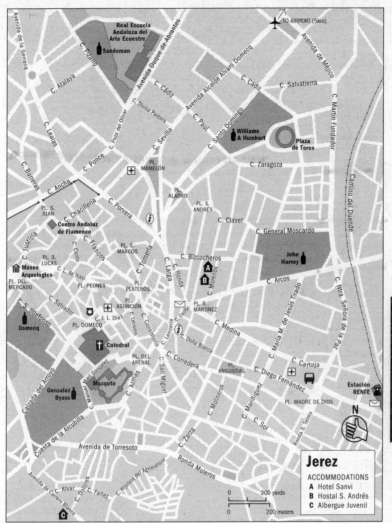

Jerez

ACCOMMODATIONS
A Hotel Sanvi
B Hostal S. Andrés
C Albergue Juvenil

Casa Pepa, Pl. Madre de Dios, 14 (tel. 956 32 49 06), around the corner from the bus station, between two tall buildings. A local meeting place and landmark. *Menú* 800ptas, entrees 450-700ptas. Open daily 11am-4pm and 7-11pm.

Dolce Vita, C. Divina Pastora, 2 (tel. 956 33 34 61), around the corner from the equestrian school. Not classy, but cheap and filling. Big pasta portions from 620ptas, burgers from 250ptas, pizza 930-1400ptas. Open M-Th 8pm-1am, F-Su 7:30pm-3am.

◤ SHERRY BODEGAS

People come to Jerez for the *jerez*. Multilingual tour guides distill the sherry-making process for you, then let you sample for free. The best time to visit is early September during the harvest; the worst is August when many *bodegas* close down. *Bodegas* are plotted on any map and the tourist office can help find the right one for you. Group reservations for hour-long tours must be made at least one week in advance; reservations for individuals are usually unnecessary. *Bodegas* open during specific hours, and most conduct tours in English. Call ahead for exact times.

Williams and Humbert, Ltd., Nuño de Cañas, 1 (tel. 956 34 65 39; fax 956 34 51 91). One of Jerez's nicest, complete with gardens and prize-winning Carthusian horses. Tours M-F 1:30pm. 400ptas, students 250ptas. Reservations required for groups.

B. Domecq, C. San Idelfonso, 3 (tel. 956 15 15 00; fax 956 33 86 74). The oldest and largest in town. Lots of cats. Tours M-F 9am and 1pm. 500ptas. Reservations required.

González Byass, C. Manuel María González, 12 (tel. 956 35 70 16; fax 956 35 70 46). The largest tour, with trained mice that climb miniature ladders in order to sip the juice. Lucky mice. English tours M-F at 10:30am, 11:30am, 12:30pm, 1:30pm, 5:30pm, and 6:30pm. 900ptas. Reservations required on weekends.

📷 SIGHTS

📷MEZQUITA. Beautiful gardens and **baños árabes** (Arab baths) lie within this 11th century mosque, while the **Torre Octagonal** rises above. Also inside, the **Cámara Oscura** offers exhibits on Jerez as well as startling views of the city. *(Near Pl. Arenal on the Alameda Vieja. Tel. 956 33 73 06. Open June-Aug. daily 10am-3pm; Sept.-May M-F 10am-6pm. Free.)*

REAL ESCUELA ANDALUZA DE ARTE EQUESTRE. Jerez's love for wine is almost matched by its passion for horses. During the first or second week of May, the Real Escuela Andaluza de Arte Equestre (Royal Andalucian School of Equestrian Art), on Av. Duque de Abrantes, sponsors a **Feria del Caballo** (Horse Fair) with shows, carriage competitions, and races of Jerez-bred Carthusian horses. During the rest of the year, shows held every Thursday at noon (also Tuesday in summer) feature a troupe of horses dancing in choreographed sequences. Dress rehearsals are almost as impressive. *(Tel. 956 30 77 98; fax 956 30 99 54. Dress rehearsal M-W and F 11am-1pm. 550ptas. Shows 1500-2400ptas, children and students 40% off.)*

CATEDRAL. Near the Mezquita is the imposing Baroque cathedral, with a Mudéjar belfry, built on the site of another mosque. *(Tel. 956 34 84 82. Open daily June-Aug. 10am-8pm; Sept.-May 10am-6pm. 200ptas, students, children, and seniors 100ptas.)*

🎵 ENTERTAINMENT

FLAMENCO. Thought to have originated in Jerez. If you're lucky, you'll catch a free, spontaneous show. Rare footage of Spain's most highly regarded flamenco singers, dancers, and guitarists is available for viewing at the **Centro Andaluz de Flamenco,** in Palacio Pemartín, on Pl. San Juan. (Tel. 956 34 92 65; fax 956 32 11 27. Open M-F 9am-2pm. Audio-visuals every hr., 9:30am-1:30pm. Free.) Most *peñas* and *tablaos* (clubs and bars that host flamenco) hide in the old town, a maze of narrow streets west of C. Larga and south of C. Porvera and C. Ancha. Most only perform for large groups, and require reservations in advance. Ask for details in the tourist office. A bit secluded but worth the trek, **El Lagá de Tío Parrilla,** Pl. Mercado, s/n (tel./fax 956 33 83 34), is the only *tablao* that hosts open shows frequently. (Shows M-Sa 10:30pm. Cover 1200-1500ptas, includes 1 drink.)

NIGHTLIFE. For more conventional nightlife, try the triangle formed by C. Santo Domingo, C. Salvatierra, and Av. Méjico, a few blocks past the Williams & Humbert bodega and near Pl. Caballo. This area thunders on weekends, as does Pl. Canterbury, a mini-mall of bars and *terrazas* located on C. Paul at C. Santo Domingo. **Cancún,** C. Parjarete, 18 (tel. 956 33 17 22), a huge, trendy *bar musical* off C. Zaragoza (a block from Pl. Canterbury), features Caribbean themes, but the usual techno-pop blasts from the speakers. (Couples, ladies, and "members" only. Free.)

FESTIVALS. Autumn is festival season, when Jerez showcases its best equine and flamenco traditions. The **Fiesta de la Bulería** in September celebrates flamenco, as does the September **Festival de Teatro, Música, y Baile.** These festivals are collectively known as the **Fiestas de Otoño,** occurring from September 10 until October 13. The largest **horse parade** in the world, with races in Pl. Arenal, is the highlight of the final week of this month-long celebration. Ask for details at the tourist office.

SANLÚCAR DE BARRAMEDA

Sanlúcar de Barrameda (pop. 62,000) sits at the mouth of the Río Guadalquivir, providing access to the **Parque Nacional Coto de Doñana** (see **Mother Nature and Family,** p. 219) and some of Spain's most pristine beaches. Home to a handful of sherry *bodegas* and a few palaces, Sanlúcar ia a cross between Spanish white-town and a European seaside resort. Its industrial outskirts are a bit of an eyesore, but it has superbly fine sand and is the third corner in the illustrious "sherry triangle," along with Jerez and El Puerto de Santa María.

7 PRACTICAL INFORMATION. Los Amarillos (tel. 956 38 50 60), on Pl. Pradillo at the end of C. San Juan, runs **buses** to: **Chipiona** (30min., every hr., 8am-9:45pm, 100ptas); **Cádiz** (1hr., 10 per day, 6:15am-6:20pm, 375ptas); **Sevilla** (2hr., 13 per day, 6:45am-9:15pm, 900ptas). **Linesur La Valenciana** (tel. 956 34 10 63) is two blocks toward the beach from Pl. Cabildo, by the tourist office. Buses run to **Chipiona** (30min., every hr., 8am-9pm, 100ptas) and **Jerez** (45min., every hr., 7:20am-10:20pm, 215ptas). Buy tickets on the bus. For **taxis,** call 956 36 11 02 or 956 36 00 04. The **tourist office** (tel. 956 36 61 10; fax 956 36 61 32) is on Calzada del Ejército, which runs perpendicular to the beach. English-speaking staff has info on Parque Nacional de Doñana. (Open June-Aug. M-F 9am-2pm and 6-9pm, Sa-Su 10am-2pm; Sept.-May M-F 10am-2pm and 5-8pm, Sa 10am-1pm.) **Emergency:** tel. 091 or 092; **medical emergency,** Ambulatorio de la S.S., Calzada del Ejército, s/n (tel. 956 36 71 65); **police,** Av. Constitución, s/n (tel. 956 38 80 11). **Post office** (tel. 956 36 09 37), C. Correos and Av. Cerro Falcón, three blocks toward the beach from the tourist office (open M-F 9am-2:30pm, Sa 9am-1pm); **postal code:** 11540.

MOTHER NATURE AND FAMILY Bust out your binoculars—the 60,000 acre **Parque Nacional Coto de Doñana** on the Río Guadalquivir delta is home to flamingos, vultures, and thousands more of your feathered favorites, along with geese (and mongeese), wild boars, and lynx. Despite a huge mining spill on a tributary of the Guadalquivir River in April of 1998 that threatened to be one of Spain's biggest ecological disasters, the park has done surprisingly well, and tourist visits have continued relatively unaffected. If ornithological delights don't entice you, the salt marshes, sand dunes, wooded areas, and beach might. Nature purists beware, though, lest you stumble upon the lair of the dreaded species *turgrupus touristicus*—the park borders the town of Matalascañas, with a concrete shopping center and hotel complex.

Access to most of the park is restricted and back-country hiking and camping are prohibited. The western end of the park is accessible from Huelva and Matalascañas. Also, boat tours on **S.S. Real Fernando** (tel. 956 36 38 13; fax 956 36 21 96) depart from **Sanlúcar** (4hr.; Apr.-Aug. Tu-Su 9:30am and 5pm; Sept.-March Tu-Su 10am; office open daily 9:30am-8pm). Call to make reservations or visit the office in the old ice factory by the dock on Av. Bajo de Guía. Those more interested in sand than life on the wild side can take the launch across the bay (8am-8pm, 400ptas) to one of the few *chiringuito* (refreshment stand)-free beaches in Spain. To get a taste of Doñana without leaving Sanlúcar, check out the **Visitor Center,** also in the ice factory (tel. 956 38 16 35; open daily June-Aug. 9am-8pm; Sept.-May 9am-2:30pm and 4-7pm).

⌐⌐ ACCOMMODATIONS AND FOOD. Few true bargains exist; it may be worth it to inquire at doorway signs reading *"se alquilan habitaciones"* (rooms for rent). **Hostal La Blanca Paloma,** Pl. San Roque, 15 (tel. 956 36 36 44), keeps spacious, clean rooms, a few with balconies (singles 2100-2500ptas; doubles 3210-4230ptas). **Pensión La Bohemia,** C. Don Claudio, 5 (tel. 956 36 95 99), just off C. Santo Domingo, offers rooms with beige bedspreads, cold showers, and no frills (singles 2200ptas, with bath 2750ptas; doubles 4200ptas, with bath 5500ptas). Sanlúcar is famous for its *langostinos* (king prawns). For a sit-down meal, head for the side streets off C. San Juan. *Terrazas* fill Pl. San Roque and Pl. Cabildo, its tree-lined neighbor. **Bar-Restaurante El Cura,** C. Amargura, 2 (tel. 956 36 29 94), between the two plazas, serves up divine *paella* (500ptas), *tapas* (from 200ptas), and entrees (400-1300ptas) in a family atmosphere (open daily 7:30am-3am).

⊕⊔ SIGHTS AND ENTERTAINMENT. Most of the sights in town are best accessed via the tourist office. Two impressive palaces compete with the enormous 14th-century **Iglesia de Nuestra Señora de la O** for the attention of sun-struck tourists. (Pl. Paz. Tel. 956 36 05 55. Open 30min. before and after mass. Mass M-Sa 7:30pm, Su noon and 8pm. Free.) The **Palacio Medina Sidonia** is inhabited by the Duque of Medina Sidonia. (Tel. 956 36 01 61. Call to arrange group visits on Sunday or Monday. Free.) The 19th-century **Palacio Infantes de Orleans** now houses the Ayuntamiento. (Tel. 956 38 80 00. Open for guided visits Th-Tu 10am-2pm. 100ptas.) Several **bodegas** tower over Sanlúcar's small streets. Check at the tourist office for the revolving schedules of the town's *bodegas* (at least one open every day, M-Sa, 12:30pm, 300ptas). The tourist office organizes cheap tours around town to both the monuments and *bodegas.* (500ptas per person.) Numerous **festivals** testify to Sanlúcar's fondness for merrymaking; the **Feria de la Manzanilla** (last week in May or first week in June) involves the most alcohol. In August, **Carreras de Caballos** (horse races) thunder along the beach, and the **Festival de la Exaltación del Río Guadalquivir** (end of August) enlivens the streets with poetry readings, a flamenco competition, dancing, and bullfights.

CHIPIONA

A quiet seaside village for nine months of the year, Chipiona (pop. 15,000) takes a summertime somersault into domestic tourism. This phenomenon began in the 19th century, when Chipiona's extremely salty and mineral-filled waters (the scent pervades the air) were reputed to have medicinal powers. A recuperative hospital was even opened along the beach to nurse ailing patients back to health; the hospital closed about 30 years ago. **Iglesia de Nuestra Señora de la O,** constructed in the 16th century, stands in the gorgeous Pl. Juan Carlos I. (Open M-F shortly before 8pm mass, Su before 9, 11am, noon, and 8:30pm mass.)

⊓ ORIENTATION AND PRACTICAL INFORMATION. Los Amarillos buses (tel. 956 37 02 92), on Av. Regla at the top of C. Peral, run to: **Sanlúcar** (30min., 15 per day, 6am-8pm, 100ptas); **Cádiz** (1½hr., 9 per day, 6am-7pm, 475ptas); **Sevilla** (2hr., 10 per day, 6:30am-8pm, 975ptas). **Linesur La Valenciana** buses (tel. 956 37 12 83) roll to **Jerez de la Frontera** (1hr., 14 per day, 8am-10:20pm, 280ptas) from Pl. San Sebastián. Follow C. Larga to reach C. Isaac Peral. The **tourist office,** Plaza de Andalucía, s/n (tel. 956 37 28 28), dispenses a free map and beach information. To get there from the bus station, exit to the main intersection and take C. Victor Pradera to C. Peral, then turn at the pharmacy onto C. Larga. The office is up ahead on the left. (Open June-Aug. M-F 10am-1:30pm and 7-9pm, Sa 11am-1pm; Sept.-May M-F 9am-2pm and 5-7pm, Sa 11am-1:30pm.) **Emergency:** tel. 091 or 092; **police** (tel. 956 37 10 88) on C. Camacho Baños. **Post office,** C. Padre Lerchundi, 15 (tel. 956 37 14 19), near Pl. Pío XII (open M-F 8:30am-2pm); **postal code:** 11550.

⛰ ACCOMMODATIONS AND FOOD. Accommodations in Chipiona seem to have conspired against budget travelers. Consider sleeping in Jerez and commuting to the beach. One luxurious option is **Hostal Gran Capitán**, C. Fray Baldomero, 3 (tel. 956 37 09 29; fax 956 37 43 35), off C. Isaac Peral, sporting a charming patio and large rooms with baths and TVs (singles 2500-3500ptas; doubles 4000-5200ptas). The municipal campground, **El Pinar de Chipiona** (tel. 956 37 23 21), on Ctra. Rota at 3km, resides 800m from the beach, with a supermarket (electricity 450ptas; 545ptas per person and per tent, 475ptas per car). C. Isaac Peral and the small streets stemming from it are dotted with bars and restaurants specializing in non-Spanish cuisine. Eateries also line Po. Cruz del Mar (at the end of C. Isaac Peral) and the area around Pl. Juan Carlos I and Pl. Pío XII. In the latter, try the scrumptious *pan montadito* (mini sandwiches on hot bread, 200ptas) at **El Rincón de Jabugo.** Another option is **Bar Toro,** Po. Maritimo Cruz del Mar, 24 (tel. 956 37 03 04), along the beachfront, which serves *tapas* (250-300ptas) and entrees (750-1500ptas) both indoors and out (open daily 9am-12:30am). The **mercado,** C. Victor Pradera, is on the left as you exit Los Amarillos bus station (open M-Sa 9am-2pm).

🌙 NIGHTLIFE. There are two things to do in Chipiona: sunbathe and party. **Bugui II** in Zona Central, **Picoco** on Po. Maritimo and **Mohama Palladium** next to the lighthouse are the three most popular discos (open summer weekends 10pm-8am). Bars cluster around these clubs, as well as opposite the tourist office on Pl. Andalucía. On the corner, **Generations Bar,** C. Larga, 38 (tel. 956 37 20 87), is American-run, with sports memorabilia on the walls and computers with **internet** access (beer 125ptas; internet 800ptas per hr; open daily 5pm-3am).

ARCOS DE LA FRONTERA

The Spanish novelist Azorín once described Arcos (pop. 33,000) by saying: "Imagine a long, narrow ridge, undulating; place on it little white houses, clustered among others more ancient; imagine that both sides of the mountain have been cut away, dropping downward sheer and straight; and at the foot of this wall a slow, silent river, its murky waters licking the yellowish stone, then going on its destructive course through the fields…and when you have imagined all this, you will have but a pale image of Arcos." The premier *pueblo blanco* on the *ruta de los pueblos blancos*, Arcos is an historic and romantic treasure.

◤ GETTING THERE

There is no train station, but Arcos is easily accesible by **bus** from: **Cádiz** (1½hr., 6 per day, 7am-6pm, 675ptas); **Sevilla** (2hr., 2 per day, 8am and 4:30pm, 905ptas)

⁊ ORIENTATION AND PRACTICAL INFORMATION

To reach the town center from the **bus station,** exit left, turn left, then continue uphill along C. Muñoz Vásquez. Walk for about 20 minutes; the street changes names more than an outlaw on the run (turning into C. Debajo del Corral, then C. Corredera, which then turns into Cuesta de Belén and finally C. Dean Espinosa (also known as Callejón de las Monjas) before it reaches the old quarter. Luckily the road runs straight (though uphill) the whole time. Mini-buses run every 30 minutes from the bus station to C. Corredera (100ptas); a taxi costs 500ptas.

Buses: C. Corregidores. **Transportes Generales Comes** (tel. 956 70 20 15) to: **Jerez** (30min., 7 per day, 7:20am-7:15pm, 280ptas); **Cádiz** (1½hr., 6 per day, 7:20am-7:15pm, 675ptas); **Ronda** (1¾hr., 4 per day, 8:20am-4pm, 950ptas); point on **Costa del Sol** (3-4hr., 1 per day, 1535-2060ptas). **Los Amarillos** (tel. 956 70 02 57) to **Jerez** (15min., 19 per day, 6:30am-7:15pm, 225ptas) and **Sevilla** (2hr., 2 per day, 7am and 5pm, 905ptas).

Taxis: tel. 956 70 13 55 or 956 70 00 66.

Tourist Office: (tel. 956 70 22 64; fax 956 70 09 00), on Pl. Cabildo. General info and free detailed map of the old city. Map of the whole town costs a whopping 100ptas. Open June-Aug. M-F 10am-2pm and 5:30-7:30pm, Sa 10am-2pm and 5-7pm, Su 10:30am-1pm; Sept.-May M-Sa 9am-2pm and 5-7pm. Also offers tours of the old city. M-Sa 10:30am, 12:30pm, 5pm, and 6:30pm; Su noon. 400ptas, children free.

Emergency: tel. 091 or 092. **Police:** (tel. 956 70 16 52), on C. Nueva.

Medical Emergency: tel. 956 70 04 98.

Post Office: C. Murete, 24 (tel. 956 70 15 60), overlooking the cliffs and the river. Open M-F 8:30am-2:30pm, Sa 9:30am-1pm. **Postal Code:** 11630.

Internet access: **@RComputer,** C. Muñoz Vásquez, 22 (tel. 956 70 11 15).

▌ ACCOMMODATIONS

Arcos has only a few budget hostels; call ahead during *Semana Santa* and in the summer to be safe. As always, the tourist office has a list of accommodations.

Hostal Callejón de las Monjas, C. Dean Espinosa, 4 (a.k.a. Callejón de las Monjas; tel. 956 70 23 02), in the old quarter behind Iglesia de Santa María. Roomy, with fans or A/C; all rooms have bath and TV. The upstairs room has its own terrace. Singles 3500-4500ptas; doubles 3500ptas, with bath 4500ptas. Visa.

Bar-Restaurant-Hostal San Marcos, C. Marqués de Torresoto, 6 (tel. 956 70 07 21), past C. Dean Espinosa and Pl. Cabildo. Run by a friendly young owner and his family and crowned by a scenic rooftop terrace. Clean rooms with private baths. Call ahead for reservations. Singles 3000ptas; doubles 4500ptas.

▐ FOOD

Restaurants huddle at the bottom end of C. Corredera, while *tapas* heaven can be found uphill in the old quarter.

Los Faraones, C. Debajo del Corral, 8 (tel. 956 70 06 12), downhill from C. Corredera. An Egyptian-Spanish couple serves Arab cuisine and Spanish staples. Extensive vegetarian *menú* 800ptas. Huge *bocadillo de falafel* 400ptas (not on menu but available on request). A/C. Open Tu-Su 9am-midnight.

Bar Típico Alcaraván, C. Nueva, 1 (tel. 956 70 33 97), down from Pl. Cabildo. Popular hangout in a beautiful 900 year-old cave. *Tapas* 250-450ptas. Beer 125ptas, mixed drinks 350-450ptas. Open daily 11:30am-4:30pm and 7:30pm-midnight.

Cafeteria Albenizb, C. Muñoz Vázquez, 10 (tel. 956 70 14 99). Lots of outdoor seating. Coffee 125-150ptas. Sandwiches 300-600ptas. Open M-Sa noon-3pm and 7-11pm.

RUTA DE LOS PUEBLOS BLANCOS If you've seen
pictures of Spain, chances are you have seen some of the perfect little towns of white houses under cloudless blue skies. These villages dot the southern reaches of Andalucia and make up a popular hiking and touring circuit known as the *ruta de los pueblos blancos* (route of the white towns). While it is the superb whitewashed houses that give the route its name, the towns are also characterized by labyrinths of narrow winding streets and plenty of medieval castles, churches and other sights. The long history of the province stretches back to before the Romans and Celts, but it was the Moors and their Arabic influence that gave the towns much of the character they still have today. Divided up into four distinct routes—northern, western, eastern, and central—the 19 *pueblos blancos* make for a memorable trip through Spanish history and culture. Arcos de la Frontera is probably the most visited of the towns, and makes for a good jumping off point for neighboring villages.

◉ ♪ SIGHTS AND ENTERTAINMENT

The most beautiful sights in Arcos are the winding white alleys, Roman ruins, and hanging flowers of the old quarter, combined with the view from ⊠**Plaza Cabildo.** The plazas earned the nickname *Balcón de Coño* because the view is so startling that people often exclaim *¡coño!* (*#%&*$!) out of disbelief. In this square stands the **Iglesia de Santa María,** a mix of Baroque, Renaissance, and Gothic styles, built between the 15th and 18th centuries. Its most impressive attribute is the well pre-served 14th-century wall-painting. A symbol of the Inquisition—a circular design within which exorcisms were once performed—is still etched into the ground on the church's left side (open M-F 10am-1pm and 3:30-6:30pm, Sa 10am-2pm; 150ptas). The late-Gothic **Iglesia de San Pedro** was built on the site of an old Arab fortress in the old quarter's northern edge. An assortment of Murillos, Zurbaráns, and Riberas decorate the interior (open M-Sa 10am-1pm and 4-7pm; 150ptas.)

An artificial **lake** made in 1960 laps at Arcos's feet, its gentle waters inviting over-heated travelers to take a dip; most choose to swim near Porto Alegre, a beach-like strip on the lake. Urban buses descend to **Mesón de la Molinera,** the beach (June-Aug. 6 per day, Sept.-May 4 per day, 9:15am-8:15pm, 100ptas). The incongruous **Mississippi Paddle Boat** (tel. 956 70 80 02) cruises around the lake on weekends at 5pm. (250ptas.) For further information on water sports at the lake, call the **Oficina de Deportes** (tel. 956 70 30 11).

Festivals in Arcos are highly spirited. A favorite is the **Toro de Aleluya,** held on the last Sunday of *Semana Santa.* Two bulls run rampant through the steep, cobbled streets as residents drink and dance flamenco.

CÁDIZ

Cádiz makes for an interesting sandwich, with a powerful ocean on one side, a placid bay on the other, and a whole lot of history in between. Founded by the Phoenicians in 1100 B.C., Cádiz (pop. 155,000) is considered the oldest inhabited city in Europe. From the 16th to the 18th century, the Spanish colonial shipping industry transformed the port into one of the wealthiest in Europe. When the New World fervor subsided, liberal politics took over as the hallmark of Cadisian life. In 1808, the city's decisive resistance to Napoleon was crucial in preserving the Span-ish nation. Residents subsequently designed the Constitución de Cádiz (1812), an assertion of democratic ideals that inspired a wave of Latin American nationalism. Sadly, it proved ineffectual in its own land. Cadisian liberalism was thwarted again during the Civil War when it fell quickly, and hard, to Franco's Nationalist army. As fitting retaliation, Cádiz continued to rekindle its immortal spirit once a year, cele-brating its extravagant *Carnaval,* the only festival of its size and kind not sup-pressed by Franco's regime. Perhaps Spain's most dazzling party, *Carnaval* makes Cádiz an imperative destination on February itineraries. During the rest of the year, the city offers a little of everything to visitors—a metropolis trimmed by golden sand beaches that put pebble-strewn eastern neighbors to shame.

▐ GETTING THERE

Trains go from: **Jerez** (45min., 12 per day, 7:45am-10:30pm, 375ptas); **Sevilla** (2hr., 12 per day, 6:35am-9:27pm, 1600ptas); **Madrid** (7hr., 2 per day, 10:05am and 4:03pm, 8000-9500ptas). Bus go from: **Algeciras** (2½hr., 10 per day, 7am-10:30pm, 1225ptas).

▐ ORIENTATION AND PRACTICAL INFORMATION

Cádiz's old town was built on the end of the peninsula, and the new town naturally grew up behind it farther inland. The old town hosts most of the cheap hostels and historic sights (not to mention the bus and train stations), while the new town is home to high-rise hotels, numerous bars and restaurants, kilometers of lovely sand, and deep blue seas. To reach **Plaza de San Juan de Dios** (the town center) from the **Comes bus station,** walk along Av. Puerto for about five minutes, keeping the port on the left; the plaza lies to the right, just after a park. From the **Los Amarillos bus stop,** walk inland about 100m. From the **train station,** walk past the fountain, keeping the port on the right, for about two blocks; Pl. San Juan de Dios is the first plaza on the left. The tangled *casco viejo* is pretty disorienting—a map is necessary. When you take the bus into new Cádiz (down the main avenue), hop off at the square with the McDonalds and the modern-looking Hotel Victoria. This square is called **Glorieta Ingeniero.**

TRANSPORTATION

Trains: RENFE (tel. 956 25 43 01), Pl. Sevilla, off Av. Puerto. To: **Pto. de Sta. María** (30min., 35 per day, 6am-10:10pm, 375ptas); **Jerez** (40min., 20-35 per day, 6:40am-10:10pm, 400ptas); **Sevilla** (2hr., 12 per day, 6am-8pm, 1100ptas); **Córdoba** (5hr., 10-12 per day, 8am-6:45pm, 2325-3700ptas); **Madrid** (5hr., 2 per day, 8am and 4:25pm, 9500ptas); **Granada** (6hr., 3 per day, 6am-3:10pm, 3800ptas); **Valencia** (10-14hr., 1 per day, 6:45pm, 5800ptas); **Barcelona** (14hr., 2 per day, 8am and 6:45pm, 6700ptas).

Buses: Transportes Generales Comes, Pl. Hispanidad, 1 (tel. 956 22 78 11). To: **Jerez de la Frontera** (1hr., 15 per day, 380ptas); **Arcos de la Frontera** (1½hr., 6 per day, 7am-6pm, 675ptas); **Vejer de la Frontera** (1½hr., 10 per day, 9am-9pm, 555ptas); **Sevilla** (2hr., 11 per day, 7am-9:30pm, 1300ptas); **Algeciras** (3hr., 13 per day, 6:45am-8:30pm, 1245ptas); **La Línea** (3hr., 4 per day, 8am-8:30pm, 1460ptas); **Málaga** (4hr., 3 per day, 7am, 9am and 4pm, 2615ptas); **Córdoba** (5hr., 1 per day, 5pm, 2275ptas); **Granada** (6hr., 2 per day, 1:30pm and 9pm, 3650ptas). **Transportes Los Amarillos** (tel. 956 28 58 52) leaves from beside the port, off Pl. San Juan de Dios, across from Po. Canalejas. Purchase tickets on the bus or at the office on nearby Av. Roman de Carranza (open M-F 9am-5pm and Sa 9am-1pm). To: **Sanlúcar** (1½hr., 9 per day, 7:15am-7:30pm, 390ptas); **Chipiona** (2hr., 9 per day, 7:15am-7:30pm, 470ptas); **Arcos** (2hr., 3 per day, 7:30am, 10:10am, and 2pm, 770ptas). Both companies reduce service on weekends. **Secorbus** (tel. 902 22 92 92) has service to **Madrid** (8hr., 6 per day, 8:10am-11:10pm, 3075ptas). Buses leave from next to Estadio Ramon de Carranza, just past Pl. Glorieta Ingeniero, in new Cádiz.

Ferry: El Vapor (tel. 956 87 02 70) leaves from the port next to the Comes station. To **Pto. de Sta. María** (45min., 5 per day, 10am-8:30pm, 275ptas).

Municipal Buses (tel. 956 26 28 06). Pick up a map/schedule and *bonobus* (discount packet of 10 tickets for 830ptas) at the kiosk across from the Comes bus station. Most lines run through Pl. España. Beach bums' favorite bus #1 (Cortadura) runs along the shore to new Cádiz (every 10min., 6:40am-1:10am, 115ptas).

Taxis: tel. 956 21 21 21.

TOURIST, FINANCIAL, AND LOCAL SERVICES

Tourist Office: Municipal, Pl. San Juan de Dios, 11 (tel. 956 24 10 01), in the mauve Pozos de Miranda building at the end of the plaza. Bright yellow "i" marks the spot. Useful free map. English spoken. Open M-F 9am-2pm and 5-8pm. On weekends, a kiosk opens in front of the main office (open Sa-Su and holidays 10am-1pm and 5-7:30pm). **Junta de Andalucía,** C. Calderón de la Barca, 1 (tel. 956 21 13 13). From the Comes bus station, cross over to Pl. España and walk uphill on C. Antonio López. Office is across Pl. Mina, on the corner of C. Calderón de la Barca and C. Zorrilla. Good regional and transport info. Free map. Open M and Sa 9am-2pm, Tu-F 9am-7pm.

Currency Exchange: Banco Central Hispano, C. Ancha, 29 (tel. 956 22 66 22). Open M-F 8:30am-2pm. On weekends, try major hotels or **Gades Tour,** Pl. España, 1 (tel. 956 22 46 08). Open M-F 10am-1pm and 5:30-8:30pm, Sa 9am-1:30pm.

Luggage Storage: Lockers at train station (400ptas), to the right on the way out to the platforms. Open daily 8am-11pm.

EMERGENCY AND COMMUNICATIONS

Emergency: tel. 091 or 092. **Municipal police:** in Campo del Sur in the new city.

Medical Assistance: Ambulatorio Vargas Ponce (tel. 062 or 956 28 38 55).

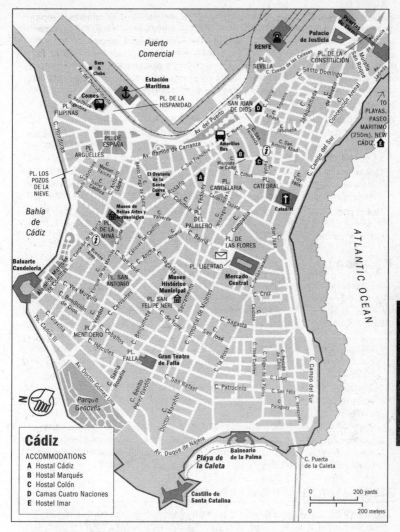

Cádiz

ACCOMMODATIONS
A Hostal Cádiz
B Hostal Marqués
C Hostal Colón
D Camas Cuatro Naciones
E Hostel Imar

Post Office: (tel. 956 21 18 78), Pl. Flores, next to the market. Open M-F 8:30am-8:30pm, Sa 9:30am-2pm. **Postal Code:** 11080.

Internet Access: Informática Café Internet, Pl. Glorieta Ingeniero, 1 (tel./fax 956 28 24 59), across from McDonald's and in front of Playa Victoria. 250ptas for 15min., 800ptas per hr. Open June-Aug. M-Sa 11am-2pm and 6-11pm, Su 6-11pm; Sept.-May M-Sa 10:30am-2pm and 5:30-10pm, Su 5:30-10pm.

▟ ACCOMMODATIONS

Most hostels huddle around the harbor, in Pl. San Juan de Dios, and just behind it on C. Marqués de Cádiz. Others scatter throughout the old town. Singles and private bathrooms are scarce but individual rooms are sometimes negotiable in the off-season. Call months in advance to find a room during February's *Carnaval;* calling a few days in advance during the summer should be fine.

Hostal Colón, C. Marqués de Cádiz, 6 (tel. 956 28 53 51), off Pl. San Juan de Dios. Spotless rooms with sinks and colorful tiles. All rooms have balconies, but the best view—the cathedral surrounded by hundreds of TV antennas—is from the terrace. Two windowless singles 2000ptas; doubles 3500ptas; triples 4500ptas.

Hostal Marqués, C. Marqués de Cádiz, 1 (tel. 956 28 58 54). Newly renovated 18th-century rooms with firm mattresses encircle a lovely courtyard. Most have balconies, except for one unloved single. Front door key. Singles 2500ptas; doubles 4000ptas, with bath 4500ptas; triples 5000ptas.

Hostal Cádiz, C. Feduchy, 20 (tel. 956 28 58 01), near Pl. Candelaria. Clean, comfy rooms, almost all triples. Fun mix of plastic and wood furniture. Ask the amicable owner for tips on cheap eateries and hip nightlife. Laundry service available. Front door key. Cheap dorm beds available in winter. Doubles 3200ptas; triples 4800ptas.

Camas Cuatro Naciones, C. Plocia, 3 (tel. 956 25 55 39), in a corner of Pl. San Juan de Dios. No dirt, no frills. Rooms facing the street get a lot of sunshine. Singles 1500ptas; doubles 3000ptas; triples 4000ptas.

Hostel Imar, Pl. Glorieta Ingeniero, 3 (tel. 956 26 05 00, fax 965 26 03 07), right on the main square in new Cádiz. Incredible location next to the beach and the luxury big-boys. Reservations a must. Doubles 5800ptas, with bath 7000ptas. Visa.

FOOD

Once you leave Pl. San Juan de Dios, finding eateries can be a trying experience. Opt for cafes and *heladerías* around Pl. Flores (also called Pl. Topete), near the post office and the municipal **market.** If you detest seafood, head to **Supermarket Champion,** next to the municipal market, off Pl. Flores (open M-Sa 9:15am-9:15pm).

Freiduría Sopranis, C. Sopranis, 2 (tel. 956 25 64 31), off Pl. San Juan de Dios. Every type of seafood imaginable. Take-out only. 1200-2200ptas per kg (feeds 4). Open daily 11am-3:30pm and 7pm-midnight.

Telepizza, Pl. San Antonio, 16 (tel. 956 80 84 84). A welcome change from the typical sit-down seafood joints. Grab a freshly made pizza (individual 750-1250ptas, 2-3 person 1000-1900ptas) and walk to the Parque Genovés on the water (or stay put and enjoy the air-conditioning). Open Su-Th 1pm-midnight, F-Sa 1pm-1am.

Bar-Restaurante Pasaje Andaluz, Pl. San Juan de Dios, 9 (tel. 956 28 52 54). Outdoor metal tables with plastic covers hardly spell "Ritz," but this casual place has a solid *menú* (900-1200ptas). Open daily 12:30-4:30pm and 8-11:30pm.

SIGHTS AND ENTERTAINMENT

CATHEDRAL. This gold-domed 18th-century masterpiece is considered the last great cathedral built by colonial riches. Its treasury bulges with opulent valuables—the *Custodia del Millón* is said to be set with a million precious stones. *(From Pl. San Juan de Dios, follow C. Pelota. Tel. 956 28 61 54. Open Tu-Sa 10am-1pm. 500ptas, children 200ptas. Mass Su at noon. Free.)*

MUSEO DE CÁDIZ. Thanks to the fusion of a Fine Arts and Provincial Archaeological Museum, Murillo, Rubens, and Zurbarán live here in unholy union with Phoenician sarcophagi. *(Pl. Mina. From Pl. San Juan de Dios, follow C. Nueva as it becomes C. San Francisco, take a left onto C. Sagasta, then a right on C. Tinte. Tel. 956 21 22 81. Open for guided tours Tu 9am-2:30pm; for public Tu 2:30-8pm, W-Sa 9am-8pm, Su 9:30am-2:30pm. 250ptas, EU citizens free.)*

PASEO. Cádiz's seaside paseo runs along the Atlantic and the bay of Cádiz (facing Puerto Santa María). Stupendous views of ships leaving the harbor recall the golden age; at the end of the *paseo*, infinite rows of antennae rising from the rooftops recall the 1950s. Exotic trees, fanciful hedges, and a few chattering monkeys enliven the adjacent **Parque Genovés.** *(Paseo accessible via Pl. Argüelles or C. Fermin Sal-vochea, off Pl. España.)*

MUSEO DE LAS CORTES DE CÁDIZ. This museum is home to an enormous, painstakingly wrought 18th-century ivory and mahogany model of the city upstairs, among other treasures. *(C. Santa Inés, 9. From Pl Mina, follow C. Zorrilla inland 5 blocks. Tel. 956 22 17 88. Open June-Aug. Tu-F 9am-1pm and 5-7pm, Sa-Su 9am-1pm; Sept.-May Tu-F 9am-1pm and 4-7pm, Sa-Su 9am-1pm. Free.)*

🏖 BEACHES

Since Cádiz was built on a peninsula, the exhaust-spewing ships on one coast don't pollute the pristine beaches on the other. **Playa de la Caleta** is the beach most convenient to the old city. Better sand and more space can be found in the new city, serviced by bus #1, which leaves from Pl. España (115ptas). The first beach beyond the rocks is the unremarkable 400m **Playa de Santa María del Mar.** Next to it, ◪**Playa de la Victoria,** stretching 2500m, has earned the EU's *bandera azul* (blue flag) for cleanliness. Get off bus #1 at Pl. Glorieta Ingeniero in front of Hotel Victoria. A more natural landscape, with fewer hotels and straw mats, belongs to **Playa de Cortadura** (5000m), where the coveted *bandera azul* also flaps proudly. Take bus #1 until it almost reaches the highway, where the bus turns around. The board-walk ends here and sunbather density falls steadily the farther one walks.

🎵 ENTERTAINMENT

For the cafe scene, try the area around **Plaza Mina,** which is especially lively on winter weekends. **Calle de Manuel Rances,** nearby off C. Antonio López, features some of the hippest bars in the old city. **Paseo Marítimo,** the main drag along Playa Victoria, has some of Cádiz's best bars. **La Jarra** (tel. 956 26 57 74), on C. José G. Agullo, is one such hotspot, blaring *música española* and American top forty late into the night. Club-rats will prefer **Punta de San Felipe,** a strip of almost ten bars and clubs, reached by walking north along the sea from Pl. España, just beyond the Comes station (take a right before the tunnel); these establishments don't get going until 4 or 5am. Look for signs on the boardwalk advertising theme parties.

Carnaval insanity is legendary. The gray of winter gives way to dazzling color as the city hosts one of the most raucous *carnavales* in the world (March 2-12 in 2000). Costumed dancers, street singers, ebullient residents, and spectators from the world over take to the streets in a week-long frenzy that makes New Orleans's Mardi Gras look like Thursday night bingo.

NEAR CÁDIZ: EL PUERTO DE SANTA MARÍA

Across the bay from Cádiz and a quick train ride from Jerez, low-key and beach-centered El Puerto de Santa María (pop. 75,000) is one of three cities (along with Jerez and Sanlúcar) that form the renowned "sherry triangle." Here, wine reigns next to God. In a final concession to vice, El Puerto boasts the only functioning casino in western Andalucía.

🛈 **PRACTICAL INFORMATION.** El Puerto's bus stop is in front of Pl. Toros (right next to the bullring), but many buses passing through drop off and pick up passengers at the train station; ask at the tourist office for specific times and departure points. **Buses** connect El Puerto to: **Sanlúcar** and **Chipiona** (20min., 10 per day, 7:45am-9pm, 215-275ptas); **Jerez** (30min., 18 per day, 7:20am-9pm, 150ptas); **Cádiz** (40min., 41 per day, 6:30am-10:30pm, 190ptas). **Trains** (tel. 956 54 25 85) depart to: **Jerez** (12min., 20 per day, 7:10am-10:40pm, 200ptas); **Cádiz** (30min., 35 per day, 6:59am-10:40pm, 375ptas); **Sevilla** (1½hr., 17 per day, 6:25am-8:20pm, 1100ptas). An **El Vapor ferry** (tel. 956 87 02 70) links El Puerto with **Cádiz,** departing from the port near the tourist office (45min., 5 per day, 250ptas). The **tourist office,** C. Luna, 22 (tel. 956 54 24 13; fax 956 54 22 46), is a few blocks up from Pl. Galeras

ANDALUCÍA

Reales and the ferry stop. From the train station, take a left on Ctra. Madrid, then a right onto C. Pozas Dulces. Follow its right branch (C. Ribera del Río) through Pl. Herrería, then turn right on C. Luna. From the bus stop in front of Pl. Toros, follow C. Santa Lucía past Pl. España to Pl. Juan Gavala. Turn right on C. Luna; the tourist office is 3½ blocks down on your left. (Open daily June-Aug. 10am-2pm and 6-8pm; Sept.-May 10am-2pm and 5:30-7:30pm.) **Emergency:** tel. 091 or 092; **medical emergency** tel. 956 54 33 02 or 956 87 11 11; **municipal police** (tel. 956 54 18 63), Ronda de las Dunas. **Post office,** Pl. Polvorista, 3 (tel. 956 85 53 22; open M-F 9am-8pm, Sa 9am-2pm); **postal code:** 11500.

⌨️📷 ACCOMMODATIONS AND FOOD. Unless you really feel like gambling, El Puerto de Santa María makes the most sense as a daytrip from Cádiz. The family-run **Pensión Santamaría,** C. Nevería/C. Pedro Muñoz Seca (*not* C. Dr. Muñoz Seca), 38 (tel. 956 85 36 31), keeps 12 clean rooms around a relaxing patio. From the tourist office, head up C. Palacios toward Pl. España and take the fourth left (singles 1750ptas; doubles 3500ptas, with bath 4000ptas; triples with bath 6000ptas). **Camping Playa Las Dunas** (tel. 956 87 22 10), Po. Marítimo La Puntilla, is a 20-minute walk along the shore from the tourist office or a painless local bus ride (#26). A cafeteria, supermarket, and clean showers await. (565ptas per adult and per tent, 490 ptas per child, 485ptas per car.) Avoid overpriced restaurants near the water. Instead, try **La Tortillería,** C. Palacios, 5 (tel. 956 87 72 77), a bar famous for its inventive *tortilla* sandwiches (open Tu-Th and Su noon-3:30pm and 8:30pm-1am, F-Sa noon-3:30pm and 8:30pm-2am). For international food, Italian **Restaurante Pasta Gansa,** on C. Puerto Escondido off C. Ribera del Rio, serves pasta dishes (700-950ptas), while **Restaurant Hong Kong** (tel. 956 85 7204 for delivery), across from the ferry dock, has a four-course Chinese *menú* (555ptas; open daily noon-4pm and 8pm-midnight; Visa, MC, AmEx).

🏛️📷 SIGHTS AND BEACHES. El Puerto's history as a point of departure for exploration and conquest has resulted in a few noteworthy monuments. Columbus's second voyage to the New World was launched here (he even had a house in El Puerto), and as business in the Americas developed, prominent families built houses along the town's winding streets. Before the boom in the 13th century, Alfonso X El Sabio constructed the **Castillo de San Marcos.** Visitors can survey the city from the castle's tower. (Open M-F 10am-1pm, Sa 11am-1:30pm. 300ptas.) **Iglesia Mayor Prioral** has a Baroque front topped with a one-armed nude and two sidekicks (open daily 10am-noon and 7:30-8:30pm; free). Two of El Puerto's *bodegas* sponsor tours: **Bodega Terry** (tel. 956 85 77 00) has standard tours. (Sept.-July M-F 9:30am, 11am, and 12:30pm; Aug. M-Tu and Th 11am. 350ptas.) **Bodega Osborne** (tel. 956 85 52 11), original sponsor of those gigantic black, bull, signs that dot the countryside (see **Bullboards,** p. 181), has an amusing promotional film in addition to the basics. (Open M-F 10:30am-1pm, 10:30 tour in English. 300ptas.) The **Fundación de Rafael Alberti,** C. Santo Domingo, 25 (tel. 956 85 07 11), displays the poet's books, correspondence, and personal belongings. (Open June-Aug. M-F 10:30am-2:30pm; Sept.-May Tu-Su 11am-2:30pm. 300ptas, seniors and students 150ptas.) El Puerto de Santa María has three beaches: **Playa La Puntilla** (accessible by city bus #8 or 26, 90ptas), **Playa Santa Catalina-Fuentebravía** (bus #35), and **Playa Valdelgrana** (also bus #35). The latter two lie west of the city and are less popular.

VEJER DE LA FRONTERA

Picture a majestic white town perched atop a hill of rippling wheat, where white-washed houses line cobbled alleys and old men discuss bullfights and politics on street corners. Free of textbook monuments and must-see sights, beautiful Vejer (pop. 13,000) invites you to sit back and soak up this truly cultural experience.

⚐ ORIENTATION AND PRACTICAL INFORMATION. Getting to Vejer can be a pain. While some buses stop at the end of **Avenida de Los Remedios,** which leads uphill into La Plazuela (10min.), many just leave you by the highway at **La Barca de Vejer,** a small town at the base of the hill. Take one of the numerous taxis waiting by the bus stop (700ptas). The alternative, a steep 20-minute uphill walk, can be arduous with a backpack. If you do make the trek, climb the cobbled track to the left of the restaurant. When you reach the top, keep walking straight; all roads lead to quiet **Plaza de España,** not to be confused with La Plazuela, which is a tiny intersection (where Av. Los Remedios and C. Juan Bueno meet).

For **bus** info, visit either the tourist office or the telephone kiosk just off La Plazuela toward Av. Los Remedios, where tickets are sold. Short-distance buses run from Av. Los Remedios to **Cádiz** (1½hr., 8 per day, 6:15am-7:15pm, 555ptas) and **Sevilla** via **Jerez** (3½hr., 1 per day, 6:45am, 1665ptas). For other destinations, descend the hill to La Barca de Vejer, with service to: **Tarifa** (1hr., 9 per day, 8am-10pm, 500ptas); **Cádiz** (1½hr., 8 per day, 8am-9:30pm, 555ptas); **Algeciras** (2hr., 9 per day, 8am-10pm, 900ptas); **Sevilla** (3½hr., 5 per day, 8:30am-5:45pm, 1575ptas); **Málaga** (4hr., 3 per day, 8am-5pm, 2005ptas). Visit the **tourist office,** C. Marqués de Tamarón, 10 (tel. 956 45 01 91). Some English spoken. (Open June-Aug. M-F 10:30am-2pm and 6-9pm, Sa 10:30am-2pm; Sept.-May M-F 9am-2:30pm and 5-9:30pm.) **Banco Central Hispano,** C. Juan Bueno, 5, off La Plazuela (open M-F 8:30am-2:30pm). **Medical emergency:** Centro de Salud (tel. 956 44 76 25), Av. Andalucía; **police** tel. 956 45 04 00. **Post office,** C. Juan Bueno, 22 (tel. 956 45 02 38; open M-F 8:30am-2:30pm, Sa 9:30am-1pm); **postal code** 11150.

▛▟ ACCOMMODATIONS AND FOOD. The best places to stay in Vejer are in *casas particulares* (private houses). One of the best is run by James Stuart, a 12-year resident of Vejer and the owner of the Magnum Bike and Surf shop (see below). Called **Casa de los Pescaitos,** Pl. España, 17 (tel. 956 44 75 75; fax 956 44 75 77; email info@discoverAndalucía.com), it has one double and two elaborate apartment suites (double 3500ptas; apartments 5500ptas). Make sure to call or email in advance—James will probably be at the shop. There are two *casas particulares* on C. San Filmo, up a stone staircase from Av. Los Remedios. The friendly Sra. Rosa Romero owns **Casa Los Cántaros,** C. San Filmo, 14 (tel. 956 44 75 92), a beautifully restored Andalucian home with a grape-vined patio. The spotless suites have sitting rooms, antique furniture, private bathrooms, and kitchen access (doubles 2500-3000ptas). Sra. Luisa Doncel keeps tidy little rooms with common bathrooms in **Calle San Filmo, 12** (tel. 956 45 02 46). If Doña Luisa is not at #12, try #16. (Singles 1500ptas; doubles 2500-3000ptas.) Where you stay may depend on which woman you meet first. The cheapest eats are *tapas* or *raciones* at the bars around the Plazuela. At **Bar El Cura,** Po. Cobijadas, 1 (tel. 956 45 07 76), at the bottom of C. Juan Bueno, locals place bets on who can make the solemn owner laugh (or at least crack a smile). Enjoy the gorgeous view around the corner while sipping *fino* (dry sherry) for a mere 50ptas. (Open daily 7am-3pm and 5:30pm-late.)

▣ SIGHTS. The best way to enjoy Vejer is by wandering along the labyrinthine streets and cliffside *paseos,* stopping occasionally for drinks or *tapas.* As for monuments, the **Castillo Moro,** down C. Ramon y Cajal from the church, offers the usual assortment of battlements and crenelated walls. (Open July-Aug. M-Sa 11am-2pm and 5-10pm; Sept.-June M-Sa 10am-2pm. A Boy Scout troop leads the way around the ramparts. Donations accepted.) The darn pretty **Iglesia del Divino Salvador,** behind the tourist office, is a choice blend of Romanesque, Mudéjar, and Gothic styles. (Open daily 11am-1pm and 7-9pm.)

Ten kilometers from Vejer on the road to Los Caños lies **El Palmar,** 7km of fine white sand and clear waters easily accessible by car. Many beach-goers hitch rides at the bend of Av. Los Remedios or catch the bus to **Conil de la Frontera** and walk southeast along the beach for 3-4km. For info on the town and outdoor activities, consult **Magnum Bike and Surf Shop,** Av. Los Remedios, 44 (tel. 956 44 75 75; bikes from 1500ptas per day, surfboards from 1000ptas per day; open M-F 10:30am-2pm and 6-9:30pm, Sa 10:30am-2pm; Visa, MC, AmEx).

🎵 **ENTERTAINMENT.** The old quarter hops at night. Leave another little piece of your heart at **Bar Janis Joplin,** on C. Marqués de Tamarón. Sit on plush wicker chairs, enjoy an amazing view, and keep an eye out for Bobby McGee. (Open nightly 9:30pm-late.) Several other popular pubs lie downhill from the Plazuela on C. Sagasta and C. Santísimo. From July to August, everyone dances among the thatched huts at *discoteca* **La Carpa** in Parque de Los Remedios, behind the bus stop. Stupendous terrace views make **Café-Bar El Arriate,** C. Corredera, 55 (tel. 956 44 71 70 or 956 45 13 05), a good place for a *copa* and *tapas* anytime. The village throws brilliant *fiestas.* As soon as the **Corpus Christi** revelry ends in June, Vejer starts anew with the **Candelas de San Juan** (June 23), climaxing with the midnight release of the *toro de fuego* (bull of fire) at midnight. A local (obviously one with a death wish) dressed in an iron bull costume charges the crowd as a bevy of attached firecrackers fly off his body in all directions. The town demonstrates its creativity again during the delirious **Semana Santa** celebrations, when a *toro embolao* (sheathed bull), with wooden balls affixed to the tips of his horns, is set loose through the narrow streets of Vejer on the Sunday of the Resurrection. The good-natured **Feria de Primavera** (two weeks after *Semana Santa,* in April) is a bit tamer, with people dancing *sevillanas* and downing cupfuls of *fino* until sunrise.

TARIFA

When the wind picks up in Tarifa (pop. 15,000), the southernmost city in continental Europe, visitors can easily understand why it is known, even to locals, as the Hawaii of Spain. Shelter-seeking residents and tourists leave miles of white sandy beaches desolate but for the few, the proud—the windsurfers. You'll see more stickered vans, Quicksilver attire, and Reefs than you could ever imagine. Still, there is more to Tarifa than just windsurfing—sandy beaches and an enchanting old city make for pleasant afternoon and evening walks.

🗺 **ORIENTATION AND PRACTICAL INFORMATION. Transportes Generales Comes** buses roll from C. Batalla del Salado, 19 (tel. 956 68 40 38; window open M-F 7:30-11am and 2:30-7pm, Sa-Su 3-8pm). Buses run to: **Algeciras** (30min., 10 per day, 6:30am-10:15pm, 220ptas); **Cádiz** (2¼hr., 8 per day, 7:25am-10:55pm, 1000ptas); **Sevilla** (4hr., 4 per day, 7:55am-5:10pm, 2050ptas). **Ferries** leave from the port to **Tangier** (1hr.; 1 per day; Sa-Th 9:30am, F 9am; 2800ptas, children 1400ptas). There is one return trip per day at 3pm (see **Tangier,** p. 664). The **tourist office** (tel. 956 68 09 93; fax 956 68 04 31), Po. Alameda, has a basic plan of the city, a list of hostels, and bus schedules. From the bus station, exit toward the castle-shaped arch, follow C. Batalla del Salado for 2½ blocks, turn right at the arch on Av. Andalucía, then left onto tree-lined Alameda. The tourist office is the small glass building under the stairwell. (Open July 15-Aug. daily 10:30am-2pm and 6-8pm; Sept.-July 14 M-F 10am-2pm and 5-7pm.) **Emergency:** tel. 091 or 092; **police** (tel. 956 68 41 86), Pl. Santa María; **medical services: Centro de Salud** (tel. 956 68 15 15). **Post office,** C. Colonel Moscardó, 9 (tel. 956 68 42 37), near Pl. San Maleo (open M-F 8:30am-2:30pm, Sa 9:30am-1pm); **postal code** 11380.

🏠 **ACCOMMODATIONS AND FOOD.** Affordable rooms line the main strip, C. Batalla del Salado. If you visit in August, call ahead or arrive early. Prices rise significantly in summer. Comfortable and clean **Hostal Villanueva,** Av. Andalucía, 11 (tel. 956 68 41 49), features a rooftop terrace with an ocean view and friendly management (singles 2500ptas; doubles 3500ptas; triples 7000ptas). The dining room downstairs serves specialty *paella* for 950ptas (open Tu-Su 1-4pm and 8-11pm). Uphill, where Av. Andalucía becomes C. Amador de los Ríos, **Hostal El Asturian** (tel. 956 68 06 19) keeps brightly tiled rooms, all with full bath. Ask for the deluxe quad that is part of an Arab castle adjoining the hostel. (Doubles 4000ptas; triples 6000ptas; quads 8000ptas.) A number of official **campgrounds** lie a few kilometers to the west on the beach (400-500ptas per person), although some people camp unofficially. Eateries cluster in the streets through the arch and downhill in the old town. **Café-Bar Central** (tel. 956 68 05 90), on C. Sancho IV El Bravo, has one of the few wind-free *terrazas* in town. It serves a wide variety of *bocadillos* (400-500ptas) and specialty drinks. (Open daily 9am-2am.) Up the street, **Ali-Baba,** C. Sancho IV El Bravo, 8, serves falafel (350ptas) and kebab (400ptas) to go (open daily 1:30-4pm and 7pm-1am).

⚅ 🔲 **SIGHTS AND ENTERTAINMENT.** Just outside the old town, next to the port, stand the ruins of the **Castillo de Guzmán el Bueno.** In the 13th century, the Moors kidnapped Guzmán's son and threatened to kill him if Guzmán didn't relinquish the castle. Surprisingly, the father did not surrender, even after they brutally sliced his son's throat right before his eyes. (Open Tu-Su 10am-2pm and 6-8pm. 200ptas, free Su afternoon.) Those with something more tranquil in mind can head 200m south to **Playa Lances** for 5km of the finest white sand on the coast. Bathers should be aware of the occasional high winds and a strong undertow. **Tarifa Spin Out Surfbase** (tel. 956 23 63 52), 9km up the road toward Cádiz, rents windsurfing boards and instructs all levels.

ALGECIRAS

Few visitors to Algeciras venture beyond the seedy, noisy port area. Moroccan migrant workers, Spanish army recruits, and an assortment of tourists, all in transit between North Africa and Spain, traffic the area day and night. But hidden in the city proper is the calmer, more attractive old neighborhood, a pleasant refuge from the chaotic port. Less harried travelers can spend a reasonably pleasant first or last night in Spain or perhaps saunter off to Gibraltar for the day.

📁 **GETTING THERE**

Buses head to Algeciras from: **Gibraltar** (40min., every 30min. 7am-9pm, 225ptas); **Málaga** (3hr., 11 per day, 1250ptas); **Sevilla** (3½hr., 4 per day, 9am-8pm, 2100ptas). Speedy TALGO 200 trains go from: **Madrid** (8¼hr., 1 per day, 8:15am, 9300ptas).

🛈 **ORIENTATION AND PRACTICAL INFORMATION**

Stretching along the coast, **Avenida de la Marina,** which turns into Av. Virgen del Carmen north of the port, is lined with travel agencies, banks, and hotels. **C. Juan de la Cierva** runs perpendicular to the coast from the port, becoming **C. San Bernardo** as it nears the **train** and **bus stations.** To reach the **tourist office** from either one, follow C. San Bernardo/C. Juan de la Cierva along the abandoned tracks toward the port, past a parking lot on the left. From the **port,** take a left onto Av. Virgen del Carmen, then a quick right onto C. Juan de la Cierva; the office is on the left. All services necessary for transit to Morocco cluster around the port, accessible by a single driveway. Be wary of imposters who peddle ferry tickets.

TRANSPORTATION
   Trains: RENFE (tel. 956 63 02 02), Ctra. Cádiz, down C. Juan de la Cierva. To **Ronda** (1½hr., 7 per day, 6:05am-9:30pm, 900-1400ptas) and **Granada** (5½hr., 4 per day, 6am-3:25pm, 2370-2565ptas). Also to **Bobadilla** (1395ptas) with connections to: **Córdoba** (5hr., 6 per day, 6am-9:30pm, 2485-3300ptas); **Málaga** (5½hr., 3 per day, 11:20am-12:20am, 2115ptas); **Sevilla** (6hr., 4 per day, 6:05am-3:25pm, 2990-3150ptas); **Madrid** (6hr., 3 per day, 3:05-9:30pm, 5200ptas).
   Buses: Empresa Portillo, Av. Virgen del Carmen, 15 (tel. 956 65 10 55). To: **Marbella** (1½hr., 10 per day, 9:30am-10pm, 760ptas); **Málaga** (3hr., 11 per day, 8am-2:15pm, 1325ptas); **Granada** (5hr., 2 per day, 8am and 2:15pm, 2505ptas); **Córdoba** (6hr., 2 per day, 8am and 3pm, 2865ptas). **Linesur La Valenciana,** Viajes Koudubia, C. Juan

de la Cierva, 5 (tel. 956 60 34 00). To: **Sevilla** (3hr., 8 per day, 6:30am-9pm, 1955ptas). **Transportes Generales Comes,** C. San Bernardo, 1 (tel. 956 65 34 56), by Hotel Octavio. To: **Tarifa** (30min., 10 per day, 7:05am-9pm, 225ptas); **La Línea,** for **Gibraltar** (45min., every 30min., 7am-9:30pm, 225ptas); **Cádiz** (2½hr., 10 per day, 7am-10:30pm, 1225ptas). **Empresa Bacoma,** Av. Marina, 8 (tel. 956 65 22 00), left of Banco Zaragozano. To **Barcelona** (19½hr., 3 per day, 10am-9pm, 9900ptas).

Ferries: To get to the ferries from the bus and train stations, walk to the end of C. Juan de la Cierva and turn left. **Tickets** are the same price in any of the dozens of travel agencies in town as at the port. Purchase tickets at the port rather than the train station. Allow 30min. to clear customs and board, 90min. with a car. In summer to: **Ceuta** (*buque ferry:* 1½hr.; 5-6 per day, 9-10 during high demand; 6:30am-5pm; 1884ptas per person, 8665ptas per car, 1870ptas per motorcycle; *embarcaciones rápidas:* 35min.; 25 per day; 6:45am-7pm; 3002ptas, under 12 1505ptas) and **Tangier** (normal ferry: 2½hr.; every hr.; 7am-7pm; 3200ptas, under 12 1600ptas, car 9900ptas, motorcycle 3000ptas, 20% discount with Eurail pass; hydrofoil service: 1hr., 3 per day, 7am-3pm, 3900ptas). Limited service in winter, and no service in bad weather.

TOURIST, FINANCIAL, AND LOCAL SERVICES

Tourist Office: (tel. 956 57 26 36; fax 956 57 04 75), C. Juan de la Cierva. It's the tube-shaped, pink-and-red building. Provides maps (free for Algeciras, 100ptas for maps of other cities). Also has a message board. Some English spoken. Open M-F 9am-2pm.

Currency Exchange: **Banco Central Hispano,** Av. Virgen del Carmen, 9-11, changes traveler's checks without commission. Open M-F 8:30am-2pm. For a daytrip to Tangier, buying **dirhams** may not be necessary (many places accept *pesetas*), and you will not be able to convert them back to *pesetas*. For longer trips, convert money in Morocco.

Luggage Storage: At Empresa Portillo bus terminal. Lockers 400ptas per day. Open daily 7:40am-9:50pm. At RENFE, 400ptas per day. Open daily 5:30am-10:30pm.

Camping Gear: Adventura Sport, Ventura Morón, 5 (tel. 956 66 92 34), off Pl. Alta. Handy place for those headed to Morocco. Hiking boots, tents, sleeping bags, etc. Open June-Aug. M-F 10am-1:30pm and 6-9pm, Sa 10:30am-2pm; Sept.-May M-F 10am-1:30pm and 5:30-8:30pm, Sa 10:30am-2pm.

EMERGENCY AND COMMUNICATIONS

Emergency: tel. 091 or 092. **Police: Municipal** (tel. 956 66 01 55), C. Ruiz Zorilla.

Post Office: C. José Antonio, 4 (tel. 956 66 36 48). Lista de Correos. Open M-F 9am-2pm, Sa 9am-1pm. **Postal Code:** 11080.

▐ ACCOMMODATIONS

Lots of convenient hostels bunch around C. José Santacana, parallel to Av. Marina and one block inland following the train tracks, and C. Duque de Almodóvar, two blocks farther from the water. Ask for a back room—local teenagers cruise the narrow streets on Vespas at ungodly hours.

Hostal Rif, C. Rafael de Muro, 11 (tel. 956 65 49 53). Follow C. José Santacana into the small market square, bear left around the large kiosk and continue up C. Rafael del Muro for 1 block. In a restored 18th-century building with a palm-studded inner courtyard, Rif is quiet, cool, and spotless. All the amenities of a hotel at hostel rates. Management dispenses info on forays into Morocco. Book exchange. Communal showers with hot water. Singles 1200-1500ptas; doubles 2400ptas; quads 4800ptas.

Hostal Residencia Versalles, C. Moutero Rios, 12 (tel 956 65 42 11), off C. Cayetano del Toro. Decently sized rooms aren't too noisy. All have phones, some with TVs (200ptas extra). Singles with shower 2500ptas; doubles with shower 3200ptas, with bath 3700ptas; triples with shower 4500ptas, with bath 4700ptas.

Hostal Residencia González, C. José Santacana, 7 (tel. 956 65 28 43). A decent bargain close to the port. Lounge with TV and nice wood carving. Singles 1500ptas, with bath 1750ptas; doubles 3000ptas, with bath 3500ptas; triples 4500ptas, with bath 5250ptas; quads 6000ptas, with bath 7000ptas.

◌ FOOD

Many outdoor cafes line C. Regino Martinez, the main drag. Welcome yourself back from Morocco with *pollo asado* (baked chicken)—or relish your last taste of it—on your way south along Av. Virgen del Carmen, near the port, and on C. Juan de la Cierva. There is a **supermarket** on the corner of C. José Santacana and C. Maroto (open daily 9am-2pm and 5-8pm). Or try the outdoor **market** at Pl. Palma, one block from Av. Virgen del Carmen (open M-Sa 8:30am-2pm).

La Alegría, C. José Santacana, 6 (tel. 956 66 65 09). Whopping portions of Moroccan cooking. Entrees 700ptas. Open daily 9am-midnight.

La Buganvilla (tel. 930 55 05 25), C. Garcia de la Torre. From the Banesto bank corner of Pl. Alta, head down C. Joaquin Costa and take an immediate left down an alley to the unmarked entrance at its end. Idyllic, mellow *tapas* bar draws a young crowd. Delicious *tapas* from 100ptas. Open M-Sa 11am-4pm and 7pm-1am.

Casa Blanca, C. Juan de la Cierva, 1 (tel. 956 57 18 89), the big green building near the tourist office. No-nonsense eatery frequented by port employees. Tortillas (400-500ptas) make a substantial meal. *Menú* 800-900ptas. Open Su-F noon-11pm.

GIBRALTAR

Anglophiles and homesick Brits will get jolly well excited over Gibraltar's fish 'n' chips, pints of bitter, and changing of the guard. Called "Gib" by locals, this colony takes its Britishness seriously, although citizens switch in and out of the Queen's English and Andalucian Spanish. Still, the tumultuous history of the Rock leaves unresolved tensions to this day—residents look up to Britain and down on mainland Spain.

The ancients considered the Rock of Gibraltar one of the Pillars of Hercules, marking the end of the world. Supernatural connections aside, it remains one of history's most contested landmarks. After numerous squabbles between Moors and Spaniards, English troops stormed Gibraltar's shores during the War of Spanish Succession; the Treaty of Utrecht (1713) solidified Britain's hold on the enclave, now one of the last outposts of Britain's empire. When a 1969 vote showed that Gibraltar's populace overwhelmingly favored its British ties (12,138 to 44), Franco sealed off the border and forbade any contact between Spain and Gibraltar. After 16 years of isolation and a decade of negotiations, the border reopened on February 4, 1985. Tourists and residents now cross with ease, but Gibraltar remains culturally detached from Spain.

Despite the peninsula's history and refreshingly heterogeneous population it's a tourist trap. Go to stand atop the imposing Rock, practice your neglected English, and stock up on duty-free liquor and tobacco (cigarettes are 90 pence a pack), then scurry back to the more picturesque Spanish coast.

▐ GETTING THERE

Neither buses nor trains enter Gibraltar, but **buses** go to the nearby town of La Línea from: **Algreciras** (45min., every 30min., 7am-9:30pm, 225ptas); **Málaga** (3hr., 1 per day, 1650ptas); **Cádiz** (3hr., 4 per day, 8am-8:30pm, 1460ptas).

▐ ORIENTATION AND PRACTICAL INFORMATION

Most buses from Spain terminate in the nearby town of **La Línea.** From the bus station, walk directly toward the Rock; the border is five minutes away. After bypassing the line of motorists, Spanish customs, and Gibraltar's passport control, catch bus #9 or 10 (40 pence or 100ptas), or walk across the airport tarmac (look both ways) and along the highway into town (20min.). Stay left on Av. Winston Churchill when the road forks with Corral Lane. Gibraltar's **Main Street,** a commercial strip lined with most services, begins at the far end of a square/parking lot past the Burger King on the left.

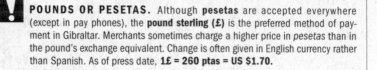

POUNDS OR PESETAS. Although **pesetas** are accepted everywhere (except in pay phones), the **pound sterling (£)** is the preferred method of payment in Gibraltar. Merchants sometimes charge a higher price in *pesetas* than in the pound's exchange equivalent. Change is often given in English currency rather than Spanish. As of press date, **1£ = 260 ptas = US $1.70.**

TRANSPORTATION

Airport: (tel. 730 26). **British Airways** (tel. 792 00) flies to London (2½hr., £150-180).

Buses: From the closest Spanish town, La Línea, to: **Algeciras** (40min., every 30min. 7am-9pm, 225ptas); **Marbella** (1¾hr., 4 per day, 7:15am-5pm, 685ptas); **Ronda** (2hr., 1 per day, 3:30pm, 990ptas); **Cádiz** (3hr., 6:30am-8pm, 5 per day, 1460ptas); **Málaga** (3¼hr., 4 per day, 7:15am-5pm, 1255ptas); **Granada** (5-6hr., 2 per day, 7:15am and 2:15pm, 2435ptas); **Sevilla** (6hr., 3 per day, 7am-4:15pm, 2575ptas); **Madrid** (7hr., 2 per day, 11:15am and 10:15pm, 3215ptas).

Ferries: Tourafrica Int. Ltd. 2a Main St. (tel. 776 66; fax 767 54). To **Tangier** (M and W 8:15am, F 6:30pm; return Tu 3pm, F 9am, Su 3pm). One-way ticket £18, under 12 £9, car £40; round-trip £30, under 12 £15, car £80.

Taxis: tel. 700 52 or 700 27.

Public Transport: There are numerous bus lines, most running from one end of the Rock to the other. Buses #9 and 10 go between the border and the Rock.

TOURIST, FINANCIAL, AND LOCAL SERVICES

Tourist Office: (tel. 749 50; fax 749 43; email gib1@gibnet.gi), Duke of Kent House, Cathedral Square, across the park from Gibraltar Museum. Free street map. Open M-F 9am-5:30pm. **Info Centre** (tel. 749 82), Main St., The Piazza. Open M-F 9:30am-5:30pm, Sa-Su 10am-4pm. There is another office at the border.

Currency Exchange: (see box above). Rates improve steadily as one proceeds along Main St. Booths charge no commission. Banks close daily at 3:30pm, reopening only on Friday 4:30-6pm. **Gib Exchange Center, Ltd.,** 6A John Mackintosh Sq. (tel. 735 17). Open M-F 9am-1pm and 3-7pm, Sa 10am-6pm.

American Express: Bland Travel (tel. 770 12), in Irish Town. Holds mail and sells and cashes traveler's checks. Open M-F 9am-6pm.

Luggage Storage: Lockers at the bus station (400ptas). Open daily 7am-10pm.

EMERGENCY AND COMMUNICATIONS

Emergency: tel. 199. **Police:** 120 Irish Town St. (tel. 725 00).

Hospital: St. Bernard's Hospital (tel. 797 00), on Hospital Hill.

Post Office: 104 Main St. (tel. 756 62). Possibly the world's easiest Poste Restante address: Name, Poste Restante, Gibraltar (Main Post Office). Open June-Aug. M-F 8:45am-2:15pm, Sa 10am-1pm; Sept.-May M-F 9am-4:30pm, Sa 10am-1pm.

Internet: At the **John McIntosh Hall Library,** Main St., 2nd fl. 75 pence per 30min.

Telephones: Red booths and pay phones don't accept *pesetas*. Try the slightly expensive **Gibtel,** 60 Main St. (tel. 756 87). Open M-F 9am-3pm, until 5pm off-season. **Telephone Code:** From Britain (00) 350. From the U.S. (011) 350. From Spain 9567. The USA Direct code is 88 00. British Telecom Direct is 84 00.

ACCOMMODATIONS

The few affordable accommodations in the area are often full, especially from July to September, and camping is illegal. If worse comes to worst, crash in La Línea, a 20-minute trudge across the border.

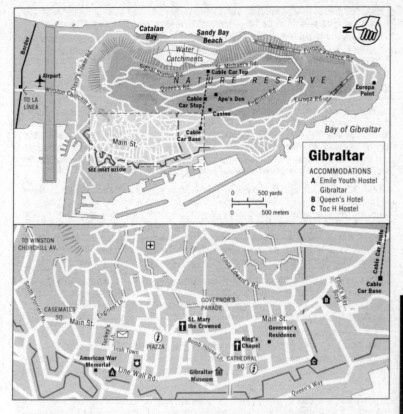

Gibraltar

ACCOMMODATIONS
A Emile Youth Hostel
    Gibraltar
B Queen's Hotel
C Toc H Hostel

Queen's Hotel, 1 Boyd St. (tel. 740 00; fax 400 30). Through Southport Gate, bear right and enter around the back. Comfortable, well-furnished rooms have phones; some have TVs. Huge bar/lounge. Breakfast included. Laundry. Free parking. Singles £18, with bath £36; twin-bed doubles £30, with bath £40; triples with bath £54. *Let's Go* users and students 20% discount. Visa, MC, AmEx.

Emile Youth Hostel Gibraltar (tel. 511 06), on Line Wall Rd., across from the square at the beginning of Main St. Cramped bunkbeds, but clean communal bathrooms. Breakfast included. Lock-out 10:30am-4:30pm and curfew 11:30pm, but the owner is friendly and flexible. Dorms £10; singles £15; doubles £25.

Toc H Hostel (tel. 734 31), Line Wall Rd. Walk toward the Rock on Main St., turn right just before the arch at Southport Gate, then left in front of Hambros Bank. A maze of plants, cats, and travelers. Warm showers during the day. Singles £5; doubles £10.

📷 FOOD

International restaurants are the easiest to find—Chinese, English, French, Indian, Spanish, and Italian cuisines are available—but you may choke on the prices. There's always the supermarket—**Safeway,** no less, in the Europort commercial complex (open M-Sa 8am-8pm).

Smith's Fish and Chips, 295 Main St. (tel. 742 54). Run by a cheerful bloke who dishes out hearty servings of fish 'n' chips, as well as some vegetarian options (£3.50-5). Open M-F 11am-6pm, Sa noon-3pm.

Maharaja Indian Restaurant (tel. 752 33), on Tuckey's Ln., off Main St. Filling meat and vegetarian entrees (from £2.70). Open daily noon-3pm and 7-11:15pm. Visa.

The Leanse, 7 Bomb House Ln. (tel./fax 417 51), off Main St., near Marks and Spencer. Kosher and international cuisine served in a cozy setting. Entrees £6-10. Open Su-F 11:30am-3:30pm and 8pm-11:30pm. Visa, MC, AmEx.

◉ SIGHTS

Top of the Rock and **Nature Reserve** are accessible by car or cable car. Cars depart every 10min. M-Sa 9:30am-6pm. £3.65, round-trip £4.90. You can buy a one-way ticket and walk down (1hr.). Tickets, sold until 5:15pm, include admission to St. Michael's Cave and Apes' Den. Nature Reserve on top. Tickets £5, £1 discount with cable car ticket, in your own car £1.50. Price includes admission to the Moorish Castle, St. Michael's Cave, the Apes' Den, the Great Siege Tunnels, and the film "Gibraltar: A City Under Siege." Moorish Castle open daily 9:30am-7pm.

APES' DEN. About halfway up the rock is the infamous Apes' Den, where a colony of Barbary monkeys cavort amusingly on the sides of rocks, the tops of taxis, and tourists' heads. These tailless monkeys have inhabited the rock since before the Moorish invasion. The British believe they'll control the peninsula only as long as these animals survive. When the ape population nearly went extinct in 1944, Churchill ordered reinforcements from North Africa, so now the monkeys can be tormented by baby-talking, picture-snapping visitors for years to come.

GREAT SIEGE TUNNELS. At the northern tip of the Rock, facing Spain, are the Great Siege Tunnels, built into the cliffside in the 1770s to defend against a Spanish assault and to allow for the mounting of the Koehler gun—the first able to fire downward. The views from the turrets are spectacular, and a talking mannequin bellows, "Halt! Who goes there?" in a full-bodied British accent.

EUROPA POINT. At the southern tip of Gibraltar, guarded by three machine guns and a lighthouse, Europa Point commands a seemingly endless view of the straits. On a clear day you can see Morocco. *(Take bus #3 or 1B from Line Wall Rd., just off Main St., all the way to the end. Departs every 15min., £0.40.)*

ST. MICHAEL'S CAVE. The ruins of a Moorish wall descend along the road from the cable car station to the south, where the spooky chambers of St. Michael's Cave were cut into the rock by thousands of years of water erosion. The deep cavern was used as a hospital during the 1942 bombardments. Now it's an auditorium with the requisite colored lights and elevator music.

♫ ENTERTAINMENT

Main St. hosts throngs of lively **pubs.** Early evening busybodies people-watch from the **Angry Friar,** 287 Main St. (tel. 715 70). Don't miss having your photo taken with the fist-shaking monk. A pint of lager, ale, or bitter goes for £1.70 to 1.90. (Open daily 9:30am-midnight. Food served 9:30am-4:15pm and 6:15pm-9:15pm.) As evening wears into night, pub-hoppers head to the **Horseshoe Bar,** 193 Main St. (tel. 774 44; pint of beer £1.80, mixed drinks £1.30; open Su-Th 9am-midnight, F-Sa 9am-1am). **Bourbon Street,** 150 Main St. (tel. 437 65), has Cajun and English cookin', a pool table, darts, and live music every night (pint of beer or mixed drinks £1.60-1.80; open M-Th 11am-midnight, F-Sa 11am-1am, Su 5:30pm-midnight).

COSTA DEL SOL

The coast has sold its soul to the Devil and now he's starting to collect. Artifice covers its once-natural charms as chic promenades and swanky hotels come between small towns and the shoreline. The Costa del Sol officially extends from Tarifa in the southwest to Cabo de Gata, east of Almería; post-industrial Málaga lies smack in the middle. To the northeast, the hills dip straight into the ocean, where rocky beaches have helped to preserve some of the natural beauty. To the southwest, water seems to wash up on more concrete than sand. That said, nothing can take away from the coast's major attraction: eight months of spring and four months of summer. News of Costa del Sol's fantastic weather has spread as far and wide. Consequently, July and August bring swarms of pale-skinned British and thick-walleted German tourists. Make reservations days in advance to avoid having to sleep on the beaches (which is not advisable for solo travelers and women). Alternatively, ask around for *casas particulares*. June is the best time to visit, when summer weather reigns and hordes of tourists don't. Private **bus lines** offer connections along the coast itself; **trains** only go as far as Málaga and Fuengirola. Railpasses are not valid, but train-prices are reasonable.

MÁLAGA

Once celebrated by the likes of Hans Christian Andersen, Málaga (pop. 531,140) has since lost much of its charm. In the hundred years since Andersen and other Romantics discovered the city, 19th-century villas have been replaced by 70s highrises, and the beach is better known for its bars than untouched sand. Yet Málaga, the second-largest city in Andalucía and a critical transportation hub for the province, brims with all the requisite historical monuments—fortress, cathedral, bullring—and buzzes with a welcoming modern atmosphere.

▐ GETTING THERE

Málaga can be easily reached by **train** from: **Sevilla** (2½hr., 5 per day, 7:40am-8:10pm, 2090ptas) or by super-fast TALGO 200 trains from **Madrid** (4hr., 6 per day, 7:10am-8:20pm, 6900-8100ptas). **Buses** go from: **Marbella** (1½hr., every 30min., 605ptas); **Granada** (2hr., 16 per day, 7am-10pm, 1180ptas); **Sevilla** (2½hr., 10 per day, 7am-midnight, 1850ptas); **Algeciras** (3hr., 11 per day, 8am-2:15pm, 1325ptas).

▐ ORIENTATION AND PRACTICAL INFORMATION

To walk to the town center from the **bus station** (20min.), exit right onto C. Perchel, walk straight through the big intersection with Av. Aurora, take a right on Av. Andalucía, and cross the bridge, Puente Tetuán. From here, the palm tree and flower-shop-lined **Alameda Principal** leads into **Plaza de la Marina.** Or take bus #4 or #21 along the same route (115 ptas). For public transportation, walk one block on C. Roger de Flor to the train station (5min.). From the **train station,** you can walk a block up Explanada de la Estación, turn left toward the bus station, and follow the directions above, or take the C-1 local train (Centro-Almeda) to Puente Tetuán (135ptas). Even better, bus #3 goes directly to Pl. Marina (115ptas). From Pl. Marina, C. Molina Lario leads to the **cathedral** and the old town. C. Marqués de Larios connects Pl. Marina to **Plaza de la Constitución,** while Po. Parque leads past the **Alcazaba.** Farther on, seaside Po. Marítimo stretches toward the lively beachfront district **El Pedregalejo,** off all street maps of the city (bus #11 or a 40min. walk).

TRANSPORTATION

Flights: (tel. 95 213 61 28 or 95 213 61 66). From the airport, bus #19 (every 30min., 200ptas) runs from the City Bus sign and stops at the bus station and the corner of C. Molina Lario and Postigo de los Abades behind the cathedral. RENFE's train connecting the city and the airport is cheaper (135ptas) and quicker (12min.). **Iberia,** C. Molina Larios, 13 (tel. 95 213 61 47; 24hr. reservations tel. 902 400 500).

Trains: Estación de Málaga (tel. 95 236 02 02), Explanada de la Estación. Take bus #3 at Po. Parque or #4 at Pl. Marina to the station. Tickets and reservations also at the less-crowded **RENFE** office, C. Strachan, 4 (tel. 95 221 31 22), off C. Molina Lario. To: **Torremolinos** (20min., every 30min., 150ptas); **Fuengirola** (30min., every 30min., 305ptas); **Córdoba** (2hr., 12 per day, 2100ptas); **Sevilla** (3hr., 3 per day, 1800ptas); **Madrid** (4hr., 5 per day, 8000ptas); **Barcelona** (13hr., 3 per day, 6700ptas).

Buses: Po. Tilos, s/n (tel. 95 235 00 61), 1 block from RENFE station along C. Roger de Flor. To: **Torremolinos** (20min., every 15min., 125ptas); **Fuengirola** (30min., every 40min., 290ptas); **Nerja** (1hr., every hr., 450ptas); **Antequera** (1hr., every hr., 525ptas); **Marbella** (1½hr., every hr., 575ptas); **Granada** (2hr., every hr., 1200ptas); **Ronda** (3hr., 4 per day, 1110ptas); **Algeciras** (3hr., 11 per day, 1250ptas); **Córdoba** (3hr., 5 per day, 1500ptas); **Gibraltar** (3hr., 1 per day, 1650ptas); **Sevilla** (3hr., 10 per day, 2200ptas); **Cádiz** (5hr., 4 per day, 2515ptas); **Madrid** (7hr., 8 per day, 2800ptas); **Murcia** (7hr., 6 per day, 3800ptas); **Alicante** (8hr., 6 per day, 4500ptas).

Taxis: Radio-Taxi (tel. 95 232 79 50 or 95 232 80 62). A taxi from the town center to the waterfront costs 850-950ptas, to the airport 1300ptas.

TOURIST, FINANCIAL, AND LOCAL SERVICES

Tourist Offices: Municipal, Av. Cervantes, 1 (tel. 95 260 44 10; fax 95 221 41 20), a little gray house along Po. Parque offering **free maps** and city info. Also has a kiosk in front of the post office on Av. Andalucía. Open M-F 8:15am-2:45pm and 4:30-7pm, Sa 9:30am-1:30pm. **Junta de Andalucía,** Pasaje de Chinitas, 4 (tel. 95 221 34 45), off Pl. Constitución at the corner of C. Nicasio. Enter the alley through the arch and take the 1st right. Brochures on the Costa del Sol and a map. Open June-Sept. M-F 9am-7pm, Sa-Su 9am-1pm; Oct.-May M-F 9am-2pm, Sa 9am-1pm.

Currency Exchange: Banco Español de Crédito, Alameda Principal, 8 (tel. 95 221 15 41), at the intersection with Pta. Mar. Open M-F 8.30am-2pm.

Luggage Storage: Lockers at the train station (open daily 7am-10:45pm) and bus station (open daily 6:30am-11pm). Both 400ptas per day.

El Corte Inglés: Av. Andalucía, 4-6 (tel. 95 230 00 00), across from the post office. City map 495ptas. Currency exchange with no commission. Travel agency books flights, trains, and boats. Supermarket, telephones, laundry service, and English language books. Open June-Aug. M-Sa 10am-10pm; Sept.-May 10am-9:30pm.

EMERGENCY AND COMMUNICATIONS

Emergency: tel. 091 or 092. **Police:** tel. 95 231 71 00.

Pharmacy: Farmacia y Laboratorio Laza, C. Molina Lario, 2 (tel. 95 222 75 97). Open M-F 9:30am-1:30pm and 5-8:30pm, Sa 10:30am-1:30pm.

Medical Services: tel. 95 230 30 34.

Post Office: Av. Andalucía, 1 (tel. 95 235 90 08), just over the Puente Tetuán. Lista de Correos. Open M-F 8:30am-8:30pm, Sa 9:30am-2pm. **Postal Code:** 29080.

Internet Access: Cibercafé Málaga, Av. Andalucía, 11 (tel. 95 204 03 03). 250ptas per 15min. Student discounts. Open M-F 8am-11pm, Sa-Su 4-11pm.

▐ ACCOMMODATIONS

Most budget establishments are in the old town, between Pl. Marina and Pl. Constitución. Try bargaining if prices seem unreasonable (above 3000ptas for a single, 4700ptas for a double). Excluding August, the market is usually slow. After dark, be wary of the neighborhoods of **Alameda de Colón, El Perchel** (toward the river from the train and bus stations), **Cruz del Molinillo** (near the market), and **La Esperanza/Santo Domingo** (up the river from El Corte Inglés).

Hostal La Palma, C. Martínez, 7 (tel. 95 222 67 72), off C. Marqués de Larios. Paternal host Antonio and equally helpful daughters keep this hostel spotless. Downstairs rooms share communal baths; upstairs doubles are brand new, with A/C, mini-terraces and private bathrooms. Singles 2000-3000ptas; doubles 3500-5000ptas; triples 3300-4500ptas; quads 4400-6000ptas.

Hostal Aurora, Muro de Puerta Nueva, 1 (tel 95 222 40 04), 5min. from Pl. Constitución. Rooms in this quiet home are cool, airy, and clean. Shared bath. Singles 1800-3000ptas; doubles 3000-4500ptas.

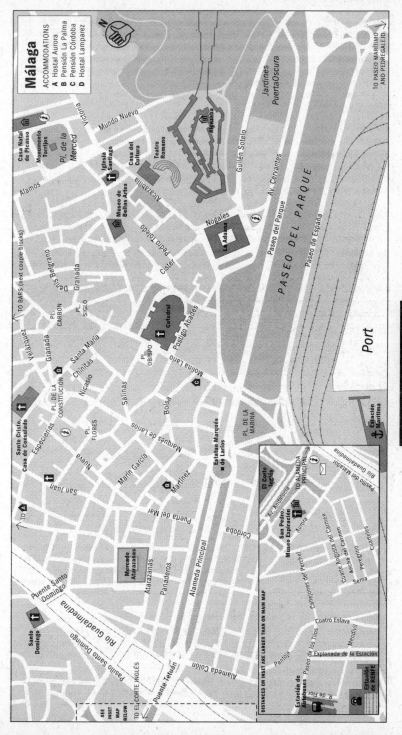

ANDALUCÍA

Málaga

ACCOMMODATIONS
A Hostal Aurora
B Pensión La Palma
C Pensión Córdoba
D Hostal Lamparez

TO PASEO MARÍTIMO
AND PEDREGALEJO

PASEO DEL PARQUE

Port

Jardines
PuertaOscura

Casa Natal
de Picasso

Monumento
Torrijos

Pl. de la
Merced

Mundo Nuevo

Victoria

Iglesia
Santiago

Casa del
Cultura

Teatro
Romano

Alcazaba

Museo de
Bellas Artes

Alamos

Pedro Toledo

Cister

Nogales

La Aduana

Guillén Sotelo

Av. Cervantes

Paseo del Parque

Paseo de España

Alcazabilla

Velázquez

TO BARS (next couple blocks)

Luis Belgrano
De

Pl.
CARBON

Granada

Pl.
SIGLO

Catedral

Postigo Abades

Santa María

Pl.
OBISPO

Molina Lario

Granada

Chinitas

Nicasio

Salinas

Bolsa

PL. DE LA
CONSTITUCIÓN

Pl. DE LA
MARINA

Santo Cristo,
Casa de Consulado

Especierías

Pl.
FLORES

Marqués de Larios

Nueva

Lexana

Marín García

Martínez

Estatua Marqués
■ de Larios

San Juan

Puerta del Mar

Alameda Principal

Mercado
Atarazanas

Córdoba

Santo
Domingo

Puente Santo
Domingo

Atarazanas

Panaderos

Pasillo Santo Domingo

Río Guadalmedina

TO A

TO EL CORTE INGLÉS

SEE
INSET
MAP
BELOW

TO EL CORTE INGLÉS

Alameda Colón

Puente Tetuán

DISTANCES ON INSET ARE LARGER THAN ON MAIN MAP

TO ALAMEDA
PRINCIPAL

El Corte
Inglés

San Pedro,
Museo Expiración

Av. Andalucía

Aurora

Pasillo del Matadero

Río Guadalmedina

Cuarte Angosta del Carmen

Ancha del Carmen

Peregrino

Callejones del Perchel

Serna

Mendívil

Cuarteles

Paseo de los Tilos

Cuatro Eslava

Pantoja

Explanada de la Estación

Estación de
Autobuses

R. de Flor

Estación
de RENFE

Estación
Marítima

Hostal Lamparez, C. Santa María, 6 (tel 95 221 94 84), off Pl. Constitución, near C. Granada. Basic, clean rooms with floral patterns that match the friendly landlady's dresses. Singles 1500-1800ptas; doubles 2600-2800ptas; triples 3500-4000ptas.

Hostal Córdoba, C. Bolsa, 11 (tel. 95 221 44 69), off C. Molina Lario. Decently sized interior rooms with antique furniture. Spotless common bathrooms. Singles 1500ptas; doubles 2700ptas; triples 4500ptas.

🍴 FOOD

Along Po. Marítimo in El Pedregalejo, beachfront restaurants specialize in fresh seafood. For a cheap snack, grab some sardines roasted over an open flame (usually in old rowboats) on the beach. The eateries around C. Granada leading out of Pl. Constitución specialize in land-bound creatures. Fresh produce fills the **market** on C. Afaranzas (open daily 8am-2pm). There is a supermarket in the basement of **El Corte Inglés** (see p. 238).

Restaurante El Tintero II, Po. Marítimo, 99 (tel. 95 220 44 64). The farthest restaurant east on the waterfront. Waiters stroll by with seafood platters while roving flamenco guitarists entertain diners. Entrees 650ptas. Open daily 11am-5pm and 7:30pm-1am.

La Acacias (tel 95 229 89 46), Playa Las Acacias, El Pedregalejo. Frantic waiters, cheap food, and sea air makes this one of the liveliest eateries on the waterfront. Entrees 600-1200ptas. Open daily 7pm-1am.

Pizzeria Il Forno, El Pedregalejo, 45 (tel 95 220 06 28). For those who enjoy the sight but not the flavors of the sea. Thin crust pizzas 600-950ptas, traditional pastas 550-850ptas. Open daily 7pm-1am.

Eco Dulces (tel 95 222 77 94), C. Compania. Fabulous bakery ideal for breakfast, picnics, afternoon snacks and midnight feasts. *Bocadillos* 175ptas, desserts 70-130ptas. Open W-M noon-3pm and 6pm-9pm.

👁 SIGHTS

ALCAZABA. With 10 major towers inside concentric walls, the Alcazaba is Málaga's most impressive sight. Guarding the east end of Po. Parque, this 11th-century structure was originally built as a fortified palace for Moorish kings. It now houses the ruins of a Roman theater and a **museum** of Moroccan art, and provides an incredible view of the harbor from its ramparts. Shifty types prowl around here at night. *(Open W-M 9:30am-8pm.)*

CATHEDRAL. Málaga's cathedral is a pastiche of Gothic, Renaissance, and Baroque styles. The cathedral's second tower, which was under construction from the 16th to 19th centuries, was never completed, hence the cathedral's nickname *La Manquita* (One-Armed Lady). The organs date from 1781. *(C. Molina Lario, s/n. Tel. 95 221 59 17. Open M-Sa 10am-12:45pm and 4-6:45pm. 200ptas.)*

CASTILLO GIBRALFARO. An Arab lighthouse was built in this Phoenician castle, which offers sweeping views of Málaga and the Mediterranean. Exploring the grounds alone can be dangerous. *(Buses to Castillo leave hourly from the plaza below, otherwise it's an uphill hike. Open daily 9:30am-8pm.)*

PICASSO FOUNDATION. Picasso's birthplace now houses the Picasso Foundation, which organizes a series of exhibitions, concerts, and lectures every October and at other times during the year. According to local officials, even though Picasso high-tailed it out of Málaga when he was quite young, he always "felt himself to be a true *malagueño.*" *(Pl. Merced. Tel. 95 221 50 05. Open M-Sa 10am-2pm and 6-9pm, Su 10am-2pm. Free.)*

MUSEUMS. Málaga's museums are on the move and, like everything else on the planet, are supposed to be ready for 2000. A **Picasso museum** will open in the Old Palace of the counts of Buenavista. *(C. San Augustin, 8. Tel. 95 221 83 82.)* The **Museo**

Arqueológico and the **Museo de Bellas Artes,** home to a premier collection of 19th-century paintings, are joining together in an as yet undecided new location (inquire at the tourist office).

🎵 ENTERTAINMENT

In summer, young *malagueños* crowd the boardwalk bars in El Pedregalejo. The **Nocturno 1 bus** takes over the Pedragalejo line daily from 12:45 to 5:45am (every hr.). A slightly older, slightly more foreign crowd drinks *copas* on C. Bolivia, parallel to and a few blocks up from the beach. Check out bar **Donde Bolivia 41,** C. Bolivia, 97, to mellow out among shrubbery, pillows, and a pool table. On weekends, crowds invade the bars in the area between C. Comedias and C. Granada, which leads out of Pl. Constitución. **O'Neill's,** C. Luis de Velazquez, 3 (tel. 95 260 14 60), has dark wooden decor, pints of Guinness (550ptas), Celtic music, and friendly bartenders imported from the Emerald Isle.

Málaga's **Semana Santa** celebrations are nearly as grandiose as those in rival Sevilla, and the **Feria de Agosto**—complete with bullfights, flamenco, and a *moraga* (sardine bake on the beach)—is among the most spectacular *fiestas* in all of Andalucía. The *Guía del Ocio* (200ptas), available at newsstands, lists special events, singles bars, and gay and lesbian entertainment.

DAYTRIPS FROM MÁLAGA

GARGANTA DEL CHORRO

The geologically inclined can rent a car and drive 50km northwest of Málaga to **Garganta del Chorro** (a.k.a. El Chorro), one of Spain's premier natural wonders. El Chorro's rocky terrain rises to 1190m, while the Río Guadalhorce, 180m below, splits the landscape in two. To truly experience El Chorro, walk the **Camino del Rey,** which leads to the bridge above the gorge, from the village of Álora.

TORREMOLINOS

Along the coast between Málaga and Marbella, Torremolinos offers the classic package-holiday trilogy: sun, sand, and *cerveza*. English is spoken, eaten, and drunk everywhere; the only trace of Spain is the pottery and lace that spill out of the souvenir shops. Visitors spend days on the wide, sandy beach, which turns into a mass of flesh in July and August. At night, they wander along **Avenida Palma de Mallorca,** the main thoroughfare, or join the hordes farther west at **La Carihuela,** a sandy expanse dotted with bars and shops. Exit the **train station,** and walk through the alleyway on the right to Av. Palma de Mallorca; turn right and the pedestrian C. San Miguel will be on the right. From the **bus station,** exit to the right and follow C. Hoyo to Pl. Costa del Sol and Av. Palma de Mallorca; C. San Miguel is on the left.

Portillo Buses (tel. 95 238 24 19) and **C-1 local trains** (tel. 95 238 57 64) depart frequently to Málaga, Fuengirola, and other destinations. The **tourist office** (tel. 95 237 11 59) is on Pl. Pablo Ruiz Picasso, uphill from Av. Palma de Mallorca. The staff speaks English, German and French. (Open daily 9am-2pm.) Hostels tend to get lost amid towering hotels and apartment complexes; some huddle on Cuesta de Tajo and on streets off Pl. Costa del Sol. Prices surge in August. **Hostal La Palmera,** Av. Palma de Mallorca, 37 (tel. 95 237 65 09), a few doors down from the post office (enter around the corner), rents airy rooms with big closets. A TV and bar spice up the reception room. (Breakfast 350ptas. Reservations suggested. Singles 2500-3000ptas; doubles 3500-5000ptas; triples 4800-7500ptas.)

FUENGIROLA

Visitors come to Fuengerola for the beach, though in August it becomes so crowded that there's barely room to swing a catfish. Since temperatures on the coast can be as much as 15°F cooler than they are a mere three blocks inland, visitors chill (relatively) in bars along Po. Marítimo and on the beach in Los Boliches, the eastern part of town. **Trains** leave for **Málaga** (40min., 315ptas) from the **RENFE** station (tel. 95 247 85 40) on Av. Jesús Santos Reino. To get to **Los Boliches,** get off one stop early. The **bus station** (tel. 95 247 50 66), on C. Alfonso XIII, runs buses to: **Marbella** (30min., every 30min., 305ptas); **Málaga** (45min., every 30min., 305ptas); **Ronda** (2hr., 5 per day, 865ptas); **Algeciras** (2hr., 11 per day, 1015ptas).

The English-speaking staff at the **tourist office,** Av. Jesús Santo Reino, 6 (tel. 95 246 74 57), provides free maps. (Open June-Aug. M-F 9:30am-2pm and 5-8pm, Sa 10am-1pm; Sept.-May M-F 9:30am-2pm and 4-7pm, Sa 10am-1pm.) Reasonable hostels hide between Pl. Constitución and the beach and in Los Boliches. **Hostal Costabella,** Av. Boliches, 98 (tel. 95 247 46 31), is only one block up from the beach, and one block seaward from RENFE's Los Boliches stop. Some rooms have beach views; all have private baths. (Singles 2000-3500ptas; doubles 3000-4700ptas.)

MARBELLA

Like your vacation spots shaken, not shtirred? Scottish smoothie Sean Connery and a host of other international jet-setters choose five-star Marbella (pop. 100,000) to dock their yachts, park their weary jets, and live the glitzy, glamorous life. Surprisingly, it's still possible to have a good time on a budget in Marbella. The city's controversial mayor has "cleaned up" the "marginal" elements (drug dealers, prostitutes, dogs, fellow politicians, etc.); best catch it now before he sets his sights on backpackers.

⌐ GETTING THERE

Marbella does not have a train station. It can be reached by bus from: **Málaga** (1½hr., every hr., 575ptas); **Ronda** (1½hr., 5 per day, 605ptas); **Algeciras** (1½hr., 10 per day, 9:30am-10pm, 760ptas); **Sevilla** (3hr., 3 per day, 8am-4pm, 1820ptas).

🛈 ORIENTATION AND PRACTICAL INFORMATION

Marbella, 56km south of Málaga, can be reached only by bus. The brand new **bus station** surveys the sea from atop Av. Trapiche. To reach the main strip, exit and walk left, make the first right onto Av. Trapiche, and follow any downhill route to the perpendicular Av. Ramón y Cajal, which becomes Av. Ricardo Soriano on the way to the super-swanky harbor of **Puerto Bonús.** C. Peral curves up from Av. Ramón y Cajal around the **casco antiguo** (old town).

TRANSPORTATION

Buses: Av. Trapiche, s/n (tel. 95 276 44 00). To: **Fuengirola** (30min., every 35min., 305ptas); **Málaga** (1½hr., every 30min., 605ptas); **Ronda** (1½hr., 4 per day, 610ptas); **Algeciras** (1½hr., 9 per day, 760ptas); **Granada** (4hr., 4 per day, 1785ptas); **Sevilla** (4hr., 3 per day, 1895ptas); **Cádiz** (4hr., 4 per day, 2005ptas); **Madrid** (7½hr., 10 per day, 3085ptas); **Barcelona** (16hr., 4 per day, 8325ptas).

Taxis: tel. 95 277 44 88.

TOURIST, FINANCIAL, AND LOCAL SERVICES

Tourist Office: (tel. 95 277 14 42), C. Glorieta de la Fontanilla. Free maps. English spoken. In the old town, **another office** (tel. 95 282 35 50) is on Pl. Naranjos. Both open June-Aug. M-F 9.30am-9pm; Sept.-May M-F 9.30am-8pm, Sa 10am-2pm.

Currency Exchange: Banco Central Hispano, Av. Ramón y Cajal, 9 (tel. 95 277 08 92). Good exchange rates. Open June-Sept. M-F 8:30am-2:30pm; Oct.-May M-F 8:30am-2:30pm. **ATMs** abound, especially near the casco antiguo.

American Express: Av. Duque de Ahumada, s/n (tel. 95 282 14 94; fax 95 286 22 92), off Po. Marítimo. Open M-F 9:30am-2pm and 4:30-8pm, Sa 10am-1pm.

Luggage Storage: At the bus station (400ptas). Open 6:30am-11:30pm.

EMERGENCY AND COMMUNICATIONS

Emergency: tel. 091 or 092. **Police:** Pl. Los Naranjos, 1 (tel. 95 282 24 94).

Hospital: Comarcal, CN-340, km187 (tel. 95 286 27 48).

Post Office: C. Jacinto Benavente, 26 (tel. 95 277 28 98), uphill from C. Ricardo Soriano. Open M-F 8:30am-2:30pm, Sa 9:30am-1pm. **Postal Code:** 29600.

Internet Access: Stop N' Go (tel. 95 286 09 99), C. Sierra Blanca, off C. Ricardo Soriano. 500ptas per 30min. Open M-F 10am-2pm and 5:30-9pm, Sa 10am-2pm.

▛ ACCOMMODATIONS AND CAMPING

If you are reservationless, especially from mid-July through August, arrive early and pray for a miracle. The area in the *casco antiguo* around Pl. Naranjos (also known as Orange Square) is loaded with quick-filling hostels.

▧ **Hostal del Pilar,** C. Mesoncillo, 4 (tel. 95 282 99 36; email hostal@marbella-scene.com), off C. Peral, an extension of C. Huerta Chica, or from the bus station off C. San Francisco. Run by a Scottish woman and an Anglophone staff who like to party with the young, international clientele. Bar downstairs is a great place to start the evening. Shared bath. Breakfast 700ptas. 1500-2500ptas per person. Roof 1000-1500ptas.

▧ **Albergue Juvenil (HI),** C. Trapiche, 2 (tel. 95 277 14 91; fax 95 286 32 27), downhill from the bus station. Just like a proper hotel, only affordable. Facilities include a large pool, garden, TV room, and basketball court. Wheelchair accessible. 800-1300ptas per person, over 26 1100-1800ptas. Tents outside 700ptas per person.

Pensión Aduar, C. Aduar, 7 (tel. 95 277 35 78). The beautiful courtyard, overflowing with flowers and songbirds, gives a sunny glow to well-kept rooms. Balconies upstairs. Singles 1700-2500ptas; doubles 2800-3600ptas.

El Castillo, Pl. San Bernabé, 2 (tel. 95 277 17 39), in the old town, a few blocks uphill from Pl. Naranjos. Medieval decor in sunny, comfortable rooms with private bathrooms. Singles 2000-2600ptas; doubles 3000-6000ptas. Visa.

Camping Marbella Playa (tel. 95 277 83 91), 2km east on N-340. On the Marbella-Fuengirola bus line; ask the bus driver to stop at the campground. 310-570ptas per person, 520-970ptas per tent. Open year-round.

◌ FOOD

Terrazas fill Pl. Naranjos but are not particularly budget-friendly—some even charge for bread. Restaurants farther uphill are less picturesque but more satisfying for the wallet. Seaside, Av. Miguel Cano and Av. Pta. Mar are both lined with lively and relatively cheap bars and cafes. The municipal **market** is on Av. Mercado, uphill from C. Peral (open M-Sa 8am-2pm). A **24-hour minimarket** beckons through the night on the corner of C. Pablo Casals and Av. Fontanilla, which intersects with Av. Ricardo Soriano.

▧ **Bodega La Venencia** (tel. 95 277 9963), Pl. Olivas. A huge restaurant, with an equally impressive terrace. Fills up each night with Spaniards who know a good deal when they see one. The menu includes a large number of vegetarian options, as well as a fantastic array of meat and fish. *Tapas* 150-300ptas. Open daily 1pm-2am.

▧ **La Casa del Té,** C. Ancha, 7 (tel. 63 916 79 18). Glass-canopied courtyard filled with cushions, paintings, and incense. Vegetarian sandwiches and crepes (275-325ptas), fruit juices (325ptas), and Indian yogurt drinks (300ptas). Open daily 5:30-11:30pm.

Bar El Gallo, C. Lobatas, 44 (tel. 95 282 79 98). One of those places where old men gather to discuss *fútbol* and politics. Cheap and filling. The most expensive dish is grilled shrimp at 550ptas. Open W-M 9am-midnight.

Picobello (tel. 952 86 19 93), C. Miguel Cano, 2 blocks from the beach. An elegant tea room with surprisingly affordable pastries, sandwiches, cheese, salads and sundaes. Teas 200ptas, coffee 140ptas. Open daily 8am-noon.

👁 ◗ SIGHTS AND BEACHES

Although visitors come to Marbella for its 320 days of sunshine per year, no visit to the city would be complete without a stroll through the **casco antiguo,** a maze of cobbled streets and ancient whitewashed facades. The thick walls of the former Arab fortress that surrounded the neighborhood are currently being restored—another of the mayor's improvements. The **Museo del Grabado Español Contemporáneo,** in a restored hospital for the poor, is a treasure-trove of engravings by Miró, Picasso, Dalí, Goya, and contemporary artists. (C. Hospital Bazán. Open M-F 10:15am-2pm and 5:30-8:30pm. 300ptas.) To the northeast is the **Parque Arroyo de la Represa,** site of the **Museo del Bonsai.** (Tel. 95 286 29 26. Open daily 10am-1:30pm and 4-7:30pm. 400ptas, botanists and under 12 200ptas.)

City buses along Av. Richard Soriano (destination San Pedro, 125ptas) bring you to chic and trendy **Puerto Banús,** buffered by imposing white yachts and row upon row of boutiques and fancy restaurants. The port has been frequented by the likes of Sean Connery, King Fahd of Saudi Arabia (who built a huge palace modeled on the White House), Antonio Banderas, and even the late Princess Diana. Throngs of Euro-chicks mill about the marina, in search of prospective husbands. The Moroccan coast is visible on exceptionally clear days.

With 22km of **beach,** Marbella offers a variety of sizzling settings, from below its chic promenade to **Playa de las Chapas,** 10km east via the Fuengirola bus. **Funny Beach,** a 10-minute bus ride along the coast, is a paradise of beach games and sports, including jet-skiing and volleyball. Ha! Because of the towering mountains nearby, Marbella's winter temperatures tend to be 5-8°F warmer than Málaga's, and beach season lasts for at least 10 months.

♫ ENTERTAINMENT

Nightlife begins around 11pm. In the *casco antiguo,* a mellow ambience suffuses the **Townhouse Bar,** C. Alamo, on an alley off C. Nueva, which leads downhill from Pl. Naranjos (opens daily at 10pm). A young international crowd socializes in **Kashmir,** C. Rafina, 8, off C. Aduar. Its smoky lounges might remind Amsterdam natives of home. (Opens daily at 10pm.) Between the beach and the old town, C. Puerta del Mar is home to several gay bars, including **Ojo,** C. Puerta del Mar, 9 (opens daily at 11pm), and the younger **Bocaccio,** C. Puerta del Mar, 17 (opens at 10pm).

On the way to the beach, **Bar Incognito,** Av. Miguel Cano, 15, serves divine, fruit-garnished cocktails at half-price during Happy Hour (350ptas; daily 9-11pm). Later in the evening, the city's entire teen population swarms to the **Puerto Deportivo** ("The Port"), an amusement park of disco-bars. **Loco's** plays loud music of all types (beer 300ptas). Attracting a slightly older crowd is **Arturo's Bar,** Local 42-43 (tel. 95 282 03 11), a rustic display of American kitsch, complete with bear-skin rugs and wall-mounted antlers. Try **La Rebotica,** next door to Locos, for a frat-party atmosphere and lots of beer.

After midnight, the actions shifts to **Puerto Banús** and the discos, which go on until dawn. Buses run there on the hour all night along Av. Ricardo Soriano (destination San Pedro, 125ptas). Cover for men: 2000ptas (women usually free); water: 1000ptas; having your attire scrutinized by a cellphone-toting promoter: priceless.

NERJA

Renowned for pristine beaches and remarkable caves, Nerja (pop. 15,000) offers the best and worst of a coastal resort town. Spectacular beaches are crowded with bikini-clad tourists and flip-flopped English-speakers. At Nerja's **Balcón de Europa,** they gather to catch a glimpse of the Costa del Sol's most stunning ocean view.

🛈 PRACTICAL INFORMATION. The **bus station,** C. San Miguel, 3 (tel. 95 252 15 04), sends buses to: **Almuñécar** (30min., 7 per day, 8am-8:30pm, 300ptas); **Málaga** (1½hr., 12 per day, 7:30am-8:25pm, 460ptas); **Granada** (2¼hr., 3 per day, 2:30-7pm,

1100ptas); **Almería** (4hr., 5 per day, 8am-7pm, 1475ptas); **Sevilla** (4hr., 2 per day, 7:30am and 2pm, 2310-2695ptas). The multilingual **tourist office,** Pta. del Mar, 2 (tel. 95 252 15 31), beside the Balcón de Europa, gives out a free map of central Nerja and sells a more detailed version (100ptas; open June-Aug. M-F 10am-2pm and 5:30-8:30pm, Sa 10am-1pm; Sept.-May M-F 10am-2pm and 5-8pm, Sa 10am-1pm). **Emergency:** tel. 091 or 092; **police** (tel. 95 252 15 45), on C. Virgen del Pilar. **Post office,** C. Almirante Ferrándiz, 6 (tel. 95 252 17 49; open M-F 8:30am-2:30pm, Sa 9:30am-1pm); **postal code:** 29780.

▮▮ ACCOMMODATIONS AND FOOD. It's worth breaking a sweat for ▨**Hostal Estrella del Mar,** C. Bellavista, 5 (tel. 95 252 04 61). From the bus station walk up the *carretera,* turn right toward "El Parador," turn left on C. General Asensio Cabanillas, and take the third right. Its spacious rooms have baths and terraces, most with ocean views (breakfast 350ptas; singles 2900-3900ptas; doubles 3700-4800ptas). Otherwise, **Hostal Residencia Mena,** C. El Barrio, 15 (tel. 95 252 05 41), conveniently located off the Balcón de Europa, has bare rooms with very small balconies and baths (July-Sept. singles 3200ptas; doubles 4500ptas; Oct.-June singles 2500ptas; doubles 3500ptas). Overpriced restaurants near and along the Balcón de Europa tempt passers-by with views, but one look at the stingy portions will repulse even the most camera-happy of tourists. On Playa de Burriana, **Merendero Montemar** serves fresh fish, English breakfasts (350ptas), and *paella* (with salad, bread, and a drink, 1000ptas). In the heart of town, **Coconuts,** C. Pintada, 11 (tel. 95 252 01 81), has two-for-one happy hour drinks (daily 8-10pm) and reasonably priced international dishes served on a tropical patio. A **market** two blocks up C. San Miguel sells produce (open daily 8am-2pm).

▨ SIGHTS. To get to the ▨**Balcón de Europa,** a promenade that overlooks Playa de la Caletilla, follow the highway uphill from the bus stop to C. Pintada, which then leads downhill to the *balcón.* Below the cliff are nifty caves, best explored from the **Paseo de los Carabineros** (off the stairs to the right of the tourist office). The walkway winds along the rocky shore to the east, past **Playa de Calahonda, Playa Carabeo,** and **Playa Burriana.** To reach the sprawling **Playa de la Torrecilla** from the *balcón,* cut through town westward to the Playa de la Torrecilla apartments; follow the shoreline from there (15min.) Much closer but more crowded is **Playa del Salón,** accessible through an alley off the *balcón,* to the right of Restaurante Marisal.

NEAR NERJA: LA CUEVA DE NERJA

One of Nerja's most popular attractions lies outside of the city. **Cueva de Nerja,** just 5km east of Nerja, has piped-in music and photographers who try to sell tourists a picture of themselves in a cave-shaped frame. The caves consist of large chambers filled with rock formations formed over millions of years by calcium deposits and sea-borne erosion. Intrepid spelunkers have recently discovered a new section of caves, reportedly four times as large as the current attraction. (Open July-Aug. 10am-2pm and 4-8pm; Sept.-June 10am-2pm and 4-6:30pm. 650ptas, children 6-12 350ptas.) One cave is used as an amphitheater for music and ballet performances during the spectacular **Festival Cueva de Nerja,** held every July. **Buses** to the caves run to and from Nerja (every hr., 8:10am-8:10pm, returns 8:45am-8:15pm, 100ptas). **Maro** is a speck of a village near the caves, with paths to nearly empty, rocky beaches and coves. For local hikes, consult the Nerja tourist office.

ALMUÑÉCAR

In the 4th century BC, a booming fish-salting industry brought prosperity to this Phoenician port town. The Romans took over 100 years later, constructing temples and an aqueduct, and naming the town **Sexi.** Though not quite as exciting as its Roman name promises, Almuñécar entices visitors with its seemingly endless boardwalks and its alluring tropical environment.

THE FIFTH BOMB In the 1960s, as Spain was debating whether to join NATO, a USAF B-52 bomber carrying five hydrogen bombs blew up during an in-flight refueling mishap, over the village of Palomares, 20km north of Mojácar. Locals looked on as U.S. personnel in radiation suits combed the town in search of the bombs. Four were recovered and identified; the fifth supposedly emerged wrapped in a plastic tarp and without a serial number (Spanish Greenpeace still doubts that it was ever found). Much of Spain boycotted the area's produce (primarily tomatoes), and anti-NATO sentiment reached new heights. To downplay the accident, the U.S. Ambassador and Franco's Minister of the Interior staged a seaside photo-op, swimming in the water before a dozen CIA agents. To top it off, the U.S. built a health clinic in the town. Palomares has since prospered, with copious harvests of tomatoes, leeks, and melons, but some locals still blame defects and illnesses on the mysterious fifth bomb.

⊓ PRACTICAL INFORMATION. Buses (tel. 950 63 01 40) run from the corner of Av. Fenicia and Av. Juan Carlos I to: **Nerja** (30min., 9 per day, 7am-9pm, 300ptas); **Málaga** (1½hr., 7 per day, 745ptas); **Granada** (1½hr., 9 per day, 8am-9pm, 845ptas); **Madrid** (7hr., 1 per day, 2300ptas). The **tourist office** (tel. 958 63 11 25; email ofi-tur@almunecar-ctropical.org), in a mauve mansion on Av. Europa, off Av. Costa del Sol, provides info and maps. From the bus station, exit right and follow Ctra. Concepción through the rotary to Av. Costa del Sol; turn left onto Av. Europa and walk past the park. The office is on the right (open M-Sa 10am-2pm and 5-8pm). **Luggage storage** at the bus station (300ptas). **Emergency:** tel. 091 or 092; **police** (tel. 958 83 86 14), at the Ayuntamiento in Pl. Constitución, up C. Puerta de Velez from Av. Europa; **medical services: Centro de Salud** (tel. 958 63 20 63), on Ctra. Málaga.

⊓⊔ ACCOMMODATIONS AND FOOD. Several convenient and reasonably priced hostels lie on Av. Europa. Situated near the tourist office and the beach along Av. Europa, **Hotel Goya** (tel. 958 63 05 50 or 958 63 11 92; fax 958 63 11 92) has large, pristine rooms with bath, TV, phone, and heating. TV lounges and a restaurant complete this luxurious hostel. (Singles 2000-3500ptas; doubles 3000-6000ptas. Visa, MC.) **Residencia Tropical** (tel. 958 63 34 58), on Av. Europa a half-block from the beach, has a bar and spotless, well-furnished rooms with private bathrooms. (Singles 2200ptas; doubles 5200ptas; Visa, MC.) Plenty of beach-front *terrazas* line Po. Puerta del Mar and Po. San Cristóbal, providing the perfect place to savor the catch of the day. Locals frequent **Bar Avenida Lute y Jesús,** Av. Europa, 24 (tel. 958 63 42 76), which specializes in *fritura de pescado* (fried fish) for 650-1000ptas (*menú* 800ptas; open daily 8am-1:30am).

⊙⊿ SIGHTS AND BEACHES. Alumñécar's historical protagonists, the Phoenicians, Romans, and Moors, fought over this subtropical paradise, and each left a distinct mark. The Moorish **Castillo de San Miguel** rests atop a massive hill at the front of Pl. Puerte del Mar. The interior may be closed in the year 2000 due to the construction of an historical museum; inquire at the tourist office. The 1900-year-old, 8km-long **aqueduct**, 3km up the Río Seco from the tourist office, watered the ancient Roman town; parts of it are still in use. Almuñécar is also home to nearly 100 different species of birds, which nest in the **Parque Ornitológico Loro Sexi,** beside El Castillo de San Miguel, 100m from the beach. (Open June-Aug. 11am-2pm and 6-9pm; 309ptas, seniors and children 206ptas; open Sept.-May 10am-2pm and 4-6pm; 412ptas, seniors and children 258ptas.) Uphill from the tourist office, **Parque El Majuelo** has 400 varieties of imported plants and great views of Roman ruins (free).

Located on the **Costa Tropical**, Almuñécar is a beach-lover's paradise. The two main beaches are separated by the jutting **Peñón del Santo.** One beach, **Puerta del Mar,** is on the left (when facing the water); the other, **San Cristóbal,** is on the right. Most streets from the bus station terminate at the beach. The easiest way to get there is via Av. Europa (signs point to Playa San Cristóbal). Walk far beyond Po.

Pta del Mar, past Apartamentos Las Goudolas, to beautiful **Playa de Velilla.** Buses to Málaga go through **La Herradura,** a suburb/beach frequented by windsurfers and scuba divers. The largest **nude beach** on the Costa Tropical is **Playa Cantarrijan.** From La Herradura, take a taxi to the beach.

ALMERÍA

Once one of the poorer cities in Andalucía, Almería is a seaside oasis undergoing a boom. Though the Franco era left the town in an economic slump, a population of migrant professionals has led to recent prosperity. These new residents swear by the city's temperate climate, flowery promenades, and granular beaches. They hope to further promote their city when Almería hosts the Mediterranean Games in 2005. Though a huge Moorish fortress presides over the city, the best parts of Almería are the kilometers of sand stretching along the sea toward Cabo de Gata, at the eastern edge of the Costa del Sol.

🚺 ORIENTATION AND PRACTICAL INFORMATION. The city revolves around **Puerta de Purchena,** a six-way intersection with a fountain, just down C. Tiendas from the old town. To reach Pta. Purchena from the **bus station** by Pl. Estación or the **train station** across the street (20min.), follow Av. Estación, turn right onto Av. Federico García Lorca, then go left onto Rbla. Obispo Orbera. Po. Almería runs out of Pta. Purchena to the port; any services you need can be found on Po. Almería or just off it. The **airport** (tel. 950 21 37 00), 9km out of town, has daily flights to Madrid and Barcelona. **Trains** (tel. 950 25 11 35), Pl. Estación, run to: **Granada** (2hr., 4 per day, 1740ptas); **Alicante** (2¼hr., 8:25am-8:15pm, 1740ptas); **Sevilla** (7-10hr., 4 per day, 4180ptas); **Madrid** (7hr., 2 per day, 4100ptas). **Buses** (tel. 950 21 00 29) leave from Pl. Barcelona to: **Mojácar** (1½hr., 5 per day, 830ptas); **Granada** (2hr., 6 per day, 1300-1600ptas); **Murcia** (3hr., 5 per day, 2125ptas); **Málaga** (3½hr., 8 per day, 1915ptas); **Sevilla** (5½hr., 3 per day, 4000ptas); **Córdoba** (6hr., 1 per day, 3000ptas); **Madrid** (8hr., 3 per day, 3000ptas); **Barcelona** (14hr., 3 per day, 7045ptas); **Valencia** (3 per day, 4070ptas).

The **tourist office,** Parque Nicolás Salmerón, s/n (tel. 950 27 43 55), distributes a map. Follow Po. Almería out of Pta. Purchena toward the port, and turn right onto Parque de Salmerón (open M-F 9am-7pm, Sa 10am-2pm). **Emergency:** tel. 091 or 061; **hospital: Hospital Torre Cardenas** tel. 950 21 21 19. **Post office** (tel. 950 24 02 31), Pl. Juan Cassinello, down Po. Almería (open M-F 8:30am-8:30pm, Sa 9:30am-2pm); **postal code:** 04080. **Internet access: Heladería La India II,** Carretera Granada, 304 (tel. 950 27 48 61), 15 min. from the center of town (8am-3pm 300ptas per hr.; 3pm-2am 600ptas per hr.).

🚹🛏 ACCOMMODATIONS AND FOOD. The tourist office provides a list of accommodations, most of which cluster around Pta. Purchena. There's an **Albergue Juvenil** (tel. 950 26 97 88) far outside the town center (35min. walk) on C. Isla Fuerteventura. From Pl. Estación, take C. Ronda, then left onto Av. Cabo de Gata. Continue straight as it becomes C. Bilbao, turn left onto C. Vinaroz, then right on C. Ubeda; Fuerteventura is on the left. (1300ptas per person, with 3 meals 2800ptas. Visa, MC.) Well-located, bright, and attractive, **Hostal Bristol,** Pl. San Sebastián, 8 (tel./fax 950 23 15 95), beside the church in Pta. Purchena, provides a TV and full bath in every room. (Call 1 week. in advance July-Aug. Singles 2700ptas; doubles 4500ptas. Visa, MC.)

Many cafes line Po. Almería. With ham chandeliers and over 70 types of *tapas* (all 100ptas), **Casa Puga,** C. Jovellanos, 7 (tel. 950 23 15 30), in the old quarter, packs them in (open M-Sa 11am-4pm and 8pm-midnight; Visa). **Augusto Cesare,** Parque Nicolás Salmerón, 17 (tel. 950 27 16 16), located along the water and down the street from the tourist office, has over 30 varieties of pizza (800-1300ptas; open Th-Tu 1-4pm and 8pm-1am). For groceries, browse the aisles of supermarket **Champon** (tel. 950 23 28 00), Po. Almería (open M-Sa 9:15am-9:15pm).

⌘ ♫ SIGHTS AND ENTERTAINMENT. Built in 995 by order of Abderramán III of Córdoba, the **Alcazaba,** a magnificent 14-acre Moorish fortress, spans two ridges overlooking the city and the sea. (From Pl. Carmen next to Pta. Purchena, follow C. Antonio Vico. Tel. 950 27 16 17. Open daily 10am-2pm and 5-8:30pm. 250ptas, free with EU passport. Guided night-tours in Spanish Tu-Th 9:15, 9:30, and 9:45pm.) The **cathedral,** in the old town, looks like a fortress due to repeated raids by Berber pirates. (Tel. 950 23 48 48. Open M-F 10am-5pm, Sa 10am-1pm. 300ptas.)

Nightlife congregates in the small streets behind the post office. A youthful crowd gathers in pub **Endanza,** while **Venue** (tel. 950 26 19 24) attracts booty-shakers with dance lessons Monday and Tuesday and live music some nights; both are on C. San Pedro off C. Padre Luque. At **Carpa,** a few miles east along the coastal road to Cabo de Gata, a half-dozen tented bars keep the beach party going all night long. Buses stop running around 11pm, but a taxi will go there for about 800ptas.

NEAR ALMERÍA: ■CABO DE GATA

Thirty kilometers east of urban Almería lies pristine **Parque Natural de Cabo de Gata-Níjar,** a 60km stretch of protected coast and inland environs. The near-desolate peninsula juxtaposes tropical and barren climates; flamingos flock to the area's salt marshes, while a desert and mountains farther inland have hosted a number of movie sets, including the *The Good, the Bad, and the Ugly.* **Grupo J. 126** (tel. 950 38 02 99) or **Ocio y Mar** (tel. 608 05 64 77) provide tourist information and guided tours of the park; contact them a day of two before arriving. Long, sandy shores await in the refreshingly low-key fishing town of **San Miguel de Cabo de Gata** (or simply **Cabo de Gata**). Farther south, the little resort of **San José** boasts one of the nicest beaches on the Spanish Mediterranean coast; it serves as serves a base for exploring the park. **Autocares Becerra** (tel. 950 22 44 03) sends buses from **Almería** to San Miguel de Cabo de Gata (1hr., every hr., 8am-9pm, 275ptas); **Autocares Bernardo** (tel. 950 25 04 22) runs to San José (45min., 3 per day, 350ptas).

MOJÁCAR

The houses of Mojácar rest on a hill, flanked by mountains of scorched earth and an expanse of turquoise Mediterranean. This small resort community thrives in July and August, when hordes of international visitors join the large contingent of expats who have made Mojácar their home. The abundance of souvenir shops and non-Spanish speakers have not diluted Mojácar's dramatic views.

⊓ ORIENTATION AND PRACTICAL INFORMATION. From the bus stop, follow the highway uphill for about 20 minutes; it eventually leads into Pl. Nueva, the town center. **Buses** leave for **Almería** (1½hr., M-Sa 4 per day, Su 3 per day, 880ptas) and **Murcia** (2½hr., 6 per day, 1400ptas). The **tourist office** (tel./fax 950 61 50 25), **post office,** and **police** are all in Pl. Nueva (tourist office open M-F 10am-2pm and 5-8pm, Sa 10am-1pm). The only reliable **ATM** can be found just below Pl. Nueva, at C. Glorieta, 3. The **Police** can be reached at tel. 950 47 20 00. **Postal code:** 046138.

⌐� ACCOMMODATIONS AND FOOD. Finding a bed in Mojácar can be difficult. To reach turn-of-the-century **Pensión Torreón,** C. Jazmín, 4 (tel. 950 47 52 59), from Pl. Nueva, follow C. Indalo, and take the second right on C. Enmedio, a left downhill along C. Unión, and a right at the end of this hill toward the hostel. Its five elegant bedrooms sit behind a breathtaking oceanview terrace. The owner can chat with you over breakfast about the mystery surrounding Walt Disney. (Doubles with shared bath 6000ptas.) To reach the intimate **Pensión La Luna,** C. Estación Nueva, 11 (tel. 950 47 80 32), walk up three flights of stairs from Pl. Nueva, continue straight ahead, and turn left at the ceramics shop past the church. The hike yields rooms complemented by spectacular mountain views. (Breakfast included. Doubles with full bath 6000ptas. Visa.) For eateries, you'll find more variety and better value in the old or new town than at the beach or in Pl. Nueva. **L'arlecchino**

IS IT A SMALL WORLD AFTER ALL?

Residents of Mojácar each tell their own mysterious version of the story of Walt Disney, whom they consider their most famous citizen. One rumor states that Disney was the product of an affair between a maid and the owner of Pensión Torreón; when his father died, Disney and his mother are said to have emigrated to California to avoid vicious gossip. Others believe that Mojacans José Guirao, Isabel Zamora, and their 12-year-old son José emigrated to California—along with many other agricultural families—during Mojácar's economic decline. Both stories state that Walt Disney was born José Guirao Zamora in 1901 in Mojácar and then migrated to California, where a farming family—the Disneys—adopted him after the death of his mother, renaming him Walt.

The story surfaced several years ago, when two American men arrived in the town to search of a birth certificate of the José Guirao Zamora. But it had mysteriously disappeared, thought to have been looted from the town hall during the Spanish Civil War. The men found no paper trace of José Guirao. Despite the absence of concrete proof, some villagers use Indalo Man to support their story. A cartoonesque figure drawn on nearby cave walls in Mojácar around 2500 BC, the Indalo Man holds a rainbow to ward off bad luck. Proud residents link Disney's success with cartoons to his native town's history of animation. They also stress that throughout his life, Disney was elusive about his upbringing. Unfortunately for Mojácar, encyclopedias say that Disney was born in 1901 in Chicago, Illinois. And while he is said to have lived in several midwestern towns as a child, there is no record of him living in either California or Spain.

(tel. 950 47 80 37), in Pl. Flores is through the Moorish arch off C. Puntica, and serves Italian and Spanish dishes on its scenic roof-top *terraza* (open daily noon-4pm and 7pm-midnight).

☎🏖 BEACHES AND ENTERTAINMENT. Mojácar's winding streets and breathtaking *miradores* (plazas with picture-perfect views) make it well-suited for romantic strolls and rosy daydreams. **Buses** run every hour between the town and beach and along the shore (9:45am-1:45pm and 3:45-11:45pm; 100ptas). In town, buses leave from the stop below Pl. Nueva. From the beach, get on at one of the stops along Av. Mediterránea.

Mojácar pulses with nightlife. **Budú Pub**, C. Estación Nueva, has a soaring rooftop terrace that may be the most romantic spot in Mojácar (open 10pm-3:30am). Along the shore, pubs turn into tented *chiringuitos* (beach bars). Go by car if you can, because buses stop running at 11pm, taxis disappear at sundown, and walking the highway is a poorly lit, dangerous alternative. Among the most popular pubs is **Pachá**, on Po. Mediterráneo, where palm trees shade the bar. The infamous **Tuareg**, on the road to Carboneras, has the highest decibel levels in town. For a midnight dip, the pool at **Master Disco** (tel. 950 46 81 33), on the highway between the beach and town, is open until 5am. Expats run more laid-back watering holes. **Time and Place**, in Pl. Flores, serves soothing cocktails, while Gordon pours Guinness and cultivates an intellectual atmosphere at **La Sartén** (a.k.a. Gordon's), on C. Estación Nueva, behind the church. **El Lord Azul**, C. Fronton, 1, plays blues and classic rock for an international crowd well into every night.

RONDA

Though the stomach-churning ascent is most people's first impression of Ronda (pop. 38,000), it's the effect on their hearts that's not soon forgotten. Everyone loves Ronda. This spectacular city, divided in two by a 100m gorge, was referred to as Arunda ("surrounded by mountains") by Pliny, Ptolemy, and pfriends, and the town was a pivotal commercial center under the Romans. In Moorish times, the Machiavellian Al Mutadid ibn Abbad annexed the town for Sevilla by asphyxiating the ruling lord in his bath. More recently, Ronda has attracted forlorn artistic types—German poet Rainer Maria Rilke wrote his *Spanish Elegies* here, and Orson Welles had his ashes buried on a bull farm outside of town. Only an hour and a half from the resorts of the Costa del Sol, Ronda draws streams of daytrippers to its numerous Moorish monuments, yet it manages to preserve a greater degree of authenticity than its more crowded neighbors. A welcome diversion in its own right, it also makes a convenient base for hiking, trekking, or exploring the *pueblos blancos* to the south.

▐ GETTING THERE

By **train** from: **Algeciras** (1½hr., 7 per day, 6:05am-9:30pm, 900-1400ptas); **Sevilla** (2½hr., 6 per day, 7am-5pm, 1235ptas). Or by **bus** from: **Marbella** (1½hr., 4 per day, 610ptas); **Jerez** (2¾hr., 4 per day, 7:45am-3:30pm, 1270ptas)

▐ ORIENTATION AND PRACTICAL INFORMATION

The 18th-century **Puente Nuevo** (new bridge) connects the city's old and new areas. On the new side of the city, **Carrera Espinel** (the main street, including the pedestrian-only walkway known as **Calle la Bola**) runs perpendicular to C. Virgen de la Paz. The **train** and **bus stations** are in the new city three blocks away from each other on Av. Andalucía. To reach the tourist office and the town center from the **train station,** turn right on Av. Andalucía and follow it through Pl. Merced past the **bus station** (it becomes C. San José) until it ends. Take a left on C. Jerez, and follow it past lush **Alameda del Tajo** (city park) and the bullring to **Plaza de España** and the new bridge. Cra. Espinel intersects C. Virgen de la Paz between the bullring and Pl. España. From the bus station, turn right and follow the directions above (10min.).

Trains: (tel. 95 287 16 73), Av. Alférez Provisional, near Av. Andalucía. **Ticket office,** C. Infantes, 20 (tel. 95 287 16 62). Open M-F 10am-2pm and 6-8:30pm. To **Algeciras** (2hr., 5 per day, 880ptas). Change at Bobadilla for: **Málaga** (2hr., 5 per day, 1225ptas); **Granada** (3hr., 3 per day, 1730ptas); **Sevilla** (3hr., 2 per day, 2155ptas).

Buses: Pl. Concepción García Redondo, 2 (tel. 95 218 70 61 or 95 287 22 62), near Av. Andalucía. To: **Marbella** (1½hr., 5 per day, 605ptas); **Málaga** (2½hr., 10 per day, 1075ptas); **Cádiz** (4hr., 3 per day, 1610ptas); **Sevilla** (5 per day, 1285ptas).

Taxis: (tel. 95 287 23 16). From the train station to the town center costs 350ptas.

Tourist Office: Pl. España, 1 (tel. 95 287 12 72). Info on Andalucía and helpful city map. Open M-F 9am-2pm and 4-7pm, Sa-Su 10am-3pm.

Currency Exchange: Banco Central Hispano , Cra. Espinel, 17, near C. Remedios. Open June-Sept. M-F 8:30am-2:30pm; Oct.-May M-F 8:30am-2:30pm, Sa 9am-1:30pm.

Luggage Storage: At the bus station (400ptas per day). Open daily 8am-10pm.

Emergency: tel. 091 or 092. **Police:** (tel. 95 287 13 69), Pl. Duquesa de Parcent.

Medical Services: Emergency Clinic: Notfall (tel. 95 287 58 52), C. Espinillo.

Post Office: C. Virgen de la Paz, 20 (tel. 95 287 25 57), across from Pl. Toros. Lista de Correos. Open M-F 8:30am-2:30pm, Sa 9:30am-1pm. **Postal Code:** 29400.

Internet Access: Zaidín Cervecería, C. Pozo, 11 (tel. 95 287 93 77), off Pl. Merced. Loud, lively bar. 600ptas for 30min., 800ptas per hr. Open daily 7-11pm.

▐ ACCOMMODATIONS AND FOOD

Most beds are concentrated in the new city near the bus station, along the streets perpendicular to Carrera Espinel—try C. Naranja and C. Lorenzo Borrego. Expect room shortages during the *Feria de Ronda* in first week in September.

Pensión Virgen del Rocio, C. Nueva, 18 (tel. 95 287 74 25), off Pl. España. Spacious, attractive rooms with baths. TV room. Breakfast 250ptas. Singles 2200-4500ptas; doubles 3500-5300ptas. Visa, MC.

Hostal Ronda Sol, C. Almendra, 11 (tel. 95 287 44 97). Brown house with brown bed-covers, matching the in-house chihuahua. Ask for a room overlooking the cool and leafy patio. Singles 1700ptas; doubles 2800ptas.

Ronda has a tons of restaurants and cafes, some of the best of which line the streets around Pl. España and those heading to Cra. Espinel. As usual, a menu in multiple languages can translate to only one thing: tourist trap.

Restaurante Royal, C. Virgen de la Paz, 40 (tel 95 287 46 43). Sit at the outside tables across the road and watch the waiters dodge traffic with your food. Large portions of tasty food. *Menú* 900ptas. Open daily noon-5pm and 7:30pm-midnight.

Cafe Mondragon, Pl. Mondragon, 6. In the old town, under the shade of an ancient tree between the church and the palace. *Bocadillos* 500ptas. Open daily 11am-10pm.

■ SIGHTS

BRIDGES. Ronda's precipitous gorge, carved by the Río Guadalevín, dips 100m below the **Puente Nuevo,** across from Pl. España. During the Civil War, political prisoners were cast into the canyon's depths from the bridge's midpoint. Two other structures bridge the unsettling gap: the innovative **Puente Viejo** was rebuilt in 1616 over an earlier Arab bridge, and the **Puente San Miguel** (a.k.a. **Puente Árabe**) is a prime Andalucian hybrid with a Roman base and Arab arches.

CASA DEL REY MORO. A colonnaded walkway leads to the Casa del Rey Moro (House of the Moorish King), which, notwithstanding its name and Moorish facade, dates from the 18th century. From the gardens in back, 365 zig-zagging steps descend to the spring, which once pumped in the town's water supply. Four hundred Christian prisoners were once employed in the arduous task of drawing water. *(C. Cuesta de Santo Domingo, 17. Open daily 10am-7pm. 600ptas.)*

PALACIO DEL MARQUÉS DE SALVATIERRA. Across the street from the Casa del Rey Moro, behind a forged iron balcony and a stone facade portraying four Peruvian Incas, stands the 18th-century Palacio del Marqués de Salvatierra. With spectacular antiques and gardens, it has belonged to the same family since 1485. *(Tel. 95 287 12 06. Open M-W and F-Sa 11am-2pm and 4-7pm, Th and Su 11am-2pm. 400ptas.)*

IGLESIA DE SANTA MARÍA. The Iglesia de Santa María la Mayor is a large 16th-century church crowned by a Renaissance belfry in the heart of Ronda's old city. The small arch just inside the entrance and the Qu'ranic verses behind the sacristy are the only vestiges of the mosque that was once here. A faint sign announces "*Julius Divo, Municipe,*" revealing the church's original incarnation as a church consecrated for Caesar. *(Off C. Marqués de Salvatierra. Tel. 95 287 22 46. Open daily 10am-7pm. 200ptas, groups 150ptas per person.)*

A WHOLE LOT OF BULL Bullfighting *aficionados* charge over to Ronda's **Plaza de Toros** (tel. 95 287 41 32), Spain's oldest bullring (est. 1785) and cradle of the modern *corrida*. The **Museo Taurino** inside tells the story of local hero Pedro Romero, the first matador to brave the beasts *a pie* (on foot), and to use the *muleta* (red cape). *(Open daily June-Sept. 10am-8pm; Oct.-May 10am-6pm. 400ptas.)* Romero killed his first bull at age 17 in 1771, the start of a glorious career: "From 1781-1799, it can be said that I killed in each year 200 bulls, whose sum totals 5600 bulls, yet I am persuaded that there may have been more." The museum displays heads of bulls, legendary for their ferocity, and bloodied matador shirts, including the shirt of Francisco Rivera ("Paquirri"), who was gored to death in 1984. Elaborate *trajes de luces,* the traditional costume of the bullfighter, are kept behind glass cases. An exhibit on 20th-century bullfighting showcases photos of Orson Welles, Ernest Hemingway, and their giddy fans. In early September, the Plaza de Toros hosts *corridas goyescas* (bullfights in traditional costumes) as part of the **Feria de Ronda.**

OTHER SIGHTS. Facing the east stands the **Minarete de San Sebastián,** part of a former mosque converted into a church after 1485, when Ronda was reconquered by the Christians. On the other side of the church lies the **Palacio de Mondragón,** once owned by Don Fernando Valenzuela, one of Carlos III's ministers. Its Baroque facade, bracketed by two Mudéjar towers, hides 15th-century Arab mosaics and displays about ancient life in Ronda. *(Tel. 95 287 84 50. Open M-F 10am-7pm, Sa-Su 10am-3pm. 250ptas, groups 150ptas per person, under 14 and handicapped free.)*

♫ ENTERTAINMENT

At night, the city congregates in pubs and *discotecas* along C. Jerez and the streets behind Pl. Socorro, including C. Pozo. **Disco-Bar Niágara,** C. Jerez, 17 (tel. 929 84 41 82), blasts its music in an aquatic atmosphere (open daily 4pm-late). For a more tranquil evening, head to **Tetería Al-Zahra,** C. Tiendas, 19 (tel. 95 287 16 98). The Islamic decor, floor pillows, and arched entryways invite long stays. Patrons sip over 100 types of tea from all over the world. (Open daily 4pm-late).

NEAR RONDA: CUEVAS DE LA PILETA

Twenty-two kilometers west of Ronda along the road to Sevilla are the **Cuevas de la Pileta** (tel. 95 216 73 43 or 95 216 72 02), a subterranean museum of bones, stalactites, stalagmites, and paleolithic paintings. Over 22,000 years ago, inhabitants colored the walls with enormous paintings of human figures, animals, and cryptic symbols. Among the most notable are the *Yegua preñada* (pregnant mare) and *Pez* (fish). In order to preserve the climate of the cave, only 25 people are admitted at a time. Wear comfortable shoes and dress warmly. Upon arrival at the caves, climb to the mouth to see if the guide is inside. If no one is around, walk to the farm below and rouse the owner, who'll make appropriate arrangements. (Open daily 10am-1pm and 4-6pm. Tours last 1¼hr. Groups of 1-4 950ptas per person, groups of 5-11 800ptas per person, groups of 12-25 700ptas per person.)

By **car,** take highway C-339 north (Ctra. Sevilla heading out of the new city). The turnoff to **Benaoján** and the caves is about 13km out of town, in front of an abandoned restaurant. Or take the **Los Amarillo bus** from Ronda to Benaoján (22min., 8:30am and 1pm, returns to Ronda 9am and 1pm, 195ptas). The approach through the Serranía de Ronda is stupendous as you wind through small Montajaque. Plan your return trip ahead of time, as there are no accommodations nearby.

ANTEQUERA

Few sunsets rival those from atop the old Moorish fortress at the crossroads of Andalucía; Antequera's (pop. 41,000) whitewashed houses spread out below. The Romans named Antequera, but older civilizations preceded them—pre-Roman *dólmenes* (funerary chambers built from rock slabs, the oldest in Europe) lie on the outskirts of town. To add to Antequera's allure, the **Sierra del Torcal,** a Mars-like wasteland of eroded rock, looms to the south, within easy striking distance. Wise travelers kick back here for a few days of inland visual splendor.

▛ GETTING THERE

Antequera can be reached by train from: **Granada** (2hr., 5 per day, 8:18am-5:25pm, 985ptas); **Sevilla** (2hr., 4 per day, 7:40am-5:40pm, 1570ptas). Or by bus from: **Málaga** (1hr., every hr., 525ptas); **Granada** (2hr., 5 per day, 3am-7pm, 910ptas).

▟ ORIENTATION AND PRACTICAL INFORMATION

From the train station, it's a 10-minute hike up a shadeless hill (Av. Estación) to the town center. At the top, continue straight past the market, turn right on C. Encarnación, and go past the Museo Municipal to reach **Plaza San Sebastían.** The **bus station** perches atop a neighboring hill. To reach Pl. San Sebastián from the bus station, walk downhill (to the right as you exit), pass the bullring to the round-about, and turn left onto Alameda de Andalucía. At the fork, follow C. Infante Don Fernando (the right branch) to the plaza. C. Encarnación connects Pl. San Sebastián to C. Calzada, which leads uphill to **Plaza San Francisco** and the market.

Trains: (tel. 95 284 32 26), on Av. Estación. To: **Málaga** (1½hr., 3 per day, 615ptas); **Ronda** (1½hr., 3 per day, 10:20am-7:15pm, 750ptas); **Granada** (2hr., 4 per day, 9:30am-8pm, 750-890ptas); **Sevilla** (2½hr., 5 per day, 9:30am-7pm, 1100-1420ptas); **Algeciras** (4hr., 3 per day, 10:20am-7:15pm, 1600ptas).

Buses: (tel. 95 284 13 65), on Po. García del Olmo, near the Parador Nacional. To: **Málaga** (45min., 3 per day, 9:30am-7pm, 475ptas); **Granada** (1hr., 5 per day, 6:30am-5:40pm, 910ptas); **Córdoba** (2¼hr., 2 per day, 9:45am and 5:45pm, 1095ptas); **Sevilla** (2¼hr., 5 per day, 8:45am-6:45pm, 1455ptas); **Jaén** (3hr., 1 per day, 3:45pm, 1445ptas); **Almería** (5hr., 2 per day, 2am and 9:30am, 2405ptas); **Murcia** (5½hr., 2 per day, 1am and 9:45am, 3225ptas).

Taxis: (tel. 95 284 10 76, 95 284 10 08, or 95 270 26 27). A cab from the center to the train or bus station costs 500ptas.

Tourist Office: Pl. San Sebastián, 7 (tel./fax 95 270 25 05). Super-helpful staff supplies free maps, transportation schedules, and info on Antequera. Open June-Aug. M-Sa 10am-2pm and 5-8pm; Sept.-May M-Sa 9:30am-1:30pm and 4-7pm, Su 10am-2pm.

Banks: Banco Central Hispano, C. Infante Fernando, 51 (tel. 95 284 04 61). Open June-Aug. M-F 8:30am-2:30pm; Sept.-May M-Sa 8:30am-2:30pm.

Emergency: tel. 091 or 092. **Police: Municipal** (tel. 95 270 81 04), on Av. Legión.

Pharmacy: on C. Encarnación, near C. Calzada. Open M-F 9:30am-1:30pm and 5-8:30pm, Sa 10am-1:30pm.

Hospital: Hospital General Básico, C. Infante Don Fernando, 67 (tel. 95 284 44 11).

Post Office: (tel. 95 284 20 83), C. Nájera. Lista de Correos. Open M-F 8am-2pm, Sa 9:30am-1pm. **Postal Code:** 29200.

ACCOMMODATIONS AND FOOD

Food and lodging in Antequera are generally cheap and splendid. Most establishments lie near C. Infante Don Fernando, between the Museo Municipal and the **market,** in Pl. San Francisco (open daily 8am-3pm). Try a nibble of the town's renowned *queso de cabra* (goat cheese). Ten-aisle **Mercadona,** C. Calzada, 18, has groceries (open M-Sa 9am-9pm; Visa, MC).

Pensión Toril, C. Toril, 3-5 (tel./fax 95 284 31 84), off Pl. San Francisco. Grandfatherly owner offers clean, bright rooms. Guests gather on patios to chat and play cards. Before sleep, feast downstairs—whopping entrees 500ptas, *menú* 800ptas, and generous drinks 100ptas. Singles 1200ptas, with bath 2000ptas; doubles 2400ptas, with bath 3000ptas. Meals served daily 1-4pm and 7:30-9:30pm.

Pensión Madrona, C. Calzada, 25 (tel. 95 284 00 14). Walk through Bar Madrona to the hostel. Newly renovated with A/C and heating in every room. This cozy, family-run hostel is filled with hand-made quilts. Restaurant/bar downstairs offers a tasty *menú* (850ptas). Singles 1600ptas, with bath 2600ptas; doubles with bath 3600ptas.

Hotel/Pensión Colón, C. Infante Don Fernando, 29 (tel. 95 284 00 10; fax 95 284 11 64). Spotless, classy joint with wood floors, un-upholstered furniture, and a labyrinth of rooms and hallways. Ritzy section has full baths, A/C, and TVs. Laundry service. Singles 1070-2200ptas, with bath 2675-3200ptas; doubles 2140-3200ptas, with bath 3850-4800ptas. Visa, MC, AmEx.

La Espuelados, C. San Agustín, 1 (tel. 95 284 13 45), on a narrow street off C. Infante Don Fernando. Pizza 650-1200ptas. Pasta (700-950ptas). Veggie options 600-1000ptas. *Menú* 1000ptas. Open daily noon-4pm and 8-11:30pm. Visa, MC.

Manolo Bar, C. Calzada, 14 (tel. 95 284 10 15), downhill from the market. Filled with Wild West paraphernalia and good-humored patrons. Ultra-cheap *tapas* (100ptas) may cost more if the staff finds you impolite. Open Tu-Th 4:30-11:30pm, F-Sa 4:30pm-3am.

La Espuela (tel./fax 95 270 26 76), in Pl. Toros. The only restaurant in the world *inside* a bullring. Not surprisingly, the prize-winning kitchen's specialty is *rabo de toro* (bull's tail). *Menú* 1800-2400ptas, worth it if you have the money. Open daily 1-4pm. Visa, MC.

■ SIGHTS

■**CUEVAS DE DÓLMENES.** Antequera's three ancient Cuevas de Dólmenes are the oldest in Europe. Giant rock slabs form the antechamber (storeroom for the dead's possessions) and burial chamber. Hefty ancients lugged the mammoth 200-ton roof of the **Cueva de Menga** (2500 BC) over five miles to the burial site. The four figures engraved on the chamber walls typify Mediterranean Stone Age art. The elongated **Cueva de Viera** (2000 BC), discovered in 1905, is also oversized—and dark. Bring a flashlight. Small, flat stones cement the circular interior walls and domed ceiling of **Cueva de Romeral** (1800 BC). *(To reach the Cuevas de Menga and Viera, follow the signs toward Granada from the town center (20min.) and watch for a small sign on C. Granada just past the gas station. To reach Cueva de Romeral from the other cuevas, continue on the highway to Granada for another 3km. Just past Almacenes Gómez, one of the last warehouses after the flowered intersection, a gravel road cuts left and bumps into a narrow path bordered by tall fir trees. Take this path across the train tracks to reach the cave. All three open Tu 10am-2pm, W-F 9am-3:30pm, Sa 9am-3pm, Su 9:30am-2pm.)*

OTHER SIGHTS. Back in town, all that remains of the **Alcazaba** are its two towers, the wall between them, and well-trimmed hedges. The view of the city is tremendous. Next to it, the towering **Colegiata de Santa María** was the first church in Andalucía to incorporate Renaissance style. *(Both open W-Su 10am-2pm. Free.)* The plaza in front of the church offers views of the massive **Peña de los enamorados (Lovers' Rock),** which looks exactly like the Sphinx lying down (tilt your head sideways). Legend has it that a Christian man and his Moorish girlfriend, fearing separation by invading soldiers, leaped to their deaths from atop the rock. Downhill, the **Museo Municipal** exhibits avant-garde 1970s paintings by native son Cristóbal Toral alongside dozens of Roman artifacts, including the graceful **Efebo,** a rare bronze statue of a Roman page; the postcards don't do him justice. *(Tel. 95 270 40 21. Open Tu-F 10am-1:30pm, Sa 10am-1pm, Su 11am-1pm. 200ptas.)*

NEAR ANTEQUERA: SIERRA DE TORCAL

A garden of wind-sculpted boulders, the Sierra de Torcal glows like the surface of a barren and distant planet. The central peak of **El Torcal** (1369m) spans over most of the horizon, but the smaller clumps of eroded rocks are even more extraordinary. Several trails circle the summit. The green arrow path (1.5km) takes about 45 minutes; the red arrow path (4.5km) takes over two hours. All but the green path require a guided tour; call the **Centro de Información** (tel. 95 203 13 89) for more details (open M-Su 10am-2pm and 3:30-5:30pm). Each path begins and ends 13km from Antequera at the *refugio* (lodge) at the mountain base. Two-thirds of the 13km can be covered by **bus;** ask the driver to let you off at the turnoff for El Torcal (repeat: "*¿Usted me puede dejar en el cruce para El Torcal?*") Buses leave from Antequera (M-F at 1 and 7pm, 170ptas); the return bus leaves from the turnoff (M-F at 4:15pm). Call **Casado buses** (tel. 95 284 19 57) for details. An easier, pricier way to go is by taxi to the *refugio* (round-trip 2700ptas). The driver will wait for an hour, giving you time to catch the sunset.

GRANADA

When Moorish ruler Boabdil fled Granada, the last Muslim stronghold in Spain, his mother berated him for casting a longing look back at the Alhambra, saying, "Weep like a woman for what you could not defend like a man." The Alhambra, a spectacular palace-fortress complex, continues to inspire melancholy in those who must depart from its timeless beauty. The age-old saying holds true: *"Si has muerto sin ver la Alhambra no has vivido"* (If you have died without seeing the Alhambra, you have not lived).

Conquered by invading Muslim armies in 711, Granada eventually blossomed into one of Europe's wealthiest, most refined cities. As Christian armies turned back the tide of Moorish conquest in the 13th century, Granada became the last Muslim outpost on the peninsula, surrounded by a unified Christian kingdom. In the latter decades of the 15th century, Fernando and Isabel's troops continually besieged the city. Meanwhile, ruling Sultan Moulay Abul Hassan, obsessing over one of his concubines, ignored his civic duties. When Queen Aïcha caught on, she drummed up local support, had her husband deposed, and thrust her young son Boabdil on the throne. Fernando and Isabel capitalized on the disarray by capturing Boabdil and the Alhambra on the momentous night of January 1, 1492. Although the Christians torched all the mosques and the lower city, embers of Granada's Arab essence still linger. The Albaícin, an enchanting maze of Moorish houses and twisting alleys, is Spain's best-preserved Arab settlement and the only part of the Muslim city to survive the Reconquest intact.

▐ GETTING THERE

Trains go to Granada from: **Sevilla** (3½hr., 5 per day, 7:40am-5:40pm, 2610ptas); **Valencia** (8½hr., 3 per day, 11:30am-10:25pm, 4900-6300ptas); **Madrid** (9hr., 3 per day, 8am-11pm, 3300-4600ptas); **Barcelona** (12½hr., 3 per day, 8am-7pm, 6200-8100ptas). **Buses** arrive from: **Málaga** (2hr., every hr., 1200ptas); **Córdoba** (3hr., 8 per day, 1515-1635ptas); **Sevilla** (3 hr., 9 per day, 8am-11pm, 2400ptas).

▐ ORIENTATION AND PRACTICAL INFORMATION

Municipal **buses** (see **Public Transportation,** below) cover practically the entire city, but the best way to explore is on foot. The geographic center of Granada is the small **Plaza de Isabel la Católica,** the intersection of the city's two main arteries, **Calle de los Reyes Católicos** and **Gran Vía de Colón.** To reach Gran Vía from the **RENFE station,** walk 3 blocks up Av. Andaluces to Av. Constitución, and take bus #3, 4, 5, 6, 9, or 11. From the bus station, take bus #3. On Gran Vía, you'll find the **catedral.** Two short blocks uphill on C. Reyes Católicos sits Pl. Nueva. Downhill, also along C. Reyes Católicos, lie Pl. Carmen, site of the **Ayuntamiento,** and Puerta Real, the six-way intersection of C. Reyes Católicos, C. Recogidos, C. Mesones, C. Acera de Darro, C. Angel Gavinet, and C. Acero del Casino. The **Alhambra** commands the steep hill up from Pl. Nueva.

TRANSPORTATION

Flights: Airport (tel. 958 24 52 37 or 958 24 52 38), 17km west of the city. A **Salidas** bus (tel. 958 13 13 09) runs from Gran Vía, in front of the cathedral (M-Sa 5 per day, 8:15am-5:30pm; Su 2 per day, 5:30 and 7pm; 425ptas). A **Taxi** to the airport costs 2000ptas. **Iberia** (tel. 958 22 75 92) to **Madrid** (45min., 2-3 per day) and **Barcelona** (1¼hr., 2-3 per day). Open M-F 9am-1:45pm and 4-7pm.

Trains: RENFE Station (tel. 958 27 12 72), Av. Andaluces. From Pl. Isabel la Católica, follow Gran Vía to the end, then bear left on Av. Constitución; or take bus #3, 4, 5, 6, 9, or 11 from Gran Vía to the stop marked Constitución 3. Turn left on Av. Andaluces; RENFE is at the end. To: **Antequera** (2hr., 5 per day, 8:18am-5:26pm, 985ptas); **Almería** (3hr., 4 per day, 10:55am-8:15pm, 1740ptas); **Ronda** (3-4hr., 3 per day, 1510-1710ptas); **Sevilla** (4-5hr., 5 per day, 8:18am-5:26pm, 2610ptas); **Madrid** (5-6hr., 2 per day, 3:40 and 11:15pm, 3200ptas); **Algeciras** (5-7hr., 3 per day, 2375ptas); **Cádiz** (7hr., 3 per day, 3595ptas); **Barcelona** (12-13hr., 2 per day, 6400ptas).

Buses: All major bus routes originate from the new bus station on the outskirts of Granada on Ctra. Madrid, near C. Arzobispo Pedro de Castro.

Alsina Graells (tel. 958 18 50 10) to: **Jaén** (1½hr., 15 per day, 900ptas); **Antequera** (2hr., 5 per day, 3am-7pm, 910ptas); **Málaga** (2hr., 16 per day, 7am-10pm, 1180ptas); **Almería** (2¼hr., 10 per day, 6:45am-7:30pm, 1300ptas); **Córdoba** (3hr., 9 per day, 7:30am-8pm, 1515ptas); **Sevilla** (3hr., 9 per day, 8am-3am, 2350ptas); **Cádiz** (4hr., 2 per day, noon and 3:30pm, 3650ptas); **La Línea** (4hr., 10 per day, 8am-12:45am, 2445ptas); **Algeciras** (5hr., 6 per day, 9am-8pm, 2550ptas); **Madrid** (5hr., 10 per day, 1945ptas). Also run to **Alpujarra** villages (3 per day, 10:30am, noon, and 5:15pm).

Bacoma (tel. 958 15 75 57) to: **Alicante** (6hr., 5 per day, 3375ptas); **Valencia** (8hr., 4 per day, 4910ptas); **Barcelona** (14hr., 3 per day, 7915ptas). All buses run 10:15am-1:45am.

Autocares Bonal (tel. 958 27 31 00) sends one bus per day to **Veleta** from Palacio de Congresos. Follow C. Acera de Darro from Pta. Real across the river to Po. Violón, or take bus #1 from Gran Vía to the last stop. Tickets sold daily 8:30-9am at Ventorillo Bar across from the *palacio*. Bus departs from the bar at 9am, returns from Veleta at 5:30pm (45min., round-trip 700ptas).

Public Transportation: (tel. 958 81 37 11). Important buses are: "Bus Alhambra" from Pl. Nueva; #10 from the bus station to the youth hostel, Camino de Ronda, C. Recogidas, and C. Acera de Darro; and #3 from the bus station to Av. Constitución, Gran Vía, and Pl. Isabel la Católica. All buses 120ptas, *bonobus* (15 tickets) 1000ptas. Handy free map at the tourist office.

Taxis: (tel. 958 28 06 54 or 958 13 23 23). Taxis abound at Pl. Nueva and Pl. Trinidad.

Car Rental: Atasa, Pl. Cuchilleros, 1 (tel. 958 22 40 04; fax 958 22 77 95). Cheapest car 46,000ptas per week with unlimited mileage and insurance. Prices rise with shorter rentals. Must be at least 20 and have had a license for at least 1 year.

TOURIST AND FINANCIAL SERVICES

Tourist Office: Oficina Provincial, Pl. Mariana Pineda, 10 (tel. 958 22 66 88; fax 958 22 89 16; email turismo@mail.valnet.es; www.dipgra.es). From Pta. Real, turn right onto C. Angel Ganivet, then take a right 2 blocks later to reach the plaza. Possibly the most helpful office in Andalucía. Free maps, posters, and brochures. English spoken. Open M-F 9:30am-7pm, Sa 10am-2pm. **Junta de Andalucía** (tel. 958 22 10 22; fax 958 22 39 27), C. Mariana Pineda. From Pta. Real, take C. Reyes Católicos to Pl. Carmen; C. Mariana Pineda is the 1st left. Free maps, hotel guide (800ptas) and brochures on hiking, hunting, and golf (400ptas). Open M-Sa 9am-7pm, Su 10am-2pm.

Currency Exchange: Banco Central Hispano, Gran Vía, 3 (tel. 958 21 73 00), off Pl. Isabel la Católica. Exchanges money and AmEx traveler's checks without commission. Open May-Sept. M-F 9am-2pm; Oct.-Apr. M-Sa 9am-2pm.

American Express: C. Reyes Católicos, 31 (tel. 958 22 45 12), between Pl. Isabel la Católica and Pta. Real. Exchanges money, cashes checks, and holds mail for members. Open M-F 9:30am-1:30pm and 2-8pm, Sa 10am-2pm and 3-7pm, Su 9am-2pm.

LOCAL SERVICES

Luggage Storage: At the train and bus stations (400ptas). Open daily 4-9pm.

El Corte Inglés: (tel. 958 22 32 40), C. Geril. Follow C. Acera del Casino from Pta. Real onto the tree-lined road. Thorough map 475ptas. Open M-Sa 10am-10pm.

Foreign Language Bookstore: Librería Flash (tel. 958 52 11 90), Pl. Trinidad. Modest selection in several languages. Open M-F 10am-2pm and 5-9pm, Sa 10am-2pm.

Laundromat: C. La Paz, 19. From Pl. Trinidad, take C. Alhóndiga, turn right on C. La Paz, and walk 2 blocks. Wash 400ptas per load; dry 100ptas for 15min. Open M-F 9:30am-2pm and 4:30-8:30pm, Sa 9am-2pm.

Swimming Pool: Piscina Neptuno (tel. 958 25 88 21), next to flamenco club Jardines Neptuno and near the intersection of C. Recogidas and Camino de Ronda. M-Sa 600ptas, Su 800ptas, children 400ptas. Open June-Sept. daily 11am-7:30pm.

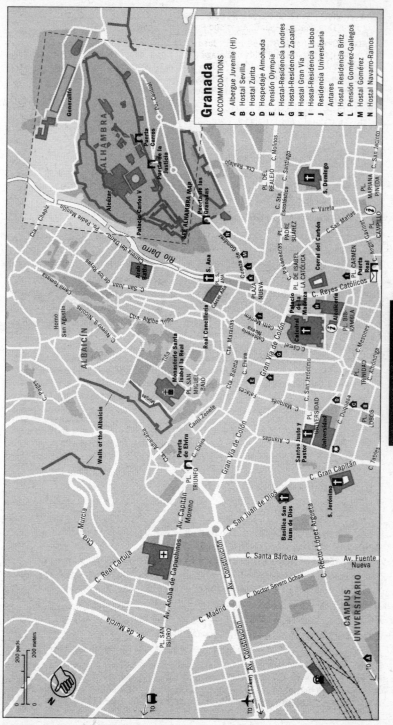

ANDALUCÍA

Granada
ACCOMMODATIONS

A Albergue Juvenile (HI)
B Hostal Sevilla
C Hostal Zurita
D Hospedaje Almohada
E Pensión Olympia
F Hostal-Residencia Londres
G Hostal-Residencia Zacatin
H Hostal Gran Vía
I Hostal-Residencia Lisboa
J Residencia Universitaria
  Antares
K Hostal Residencia Britz
L Pensión Gomérez-Gallegos
M Hostal Gomérez
N Hostal Navarro-Ramos

EMERGENCY AND COMMUNICATIONS

Emergency: tel. 091 or 092. **Police:** C. Duquesa, 21 (tel. 958 24 81 00). English spoken.

Pharmacy: Farmacia Gran Vía, Gran Vía, 6 (tel 958 22 29 90). Open M-F 9:30am-2pm and 5-8:30pm.

Medical Assistance: Clínica de San Cecilio, C. Dr. Oloriz, 16 (tel. 958 28 02 00 or 958 27 20 00), on the road to Jaén. **Ambulance:** tel. 958 28 44 50.

Post Office: (tel. 958 22 48 35; fax 958 22 36 41), Pta. Real, on the corner of C. Acera de Darro and C. Angel Ganinet. Lista de Correos and **faxes.** Open M-F 8am-9pm, Sa 9:30am-2pm. Wires money M-F 8:30am-2:30pm. **Postal Code:** 18009.

Internet Access: Madar Internet, C. Caldevera Nueva, 12 (tel. 656 48 69 93). Open M-Sa 10am-midnight, Su noon-midnight. 400ptas per hr., students 300ptas. **Net,** C. Santa Ecolástica, 13 (tel. 958 22 69 19), up C. Pavaneras from Pl. Isabel la Católica. English spoken. 400ptas per hr. Open M-Sa 9am-11pm, Su 4-11pm.

▶ ACCOMMODATIONS AND CAMPING

Granada has more cheap accommodations than shoe stores. Finding lodgings is a problem only during *Semana Santa* when you must call ahead.

NEAR PLAZA NUEVA

Hostels line Cuesta de Gomérez, the street leading uphill to the Alhambra, to the right of Pl. Nueva. Crashing in this area is wise for those planning to spend serious time at the Alhambra complex, but these spots tend to fill up the quickest.

■ **Hostal Residencia Britz,** Cuesta de Gomérez, 1 (tel. 958 22 36 52), on the corner of Pl. Nueva. Large rooms with luxurious beds and green-tiled bathrooms. Laundry 600ptas. 24hr. reception. Singles 2300ptas; doubles 3900ptas, with bath 5400ptas. 6% discount for *Let's Go* readers if you pay in cash and show them the book. Visa, MC.

Hostal Gomérez, Cuesta de Gomérez, 10 (tel. 958 22 44 37). Clean rooms with firm beds. Multilingual (English, French, and Italian) owner will assist guests planning longer stays. Laundry 1000ptas per load. Singles 1600ptas; doubles 2700ptas; triple 3700ptas. 100-200pta *Let's Go* discount in the off-season.

Pensión Gomérez-Gallegos, Cuesta de Gomérez, 2, 3rd fl. (tel. 958 22 63 98). Small hostel with large rooms, some balconies, and numerous drooping plants. One clean and roomy shared bath. Ask about discounts on longer stays. Singles 1500-1800ptas; doubles 3000-3500ptas; triples 5000ptas.

Hostal Navarro-Ramos, Cuesta de Gomérez, 21 (tel. 958 25 05 55). Comfortable and cool in the evening. Small balconies in some rooms. Showers 150ptas. Singles 1575ptas; doubles 2500ptas, with bath 3900ptas; triples with bath 5300ptas.

NEAR THE CATHEDRAL/UNIVERSITY

The area along C. Mesones and C. Alhóndiga is close to the cathedral, Pta. Real, and Pl. Isabel la Católica. Hostels cluster around Pl. Trinidad, a cozy square at the end of C. Mesones when coming from Pta. Real. Many *pensiones* around C. Mesones cater to students during the academic year but free up during the summer. The ones listed below are open year-round.

■ **Hospedaje Almohada,** C. Postigo de Zarate, 4 (tel. 958 20 74 46). Walk 1 block from Pl. Trinidad along C. Duquesa; it's to the right down C. Málaga (no sign, but a big red door). A successful experiment in communal living: guests enjoy socializing in the court-yard, living room, and kitchen. Laundry 500ptas per load. Singles 1800ptas; doubles 3500ptas. Longer stays common and encouraged (33,000-36,000ptas per month).

■ **Hostal Zurita,** Pl. Trinidad, 7 (tel. 958 27 50 20). Beautiful rooms, high-quality beds, remote-controlled A/C, and 24hr. hot water. Double-paned balconies keep out noise, while the chirping of Zurita's many caged birds soothes the soul. Singles 1875ptas; doubles 3750ptas, with bath 5000ptas; triples 5000ptas, with bath 5500ptas.

Hostal-Residencia Zacatín, C. Ermita, 11 (tel. 958 22 11 55). Enter through the Alcaicería archway from C. Reyes Católicos; C. Ermita is on the left. Ideal location. Rooms are amply sized; baths are immense. Singles 1700ptas, with bath 2500ptas; doubles 3000ptas, with shower 3400ptas, with bath 4100ptas.

Hostal-Residencia Lisboa, Pl. Carmen, 29 (tel. 958 22 14 13 or 958 22 14 14; fax 958 22 14 87). Take C. Reyes Católicos from Pl. Isabel la Católica; Pl. Carmen is on the left. Rooms have phones and fans. Singles 2600ptas, with bath 3900ptas; doubles 3900ptas, with bath 5600ptas; triples 5200ptas, with bath 7500ptas. Visa, MC.

Hostal Sevilla, C. Fábrica Vieja, 18 (tel. 958 27 85 13). From Pta. Real, follow C. Alhóndiga into C. Fábrica Vieja. Spotless, well-furnished, and cool rooms. Singles 2000ptas, with bath 2700ptas; doubles 3000ptas, with bath 4200ptas; triples 4500ptas.

ALONG GRAN VÍA DE COLÓN

Hostels are sprinkled along Gran Vía. In all cases, rooms with balconies over the street are much noisier than those that open onto an inner patio.

■ **Residencia Universitaria Antares,** C. Cetti Meriém, 10 (tel. 958 22 83 13), on the corner of C. Elvira, 1 block from Gran Vía. Spotless and cheap in a great location, 1 block from the cathedral. All rooms have balconies and sinks, and there are plenty of shared bathrooms. Winter heating. Singles 1500ptas; doubles 3000ptas; triples 4500ptas.

Hostal Gran Vía, Gran Vía, 17 (tel. 958 27 92 12), about 4 blocks from Pl. Isabel la Católica. Clean, bright rooms. Singles with shower 2500ptas; doubles 3000ptas, with shower 3500ptas, with bath 4000ptas; triples with bath 6000ptas.

Hostal-Residencia Londres, Gran Vía, 29, 5th fl. (tel. 958 27 80 34). Pretty rooms and a big patio with views of the Alhambra. 1 large bathroom for every 2 bedrooms. Singles 2500ptas; doubles 3200ptas; 1500ptas per additional person.

Pensión Olympia, Alvaro de Bazán, 6 (tel. 958 27 82 38). From Pl. Isabel, walk 6 blocks down Gran Vía and make a right. The cheaper version of Hostal Gran Vía (with the same owner). Communal bathrooms. Singles 2000ptas; doubles 3000ptas.

ELSEWHERE

Albergue Juvenil Granada (HI), Ramón y Cajal, 2 (tel. 958 27 26 38 or 958 28 43 06; fax 958 28 52 85). From the bus station take bus #10; from the train station #11; ask the driver to stop at "El Estadio de la Juventud." It's the peach building across the field on the left. Spacious rooms with comfortable beds. All rooms are either doubles with baths or triples. 24hr. reception. Towels 175ptas. Dorms 1300ptas, over 26 1600ptas; to join non-HI guests can pay an extra 300ptas per night for 6 nights.

CAMPING

Buses serve five campgrounds within 5km of Granada. Check the departure schedules at the tourist office, sit up front, and ask bus drivers to alert you to your stop.

Sierra Nevada, Av. Madrid, 107 (tel. 958 15 00 62, fax 958 15 09 54). Take bus #3 or 10. Lots of shady trees, modern facilities, and free hot showers. If you arrive when the town fair is here, stay elsewhere or you'll have clown nightmares. 560ptas per person, per tent, and per vehicle. Children under 10 460ptas. Open Mar.-Oct.

María Eugenia, Ctra. Nacional, 342 (tel. 958 20 06 06), at km 436 on the road to Málaga. Take the Santa Fé or Chauchina bus from the train station (every 30min.). 425ptas per person, per tent, and per car. Children 325ptas. Open year-round.

Los Alamos (tel. 958 20 84 79), next door to María Eugenia. Showers 50ptas. 1300ptas per person, per tent, and per car. Children 300ptas. Open Apr.-Oct.

ANDALUCÍA

⬛ FOOD

Granada offers a variety of ethnic restaurants to emancipate your taste buds from the fried-fish-and-pig-products doldrums. Cheap and tasty North African cuisine can be found in and around the **Albaicín**. Near Pl. Nueva and Pl. Trinidad, the usual *menú* fare awaits. The adventurous eat well in Granada—*tortilla sacromonte* (omelette with calf's brains, bull testicles, ham, shrimp, and veggies), *sesos a la romana* (batter-fried calf's brains), and *rabo de toro* (bull's tail) are common. Picnickers can gather fresh fruit and vegetables at the **market** on C. San Augustín. Get groceries at **Supermercado T. Mariscal**, C. Genil, next to El Corte Inglés (open M-F 9:30am-2pm and 5-9pm, Sa 9:30am-2pm).

NEAR PLAZA NUEVA

The places around Pl. Nueva are great stops on a *tapas* route. *Tapas* are **free** in Granada (with a drink).

La Nueva Bodega, C. Cetti Meriém, 9 (tel. 958 22 59 34), out of Pl. Nueva on a small side street off C. Elvira. Popular with locals and tourists. *Menús* 825-1400ptas. *Bocadillos* 300ptas. Open daily noon-midnight.

Bodega Mancha, C. Joaquin Costa, 10, and **Bodega Castañeda**, C. Almireceros 1-3, are off C. Elvira leading from Pl. Nueva. Drink and eat with the local good old boys. *Bocadillos* (under 300ptas) and *tapas* are the preferred fare in these dens of Dionysus. The pork aroma unsettles the stomach more than the wine and sherry (175-200ptas). Both open daily 8am-4pm and 6pm-1am, Sa-Su noon-4pm and 6pm-3am.

Restaurante Boabdil (tel. 958 22 81 36). Serves lunch and dinner in a little outdoor nook on C. Elvira. A variety of entrees (725ptas) includes staples like *paella* and macaroni and cheese. Open F-W 1-5pm and 8pm-midnight, Th 8pm-midnight. Visa, MC.

Restaurante Alcaicería, C. Oficios, 6 (tel. 958 22 43 41), between the cathedral and C. Reyes Católicos. Eat outdoor in a corner of the souvenir market. *Menú* 1500ptas, entrees 750-2000ptas. Open daily noon-4pm and 8pm-midnight. Visa, MC.

THE ALBAICÍN

Wander the romantic, winding streets of the Albaicín and you'll discover a number of budget bars and restaurants on the slopes above Pl. Nueva. C. Calderería Nueva, off C. Elvira leading from the plaza, is crammed with teahouses and cafes.

▨ **Naturi Albaicín,** C. Calderería Nueva, 10 (tel. 958 22 06 27). Excellent vegetarian cuisine by the owner who wrote the book on "healthy living." Tasty options include *berenjenas rellenas* (stuffed eggplant), quiche, and *kefir* (a yogurt drink). *Menús* 950-1150ptas. Open Sa-Th 1-4pm and 7-11pm, F 7-11pm.

Las Cuevas, Placeta de San Gregorio, 30, (tel. 958 22 68 33), at the top of C. Calderería Nueva. A delightful selection of local entrees served at outdoor tables. Entrees 650-900ptas, *raciones* 600-1200 ptas. Open daily noon-4am.

El Ladrillo II (tel. 958 29 26 51), C. Panaderos, off Cuesta del Chapiz near the Iglesia El Salvador, high on the Albaicín. Consume immense rations of delicious, fresh seafood to the sound of *sevillanas*. Thunderous evening hangout. Open daily 12:30pm-1:30am.

Los Chirimías (tel. 619 96 28 79), Po. Padre Manjón, up C. Acera de Darro from Pl. Nueva. Pizzas 550-775ptas, *menú* 775-2250ptas. Open daily 12:30pm-2am.

Medina-Zahara, C. Calderería Nueva, 12 (tel. 958 22 15 41). Mediterranean take-out joint makes delicious samosas (275-325ptas) and falafel (325ptas).

GRAN VÍA

Restaurante Chino Estrella Oriental, C. Alvaro de Bazán, 9 (tel. 958 22 34 67), 5 blocks down Gran Vía from Pl. Isabel la Católica. Bright-red Pagoda facade welcomes all to cheap, tasty *menús* (695ptas). Free delivery with order of 1500ptas or more. Open daily 12:30-4:30pm and 8pm-12:30am. Visa, MC.

THE ALHAMBRA COMPLEX

> Give him alms, woman!
> For there is nothing crueler in life
> than to be blind in Granada.
> —Francisco de Icaza, inscribed in the Torre de la Pólvora

From the streets of Granada, the Alhambra appears simple, blocky, faded—a child's toy castle planted in the foothills of the Sierra Nevada. Up close, however, you will discover an astoundingly elaborate and detailed piece of architecture; one that magically meshes water, light, carved wood, stucco, ceramics, and sheepskin paintings to create a fortress-palace of rich aesthetic and symbolic grandeur. *(Take C. Cuesta de Gomérez off Pl. Nueva, and be prepared to pant (20min.; no unauthorized cars 9am-9pm). Or take the cheap, quick Alhambra-Neptuno microbus (every 15min., 120ptas) from Pl. Isabel la Católica or Pl. Nueva. Tel. 958 22 15 03; fax 958 21 05 84. Open Apr.-Sept. daily 8:30am-8pm; Oct.-Mar. M-Sa 9am-5:45pm. Nighttime visits June-Sept. T, Th, and Sa 10-11:30pm; Oct.-May Sa 8-10pm. 1000ptas, free for the handicapped and children under 8. Limited to 8400 visitors per day June-Sept., 6800 Oct.-May, so get there early to stand in line. Enter the Palace of the Nazarites (Alcázar) during the time specified on your ticket, but stay as long as desired.)*

THE ALCAZABA. The Christians drove the first Nazarite King Alhamar from the Albaicín to this more strategic hill. There he built the fortress Alcazaba, the section of the Alhambra with the oldest recorded history. A dark, spiraling staircase leads to the **Torre de la Vela** (watchtower), where visitors get a great 360° view of Granada and the surrounding mountains. The tower's bells were rung to warn of

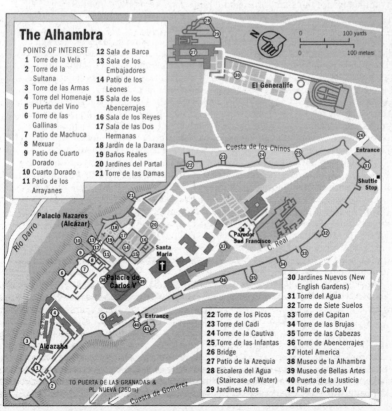

The Alhambra

POINTS OF INTEREST
1 Torre de la Vela
2 Torre de la Sultana
3 Torre de las Armas
4 Torre del Homenaje
5 Puerta del Vino
6 Torre de las Gallinas
7 Patio de Machuca
8 Mexuar
9 Patio de Cuarto Dorado
10 Cuarto Dorado
11 Patio de los Arrayanes
12 Sala de Barca
13 Sala de los Embajadores
14 Patio de los Leones
15 Sala de los Abencerrajes
16 Sala de los Reyes
17 Sala de las Dos Hermanas
18 Jardín de la Daraxa
19 Baños Reales
20 Jardines del Partal
21 Torre de las Damas
22 Torre de los Picos
23 Torre del Cadi
24 Torre de la Cautiva
25 Torre de las Infantas
26 Bridge
27 Patio de la Azequia
28 Escalera del Agua (Staircase of Water)
29 Jardines Altos
30 Jardines Nuevos (New English Gardens)
31 Torre del Agua
32 Torre de Siete Suelos
33 Torre del Capitan
34 Torre de las Brujas
35 Torre de las Cabezas
36 Torre de Abencerrajes
37 Hotel America
38 Museo de la Alhambra
39 Museo de Bellas Artes
40 Puerta de la Justicia
41 Pilar de Carlos V

ANDALUCÍA

impending danger and to coordinate the Moorish irrigation system. During an annual festival, custom dictates that any local girl who scrambles up the tower and rings the bell by hand will receive a wedding proposal within a year. Exit through the **Puerta del Vino** (wine gate), the original entrance to the medina, where inhabitants of the Alhambra once bought tax-free wine (alas, no more).

THE ALCÁZAR. Follow signs to the *Palacio Nazaries* to see the Alcázar, a royal palace built for the Moorish rulers Yusuf I (1333-1354) and Muhammed V (1354-1391). An unexplained force allegedly murdered Yusuf I in an isolated basement chamber of the Alcázar; his son Muhammed V was left to complete the palace.

The entrance leads into the **Mexuar,** a great pillared council chamber. Note the glazed tile arrangements that reiterate the Nazarite mantra: "There is no victor but God." The Mexuar adjoins the **Patio del Cuarto Dorado (Patio of the Gilded Hall).** Off the far side of the patio, foliated horseshoe archways of diminishing width open onto the **Cuarto Dorado (Gilded Hall),** decorated by Muhammed V. Its painstakingly carved wooden ceiling, inlaid with ivory and mother-of-pearl, displays polygonal figures and colorful ceramic *dados.*

Next is the **Patio de los Arrayanes (Courtyard of Myrtles),** an expanse of emerald water filled with goldfish and bubbling fountains. Stand at the top of the patio for a glimpse of the 14th-century **Fachada de Serallo,** the palace's elaborately carved facade. The long and slender **Sala de la Barca (Boat Gallery),** with an inverted boat-hull ceiling, flanks the courtyard.

In the elaborate **Sala de los Embajadores (Hall of Ambassadors),** adjoining the Sala de la Barca to the north, Fernando and Columbus discussed finding a new route to India. Every surface of this magnificent square hall is intricately wrought with symbolic inscriptions and ornamental patterns. The dome, carved of over 8000 pieces of wood and inlaid cedar, depicts the seven skies of paradise mentioned in the Qu'ran (the ceiling style is called *mozárabe*).

From the Patio de los Arrayanes, the Sala de los Mocárabes leads to the **Patio de los Leones (Courtyard of the Lions),** the grandest display of Nazarite art in the palace. The grandeur continues: a rhythmic arcade of arches and marble columns borders the courtyard, and a fountain supported by 12 marble lions babbles in the middle.

Moving counter-clockwise around the courtyard, the next room is the **Sala de los Abencerrajes.** Here, Sultan Abul Hassan piled the heads of his first wife's 16 sons so that Boabdil, son by his second wife, could inherit the throne. The rust-colored stains in the basin are said to mark the indelible traces of the butchering. Light bleeds into the room through the intricate domed ceiling, which features an eight-pointed star—a design said to represent terrestrial and heavenly harmony.

Through dripping stalactite archways, at the far end of the courtyard from the Patio de los Leones, lies the **Sala de los Reyes (Hall of Kings).** Fixed to the walls with bamboo pins, detailed sheepskin paintings depict important assemblies and hunts. On the remaining side of the courtyard, the resplendent **Sala de las Dos Hermanas (Chamber of the Two Sisters)** has a staggering honeycomb dome (Mozárabe style), comprised of thousands of tiny cells. From here a secluded portico, **Mirador de Daraxa (Eyes of the Sultana),** overlooks the Jardines de Daraxa.

Passing the room where American author Washington Irving resided in 1829, a balustraded courtyard leads to the 14th-century **Baños Reales (Royal Baths),** the center of court social life. Light shining through star-shaped holes in the ceiling once refracted through steam, creating indoor rainbows. (Baths currently closed in summer for conservation studies and archaeological bubble baths).

TOWERS AND GARDENS. Just outside the east wall of the Alcázar in the **Jardines del Partal,** lily-studded pools flow beside terraces of roses. The **Torre de las Damas (Ladies' Tower)** soars above it all, a series of six towers traversing the area between the Alcazaba and El Generalife, one for captives, one for princesses, etc.

EL GENERALIFE. Over a bridge, across the **Callejón de los Cipreses** and the shady **Callejón de las Adelfas,** are the vibrant blossoms, towering cypresses, and streaming waterways of El Generalife, the sultan's vacation retreat. In 1313 Arab engi-

A ROSE BY ANY OTHER NAME...

Alahambra: Derived from Calatahamrá (red fort), some say the once white castle got this name from the distinctly red earth. Others, noting that the structure was built at night, argue that the name comes from the flicker of torches upon the castle walls.

Palacio de los Leones: Lions were thought to represent fertility and manliness—a desired symbol for a room that housed the palace harem, which included wives (several per Nazarite king) and numerous concubines.

Torre de las Damas (Ladies' Tower): Legend has it that Boabdil fled to this tower to hide from his angry, adulterous father Moulay Abul Hassan.

Torre de las Infantes (Tower of Princesses): Best told by Washington Irving, local lore reports that this tower earned its name from three naughty princesses—Zoraida, Zaida, and Zorahaida—who fell head-over-heels in love with three Christian prisoners.

Sala de Los Abencerrajes: In this vast (blood) stained room, Sultan Abul Hassan chopped off the heads of all 16 sons from his first marriage, thus terminating the lineage and ensuring Boabdil's succession to the throne.

Sala de dos Hermanas (Room of Two Sisters): Experts agree that the name derives from two chunks of marble in the floor along the fountain.

Court of Myrtles or Court of the Pools: An architectural gem, the Court gets its name from the reflective, mirror-like ponds that add space and volume to the castle.

neers changed the Darro's flow by 18km and employed dams and channels to prepare the soil for Aben Walid Ismail's design of El Generalife. Over the centuries, the estate passed through private hands until it was finally repatriated in 1931. The two buildings of El Generalife, the **Palacio** and the **Sala Regia,** connect across the **Patio de la Acequia (Courtyard of the Irrigation Channel),** embellished with a narrow pool fed by fountains that form an aquatic archway. Honeysuckle vines scale the back wall, and shady benches invite long rests.

PALACIO DE CARLOS V. After the Reconquest drove the Moors from Spain, Fernando and Isabel restored the Alcázar. Little did they know that two generations later Emperor Carlos V would demolish part of it to make way for his Palacio, a Renaissance masterpiece by Pedro Machuca (a disciple of Michelangelo). Although the building is glaringly incongruous amid all the Moorish splendor, experts agree that the Palace is one of the most beautiful Renaissance buildings in Spain. A square building with a circular inner courtyard wrapped in two stories of Doric colonnades, it is Machuca's only surviving effort. Inside, the **Museo de La Alhambra** contains the only original furnishings remaining from the Alhambra. *(Tel. 958 22 62 79. Open Tu-Sa 9am-2:30pm. 250ptas, free for EU citizens.)* Upstairs, the **Museo de Bellas Artes** displays mostly religious sculpture and paintings of the Granada School dating from the 16th century to the present. *(Tel. 958 22 48 43. Open June-Aug. Tu 2:30-6pm, W-Sa 9am-6pm; Sept.-May Tu 2:30-7:45pm, W-Sa 9am-7:45pm, Su 9am-2pm.)*

👁 SIGHTS IN THE CATHEDRAL QUARTER

CAPILLA REAL. Downhill from the Alhambra's Arab splendor, the Capilla Real (Royal Chapel), Fernando and Isabel's private chapel, exemplifies Christian Granada. During their prosperous reign, they funneled almost a quarter of the royal income into the chapel's construction (which lasted from 1504 to 1521) to produce their proper burial place. Their efforts did not go unrewarded; intricate Gothic carvings and meticulously rendered statues, as well as **La Reja,** the gilded iron grill of Master Bartolomé, now mark the resting place of the couple. Behind La Reja rest the elaborate, almost lifelike marble figures of the royals themselves. Fernando and Isabel's feet face visitors as they enter; beside them sleeps their daughter Juana la Loca (the Mad) and her husband Felipe el Hermoso (the Fair). To the horror of the rest of the royal family, Juana insisted on keeping the body of her husband with her for an unpleasantly long time after he died. Friends had a

ANDALUCÍA

hard time convincing the insanely jealous wife that Felipe was actually dead. The lead caskets, where all four monarchs were laid to rest, lie in the crypt directly below the marble statues, accessible by a small stairway on the left. The smaller, fifth coffin belongs to the hastily buried child-king of Portugal, Miguel, whose death allowed Carlos V to ascend the throne.

SACRISTY. Next door in the sacristy, Isabel's private **art collection,** the highlight of the chapel, favors Flemish and German artists of the 15th century. The glittering **royal jewels**—the queen's golden crown and scepter and the king's sword—shine in the middle of the sacristy. *(Open Apr.-Sept. M-Sa 10:30am-1pm and 4-7pm; Oct.-Mar. M-Sa 10:30am-1pm and 3:30-6:30pm, Su 11am-1pm. 300ptas.)*

CATHEDRAL. The adjacent cathedral was built from 1523-1704 by Fernando and Isabel upon the foundation of the major Arab mosque. The first purely Renaissance cathedral in Spain, its massive Corinthian pillars support an astonishingly high (45m) vaulted nave. *(Tel. 958 22 29 59. Open daily Apr.-Sept. 10:30am-1:30pm and 4-7pm; Oct.-Mar. 10:30am-1:30pm and 3:30-6:30pm. Closed Sunday morning. 300ptas.)*

OTHER SIGHTS. The 16th-century **Hospital Real** is divided into four tiled courtyards. Above the landing of the main staircase, the Mudéjar-coffered ceiling echoes those of the Alhambra. *(C. San Juan de Dios. Open M-F 9am-2pm. Free.)* The 14th-century **Monasterio de San Jerónimo** is around the corner. Though badly damaged by Napoleon's troops, it was later restored. *(Tel. 958 27 93 37. Open daily Apr.-Sept. 10am-1pm and 4-7pm; Oct.-Mar. 10am-1pm and 3-6:30pm. 300ptas.)*

THE ALBAICÍN. The Albaicín is the fascinating old Arab quarter where the Moors built their first fortress. After the Reconquest, a small Moorish population clung to the neighborhood on this hill until their expulsion in the 17th century. The abundance of North African cuisine and the recent construction of a mosque near Pl. San Nicolas attest to a continued Arab influence in Granada. A labyrinth of steep slopes and dark narrow alleys, the Albaicín warrants caution at night. *(Bus #12 runs from beside the cathedral to C. Pagés at the top of the Albaicín. There is another bus that departs from Pl. Nueva and weaves its way to the top. From here, walk down C. Agua through Pta. Arabe.)*

The best way to explore this maze is to proceed along C. Acera de Darro off Pl. Nueva, climb the Cuesta del Chapiz on the left, then wander aimlessly through Muslim ramparts, cisterns, and gates. On Pl. Nueva, the 16th-century **Real Cancillería** (or **Audiencia**), with a beautiful arcaded patio and stalactite ceiling, was the Christians' Ayuntamiento. Farther uphill are the 11th-century **Arab baths.** *(C. Acera de Darro, 31. Tel. 958 22 23 39. Open Tu-Sa 10am-2pm. Free.)* The **Museo Arqueológico** showcases funerary urns, Classical sculpture, Carthaginian vases, Muslim lamps, and ceramics. *(C. Acera de Darro, 41. Tel. 958 22 56 40. Open Tu 3-8pm, W-Sa 9am-8pm, Su 9am-2:30pm. 250ptas, free for EU members.)* The terrace adjacent to **Iglesia de San Nicolás** affords the city's best view of the Alhambra, especially in winter when snow adorns the Sierra Nevada behind it.

🎵 ENTERTAINMENT

Entertainment listings are near the back of the daily paper, the *Ideal* (120ptas), under *Cine y Espectáculos;* the Friday supplement lists bars and special events. The *Guía del Ocio,* sold at newsstands (100ptas), lists clubs, pubs, and cafes. The tourist office also distributes a monthly guide, *Cultura en Granada.*

FLAMENCO AND JAZZ

The most "authentic" flamenco performances, which change monthly, are advertised on posters around town. Tourists and locals alike flock to **Los Jardines Neptuno** (tel. 958 52 25 33), C. Arabial, near the Neptuno shopping center at the base of C. Recogidas. Rows of plastic chairs fill this huge, enclosed theater. (Cover 3500ptas, includes 1 drink). A smoky, intimate setting awaits at **Eshavira** (tel. 958 20 32 62), C. Postigo de la Cuna, in an alley off C. Azacayes, between C. Elvira and

Gran Vía. This joint is *the* place to go for flamenco, jazz, or a fusion of the two. Photos of Nat King Cole and other jazz greats plaster the walls. (min. 1 drink; call for schedule.)

PUBS, BARS, AND CLUBS

Pubs and bars spread across several neighborhoods, genres, and energy levels. Perhaps the most boisterous crowd belongs to C. Pedro Antonio de Alarcón, running from Pl. Albert Einstein to Ancha de Gracia.

Taberna El 22, Pl. Santa Gregorio, 5. Close to Pl. Nueva, at the top of C. Calderería Nueva. A young and mellow throng of vacationers lounge on the cobblestone patio. *Caña* 150ptas; wine 175 ptas. Open daily noon-3pm and 9pm-3am.

Kasbah, C. Calderería Nueva, 4 (tel. 958 52 31 73). Seductively scented. Offers silky pillows, romantic nooks, and tasty Marroqua beverages (275ptas). Perfect for a laid back, shoeless Saturday night. Open 3pm-3am.

Campo del Principa (tel. 508 00 42 00), up C. Pavaneras from Pl. Isabel la Católica. Take a left at Pl. Realejo, the 1st right on C. Molinos, the 2nd alley on the left, then the 1st right. *Tapas* and *terrazas* attract friendly folks. Open daily 1-4pm and 8pm-1am.

Cine/Disco Granada 10, C. Cárcel Baja, 14 (tel. 958 22 40 01), 3 blocks from Pl. Isabel la Católica along Gran Vía. Only room to wiggle—but perhaps that's enough. Really gets going at 2am. Cover 700-1000ptas, includes 1 drink. Open daily 9pm-4am.

Iguazu, from C. Pedro Antonio, head up C. Socrates and turn right into the orange breezeway. A hip and intimate setting for merengue or salsa beats. Open daily 8pm-4am.

Bar-Rama, along C. Pedro Antonio de Alarcon. Known as **"Chupitos"** for the shot-sized concoctions they serve—some with such appetizing names as *"Aborto de gallona"* (chicken abortion) and *"Vomito Lagarto"* (lizard vomit). Open daily 9pm-4am.

Casa de Yanguas, in the Albaicín. Follow Cuesta del Chapiz to its end near C. San Buenaventura. Refined patrons casually sip beer (200ptas) amid contemporary art in fountained Moorish patios. Open daily 8pm-3am.

Babylon, Placeta Sillería, 5, off C. Reyes Católicos before Pl. Nueva. Pumps Reggae, hip-hop, and funk. Moonlights as a speakeasy for foreign students.

FESTIVALS

A number of festivals sweep the city during the summer. Granada's **Corpus Christi** celebrations, processions, and bullfights are famous (May or June). Every May, avant-garde theater groups from around the world make a pilgrimage to Granada for the **International Theater Festival** (tel. 958 22 93 44). The **Festival Internacional de Música y Danza** (mid-June to early July) sponsors open-air performances of classical music and ballet in the Alhambra's Palacio de Carlos V (tickets 1000-6000ptas).

DAYTRIPS FROM GRANADA

LA CARTUJA

On the outskirts of Granada stands La Cartuja, a 16th-century Carthusian monastery and the pinnacle of Baroque artistry in Granada. Marble with rich brown tones and swirling forms (a stone unique to nearby Lanjarón) marks the sacristy of Saint Bruno. To reach the monastery, take bus #8 from the front of the cathedral. (Tel. 958 16 19 32. Open Apr.-Sept. M-Sa 10am-1pm and 4-8pm, Su 10am-noon; Oct.-Mar. M-Sa 10am-1pm and 3:30-6pm, Su 10am-noon. 300ptas.)

FUENTE VAQUEROS

Poet and playwright Federico García Lorca, famed for his works *Bodas de Sangre* and *Romancero Gitano*, was born outside the tiny town of Fuente Vaqueros; he was shot by right-wing forces near Granada at the outbreak of the Civil War. For

ANDALUCÍA

Lorca fans, Fuente Vaqueros is a must-see. Walk through the restored **Casa-Museo,** Lorca's house-turned-museum, to see everything from the piano where the master played to the bed in which he was born. Upstairs in the **granero** gaze upon photos of Lorca with Dalí and original costumes from performances of his plays around the world. (Tel. 958 51 64 53; fax 958 24 73 38. Open Oct.-Mar. Tu-Sa 10am-1pm and 4-7pm; Apr.-Sept. Tu-Sa 10am-1pm and 5-8pm. 200ptas. Tours every hr.) Buses run hourly from the Granada train station (25min., 160ptas). From the bus stop, turn right on Po. Prado and left on C. Poetra Lorca; follow signs for "Casa-Museo."

SIERRA NEVADA

The peaks of Mulhacén (3481m) and Veleta (3470m), the highest in Spain, sparkle with snow and buzz with tourists for most of the year. Ski season runs from December to April. During the summer, the bare mountains are arguably less attractive, as black slate slopes are dotted by patches of yellow-green moss; nevertheless, tourists hike, parasail, and take jeep tours. Before you go, check road and snow conditions (tel. 958 24 91 19; English spoken) and hotel vacancies. If you plan to hike extensively, head to **Librería Flash** in Granada for their indispensable 800pta map of the Sierra (see p. 256).

VELETA

Near the foot of Granada's Alhambra, the highest road in Europe begins its long, gradual ascent to one of Europe's highest peaks, Veleta. The road begins in the arid countryside, then scales the daunting face of the Sierra. Due to snow, cars can cruise to the very top of Veleta only in August and September.

Veleta has 39 slopes and 61 square km of skiing area, with a vertical drop of 1300m. Lift tickets cost 2325ptas in *temporada alta* (winter) and 2025ptas in *temporada baja* (off-season). **Ski rentals** are available in the Gondola Building and in Pl. Prado Llano (full equipment 2500ptas per day). This ski resort is the southernmost in Europe—wear sunscreen or suffer DNA mutations. The cheapest accommodation is the **Albergue Universitario** (tel. 958 48 01 22), the yellow building at the Veleta bus stop. (Breakfast included. Reserve early in winter. Singles 2000ptas; doubles with sinks 5000ptas.) The **bar** downstairs (tel. 958 48 10 03) serves *bocadillos* (350-450ptas) and a hearty *menú* (1300ptas).

The **Autocares Bonal bus** (tel. 958 27 31 00) from **Granada** to Veleta is a bargain (9am; returns 4:30pm from Albergue; round-trip 800ptas). Buy tickets in the bar El Ventorrillo, next to the bus stop (see **Granada,** p. 255). Call **Cetursa** (tel. 958 24 91 11) for info on outdoor activities.

LA ALPUJARRA

La Alpujarra's secluded white villages are perched along the southern slopes of the Sierra Nevada. Although its roads are now paved and the towns well-traveled, a medieval Berber influence is still evident in the region's architecture. Low-slung houses rendered from earth and slate resemble only those in Morocco's Atlas Mountains. After the fall of Granada, the Berbers were exiled to La Alpujarra, where Christian-Muslim conflicts resumed. Legend has it that in a gory battle at Bananco de la Sangre, Christian blood trickled uphill to avoid contamination with the heathens' blood below. Finally, in 1610 John of Austria ousted the Moors from La Alpujarra and ended their reign on the peninsula. On the heels of the Muslims, settlers from Galicia and Asturias brought Celtic and Visigothic traditions found nowhere else in Andalucía. The legacy of Moorish defiance lives on and peaks during Trevélez's **Fiestas de Moros y Cristianos,** a dramatization of the Moorish-Christian conflict, usually held in early June.

Although tourists have recently discovered the beauty of these settlements and the surrounding region's numerous hiking trails, the Alpujarras remain among Spain's poorest areas. Until the 1950s, travel was possible only by foot or mule, and the area still suffers from severe drought, unemployment, and low literacy rates. Nevertheless,

BUDDHISM IN BUBIÓN Bubión has a distinctly Buddhist slant. It was the birthplace of Osel, the Spanish reincarnation of the Tibetan lama Yeshe and one of the first lamas born in the West. Visitors from around the world (among them the Dalai Lama himself) come to meditate at the Buddhist retreat **Osel-Ling** (clear light), high in the mountains above Bubión. Osel is now in India, but his retreat is currently organizing courses in Buddhist studies and opens its *sala de meditación* to the public from 3 to 6pm (free). For more information, call 958 34 31 34.

the region's slow-paced lifestyle, preserved beauty, and deep roots in cultural traditions make for a refreshing visit—not to mention the crop of adventure tourism organizations eagerly waiting to show you a more adrenaline-oriented side of La Alpujarra.

Alsina Graells buses zoom from Granada to many of the elevated towns, including Lanjarón, Pampaneira, Bubión, Capileira, and Trevélez. Bus drivers will often stop to let travelers off at intermediate points. Although these buses are the only form of public transportation between the villages, **hiking** is a tradition in the Alpujarra. The locals, aware of the transportation problem, often sympathize with **hitchers.**

LANJARÓN

Lanjarón (pop. 4300) is Spain's version of Evian, France. Famed throughout the country for mineral water, Lanjarón once attracted Spaniards in droves when mineral water was thought to have medicinal value. A mere 45km daytrip from Granada, Lanjarón still abounds with accommodations. **Hostal Dólar,** Av. Andalucía, 5 (tel. 958 77 01 83), offers bright and clean rooms (singles 1700ptas; doubles 3000ptas, with bath 3600ptas).

PAMPANEIRA

As the road winds in serpentine curves up to Pampaneira, the lowest of the high Alpujarran villages (1059m), the landscape quickly becomes harsh. Pampaneira is the most tourist-accommodating town in La Alpujarra, and the first in a trio of hamlets overlooking **Poqueira Gorge,** a massive ravine cut by the Río Poqueira. Pampaneira makes a great springboard for climbing to **Bubión** (40min.) and **Capileira** (1¾hr.). For more info on the region's natural wonders, visit **Nevadensis** (tel. 958 76 31 27; fax 958 76 33 11; email nevadensis@arrakis.es) in Pampaneira's main square. A local organization associated with the Parque Natural de La Sierra Nevada, it arranges for rural accommodations, horseback riding, and other services. (Open M-Sa 10:30am-2:30pm and 5-7pm.) **Hostal Pampaneira** (tel. 958 76 30 02), just off the highway in front of the bus stop, provides large, heated rooms with polished chestnut furniture, all with bath (singles 2000ptas; doubles 3500ptas; triples 4500ptas; Visa, MC). Downstairs, the **restaurant** serves a mean bowl of stew for 350ptas (entrees 650-1200ptas; Visa, MC).

BUBIÓN

Bubión, a steep 3km (40min.) hike from Pampaneira, beams with Berber architecture, village charm, and three contemporary art galleries. For info, check out **Rustic Blue,** Barrio La Ermita, s/n (tel. 958 76 33 81; fax 958 76 31 34). The helpful staff organizes excursions, cooking lessons with Irish mountaineer/chef Conor Clifford, and lodging. (Open M-F 10am-2pm and 5-8pm, Sa 10:30am-1:30pm. English spoken.) **Las Terrazas** (tel. 958 76 30 34), Pta. Sol, has spotless rooms with tiled floors, Alpujarran bedspreads, and baths (singles 2500ptas; doubles 4000ptas). Locals rave about the food at **Restaurante La Artesa,** on the main road in front of the bus stop (*menús* 1100-1500ptas; open daily 1:30-4pm and 8-11pm).

CAPILEIRA

Capileira (1436m) is perched atop the Poqueira Gorge (2½hr. from Granada and a 1hr. hike from Bubión) and makes a good base for exploring the neighboring villages and the back side of the Sierra Nevada. Cobblestone alleys wind up the slope while peaks loom above and the valley plummets below. Enjoy the vista from your bedroom window at **Mesón-Hostal Poqueira,** C. Dr. Castillo, 6 (tel. 958 76 30 48). Rooms are pleasant and fresh, with baths and central heating. (Singles 2100ptas; doubles 3300ptas; triples 4200ptas.) A scrumptious and filling 1200pta *menú* is served at the restaurant (open Tu-Su). **Supermercado Rubies,** downhill from the bus station, supplies provisions (open M-Sa 9am-2pm and 5-9pm, Su 9am-2pm).

TREVÉLEZ

Rural isolation and lots of pork characterize Trevélez, continental Spain's highest community (1476m). Despite its Alpujarran charms, the town is best known for its cured pork, whose special qualities will probably elude all but the true connoisseur. Ham here is cured in the cool and dry winter, then sweated in the summer months, producing a unique flavor. Steep roads weave in and out of three distinct *barrios* (upper, middle, lower) amid the sounds of rushing water carefully channeled down thousand-year-old Moorish irrigation systems. In fact, some Moors were spared from the Inquisition because the Christians could not operate the channels without them.

Trevélez is a logical base for the ascent to **Mulhacén.** Every August, throngs of locals climb to pay homage to the **Virgen de las Nieves (Virgin of the Snow),** whose shrine is at the peak. Those summit-bound should head north on the trail leaving the upper village; avoid the lower trail that follows the swampy Río Trevélez. Continue past the Cresta de los Postreros for a good 5½ hours and you will reach the Cañada de Siete Lagunas (the largest lake should be directly in front of you); go right to see a famous cave-refuge. To reach Mulhacén, go up the ridge south of the refuge. It is not advisable to hike Mulhacén the same day you visit the lake.

Despite numerous signs near the bus stop advertising nearby *camas* (beds), the steep walk to **Hostal Fernando** (tel. 958 85 85 65), on C. Pista, 1km uphill on the left side of town from the bus stop, is well worth it. The friendly management keeps attractive, heated rooms with unbeatable views of the mountains from the terrace. (Singles 2500ptas; doubles 4000ptas.) They also rent apartments by the day for two (5000ptas) and four people (7000ptas). For food, try **La Fragua** (tel. 958 85 85 73), C. Carcel, which overlooks the town and valley (*menú* 750ptas).

JAÉN

Olive trees and wheat fields—barely visible from city's steep, crowded streets—streak Jaén's surrounding hills. Unfortunately, that is just about all Spain's bustling olive capital has to offer. Still, the city may be a necessary stopover—Baeza and Cazorla, two considerably more appealing destinations, lie only an hour away.

◗ ORIENTATION AND PRACTICAL INFORMATION. Jaén centers around **Plaza de la Constitución,** roaring with autos and mopeds. C. Bernabé Soriano leads uphill from the plaza to the cathedral and the old section of town. C. Roldán y Marín and C. Virgen head downhill and become Po. Estación and Av. Madrid, respectively. To reach the town center from the bus station, exit from where the buses arrive and follow Av. Madrid uphill to Pl. Constitución (5min.). From the train station, turn right on Po. Estación, which becomes C. Roldán y Marín. If you're not up for the 25-minute walk, take the #1 bus along Po. Estación (90ptas).

Trains (tel. 953 27 02 02) leave from Po. Estación at the bottom of the slope and go to: **Córdoba** (1½hr., 1 per day, 8am, 1155ptas); **Sevilla** (3hr., 1 per day, 8am, 2210ptas); **Madrid** (4-5hr., 3 per day, 6am-5pm, 3000ptas). **Buses** (tel. 953 25 50 14), Pl. Coca de la Piñera, are much more efficient. They head to: **Úbeda** (30min., 12 per day, 8:30am-8:45pm, 545ptas); **Baeza** (1hr., 12 per day, 8:30am-8:45pm, 455ptas); **Granada** (1½hr., 14 per day, 7:30am-9pm, 915ptas); **Cazorla** (2hr., 2 per day, noon and 4:30pm, 945ptas); **Málaga** (3hr., 3 per day, 7:30am-noon, 2040ptas). The **tourist office,** C. Arquitecto Berges, 1 (tel./fax 953 22 27 37), off C. Roldán y Marín, on the left when heading downhill, is just like every other tourist office in Spain (open M-F 9am-7pm, Sa 9am-1pm). **Banco Central Hispano,** in Pl. Constitución (open M-F 8:30am-2:30pm). **Emergency:** tel. 091 or 092; **police** tel. 953 26 18 50.

▐▌ ACCOMMODATIONS AND FOOD. Quality budget beds are scarce in Jaén. At the **Hostal La Española,** C. Bernardo López, 9 (tel. 953 23 02 54), vines canopy the dining room and a staircase spirals its way upwards. Everything, including the sagging beds, exudes antiquity. To get to the hostel, follow the street across from the cathedral's side entrance and turn left onto the alley Bernardo López. (Singles 2000ptas; doubles 3500ptas, with bath 4000ptas.) **Pensión Carlos V,** Av. Madrid, 4 (tel. 953 22 20 91), downhill from Pl. Constitución, is more mainstream (singles 2500ptas; doubles 3700ptas). C. Nueva, a pedestrian street down C. Roldán y Marín, offers several palatable restaurant options. **Yucatán,** C. Bernabé Soriano, 1 (tel. 953 24 17 28), has tasty *bocadillos* (300-500ptas), burgers (300-350ptas), and entrees (900-1000ptas), served indoors or out (open daily 8am-2am). **Supermarket Simago** is off Pl. Constitución on C. San Clement (open 9am-9pm).

◙ ▐▌ SIGHTS AND ENTERTAINMENT. The Renaissance **Catedral de Santa María,** on C. Bernabé Soriano uphill from Pl. Constitución, was designed by Andrés de Valdelvira (open daily 8:30am-1pm and 5-8pm; free). The **Museo de la Catedral** displays sculptures by Martínez Montañés and canvases by Alonso Cano (tel. 953 22 46 75; open M-Sa 10am-1pm and 5-8pm, Su 10am-1pm; 200ptas). Jaén's most imposing and least accessible sight is the **Castillo de Santa Catalina** (tel. 953 21 91 16), a 3km climb from the center of town. From the cathedral, take C. Maestra, which leads to C. Madre de Dios and continues to C. San Lorenzo. Turn left on Ctra. Circumvalación, which becomes Ctra. Neveral; this leads to the castle. Those who don't feel like walking can take a cab (900ptas) from the bus station to the *castillo*. (Open M-Tu and Th-Su 10:30am-1:30pm. Free.) The Renaissance **Palacio de Villadompardo** (tel. 953 23 62 92), in Pl. Santa Luisa Marillac, contains Arab baths. The recently restored 11th-century baths, though not as elaborate as those in Granada, are Spain's largest. Follow C. Maestra from the cathedral to C. Martínez Molina. (Open Tu-F 9am-8pm, Sa-Su 9:30am-2:30pm. Free.) Centuries-old **Peña Flamenca Jaén,** C. Maestra, 11 (tel. 953 23 17 10), uphill from the cathedral, serves up drinks and flamenco, indoors and out. **Del Posito,** a cafe bar tucked in a plaza below Yucatán, has the most popular outdoor tables in town.

BAEZA

Quiet, tourist-free Baeza (pop. 17,000) and its surroundings are old Spain at its best. A former Moorish capital and the first Andalucian town to fall during the Reconquest, Baeza flaunts its Renaissance heyday with exceptionally well-preserved monuments on nearly every street. Thanks to the limited lodging options, the town remains uncorrupted, and those who spend the day here will satisfy their quest for quintessential Spain. Baeza's poet, Antonio Machado, immortalized Baeza in his works when he said, *"Campo de Baeza, soñaré contigo cuando no te vea."* (Countryside of Baeza, I shall dream of you when I see you no more).

▐ ORIENTATION AND PRACTICAL INFORMATION. Plaza de España, which marks the center of town, leads downhill to Pl. Constitución. **Trains** leave **Estación Linares-Baeza** (tel. 953 65 02 02), 13km from town on the road to Madrid, for **Madrid** (7 per day, 7am-11:30pm, 2500ptas) and **Málaga** (3 per day, 6:40am-5pm, 2900ptas). The **bus station** (tel. 953 74 04 68), at the top of Av. Alcalde Puche Pardo, which becomes C. Julio Barrel, offers service to: **Úbeda** (15min., 15 per day, 8:20am-7:30pm, 105ptas); **Jaén** (1hr., 11 per day, 7:10am-7pm, 455ptas); **Cazorla** (1½hr., 2 per day, 1pm and 5:30pm, 500ptas); **Granada** (2-3hr., 7 per day, 7:55am-6:55pm, 1335ptas); **Málaga** (4hr., 1 per day, 8:10am, 2465ptas). To get to Pl. España from the bus station, follow C. Julio Burrel to C. San Pablo (on the right), and continue to the plaza. The **tourist office,** Pl. Pópulo, s/n (tel. 953 74 04 44), offers free maps of Baeza and info on tours of Andalucía (open M-F 9am-2:30pm, Sa 10am-1pm). **Emergency:** tel. 091 or 092; **police,** C. Cardenal Benavides, 5 (tel. 953 74 06 59); **medical services: Centro de Salud Comarcal** (tel. 953 74 09 17), on Av. Alcalde Puche Pardo.

Post office, C. Julio Burell, 19 (tel. 953 74 08 39; open M-F 8:30am-2:30pm); **postal code:** 23440; **internet access: Speed Informática,** Pl. Constitución, 2 (tel. 953 74 70 75; 250ptas per hr.; open M-F 9am-1:30pm and 4-7pm).

▮▮ ACCOMMODATIONS AND FOOD. Hostels are scarce—call ahead to ensure a room. **Hostal el Patio,** C. Romanones, 13 (tel. 953 74 02 00), has a delightful lounge complete with plants and a mini-zoo (singles 1500ptas, with shower 2000ptas; doubles 3000ptas, with bath 4000ptas). **Hostal Residencia Comercio,** C. San Pablo, 21 (tel. 953 74 01 00), provides large, attractive rooms with showers or baths (singles with shower 1600-1700ptas, with bath 1800-1900ptas; doubles with shower 3100-3300ptas, with bath 3500-3800ptas). A plethora of bars and restaurants line Pl. Constitución and neighboring streets. **Café Las Vegas** (tel. 953 74 00 87), on the plaza's southwest corner on Portales Tundidores, has choice *bocadillos* (275-375ptas) and entrees (850-950ptas). **Helados los Valencianos,** C. Gaspar Becerra, 10 (tel. 953 74 15 05), might just make the best ice cream in Spain. Their stand in the plaza sells cones (50-200ptas) and cool lemon and orange *granizados* (150-300ptas; open daily 10:30am-3pm and 5pm-1am). **Supermarket,** Portales Carboneria, 15, has groceries (open M-Sa 9am-2pm and 5-9pm, Su 10am-1pm).

▣ SIGHTS. A stroll through the **Barrio Monumental** yields a sight on every corner. Follow C. Romanones up the stairs next to the tourist office before it opens onto Pl. Santa Cruz; the **Antigua Universidad** (founded in 1595) stands on the left. Ask someone to let you into the courtyard, where poet Antonio Machado used to teach French (open Tu-Su 10am-1pm and 4-6pm; free). Across from it survives the **Palacio de Jabalquinto,** featuring a gracefully decaying courtyard punctuated with ancient stonework and orange trees (open Tu-Su 10am-1pm and 4-6pm; free). To the right of the Antigua Universidad looms the 13th-century Romanesque **Iglesia de Santa Cruz,** Baeza's oldest church, with its frescoes of La Virgen, Santa Catalina, and the martyr San Sebastián (open M-Sa 11am-1pm and 4-6pm, Su noon-2pm). Adjacent to the *palacio,* the **seminario's** facade bears the names of some egotistical graduates and a caricature of an unpopular professor, rumored to be painted in bull's blood. Across the Pl. Santa María from the seminary looms the **Santa Iglesia Catedral,** home to *La Custodia de Baeza,* Spain's second-most important (after Toledo's) Corpus Christi icon (open daily June-Aug. 10:30am-1pm and 5:15-7pm; Sept.-May 10:30am-1pm and 4:15-6pm).

ÚBEDA

Fifteen minutes from Baeza and two hours from Granada and Córdoba, the cobbled streets of Úbeda's monument district dip between ivied medieval walls and old churches and palaces. A stop on the crucial 16th-century trade route linking Castilla to Andalucía, the town (pop. 35,000) prospered from American gold on its way from Sevilla. The *barrio antiguo,* surrounded by friendly, newer neighborhoods, is one of the best-preserved gems of Spanish Renaissance architecture.

▮ ORIENTATION AND PRACTICAL INFORMATION. Úbeda centers around **Plaza de Andalucía.** From here, the **barrio antiguo** stretches downhill along C. Doctor Quesada (which leads to C. Real) and surrounding streets. There's **no train service** to Úbeda. The nearest station is **Estación Linares-Baeza** (tel. 953 65 02 02), 40 minutes northwest by bus. **Buses** leave Úbeda from C. San José, 6 (tel. 953 75 21 57). **Alsina Graells** travels to: **Baeza** (15min., 15 per day, 10am-6pm, 105ptas); **Estación Linares-Baeza** (30min., 8 per day, 255ptas); **Jaén** (1hr., 11 per day, 7am-6:45pm, 545ptas); **Cazorla** (1hr., 4 per day, 10am-6pm, 430ptas); **Granada** (2-3hr., 7 per day, 7:45am-6:45pm, 1420ptas). **Bacoma** goes to **Córdoba** (2½hr., 3 per day, 9:45am-3:30pm, 1350ptas) and **Sevilla** (5hr., 1 per day, 9:45am, 2615ptas). To reach Pl. Andalucía from the **bus station,** go right from the front of the station, walk one block downhill, turn left on Av. Cristo Rey, which turns into C. Obispo Cobos and then C. Mesones, and continue to the plaza (5min.).

The **tourist office** in the **Centro Cultural Hospital de Santiago**, C. Obispo Cobos, s/n (tel./fax 953 75 08 97), on the way from the bus station to Pl. Andalucía, offers books, brochures, and a map with English translations (open June-Aug. M-F 9am-2:30pm; Sept.-May M-F 9am-2:30pm, Sa 11am-1pm). **Banco Central Hispano,** C. San Fernando, 28 (tel. 953 75 04 43), uphill from Pl. Andalucía, has an **ATM** (open May-Sept. M-F 8:30am-2:30pm; Oct.-Apr. M-F 8:30am-2:30pm, Sa 8:30am-1pm). **Luggage storage** at the bus station (300ptas). **Emergency:** tel. 091 or 092; **police** tel. 953 75 00 23; **medical services: Centro de Salud** (tel. 953 75 11 03), on C. Explanada, off Av. Ramón y Cajal. **Post office,** C. Trinidad, 4 (tel. 953 75 00 31), along the Hospital de Santiago (open M-Sa 9am-2pm); **postal code:** 23400.

⊓⊓ ACCOMMODATIONS AND FOOD. Úbeda's best bargain is the ⊠**Hostal Castillo,** Av. Ramón y Cajal, 20 (tel. 953 75 04 30 or 953 75 12 18), with comfy singles upstairs and a popular bar and affordable restaurant downstairs (singles 2200-2400ptas, with bath 2400-2700ptas; doubles 3400-3600ptas, with bath 4600-4900ptas; triples from 6300ptas). The ritzier **Hostal Victoria,** C. Alaminos, 5, 2nd fl. (tel. 953 75 29 52), features glistening private bathrooms, color TVs, and A/C. From the bus station, walk down C. Mesones past Hospital de Santiago and turn right on C. Alaminos. (Singles 2400-2700ptas; doubles 4300-4900ptas.) For food, C. Rastro leading from Pl. Andalucía has many *terrazas* with combination platters under 1000ptas and entrees for around 600ptas. **Restaurante Castille-Victoria,** Av. Ramon y Cajal, 20 (tel. 953 75 12 18), inside Hostal Castillo, serves a great *menú* for 1100ptas (open daily 2-4pm). **Helados los Valencianos,** C. Obispo, 1, and Av. Ramón y Cajal, 18 (next to Hostal Castillo), serves delicious *granizados* (40-325ptas) and ice cream cones (100-300ptas; open daily 9am-1:30am). The **market** is down C. San Fernando from Pl. Andalucía (open M-Sa 7am-2:30pm).

⊠ SIGHTS. A walk through historic Úbeda should begin with the **Hospital de Santiago** (tel. 953 75 08 42), right by the bus station. The building is a worthy sight in its own right. Inside, it houses a modern art museum, holds concerts, and has information on cultural events. (Open M-F 8am-3pm and 3:30-10pm, Sa 8am-3pm. 225ptas, children and seniors 75ptas.) From Pl. Andalucía, C. Real leads downhill to C. Juan Montilla, which continues to **Plaza de Vázquez de Molina,** the center of historic Úbeda. Two stone lions at the head of a garden-lined pathway guard the **Palacio de las Cadenas,** now the Ayuntamiento. Across the pathway is the Gothic **Colegiata de Santa María de los Reales Alcázares,** its side chapels embellished with wrought-iron grilles. Uphill from Pl. Vásquez de Molina along C. Juan Ruíz Gonzales is Pl. 1 de Mayo, in front of **Iglesia de San Pablo.** The **Museo Arqueológico,** C. Cervantes, 6 (tel. 953 75 37 02), uphill from the church, narrates Úbeda's history through prehistoric, Roman, Moorish, and Castilian times. (Open Tu-Su 10am-2pm and 5-7pm. 250ptas, EU citizens free with passport.) A walk downhill leads to a stunning view of the olive-laden **Guadalquivir valley** and the ruins of the **muralla,** an old Moorish wall.

CAZORLA

Nestled between foreboding cliffs and two ancient castles, Cazorla (pop. 9000) is one Andalucian *pueblo blanco* (white town) that should not be missed. Though most tourists pass through on their way to the **Parque Natural de las Sierras de Cazorla, Segura, y las Villas,** one of the largest national parks in Europe (1hr. away), a hike through the mountainous town itself provides exceptional views of the Guadalquivir valley. That said, the national park's 210,000 hectares of protected mountains and waterways offer some of the best hiking, mountain biking, and horseback riding in Andalucía, and possibly even Spain.

⊠ ORIENTATION AND PRACTICAL INFORMATION. To reach **Plaza de Corredera** from the bus stop, face the peaks and walk down C. Dr. Muñoz to the right (5min.). Farther downhill is Pl. Santa María and the **barrio antiguo. Buses** (tel. 953

75 21 57) leave from Pl. Constitución to: **Granada** (2hr., 2 per day, 7am and 5:30pm); **Jaén** and **Úbeda** (2hr., 2 per day, 7am and 5:30pm, 950ptas); **Río Ebros** (2 per day, 5:45am and 3pm). Buy tickets in the unmarked booth in the plaza. The helpful **tourist office,** Po. Santo Cristo, 17 (tel. 953 71 01 02; fax 953 72 00 60), up a garden-lined walkway from Pl. Constitución, has free maps (open M-F 10am-2pm). **Emergency:** tel. 091 or 092; **police** (tel. 953 72 01 81), on Pl. Corredera; **medical services: Centro de Salud,** Av. Ximenez de Rada, 1 (tel. 953 72 10 61 or 953 72 20 00), a few kilometers away. **Post office,** C. Mariano Extremera, 2 (tel. 953 72 02 61), uphill on the left from Pl. Corredera (open M-F 8:30am-2:45pm, Sa 8:30am-1pm); **postal code:** 23470.

■■ **ACCOMMODATIONS AND FOOD.** From the far end of Pl. Corredera, walk uphill on C. Carmen to reach the ■**Albergue Juvenil Cazorla (HI),** Pl. Mauricio Martinez, 6 (tel. 953 72 03 29; fax 953 72 02 03). This sparklingly clean hostel has a TV lounge, outdoor patios, a heaven-sent pool (open July-Aug.), an English-speaking staff, and spacious rooms for one to six people. (Sheets provided. HI members 1300ptas, over 26 1800ptas; nonmembers add 300ptas. Prices drop 500-700ptas Sept. 15-June 15.) **Hostal Betis,** Pl. Corredera, 19 (tel. 953 72 05 40), has firm beds and great views of the valley (singles with bath 1300-1500ptas; doubles 2500-2800ptas, with bath 2700-3000ptas). Open-air bar-restaurants serving such traditional platters as *rin-ran* (a cold soup of potatoes, red peppers, olives, and fish) line Pl. Corredora and Pl. Santa María. Set in a 16th-century house on Pl. Santa María, **La Cueva** (tel. 953 72 12 25) cooks veggies and roast rabbit (among other things) in its ancient hearth (*menú* 1200ptas, entrees 800ptas; open daily noon-midnight; Visa, MC). Cazorla's **market** is at Pl. Mercado, downstairs from C. Dr. Muñoz (open M-F 9am-noon). A **supermarket** sits in Pl. Corredera (open M-F 9am-noon and 6-9pm, Sa 9am-noon).

■■ **SIGHTS AND HIKING.** Cazorla offers many opportunities for scenic strolls. The **Castillo de la Yedra** (tel. 953 71 00 31), started by the Romans, provides a pretty vista of Cazorla from its solitary peaks. The castle also houses an art museum (open June-Aug. Tu-Su 9am-2:30pm; Sept.-May Tu-Su 10am-1pm and 4-8pm; free). For longer excursions, stop by **Quercus,** C. Juan Domingo, 2 (tel. 953 72 01 15; fax 953 71 00 68), where English-speaking tour operators provide info on the **Parque Natural de las Sierras de Cazorla, Segura, y las Villas.** (Open daily 9am-2pm and 5-9pm, holidays 10am-2pm and 6-9pm. Map 375ptas.) Buses run from Cazorla to the park (1hr., June-Aug. 6:30am and 2:40pm, Sept.-May 5:45am and 3pm, 400ptas), but service is subject to change. Carecesa buses departs from Pl. Constitución and go to the **Torre del Vinagre Visitor Center,** near the trailhead of the popular **Sendero Cerrada de Elias/Río Borosa,** which has four- or 12km trails up a river canyon carved with natural pools. The center rents **horses** (1500ptas per hr., in groups of 4 or more) and **mountain bikes** (1200ptas per ½-day, 2000ptas per day). The last bus back to Cazorla leaves Torre del Vinagre at 4:30pm.

EAST COAST

VALENCIA

Valencia's rich soil has earned the region its nickname *"Huerta de España"* (Spain's Orchard). Spring and autumn river floods transport soil down the alluvial plain, nurturing Valencia's famous orange and vegetable groves, while irrigation networks designed by the Moors continue to nourish Valencia's farmlands. Dunes, sandbars, jagged promontories, and lagoons mark the grand coastline, and lovely fountains and pools grace the cities' carefully landscaped public gardens.

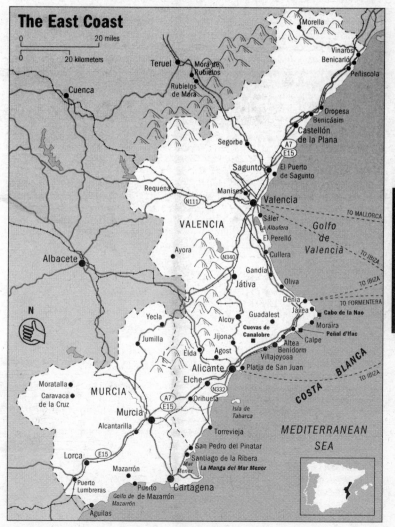

The East Coast

0   20 miles

0   20 kilometers

Valencia's past is a tangle of power struggles between the Phoenicians, Carthaginians, Greeks, Romans, and Moors. The region first fell under Castillian control when El Cid expelled the Moors in 1094; he ruled it in the name of Alfonso VI until his death five years later. Without El Cid's powerful influence, the city again fell to the Moors, remaining an Arab stronghold until 1238. In the 1930s, Valencia was again besieged, this time by Franco's troops. The *valencianos* resisted with characteristic strength; as a result Valencia was the last region incorporated into Franco's Spain. In 1977, with the reinstitution of the Bourbon monarchy, the region finally regained its autonomy.

Valenciano, the regional language spoken sparingly in the north and inland, is similar to Catalán. Although Valencia's regionalism is not as intense as Cataluña's, the Generalitat's recent mandate that all students enroll in one course of *valenciano* reflects a resurgence of regionalism. Local *fiestas*, spectacles of fire and fireworks, celebrate Valencia's vitality. From the furor and artistry invested in the effigies at Valencia's *Las Fallas* (March), to the artful displays during San Juan (June), to the reckless, adrenaline of *Nit de l'Alba* (August) in Elche, Valencia's festivals are some of the craziest in Spain. *Paella*, the pride of Spanish chefs everywhere, was first concocted somewhere in the rice fields around Valencia. In fact, Valencia boasts over 200 such rice dishes. Among its culinary treats, Valencia also serves tangy oranges, tasty olives, and a sweet, milky refreshment made of pressed *chufa* (almonds).

HIGHLIGHTS OF VALENCIA

■ Valencia's festival of **Las Fallas,** a pyromaniac's dream (see p. 279).
■ *Paella* (and other rice-based specialties) straight from the source (see p. 278).
■ Nightlife in the capital city of **Valencia** (see p. 274) and **Alicante** (see p. 285).
■ The hilltop medieval fortress town of **Morella** (see p. 282)–if you can get there.

VALENCIA

Valencia is a stylish, cosmopolitan, and business-oriented nerve center—a striking contrast to the surrounding orchards and mountain ranges. Fountained parks and gardens soothe the city's congested environment, and soft-sanded beaches nearby complement its frenetic day and nightlife. Unique architectural surprises hide behind the crowded city center, built by a self-conscious government trying to establish the province as a tourist destination for the 21st-century.

▐ GETTING THERE

The most convenient way to get to Valencia is by train. **Trains** run from: **Alicante** (1½hr., 12 per day, 1400-3000ptas); **Barcelona** (2¾-3½hr., 18 per day, 7am-10:30pm, 3300-4900ptas); **Madrid** (3½.-5½hr., 11 per day, 7am-8pm, 440-560ptas); **Zaragoza** (5½hr., 3 per day, 12:38am-3:40PM, 2475-4200ptas); **Granada** (8½hr., 3 per day, 8:15am-9:45pm, 4900-5100ptas).

▐ ORIENTATION AND PRACTICAL INFORMATION

Since **Estación del Nord** is close to the city's center, Valencia is best approached by train. **Avenida Marquéz de Sotelo** runs from the train station to **Plaça del Ayuntamiento,** the center of town. Just about everything of interest, except for the university and beaches, is in the **casco antiguo** (old quarter), nestled in a bend of the Río Turia. Valencia's geographical sprawl make unaided tours futile; although few maps do it justice, the tourist office's is best.

TRANSPORTATION

Flights: Airport (tel. 96 159 85 15), 15km from the city. *Cercanías* trains run between the airport and train station (32min.; M-F every 30min., 150ptas; Sa-Su every hr., 170ptas). Domestic and international destinations. **Iberia,** C. La Paz, 14 (tel. 96 352 75 52; 24hr. info and reservation tel. 902 400 500). Open M-F 9am-2pm and 4-7pm.

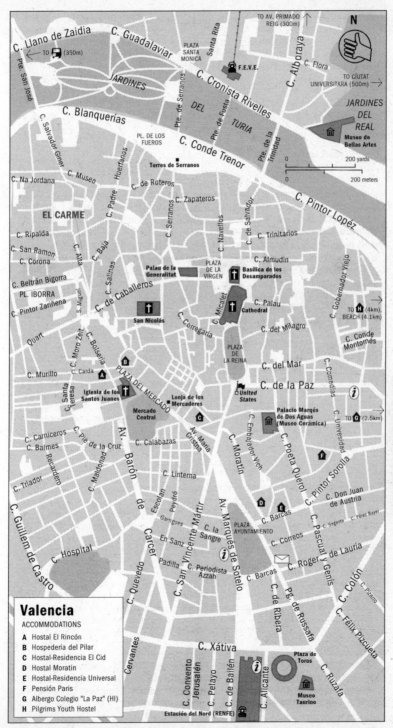

N

TO AV. PRIMADO
REIG (300m)

C. Llano de Zaidia
C. Guadalaviar
PLAZA
SANTA
MONICA
Santa Rita
F.E.V.E.
C. Alboraya
C. Flora

TO 🚌 (350m)
Pte. San José

JARDINES
DEL
TURIA
C. Cronista Rivelles
Pte. de Serranos
Pte. de Fusta
Pte. de la Trinidad

TO CÍUTAT
UNIVERSITARA (500m)

JARDINES
DEL
REAL
Museo de
Bellas Artes

C. Blanquerías
C. Salvador Giner
PL. DE LOS
FUEROS
C. Conde Trenor

C. Na Jordana
C. Museo
Torres de Serranos
C. de Roteros
C. Zapateros
C. Pintor Lopéz

EL CARME
C. Ripalda
C. San Ramon
C. Corona
C. Beltrán Bigorra
PL. IBORRA
C. Pintor Zariñena
Quart
C. Murillo

C. Padre Huerfanos
C. Baja
C. Alta
C. Salinas
C. Serranos
C. Navellos
C. de Salvador
C. Trinitarios
C. Almudin

Palau de la
Generalitat
PLAZA
DE LA
VIRGEN
Basilica de los
Desamparados

C. de Caballeros
S. Miguel
C. Moro Zeit
C. Bolseria
C. Carda

San Nicolás
C. Corregaria
C. Micalet
Cathedral
C. Palau
C. del Milagro
C. Gobernador Viejo

TO 🏛 (4km),
BEACH (4.1km)
C. Conde
Montornés

PLAZA
DE
LA REINA
C. del Mar
C. de la Paz
C. Comedias
ℹ

EAST COAST

B
A
PLAZA DEL MERCADO
Iglesia de los
Santos Juanes
Lonja de los
Mercaderes
United
States
C
Mercado
Central

Palacio Marqués
de Dos Aguas
(Museo Cerámica)
C. Universidad
TO G (2.5km)

C. Santa Teresa
C. Carniceros
C. Balmes
C. Triador
Recaredo
C. Pie de la Cruz
AV. BARÓN de
C. Calabazas
AV. María Cristina
C. Linterna
C. Embajador Vich
C. Moratin
C. Poeta Querol
F
C. Pintor Sorolla
C. Don Juan
de Austria

Escolan
Peydró
Garrigues
En Sanz
Padilla
Carcel
C. Quevedo
C. San Vincente Mártir
AV. Marques de Sotelo
C. la Sangre
C. Periodista
Azzah
D
C. Barcas
E
PLAZA
AYUNTAMIENTO
C. Barcas
C. Correos
✉
C. Pascual i Genís
C. Sagasta
C. Pérez Bayer
C. Roger de Lauria
C. Colón
C. Pizarro

C. Guillem de Castro
C. Hospital

Cervantes
C. Convento
Jerusalén
C. Pelayo
C. de Bailén
C. de Ribera
Pg. de Russafa
C. Felix Pizcueta
C. Ruzafa

C. Xátiva
Plaza de
Toros
ℹ
Museo
Taurino
C. Alicante

Estación del Nord (RENFE)

0 _____ 200 yards
0 _____ 200 meters

Valencia

ACCOMMODATIONS

A Hostal El Rincón
B Hospedería del Pilar
C Hostal-Residencia El Cid
D Hostal Moratin
E Hostal-Residencia Universal
F Pensión Paris
G Albergo Colegio "La Paz" (HI)
H Pilgrims Youth Hostel

Trains: Estación del Nord, C. Xàtiva, 24. Ticket windows open 7:30am-9:30pm. **RENFE** (24hr. tel. 96 352 02 02) to: **Alicante** (2hr., 9 per day, 1375-3000ptas); **Barcelona** (3-4hr., 18 per day, 3300-4900ptas); **Madrid** (5-7½hr., 12 per day, 2890-5600ptas); **Sevilla** (9hr., 2 per day, 5300ptas). *Cercanías* service Gandía, Játiva, Sagunto, Alicante, and the airport (prices range 135-550ptas).

Buses: Estación Terminal d'Autobuses, Av. Menéndez Pidal, 13 (tel. 96 349 72 22), across the river, a 25min. walk from the city center. Municipal bus #8 (110ptas) runs between Pl. Ayuntamiento and the train station. **Auto Res** (tel. 96 349 22 30) sends 3 regular and 12 express buses per day to **Madrid** (4-5hr., 2865-3165ptas). **Bacoma** (tel. 96 347 96 08) runs to: **Granada** (8hr., 6 per day, 4910ptas); **Málaga** (11hr., 5 per day, 6025ptas); **Sevilla** (11hr., 2 per day, 6380ptas). **Enatcar** (tel. 96 340 08 55) runs to **Barcelona** (4½hr., 10 per day, 7am-1am, 2900ptas). **Ubesa** (tel. 96 340 08 55) stops along the Costa Blanca on its way to **Alicante** (2¼-3hr., 9 per day, 1980ptas). **Eurolines** (tel. 96 349 38 22) has international service.

Ferries: Trasmediterránea, Estació Maritima (tel. 902 45 46 45). Take bus #4 from Pl. Ayuntamiento or #1 or 2 from the bus station. Boats run to Mallorca and Ibiza. Buy tickets at a travel agency, or on the day of departure at the port. Ask a travel agent about **Balearia/Flebasa's** (tel. 96 578 40 11) Denia-Eivissa service. See **By Boat,** p. 472.

Public Transportation: EMT Office, C. En Sanz, 4 (tel. 96 352 83 99). Bus **map** available at the tourist office and at the EMT office. Open M-F 8am-2pm. **EMT buses** run out of Pl. Ayuntamiento. Bus #8 runs to the bus station; bus #19 (in summer also #20, 21, 22) to Las Arenas and Malvarrosa. Buy tickets (110ptas) on board; 10-ride ticket (690ptas) or 1-day pass (500ptas) available at newsstands. Service stops at 10:30pm. Late-night buses run through Pl. Ayuntamiento (every 45min., 11pm-1:38am).

Taxis: tel. 96 370 33 33 or 96 357 13 13.

TOURIST AND FINANCIAL SERVICES

Tourist Office: Regional, Estación del Nord, C. Xàtiva, 24 (tel. 96 352 85 73), on the right of the train tracks (inside the station) as you disembark. Lots of pamphlets and maps. Open M-F 9am-6:30pm. The **main regional branch** with similar information is on C. Paz, 46-48 (tel. 96 398 64 22). Open M-F 10am-6pm, Sa 10am-2pm. **City Office,** Pl. Ayuntamiento, 1 (tel. 96 351 04 17; tourist info tel. 96 352 40 00), has Ajuntament-sponsored info. Open M-F 8:30am-2:15pm and 4:15-6:15pm, Sa 9am-12:45pm.

Budget Travel: IVAJ, C. Hospital, 11 (tel. 96 386 97 57). From the train station, head left on C. Xàtiva, which becomes C. Guillem de Castro, and turn right on C. Hospital. Several travel handbooks in English. Expect a line. ISIC 700ptas. HI cards 1800ptas. Open June-Aug. M-F 9am-2pm, Sept.-May M-F 9am-2pm and 5-7pm.

Currency Exchange: Banco Central Hispano, C. Barcas, 8 (tel. 96 353 81 00), offers decent exchange rates. 24hr. **ATMs** are everywhere.

American Express: Duna Viajes, C. Cirilo Amorós, 88 (tel. 96 374 15 62; fax 96 334 57 00). From the tip of Pl. Ayuntamiento, take C. Barcas, which becomes C. Don Juan de Austria, then C. Sorní. When you reach Pl. América, take C. Cirilo Amorós on the right. No commission on AmEx traveler's checks. Accepts wired money. Will hold mail and provide **fax** service for cardholders. Open June-Aug. M-F 10am-2pm and 5-8pm, Sa 10am-1:30pm; Sept.-May M-F 9:30am-1:30pm and 4:30-7:30pm.

LOCAL SERVICES

Luggage Storage: At the bus station, lockers 200-400ptas. At the train station, lockers 300-600ptas. Both open daily 7am-10pm.

El Corte Inglés: C. Pintor Sorolla, 26 (tel. 96 351 24 44). From Pl. Ayuntamiento, go down C. Barcas; when the street become pedestrian-only, it is on the left. Currency exchange, free map, English books, groceries. Open daily 10am-9:30pm.

English Bookstore: The English Book Centre, C. Pascual y Genis, 16 (tel. 96 351 92 88), off C. Barcas from Pl. Ayuntamiento. Open M-F 10am-1:30pm and 4:30-8pm, Sa 10am-1:30pm; June-Aug. Sa 6-8pm as well. Visa, MC, AmEx.

Laundromat: Lavandería El Mercat, Pl. Mercado, 12 (tel. 96 391 20 10). Self-service wash and dry 1000ptas. Open M-Sa 10am-2pm and 5-8:30pm, closed Sa in August.

EMERGENCY AND COMMUNICATIONS

Emergency: tel. 091 or 092. **Ambulance:** tel. 085.

24-Hour Pharmacy: Check listing in the local paper *Levante* (125ptas) or check the *farmacias de guardia* schedule posted outside any pharmacy.

Hospital: Hospital Clínico Universitario, Av. Blasco Ibañez, 17 (tel. 96 386 26 00), at the corner of C. Dr. Ferrer. Take bus #41, 71, or 81 from Pl. Ayuntamiento. An English-speaking doctor is often on duty.

Post Office: Pl. Ayuntamiento, 24 (tel. 96 351 67 50). Open M-F 8:30am-8:30pm, Sa 9:30am-2pm. **Postal Code:** 46080.

Internet Access: Agora Internet, C. Paz 33 (tel. 96 351 04 44). 5 fast computers. 500ptas per 30min.; students 400ptas. **Quisiera,** Dr. Ute Zaragoza, 46 (tel. 902 14 71 47), between the Benimaclet and Zaragoza metro stops. 240ptas for 10min.

ACCOMMODATIONS

Since Valencia's accommodations are geared more towards businessmen than tourists, rooms are plentiful during the summer. During the papier-mâché orgy of *Las Fallas* (Mar. 12-19), reserve well in advance. The best options cluster around **Plaza del Ayuntamiento** and **Plaza del Mercado.** Last resort options are off C. Xátvia, near the train station. Avoid the areas by the *barrio chino* (red light district) around Pl. Pilar.

NEAR THE BEACH

Pilgrim's Youth Hostel, Pl. Hombres del Mar, 25 (tel. 96 356 42 88; fax 96 355 33 08; email albergue@ran.es). From Estació Nord, take the metro to Benimaclet, then switch to L4 toward Av. Dr. Lluch. Get off at Las Arenals; the hostel entrance is on the other side of the building. 2 blocks from the beach. Communal atmosphere and modern comforts: A/C, massages, TV, free load of laundry, kitchen access, free email, and internet access (500ptas per 30min.; 30min. free with *Let's Go*). Reception open 24hr. Quiet time 11pm. Dorms 1000ptas, over 26 1500ptas, over 30 2000ptas. Prices reflect a *Let's Go* discount. Reserve ahead. Visa, MC for payments over 3000ptas.

Alberg Colegio "La Paz" (HI), Av. Puerto, 69 (tel. 96 369 01 52), nearly halfway between the city and the port. Take bus #19 from Pl. Ayuntamiento (next to Citibank); get off at the 2nd stop on Av. Puerto (20min. walk to the beach). Peaceful ambiance partially makes up for saggy beds and not quite spic-and-span rooms. 2-4 people and a bathroom in every room. HI membership required. Breakfast included. Sheets 400ptas for 5 days. Lockout 10am-3pm. Curfew 2-3am. Reception daily 9am-2pm and 3pm-2am. Dorms 1400ptas, over 26 1800ptas. Open July-Sept. 15.

NEAR PLAZA DEL AYUNTAMIENTO

Hostal-Residencia El Cid, C. Cerrajeros, 13 (tel. 96 392 23 23). From the train station, pass Pl. Ayuntamiento and take the 2nd left off C. Vicente Mártir. Spotless, homey rooms with fans. Singles 1700ptas; doubles 3000ptas, with shower 3500ptas, with bath 4000ptas.

Hostal-Residencia Universal, C. Barcas, 5 (tel. 96 351 53 84), off Pl. Ayuntamiento. 3 floors of spacious, clean rooms with balconies, ornate ceilings, and tiled floors. English and French spoken. Keys for 24hr. access. Singles 2300ptas; doubles 3600ptas, with shower 4200ptas; triples 5100ptas.

Pensión Paris, C. Salvá, 12 (tel. 96 352 67 66). From Pl. Ayuntamiento, turn right at C. Barcas, left at C. Poeta Querol, and take the 2nd right onto C. Salvá. 13 spotless rooms complemented by lace curtains and balconies. Singles 2500ptas; doubles 3600ptas, with shower 4200ptas, with bath 4800ptas; triples 5400ptas.

EAST COAST

Hostal Moratin, C. Moratin, 15 (tel./fax 96 352 12 20). From Pl. Ayuntamiento, take C. Barcas, and take the first left on C. Moratin. Well located with solid, clean rooms and a rooftop terrace. Bathrooms and walls sparkle like teeth on a toothpaste commercial. Breakfast 300ptas. Keys distributed for 24hr. Singles with shower 2900ptas, with bath 3500ptas; doubles with shower 4500ptas, with bath 5500ptas; triples with shower 6750ptas, with bath 10,500ptas. Visa, MC, Maestro.

NEAR PLAZA DEL MERCADO

Hostal El Rincón, C. Carda, 11 (tel. 96 391 79 98 or 96 391 60 83). From Pl. Ayuntamiento, Pl. Mercado extends past the market building and continues as C. Carda. Most of the 54 rooms are newly renovated and spotless; try for those with private bath. Singles 1500ptas, with bath 2000ptas; doubles 2800ptas, with bath 3600ptas.

Hospedería del Pilar, Pl. Mercado, 19 (tel. 96 391 66 00), past the market and Llonja, on the far right-hand side. Noisy and big. Room size varies, but all have hot water and tiled bathrooms. Singles 1600ptas, with bath 2140ptas; doubles 2995ptas, with bath 3850ptas; triples 3900ptas, with bath 4815ptas.

⬤ FOOD

Paella may be Valencia's most famous dish, but it is actually just one of 200 Valencian rice dishes. Other specialties include *arroz a banda* (rice and fish with garlic, onion, tomatoes, and saffron), *all i pebre* (eels fried in oil, paprika, and garlic), and *sepia con salsa verde* (cuttlefish with garlic and parsley). Buckets of fresh fish, meat, and fruit are sold at the **Mercado Central,** on Pl. Mercado (open June-Aug. M-Th 7am-2pm, F-Sa 7am-3pm; Sept.-May M-Th 7am-2pm, F 7am-2pm and 5-8pm). For **groceries,** glide up to the 5th floor of **El Corte Inglés,** C. Pintor Sorolla, 26 (tel. 96 351 24 44; open M-Sa 10am-9:30pm).

▧ **Restaurante La Utielana,** Pl. Picadero Dos Aguas, 3 (tel. 96 352 94 14). Take C. Barcelonina off the tapered end of Pl. Ayuntamiento, turn left at its end into and across Pl. Rodrigo Botet, turn right onto C. Procida, and duck into a little alley/plaza on the left (look for the La Utielana sign). Choose from a super scoop of scrumptious seafood *paella* (375ptas) or any of the other tasty meals (all under 825ptas). A/C. Open Sept.-July M-F 1:15-4pm and 9-11pm, Sa 1:15-4pm. Visa.

La Lluna (tel. 96 392 21 46), C. Sant Ramón, in El Carme district. From Pg. Guillem de Castro, take C. Corona, then the 1st left onto C. Beneficia; C. Sant Ramón is on the right. A veggie restaurant to moon over. A/C. 4-course *menú* (served weekday afternoons) 900ptas. Entrees 400-575ptas. Open M-Sa 1:30-4pm and 8:30-11:30pm.

La Pappardella, C. Bordadores, 5 (tel. 96 391 89 15). Face the cathedral, and the restaurant is on the right. Sit among a lively, chic crowd, while enjoying fresh pasta dishes (675-1100ptas) on the outdoor terrace. Open W-M 2-4:30pm and 9pm-midnight.

◉ SIGHTS

Touring Valencia on foot is complicated. Most of the sights line the Río Turia or cluster near Pl. Reina, which is linked to Pl. Ayuntamiento by C. San Vicente Mártir. EMT bus #5, dubbed the **Bus Turistic** (tel. 96 352 83 99), makes a loop around the old town sights (110ptas; 1-day pass 500ptas for all buses).

▧**CIUDAD DE LAS ARTES Y LAS CIENCIAS.** In an effort to aid its weak tourism industry, Valencia has recently completed what the city calls "the largest urban complex under development in Europe." Built along the dried-up bed of the Río Turia, this mini-city has already become the fourth biggest tourist destination in Spain. The complex consists of L'Hemisfèric (an IMAX theater), a planetarium, an oceanographic park (an underwater city and aquarium), and a performing arts center. Designed by *valencianos* Santiago Calatrava and Félix Candela, the complex is finished, except for the performing arts center, which will be completed during the summer of 2000. *(South along the riverbed bank off the highway to Salér. General*

PYROMANIAC'S PARADISE Fire, fire! If you can choose any time of year to come to Valencia, make it March 12 to 19, when Valencia's most illustrious event, **Las Fallas,** grips the city. The city explodes with festivity, including parades, bullfights, fireworks, and street dancing. Neighborhoods compete to build the most elaborate and satirical papier-mâché effigy; over 300 such enormous *ninots* spring up in the streets. On the final day—*la nit del foc* (fire night)—Valencians burn all the *ninots* simultaneously in one last, clamorous inferno meant to bring luck for the agricultural season and to exorcise the social ills satirized by the papier-mâché giants.

info tel. 963 52 60 23. L'Hemisfèric tel. 902 10 00 31. www.cac.es. IMAX shows 1000ptas, weekdays children and students 700ptas. For more information on the route to the Ciudad de las Artes y las Ciencias, ask at the tourist office.)

◪**CATHEDRAL.** The cathedral was begun in the 13th century on the site of the desecrated Arab mosque, and was finished in 1482. The three different entrances display a melange of architectural styles, including Gothic, Baroque, and Romanesque. French novelist Victor Hugo once counted 300 bell towers in Valencia from atop the **Miguelete** (the cathedral tower); there are actually only about a hundred. The **Museo de la Catedral** squeezes a great many treasures into very little space. Check out the overwrought tabernacle made from 1200kg of gold, silver, platinum, emeralds, and sapphires, a Holy Grail, two Goyas, and the *Crucifijo de Marfil* (crucifix) statues depicting "man's passions." *(Pl. Reina. Cathedral tel. 96 391 01 89. Open daily 8am-2pm and 5-8pm. Closes earlier in winter. Free. Tower open daily 10am-1pm and 4:30-7pm. 200ptas. Museum tel. 96 391 81 27. Open Mar.-Nov. M-F 10am-1pm and 4:30-7pm, Sa 10am-1pm; Dec.-Feb. M-Sa 10am-1pm. 200ptas.)*

MUSEU PROVINCIAL DE BELLES ARTES. This compelling museum displays superb 14th- to 16th-century Valencian art. The collection also includes works by Spanish and foreign masters, including a Hieronymous Bosch triptych, El Greco's *San Juan Bautista,* Velázquez's self-portrait, Ribera's *Santa Teresa,* and a slew of Goyas. *(C. Sant Pius V, next to the Jardines del Reial. Tel. 96 360 57 93. Open T-Su 10am-2pm and 4-7:30pm. Free.)*

INSTITUTO VALÈNCIA DE ARTE MODERNO (IVAM). The instituto is home to a permanent collection of abstract works by 20th-century sculptor Julio González and temporary exhibits of cutting-edge art and photography. *(C. Guillem de Castro, 118, west across the old river. Tel. 96 386 30 00. Open Tu-Su 10am-7pm. 350ptas, students 175ptas; Sunday free.)*

PARKS. The city maintains impressive parks on the outskirts of the historic district. Horticulturists will marvel at the **Jardín Botànico,** a university-maintained, open-air garden which cultivates 43,000 plants of 300 precisely labeled species from around the world. *(C. Beato Gaspar Bono, 6, on the western end of Río Turia. Tel. 96 391 16 57. Open Tu-Su 10am-9pm. 50ptas.)* One block farther, a series of pillared and manicured public recreation areas marks the banks of the now diverted Río Turia. These areas end with hundreds of children climbing on a gigantic rendition of Lilliput. *(Open daily 10am-2pm and 5-9pm. Free.)*

OTHER SIGHTS. The elliptical **Basilica Virgen de los Desamparados** houses a resplendent golden altar. *(Behind the cathedral on Pl. Virgen. Open for mass M-F 7am-2pm and 5-9pm, Su 7:30am-2:30pm and 5-9:30pm. Free.)* The old **Lonja de la Seda (Silk Exchange)** is one of the foremost examples of Valencian Gothic architecture and a testament to Valencia's prominence in the medieval silk trade. *(Pl. Mercado. Tel. 96 352 54 78. Open Tu-Sa 9am-2pm and 5-9pm, Su 9am-1:30pm. Free.)* The 15th-century **Torres de Serranos,** from which boiling oil was dumped on invaders, guards the edge of the historic district. *(Pl. Fueros. Open Tu-F 9am-2pm and 4:15-8pm, Sa 9am-1:30pm. Free.)*

EAST COAST

BEACHES

Sand-seekers will be disappointed with the crowded beaches along Valencia's coast. The most popular beaches are **Las Arenas** and **Malvarrosa,** both on bus #19's route from Pl. Ayuntamiento (also #20, 21, and 22 in summer). Equally crowded but more attractive is **Salér,** a long, pine-bordered strand 14km from the city center. Cafeterias and snack bars line the shore, and shower and bathroom facilities lie nearby. **Autobuses Buñol buses** (tel. 96 349 14 25) go to Salér (on the way to El Perello) from the intersection of Gran Vía Germanias and C. Sueca. To get to the bus stop, exit the train station, and take the street to the right (between the station and the bullfighting stadium) to Gran Vía Germanias. The bus stop is one block down (25min., every 30min., 160ptas).

ENTERTAINMENT

Use your siesta wisely—Valencia's nightlife will keep you drinking and dancing until sunrise. Bars and pubs around the **El Carme** district, just beyond the market, start hopping at 11:30pm. Follow Pl. Mercado and C. Bolsería (bearing right) to Pl. Tossal, where outdoor terraces, upbeat music, and *agua de Valencia* (orange juice, champagne, and vodka) entertain the masses.

Bar Sant Jaume and **Café Infanta**, both in Pl. Tossal, stay lively late into the night. American students and expats frequent two Irish pubs. One is **Finnegan's,** at Pl. Reina in front, and to the right, of the cathedral. The other is **The Black Sheep,** Pl. Porta de la Mar, 6, in the plaza on the old-city side of the huge bridge that looks like the dorsal fin of a fish; Wednesday is student night (pints of Guinness and Kilkenny 350ptas). Both stay open until around 2am, when disco life begins.

Discos dominate the university area, particularly on **Avenida Blasco Ibañez.** Young 20-somethings begin dancing at the pubs off Av. Ibañez at Pl. Xúquer. In the summer, the most popular disco is **Caballito de Mar,** C. Eugenia Viñes, 22 (tel. 96 371 07 63), at Playa de Malvarrosa (open June-Sept. 2am-7am; cover 1000ptas). Discos don't draw a crowd until 3am at the earliest. For more info, consult the *Qué y Dónde* weekly magazine, available at newsstands (150ptas), or *Levante's* weekly entertainment supplement, *La Cartelera* (125ptas).

Movie selections are varied. Vintage and foreign films, many in English, show at the **Filmoteca,** Pl. Ayuntamiento, 17 (tel. 96 351 23 36). Look in *Qué y Dónde* for films marked *V.O. subtitulado* (in their original languages). The **Plaza de Toros** (tel. 96 351 93 15; www.plazadetorosvalencia.com), next to the train station, stages **bullfights** three to four nights a week from 7 to 11pm. (Tickets 1700-13,200ptas.)

Valencia's most famous festival is *Las Fallas* (see **Pyromaniac's Paradise,** above). During **Semana Santa,** the streets clog with lavishly attired monks enacting Biblical scenes and children performing the miracle plays of St. Vincent Ferrer. The **Fira de Juliol** (July Fair) brings fireworks, cultural events, riverside concerts, bullfights, and a *batalla de flors*—a violent skirmish in which girls on passing floats throw flowers at the crowd, which in turn flings them back.

DAYTRIPS FROM VALENCIA

SAGUNTO (SAGUNT)

The residents of Sagunto are thought to be the most courageous in Spain. Their reputation dates back to the third century BC, when the citizens of Phoenician-controlled Sagunto (called Saguntum) held out for eight months against Hannibal's besieging Carthaginians. Some sources say that on the brink of annihilation, Sagunto's women, children, and elderly threw themselves into a burning furnace, while others insist that the residents chose starvation over defeat. Sagunto's monuments reflect the extensive list of those who have since conquered the region. By 1874, Sagunto had learned the hard way the art of surrendering; it became the first town to recognize Alfonso XII's restoration of the Bourbon monarchy.

EAST COAST

Frequent **RENFE Cercanías trains** (tel. 96 266 07 28) from Valencia (the C-6 line) stop in Sagunto (30min.; every 30min.; 8am-9pm, M-F 320ptas, Sa-Su 360ptas), as do Vallduxense **buses** (tel. 96 466 18 50; 45min., every 30min., 275ptas). The highlight of the old town is its refurbished medieval **castle** (open June-Sept. Tu-Sa 10am-8pm, Su 10am-2pm; Oct.-May Tu-Sa 10am-2pm and 4-6pm, Su 10am-2pm). Along the way, heading into town, is the once-crumbling **Roman Theater,** which has survived a controversial restoration process to become an impressive modern performance stage, built entirely on the still-visible skeleton of the Roman structure. By the port (4km from the town center), **beaches,** including **Puerto de Sagunto,** the recent recipient of an EU beach award, attract summer travelers. **Buses** to the beaches leave from Av. Santos Patronos next to the tourist office (every 20min., 100ptas).

MANISES

If ceramic artistry floats your boat, you'll love the small town of Manises, famous for its hand-decorated ceramics. Venders push their colorful wares in the main square, and many houses in the town display the region's talents with hand-painted tiling. **Cercanías trains** from Valencia along the C-4 line are a quick bet (20min., every 30min., M-F 155ptas, Sa-Su 175ptas) as are **CVT buses** (tel. 96 211 00 08), which depart from Valencia's bus station (30min., every 10min., 105ptas).

L'ALBUFERA

Spain's largest lagoon, L'Albufera, is 13km south of Valencia. L'Albufera is exactly what you'd expect from a nature enclave so close to the business-minded Valencia—motorized boat tours weave around reeds while flying fish serenade cruisers. **Autobuses Buñol Buses** (tel. 96 349 14 25) depart from the corner of Gran Vía de Germanía and C. Sueca in Valencia, stopping here on the way to El Perello (40min., every 30min., 165ptas). To catch the return bus, walk with your back to the lagoon and cross the bridge on the right.

CULLERA

The rapidly growing town of Cullera stretches beneath the protective glare of its 13th-century **castle,** recently reopened but still undergoing reconstruction. Those who complete the 15-minute zig-zag hike are rewarded with a 360-degree postcard-worthy view of the mountains, verdant rice paddies, the sea, the river, and the city beyond. Attached to the castle, the 19th-century **Santuari de la Verge** displays sundry religious treasures "collected" by castle residents over the years. (Both castle and sanctuary open June-Aug. 10:30am-1:30pm and 5:30-8:15pm. Free.) Cullera lies on the **Cercanías train** line between Valencia and Gandía (35min., every hr., M-F 320ptas, Sa-Su 360ptas). From the train station, take the bus into the city (105ptas) and ask the bus driver to let you off near Pl. Virgen and point you toward Pl. Mercado. From the Pl. Mercado go up the stairs in the back and continue up C. Calvari at the top. This road narrows as it climbs to the castle.

EAST COAST

EL SEXENNI When the epidemic plague of the 1620s returned in 1672, the people of Morella faced extinction. After exhausting the scientific options, city leaders turned to religion for salvation. They asked for help from the Virgin of Vallivana, leading a prayer procession over 20km to the Sanctuary of Vallivana. When they returned the plague had left town, never to return. To thank the Virgin and remind future generations of the miracle, the town vowed to hold festivities to honor her every six years, beginning in 1678. The tradition continues today: Morella will celebrate its 51st *Sexenni* in the year 2000, with 9 days of festivities in the 2nd half of August.

MORELLA

Once upon a time, in a land far, far away, amidst the rolling green hills of Valencia, there was a castle perched atop a lone rock. In the castle lived a beautiful princess, imprisoned in its towers for eternity by her wicked stepmother and guarded by an evil dragon. She spent her days looking mournfully out her small window past the surrounding countryside to the neighboring kingdom of her handsome prince, knowing in her heart that she would never see him again... Actually, there was no handsome prince, no wicked stepmother, no evil dragon, and no beautiful princess. However, there is an incredible castle, perched atop a lone rock, amidst the rolling hills of Valencia.

⚐ PRACTICAL INFORMATION. Morella is somewhat difficult to reach from Valencia. Visitors must pass through **Castelló**, which is on the **Cercanías train** line (1hr.; every 30min.; 6:10am-10:20pm; M-F 495ptas, Sa 550ptas). From Barcelona, the **RENFE** Mediterranean line stops in Castelló (2½hr., 17 per day, 2065-2600ptas). From Castelló, **Autos Mediterráneo** (tel. 964 22 00 54 or 964 22 05 36) runs **buses** to Morella from in front of their Pl. Fadrell office (2½hr.; from Castelló to Morella M-F 7:15am and 3:30pm, Sa 3:30pm; returning M-F 7:30am and 4pm, Sa 4pm; 1065ptas one-way). To get from the train station to the bus stop in Castelló, walk through the park across from the station and bear right; it is about 20 minutes to the plaza.

▊▊ ACCOMMODATIONS AND FOOD. Difficult transportation may force travelers to stay overnight in Morella. Try **Fonda Moreno,** C. San Nicolás, 12 (tel. 964 16 01 05), with its ancient rooms and wood ceilings (doubles 2000ptas). Downhill from the bus stop is **Hostal-Residencia La Muralla,** C. Muralla, 12 (tel. 964 16 02 43), with palatial singles and standard doubles, complete with private bath (breakfast 400ptas; singles 3000ptas; doubles 3900ptas; Visa, MC). Morella's cuisine is filled with *rufas* (truffles) dug up from the local turf. Specialties include *paté de trufas* (truffle pâté) and *cordero relleno trufado* (lamb with truffle stuffing). Eat in style at **Restaurante Casa Roque,** Cuesta de San Juan, 1 (tel. 964 16 03 36), the best trufflejoint in town (open Tu-Su 1-4pm and 8:30-11pm).

▨ SIGHTS. The **▨Castell de Morella** (tel. 964 17 31 28), atop a massive rock, dazzles even the most seasoned of castle-goers. Celts, Romans, and Moors all chose Morella for its natural defenses. El Cid stormed the summit in 1084, and Don Blasco de Aragón took the town in the name of Jaume I in 1232. Civil wars in the 19th century damaged the castle, but the resulting craters only add to the castle's allure. (Entrance on C. Hospital, uphill from the basilica. Open June-Aug. 10:30am-7:30pm, Sept.-May 10:30am-6:30pm. 200ptas, students 100ptas.) In Pl. Arciprestal, on the way to the castle, the Gothic **Basílica Santa María la Mayor** hovers over a windy stairwell, an overgrown organ, an eerie gold altarpiece, and a ghostly statue of *Nuestra Señora de la Asunción.* (Open June-Aug. 11am-2pm and 4-7pm; Sept.-May noon-2pm and 4-6pm. Basilica free; museum inside costs 150ptas.) Exit the city from Puerta de San Miguel, turn left, and walk five-minutes to the remnants of the 13th-century Gothic **aqueduct,** which has 16 towers and six gates.

JÁTIVA (XÀTIVA)

Once the second most populated city in Valencia, Játiva, a town of palaces and churches, still retains traces of its opulent past. The birthplace of the Borgia Popes Calixtus III and Alexander VI and later home of the Baroque painter José Ribera, the town was prosperous and well-known. Unfortunately for Játiva, the last person of note to pass through was Felipe V, who burned it to the ground in the 18th century. With an imposing, mountainous backdrop and land that lends itself to orchards and vineyards, Játiva is now a small, pleasant city that snares few tourists and loses its locals to coastal neighbors during the hot summer months.

🔢 ORIENTATION AND PRACTICAL INFORMATION. Sixty-four kilometers south of Valencia and 102km north of Alicante, land-locked Játvia is easily accessible by train. **Alameda de Jaume I** divides the town into two parts: the new village and the old village, located at the foot of the hill with the castles and ancient walls. To reach the old village and the tourist office from the train station, walk straight out of the station up Baixada de L'Estació and turn left at its end. **RENFE trains** (tel. 96 352 02 02) run from the station to: **Gandía** (45min., every 30min., 495-550ptas), via Silla; **Valencia** (1hr., every 30min., 380-435ptas); **Madrid** (3hr., 2 per day, 5200ptas); **Barcelona** (4hr., 8 per day, 4800ptas); **Granada** (2 per day, 5000ptas). Buses also service Sevilla and Málaga. **Buses** stop at the corner of Av. Cavaller Ximén de Tovia and C. Don Carles Santhou, near the train station. **Chambitos** (tel. 96 219 20 36) goes direct to **Gandía** (1¼hr., 1 per day, 400ptas). The **tourist office,** Alameda Jaume I, 50 (tel. 96 227 33 46), across from the Ajuntament, speaks English and has pamphlets, a map, and a restaurant guide (open June 15-Sept. 15 Tu-F 10am-2:30pm and 5-7pm, Sa-Su 10am-2pm; Sept. 16-June 14 Tu-F 9am-2pm and 4-6pm, Sa-Su 10am-2pm). **Emergency:** tel. 091 and 092; **police,** on Baixada del Carme at Alameda Jaume I, 33; **Hospital Lluis Alcanyis** (tel. 96 228 95 00; emergency tel. 96 228 95 21), Ctra. Alzira, 2km from the town center. **Post office,** Av. Alameda Jaume I, 33 (open M-F 8:30am-2:30pm, Sa 9:30am-1pm); **postal code:** 46800.

🔢🔢 ACCOMMODATIONS AND FOOD. If you plan on staying the night, try **Margallonero,** Pl. Mercat, 42 (tel. 96 227 66 77). From the train station, turn left on Alameda Jaume I, take the first right onto C. St. Francese, go straight up the ramp onto C. Alos, and take the first left on C. Botigues, which runs into Pl. Mercat. Margallonero has flowery rooms with sinks and shared bath. (1400ptas per person.) For meals **Casa Floro,** Pl. Mercat, 46 (tel. 96 227 30 20), next door to the Margallonero, serves a tasty four-course *menú* for 1400ptas (open M-Sa 1-3pm). Tuesday and Friday are **market** days in Pl. Mercat (open 8am-1pm). The **Mercadona supermarket** is on Av. Abu Masaif, just off Baixada de L'Estació (open M-Sa 9am-9pm).

🔢🔢 SIGHTS AND ENTERTAINMENT. The striking ramparts atop the hill in back of town lead to the awe-inspiring ▥**castle,** a 2km climb from the town. The castle has two sections: the **castell machor,** on the right as you come in, and the pre-Roman **castell chicotet.** The former, used from the 13th through the 16th centuries, bears the scars of many sieges and earthquakes. Its arched, stone **prison** has held some famous wrongdoers, including King Fernando el Católico and the Comte d'Urgell, would-be usurper of the Aragonese throne. Referred to in Verdi's *Il Trovatore,* this castle is where Comte spent his final years—he is now buried in its chapel. (Open Tu-Su 10am-7pm; in winter Tu-Su 10am-6pm. 300ptas, students and seniors 150ptas.) Exit the tourist office to the right, take the first right and ascend Portal de Lleo and C. Peris Urios to find **Colegiata de Santa María,** a giant church known as **La Seu.** In front are two bronze sculptures of the town's popes. Constructed from 1596 to 1920, the ornate *colegiata* operates as a religious museum— paintings and figurines lurk in nooks and crannies and on the ceiling. (Open daily 9:30am-1:30pm. Museum 100ptas.) From La Seu, cross the plaza where C. Corretgeria runs to the right of the 15th-century hospital to get to the **Museu Municipal l'Almodí,** C. Corretgeria, 46 (tel. 227 65 97), off Pl. Calixto III. The museum, in a 16th-century palace, holds four floors of Spanish paintings, including three Riberas. The townspeople avenged Felipe V's 1707 destruction of the town by hanging his portrait upside down; it remains that way today. (Open June-Aug. Tu-F 10am-2:30pm and 4-6pm, Sa-Su 10am-2:30pm; Sept.-May Tu-Su 10am-2pm. 75ptas.)

GANDÍA

Centuries before the EU began blue-flagging the Mediterranean's best beaches, the powerful Borjas family had already discovered Gandía (pop. 53,000). Five centuries later, the city still cashes in on agricultural products, though most of its income comes from Gandía's beaches and condos.

■ **ORIENTATION AND PRACTICAL INFORMATION.** Everything you need is a stone's throw from the train station on **Marqués de Campo.** Everything you want is at the **beach,** 4km away. **RENFE** (tel. 96 352 02 02) trains depart from Marqués de Campo to **Valencia** (1hr., every 30min., 495ptas) and **Játiva** (380ptas). Trains also run from Valencia to **Platja i Grau de Gandía,** Gandía's beach (3-4 per day, 495ptas). **UBESA,** C. Magistrado Catalán, 3 (tel. 96 296 50 66; in Valencia tel. 96 340 08 05) runs buses to: **Valencia** (1¼hr., 9-12 per day, 710ptas); **Alicante** (3hr., 9-12 per day, 1185ptas); **Barcelona** (7-8hr., 1 per day, 3600ptas). Buses also stop in **Denia** (320ptas), **Calpe** (540ptas), **Altea** (640ptas), and **Elche** (1280ptas). **Auto Res,** Marqués de Campo, 12 (tel. 96 287 10 64), across from the train station, runs buses to the beach at Pg. Marítim en route to **Madrid** (5½hr., 7 per day, 3300ptas).

Tourist office (tel. 96 287 77 88), Marqués de Campo, across from the train station, offers a detailed free map (English spoken; open June-Aug. M-F 10am-2pm and 4:30-7:30pm, Sa 10am-1pm; Sept.-May M-F 10am-2pm and 4-7pm, Sa 10am-1pm). Another **branch** (tel. 96 284 24 07) is at Pg. Marítim on the water (open Mar. 15-Oct. 15 M-Sa 10am-2pm and 5-8pm, Su 10am-1pm; Oct. 16-Mar. 14 Su 10am-1pm). **Emergency:** tel. 091 or 092; **police:** tel. 96 287 88 00; **hospital:** (tel. 96 295 92 00), C. Sant Pere and Pg. Germanies. **Post office,** Pl. Jaume I, 7 (tel. 96 287 10 91), a few blocks behind the Ajuntament (open M-F 8:30am-2:30pm); **postal code:** 46700.

■ **ACCOMMODATIONS AND FOOD.** HI cardholders rejoice at the Platja de Piles hostel (see **Near Gandía,** below), especially given the number of expensive hostels in town. Make reservations well in advance during the summer, especially in August and on weekends. **Hotel Europa,** C. Levante, 12-14 (tel. 96 284 07 50), is the least expensive of the beachfront establishments. From the tourist office, hop on the **La Marina** bus and ask to be let off at the C. Levante stop (110ptas), then walk down C. Ermita, which becomes C. Levante. (Breakfast 350ptas. Singles with bath 3000ptas; doubles with shower 4000ptas, with bath 5000-5500ptas.) Or try **Hotel Mavi,** C. Legazpi, 18 (tel. 96 284 00 20), across from the train station and 2½ blocks from the beach. Take the bus to Platja de Gandia (125ptas). The rooms are unexciting but clean. (Doubles 5000ptas. Visa, MC.) The tourist office has info on the 2 campsites near the beach. One is **L'Alqueria** (tel. 96 284 04 70), on the La Marina bus route between Gandía and the beach (600ptas per person; 750ptas per tent; open March-Sept.). Before hopping on the bus to the beach, stock up at **Supermarket Macedona,** C. Perú, across from the La Amistad stop (open M-Sa 9am-9pm). **Polleria Asador Josman,** C. Ermita, 16 (tel. 96 284 05 30), 100m down the street from Hotel Europa, toward the bus stop, serves chicken, chicken, and more chicken (open June-Aug. M-Sa 9am-3pm and 7-10pm, Su 9am-3pm; Sept.-May F and Su 9am-3pm, Sa 9am-3pm and 6-8pm).

■ **BEACHES.** There is not much here aside from the **beach,** but who cares? Wedged between the blue sea and the tiled Pg. Marítim, fine sands stretch for several kilometers from the port to the condos. **La Marina buses,** Marqués de Campo, 14 (tel. 96 287 18 06), next to the tourist office, run to the beach along Pg. Marítim (every 12min., last bus 12:30am, 125ptas).

NEAR GANDÍA: PLATJA DE PILES

Just 10km south and a short bus ride away from Gandía, Platja de Piles offers beach and more beach, plus a fantastic youth hostel. From Gandía, **La Amistad,** Av. Marqués de Campo, 9 (tel. 96 287 44 10), runs to and from Platja de Piles (8 per day, 105ptas). Buses depart from outside the train station, across from the supermarket. While in Platja, spend the night at ◪**Alberg Mar i Vent (HI)** (tel. 96 283 17 48 or 283 17 25), on C. Dr. Fleming. Walk down the street from the bus stop, then follow the signs to the hostel. Even *Let's Go* cannot do justice to this hostel/beachfront resort. It has a weight room, pool table, outdoor patio, and basketball/soccer court. The relatively uncrowded beach is literally just out the back door. Dishware, microwave, and fridges are available until late at night. **Bike** (500ptas per

EAST COAST

day) and **kayak rental** (700ptas per hr.), and windsurfing lessons are also available. (No alcohol. Washing machine and library. 3-day max. stay, flexible if uncrowded. Curfew weeknights 2am, Sa 4am. Open Feb. 15-Dec. 15. Call well in advance for reservations. Sheets 300ptas for entire stay. Dorms 800ptas, with breakfast 900ptas, with full board 1900ptas; over 26 300-500ptas extra.) Grab a bite at **Spinach,** Av. del Mar, 33 (tel. 96 283 15 86), around the corner from the bus stop. Fresh fruit shakes and tasty crepes (325-825ptas) won't make that bikini look any better. (Open daily June-Aug. noon-2am; Sept.-May F-Su noon-2am.)

ALICANTE (ALACANT)

Sun-drenched Alicante (pop. 250,000) is somehow both dutifully entertaining yet quietly charming—the best sort of resort town. While a multifaceted nightlife energizes the city, Alicante's famous, mosaic-lined waterside Explanada relaxes it at sunset. The sizeable Playa Postiguet sprawls a few feet from the town's center, where lanky palms line the avenues and fountained plazas. High above the rows of sun-darkened bodies, the ancient *castillo,* spared by Franco, guards the wicked tangle of streets in the cobblestoned *casco antiguo.*

▐ GETTING THERE

Trains to Alicante are generally cheaper and more frequent than buses. They run from: **Murcia** (1½hr., 9-17 per day, 6am-10pm, 540ptas); **Valencia** (2hr., 9 per day, 7am-9pm, 2000ptas); **Almería** (2½hr., 5 per day, 8am-8pm, 1740ptas); **Madrid** (4hr., 7 per day, 8am-8pm, 6000ptas). **Buses** run from **Granada** (8hr., 4 per day, 4910ptas).

▌ ORIENTATION AND PRACTICAL INFORMATION

Originating at the train station, **Avenida de la Estación** becomes **Avenida Alfonso X el Sabio** after passing through Pl. Luceros. **Explanada d'Espanya** stretches along the waterfront between Rbla. Méndez Núñez and Av. Federico Soto, which reach back up to Av. Alfonso X El Sabio. Together these form the grid of streets which constitutes the center of town.

TRANSPORTATION
Flights: Aeroport Internacional El Altet (tel. 96 691 90 00), 10km from town. **Alcoyana** (tel. 96 516 79 11) bus C-6 runs to the airport from Pl. Luceros (every 40min., 140ptas). **Iberia** (24hr. tel. 902 40 05 00) and **Air Europa** (tel. 902 24 00 42).

Trains: RENFE, Estació Término (tel. 96 592 02 02), on Av. Salamanca, at the end of Av. Estación. Info open daily 7am-midnight. Many destinations require a transfer. Direct service to: **Elche** (30min., 235ptas); **Murcia** (1½hr., every hr., 540-620ptas); **Valencia** (1½hr., 12 per day, 1400-3000ptas); **Madrid** (4hr., 9 per day, 3200-4700ptas); **Barcelona** (4½-6hr., 7 per day, includes 2 super-fast Euromed trains, 4400-6600ptas). **Ferrocarriles de la Generalitat Valenciana,** Estació Marina, Av. Villajoyosa, 2 (tel. 96 526 27 31), on Explanada d'Espanya, by the beginning of the beach. Service along the Costa Blanca day and night (see **Costa Blanca: Getting There and Away,** p. 289, for more info). In summer the **Trensnochador** (night train; tel. 96 526 22 33) runs to beaches near Alicante (F-Sa every hr., Su-Th 10:30pm-6am; round-trip 150-700ptas).

Buses: C. Portugal, 17 (tel. 96 513 07 00). To reach Explanada d'Espanya from the station, turn left on Carrer d'Italia and take the 3rd right on Av. Dr. Gadea, then turn left at the waterfront. **UBESA** (tel. 96 513 01 43) runs to: **Altea** (540ptas); **Calpe** (640ptas); **Jávea** (895ptas); **Dénia** (1025ptas); **Valencia** (1980ptas). **Mollá** (tel. 96 513 08 51) goes to **Elche** (M-Sa every hr., Su every other hr., 210ptas). **Enatcar** (tel. 96 513 06 73) runs to: **Granada** (6hr., 5 per day, 3375ptas); **Madrid** (6½hr., 7 per day, 3000ptas); **Málaga** (8hr., 5 per day, 4500ptas); **Barcelona** (8hr., 6 per day, 4700ptas); **Sevilla** (10hr., 2 per day, 6000ptas). **Linebús** (tel. 96 522 95 04) to **Brussels** (1 per day, 7:30am, 13,000ptas); **Amsterdam** (1 per day, 7:30am, 14,000ptas); **Paris** (1 per day, 11:30am, 15,675ptas).

Ferries: Flebasa lines leave from nearby **Dénia** (see p. 291).

Taxis: tel. 96 525 25 11.

Public Transportation: In 1999 Alicante introduced a new numerical bus system, **TAM** (tel. 96 514 09 36). Consult the tourist office for info and schedules.

TOURIST, FINANCIAL, AND LOCAL SERVICES

Tourist Office: Main city office, C. Portugal, 17 (tel. 592 98 02), at the bus station (open M-Sa June-Aug. 9am-2:30pm and 5-8pm; Sept.-May 9am-2:30pm). **2nd office** (tel. 96 520 03 77) on Playa Postiguet. English spoken. Open June-Aug. M-F 10am-8pm, Sa 10am-2pm; Sept.-May M-Sa 10am-2pm. **Regional office,** Explanada d'Espanya, 2 (tel. 96 520 00 00; fax 96 520 02 43). Info on the entire coast. English spoken. Open June-Aug. M-F 10am-8pm, Sa 10am-2pm and 3-8pm; Sept.-May M-F 10am-7pm, Sa 10am-2pm. Also an **airport branch** (tel. 96 691 91 00), a branch by the **Ayuntamiento** (tel. 900 21 10 27), and one by **Playa Postiguet** (tel. 96 520 03 77).

Budget Travel: TIVE, Pl. San Cristobal, 8 (tel. 96 521 16 86). ISIC 700ptas. HI card 1800ptas. Open M-F 9am-1:30pm and 5-8pm.

El Corte Inglés: Maisonnave, 53 (tel. 96 511 30 01). Open M-Sa 10am-9:30pm.

Luggage Storage: At the bus station (200-500ptas per bag) and the train station (400ptas per bag). Both open M-Sa 8am-8:30pm, Su 10am-1pm and 3:45-7pm.

EMERGENCY AND COMMUNICATIONS

Emergency: tel. 091 or 092. **Police: Comisaría,** C. Médico Pascual Pérez, 33 (tel. 96 514 22 22).

Hospital: Hospital General, C. Maestro Alonzo, 109 (tel. 96 593 83 00).

Post Office: Pl. Gabriel Miró, 7 (tel. 96 521 99 84), off C. San Fernando. Lista de Correos. Open M-F 8:30am-8:30pm, Sa 9:30am-2pm. 2nd **branch,** Bono Guarner, 2 (tel. 96 522 78 71), next to the RENFE Station. Same hours. **Postal Code:** 03070.

Internet Access: Battlezone, C. Campos Vassallo, 9 (tel. 96 514 51 97). Mornings 300ptas per hr., evenings 400ptas per hr. Open June-Aug. M-Th 11am-3pm and 4:30-11pm, F-Su 11am-3pm and 4:30pm-midnight; Sept.-May M-Th 4:30-10pm, F 4:30pm-midnight, Sa 11am-2pm and 4pm-midnight, Su 10am-2pm and 4-10pm.

▚ ACCOMMODATIONS AND CAMPING

Although there seem to be hostels on every corner, the number of truly desirable rooms is minimal. The best places can be found in the new section of town. Good, cheap rooms require an early arrival or a reservation. In winter, prices drop significantly. If everywhere you go is full, try the tourist office's accommodations list.

Pensión Les Monges Palace, C. Monjas, 2 (tel. 96 521 50 46), behind the Ayuntamiento. In the center of the historic district a few blocks from the beach. Palace indeed: impeccable taste and charm have made it a budget traveler's dream. Immaculate rooms are well decorated, and the newly constructed downstairs section features satellite TVs. A real Dalí hangs in the living room. A/C (700ptas per day), parking (900ptas per day). Hair dryer, TV, and excellent mattress in each room. Winter heating. Singles with sink 2100ptas, with shower 2400ptas, with bath 3200ptas; doubles with sink 3900ptas, with shower 4200ptas, with bath 5000ptas; triples with sink 5000ptas, with shower 5500ptas, with bath 6000ptas. Visa, MC.

Habitaciones México, C. General Primo de Rivera, 10 (tel. 96 520 93 07; email mexrooms@lix.ctv.es), off the end of Av. Alfonso X El Sabio. Wins the award for "Nicest Hostel Owner." Just like home, with free use of kitchen and email, book swap, and TV room. Internet 800ptas per hr. Laundry 1000ptas per load. Singles 1900ptas, with bath 2200ptas; doubles 3600ptas, with bath 4200ptas; triples with bath 6000ptas.

Residencia Universitaria (HI), Av. Orihuela, 59 (tel. 96 511 30 44). Take bus #03 (100ptas). Not near nightlife, but spectacular, spotless facilities. Hybrid college dormitory/1-star hotel. Individual rooms with private bath and A/C, cheap snack bar, big-screen TV, free laundry, pool table, and foosball. 3-day max. stay. Call well in advance. Dorms 800ptas, with breakfast 900ptas, with 3 meals 1900ptas; over 26 dorms 1100ptas, with breakfast 1400ptas, with 3 meals 2400ptas. July-Sept. only.

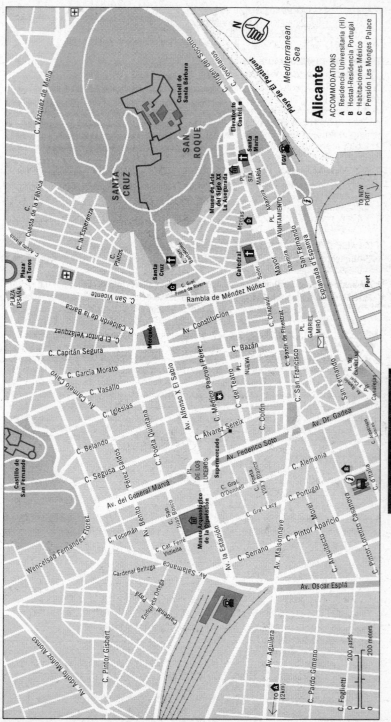

Alicante

ACCOMMODATIONS
A Residencia Universaria (HI)
B Hostal-Residencia Portugal
C Habitaciones México
D Pensión Les Monges Palace

Mediterranean Sea

N

Castell de Santa Bárbara

SAN ROQUE

SANTA CRUZ

Castillo de San Fernando

C. Vázquez de Mella

C. Virgen del Socorro

C. Covadonga

Elevator to Castell ■

Santa María
PL. STA. MARÍA

FGV

Museu de Arte del Siglo XX La Asegurada

C. Cuesta de la Fábrica

C. la Esperanza

C. Adolfo Blanca

C. Prados

Monjas

PL. AYUNTAMIENTO

D

Santa Cruz

Catedral

C. Labradores

C. Gral. Primo de Rivera

Mayor

Altamira

San Fernando

Soler

Plaza de Toros

PLAZA EPSAÑA

C. San Vicente

Rambla de Méndez Núñez

Av. Constitución

C. Chapaull

PL. GABRIEL MIRÓ

Esplanada d'Espanya

Port

TO NEW PORT

Mercado

C. Calderón de la Barca

C. El Pintor Velázquez

C. Capitán Segura

C. García Morato

C. Vasallo

C. Iglesias

Av. Carmelo Calvo

C. Poeta Quintana

C. Alfonso X El Sabio

C. Médico Pascual Pérez

C. del Teatro

PL. NUEVA

C. Bazán

C. Barón de Finestrat

C. San Francisco

C. Álvarez Sereix

C. Colón

Av. Dr. Gadea

PL. DE CANALEJAS

San Fernando

Parq. de Canalejas

C. Belando

C. Segusa

Av. Pérez Galdos

Av. del General Marvá

PL. DE LOS LUCEROS

Supermercado

Av. Federico Soto

C. Gral. O'Donnell

C. poeta Vila y Blanco

C. Gral. Lacy

C. Alemania

C. Portugal

B

C. d'Italia

Wenceslao Fernández Flórez

C. Tucumán

Av. Benito

C. San Juan Bosco

C. Cat. Ferré Vidiella

Museu Arqueológico de la Diputación

C. Serrano

C. Maisonnave

C. Pintor Morel

C. Pintor Aparicio

C. Arquitecto

C. Pintor Lorenzo Casanova

Cardenal Belluga

Cardenal Payá

Enriqueta Ortega

Av. Salamanca

Av. la Estación

Av. Oscar Esplá

C. Pintor Gisbert

Av. Adolfo Muñoz Alonso

C. Foglietti

C. Pardo Gimeno

Av. Aguilera

TO A (2km)

0   200 yards
0   200 meters

EAST COAST

Hostal-Residencia Portugal, C. Portugal, 26 (tel. 96 592 92 44), across from the bus station. Friendly atmosphere nurtured by Ramón and his staff. The functional dining room/lounge has a color TV. Steamy interior rooms have fans and good beds. TV 400ptas. Singles 2400ptas; doubles 3800ptas, with bath 4500ptas.

Camping: Playa Mutxavista (tel. 96 565 45 26), 2nd-class site near the beach. Take bus #21. 520ptas per person and per tent. Open year-round.

🍴 FOOD

Most tourists refuel along the main pedestrian thoroughfares. The smaller, cheaper, family-run *bar-restaurantes* in the old city are less-touristed. The most popular *terrazas* stuff C. San Francisco with cheap *menús* and *tapas;* locals and tourists devour *tapas* on C. Mayor. The **market** is near Av. Alfonso X El Sabio (open M-Sa 8am-2pm). Buy basics at **Supermarket Mercadona,** C. Alvarez Sereix, 5 (tel. 96 521 58 94), off Av. Federico Soto (open M-Sa 9am-9pm).

Café Mediterraneo (tel. 96 514 08 40), corner of C. Alberola-Romero and C. Altamira, 2 blocks from the Explanada. A low-key, bustling, bright cafe that bursts with locals. Four-course *menú* 1000ptas. Open M-Sa 1-4 and 8-11pm.

Capitol, C. Bazan, 45 (tel. 96 520 05 92), between Av. Alfonso X El Sabio and the Explanada. Four-course *menú* 1150ptas. Open daily 1-4:30pm; Tu-Sa also 8-11pm. Closed the first half of Aug.

La Venta del Lobo, C. San Fernando, 48 (tel. 96 514 09 85), 2 blocks toward the center from Av. Dr. Gadea. Prepares regional specialties from all over Spain. Four-course *menú* 1125ptas. Entrees 400-900ptas. Open Tu-Sa 1-4pm and 8:30pm-midnight, Su 1-4pm.

👁️ 📷 SIGHTS AND BEACHES

CASTELL DE SANTA BÁRBARA. Complete with drawbridges, dark passageways, and hidden tunnels, Castell de Santa Bárbara keeps silent guard over Alicante's beach. Built by the Carthaginians and recently renovated, the 200m high fortress has a dry moat, dungeon, ammunition storeroom, and an all-encompassing view of Alicante. A paved road from the old section of Alicante leads to the top; most people take the **elevator** from a hidden entrance on Av. Jovellanos, across the street from Playa Postiguet and near the white crosswalk over the road. *(Tel. 96 526 31 31. Open Apr.-Sept. 10am-7:30pm; Oct.-Mar. 9am-6:30pm. Free. Elevator 400ptas.)*

OTHER SIGHTS. Bronze Age dowries and Roman statues found throughout the province coexist inside the **Neoclassical Museu Arqueológic de la Diputación.** *(Pl. Gomez Ulla. Take bus #02.)* Skipping ahead a few centuries, a crowd of Valencian modernist art pieces, along with a few Mirós, Picassos, Kandinskys, and Calders fraternize in the **Museu de Arte del Siglo XX La Asegurada.** *(Pl. Santa Maria, 3, at the east end of C. Mayor. Tel. 96 514 07 68. Open May.-Sept. Tu-Sa 10:30am-1:30pm and 6-9pm, Su 10:30am-1pm; Oct.-Apr. Tu-Sa 10am-1pm and 5-8pm, Su 10am-1pm. Free.)*

BEACHES. Alicante's own **Playa del Postiguet** attracts a disturbing number of sun-seekers. Six-kilometer-long **Playa de San Juan** and **Playa del Mutxavista** are popular options. *(For San Juan, take TAM buses #21, 22, or 31. For Mutxavista, take #21. All depart every 15min., 105ptas. Or take the Alicante-Dénia train (20min., every hr., 105ptas.) from the main station.)* The regional tourist office also has a listing of *bandera azul* (blue flag) beaches (an award given by the EU) on the Alicante-Dénia rail line.

🎵 ENTERTAINMENT

Warm-weather nightlife centers on the **Playa de San Juan.** A **taxi** for up to four people from Alicante to Playa San Juan costs about 1000ptas. The **Buhobus** runs to Playa San Juan (TAM #21 and 21c, every 20min., 100ptas). In July and August, **Ferrocarriles de la Generalitat Valenciana** runs special **Trensnochador** night trains from

Estació Marina to several points along the beach (see **Trains,** p. 285, for more info). Pick up a schedule, along with discounts on cover charges, at the tourist office. At the "Discotecas" night train stop and all along Playa San Juan, discos are packed until dawn; *bares-musicales* line side streets off the beach to the right of the same train stop. The "Disco Benidorm" stop (round-trip 650ptas), in package-tour crazy Benidorm, has hard-core *discotecas* like **Penélope, Pachá, KU, KM,** and **Insomnia** (open nightly until 9am; cover from 1500ptas), as well as a number of others in the town center and along the beach that don't charge a cover.

For those in search of parties closer to home, Alicante itself offers a number of popular *discotecas* and bars. The **new port** throbs with masses of tourists and sunglass vendors in the shadow of posh yachts. In the fall and winter, the old section of town, **El Barne,** overflows with students. Popular with just about everyone is **Celestial Copas** on C. San Pascual. **Rosé** on C. San Juan Bosco also attracts a gay crowd, while **Desdén** on C. Santo Tomás attracts an astronomical number of Americans. Closer to the water is **Buggatti** (tel. 96 521 06 46), C. San Fernando, 37 (cover 1500ptas, includes one drink; women usually get in free; open nightly until 5:30am). On the Explanada, at Pl. Canelejas, **Petit Pachá** welcomes those who don't want to brave its bigger brother in Benidorm.

From June 20 to 29, hedonistic celebrations erupt for the **Festival de Sant Joan.** *Fogueres* (symbolic or satiric effigies) are paraded around the *casco antiguo*, then burned in a bonfire on the 24th. The revelry continues with breathtaking and hazardous nightly fireworks and street decorations. The **Verge del Remei** procession takes place on August 3; pilgrims trek to the monastery of Santa Faz the following Thursday. Alicante honors *La Virgen del Demedio* all summer with the **Fiestas del Verano,** when concerts and theatrical performances are often held in the new open-air theater on the port; inquire at the tourist office for a schedule.

DAYTRIPS FROM ALICANTE

ISLA TABARCA. This island, 15km south of Alicante, was once home to one of Spain's prisons. Today it is a natural reserve and a great place for **scuba diving.** One of the most reliable scuba companies is **Cruceros Kon Tiki** (tel. 96 521 63 96) which leaves for Tabarca from the Explanada d'Espanya in Alicante (30min.; July-Aug. 4 per day, 10:30am-3:30pm; Sept.-June 1 per day; round-trip 1700ptas). For more info on the island, tel. 902 10 09 10.

COVAS DE CANALOBRE. These spectacular, stalagmited caves are situated 24km north of Alicante, above the tiny village of **Busot.** (Tel. 96 569 92 50. Open daily June 21-Sept. 10:30am-7:50pm; Oct.-June 20 11am-5:50pm. 600ptas.) To get there, take **Alcoyana bus** C-14 (tel. 96 526 78 00; 3 per day, 100ptas).

COSTA BLANCA

The "white coast" that extends from Dénia through Calpe, Alicante, and Elche, derives its name from the fine, white sand of its shores. A varied terrain of hills blanketed with cherry blossoms, craggy mountains, lush pine-layered hillsides, and natural lagoons surrounds densely inhabited coastal towns. Altea, Calpe, Dénia, and especially Jávea offer relief from the disco-droves that energize Alicante and Benidorm, although even these towns are not tourist-free.

▐ GETTING THERE AND AWAY

UBESA (in Valencia tel. 96 340 08 55; in Gandía tel. 96 296 50 66; in Dénia tel. 96 643 50 45; in Calpe tel. 96 583 90 29; in Alicante tel. 96 513 01 43) runs inexpensive **buses** between Alicante and Valencia (every hr., 6:30am-9pm). From **Valencia** buses run to: **Gandía** (1½hr., 12 per day); **Dénia** (2hr., 9 per day); **Jávea** (2hr., 5 per day); **Calpe** and **Altea** (3-3½hr., 10 per day); **Alicante** (4½hr., 13 per day, 6:30am-6pm). From **Alicante** buses run to: **Altea** (1¼hr., 18 per day); **Calpe** (1½hr., 18 per day); **Jávea** (2½hr., 5 per day); and **Dénia** (2½hr., 14 per day). Only buses that leave before 6pm make it all the way to Valencia.

E A S T C O A S T

Ferrocarrils de la Generalitat Valenciana (general info tel. 96 592 02 02; in Alicante tel. 96 526 27 31), with its Alicante-Dénia line, competes with UBESA and offers similar prices and frequencies, but adds stops at San Juan and El Campello, beaches near Alicante. Trains depart Alicante every hour on the hour from 6am to 9pm to **Altea** (1½hr.). Trains leaving on even-numbered hours continue to **Calpe** (1¾hr.) and **Dénia** (2¼hr.). From Dénia and Calpe, trains return to **Alicante** every two hours (6:25am-7:25pm), while from Altea trains depart every hour (6:24am-10:24pm). Railpasses are not valid on these trains. **Trensnochador** (tel. 96 526 22 33), the night train running out of Alicante, goes as far as Altea in the summer (F-Sa every hr., Su-Th every other hr., 10:20pm-6am).

ALTEA

A whitewashed beach town on a small hill, Altea is a relaxing and pleasant daytrip from Alicante. From the pebbled beach, narrow, stone streets and steps wind up to **Plaza de la Iglesia.** Shaded by the cobalt dome of the church of the **Virgen del Consuelo,** the square commands breathtaking views of the turquoise Mediterranean. An extended meal or drink here is reason enough to visit—the crooked streets lead to other squares that offer glimpses of the sea framed by bright white houses. During the last week of September the city erupts with music, gunpowder, and dance for the **Fiestas de Moros y Cristianos.**

Both trains and buses stop at the foot of the hill and along the coast on C. La Mar (coming out of the station, head left to go toward the center). If arriving by bus from Alicante, get off at the 1st stop; if arriving from Valencia, get off at the 2nd stop. The **tourist office** is on C. Sant Pere, 9 (tel. 96 584 41 14; fax 96 584 42 13), parallel to C. La Mar. From the train station or the bus stop, walk 50m toward the sea to C. Sant Pere. (Open M-Sa 10am-2pm and 5-8pm.) **Emergency:** tel. 091 or 092; **ambulance** tel. 96 584 35 32. **Post office** (tel. 96 584 01 74), on Av. Alt Rei en Jaume I, in the old town on the hill (open M-F 9am-2pm).

CALPE (CALP)

Stepping into Calpe is like stepping into a Dalí landscape mobbed with sun-seeking package vacationers. Sixty-two kilometers northeast of Alicante, the whitewashed town cowers beneath the **Peñó d'Ifach** (327m), a gargantuan, flat-topped rock protrusion whose precipitous face drops straight to the sea. Farther north are the cliffs and caves of the easterly **Cabo de la Nao,** from which you can see Ibiza. Around the bend from the *cabo,* a castle and watch-tower have protected the old fishing village of **Moraira** from pirates for centuries (buses run from Calpe).

Commercialized Calpe attracts hordes of *madrileños* and other European bourgeoisie. The main avenue, **Gabriel Miró,** descends to the blue-flagged (EU praised) **Platja Arena-Bol,** which gets deep quickly (a plus), but has a rocky, floral bottom (a minus). **Platja Levante,** beyond the Peñó, and the cove of **Calalga** also bear the flapping *bandera azúl.* A free **tourist train** (tel. 96 583 69 20), leaving from the train station, gives rides around the city (M-F 6pm). Leaving from the port, **boats** take tourists out on recreational rides. **UBESA buses** stop 2km from the beach at C. Capitán Pérez Jorda. To get to town, head across the intersection and curve downhill to the left on Av. Masnou or take an **Autobuses Ifach bus** past the bus station and to the beach (1 per hr., 110ptas). The **tourist office,** Av. Ejércitos Españoles, 62 (tel. 96 583 69 20), on the street that runs from the old town along the beach, has all the info you need on Costa Blanca beaches (open June-Aug. M-Sa 9am-9pm, Su 10:30am-2pm; Sept.-May hours vary).

Hang your hat at the bright and comfortable English-run **Pensión Céntrica** (tel. 96 583 55 28), Pl. Ifach. With your back to the water, turn right off Av. Gabriel Miró at the Banesto bank. TV lounge and carpeted floors are refreshing after a day in the sun. (1500ptas per person.) Backpackers can try **Camping La Merced,** Urb. La Merced, 1E (tel. 96 583 00 97), a second-class site 400m from Playa la Fossa-Levante (520ptas per person and per tent). The most reasonably priced **restaurants** line the steep incline toward the old town.

ELCHE (ELX)

An oasis-like city surrounded by one of Europe's only palm forests, Elche, 23km from Alicante, is a tropical paradise. Locals, however, have no time to lounge—they're busy supplying Spain with their highly regarded footwear. The **Dama de Elche,** Spain's finest example of pre-Roman sculpture, hails from here although it now rests at the Museo Arqueológico Nacional in Madrid (see **Museums,** p. 106). At the corner of Av. Ferrocarril and Po. Estación begins the **Parque Municipal,** where doves and palm trees glide and sway above subtropical flora and imitation Arabic fountains (open June-Aug. 7am-midnight; Sept.-May 7am-9pm). A mini-train (every 30min., 300ptas) tours the parks and another baby palm forest across the street. Of Elche's parks and public gardens, the most beautiful is definitely the **Hort del Cura (Orchard of the Priest),** where magnificent trees shade colorful flower beds (open June-Aug. 9am-9pm; Sept.-May 9am-6pm; 300ptas).

Both the train station, **Estación Parque,** and the **bus station** (tel. 96 545 58 58), are on Av. Llibertat. Buses serve **Alicante** and the private, quietly rolling sand dunes of **La Marina d'Elx** (M-Sa 6 per day, 210ptas), as well as other local routes. The best way to get to Elche from Alicante or Murcia is by **Cercanías train,** although buses also run (see **Getting There and Away,** p. 289). To get to the town center from the bus and train stations, go left leaving either station and left again on Po. Estación. The **tourist office** (tel. 96 545 27 47) is on Pl. Parc, at the end of Pg. Estación (open M-F 10am-7pm and 4:15-7:45pm, Sa-Su 10am-2pm).

DÉNIA

Halfway between Valencia and Alicante on the promontory that forms the Golfo de Valencia, Dénia (named by the Greeks for Diana, goddess of the hunt, the moon, and purity) is an upscale family resort. Though there is little here for budget travelers, Dénia's harbor serves as an important ferry connection to the Balearic Islands. In the summer the town goes nuts with several wild festivals.

■ **PRACTICAL INFORMATION.** The **train station** (tel. 96 578 04 45) is on C. Calderón. The **UBESA bus station** is on Pl. Arxiduc Carles. Local buses leave from the tourist office to nearby beaches (105ptas). To head Balearic-ward by sea, consult **Flebasa Lines** (tel. 96 578 40 11), Puerto de Dénia. Boats go to **Eivissa** and **Palma** (5475ptas). **Pitra car ferries** (tel. 96 642 31 20) also depart from Estació Marítime in Dénia to **San Antonio** (5475ptas) and **Palma** (Tu and F only, 10,950ptas round-trip), both on Mallorca. For full transportation info, see **Getting There and Away,** p. 472.

Most **tourist services,** including local buses, trains, ferries, the tourist office, and the **post office,** are clustered on **Calle Patricio Fernandez,** running straight to the port. Turn left out of the Enactean/UBESA bus office and turn left out of the plaza onto C. Patricio Fernandez to reach the center of town. The **tourist office,** C. Glorieta Oculista Baigues, 9 (tel. 96 642 23 67), 30m inland from Estación Marítime, directs travelers to beach and bed options (open July-Sept. daily 10am-2pm and 5-8pm; Oct.-June M-Sa 10am-2pm and 5-8pm, Su 10am-2pm).

■ **ACCOMMODATIONS AND FOOD.** Dénia loves large wallets. The tourist office has a list of accommodations; among the less expensive options is **Hostal Comercio,** C. de la Vía, 43 (tel. 96 578 00 71), between the tourist office and the bus station. Its spacious rooms have A/C, TVs, phones, and tiled baths. (Singles 4200ptas; doubles 7000ptas.) Among several campgrounds, **Camping Las Marinas,** C. Les Bovetes Nord, 4 (tel. 96 647 41 85 or 96 575 51 88), is a 3km bus ride (105ptas) from Platja Jorge Joan (500ptas per person and per tent; open Nov.-Sept.). The **supermarket,** C. Carlos Senti, 7 (tel. 96 578 22 61), is just off C. Patricio Fernandez (open M-Sa 9am-8:30pm). Restaurants hover around C. Marqués de Campo. For un-Spanish food at a budget price, try **Restaurante Chino Pu-Chang,** C. Patricio Fernandez, 79. The all-inclusive *menú* costs 700ptas (open daily noon-4:30pm and 7pm-midnight).

EAST COAST

▣ ◪ **SIGHTS AND ENTERTAINMENT.** An 18th-century **castle** (tel. 96 642 06 56) sprawls across the hill overlooking the marina (open June-Sept. 10am-1:30pm and 4:30-8pm; Oct.-May 10am-1pm and 3-6:30pm; 300ptas). A tourist train chugs to the castle from outside the tourist office (every 30min., 10am-1pm and 5-8pm, 500ptas includes ride and entrance to castle). Dénia holds a mini **Fallas festival** from March 16 to 20, burning effigies on the final midnight. During **Festa Major** (early July), locals prove they're just as gutsy as their fellow countrymen in Pamplona—bulls and fans dive simultaneously into a pool of water, a feat known as **Bous a la mar.** During the second week of July, the **Fiestas de la Santísima Sangre (Holy Blood)** feature street dances, concerts, mock battles, and wild fireworks over the harbor. The colorful parades and religious plays of the **Moros y Cristianos** celebration take place between August 14 and 17.

JÁVEA (XÀBIA)

Jávea's wide, sheltered position hides tranquil waters free from rambunctious tourists—for now, the town still lives up to its nickname as the "Jewel of the Costa Blanca." Although a municipal bus runs 2km inland to the port and then on to a larger beach, Jávea's hidden beauties—its coves, capes, and cliffs—are only accessible by bike, car, or foot. A number of secluded coves line the coast south of the port. The most populated beaches, **Playa La Granadella, Playa de Ambolo** (clothes optional), and **Playa La Barraca,** are serene and accessible. Jávea's **Moros y Cristianos festival** erupts the second half of July; fireworks jolt wide-eyed tourists roaming among costumed Moors and Christians.

Inconvenient transportation to Jávea has spared the town from tourist havoc. **UBESA buses** stop at C. Príncipe de Asturias but only arrive five times per day. To get to the port, take the **municipal bus** (tel. 96 642 14 08) from there (every 30min., 8am-2pm and 4-10pm, 110ptas). If you don't feel like waiting, continue walking down Av. Alicante, which runs directly to the port (20min.). In addition, **Autocarres Carrió** runs between Denia and Jávea (6 per day, 140ptas). The **tourist office,** Pl. Almirante Bastarreche, 11 (tel. 96 579 07 36; fax 96 579 60 57), is at the port.

Jávea's remote location may necessitate spending the night. If so, **Pensión La Favorita,** C. Magallanes, 4 (tel. 96 579 04 77), will be your favorite too, with comfortable rooms near the port (singles 2800ptas; doubles 4500-6500ptas). To get to the hostel, follow the signs near the tourist office. **Camping Jávea,** Partida Plà, 7 (tel. 96 579 10 70), is a second-class site between the town and the port. **Restaurants** with reasonable *menús* line C. Andrés Lambert, away from the port.

MURCIA

Four centuries ago, a bizarre wave of plagues, floods, and earthquakes wreaked havoc throughout Murcia. Despite their utter desecration of some areas, the earthquakes uncovered a rich supply of minerals and natural springs. Thermal spas, pottery factories, and paprika mills pepper the lively coastal towns, and orange and apricot orchards bolster Murcia's reputation as the "Huerta de Europa" (Europe's Orchard). Overlooked by most vacationers, this unjaded region of the Mediterranean coast is Spain at its casual, flourishing best.

With Valencia to the north, the Mediterranean to the east, and Andalucía to the west, Murcia is a mosaic of regional cultures. The diverse physical appearance of *murcianos* dates to the intermarriages and interbreeding of fair-haired Visigoths with the Alfonso X El Sabio's dark-haired and olive-skinned Castilian troops.

HIGHLIGHTS OF MURCIA

■ **Lorca's** collage of architecture (see p. 294).
■ The glorious beaches of **La Manga del Mar Menor** (see p. 294).

MURCIA

Residents of Murcia will tell you that their city is a pleasant place to visit in the fall, winter, and spring, when the city thrives on the energy of its university. In summer Murcia is plagued with dry, oppressive heat that forces even the most patriotic of residents to the nearby Mediterranean. Though the city offers tree-lined streets, manicured gardens, and a few sights, its most appealing feature is the abundance of beachward buses and frequent trains to nearby Lorca.

🔂 ORIENTATION AND PRACTICAL INFORMATION. The **Río Segura** divides the city, with sights and services in the northern half and the train station in the south (take bus #9 or 11 between the two). The cathedral is in **Plaza Cardenal Belluga**, at C. Trapería's end, while the bus station is to the west of town (10min. walk). **Aeropuerto San Javier** (tel. 968 17 20 00) has flights to Barcelona, Madrid, and London. **RENFE trains** (tel. 968 25 21 54), at Pl. Industria, head to: **Lorca** (1hr., 1 per hr., 540ptas); **Alicante** (1½hr., 9-17 per day, 540ptas); **Valencia** (3-4½hr., 4 per day, 2000-3500ptas); **Madrid** (4-5hr., 3 per day, 5200ptas); **Barcelona** (7-10hr., 2 per day, 6400ptas). **Buses** (tel. 968 29 22 11) leave from C. San Andrés, behind the Museo Salzillo, to: **Elche** (50min., 600ptas); **La Manga de Mar Menor** (1hr., every hr., 375ptas); **Lorca** (1½hr., 10 per day, 800ptas); **Alicante** (1½hr., 9-17 per day, 600ptas); **Valencia** (3¾ hr., 3-7 per day, 1850ptas); **Almería** (4hr., 9 per day, 2150ptas); **Granada** (4-5hr., 6 per day, 2480ptas); **Sevilla** (7-9hr., 3 per day, 4900ptas); **Córdoba** (9hr., 1 per day, 4150ptas); **Madrid** (12 per day, 3165ptas); **Barcelona** (7 per day, 5275ptas). Municipal buses (100ptas) cover the city and outskirts. Bus #9 runs a circular route past the train and bus stations.

The **tourist office,** C. San Cristobal, 6 (tel. 968 36 61 00), is behind the casino (open Aug. M-F 9:30am-2:30pm; June-July M-F 9:30am-2:30pm and 5:30-7:30pm, Sa 11am-1:30pm; Sept.-May M-F 9am-2pm and 5-7pm, Sa 11am-1:30pm). **Emergency:** tel. 091 or 092; **police** (tel. 968 26 66 00), on Av. San Juan de la Cruz; **Hospital Morales Meseguer,** Av. Marqués de Vélez, 22 (tel. 968 36 09 00). **Post office,** Pl. Circular, 8a (tel. 968 24 10 37), where Av. Primo de Ribera connects to the plaza (open M-F 8:30am-8:30pm, Sa 9:30am-2pm); **postal code:** 30008.

📷🍴 ACCOMMODATIONS AND FOOD. When Murcia steams up and empties out in summer, finding a room is the only breeze in town; winter competition is a bit stiffer. A great option is **Hostal-Residencia Murcia,** C. Vinadel, 6 (tel. 968 21 99 63), off Pl. Sta. Isabel; take bus #11 from the train station. TVs, phones, and steamy baths spice up rooms. (Singles 2500ptas, with bath 3000ptas; doubles 5000ptas, with bath 7000ptas.) Or try **Hostal Legazpi,** Av. Miguel de Cervantes, 8 (tel. 968 29 30 81; fax 968 29 91 27). Take bus #9 or 11 from the train or bus station to the last Ronda Norte stop, and turn the corner to the right. Ample rooms have TVs and fans. (Parking 500ptas per day. Singles 2200ptas, with bath 3000ptas; doubles 4400ptas, with bath 4800ptas.) *Murcianos* must suffer a vitamin surplus from the veggies produced in the surrounding countryside. Sample the harvest at the **market** on C. Verónicas (open M-Sa 9am-1pm). For more veggies, head to **Tío Sentao,** C. La Manga, 12 (tel. 968 29 10 13), hidden off Pl. Agustinas, one block from the Convento de Agustinas. From the bus station, take a right on C. Dr. Jesús Quesada, a left at Pl. San Agustín, and then right on C. Sta. Cecilia. Turn right on C. Doctrinos, left on C. Baeza, and then left on C. La Manga; Tío Sentao is a family restaurant serving authentic Murcian fare. (*Menú* 1000ptas. Open daily 1-4pm and 8-11pm.)

🎭🎶 SIGHTS AND ENTERTAINMENT. The palatial **Casino de Murcia (Casino Cultural),** C. Trapería, 18 (tel. 968 21 22 55), began as a gentlemen's club for the town's 19th- and 20th-century bourgeoisie. Rooms inside were designed according to a particular theme, including the Versailles ballroom, English billiard room, Arabic patio, and Oxford library. (Open daily 10am-9pm. 100ptas.) The **⬛Museo de Arqueología de Murcia,** Gran Vía Alfonso X El Sabio, 9 (tel. 968 23 46 02), one of the finest in Spain, chronicles provincial history from prehistoric times. (Open July-

Aug. M-F 9am-2pm; Sept.-June M-F 9am-2pm and 4-8pm, Sa 10am-1:30pm. 75ptas.) The **Museo Taurino** (tel. 968 28 59 76), within the Jardín del Salitre between Pl. Circular and the bus station, displays bullfighting memorabilia, matador costumes, and mounted bulls' heads that pay homage to particularly valorous beasts. Of questionable taste is the enshrinement of José Manuel Calvo Benichon's shredded, bloody shirt, worn the day he was gored to death in Sevilla by his 598kg opponent. (Open June-Aug. M-F 10am-2pm and 5-8pm; Sept.-May 10am-2pm and 5-8pm, Su 11am-2pm. Free.) Just outside of Murcia, the Río Espuña courses through rocky mountains dotted with the pines and sagebrush of the **Parque Natural Sierra Espuña** (highest elevation 1585m). The flowers explode into dazzling color in springtime, the best season to visit the park. On Thursday, Friday, and Saturday nights, local university students study the effects of alcohol at **bars** near C. Saavedra Fajardo (near the main campus). On the day before Easter, the **Fiesta de Primavera** starts a week-long harvest celebration that brings jazz and theater to Murcia's streets.

NEAR MURCIA: ◼LORCA

A stroll through Lorca, from the colorful, modern train station to the crumbling medieval castle, leads you through centuries of aesthetic and economic variety. Medieval ghettos, Renaissance artistry, Baroque glory, post-Franco urban expansion, and contemporary elitism demarcate the town's neighborhoods.

Battles between Romans and Visigoths, and later Christians and Muslims, left Lorca without the orchards that extend through the rest of the region. Yet each conquering force left its own peculiar imprint on the **castillo** atop Lorca's central hill, a 20-minute walk from Pl. Espanya (stick to the main road when heading up; always open and free). The Moors built the **Torre Espolón** shortly before the city fell to Alfonso el Sabio of Castilla, who in self-adulation ordered the construction of the **Torre Alfonsín.** The ruins of Lorca's first church, the **Ermita de San Clemente,** deteriorate at the castle's eastern edge. When Granada fell in 1492, inhabitants left the fortresses and moved to the bottom of the slope, leaving in their wake three idyllic churches—**Santa María, San Juan,** and **San Pedro.** Starting anew, Lorcans erected six monasteries and the **Colegiata de San Particio.** One of many well-preserved private residences, **Casa de Guevarra,** a pharmacy in the 16th-century, has wreathed columns and intricate carvings (open M-F 11am-1pm and 5-7pm).

RENFE Cercanías trains (tel. 968 44 28 50) run to **Lorca Sutullena Station,** Av. Estació, parallel to C. Juan Carlos I (1hr., every hr., 8:45am-9:45pm, 540-575ptas). Next door, the **bus station** (tel. 968 46 92 70) sends **Trapemusa** buses to **Murcia** (every hr., 625ptas), Barcelona, Granada, Alicante, Valencia, Almería, and Málaga. The **tourist office** (tel. 968 46 61 57) is just before the Casa de Guevarra on C. Lópes Gisbert. To get there from the train station, take the pedestrian path to C. Juan Carlos I, head down C. Juan Carlos I to the right, then left on C. E. García Navarro and right onto C. Gisbert. (Open M-F 9am-2pm and 5-8pm, Sa 10:30am-1:30pm.) **Luggage storage** is available in the bus station (daily 6am-11pm, 400ptas).

NEAR LORCA: ÁGUILAS

Tourists delight in the fortified medieval town of Águilas (tourist office tel. 968 41 33 03), 45 minutes from Lorca and one and a half hours from Murcia along the *Cercanías* train line (5 per day, 140ptas from Lorca, 740ptas from Murcia). Its popularity is a result of its 35 coves, picturesque beaches, pier on the Bay of Hornillo, and **Tower of Cope** (on the wonderfully named Cape of Cope).

LA MANGA DEL MAR MENOR

A geographic fluke created the popular vacation spot known as La Manga (the sleeve) of the Mar Menor. Centuries of marine deposits settled over a small volcanic ridge and then solidified into a 19km strip of land separating the calm, tepid Mar Menor from the luxurious breaks of the Mediterranean. Windsurfers take advantage of the waveless sea, while beach-lovers relax in the white sands and crystal waters of the Mediterranean. The two seas are only a somersault apart, and the strip's 40km beach and lack of industry provides a relaxing getaway.

▨ **ORIENTATION AND PRACTICAL INFORMATION.** La Manga has one main road, **Gran Vía,** that runs its length. Addresses are indicated by km point (km 0 is at the mainland pole), plazas, and *urbanizaciones* (tourist complexes). Local **buses** zip back and forth along La Manga (every 20-30min., after 4am every hr., 150ptas). **Autobuses Gimenez Hermanos/Lycar** (tel. 968 29 22 11) runs to and from **Murcia** (5-6 per day, 650ptas) and makes several stops along the strip. **Autocares Costa Azúl** (tel. 968 50 15 43) goes to **Alicante** (2½hr., 1 per day, 930ptas); **Autobuses Enatcar** cruises to **Madrid** (7hr., 4 per day, 3755ptas). The Enatcar office is next to Bar La Parada, across from the bus stop. The **tourist office,** Gran Vía, Salida 2, km 0 (tel. 968 56 33 55), has a map and accommodations list. **Serma, C.B.** (tel. 968 56 41 19), in Pl. Cavanna, rents **bikes** (1400ptas per day) and **scooters** (5000ptas per day; open daily 10am-2pm and 5-9pm). The **Escuela de Vela Pedruchillo,** km 8-9 (tel. 968 14 04 12), sells water sports equipment (open daily 10am-2pm and 4-8pm). **Emergency:** tel. 091 or 092; **medical emergencies:** tel. 968 14 20 60. The **post office,** is in Pl. Cavanna, next to the Enactcar office (open M-F 10am-2pm).

▨▨ **ACCOMMODATIONS AND FOOD.** The closest thing to a budget accommodation on La Manga is the **Albergue Juvenil Deportivo,** Urbanización Hawaii V, km 8-9 (tel. 968 14 07 42), in the Grimanga Club. Bunk beds, locker-room showers, and rambunctious summer campers are an unfortunate addition, but the front door opens onto one of the nicest beaches in Spain, **Playa de Pedrucho.** (Dorms 1500ptas, with 3 meals 3200ptas.) Also in Hawaii V, **Restaurante Philadelphia** (tel. 968 14 37 15) dishes out mountainous platters of Murcian dishes (open daily 10am-2am).

BARCELONA

Paris, London, and New York have been described as *noir* cities, best captured in black-and-white. Barcelona, on the other hand, must be seen in vivid colors. Unsurprisingly, its fantastic contemporary style and its frenetic trendiness has made Barcelona Europe's fastest growing center of tourism. Unique Modernist architecture and the 1992 Summer Olympics won Barcelona worldwide admiration as the vibrant, festive city of the future. Today, the city enters the 21st century with an ultra-hip, ultra-modern culture tinged with Catalán individualism.

Barcelonenses have long been the privileged class of Spain. During the Middle Ages, the city was the commercial center of a vast Mediterranean empire. Barcelona suffered financial decline in the 15th century as both the discovery of America and Sevilla's trade monopoly shifted commercial routes away from the Mediterranean. The Industrial Revolution's textile mills, however, propelled Barcelona's turn of the century economic boom. During the *febre d'or*, the gold fever of 1875-1885, the city's financial moguls geographically separated the aristocracy from the proletariat. As the twentieth century approached, Josep Batlló, Antoni Amatller, and their compatriots commissioned architects like Montaner, Cadafalch, and the legendary Antoni Gaudí to build private residences in *L'Eixample*, a spacious, gridded "upper" Barcelona, higher in elevation and status than the tangled, lower-class Barri Gòtic (Gothic Quarter).

The result of these new architectural pursuits was *Modernisme*, an artistic movement that incorporated tradition and innovation. After the suffocating years of Franco's fascist regime, Barcelona swiftly reclaimed its role as the world's premier showcase of avant-garde architecture. Today, brilliantly daring buildings and parks stud the cityscape, battling one another for attention. Amid the graceful Gothic churches, wrought-iron balconies, and grand European avenues, you will find not only Gaudí's flights of fancy, but also the city's latest architectural triumphs—the angular, glassy-white Museum of Contemporary Art and the Maremagnum, a mall that juts precariously into the water.

HIGHLIGHTS OF BARCELONA

- The **Ruta del Modernisme** (see p. 314), especially Gaudí's Parc Güell, Casa Milà, and Sagrada Familia Cathedral.
- **People-watching,** day or night, at a sidewalk cafe on **Las Ramblas,** Barcelona's most famous street (see p. 315).
- Three great museums—the **Museu Picasso** (see p. 321), the **Museum of Contemporary Art (MACBA)** (see p. 321), and the **Museu d'Historia de la Ciutat** (see p. 321).
- Barcelona's never-ending **nightlife** (see p. 323).
- The eerie rock formations at the mountaintop monastery of **Montserrat** (see p. 328).

◧ GETTING THERE AND AWAY

BY PLANE

All domestic and international flights land at **El Prat de Llobregat** airport (tel. 93 298 38 38), 12km southwest of Barcelona. The **Aerobus** conveniently links the airport to Plaça de Catalunya, the center of town (40min.; every 15min.; to Pl. Catalunya M-F 6am-midnight, Sa-Su 6:30am-midnight; to the airport M-F 5:30am-11:15pm, Sa-Su 6am-11:20pm; 485ptas).

RENFE trains provide slightly cheaper transportation to and from the airport (20min.; every 30min.; 6:13am-10:40pm from airport, 5:40am-10:13pm from Pl. Catalunya; M-Sa 305ptas, Su 350ptas). The most useful stops are **Estació Barcelona-Sants** and **Plaça de Catalunya.** Tickets are sold at the red automatic machines. In

Sants, buy tickets at the "Aeroport" window (open 5am-11pm). After 11pm, get them from the ticket machines or the Recorridos Cercanías window.

The city **bus** offers the only inexpensive late-night service. Take bus EN from the airport to Pl. Espanya (every hr.; airport to Pl. Espanya 6:20am-2:40am, Pl. Espanya to airport 7am-3:15am; 145ptas). The stop in Pl. Espanya is on the corner of Gran Vía de les Corts Catalanes and Av. Reina María Cristina. A **taxi** ride between Barcelona and the airport costs 2000-3500ptas.

Three **national airlines** serve all domestic and major international destinations. **Iberia/Aviaco,** C. Diputació, 258 (24hr. reservation and info tel. 902 40 05 00), has the most extensive coverage. Iberia/Aviaco usually offers student discounts (except on already reduced fares). **Air Europa** (24hr. reservation and info tel. 902 24 00 42) and **Spanair** (tel. 902 13 14 15) offer fares that are often cheaper.

All major **international airlines** serve Barcelona. **British Airways,** Pg. Gràcia, 85, 3rd fl. (tel. 93 215 69 00), **TWA,** Consell de Cent, 360, 5th fl. (tel. 93 215 81 88), and most other airlines have offices in Barcelona. For more information on international reservations, visit a travel agency in Barcelona.

BY TRAIN

Barcelona has three main train stations. When in doubt, go to Estació Barcelona-Sants as all domestic trains leaving França pass through here as well; all trains leaving Barcelona-Sants do not necessarily pass through França.

Estació Barcelona-Sants: (tel. 93 490 02 02), in Pl. Països Catalans. M: Sants-Estació. Barcelona-Sants is the main terminal for domestic and international traffic. For late arrivals, the N14 Nitbus shuttles to Pl. Catalunya (every hr., 11:30pm-4:30am, 160ptas). Currency exchange (open 8am-9:30pm), ATMs, pharmacy, tourist office. Station open daily 6am-11pm.

RENFE: (tel. 93 490 02 02, open daily 7am-10pm; international tel. 93 490 11 22). RENFE has service to: **Valencia** (4hr., 15 per day, 3500-7200ptas); **Montpellier, France** with connections to Geneva and Paris (5hr,, 2 per day, 12,608-43,800ptas); **Madrid** (7-8hr., 6 per day, 4900-7000ptas); **Sevilla** (12hr., 4 per day, 6700-26,700ptas); **Milan** (13hr., 1 per day, 12,608-43,800ptas). Student discounts are available with a youth card.

Trenes Euromed: A subsidiary of RENFE offering high-speed service along Spain's Mediterranean coast. Trains leave from Barcelona-Sants for **Valencia** (3hr., 6 per day, 4900ptas) and **Alicante** (4¾hr., 3 per day, 6600ptas), stopping in smaller towns along the way.

Estació França: (tel. 93 319 64 16), on Av. Marqués de L'Argentera. M: Barceloneta. Services a few domestic and international destinations. Open daily 6am-11:30pm.

Ferrocarrils de la Generalitat de Catalunya (FFCC): (tel. 93 205 15 15; www.fgc.catalunya.net). Commuter trains with main stations at Pl. Catalunya and Pl. Espanya. Service to **Montserrat** (from Pl. Espanya). Symbols resembling two interlocking "V"s mark connections with the metro. The commuter line charges the same as the metro until Tibidabo. T1 passes valid on FFCC trains.

BY BUS

Most—but not all—buses arrive at the **Estació del Nord,** C. Ali-bei, 80 (tel. 93 265 65 08; info office open daily 9am-9pm). M: Arc de Triomf (exit to Nàpols). Buses are offer cheaper and more direct than trains.

Enatcar, Estació del Nord (tel. 93 245 25 28 or 93 245 88 56; www.enatcar.es). Open daily 6am-1am. To **Valencia** (4hr., 10 per day, 2690ptas) and **Madrid** (8hr., 5 per day, 2690ptas).

Sarfa, Estació del Nord (tel. 93 265 11 58 or 93 263 11 79). Sarfa buses stop at many beach towns along the **Costa Brava,** north of Barcelona. Open daily 8am-8:30pm.

Linebús, Estació del Nord (tel. 93 232 10 92). Open M-F 8am-2pm and 3-8pm, Sa 8:30am-1:30pm and 4:30-8pm. Discounts for travelers under 26. To **Paris** (14hr., 6 per week, 11,950ptas) and **London** (25hr., 3 per week, 14,775ptas). Also has daily service to southern France and Morocco.

BARCELONA

TO MUSEU-MONESTIR
DE PEDRALBES

Ⓜ PALAU REIAL

Av. Pedralbes

Passeig Manuel Girona

Ronda General Mitre

C. les Escales

C. Modolell

Via Augusta

N

PLAÇA
PAPA PIUS
XII

PLAÇA PRAT
DE LA RIBA

Ⓜ PLAÇA DE LA
REINA MARIA
CRISTINA

MARIA CRISTINA

Avinguda Sarrià

Av. Diagonal

Gran Via de Carles III

Parc de Poeta
Eduard de
Marquina

C. Calvet

C. Muntaner

PL. DE
FRANCESC
MACIÀ

**United
Kingdom**

0 ⊢ 450 yards
0 ⊢ 450 meters

Travessera de les Corts

Ⓜ LES CORTS

Av. Madrid

C. Brasil

C. Joan Güell

C. Numancia

C. d'Entença

L'EIXAMPLE

Ⓜ PLAÇA DEL CENTRE

C. Berlin

Av. la Infanta Carlota

C. Còrsega

C. Rosselló

C. Provença

C. Mallorca

PLAÇA DEL SANTS

Ⓜ

MERCAT NOU

C. Sants Creu Coberta

Ⓜ

Estació de
Sants

Ⓜ SANTS ESTACIÓ

ⓘ

PL.
PAÏSOS
CATALANS

Avinguda Roma

C. Vallespir

Parc de la
Espanya
Industrial

C. Sagunt

C. Obrielles

C. Guadiana Premià

C. Gavà la Bordeta

C. Molines

Ⓜ TAFRAGONA

C. de València

Ⓜ
HOSTAFRANCS

C. d'Aragó

C. de Tarragona

Parc de
Joan Miró

TIVE

C. de Rocafort

C. Calàbria

C. Viladomat

C. Comte Borrell

C. Comte d'Urgell

C. Villarroel

C. Casanova

C. de la Diputació

ESPANYA

Av. la Reina Maria Cristina

Av. Paral·lel

ROCAFORT

Ⓜ URGELL

Gran Via Corts Catalanes

TO AIRPORT
✈ ←

Gran Via Corts Catalanes

PLAÇA
D'ESPANYA

C. de Vilamari

C. Sepúlveda

C. Floridablanca

Ronda de Sant Antoni

Joaquim Costa

PLAÇA
DE SANT
JORDI

Av. Marqués de Comillas

Poble
Espanyol

PL. DE LES
CASCADES

Palau
Alfonso
XIII

Pg. los Cascades

C. de Lleida

C. de Tamarit

C. Manso

Mercat de
Sant Antoni

EL RAVAL

C. Hospital

Museo de
Arqueológia

Palau
Nacional

Ⓜ
POBLE SEC

Pg. l'Exposició

C. Blai

C. Magalhães

Ronda de Sant Pau

C. Sant Pau

PLAÇA
EUROPA

Jardins de
Joan
Maragall

Av. l'Estadi

Pg. Olímpic

C. Nou de la

Palau
Sant Jordi

Fundació
Miró ■

Av. Miramar

Funicular

Ⓜ PARAL·LEL

Estadi
Olímpic

Camí dels Tres Pins

Pg. Montjuïc

Ctra. Montjuïc

**Museu
Maritim**

MONTJUÏC

Ctra. Mondials

Cablecar

Jardins de
Miramar

Pg. Josep Carner

Teleférico

Castell de Montjuïc

TO Ⓖ , AEROPORT
PRAT DE LLOBREGAT ✈ ←

Barcelona

ACCOMMODATIONS

A Albergue de Monserrat (HI)
B Pensión San Medín
C Hostal Bonavista
D Hostal Residencia Windsor
E Hostal Residencia Oliva
F Hostal de Joves Municipal
G Camping

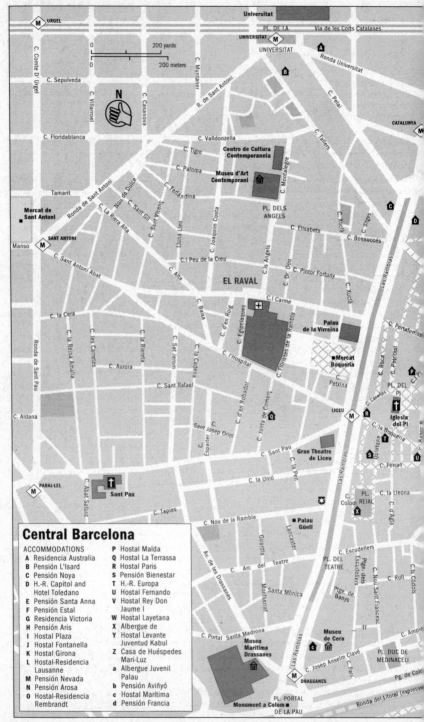

Central Barcelona

ACCOMMODATIONS
A Residencia Australia
B Pensión L'Isard
C Pensión Noya
D H.-R. Capitol and
    Hotel Toledano
E Pensión Santa Anna
F Pensión Estal
G Residencia Victoria
H Pensión Aris
I   Hostal Plaza
J   Hostal Fontanella
K Hostal Girona
L Hostal-Residencia
    Lausanne
M Pensión Nevada
N Pensión Arosa
O Hostal-Residencia
    Rembrandt

P Hostal Malda
Q Hostal La Terrassa
R Hostal Paris
S Pensión Bienestar
T H.-R. Europa
U Hostal Fernando
V Hostal Rey Don
    Jaume I
W Hostal Layetana
X Albergue de
Y Hostal Levante
    Juventud Kabul
Z Casa de Huéspedes
    Mari-Luz
a Albergue Juvenil
    Palau
b Pensión Aviñyó
c Hostal Marítima
d Pensión Francia

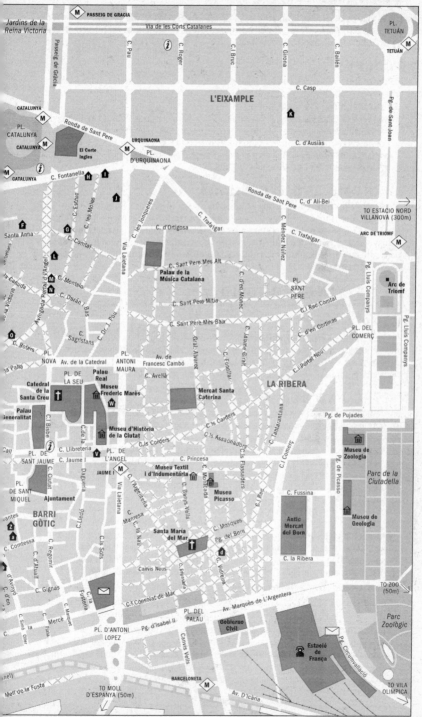

Julià Vía, Estación del Nord (tel. 93 232 10 92). To: **Marseille** (10hr., 5 per week, 7100ptas); **Paris** (15hr., 6 per week, 12,000ptas); **Frankfurt** (19hr., 4 per week, 14,300ptas). Youth discounts available.

BY FERRY

For more info on ferries to the Balearic Islands, see **Islas Baleares,** page 472.

Trasmediterránea, Estació Marítima-Moll Barcelona (tel. 902 45 46 45; fax 93 295 91 34), Moll de Sant Bertran. M: Drassanes. From the metro, head down Las Ramblas to the Columbus monument. Columbus points straight toward the Estació Marítima. Cross Ronda Litoral and pass the Aduana building on the left. During the summer, boats embark most days from Barcelona to the Balearic Islands. Get tickets from any travel agency. Open M-Sa 8am-2pm and 7-11pm.

BY THUMB AND RIDESHARE

Those who hitch to France often take the metro to Fabra i Puig and then walk along Av. Meridiana to highway A-7. Those en route to Tarragona and Valencia take bus #7 from Rambla Catalunya on the Gran Vía side—it's easy to access the *autopista* (toll road, marked by the letter A) from here. Hitchhiking on *autopistas* is illegal. Hitchhiking is permitted (although not recommended) on national highways (marked by N).

▣ GETTING AROUND

MAPS

El Corte Inglés's free map, distributed in their stores and at mobile and stationary info centers, is accurate and highly informative. The Barcelona **tourist office** (in Pl. Catalunya or Pl. Sant Jaume) also has good maps of the city (100ptas) with the best enlargement of the streets of the Barri Gòtic you'll find anywhere.

METRO AND BUS

Barcelona's extensive public transportation system (info tel. 010; tel. 93 318 70 74 for claims) is quick, cheap, and extensive. The useful *Guía d'Autobusos Urbans de Barcelona,* available free at tourist offices and in metro stations, maps out all of the city's bus routes and the five metro lines. If you plan to use the metro and bus systems extensively, consider buying a **T1 Pass** or a **T-DIA Card.** The T1 Pass (795ptas), valid for 10 rides on the bus, metro, and most FFCC trains, is a great deal (especially since multiple people can share one pass). The T-DIA Card (575ptas), good for one day of unlimited bus or metro travel, is not worthwhile unless you plan to take eight or more trips per day.

Metro: Automatic vending machines and ticket windows sell metro passes. Hold on to your ticket or pass until you leave the metro—an official with a white and red pinstripe shirt may stop you and ask to see it. Riding without a ticket carries a hefty 5000pta fine. Trains run M-Th 5am-11pm, F-Sa 5-2am, Su 6am-midnight. 145ptas.

Buses: Go just about anywhere. Usually run from 5am-10pm. 145ptas.

Nitbus: (tel. 93 395 31 11). Since both the regular bus system and metro close early, at night you'll have to ride the Nitbus. Runs from 10pm to 4am. 160ptas.

Bus Turístic: The clearly marked Bus Turístic stops at 25 points of interest along two different routes. You can get on and off either of the routes as often as you wish. The easiest place to hop on the Bus Turístic is Pl. Catalunya, in front of El Corte Inglés. The bus is great for those only staying a few days. Many of the museum and sights covered by the tour bus are closed on Mondays. Buses run Mar. 28-Jan. 6 every 10-30min., 9am-9:30pm. Purchase tickets on the bus or at the Plaça de Catalunya tourist office. Full day pass 1800ptas, children age 4-12 1100ptas; 2 day pass 2300ptas.

TAXIS

Taxis are everywhere in Barcelona. A *libre* sign in the windshield or a lit green light on the roof means they are vacant; red means they are occupied. Cabs can be summoned by phone (tel. 93 330 03 00 or 93 300 11 00; for disabled travelers tel. 93 358 11 11 or 93 357 77 55). The first six minutes or 1.9km cost 300ptas; each additional kilometer costs 110ptas (depending on when you ride).

CAR RENTAL

Docar, C. Montnegre, 18 (24hr. tel. 93 439 81 19). Free delivery and pickup. From 4480ptas per day, 23ptas per km. Insurance included. Open M-F 8:30am-2pm and 3:30-8pm, Sa 9am-2pm.

Tot Car, C. Berlín, 97 (tel. 93 430 01 98, fax 93 419 22 94). Free delivery and pickup. From 4280ptas per day, 21ptas per km. Insurance included. Open M-F 8am-2pm and 3-8pm, Sa 9am-1pm.

BICYCLE AND MOPED RENTAL

Vanguard Rent a Car, C. Londres, 31 (tel. 93 439 38 80; fax 93 410 82 71). Mopeds Tu-Th 4740ptas per day, F-M 7280ptas per day. Insurance, helmet, and IVA included.

Biciclot, C. Sant Joan de Malta, 1 (tel. 93 307 74 75). M: Clot. Leave through the Aragó-Meridiera exit, and turn 180 degrees at the top of the steps; take the 2nd right, the 2nd left (C. Verned), then the 2nd right onto C. Sant Joan de Malta. 10-speeds or mountain bikes 500ptas per hr., 2000ptas per day. Tandem 1000ptas per hr., 4000ptas per day. Multi-day and group rates available. Open M-F 9am-2pm and 5-8pm, Sa 10am-2pm.

✷ ORIENTATION

Barcelona's layout is quite simple. Imagine yourself perched atop Columbus's head at the **Monument a Colom** (on **Passeig de Colom,** which runs parallel to the shore), viewing the city with the Mediterranean at your back. From the harbor, the city slopes upward toward the mountains. Keep this in mind to help you re-orient yourself. From the Columbus monument, the city's main thoroughfare, **Las Ramblas,** runs away from the harbor, directly to **Plaça de Catalunya,** the city's center.

To the east of Las Ramblas (to the right, with your back to the sea) spans the **Barri Gòtic,** enclosed on the other side by **Vía Laietana. Carrer de Ferran** bisects the Barri Gòtic into northern (upper) and southern (lower) halves. East of Vía Laietana lies the maze-like neighborhood of **La Ribera,** which borders **Parc de la Ciutadella** and the **Estació de França train station.** Beyond Parc de la Ciutadella (farther east) is the **Vila Olímpica,** with its twin towers (the tallest buildings in Barcelona) and a shiny assortment of malls, discos, and hotels.

On the west side (to the left, with your back to the sea) of Las Ramblas is **El Raval.** The southern half of El Raval comprises Barcelona's shrinking red-light district. In the background (farther west) rises **Montjuic,** a picturesque hill crammed with gardens, museums (including the Fundació Miró), the '92 Olympic grounds, the Montjuïc castle, and other tourist attractions.

Directly behind you as you sit atop the Monument a Colom is the **Port Vell** (Old Port) development, where a wavy bridge leads across to the ultra-modern shopping and entertainment complexes **Moll d'Espanya** and **Maremagnum.**

L'Eixample, the gridded neighborhood created during the urban expansion, fans outward from Pl. Catalunya toward the mountains. **Gran Vía de les Corts Catalanes** defines its lower edge and **Passeig de Gràcia,** L'Eixample's main commercial street, bisects the neighborhood. **Avinguda Diagonal** marks the upper limit of the grid-planned neighborhoods, separating L'Eixample from **Gràcia,** an older neighborhood in the foothills. The peak of **Tibidabo,** the northwest border of the city and the highest point in Barcelona, offers the most comprehensive view of the city.

> ▼ Barcelona is fairly safe, even at night, but secure your valuables. Be careful in
> Plaça Reial and the Barri Gòtic and along Las Ramblas and C. Escudellers. The
> deeper into El Raval you venture, the more unsafe it becomes, especially at night.
> Most areas with active nightlife (see p. 323) are well patrolled and well lit.

✷ PRACTICAL INFORMATION

TOURIST AND FINANCIAL SERVICES

Tourist Info: (tel. 010, 906 30 12 82, or 93 304 34 21; www.barcelonaturisme.com).
Barcelona has 4 main tourist offices and numerous mobile info stalls.

Informacio Turistica at Plaça Catalunya, Pl. Catalunya, 17-S, below Pl. Catalunya. M: Catalunya. The biggest, best, and busiest tourist office. Provides multilingual advice, maps,
pamphlets, transportation passes, hotel info, currency exchange, telephone cards, and
souvenirs for purchase. Open daily 9am-9pm.

Informacio Turista at Plaça Sant Jaume, Pl. Sant Jaume, 1. M: Jaume I. Open M-Sa 10am-
8pm, Su 10am-2pm.

Estació Central de Barcelon-Sants, Pl. Paisos Catalans, in the Barcelona-Sants train station.
M:Sants-Estació. Open June-Aug. M-F 8am-8pm; Sept.-May M-F 8am-8pm, Sa-Su 8am-
2pm.

Aeroport El Prat de Llobregat (tel. 93 478 47 04), in the international terminal. Open M-Sa
9:30am-8:30pm, Su 9:30am-3pm.

Mobile info offices dot the city in the summer. Open Mar.-June 10am-8pm.

Tours: In addition to the **Bus Turístic** (see **Metro and Bus,** p. 302), Barcelona's tourist
offices offer walking tours from Pl. Catalunya. Open Sa-Su at 10am (English) and noon
(Spanish and Catalán). 950ptas, children 4-12 500ptas.

Budget Travel Offices: Many cluster near the university.

Unlimited Student Travel (USIT), Rda. Universidad, 16 (info and sales tel. 902 32 52 75;
www.unlimited.es), 1½ blocks from Pl. Catalunya. M: Catalunya. Also at C. Rocafort, 116-
118, 2 blocks from the metro. M: Rocafort. Expect a long wait in summer. Open M-F 10am-
8pm, Sa 10am-1:30pm. Bring an ISIC card.

Centre d'Informació Assesorament per a Joves, C. Ferrán, 32 (tel. 93 402 78 00). More of
a student assistance office than a travel agency. No tickets for sale, but plenty of free
advice and a bulletin board with youth events. Excellent library of travel guides. Open M-F
10am-2pm and 4-8pm.

Currency Exchange: As always, **ATMs** give the best rates (with no commission). The next
best rates are available at **banks.** General banking hours M-F 8:30am-2pm. **Banco de
Espanya,** Pl. Catalunya, 17 (tel. 93 482 47 00) and the **American Express office** (see
below) charge no commission on traveler's checks. Change U.S. dollars at **Estació de
Barcelona-Sants** (tel. 93 490 77 70) for no commission. Open daily 8am-10pm.

American Express: Pg. Gràcia, 101 (24hr. traveler's check info tel. 900 99 44 26; fax 93
415 37 00). M: Diagonal. The entrance is around the corner on C. Rosselló. Mail held
free for cardholders. Open M-F 9:30am-6pm, Sa 10am-noon.

LOCAL SERVICES

Luggage Storage: Estació Barcelona-Sants. M: Sants-Estació. Small lockers 400ptas,
large lockers 600ptas. Open 4am-midnight. **Estació França.** M: Barceloneta. Small
lockers 400ptas, large lockers 600ptas. Open 6am-11pm. **Estació del Nord.** M: Arc de
Triomf. Lockers 300-600ptas. Open 24hr.

El Corte Inglés: Pl. Catalunya, 14 (tel. 93 306 38 00), Av. Diagonal, 471-473, and Av.
Diagonal, 617. Behemoth department store. Gives out a great map. Also has English
books, haircutting, rooftop cafeteria, supermarket, currency exchange, and telephones.
Open M-Sa 10am-9:30pm.

English Bookstores: LAIE, Av. Pau Claris, 85 (tel. 93 318 17 39), 1 block from the Gran
Vía. M: Urquinaona or Pl. Catalunya. Open M-F 10am-9pm, Sa 10:30am-9pm. **The
Bookstore,** C. La Granja, 13 (tel. 93 237 95 19), in Gràcia off Travesera del Dalt. M:
Lesseps. Best used bookstore around, run by an eccentric British expat. Trade-ins
accepted. Open M-Sa 11am-1:30pm and 2:30-7pm.

Library: Biblioteca Sant Pau, C. Hospital, 56 (tel. 93 302 07 97). M: Liceu. Take C. Hospital off Las Ramblas and walk through the stone courtyard a few blocks down; the library is on the left. Do not confuse it with the Catalunyan library (in the courtyard on the left) which does not admit foreign visitors. Open M-F 10am-2pm and 3:30-8:30pm, Sa 10am-2pm. Closed for 3 weeks in Sept. **Institut d'Estudis Norteamericans,** Vía Augusta, 123 (tel. 93 240 51 10). Open Sept.-July M-F 9am-2pm and 4-7pm.

Religious Services: Jewish services, Comunidad Israelita de Barcelona, C. Avenir, 29 (tel. 93 200 33 75). **Muslim services,** Comunidad Musulmana, Mezquita Toarek Ben Ziad, C. Hospital, 91 (tel. 93 441 91 49). Services daily at prayer times.

Gay and Lesbian Services: Cómplices, C. Cervantes, 2 (tel. 93 412 72 83). M: Liceu. From C. Ferrán, take C. Avinyó and then the 2nd left. A gay and lesbian bookstore with publications in English and Spanish. Also provides a map of Barcelona's gay and lesbian bars and discos. Open M-F 10:30am-8:30pm, Sa noon-8:30pm.

Laundromat: Tintorería San Pablo, C. San Pau, 105 (tel. 93 329 42 49). M: Liceu. Wash, dry, and fold 1600ptas; do-it-yourself 1200ptas. Open M-F 9am-1:30pm and 4-8pm. **Tintorería Ferran,** C. Ferran, 11. M: Liceu. Ferran runs off Las Ramblas, just below Liceu. 1500ptas for full service. Open daily 8:30am-2pm and 4:30-7:30pm.

EMERGENCY AND COMMUNICATIONS

Emergency: National Police: tel. 091; **Local Police:** tel. 092.**Medical:** tel. 061

Police: Las Ramblas, 43 (tel. 93 301 90 60), across from Pl. Reial and next to C. Nou de La Rambla. M: Liceu. Multilingual officers. Open 7am-midnight.

Crisis Services: Oficina Permanente de Atención Social (24hr. toll-free tel. 93 319 00 42). **AIDS Info: Association Ciutadana Anti-SIDA de Catalunya,** C. Tantarantana, 4 (tel. 93 317 05 05). Open M-F 10am-2pm and 4-7pm.

Late-Night Pharmacy: Pharmacies open late on a rotating basis. Check pharmacy windows for current listings.

Hospitals: Barcelona Centro Médico (BCM), Av. Diagonal, 612, 2nd fl., #14 (tel. 93 414 06 43), coordinates referrals, especially for foreigners. **Hospital Clínic,** Villarroel, 170 (tel. 93 454 60 00). M: Hospital Clínic. Main entrance at the intersection of C. Roselló and C. Casanova. **Hospital de la Santa Creu i Sant Pau** (tel. 93 291 90 00; emergency tel. 93 291 91 91), at the intersection of C. Cartagena and C. Sant Antoni Moria Claret. M: Hospital de Sant Pau.

Post Office: (tel. 93 318 38 31), in Pl. Antoni López, at the end of Vía Laietana, portside. M: Jaume I or Barceloneta. **Fax** and Lista de Correos. Open M-F 8:30am-9:30pm. A little shop in the back of the post office building, across the street, wraps packages for mailing (about 300ptas). Open M-Sa 9am-2pm and 5-8pm. **Postal Code:** 08003.

Internet Access: The hotmail-obsessed will rejoice at the city's many internet cafes.

Email from Spain, Las Ramblas, 42 and Pje Bacardí, 1 (tel. 93 481 75 75). M: Liceu. Convenient, but busy. 600ptas for 30min., 1000ptas per hr. Books of tickets are a much better deal. Open M-Sa 10am-8pm.

Café Interlight, Av. Pau Claris, 106 (tei. 93 301 11 80; email interlight@bcn.servicom.es). M: Catalunya. From the metro, go up Pg. Gràcia, turn right onto Gran Vía des Corts Catalans, and take the first left onto Av. Pau Claris. Interlight is on the right, marked by a hanging "@" sign. Suave Danish owner provides affordable and fast internet access in a cool, futuristic environment. 500ptas for 30min, 800ptas per hr.; students with ID 700ptas per hr. Open June-Aug. M-Sa 9am-10pm; Sept.-May M-Sa 11am-10pm, Su 5-10pm.

El Cafe de Internet, Gran Vía de les Corts Catalanes, 656 (tel. 93 412 19 15; www.cafeinternet.es). M: Catalunya. From the metro, walk up Pg. Gràcia and turn right onto Gran Vía. The cafe is 1½ blocks down on the right. Features live concerts, poetry readings, slide shows, and art exhibits. Trendy restaurant offers access for 600ptas for 30min., 800ptas per hr. with student ID. Monthly email packages also available. Daily menu 900-1050ptas. Open M-W 8am-midnight, Th-Sa 8am-2pm. Internet access until 10pm.

Oh! Net i Kiosk Internet, Las Ramblas, 99. M: Liceu. Blue and green machine in the archway of the Cultural Center, a few doors up Las Ramblas from La Boquería market and the Liceu metro. Machine charges 100ptas for 4min. Expensive, but always open. Identical machines in Pl. Catalunya info office.

Telephones: Get phone cards at tobacco stores, tourist offices, post offices, and some newsstands on Las Ramblas. **Private phone service** (tel./fax 93 490 76 50), at Estació Barcelona-Sants. M: Sants-Estació. **Fax** services (1st page 250ptas, each additional page 100ptas). Open M-Sa 8am-9:45pm. For collect calls dial 1009; for information dial 1003. For general info on the Spanish phone system, see **Keeping in Touch**, p. 68.

ACCOMMODATIONS AND CAMPING

Ciutat Vella, the region of Barcelona between Pl. Catalunya and the water consisting of the **Barri Gòtic, Las Ramblas, El Raval,** and **La Ribera,** offers a wealth of budget accommodations. Still, visitors without reservations will end up scrambling in summer, when tourists flood every corner of the city. Signs with a large "P" or "H" mark the location of hostels. *Albergues* (youth hostels), which offer basics at the lowest prices, are the best places to meet fellow backpackers. For all listings, prices are for summer unless noted otherwise. All hostels offer 24hr. access.

LOWER BARRI GÒTIC

The following hostels are centrally located in the areas of the Barri Gòtic south of C. Portaferrissa. They are generally lower in price—and often lower in quality. Though atmospheric (and popular among backpackers), these streets can be a little unnerving at night. Avoid C. Escudellers when heading to these hostels.

■ **Hostal Fernando,** C. Ferràn, 31 (tel. 93 301 79 93). M: Liceu. This hostel sparkles with cleanliness and charm. Friendly, multilingual staff. Recent renovations and an internet kiosk make it one of the best hostels in the area. Most rooms have bunk beds. Dorms 1900ptas; doubles with bath 6000ptas; triples with bath 7000ptas. Visa, MC.

■ **Albergue de Juventud Kabul,** Pl. Reial, 17 (tel. 93 318 51 90; fax 93 301 40 34). M: Liceu. Head to the port on Las Ramblas, pass C. Ferràn, and turn left onto Pl. Reial; Kabul is on the near right corner of the *plaça*. Legendary among European backpackers. Common area offers satellite TV, a breakfast/snack bar, email kiosks, pool table, and a 24hr. party. Those looking for sobriety or a good night's sleep might consider going elsewhere. 130 beds. Sheets 200ptas. 4.5kg laundry 800ptas. Free lockers; safe deposit boxes with key deposit. Key deposit 1000ptas. Flexible 5-day max. stay. Multilingual receptionist (24hr.). Dorms 1900ptas.

Hostal Malda, C. Pí, 5 (tel. 93 317 30 02). M: Liceu. Take C. Portaferrissa (on the right with your back to the sea) from Las Ramblas, take the fourth right onto C. Pí, and enter at the green "Galleries Maldo" sign. Offers clean, nicely furnished, dark rooms. The dining room has a travel library. One of the best deals in the Barri Gòtic. Singles 1500ptas; doubles 3000ptas, with bath 3500ptas; triples 4000ptas.

Hostal Paris, Cardenal Casañas, 4 (tel. 93 301 37 85; fax 93 412 70 96), on Las Ramblas across from the metro. M: Liceu. Centrally located hostel with standard rooms. Common room with TV. Singles 2800ptas, with bath 5000ptas; doubles 4800ptas, with bath 6000ptas. Visa, MC.

Hostal Levante, Baixada de San Miguel, 2 (tel. 93 317 95 65; fax 93 317 05 26; email hostallevante@mx3.redestb.es). M: Liceu. Walk down C. Ferràn, turn right on C. Avinyó, and take the first left onto Baixada de San Miguel. Shabby entrance, but rooms inside are up to par. Wooden interior, large windows, good ventilation, clean shared bathrooms, excellent TV lounge, and knowledgeable owner. Safe available 7am-10pm. Reception 24hr. Singles 3000ptas; doubles 4600ptas, with bath 5800ptas. Visa, MC.

Hostal Avinyó, C. Avinyó, 42 (tel. 93 318 79 45; fax 93 318 68 93). M: Drassanes. Unassuming entrance leads to cheery rooms, all with either street-side balconies or windows off a courtyard. Recently renovated. Doubles 3200ptas, with shower 4400ptas; triples 4800ptas, with bath 6600ptas; quads 6400ptas, with bath 7200ptas. Visa, MC.

Hostal-Residencia Rembrandt, C. Portaferrisa, 23 (tel./fax 93 318 10 11). M: Liceu. From the port, walk up Las Ramblas and turn right onto C. Portaferrisa. Large windows, 3 tiled patios, and a dining area. Rooms have themes ranging from "little kid" to "ritzy." Reservations accepted. Breakfast 400ptas. Singles 3000ptas; doubles 4800ptas, with bath 6000ptas; triples 7000ptas.

Pensión Bienestar, C. Quintana, 3 (tel. 93 318 72 83), on a quiet, narrow street 2 blocks from Las Ramblas. M: Liceu. From Las Ramblas (heading away from the port), turn right onto C. Ferrán and then left on C. Quintana. 30 dim and simple rooms, brightened up by a central patio. Bathrooms vary from roomy to claustrophobic. Hot water only 8am-midnight. Singles 2000ptas; doubles 3000ptas; triples 4500ptas.

Hotel Call, Arco San Ramón del Call, 4 (tel. 93 302 11 23; fax 93 301 34 86). M: Liceu. From Las Ramblas, take C. Boqueria to its end, then veer left onto C. Call; the hotel is on the first corner on the left. Look for the neon "Hotel" sign. Phone and bathroom in every *habitación*. Ask for a room with a balcony—almost all are windowless. Singles 3800ptas; doubles 5000ptas; triples 7000ptas; quads 7500ptas. Plus IVA. Visa, MC.

Albergue Juvenil Palau (HI), C. Palau, 6 (tel. 93 412 50 80). M: Liceu. From Las Ramblas, take C. Ferrán to C. Enseyança, which eventually becomes C. Palau. A small, tranquil refuge in the heart of the Barri Gòtic. Offers kitchen and common room where you swap stories with fellow backpackers, read a complimentary magazine, or watch TV. 2-8 people per room. 40 beds. Breakfast included. Showers available 8am-noon and 4-10pm. Sheets 200ptas. Flexible 5-night max. stay. Reception daily 7am-3am. Curfew 3am, kitchen closes at 10pm, common room at midnight. Dorms 1600ptas.

Casa de Huéspedes Mari-Luz, C. Palau, 4 (tel. 93 317 34 63), next to Albergue Juvenil Palau. M: Liceu. Take C. Ciutat to C. Templaris, then take the 2nd left. Narrow hallways are flanked by ultra-clean, barracks-style bedrooms for 4-5 people. Kitchen use with permission. Lockers in rooms. Laundry 800ptas per load. Keys for 24hr. entry. Reservations accepted. Dorms 1700ptas. Visa, MC.

Hostal-Residencia Europa, C. Boquería, 18 (tel. 93 318 76 20). M: Liceu. A popular spot with a fabulous location—only a few feet off Las Ramblas. Rooms are basic, but the lounge has a TV and vending machine. Singles 3200ptas, with bath 5800ptas; doubles 5800ptas, with bath 7800ptas.

Hostal Layetana, Pl. Ramón Berenguer el Gran, 2 (tel. 93 319 20 12), less than a block from the metro, on the left as you walk away from the sea. M: Jaume I. Balconies open onto the cathedral or a fashionable plaza. Living room with terrace. Showers 200ptas. Singles 2500ptas; doubles 4000ptas, with bath 5600ptas. Plus 7% IVA. Visa, MC.

Hostal Marítima, Las Ramblas, 4 (tel. 93 302 31 52), down a tiny alley off the port end of Las Ramblas. M: Drassanes. Follow the signs to Museo de Cera, which is next door. Though the hostel has a prime location and comfortable rooms, it can be noisy. Laundry: wash 800ptas, no dryer. Singles 2000-2500ptas; doubles 4000-5000ptas.

Hotel Rey Don Jaume I, C. Jaume I, 11 (tel. 93 310 62 08). M: Jaume I. Every room has a bathroom and telephone, every bed a double mattress. Multilingual staff. Singles 4700ptas; doubles 6900ptas; triples 9500ptas. Visa, MC, AmEx.

UPPER BARRI GÒTIC

This section of the Barri Gòtic includes the area south of Pl. Catalunya, bounded by C. Fontanella to the north and C. Portaferrisa to the south. **Portal de L'Angel,** the better-behaved little brother of Las Ramblas, is a broad pedestrian avenue running through the middle, southward from Pl. Catalunya. A bit pricier than those in the Lower Barri Gòtic, accommodations here are safer, more modern, and just a few minutes from Las Ramblas. Reservations are almost obligatory in June, July, and August. The nearest metro stop is Pl. Catalunya unless otherwise specified.

■ **Hostal Fontanella,** Vía Laietana, 71 (tel./fax 93 317 59 43). M: Urquinaona. From the metro, head down Vía Laietana. "Pretty," with soft lights, floral bouquets, flowing curtains, and embroidered towels. Hotel-quality beds and baths. Singles 2900ptas, with bath 3800ptas; doubles 4800ptas, with shower 5500ptas, with bath 6600ptas. Reservations with deposit. Visa, MC, AmEx.

■ **Hotel Toledano/Hostal Residencia Capitol,** Las Ramblas, 138 (tel. 93 301 08 72; fax 93 412 31 42; email toledano@idgrup.ibernet.com), just off Pl. Catalunya. This family owned, split-level hotel/hostel has been making tourists happy for 78 years. Rooms border on luxurious, with cable TV, phones, and some balconies. English-speaking owner. 4th floor hostel singles 2900ptas; doubles 4600ptas, with shower 5200ptas; triples 5900ptas, with shower 6500ptas; quads 6800ptas, with shower 7400ptas. 5th-floor hotel: singles 3600ptas; doubles 6900ptas; triples 8600ptas; quads 9600ptas. Plus 7% IVA. Visa, MC, AmEx.

Hostal-Residencia Lausanne, Av. Portal de L'Angel, 24 (tel. 93 302 11 39). Peaceful hostel is almost as fancy as its imperial facade and entryway. All rooms have new wallpaper, renovated baths, and a TV lounge. Front balcony overlooks a shopping promenade. Ask for a room with a view. Doubles 4500-5000ptas, with shower 7500ptas; triples with shower 8000ptas, with bath 9600ptas.

Pensión Nevada, Av. Portal de L'Angel, 16 (tel. 93 302 31 01), just past Hostal Residencia Lausanne. Enter under the "Raphael Roca Optico" sign. Great location. Bedrooms are just like home, complete with matching throw pillows, firm beds, flowers, and balcony. TV in common room. Single 3700ptas; doubles 6000ptas.

Pensión Estal, C. Santa Anna, 27 (tel. 93 302 26 18). From the metro, take the Las Ramblas exit and then the 1st left onto C. Santa Anna. Some of these tiny, simple rooms offer views of Iglesia de Santa Anna. French-speaking owner takes great pride in his establishment. Space-age windows shut out all sound, ensuring a good night's sleep. Singles 3500ptas, with bath 5500ptas; doubles 4500ptas, with bath 6500ptas.

Hostal Plaza, C. Fontanella, 18 (tel./fax 93 301 01 39). C. Fontanella stems right out of Pl. Catalunya at El Corte Inglés. The Texan couple that runs this hostel loves students. Americana decorates 18 rooms and a plush lounge. Room quality varies, but bathrooms are all great. Phone, fax (300ptas), TV, internet (600ptas for 30min.), and kitchen. Laundry 1500ptas for 5kg. Reception closed 2-5pm. Singles 4500ptas, with shower 5000ptas, with bath 6000ptas; doubles with shower 7000ptas, with bath 8000ptas; triples with shower 10,100ptas, with bath 11,000ptas. Visa, MC, AmEx.

Pensión Santa Anna, C. Santa Anna, 23 (tel. 93 301 22 46), near Pensión Estal. M: Catalunya. What this place lacks in ambiance and water temperature it makes up for with friendly management, clean facilities, and great eateries nearby. Singles 2500ptas; doubles 5000ptas, with bath 6000ptas; triples 7000ptas.

Pensión Noya, Las Ramblas, 133 (tel. 93 301 48 31), above the noisy Nuria restaurant. This 10-room hostel loves backpackers. Bathrooms are cramped. No heat in winter. Hot water 8am-midnight. Singles 2200ptas.; doubles 4200ptas; triples 6000ptas.

Residencia Victoria, C. Comtal, 9 (tel. 93 317 45 97). From Pl. Catalunya, take the 1st left onto Av. Portal de L'Angel, then a left on C. Comtal. Large rooms are complemented by a social lounge, outdoor terrace, kitchen, TV, and small library. Rooms could be cleaner. Laundry 300ptas. Singles 2500-3000ptas; doubles 5000ptas. Plus 7% IVA.

Pensión Arosa, Av. Portal de L'Angel, 14 (tel. 93 317 36 87; fax 93 301 30 38), next to Pensión Nevada. Enter by the tie shop. Definitely the pinkest *pensión* in town. Rooms are airy but small. 2000ptas per person. Visa, MC, AmEx.

Pensión Aris, C. Fontanella, 14 (tel. 93 318 10 17), near Hostal Plaza. Huge, clean, and sparse rooms. Laundry 500-1000ptas. Singles 2500ptas; doubles 4000ptas, with bath 5000ptas; triples 5000ptas, with bath 6000ptas.

EL RAVAL

Hostels in El Raval, west of Las Ramblas are fewer and somewhat less-touristed.

■ **Pensión L'Isard,** C. Tallers, 82 (tel. 93 302 51 83), near MACBA, the new contemporary art museum. M: Universitat. Take the C. Pelai exit from the metro, turn left at the end of the block, and then left at the pharmacy. Ultra-tidy rooms. Ask for a room with a balcony. Singles 2000ptas; doubles 4000ptas, with bath 5000ptas; triples 5400ptas.

Hostal La Terrassa, Junta de Comerç, 11 (tel. 93 302 51 74; fax 93 301 21 88). M: Liceu. From the metro, take C. Hospital, and turn left after Teatre Romea. Fifty small, clean rooms. The social courtyard is a rarity among non-youth hostels. Doubles 3600ptas, with shower 4400ptas; triples with shower 5700ptas. Visa, MC.

Residencia Australia, Ronda Universitat, 11 (tel. 93 317 41 77). M: Universitat. The English-speaking owner cares about guests and her rooms reflect it—all have embroidered sheets, curtains, and fans. Not exactly a 24hr. party—quiet time after 10pm. Curfew 4am. Singles 3000ptas; doubles 4400ptas, with bath 5400ptas. Visa, MC.

L'EIXAMPLE

Barcelona's most beautiful accommodations lie along L'Eixample's wide, safe *avingudas*. Most hostels have colorfully tiled interiors and Modernista elevators styled with wood and steel. Rooms here have high ceilings and lots of light.

⊠ Hostal Residencia Oliva, Pg. Gràcia, 32, 4th fl. (tel. 93 488 01 62 or 93 488 17 89), on the intersection of C. Diputació. M: Pg. Gràcia. Treat yourself. Elegantly wood-worked bureaus, bed frames, and mirrors give the hostel ambiance; color TVs in rooms make it entertaining. Some windows overlook the *manzana de discordia*, where Puig, Domènech, and Gaudí compete for aesthetic prominence (see p. 318). Reservations a must. Singles 3200ptas; doubles 6000ptas, with bath 7000ptas.

Hostal Girona, C. Girona, 24, 1st fl. (tel. 93 265 02 59; fax 93 265 85 32), located between C. Casp and C. Ausias Marc. M: Urquinaona. Carpeted hallways, immense wooden doors, and TVs go for a surprisingly small price. Singles 3000ptas; doubles with shower 6000ptas. Visa, MC.

Hostal Residencia Windsor, Rambla Catalunya, 84 (tel. 93 215 11 98), near the intersection of C. Mallorca. M: Pg. Gràcia. With crimson carpets and palatial decor, this hostel lives up to its royal name. Balcony rooms are gorgeous. Singles 3700ptas, with bath 4500ptas; doubles 6100ptas, with bath 7500ptas. Plus 7% IVA.

GRÀCIA

In Gràcia, a five to ten-minute walk from M: Diagonal, locals outnumber travelers. Berlitz-Spanish won't help in this quiet, Catalán-dominated area. The accommodations listed here are small and well kept. Quaint neighborhood bars and *pastelerías* have given Gràcia its reputation as Barcelona's "undiscovered" quarter.

Hostal Bonavista, C. Bonavista, 21 (tel. 93 237 37 57). M: Diagonal. Head toward the fountain at the end of Pg. Gràcia and take the first right; the hostel is just off the traffic circle. Well-kept rooms. Common room with flashy TV. Showers 300ptas. No reservations. Singles 2300ptas; doubles 3500ptas, with bath 4500ptas. Plus 7% IVA.

Pensión San Medín, C. Gran de Gràcia, 125 (tel. 93 217 30 68; fax 93 415 44 10). M: Fontana. Embroidered curtains and ornate tiling adorn this family-run *pensión*. Newly renovated rooms have nice furniture and phones. Common room with TV. Singles 3000ptas, with bath 4000ptas; doubles 6000ptas, with bath 7000ptas. Visa, MC.

ELSEWHERE

⊠ Pensión Francia, C. Rera Palau, 4 (tel. 93 319 03 76). M: Barceloneta. From Estació de França, turn left onto the main avenue (Av. Marquès de l'Argentera); C. Rera Palau is the 5th right. From the metro, head toward town, cross Pl. Palau, and turn right onto Av. Marqués de l'Argentera; C. Rera Palau is the 2nd left. A diamond in the rough, near the Museu Picasso but a bit off Las Ramblas. Singles 1800ptas; doubles 4000ptas, with shower 4500ptas, with bath 6000ptas; triples with shower 5500ptas; quads with shower 6000ptas. Visa, MC.

Albergue Mare de Déu de Montserrat (HI), Pg. Mare de Déu del Coll, 41-51 (tel. 93 210 51 51; fax 93 210 07 98), beyond Parc Güell (way out there). Bus #28 from Pl. Catalunya and Nitbus N-4 stops across the street from the hostel. Otherwise, from M: Vallcarca, walk up Av. República Argentina and across C. Viaducte de Vallcarca; signs point the way up the hill. This 180-bed government-sponsored hostel has its own private woods and a hilltop view of Barcelona. HI members only. Breakfast included. Sheets 350ptas. Flexible 3-day max. stay. Reception daily 8am-11pm. Lockout 10am-2pm. Midnight curfew, but doors open every 30min. midnight-3am. Wheelchair accessible. Reservations accepted. Dorms 1800ptas, over 25 2325ptas. Visa, MC, AmEx.

Hostal De Joves Municipal (HI), Pg. Pujades, 29 (tel./fax 93 300 31 04). M: Arc de Triomf. From the metro, exit to C. Nápols, walk toward Parc de la Ciutadella, and turn left on Pg. Pujades. 68 beds and 6 bathrooms. No locks on doors. Breakfast included. Showers 7-9:30am and 3-10:30pm. Sheets 350ptas. Laundry: 500ptas wash, 700ptas dry. 5-day max. stay. Reception daily 8-10am and 3pm-midnight. Lockout 10am-3pm. Curfew midnight, but doors open briefly at 1 and 2am. Dorms 1500ptas.

CAMPING

Although there are no campsites within the city, intercity buses (200ptas) run to all the following locations in 20 to 45 minutes. For more information, contact the **Associació de Càmpings de Barcelona,** Gran Vía Corts Catalanes, 608 (tel. 93 412 59 55). All sites listed here are wheelchair accessible.

El Toro Bravo (tel. 93 637 34 62), 11km south of Barcelona, accessible by bus L95 from Pl. Catalunya. Provides laundry facilities, currency exchange, pool, and supermarket. Reception daily 8am-1:30pm and 4:30-8pm. 675ptas per person, 490ptas per child; 725ptas per tent. 7% IVA not included. Visa, MC, AmEx.

Filipinas (tel. 93 658 28 95), 1km down the road from El Toro Bravo, accessible by bus L95. The same prices and services as El Toro Bravo. Visa, MC, AmEx.

La Ballena Alegre (tel. 93 658 05 04), 1km farther down the road from Filipines, 13km from Barcelona, accessible by bus L95. Same services as its competitors. Reception 24hr. 575ptas per person, 270ptas per child, 1375ptas per tent (without car). Open Feb.16-Dec. 14. Credit cards accepted.

ⓕ FOOD

Barcelona's restaurants are a refreshing combination of cosmopolitan style and Catalán cuisine. For the cheapest meals, look out for 850-1050ptas *menús* posted in the restaurants on the Barri Gòtic's side streets. Small, family-owned eateries a bit off the beaten track serve basic, more "authentic" dishes. Bars and cafes closer to the port get more crowded and hectic. On Las Rambas, leisurely *al fresco* meals are a good excuse for people-watching. Consult the weekly *Guía del Ocio* (available at newsstands, 125ptas) for additional dining options. The *Guía* provides listings by specialty for hundreds of restaurants (though many are somewhat overpriced) and also includes sections on *servicio a domicilio* (delivery), *para llevar* (take-out), *abiertos en domingo* (restaurants open Sundays), and *cenar de madrugada* (late-night dining). Be aware that food options shrink drastically in August, when restauranteurs and bar owners close up shop and take their vacations. Most un-touristed restaurants close Sunday.

BASICS

For a truly low-budget meal, try concocting your own dinner or picnic lunch with groceries from the *Boqueria* street market, the supermarket, or Barcelona's *patisserías* (bread and pastry shops).

Groceries: La Boquería, officially Mercat de Sant Josep, off Las Ramblas outside of the Liceu metro station (Mercat exit). Barcelona's best market, with fresh fish and produce in an all-steel modernist structure. Lowest prices around for fruit, cheese, and wine. Open M-Sa 7am-8pm. **Champion Supermarket,** Las Ramblas, 113 (tel. 93 302 48 24). M: Liceu. From Liceu, walk up Las Ramblas and look to the left. Stocks essentials and has an inexpensive *menú* and salad bar. Open M-Sa 9am-9pm.

Fast Food, Spanish Style: PANS & Co. PANS franchises abound in Barcelona (including an all-night branch at Maremagnum). Decidedly mass-produced, but reasonably priced. *Bocadillos* (300-695ptas) and other deli-type food. Hours vary by branch.

LOWER BARRI GÒTIC

Some of the liveliest between-meal hangouts cluster around Església Santa María del Pí. Relax at the *terrazas* for drinks and ice cream. From Las Ramblas, enter Llano de la Boqueria and turn left at the Banco Central Hispano onto C. Cardenal Casanyes, which leads into Pl. Pí.

▨ **Peimong,** C. Templaris, 6-10 (tel. 93 318 28 73). M: Liceu. From Las Ramblas, take C. Ferrán. At Pl. Sant Jaume, turn right onto C. Ciutat, and take the 2nd right on C. Templaris. Meat-lovers of the world unite! Generous portions of hen, goat, veal, duck, and fish (750ptas and under). Open Tu-Su 1-5pm and 8pm-midnight.

▨ **Juicy Jones,** Cardenal Casañas, 7 (tel. 93 302 43 30). M. Liceu. Head down Las Ramblas from the metro and take the first left (almost a U-turn) on Cardenal Caseñao. Let the aura of this psychedelic restaurant seep in as you enjoy some of the best vegetarian cuisine around. Amazing *menú* 1000ptas. Open 1pm-midnight.

Irati, C. Cardenal Casañas, 17 (tel. 93 302 30 84). An excellent Basque restaurant that attracts droves of hungry *tapas*-seekers. Bartenders pour *sidra* (cider) with the bottle high above the glass and parade new platters of treats every 5min. Specialties include *anchoa rellena* (anchovies stuffed with ham and cheese) and *turutu* (fried chicken, bacon, ham, and cheese). All *tapas* 140ptas (they count the toothpicks). Open Tu-Sa noon-midnight, Su noon-5pm, but *tapas* only noon-3pm and 7-11pm. Visa, MC.

Restaurante Bidasoa, C. Serra, 21 (tel. 93 318 10 63). M: Drassanes. From the metro, take C. J. A. Clavé, and then take the 3rd left. Locals greet the owner with hugs and kisses—and for good reason. Forty years of practice have produced many delectable permutations of soup, salad, and meat and fish dishes (600ptas or under). Open Tu-Su noon-3:30pm and 8pm-midnight. Closed Aug.

Les Quinze Nits, Pl. Reial, 6 (tel. 93 317 30 75). Don't be dissuaded by the long line—it moves quickly. Savory Catalán cuisine served in a classy atmosphere rewards those who wait. Prices are surprisingly affordable. Appetizers 195-690ptas. Entrees 640-1150ptas. Open daily 1-3:45pm and 8:30-11:30pm. Visa, MC.

La Fonda, C. Escudellers, 10 (tel. 93 301 75 15). M: Drassanes or Liceu. C. Escudellers branches off Las Ramblas between Liceu and Drassanes. Another long line, for another great Catalán restaurant. Open daily 1-3:30pm and 8:30-11:30pm. Visa, MC, AmEx.

El Gallo Kiriko, C. Avinyó, 19 (tel. 93 412 48 38). M: Liceu. Walk down C. Ferrán from Las Ramblas; C. Avinyó is the 4th right. Enjoy Pakistani rice, couscous dishes, and fruit shakes. A 4th-century stone wall in the back room takes you back to Barcelona's Roman origins. Several vegetarian options. Most dishes under 500ptas. 5% discount for ISIC holders. Open daily noon-1am. Visa, MC accepted, but not with youth discount.

El Gran Café, C. Avinyó, 9 (tel. 93 318 79 86). M: Liceu. Walk down C. Ferrán from Las Ramblas; C. Avinyó is the 4th right. Four stylish floors, each with posh turn-of-the-century decor. Expensive, but a Barcelona mainstay. Accommodating waitstaff treats patrons like royalty. Great wine selection. Entrees 1150-1950ptas. Lunchtime *menú rapido* 1200ptas. Open M-Sa 1-4pm and 9-11:30pm. Visa, MC, AmEx.

Restaurant Pitarra, C. Avinyó, 56 (tel. 93 301 16 47). M: Drassanes. From the metro, take C. J. A. Clavé and take the 3rd left after a church. Art lives on in this former home of the great Catalán poet-dramatist, Pitarra—today Queen Sofía's former chef cooks up incredible dishes. Phenomenally attentive waiters in tuxes. Entrees 875-2800ptas. Open M-Sa 1-4pm and 8:30-11pm. Visa, MC, AmEx.

UPPER BARRI GÒTIC

In the upper Barri Gòtic, the interiors of old buildings are continually being disemboweled to make room for classy cafes and restaurants. Thanks to free-market competition, the more cafes that pop up, the cheaper they get.

▨ **Els Quatre Gats,** C. Montsió, 3 (tel. 93 302 41 40). M: Catalunya. From the metro, go down Av. Portal de L'Angel and take the 2nd left. Modernista hangout of Picasso; he loved it so much that he designed a new menu (on display at Museu Picasso; see p. 321). *Tapas* (150-650ptas) are the best way to go. Entrees about 2000ptas. Live music 9pm-1am. Open M-Sa 9am-2am, Su 5pm-2am. Closed August. Visa, MC, AmEx.

The Bagel Shop, C. Canuda, 25 (tel. 93 302 41 61). M: Catalunya. From the metro, walk down Las Ramblas and take the first left onto C. Canuda. Barcelona meets New York City. Choose from an enormous selection of freshly baked bagels and spreads (80-625ptas). The artwork on the walls changes monthly. Open M-Sa 9:30am-9:30pm.

Cafe D'Estiu, Pl. Sant Lu, 5-6. M: Jaume I. Walk up C. Libreteria from the metro and follow the signs to Museu Marés. A tiny outdoor cafe, located in a peaceful courtyard, provides relief from the bustle of Barri Gòtic. Limited menu. Open Tu-Su 10am-10pm.

Café de Ciutat Vella, Carrer del Pí, 5 (tel. 93 302 10 21). Trendy music, trendier patrons, and the trendiest coffee drinks around. Hot and cold coffee concoctions 110-475ptas. Hot chocolates 200-275ptas. Pastries from 100ptas. Open M-Sa 9am-9pm.

Restaurante Self Naturista, C. Santa Anna, 11-17 (tel. 93 318 26 84), off Las Ramblas. M: Catalunya. A self-service vegetarian cafeteria that feels like a fast food restaurant. Desserts and salads may spill over the counter, but portions are small. Entrees under 500ptas. Lunch *menú* 930ptas. Open M-Sa 11:30am-10pm.

EL RAVAL

Students and workers congregate in this neighborhood to the west of Las Ramblas. Typical Catalán joints feature a simple space, basic food, lots of noise, and unlimited bread and wine. C. Tallers and Sitges overflow with inexpensive restaurants, while establishments off C. Lluna and Joaquín Costa serve Galician fare.

▨ **Restaurante Riera,** C. Joaquín Costa, 30 (tel. 93 443 32 93). M: Liceu or Universitat. Off C. Carme coming from Liceu, or off Ronda de Sant Antoni from Universitat. The Riera family supplies a feast fit for a hungry king. 3-course gorge-fest plus dessert offered day and night (750ptas). Open daily 1-4pm and 8-11:30pm.

Restaurante Chino, C. Tallers, 70 (tel. 93 317 49 30). M: Catalunya or Universitat. Take C. Tallers from Pl. Universitat or Las Ramblas. More pan-Asian than Chinese, this restaurant offers a filling, inexpensive *menú* (M-F lunchtime, 725ptas). Or try their spicy Thai menu (M-F lunchtime, 850ptas). Open daily noon-5:30pm and 8pm-midnight.

Bar Restaurante Los Toreros, C. Xuclá, 3-5 (tel. 93 318 23 25), on a narrow alley between C. Fortuny and C. Carme, both off Las Ramblas. M: Catalunya. The floors have faded from red to brown, but the traditional lunch *menú* still pleases (900ptas, Sa 1100ptas). New nighttime *tapas menú* is extremely popular (2000ptas, drinks included). Open Tu-Sa 9am-midnight, Su 9am-5pm. Lunch *menú* available 1-4pm.

Restaurante Can Lluís, C. Cera, 49 (tel. 93 441 11 87). M: San Antoni. From the metro, head down Ronda S. Pau, and take the 2nd left on C. Cera. A Barcelona mainstay for over 100 years, Can Lluís is a fine place for an authentic Catalán meal. The menu will put your Catalán skills to the test. The 3-course midday *menú* is an excellent value at 950ptas. Open M-Sa 1:30-4pm and 8:30-11:30pm. Visa.

Pla dels Angels, C. Ferlandina, 23 (tel. 93 443 31 03), right across from MACBA. Eating indoors is a far better deal. A delightful lunchtime *menú* (950ptas) comes with a buffet selection of salads, pasta, cheeses, and dessert; bread and drinks are not included. Pastas 775-950ptas. Open daily noon-4pm and 8-11:30pm.

Raim D'or Can Maxim, C. Bonsuccés, 8 (tel. 93 302 02 34), off Las Ramblas (to the right as you face the port). M: Catalunya. Multilingual staff and menu. Specialties include oily *torrades* (475-700ptas) and pizzas (650-925ptas). Lunch *menú* 1100ptas. Open Oct.-Aug. M-Sa 9am-5pm and 8pm-midnight. Visa, MC, AmEx.

Bar Restaurante Romesco, C. Sant Pau, 28 (tel. 93 318 93 81). M: Liceu. From the metro, walk up Las Ramblas and turn left onto C. Sant Pau. Take the first right; Romesco is immediately on the left. This small diner serves simple, inexpensive food. *Frijoles* (beans) and *crema catalana* are their specialties, and their fries are among the best in Barcelona. Fish, chicken, and meat dishes 375-800ptas.

Bar Universitat de Barcelona, M: Universitat. Enter the medieval courtyard through the main university entrance on Gran Vía Corts Catalanes between C. Aribau and Balmes, then turn left; the Bar is below eye level on the right. Student cafe with prices so cheap you'll think they're misprints. Don't order in *inglés*, and you'll blend right in. *Bocadillos* and other typical fare 170-350ptas. Entrees under 550ptas. Open 8am-8pm.

Restaurante Biocenter, C. Pintor Fortuny, 25 (tel. 93 301 45 83), off Las Ramblas and across the street from the store of the same name. M: Catalunya. Bustling, self-serve vegetarian restaurant. *Menú* with unlimited soup and salad, vegetarian entree, and dessert 1200ptas. Open M-Sa 9am-noon and 1-5pm.

LA RIBERA

East of Vía Laietana, La Ribera is home to the Museu Picasso and numerous bars and small restaurants. Once filled with fishermen, the neighborhood is still far from touristed. Menus are available only in Spanish and Catalán, but if you guess right (hint: *cesos* means brains), you'll get one of the city's best bargains.

LLuna Plena, C. Montcada, 2 (tel. 93 310 54 29). M: Jaume I. From the metro, take C. Princesa; turn left onto C. Montcada. The restaurant looks like an old brick smokehouse. Expensive for dinner, but afternoon *menú* (1000ptas) is a steal. Reservations accepted. Open Tu-Sa 1-4pm and 8-11:30pm, Su 1-4pm. Closed Aug. Visa, MC.

La Habana Vieja, C. Baños Viejos, 2 (tel. 93 268 25 04). C. Baños Viejos is parallel to C. Montcada. Feast on delicious Cuban cuisine in a small wooden-beamed house. Large portions are perfect for sharing among friends. *Arroz cubano* 600-900ptas. Meat dishes 1600-2000ptas. Open M-Sa 8:30am-11pm. Visa.

Nou Celler, C. Princesa, 16 (tel. 93 310 47 73). M: Jaume I. From the metro at Pl. Angel, take C. Princesa. Tavern-like atmosphere minus the touristy tackiness. Eclectic list of specials. Sandwiches 275-375ptas. *Menú* 1000ptas. Open M-Sa 8am-1am, Su 2pm-midnight. Closed June 19-July 17. Visa, MC, DC.

Nice-Café Milena, Vía Laietana, 6 (tel. 93 319 23 61), at the corner of Vía Laietana and C. Joan Hassan. M: Jaume I. Popular local restaurant serves moderately priced dishes. *Paella* 950-1375ptas. Pizzas 725-875ptas. Weekday lunch *menú* 900ptas, dinner *menú* 1600ptas, weekend *menú* 1395ptas. Open daily 7:30am-1am. Visa, MC, AmEx.

L'EIXAMPLE

When dining uptown, expect restaurants to be more expensive and the ambiance more elegant. For cheaper fare, try the area's *patisserías*, which sell delicious croissants and desserts.

Comme-Bio, Gran Vía de les Corts Catalanes, 603 (tel. 93 301 03 76), at the corner of Corts Catalanes and Rambla Catalunya. M: Catalunya. Fancy organic groceries in front, restaurant behind. The all-veggie menu is quite creative—the delicately spiced dishes will certainly please your palate. Salads 550-995ptas. Pastas 1200ptas and up. Pizzas 825-975ptas. Open M-Sa 9am-midnight, Su noon-midnight. Visa, MC.

ba-ba-reeba, Pg. Gràcia, 28 (tel. 93 301 43 02). M: Pg. Gràcia. Offers a wide selection of *tapas* and Catalunyan *pa* (bread). So many *tapas*, so little time (most under 500ptas). Outdoor dining on the *passeig* recommended. Open daily 8am-2am.

GRÀCIA

You know you are in mellow Gràcia when you hear fellow diners speaking Catalán instead of Spanish, English, French, or German. The food is likewise authentic.

El Glop de la Rambla, R. Catalunya, 65 (tel. 93 487 00 97). M: Pg. Gràcia. Other locations sprinkled throughout L'Eixample. This rustic tavern is famous among locals for its *chorizo* (Spanish sausage) cooked over an open flame. Outdoor seating available. Lunch *menú* 1000ptas. Open M-Sa 8am-1am, Su 11am-1am. Visa, MC.

El Tastavins, C. Ramon y Cajal (tel. 93 213 60 31), near Pl. Sol. M: Joanic. Admire work by local artists (even caricatures of the owners) while enjoying Catalán mainstays. Lunch *menú* 950ptas. Open Tu-Sa 12:30pm-5pm and 8:30pm-1am, Su 12:30-5pm.

Can Suñé, C. Mozart, 20 (tel. 93 218 54 86). M: Diagonal. From C. Gran de Gràcia, take C. Goya, then take the 2nd right. A petite, family-run restaurant where neighbors gather to spin yarns. Open Tu-Su 8am-midnight.

Xavi Petit, C. Bonavista, 2 (tel. 93 237 88 26), off C. Gran de Gràcia. M: Diagonal. Funky crêpes can be a meal or just dessert (550-750ptas). Crêpe-less afternoon *menú* 950ptas. *Tapas* 350-550ptas. Open M-F 8am-11:30pm, Sa 8pm-midnight.

◐ SIGHTS

Barcelona's Modernista treasures dominate the city (see **Ruta del Modernisme,** below). Las Ramblas—everyone's favorite street—and the lovely Barri Gòtic are the traditional tourist areas. But don't neglect vibrant La Ribera and El Raval, the upscale avenues of L'Eixample, the panoramic city views from Montjuïc and Tibidabo, Gaudí's Parc Güell, and the harbor-side Port Olimpíc.

RUTA DEL MODERNISME

Barcelona's hyper-organized tourist administration has designed a Gaudí-dominated route that covers prominent Modernista architecture all over the city. **Ruta del Modernisme passes** (600ptas, students 400ptas) are an excellent deal that allows economical access to Barcelona's architectural masterpieces. The pass, good for a month, gives holders a 50% discount on entrance to Palau Güell, La Sagrada Familia, Casa Milà (La Pedrera), Palau de la Música, Casa-Museu Gaudí, Fundació Antoni Tápies, and the Museu d'Art Modern. Purchase passes at **Casa Lleó Morera,** on the corner of Pg. Grácia and C. Consedel (tel. 93 488 01 39; see p. 318). Included with the pass is a booklet explaining each sight and a good map that indicates all 50 stops on the tour.

The best way to approach this macro-museum of Catalán architecture is with the *Ruta del Modernisme* booklet and handy pamphlet guides available free at the tourist office. Although the city has many fascinating Modernista sights, the highlights include: **Palau Güell;** the fairy-tale **Parc Güell** (see p. 319); **Palau de la Música Catalana** (see p. 317); **Casa Calvet** (if you can peek in); the houses along the **Manzana de Discordia** (see p. 318); the amazing **Casa Milà (La Pedrera);** the enormous **Templo Expliatorio de la Sagrada Familia** (see p. 317); **Els Quatre Gats** (see **Food,** p. 312); **Casa Vicens** (see p. 320); and the **Museo de Arte Moderno** (see **Museums,** p. 322). Since many of these sights have mandatory hour-long tours, visiting all of them on the same day is nearly impossible. During the summer, the easiest—and cheesiest—way to sight-see is to hop on the **Bus Turístic** (see p. 302).

MARVELOUS MODERNISME In the late 19th and early 20th centuries, Barcelona's flourishing bourgeoisie commissioned a new class of architects to build their houses, reshaping the face of L'Eixample with Modernista architecture that employed revolutionary shapes, materials, and spaces to reflect the signs and symbols of Catalunya. **Antoni Gaudí's** serpentine rooftops, warrior-like chimneys, and skeletal facades are perhaps the most famous examples of this Modernisme style. A staunch regionalist, Gaudí incorporated an array of Catalán symbols and myths in his organic architecture. He carefully designed every feature of his buildings, down to the furniture, colorful ceramic mosaics, and elaborate light fixtures. Even his methods were unconventional, and although most of Gaudí's creations seem fantastical, they are architectural breakthroughs that have since been imitated only by advanced computer technology and mathematics. Fellow Modernista luminaries include **Luis Domènech i Montaner,** noted for his heavily decorated surfaces exemplified by the Palau de la Musica Catalana and Casa Lleó i Morera, and **José Puig i Caldafach,** who developed an antiquarian style uniting local and foreign traditions.

LAS RAMBLAS

Las Ramblas's pedestrian-only median strip is a veritable urban carnival, where street performers dance, fortune-tellers survey palms, human statues shift poses, vendors sell birds, and artists sell caricatures—all, of course, for a small fee. The wide, tree-lined boulevard dubbed "Las Ramblas" actually comprises five distinct segments (Canaletes, Estudis, Sant Josep, Capuxtins, and Santa Monica) that together form one long boulevard. The sights below are arranged beginning with Pl. Catalunya in the north to the port in the south.

UPPER LAS RAMBLAS. A port-ward journey begins at the **Font de Canaletes** (more a pump than a fountain), where visitors who wish to eventually return to Barcelona are supposed to sample the water. The upper part of Las Ramblas has been dubbed "Rambla de las Flores" for the numerous flower vendors that inhabit it. Halfway down Las Ramblas by **La Boqueria,** the traditional food market (see p. 310), **Joan Miró's** small pavement **mosaic** brightens up the street.

GRAN TEATRE DEL LICEU. The Gran Teatre del Liceu has been Barcelona's opera house for over a century. It was once one of Europe's leading stages, nurturing the likes of José Carreras. Ravaged by a fire in January 1994, the Teatre reopened for performances in 1999 (see **Music,** p. 326). *(Las Ramblas, 61, on the corner of C. Sant Pau.)*

◙PALAU GÜELL. Antoni Gaudí's Palau Güell has one of Barcelona's most spectacular interiors, crossing a Modernista apartment building with a haunted house. The rooftop chimneys display Gaudí's first use of the *trencadís*, the covering of surfaces with irregular shards of ceramic or glass. *(C. Nou de la Rambla, 3-5, 2 blocks from the Teatre Liceu. Tel. 93 317 51 98. Open M-Sa 10am-2pm and 4-8pm. 400ptas, students 200ptas. Only a few tours per hour, so come early.)*

MONUMENT A COLOM. At the port end off Las Ramblas, the Monument a Colom towers above the city. When Renaixença enthusiasts "rediscovered" Spain's role in the discovery of the Americas, they convinced themselves that Colom was really Catalán. The fact that the statue proudly points toward Libya, not the Americas, is symbolic of the people's mistake; history shows that Columbus was actually Genoese. At night, spotlights turn the statue into a firebrand. *(Portal de la Pau. Tel. 93 39 02 52 24. Elevator to the top open June-Sept. 9am-8:30pm; Oct.-Mar. M-F 10am-1:30pm and 3:30-7:30pm, Sa-Su 10am-6:30pm; Apr.-May 10am-1:30pm and 3:30-7:30pm, Sa-Su 10am-7:30pm. 250ptas, children 150ptas.)*

AROUND THE PORT. Farther down Las Ramblas toward the port, Barcelona's drive to refurbish its seafront has resulted in the **Vila Olímpica** and the expansion of **Port Vell,** the port complex and waterfront area near Monument a Colom. After moving the coastal road underground, the city opened **Moll de la Fusta,** a wide pedestrian zone that leads down to the docks past scenic (but pricey) restaurant-cafes and the **Museu de la Historia de Catalunya** (see **Museums,** p. 322). The wavy, modern bridge **Rambla de Mar** links the cobblestone docks of the Moll de la Fusta with the bright **Maremagnum** mall (see **Shopping,** p. 327).

◙L'AQUÀRIUM DE BARCELONA. Barcelona's new aquarium is state of the art, featuring an 80m-long glass tunnel and moving walkway through a tank of sharks and tropical fish. *(In Moll d'Espanya del Port Vell, next to Maremagnum and the cinema. M: Barceloneta. Tel. 93 221 74 74. Open July-Aug. 9:30am-11pm; Sept.-June 9:30am-9pm. Whopping 1400ptas per person, students 10% off. Admission up to 1hr. before closing.)*

BOAT TOURS. Tours sail from Portal de la Pau, in front of the Monument a Colom. **Las Golondrinas** (tel. 93 442 31 06) ferries steam around Montjuïc to **Rompeolas** and **Port Vell** (35min.; July-Aug. every 30min., noon-7:30pm; Sept.-June every hr., M-F noon-6pm, Sa-Su noon-7:30pm; 485ptas). A longer excursion includes a tour of Port Olímpic (2hr., July-Aug. every 30min. noon-7:30pm; Sept.-June 3 per day, 11am-4:30pm; round-trip 1275ptas, students 900ptas).

BARRI GÒTIC

While the weathered, narrow streets of the Barri Gòtic, including **Carrer de la Pietat** and **Carrer del Paradis,** have preserved their medieval charm, the ever-growing tourist economy has infused a new, multilingual liveliness into the area.

PLAÇA DE SANT JAUME. Any tour of the "Old Quarter" should begin in the handsome Plaça de Sant Jaume, Barcelona's political center since Roman times. Two of Catalunya's most important buildings have dominated the square since 1823: the **Palau de la Generalitat,** the headquarters of Catalunya's autonomous government, and the **Ajuntament,** the Spanish government's seat of power. Fittingly, the two buildings face each other across the *plaça. (Palau de la Generalitat open the 2nd and 3rd Sunday of each month 10am-2pm. 30min. tours in English, French, Spanish, and Catalán. Ajuntament open Sa-Su 10am-2pm. Free.)*

ESGLÉSIA CATEDRAL DE LA SANTA CREU. The jagged spires of the 14th-century Gothic Església Catedral de la Santa Creu are a sight in themselves. The church was begun in 1298, but the facade was not completed until the 1880s. Barcelona's patron saint and Christian martyr, Santa Euália, naps below the altar in the church **crypt.** The cathedral's lovely **cloister** has magnolias growing in the middle and geese waddling around the periphery. *(In Pl. Seu, past the Generalitat and up C. Bisbe. Cathedral open daily 8am-1:30pm and 4-7pm. Cloister open 9am-1:15pm and 4-7pm. Free. Elevator to the rooftop M-F 9:30am-12:30pm and 4-6:30pm, Sa-Su 9:30am-12:30pm; 200ptas. Entrance to Choral Chamber 125ptas.)*

OTHER SIGHTS. Palaces and museums congregate on C. Comtes, on the opposite side of the Catedral. The former home of the royal family, the **Palau Reial** (Royal Palace), is the pearl of the plaça. Inside, the **Museu d'Historia de la Ciutat** (see **Museums,** p. 321) and **Museu Frederic Marès** hold court. *(The royal palace can be visited with admission to the history museum.)* Also in the Barri Gòtic is the lively student hangout **Plaça del Pí** and the picturesque old **Església del Pí,** just off Las Ramblas. *(From Las Ramblas, follow C. Cardenal Casañas.)*

LA RIBERA

In the 18th century, Felipe V demolished much of La Ribera to make space for the Ciutadella. The remaining neighborhood has since evolved into Barcelona's bohemian nucleus, complete with art galleries, chic eateries, and exclusive bars.

◼PALAU DE LA MÚSICA CATALANA. Modernista architect Luis Domènech i Montaner designed this fabulous, must-see palace. The music hall glows with tall stained-glass windows, an ornate chandelier, marble reliefs, *preciosa* woodwork, and ceramic mosaics. Concerts include all varieties of symphonic and choral music. *(C. Sant Francesc de Paula, 2, off Vía Laietana near Pl. Urquinaona. Head up Vía Laietana to the intersection of C. Ionqueres. Tel. 93 268 10 00. Open M-F 10am-9pm. Mandatory tours in Spanish, Catalán, and English every 30min., 10:30am-3pm. 700ptas, students 500ptas; 350ptas with Ruta del Modernisme pass. Concert tickets 1000-26,000ptas. Box office open M-Sa 10am-9pm, Su from 1hr. prior to the concert. No concerts in August.)*

OTHER SIGHTS. La Ribera's streets converge at the foot of the **Església Santa María del Mar's** octagonal towers. As its name suggests, this 14th-century Gothic church once stood on the Mediterranean coastline. *(Tel. 93 310 23 90. Open M-Sa 9am-1:30pm and 4:30-8pm, Su 9am-2pm and 5-8:30pm.)* **Carrer de Montcada,** beginning behind the church, validates Barcelona's local reputation as *"la ciudad del diseño"* (the city of design). Museums, art galleries, workshops, and Baroque palaces that once housed Barcelona's 16th-century bureaucrats are packed into just two blocks. The **Museu Picasso** now inhabits the Palau de Agüilar (see **Museums,** p. 321). **Galeria Maeght** (#26), one of several prestigious art galleries on the block, was once the manor of a medieval aristocrat (see **Art Galleries,** p. 324).

PARC DE LA CIUTADELLA AND VILA OLÍMPICA

PARC DE LA CUITADELLA. Barcelona's military resistance to the Bourbon monarchy in the early 18th century convinced Felipe V to quarantine Barcelona's influential citizens in the Ciutadela, a large citadel on what is now Pg. Picasso. The city razed the fortress in 1868 and replaced it with the peaceful promenades of Parc de la Ciutadella. Host of the 1888 Universal Exposition, the park now harbors several museums, well-labeled horticulture, the wacky **Cascada** fountains, a **pond,** and a zoo. Buildings of note include Domènech i Montaner's Modernista **Castell dels Tres Dragons** (now **Museu de Zoología**), the **geological museum** (a few buildings down P. Picasso from M. Zoología), and Josep Amergós's **Hivernacle.** Expo '88 also inspired the small Arc de Triomf, just across Pg. Pujades from the park. Little Snowflake *(Copito de Nieve)*, the world's only albino gorilla behind bars, vegetates in the **Parc Zoològic**, on the end of the park closer to the sea. In the center of the park, on Pl. Armes, is the **Museu d'Art Modern** (see p. 322). *(M: Barceloneta or Arc de Triomf. Rowboat rental 10am-7pm; 250ptas per person for 30min. Parc Zoològic tel. 93 221 25 06. Open June-Aug. 9:30am-7:30pm; Sept.-May 10am-5pm. 1500ptas, children 3-12 950ptas.)*

VILA OLÍMPICA. The Vila Olímpica, beyond the east side of the zoo, was built (on top of what was once a working-class neighborhood) to house 15,000 athletes and entertain millions of tourists for the 1992 Summer Olympics. These days, it is a yuppie village that's home to several public parks, a shopping center, and business offices. Toward the Mediterranean, **Port Olímpic** flaunts twin towers, a huge fish-inspired sculpture, a long pier, and waves of upscale bars and restaurants, both indoors and out. In the area called **Barceloneta,** mediocre beaches—good for little more than catching a tan—stretch out from the port. Barcelona's quaint old fishing quarter stretches lazily along the waterfront, although pricey seafood restaurants are now moving into what many have begun to consider a neighborhood of the future. *(From M: Ciutadella/Vila Olímpica, walk along the waterfront on Ronda Litoral toward the two towers.)*

L'EIXAMPLE

The Catalán Renaissance and the growth of Barcelona during the 19th century pushed the city past its medieval walls and into ordered modernity. Ildefons Cerdà, a Catalán architect, drew up an aerial plan for a new neighborhood, which called for a geometric grid of squares, softened by octagonal intersections with cropped corners. Cerdà's wide avenues and diagonal corners were an attempt to relieve the stress that had festered in the overcrowded Barri Gòtic. The original plan also called for three-sided city blocks that facilitated air circulation and imitated Catalán country-side *massas* (neighborhoods). Unfortunately, virtually every block was immediately enclosed by a fourth wall, thus sullying the genius of Cerdà's original design. The resulting **Eixample** (pronounced uh-SHOMP-luh) neighborhood gave rise to *passeigs* (streets) lined with high-brow shopping and other, more fantastic, must-see designs (see **Marvelous Modernisme,** p. 314).

▒LA SAGRADA FAMILIA. Only Gaudí's genius could draw thousands of tourists to a half-finished church. The architect himself estimated that the **Temple Expiadori de la Sagrada Familia** would take 200 years to complete. For 43 years, Gaudí obsessed over La Sagrada Familia, even living in the complex for the last eleven years of his life; in 1926, virtually forgotten by the public, he was run over by a trolley. Since then, construction has progressed erratically and controversially. A furor has arisen over recent additions, including sculptor Josep Subirach's Cubist Passion Facade on C. Sardenya (the facade you see as you enter), which some argue clashes with the rest of the structure. Of the church's three proposed facades, only the first (actually one of the smaller ones), the nativity facade, was finished under Gaudí. Elevators and a maze of staircases lead to the church's towers and bridges. The **museum** displays a model of the structure as it was meant to be completed and various artifacts relating to La Sagrada Familia's construction. *(C. Marinara, between C. Mallorca and C. Provença. M: Sagrada Familia. Tel. 93 207 30 31. Open Apr.-Aug. 9am-8pm. Sept.-Oct. and Mar. 9am-*

7pm; Nov.-Feb. 9am-6pm; Tours Apr.-Oct. 11:30am, 1, 4, and 6:30pm, Nov.-Mar. 11:30am and 1pm. Admission to church and museum 800ptas. Elevator 200ptas.)

⛫MANZANA DE LA DISCÒRDIA. A short walk from Pl. Catalunya, the odd-numbered side of Pg. Gràcia between C. Aragó and Consell de Cent is popularly known as *la manzana de la discordia* (block of discord), referring to the clashing, aesthetic competition of the three buildings on the block. In the herd of L'Eixample, the block offers an overview of the Modernista style. Regrettably, the bottom two floors of **Casa Lleó i Morera,** by Domènech i Montaner, were destroyed to make room for a fancy-schmancy store. Here, you can buy the **Ruta del Modernisme pass** and take a tour of the upstairs, where sprouting flowers, stained glass, and legendary doorway sculptures adorn the interior. Puig i Cadafalch opted for a geometric, Moorish-influenced pattern on the facade of **Casa Amatller** at #41. Gaudí's balconies ripple and tiles sparkle in blue-purple glory on **Casa Batlló,** #43. Experts and tourists alike debate the meaning of Battllo's forboding facade; the most popular theory is that the rooftop represents Cataluña's patron Sant Jordi slaying a dragon (the chimney plays the lance). Also of interest is **Fundació Antoni Tàpies,** designed by Domènech, around the corner from *la manzana.*

⛫CASA MILÀ (LA PEDRERA). Modernisme buffs argue that the spectacular Casa Milà apartment building, an undulating mass of granite popularly known as *La Pedrera* (the Stone Quarry), is Gaudí's most refined work. Note the intricate ironwork around the balconies and the irregularity of the front gate's egg-shaped window panes. The roof sprouts chimneys resembling armored soldiers, one of which is decorated with broken champagne bottles. Rooftop tours provide a closer look at the "Prussian helmets" (spiral chimneys inspired by the helmets worn in Wagner's operas). The winding brick attic (recently restored along with the rooftop in a multi-million-*peseta* project) has been transformed into the **Espai Gaudí,** a multimedia presentation of Gaudí's life and works. Opened in the summer of 1999, a refurnished and restored apartment awaits one floor below, exhibiting the fine, captivating interior of Gaudí homes. *(Pg. Gràcia, 92. Enter around the corner on C. Provença. Tel. 93 484 59 95. Open daily 10am-8pm. Tour M-F at noon and 6pm, Sa-Su 11am. 600ptas, students 350ptas; with apartment 1000ptas.)*

MONTJUÏC

Throughout Barcelona's history, whoever controlled Montjuïc (Hill of the Jews) controlled the city. Dozens of despotic rulers have modified the **fortress,** built atop the ancient Jewish cemetery; Franco made it one of his "interrogation" headquarters. Somewhere deep in the recesses of the structure, his *beneméritos* ("honorable ones," a.k.a. the Guardia Civil) shot Catalunya's former president, Lluís Companys, in 1941. The fort was not available for recreational use until Franco rededicated it to the city in 1960. A huge stone monument expresses Barcelona's (forced) gratitude for the return of the fortress. Since reacquiring the mountain, Barcelona has made it a tourist attraction, even choosing it as the site of the 1992 Olympics. To get to **Parc de Montjuïc,** take the metro to Pl. Espanya (M: Espanya) and catch bus #50 either at Av. Reina María Cristina (flanked by two large brick towers) or as it heads up the hill (every 10min.). Scenic outdoor escalators (installed for the Olympics) lead up to the Montjuïc from the Palau Nacional.

PALAU NACIONAL. The **Fonts Luminoses** (Illuminated Fountains), dominated by the huge central **Font Mágica** (Magic Fountain), are visible from Pl. Espanya up Av. Reina María Cristina. During the summer, they are employed in a weekend audio-visual show that illuminates the whole mountainside and the **Palau Nacional,** located directly behind the fountains (Apr. 30-Oct. 3 Th-Su, every ½hr., 9:30-11:30pm). The palace was designed in what was considered the "international style" by German architect Pavelló Mies van der Rohe at his country's Expo pavilion in 1929. Now it houses the **Museu Nacional d'Art de Catalunya** (see **Museums** p. 321), with its exquisite Romanesque and Gothic art collections. Just below the hillside to the left when facing the palace lies the intriguing **Museum of Archaeology** (see **Museums** p. 322).

OLYMPIC AREA. In 1929, Barcelona inaugurated the **Estadi Olímpic de Montjuïc** in its bid for the 1932 Olympic games. Over 50 years later, Catalán architects Federic Correa and Alfons Milà, who were also responsible for the overall design of the **Anella Olímpica** (Olympic Ring) esplanade, renovated the shell with the help of Italian architect Vittorio Gregotti. *(Tel. 93 426 20 89. Open daily 10am-8pm. Free.)* Designed by Japanese architect Arata Isozaki, the **Palau d'Esports Sant Jordi** is the most technologically sophisticated of the Olympic structures. *(Tel. 93 426 20 89. You must call in advance to visit.)* To re-live the Olympics, swim in the **Olympic pools** (see **Pools and Beaches,** p. 327) or visit the **Galeria Olímpica,** at the south end of the stadium. *(Galeria tel. 93 426 06 60. Open Apr.-Sept. Tu-Sa 10am-2pm and 4-8pm, Su 10am-2pm; Oct.-Mar. Tu-F 10am-1pm and 4-6pm, Su 10am-2pm. 390ptas, students 340ptas.)* About 100m down the road from the stadiums is the **Fundació Miró** (see **Museums,** p. 322).

CASTELL DE MONTJUÏC. At the top of Montjuïc mountain, this historically rich castle watches over the port. From the castle's exterior ramparts, gaze over the bay and the city. Inside, the Museu Militar has a large armaments display. From Barcelona, take the **funicular** to Av. Miramar. *(Pl. Raquel Meller. M: Parallel. Tel. 93 298 70 00. July 19-Sept. 23 10:45am-10pm, every 10min.; Sept. 24-July 18 10:45am-8pm; 225ptas, round-trip 375ptas.)* Then take the **teleferic cable car** to the top *(June 19-Nov. 1 M-F 11:15am-8pm, Sa-Su 11:15am-9:30pm; Nov. 2-June 18, M-F 11:15am-6:30pm, Sa-Su 11:15am-7:30pm.)*

POBLE ESPANYOL. This "town" features replicas of famous buildings and sights from every region of Spain. While this pseudo-town may sound great, it is pretty much just an artificial souvenir bazaar with several mediocre restaurants and a few discos. *(On Av. Marqués de Comillas, to the right when facing the Palau Nacional. Tel. 93 325 78 66. Open Su 9am-midnight, M 9am-8pm, Tu-Th 9am-2am, F-Sa 9am-4am. 950ptas, students with ID 760ptas. 1000pta cover at discos.)*

GRÀCIA

Just beyond L'Eixample, lovely, untouristed Gràcia is the real thing. The neighborhood charms and confuses with its narrow alleys and numerous plazas.

⧉PARC GÜELL. On a hill at the northern edge of Gràcia lies one of Barcelona's greatest treasures and the world's most enchanting public park. The park was designed entirely by Gaudí, and—in typical Gaudí fashion—was not completed until after his death. Gaudí intended Parc Güell (named after Eusebi Güell, its commissioner) to be a garden city, and its multicolored dwarfish buildings and sparkling ceramic-mosaic stairways to house the city's elite. But when only two aristocrats signed on, it became a park instead. The front entrance puts you face to face with a gaping, multicolored lizard. Some believe that the animal is a reference to the shield of the French city of Nîmes, the northern boundary of Old Cataluña. Two mosaic staircases flank the curious creature, leading to a towering Modernista pavilion that Gaudí originally designed as an open-air market for the park's would-be residents. The longest park bench in the world, a multicolored serpentine wonder made of tile shards, decorates the top of the pavilion. From here, sweeping paths supported by columns (meant to resemble palm trees) swerve through hedges and ascend to the park's summit, which commands tremendous views of the city. In the midst of the park is the **Casa-Museu Gaudi** (see **Museums,** p. 322). *(The easiest way to reach the park is by bus #24 from Pg. Gràcia, which stops at the upper park entrance. If a mild uphill hike does not disturb you, the most scenic way to enter the park is to take the metro to Vallarca, walk straight out of the metro down Av. L' Hospital Militar, turn left onto Baixada de la Gloria, and take the outdoor escalators uphill to the park's back entrance. Park tel. 93 219 38 11. Open May-Aug. 10am-9pm; Apr. and Sept. 10am-8pm; Mar. and Oct. 10am-7pm; Nov.-Feb. 10am-6pm. Free.)*

PLAÇAS. Gràcia has several notable plaças. The first of these is **Plaça Rius i Taulet,** home to the **Torre del Reloj** (Clocktower), an emblem of the Revolution of 1868. **Plaça del Diamant,** on nearby C. Astúries, was made famous by Mercè Rodoreda's novel. The most popular plaza is **Plaça del Sol,** skirted by cafes and bars and crowded with young locals at night. Here, activism is in the air: protest graffiti and banners fill the plaza, touching on everything from Catalán independence to the Zapatista uprising in Chiapas, Mexico.

CASA VICENS. Modernisme brushed Gràcia in one of Gaudí's youthful experiments, Casa Vicens. The *casa* illustrates the colorful influence of Arabic architecture and a rigidness of angles that is uncharacteristic of Gaudí's later works. *(C. Carolines, 24-26. The interior is currently closed to the public.)*

SARRIÀ AND PEDRALBES

The northwestern neighborhood of Sarrià is home to Barcelona's old money—residents still talk about "going down to Barcelona." The last *barri* to lose its independence, Sarrià finally merged with Barcelona in 1921. A walk through the peaceful streets reveals elegant mansions, manicured gardens, and exclusive private schools, all signs of a privileged life.

MONESTIR DE PEDRALBES. The artistic high-water of this Gothic church and 14th-century cloister is in the **Capella Sant Miguel,** where murals by Ferrer Bassa depict the seven joys of Mary, as well as several of her sorrows. The monastery received a part of the Museo Thyssen-Bornemisza collection when the Madrid museum was purchased by Spain in 1993. *(Baixada del Monestir, 1. At the end of Pg. Reina Elisenda. Tel. 93 280 14 34. Open Tu-Su 10am-2pm. 300ptas, students 175ptas.)*

TIBIDABO

This neighborhood's curious name comes from the Latin *tibi dabo* (meaning "I will give you"). The inspiration for the name is in the Gospel of St. Matthew when the devil tempts Jesus by saying "All this I will give to you if you fall prostrate and worship me." The "all this" is undoubtedly in reference to the incredible view this area affords of Barcelona, the Pyrenees, the Mediterranean, and even, on clear days, Mallorca. The souvenir shop and telescopes tucked away in the spires of the huge **Temple del Sagrat Cor (Church of the Sacred Heart)** make its religious function appear an afterthought *(round-trip elevator ride 75ptas).* The adjacent **Parc d'Atraccions** is a favorite among Barcelona's youngsters. *(Tel. 93 211 79 42. Open June W-F 10am-6pm, Sa-Su noon-8pm; July-Aug. M-F noon-10pm, Sa-Su noon-1am. Unlimited use of 12 rides 1900ptas, no rides 700ptas.)* Riding the elevator up the nearby **Torre de Collserola** communications tower (560m above sea level) can be almost as scary as the amusement park *(500ptas).*

There are several easy ways to get to Tibidabo. The Tibibús runs from Pl. Catalunya to the Torre de Collserola (June 9-Sept. 9 every 30min., from 30min. before park opening until 30min. after closing, Sept. 10-June 8 Sa-Su and holidays every hr. 270ptas.) An FFCC train from Pl. Cataluyna runs to Av. Tibidabo (round-trip 1900ptas including funicular and park entrance fee.) To reach the mountaintop, take the city bus on weekdays (runs every 20min., starting at 7am) and take the Tramvia Blau (Blue Train) on weekends (runs during the same hours as the amusement park). At the top of the street take the funicular (every 30min. during park hours, 200ptas).

🏛 MUSEUMS

> When I was a child, my mother said to me, 'If you become a soldier, you'll be a general. If you become a monk, you'll end up as the pope.' Instead, I became a painter and wound up as Picasso.
>
> —Pablo Picasso

In Barcelona, museums seem to spring up almost daily, providing an opportunity to explore the city's architectural feats, admire the works of accomplished Catalán artists, and delve into the world of modernism and contemporary art. Many museums offer **free admission** the first Sunday of each month; almost all close on Mondays. While this section includes all major museums, art-buffs should consult *Guía del Ocio* (125ptas at newsstands) or *Metropolitan* for additional listings.

◾MUSEU PICASSO. This truly incredible museum traces the development of Picasso as an artist, with a collection of his early works that weaves through the Gothic Palau Berenguer Dagueria. Although the museum offers little from Picasso's middle years, it boasts the world's best collection of work from his formative period in Barcelona. The collection also includes lithographs, ceramics, pencil sketches by an 11-year-old Picasso, and an excellent display of the artist's Cubist interpretations of Velázquez's *Las Meninas* (which hangs in the Prado). The collection was started in 1968 with a donation from one of Picasso's friends; it was later expanded by Picasso himself and by relatives, after his death. *(C. Montcada, 15-19. M: Jaume I. Walk down C. Princesa from the metro, and turn right on C. Montcada. Tel. 93 319 63 10. Open Tu-Sa 10am-8pm, Su 10am-3pm. 700ptas, students 400ptas, under 16 free. Free first Sunday of each month.)*

◾MUSEU D'ART CONTEMPORANI (MACBA). With its gentle curves and large, angular windows, this gleaming white edifice, constructed by American architect Richard Meier, is a stark contrast to its run-down surroundings. MACBA is a world-class museum and one of Barcelona's best. Eclectic and often interactive exhibits focus on three-dimensional art, photography, video, and graphic work from the past 40 years. The MACBA also has excellent rotating exhibits. *(Pl. dels Angels, 1. M: Universitat or Catalunya. Tel. 93 412 08 10; www.macba.es. Open M and W-F 11am-8pm, Sa 10am-8pm, Su 10am-3pm. 750ptas, students 550ptas, 16 and under free. Wednesdays 375ptas.)*

MUSEU D'HISTORIA DE LA CIUTAT. Exhibits in this museum display the history of Barcelona, from its Roman foundations through 6th-century Visigoth takeover and medieval development to the modern day. The fantastic history of the city unfolds as you descend to the original Roman ruins in the basement and continue on through the other exhibits. The upper floors are home to the **Capella de Santa Agueda,** which was built to store the king's holy relics. *(In Pl. del Rei. M: Jaume I. Walk up C. Jaume I and take the first right. Enter on C. Verguer. Tel. 93 315 11 11. Open June-Sept. Tu-Sa 10am-8pm, Su 10am-2pm; Oct.-May Tu-Sa 10am-2pm and 4-8pm, Su 10am-2pm. 1000ptas, students 700ptas. Free first Saturday of the month 3-8pm.)*

FUNDACIÓ JOAN MIRÓ. Designed by Miró's friend Josep Luís Sert and tucked into the side of Montjuïc, the Fundació links interior and exterior spaces with massive windows and outdoor patios. Sky lights illuminate an extensive collection of statues, paintings, and tapestries from Miró's career, including the stunning *Barcelona Series*, which depicts Miró's personal reaction to the Spanish Civil War. Room 13 displays experimental work by young artists. The Fundació also sponsors music recitals and film festivals. *(In Parc de Montjuïc. On Av. Miramar, 71-75, at Pl. Neptú. M: Espanya, then bus #50 from Pl. Espanya. Tel. 93 329 19 08. Open July-Sept. T-W and F-Sa 10am-8pm, Th 10am-9:30pm, Su 10am-2:30pm; Oct.-June T-W and F-Sa 10am-7pm, Th 10am-9:30pm, Su 10am-2:30pm. 800ptas, students and seniors 450ptas.)*

MUSEU NACIONAL D'ART DE CATALUNYA (MNAC). Besides housing the world's finest collection of Catalán Romanesque art, the museum also displays Gothic altarpieces and paintings of Cataluña's medieval churches, retrieved from museums around the world. *(In Palau Nacional, Parc de Montjuïc. M: Espanya, then bus #50; or walk up Av. Reina M. Cristina and take the escalators. Tel. 93 423 71 99. Open Tu-W and F-Sa 10am-7pm, Th 10am-9pm, Su 10am-2:30pm. 800ptas, 900ptas with temporary exhibits. 50% off with youth card.)*

FUNDACIÓ ANTONI TÀPIES. Tàpies's bizarre wire sculpture atop Domènech's red brick building announces this collection of contemporary art. The top floor is dedicated to famous Catalán artists. The other two floors feature special exhibits of other modern artists. *(C. Aragó, 255, around the corner from the Manzana de la Discordia and between Pg. Gràcia and Rbla. Catalunya. M: Pg. Gràcia. Tel. 93 487 03 15. Library upstairs open by appointment only. Open Tu-Su 11am-8pm. 700ptas, students 300ptas.)*

MUSEU D'ART MODERN. This museum, a part of MNAC, houses a potpourri of paintings and sculptures, all by 19th-century Catalán artists. Noteworthy works include Casas's *Plein Air*, Blay Fabregas's *Els Primers Freds*, Josep Llimona's *Desconsol*, and Isidre Nonell's paintings of Gypsy women. The museum also displays furniture designed by Gaudí. *(In Pl. Armes, in the Parc de la Ciutadella. M: Arc de Triomf. Tel. 93 319 57 28. Open Tu-Sa 10am-7pm, Su 10am-2:30pm. 600ptas, students 400ptas.)*

CENTRE CULTURAL DE LA FUNDACIÓ "LA CAIXA". Stroll through Puig i Cadafalch's **Casa Macaya** and admire the *fundació's* collection of modern art and photography. *(Pg. Sant Joan, 108, between C. Provença and C. Mallorca. M: Verdaguer. Tel. 902 222 30 40. Open Tu-Sa 11am-8pm, Su 11am-3pm. Free.)*

MUSEU DEL ARQUEOLÒGIA DE CATALUNYA. The exhibits cover prehistoric times up to the constitution of Catalunya. Several rooms feature a collection of Carthaginian art from Ibiza and excavated relics from the Greco-Roman city of Empúries (near Girona). *(Parc de Montjuïc, Pg. Santa Madrona, 39-41. Next to the Palau Nacional. M: Espanya, then bus #55. Tel. 93 424 61 77. Open Tu-Sa 9:30am-7pm, Su 10am-2:30pm. 400ptas.)*

MUSEU D'HISTORIA DE CATALUNYA. This high-tech and hands-on museum guides visitors through Catalunya's history, from Roman times through the 20th century. Computer screens, original film clips, and music stations help narrate the region's tumultuous past. *(Pl. Pau Vila, 3. M: Barceloneta. Tel. 93 225 47 00. Open Tu-Th 10am-7pm, F-Sa 10am-8pm, Su 10am-2:30pm. 500ptas, students 250ptas.)*

MUSEU DE LA MÚSICA. This exhibit of antique instruments, including a particularly good guitar collection, is housed in Puig i Cadafalch's Casa Baró de Quadras. *(In Casa Vidal-Quadras, Av. Diagonal, 373. M: Diagonal. Tel. 93 416 11 57. Open Tu-Su 10am-2pm, W 10am-8pm. 400ptas. Wednesday afternoons and first Sunday of the month are free.)*

PALAU DE LA VIRREINA. Once the residence of a Peruvian viceroy, this 18th-century palace displays temporary photography, music, and graphics exhibitions. More importantly, it serves as the headquarters for info on Barcelona's festivals. *(Las Ramblas, 99, on the corner of C. Carme. M: Liceu. Tel. 93 301 77 75. Open Tu-Sa 11am-8:30pm, Su 11am-2:30pm. 500ptas, students 250ptas.)*

MUSEU FREDERIC MARÈS. Founded in 1946, this museum is home to the personal collection of the sculptor Marès. The first floor houses an almost overwhelming collection of crucifixes and other biblical motifs. The 2nd and 3rd floors contain an eclectic collection of commonplace 15th- to 20th-century objects, including canes, ashtrays, and pipes. *(Pl. Sant Lu, 5-6, in the Palau Reial. Tel. 93 310 58 00. M: Jaume I. Open Tu and Th 10am-5pm, W and F 10am-7pm, Su 10am-3pm. 300ptas, students 150ptas. Wednesday afternoon and first Sunday of the month free.)*

CENTRE DE CULTURA CONTEMPORÀNIA DE BARCELONA (CCCB). This cultural center investigates modern urban design and sponsors temporary exhibits, dance performances, concerts, workshops, and lectures. *(Casa de Caritat, C. Montalegre, 5. M: Catalunya or Universitat, next to the MACBA. Tel. 93 306 41 00. Open Tu-Sa 11am-8pm, Su 11am-7pm. 600ptas, students 400ptas, children under 16 free.)*

ART GALLERIES

One of the capitals of cutting-edge art, Barcelona showcases many of the latest artistic trends. Many private galleries display the works of both budding artists and renowned masters. The *Guía del Ocio* (125ptas at local newsstands) is the best source for the latest exhibits and events. The **Palau de la Virreina** has information on cultural events. *(Las Ramblas, 99. Between La Boqueria market and C. Carme. M: Liceu. Tel. 93 301 77 75. Open M-F 10am-2pm and 4-8pm.)* **Centro de Informacion Cultural** distributes *Metropolitan*, Barcelona's only cultural magazine in English. *(Las Ramblas, 118. Tel. 93 302 15 22, ext. 266; open M-F 11am-2pm and 4-8pm, Sa 10am-2pm.)*

♫ ENTERTAINMENT

Nightlife in Barcelona begins with a 5pm stroll and winds down nearly fourteen hours later. After the *siesta*, the masses flood Las Ramblas or stroll portside, while youngsters model the latest fashions on C. Portal l'Angel and Portaferrissa. To recharge, the theater crowd makes conversation in cafes and *tapas* bars around Liceu, and foreign 20-somethings order *copas* in Pl. Reial. Farther away from the Barri Gòtic, upper-class adults cruise L'Eixample, while students head for the bars and cafes in Gràcia. Most people eat dinner between 9 and 11pm, Barcelona's bar scene begins around 10pm, and the discos start to fill after 2am.

Consult the weekly *Guía del Ocio* (www.guiadelociobcn.es), available at newsstands for 125ptas, for info on movies (*ciné*), live concerts (*múscia*), bars and discos (*Tarde/Noche* section), and cultural events.

BARS AND DISCOS

After dinner, *bar-restaurantes* and *cervecerías* (tapas and non-tapas bars) fill up along Las Ramblas and throughout the Barri Gòtic. As a general rule, the farther from Las Ramblas and the narrower the street, the less-touristed the bar. Slabs of meat swinging from the ceiling and *fútbol* on a little TV are the standard signs of a local hangout.

Barcelona's clubs do not heat up until around 2am, and most don't wind down until dawn (some discos stay open until 9am). If you are planning on clubbing, make sure to dress for the occasion; some of the more popular spots may discriminate on the basis of looks and clothes. Men may have to pay ridiculously high covers, often invented by bouncers to keep the ratio of men to women low. Even once you are inside a disco, partying isn't cheap. Expect to pay around 500ptas for a beer and 800ptas and up for mixed drinks; prices are higher at Maremagnum, Port Olympic, and other tourist-oriented spots. Below is a list of Barcelona's best bars and discos. Just keep in mind that what's popular changes on a daily basis—talk to locals for an up-to-the-minute report.

BARRI GÓTIC

Here, cookie-cutter *cervecerías* and *bar-restaurantes* can be found every five steps. Though nightlife in the Barri Góthic is not disco-oriented, it is still exciting.

🏛 **Les Bosq des Fades** (tel. 93 317 26 49), just off Las Ramblas near the water and next to the *Museu de Cera* (wax museum). M: Drassanes. A fairy-tale world, complete with gnarly trees, small bridge, and plush side rooms. Perfect for a drink with that special someone. Open weeknights until 1:30am, F and Sa until 2:30am.

Schilling, C. Ferrán, 23 (tel. 93 317 67 87). M: Liceu. Though columns and chandeliers cry out "exclusive," this chic bar is surprisingly diverse. Mixed gay and straight crowd. Beer 295ptas. Glass of wine 200ptas. Open M-F 9am-2am, Sa-Su 11am-2am.

Cafe d l'Opera, Las Ramblas, 74 (tel. 93 317 75 85 or 302 41 80). M: Liceu. A drink at this Barcelona institution was once a post-opera tradition for bourgeois *Barcelonenses* Today, the cafe caters to all types. Outdoor seating available. *Bocadillos* 350-660ptas. Beer 325-560ptas. 4-person *sangría* 1690ptas. Open daily 8am-2:30am.

Harlem Jazz Club, C. Comtesa de Sobradiel, 8 (tel. 93 310 07 55). M: Liceu. Between Pl. Reial and Vía Laietana. Not quite Louis Armstrong, but still pretty damn good. Live jazz every night. This club, which doesn't hop until midnight, is thoroughly packed by 1:30am. Su-Th free, Sa 500ptas with drink. Open daily 10pm-4am.

Margarita Blue, C. J. A. Clavé, 6 (tel 93 317 71 76), off Las Ramblas, a block from the port. M: Drassanes. With blue margaritas and swinging jazz tunes, this Mexican-themed bar draws a lively 20- and 30-something crowd. Margaritas 350ptas before 10:30pm, 450ptas after. Open M-W 11:30pm-2am, Th-F 11:30pm-3am, Sa-Su 7pm-3am.

Karma (tel. 93 302 56 80), on Pl. Reial. Karma is lively, indoors and out. A mixed crowd, from late-teens to early-thirties, lives it up for the next life. Beer 400-500ptas. Cover Th-Sa 1000ptas. Open 11:30pm-5am.

Jamboree, Pl. Reial, 17 (tel. 93 301 75 64). M: Liceu or Drassanes. From Las Ramblas, take C. Colom to Pl. Reial; Jamboree is on the right. Jazz, blues, soul, reggae, pop-funk, and jazz-funk. More spirited dancing upstairs. Concerts M-Sa 11pm-1am and dancing until 5am. 1500ptas with drink included, more when well-known musicians play.

EL RAVAL

More traditional, more local, these un-pretentious hangouts line the streets of El Raval, to the west of Las Ramblas (to the right when facing the sea)

🔊 **La Oveja Negra,** C. Sitges, 5 (tel. 93 317 10 87). M: Catalunya. From Pl. Catalunya, go down Las Ramblas and take the first right onto C. Tallers; C. Sitges is the first left. Also known as the Black Sheep, this is most popular tavern in town. Locals and backpackers fraternize over foosball and pitchers of beer. Beer 325ptas. Large *sangría* 1000ptas for 1.5L. Open M-Th 9am-2:30am, F 9am-3:30am, Sa-Su 5pm-3am.

Casa Almirall, C. Joaquim Costa, 33. A cavernous bar with a decaying ceiling and weathered couches, Casa Almirall is the oldest bar in Barcelona. The bartenders serve *absenta* (absinthe; 500ptas), the licorice-flavored liquor banned in France for its eerie effects on the mind. Beer 250ptas. Open daily 7pm-3am.

LA RIBERA

In La Ribera, tourist traps give way to inexpensive local hangouts. Be prepared to order and mingle in Spanish or Catalán.

Xampanyet, C. Montcado, 15. M: Jaume I. From the metro, cross Vía Laietana, walk down C. Princessa, and turn right on C. Montcado. Xampanyet is on the right after the Museu Picasso. Juan Carlos, the 3rd-generation proprietor, treats everyone like family. The house special—*cava* (Spanish champagne) and anchovies—served at the colorful bar. *Cava* 110ptas and up, bottles 800ptas and up. Open Tu-Sa noon-4pm and 6:30-11:30pm, Su 6:30-11:30pm.

Euskal Etxea, Placeta Montcada, 1-3 (tel. 93 310 21 85), down the street from the Museu Picasso. Celebrate Spain's regional diversity in this "Basque House." *Tapas* and cheap wines (135-145ptas; in traditional Basque glasses) served after 7:30pm. Open M-Sa 8am-5pm and 8-11:30pm, Su 8-11:30pm.

L'EIXAMPLE

A mod crowd: leave your shorts and sneakers at home or face the fashion police. A slew of *bares-musicales*, disco bars, and other hybrids lie between Pg. Gràcia and C. Aribau and between C. Rossell and C. València.

Velòdrom, C. Muntaner, 213 (tel. 93 430 60 22). M: Diagonal. Pre-party crowd. Students meet to drink in cushioned booths and shoot pool in this well-worn hangout. *Jarras* (mugs) of beer 275ptas, other sizes 150ptas. M-Sa 6pm-2am.

La Bodegueta, Rbla. Catalunya, 100 (tel. 93 215 48 94), on the corner of Rbla. Provença, a block away from La Pedrera. M: Diagonal. Before dinner, this wine bar hops with chic Barcelonans sampling local wine (135ptas) and *cava* (325ptas) with their cheese and pâté. Dress for success. Open M-Sa 7am-2am.

MONTJUÏC

Lower Montjuïc is home to Barcelona's epic "disco theme park."

Poble Espanyol, Av. Marqués de Comillas (tel. 93 322 03 26). M: Pl. Espanya. The numbers are impressive: 12 restaurants, 15 bars, 3 *bares-musicales,* and a few large *discotecas.* Dancing starts at around 1:30am and doesn't end until 9am. Open in July-Aug. nightly; in Sept.-June Th-Sa.

PORT OLÍMPIC

Tracing the coast and marked by the two tall, rectangular Olympic towers, the Olympic Village brims with glitzy restaurants and throngs of European dance fiends. Twenty or so bars and clubs occupy the strip, but many revelers choose to dance on the port itself. If you don't like the music in one club, take five steps to the next. Any music that you desire can be found in this tourist-oriented festival of dance, drink, and late-night snacks. Things begin at midnight and wind down at 6am. From the metro stop Ciutadella-Vila Olímpica (L4), walk down C. Marina toward the twin towers. Bonus: there's **no cover anywhere.**

MAREMAGNUM

At 1am the adults go home, the children go to bed, and Barcelona's contingent of international students begins to party. To get to Maremagnum, walk down Las Ramblas and cross over the wavy bridge to the mall, where there's something for everyone. The venues listed below are only examples of the hopping clubs Maremagnum offers. You'll do best if you explore all floors of the disco complex before following your ears to the hotspot of your choice.

Nayandei (tel. 93 225 81 37), on the top floor. Indoor/outdoor dance floors mix the decades, with tunes from the 60s and 70s in one disco, and thumping 90s dance music in the other. Nayandei sometimes hands out fliers for free 2nd drinks, valid Su-Th. No cover. Beer 800ptas. Mixed drinks 1100ptas. Open daily 9pm-5:30am.

Sub 34.3 (tel. 93 225 81 58), on the middle floor. Take a submarine into the depths of the ocean and grind to thumping pop or house. The sub theme is all-pervasive (including the bathrooms and the ceiling, with its small rotating sharks) and mildly amusing. Beer 300ptas. Mixed drinks 1000ptas. Open daily midnight-5am.

Mojito Bar (tel. 93 225 80 14). *The* place for Caribbean music, merengue, and salsa. Free classes available on weekends. Coke 600ptas. Beer 600ptas. *Mojito* (Hemingway's favorite drink, made with crushed mint, lemon, and lots of alcohol) 900ptas. Open daily midnight-5am.

Distrito Marítimo, Moll de la Fusta, Edicles, 1 (tel. 93 221 55 61). Techno music and gay and straight patrons flood the outdoor terrace. Open F-Sa midnight-3:30am.

ELSEWHERE

Most of the biggest and best *discotecas* are outside Pl. Catalunya.

Zeleste, C. Almogàvers, 122 (tel. 93 486 44 22), in an old warehouse. M: Marina. Walk 15min. from Pg. Lluís Companys, or take the Nitbus (11pm-4:30am). This dance club sometimes has live performances and rooftop dancing for an additional charge. Cover 1000ptas, F and Sa 900ptas. Concert price varies. Open 1-5am.

KGB, C. Alegre de Dalt, 55 (tel. 93 210 59 06). M: Joanic. From the metro, walk along Pi i Maragall, and take the first left. Loud rock and roll delivered to a mixed crowd of students and Soviet secret agents. No microfiche. Occasional live music. Cover 1000ptas, includes 1 drink. Open F-Su 1-8am.

Les Carpes del Cel, Castelldefels "Canal Olímpic," on Autovia A-16, Castelldefels Platja exit. Huge outdoor disco complex with 3 separate dance-floor tents, each pumping different types of music. 18 bars, plus other amusements. Cover 1000ptas, includes 1 drink. Open June 19-Sept. 19 10:30pm-5am.

Otto Zutz, C. Lincoln, 15 (tel. 93 238 07 22), uptown near Pl. Molina where C. Balmes intersects Vía Augusta. M: FFCC Muntaner. 3 floors, 6 bars. Live music F midnight-2am. The beautiful people don't show up until after 3am. Cover a negotiable 2000ptas, includes 1 drink. Open W-Sa midnight-5am.

La Boite, Av. Diagonal, 477 (tel. 93 419 59 50). M: Hospital Clinic. More emphasis on dance than decor. Big names sometimes come to perform in the intimate disco setting. Live jazz, soul, and blues Tu, Th, and F. Open daily 11pm-5:30am.

Fibra Óptica, C. Beethoven, 9 (tel. 93 202 00 69). M: Hospital Clinic. From the metro, walk up C. Comte Urgell, turn left at Diagonal; the club is in Pl. Wagner, 1 block up on the right. A 30-something crowd hits this ultra-popular disco. Cover around 2000ptas, includes 1 drink. Open M-F midnight-5am, Sa-Su midnight-9:30am.

MUSIC

The **Gran Teatre del Liceu,** Las Ramblas, 51-59 (tel. 93 485 99 00; www.liceubarce-lona.com), founded in 1847, was one of the world's leading opera stages until its interior was destroyed by a fire in 1994. It recently reopened after extensive repairs (see **Sights,** p. 315). **Palau de la Música Catalana** stages choral and symphonic concerts throughout the year (see **Sights,** p. 316). **Rock concerts** are held in the main soccer stadium, the Olympic stadium, and in the sports palace Sant Jordi. Get tickets in the booth on Gran Vía at C. Aribau, next to the university (open M-Sa 10:30am-1pm and 4:30-7pm). Parks and museums (including Parc Güell, Parc de la Ciutadella, Fundació de Joan Miró, Fundació la Caixa, and the Centre de Cultura Contemporània) also host concerts and recitals. Consult the Palau de la Virreina office for more information (see **Art Galleries,** p. 322). Some concerts take place at other venues; contact the tourist office (see **Tourist and Financial Services** p. 304), or check local periodicals (including the *Guía del Ocio*) for listings and ticket info.

THE SARDANA

The sardana, Catalunya's regional dance, is quite popular in Barcelona. It is a communal dance in which men and women join hands in a closed circle and perform a series of long and short steps; travelers are welcome to participate, as long as they observe the dance's solemn atmosphere. Dances take place Saturdays at 6:30pm and Sundays at noon in front of the cathedral, Pl. Sagrada Família, or near Parc de la Ciutadella's fountains. Dances are also held in Pl. Sant Jaume on Sundays at 6:30pm, at Parc de l'Espanya Industrial on Fridays at 7:30pm, and elsewhere in the city on Tuesdays, Thursdays, and Fridays. Consult papers for current info.

THEATER

Barcelona offers many options for theater aficionados though most performances are in Catalán (*Guía del Ocio* lists the language of the performance). Reserve tickets through **TelEntrada** (24hr. tel. 902 10 12 12; www. telentrada.com) or any branch of **Caixa Catalunya** bank (open M-F 8am-2:30pm).

The **Grec-Barcelona** summer festival (www.grecbcn.com) turns Barcelona into an international theater, music, and dance extravaganza from late June to mid-August. For info about the festival, ask at the tourist office or contact **Institut de Cultura de Barcelona (ICUB),** Palau de la Virreina, Ramblas 99 (tel. 93 301 77 75; open M-F 10am-2pm and 4-8pm). Some of the major venues (such as the **Teatre Grec** and the **Convent de Sant Augusti**) are open-air theaters. Tickets can be purchased through **TelEntrada,** or at the Pl. Catalunya **tourist office.**

Major venues for theatrical performances include the **Teatre Nacional de Cataluya,** Pl. del Arts, 1 (tel. 93 246 00 41; M: Monumental or Glòries i Marina), near the intersection of Av. Diagonal and Av. Meridiana; **Teatre de l'Eixample,** C. Arago, 140 (tel. 93 323 39 50 or 93 451 34 62; M: Urgell), which showcases flamenco; and **Teatre Lliure,** C. Montseny, 47 (tel. 93 218 92 51; M: Fontana), in Gràcia, which features innovative contemporary productions.

FILM

Most screens display the latest Hollywood features, some of which are in the original English. The *Cine* section in *Guía del Ocio* denotes these subtitled films with *V.O. subtitulada (version original);* other foreign films are dubbed, usually in Catalán. Many theaters have a bargain ticket day (usually Monday). **Filmoteca,** Av. Sarrià, 33 (tel. 93 410 75 90; M: Hospital Clínic), screens classic, cult, and otherwise exceptional films (both foreign and domestic, 400ptas). **Méliès Cinemas,** Villarroel, 102 (tel. 93 451 00 51; M: Urgell), shows classics (Tu-Su 600ptas, M 400ptas). For new releases, try **Maremagnum, Moll d'Espanya** (tel. 93 405 22 22), which has 8 screens (Tu and Th-Su 750ptas, W 600ptas). **Icaria-Yelmo**, C. Salvador Espira, 61 (tel. 93 221 75 85), in the Olympic Village, boasts 15 screens (750ptas, M 575ptas). The new **IMAX Port Vell** (tel. 93 225 11 11), on the Moll d'Espanya next to the aquarium and Maremagnum, features an IMAX screen, an Omnimax 30m in diameter, and 3-D projection. Get tickets at the door, through ServiCaixa automatic machines, or by phone (1000-1500ptas).

FÚTBOL

For the record, the lunatics that run around the city covered head to toe in red and blue didn't just escape from a nearby asylum—they are **F.C. Barcelona** fans. Grab some face paint and head to the 110,000-seat **Nou Camp**, which has a box office on C. Aristedes Maillol, 12-18 (tel. 93 496 36 00). **R.C. Deportivo Espanyol**, a.k.a. *los periquitos* (parakeets), Barcelona's second professional soccer team, spreads its wings at **Estadi Olímpic**, Pg. Olímpic, 17-19 (info tel. 93 405 02 97). Obtain tickets for both from Banca Catalana or by phoning TelEntrada (24hr. tel. 902 10 12 12).

BULLFIGHTS

Although the best bullfighters rarely venture out of Madrid, Sevilla, and Málaga, Barcelona's **Plaça de Toros Monumental** (tickets tel. 93 253 38 21), on Gran Vía at Pg. Carles I (M: Monumental), is an excellent facility, complete with Moorish and Modernista influences. Bullfights usually take place during the tourist season (June-Oct. Sundays at 6:30 or 7pm). Tickets available at local travel agencies or ServiCaixa ("la Caixa" banks; tel. 902 33 22 11; 2400-12,500ptas). The box office also sells tickets just before the start of the *corrida*.

RECREATIONAL SPORTS

The tourist offices can provide info about swimming, cycling, tennis, squash, sailing, hiking, scuba diving, white-water rafting, kayaking, or just about any sport. Info is available over the phone (tel. 93 402 30 00 or 93 402 30 40, no English). Though Barcelona tends to ignore its beaches, there's plenty of nearby sand.

Swimming Pools and Workout Facilities: Piscinas Bernat Picornell, Av. l'Estadi, 30-40 (tel. 93 423 40 41). M: Espanya, then bus #50 up Montjuïc. Not just Olympic-sized; this was the actual Olympic pool in 1992. Open M-F 7am-midnight, Sa 7am-9pm, Su 7:30am-2:30pm. 1300ptas for all pools for 1 day. **Club Sant Jordi,** C. París, 114 (tel. 93 410 92 61). M: Sants. Passes are available for other facilities including the sauna, weights, and stairmaster. Bring your passport. Open M-F 7am-5pm, Sa 8am-6pm, Su and holidays 9am-2pm. Pool 500ptas per hr., closed Aug. 1-15.

Beaches: Several lie between Vila Olímpica and the sea, all accessible from M: Ciutadella. The closest and most popular is **Platja Barceloneta**, off Pg. Marítim. **Sitges** (see p. 330) is a popular daytrip. **Castelldefels,** 20min. from Barcelona on the same train line as Sitges, is an enormous beach good for young children–the water takes its time to get deep. The L93 bus leaves Barcelona's Pl. Espanya for Castelldefels (180ptas).

SHOPPING

There's a lot of style walking around Barcelona. Unfortunately, the city's reputation as a fashion capital has led to outlandish prices in the elegant shops along **Passeig Gràcia** and **Rambla Catalunya**—but, hey, it's fun to look. Some of the stores on C. Portaferrissa and Av. Universitat are more affordable. Shoes, leather goods, and clothing can often be cheaper than at home—the farther from Las Ramblas, the better; Gràcia has some of the city's best bargains.

Carrer Banys Nous, off Pl. Pí, in the Barri Gòtic. Antique heaven. Prices and quality vary. Painters gather in Pl. Pí to sell their work Sa 11am-8pm, Su 11am-2pm.

Carrer Pelai, between Pl. Catalunya and Pl. Universitat. Home to Zara's flagship store and other chic-but-cheap clothing and footwear.

Carrer Portaferrissa, between Las Ramblas and Av. Portal de l'Angel. Naf-Naf and Pull & Bear join other post-Generation-X clothing stores. Shoe stores galore and a maze of indoor malls. Swarming with teens M-F, especially 5:30-8pm.

Maremagnum, the ultra-modern mall complex at **Port Vell,** has shops and restaurants. Open daily 9am-9pm.

VIPS, Rbla. Catalunya, above Pl. Catalunya. A super-sized store, this late-night locale is crammed with books, records, food, alcohol, and a cafe. Open M-Th 8am-2am, F 8am-3am, Sa-Su 9am-3am.

FIESTAS

Fiestas are abundant in Barcelona. For more info on all festivals, call 93 301 77 75 (open M-F 10am-2pm and 4-8pm). Before Christmas, **Feria de Santa Llúcia** fills Pl. Catedral and the area around the Sagrada Familia with stalls and booths. Barcelonans wildly celebrate **Carnaval** on February 7 to 13, but many head to the even more raucous celebrations in Sitges and Vilanova i la Geltrù. Soon thereafter, the **Festa de Sant Jordi** (St. George), April 23, feasts in honor of Catalunya's patron saint. This is Barcelona's St. Valentine's Day; men give women roses, and women give men books. On May 11, the **Festa de Saint Ponç,** a traditional market of aromatic and medicinal herbs and honey, sets up in Carrer Hospital, close to Las Ramblas. Barcelona erupts on June 23, the night before **Día de Sant Joan.** Bonfires roar throughout the city, unsupervised children play with fireworks, and the fountains of Pl. Espanya and Palau Reial light up in anticipation of fireworks on Montjuïc. On August 15-21, city folk jam at Gràcia's **Fiesta Mayor.** Lights blaze in the plazas and streets, and rock bands play all night.

On September 11, the **Fiesta Nacional de Catalunya** brings traditional costumes, dancing, and Catalán flags hanging from balconies. The **Feria de Cuina i Vins de Catalunya** brings wine and *butifarra* (sausage) producers to the Rbla. Catalunya. For one week you can sample fine food and drink for a small fee. On September 24, during the **Festa de la Verge de la Mercè,** fireworks light up the city while the traditional *correfocs* (parades of people dressed as devils) whirl pitchfork-shaped sparklers and the city's residents hurl buckets of water at the demons. The beginning of November marks the **Fiesta del Sant Çito,** when locals and tourists alike roll up their sleeves and party on Las Ramblas. Finally, from October through November, a **Festival Internacional de Jazz** hits the city's streets and clubs.

NEAR BARCELONA

MONTSERRAT

An hour northwest of Barcelona, the mountain of Montserrat, whose unmistakable profile protrudes from the flat Río Llobregat Valley, makes an easy daytrip. Its popularity began in the 9th century when a mountaineer wandering the crags of Montserrat had a blinding vision of the Virgin Mary. His story spread, attracting pilgrims to the mountain in droves. In 1025 an opportunistic bishop-abbot named Oliba founded a monastery to worship the Virgin, who had become the spiritual patroness of Catalunya. Nowadays 80 Benedictine monks tend the building, most of which dates from the 19th century (although two wings of the old Gothic cloister survive). During the Catalán *Renaixança* of the early 20th century, politicians and artists, such as poets Joan Maragall and Jacint Verdaguer, turned to Montserrat as a source of Catalán legend and tradition. In the Franco era, it became a center for Catalán resistance—Bibles were printed here in Catalán, and nationalist demonstrations were held on the mountain. Today, the site attracts both devout worshipers and everyday tourists, who come to see the Virgin of Montserrat, her ornate basilica, the accompanying art museum, and perhaps most of all, the panoramic views of the mountain's awesome rock formations.

🛈 PRACTICAL INFORMATION. FFCC trains (tel. 93 205 15 15) to Montserrat leave from M: Espanya in Barcelona (1hr., every hr. on the half hour 6:30am-11:30pm, one-way 1185ptas, same day round-trip 1855ptas); be sure to get off at Aeri de Montserrat, *not* Olesa de Montserrat. The train stops at the base of the mountain, where you can take the heartstopping **Aeri cable car** up to the monastery (every 15min. M-F 9:45am-1:45pm and 3-6:15pm, Sa-Su 2:20-6:35pm, price included in train fares or 925ptas round-trip by itself). Exit the upper cable car station, turn left and walk to **Plaça Creu,** Montserrat's commercial area.

The info booth in Plaça Creu (tel. 93 835 02 51) provides **maps,** schedules of daily religious services, and advice (in a number of languages) on mountain navigation (open July-Sept. daily 10am-7pm; Oct.-June M-F 9am-6pm, Sa-Su 10am-7pm). If you've got a few extra *pesetas,* pick up the *Official Guide to Montserrat* (825ptas). Other conveniences in Pl. Creu include **currency exchange** with poor rates (open June-Sept. M-F 9:15am-2pm; Oct.-May M-F 9:15am-2pm, Sa 9:15am-1:30pm), **ATMs,** and a **post office** (open June-Sept. M-F 9am-12:45pm and 2-5:30pm, Sa 9-11:30am). **Ambulance** or **mountain rescue team,** tel. 93 877 77 77; **police: Guardia Civil,** (tel. 93 877 77 77), in the main square.

🍴 ACCOMMODATIONS AND FOOD. For those who choose to spend the night, apartments for up to 10 people are available through **Administración de les Celles** (tel. 93 835 02 01; fax 93 835 06 59), in the far plaza (open daily 9am-1pm and 2-6pm; after 6pm, they're at the Hotel Abat Cisneros reception). The office runs three *hostales* and a three-star hotel. **Abat Marcet,** nicest of the three hostels, has rooms to accommodate one to four people. Every room comes with private bath and a microwave. (Singles 1650-4680ptas; doubles 2580-4950ptas.) Rooms at **Abat Oliba,** all with bath, accommodate two to seven people but are closed during the low season (doubles 3580-3900ptas; quads 5600ptas-6100ptas). **Hotel Monestir** is the oldest of the three and has shared baths (singles 2050-3290ptas, with bath 2935-4285ptas; doubles 3535-6015ptas, with bath 5100-7580ptas.)

As food options are less than thrilling, the prudent beat a path to the **supermarket,** on the right as you go up Pl. Creu. The **Forn Pastissería** sells meat, cheese, and baked goods to appreciate on the quiet mountain paths (open M-F 9am-5:45pm, Sa 9am-7:45pm, Su 9am-6:45pm). Other options include the informal **Bar de la Plaça,** in the building past the info booth, which serves up *bocadillos* (365-510ptas) and other treats. (Roast chicken 975ptas; hamburgers 445ptas. Open Su-F 9:30am-7:30pm, Sa 9:30am-8pm.) **Bar-Snack de Montserrat** is cafeteria-style with an open dining hall. (*Bocadillos* 410-445ptas. Open Apr.-Nov. Su-F 8:45am-6:45pm, Sa 8:45am-7:30pm. Platters from 950ptas; daily noon-4pm.)

🔲 SIGHTS. Above Pl. Creu, the entrance to the **basilica** looks out onto Pl. Santa Noría. To the right of the main chapel, a special route through the **side chapels** leads to the glimmering 12th century Romanesque **La Moreneta** (the black Virgin Mary), Montserrat's venerated icon of Mary and child. (Route open summer daily 9-10:30am, noon-6:15pm, and 7:30-8:30pm.) Legend has it that St. Peter hid the figure, which was carved by St. Luke, in Montserrat's caves. Removed from Montserrat after the Napoleonic Wars and the Spanish Civil War, the solemn little figure found its way back—it is now showcased in an elaborate silver case. For good luck rub the orb in Mary's outstretched hand. Songs by the renowned *Escalonia* (a boys' choir) ring through the basilica. (Performances daily 1pm, except for July.)

Also in Pl. Santa María, the **Museo de Montserrat** exhibits a variety of art, ranging from a mummified Egyptian woman to several Picassos—including *Sardana of Peace,* painted just for Montserrat, and his *Old Fisherman,* completed when he was 14. The museum's Impressionist paintings are its highlights. Look for works by Catalán artists like Joaquim Mir and Ramón Casas, whose famous *Madeline Absinthe* is one of many evocative portraits. (Open summer daily 9am-6pm; winter 9:30am-6:30pm. 500ptas, students 300ptas.)

BARCELONA

🚶 **WALKS.** A visit to Montserrat is not complete without a meditative walk along the "mountain of a hundred peaks." Some of the most beautiful areas of the mountain are accessible only on foot. Visitors have two options: down or up. To go down, the **Santa Cova** funicular descends from Pl. Creu to paths which wind along the sides of the mountain to ancient hermitages (every 20min., summer daily 10am-1pm and 2-6pm, winter Sa-Su only, round-trip 360ptas). Take the **St. Joan funicular** up for more inspirational views of Montserrat (Mar.-Oct., every 20min., 10am-7pm, round-trip 895ptas). The dilapidated **St. Joan monastery** and **shrine** are only a 20min. tromp from the highest station. But the real prize is **Sant Jerónim** (the area's highest peak at 1235m), with its mystical views of Montserrat's celebrated rock formations—these enormous domes and serrated outcroppings resemble human forms including "The Bewitched Friars" and "The Mummy." The hike is about two hours from Pl. Creu (or a 1hr. trek from the terminus of the St. Joan funicular). The paths are long and winding though not all that difficult—after all, they were made for guys wearing long brown robes. En route, make sure you take a sharp left when, after about 45 minutes, you come to the little old chapel—otherwise you're headed straight for a helicopter pad. On a clear day the hike offers spectacular views of Barcelona and environs.

SITGES

Forty km south of Barcelona, the resort town of Sitges has earned considerable fame for its prime tanning grounds, lively cultural festivals, thriving gay community, and wired nightlife. Long considered a watered-down Eivissa (Ibiza City), Sitges has better beaches than the notorious Balearic hotspot (though it may be a bit less picturesque and certainly less flamboyant). However, you won't find crazier beach-oriented nightlife than this on mainland Spain. Sitges's booming status has recently begun to attract pro-soccer players and movie stars.

📋 **PRACTICAL INFORMATION. Cercanías Trains** (tel. 93 490 02 02) run from Barcelona-Sants and M: Gràcia to Sitges (40min.; every 15min.; M-F 310ptas, Sa-Su 355ptas) and continue on to **Vilanova** (7min.; every 15min. until 11:45pm; M-F 150ptas, Sa-Su 160ptas). The last train back from Sitges to Barcelona is at 10:25pm. To access the beaches between towns, rent a car at **Car Office**, Oasis Local, 14 (tel. 93 811 12 12), at the corner of C. Vilafranca and Vilanova, up C. Carbonell from the train station. For a super map and info on accommodations, try the **tourist office** (tel. 93 894 42 51; email info@sitgestur.com), on Pg. Vilafranca. From the station, turn right onto C. Carbonell and go downhill until you see the sign with the big "i." (Open W-M 10am-1pm and 5:30-9pm; in summer another branch by the museums on C. Fohollar.) **Emergency:** tel. 062; **police** (tel. 93 811 76 25); **medical assistance** (tel. 93 894 64 26; emergency tel. 894 39 49), way uptown on C. Samuel Barrachina. **Post office** (tel. 93 894 12 47), in Pl. Espanya (open M-F 8:30am-2:30pm, Sa 9:30am-1pm; no packages Sa); **postal code:** 08870. **Internet access** and **fax** service available at **El Patí**, C. Illa de Cuba, 29 (tel. 93 894 76 76; 500ptas per 30min.; open M-Sa 9am-2pm and 5-10pm, Su 10am-2pm).

🛏 **ACCOMMODATIONS.** Accommodations are expensive and extremely difficult to find in high season, so consider daytripping from Barcelona. If you plan to stay, reserve early. **Hostal Parelladas,** C. Parellades, 11 (tel. 93 894 08 01), one block from the beach, which offers standard rooms and an airy terrace, is dirt cheap for Sitges (singles 2700ptas; doubles with bath 5500ptas). **Hostal Internacional,** C. Sant Francesc, 52 (tel. 93 894 26 90), provides clean, bright rooms (doubles 5000ptas, with bath 6000ptas). **Casa Julián,** C. Carbonell, 2 (tel. 93 894 03 06), at the corner of C. Sant Francesc, has slightly more expensive rooms (singles 3700ptas, doubles 5400ptas; open June 20- Sept. 20). For more options, consider neighboring Vilanova (see below), seven minutes away on the Cercanías train. Staying in Vilanova, however, may be difficult—the last train from Sitges to Vilanova runs at 11:45pm, before the nightlife gets going.

☐ FOOD. Chickens roasting on an open fire at **Restaurante La Oca,** C. Parelladas, 41 (tel. 93 894 79 36), attract long lines of hungry tourists. Try the succulent *half-pollo al ast* (roasted chicken) for 750ptas, or grab a whole one for 850ptas (open daily 1pm-midnight). Take part in the immense popularity of **Mont Roig Café,** C. Montroig, 11-13, just off Parellades, by dining in the spacious indoor lounge or shady outdoor patio. (Sandwiches 325-500ptas, hamburgers 675-875ptas, salads 600ptas. Open Su-F 9am-3am, Sa 9am-3:30am). The baguette fast-food stop **Bocapà,** also on C. Montroig, is a cheaper option, with a large variety of *bocadillos* (295-475ptas) and a 495pta *menú* (open Su-Th 10am-1am, Sa 10am-2am; Visa, MC). At the spiritual bookstore-cafe **Hatuey,** C. Sant Francesc, 44 (tel. 93 894 52 09), you can sip specialty teas and drinks while pondering man's evolution from primate to TV-headed yuppie (open daily 9am-3am).

☑ SIGHTS. Plenty of soothing sand pacifies vacationing families and 20-somethings. The **beach** is a 10-minute walk from the train station on any street. In summer, the main beaches can get crowded; a short walk leads to quieter areas.

Back in town, **Carrer Parellades,** with shopping, eating, and drinking galore, is the main tourist drag. Although beachgoers may consider cultural activities to be as frightening as rain, Sitges has some can't-miss beachside attractions. Check out Morell's whimsical **Modernista clock tower,** Pl. Cap de la Vila, 2, above Optica at the intersection of Parellades and Sant Francesc. Behind **Església del Evangelista** on C. Fonollar, the **Museu Cau Ferrat** (tel. 93 894 03 64) hangs over the water's edge. Once home to Catalán modernist Santiago Russinyol and a rendezvous point for young Catalán artists Picasso and Ramón Casas, the building is a shrine to Modernista iron, glasswork, and painting. Next door, the **Museu Maricel del Mar** (tel. 93 894 03 64) has a selective collection of medieval painting and sculpture. The **Museu Romàntic,** C. Sant Gaudenci, 1 (tel. 93 894 29 69), off C. Bonaire from the waterfront, is a 19th-century bourgeois house filled with period pieces, like music boxes and 17th- to 19th-century dolls. (All 3 museums open June 15-Oct. 15 Tu-Su 9:30am-2pm and 5-9pm; Oct. 16-June 14 Tu-F 9:30am-2pm and 4-6pm, Sa 9:30am-7pm, Su 9:30am-3pm. Combo entrance 900ptas, students 500ptas; otherwise 500ptas per museum, students 250ptas.) Across the street from the two museums the stately **Palau Maricel** (tel. 93 894 03 64), on C. Fonollar, built in 1910 for American millionaire Charles Deering, rivals Richie Rich's playpad (open in summer only, hours vary; classical concerts on select days July-Aug. 8pm; 800ptas, includes a glass of *cava*).

☑ ENTERTAINMENT. Late-night foolhardiness clusters around **Carrer Primer de Maig** (which runs directly from the beach) and its continuation, **Carrer Marques Montroig.** The wild ones get even crazier at the "disco-beach" **Atlántida** (tel. 93 894 26 77), in Sector Terramar, and then shuffle their feet at the legendary **Pachá** (tel. 93 894 22 98), on Pg. Sant Didac in nearby Vallpineda. Buses run all night to the two discos from C. Primer de Maig (midnight to 4am). Other popular digs include **Ricky's,** Sant Pau, 25 (tel. 93 894 96 81) and **Otto Zutz,** on Port d'Aiguadoc, to the left of the museums when facing the water. C. Boraire is also home to some late night action. **Road House 66,** C. Boraire, 12, has salsa on Saturday from 11:30pm to 3am.

Sitges celebrates holidays with all-out style. During the **Festa de Corpus Christi** on June 6, townspeople collaborate to create intricate fresh-flower carpets. For *papier-mâché* dragons, devils, and giants dancing in the streets, visit during the **Festa Major,** held August 23 to 25 in honor of the town's patron saint Bartolomé. Nothing compares to the **Carnaval,** on Sunday and Tuesday of the first week of Lent, when Spaniards crash the town for a frenzy of dancing, outrageous costumes, and vats of alcohol. On the first Sunday of March, a pistol shot starts the **Rallye de Coches de Epoca,** an antique car race from Barcelona to Sitges. June brings the **International Theater Festival** (1500-3500ptas per show), July and August the **International Jazz Festival** (1700ptas per concert), and mid-October the one- to two-week **Festival Internacional de Cine Fantástico de Sitges.**

BARCELONA

NEAR SITGES: VILANOVA I LA GELTRÙ

Catalunya's most important port after Barcelona and Tarragona, **Vilanova i la Geltrù** is actually two cities in one: an industrial center and a well-groomed beach town. Since there's little in the dusty uptown areas except for a couple of old churches and stone facades, most visitors spend the day on the beach (10min. from the train station). In the evening, Vilanovans generally forgo late-night madness for beach volleyball or soccer at Parc de Ribes.

Cercanías Trains run from Vilanova to **Sitges** (7min.; every 15min.; M-F 150ptas, Sa-Su 160ptas), continuing to **Barcelona** (50min.; M-F 305ptas, Sa-Su 355ptas) and **Tarragona** (10 per day). Many also continue to **Port Aventura** (10min., 5-7 per day, 130ptas) and **Valencia** (30min.-2hr., delay due to necessary connection on 3-8pm trains, 330ptas). **Mon Bus** (tel. 93 893 70 60) also connects Vilanova to **Sitges** (185ptas), **Vilafranca** (255ptas), and **Barcelona** (450ptas, 800ptas roundtrip). The **train station** doubles as the **bus station**. A **taxi** ride between Vilanova and Sitges costs around 1500ptas. To get to the beaches, exit the station, turn left on C. Forn de Vidre, take the third left onto the thoroughfare Rambla de la Pau, head under the overpass, and follow the *rambla* all the way to the port. The **tourist office** (tel. 93 815 45 17), with an excellent **map** and lodgings advice, is about 50m to the right, in a small park called Parc de Ribes Roges (open July-Aug. M-F 10am-8pm, Sa 10am-2pm; Sept.-June 10am-2pm and sometimes 4-7pm, unpredictably). To the right, past the tourist office, is **Platja de Ribes Roges;** to the left is the smaller **Platja del Far.** Expect fine sands, sun, and tons of company.

If you decide to stay in town, the popular **Can Gatell,** C. Puigcerdà, 6-16 (tel. 93 893 01 17), has clean rooms. With your back to the station, head down C. Victor Balaguer, the leftward of the two parallel streets; at the end, turn right onto Rbla. Ventosa, and hang a quick left at the sign. (Singles 4500ptas; doubles 7000ptas; triples 9450ptas.) The hostel's four-course 1300pta *menú* (served M-F) is popular with locals. A less expensive alternative is **Supermarket Condis,** Av. Gairraf, 23, down the street from Can Gatell (open M-Sa 9am-9pm).

NORTHEASTERN SPAIN

CATALUÑA (CATALUNYA)

From rocky Costa Brava to smooth Costa Dorada, the lush Pyrenees to chic Barcelona, Cataluña is a vacation in itself and it's got the brochures to prove it. Cataluña has also been graced with the nation's richest resources, making it one of the most prosperous regions in Iberia. To top it off, *catalanes* are famous for their strong work ethic. As the saying goes, "El Català de les pedres fa pa" (a Catalán can make bread out of stones).

Colonized first by the Greeks and the Carthaginians, Cataluña was later one of Rome's favored provinces. Only briefly subdued by the Moors, Cataluña's counts achieved independence in AD 874 and gained recognition as sovereign princes in 987. After nabbing the throne of Aragón in 1137, Cataluña became part of Spain, but Catalán legal codes remained in effect. King Felipe V was finally able to suppress Cataluña in the early 18th century when the *catalanes* sided against him in the War of Spanish Succession (1702-1714). In the late 18th century, the region's fortunes revived when it developed into one of Europe's premier textile manufacturers, opening trade with the Americas. Nineteenth-century industrial expansion nourished arts and sciences, ushering in an age known as the Catalán *Renaixença* (Renaissance). The 20th century gave birth to the Modernist movement and an all-star list of artists and architects, including Picasso, Miró, Dalí, and Antoni Gaudí. Home to staunch opponents of the Fascists during Spain's Civil War, Cataluña lost its autonomy in 1939. During his regime, Franco suppressed Catalán language instruction (except in universities) and limited Catalán publications.

Since Cataluña regained autonomy in 1977, Catalán media and arts have flourished. Today, Catalán is once again the region's official language (though Cataluña is almost entirely bilingual). While some worry that the use of Catalán will discourage talented Spaniards from working or studying in Cataluña, effectively isolating the principality, others argue that extensive regional autonomy has generally led to progressive ends. Cataluña's regional pride rivals that of País Vasco. Many *catalanes* will answer inquiring visitors in Catalán, even if asked in Castilian (the politically and technically correct name for "Spanish"). Lauded throughout Spain, Catalán cuisine boasts *pan con tomate*, bread smeared with olive oil, tomato, and garlic, and *ali-oli*, a garlic and olive oil sauce. Lovers exchange books and roses to honor the region's patron, St. George, on the *Fiesta de Sant Jordi* (April 23). On September 11, *catalanes* whoop it up for *Diada (La Fiesta Nacional de Catalunya)*, a celebration of the region's political autonomy.

HIGHLIGHTS OF CATALUÑA

■ The fascinating history and friendly people of seaside **Tossa de Mar** (see p. 337).
■ The jumbled streets of historic, charming, and under-touristed **Girona** (see p. 345).
■ **Teatre Museu Dalí**, Salvador Dalí's self-built monument (see p. 352).
■ The small yet bustling town of **Vielha** in the midst of the Pyrenees (see p. 361).

COSTA DORADA

TARRAGONA

Tarragona's strategic position made the city a provincial Roman capital under Augustus; today an amphitheater and other ruins pay homage to the city's imperial days. Cataluña's second most important port, Tarragona has earned a reputation as the younger sibling of Spain's urban elites. Ironically, the vestiges of Tarragona's august past are the city's most compelling attractions.

▐ GETTING THERE

Trains are the best transportation option; try and get on a Talgo or Euromed train— they're much faster. Trains connect to Tarragona from: **Barcelona** (1½hr., 20 per day, 6am-10pm, 645-820ptas); **Valencia** (2-3hr., 20 per day, 2:20am-9:55pm, 2600-400ptas); **Zaragoza** (3½hr., 14 per day, 12:38am-4:54pm, 2000-2600ptas).

▐ ORIENTATION AND PRACTICAL INFORMATION

Most sights are clustered on a hill, surrounded by the remnants of Roman walls. At the foot of the hill, **Ramblas Vella** and **Nova** (parallel to one another) are the main thoroughfares of the new city. Rambla Nova runs from **Passeig de les Palmeres** (which overlooks the sea) to **Plaça Imperial Tarraco,** the monstrous rotunda and home of the bus station. To reach the center of the old quarter from the train station, turn right and walk 200m to the killer stairs parallel to the shore.

Trains: (tel. 977 24 02 02), on Pl. Pedrera by the water. Info open daily 6am-9pm. The best transportation option. To: **Barcelona** (1hr., 30-40 per day, 6000ptas); **Sitges** (1hr., 23 per day); **Valencia** (2-3hr., 15 per day, 3100ptas); **Zaragoza** (3½hr., 10 per day); **Alicante** (4½hr., 7 per day, 5000ptas); **Madrid** (6½hr., 7 per day, 5000ptas).

Buses: (tel. 977 22 91 26), Pl. Imperial Tarraco. **Transportes Bacoma** (tel. 977 22 20 72) serves most destinations. To: **Barcelona** (1½hr., 3 per day, 785ptas); **Valencia** (3½hr., 6 per day, 225ptas); **Alicante** (6hr., 6 per day, 3740ptas).

Public Transportation: EMT Buses (tel. 977 54 94 80) run all over Tarragona. Buses run daily 6am-11pm. 105ptas, 10-ride "bono" ticket 680ptas.

Taxi: Radio Taxi (tel. 977 22 14 14).

Tourist Office: C. Major, 39 (tel. 977 24 52 03; fax 977 24 55 07), below the cathedral steps. Crucial free map and a guide to Tarragona's Roman ruins. Open June-Sept. M-F 9:30am-8:30pm, Sa 9:30am-2pm and 4-8:30pm, Su 10am-2pm; Oct.-May M-F 10am-2pm and 4:30-7pm, Sa-Su 10am-2pm. **Information booths:** Pl. Imperial Terraco, at the bottom of Rambla Vella; another at the intersection of Av. Catalunya and Vía de L'Impera Romi; a third at the corner of Vía Augusta and Pg. Sant Antoni. Open July-Oct. daily 10am-2pm and 4-8pm; Nov.-June Sa-Su 10am-2pm.

Luggage Storage: 24hr. lockers at the train station. June-Aug. 400ptas; Sept.-May 600ptas.

Emergency: dial 091 or 092. **Police: Comisaría de Policía** (tel. 977 23 33 11), on Pl. Orleans. From Pl. Imperial Tarraco on the inland end of Rambla Nova, walk down Av. Pres. Lluis Companys, and take the 3rd left to the station.

Medical Assistance: Hospital de Sant Pau i Santa Tecla, Rambla Vella, 14 (tel. 977 23 80 54). **Hospital Joan XXIII** (tel. 977 29 58 00), on C. Dr. Mallafré Guasch.

Post Office: Pl. Corsini, 12 (tel. 977 24 01 49), below Rambla Nova off C. Canyelles. Open M-F 8:30am-8:30pm, Sa 9am-2pm. **Postal Code:** 43001.

Internet Access: Biblioteca Pública, C. Fortuny, 30 (tel. 977 24 05 44). Free with passport.

Cataluña

ACCOMMODATIONS AND CAMPING

Although Tarragona is not known for its abundance of cheap beds, deals can be found near Pl. Pedrera (by the train station) and by Pl. Font, in the old quarter (parallel to Rambla Vella).

Pensión Marsal, Pl. Font, 26 (tel. 977 22 40 69), in the heart of the historic town. Unassuming entrance through a cafe. Tidy rooms with private baths, nice beds, and fans. Breakfast included. Singles 2500ptas; doubles 5000ptas. Visa, MC, AmEx.

Residencia Juvenil Sant Jordi (HI), C. Pres. Lluis Companys, 5 (tel. 977 24 01 95). Go left after leaving the train station, take the 1st right, and catch bus #2 in front of Bar Fa; it stops on C. Presidente Lluis Companys, 2 blocks from the bus station. Common room features TV and table tennis. Laundry 300ptas; drying 200ptas. Breakfast included. Sheets and towels 500ptas. July-Aug. singles 2800ptas; doubles 2050ptas per person.

Camping: Several sites line the road toward Barcelona (Vía Augusta or CN-340) along the beaches north of town. Take bus #9 (every 20min., 105ptas) from Pl. Imperial Tarraco. The closest is **Tarraco** (tel. 977 29 02 89), at Platja de l'Arrabassada. Well-maintained facilities by beach. Reception 24hr. 530ptas per person and per car; 390ptas per tent. Open Apr.-Sept.

FOOD

Pl. Font and Ramblas Nova and Vella are full of cheap *menús* (800-1200ptas) and greasy *platos combinados*. Tarragona's **indoor market,** is at Pl. Corsini next to the post office (open M-W and Sa 7am-2pm, Th-F 7am-2pm and 5:30-8:30pm). For **groceries,** turn to **Simago,** C. Augusta at Comte de Rius, between Ramblas Nova and Vella (open M-Sa 9am-9pm).

La Teula, C. Merceria, 16 (tel. 670 95 71 54), in the old city off Pl. Santiago Rusiñol. Great for salads (450-600ptas) and savory sandwiches (675-1000ptas). Lunch *menú* 975ptas. Open Tu-Sa 11am-4pm and 8pm-midnight.

Restaurant El Caserón, Trinquet Nou, 4 (tel. 977 23 93 28), parallel to Rambla Vella (off Pl. Font). Ceiling fans cool travelers and home-cooked meals fill stomachs. Entrees 800-1400ptas. Open M-Sa 1-3:30pm and 8:30-10:30pm, Su 1-3:30pm.

◫◉ SIGHTS AND BEACHES

Tarragona's status as provincial capital transformed the small military enclosure into a glorious imperial port. Countless Roman ruins stand silently amid 20th-century hustle and bustle.

ROMAN RUINS. Below Pg. Palmeres is the **Amfiteatre Romà**, where gladiators once killed wild animals and each other. Above the amphitheater, across Pg. Sant Antoni, is the entrance to the **Museu de la Romanitat**, which houses the **Pretori** and the **Circ Romans.** The Pretori was the governor's palace in the first century BC. Rumor has it that Pontius Pilate was born here. The Circ Romans, connected by vaults that both the Romans and Franco's troops used as dungeons, was once a chariot race track that extended across the old city. Most of it is buried, but some sections are still visible in the basements of restaurants and apartment buildings. To see what remains of the second-century BC walls, stroll through the **Passeig Arquelògic.** The walls originally stretched to the sea and fortified the entire city. The scattered **Fòrum Romà** lies near the post office on C. Lleida, clearly demonstrating how far the walls extended. *(All monuments and museums open June-Sept. Tu-Su 9am-9pm; Oct.-May Tu-Su 10am-1:30pm and 4-6:30pm. Joint ticket to Amfitheatre, Museu de la Romanitat, Pg. Arquelògic, and Forum 300ptas, students 100ptas, under 16 free.)*

MUSEUMS. The **Museu Nacional Arqueològic** displays ancient utensils, statues, and mosaics, including a ravishing *Cap de Medusa.* *(Across Pl. Rei from the Pretori. Tel. 977 23 62 09. 400ptas, students 200ptas; includes admission to the Necropolis.)* For a bit of the macabre, creep over to the **Museu i Necròpolis Paleocristians.** The huge early Christian burial site has yielded a rich variety of urns, tombs, and sarcophagi, the best of which are in the museum. *(Av. Ramón y Cajal, 78. At Pg. Independència on the edge of town. Tel. 977 21 11 75. 400ptas, students 200ptas; includes admission to Museu Arqueològic.)* If you've had too much Roman roamin', try a visit to the **Casa-Museu Castellarnau.** It housed the Viscounts of Castellarnau, 18th-century nobles. *(Descend the steps in front of the cathedral and take the 3rd right onto C. Cavellares. Tel. 977 24 22 20. 300ptas.)*

OTHER SIGHTS. The **Pont del Diable (Devil's Bridge)** is a well-preserved Roman aqueduct. *(Take municipal bus #5 (every 20min., 105ptas) from the corner of C. Christòfor Colom and Av. Prat de la Riba or from Pl. Imperial Tarraco.)* Lit by a huge rose window is the Romanesque-Gothic **cathedral.** *(C. Major near Pl. Seu. Open June-Aug. M-Sa 10am-7pm; Sept.-May M-Sa 10am-12:30pm and 3-6pm. 300ptas, students 150ptas.)*

BEACHES. The hidden access to **Platja del Miracle,** the town's main beach, is along Baixada del Miracle, starting off Pl. Arce Ochotorena, beyond the Roman theater. A bit farther away are the larger beaches, **l'Arrabassada,** with dirt-like sand, and the windy **Llarga.** *(Take bus #1 or 9 from Pl. Imperial Tarraco or any of the other stops.)*

♫ ENTERTAINMENT

Tarragona's nightlife is a smaller-scale version of Barcelona's. Between 5pm and 9pm, Ramblas Nova and Vella (and the area in between) are packed with strolling families. Around 9pm, the bars liven up. **Puerto de Portivo** is the most popular spot. From Rambla Vella, take C. Sant Francese, which becomes C. Unío; bear left at Pl. General Prim and follow C. Apodaca to its end. Cross the tracks and keep walking. **Pau de Protectorat** is also a popular street. When these bars close around 2am, everyone heads to the new **Port Esportiu,** across the train tracks, for dancing.

July and August usher in the **Fiestal de Tarragona** (tel. 977 24 47 95; 24hr. tickets tel. 902 33 22 11). The **Auditori Camp de Mart** near the cathedral holds film screenings and rock, jazz, dance, and theater performances. A booth on Av. Catalunya at Portal del Roser sells tickets until 9pm for the 10:30pm performances (1000-2500ptas). Arrive one hour before the performance. On even-numbered years, the first Sunday in October brings the **Concurs de Castells,** featuring tall stacks of people called "human towers." They also appear amid beasts and fireworks during the annual **Festa de Santa Tecla** (September 23).

NEAR TARRAGONA: PORT AVENTURA AMUSEMENT PARK

Catalán youth are all a-buzz over Port Aventura (tel. 902 40 44 40), Spain's latest and greatest theme park. Although Disney veterans will find Port Aventura strangely familiar, it makes for a refreshing break from museum and history-heavy itineraries. Spain's take on the Disney original includes five "lands" surrounding a lagoon, each representing a region of the world: the Mediterranean, Polynesia, China, Mexico, and the "Far West." The park's blockbuster attractions are its high-speed roller coasters. Although prices for food are predictably high, Mexico's self-service cantina (entrees 600-900ptas) won't break the bank, and it ain't bad for ambience either. About half the trains on the Barcelona-Tarragona-Tortosa line stop at Port Aventura (1½hr., 11 per day; 150ptas). A taxi from Tarragona costs 2000ptas (10min.). (Open daily Mar. 26-June 19 10am-8pm; June 20-Sept. 13 10am-midnight; Sept. 14-Jan. 11 10am-8pm. 4300ptas for 1 day, 6300ptas for 2 days. Seniors and children 3200ptas for 1 day, 4900ptas for 2 days. Nighttime 3300ptas, seniors and children 2000ptas. Admission fee includes all rides and shows.)

COSTA BRAVA

The Costa Brava's jagged cliffs cut into the Mediterranean Sea from Barcelona to the French border. Though rugged by name, the Brave Coast is tamed in July and August by the planeloads of Europeans dumped onto its once tranquil beaches (you'll make the most friends if you speak German). In early June and late September the water is still warm and the beaches less crowded. Unlike its counterparts, Costa Blanca and Costa del Sol, Costa Brava offers more than just high-rises and touristy beaches. The rocky shores have traditionally attracted artists, like Marc Chagall and Salvador Dalí, a Costa Brava native. Dalí's house in Cadaqués and his museum in Figueres display the largest collections of his work in Europe. In the winter Costa Brava lives up to its name, as fierce winds sweep the coast, leaving behind tranquil, boarded-up beach towns.

▐ GETTING THERE

Transportation on the Costa Brava is fickle, with frequent service during July and August, less service the rest of the tourist season (May-June and Sept.-Oct.), and little to no service in winter. **RENFE trains** stop at the southern tip of the coast at Blanes, Figueres, and again at Llançà and Portbou (near the French border). **Buses** are the preferred mode of transportation, often running along beautiful winding roads, although the few trains that run are usually faster and slightly cheaper.

TOSSA DE MAR

Falling in love in (and with) Tossa is easy. In 1934, French artist Marc Chagall commenced a 40-year love affair with this seaside village, deeming it "Blue Paradise." When *The Flying Dutchman* was filmed here in 1951, Ava Gardner fell hard for Spanish bullfighter-turned-actor Mario Cabrera, much to the chagrin of Frank Sinatra, her husband at the time. Like most coastal cities, Tossa (pop. 3800) suffers from the usual tourist industry blemishes: souvenir shops and crowded beaches. That said, Tossa stands out, framed by reddened cliffs and small-town sincerity long since abandoned by the larger resort towns. Tossa also hosts some impressive sights, most notably a sun-baked cluster of 12th- to 14th-century buildings that knot themselves inside stone-walled Vila Vella. These walls were originally raised at the end of the 12th century, reconstructed in 1387, and are continually being restored for your enjoyment.

▐▀ GETTING THERE

Buses run to Tossa de Mar from **Lloret** (20min., every 30min., 7:45am-8:15pm, 180ptas) and **Girona** (1hr., 2 per day, 625ptas).

▐ ORIENTATION AND PRACTICAL INFORMATION

Buses arrive at **Plaça de les Nacions Sense Estat,** at the corner of Avinguda Pelegrí and Avinguda Ferrán Agulló; the town slopes gently down from there to the waterfront. Walk away from the station on Av. Ferrán Agulló, turn right on Avinguda Costa Brava, and continue until your feet get wet (10min). **Passeig del Mar,** at the end of Av. Costa Brava, curves along the **Platja Gran** (Tossa's main beach) to the foot of the old quarter.

Buses: Av. Pelegrí at Pl. Nacions Sense Estat. **Pujol i Pujol** (tel. 972 36 42 36) to **Lloret del Mar** (20min., June-Aug. every 30min., Sept.-May every hr., 7:45am-8:15pm, 180ptas). **Sarfa** (tel. 972 34 09 03) to **Girona** (1hr., in summer 2 per day, off-season 1 per day, 615ptas) and **Barcelona** (3½hr., M-F 9 per day, 7:40am-6:40pm, Su 8 per day, 6:10am-7:10pm, 1120ptas).

Ferries: Round-trip ferries are often more economical than the bus service. For a one-way trip, take the bus. **Crucetours** (tel. 972 36 60 37) runs from the main beach to **St. Feliu** (45min., July-Aug. 5 per day, 9:30am-9pm, 725ptas, round-trip 1250ptas). Check with the booth near the Vila Vella end of the Platja Gran for info.

Car Rental: Viajes Tramontana, Av. Costa Brava, 23 (tel. 972 34 28 29). **Europcar** and **Avis** operate from the same storefront. One-day rentals start at 6700ptas. Must be 18 with a license to rent from Viajes Tramontana; for Europcar and Avis, min. age is 25.

Mountain Bike and Moped Rentals: Road Runner, Av. de la Palma, s/n (tel. 972 34 05 03). Bring passport and license (for moped). Mountain bike rental 600ptas per hr., moped rental 1950ptas for 2hr. Open Apr.-Oct. daily 9:30am-9pm.

Tourist Office: Av. Pelegrí, 25 (tel. 972 34 01 08; fax 972 34 07 12), in the bus terminal at Av. Ferrán Agulló and Av. Pelegrí. Handy, thoroughly indexed map. English spoken. Open June 15-Sept. 15 M-Sa 9am-9pm, Su 10am-1pm; May and Oct. M-Sa 10am-1pm and 4-8pm; Sept. 16-June 14 M-F 10am-1pm and 4-7pm, Sa 10am-1pm.

Currency Exchange: Banco Central Hispano, C. Ferran Agulló, 2 (tel. 972 34 10 65). **ATM.** Open June-Aug. M-F 8:30am-2:30pm; Sept.-May M-Sa 8:30am-2:30pm.

Police: Municipal police, C. Església, 4 (tel. 972 34 01 35) in the Ajuntament. English spoken. They'll escort you to the **24hr. pharmacy.**

Medical Services: Casa del Mar, Av. Catalunya (tel. 972 34 18 28). Primary health services and immediate attention. Nearest hospital is in Blanes.

Post Office: C. Maria Auxiliadora, s/n (tel. 972 34 04 57), down Av. Pelegrí from tourist office. Open M-F 8:30am-2:30pm, Sa 9:30am-1pm. **Postal Code:** 17320.

Internet: La Lluna (tel. 972 34 30 27), Av. Sant Raimon de Penyafort. Before 8pm, 300ptas for 15min., 75ptas for each additional 5min; after 8pm, 400ptas for 15min., 100ptas for each additional 5min. Open May-Oct. 3pm-midnight, closed Nov.-Apr.

ACCOMMODATIONS

Tossa is a seasonal town, and therefore many hostels, restaurants, and bars open only from May to October. In the summer and during festivals, Tossa fills quickly. Make reservations in advance, as some establishments are booked solid in July and August. The **old quarter** hotels are the only ones worth considering.

■ **Pensión Pepi**, C. Sant Miguel, 10 (tel. 972 34 05 26). Turn left off Av. de Pelegrí onto Maria Auxiliadora and veer right onto Sant Miguel towards Plaça de L'Antic Hospital. Pleasant owner makes guests feel at home. Carpets and lace curtains in virtually every room, each with private bath. Breakfast 300ptas. July-Aug. singles 1500ptas, doubles 4000ptas; Sept.-June singles 1400ptas, doubles 3000ptas. Visa, MC.

■ **Fonda/Can Lluna**, C. Roqueta, 20 (tel. 972 34 03 65). Turn right off Pg. Mar onto C. Peixeteras, walk through C. Estalt until it ends, go left, and then head straight. Delightful family offers immaculate rooms, all with private baths. Breakfast included—eat on the rooftop terrace and enjoy the lovely view. Winter heating. Washing machine 600ptas. In the high season, either show up in the morning or call 1-2 days prior to arrival. Open all year. July-Aug. 1900ptas per person; Sept.-June 1750ptas.

Pensión Moré, C. Sant Telmo, 9 (tel. 972 34 03 39). Downstairs, a dim and cozy sitting room. Upstairs, large rooms with basins and views of the old quarter. July-Aug. singles and doubles 1500-1600ptas; Sept.-June 1400ptas per person.

Camping: Closest site is **Can Martí** (tel. 972 34 08 51; fax 972 34 24 61), at the end of Rambla Pau Casals, off Av. Ferrán Agulló, 15min. from the bus station. July-Aug. 750ptas per person, 755ptas per tent, 500ptas per car; May 15-June 30 and Sept. 1-15 600ptas per person, 650ptas per tent, 400ptas per car.

FOOD

The old quarter is home to the best cuisine and ambience in Tossa. Restaurants catering to tourists serve up *menús* at reasonable prices. Most places specialize (though not exclusively) in local seafood. If you need groceries, **Megatzems Palau,** C. Enric Granados, 4 (tel. 972 34 08 58), the first left after Club Nàutic along the beachside road, will debit your Visa or MC for your daily bread. (Open June-Aug. daily 8am-10pm; Sept.-May M-Sa 8am-2pm and 4:30-8:30pm, Su 8am-2pm.)

■ **Restaurant Marina**, C. Tarull, 6 (tel. 972 34 07 57). Faces the Església de Sant Vincenç—look for the striped awning and tables out front. Cooks up a *paella* that's as good as it gets. Vegetarian options available too. *Menú* 1350ptas. Open *Semana Santa* to Oct. daily 11am-11pm.

Pizzeria Anna, Pont Vell, 13 (tel. 972 34 28 51). Turn right on Pont Vell from Pg. Mar; it's the small restaurant on the left-hand corner. Though homesick Italians might be a little disappointed, the seafood-sick traveler will be in heaven. Seating inside and out. Pasta (650-775ptas), pizza (750-975ptas). Open daily 11am-11pm. Visa, MC, AmEx.

SIGHTS AND ENTERTAINMENT

Inside the walled fortress of the **Vila Vella,** a spiral of medieval alleys leads to tiny Pl. Pintor J. Roig y Soler, where the **Museu Municipal** has a nice collection of 20s and 30s art, including—because the artist had a house here—one of the few Chagall paintings still in Spain. It will also be hosting a special Dalí exhibit in 2000. Tossa's Roman mosaics, dating from the 4th to the 1st century BC, and other artifacts from the nearby **Vila Romana** are displayed in the museum, originally a 12th-century palace. (Tel. 972 34 07 09. Open June-Sept. Tu-Su 10am-7pm; Oct.-May Tu-Su 10am-1pm and 3-6pm. 1000ptas.)

All of Tossa's **beaches** are nice, though each has its fair share of visitors. **Calas** (small coves) are accessible by foot and less crowded. **Hikers** pass through on the GR-92 but several shorter trails and **mountain bike paths** also criss-cross the area. The tourist office pamphlet provides lots of information. Several companies, like **Fonda Cristal** (tel. 972 34 22 29), send **glass-bottom boats** to nearby beaches and caves (1hr., 8 per day, 1000ptas per person). Tickets are available at booths on the Platja Gran. **Club Aire Libre** (tel. 972 34 12 77), on the highway to Lloret, organizes various excursions, including canoeing and kayaking (both 2000ptas), water skiing (4250ptas for 2 lessons), scuba diving (44,000ptas for 5-day certification course), sailing (1700ptas per hr.), and windsurfing (1600ptas per hr.). Bars line the streets of the old quarter. Many occasionally offer live music. **Bar El Pirata**, C. Portal, 32 (tel. 972 34 14 43), has outdoor tables overlooking the sea (open Apr.-Oct. daily 10am-3am).

PALAFRUGELL

Forty kilometers east of Girona, Palafrugell serves as the budget traveler's base for trips to nearby beach towns **Calella, Llafranc,** and **Tamariu,** which cater to wealthy Europeans whose idea of a budget accommodation is any hotel that doesn't leave mints on the pillow. To save some *pesetas*, stay in admittedly bland (and beachless) Palafrugell and daytrip to nearby beaches. Minuscule Tamariu is isolated from the other two beach towns, and is therefore likely to be the least crowded. Calella is the largest and liveliest of the three, and is connected to Llafranc by one of several **Caminos de Ronda,** a series of stone footpaths allowing exploration of the coast.

GETTING THERE

Buses run to Palafrugell from: **Figueres** (4 per day, 10am-6pm, 760-900ptas); **Sant Feliu** (5 per day, noon-8:30pm, 450ptas); **Girona** (15 per day, 7:45am-8:30pm, 535ptas); **Barcelona** (13 per day, 8:30am-10:30pm, 1530-1715ptas).

ORIENTATION AND PRACTICAL INFORMATION

To get from the bus station ticket office to the center of town, turn right and walk down Carrer Torres de Jonama to Carrer de Pi i Maragall. Then turn right and walk past the Guardia Civil and the market until you hit **Plaça Nova.** Back up C. Pi. Maragall to your right lies the center of the city and Pl. Esglesia. To get to nearby towns, take a bus, spin away on moped or mountain bike, or take a pleasant, if lengthy, walk through the countryside (1hr. to each coastal town).

TRANSPORTATION

Buses: Sarfa, C. Torres Jonama, 67-79 (tel. 972 30 06 23). Prices rise on weekends. To: **Calella** and **Llafranc** (in summer 11-24 per day, in winter 4-5 per day, 145ptas); **Tamariu** (in summer 3-4 per day, 140ptas); **Sant Feliu** (45min., 16 per day, 260-320ptas); **Girona** (1hr., 15 per day, 515-560ptas); **Figueres** (1½hr., 3-4 per day, 760-900ptas); **Barcelona** (2hr., 12 per day, 1500-1725ptas).

Taxis: Ràdio Taxi (tel. 972 61 00 00). 24hr. service throughout the area.

Bike Rental: Bicismarca, C. Barrisi Buixo, 55 (tel. 972 30 44 47). 500ptas for 2hr., 1200ptas for ½-day, 1700ptas per day.

TOURIST, FINANCIAL, AND LOCAL SERVICES

Tourist Office: Can Rosés, Pl. L'Església (tel. 972 61 18 20; fax 972 61 17 56). First right off C. Cavallers walking away from Pl. Nova. The *Guía Municipal* is indispensable. A larger **branch** is at C. Carrilet, 2 (tel. 972 30 02 28; fax 972 61 12 61). From the bus station go left on C. Torres i Jonama, left again at the traffic circle, and walk about 200m. In an inconvenient location, but loaded with info. Both open Apr.-Sept. M-Sa 10am-1pm and 5-8pm, Su 10am-1pm; Oct.-Mar. M-Sa 10am-1pm and 4-7pm, Su 10am-1pm; Carrilet branch open July-Aug. M-Sa 9am-9pm, Su 10am-1pm. **Branch** in **Llafranc,** C. Roger de Llúria (tel. 972 30 50 08). Open July-Aug. daily 10am-1pm and 5-9pm; Apr.-June and Sept. M-Sa 10am-1pm and 5-8pm. Branch at **Tamariu,** C. Riera (tel. 972 62 01 93). Open June-Sept. M-Sa 10am-1pm and 5-8pm, Su 10am-1pm.

Currency Exchange: Banco Central Hispano, at the corner of C. Valls and Cavallers off Pl. Nova. **ATM.** Open June-Aug. M-F 8:30am-2:30pm, Sept.-May M-Sa 8:30am-2:30pm.

Luggage Storage: At the Sarfa bus station 200ptas per bag. Open daily 6:30am-8:30pm.

EMERGENCY AND COMMUNICATIONS

Emergency: tel. 091 or 092. **Municipal police:** (tel. 972 61 31 01), Av. Josep Pla and C. Cervantes. Call them for 24hr. **pharmacy** info.

Medical services: Centro de Atención Primaria, C. d'Angel Guimerà, 6 (tel. 972 61 06 07). Open 24hr.

Post Office: C. Torres Jonama, 14 (tel. 972 30 06 07). Lista de Correos. Open M-F 8:30am-2:30pm, Sa 9:30am-1pm. **Postal Code:** 17200.

Internet Access: Internet Papereria Palé, C. Cavallers, 16 (tel. 972 30 12 48). 175ptas for 1st 15min., 550ptas per hr., 10hr. ticket for 5000ptas.

▐ ACCOMMODATIONS

Though there are only three options, accommodation prices are reasonable and room quality high in Palafrugell. Be sure to call ahead on summer weekends.

Fonda L'Estrella, C. Quatres Cases, 13-17 (tel. 972 30 00 05), at the corner of C. La Caritat, a right off C. Torres Jonama. High-ceilinged, well-lit rooms with sinks off a Moorish courtyard bursting with plant life. Breakfast in the garden 500ptas. Singles 2300ptas; doubles July-Aug. 4200ptas, Sept.-June 4000ptas.

Residencia Familiar, C. Sant Sebastià, 29 (tel. 972 30 00 43). C. Quatres Cases crosses Pl. Nova and turns into C. Sant Sebastià. Splattered halls are straight out of a Jackson Pollack painting. Fortunately, rooms, with sinks, are not. Singles 2000ptas; doubles 4000ptas; less for longer stays and off-season. Open *Semana Santa* to Oct.

Hostal Plaja, C. Sant Sebastià, 34 (tel. 972 30 05 26). Grand, frescoed foyer gives way to a broad courtyard surrounded by spotless rooms, all with balconies, clotheslines, new beds, and bathrooms. July-Aug. singles 3000ptas, with breakfast 3400; doubles 5500ptas, with breakfast 6500ptas. Dec.-June singles 2800ptas, with breakfast 3200ptas; doubles 5000ptas, with breakfast 6000ptas. Visa, MC.

Camping: Camping Moby Dick, C. Costa Verda, 16-28 (tel. 972 61 43 07), on bus route off Av. Costa del Sol in Calella. No white whale in sight, but it is close to the water (5min.). Plenty of shade from abundant pine trees. Nice showers. 530ptas per person, 540ptas per car and per tent. Cheaper in off-season. Open *Semana Santa*-Oct. 15.

◖ FOOD

Restaurants near the beach are predictably expensive. For daytrips, try shopping at **Super Stop,** C. Torres Jonama, 33 (open July-Aug. M-Sa 8:30am-2pm and 5-9pm, Su 9am-2pm; Sept.-June M-Sa 8:30am-1:30pm and 5-8:30pm, Su 9am-2pm).

Restaurant el Rebost del Pernil, C. Mayor, 3 (tel. 972 61 06 95). A delicious option. Wide-ranging *menú del día* (M-F, 1100ptas) features outstanding versions of Catalán classics. Open June-Sept. noon-midnight; Oct.-May 1-4:15pm and 7:30pm-midnight. Visa, MC, AmEx, Maestro.

Restaurante La Taverna, Giralt/Subiós, 3 (tel. 972 30 04 30). Straight ahead from the tourist office (with the church to the right) and around the corner to the left. Secluded restaurant and bar satisfies with tasty dishes. English tavern-like menu offers grilled bass fish (1500ptas), beefsteak (750ptas), and grilled chicken and chips (550ptas). Open Tu-Su 1-4pm and 7:30pm-midnight. Visa, MC, Maestro.

Restaurant Bar L'Espasa, C. Fra Bernat Boil, 14 (tel. 972 61 50 32), on the seaside walk from Calella to Llafranc. Delicious food complemented by great views. Specializes in seafood stews and *arroz negro* (black rice). *Menú* 1100ptas. Open daily 1-4pm and 8-11pm. Open June-Sept. Visa, MC.

📷 🎵 SIGHTS AND ENTERTAINMENT

Besides nearby beaches, Palafrugell boasts one of the world's few cork museums. The **Museu del Suro,** C. Tarongeta, 31 (tel. 972 30 39 98), has everything you wanted to know (and more) about cork. (Open July-Aug. Tu-Sa 10am-1pm and 5-9pm, Su 10:30am-1:30pm; Sept.-June Tu-Sa 5-8pm, Su 10:30am-1:30pm. 200ptas, seniors and students 100ptas. English explanations available.) For an outdoor adventure, take a 40-minute walk up the road from Llafranc to the **Ermita de San Sebastià.** Crowning the mountain of the same name (50m from the lighthouse), it offers views of the entire Palafrugell valley, beaches, and sea.

Palafrugell's Friday evening **passeig** ends up at the *plaça,* where young and old dance the traditional Catalán *sardana* at about 10:30pm in July and August. Don't be afraid to join in. For more familiar dancing, check out **Discoteca X qué** (pronounced *por qué*), 1km down the old road to Calella (open F-Su 1pm-3am). The tourist office prints a monthly bulletin of upcoming events. The town's biggest party takes place July 19-21, when the dance-intensive **Festa Major** bursts into the streets. Calella honors **Sant Pere** on June 29 and **Tamariu** celebrates on August 15.

DAYTRIPS FROM PALAFRUGELL

CALLELA

The tourist office in Palafrugell provides maps of paths and trails that criss-cross the area, including the **Camino de Ronda** (incredible climbs near the coast from Callela to Llafranc; usually 1½hr.). **Jardí Botànic de Cap Roig** (tel. 972 61 53 45), the botanical garden in front of Hotel Garbí, provides an excellent view of the coast. (Open daily June-Aug. 9am-8pm; Sept.-May 9am-6pm. 300ptas.) Russian Colonel Nicolas Voevodsky built the **seaside castle** after fleeing the Bolshevik Revolution. He and his wife planted and pruned a splendid maze of paths and flower beds with their own hands. The first sign for the castle points to the right at the fork of Av. Costa Daurada and C. Consolat del Mar. The castle also hosts the **Festival de Jazz de la Costa Brava** in July and August. The town **tourist office** is at C. Voltes, 6 (tel. 972 61 44 75; open daily July-Aug. 10am-1pm and 5-9pm; Apr-June and Sept. 10am-1pm and 5-8pm). **Poseidón Nemrod Club,** Port Peleği (tel. 972 61 53 45) offers **scuba diving** courses and equipment.

SANT FELIU DE GUÍXOLS

Due to its perilous yet panoramic nature, the 23km road between Tossa de Mar and Sant Feliu (pop. 18,000) is a favorite of photographers and daredevils alike. Cork production was once Sant Feliu's main industry; today tourism takes center stage. The town sees its share of visitors, but luckily the smell of the sea still overpowers that of Coppertone. Sant Feliu's sandy beaches and reasonably priced hostels make it a fine place to work on that tan.

🔼 ORIENTATION AND PRACTICAL INFORMATION. Sarfa buses arrive at the **bus station** on Ctra. Gerona. A tree-lined promenade and pedestrian path, **Passeig del Mar,** runs parallel to the beach. The main plaza, **Plaça Mercat,** is right off Pg. Mar and Av. Juli Garreta. If entering by sea, you'll disembark mid-beach in front of Passeig del Mar. Teisa buses stop and depart at Pl. Monestir across from the English-speaking tourist office.

Sarfa, Ctra. Gerona, 35 (tel. 972 32 11 87), runs **buses** to **Palafrugell,** on the Girona line (45min., 13 per day, 9:50am-9:50pm, 255-290ptas) and **Barcelona** (1½hr., 12 per day, 7:10am-10:10pm, 1280-1444ptas). Prices rise on weekends. **Teisa** (tel. 972 20 48 68), down the stairs from the bus stop on the left, sends buses from Pl. Monestir to **Girona** (45min., 3 per day, 10:15am-10:30pm, 445ptas). **Crucetours Ferry** (tel. 972 36 60 37) has a stand on the beach and sails July-Aug. to: **Tossa** (45min., 5 per day, round-trip 1250ptas); **Lloret** (1¼hr., 1 per day, round-trip 1550ptas); and other beaches to the north and south. The **tourist office,** Pl. Monestir, 54 (tel. 972 82 00

51), up Av. Juli Garetta, has a good map and info about accommodations (open July-Sept. M-Sa 10am-2pm and 4-8pm, Su 10am-2pm; Oct.-June M-Sa 10am-1pm and 4-7pm, Su 10am-2pm). **Banco Central Hispano** is on Pg. Mar, 26-27 (open June-Aug. M-F 8:30am-2:30pm; Sept.-May M-F 8:30am-2:30pm, Sa 9:30am-1pm; ATM). **Luggage storage** is available at the Sarfa bus ticket window (200ptas per bag; open 6:30am-8:30pm). **Municipal police** (tel. 972 82 09 33), on C. Callao, on the outskirts of town. **Post office,** Ctra. Gerona, 15 (tel. 972 32 11 60; open M-F 8:30am-2:30pm, Sa 9:30am-1pm); **postal code**: 17220.

▓▓ ACCOMMODATIONS AND FOOD. Many hotel owners discount prices for stays of five days or more. Reservations are suggested for July and August. **Hostel Geis,** C. Especiers, 27 (tel. 972 32 06 79), is off Pl. Mercat. A cheerful owner keeps neater than neat rooms, all with blue-tiled bath and winter heating. (Breakfast 400ptas. July-Aug. singles 2250ptas; doubles 4250ptas. Sept.-June singles 2000ptas; doubles 4000ptas. Visa, MC.) It's not Switzerland, but at **Hostal Zürich,** Av. Juli Garreta, 43-45 (tel. 972 32 10 54), friendly, English-speaking owners rent huge, pleasant rooms with lots of light, some with balconies, some with TV. (Breakfast included. Singles 3500ptas; doubles 6000ptas, with bath 7000ptas. Visa, MC.) Clean rooms with sinks and big windows are 10 minutes from the beach at **Pension El Gas Vell,** C. Sta. Magdalena, 29 (tel. 972 32 10 24). Follow C. Especiers to its end and bear right, taking the first left on C. Mall; C. Sta. Magdalena is six blocks down. Ring the doorbell by the restaurant of the same name. (Singles 2000ptas; doubles 3750ptas, with bath 4600ptas; triples 5000ptas.)

An excellent **market** is in Pl. Mercat (open June-Aug. daily 8am-2pm; Sept.-May Tu-Su 8am-2pm). For groceries, **Centi Supermercat** is at the end of C. Concepción (open M-Sa 9am-9pm, Su 9am-1:30pm). For lip-smacking *tapas*, check out **Bar El Gallo,** C. Especiers, 13 (tel. 972 82 23 44). Snack on grilled sardines (450ptas) or go for the *tapeo menú* (4000ptas for two), which tops off six different *tapas* with a dessert crepe. (Open daily 10am-3pm and 5:30-11pm. Gamble while you eat at **Nou Casino La Costancia,** Rambla Portalet, 2 (tel. 972 32 23 01), a cafe-bar with 2 slot machines (open daily June-Sept. 9am-1am; Oct.-May 9am-11pm).

▓▓ SIGHTS AND ENTERTAINMENT. Little remains to distinguish Sant Feliu from other mildly pretty Costa Brava towns, since most traces of its 1000-year history have been obliterated by successive invaders. Still, the church and monastery at Pl. Monestir is an architectural potpourri, combining the remains of several buildings. The **Torre de Fum** stands over Visigothic and Roman walls, and houses a Romanesque crucifixion. (Open daily 8-11am for mass. Free.) Behind the tourist office is the **Museu d'Història de la Ciutat,** with changing exhibits, artifacts, and fun info about cork. (Open June-Aug. Tu-Sa 11am-2pm and 6-9pm, Su 11am-2pm; Sept.-May Tu-Sa 11am-2pm and 5-8pm, Su 11am-2pm. Free.)

If you've come for the **beaches**...scratch that. So, you've come for the beaches. Sant Feliu's is sandy and pleasant enough. It's a 30-minute walk to the **Platja de Sant Pol.** Alternatively, Crurisa **buses** go from Pl. Monestir and Pg. Mar. (10min., July-Aug. depart every 30min., Sept.-June 6 per day, 100ptas.) With no commercial docking, the cove has unmediated access to the sea. Next to Sant Pol, a 2km path scampers across the rocky hills, past picturesque coves and lagoons, to **La Conca,** another popular beach.

In summer, locals dance *sardanas* one block from the beach in Pl. Espanya. (July-Sept. Friday 10:15pm.) Throughout July, August, and September, a wide range of music and theater performances take place all over Sant Feliu in the Festival Internacional de la Porta Ferrada, the oldest in Cataluña. Many events are free; get a schedule from the tourist office. Every June and July restaurants throughout town are filled with locals competing in the Mostro de Cançó de Taverna. During this festival, groups of men compete over a few accordion-assisted ditties and then enjoy a meal of bluefish complimented by copious amounts of wine.

L'ESCALA

L'Escala (pop. 6000, in summer 70,000) is mostly just a string of tacky souvenir shops 45 minutes north of Palafrugell. However, the beaches and ruins make for a worthwhile daytrip. Sandy expanses with room for you and your towel lie outside of town. The beach crowd slims somewhat beyond the Greek and Roman ruins of **Empúries.**

▨ ORIENTATION AND PRACTICAL INFORMATION. Sarfa **buses** (tel. 972 77 01 29) stop in front of the tourist office. With your back to the office, the ruins are to the left (walk down Rda. del Pedró) and the heart of the town is straight ahead (down Av. Ave Maria). Tickets available on the bus. To: **Palafrugell** (35min., 5 per day, 7:10am-6:55pm, 365ptas); **Figueres** (55min., 5 per day, 7:10am-7:05pm, 440ptas); **Girona** (2hr., 2 per day, 7:30am and 2:30pm, 555ptas). The HI arranges **mountain bike rental** if you contact them in advance, and **Cicles JK**, Av. Ave Maria, 9 (tel. 972 77 40 47), rents bikes. (450ptas per hr., 1700ptas per day. Open daily 9am-1pm and 4-8pm.) The **tourist office,** Pl. Escoles, 1 (tel. 972 77 06 03; fax 972 77 33 85), has a decent map, info on tourist sites, and **fax** service (open June-Sept. M-Sa 9am-8:30pm, Su 10am-1pm; Oct.-June M-F 10am-1pm and 4-7pm). A **Banco Central Hispano** with **ATM** sits at C. Maranges, 16 (open June-Aug. M-F 8:30am-2:30pm; Sept.-May M-Sa 8:30am-2:30pm). **Municipal police,** C. Pintor Joan Massanet, 24 (tel. 972 77 48 18), next to the tourist office; **medical emergencies** tel. 908 09 43 33. **Post office** (tel. 972 77 16 51), next to the tourist office (open M-F 8:30am-2:30pm, Sa 9:30am-1pm); **postal code:** 17130.

▧▧ ACCOMMODATIONS AND FOOD. Although there are plenty of options, finding a cheap room in L'Escala is difficult. The **Alberg de Juventut,** Les Coves, 41 (tel. 972 77 12 00), is a 15 minute walk from the Empúries ruins and three minutes from the beach in a grove of trees. Facing the tourist office, follow the road on the right toward the coast; follow signs or ask bus drivers to stop near the ruins. The hostel has friendly owners, English books, TV, and lots of beds in each room. (Apr.-Sept. dorms 1800ptas, over 25 2325ptas. Oct.-Mar. dorms 1575ptas, over 25 2000ptas. Breakfast included. Lunch and dinner offered. HI members only; cards available at the hostel. To guarantee reservations, call Barcelona's youth office at tel. 93 483 83 63, 1 month in advance. Another option is **Pensió Torrent,** Carrer Riera, 28 (tel. 972 77 02 78). From Pl. Escoles walk downhill one block on C. Pintor, turn left, and follow the street around the corner. The hostel has whitewashed rooms with bath and tiled floors (doubles 3600ptas; off-season 3000ptas).

The town **market** is held daily from 7:30am to 1:30pm in **Plaça Victor Català.** Alternatively, fill your basket at **MAXOR,** Pl. Les Escoles Ronda Pedró, 2, across the street from the tourist office (open M-Sa 8am-10pm, Su 9am-2pm). ▨**Restaurante-Snack Galan,** C. d. L'Usach, 3 (tel. 972 77 30 54), on a small street off C. de la Torre to the left, is the perfect place to grab a sandwich. (*Menú* 1000ptas. Open daily 1-3:30pm and 7-10:30pm; closed in Nov.) Although slightly pricey, the English menu at **Restaurant El Gotim,** C. Puig Sureda, 16-18, insures that you know what you're ordering. (Entrees 550-650ptas. Open M-F 1-4pm and 6-10pm, Sa-Su 1-4pm and 7-10pm; closed Sa-Su in winter.)

NEAR L'ESCALA: EMPÚRIES

Just 1km north of L'Escala are the ruins of Empúries. In the 7th century BC, Greek traders landed on a small island on the northeast Iberian coast. As the settlement grew, it moved to the mainland and became the prosperous colony of Emporion (meaning "marketplace"); it fell into Roman hands four centuries later. Remnants of both Greek and Roman cities, including some gorgeous mosaic floors and a Visigothic basilica, fill Empúries's 40 hectares of ruins. Excavation of the ruins continues, backed by profits from the 1992 Olympic Games. The Olympic torch formally entered Spain through this ancient Greek port city. The small but wealthy **Museu Monogràfic d'Empúries** (tel. 972 77 02 08) showcases a large collection of ceramics and Etruscan wares. (Ruins and museum open daily June-Sept. 10am-

8pm; Oct.-May 10am-6pm. 400ptas, seniors and students free. Audiovisual program screened every 30min. from 10:30am until closing, 300ptas. Audio tape 600ptas.) Explanatory signs through the ruins indicate the ancient urban plan without marring the aura of fountains, mosaics, and columns against a backdrop of cypress trees and the breezy Mediterranean. Half a kilometer north of the ruins is the entrance to the **Parc Natural deis Aiguamolls de l'Empordà**, a protected habitat with miles of marshland and lakes, filled with plant and animal species. For more info on the park, contact **El Cortalet** (tel. 972 25 42 22).

If you can't bear a 30-minute walk, take the little blue train, *Carrilet*, from **La Punta** in L'Escala (between the main beach and **Port d'en Perris**) to St. Martí d'Empúries, and ask to get off at the ruins (every hr., June 15-Sept. 15, 250ptas).

GIRONA

Girona (pop. 70,500) is a world-class city. Unfortunately, it is still waiting for the rest of the world to notice it. A Roman settlement, and later an important medieval center, Girona was one of the few Spanish cities where Christians, Arabs, and Jews were able to peacefully coexist. This multiculturalism was a result of the city's geographical location, as Girona served as a gateway to the rest of Europe by land and to the Orient by sea. It was also the founding place of the renowned *cabalistas de Gerona*, a group who appeared in Girona in the 12th century and were known for their Jewish mysticism and the oral tradition of the *Kabbala*. Today the city is divided by the Riu Onyar, which separates the Baroque arches and Romanesque buildings of the old city from the Spanish dwellings of the new.

▐▘ GETTING THERE

Trains run to Girona from **Barcelona** (1hr., 22 per day, 6am-9:20pm, 775-985ptas) and **Figueres** (45min., 21 per day, 6:11am-8:58pm, 375ptas). **Buses** go from **Lloret** (15min., 6 per day, 7:30am-7:10pm, 350ptas).

▨ ORIENTATION AND PRACTICAL INFORMATION

The **Riu Onyar** separates the new city from the old. The **Pont de Pedra** connects the two banks and leads directly into the old quarter by way of Carrers Ciutadans, Peralta, and Força, off of which are located the cathedral and **El Call**, the historic Jewish neighborhood. **RENFE** and **bus terminals** are situated off Carrer de Barcelona, in the modern neighborhood. To get to the old city from the stations, head straight out through the parking lot, turning left on C. Barcelona. Follow C. Barcelona for two blocks until it forks at the traffic island. Take the right fork via C. Santa Eugenia to Gran Vía de Jaume I, and continue straight across at the Banco Central Hispano to get on Carrer Nou, which runs directly to the Pont de Pedra.

TRANSPORTATION

Trains: RENFE (tel. 972 20 70 93), in Pl. Espanya. Info open daily 6:30am-10pm. To: **Figueres** (45min., 21 per day, 6:15am-10:46pm, 325ptas); **Portbou** (1hr., 12 per day, 6:15am-10:46pm, 250ptas); **Barcelona** (1¼hr., 21 per day, 6:12am-9:29pm, 1265ptas); **Madrid** (9-10½hr., 1 per day, 9:05am, 6000-7500ptas); **Paris** (11hr., 1 per day, 9:17pm, 16900ptas).

Buses: (tel. 972 21 23 19), around the corner from the train station. Info open daily 6am-10pm. **Sarfa** (tel. 972 20 17 96) runs to **Tossa de Mar** (1hr., July-Aug., 2 per day, Sept.-June, 1 per day, 625ptas) and **Palafrugell** (1hr., 12 per day, 525ptas), for connections to Begur, Llafranc, Calella, and Tamariu. **Teisa** (tel. 972 20 02 75) drives to: **St. Feliu** (45min., 9-15 per day, 435-500ptas); **Olot** (1¼hr., 6-16 per day, 625-725ptas); **Ripoll** (2hr., 3 per day, 1100-1400ptas); **Lerida** (3½hr., 2-4 per day, 2155ptas). **Barcelona Bus** (tel. 972 20 24 32) express to **Barcelona** (1½hr., 3-4 per day, 1100-1200ptas) and **Figueres** (1hr., 7 per day, 400-480ptas).

Taxis: (tel. 972 20 33 77 or 972 22 10 20). Try Pl. Independència and Pont de Pedra.

Car Rental: Most companies cluster around C. Barcelona, near the train station. Must be over 21 (for most) and have had a license for at least 1-2 years. **Hertz** (tel. 972 21 01 08), in the train station. Min. age 25. Rentals start at 5000ptas for 1 day with unlimited mileage. Open M-F 8am-1pm and 4-8pm, Sa 8am-1pm.

TOURIST, FINANCIAL, AND LOCAL SERVICES

Tourist Office: Rambla Llibertat, 1 (tel. 972 22 65 75; fax 972 22 66 12), in a red building directly on the left as you cross Pont de Pedra from the new town. Loads of info on the city and region. English spoken. Open M-F 8am-8pm, Sa 8am-2pm and 4-8pm, Su 9am-2pm. The **train station branch** (tel. 972 20 70 93) is to the right of the RENFE ticket counter. Open M-F 8:30am-1:30pm.

Currency Exchange: Banco Central Hispano, on the corner of C. Nou and Gran Vía de Jaume I, and in the old city on Pujada Pont de Pedra, just after crossing the bridge on the right. **ATMs.** Both open M-F 8:30am-2:30pm, Sa 9:30am-1pm.

Luggage Storage: Lockers in train station (600ptas). Open daily 5:30am-11pm.

Hipercor (El Corté Inglés's Not-So-Chic Cousin): (tel. 972 24 44 44). On C. Barcelona; take a right out of train station (15min.). Groceries, telephones, currency exchange, English books, and cafeteria. Open M-Sa 10am-10pm.

English Bookstore: Gerona Books, C. Carme, 63 (tel. 972 22 46 12). Rambla Llibertat runs into C. Carme as you walk with the river on your right. New and used, fiction and classics. Open July M-F 9am-2pm; Sept.-June M-F 9am-1pm and 4-8pm.

EMERGENCY AND COMMUNICATIONS

Emergency: tel. 091 or 092. **Police: Policía Municipal,** C. Bacià, 4 (tel. 092). From Banco Central Hispano, turn right on the Gran Vía, then right on Bacià.

Hospitals: Hospital Municipal de Santa Caterina, Pl. Hospital, 5 (tel. 972 18 26 00).

Post Office: Av. Ramón Folch, 2 (tel. 972 20 32 36), at the start of Gran Vía de Jaume I. Turn right on Gran Vía coming from the old city. **Second office,** Ronda Ferrán Puig, 17 (tel. 972 22 34 75). Lista de Correos only. Both open M-F 8:30am-8:30pm, Sa 9:30am-2pm. **Postal Code:** 17070.

Internet Access: Ciberxuxes, C. Carme, 55 (tel. 972 22 61 91). Rambla Llibertat runs into C. Carme as you walk with the river on the right. 300ptas for 1st 30min., 500ptas for 1st hr., 100ptas for each additional 15min. Open M-F 9am-1pm and 5-8pm.

▍ ACCOMMODATIONS

Rooms are only hard to find in June and August. Most budget accommodations are sprinkled around the old quarter; they are both reasonably priced and well-kept.

Alberg-Residència Cerverí de Girona (HI), C. Ciutadans, 9 (tel. 972 21 81 21; fax 972 21 20 23), on the street running left after Pont de Pedra. A college dorm during the year, it's ultra-modern inside. 8 beds are available Oct.-June; 82 beds July-Sept. Sleek sitting rooms with TV/VCR; rooms of 3 and 8 beds with lockers. High-spirited staff, high-fashion sheets. Breakfast included. Other meals 750-800ptas. Sheets 350ptas. Laundry 500ptas. Members only, but HI cards for sale. Make reservations at the Barcelona office (tel. 93 483 83 63) in Aug. Dorms 1800ptas, over 25 2275ptas.

Pensió Viladomat, C. Ciutadans, 5 (tel. 972 20 31 76), next door to the Youth Hostel. Clean, well-furnished rooms and bathrooms. Some rooms with balconies. Singles 2000ptas; doubles 4000ptas, with bath 6000ptas, 6500ptas in July-Aug.

Pensió Pérez, Pl. Bell-lloc, 4 and **Pensió Borras,** Trav. Auriga, 6 (tel. 972 22 40 08). Keep straight after crossing Pont de Pedra into the old quarter onto C. Nou del Teatre; Pl. Bell-lloc is on the right. To Pensió Borras from Pérez, take a right out the door and follow the street around the corner, making a left at its end. The Pensió is 10m on the right. Energetic owner offers simple rooms with bright white walls. Singles 1600ptas, with bath 2000ptas; doubles 2800ptas, with bath 3300ptas; triples 4000ptas.

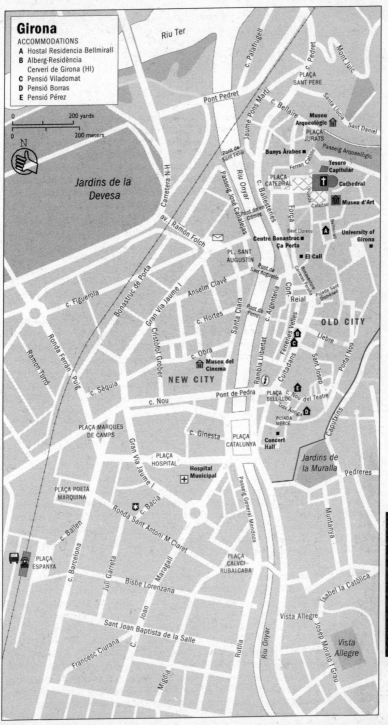

Girona

ACCOMMODATIONS
A Hostal Residència Bellmirall
B Alberg-Residència
  Cerverí de Girona (HI)
C Pensió Viladomat
D Pensió Borras
E Pensió Pérez

0   200 yards
0   200 meters

N

Riu Ter

c. Patafrugell

c. Pedret

Mont Juïc

PLAÇA
SANT PERE

Pont Pedret

Jaume Pons Martí

c. Bellaire

Santa Llúcia

Museu
Arqueològic

PLAÇA
JURATS

Sant Daniel

Pont de
Sant Feliu

Passeig Arqueològic

Carretera N-II

Riu Onyar

Banys Àrabes ■

Ferran Catòlic

Tesoro
Capitular

Jardins de la
Devesa

Passeig José Calalejas

PLAÇA
CATEDRAL

Cathedral

av. Ramón Folch

Pont de en
Gómez

C. Ballesteries

Força

Museu d'Art

Catedral

Sant Llorenç

Bellmirall

Centre Bonastruc
Ça Porta

University of
Girona

PL. SANT
AUGUSTÍN

El Call ■

Bonastruc de Porta

c. Figuerola

Gran Via Jaume I

Anselm Clavé

Pont de
Sant Augustín

C. Argenteria

Cort

Reial

Ronda Ferràn Puig

Ramon Turró

Cristòfol Grober

c. Hortes

Santa Clara

Pont de
Ferrro

Ferreries Velles

OLD CITY

B

C. Obra

C. Sèquia

Museu del
Cinema

Rambla Libertat

Ciutadans

Llebre

Sant Josep

Portal Nou

NEW CITY

Pont de Pedra

i

C

E

c. Nou

PLAÇA MARQUES
DE CAMPS

c. Ginesta

PLAÇA
CATALUNYA

PLAÇA
BELL-LLOC

C. Nou del Teatre

Trav. Auriga

D

Gran Via Jaume I

PLAÇA
HOSPITAL

Hospital
Municipal

Concert
Hall

PUJADA
MERCÉ

Caputxins

Jardins de
la Muralla

Pedreres

PLAÇA POETA
MARQUINA

c. Bacia

Passeig General Mendoza

Ronda Sant Antoni M.Claret

Muntanya

c. Ballen

c. Barcelona

Juli Garreta

Maragall

Joan

PLAÇA
CALVCI
RUBALCABA

PLAÇA
ESPANYA

Bisbe Lorenzana

Isabel la Catòlica

Sant Joan Baptista de la Salle

Riu Onyar

Rutlla

Vista Allegre

Josep Morató Grau

Francesc Curana

C.

Migdia

Vista
Allegre

Hostal Residencia Bellmirall, C. Bellmirall, 3 (tel. 972 20 40 09). Go straight from the door on the right side of the cathedral (angle left) until the blue sign appears on the right. The delightful stone rooms are the creation of 2 Gironese artists. Unfortunately, creativity comes at a price. Breakfast included. Call ahead for reservations May-Sept. Singles 4990ptas, with bath 5280ptas; doubles 7920ptas, with bath 8580ptas.

FOOD

Considered home to some of the best Catalán cuisine, Girona abounds with innovative specialties. The city has many excellent yet inexpensive restaurants. Some of the best places huddle near the cathedral and along Carrer Cort Reial. Others are found on Pl. Independència, at the end of C. Santa Clara in the modern section of the city. In the old quarter, even more cater to university students. Girona's permanent **market** is in Pl. Clave, on the new side of the city near the river (open M-Sa 8am-1pm). In summer, a second location opens near the Polideportivo in Parc de la Deversa (open Tu and Sa 8am-1pm). A block from C. Nou (off the Gran Vía) is **Supeco,** C. Sequia, 10 (tel. 972 21 45 16), a basic supermarket (open M-Sa 9am-1:30pm and 5-8:30pm).

Café Le Bistrot, Pujada Sant Domènec, 4 (tel. 972 21 88 03), a right off C. Ciutadans. Hipsters crowd outdoor marble tables to munch and people-watch. Freshly made pizzas (500-675ptas) and crepes (550-600ptas). Lunchtime *menú* 1200ptas; abridged version 950ptas. Open M-Th 1-5pm and 7pm-1:30am, F-Sa 1-5pm and 7pm-1am. Closed some Mondays in winter.

L'Anfora, C. Força, 15 (tel. 972 20 50 10). Upstairs dining hall was once the secret site of Jewish religious ceremonies. Times have changed: downstairs, large hunks of decidedly un-kosher ham hang over the bar. Entrees 1000-1500ptas. Multilingual lunch *menú* 1300ptas. Open M-Sa noon-4pm and 7-11pm. Visa, MC.

Granje Mora, C. Corte Reial, 18 (tel. 972 20 22 38). Fun, down-to-earth owners have made this a Girona institution for 60 years. Delicious sandwiches (150-500ptas) and ice-cream drinks (100ptas). Open daily noon-4pm and 7-11pm.

Restaurant Vegetariano La Polenta, C. Corte Reial, 6 (tel. 972 20 93 74). Vegetarian fare with an international accent. Catalán rice dishes, Italian pasta, sushi, and pita sandwiches. Plenty of lacto-free choices. Entrees 575-700. *Menú* (lunch only) 1100ptas. Open M-Sa 1-4pm.

SIGHTS

The narrow, winding streets of the medieval old city, interspersed with steep stairways and low arches, is ideal for wanderers. Start your self-guided historical tour at the Pont de Pedra and turn left at the tourist office down tree-lined Rambla de la Llibertat. Continue on C. Argenteria, bearing right across C. Cort Reial. Up the flight of stairs, C. Força begins on the left.

EL CALL. This was once the medieval Jewish neighborhood ("Call" comes from *kahal*, meaning "community" in Hebrew). The site of the last synagogue in Girona now serves as a museum linking the baths, butcher shop, and synagogue, all of which surround a serene central patio. The center is named for Girona-born Rabbi Moshe ben Nahman (Nahmanides), best known for his studies of Jewish mysticism and the oral tradition known as the *Kabbalah*. For more information on El Call, see **Rebuilding Sepharad,** p. 349. *(El Call begins at C. Sant Llorenç and is centered along C. Força. The entrance to the Centre Bonastruc Ça Porta is off C. Sant Llorenç about halfway up the hill. Tel. 972 21 67 61. Open June-Oct. M-Sa 10am-8pm, Su 10am-3pm; Nov.-May M-Sa 10am-6pm, Su 10am-2pm. Free. The tourist office also offers guided tours of El Call in July and August for 800ptas.)*

CATHEDRAL COMPLEX. Farther uphill on C. Força and around the corner to the right, Girona's imposing Gothic **cathedral** rises a record-breaking 90 steps (making its Rococo stairway the largest in Europe) from the plaza below. The **Torre de Charlemany** and the cloister are the only structures left standing from the 11th century; the rest of the building dates from the 15th and 16th centuries. The most unique feature of the cathedral is its interior, where the three customary naves have been compressed into one, producing the world's widest Gothic **nave** (22m).

A door on the left leads to the trapezoidal cloister and the **Tesoro Capitular,** containing some of Girona's most precious possessions. The *tesoro's* (and possibly Girona's) most famous piece is the **Tapis de la Creació,** a 15th-century tapestry depicting the creation story and covering the entire wall of Room IV. *(Tesoro tel. 972 21 44 26. Cathedral and Tesoro open July-Aug. Tu-Sa 10am-2pm and 4-7pm; Sept.-June Tu-Sa 10am-2pm and 4-7pm, Su 10am-2pm. Tesoro and cloister 400ptas.)*

WALKS. Near the **University of Girona** is the start of the extremely beautiful **Passeig de la Muralla.** Railed steps lead onto the city walls for an impressive view of old Girona. The walk ends two blocks to the left of the Pont de Pedra. Another nice walk is the **Passeig Arqueològic,** partly lined with cypresses and flower beds, which skirts the medieval wall on the east side of the river and overlooks the city.

NEW CITY. The commercial New City seems a world away from the tourist's Girona. Of interest is the Museu del Cinema, along the river. The museum chronicles the invention of movies, from the rise of shadow theater to early special effects, in wacky interactive exhibits. *(Sèquia, 1. One block north of C. Nou off C. Santa Clara. Tel. 972 41 27 77; fax 972 41 30 47. Open Tu-Su 10am-8pm; Oct.-May 10am-6pm. 500ptas, students 200ptas.)*

OTHER SIGHTS. Inspired by Muslim bath houses, the graceful 12th-century **Banys Àrabs** once contained saunas and baths of varying temperatures. *(From the cathedral, with your back to the stairs, take a right on C. Ferran Catòlic. Tel. 972 21 32 62. Open Apr.-Sept. M-Sa 10am-7pm, Su 10am-2pm; Oct.-Mar. daily 10am-2pm. 200ptas, students 100ptas.)* The **Museu Arqueològic** is housed in the 11th- to 12th-century Romanesque **Monasterio de Sant Pere de Galligants,** the final resting place of medieval tombstones that once marked Jewish burial sites. *(Left from the Banys Àrabs and straight ahead through the gates of Pl. Jurats. Tel. 972 20 26 32. Open June-Aug. Tu-Sa 10:30am-1:30pm and 4-7pm, Su 10am-2pm; Sept.-May Tu-Sa 10am-2pm and 4-6pm. 200ptas. Sunday free. 30-day pass for the old city's six museums is available at any of the museums or the tourist office for 800ptas.)* The **Museu d'Art** has an impressive art collection, including a 12th-century Romanesque wood sculpture and remnants of the medieval stained-glass industry. *(Pujada de la Catedral. Tel. 972 20 95 36. Open March-Sept. M-Sa 10am-7pm, Su 10am-2pm; Oct.-Feb. 10am-6pm, Su 10am-2pm. 300ptas. Su free.)*

REBUILDING SEPHARARD Though Girona has a reputation for tolerance, the Jews of Girona were still victims of discrimination, ostracism, and eventual expulsion. Despite it all, they contributed ineradicably to the city's culture. The *aljama* (Jewish quarter) in Girona, once populated by 300 people, became a leading center for the study of the **Kabbala,** a mystical reading of the Torah in which number values are assigned to each Hebrew letter and numerical sums are interpreted to reveal spiritual meaning. Operating like a tiny, independent country within the city (inhabitants answered to their King, not the city government), El Call was protected by the crown of Cataluña in exchange for financial tribute. Until the 11th century, Christians and Jews coexisted peacefully, occasionally even intermarrying. Unfortunately, this did not last. Historical sources cite attacks and looting of the Jewish quarter in eight separate years, the first in 1276 and the last in 1418. Eventually, almost every entrance to El Call was blocked off. The reopening of the streets of El Call began only after Franco's death in 1975. In recent years, eight Spanish mayors have created a network called *Caminos de Sepharad,* an organization aimed at restoring Spain's Jewish quarters and fostering a broader understanding of the Sephardic legacy.

♫ ENTERTAINMENT

The **Rambla** and **Plaça de Independencia** are the places to see and be seen. Some summer Fridays inspire spontaneous *sardanas*, traditional Catalán dances involving 10 to 12 musicians serenading a ring of dancers.

BARS AND CLUBS. Locals usually end their days with a *passeig* (walk), dinner, and then bar-hopping, which generally takes place in the new city. Bars near **Pl. Ferrán Catòlic** draw big crowds, but during the summer, **Parc de la Devesa,** across the river from the old town and several blocks to the left, has all the cachet and often live music as well. Of Girona's four discos, the most popular is **La Sala de Cel,** C. Pedret, 118 (tel. 972 21 46 64), off Pl. Sant Pere, in the north quarter of the city (open Sept.-July Th-Su; cover 2000ptas, includes 2 drinks). Artsy folk mill around the oh-so-cute bars and cafes in the old quarter. Enter on C. Ferreires Vellas, parallel to C. Ciutadans, to try the **Cafe del Lliberia,** C. Ciutadans, 15 (tel. 972 20 48 18), which caters to chic intellectual types (drinks 600-850ptas; open M-Sa 8:30am-2am, Su noon-2am). Low tables and cozy nooks fill the unmarked **La Terra,** C. Ballesteries, 23 (tel. 972 21 57 64). Try their flavored alcoholic slushies (400ptas)— everyone else does. (Open Su-W 6pm-1am, Th-Sa 6pm-2am, 3am in summer.)

FESTIVALS. During the second half of May, **flower exhibitions** spring up in the city, local monuments swim in blossoms, and the courtyards of Girona's fine old buildings open to the public. From July through September, the city hosts the **Festival de Noves Músiques,** a series of six concerts in La Mercè (Sa 7pm and Su noon, 1000ptas). The complete *sardana* guide, the *Guia d'Aplecs Sardanistes de les Comarques Gironines*, is available at the tourist office, along with a complete listing of observed holidays and festivals. Like the rest of northern Spain, Girona lights up for the **Focs de Sant Joan** on June 24, an outdoor party featuring fireworks and campfires.

FIGUERES (FIGUERAS)

In 1974, Salvador Dalí chose his native Figueres (pop. 37,000) as the site for a magnificent museum to house his works, instantly catapulting the city to international fame. Ever since, a multilingual parade of Surrealism fans has been awed and entranced by Dalí's bizarre perspectives and erotic visions. Though a beachless sprawl, Figueres hides other quality museums and some pleasant cafes. It is also a convenient base for visiting the Costa Brava.

⌐ GETTING THERE

Trains run to Figueres from: **Girona** (30min., 21 per day, 6:12am-10:46pm, 325ptas); **Portbou** (1hr., 19 per day, 5:47am-8:35pm, 295ptas); **Barcelona** (1½hr., 20 per day, 6:06am-9:20pm, 1150-1350ptas).

⟁ ORIENTATION AND PRACTICAL INFORMATION

Trains and buses arrive at **Plaça Estació** on the edge of town. Cross the plaza and bear left on Carrer Sant Llàtzer, walk several blocks to Carrer Nou, and take a right to Figueres's tree-filled Rambla. To reach the **tourist office,** walk up the Rambla and continue on Carrer Lasauca straight out from the left corner. The blue all-knowing **"i"** beckons across the rather treacherous intersection with Ronda Frial.

TRANSPORTATION

Trains: (tel. 972 20 70 93). To: **Girona** (30min., 21 per day, 6:11am-8:58pm, 375ptas); **Portbou** (30min., 12 per day, 6:42am-11:16pm, 250ptas); **Barcelona** (1½hr., 21 per day, 6:11am-8:58pm, 1265ptas).

Buses: All lines leave from the **Estació Autobuses** (tel. 972 67 33 54), Pl. Estació. **Sarfa** (tel. 972 67 42 98) runs to **Llançà** (25min., 4 per day, Sept.-June 2 per day, 300ptas) and **Cadaqués** (1¼hr., July-Aug. 5 per day, Sept.-June 2-3 per day, 490ptas). **Barcelona Bus** (tel. 972 50 50 29) drives to **Girona** (1hr., 4-6 per day, 475ptas) and **Barcelona** (2¼hr., 4-6 per day, 1750ptas).

Taxis: (tel. 972 50 00 08). Taxis line up on the Rambla and outside the train station.

Car Rental: Europcar, Pl. Estació, 16 (tel. 972 67 34 34; fax 972 50 21 52). Min. age 25. All-inclusive rental from 8900ptas per day.

TOURIST, FINANCIAL, AND LOCAL SERVICES

Tourist Office: (tel. 972 50 31 55), Pl. Sol. Good map and list of accommodations. Open July-Aug. M-Sa 8am-9pm, Su 9am-6pm; April-June and Oct. M-F 8:30am-3pm and 4:30-8pm, Sa 9:30am-1:30pm and 3:30-6:30pm; Sept. and Nov.-April M-F 8:30am-3pm. Two **branch offices** in summer, one in front of the bus station (open mid-July-mid-Sept. M-Sa 9:30am-1pm and 4-7pm), and the other in a yellow mobile home by the Dalí museum (open July-Sept. 15 M-Sa 10am-2:30pm and 4:30-7pm).

Currency Exchange: Banco Central Hispano, Rambla, 21. **ATM.** Open M-F 8:30am-2pm.

Luggage Storage: At the train station, large lockers 600ptas. At the bus station 300ptas. Both open daily 6am-10pm.

EMERGENCY AND COMMUNICATIONS

Emergency: tel. 088. **Police: Mossos d'Esquadra** (tel. 972 67 50 89), on C. Ter.

Post Office: C. Santa Llogaia, 60-62 (tel. 972 50 54 31). Open M-F 8:30am-2:30pm, Sa 9:30am-1pm. **Postal Code:** 17600.

Internet Access: Netway, Pl. Tarradella, 14 (tel. 972 67 70 65). Follow C. Monturiol straight off the Rambla (away from the tourist office), stay to the left of Plaça Palmera, and turn left onto C. Pella i Forjas at the Caixa Catalunya. Netway is visible straight through Pl. President Terradellas. 400ptas per 30min. Open M-F 9am-1pm and 3-7pm.

IS THAT A MELTING CANDLE IN YOUR POCKET, OR ARE YOU JUST A ROTTING DONKEY?

From an early age, Salvador Dalí was plagued by nightmares and insecurities. By age 15, Dalí already had high hopes for himself: "I'll be a genius and the world will admire me." Although Dalí appeared to be confident in his talents, he was not equally confident in other aspects of his life. Sexually inexperienced until a late age, Dalí was sexually ambiguous and had a fear of sexual contact and impotence. This fear was one of the two central subjects of his work; the other, interestingly enough, was landscapes. Dalí was also influenced by Sigmund Freud, and sought to connect the unconscious with the conscious in his paintings. Surrealism itself attempted to explore the language of dreams in order to tap the unconscious. Although Dalí's paintings can be confusing at first, aspects of their symbol-language are consistent enough to be translated. Here a few examples:

Look carefully at Dalí's **women**. Those that are portrayed in a cubist style are that way because they pose no threat to Dalí.

Most of Dalí's **landscapes** are of the rocky shores of Cadaqués.

A rotting **donkey** or **fish** is Dalí's symbol of the bourgeoisie.

The **crutches** propping up bits of soft flesh are symbols of masturbation.

The **grasshopper** is a symbol of terror, as Dalí had a great fear of the insect.

Staircases are a Freudian image, representing the fear of intercourse.

A **melting candle** is a symbol of impotence.

Lions represent animal aggression and **knives** are meant to be phallic symbols.

A **fish hook** (found in Dalí's head) is a symbol of his entrapment.

When asked about the **clocks** he said, "the famous soft watches are nothing else than the tender, extravagant, solitary, paranoia-critical Camembert of time and space." (*Conquest of the Irrational*, 1969.)

ACCOMMODATIONS

Finding a place to sleep in Figueres can be a surreal experience. Affordable accommodations hide in unlikely spots. Some cluster on Carrer Jonquera, but they necessitate a trek northeast from the Dalí museum; others are on C. Pep Ventura. The tourist office has an annually updated list of all *pensiones*.

Alberg Tramuntana (HI), C. Anciet de Pagès, 2 (tel. 972 50 12 13; fax 972 67 38 08), 1 block behind the tourist office. A backpacker's dream—friendly hosts, fax service, VCR, library, board games, bike rentals, and laundry. Members only, but HI cards for sale. Breakfast included. Sheets 350ptas. Laundry service 500ptas. Reception daily 8am-2pm and 4-11pm. Lockout M-F 2-4pm, Sa-Su 1-7pm. Curfew midnight; in summer open for 10min. at 1, 2, 3, and 4am. Reserve 1 month in advance through the Barcelona office (tel. 93 483 83 63) or call the hostel 2-3 days prior to arrival. July-Sept. dorms 1800ptas, over 26 2325ptas; Oct.-June 1575ptas, over 26 2000ptas. Visa, MC, AmEx. Closed mid-Jan. to mid-Feb and Oct. 15-30.

Pensión Mallol, C. Pep Ventura, 9 (tel. 972 50 22 83). Follow the Rambla toward the tourist office, turn right on Castell at its end, and take the 2nd left. The friendly owner holds cleanliness sacred. Singles 1950ptas; doubles 3300ptas. Visa.

La Viña, C. Tins, 18 (tel. 972 50 00 49). Left off the Rambla (when heading away from the tourist office) onto C. Enginyers, then turn onto C. Tins. Bare rooms and cold showers are perfect for the ultimate penny-pincher. Singles 1200ptas, doubles 2400ptas.

FOOD

Restaurants near the Dalí museum serve overcooked *paella* to the masses; better choices surround the Rambla. The **mercado** is at Pl. Gra and nearby Pl. Catalunya (open Tu, Th, and Sa 7am-1pm). Mass-buy mass-produced goods at the mass-supermarket **MAXOR**, Pl. Sol, 5 (tel. 972 51 00 19; open July-Sept. M-F 8am-9pm, Sa 8am-9pm; Oct.-June M-Sa 8am-8:30pm; Visa, MC).

Restaurante La Pansa, C. l'Emporda, 8 (tel. 972 50 10 72). The back faces the youth hostel. A comfortable restaurant, extremely popular with workmen on their lunchbreaks. *Menú* 1000ptas. Open M-Sa 1-3:30pm and 8-10pm.

Restaurante La Torrada, La Rosa, 6 (tel. 972 50 95 66), left off the Rambla on C. Vilatant, then the 2nd right. Fun music and pine stools await those who pop in for a meal. *Menú* 1000ptas. Open W-M 1-3:30pm and 8pm-midnight. Closed July 1-14.

La Torrada II, C. Mestre Falla, 15 (tel. 972 67 58 26), up the street from the youth hostel. The *menú* (900ptas) is fresh and delicious. Open W-M 7am-3:30pm and 6pm-2am.

SIGHTS AND ENTERTAINMENT

TEATRE-MUSEU DALÍ. Despite his reputation as being a fascist self-promoter, Dalí's self-built theater/museum/monument-to-himself is undeniably a masterpiece. It's all here: Dalí's naughty cartoons, his dramatically low-key tomb, and many paintings of Gala, his wife and muse, one of which, when viewed through a telescope (10ptas), transforms into a portrait of Abraham Lincoln. The treasure trove of paintings includes the remarkable *Self Portrait with a Slice of Bacon*, and several other artists' works as well. The museum is chock-full of interesting art, though not all the works are on the walls; look up. (*From the Rambla, take C. Girona from the end farthest from the tourist office, which goes past Pl. Ajuntament and becomes C. de la Jonquera. A flight of steps by a Dalí statue leads to the museum. Tel. 972 51 19 76; fax 972 50 16 66. Open Oct.-June 10:30am-5:15pm and 10pm-12:30am; July-Sept. 9am-7:15pm and 10pm-12:30am. 1000ptas, seniors and students 800ptas.*)

CASTELL DE SANT FERRAN. Are the crowds too much? Head over to the massive 18th-century Castell de Sant Ferran, the largest stone fortress in Europe at 12,000 square meters. *(Av. Castell de Sant Ferran. Tel. 972 50 26 53. Open daily June 15-Sept. 10:30am-7pm; Oct.-June 14 Tu-Su 10:30am-2pm. 350ptas, includes an audio tape.)*

MUSEU DE L'EMPORDÀ. A pleasingly random assortment of archaeological finds and paintings from the 19th-century Catalán Renaissance fills this museum. *(Rambla, 2. Tel. 972 50 23 05. Open July-Sept. Tu-Sa 10:30am-2pm and 3:30-7pm, Su 10am-2pm; Oct.-June M-Sa 11am-1pm and 3-7pm, Su 11am-1:30pm. 300ptas, seniors and students 150ptas, under 18 free. Free entry with ticket from Teatre-Museu Dalí.)*

ENTERTAINMENT. In September, Figueres features classical and jazz music at the **Festival Internacional de Música de l'Empordà.** *(Tickets available at Caixa de Catalunya. Call 972 10 12 12 or get a brochure at the tourist office.)* From September 9-12, the **Mostra del Vi de L'Alt Empordà,** a tribute to regional wines, brings a taste of the local vineyards to Figueras. Around May 3, the **Fires i Festes de la Santa Creu** sponsors cultural events, art and technology exhibitions, and parties. Merrymaking at the **Festa de Sant Pere,** held June 28-29, honors the town's patron saint.

NEAR FIGUERES: CADAQUÉS

The whitewashed houses and small bay of Cadaqués (pop. 1800) have attracted artists, writers, and musicians ever since Dalí built his summer home here in the 1930s. To preserve the town's facade, an affluent crowd of property owners and renters just say no to condos, big hotels, and trains. The rocky beaches attract their share of tourists, but Cadaqués preserves a pleasantly laid-back atmosphere.

▟ ORIENTATION AND PRACTICAL INFORMATION. The bus to Cadaqués halts at a small stone tower beneath a miniature two-fisted Statue of Liberty. With your back to the Sarfa office, walk right and downhill along Av. Caritat Serinyana to the waterfront **Plaça Frederic Rahola.** Once there, a signboard map with indexed services and accommodations will orient you. Cadaqués has no train station, but Sarfa **buses** (tel. 972 25 87 13) run to: **Figueres** (1hr., 3-5 per day, 490ptas); **Girona** (2hr., 1-2 per day, 940ptas); **Barcelona** (2½hr., 2-5 per day, 2045ptas). Buses stop at the junction of Ctra. Port Lligat and Av. Caritat Serinyana, which leads to the town center. **Escola de Vela Ones** (tel. 939 31 02 84; ask for Xavi) sets up shop on the beach directly in front of the tourist office and rents **mountain bikes** (900ptas per hr., 1900ptas per ½-day, 2500ptas per day), kayaks, and wind-surfing gear (open July-Sept. 15 daily 10am-8pm). The **tourist office,** C. Cotxe, 2 (tel. 972 25 83 15; fax 972 15 95 42), off Pl. Frederic Rahola opposite the *passeig*, gives out an adequate map (open July-Aug. M-Sa 10am-2pm and 4-9pm, Su 10am-1pm; Sept.-June M-Sa 10:30am-1pm and 4-8pm). **Banco Central Hispano** (tel. 972 25 78 36) is on C. Caritat Serinyana, 4 (open M-F 8:30am-2:30pm). **Emergency: local police** (tel. 972 15 93 43), Pl. Frederic Rahola, beside the promenade; **medical assistance** tel. 972 25 88 07. **Post office** (tel. 972 25 87 98), on Av. Rierassa off C. Caritat Serinyana (open M-F 8:30-11:30am, Sa 9am-11pm); **postal code** 17488.

▟▟ ACCOMMODATIONS AND FOOD. Hostal Cristina, C. Riera, s/n (tel. 972 25 81 38), right on the water, has bright, newly renovated rooms. (Mid-July to Aug. singles 2000ptas, with bath or terrace 3000ptas; doubles 4000ptas, with bath 6000ptas, with TV 8000ptas; Sept. to mid-July doubles with bath or terrace 5000ptas. Visa, MC.) **Hostal Marina,** C. Riera de Sant Vicenç, 3 (tel. 972 25 81 99), has clean, airy rooms, some with balconies. (Singles 2300ptas, with bath 4000ptas; doubles 4300ptas, with bath 7000ptas. Breakfast 500ptas. Open Apr.-Dec. Visa, MC.) **Camping Cadaqués,** Ctra. Portlligat, 17 (tel. 972 25 81 26), is on the left on the way to Dalí's house; follow the signs for Hotel Port Lligat. The campsite is 100m from the beach and has a pool, supermarket, and bungalows. (550ptas per person, 695ptas per tent, 550ptas per car. Plus 7% IVA. Open June-Sept. 15.) Cadaqués harbors the usual slew of overpriced, unexciting tourist **restaurants** on the waterfront.

Head into the back-streets for more interesting options. Check out the family-run **Can Pelayo** (tel. 972 25 83 56), on C. Pruna. Veer left around Plaça Dr. Pont off Riba Pitxot (along the water) and it's the first street on the right. They serve good fish and even better fried veggies. *Menú* 1700ptas + 7% IVA. (Open Dec.-Oct. 14 daily 1-4pm and 8-11:30pm. Visa, MC.). Otherwise, pack a picnic from **Super Auvi,** Riera, s/n (tel. 972 25 86 33; open July 15-Aug. M-Sa 8am-9pm, Su 8am-2pm; Sept.-July 14 M-Sa 8am-2pm and 4-9pm, Su 8am-2pm).

📷 📂 **SIGHTS AND ENTERTAINMENT.** The **Centre d'Art Perrot-Moore,** C. Vigilant, 1 (tel. 972 25 82 31), near the town center, houses many Dalí masterpieces, including an erotic fantasy room (no children permitted) and mixed media from the Disney version of Dante's *Divine Comedy.* Also check out the impressive Picassos, backdrops for a 1953 García Lorca play, and his practice sketches for the phenomenal *Guernica.* (Open July-Aug. daily 10:30am-1:30pm and 4:30-8:30pm; Apr.-June and Sept.-Oct. M-Sa 10:30am-1:30pm and 4-8pm, Su 10:30am-1:30pm. 800ptas, students and children 500ptas.) The **Museu de Cadaqués,** C. Monturiol, 15 (tel. 972 25 88 77), has changing exhibits, often on a Dalí theme. (Open daily mid-June to Sept. 11am-1:30pm and 3-8pm. 800ptas, students and children 500ptas.) From there it is a pleasant walk (30min.) to 📷**Casa-Museu Salvador Dalí** (tel. 972 25 80 63), in Port Lligat, the home where Dalí and his wife Gala lived until her death in 1982. A pop-art Alhambra, the building flaunts Dalí's favorite lip-shaped sofa and more stuffed snakes and swans than you bargained for. To get there, follow the signs to Port Lligat (take the right fork with your back to the statue of liberty); eventually Casa de Dalí signs appear. (Open daily June 15-Sept. 15 10:30am-9pm; Mar. 15-June 14 and Sept. 16-Nov. Tu-Su 10:30am-6pm. Multilingual tours every 10min.; ticket office closes 45min. before closing. 1200ptas; seniors, students, and children 700ptas.).

PORTBOU

Perched on the Spanish and French border, Portbou (pop. 1500) was a virtually non-existent fisherman's village until the Barcelona-Cerbère railroad was constructed in 1872, bringing life, albeit an industrial one, to the town. And while most visitors will see little more than the train station, Portbou is not so bad. Nestled between two mountains, Portbou offers a magnificent view of the sea, a clean pebble beach, and tree-lined streets.

🏂 **ORIENTATION AND PRACTICAL INFORMATION.** The train station lies above the town, and its only exit, down a set of stairs, leads onto C. Mercat. Go through Pg. Enric Granados and bear left; the tourist office and the beach are straight ahead. **RENFE trains** (tel. 972 39 00 99) go to: **Figueres** (30min., 21 per day, 5:47am-10:35pm, 250ptas); **Girona** (1hr.:, 21 per day, 5:47am-10:35pm,

THE LAST DAYS OF BENJAMIN Although Portbou may seem fairly insignificant on the cultural landscape, it gained notoriety in the 1940s as the site where the extremely influential literary and cultural critic Walter Benjamin died. Benjamin, a social theorist of the Frankfurt school and close friend of Bertold Brecht, left behind a profound legacy. A pessimistic Marxist, he elucidated the relationship between literature and social structures. Of German-Jewish descent, Benjamin was fleeing the Nazis in 1940 when he arrived at the border town of Portbou. Because of Spanish Fascist sympathy with the Nazi cause, Benjamin was detained there and not permitted to enter Spain. He retired to the Pensión at Restaurante Internacional and killed himself upstairs by overdosing on morphine. Local lore, however, claims that Benjamin was murdered by the Nazis. Regardless of the way he died, a lovely memorial to Benjamin sits above the town, right outside the cemetery where his grave lies. The **Civic Center**, Méndez Núñez, 2 (tel./fax 972 39 04 06), has a Walter Benjamin Documentation Center; exhibitions on the philosopher are held often.

550ptas); **Barcelona** (2¾hr., 12 per day, 5:47am-1035pm, 13000-2500ptas) via every town with a station in western Cataluña and Collioure, France. The **tourist office**, Paseo Lluís Companys, s/n (tel. 972 21 25 16; fax 972 21 25 12) sits beachside (open Apr.-June 15 M-Sa 9am-1pm and 3-5pm, Su 9am-2pm; June 16-Sept. M-Sa 9am-2pm and 3-8pm, Su 9am-2pm). **Banco Central Hispano**, C. Mercal, 13, on the street from the train station, **exchanges currency** and has an **ATM** (open Oct.-Apr. M-F 8:30am-2:30pm, Sa 8:30am-1pm; May-Sept. M-F 8:30am-2:30pm); **luggage storage** in lockers at the train station (600ptas). **Police** (tel. 972 39 00 90), in the town hall, at the end of Pg. Sardanes near the end of the beach. **Post office,** Pg. Enric Granades, 10 (tel. 972 39 01 75; open M-F 8:30am-2:30pm, Sa 9:30am-1pm); **postal code:** 17497.

▮▮▮ ACCOMMODATIONS AND FOOD. Hostal Juventus, Av. Barcelona, 3 (tel. 972 39 02 41). From the train station, head straight down to the water, past beachside cafes on Passeig Sardana for one block, and take the last right. Simple rooms with sinks and a large common bathroom. Singles 2000ptas; doubles 4000ptas; triples 6000ptas. Hungry? Buy fresh fruits, vegetables, meat, and fish at **Mercat Municipal,** Passeig d'enric Granados, 1 (open daily 8am-1pm). Philosophy and literary theory buffs might try **Restaurant International,** C. Del Mar, 5, left off C. Mercat as you exit the station. Philosopher and theorist Walter Benjamin ate his last meal here and died upstairs (see **The Last Days of Benjamin,** p. 354). Restaurants by the waterfront offer typical tourist fare at high prices.

CATALÁN PYRENEES

While the Costa Brava and Barcelona attract beach-goers and city-dwellers in droves, the jagged green mountains, simple Romanesque churches, and tranquil towns of the Catalán Pyrenees draw a different type of tourist. Hikers and high-brow skiers, most from Spain and France, come in search of outdoor adventures. Tourist offices distribute pamphlets with information on local winter sports and scenic areas. Skiers will find the English-language guide *Snow in Catalonia* (free at tourist offices) especially useful. *Ski España* lists vital stats of all ski stations in Spain. For those coming from the east, **Ripoll** is the point of entry to the Pyrenees, while those coming from the west and south enter through **Lérida** (Lleida), the town that provides the only public transportation (bus) to the lakes and trails of the national park. The Catalán Pyrenees are best explored with a car.

RIPOLL

Although the industrial city of Ripoll (pop. 11,000) is not full of charm and excitement, it serves as a good base for visiting the **Monasterio de Santa María de Ripoll** and nearby **Sant Joan de las Abadesses.** If a good Romanesque portal floats your boat, Ripoll may be the town for you.

▮ PRACTICAL INFORMATION. RENFE, Pl. Mova, 1 (tel. 972 70 06 44), runs **trains** to **Puigcerdà** (1hr., 5 per day, 8:56am-8:54pm, 400ptas) and **Barcelona** (1½hr., 5-12 per day, 6:32am-8:04pm, 775ptas). The bus station next door sends **Teisa buses** (tel. 972 70 20 95) to: **Sant Joan de las Abadesses** (15min., 4 per day, 250ptas); **Barcelona** (1½hr., 1 per day, 1700ptas); **Girona** (2hr., 6 per day, 1000ptas), via **Olat**. The **tourist office** (tel. 972 70 23 51), next to the monastery on Pl. Abat Oliba, gives out mediocre maps (open June 12-Sept. 15 M-Sa 10am-noon and 4-6pm, Su 10am-noon; Sept.16-June 11 M-Sa 10am-noon and 4-6pm, Su 10am-2pm). **Banco Central Hispano,** on Pl. Sant Eudald, off Pl. Gran (open M-F 8:30am-1:30pm and W 4-7pm). **Emergency:** tel. 088; **police**, Pl. Ajuntament, 3 (tel. 972 70 06 00). **Post office,** C. Sant Bartolomeu, 6 (tel. 972 70 07 60), at the corner of C. Progrés (open M-F 8am-2:30pm, Sa 9:30am-1pm); **postal code:** 17500.

ISN'T IT ROMANESQUE?

Romanesque castles, churches, and monasteries are everywhere in the Pyrenees. This style emerged after the breakup of the Carolingian Empire in the late 10th century and dominated Europe until the end of the 13th century. Romanesque architecture mixed Roman building traditions (such as vaulted roofs) with newer techniques (such as massive masonry to uphold barrel vaults). The buildings are characterized by their rounded arched doors and windows and modest (compared to Gothic) heights. Benedictine monks and the Knights Templar hired builders to spread Romanesque influence far and wide, making it the first truly pan-European architectural style. The increasing popularity of the Camino de Santiago contributed further to the propagation of the style.

ACCOMMODATIONS AND FOOD. For those in search of a place to sleep, the luxurious **Fonda La Paula,** C. Berenfuer, 4 (tel. 972 70 00 11), on Pl. Abat Oliba alongside the tourist office, has big rooms with TVs and bathrooms (singles 3000ptas; doubles 4500ptas; 7% IVA not included). Restaurants surround Pl. Gran. Follow C. Bisbe Morgades and take a right before the river on C. Mossen; the plaza is to the left. **Restaurante La Perla,** Pl. Gran, 4 (tel. 972 70 00 11), serves entrees from 750-1500ptas (open M-Sa 1-5pm and 8pm-midnight, Su 1-5pm; Visa, MC). Stock up on groceries at **Maxim,** C. Progress, 32-37 (tel. 972 70 26 32; open M-Th 9am-1:30pm and 4:30-9pm, F-Sa 9am-9:30pm, Su 10am-2pm; Visa, MC, AmEx).

SIGHTS. Almost everyone who comes to Ripoll comes to see the incredibly intricate 11th-century portal of the ■**Monasterio de Santa Maria.** To reach the monastery, take a left on C. Progrés from the train and bus stations, then follow it until it merges with C. Estació. Take the first left after the "metal dancers" onto Pont d'Olot, cross the river, and continue straight on C. Bisbe Morgades to the Pl. Ayuntament and Pl. Abat Oliba. Founded in AD 879 by Count Guifré el Pelú (Wilfred the Hairy), it was once the most powerful monastery in Cataluña. The curved doorway, nicknamed the "Stone Bible," depicts survival scenes from the Old and New Testaments as well as a hierarchy of the cosmos and a 12-month calendar. Explanatory panels (in Catalán) attempt to decode the doorway. Adjoining it is a beautiful two-story Romanesque and Gothic **cloister.** (Church open daily 8am-1pm and 3-8pm. Free. Cloister open 10am-1pm and 3-7pm. 100ptas.) To the left of the church and up a long spiral staircase is the bizarre **Museu Enogràfic de Ripoll** (tel. 972 70 31 44), complete with birds' nests, slightly worn 19th-century socks, and a noisy model of a forge. (Open Mar. 21-Sept. 20 daily 9:30am-1:30pm and 3:30-7pm; Sept. 21-Mar. 20 Tu-Su 9:30am-1pm and 3:30-6pm. 300ptas, students and seniors 200ptas.)

NEAR RIPOLL: SANT JOAN DE LES ABADESSES

Wilfred the Hairy was nothing if not an equal-opportunity employer. After founding Ripoll's first monastery, he went on to endow a convent 10km away, to which he appointed his daughter Emma as the first abbess in 887. A town (pop. 3700) developed around the nuns, but unfortunately some of his successors were not so keen on female independence; their community was suppressed in the 11th century and it took 100 years before anyone was allowed to move back. The Augustinians who eventually took over turned the convent into a monastery. Today it contains a Romanesque **church** with the **Santíssim Misteri,** a 13th-century seven-piece colored sculpture. One piece depicts Christ's removal from the cross; on Christ's forehead is a piece of Holy Bread, preserved for 700 years. (Open daily Mar.-Apr. and Oct. 10am-2pm and 4-6pm; May-June and Sept. 10am-2pm and 4-7pm; July-Aug. 10am-7pm; Nov.-Feb. M-F 10am-2pm, Sa-Su 10am-2pm and 4-6pm. 200ptas, includes a visit to the attached museum.)

TEISA buses (tel. 972 74 02 95) connect Sant Joan to Ripoll (15min., 5-7 per day, 250ptas). The **tourist office,** Pl. l'Abadia, 9 (tel. 972 720 599), is next door to the monastery alongside a lovely 15th-century cloister (open daily 10am-2pm and 4-7pm). **Banco Central Hispano** is on C. Comella, 4 (open M-F 8am-2pm). **Hostal Restau-**

rant Nati, C. Perre Rovira, 3 (tel. 972 72 01 14), has simple rooms with TVs, sinks, and saggy beds (2000ptas per person; Visa, MC). **Janpere Hostal,** C. Mestre Andrew, 3 (tel. 972 72 00 77), has tile floors and clean rooms (3000ptas per person with bath and TV; 5800ptas for bath, room, breakfast and dinner). Friendly **Restaurant La Ramba,** Rambla Count Guifré, 1 (tel. 972 72 02 94), has tables on the *rambla* and serves a 1500pta *menú* (open daily 1-4pm and 8-10pm; Visa, MC, Maestro). Or shop at **Supermercado Super Avui** (tel. 972 72 02 67), on the corner of Av. Conte Guife and C. Comella (open M-Sa 9am-2pm and 5-9pm, Su 9am-2pm).

NÚRIA

Núria, set in a small valley near the French border, is best known for its vista-filled hiking trails. The surrounding mountains are inaccessible by train or car. For centuries, only the pious and infertile (see **Our Virgin of Fertility Drugs,** p. 358) made it through the high passes to the Santuario de Sant Gil. In 1931, however, the valley installed a second-hand cable car, the *Cremallera* (Zipper), to make Núria a major ski resort. Unfortunately, as bigger mountains with longer slopes appeared, the resort lost its popularity. In recent years it has been revived, offering right-at-your-doorstep hiking and skiing. The bland modern complex sits aside a blatantly artificial lake which meshes poorly with the rest of Núria's pristine countryside.

In summer, vacationers picnic along the shores of Núria's "lake," ride **horseback** along its trails, and use the valley as a base for **hiking** up to the snow-capped peaks of **Puigmal** (2913m; 5-6hr.) and **Eina** (around 1000m; 3hr.). Less ambitious trekkers can follow the path to neighboring **Queralbs** (2-3hr.), which passes alongside waterfalls and gorges carpeted with wildflowers (the way back up to Núria from Queralbs is significantly more challenging than the way down). In winter, ten **ski trails** offer slopes ranging from *molt facil* (very easy) to *molt dificil* (very difficult or expert). The *Cremallera* leaves from the Ribes de Freser stop on the Ripoll-Puigcerdà train line, climbing over 1000m through virgin mountain faces spotted with stubborn sheep, goats, and pine trees (45min., 6-11 per day depending on season, round-trip 2200ptas; closed Nov.; tel. 972 73 20 20 for more info).

🕐📶🛒 **PRACTICAL INFORMATION, ACCOMMODATIONS, AND FOOD.** From Núria's station, a cable car (included in the price of a *Cremallera* ticket) whisks passengers straight to **Alberg de Joventut Pic de l'Aliga** (tel. 972 73 20 48; reservations tel. 93 483 83 63). The alternative route is an arduous 20-minute climb. (Reservations recommended; breakfast included; dorms 1800ptas, over 25 2375ptas). The **Bar Finistrelles,** downstairs from the souvenir store in the main complex, sells sandwiches (400ptas) and entrees (1000ptas). The complex also offers other services, including **ski rentals, ATMS, telephones,** and **lockers** (300ptas).

If you find the shiny artificiality of Núria a little spooky, escape to the more honest village of **Queralbs** (pop. 80 in winter, 500 in summer) and check out the sublime views from beside Queralbs's medieval rubble or the lovely 10th-century Romanesque church. There's one official *pensión* in town, **Hostal L'Avet,** C. Mayor, 21 (tel. 972 72 73 77; singles with bath 3000ptas, doubles with bath 4800ptas; 4800ptas per person with breakfast and dinner included). However, **Cans Constans** (tel. 972 72 70 13), just off the main road at the entrance to Queralbs, rents four-person apartments with fireplaces for 6000ptas per night. The *Cremallera* stops in Queralbs on its journey between Ribes and Núria.

PUIGCERDÀ

A challenge for foreign tongues, Puigcerdà (pop. 7000; Pwee-chair-DAH) has a refreshingly genuine feel to it, especially compared to some of the more touristy towns that dot the Pyrenees. Although the town itself is nothing to write home about, it commands an undeniably beautiful view of the valley and serves as the best vantage point from which to explore the region of Cerdanya. Hikers, bikers, and skiers will find plenty to do in the area. Puigcerdà is best known for appearing in the 1993 *Guiness Book of World Records* for the world's longest *butifarra* (sausage), a Freudian nightmare measuring 5200 meters.

OUR VIRGIN OF FERTILITY DRUGS The Vall de Núria was just another remote mountain pass when recluse Gil of Nimes settled here in 700. At some point he carved an elaborate statue of the Virgin and child. Almost 400 years later, that statue, along with Gil's bell and cooking pot, were discovered by a local shepherd, and the hermit's isolated sanctuary became a pilgrimage destination. In a twist of events on which it is best not to speculate, some daredevil pilgrim discovered that her fertility increased if she put her head in the pot while simultaneously ringing the bell. Ever since, barren women have been doing the same—one chime for each desired child. Visitors today can stick their own heads in the progeny-producing pot.

◪ **ORIENTATION AND PRACTICAL INFORMATION.** Puigcerdà's center is at the top of a hill. **Plaça Ajuntament,** to the west, is nicknamed *el balcón de Cerdanya*, as it offers a commanding view of the valley and the less picturesque **train station** at the foot of the western slope. Buses stop at the train station and then Pl. Barcelona, where it's best to get off. To reach Pl. Ajuntament from the absolutely inconvenient train station, walk past the stairs in the station's *plaça* until you reach the first real flight of stairs (between two buildings). Walk up and turn right at the top; then look for the next set of stairs on your left, just before a sign for C. Hostal del Sol. Climb these to the top and turn left on C. Raval de les Monges, where the final set of stairs winds up to the right. From the *plaça* walk one block on Carrer Alfons I to **Carrer Major,** the principal commercial street. Turn left on C. Major to Pl. Santa María. From Pl. Santa Maria with your back to the bell tower head out diagonally to the left to Pl. Barcelona.

RENFE trains (tel. 972 88 01 65) run to: **La Molina** (20min., 6 per day, 350ptas); **Núria** (6 per day, round-trip train and *Cremallera* 2550ptas); **Ripoll** (1¼hr., 6 per day, 400ptas); **Barcelona** (3hr., 6 per day, 1100ptas). **Alsina Graells buses** (tel. 973 35 00 20) run to **La Seu d'Urgell** (1hr., 2-3 per day, 580ptas) and **Barcelona** (3hr., 1-4 per day, 1758ptas). From **La Seu** there is passage to **Andorra.** Buses depart in front of the train station and from Pl. Barcelona; purchase tickets on board. See schedule in Bar Estació, to the right as soon as you walk into the bus station. **Taxis** (tel. 972 88 00 11) wait on Pl. Cabrinetty. For **bike rental,** try **Top-Bikes,** Pl. d'Avenes, 21 (tel. 972 88 20 42; 800ptas per hr., 1500ptas per 4hr., 2500ptas per day; Visa, MC). The **tourist office,** C. Querol, 1 (tel./fax 972 88 05 42), a right turn off Pl. Ajuntament with your back to the view, has a friendly English-speaking staff that gives out good maps and helpful lodging, entertainment, and daytrip listings. (Open July-Sept. 15 M-Sa 9am-2pm and 3-8pm, Su 9am-2pm; Sept. 16-June Tu-F 10am-1pm and 4-7pm, Sa 10am-1:30pm and 4:30-8pm, Su 10am-2pm.) **Banco Central Hispano,** on Pl. Cabrinetty (open M-F 8:30am-2:30pm). **Emergency:** tel. 091 or 092; **municipal police,** Pl. Ajuntament, 1 (tel. 972 88 19 72); **hospital: Centre Hospitalari** (tel. 972 88 01 50 or 972 88 01 54), in Pl. Santa María (English spoken). **Post office,** Av. Coronel Molera, 11 (tel. 972 88 08 14), off Pl. Barcelona on the left after 1½ blocks (open M-F 8:30am-2:30pm, Sa 9:30am-1pm); **postal code:** 17520.

◪◪ **ACCOMMODATIONS AND FOOD.** Since many visitors daytrip to Puigcerdà, rooms come easily, if not cheaply. Most cheaper *pensiones* hole up off Pl. Santa María, in the old town. **Mare de Déu de les Neus (HI)** (tel. 972 89 20 12; reservations tel. 93 483 83 63), on Ctra. Font Canaleta, 500m from the La Molina RENFE station and 4km from the slopes, has modern facilities and a beautiful location. In winter a bus goes up every 30min. (Breakfast included. Sheets 350ptas. Jan.-Nov. dorms 1700ptas, over 25 2275ptas; Dec. dorms 1800ptas, over 25 2375ptas. Reserve in high season. Visa, MC, AmEx.) **Alfonso Habitaciones,** D'Espanya, 5 (tel. 972 88 02 46), a left off C. Alfons I when heading away from the church, has clean rooms with colorful bedspreads (singles 4000ptas, with bath 6000ptas; doubles with bath and breakfast 7000ptas). **Camping Stel** (tel./fax 972 88 23 61) offers full-service camping, 1km from Puigcerdà on the road to Llivia (*parcela*, including tent and car, 1950ptas; 615ptas per person; open June 19-Sept. 29, weekends in winter).

The neighborhood off C. Alfons I is filled with markets and inexpensive restaurants. For supplies, try the **supermarket** diagonally across from the post office (open Tu-Sa 9am-1pm and 4:30-8:30pm, Su 10am-2pm). **🏵Cantina Restaurant Mexicà**, P. Cabrinetty, 9 (tel. 972 88 16 58), offers truly excellent food. Friendly staff welcomes fans of Mexican food. (Entrees 400-1800ptas. Open M-Tu and Th-F 7:30pm-midnight, Sa-Su 1-4pm and 7:30-midnight. Visa, MC, Maestro.) A more traditional option is **Bar-Restaurant El Meson**, Pl. Cabrinetty, 11 (tel. 972 88 19 28; *menú* 900ptas; *bocadillos* 250-400ptas; open daily 1-3 and 8-10pm).

🏵 🎵 SIGHTS AND ENTERTAINMENT. Puigcerdà calls itself the "capital of snow." **Ski** in your country of choice (Spain, France, or Andorra) at one of 19 ski areas within a 50km radius. The closest one on the Spanish side is at **La Molina.** The area is also popular for **biking;** the tourist office has a brochure with 17 potential routes mapped out. Between ski runs and two-wheeled exploration, dash over to the **campanario,** the octagonal bell tower in Pl. Santa María. This 42m-high 12th-century tower is all that remains of the **Església de Santa María,** and it is an eerie reminder of the destruction wreaked by the 1936 Civil War. (Open July-Sept. daily 11am-2pm and 4-8pm; Oct.-June weekends. Free.) **Església de Sant Domènec,** on Pg. 10 d'Abril, contains several Gothic paintings considered to be among the best of their genre (open 9:30am-8pm).

PARC NACIONAL D'AIGÜESTORTES

The great Parc Nacional d'Aigüestortes, tucked away in its northwestern corner in the province of Lleida (Lérida), is Cataluña's only national park. On a sunny spring day, the snow-capped peaks and wildflower-dusted meadows are a sight to behold. A 2500m range divides the park into western and eastern halves, known respectively as the Estany de Sant Maurici and the Aigüestortes. The halves can be reached separately only by motor vehicle. With over 10,000 hectares and 50 ice-cold mountain lakes, the park merits at least two days—if you rely on public transport, it's hard to do it in fewer than three. Cars can go only as far as the park entrance, 1km outside Espot; when that lot fills, cars must park in Espot.

Don't rely on the freebie park maps from info offices. The offices sell a better, more detailed map (1000ptas; also available in area stores) that is worth the extra cash. The red *Editorial Alpina* guides, one each for Montardo, Vall de Boí, and Sant Maurici, are also an option (800ptas at bookstores). The park brochure, available at tourist offices, is useful. For more info, contact the park tourist offices (in Espot tel. 973 62 40 36; in Boí tel. 973 69 61 89; general info tel. 973 69 40 00). The park's five *refugios* (government-maintained dormitories; about 1300ptas per person) and *Casas de Pagés* (lodging in private homes) are good but pricey accommodation options. The mountains are deceptively placid from afar, but the sometimes unpredictable weather can be dangerous, especially in winter.

AIGÜESTORTES AND VALL DE BOÍ

Because the western half of the park is close to Lérida, it's more popular with casual strollers than the eastern half. To savor the park's two halves, take the main trail along the Riu de Sant Nicolau from Aigüestortes to the **Portarró de Espot,** the gateway between the two sides. The westward descent to Estany de Sant Maurici is steep and covered in patches of snow at higher altitudes. This six- to eight-hour hike crosses the whole park, passing the **Estany Llong.** Near its western tip lies the park's first *refugio*, also called **Estany Llong** (tel. 629 37 46 52; open mid-June to mid-Oct. and weekends in winter; 725ptas per person, over 18 970ptas).

Entering the park from its west side isn't much easier than the eastern approach. When it's running (July-Sept.), the **Alsina Graells** (tel. 973 26 85 00 or 93 265 68 66) bus from Lérida drops explorers off in **Boí** (pop. 150), 7km from the park's entrance. **Taxis** (tel. 973 69 60 36) go from the town's *plaça* to the park (500ptas per person). The helpful **park info office** (tel. 973 69 61 89) is near the bus stop on the *plaça* (open daily 9am-1pm and 3:30-6:45pm). **Guardia Civil** (tel. 973 69 00 06); **emergency** (tel. 973 69 11 59).

Despite the nearby ski resort in **Taüll,** Boí maintains its pastoral feel. Low arches and cobblestone streets surround several family-run accommodations. The proprietor at **Casa Guasch** (tel. 973 69 60 42) lets simple rooms. Leave the plaza through the stone arch, turn right through the next arch, then bear left and turn left again where the street ends. Look for the entrance on the left. The family knows the mountains well and can give you pointers in Spanish or Catalán. (Kitchen access 200ptas per person per day. 1500ptas per person. Open Dec.-March.)

ESPOT AND ESTANY DE SANT MAURICI

The official gateway to the eastern half of the park is the quiet little town of **Espot.** Espot is actually a good 4.5km from the entrance proper, an arrangement that respects the tranquility of the park but disturbs that of the traveler. The only consolation is that the uphill hike to the entrance is quite scenic. Unfortunately, the **Alsina Graells bus** (tel. 973 26 85 00 or 93 265 68 66) from Barcelona or Lérida—the only mass transit in the area—only comes within 7km of the *other* side of Espot, on Highway C-147 at the La Torrassa crossing (3hr., M-Sa 1 per day, 4:30pm, 1820ptas). A **jeep service** (tel. 973 62 41 05) goes into the park from Espot and will even collect travelers from the bus stop (1000ptas to Espot; seats 7-8). From Espot, jeeps run to Estany Sant Maurici (600ptas per person) and to Amitges (round-trip 2000ptas), in the north of the park by the best and biggest **refugio** (tel. 93 315 23 11 or 973 25 01 09; open Feb. 13-28 and June 12-Sept. 26; call ahead). The **park info office** (tel. 973 62 40 36; medical emergencies tel. 973 62 10 05), on the main road (on the right as you enter town), provides good brochures and advice (open daily 9am-1pm and 3:30-6:45pm).

A night's rest in Espot allows hikers to start early. Many local residences take in travelers; inquire at the tourist office. **Residència Felip** (tel. 973 62 40 93) provides lovely rooms and breakfast. Cross the main bridge, follow the road two blocks, and then turn left. (Sept.-June 2000ptas per person; Aug. 3000ptas). **Càmping la Mola** (tel. 973 62 40 24) and **Càmping Sol i Neu** (tel. 973 62 40 01), both on the way to Espot, have good facilities and pools (both open June-Sept. and *Semana Santa;* 580ptas per person, per tent, and per car).

VAL D'ARAN

Some of the Catalán Pyrenees's most dazzling peaks cluster around Val d'Aran, in the northwest corner of the province. The peaks have proven to be sizeable barriers to outside infiltration—though geographically just miles away from Aragon, Val D'Aran seems to be culturally another world.

BAQUIERA-BERET

Though increasingly popular in summer, the Val d'Aran is best known for its chic ski resorts—the Spanish royal family's favorite slopes are those of **Baquiera-Beret.** Girls, it's probably as good a place as any to have a chance encounter with the very eligible Prince Felipe (see **SWM Seeking,** p. 361). Currently, about 80 alpine trails and a few cross-country ones wind down the surrounding peaks. Although budget accommodations have disappeared at the ski station itself, the town of Salardú, a few kilometers away, has a youth hostel, **Albergue Era Garona (HI)** (tel. 973 64 52 71; reservations tel. 934 83 83 63), accessible by high-season shuttle bus from Vielha. (Breakfast included. Sheets 350ptas. Dorms 1800ptas, over 25 2375ptas.) Vielha itself is only 12km from Bacquiera-Beret, and the two are connected by a shuttle bus in July and August. Check at the tourist office for schedules. For skiing info and reservations, contact the **Oficeria de Baquiera-Beret** (tel. 973 64 44 55; fax 973 64 44 88) or the tourist office in Vielha (tel. 973 64 01 10).

SWM SEEKING... Tall, dark, handsome, rich, famous, respected, powerful, and searching for life partner. Enjoys water sports (competed on the Olympic sailing team). Was educated at Georgetown. Looking for that special someone—attractive, charismatic, and preferably of noble lineage—to share interests and raise a family.

His name is Felipe, the Prince of Asturias and heir to the Spanish throne. With his 30th birthday just behind him and his two older sisters recently married, all eyes are on Felipe. Whom will he choose to be his queen when he takes over one of Europe's few powerful monarchies? The competition is fierce. Lovely ladies from wealthy families are stalking the streets of Madrid and the slopes of the Val d'Aran, but so far there are no front runners. Cross your fingers and pack something nice—you could be the next queen of Spain.

VIELHA

The biggest town in the valley, Vielha (pop. 3700) suffers from its share of multi-story architectural blunders but welcomes hikers and skiers to its lively streets with every sort of service the outdoorsy-type might desire.

⚑ PRACTICAL INFORMATION. Alsina Graells (tel. 973 26 85 00) runs **buses** to Vielha from **Lérida** (3hr., 2 per day, 8:45am and 5pm, 1550ptas) that continue on to **Barcelona** (5½hr., 3325ptas). **Taxis** are at tel. 973 64 01 95. The **tourist office,** C. Sarriulèra, 6 (tel. 973 64 01 10; fax 973 64 05 37), is one block upriver from the *plaça*. The staff helps hikers, skiers, and Romanesque-seekers alike. (Open July-Sept. 15 daily 9am-1pm and 4-8pm; Sept. 16-June M-Sa 10am-1pm and 4:30-7:30pm.) **ATMs** pepper Av. Castiéro, which intersects the river. **Guardia Civil** tel. 973 64 00 05; **emergency** tel. 091 or 092. **Post office,** C. Sarviulèra, 2 (tel. 973 64 09 12), by the tourist office (open M-F 8:30am-2:30pm, Sa 9:30am-1pm); **postal code:** 25530.

⚑⬛ ACCOMMODATIONS AND FOOD. Several inexpensive *pensiones* cluster at the end of Camin Reiau, off Pg. Libertat (which intersects Av. Casteiro at Pl. Sant Antoni). The best of the bunch is **Casa Vicenta,** Camin Reiau, 3 (tel. 973 64 08 19), which has sparkling rooms with private baths (Sept.-June singles 2000ptas; doubles 3500ptas; July-Aug. singles 3000ptas, doubles 4500ptas). **Pensión Busquets,** C. Mayor, 11 (tel. 973 64 02 38), in the old part of town, has homey rooms (Aug.-Sept. and Dec.-Mar. 2000ptas per person; Apr.-July and Oct.-Nov. 1800ptas). **Grill Des Isards,** C. La Palha, 9 (tel. 973 630 28 69 15 or 973 606 29 43 27), serves up the town's best food (*menú* 1300ptas; open M-Sa 1-4pm and 7:30-11pm, Su 10am-11pm). **Bar-Restaurante Vidal,** C. Mayor, 6A (tel. 973 64 07 40), cooks a 1200pta *menú* (open daily 1-4pm and 9-11:30pm).

⬛⬛ SIGHTS AND ENTERTAINMENT. The **Iglesia de San Miguel,** a simple 12th-century Romanesque church, houses the intricately carved *Crist de Mijaran.* (Open daily 11am-8pm.) Also in Vielha is the **Museu de Val d'Aran** (tel. 973 64 18 15), on C. Mayor, with an ethnographic collection that attempts to shed light on Aranese culture. (Open Tu-F 5-8pm, Sa 10am-1pm and 5-8pm, Su 10am-1pm. 200ptas.)

Vielha is a good base for all sorts of outdoor activities. **Camins,** Av. Pas d'Arro, 5 (tel. 973 64 24 44; fax 973 64 24 97; email camins-guias.pirineo@lrd.servicom.es), has a helpful staff that can answer questions, organize treks into the Aigüestortes National Park and the surrounding mountains (starting at 2000ptas), lead rafting and horseback trips, and rent mountain bikes (½day 2000ptas, full-day 2600ptas.).

NORTHEASTERN SPAIN

ANDORRA

Welcome to Andorra, the forgotten European country. In this small Pyrenean nation the serenity of the stunning landscapes vie for attention with the energy of its neon-lit capital. Pragmatists might say Andorra (pop. 65,000; 464 sq. km) offers the best of both worlds, though some may beg to differ. Known officially as Principat d'Andorra (Principality of Andorra), it is ruled by two co-princes—the French president and the Bishop of Urgell—and a popularly elected *Consell General* who represents the seven parishes and retains the bulk of the power.

According to legend, Charlemagne founded Andorra in 784 as a reward to the valley's inhabitants for having led his army against the Moors. For the next 12 centuries, Andorra played the rope in a game of tug-o'-war between the Spanish Counts of Urgell, the Church of Urgell, and the French King. Not until 1990 did Andorra create a commission to draft a democratic constitution, adopted on March 14, 1993. Andorra today is far less progressive than other western European nations. In the 1993 election, only the 10,000 native Andorrans (out of 65,000 total inhabitants) were granted the vote; women have only had suffrage since 1970.

Sandwiched between France and Spain, Andorra struggles to assert its identity. Its citizens are comfortably trilingual, though Catalán is the official language. The country has no currency of its own. All establishments are required to accept both *pesetas* and *francs*, although *pesetas* are more prevalent. In fact, currency seems to flow like water, as the absence of a sales tax (and the abundance of duty-free shops) draws consumers from all over Europe. With Andorran towns spaced mere minutes apart and an extensive local bus system, a single day can include wading through aisles of duty-free perfume, hiking through a pine-scented valley, eating in an informal country restaurant, and relaxing in a luxury spa.

▐ GETTING THERE AND GETTING AWAY

The only way to get to Andorra is by car or bus, as the country has no airport or train station. Visitors are required to show a valid passport or an EU identity card to enter the country. All traffic from France must enter Andorra through the town of **Pas de la Casa;** the gateway town on the Spanish side is **La Seu d'Urgell. Andor-Inter/Samar buses** (in Madrid tel. 91 468 41 90; in Toulouse tel. 61 58 14 53; in Andorra tel. 82 62 89) run to **Madrid** (9hr.; Tu, Th, and Su; 4900ptas). **Alsina Graells** (tel. 82 65 67) runs to **Barcelona** (4hr., 6 per day, 2800ptas). **Eurobus** also runs to **Barcelona** (3hr., 4 per day, 6:15am-7:30pm, 2800ptas). All buses arrive at and depart from **Estació d'Autobusos,** on C. Bonaventura Riberaygua. To get to the station from Pl. Princep Benlloch, follow Av. Meritxell past the tourist office to the other side of the river. Make an immediate right after crossing the river and then an immediate left. Take the fourth right and go straight for four to five blocks (20min.). To go anywhere else in Spain, you must first go to La Seu d'Urgell on **La Hispano-Andorra** buses (tel. 82 13 72; 30min., 5-7 buses per day, 340ptas), which leave from in front of Pyrénées, Av. Meritxell, 11. From La Seu, **Alsina Graells buses** (tel. 82 65 67 in Andorra) continue to the rest of Spain via **Puigcerdà** (1hr., 2 per day, 570ptas) and **Lérida** (2½hr., 2 per day, 1650ptas).

▐ GETTING AROUND

Driving in Andorra la Vella is a nightmare. The main road turns into a parking lot even though red-clad traffic officers attempt to keep traffic moving. Drivers will find a map totally useless—it's best to follow signs. Desert the car in one of the

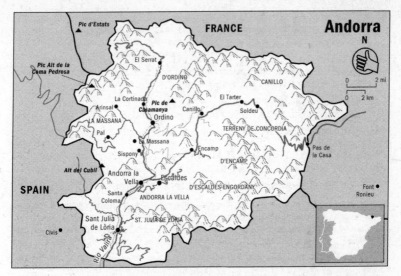

city's free parking lots. The first parking lot on the road from Spain is located at the intersection of C. Moll and C. Prat de la Creu, across from the Holiday Inn.

Efficient **intercity buses** connect villages along the three major highways that converge in Andorra la Vella. The entire country is navigable in an hour or two via public transportation; most towns are only 10 minutes away. Bus rides cost between 90 and 590ptas. All buses make every stop in the city, so don't worry about finding the right bus—just pay attention to the direction sign in the front window. The tourist office has schedules, and bus stops are easy to find.

ANDORRA LA VELLA

Andorra la Vella (pop. 20,000), the country's capital, is little more than a narrow, cluttered road flanked by shop after duty-free shop and sprinkled with American fast food chains. This city is anything but *vella* (old), as most of the old buildings have been upstaged by electronics and sporting goods stores. After doing a little shopping, you're best off escaping to the countryside.

🛈 ORIENTATION AND PRACTICAL INFORMATION

Avinguda Meritxell, the main artery, runs through the city, beginning at Pl. Princep Benlloch in the heart of the tiny **barri antic** (old quarter) and continuing through the modern city's heart, across the Riu Valira, and becoming the main highway to parishes northeast of the capital. West of Pl. Princep Benlloch (to the right when facing the Eglésia de Sant'Esteve) Av. Meritxell becomes **Avinguida Princep Belloch**.

TRANSPORTATION
Taxis: (tel. 86 30 00). Flag one of these yellow-and-white puppies down.
Car Rental: Europcar, Av. Tarragona, 42 (tel. 82 00 91; fax 82 06 42), at the bus station. Must be over 21. Prices start at 4500ptas per day, 35ptas per km, or 18,500ptas for 3-day weekend (1000km limit). Open M-Sa 8:30am-7pm. Visa, MC.

TOURIST, FINANCIAL, AND LOCAL SERVICES
Tourist Office: (tel. 82 02 14; fax 82 58 23), on Av. Doctor Villanova. From the bus stop on Av. Princep Benlloch, continue east (away from Spain) just past the *plaça* on your

left, and take C. Dr. Villanova, which curves down to the right. The office is on the left just before the hill. Multilingual staff has bucket-loads of brochures—the *Sports Activities* and the *Hotels i Restaurants* guides are especially useful. Open July-Sept. M-Sa 9am-1pm and 3-7pm; Oct.-June M-Sa 10am-1pm and 3-7pm, Su 10am-1pm.

Currency Exchange: Banc Internacional, Av. Meritxell, 32 (tel. 88 44 89). 500ptas commission. Exchanges traveler's checks. Open M-F 9am-1pm and 3-5pm, Sa 9am-1pm.

American Express: Viatges Relax, C. Mossèn Tremosa, 2 (tel. 82 20 44). From Pl. Princep Benlloch, take the first left off Av. Meritxell. Open M-F 9am-1pm and 3:30-7pm.

Weather and Ski Conditions: In Spanish tel. 84 88 52; French tel. 84 88 53.

EMERGENCY AND COMMUNICATIONS

Emergency: call 116 or 110. **Police:** C. Prat de la Creu, 16 (tel. 87 20 00).

Hospital: Clinica Nostra Senyora de Meritxell (tel. 87 10 00), Av. Fiter I Rossell.

Post Offices: Both at the east end of town, on the other side of the river from Pl. Princep Benlloch. **Spanish Post Office,** Carrer Joan Maragall, 10 (tel. 82 20 57). Lista de Correos upstairs. Open M-F 8:30am-2:30pm, Sa 9:30am-1pm. **French Post Office,** *La Poste,* C. Pere d'Urg, 1 (tel. 82 04 08). Poste Restante. Open M-F 8:30am-2:30pm.

Internet Access: Bavaria (tel. 81 26 12), Pl. Rotunda, across from the tourist office. 600ptas for 30min., 1100ptas per hr. Open daily 8:30am-1am.

Telephones: Purchase an STA *teletarjeta* (telecard) at the tourist office, post office, or kiosk (500ptas minimum). Collect calls not available; AT&T does not maintain an access network with Andorra. **Directory assistance:** dial 111.

COUNTRY CODE	The country code for Andorra is 376

▌ ACCOMMODATIONS AND CAMPING

It's as easy to find a place to drop as it is to find a place to shop. Cheap hostels are just about everywhere in Andorra la Vella.

Pensió La Rosa, Antic Carrer Major, 18 (tel. 82 18 10), off Av. Princep Benlloch. Friendly owners; immaculate rooms. Breakfast 350ptas. Singles 1700ptas; doubles 3000ptas.

Hotel Costa, Av. Meritxell, 44 (tel. 82 14 39), above Restaurant Marti. Big rooms, some with views of the city. Large lounges. Singles 1500ptas; doubles 3000ptas. Visa, MC.

Camping: Camping Valira (tel. 82 23 84), Av. Salou, located behind the **Estadi Comunal d'Andorra la Vella.** Shade, video games, hot showers, and an indoor pool. 525ptas per person, per tent, and per car. Call ahead. 2½km down the road, **Camping Santa Coloma,** Av. Verge del Remei, 11.13 (tel. 82 88 99), charges 550ptas per person, per tent, and per car, and has no video games.

◐ FOOD

Andorra's restaurants serve decent meals, but the city is better known for its supermarkets. Check out one of the amazing three-story supermarkets in nearby Santa Coloma (you can't miss them) or the **Grans Magatzems Pyrénées,** Av. Meritxell, 11, the country's biggest department store, with an entire aisle dedicated to chocolate bars alone (open M-F 9:30am-8pm, Sa 9:30am-9pm, Su 9:30am-7pm).

Restaurant Ca La Conxita, Placeta Monjó, 3 (tel. 82 99 48). From C. Mayor heading toward the river, take the 1st right on Ana M. Janer, then the 1st left and 1st right. Candlelit restaurant. Entrees 900-2200ptas. Open M-Sa 1-3pm and 9:30-11pm. Visa, MC.

Restaurant Marti, Av. Meritxell, 44 (tel. 82 09 46). Good, cheap basics. *Menú A* with 3 courses (1100ptas) or *Menú B* with 4 courses (1425ptas). Open daily noon-4pm and 8-10pm. Visa, MC.

👁 🎵 SIGHTS AND ENTERTAINMENT

Although there is more to Andorra la Vella than shopping, there isn't *much* more.

CASA DE LA VALL. Sixteenth-century Casa de la Vall (House of the Valleys), is the home of Andorra's pocket-sized parliament. Each of Andorra's seven parishes holds a key to the "seven-keyed" cupboard containing General Council documents. *(Down the stone alley off Pl. Princep Benlloch and past the church. Tel. 82 91 29. Open M-F 9am-1pm and 3-7pm. Guided tours only; call or stop by to book a spot.)*

ENTERTAINMENT. The tourist office offers information and sells tickets for Andorra la Vella's annual **Festival Internacional de Música i Dansa,** which showcases an international array of ballet, jazz, and classical concerts. The city's annual **festival** colors the capital on the first Saturday, Sunday, and Monday in August. The tourist office's monthly *Un mes a Andorra* lists cultural activities. *7 dies a Andorra*, the free weekly, lists useful phone numbers and entertainment info.

AROUND ANDORRA

If you haven't come to Andorra for the shopping, you've definitely come for the excursions. Escape the polluted air that drips over Andorra la Vella to ski, bike, fish, climb, ride, or just bask in the serenity of the rural *parròquias* (parishes).

ORDINO

Ordino (pop. 2219; alt. 1,304m), 5km northeast of La Massana, has yet to fall victim to the strip-mall craze that has hit the rest of the country. The least populated of Andorra's seven parishes, Ordino is conveniently located for hiking and skiing and is distinguished by the presence of a **seignorial mansion,** the home of Andorran aristocrats. The D'Areny i Plandolit family accrued a small fortune in the region's iron industry, and their 17th-century home is now a **museum** (tel 83 69 08; open M-Sa 9:30am-1pm and 3-6:30pm, Su 10am-2pm for guided visits; 300ptas). The **bus** from Andorra la Vella to La Massana continues on to Ordino (130ptas). The **tourist office** (tel. 73 70 80), C. Nou Desvio, supplies comprehensive brochures on hiking and skiing in the area (open M-Sa 9am-1pm and 3-7pm, Su 9am-noon; July-Sept. Su 9am-7pm). The stone-faced **Hotel Quim** (tel. 83 50 13), on the *plaça*, contains homey, comfortable rooms (doubles 3000ptas).

CANILLO

The tiny town of Canillo (pop. 952, alt. 1400-2813m), in the center of the country, suffers from the same architectural short-sightedness as the rest of Andorra, but is surrounded by fine scenery and the country's best skiing. The colossal **Palau de Gel D'Andorra** (tel. 85 15 65) is an eclectic recreational facility almost as monumental as the mountains themselves. The palace's marvels, including a swimming pool, ice-skating rink ("ice disco" at night), and squash courts, are accessible with individual tickets. In winter, you can swim outdoors in the palace's heated pool while snow melts around its edges. (Palace open daily 10am-midnight. Each facility has its own hours. 650ptas each or 1300ptas for all in one day. Equipment rental 350ptas.) The closest hostel is **Hotel Comerç** (tel. 85 10 20), on the road to Andorra La Vella, with bare rooms at bare prices (singles 1450ptas; doubles 2900ptas).

NEAR ANDORRA LA VELLA

Encamp houses the **Museu Nacional de l'Automòbil** (tel. 83 22 66), with 80 antique cars, motorbikes, and bicycles all revved up with nowhere to go. (Open Tu-Sa 9:30am-1:30pm and 3-6pm, Su 10am-2pm. 300ptas, seniors and students 150ptas.) Slink toward **Escaldes-Engordany,** just outside Andorra la Vella, for the expensive pleasures of the **Caldea Spa,** Parc de la Mola, 10 (tel. 80 09 99). Housed in a glass steeple, the "Centre Termolúdic" offers steam baths, hydro and human massages, tanning beds, and decadent dips in faux Roman baths. (Admission 2500ptas per 3hr., not including fees for each service. Open daily 10am-9pm.)

OUTDOOR ACTIVITIES

◪ HIKING

You're broke, out of shape, and covered by a thickening layer of dirt, city exhaust, and last night's *sangría*. It's time to strap on your hiking boots and take a hike. The melted snow opens up a whole new country—one boasting glacial legacies, navigable peaks, rolling forests, wild meadows, and scenic vistas. Like most everything else in Andorra, all the routes are close together, and most can be tackled by even the least seasoned outdoors enthusiast. An extensive network of hiking trails traverses the country, and trails range from short and sweet to long and rewarding. The tourist office brochure *Sports Activities* includes suggested itineraries, potential routes, and bike rental locations, and is helpful for planning excursions.

The *Grandes-Randonnées* trails #7 and 11 traverse nearly all of the country. La Massana is home to Andorra's tallest peak, **Pic Alt de la Coma Pedrosa** (2946m). Ordino is another base for trails of varying difficulty levels: an easy four-hour hike tours the lakes of **Tristaina;** a very difficult eight-hour climb brings summit-oriented hikers to **Pic de Casamanya** (2740m), **Coll d' Arenas** (2539m), **Pic de l'Estanyó** (2915m), **Pic de la Cabaneta** (2863m), and **Pic de la Serrera** (2913m), a route that can also be split up into more manageable portions. *Sports Activities* sketches out 52 itineraries, ranging from 15-minute strolls to longer affairs, and lists cabin and refuge locations within the principality.

Andorra's countryside, with an array of clearly marked trails, lends itself to **mountain biking.** One loop trail begins and ends in Andorra la Vella, passing through La Comella for an aerial view of lazy shoppers (11km). **Club Hipic L'Aldosa** (tel. 83 73 29), in La Massana, has **horses** available for excursions. For more organized trips, try the **La Rabassa Sports and Nature Center** (tel. 84 34 52), in the parish of Sant Juliàde Lòria, in the southwest corner of Andorra. In addition to *refugio*-style accommodations, the center offers mountain biking, guided hikes, horseback riding, archery, and all sorts of field sports.

◪ SKIING

In the winter, Andorra offers skiing opportunities galore. The four outstanding resorts within its boundaries all rent equipment and attract the masses. **Pal** (tel. 73 70 00), 10km from La Massana, is a biggie. Four buses leave for Pal from La Massana daily; the last bus returns at 5pm (255ptas). Seven buses run daily from La Massana to nearby **Arinsal** (tel. 83 58 22); the last one returns at 7:45pm (160ptas). On the French border, **Pas de la Casa Grau Roig** (tel. 85 69 92) boasts 600 hectares of skiable land, with 48 trails for all levels of ability. The resort provides 27 lifts, lessons, two medical centers, and night skiing. **Soldeu-El Tarter** (tel. 85 11 51) occupies 840 hectares of skiable area between Andorra la Vella and Pas de la Casa. **Free buses** transport skiers from their hotels in Canillo. Andorra's tourist office publishes a winter edition of *Andorra: The Pyrenean Country,* a guide to the ski resorts. **SKI Andorra** (tel. 86 43 89) or the tourist offices can answer questions.

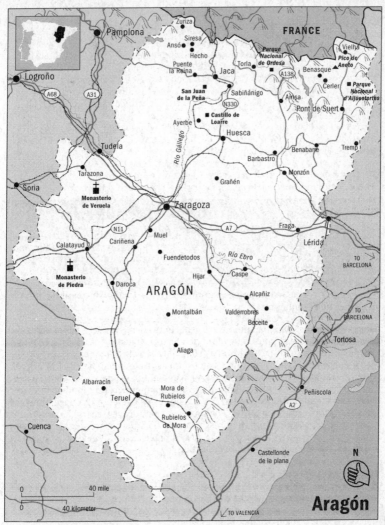

Aragón

ARAGÓN

Upon first observation, Aragón seems a region whose landscapes ought not to fit together. In the south, a sun-baked assemblage of hardworking towns and flaxen plains, scattered with fine examples of ornate Mudéjar architecture (a Moorish-Christian mix), gives way to prosperous and industrious Zaragoza. Up north the stunning snow-capped peaks of the Pyrenees peer down on tiny medieval towns and their remarkable Romanesque architecture.

The harsh terrain and climate, coupled with the region's strategic location, produced a martial culture. Established as a kingdom in 1035 and united with enterprising Cataluña in 1137, Aragón forged a far-flung Mediterranean empire that brought Roussillon, Valencia, Murcia, the Balearic Islands, Naples, Sicily, and even the Duchy of Athens under its sway. Aragón retained the privileges of internal government even after its union with Castilla in 1469, and it held those privileges until Felipe II marched into Zaragoza in 1591 and brought the region to its knees. Economic decline followed political humiliation; as eyes turned to the New World, people (and capital) moved to the coast in search of riches. Today, Aragón is back on its feet economically, although much of the region is still relatively tourist-free. Only some areas of the rural Pyrenees and the **Parque Nacional Ordesa y Monte Perdido,** with its dramatic peaks and copious hiking and skiing opportunities, attract many visitors, and even those are mostly urban Spaniards escaping the city heat during July and August.

Aragonese cuisine is as hearty as the people who make it. *Migas de pastor* (bread crumbs fried with ham) and lamb chops are ubiquitous; more surprising treats include *chilindrón* (lamb and chicken stewed with red peppers) and *melocotones al vino* (sweet native peaches steeped in wine). The *Guía de servicios turísticos de Aragón,* available at any tourist office in the province, makes roaming easy, with information on accommodations and tourist offices.

HIGHLIGHTS OF ARAGÓN

■ **Zaragoza's** breathtaking **Basílica de Nuestra Señora de Pilar** (see p. 372).

■ Exploring and bounding through the **Castillo de Loarre** (see p. 380).

■ Hiking among the snow-covered peaks of **Parque Nacional de Ordesa** (see p. 382).

■ A summertime visit to the adorable little Pyrenean town of **Ansó,** with a warm bed and a hearty meal at a *casa rural* (see p. 381).

ZARAGOZA

Whoever said God and mammon can't peacefully co-exist never visited Zaragoza (pop. 700,000). Firmly conscious of its rich historical and artistic heritages, yet a thoroughly modern city, Zaragoza has somehow achieved harmony. The city has also managed to attract several big names. Augustus founded the city in 14 BC as a retirement colony for Roman veterans, naming it Caesaraugusta after himself. Eventually shortened to Zaragoza, the city gained everlasting fame years later when the Virgin Mary dropped in for a visit; it has been a pilgrimage site ever since. Centuries later, industrial, not spiritual, vibes drove General Motors to set up shop here, augmenting the already strong manufacturing sector. Zaragoza hums with prosperity, blessed by a beloved patron saint, *Nuestra Señora del Pilar,* and the convenience of low price tags.

⌐ GETTING THERE

Trains run to Zaragoza from **Valencia** (5hr., 2 per day, 9:15am and 3:25pm, 2475ptas) and **Barcelona** (5hr., 7 per day, 7:30am-11pm, 4000ptas). **Buses** go from **Pamplona** (2-3hr., 6 per day, 7:15am-8:30pm, 1450-1650ptas).

⚹ ORIENTATION AND PRACTICAL INFORMATION

Bordered to the north by the Río Ebro, Zaragoza is laid out like a slightly damaged bicycle wheel. Five spokes radiate from the hub at **Plaza Basilio Paraíso.** Facing the center of the plaza with the IberCaja bank building at your back, the spokes going clockwise are: Po. Sagasta; Gran Vía, which turns into Po. Fernando el Católico; Po. Pamplona, which leads to Po. María Agustín and the **train station;** Po. Independencia, which ends at **Plaza de España** (the entrance to the *casco viejo*); and Po. Constitución. To get to Pl. Paraíso from the train station, start upstairs, bear right down the ramp, and walk across Av. Anselmo Clavé. Head one block down C. General Mayandía and turn right onto Po. María Agustín. Go seven blocks; the street becomes Po. Pamplona and ends at Pl. Paraíso.

The *casco viejo* lies at the end of Po. Independencia and stretches between Pl. España and **Plaza del Pilar,** along the river. Several key museums and sights frame

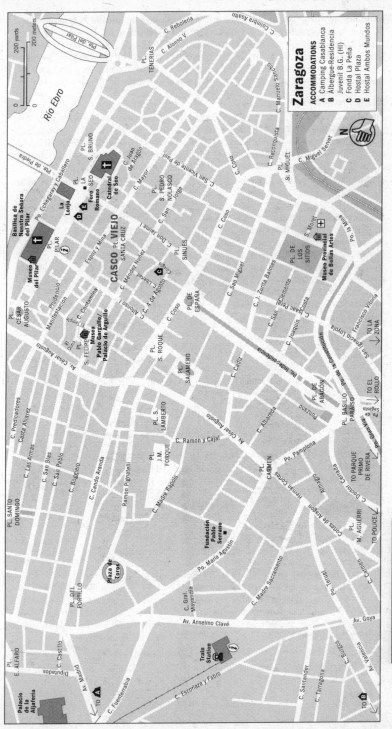

Pl. Pilar, the most central being the grandiose **Basílica de Nuestra Señora del Pilar.**
Its blue-and-yellow tiled domes make a good reference point. To reach Pl. Pilar
from Pl. Paraíso, walk down Po. Independencia to Pl. España and continue onto C.
Don Jaime I (a bit to the right), which runs to the plaza. The user-friendly bus system and city map blow-ups at major intersections make touring easy. The narrow
streets to either side of C. Conde de Aranda may be unsafe at night.

TRANSPORTATION

Airplanes: Airport (tel. 976 71 23 00). Flights to major Spanish and European cities. **Iberia,** C. Bilbao, 11 (tel. 976 21 34 18; reservations tel. 902 400 500). Open M-F
9:30am-2pm and 4-7pm, Sa 9:30am-1:30pm. **Ebrobus,** Pl. Aragón, 10 (tel. 976 32 40
09), off Pl. Paraíso at the beginning of Po. Independencia, runs to the airport (30min.,
5-7 per day, 5am-9pm, 200ptas). A taxi to the airport costs about 2000ptas.

Trains: Estación Portillo (24hr. tel. 976 28 02 02), Av. Anselmo Clavé. Taxi to Pl. Pilar
(500ptas) or bus #21 from Po. María Agustín. Info booth open 8am-9pm. The **RENFE**
office, C. San Clemente, 13 (tel. 976 28 02 02), is helpful. From Pl. Paraíso, follow Po.
Independencia 4 blocks, then turn right. Open M-F 9am-1:30pm and 4:30-8pm, Sa
9:30am-1pm. To: **Tudela** (45min., 7-15 per day, 6:30am-9:05pm, 505-580ptas);
Logroño (2¼hr., 4 per day, 6:30am-7:30pm, 1240-1400ptas); **Pamplona** (2¼hr., 5
per day, 12:02pm-4:15am, 1420ptas); **Jaca** (3hr., 2 per day, 7:15am and 3:20pm,
1375-1400ptas); **Teruel** (3hr., 3 per day, 7:50am-7:25pm, 1375-1400ptas); **Madrid**
(3hr., 8 per day, 6am-3am, 3100-3800ptas); **San Sebastián** (4hr., 2 per day, 1:45pm
and 5pm, 2800ptas); **Barcelona** (4hr., 7 per day, 12:20-9pm, 3100-3800ptas);
Valencia (6hr., 2 per day, 7:50am and 3:40pm, 2475-2580ptas).

Buses: Various bus companies dot the city, each with private terminals.

Agreda Automóvil, Po. María Agustín, 7 (tel. 976 22 93 43). Bus #21 stops in front. From
station, turn right and follow Po. María Agustín to Pl. Paraíso. Info open 7:30am-9pm. To:
Soria (2½hr.; M-Sa 5 per day, 7:30am-4:30pm; Su 1 per day, 9am; 1100ptas); **Barcelona**
(3½hr., 15-18 per day, 1am-9:30pm, 1640ptas); **Madrid** (3½hr., 15-18 per day, 4:15am-
10:30pm, 1740ptas). **Second Terminal,** Av. Valencia, 20 (tel. 976 55 45 81). Enter on
C. Lérida (bus #38). To: **Daroca** (1½hr., 2-3 per day, 7:15am-6:30pm, 720ptas).

La Oscense, Po. María Agustín, 7 (tel. 976 22 93 43). Shares terminal with Agreda
Automóvil. To **Jaca** (2¼hr., 4-6 per day, 7:15am-7:15pm, 1455ptas).

Therpasa, C. General Sueiro, 22 (tel. 976 34 31 58). From station, turn left onto C. General
Sueiro and follow for 1½ blocks, then turn left onto C. San Ignacio; after 2 blocks, turn right
into Pl. Paraíso. To **Tarazona** (1½hr., 4-5 per day, 8am-6:30pm, 670ptas).

CONDA, Av. Navarra, 79 (tel. 976 33 33 72). From station, turn right and follow Av. Navarra,
bearing left onto Av. Madrid. Cross the highway on the blue pedestrian bridge. After 2
blocks, turn right on Po. María Agustín and continue along Po. Pamplona to Pl. Paraíso. Or
take bus #25 to Po. Pamplona. To: **Tudela** (1hr., 6 per day, 7:15am-8:30pm, 700ptas);
Pamplona (2½hr., 8 per day, 7:15am-8:30pm, 1660ptas); **San Sebastián** (3¼hr., 4 per
day, 7:15am-7pm, 2350ptas).

Grupo Autobús Jimenez, C. San Juan Pablo Bonet, 13 (tel. 976 27 61 79). To get to the
station, take bus #33 from Pl. España; find the road sign for C. San Juan Pablo Bonet after
2 stops on Po. Sagasta. To **Logroño** (2hr., 3-6 per day, 7:15am-10pm, 1430ptas) and **Teruel** (3hr., 3-4 per day, 7am-7:30pm, 1340ptas).

Public Transportation: Red **TUZSA buses** (tel. 976 41 39 00) cover the city (85ptas, 10-
ride 550ptas, tickets available at any kiosk). Tourist office offers a free map of routes.
Bus #21 runs from near the train station to Po. Pamplona, Pl. Paraíso, Pl. Aragón, Pl.
España, Pl. Pilar, and then up C. San Vincente de Paúl. Bus #33 is more central, going
through Po. Sagasta, Pl. Paraíso, Po. Independencia, and Pl. España.

Taxis: Radio-Taxi Aragón (tel. 976 38 38 38). From train station to Pl. Pilar 500ptas.

Car Rental: Avis, Po. Fernando El Católico, 9 (tel. 976 35 78 63). From Pl. Paraíso, take
Gran Vía, which becomes Po. Fernando El Católico. Around 10,600ptas per day. Must
be at least 25. Open M-F 8am-1pm and 4-8pm, Sa 8am-12:45pm. **Second office** in
the train station. Open M-F 8:30am-1pm and 4-7:30pm, Sa 8:30am-1pm.

TOURIST AND FINANCIAL SERVICES

Tourist Office: Main Branch (tel. 972 20 12 00 or 902 22 12 12; fax 972 20 06 35), Pl. Pilar, in the black glass cube across from the basilica. Multilingual staff. Request the tourist map, the guide *Paseos del Color* (thematically organized walking tours), and the *guía de TAPAS*. Open M-Sa 10am-8pm, Su 10am-2pm. **Another branch** at train station. Open M-Sa 11am-2:30pm and 4:30-8pm.

Currency Exchange: Banks line Po. Independencia; **ATMs** are everywhere. **Banco Central Hispano**, Pl. Aragón, 6, has good rates on traveler's checks.

American Express: Viajes Turopa, Po. Sagasta, 47 (tel. 976 38 39 11; fax 976 25 42 44), 6 blocks from Pl. Paraíso. Bus #33 from Pl. España stops nearby. Cardholder mail held. Open M-F 9am-1:30pm and 4-8pm, Sa 9:30am-1pm.

LOCAL SERVICES

El Corte Inglés: Po. Sagasta, 3 (tel. 976 21 11 21), and Po. Independencia, 11 (tel. 976 23 86 44). Supermarket, telephones, and a free map. Open M-Sa 10am-9:30pm.

Luggage Storage: At the **train station** (small 300ptas, large 400ptas). Open 24hr. At **Agreda Automóvil** bus station, Po. María Agustín, 7 (200ptas). Open daily 8am-8pm. At the other **Agreda Automóvil,** Av. Valencia, 20 (100ptas per piece per day). Open M-F 10am-2:30pm and 4:30-8pm. At **Therpasa** bus station (100ptas). Open M-F 9am-1pm and 4:15-7:30pm, Sa 9am-12:45pm.

English Bookstore: Librería General, Po. Independencia, 22 (tel. 22 44 83). Large selection of classics. Open June-Aug. M-F 9:30am-1:30pm and 4:30-8:30pm, Sa 10am-2pm; Sept.-May M-Sa 9:30am-1:30pm and 4:30-8:30pm. Visa, MC, AmEx.

Laundromat: Lavandería Rosseli, C. San Vicente de Paul, 27 (tel. 976 29 90 34). From Pl. España, turn right on C. Coso, go 4 blocks, then head left 4½ blocks. Wash and dry 990ptas per load. Open M-F 8:30am-1:30pm and 5-8pm, Sa 8:30am-1:30pm.

EMERGENCY AND COMMUNICATIONS

Emergency: tel. 091 or 092. **Police:** Domingo Miral, s/n (tel. 091 or 092).

Medical Services: Hospital Miguel Servet, Po. Isabel La Católica, 1 (tel. 976 35 57 00). **Emergency: Ambulatorio Ramón y Cajal,** Po. María Agustín, 12 (tel. 976 43 41 11).

Post Office: Po. Independencia, 33 (tel. 976 22 80 09 or 976 22 69 52), 1 block from Pl. Aragón on the right. **Fax** and Lista de Correos (downstairs at window 4). Open M-F 8:30am-8:30pm, Sa 9:30am-2pm. **Another branch** next to train station at C. Clavé. Open M-F 8:30am-8:30pm, Sa 9:30am-1pm. **Postal Code:** 50001.

Internet Access: Pub Via Sacra, Arzobispo Domenech, 12 (tel. 976 22 04 73). From Pl. Paraíso, follow Gran Vía for 2 blocks, then make a left on Arzobispo Domenech. 500ptas for 30min., 800ptas per hr. Open daily 6pm-3am.

▐ ACCOMMODATIONS AND CAMPING

Hostels and *pensiones* pepper the narrow streets of the *casco viejo*, especially within the rectangle bounded by C. Alfonso I, C. Don Jaime I, Pl. España, and Pl. Pilar, and in the area to the right of the train station exit. Be wary the week of October 12, when Zaragoza celebrates the *Fiesta de la Virgen del Pilar*. Make reservations as early as possible and expect to pay as much as double the rates listed below. *Ferias* (trade shows) are held from February through April. The biggest is the agricultural machinery show, FIMA, usually in late April, when you may have to scour everything within a 100km radius to find a room.

Albergue-Residencia Juvenil Baltasar Gracián (HI), C. Franco y Lopez, 4 (tel. 976 55 15 04). Take bus #22 from the train station, or turn right out of the station onto Av. Clavé, take the 2nd right onto C. Burgos, walk 6 blocks, then turn right onto C. Franco y Lopez. Fifty beds in sparkling rooms of 2, 4, and 8. Must call ahead for reservations. Midnight curfew. Dorms 1055ptas, over 26 1425ptas.

Hostal Ambos Mundos, Pl. Pilar, 16 (tel. 976 29 97 04; fax 976 29 97 02), at C. Don Jaime I. Comfortable, tidy rooms with bright bedspreads, showers, and sinks. Ask for a room with a balcony overlooking the plaza. Breakfast 350ptas; other meals 1200ptas. Singles 2500ptas; doubles 4500ptas.

Fonda La Peña, C. Cinegio, 3 (tel. 976 29 90 89). Decent rooms, all with bath, kept by pleasant owners. No reservations. Singles 1500ptas; doubles 3000ptas.

Hostal Plaza, Pl. Pilar, 14 (tel. 976 29 48 30 or 976 28 48 39; fax 976 39 94 06). Immaculate rooms on the pricier side, all with phones and TV. English and French spoken. Singles 3500ptas, with shower 4500ptas; doubles with bath 5900ptas.

Camping: Casablanca (tel. 976 75 38 70), Barrio Valdefierro, down Cra. Madrid. Bus #36 from Pl. Pilar or Pl. España to the suburb of Valdefierro. Ask the driver to let you off at the campsite, as it's notoriously difficult to find. By car, take the road to Madrid to the Valdefierro Exit (km 316, from there follow the signs). Good facilities, including a pool open in summer. July-Aug. 600ptas per person, per tent, and per car; Sept-Oct. 15 and Apr.-June 545ptas.

⬛ FOOD

Hungry budget travelers will love Zaragoza's *casco viejo. Tapas* bars, inexpensive restaurants, and *bocadillo* factories crowd the area known as **El Tubo** (C. Mártires, C. Cinegio, C. 4 de Agosto, and C. Estébanes). The tourist office gives out a *guía de TAPAS,* which lists *tapas* bars, many clustered around Pl. Santa Marta (to the right and behind the Catedral del Seo). The **market** thrives in the long green building on Av. César Augusto off Pl. Pilar (open M-Sa 9am-2pm and 5-8pm). Zaragoza's oldest bakery, **Fantoba,** C. Don Jaime, 21 (tel. 976 29 85 24), tempts with scrumptious pastries and chocolate-dipped fruits (open M-Sa 10am-2pm and 5-9pm). **Supermarket** shoppers can refuel at **Galerías Primero,** C. San Jorge, the continuation of C. Merdeo Nuñez (open M-Sa 9am-2pm and 5-8:30pm).

Bar Los Amigos, C. Mártires, 8 (tel. 976 39 25 14), off Pl. España. A snug hole in the wall with a massive selection of sandwiches at unbeatable prices (250-475ptas). Tantalizing *tapas* platter. Open daily noon-3pm and 7-11pm.

Casa Pascualillo, C. Libertad, 5 (tel. 976 39 72 03). In the El Tubo district, off C. Méndez Nuñez. Filling, homestyle meals served in a lively atmosphere. *Menú* 900ptas. Open Tu-Sa 1-4pm and 8-11pm, Su 1-4pm. Visa, MC, AmEx.

La Zanahoria, C. Tarragona, 4 (tel. 976 35 87 94). From Pl. Paraíso, take Gran Vía, turn right on Av. Goya, then take the 1st left after crossing Av. Teruel/Valencia. Yuppie vegetarians enjoy excellent salads and quiches. *Menú* 1000ptas, entrees 950ptas. Open daily 1:30-4pm and 9-11:30pm. Visa, MC.

⬛ SIGHTS

PLAZA DEL PILAR

Pl. Pilar, a vast square surrounded by a unique combination of architectural styles, is Zaragoza at its best. It is also the perfect place to begin a tour of the old city.

⬛BASÍLICA DE NUESTRA SEÑORA DEL PILAR. The Basílica de Nuestra Señora del Pilar, the patroness after whom millions of Spanish women are named, dominates Pl. Pilar. Its massive Baroque structure (begun in 1681) defines the skyline with brightly colored tiled domes; the inside is even more incredible, with frescoes by Goya, González Velázquez, and Francisco Bayeau. Evidence of the miraculous abounds. Two bombs (now on display) were dropped on the basilica during the Civil War but failed to explode, obviously due to the divine intervention of the Virgin. A small piece of the basilica's original pillar is surrounded by a gold plate, which the faithful—like Pope John Paul II (who visited in 1986)—kiss. The **Museo del Pilar** exhibits the glittering *joyero de la Virgen* (Virgin's jewels) and preliminary paintings of the ceiling frescoes. Don't leave without seeing the panoramic view of Zaragoza from one of the towers. The **elevator** is located in the corner, on the left when facing the Museo del Pilar. *(Basilica open daily 5:45am-9:30pm. Free. Museum tel. 976 39 74 97. Open daily 9am-2pm and 4-6pm. 200ptas. Elevator open June-Aug. Sa-Th 9:30am-2pm and 4-7pm; Sept.-May Sa-Th 9:30am-2pm and 4-6pm. 200ptas.)*

OTHER SIGHTS. On the left as you exit the basilica is Zaragoza's town hall. Next to the town hall is the Renaissance **La Lonja,** which hosts occasional art exhibits. *(Open M-Sa 10am-2pm and 5-9pm, Su 10am-2pm.)* In front of La Lonja is an outdoor **monument** where statues portray scenes from Goya's paintings. On the other side of C. Don Jaime I, a large glass-and-marble cube houses the entrance to the **Foro Romano.** Excavated ruins lurk underground, along with a 19-minute movie (in Spanish) on the site's history. *(Tel. 976 39 97 52. Open Tu-Sa 10am-2pm and 5-8pm, Su 10am-2pm. Visits begin on the hr. 400ptas, students 200ptas, over 65 and under 8 free.)*

ELSEWHERE

Zaragoza's sights are not limited to Pl. Pilar. Other points of interest are spread throughout the city. When in doubt, head to the tourist office.

▨PALACIO DE LA ALJAFERÍA. Following the Muslim conquest of the Iberian Peninsula in the 8th century, a crisis over succession smashed the kingdom into petty tributary states called *taifas.* The Palacio de la Aljafería is the principle relic of Aragón's Moorish *taifa.* Renovations have somewhat encumbered the building's original grace, but its awesome stone exterior and exquisite interior still impress. The ground floor has a distinctly Moorish flavor that contrasts starkly with the Gothic second floor. The fortified tower imprisoned *el trovador* in García Gutierrez's drama of the same name, the inspiration for Verdi's opera *Il Trovatore.* *(C. Castillo. Take bus #21 and 33. Or head left on C. Coso from Pl. España; facing the casco viejo, continue onto Conde Aranda, make a right onto Pl. Maria Agustín and a left onto C. Aliaferia. Tel. 976 28 95 28. Open Apr. 15-Oct. 15. M-W and Sa 10am-2pm and 4:30-8pm, F 4:30-8pm, Su 10am-2pm; Oct. 16-Apr. 14 M-W 10am-2pm and 4-6:30pm, F 4-6:30pm, Su 10am-2pm. 300ptas, students and seniors 150ptas, under 12 free.)*

MUSEO PROVINCIAL DE BELLAS ARTES. In addition to an extensive collection of medieval Aragonese paintings, the Museo Provincial de Bellas Artes (within the Museum of Zaragoza) hangs a selection of works by Goya, including a collection of excellent drawings. *(Pl. Los Sitios, 6. From Pl. España, follow Po. Independencia about 5 blocks, turn left and go 5 more blocks on C. Joaquín Costa. Turn left at Pl. Sitios; the museum is on the right. Tel. 976 22 21 81. Open Tu-Sa 10am-2pm and 5-10pm, Su 10am-2pm; special exhibits 4-8pm. Free.)*

MUSEO PABLO GARGALLO. The Museo Pablo Gargallo, dedicated to one of the most innovative sculptors of the 1920s, houses a small but marvelous collection of his works in the graceful **Palacio de Arguillo,** which was built in 1670. *(From Pl. España, walk down C. Don Jaime I and turn left on C. Ménendez Nuñez. The museum is 5 blocks down in Pl. San Felipe. Open Tu-Sa 10am-2pm and 5-9pm, Su 10am-2pm. Free.)*

FUNDACIÓN PABLO SERRANO. House many bronze sculptures by the fascinating Pablo Serrano (1908-1985). Look for *Gran pan partido (Big Bread Parted)* and sculptural reinterpretations of works by Picasso, Velázquez, and Goya. *(Po. María Agustín, 26. Open June-Aug. M and W-Sa 10am-2pm and 6-9pm, Su 10am-2pm; Sept.-May M and W-Sa 10am-2pm and 5-8pm, Su 10am-2pm. Free.)*

♫ ENTERTAINMENT

Young Zaragozans brag that their city has *mucha marcha* (lots of nightlife). They're right. The scene begins in **La Zona**—the streets bounded by Po. Constitución, C. León XIII, Po. Damas, and Camino de las Torres. Gulping beer from *litros* (about 400ptas) is the primary sport around **El Rollo,** the zone bounded by C. Moncasi, C. Bonet, and C. Maestro Marquina at the southern end of Po. Sagasta. University students storm Po. Sagasta and its offshoot, C. Zumalacárregui. Around midnight, herds of *casco viejo*-goers move into the market area around Pl. San Felipe. Gay bars and discos are situated around the west side of the *casco viejo:* **Atuaire,** C. Contamina, 13, and **Sphinx,** C. Ramón y Cajal, are long-standing favorites. **La Casa del Loco,** C. Mayor, 16, has frequent concerts and a range of music for its international, 20- to 30-year-old crowd (open around 10pm-5am; free). **Oasis,** C. Boggiero, may open its doors to people of all ages, but it also opens their wallets (1100ptas for men, includes 1 drink; free for women. Open 1pm-7am.) **Kitsch,** C. Fernando el Católico, is full of 20-somethings (cover 1000-1500ptas).

The city erupts for a week of unbridled craziness around October 12 in honor of *La Virgen Santa del Pilar,* one of the few full-blown autumn *fiestas.* You may not find lodging, but then again, you may not need it. City patrons **San Valero** (Jan. 29) and **San Jorge** (Apr. 23) are also celebrated.

DAYTRIPS FROM ZARAGOZA

Ask at the Zaragoza tourist office for info on excursions like the *Ruta del Vino* (wine route) and the *Ruta de Goya.* **Teruel** (p. 376) and **Tarazona** (p. 375) are both good daytrips from Zaragoza. Fans of all things Romanesque should inquire about visits to the **Cinco Villas** (five villages).

MONASTERIO DE PIEDRA

An oasis of waterfalls and trees springs out of the dry plain around the Monasterio de Piedra, about 110km southwest of Zaragoza. Founded in 1195 by an order of Cistercian monks from Tarragona, and abandoned under government orders in 1835, the monastery is now a three-star hotel. The 12th-century **Torre del Homenaje,** the only part of the existing building that hasn't been restored, still towers over the valley. (Tel. 976 84 90 11. Open daily 9am-9pm.) The main attraction is the surrounding park and the **Río Piedra,** which casts off waterfalls and lakes as it plunges down the valley. Follow the path leading through, under, and around this aquatic paradise. (Park open daily 9am-nightfall. 1000ptas for monastery and park.) **Aragón Tours** buses, C. Almagro, 18 (tel. 976 21 93 20), leave from Zaragoza to the monastery (July-Oct. 15; Tu, Th, Sa 9am; return same day at 5pm; round-trip 2220ptas).

DAROCA

Burros and wagons still wander the streets of Daroca (pop. 2400). The town rests in a dramatic gorge; its burnt-sienna roofs match the surrounding cliffs. The town's main artery, **Calle Mayor,** runs uphill from the **Puerta Baja** (lower gate) to the **Puerta Alta** (upper gate). Daroca's walls, four km in circumference, were started in the 9th century; at one time they were home to 114 towers. Dirt paths trace along the walls and reward hikers with a sentry's-eye view of the town and surrounding valleys. **La Ruta de Castillo** reveals a spectacular view of Daroca and neighbors (45min.); **La Ruta de las Murallas** does the whole tour in two hours. Both routes start outside Puerta Alta; the tourist office has a map.

Buses to **Zaragoza** (1½hr., 3 per day, 8-4:30pm, 720ptas) and **Teruel** (M-Sa 4 per day, 8:15am-7:40pm) depart from **Mesón Felix,** C. Mayor, near Puerta Baja. Buses arriving in Daroca, the last stop on the Agreda Automóvil line, halt near Puerta Baja. The **tourist office,** Pl. España, 4 (tel. 976 80 01 29), is opposite Colegiata de Santa María. From Puerta Alta, walk down C. Mayor for four or five blocks and hang a right on C. San Juan de la Huerta. (Open June-Aug. M-F 9:30am-2pm and 6-8pm, Sa-Su 11am-2pm and 5-6pm; Sept.-May M-F 11am-2pm, Sa-Su 11am-2pm and 5-6pm.) Although Daroca works best as a daytrip, sleepy travelers should try the comfortable **Pensión El Ruejo,** C. Mayor, 88 (tel. 976 80 09 62), with modern rooms, heating, A/C, a disco, and a flowering courtyard. Inquire at the bar downstairs after 9am (singles 2000ptas; doubles 3500ptas, with bath 4500ptas). The **restaurant** on the first floor serves a satisfying 1100pta *menú.* Picnickers can stock up at **%Día,** the supermarket on C. Mayor (open M-Sa 9:30am-2pm and 5-8pm).

The main sight in town is the icon-filled museum of the **Colegiata de Santa María,** a 16th-century Renaissance church. To get there, take C. Juan de la Huerta from C.

Mayor. (Open June-Aug. Tu-Sa 11am-1pm and 5:30-8pm, Su 1hr. before Mass at 11:30am and 7pm; Sept.-May Tu-Sa noon-1pm and 5:30-7pm, Su 1hr. before Mass at 11:30am and 6pm. Museum 300ptas. The tourist office arranges guided tours.) Little Daroca puts on a good party during its week-long **Fiesta de Corpus Christi,** held every year in late May or early June. The town also hosts the annual **International Program for Ancient Music** during the first two weeks of August. Musicians from the world over gather to teach, learn, and give free concerts.

TARAZONA

Because of the predominance of Moorish architecture, Tarazona (pop. 10,500) is known as the "Mudéjar City." Some even liken the winding streets of *El Cinto,* the medieval quarter, to those in Toledo—Tarazona, though, is much less touristed and the Arab influence somewhat less apparent. The town makes a nice daytrip from Zaragoza, especially during the **Tarazona Foto** festival (mid-July to mid-Aug.).

7 PRACTICAL INFORMATION. Therpasa buses (tel. 976 64 11 00) run from the station on Av. Navarra to **Soria** (1hr., 4-8 per day, 7:45am-9:45pm, 550ptas) and **Zaragoza** (1hr., 4-7 per day, 7am-9pm, 670ptas). **Conda buses** leave from Parque de Estación (up C. Carrera Zaragoza from Pl. San Francisco) to **Tudela** (1hr., M-Sa 5 per day, 8am-6:30pm, 225ptas); buy tickets on the bus. The very helpful **tourist office,** C. Iglesias, 5 (tel. 976 64 00 74), sits alongside the cathedral. From the Therpasa bus station, turn right on Av. Navarra, and at the circular Pl. San Francisco follow the Soria/Zaragoza signs on C. Martínez to the tree-shaded Pl. Seo; turn left and go up the steps. (Open M-F 9am-1:30pm and 4:30-7pm, Sa-Su 10am-2pm and 4-7pm.) **Banco Central Hispano,** in Pl. San Francisco (open May-Sept. M-F 8:30am-2:30pm; Oct.-Apr. M-F 8:30am-2:30pm, Sa 8:30am-1pm); **luggage storage,** at the Therpasa bus station (open daily 7am-1pm and 2-10pm; free). **Medical emergencies: Ambulatorio San Atilano,** Av. Paz, 29 (tel. 976 64 12 85); **municipal police** (tel. 976 64 16 91, emergency tel. 091 or 092), on Pl. San Francisco, provides maps when the tourist office is closed. **Post office** (tel. 976 64 13 17), at Pl. Seo downhill from the cathedral (open M-F 8:30am-2:30pm, Sa 9:30am-1pm); **postal code:** 50500.

ʄ☐ ACCOMMODATIONS AND FOOD. Options for lodging are scant, but **Hostal Palacete de los Arcedianos,** C. Marrodán, 16 (tel. 976 64 09 45 or 919 94 60 22), is pleasant. To get there, start with your back to the bank in Pl. San Francisco and head right along the river on Po. Constitución. Take the second right onto C. Marrodán, and enter through the doorway on the left under the Centro de Estudios sign. Comfortable rooms and tidy bathrooms lie off a stairway with a vaulted ceiling (singles 3000ptas; doubles 4500ptas). A second option and probably a more comfortable one, with TVs, bathrooms, and A/C, is **Brujas de Becquer Hotel,** Teresa Cajul, 30 (tel. 976 64 04 04 or 976 64 04 00; fax 976 64 01 48; singles 4200ptas; doubles 6250ptas; prices decrease Nov.-May; Visa, MC, AmEx, traveler's checks). **Día,** on the corner of C. Quiñones and C. Visconti, just off Pl. San Francisco, sells groceries (open M-Sa 9am-2pm and 5:30-8:30pm). Restaurant options include **Hotel/ Restaurante Ituri-Asso,** C. Virgen del Río, 3 (tel. 976 64 31 96), with a tasty and original *menú* for 1200ptas (open M-F 1-4 and 9-11pm, Sa 1-4 and 9-11:30pm, Su 1-4pm; Visa, MC, AmEx). **S'ha Feito...Taverna,** Pl. Toros, 18, is a new bar with faux historic decor. It is run by hip youngsters serving traditional Aragonese *tapas* and *bocadillos* (300-550ptas; open M-F noon-4pm and 6-11pm, Sa-Su noon-11pm).

▣ SIGHTS. The splendid Gothic 13th- to 15th-century **▨cathedral** is undergoing painstaking restorations. The glorious towers, belfry, lantern, and plasterwork in the inner cloister are fine examples of *Mudéjar* work. The cloister may be open by the time you read this, but the interior could take up to 15 years to complete. The quirky, octagonal **Plaza de Toros Vieja** was built in the 18th century to include private residences. To get there from the cathedral, follow signs to Soria/Zaragoza down C. Laureles, turn right at the Olympia Gym, and pass through the arch.

NORTHEASTERN SPAIN

Tarazona was a seasonal residence of Aragonese kings until the 15th century. Their Alcázar has since served as the **Palacio Episcopal,** usually closed to visitors. Now the bishop's workplace, the palace lies across the bridge from the Pl. Toros Vieja; go left one block and then up the zig-zagging stairs of the Recodos and Rúa Baja. Opposite the Palacio Episcopal, in the heart of *El Cinto* (the medieval quarter), rises the **Iglesia de Santa Magdalena,** with a graceful *Mudéjar* tower that hovers over the old town. To enter, take a left up Cuesta del Palacio from the Palacio Episcopal and take the first left (open only for mass; inquire at tourist office).

NEAR TARAZONA: MONASTERIO DE VERUELA

Travelers with cars can visit the enchanting walled monastery of Veruela, which slumbers in the Sierra de Moncayo, 15km south of Tarazona. Its golden stone walls guard a Romanesque-Gothic church (tel. 976 64 90 25) and a transcendentally peaceful cloister. Nineteenth-century poet Gustavo Adolfo Bécquer wrote his *Cartas desde mi celda (Letters from My Cell)* within these walls. (Grounds open Apr.1-Sept.30 Tu-Su 10am-2pm and 4-7pm; Oct.1-Mar.31 Tu-Su 10am-1pm and 3-6pm. 300ptas.) **Buses** on their way to Alcalá de Moncayo might stop at the monastery if you ask the driver before departure from Tarazona. Buses also run to Vera de Moncaya, 4km from the monastery. For more info, ask at the tourist office in Tarazona.

TERUEL

A sleepy town that becomes even sleepier during the afternoon *siesta*, the provincial capital of Teruel (pop. 28,000) practices traditional Spanish habits that belie its cosmopolitan history. From the 12th to the 15th centuries, Muslims, Jews, and Christians lived here in cultural collusion. The resulting Mudéjar architecture blends characteristically Arab patterns with Gothic and Romanesque touches. An easy stopover between Valencia and Zaragoza, Teruel doesn't really reach its prime until July, when citizens celebrate the resilience of their dear *torico* (iron bull) in an 168-hour anarchic liquor fest.

7 **ORIENTATION AND PRACTICAL INFORMATION.** Teruel's somewhat nonsensical layout can be confusing. The *casco viejo* perches on a hilltop, linked to modern Teruel by bridges. The center of the *casco* is **Plaza de Carlos Castell,** affectionately known as **Plaza del Torico.** To reach Pl. Torico from the **train station,** take the staircase from the park and follow signs to the *centro*. To get to Pl. Torico from the new **bus station,** get on C. Judería and make the second left onto C. Hartzembusch, which zigzags to the plaza. **Trains** leave from Camino de la Estación, 1 (tel. 978 61 02 02), down the stairs from Pl. Ovalo. To: **Mora de Rubielos** (45min., 3 per day, 6:35am-6:17pm, 400ptas); **Rubielos de Mora** (50min., 1 per day, 7:30am, 400ptas); **Valencia** (2¾hr., 3 per day, 7:30am-6:20pm, 1240-2200ptas); **Zaragoza** (3hr., 3 per day, 6:35am-6:17pm, 1375ptas). **Buses** leave from the new **station** (tel. 978 60 10 14), Ronda de Ambeles, only a few blocks from the *casco viejo*. **La Rápida** (tel. 978 60 20 04) to **Barcelona** (5½-6½hr., 1 per day, 8:30am, 3186ptas). **Samar** (tel. 978 60 34 50) to **Valencia** (2-3hr.; 3-5 per day; M-Sa 7:15am-7pm, Su 8am-7pm; 1120ptas) and **Madrid** (5hr., 2-3 per day, M-F 7:30am-5pm, 2345ptas). **Magallón** (tel. 976 41 72 52) and **Jiménez** (tel. 978 60 10 40) to **Zaragoza** (Magallón: M-Sa 2 per day, 6:30am and 2:30pm; Su 1 per day, 3:30pm; Jiménez: 4 per day, 7am-7pm). **Ruelilla** (tel. 978 60 57 01) to **Albarracín** (45min., 1 per day, M-F 5:30pm, Su 2:15pm). **Furio** (tel. 964 60 01 00) to **Mora de Rubielos** (1hr., 1 per day, 2:30pm) and **Rubielos de Mora** (1½hr., 1 per day, 2:30pm). To rent a car, call **BMW** (tel. 978 60 65 36).

The **tourist office** is at C. Tomás Nogues, 1 (tel. 978 60 22 79). From Pl. Torico, follow C. Ramón y Cajal (C. San Juan) and take the first left; the office is one block away on the right. (Open June-Aug. M 9am-2:30pm, Tu-Sa 8am-2pm and 4:30-9:30pm, Su 10am-2pm; Sept.-May M and Sa 9am-1:30pm, 5-7:30pm, Tu-F 8am-2:30pm and 4:30-7:30pm). **Luggage storage** is available at lockers in the train station (400ptas) or at the bus station (100ptas per piece per day; both open daily 6:30am-10:30pm). **Banco Central Hispano,** Pl. Torico, 15 (open M-F 8:30am-2:30pm; Oct.-

STAR-CROSSED LOVERS The tombs of Diego de Marcilla and Isabel de Segura in the **Mausoleo de los Amantes,** next to Torre San Pedro, are the source of Teruel's nickname: *ciudad de los amantes* (city of lovers). The story began when Diego left Teruel to make his fortune and prove his worth to Isabel's affluent family. Five years later, he returned a rich man, just in time to watch Isabel marry his childhood rival. Diego begged for one last kiss but was refused; he immediately died of grief. At the funeral, Isabel kissed the corpse and overcome with sorrow, died herself. The lovers are commemorated with life-size statues of the lovers, reaching out over to touch hands, but not quite making it. For a peek at the lover's remains, duck down near their heads. (From Pl. Torico, take the alleyway to the left of the purple *modernista* house. Stairs lead directly to the mausoleum. Open M-Sa 10am-2pm and 5-7:30pm, Su 10:30am-2pm and 5-7:30pm. 50ptas.)

May also Sa 8:30am-1pm). **Emergency:** tel. 091 or 092. The **post office,** C. Yagüe de Salas, 17 (tel. 978 60 76 86), can send **faxes** (open M-F 8:30am-8:30pm, Sa 9:30am-2pm); **postal code:** 44001; **internet access: Pub Lennon,** C. San Andres, 23 (tel. 978 60 19 70; 700ptas per hr.; open daily June-Aug. 7pm-2am, Sept.-May 3pm-2am).

⌂⌂ ACCOMMODATIONS AND FOOD. Lodgings are scarce during August and *Semana Santa* and impossible during *fiesta*-time in early July. Try **Hostal Aragón,** C. Santa María, 4 (tel. 978 60 13 87). Head in the direction the Torico faces, and take the first left as you leave Pl. Torico. It offers attractive hotel-quality rooms at hostel prices; all rooms have TV. (English spoken. Singles 2000ptas, with bath 3000ptas; doubles 3200ptas, with bath 4900ptas; triples with bath 7000ptas.) Or **Fonda el Tozal,** C. Rincón, 5 (tel. 978 60 10 22), two blocks past Hostal Aragón. Under constant restoration, the building dates from the early 1500s. (Singles 1500ptas, with bath 2500ptas; doubles 3000ptas, with bath 4500ptas; triples 4500ptas, with bath 6000-6500.) Teruel is famous for its salty, flavorful cured ham, *jamón de Teruel,* featured in *tapas* bars in Pl. Torico. Restaurant standards and prices are high; the *casco viejo* is the place to look. **Restaurante La Parrilla,** C. Esteban, 2 (tel. 978 60 59 17), two blocks uphill from the tourist office, has a magnificent 1300pta *menú* with succulent meats grilled on a stone fireplace (open M-Sa 2-5pm and 8-11:30pm, Su noon-5pm; Visa, MC). There is a **market** on Pl. Domingo Gascón; from Pl. Torico, take C. Joaquín Costa/Tozal (open M-Sa 8am-1:30pm).

◉ SIGHTS. The mother of all of Teruel's Mudéjar monuments is the 13th-century **▨Catedral de Santa María de Mediavilla.** The magnificently decorated brick tower is a mere preface to the 14th-century stylized *artesonado mudéjar* (Mudéjar coffered ceiling) roofing the central nave. (All roads left of Pl. Torico lead one block away to Pl. Catedral. Open daily 11am-2pm and 4-8pm. 300ptas with mandatory guide.) Muslim artisans built the brick-and-glazed-tile **Torres Mudéjares** (Mudéjar Towers) between the 12th and 15th centuries, then Christian churches adapted Almohad minarets to their own purposes. The most intricately designed of the three towers are the richly tiled, 14th-century **Torre de San Martín,** in Pl. Pérez Prado near the post office, and the 13th-century **Torre de San Salvador,** on C. Salvador. In the latter, 123 skinny steps climb through several chambers to the panoramic belltower above (San Salvador open July-Sept. daily 11am-2pm and 5-7pm; Oct.-June Sa 11am-2pm and 5-7pm, Su 11am-2pm. 200ptas.) Behind the cathedral, the ethnographic- and archaeology-oriented **Museo Provincial** rests in the 16th-century porticoed Casa de la Comunidad. (Pl. Fray Anselmo Polanco. Tel. 978 64 74 00. Open Tu-F 10am-2pm and 4-7pm, Sa-Su 10am-2pm. Free.)

DAYTRIPS FROM TERUEL

Protected by ancient walls, medieval townships in Teruel's countryside stand amid acres of wild land. Getting to these mystical hamlets is less of an ordeal now that **Regionales** trains from Teruel, Valencia, and Zaragoza make the journey. Only one bus per day ventures from Teruel and returns the next morning. Unless you have a car—there is only one rental agency in Teruel—you'll have to spend the night. The almighty *Guía de servicios turísticos*, available at any Aragonese tourist office, has information on accommodations in the area.

RUBIELOS DE MORA. Local connoisseurs insist that the most exquisite of the medieval towns around Teruel is Rubielos de Mora (pop. 600), 15km east of Mora de Rubielos. Residents live in an unrestored and unscathed architectural set-piece from medieval days, complete with two city gates and a 16th-century town hall (with the usual courtyard and dungeon). The **tourist office** is in the Ayuntamiento building, Pl. Hispano América, 1 (tel. 978 80 40 96; open July-Aug. 10am-2pm and 5-7pm; Sept.-June M-F 10am-2pm). **Trains** run to Rubielos de Mora from **Teruel** (1 per day) and **Valencia** (1 per day).

MORA DE RUBIELOS. Forty-two km east of Teruel, Mora de Rubielos has the area's largest and best-preserved 15th-century castle. The **bus** is the best way to get here—**Furio** vehicles (tel. 964 60 01 00) roll into town from Valencia and Teruel. Though the station is 14km away, **trains** run to Mora de Rubielos from **Valencia** (3 per day), **Zaragoza** (3 per day), and **Teruel** (3 per day). In the summer, a **tourist office** (tel. 978 80 00 00) sets up on C. Diputación.

ALBARRACÍN. Thirty-five km west of Teruel, the former Moorish city of Albarracín (pop. under 1000) still lives off the fading grandeur of its stone houses, small churches, and dispersed towers. The **tourist office,** Pl. Mayor, 1 (tel. 978 71 02 51), will direct you to tours of the *pinturas rupestres,* post-Paleolithic cave paintings dating from 5000 BC. (Open July-Sept. M-Sa 10am-2pm and 5-7:30pm, Su 10am-2pm. Free tours daily at 2:30 and 5:30pm. Oct.-June consult the **Ayuntamiento** at tel. 978 71 02 51; open M-F 9am-3pm.)

ARAGONESE PYRENEES

Historians look at the Aragonese Pyrenees, note the infrequency with which northern enemies have invaded Spain, and say it all makes sense. Everyone else looks and can't say a word. Their jagged cliff faces, deep gorges, icy rivers, and alpine meadows have awed humans for centuries. Despite limited train and bus transportation, the area draws both casual hikers and mountaineering veterans to its famous peaks. To truly enjoy the area, explore the cobbled streets and meandering trails of outlying villages and valleys. The region's spectacular features crescendo at the magical **Parque Nacional de Ordesa**. In summer, the Aragonese Pyrenees are a climber's fantasy. In winter, skiers find their own bliss. Five major resorts—Astún, Panticosa, Formigal, Cerler, and Candanchú—lie at their pole-tips. The pamphlets *Ski Aragón* and *El Turismo de Nieve en España,* free at tourist offices, give the low-down on each one. **Huesca** and **Jaca** provide limited access to the area by bus, but the most efficient and enjoyable way to explore the valleys is by car.

JACA

For centuries, pilgrims bound for Santiago would cross the Pyrenees into Spain, nest in Jaca (pop. 14,000) for the night, and be off by sunrise. They had the right idea. Although Jaca served a brief stint as capital of Aragón (1035-1095), there is little to do here but organize excursions into the Pyrenees and nearby ski resorts.

◪ ORIENTATION AND PRACTICAL INFORMATION. Buses drop passengers on Av. Jacetania, at the edge of the city center. From the **bus station,** walk straight through the plaza to C. Zocotin and go straight for two blocks to reach the city's central artery **Calle Mayor**. The shuttle bus from the **train station** drops passengers off at the **Ayuntamiento,** in the middle of C. Mayor, or at the intersection of C. Mayor and Av. Regimiento de Galicia. Shuttle buses run from downtown to the **train station** roughly 30min. before each train leaves. They depart from the Ayuntamiento on C. Mayor or, if C. Mayor is closed, from the taxi stop next to C. Mayor and the bus station. If you're walking to town from the station, take Av. Juan XXIII until its end, turn left on C. Francia and continue straight for about 6 blocks as it becomes C. Primer Viernes; then make a left onto C. Mayor. **RENFE,** C. Estación, s/n (tel. 974 36 13 32; ticket booth open 10am-noon and 5-7pm) runs to **Zaragoza** (3hr., 2 per day, 7:36am-6:12pm, 1325ptas) and **Madrid** (7hr., 1 per day, 3:30pm, 4200ptas). **La Oscense buses** (tel. 974 35 50 60) run to: **Zaragoza** (2hr., 1 per day, 1460ptas); **Pamplona** (2hr., 1 per day, 4:30pm, 860ptas); **Sabiñánigo** (20min., 1 per day, 11am, 185ptas), where **Empresa Hudebus** (tel. 974 21 32 77) connects to **Torla,** near Ordesa and Aínsa. **Josefa Escartín** (tel. 974 36 05 08) runs 1 bus (M-Sa 6:30pm) to: **Hecho** (55min., 400ptas); **Siresa** (1hr., 425ptas); **Ansó** (1½hr., 500ptas). **Taxis** (tel. 974 36 28 48) line up at the intersection of C. Mayor, Av. Regimiento Galicia, and Av. Viernes de Mayo. For **car rental,** try **Europcar** (tel. 974 35 50 60), in Huesca. You must be 21 and have had a license for at least one year.

The English-speaking staff at the **tourist office,** Av. Regimiento de Galicia, 2 (tel. 974 36 00 98), off C. Mayor, offers useful maps and hiking advice. (Open July-Aug. M-F 9am-2pm and 4:30-8pm, Sa 10am-1:30pm and 5-8pm, Su 10am-1:30pm; Sept.-June M-F 9am-1:30pm and 4:30-7pm, Sa 10am-1pm and 5-7pm.) For **ski rental,** head to **Nieve Sport,** Av. Francia, 33 (tel. 974 36 35 72). For **adventure tourism,** try **Alcorce,** Av. Regimiento Galicia, 1 (tel./fax 974 36 39 72; email alcorce-pirineos@encomix.es), across from the tourist office, which organizes hiking, rock climbing, spelunking, and rafting trips. (Guided hiking trips start at 3000ptas per person per day; rafting at 5500ptas. Open M-Sa 10am-1:30pm and 5-8:30pm, later July-Aug.) A **Banco Central Hispano** is on C. Primer Viernes de Mayo, at the corner of C. Mayor (open M-F 8:30am-2:30pm). For **ski conditions,** call **Teléfono Blanco** (tel. 976 20 11 12) or the resorts. **Police,** C. Mayor, 24 (tel. 091 or 092), in the Ayuntamiento; **medical services: Centro de Salud,** Po. Constitución, 6 (tel. 974 36 07 95). **Post office,** C. Correos, 13 (tel. 974 36 00 85), off Av. Regimiento de Galicia, across from the tourist office (open M-F 8:30am-2:30pm, Sa 9:30am-1pm); **postal code:** 22700.

▐▐ ACCOMMODATIONS, CAMPING, AND FOOD. Jaca's hostels and *pensiones* cluster around C. Mayor and the cathedral. Lodgings are scarce only during the bi-annual *Festival Folklórico* in late July and early August. For Santiago-bound pilgrims, the **Albergue de Peregrinos** is on C. Hospital. Other visitors might try the **Albergue Juvenil de Escuelas Pias (HI),** Av. Perimetral, 6 (tel. 974 36 05 36). From C. Mayor, turn left onto C. Regimiento de Galicia and left again on Av. Perimetral. On the right side of the road after the long bend, turn off on the unmarked dirt driveway before the sports center. The hostel has rows of red-shuttered bungalows, rooms with 2, 3, or 4 beds and sinks, and clean bathrooms. (Breakfast 250ptas. Midnight curfew. 1300ptas per person, over 26 1500ptas. Nonmembers pay 400ptas more.) Or try **Habitaciones Martínez,** C. Mayor, 53 (tel. 974 36 33 74), above a bar. To avoid the smell of cigarettes, request a balcony. (Singles 1500ptas; doubles 3000ptas.) **Camping Peña Oroel** (tel. 974 36 02 15), 3½km down the road to Sabiñánigo, has wooded grounds along a riverbank, complete with a market and swimming pool. (650ptas per person, per tent, per car. Open *Semana Santa* and mid-June to mid-Sept.)

Restaurants offering *menús* and *tapas* are located off C. Mayor; those lining Av. Primer Viernes de Mayo serve *bocadillos* and *platos combinados*. Groceries are available at **Supermercado ALDI,** C. Correos, 9, next to the post office (open M-Sa 9:30am-1:30pm and 5-8pm). **Restaurante Vegetariano El Arco,** C. San Nicolas, 4, off the bus station plaza, serves a tasty vegetarian *menú* (1200ptas) which changes daily (entrees 850ptas; open M-Sa 1:30-3pm and 8:30-11pm).

NORTHEASTERN SPAIN

⚄🖾 SIGHTS AND ENTERTAINMENT. The pentagonal fortress referred to as **La Ciudadela** (tel. 974 36 04 43) or Castillo de San Pedro lines Av. Primer Viernes de Mayo. Begun by King Felipe II in 1595, the citadel originally served to protect Jaca from French Huguenot attacks. It was last used during the Civil War, when the original canons were melted down for ammunition. (Open daily July-Aug. 11am-12:30pm and 5-6:30pm; Sept.-June 11am-noon and 5-6pm. By tour only. 300ptas, under 15 100ptas.) The Romanesque **cathedral** (tel./fax 974 35 63 78) is modestly noteworthy and houses the **Museo Diocesno.** Started in 1063, it served as the model for most local churches. (Cathedral open daily 10am-1:30pm and 4-8pm. Free. Museum open daily June-Oct. 10am-2pm and 4-9pm; Sept.-May 11am-1:30pm and 4-6:30pm. 300ptas.) Jaca's biggest **fiesta** (in honor of **Santa Orosia**) falls on June 23-29.

DAYTRIPS FROM JACA

MONASTERIO DE SAN JUAN DE LA PEÑA. The spectacular **Monasterio de San Juan de la Peña** (tel. 974 35 51 19 or 974 35 51 45; fax 974 35 50 89) is difficult to reach—it was designed that way. Determined hermits hid the original monastery in a canyon 22km from Jaca and maintained such extreme privacy that invading Moors never discovered it or the Holy Grail (supposedly concealed here for three centuries). It's worth a visit, both for the 10th-century underground church carved directly into the rock and the 12th-century cloister dwarfed by a massive boulder. The stunning carved capitals of the cloister's columns are among the best preserved around. Don't confuse the monastery with the uninteresting 17th-century *monasterio nuevo* 1km uphill. (Open Nov.1-Mar. 15 11am-2:30pm and 4-5:30pm; Mar. 16-May 31 10am-2:30pm and 4-7pm; June 1-Aug. 31 10am-8pm; Sept. 1-Oct. 31 10am-2:30pm and 4-7pm.) **Viages Arán,** C. Mayor, 46 (tel. 974 35 54 80), schedules bus trips to San Juan July 15 through August, usually on Thursdays (1300ptas). For 5000ptas round-trip, **taxis** (tel. 974 36 28 48) will make the journey, with a one-hour wait at the monastery.

🖾CASTILLO DE LOARRE. The power and magnificence of **El Castillo de Loarre** (5km from the town of Loarre and 70km from Jaca) is visible for kilometers in each direction. A maze of history sits above the fields, every inch of which is open to exploration. No tours or guides shuffle people through the castle; each visitor is free to investigate, meander, or just sit and ponder the wonder of it all. In the 11th century, King Sancho Ramírez built this marvelous castle in an effort to protect himself from Moorish attacks. He succeeded—sharp cliffs at its rear and 400m of thick walls to the east make the castle nearly impenetrable. The building's outer walls follow the turns and angles of the rock so closely that a nighttime attacker might have seen only the silhouette of the awesome stone monolith. A crypt, which opens to the right of the steep entrance staircase, holds the remains of Demetrius, the French saint who died in Loarre. You can climb up to the battlements of both towers, but be careful when climbing the wobbly steel rungs to the roof or descending into the dark and doorless basement. (Open May-June daily 10am-1:30pm and 4-6pm; July-Aug. daily 10am-8pm; Sept.-April W-Su 11am-2:30pm. Free.)

Reaching the castle requires a little ingenuity. **La Oscence** (tel. 974 35 50 60) sends one **bus** (1hr., M-Sa 1 per day, 7:15am, 665ptas) from Jaca to the town of **Loarre,** 5km from the castle; the return bus at 5pm stops only in Ayerbe, 7km away from Loarre. **Trains** go only to Ayerbe. From there, you can request a taxi or trek the two hours to the town of Loarre.

VALLE DE HECHO

The craggy Valle de Hecho and its picturesque hamlets, just 40km west of Jaca, are the hiking areas closest to the city. From early July to early August, villages in the valley host the **Simposio de Escultura y Pintura Moderna.** Artists come from far and wide, turning the surrounding hills into a huge open-air museum. The valley is best visited during July and August as it is too tranquil the rest of the year. A **Josefa**

Escartin (tel. 974 36 05 08) bus leaves Jaca Monday through Saturday at 6:30pm, stopping at **Hecho** (7:25pm) and **Siresa** (7:40pm) and continuing to **Ansó** (8:10pm). Every morning except Sunday the bus returns from Ansó (6am) via Siresa (6:30am) and Hecho (6:45am) on its way to Jaca.

HECHO (ECHO)

Hecho (pop. 670) is the valley's geographical and administrative center, a serious title that doesn't seem to suit the relaxed and peaceful city. The **Ayuntamiento** (tel. 974 37 53 29) provides information for tourists. A **bank** is behind Pl. Fuente—follow Traversia Muro and turn left (open M-F 8:30am-2pm, Sa 8:30am-1pm). the **post office** sits in a small square off C. Mayor (open M-F 8:30am-2:30pm, Sa 9:30am-1pm). **Supermercado Aldi**, on C. Mayor, stocks provisions (open M-Sa 10am-2pm and 5-8pm). Ansó and nearby campgrounds provide better **accommodations** options, but the best deal in town is **Casa Blasquico**, Pl. Fuente, 1 (tel. 974 37 50 07), a white house with balconies and wood panelling facing the bus stop. The proprietor's cooking skills are formidable, as is her command of English and French. (Meals 1700ptas. Doubles 3500ptas, with bath 6000ptas. Visa. Call ahead July-Aug.) **Camping Valle de Hecho** (tel./fax 974 37 53 61), at the entrance to Hecho from the southern valley on the left off Crta. Fuente la Reina, has clean facilities in a lovely location. *Literas* (1000ptas) are also available in the *albergue* on the same site. The knowledgeable staff organizes excursions. (500ptas per person, per car, and per tent. 7% IVA not included. Visa.) The **Compania de Guías Valle de Echo** (tel. 974 37 52 18; or ask at the bar next to Casa Blasquico), leads hiking trips (7900ptas for a 2-day trip to the Selva de Oza) and rents cross-country skis (2000ptas per day).

VALLE DE ANSÓ

Slightly farther down the road from Jaca, the town of Ansó is set in one of the most appealing valleys in the Pyrenees. Cobblestone streets intertwine with shops and friendly pubs, while pleasant accommodations dot the town. Like Hecho, this valley lives for July and August, when it receives the bulk of its visitors. The best treks leave from Zuriza, farther up the valley than the little town of Ansó.

ANSÓ

Tiny Ansó's (pop. 530) cobblestone streets and matching stone houses are peacefully removed from the rest of the world. Near inviting mountains and lakes, this tiny town is well worth a stop. The city relives its past during the **Fiesta del Traje,** the last Sunday in August, when residents don traditional garb for a day. At the **Museo de Etnología** (tel. 974 34 00 22) inside the **Iglesia de San Pedro,** mannequins model customary dress next to spinning wheels and looms. (Open July-Aug. M-F 10:30am-1:30pm and 3:30-8pm; mid-Sept.-June daily 11am-12:30pm. For more info, talk to the priest in the stone house in front of the church. 200ptas.)

The **Josefa Escartín** (tel. 974 36 05 08) **bus** from Jaca stops at C. Mayor, departing for Jaca again the next day (1½hr., M-Sa 1 per day, 6:30am, 390ptas). Those who spend the night are in for a treat. The friendly owners of ▓**Posada Magoria,** C. Chapitel, 8 (tel. 974 37 00 49), have restored a traditional stone house with wide-planked wood floors and antique-filled rooms. They make their own yogurt, bake bread, and grow vegetables, serving it all at family-style meals. (Breakfast 700ptas, dinner 1800ptas. Call ahead in July and Aug. 2400ptas per person.) Around the corner of the wide cobbled street (look for the sign) is the newer, more standard hostel **Posada Veral,** C. Cocorro, 6 (tel. 974 37 01 19; *menú* 1500ptas for guests only; breakfast 375ptas; singles 1800ptas; doubles 3400ptas, with bath 3800ptas).

ZURIZA AND ENVIRONS

Around Zuriza the terrain alternates between the shallow **Agujero de Solana** (Hole of Solana) and the steep summit of **Escoueste**. From the town, you can also make the arduous trek to **Sima de San Martín,** on the French border. To enjoy the area without straining yourself, walk 2km south of Ansó to the fork in the road. Just above the tunnel toward Hecho is the striking, weather-sculpted rock formation called **El Monje y la Monja (The Monk and the Nun).** Sweep all lurid thoughts from your mind and enjoy the view. Fifteen km north of Ansó, **Camping Zuriza** (tel. 974 37 01 96 or 974 37 00 77), which lies on a mountain stream 2km away from the Río Veral, is great for fishing, rafting, or kayaking. The site also provides a **supermarket** and **hostel.** (Hot showers included. Breakfast 350ptas, dinner 1400ptas. Mountain bike and ski rental. Campsite 450ptas per person and per car; individual tents 400ptas, group tents 450ptas; add 7% IVA. Hostel doubles 4000-4500ptas, with bath 5500-6000ptas; bunk in *literas* 1000ptas. Visa, MC.) From the campground, it's a dayhike (3½hr.) to the **Mesa de los Tres Reyes,** a series of peaks close to the borders of France, Navarra, and Aragón (hence "los tres reyes").

▨PARQUE NACIONAL DE ORDESA

The beauty of Ordesa will reduce even the seasoned traveler to stupefied monosyllables. Extremely well-maintained trails cut across idyllic forests, jagged rock faces, snow-covered peaks, rushing rivers, and magnificent water-falls. Located just south of the French border, Ordesa includes the canyons of Ordesa, Añisclo, Escuaín, and Pineta. The park has trails for hikers of all levels of experience, and as a result attracts huge crowds in July and August. It is easiest to enter Ordesa through the village of Torla.

▨ PRACTICAL INFORMATION. La Oscense (tel. 974 35 50 60) sends a **bus** from Jaca to **Sabiñánigo** in July (30min., M-Sa 10:15am and 6:15pm, Su 10:15am, 110ptas). Sabiñánigo is also easily accessible by **train;** all trains on the Zara-goza-Huesca-Jaca line stop here. From there **Empresa Hudebus** (tel. 974 21 32 77) runs to **Torla** (55min.; Sept.-June 1 per day, 11am; July-Aug. 2 per day, 11am and 6pm; 355ptas). A bus shuttles between Torla and Ordesa during July and August (every 15min., round-trip 200ptas). In the off-season you'll have to either hike the 8km to the entrance or call a cab (tel. 974 48 62 43; 1500-2000ptas). To leave the area, catch the bus as it passes through Torla at 3:30pm on its way back to Sabiñánigo. Since parking is limited, drivers should arrive at the park early in the day.

The **visitor center "El Parador"** awaits beyond the Ordesa park entrance. The staff sells maps (400ptas) and gives out lots of info about the park and its vari-ous hikes. (Open daily July-Aug. 9am-1pm and 3:30-7pm; Apr.-May 9am-2pm and 3:30-6pm; June 9am-1:30pm and 4-7pm.) In Torla, consider buying the indispensable *Editorial Alpina* guide (675ptas). Across from Refugio L'Ata-laya, **Compañia de Ordesa** (tel. 974 48 64 17) rents mountain bikes and organizes excursions (rafting 6100ptas per person; kayaks 8000ptas per person). **Police: Guardia Civil** (tel. 974 48 61 60). **Post office:** on C. Francia at Pl. Ayuntamiento, behind a tiny door (open M-Sa 9-11am); **postal code:** 22376.

▨▨ ACCOMMODATIONS, CAMPING, AND FOOD. Within the park, many **refugios** (mountain huts, usually without facilities) allow overnight stays. The 120-bed **Refugio Góriz** (tel. 974 34 12 01), a four-hour walk from the park's park-ing lot, has winter heating and meager hot showers (1000ptas per person). The town of Torla has a greater range of accommodations, but it tends to fill up fast in July and August—reserve ahead. Ascend cobblestoned C. Francia, and on the right after one block, you'll find **Refugio L'Atalaya,** C. Francia, 45 (tel. 974 48 60 22), under some wooden beams. Its 31 mats go for almost nothing

FAR TREK On your way to Berlin? A *Gran Recorrido* (Great Hike) trail will get you there—eventually. One of the most beautiful and rugged stretches of the pan-European *Gran Recorrido* network treks east to west just below the French-Spanish border. Strung together by old mountain roads, animal tracks, and forest paths, the Aragonese portion of **GR-11** passes by clear mountain lakes and under, over, and through snow-covered peaks (the highest being Mt. Aneto, at 3404m). Though some parts of GR-11 are pretty gentle, the full trek across Aragon requires hiking experience, especially when snow cover is extensive. The border-to-border route takes eight to ten days. For detailed info on this and other GR trails, consult tourist offices in the area or the **Federación Aragonesa de Montañismo** at C. Albareda, 7 (tel. 976 22 79 71) in Zaragoza, or pick up a detailed and trail-specific *Topoguía* guide. The extremely useful *Editorial Alpina* also has a good map of the route.

(kitchen and dining area available for use; owner's own *menú* 1400ptas; breakfast 500ptas; mats 1000ptas per person). The newer **Refugio Briet** (tel. 974 48 62 21), across the street, has similar facilities and prices (*menú* 1400ptas; lodging 1000ptas per person), but its separate bunks are dispersed through two rooms.

Three campgrounds lie outside Torla. Both **Camping Río Ara** (tel. 974 48 62 48) and **Camping San Anton** (tel. 974 48 60 63) are small and pretty (460ptas per person, per tent, and per car; open Apr.-Oct.). Midway between the two is more upscale **Camping Ordesa** (tel. 974 48 61 46; 630ptas per person, 660ptas per tent and per car; IVA not included; 30% off in low season; open Apr.-Oct.). For food, stock up at **Supermercado Torla,** on C. Francia, near Refugio Briet (open daily Feb.-Nov. 8am-2pm and 4-8pm; Dec.-Jan. 10am-2pm and 4-8pm), or try **Restaurante Bar El Rebeco** (tel. 974 48 60 68), up C. Francia and a right at the parking lot, which serves a 1550pta *menú* (entrées 700-2000ptas; open June-Oct. 8-10:30pm.)

⚑ HIKING. If you have only a day to spend in Ordesa, the **Soaso Circle** is the most practical hike, especially for inexperienced mountaineers. Frequent signposts along the wide trail clearly mark the five-hour journey, which traverses forests, waterfalls, cliffs, and plateaus. Be forewarned that it gets slippery and rather dangerous when wet. Check weather forecasts before starting out, and remember that heavy snow can make the trail impassable in winter. Less intrepid types may want to cut the hike to about two hours and return to the parking lot rather than continue past the Gradas de Soaso waterfall to **Refugio Góriz.** However, the views from *Cascada del Cueva* and especially *Cascada del Estrecho* are well worth the 10-minute hike past the *aparcamiento* sign. Whichever route you choose, try to arrive at the park early in the day during July and August because by noon the entire Soaso Circle can resemble Picadilly Circus.

NEAR ORDESA: AÍNSA (L'AINSA)

A pleasant stopover about an hour away from Ordesa, Aínsa hides within its bland new town a perfectly preserved and enchanting medieval quarter, where flowers spill over stone walls into the streets. A thousand years ago Aínsa was the capital of the Kingdom of Sobrarbe (incorporated into Aragón in the 11th century), and the ruins of its 11th-century **castle** on Pl. Mayor remind visitors of its history. In 1181, priests consecrated the **Iglesia de Santa María,** across the plaza from the castle, where you can climb the tower for 100ptas (not for the tall or claustrophobic).

Compañía Hudebus (tel. 974 21 32 77) runs **buses** from Sabiñánigo to Aínsa, stopping in Torla along the way (2hr., 11am, returning at 2:30pm, 730ptas). **Compañía Cortés** (tel. 974 31 15 52) sends a bus from Aínsa to **Barbastro** (1 per day, 7am), where buses connect to Benasque. The **tourist office,** Av. Pirenáica, 1 (tel. 974 50 07 67), at the highway crossroads, advises on transport, lodgings, and excursions (open July-Aug. 10am-2pm and 4:30-8:30pm; Sept.-June Tu-Sa 10am-2pm and 4:30-8:30pm, Su 10am-2pm). Though Aínsa is not as well situated for hiking as Torla or Benasque, the companies in town can arrange countless outdoor activities.

Behind the church in the old town is the pleasant **Casa Rural El Hospital,** C. Sta. Cruz, 3 (tel. 974 50 07 50; doubles with bath, TV, and A/C 4000-4500ptas). Other budget lodgings congregate just uphill from the bus station, and **Camping Aínsa,** Ctra. Aínsa-Campo, km 1.8 (tel. 974 50 02 60), is just outside of town (575ptas per person and per car, 550ptas per tent). The supermarket **Alimentación M. Cheliz,** on Av. Ordesa at the new town's main intersection, stocks essentials (open July-Sept. 9am-9pm and Oct.-June 9am-2pm and 4-8pm). **Restaurante Brasería** (tel. 974 50 09 81), at the *castillo* end of Pl. Mayor, offers a succulent *menú* (1600ptas) among other delights (open daily 1:30-4pm and 8:30-11pm; Visa, MC).

VALLE DE BENASQUE

The Valle de Benasque is a haven for no-nonsense hikers, climbers, and skiers. Countless trails wind through the surrounding peaks, and the area teems with *refugios*, allowing for longer expeditions. Casual hikers are often scared away by the valley's reputation for serious mountaineering—the area has the Pyrenees' highest peak—but there is something here for even the most mild adventurer. With its many excursion companies and nearby trailheads, the town of Benasque (pop. 1100) offers an excellent base for outdoor activities. Although the town is growing commercially, its few cobblestone streets remain quiet.

▓▐▐ PRACTICAL INFORMATION, ACCOMMODATIONS, AND FOOD. La Alta Aragonesa (tel. 974 21 07 00) runs **buses** between Huesca and Benasque (3hr., 1-2 per day, 1300ptas). To find the **tourist office** (tel./fax 974 55 12 89) and its volumes of hiking info, face the Hotel Aragüells at the main highway intersection and continue one block down the alley, angling to the right. (Open July-Aug. and *Semana Santa* daily 9:30am-1:30pm and 4:30-8pm; Sept.-June Tu-F 10am-2pm and 5-8pm, Sa 5-9pm, Su 9:30am-1:30pm.) **The Guardia Civil** (tel. 974 55 10 08). **Post office** (tel. 974 55 20 71), in the Ayuntamiento building (open M-F 9am-noon, Sa 10am-noon, only for stamps); **postal code:** 22440.

Fonda Barrabés, C. Mayor, 5 (tel. 974 55 16 54), a left from the bus stop and straight ahead 200m, is a clean and comfortable hostel with a restaurant. (Bunks 900-1000ptas; singles 1700ptas; doubles 3300ptas; triples 4500ptas. Visa.) **Camping Aneto** (tel. 974 55 11 41), 3km out of town up the hill past the Cerler turnoff, has both summer and winter facilities (440ptas per person, tent, or car). **Restaurante-Crêperie Les Arkades** (tel. 974 55 12 02), hiding down a street between the post office and church, flips all kinds of crepes (400-500ptas) and other entrees (open daily 1-4pm and 8pm-midnight; *creperie* open Dec.-Apr. 5:30pm-midnight).

▟ HIKING. If you start early from Benasque, you can hike just over 8km down the valley road, cross the river on the camping area bridge, and climb up, up, and away, following the falls of the Río Cregueña. Four sweaty hours later you'll reach **Lago de Cregueña** (2657m), the largest and highest lake in the **Maladeta** massif.

To scale **Mount Aneto** (3404m), the highest of the Pyrenees, acquire some climbing skills and gear and then head out at 5am with the experts from the **Refugio de la Renclusa** (tel. 974 55 21 06; open June 22-Sept. 24). To reach the *refugio*, take the main road north for about 15km until the paved road ends. From there it's a 45-minute hike. Many companies in Benasque also organize trips. If lugging heavy equipment up a mountain isn't your idea of fun, head downhill to the road and follow signs to **Forau de Aigualluts,** a lovely pond at the base of a waterfall (30min.).

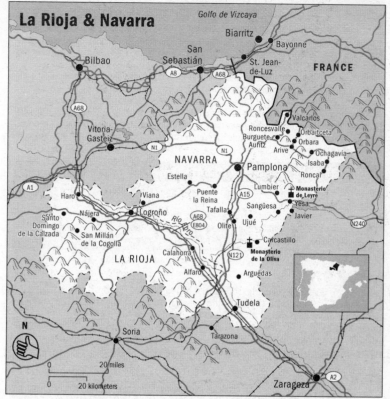

La Rioja & Navarra

Golfo de Vizcaya

LA RIOJA AND NAVARRA

The spirit of the Navarrese emanates from the rustic Pyrenean *pueblos* on the French border, through bustling Pamplona, to the dusty villages in the south. Bordered by Basque Country to the west and Aragón to the east, Rioja and Navarra's little-visited villages greet tourists with open arms and a toast of La Rioja wine.

Navarra has long experienced the difficulties of Spain's on-again, off-again regionalism. It gained regional autonomy in 1512, only to see it revoked in 1833. To avoid another devastating loss, they sided with the "winners" in the 20th century, allying themselves with Franco's Nationalist forces, victors of the Spanish Civil War. Unfortunately, as a result they found themselves under a regime with no toleration for regional differences. The Navarrese have continued to support regionalist causes since the fall of Franco and the subsequent reestablishment of provincial autonomy in 1983. Many of the region's northern inhabitants identify themselves as Basque and some are concerned with their regional exclusion from both País Vasco and the Basque independence movement.

For one week each July, Navarra becomes the most touristed region in Europe; the festival of *San Fermín* supports the region's tourist industry for the rest of the year. An extensive network of government-approved *casas rurales* host tourists in lovely private homes, and home-cooked meals are often available. The region's epicurean specialty is *trucha a la Navarra* (trout stuffed with ham).

Tucked under Navarra, La Rioja is famous for one thing: great wine. "Rioja" is an internationally acclaimed wine classification with an 800-year tradition; both the

1994 and 1995 grapes received the highest ratings possible. The name derives from the Ebro tributary Río Oja, whose waters trickle through the vineyards. When ordering wine, asking for *"vino"* will get you the wine of the year, ordering *"crianza"* delivers higher-quality wine at least three years old, while a request for *"gran reserva"* brings the *crème de la crème* (and you'll pay for it).

Logroño, capital of La Rioja, lies in the region's center. The best *bodegas* (wine cellars) siphon off the lands in western Rioja Alta, around Haro. *El Camino de Santiago* (St. James's Way) passes through much of La Rioja, and tourist offices can provide useful information on the route. The mountainous Sierra region, with tranquil fields at the feet of towering peaks, lines La Rioja's southern border, where dinosaur tracks have been discovered; ask at any tourist office about the *Ruta del dinosaurio.*

HIGHLIGHTS OF LA RIOJA AND NAVARRA

■ Without a doubt, the world-famous **Fiesta de San Fermín (Running of the Bulls)** in **Pamplona** (see p. 396).
■ The fantastic views of and from the **Palacio Real** in Olite (see p. 398).
■ **Ochagavía,** exactly what a mountain village should be (see p. 405).
■ The darling towns and prime skiing grounds of the **Valle del Roncal** (see p. 406).

LOGROÑO

With characteristic hyperbole, the tourist office brochure proclaims that Logroño (pop. 124,000) feeds both the body and the soul. Although the Camino de Santiago makes a stop here, the soul finds little but bustling commerce for spiritual nourishment. The body, however, will have something to write home about. In Logroño, the best entry point into the vineyard towns of La Rioja, bars are around every corner in the old city, serving the region's fine wines and savory, inexpensive *tapas.*

▐ GETTING THERE

Trains run to Logroño from **Burgos** (2hr., 4 per day, 1800ptas); **Zaragoza** (2¼hr., 4 per day, 6:30am-7:30pm, 1300ptas). **Buses** go from **Pamplona** (1hr., 4-12 per day, 7:30am-7pm, 1000ptas) and **Bilbao** (1¾hr., 3-5 per day, 8:30am-7:30pm, 1455ptas).

▊ ORIENTATION AND PRACTICAL INFORMATION

Both the old and new towns radiate from the **Parque del Espolón,** a tree-lined set of gravel paths with a fountain at the center. The **casco antiguo** stretches between the park and the Río Ebro, on the far north side of the city. To reach the park from the **train station,** cross the major traffic artery of **Avenida de Lobete** and angle left on Av. España. At the **bus station** (the next major intersection), turn right onto C. General Vara de Rey, which leads north to the park (8min.) and the *casco antiguo.*

TRANSPORTATION

Trains: RENFE (tel. 941 24 02 02), Pl. Europa, off Av. España on the south side of town. Bus service is more frequent. Info open daily 7am-11pm. To: **Calahorra** (40min., 3-4 per day, 7:30am-8:11pm, 455ptas); **Haro** (45min., 2 per day, 10:05am and 4:40pm, 395-1100ptas); **Burgos** (2hr., 2-3 per day, 3:46-6:46pm, 1800ptas); **Zaragoza** (2-2½hr., 4-6 per day, 7:30am-8:11pm, 1220-1800ptas); **Bilbao** (4hr.; 1-2 per day; M-F 3:46 and 6:55pm, Sa 3:50pm; 1800ptas); **Madrid** (5½hr., M-Sa 1 per day, 3:20pm, 4000ptas); **Barcelona** (7hr., 3 per day, 12:40-4:18pm, 4100-4200ptas).

Buses: (tel. 941 23 59 83), Av. España, on the corner of C. General Vara and Av. Pío XII. Several companies; check info board for the appropriate counter. Info open daily 6am-11pm. To: **Haro** (1hr., 3-6 per day, 7:30am-7:15pm, 345ptas); **Santo Domingo de la Calzada** (1hr.; 3-9 per day; M-F 7:15am-8:30pm, Sa 8:30am-8pm, Su 11am-10:30pm; 365ptas); **Soria** (1½hr.; 5 per day; M-Sa 6:45am-7pm, Su 9:30am-10pm;

825ptas); **Bilbao** (2hr.; 3-5 hr.; M-Sa 8:30am-7:30pm, Su 11am-9pm; 1455ptas); **Burgos** (2hr., 4-7 per day, 8:30am-9:45pm, 850ptas); **Pamplona** (2hr., 3-5 per day, 7am-7pm, 905ptas); **Vitoria-Gasteiz** (2hr.; 4-6 per day; M-F 7am-8pm, Sa 10:30am-8pm, Su 10:30am-8:45pm; 970-1035ptas); **Zaragoza** (2hr., 4-11 per day, 9am-9pm, 1450ptas); **Madrid** (4hr., 5-6 per day, 6:45am-7pm, 2550ptas); **Barcelona** (6hr., 2-4 per day, 1:30pm-1:14am, 3930ptas).

Public Transportation: All buses run to Gran Vía, one block from Parque Espolón; lines #1 and 3 pass the bus station. All rides 75ptas.

Taxis: (tel. 941 22 21 22). Stands at the bus station and the northwest corner of the park. **Radio Taxi** (tel. 941 50 50 50).

Car Rental: Avis, Gran Vía, 67 (tel. 941 20 23 54), left off C. General Vara. Must be 25 years old and have had a license for at least 1 year. Open M-F 9am-1:30pm and 4-7pm, Sa 10am-1:30pm. Visa, MC, AmEx.

TOURIST, FINANICAL, AND LOCAL SERVICES

Tourist Office: (tel. 941 26 06 65; fax 941 25 60 45), Po. Espolón, at the south end of Parque Espolón. Take a left off C. General Vara coming from the bus and train stations. Gives out maps and helpful advice in English. Open June 15.-Oct. M-Sa 10am-2pm and 4:30-7:30pm, Su 10am-2pm; Nov.-May M-F 9am-2pm.

Currency Exchange: Banco Central Hispano, on C. General Vara at the corner of Parque Espolón. **ATM.** Open M-F 8:30am-2:30pm; Oct.-Apr. also Sa 8:30am-1pm.

Luggage Storage: At the bus station (200ptas; open daily 6am-11pm) and train station (400ptas; open 7am-11pm).

EMERGENCY AND COMMUNICATIONS

Emergency: tel. 091 or 092.

Medical Services: Hospital de la Rioja, Av. Viana, 1 (tel. 941 29 11 94), on the edge of town in the direction of Pamplona.

Post Office: (tel. 941 26 02 34 or 941 22 89 06), Pl. San Agustín, next to the museum. Open M-F 8:30am-8:30pm, Sa 9:30am-2pm. **Postal Code:** 26070.

Internet Access: Centro MAIL, Av. Dr. Mújica, 6 (tel. 941 20 78 33). 100ptas per 15min. Open M-Sa 10am-2pm and 5-9pm, Su noon-2pm and 5-9pm.

▼ ACCOMMODATIONS AND CAMPING

The *casco antiguo* brims with budget *pensiones* and hostels. Try C. San Juan, the second left past Parque Espolón from the stations, and C. San Agustín and C. Laurel, a little deeper into the old quarter past the far corner of the park. Reservations are crucial for the *fiesta* week around September 21.

Residencia Universitaria (HI), C. Caballero de la Rosa, 38 (tel. 941 29 11 45 or 941 26 14 22). From the stations, take a right off C. General Vara onto Mura de Cervantes, which becomes Av. Paz. Go about 10 blocks, and make a left on C. Caballero de la Rosa. Buses #1A and 4 stop nearby. 25-30min. walk from the *casco antiguo*. Common room with TV. Clean doubles, each with bath. Breakfast 200ptas. Call ahead. Dorms 1000ptas, with sheets 1350ptas. Open July-Sept.

Fonda Bilbaína, C. Capitán Eduardo Gallarza, 10, 2nd fl. (tel. 941 25 42 26). Take C. Sagasta into the *casco antiguo*, turn left on C. Hermanos Moray and then right on C. Capitán Eduardo. High ceilings, shiny floors, and bright rooms, some with balconies. Singles 1700ptas; doubles 3000ptas, with shower 3500ptas, with bath 4000ptas.

Pensión La Cortijana, C. Cigueña, 28 (tel. 941 23 03 44). Head away from the *casco antiguo* on Av. Paz and turn left. Walk around the first corner and the hostel is on the right. Pleasant, clean rooms. Singles 1500ptas; doubles 3000ptas; *pensión completa* (with breakfast and dinner) 2850ptas.

Camping La Playa, Av. Playa, 6 (tel. 941 25 22 53), off the main highway, across the river from the *casco antiguo*. Riverbank site with beach. Municipal pool next door, open after July 15 (free). Laundromat. 600ptas per person, per tent, per car. Open June-Sept.

◯ FOOD

Logroñeses take their grapes seriously. Wine is the beverage of choice; don't even try ordering anything else. Head to C. Laurel and C. San Juan, brimming with bars and cafes—many have little windows so passers-by can sample the goodies. The local market, **Mercado de San Blas,** is in a large concrete building on C. Capitán Eduardo Gallarza. Take a right off C. Mura de la Francisco de la Mata, along the park (open M-Sa 7:30am-1:30pm and 4-7:30pm). For half a block's worth of groceries, head to supermarket **Champión,** Av. La Rioja, a left off C. Miguel Villanueva past the tourist office (open M-Sa 9:15am-9:15pm).

Bar Soriano, Travesía de Laurel, 2 (tel. 941 22 88 07), where C. Laurel makes its 90° turn. Borders on the transcendent. Bartenders shovel shrimp and mushrooms out the window to eager crowds in the street. The specialty *pintxo* is *champiñones con gambas* (140ptas). Open daily 11am-3am.

Mesón Julio, C. Laurel, 23 (tel. 941 20 96 58), serves an excellent *menú* (1375ptas) complete with fresh bread in a tight but tidy dining room. Entrees 800-1600ptas. Wine 900-3200ptas. Open Mar.-Oct. M-F 1:30pm-3am; Nov.-Feb. Tu-F 1:30pm-3am.

Bocatas Riojas, C. Portales, 39 (tel. 941 25 40 55), across from the cathedral. Stuffs just about anything between two slices of hot bread—try the *logroñesa* with tomato, bacon, and cheese (375ptas) or the *cordobés* with tomato and a skewer of spicy grilled beef (400ptas). Open Su-F 9am-midnight, Sa 9am-4am.

◉ ♫ SIGHTS AND ENTERTAINMENT

MUSEO DE LA RIOJA. This pleasant museum has an interesting collection spanning the last eight centuries of art. While Renaissance paintings and Impressionist works line the staircase, most rooms are filled with religious sculptures and paintings. The collection originates from the 1835 state seizure of regional monasteries' and convents' artwork and wealth. (*Pl. San Agustín, 23, along C. Portales. Tel. 941 29 12 59. Open Tu-Sa 10am-2pm and 4-9pm, Su 11:30am-2pm. Free.*)

OTHER SIGHTS. The ornate Chirrugueresque towers of the **Catedral de Santa María de la Redonda** dominate the Pl. Mercado in the *casco antiguo*. (*From C. General Vara turn left on C. Portales; the cathedral is two blocks away on the right. Open M-Sa 7:45am-1:15pm and 6:30-10pm, Su 8:15am-1:15pm and 6:30-9pm. Free.*) The grassy knolls along the **Río Ebro** make for a nice walk. A pedestrian path and the bridges **Puente de Hierro** and **Puente de Piedra** cross the river.

NIGHTLIFE AND FESTIVALS. At night, the **partying** begins in the *casco antiguo* along C. Laural and after midnight moves to C. Mayor along Pl. Mercado, C. Sagasta, and C. Carnicerías. Dusk-till-dawn revelry characterizes the **Fiestas de San Bernabé** (June 11), which are capped by an awesome fireworks display. The big party is September 20-26, around the **Fiesta de San Mateo** on September 21, which coincides with the **Fiestas de la Vendimia,** celebrating the grape harvest, when citizens make a ceremonial offering of crushed grapes to the Virgen de Valvanera.

HARO

Haro's main attractions are wine, wine, and more wine. In this small, pleasant city (pop. 9500), 17 *bodegas* dominate. Needless to say, Haro lives off its wine industry. But along with the *bodegas* and a wine museum, the city also maintains two fantastic churches and a welcoming atmosphere, making a visit worthwhile.

THAT'S A WHOLE LOT OF EGGS A visit to one of the many *bodegas* in Haro will make any visitor appreciate the art of wine-making. After the grape juice has been gathered and put into 18,000-liter barrels, workers must ensure that all the grape leftovers are removed from the juice. Every morning, one man breaks between 1000 and 2000 eggs, separating the whites from the yolks. These egg yolks are then poured into the barrel (about 540 eggs per barrel), creating a thick film on the top. This film slowly begins to sink, and after 35 days it has removed any grape debris. The yolks are then donated to neighborhood bakeries to be used in cakes.

Ⅱ PRACTICAL INFORMATION. RENFE trains (tel. 941 31 15 97) run to **Logroño** (35min., 5 per day, 12:57-7:30pm, 455-900ptas), **Bilbao** (2hr., 4 per day, 1000ptas), and **Zaragoza** (2½hr., 2 per day, 12:57 and 7:30pm, 2400ptas). To reach Pl. Paz from the train station, take the road downhill, turn right and then left across the river, and follow C. Navarra uphill to the plaza (35min.). Haro's **bus station** (tel. 941 31 15 43) is between C. Castilla and Av. Santo Domingo. Buses go to: **Santo Domingo de la Calzada** (30min.; 4 per day; M-F 7:30am-5:30pm, Sa noon-5pm, Su 1 per day, 8:30pm; 160ptas); **Vitoria** (45min.; 5-7 per-day; M-F 8am-9pm, Sa 10:55am-9pm, Su 10:55am-10pm; 550ptas); **Logroño** (1hr.; 6-7 per day; M-F 7:45am-8:30pm, Sa 8:45am-6pm, Su 8:45am-7pm; 345ptas); **Bilbao** (1hr.; 4-6 per day; M-Sa 9:15am-8:25pm, Su 11:35am-8pm; 1035ptas). To reach Pl. Paz from the bus stop, follow signs to *centro ciudad* along C. Ventilla (on the right side of the station) and continue diagonally left across Pl. Cruz onto C. Arraball, which leads straight into Pl. Paz.

The bilingual staff at the **tourist office** (tel. 941 30 33 66), Pl. Monseñor Florentino Rodríguez, dispenses information and maps. With your back to the Ayuntamiento, take C. Vega from the far left corner of Pl. Paz. The office is in the plaza to the left around the bend. (Open June-Oct. 15 M-Sa 9:30am-1:30pm and 4-7pm, Su 10am-2pm; Oct. 15-May Tu-F 10am-2pm, Sa 10am-2pm and 4:30-7:30pm.) **Bank of Central Spain,** C. Vega, 20 (tel. 941 31 11 84), offers **currency exchange** with no commission (open M-F 8am-2pm). **Post office,** on Av. La Rioja; **postal code:** 26200.

🏠🍴 ACCOMMODATIONS AND FOOD. Haro is a good daytrip from Logroño, but for those sticking around, **Hostal Las Conchas,** C. Vega, 1 (tel. 941 31 00 22), has spotless rooms with white bedspreads, flowered curtains, and TVs. (Singles 3000ptas; doubles 4000ptas, with bath 5000ptas; triples with bath 6000ptas.) **Hostal Aragón,** C. Vega, 9 (tel. 941 31 00 04), between the tourist office and Pl. Paz, has spacious old rooms with high ceilings and wood floors, but there's only one shower for all the rooms. (Singles 2500ptas; doubles 3900ptas.) **Camping de Haro** (tel. 941 31 27 37), Av. Miranda, is on the train station side of the river, left of the bridge from town (Jan.-June 15 410ptas per person, per tent, and per car; June 16-Dec. 485ptas; plus 7% IVA). For an excellent lunch, join Haro's upper crust at **Mesón Atamauri,** Pl. Juan García Gato, 1 (tel. 941 30 32 20), right off C. Vega (entrees 1000-2000ptas; *menú* 400ptas; open daily 1:30-3:30pm and 8:30-11:30pm). For cheaper eats, munch on *tapas* in the **La Herradura** quarter or on C. Vega.

📷🎭 SIGHTS AND ENTERTAINMENT. Seventeen *bodegas* overwhelm the town of Haro, the heart of La Rioja's wine industry. Most offer free tours of their facilities in English and Spanish between 9am and 2pm, although reservations are almost always required. Only **Bodegas Muga** (tel. 941 31 04 98), across the river and under the train tracks, can be visited without calling ahead. (Tours M-F June-Aug. 10, 11am (English), and noon; in Sept.-May 11am and 4pm. The tourist office has additional information on visiting *bodegas*.) If you're interested in buying some of Haro's wine, try the **wine shops** on C. Santo Tomás. Most charge 200-500ptas per bottle, but some vintages can run up to 3500ptas.

For those craving a little religion with their wine, the **Basílica de Nuestra Señora de La Vega** has beautiful stained-glass windows and a frescoed dome. From the tourist office, turn left and follow C. Vega for about three blocks. (Tel. 941 31 28

73. Open daily 8am-1pm and 5-8:30pm.) Past the basilica, in the Estación Etnológica, the **Museo del Vino** has sleek exhibits in Spanish on everything you wanted to know about wine. (Tel. 941 31 05 47. Open M-Sa 10am-2pm and 4-8pm, Su 10am-2pm. 300ptas, Wednesday free.)

Join the locals and *ir de vinos* ("go for wines") in the evening in **La Herradura,** the area around C. Santo Tomás, off Pl. Paz. Ask for *vino* and you'll get the vintage of the year (about 50-75ptas); for higher quality, order *crianza*, more than three years old (about 150ptas). Haro parties on June 24-29, culminating in the **Batalla del Vino** (June 29), when participants spray wine at innocent bystanders. The **Fiesta Mayor,** on and around September 8, is more sedate.

NEAR HARO: SANTO DOMINGO DE LA CALZADA

A symbolically important stop along the Camino de Santiago, Santo Domingo de la Calzada (pop. 5741) was founded with the sole purpose of aiding pilgrims. Eleventh-century Saint Dominic retired to the woods southwest of Logroño in search of solitude. Yet day after day he witnessed the trials of pilgrims attempting to cross the river. Admiring their courage, he decided to do something to help. So he built a bridge for them, created a road (*calzada*, or causeway) through the woods, and converted his hermitage into a hospice. Soon, business was booming and Santo Domingo became an important stop along the Camino. King Alfonso VI noticed the work of the hermit and donated resources for the construction of the grand ◨**Catedral de Santo Domingo,** even setting the first stone himself. The lavish *retablo* (altarpiece) was removed for restoration in 1994, and exquisite Romanesque pillars were discovered behind where the altarpiece had once stood. Consequently the *retablo* has been moved to a side chapel to preserve the stylistic cohesiveness of the Romanesque church. (Tel. 941 34 00 33. Open M-Sa 10am-6:30pm. 250ptas, over 65 and pilgrims 150ptas, under 18 100ptas.)

Not far from the cathedral, but over 100 steps up, awaits an outstanding view of the city and neighboring lands from the **Tower of the Cathedral.** The present tower is actually the third to stand in its place; the first was destroyed atop the cathedral by lightning and the second was considered unsafe. The present one (73m high) was finished in 1766 and is supported by a base of lime, wood, and cattle horns. (Open M-Sa 11am-2pm and 5-8pm. 125ptas. Be careful climbing the steps.

Buses run from Pl. Beato Hermosilla to **Haro** (20min., M-Sa 2-5 per day, 8am-7:30pm, 160ptas) and **Logroño** (1hr., M-Sa 9 per day, Su 3 per day, 360ptas). To reach the cathedral from the **bus stop** at Pl. Beato Hermosilla, cross Av. Juan Carlos I and follow C. Alcalde Rodolfo Varona. Take the next left (unmarked C. Pinar) for one block, then turn right on C. Hilario Perez, which ends at Pl. Santo, bordered by the cathedral and pilgrim hospice-turned-parador. The town's **tourist**

A FEATHERY REMINDER Wandering through the Cathedral of Santo Domingo, the visitor may be surprised to hear the crowing of a rooster. That white rooster lives with an accompanying white hen in an elegant pen in the cathedral wall. The birds are there to remind visitors of the tale of the miracle of Santo Domingo, known as "the cock that crows after it has been roasted." As the legend goes, an innkeeper's daughter fell madly in love with a pilgrim named Hugonell; but her passions were unrequited. The rejected, heartbroken girl slipped a silver cup into Hugonell's bag and reported the "robbery" to the mayor. Hugonell was found guilty and hanged. When his distraught parents visited the gallows, they heard their son's voice insisting that he was alive and that Santo Domingo had saved him. They rushed to the mayor's house and related the bizarre series of events. The skeptical mayor, his meal of fowl and greens interrupted, scoffed and insisted that Hugonell was as dead as the roasted cock and hen on his plate. The mayor ate his words when the cooked birds suddenly bounded off the plate and crowed Hugonell's innocence. The two white birds in the chapel are donated and switched every month. Next to the pen and beneath the window is a piece of the gallows from which Hugonell was hanged.

office sits in Casa de Trastámara, C. Mayor, 70 (tel. 941 34 33 34; fax 941 34 12 31). From Pl. Santo, face the cathedral, and go left onto C. Mayor. (Open M-Sa 10am-2pm and 4:30-7:30pm, Su 10am-2pm.) Unless you're planning to withdraw in contemplation, Santo Domingo is best as a daytrip. Persistent non-pilgrims can try **Hostal Miguel,** C. Juan Carlos I, 23 (tel. 941 34 32 52), which is clean and comfy and has big windows (singles 2000ptas; doubles 3500ptas). Several restaurants cluster near the cathedral on C. Mayor and adjoining plazas, luring hungry pilgrims with generous *menús.* A pleasant pink dining room awaits in **Restaurante/Cafetería Río,** Alberto Etchegoyen, 2 (tel. 941 34 02 77), which specializes in meat and fish. From the bus stop, take Av. Juan Carlos I, and turn right. (*Menú* 100ptas. Open noon-4pm and 7-10pm. Visa, MC.)

PAMPLONA (IRUÑA)

Long, long ago, Pamplona's fiesta in honor of its patron saint San Fermín was just another religious holiday. These days *San Fermines,* July 6-14, is the most talked about holiday in Spain and on the European backpacker circuit. Ever since Nobel-prize-winning author Ernest Hemingway brought the city international attention with *The Sun Also Rises,* hordes of visitors from around the world have come to witness and experience the legendary running of the bulls. At the bullring, a statue of Hemingway welcomes fans to Europe's premier festival, an eight-day extravaganza of dancing, dashing, and of course, drinking.

Though *San Fermines* may be the city's only irresistible attraction, Pamplona (pop. 180,000) is a pleasant place to visit the other 357 days of the year as well. Lush parks, a lovely Gothic cathedral, a massive citadel, and the winding streets of the *casco antiguo* entertain those who show up in the "off-season." Although Pamplona is the capital of the province of Navarra, its roots are truly Basque. The Basques had settled the area even before the Roman "founders" (who named the city after Pompey the Great) put its name on western maps.

▐ GETTING THERE

Trains run to Pamplona from **Madrid** (5hr., 2 per day, 9am and 5pm, 5500ptas); **Barcelona** (6hr., 4 per day, 7:30am-9:30pm, 4100ptas). **Buses** are the best way to get there from **San Sebastián** (1hr., 7 per day, 7am-9:15pm, 780ptas). During the festival transportation increases; there are several buses and trains a day from **France.**

▐ ORIENTATION AND PRACTICAL INFORMATION

The **casco antiguo,** in the northeast quarter of the city, houses almost everything of interest in Pamplona. **Plaza del Castillo,** marked by a bandstand, is Pamplona's center. From the **bus station,** turn left onto Av. Conde Oliveto. At the traffic circle on Pl. Príncipe de Viana, take the second left onto Av. San Ignacio, follow it to the end of the pedestrian thoroughfare Po. Sarasate, and bear right. From the **train station,** take bus #9 (95ptas); disembark at the last stop, cut across Po. Sarasate, and walk diagonally left to Pl. Castillo. North of Pl. Castillo, the Baroque **Casa Consistorial (Ayuntamiento)** makes a handsome marker in the swirl of medieval streets.

TRANSPORTATION

Flights: Aeropuerto de Noaín (tel. 948 31 71 82), 6km away, accessible only by taxi (about 1200ptas). To **Barcelona** (30min., M-F 4 per day) and **Madrid** (7 per day).

Trains: Estación RENFE (tel. 948 13 02 02), off Av. San Jorge. Take bus #9 from Po. Sarasate (20min., 95ptas). Info open daily 6am-10pm. Another more accessible **office,** C. Estella, 8 (tel. 948 22 72 82), is located near the bus station. Exit the bus station and go around the right corner; the office is across the parking lot. Open M-F 9am-1:30pm and 4:30-7:30pm, Sa 9:30am-1pm. Pamplona is miserably connected by rail, and reservations are often mandatory on longer trains during *San Fermines;* the bus is faster and easier. To: **Olite** (40min., 1-4 per day, 7:25am-8:05pm, 380ptas); **Vitoria-Gasteiz** (1¼hr., 1-4 per day, 8:35am-7:35pm, 585ptas); **Tudela** (1½hr., 4-8 per day, 7:25am-6:50pm, 800-1300ptas); **Zaragoza** (2hr., 1 per day, 6:50pm, 1565-1900ptas); **San Sebastián** (2hr., 2 per day, 5:40am-7:10pm, 1195-1500ptas); **Madrid** (5hr., 8 per day, 4200ptas); **Barcelona** (6-8hr., 3 per day, 12:23-8:05pm, 4100-5300ptas); **Paris** (13-15hr., 7 per day, 9:30am-11:15pm, 11,500ptas).

Buses: Estación de Autobuses (tel. 948 22 38 54), at the corner of C. Conde Oliveto and C. Yanguas y Miranda. Info open daily 6am-10pm. Nearly 20 companies. **La Tafallesa** (tel. 948 22 28 36) to **Olite** (50min., 7 per day, Su-F 8:15am-8:30pm, Sa 8:15am-9:30pm, 360-390ptas) and **Roncal** (2hr.; M-F 1 per day, 5pm; Sa 2 per day, 1pm and 5pm; 880-900ptas). **La Ronclesa** (tel. 948 22 20 79) to **San Sebastián** (1 hr., 7-8 per day, 7am-10:45pm, 780ptas) and **Jaca** (1¾hr., 2 per day, 8:30am and 3:30pm, 855-875ptas). **Conda** (tel. 948 22 10 26) to: **Tudela** (1½hr., 5-7 per day, 7:15am-8:45pm, 800-900ptas); **Zaragoza** (2-3hr., 6 per day, 7:15am-8:30pm, 1450-1650ptas); **Madrid** (5hr., 4-5 per day, 7am-9:30pm, 3140-3300ptas). **La Burendesa (ALSA)** (tel. 948 22 17 66) to **Vitoria-Gasteiz** (1½hr., 6-13 per day, 7am-8:30pm, 890ptas) and **Bilbao** (2hr., 4-7 per day, 10:30am-8pm, 1520-1535ptas). **Bilman** to **Barcelona** (5½hr., 3-4 per day, 9am-4:40pm, 2820ptas). **La Estellesa** (tel. 948 22 22 23) to **Logroño** (1hr., 4-12 per day, 7:30am-7pm, 1000ptas).

Public Transportation: 14 buses cover the city. The tourist office has a list of routes. Bus #9 runs from Po. Sarasate to the train station (20min., every 10-15min., 6:30am-10:30pm, 95ptas). During *San Fermines* some routes run nights (150ptas).

Taxis: (tel. 948 23 21 00 or 948 23 23 00), available at Pl. Castillo and Taconera.

Car Rental: Nal-Car (tel. 948 22 35 69), in Hotel Tres Reyes, on Jardines de la Taconera. 6500ptas per day for rentals over 3 days. Open M-F 9am-1pm and 4-7:30pm, Sa 9am-noon. Visa, MC, AmEx. **Europcar,** Hotel Blanca Navarra, Av. Pío XII, 43 (tel. 948 17 60 02). Take bus #1, 2, or 4 and get off after the traffic circle on the way out of town. Minimum age 21. 56,000ptas per week. Open M-F 9am-1pm and 4-7:30pm, Sa 9am-1pm.

TOURIST AND FINANCIAL SERVICES

Tourist Office: C. Hilarión Eslava, 1 (tel. 948 20 65 40; fax 948 20 70 36). From Pl. Castillo, take C. San Nicolas, turn right on C. San Miguel, and walk straight through Pl. San Francisco. Map and minute-by-minute guides to the festivities. English spoken. Info about currency exchange, public baths, and campsite buses is posted on a bulletin board outside. Open during *San Fermines* daily 10am-5pm; July-Aug. M-Sa 10am-2pm and 4-7pm, Su 10am-2pm; Sept.-June M-F 10am-2pm and 4-7pm, Sa 10am-2pm.

Currency Exchange: Reception desk at **Hotel Tres Reyes** (tel. 948 22 66 00), Jardines de la Taconera, changes money 24hr. From the bus station, turn right, bear left at the second fork, and then left again; the hotel is to the left where the road forks. **Banco Central Hispano,** Pl. Castillo, 21 (tel. 948 20 86 00), and in Pl. Vinculo on the corner of C. Estella and C. Alhondiga, has **ATMs.** Open May-Sept. M-F 8:30am-2:30pm; Oct.-Apr. M-F 8:30am-2:30pm, Sa 8:30am-1pm; *San Fermines* 9:30am-noon.

LOCAL SERVICES

Luggage Storage: At the **bus station.** Bags 200ptas per day, large packs 300ptas per day. Open M-Sa 6:15am-9:30pm, Su 6:30am-1:30pm and 2-9:30pm. Closes for *San Fermines*, when the Ayuntamiento, around the corner at C. Garcia Jimenez and C. Yanguas y Miranda, opens storage. 300ptas each time you check on your luggage. Open 24hr. **RENFE** (tel. 948 13 02 02) has lockers. 400ptas per day. Buy tokens at the ticket counter daily 7am-10pm.

Laundromat: Lavomatique, C. Descalzos, 28 (tel. 948 22 19 22). From Pl. San Francisco follow C. Hilarión Eslava to the end, then turn right. Wash, dry, and soap for 1000ptas. Open M-F 4:30-8:30pm; closed during *San Fermines.*

Public Toilets and Baths: Squat **toilet booths** are set up for *San Fermines,* but the permanent bathrooms in the **Jardines de Taconera** are more comfortable. **Casa de Baño,**

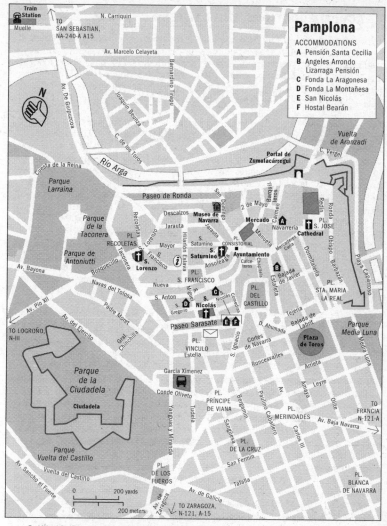

Pamplona

ACCOMMODATIONS
A Pensión Santa Cecilia
B Angeles Arrondo
  Lizarraga Pensión
C Fonda La Aragonesa
D Fonda La Montañesa
E San Nicolás
F Hostal Bearán

C. Hilarión Eslava, 2 (tel. 948 22 17 38), at the corner of C. Jarauta. Showers 110ptas, towel 40ptas, soap 40ptas. Open Tu-Sa 8am-8pm, Su 8am-2:30pm.

EMERGENCY AND COMMUNICATIONS

Emergency: tel. 091, 092, or 112. **Municipal Police,** C. Monasterio de Irache, 2.

24-Hour Pharmacy: Check the *Diario de Navarra* listings or call 948 22 21 11.

Medical Services: Hospital de Navarra (tel. 948 42 21 00), C. Irunlarrea. The **Red Cross** sets up stands at the bus station and the *corrida* during *San Fermines*.

Post Office: Po. Sarasate, 9 (tel. 948 21 26 00). Open M-F 8:30am-8:30pm, Sa 9:30am-2pm; *San Fermines* M-Sa 8:30am-2pm. **Postal Code:** 31001.

Internet Access: iturNet cibercafé, C. Iturrama, 1 (tel. 948 25 28 20), on the corner of C. Abejeras. Bus #2 stops on C. Iturrama. From the bus station, take a left on C. Yanguas y Miranda, then head across Pl. Fueros to C. Abejeras. 500ptas per hr. Open M-Sa 10am-2pm and 4:30-10pm; closed Saturdays during *San Fermines*. Visa, MC.

▌ ACCOMMODATIONS AND CAMPING

If you are planning on finding a hotel room during *San Fermines*, good luck. If there was a lucky convergence of stars on the day of your birth and you have truckloads of cash, you *may* find a room during the first few days of the festival. Diehard *sanferministas* book their rooms a year in advance. In most cases, you must reserve several months ahead and pay rates (up front) up to four times higher than those listed (anywhere from 4000-8000ptas per person in most budget hostels). Arriving several days before the *fiestas* may help, because some hostels don't accept reservations in advance. Early in the week, people accost visitors at the train and bus stations, offering couches and floor space. Be wary—accommodations and prices vary tremendously, and you might find yourself blowing your money to sleep on a dirty floor in a bad part of town. Check the newspaper *Diario de Navarra* for **casas particulares.** Many who can't find rooms sleep outside on the lawns of the Ciudadela, Pl. Fueros, Pl. Castillo, and on the banks of the river. Veteran park-sleepers recommend extreme caution; *Let's Go* does not recommend sleeping outside. If you can't leave your backpack at the train station or Ayuntamiento (they fill fast), sleep on top of it. Parking is free on most streets during *San Fermines* (see p. 396) and many sleep right in the back seat.

During the remainder of the year, finding a room is no problem. Accommodations that define the word "budget" line C. San Nicolás and C. San Gregorio off Pl. Castillo. Be aware that most hostel owners follow separate price schedules for *temparada alta (San Fermines)*, *temparada media* (summer), and *temparada baja* (rest of the year).

Pensión Santa Cecilia, C. Navarrería, 17 (tel. 948 22 22 30). From C. Chapitela (off Pl. Castillo), take the 1st right on C. Mercaderes, then turn left at a 45° angle. The hostel is on the left. Comfort lies behind the impressive (and spooky) portal. Rooms have high ceilings and winter heating. Laundry 1000ptas. *San Fermines* dorms 5000ptas. Rest of year singles 2500ptas; doubles 4000ptas; triples 5600ptas. Visa, MC.

Angeles Arrondo Lizarraga Pensión, C. Estafeta, 25, 5th fl. (tel. 948 22 18 16). Look for the green and white CAMAS sign. Cozy rooms with clean, colorful bathrooms. *San Fermines* 4000-6000ptas per person. Rest of year singles 1500ptas; doubles 3000ptas.

Fonda La Aragonesa, C. San Nicolás, 22 (tel. 948 22 34 28). For the reception desk, walk across the street to Hostal Bearán. Simple rooms, shiny hallways, and aromatic bathrooms. *San Fermines* doubles 9000ptas. July-Sept. doubles 3500ptas. Oct.-June singles 2000ptas; doubles 3000ptas. Visa, MC, AmEx.

Hostal Bearán, C. San Nicolás, 25 (tel. 948 22 34 28). Squeaky-clean salmon-colored rooms with phone, TV, bath, safebox, and a whopping pricetag. *San Fermines* singles 13,000ptas; doubles 15,000ptas. July-Sept. singles 5500ptas; doubles 6500ptas. Oct.-June singles 4500ptas; doubles 5500ptas. Visa, MC, AmEx.

Fonda La Montañesa, C. San Gregorio, 2 (tel. 948 22 43 80). You can't beat the price. No reservations are accepted during the fiesta, so show up early in the morning. No winter heating. *San Fermines* dorms 5000ptas. Rest of year dorms 1600ptas.

San Nicolás, C. San Nicolás, 13 (tel. 948 22 13 19), next to the restaurant. Helpful staff keeps pleasant rooms. *San Fermines* dorms 5000ptas. Rest of year dorms 1500-2000ptas. Visa, MC, AmEx.

Camping: Camping Ezcaba (tel. 948 33 03 15), in Eusa, 7km outside Pamplona on the road to Irún. From Pl. Toros, La Montañesa bus runs to Eusa (4 per day, 9:10am-8:30pm). Get off at the gasoline station, the last stop. Capacity 714 campers, although it fills fast during *San Fermines*. No reservations accepted. 450ptas per person, per tent, and per car. Open June-Oct.

▐ FOOD

While *San Fermines* draws street vendors selling everything from roast chicken to *churros*, the tiny neighborhoods of Pamplona advertise hearty *menús* throughout the year. Try the side streets near Pensión Santa Cecilia, the area above Pl. San Francisco, and C. Jarauta and C. Descalzos, near Po. Ronda. C. Navarrería and Po. Sarasate house *bocadillo* bars. Bars in Pl. Castillo serve sandwiches and pizza, but service is horrendous during the festival. The *barracas políticas* (bars organized by political interest groups that don't expect any interest in their platforms), located next to the amusement park in the Ciudadela, offer cheap drinks and cheap idealology. Many cafes and restaurants close for one to two weeks after *San Fermines* to recover.

The **market,** C. Mercado, is to the right of Casa Consistorial's facade and down the stairs (open M-Sa 8am-2:30pm). For a **supermarket,** check out **Vendi** at the corner of C. Hilarión Eslava and C. Mayor (open M-F 9am-2pm and 5:30-7:30pm, Sa 9am-2pm; *San Fermines* M-Sa 9am-2pm; Visa, MC).

■ **Restaurante Sarasate,** C. San Nicolás, 19-21 (tel. 948 22 57 27), above the seafood store. Healthy vegetarian cuisine. Simply scrumptious. Lunchtime *menú* 1300ptas. Open M-Th 1:15-4pm and 8:15-11pm, F-Sa 1:15-4pm and 9-11pm.

Restaurante San Fermín, C. San Nicolás, 44-46 (tel. 948 22 21 91). Tranquil upstairs dining room. *The* place to celebrate your brush with death. Locals rate it as one of the best. Entrees 1000-2000ptas. Weekday *menú* 1700ptas, Sa-Su 3200ptas. Open M-F 1-3:30pm and 9-11:30pm, Sa 1-3:30pm and 8:30-11:30pm; *San Fermines* M-Sa 1-4:30pm and 8:30pm-12:30am, Su 1-3:30pm. Visa, MC, AmEx.

Bar-Restaurante Lanzale, C. San Lorenzo, 31 (tel. 948 22 10 71), between C. Mayor and C. Jarauta, above Pl. San Francisco. Pleasant, spacious dining room serves up a changing *menú* (1100ptas) and delicious desserts. Entrees 600-1000ptas. Open M-Sa 1:30-3:30pm and 9-11pm. Bar open daily 10am-midnight. Visa, MC, AmEx.

Hong Kong, C. San Gregorio, 38 (tel. 948 22 66 35). Look for the red balcony. Ignore the cheesy Chinese pop music. *Menú* 850ptas. Entrees 800-1300pta. Open daily noon-4pm and 8pm-midnight.

Bar Restaurant Tudela, Tudela, 9 (tel. 948 22 20 24), near the bus station. Entrees 575-1450ptas. Open M-F 1-3:30pm and 9:30pm-midnight, Sa-Su 9:30pm-midnight; *San Fermines* 1-3:30pm and 9:30pm-midnight. Visa, MC, AmEx.

◉ SIGHTS

CATHEDRAL AND CHURCHES. Pamplona's rich architectural legacy gives ample reason to visit all year long. The recently restored late 14th-century **Gothic cathedral** houses an ornate alabaster mausoleum where Carlos III and his wife Queen Leonor are entombed. Off the lovely cloister is a five-chimneyed kitchen (1335), one of four of its kind in all of Europe. *(At the end of C. Navarrería. Tel. 948 21 08 27. Open M-F 10am-1:30pm and 4-7pm, Sa 10am-1:30pm. Tours at 10:30am, 11:30am, 12:30pm, and 5pm. 500ptas.)* Church lovers will also enjoy the Gothic 13th-century **Iglesia de San Saturnino,** near the Ayuntamiento, and **Iglesia de San Nicolás,** in Pl. San Nicolás. *(Both open daily 9am-12:30pm and 6-8:30pm. Free.)* For a peek at San Fermín himself, head to **Iglesia de San Lorenzo.** *(C. Mayor, 74. Open daily 8am-12:30pm and 6:30-8pm.)*

CIUDADELA. The pentagonal Ciudadela was built by Felipe II in an effort to secure the city's safety. Today it is part of a grassy park that hosts free exhibits and concerts in the summer. Its impressive walls even scared off Napoleon, who refused to launch a frontal attack and staged a trick snowball fight instead. When Spanish sentries joined in, the French entered the city through its gates. To get to the **walls** from the old quarter, pick up C. Redín at the far end of the cathedral plaza. A left turn follows the walls past the **Portal de Zumalacárregui** and along the Río Arga. Bear left through the gardens of **Parque de la Taconera**—where some random peacocks and assorted wildlife hang out—until reaching the Ciudadela. *(Av. Ejercito. Open daily 7am-10pm; closed during San Fermines. Free.)*

MUSEO DE NAVARRA. The Museo de Navarra shelters beautifully preserved 4th- and 5th-century Roman mosaics, murals from all over the region, and a nice collection of 14th- to 20th-century paintings, including Goya's portrait of the Marqués de San Adrián. *(In the casco antiguo, up C. Santo Domingo from Casa Consistorial. Tel. 948 42 64 92. Open Tu-Sa 10am-2pm and 5-7pm, Su 11am-2pm; San Fermines Tu-Su 11am-2pm. 300ptas, students 150ptas, Saturday afternoon and Sunday free.)*

♫ ENTERTAINMENT

Throughout the year, **Plaza de Castillo** is the social heart of the city. Hemingway's favorite haunt was **Café-Bar Iruña**, the backdrop for much of *The Sun Also Rises*. Though the *café* maintains a timeless feel, its prices are very 21st century *(café con leche* 225ptas; good *bocatas* 600ptas; open daily 5pm-3am).

The young and restless booze up at bars in the *casco antiguo*. C. de Jarauta is a nighttime favorite, as well as C. San Nicolás and C. San Gregorio. **Bodegan La Ribera,** C. Navaria, 11, is a good place for cheap beers (175ptas) and poolside rock 'n' roll. Bars on the opposite side of the street draw an older but equally hip crowd. Claustrophobes escape the cramped streets of San Gregorio and San Nicolás to bars in **Barrio San Juan,** beyond Hotel Tres Reyes on Av. Bayona; many draw a gay clientele.

> **!** Although Pamplona is usually a very safe city, crime skyrockets during *San Fermines,* when assaults and muggings do occur. Unfortunately, some come to the fiesta to take advantage of tourists. Do not roam alone at night, and be extremely cautious in the parks and shady streets of the *casco antiguo.* Enthused revelers who pass out in parks can say good-bye to their wallets and money belts.

▧ LOS SAN FERMINES (JULY 6-14)

> "My gosh! I'm sleepy now, doesn't this thing ever stop?"
> "Not for a week," was the seasoned response.
> *— The Sun Also Rises*

Visitors from the world over crowd Pamplona for the *Fiestas de San Fermín—* known to most as "The Running of the Bulls"—in search of Europe's greatest party. Pamplona delivers, with an eight-day frenzy of parades, bullfights, parties, dancing, fireworks, concerts, and wine. Pamplonese, uniformly clad in white garb with red sashes and bandanas, literally throw themselves into the merry-making, displaying obscene levels of physical stamina and alcohol tolerance.

Around 11am, the whole city crowds its way into the plaza around the Ayuntamiento. The mass sings and chants *"San Fermine!"* with *pañuelos* flying until the mayor appears at noon. He fires the first rocket *(chupinzao)*, from the Ayuntamiento's balcony, and a barbaric howl explodes from the sea of expectant *sanferministas* in the plaza below. Champagne rains (be wary of flying corks) along with eggs, ketchup, wine, and flour. Within minutes the streets of the *casco antiguo* flood with improvised singing and dancing troupes. The *peñas*, societies more concerned with beer than bullfighting, lead the hysteria. At 5pm on the 6th and at 9 or 9:30am every other day, they are joined by the *Comparsa de Gigantes y Cabezudos*, a troupe of *gigantes* (giant wooden monarchs) and *zaldikos* (courtiers on horseback). *Kilikis* (swollen-headed buffoons) run around chasing little kids and hitting them with play clubs. These misfits, together with church and Ayuntamiento officials, escort San Fermín on his triumphant procession through the *casco antiguo*. The saint's 15th-century statue is brought from the Iglesia de San Lorenzo at 10am on July 7, the actual day of *San Fermín*.

THE RUNNING OF THE BULLS

The running of the bulls, called the *encierro*, is the focal point of *San Fermines*. The ritual dates back to the 14th century, when it served the practical function of getting the bulls from their corrals to the bullring. These days, the first *encierro* of

RUNNING SCARED

So, you're going to run danger. No one wants to see you end up on evening news programs around the world, so here are a few words of *San Fermines* wisdom:

■ Research the *encierro* before you run. The tourist office dispenses a pamphlet that outlines the exact route of the three-minute run and offers tips for inexperienced runners. You should also watch it once on TV to get a glimpse of what you're in for, and once in person to experience the crush and hysteria first-hand. Check out the tourist office for exhibitions on the event's tradition and history.

■ Do not stay up all night drinking and carousing. Not surprisingly, hung-over foreigners have the highest rate of injury. Experienced runners get lots of sleep the night before and arrive at the course no later than 7am. Many locals recommend arriving at 6am. Access to the course closes at 7:30am.

■ Wear proper clothing (nothing loose or baggy) and appropriate shoes. Do not carry anything with you (especially a back pack or video camera).

■ Give up on getting near the bulls and concentrate on getting to the bullring in one piece. Although some whack the bull with rolled newspapers, runners should never distract or touch the animals; anyone who does is likely to anger the bull and locals alike.

■ Try not to cower in a doorway; people have been trapped and killed this way.

■ Be particularly wary of isolated bulls—they seek company in the crowds.

■ If you fall, STAY DOWN. Curl up into a fetal position, lock your hands behind your head, and **do not get up** until the clatter of hooves has passed.

the festival takes place at 8am on July 7 and is repeated at 8am every day for the following seven days. Hundreds of bleary-eyed, hung-over, hyper-adrenalized runners flee from very large bulls as bystanders cheer from barricades, windows, balconies, and doorways.

A rocket marks the release of the bulls onto the 825m course. One to three animals are released from their pens as runners scurry away. If you want to participate in the bullring excitement, you can line up by the Pl. Toros well before 7:30am and run in *before* the bulls are even in sight (though such a "cowardly" act will bring only booing from the locals). Then you can "play" with the bulls in a mass of 350 people or so. Three to six steers accompany the six to nine bulls—watch out, they have horns, too. Both the bulls and the mob are dangerous. Terrified runners, all convinced the bull is right behind them, flee for dear life and react without concern for those around them. Experienced runners, many of whom view the event as an athletic art form, try to get as dangerously close to the bull as possible. The course has three sharp turns which the fast-running bulls have difficulty cornering; when their legs slide out from under them, they falter, creating a pile of bull. One of the turns is often left unbarricaded—here, a human wall, held together by linked arms, is the sole reinforcement.

After cascading through a perilously narrow opening (where a large proportion of the injuries occur), the run pours into the bullring, amid scores of appreciative spectators. Hemingway had the right idea: don't run—watch the *encierro* from the bullring instead. Music, waves, chanting, and dancing pump up the spectators until the headline entertainment arrives. Bullring spectators should arrive around 6:45am. Tickets for the Grada section of the ring are available before 7am (M-F 450ptas, Sa-Su 600ptas). You can watch for free, but the free section is overcrowded, and it can be hard to see and breathe.

To watch one of the bullfights, you must wait in the line that forms at the bullring around 8pm every evening (tickets start at 2000ptas). As one bullfight ends, tickets go on sale for the next day. Though the *sol* section can get pretty darn hot, it is cheaper and generally more fun.

THE REST OF THE DAY

Once the running is over, the insanity spills into the streets, gathering steam until nightfall when it explodes with singing in the bars, dancing in the alleyways, spon-

NORTHEASTERN SPAIN

taneous parades, and a no-holds-barred party in Pl. Castillo, which quickly becomes Europe's biggest open-air dance floor. The right attire for this dance-a-thon includes sturdy shoes (there's glass everywhere), a white t-shirt (that will soon be soaked with wine), a red *pañuelo* (bandana), and a cheap bottle of champagne (to spray, of course). English speakers often congregate where C. Estafeta hits Pl. Toros, an outdoor consortium of local *discotecas*. A word to the wise: avoid the fountain-jumping (you'll know it when you see it). It is *not* a traditional part of the festivities—it was inaugurated by Americans, Aussies, and Kiwis—and several people have died in recent years. The truly inspired partying takes place the first few days of *San Fermines*. After that, the crowds thin, and the atmosphere goes from dangerously crazed to mildly insane. The party begins (or ends) each day at 6am, when bands march down the streets, waking everyone for the running. In between, the city eases the transition with concerts, outdoor dances, and a host of other performances. The end of the festivities culminates at midnight of July 14 with the singing of *Pobre de mí* (Poor Me): *"Pobre de mí, pobre de mí, que se han acabao las Fiestas de San Fermín."*

Nearby towns sponsor *encierros* as well: **Tudela** holds its festival during the week of July 24, **Tafalla** during the week of August 15, and **Sangüesa** for a week beginning September 11. Many Pamplonese opt to take part in a festival less touristed than their own.

OLITE

Olite (pop. 3000) was a city fit for kings in the early 15th century. Its proximity to Pamplona (35min.) and its Gothic, Baroque, and medieval architecture may make it fit for you too. The **Palacio Real** (tel. 948 74 00 35; fax 948 26 02 41), former palace of the Navarrese kings, is Olite's crown jewel. In the early 15th century, Carlos III made this sumptuous palace the focus of Navarrese court life. Although the 1937 restoration was far from subtle, the palace's spiral staircases, lookout points, and abundant towers are still fun to explore. (Open daily July-Aug. 10am-2pm and 4-8pm; Apr.-June and Sept. 10am-2pm and 4-7pm; Oct.-Mar. 10am-2pm and 3:30-5:30pm. Closed Dec. 25 and Jan. 1. 350ptas, students 250ptas, seniors and children 200ptas. Guided tours in Spanish every hr. on weekends.) Sandwiched between the Palacio Real and the **Palacio Viejo** (now a *parador*), at the base of Pláza de Carlos III, is the **Iglesia de Santa María,** noted for its 14th-century Gothic facade and belfry (mass at 10am and 6pm). **Iglesia de San Pedro** is fitted with an octagonal tower; turn right on Rua Villavieja from the Palacio Real and follow it to its end. (Ask in the tourist office about guided visits.) Every 2nd-to-last weekend in August, the palace plays the backdrop for a medieval festival featuring concerts, theater, and dance. September 13-20 ushers in the **Fiesta de la Cruz,** a week of dancing and bull-tormenting.

Those with their own wheels can drive 18km from Olite up a winding road to the medieval hilltop town of **Ujué** (pop. 240), crowned by an 11th-century church with stunning views. From Olite you can also head to the Cistercian **Monasterio de la Oliva,** 34 km in the opposite direction.

▓ PRACTICAL INFORMATION. Trains (tel. 948 70 06 28) run to **Pamplona** (40min., 2-4 per day, 7:50am-4:05pm, 410ptas), Tudela, and other points on the Vitoria-Gasteiz-Zaragoza line. To get from the **RENFE station** to Pl. Carlos III, take C. Estación to Bar Orly, walk through the archway and follow Rua San Francisco past **Plaza Teobaldos** and through another arch to **Plaza Carlos III.** The bus is far more convenient and less expensive. **Conda** (tel. 948 22 10 26) and **La Tafallesa** (tel. 948 22 28 86) run buses to **Pamplona** (35min., 6-12 per day, 7am-8:30pm, 360ptas). There are 4-7 buses per day from Pamplona to Olite (8:15am-7:30pm, 360ptas). Conda also runs to **Tudela** (5-7 per day, 460ptas). La Tafallesa stops at Bar Orly; to reach Pl. Carlos III, follow the instructions from the train station. Conda stops at the Carretera; to reach Pl. Carlos III, follow C. El Portillo for a block. The staircase leading underground from the middle of Pl. Carlos III goes to the **tourist office** (tel./

fax 948 74 17 03; open Apr.-Sept. M-F 10am-2pm and 4-7pm, Sa-Su 10am-2pm; Oct.-Mar. daily 10am-2pm); **banks** with **ATMs** are in Pl. Carlos III. **Emergency:** tel. 112. **Post office** (tel. 948 74 05 82), on the far end of the plaza from the palace (open M-Sa 9-11:30am); **postal code:** 31390.

⌐▐⌐ ACCOMMODATIONS AND FOOD. The luxurious air of the court lingers in many of Olite's restaurants and accommodations. **Fonda Gambarte,** Rua Seco, 13, 2nd fl. (tel. 948 74 01 39), off Pl. Carlos III, has basic doubles (3500ptas) and a downstairs **restaurant** (2-course *menú*, 1200ptas; open M-F 1-3:30pm and 8:30-10:30pm; Visa). A more expensive but newly renovated option is **Carlos III El Noble**, Rúa de Medíos, 1 (tel. 948 74 06 44), right off Pl. Carlos III, near the tourist office. All doubles with TV, fan, and clean bathrooms. (July-Aug. 8000ptas; off-season 6500ptas; breakfast 700ptas; dinner 2000ptas; add 7% IVA; Visa, MC.) **Camping Ciudad de Olite** (tel. 948 74 06 04; fax 948 74 10 14), one km outside of town on C. de Sta. Brígida, provides adequate accommodations at 425ptas per person and car, 475ptas per tent. There are several **supermarkets** on C. Mayor, off Pl. Carlos III, and a small street **market** on Po. Doña Leonor and Pl. San Antón, at the end of R. Mayor (Wed. 9am-1:30pm).

TUDELA

A somewhat homely modern city with an attractive historic center, Tudela (pop. 26,000) offers enticing versions of standard regional attractions—ghostly medieval churches and elegant old mansions in a labyrinthine *casco antiguo*. A major Muslim center until Christian King Sancho the Strong outmuscled the Moors in 1114, Tudela hosted eminent Muslim and Jewish populations throughout the Middle Ages. Nowadays, solid transportation connections make Tudela a potential hub for exploring Navarra and nearby destinations in Aragón.

◪ ORIENTATION AND PRACTICAL INFORMATION. Old town and new meet in **Plaza de los Fueros,** erstwhile sight of bullfights. To get to Pl. Fueros from the combined **bus and train station,** cross the plaza up Cuesta de la Estación, make the second right onto Av. Zaragoza, go straight for five blocks, and then turn left onto C. Gaztambide-Carrera, which leads to the plaza. The **Casa del Reloj,** with its ornate clock tower, presides over the city's west end. Right (north) of the plaza when facing the clock is the *casco antiguo*, overlooked by the **Castillo de Sancho el Fuerte** and the **Monumento al Corazón de Jesús,** which crown a hill at the edge of town.

Two **RENFE** train lines (tel. 948 82 06 46) run through Tudela: one connects La Miranda to Zaragoza via Castejón de Ebro; the other connects Zaragoza to Vitoria-Gasteiz via Pamplona. The trains go to: **Zaragoza** (7 per day, 6:40am-9:27pm, 1100ptas); **Miranda** (1 per day, 3:38pm, 1420ptas); **Pamplona** (1 direct per day, 5pm, 820ptas); **Vitoria** (none direct, 1420ptas). Conda **buses** (tel. 948 82 03 42) run to: **Pamplona** (1½ hr., 6-7 per day, 8am-9:30pm, 845ptas); **Olite** (1hr., 5 per day, 8am-6pm, 475ptas); **Tarazona** (1hr., M-Sa 5 per day, 10:15am-7:30pm, 220ptas); and to **Madrid** (3 per day, 10:30am-7pm, 2480ptas), Soria, Zaragoza, and San Sebastián. Buses run back to Tudela from: Pamplona (5-7 per day, 7:15am-8:45pm); Tarazona (6 per day, none on Su, 7:15am-6:30pm); Madrid (3 per day, 8am-7pm).

The **tourist office** (tel. 948 84 80 58), on Pl. Vieja alongside the cathedral, has a **fax** machine and a great **map.** To get there from Pl. Fueros, head sharply right when facing the clock tower onto C. Concarera. Cross Pl. San Jaime to the street in the far right corner, follow it around the corner, and look on your right. (Open Apr.-Oct. M-F 9am-3pm and 4-7pm, Sa-Su 10am-2pm; Nov.-Mar. M-F 9am-3pm, Sa 10am-2pm.) **Banco Central Hispano** is on C. Gaztambide, right off P. de los Fueros, and has an **ATM** (open M-F 8:30am-1:45pm); **luggage storage** is in lockers at the station (400ptas per day; open 24hr. on the train station side). **Municipal police** (**emergency** tel. 112), on C. Carcel Vieja. **Post office,** C. Juan Antonio Fernandez, 4 (tel. 948 82 04 47; turn left at the end of C. Eza D. Miguel, off Pl. Fueros; open M-F 8:30am-2pm, Sa 9:30am-1pm); **postal code:** 31500.

▓▓ ACCOMMODATIONS AND FOOD. Tudela does not abound with budget options. **Hostal Remigio,** C. Gaztambide, 4 (tel. 948 82 08 50), on the way from the train and bus station to Pl. Fueros, has sleek modern rooms, firm beds, and pristine bathrooms. (Breakfast 425ptas, *menú* 1500ptas. Singles 1900ptas, with bath 2800ptas; doubles 3800ptas, with bath 5100ptas. Higher rates July, Aug., and *Semana Santa*. Visa, MC, AmEx.) **Bar/Casa de Huéspedes Estrella,** C. Carnicerias, 14 (tel. 948 41 04 42), off C. Yanguas y Miranda from the northwest corner of Pl. Fueros, offers rooms overlooking a pleasant plaza. Ask in the bar about rooms (reception 9am-3pm and 6pm-midnight; doubles 3200ptas.) Chow down at the Chinese restaurant **Gran Mundo,** Av. Zaragoza, 51 (tel. 948 82 05 19), one block past Cuesta de Estación. The lunchtime *menú* is 795ptas; entrees 550-1300ptas. Visa. Picnickers can shop at **Supermercado Consum,** Av. Pamplona, 10 (open M-F 9am-1:30pm and 5-8pm, Sa 9am-2pm and 5-8pm; Visa, MC), or pick up fresh produce at the **mercado** on C. Concarera, off the plaza (open M-F 8am-1:30pm and 5-8pm, Sa 8am-2pm).

▓▓ SIGHTS AND ENTERTAINMENT. Tudela's airy Gothic ▓**cathedral,** built on the site of the town's old mosque, rises from Pl. Vieja in the *casco antiguo*, across from the tourist office. An amalgam of styles from different periods, the cathedral features a Romanesque cloister, several 15th-century Gothic *retablos* (altarpieces), and a chilling Last Judgment tympanum over the west portal. (Cathedral open Tu-Sa 9am-1pm and 4-7pm, Su 9am-1pm. Admission to the cloister 100ptas.)

While the cathedral is the highlight, strolling through the *casco antiguo* can be a pleasure. Points-of-interest include the 12th-century **Iglesia de la Magdalena** to the northeast, the ominous creation that is visible from the entrance to the city. The imposing mansion of the 16th-century **Palacio del Marqués de San Adrián** is next to P. Judería, a left off Muro heading towards the train tracks and out of town. The 18th-century **Palacio del Marqués de Huarte,** home to a Rococo carriage, is on Herrerías, which is a left jog from Yanguesa y Miranda off P. Fueros, and the lovely Romanesque portico of the **Iglesia de San Nicolás** is straight in front of the end of Rua behind the tourist office.

Tudela's **nightlife** is lively and nomadic. Early in the evening, friends gather in bars and cafes between Pl. Fueros and the cathedral. Then it's on to **Calle San Marcial,** east of the plaza, and **Calle Aranaz y Vides,** north from the bus station toward the old town, where pits of revelry carry on into the wee hours.

NEAR TUDELA: BARDENAS REALES

The awesome desert **Bardenas Reales,** with textured hills and cliffs wrought by erosion, covers over 400 square km near the beginning of the Tudela-Pamplona road. The vistas are best contemplated from a mountain bike or car. To rent a bike, take the bus from Tudela to Pamplona and ask to be let off in the unremarkable, sunblasted town of **Arguedas** (20min., 125ptas). There, **Ciclos Marton,** C. San Ignacio, 2 (tel. 948 83 15 77 or 948 83 00 85), has mountain bikes for full-day rental (2000ptas for first day, 1000ptas each additional day). Cyclists should remain on the official roads to prevent damage and/or injuury. Don't forget that Bardenas is a desert; call ahead (tel. 948 84 80 58) about weather conditions as the heat can sometimes be prohibitive. The tourist office in Tudela provides tips and directions. We can recommend that you bring *agua*.

ESTELLA

Hiding between the robust cities of Logroño and Pamplona, charming Estella (pop. 13,000) snuggles into a bend in the Río Ega. What it lacks in size and glamor, it makes up for in hospitality toward the faithful. With tell-tale walking sticks in hand, pilgrims traversing the Camino de Santiago have been descending upon Estella since the town's founding expressly for that purpose in 1090. A number of monuments attest to Estella's medieval prominence.

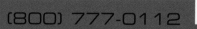

⚑ ORIENTATION AND PRACTICAL INFORMATION. Two streets form a cross through the heart of town, which in turn is bounded by the river. **Calle San Andrés/ Calle Baja Navarra** runs north-south from the bus station on Pl. Coronación to **Plaza de los Fueros. Paseo de la Inmaculada Concepción** runs east-west from C. Dr. Huarte to the **Puente (bridge) del Azucarero,** which spans the river and leads to the old town, where most sights and the tourist office await. To get to the *puente* from the bus station, go right and then follow the river road to the left.

All **buses** running from the station on Pl. Coronación belong to **La Estellesa** (tel. 948 55 01 27). Buses go to: **Logroño** (50min., 5-9 per day, 8:30am-8:30pm, 495ptas); **Pamplona** (1hr., 6-12 per day, 6:50am-8pm, 430-505ptas); **San Sebastián** (1½-2hr., 4-5 per day, 8:45am-7:45pm, 1210ptas); **Zaragoza** (2½hr., M-Sa 1 per day, 8:30am, 1640ptas). The **tourist office,** C. San Nicolás, 1 (tel./fax 948 55 63 01), is a straight shot from the bridge through Pl. San Martín, around the corner to the right. The staff has a map and info on the *camino* and surrounding areas. (Open Mar.-Sept. M-Sa 9am-8pm, Su 10am-2pm; Oct.-Apr. daily 10am-5pm.) **Emergency:** 112; **police,** Po. Inmaculada, 1 (tel. 948 54 82 00). **Post office,** Po. Inmaculada, 5 (tel. 948 55 17 92; open for stamps and Lista de Correos M-F 8:30am-2:30pm, Sa 9:30am-1pm); **postal code:** 31200.

⌂⌘ ACCOMMODATIONS, CAMPING, AND FOOD. Near Pamplona, Estella is a good place to catch some shut-eye during *San Fermines*. Reservations are advisable during its own August *encierro* (running of the bulls). **Pensión San Andrés,** Pl. Santiago, 50 (tel. 948 55 04 48), overlooks a pretty plaza. The first left off C. Baja Navarra after crossing Po. Inmaculada, down C. Mayor, leads you there. San Andrés adorns his tidy rooms with TVs and woven bedspreads, and some with refrigerators. (Breakfast 350ptas. July-Aug. and *Semana Santa* singles 1600ptas; doubles 3500ptas, with bath 5000ptas. Sept.-June singles 1600ptas; doubles 3200ptas, with bath 4000ptas.) **Fonda Izarra,** C. Calderería, 20 (tel. 948 55 06 78), off Pl. Fueros, offers simpler rooms (breakfast 250ptas; summer doubles 4000ptas; off-season 3500ptas; Visa). **Camping Lizarra** (tel. 948 55 17 33; fax 948 55 47 55) is on C. Ordoiz, left from the tourist office and 1km down-river. The grounds have a supermarket, a pool, and mountain bike rentals. (675ptas plus I.V.A. per half *parcela*, with tent, car, and electricity; 495ptas per extra person.)

Estella is known throughout the region for its *gorrín asado* (roast piglet, also called *gorrín de Estella*). Picnickers can stock up at **Supermarket Vendi,** C. Zapatería, at the corner of C. Navarrería and C. Mayor. To get there, take the first right off C. Baja Navarra after Po. Inmaculada Concepción, then go straight three blocks. (Open M-F 9am-2pm and 4:30-8:30pm, Sa 8am-2pm.) **Restaurante Casanova,** C. Fray Wenceslao de Oñate, 7 (tel. 948 55 28 09), upstairs on the left as you enter Pl. Fueros, has overwhelming portions that are sure to slow any pilgrim's progress. The lunch and dinner *menú* are 1200ptas M-F, 1900ptas Sa-Su; entrees 500-1700ptas. (Open in summer daily 1-3:30pm and 8:30-11pm; off-season M 1-3:30pm, Tu-Su 1-3:30pm and 8:30-11pm.) Looking out on Plaza Fueros and its occasional live music, **Café Bar Florida**, Pz. de los Fueros, 18 (tel. 948 55 00 15), serves great fresh pizzas (800ptas), pastas (500ptas) and *bocatas* (sandwiches, 350-500ptas). Serves food 10am-9pm, open until 11pm.

◉♪ SIGHTS AND ENTERTAINMENT. In the "modern" quarter, the 12th-century **Iglesia de San Miguel** commands a view of the town from the hilltop Pl. San Miguel. Its highlight is its ornately carved stone portal depicting St. Michael fighting dragons, weighing souls, and generally taking care of business. Up the stairs and opposite the tourist office, the **Iglesia de San Pedro de la Rúa** towers above **Calle de la Rúa,** the main street of the original mercantile center. The bulbous 12th- to 13th-century late Romanesque/early Gothic church has an unusual half-destroyed cloister. Left from the tourist office at the end of C. Rúa lurks the **Iglesia del Santo Sepulcro,** whose 14th-century facade features a monstrous Satan swallowing the damned by the mouthful. (Outside of mass hours, the San Miguel and San Pedro churches can be visited only by taking tours in Spanish. 30min. tour of San Pedro 200ptas. 30min. tour of San Pedro, San Miguel, and the outside of Santo Sepulcro 400ptas.)

Across from San Pedro and next to the tourist office, the oldest representation of Roland in the world jousts with Farragut the Moor on the columns of the 12th-century Romanesque **Palacio de los Reyes de Navarra,** now the **Museo Gustavo** (tel. 948 54 60 37). Inside are the works of painter Gustavo de Maesta, who spent his last years in Estella. (Open Tu-Sa 11am-1pm and 5-7pm, Su 11am-1pm. Free.)

The week-long **Fiestas de la Virgen del Puy y San Andrés** kick off the Friday before the first Sunday in August. Estella has an *encierro* with baby bulls, smaller and less ferocious than Pamplona's. Kiddie entertainment, a fair, and Navarrese dancing and *gaitas* (bagpipes without the bags) round out the *fiestas.*

NAVARRESE PYRENEES

Navarra encompasses the most topographically diverse range of the Pyrenees. While forbidding peaks dominate the eastern Valle de Roncal, the mountain slopes to the west are diminished in ferocity and height, allowing easier access to the streams, waterfalls, and green meadows dotting the area. Mist and fog obscure visibility at high altitudes, creating either a dreamy atmosphere or slightly nerve-racking driving conditions, depending on your point of view.

While most inhabitants raise cattle or log, tourism is also a booming business. **El Camino de Santiago** is the celebrated cross-kingdom super-trek of intrepid pilgrims clambering over from France (see **Pilgrim's Progress,** p. 454). The most popular pilgrim route crosses the border at Roncesvalles and winds down through Pamplona on the way to Santiago de Compostela in Galicia. Many free and cheap **refugios** cater to certified modern-day pilgrims along the way. To join the fun, get the best available guide, the *Guía práctica del peregrino* (pilgrim's guide; in Castilian, French and Spanish), published by Ediciones Everest (2500ptas). We also highly recommend picking up a copy of the useful *Guía de alojamientos de turismo rurales* (free in any of Navarra's tourist offices), which lists *casas rurales,* beautiful rural houses that lodge travelers. As a rule, these homes are welcoming places to stay and great budget options, usually costing between 3200 and 4400ptas for a double. For reservations, call the multilingual tourist office (tel. 948 20 65 40).

Pamplona is a sensible base for those depending on public transportation; you can head east toward Valle de Roncal (via Sangüesa), or north toward Roncesvalles. **Buses** are one-a-day affairs (if that) throughout most of the area.

SANGÜESA

At first glance, Sangüesa (pop. 4700), set in the arid foothills 44km east of Pamplona, isn't much to look at. Yet Sangüesa's beautiful churches and streets demand a second chance. The town, an entry point for some spectacular nearby sights (both natural and manmade) and is often a necessary stop-over for pilgrims.

Sangüesa earns its place on the Camino due to the **Iglesia de Santa María,** on C. Mayor by the bus stop. Its portal is a veritable triumph of Romanesque sculpture. The central relief depicts the Day of Judgment, with fanged devils casting the damned into the cavernous mouth of Lucifer. The woman nursing a toad on one breast and a snake on the other is a conventional iconographic rendering of Lust. Inside is a hairy Baroque Madonna whose human locks change every 10-15 years. St. James, made of Gothic stone, stands atop a large conch before the **Iglesia de Santiago** Ttel. 948 87 01 32. Churches open for mass only. Ask at the tourist office about guided visits or call 948 43 04 97. 300ptas for Santa María only, 450ptas for tour of all monuments.)

A traditional **metalsmith,** at C. Alfonso el Batallador, 9, lets visitors into his forge. Ask for a guided tour and he will arrange for it. In July and August, the town hosts a series of **medieval dinners,** when hucking half-eaten bones is totally kosher.

⁊ PRACTICAL INFORMATION. Veloz Sangüesina **buses** (tel. 948 87 02 09) go to and from Pamplona (45 min., M-Sa 3 per day, Su 4 per day, 8am-6pm, 425ptas). La Tafallesa (tel. 948 22 28 86) heads to Javier and Yesa on the Pamplona-Uztátroz route (M-Sa 1 per day). Inquire at the tourist office. All buses deposit passengers on C. Mayor. For **taxis,** ring 948 87 02 22. The helpful, English-speaking **tourist office,** C. Mayor, 2 (tel./fax 948 87 14 11), has maps and lots of info on the surrounding area (open in summer M-F 10am-2pm and 4-7pm, Sa-Su 10am-2pm; off-season daily 10am-4pm). **Emergency:** tel. 088 or 112; **medical services: Centro de Salud** (tel. 948 87 14 09), on the road to Cantolagua; **police: Guardia Civil** tel. 091 or 092. **Post office,** Fermín de Lubián, 17 (tel. 948 87 04 27), at the end of C. Mayor beyond Pl. Fueros (open M-F 8am-2pm); **postal code:** 31400.

⁊⚁ ACCOMMODATIONS, AND FOOD. Although expensive, **Pensión Las Navas,** C. Alfonso el Batallador, 7 (tel. 948 87 00 77), is, unfortunately, the cheapest place in town. Dusty rooms with saggy beds, all with baths. Prices are subject to change. (Singles 2675ptas; doubles 5300ptas; closed Sept. 18-Oct. 10). The **Albergue de Pereginos** (tel. 948 34 03 02), free and for pilgrims only, rests on C. Enrique Labrit. Ask at the tourist office for a guide to *casas particulares.* **Camping Cantolagua** (tel. 948 43 03 79) is located near the Ciudad Deportivo (400ptas per person, per car, and per tent; 7% I.V.A. not included). The town's **market,** Pl. Toros, bustles at the end of C. Alfonso el Ballatador away from C. Mayor (Fridays 9am-2pm). **Autoservicio Lozano Hermanos,** C. Mayor, 80, is the supermarket in town. **Restaurante Las Navas** (downstairs from the Pensión) has great **bocadillos** (375-500ptas; open 10:30am-11pm).

DAYTRIPS FROM SANGÜESA

▨GORGES. Two fantastic gorges lie within 12km of Sangüesa. The **Foz de Lumbier** (Lumbier Gorge) is outside the little town of **Lumbier.** Fifty-meter walls tower on one side of this yawning gorge on the Río Irati. A path alongside leads through old railway tunnels. Rio Irati (tel. 948 22 24 70) runs **buses** to the town from Pamplona (1hr., M-F 3 per day, Sa 1 per day, 365-410ptas). A 12km ride from Lumbier brings you to **Iso** and the mouth of an even more impressive gorge, the 6km **Foz de Arbayún.** A lookout affords gorgeous views and glimpses of swooping **griffin vultures.** From Iso, a short path in the chasm leads along the Río Salazar, until it gets too narrow. No buses go directly to Iso. Ask the tourist office in Sangüesa for transportation information; if you have a car, look for the signs off N-240 in the direction of Pamplona.

CASTILLO DE JAVIER. Eight km from Sangüesa by the entrance of the small village of **Javier** is the restored **Castillo de Javier,** the birthplace of San Francisco Xavier (Javier). On the border between Navarra and Aragón, this picture-perfect castle has changed hands many times over the last millennium. Today it's safely in the Jesuits' possession. Its Chapel of the Holy Christ houses a 14th-century effigy that suffered a spontaneous blood-sweating fit at the moment of San Francisco Xavier's death. (Open daily 9am-1pm and 4-7pm, although last entrances at 12:30pm and 6:30pm. Free, but donations requested. Occasional tours in Spanish.) **La Tafallesa** (tel. 948 22 28 86) runs a bus from Pamplona to Javier (1hr., M-F at 5pm, Sa at 1:30pm, 500ptas), and on to nearby Yesa (510ptas); it also stops in Sangüesa, 45 minutes from Pamplona. Buses return Monday through Saturday at 8am.

MONASTERIO DE LEYRE

Windswept and austere, the Monasterio de Leyre (50km from Pamplona) silently surveys the foothills of the Pyrenees and the fabricated lake, Lago de Yesa. It lies about one hour away from Pamplona, off the highway to Huesca. If you don't have your own wheels, it's a 5km uphill slog from Yesa. Here hang-gliders launch themselves off the hills where great wealth and power once presided. In the 12th century, medieval Navarrese kings took up residence in the **monasterio medieval.** Because monks still live at Leyre, you can enter neither this part nor the 20th-century **monasterio nuevo.** However, the dank, subterranean **cripta** eagerly welcomes the public. The architectural highlight of the monastic complex is the ghoulish 12th-century **Portal de la Iglesia.** Outside the monastery is a path to the **Fuente de San Virila.** The fountain occupies the site where, according to legend, the abbot of San Virila fell into a 300-year trance induced by the singing of a nightingale. (Monastery tel. 948 88 40 11. Open daily Apr.-Oct. 10:15am-2pm and 3:30-7pm; Nov.-Mar. M-Sa 10:15am-1:30pm and 3:30-6pm, Su 10:15am-1:30pm and 3:30-6pm. 225ptas, children 50ptas. Guided tours when there are enough people. Mass with Gregorian chanting M-Sa 9am and Su at noon.)

Connected to the monastery, the **Hospedería de Leyre** (tel. 948 88 41 00; fax 948 88 41 37) offers comfortable rooms that, with cozy beds, TVs, and private bathrooms, make the monks' cells look like, well, monks' cells. (Breakfast 700ptas, *menú* 1550ptas. July-Aug. and *Semana Santa* singles 4500ptas; doubles 8800ptas; the rest of the year singles 4150ptas; doubles 7250ptas.) Cheaper shut-eye, a **supermarket,** and **banks** await at the bottom of the hill in Yesa.

RONCESVALLES AND AURITZ-BURGUETE

The first stop in Spain on the Camino de Santiago, **Roncesvalles'** mist-enshrouded ten-odd buildings rest amid miles of thickly wooded mountains. This itty-bitty town (pop. 31), 48km from Pamplona, 20km from France, and eons from reality, lives off legends and the accompanying tourists. Charlemagne's favorite soldier Roland was supposedly slain just up the hill in AD 778, at the hands of the ambushing Basque-Navarrese, who were perturbed that Charlemagne had razed the walls of Pamplona. **Puerto Ibañeta** (1057m), less than 2km up the main road from the monastery, supposedly marks the spot where he breathed his final breath. The heavily restored **Capilla de Sancti Spiritus** stands over the remains of the bone heap (courtesy of dead soldiers and pilgrims), where Roland's tomb may be. The tiny 12th-century **Capilla de Santiago** is next door to the left. (They can only be visited by guided tours; see below.)

Inside the **Colegiata** (tel. 948 76 00 00), up the driveway from the *capilla*, tombs of King Sancho El Fuerte (the Strong) and his bride rest in solitary splendor, lit by the huge stained-glass windows of the **Capilla de San Agustín.** (*Capilla* and claustro open M-F 10:30am-1:30pm, Sa-Su 10am-2pm and 4-7pm. 225ptas; students, seniors, and pilgrims 150ptas.) In the decisive battle of the Navas de Tolosa, Sancho reputedly broke the chains protecting the Arab king Miramomolin with his own hands then promptly decapitated him. The heavy iron chains hanging from the walls of the chamber are represented in Navarra's flag. The monastery's lovely French Gothic **church,** endowed by the Sancho and consecrated in 1219, is its main attraction. (Open daily 8am-8pm. Free. Guided visits including other monuments 425ptas; students, seniors, and pilgrims 325ptas. Call 948 79 04 80 for more info.)

🚌 **PRACTICAL INFORMATION.** La Montañesa **buses** (tel. 948 22 15 84) run from Pamplona to Roncesvalles (1¼hr., M-F 6pm, Sa 4pm, 525ptas); the return bus leaves Roncevalles M-Sa at 7:10am. The bus stops in Burguete each way. A **tourist office** (tel. 948 76 03 01) in Roncesvalles, in the mill behind Casa Sabina Hostería, has maps and guides to the Camino de Santiago (open M-Sa *Semana Santa*-July and Sept.-Oct. 10am-2pm and 3-6pm; Nov.-*Semana Santa* 10am-5pm; July-Aug. 10am-6pm; Su all year 10am-2pm). For a **Banco Central Hispano** (open M-F 8:30am-2:30pm; Oct.-Apr. Sa 8:30am-1pm, May-Sept. Sa closed) a supermarket, and more eating options, head to nearby **Burguete** (2km south); there is hardly any food for sale in Roncesvalles.

🛏️ **ACCOMMODATIONS AND FOOD.** The **monastery** in Roncesvalles has free lodging for official pilgrims—enter the door to the right as you face the monastery. The attached **Oficina de Peregrinos** (tel. 948 76 00 00) gives out credentials. **Albergue Juvenil Roncesvalles (HI)** (tel. 948 76 03 02; fax 948 76 03 62) is in an 18th-century hospital tucked to the right behind the monastery. (Breakfast 200ptas. 1500ptas per person, with *pensión completa* 3050ptas—not always available; over 26 1900ptas, with *pensión completa* 3450ptas. Members only. Call in winter, as the hostel may be closed.)

In nearby **Burguete,** accommodations are numerous and several *casas rurales* line the street. Those following the **Camino de Hemingway** will want to check out the **Hostal Burguete,** San Nikolas, 59 (tel. 948 76 00 05). The big boy slept here and did a little writing on his way back to Paris from *San Fermines.* By the looks of it, the place hasn't changed much—high, plump beds in spacious, old-fashioned rooms. (Breakfast 400ptas, *menú del día* 1350ptas. Singles 2900ptas; doubles with sink 4400ptas, with bath 5600ptas. Open Mar. 15-Dec. 15.) **Camping Urrobi** (tel. 948 76 02 00), 2½ kilometers downhill from Burguete in Espinal, has a grocery store and recreational facilities. (450ptas per person, per tent, and per car; open Apr.-Oct.)

VALLE DE SALAZAR: OCHAGAVÍA

On the banks of the Río Andena, **Ochagavía** (pop. 600) is that perfect picturesque mountain village urbanites dream about. Forty kilometers from Pamplona, the Valle de Salazar's biggest town spans both sides of a cheerful river. Ochagavía's cobbled streets and whitewashed houses lead to forested mountains that make it a great base for hiking, trout fishing, and cross-country skiing. The charming 12th-century **Hermita de Muskilda** (tel. 948 89 00 38) is a 30-minute hike away; follow the stone path behind the church or the road to the left just outside of town if you've got wheels. From the *hermita* there are beautiful views of the valley. (July-Aug. open daily 11am-1pm and 4-7pm; Sept.-June Sa-Su 11am-1pm and 4-6pm, although schedule may vary.)

Hikers will find the climb up the Pico de Orhy (2021m) fairly easy. The trail leaves from the parking lot at Puerto de Larrau, 9km north of Ochagavía on the highway to France. The ascent from *el puerto* takes about one hour. Another good hike is along the Río Irati, through the **Selva de Irati** to **Orbaitzeta.** Leave your car at the Ermita de las Nieves, 24km from Ochagavía, and make the 20km hike to Orbaitzeta (6hr. one-way but one needn't make the whole hike). **Cross country skiers** can enjoy two circuit trails starting a little farther down the same highway.

Río Irati (tel. 948 22 14 70) runs **buses** to and from Pamplona (M-Sa 1 per day, 7am, 825ptas). The **tourist office** (tel./fax. 948 89 06 41), on the main road, is in the same building as a nature center (tourist office open *Semana Santa*-Oct. M-Sa 10am-2pm and 4:30-7:30pm, Su 10am-2pm; Nov.-*Semana Santa* Sa-Su 10am-2pm and 4:30-7:30pm). Several **ATMs** are located on the main road. **Emergency** tel. 112; **pharmacy,** C. Urrutia, 31 (tel. 948 89 05 06). **Post office,** C. Labaria, s/n (tel. 948 89 04 52), next to the Ayuntamiento (open M-Sa 10am-11:30pm).

Hostal Orialde (tel. 948 89 00 27), across the river from the main road on the edge of town, has attractive, spacious rooms (breakfast 350ptas, *menú* 1500ptas; singles 2800ptas, doubles 3500ptas, with bath 4800ptas; 7% I.V.A. not included). Ask

TRADITIONS OF NAVARRA (WITHOUT HORNS)
Yes, yes, everyone knows about the "encierros" in Navarra, but there are more traditions than just bull chases man...man stabs bull. Not only does the area have regular axe-cutting and stone-lifting contests (*aitzkolaris* and *harrijusotza-iles*), but they annually partake in an angelic flight and a "peace treaty" with France.

Every Easter Sunday in the Pl. Fueros in Tudela, thousands of people crowd in to catch a glimpse of their angel sent from heaven. Atop the Casa del Reloj building, a (man-made) heaven rests. From this heaven, a small child dressed as an angel descends from a cloud (and rope) to the center of the plaza. When the child reaches the awaiting black-veiled Virgin statue, to the cheers and encouragement of the crowd, she unmasks the virgin.

At the Piedra de San Martín border, every July 13th, the Mayors of the French Valley Baretous wait with three cows. The French present the gifts to the Mayors of the Roncal Valley. Both Mayors renew peace vows and nominate the overseer of the grazing land between the countries. Although the event at one time was a meaningful statement and gesture, it is now a tradition based on brotherhood and a cause for celebration.

at the tourist office or look for the "CR" signs advertising one of the town's 25 *casa rurales*. **Camping Osate** (tel. 948 89 01 84), at the entrance to town, provides a modern campsite on the river and rents **mountain bikes** (475ptas per person and per car, 425ptas per tent; 1000ptas per day for bike).

VALLE DE RONCAL

Carved by the Río Esca, Valle de Roncal is a particularly handsome valley stretching from the French border. With its darling towns, inviting *casas rurales*, prime **hiking** and **cross-country skiing** grounds, and overall laid-back air, Valle de Roncal is a showcase of the best the Navarran Pyrenees have to offer.

RONCAL

Smack in the center of the Valle de Roncal, the diminutive town of **Roncal** (pop. 300) puffs up with pride over its famed *queso Roncal*, a sharp cheese made from sheep's milk, and its own Julián Gayarre (1844-1889), a "world-renowned" tenor. **Casa Museo Julián Gayarre** (tel. 948 47 51 80), on C. Arana, is a museum in the singer's birth-house, showcasing his personal belongings and assorted memorabilia. (Open Apr.-Sept. Tu-Su 11:30am-1:30pm and 5-7pm; Oct.-Mar. Sa-Su 11:30am-1:30pm and 4-6pm. 200ptas.)

La Tafallesa (tel. 948 22 28 86) **buses** run from Pamplona (depart M-F 5pm, Sa 1pm), through Javier, and on to Roncal (2hr., 880ptas from Pamplona); buses also return to Pamplona and Javier from Roncal (depart M-Sa 7am). There is an extremely helpful **tourist office** (tel. 948 47 51 36) on Roncal's main road. Ask about nearby hiking and *casas rurales*. (Open June-Sept. daily 10am-2pm and 4:30-7:30pm; May-June and Oct.-Dec. M-Sa 4:30-7:30pm, Su 10am-2pm.) **Banco Central Hispano** is across the street (open May-Sept. M-F 8:30am-2:30pm; Oct.-Apr. M-Sa 8:30am-1pm; no commission); the **Guardia Civil** is at tel. 948 47 50 05; in an **emergency**, call 122; a **pharmacy** is next door to the tourist office (open M-F 10am-2pm and 5-7:30pm, Sa 10am-2pm); a couple of **supermarkets** and telephones cluster by the bridge at the base of the town.

Try one of the splendid *casa rurales* for a night's rest. **Casa Villa Pepita**, Po. Julián Gayarre, 4 (tel. 948 47 51 33), south of the bridge on the main road, has adorable rooms (singles 1650ptas; doubles 3400ptas, with bath 4400ptas; breakfast 350ptas, meals 1300ptas). If Pepita is full, the owner will gladly direct you to another *casa rural*.

ISABA AND ENVIRONS

The more populous village of **Isaba** (pop. 542) straddles the highway 7km north of Roncal. The **tourist office** (tel. 948 89 32 51) is right off the main road (open in summer Tu-Sa 10am-2pm and 5-8pm, Su 10am-2pm; off-season Tu-Su 10am-2pm). **Phones** and **ATMs** huddle at the southern end of town. **Albergue Oxanea**, C. Bormapea, 47 (tel. 948 89 31 53), is left up the stone staircase, opposite the Centro de Salud. Wooden *literas* (bunks) fit eight and 14 to a room, and there's a TV/VCR room. (Hot showers included. Breakfast 300ptas. Other meals 1285ptas. 1200ptas per night, 1000ptas with own sleeping bag. 7% I.V.A. not included.) **Camping Asolaze** (tel. 948 89 30 34), 6km toward the French border, houses a restaurant and a store and offers *literas* (1000ptas per person, sheets 200ptas), in addition to regular plots of earth (500ptas per person and per car, 505ptas per tent; doubles with bath 4000ptas; Visa, MC, Maestro). Eight km north of Isaba, the earth opens up into the idyllic **Valle de Belagua. Refugio Angel Oloron** (tel./fax. 948 39 40 02) is open year-round and offers *literas* (1100ptas), breakfast (300ptas), and other meals (1500ptas). The refuge is located at km 19 on the highway to France from Isaba, and the drive offers grade-A views. Check also in the guide to *Casas Rurales* (see p. 402) for local houses offering lodging.

A standard yet stunning hike goes from Isaba to Zuriza (5-6hr.). Shorter, but steeper, are the ascents from Collado Argibiela to **Punta Abizondo** (1676m) and **Peña Ezkaurre** (2050m). Ask the tourist office for routes of differing durations and difficulty. Ski trails run north of Isaba, at the **Estación de Ski Larra-Belagna** (tel. 608 16 51 67 or 948 39 40 02). The **Escuela de Esquí Valle del Roncal**, with offices in Hotel Isaba (tel. 948 89 32 66), offers lessons and skis (4000ptas per hr. lesson for one person; 4500ptas for two people; group lessons available). A village festival runs July 25-28 and Sept. 15 in Isaba.

PAÍS VASCO (EUSKADI)

As the Basque saying goes, "Before God was God and the rocks were rocks, the Basques were Basque." País Vasco is officially composed of the provinces Guipúzcoa, Alava, and Vizcaya, but those who identify themselves as Basque are not restricted by boundaries. Instead, the Basque country is often thought to expand into Navarra and southwestern France. The varied landscape of País Vasco resembles a nation complete unto itself, combining cosmopolitan cities, verdant hills, industrial wastelands, and quaint fishing villages. The people are bound by their deep attachment to the land, an almost spiritual appreciation of fine food and drink, and immense cultural and national pride.

Many believe that the Basques are the native people of Iberia, as their culture and language date back several millennia. Today's nationalistic sentiment stems from the 18th-century abolition of the Basque *fueros* (ancient rights of self-government) and the Basques' military defeat in the late 19th-century Carlist wars. During Franco's regime, attempts to suppress Basque identity were seen as threats to their traditional values, provoking renewals of pre-modern identities. Euskadi ta Askatasuna (ETA) began an anti-Spanish terrorist movement that has lasted over 30 years, despite the fact that most Basque National-

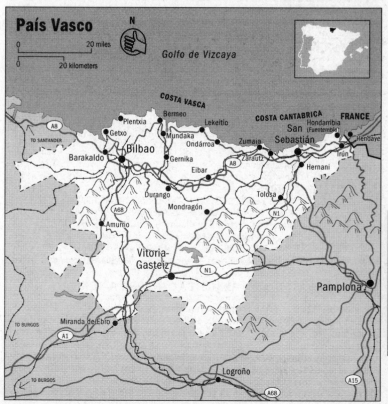

País Vasco

N

0   20 miles

0   20 kilometers

Golfo de Vizcaya

COSTA VASCA

Plentxia

Bermeo

Lekeitio

COSTA CANTABRICA   FRANCE

A8

Getxo

Mundaka

Ondárroa

Zumaia

San
Sebastián

Hondarribia
(Fuenterrabia)

Hendaye

TO SANTANDER

Barakaldo

Bilbao

Gernika

Zarautz

A8

Irún

Hernani

Eibar

Durango

Tolosa

A68

Mondragón

N1

Amurrio

Vitoria-
Gasteiz

N1

Pamplona

TO BURGOS

Miranda de Ebro

A1

TO BURGOS

Logroño

A68

A15

ists are critical of ETA and the affiliated party, Euskal Herritarrok. Demonstrations and other forms of Nationalist activity do, however, occur. Although violence has generally been directed at Spanish government officials, beginning in 1996 ETA targeted heavily touristed areas in order to arouse international attention; a cease-fire was declared in 1998 and has held thus far.

The desire to preserve their cultural identity is common among Basques. Although Castilian Spanish is the predominant language, Basque *(euskera)* has enjoyed a resurgence of popularity since Franco's death. Other traditions such as *cesta punta* or *pelota vasca* (known outside of Spain as *jai-alai*) continues to thrive. Basque cuisine is some of Iberia's finest, including *bacalao a la vizcaína* (salted cod in a tomato sauce), dishes *a la vasca* (in a delicate parsley-steeped white wine sauce), and *chipirones en su tinta* (baby squids in their own ink). *Tapas* in País Vasco, considered regional specialties, are called *pintxos;* locals wash them down with *sidra* (cider) and the local white wine, *txakoli.*

HIGHLIGHTS OF PAÍS VASCO

■ *Pintxos* at **San Sebastián's** bars after a day at the beautiful beach (see p. 413).
■ A walk along the marina in refreshing seaside **Hondarribia** (see p. 416).
■ Frank O. Gehry's shiny new **Guggenheim Museum Bilbao** (see p. 421).
■ The educational and powerful **Guernica Museum** (see p. 424).

SAN SEBASTIÁN (DONOSTIA)

Glittering on the shores of the Cantabrian Sea, San Sebastián (pop. 170,000) is a cool, elegant city. By the beginning of the 19th century the city had become one of Spain's great ports, but much of the city was destroyed during the Peninsular War—in 1813 Anglo-Portuguese troops set fire to it after taking it from the French. The city's damaged walls were finally torn down in 1863 and construction of a new San Sebastián began. Today the city stands as a stronghold of Basque nationalism. Basque efforts for separatism have been fueled by a strong economy, which is rooted in a thriving tourist industry. The city gained international fame when Queen Isabel II made it her summer residence in 1846. Its popularity has been increasing ever since, particularly among landlocked Spaniards desperate to escape the heat of central Spain. Vacationers come for its world-famous beaches, *tapas*, and bars, as well as its strong sense of regional culture.

▐ GETTING THERE

Buses to San Sebastián are cheaper and more frequent than trains. They run from: **Pamplona** (1hr., 7-8 per day, 7am-10:45pm, 780ptas); **Bilbao** (1hr., 8-23 per day, 6:30am-10pm, 1100ptas); **Burgos** (3½hr., 7 per day, 3:15am-10pm, 1825ptas). Trains run from: **Madrid** (6-7hr., 5 per day, 9:20am-10:45pm, 4600-4900ptas); **Barcelona** (8hr., 4 per day, 10am-9:50pm, 4900ptas).

▐ ORIENTATION AND PRACTICAL INFORMATION

Street and plaza signs are usually in both *castellano* and *euskera*. The street guide on the tourist office map gives both versions in its index, so don't despair if you see "kalea" and "tx" everywhere. The **Río Urumea** splits San Sebastián in two. The city center, most monuments, and the two most popular beaches are on the peninsula on the west side of the river. The tip of the peninsula is **Monte Urgulla**. Inland is the **parte vieja** (old city), where nightlife rages and budget accommodations and restaurants cluster. South of the *parte vieja*, at the base of the peninsula, is the commercial district. The **bus station** lies in

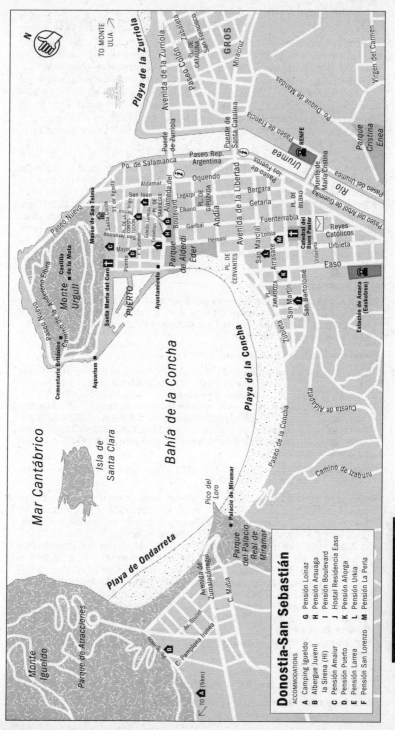

Mar Cantábrico

Isla de Santa Clara

Bahía de la Concha

Playa de Ondarreta

Playa de la Concha

Monte Igueldo

Parque de Atracciones

Pico del Loro

Palacio de Miramar

Parque del Palacio Real de Miramar

Av. Brunet

C. Pamplona Irunea

C. Matia

Avenida de Zumalacárregui

Camino de Izaburu

Paseo de la Concha

Cuesta de Aldapeta

TO (5km)

Playa de la Zurriola

TO MONTE ULIA

Avenida de la Zurriola

Paseo Colón

PL. DE CATALUÑA

San Francisco

Zabaleta

GROS

Miracruz

Virgen del Carmen

Po. Duque de Mandas

Parque Cristina Enea

Río Urumea

Paseo del Árbol de Guernica

Puente de María Cristina

Puente de Guernica

Paseo de Francia

RENFE

Puente de Santa Catalina

Santa Catalina

Paseo de los Fueros

Puente de Zurriola

Po. de Salamanca

Paseo Rep. Argentina

Oquendo

Aldamar

3? de Agosto

Santa Corda

San Juan

Alameda del Boulevard

Legazpi

Elkano

Garibai

Hernani

PL. DE LA CONST.

Embeltran

F. Calbeton

Mayor

Puerto

Iñigo

Narrica

San Lorenzo

Esterlin Lorenzo

Museo de San Telmo

Paseo Nuevo

Castillo de la Mota

Santa María del Coro

Cementerio Británico

Camino de Andereno Elbira

Paseo Nuevo

Monte Urgull

PUERTO

Aquarium

Ayuntamiento

Parque de Alderdi Eder

PL. DE CERVANTES

PL. DE ZARAGOZA

Bergara

Getaria

Andía

PL. DE GIPUZKOA

SARRIEGI

Fuenterrabia

Loiola

San Marcial

Arrasate

San Martín

San Bartolomé

Zubieta

Avenida de la Libertad

PL. DE BILBAO

Catedral del Buen Pastor

Reyes Católicos

Urbieta

Easo

Urdaneta

Estación de Amara (Euskotren)

Avenida de

NORTHEASTERN SPAIN

Donostia-San Sebastián

ACCOMMODATIONS

A Camping Igueldo
B Albergue Juvenil
    la Sirena (HI)
C Pensión Amaiur
D Pensión Puerto
E Pensión Larrea
F Pensión San Lorenzo

G Pensión Loinaz
H Pensión Arsuaga
I Pensión Boulevard
J Hostal Residencia Easo
K Pensión Añorga
L Pensión Urkia
M Pensión La Perla

WHAT THE DEVIL ARE THEY TXPEAKING?

Linguists still cannot pinpoint the origin of *euskera*. Its commonalities with Caucasian and African dialects suggest that prehistoric Basques may have migrated from the Caucasus mountains through Africa. Referred to by other Spaniards as *la lengua del diablo* (the devil's tongue), *euskera* has come to symbolize cultural self-determination. Only half a million natives speak the language, chiefly in País Vasco and northern Navarra. During his regime, Franco banned *euskera* and forbade parents to give their children Basque names (like Iñaki or Estibaliz). Since his death, there has been a resurgence of everything from *euskera* TV shows to *ikastolas* (Basque schools). As a result, it is a language of the old and the young.

the south of the city on Pl. Pío XII. Av. de Sancho el Sabio runs to the right (north) straight toward the cathedral, ocean, and old town. East of the river lie the **RENFE station, Barrio de Gros,** and **Playa de la Zurriola.** Both sides of the river are connected by three bridges: Puentes Zurriola, Santa Catalina, and María Cristina (listed from north to south). To get to the *parte vieja* from the train station, head straight to Puente María Cristina, cross the bridge, then turn right at the fountain and walk four blocks north to Av. Libertad. Turn left and follow it to the port; the *parte vieja* fans out to the right, and Playa de la Concha to the left.

TRANSPORTATION

Flights: Airport in Hondarribia (Fuenterrabía), 20km east of the city. **Interurbanos** buses to Hondarribia pass by the airport (45min., every 15min., 7:45am-11pm, 200ptas). Taxi 3200ptas. To **Madrid** (4 per day) and **Barcelona** (3 per day). **Iberia** (tel. 943 64 12 67) has an office at the airport.

Trains: San Sebastián has two train stations.

RENFE, Estación del Norte (tel. 943 28 30 89), on Po. Francia, on the east side of Puente María Cristina. Info open daily 7am-8pm. To: **Vitoria-Gasteiz** (1¾hr., 3-14 per day, 6:57am-11:07pm, 1500-1600ptas); **Pamplona** (2hr., 2-12 per day, 10:35am-10:59pm, 1500ptas; the bus costs half as much and takes half the time); **Burgos** (3½hr., 7 per day, 8:32am-11:07pm, 2400-2600ptas); **Zaragoza** (4hr., 5 per day, 10:35am-11:07pm, 2700-3900ptas); **Madrid** (8hr., 4 per day, 8:32am-11:07pm, 4600-4800ptas); **Barcelona** (9hr., 2 per day, 10:35am and 10:59pm, 4700-4900ptas); **Paris** (8-11hr., 3 per day, 7:30am-9:10pm, 11,000ptas).

Estación de Amara (Euskotren) (tel. 943 45 01 31), Pl. Easo. Commuter trains to **Irún** (30min., 7:47am and 10:17am, 200ptas).

Buses: Several private companies run from different points in the city. Most buses pass through the central station on Pl. Pío XII, about 13 blocks south of Av. Libertad on Av. Sancho el Sabio. Public bus #28 goes to the city center from the bus station. Buy tickets at the office of each company. **PESA,** Av. Sancho el Sabio, 33 (tel. 902 10 12 10), to **Bilbao** (1¼hr., every 30min., 6:30am-10pm, 1060-1200ptas) and **Vitoria-Gasteiz** (2hr., 1-4 per day, 8:15am-6pm, 1010-1100ptas). **Continental Auto,** Av. Sancho el Sabio, 31 (tel. 943 46 90 74), to **Burgos** (3-3½hr., 6-7 per day, 9am-8:30pm, 1825-1950ptas) and **Madrid** (6hr., 3-17 per day, 3685-4000ptas). **La Roncalesa,** Po. Vizcaya, 16 (tel. 943 46 10 64), to **Pamplona** (1hr., 7 per day, 7am-9:15pm, 780ptas). **Vibarsa,** Po. Vizcaya, 16 (tel. 902 10 13 63), to **Barcelona** (7hr., 3-5 per day, 7:20am-11:20pm, 2450-2600ptas). **Turytrans** (tel. 943 46 23 60), to **Paris** (11 hr., 3-5 per week, 8:40am-3:10pm, 7600-8000ptas). **Interurbanos** (tel. 943 64 13 02), Pl. Guipozcoa (pay on board), to **Irún** (35min., every 15min., 165ptas) and **Hondarribia** (45min., every 15min., 200ptas).

Public Transportation: List of 19 routes at the tourist office, or call 943 28 71 00. Each trip 110ptas. Bus #16 goes from Alameda del Boulevard to campground and beaches.

Taxis: Santa Clara (tel. 943 31 01 11) or **Donostia** (tel. 943 40 40 40).

SAN SEBASTIÁN ■ 411

Car Rental: Europcar (tel. 943 32 23 04; fax 943 29 07 00), Estatión de RENFE. Must be 21 or over. Open M-F 8am-1pm and 4-7:30pm, Sa 9am-1pm.

Mountain Bike Rental: Comet, Av. Libertad, 6 (tel. 943 42 66 37). Half-day 2500ptas, full day 3000ptas, 2000ptas per additional day. Open M 4-7:30pm, Tu-F 10am-1pm and 4-7:30pm, Sa 10am-1:30pm and 4-7:30pm. Visa, MC, AmEx.

TOURIST, FINANCIAL, AND LOCAL SERVICES

Tourist Office: Municipal: Centro de Atracción y Turismo (tel. 943 48 11 66; fax 943 48 11 72), C. Reina Regente, in the vast Teatro Victoria Eugenia. From the train station, turn right immediately after crossing Puente María Cristina. Continue until reaching Puente Zurriola; C. Reina Regente will be on the left. From the bus station, go down Av. Sancho el Sabio. At Pl. Centenario, bear right on C. Prim, take a left on Av. Libertad, and follow it to the end. English- and French-speaking staff, map, transit and accommodations info, and a bulletin board. Open June-Sept. M-Sa 8am-8pm, Su 10am-1pm; Oct.-May M-Sa 9am-2pm and 3:30-7pm. **Regional: Oficina de Turismo del Gobierno Vasco** (tel. 943 42 62 82), Po. Fueros, is farther down the river from the municipal office, near the train station. Open June-Aug. M-F 9am-1:30pm and 3:30-6:30pm, Sa-Su 9am-1pm; May-Sept. M-F 9am-1:30pm and 3:30-6:30pm, Sa 9am-1pm.

Luggage Storage: Lockers at **RENFE station.** 400ptas per day. Open daily 7am-11pm. At **Continental Auto.** 300ptas per day. Open daily 7am-noon and 3-8:30pm.

English Bookstore: Donosti, Pl. Bilbo, 2 (tel. 943 42 21 38), 1 block west of Puente María Cristina near the cathedral. Excellent selection. Open M-F 9am-1pm and 4:30-8pm, Sa 9am-1pm. Visa, MC, AmEx.

Laundromat: Lavomatique, C. Iñigo, 13 (tel. 943 42 38 71), off C. San Juan. Self-service. 575ptas wash, 400ptas dry. Soap 60ptas. Ironing 75ptas for 15min. Open M-F 10am-1pm and 4-7pm, Sa-Su 10am-1pm.

Hiking Info: Club Vasco de Camping, San Marcial, 19 (tel. 943 42 84 79), 1 block south of Av. Libertad. Organizes excursions. Open M-F 6am-8:30pm. **Izadi,** Ramón Maria Lili, 2 (tel. 943 29 35 20). Sells hiking guides and maps, some in English. Organizes tours and rents skis, wetsuits, and hiking equipment. Open M-Sa 10am-1pm and 4-8pm.

EMERGENCY AND COMMUNICATIONS

Emergency: tel. 091 of 092. **Police: Municipal** (tel. 943 45 00 00), C. Easo.

Medical Services: Casa de Socorro, Bengoetxea, 4 (tel. 943 44 06 33).

Post Office: (tel. 943 46 34 17; fax 943 42 43 90), C. Urdaneta, the street just south of the cathedral. Open M-F 8:30am-8:30pm, Sa 9:30am-2pm. Lista de Correos at window #11. **Postal Code:** 20006.

Internet Access: Netline, C. Urdaneta, 8 (tel. 943 44 50 76). 8 computers with a lengthy wait. 250ptas for 15min., 400ptas for 30min., 750ptas per hr. Open M-Sa 10am-10pm. **Airtel,** C. Euso, 25 (tel. 943 42 04 24; fax 943 42 02 45). 5 computers and A/C. 150ptas per 15min. First 2 print-outs free, 10ptas per additional printout. Open June-Aug. M-F 9:30am-1pm and 4-7:30pm, Sa 10am-1pm; Sept.-May M-F 9:30am-1pm and 4-7:30pm, Sa 10am-1pm and 4-8pm.

⌐ ACCOMMODATIONS AND CAMPING

Desperate backpackers will scrounge for rooms in July and August—particularly during *San Fermines* (July 6-14) and *Semana Grande* (starts Sunday during the week of Aug. 15); September's film festival is not much better. To make matters worse, many places don't take reservations in summer. Budget options center in the *parte vieja* and around the cathedral; there are often a few per entryway—look for signs in doorways. Solo travelers should be prepared to pay for a double, as single rooms are virtually impossible to come by, especially in summer. The tourist office has lists of budget accommodations, and most hostel owners know of **casas particulares**—don't be afraid to ask for help. Owners of *casas particulares* often solicit guests at the RENFE station. Be wary—this is illegal.

PARTE VIEJA

A bit of a hike from the bus and train stations, the *parte vieja* is brimming with reasonably priced *pensiones*. Its proximity to Playa de la Concha and the port makes this area a prime nightspot; scores of *pensiones* offer a night's sleep above loud *pintxos (tapas)* bars. Call in advance for reservations.

■ **Pensión Amaiur,** C. 31 de Agosto, 44, 2nd fl. (tel. 943 42 96 54 or 616 38 89 88). From Alameda del Boulevard, go up C. San Jerónimo to the end and turn left. Look for the flower-obscured facade. Pastel rooms, all with satellite TV, face the street or mountains. Delightful English- and French-speaking owner. *Semana Santa* and June 22-Sept. 21 doubles 5500ptas; triples 7500ptas. Apr.-June and Oct. doubles 4000ptas; triples 5200ptas. Nov.-Mar. doubles 3300ptas; triples 4200ptas. *Let's Go* discount 300ptas.

■ **Pensión Loinaz,** C. San Lorenzo, 17 (tel. 943 42 67 14), off C. San Juan. Friendly English-speaking owners offer bright rooms with big windows. Laundry 1000ptas. July-Aug. doubles 4200-4700ptas; triples 6200ptas. Apr.-June doubles 3200ptas; triples 4500ptas. Sept.-March doubles 2700ptas; triples 3800ptas. Singles sometimes available. 3-bedroom apartment available upstairs for groups. *Let's Go* discount 500ptas.

Pensión San Lorenzo, C. San Lorenzo, 2 (tel. 943 42 55 16), off C. San Juan. Cozy rooms and a fully equipped kitchen. June-Oct. 1500-2000ptas per person. Nov.-May singles 1500ptas; doubles 2800ptas; triples 3900ptas; quads 5000ptas.

Pensión Larrea, C. Narrica, 21, 1st fl. (tel. 943 42 26 94). Appealing rooms with sparkling bathrooms. July-Aug. singles 3000ptas; doubles 5000ptas; triples 6000ptas. Sept.-June singles 2500ptas; doubles 3500ptas; triples 5000ptas. Open Mar. 21-Oct.

Pensión Boulevard, Alameda del Boulevard, 24 (tel. 943 42 94 05). Beautiful, modern rooms, all with radios, some with balconies. June-Aug. 2000ptas per person; Sept.-May singles 2500ptas; doubles 3000ptas, with bath 4500ptas; triples 4000ptas.

Pensión Puerto, C. Puerto, 19, 2nd fl. (tel. 943 43 21 40), off C. Mayor. Clean rooms with big closets and some balconies. 3000-4000ptas per person.

Pensión Arsuaga, C. Narrica, 3, 3rd fl. (tel. 943 42 06 81), off Alameda del Boulevard. Charming, homey rooms. Doubles 5000ptas; triples 7850ptas.

OUTSIDE THE OLD CITY

Most of these hostels lie in the heart of the commercial zone. They tend to be quieter than those elsewhere in the city, yet are still fairly close to the port, beach, bus and train stations, and all of the action in the *parte vieja*.

Albergue Juvenil la Sirena (HI), Po. Igueldo, 25 (tel. 943 31 02 68; fax 943 21 40 90), near the beach at the far west end of the city. Bus #24 runs from the train and bus stations to Av. Zumalacárregui (the stop in front of the San Sebastián Hotel). Bus #5 drops you off 1 street away on C. Matia. From Av. Zumalacárregui, take the street that angles toward the mountain (Av. Brunet) and turn left at its end. The hostel is the big pink building. Clean, modern, dorm-style rooms and a multilingual staff. HI members and ISIC-carriers only. Breakfast included. Sheets 385ptas. Luggage storage, laundry facilities, and kitchen available. Best to arrive before 11am. Lockout 11am-3pm. Curfew June-Aug. daily 2am; Sept.-May Su-Th midnight, F-Sa 2am. June-Aug. 1950ptas, over 26 2200ptas; Sept.-May 1600ptas, over 26 1950ptas. Visa.

Pensión Urkia, C. Urbieta, 12, 3rd fl. (tel. 943 42 44 36). C. Urbieta borders the cathedral on the west; the hostel is one block north at C. Arrasate. Polished knick-knacks and gilt mirrors in the foyer. Rooms with lovely blue and white linens, full bathrooms, and TV. July-Sept. doubles 5300ptas. Oct.-June singles 3000ptas; doubles 3745ptas.

Pensión La Perla, C. Loiola, 10, 2nd fl. (tel. 943 42 81 23), on the street directly ahead of the cathedral. Friendly, English-speaking owner. Grand stairway leads to attractive rooms with polished floors. All rooms have bath and TV; #7 is a gem. July-Sept. singles 4000ptas; doubles 6000ptas. Oct.-June singles 3225ptas; doubles 3750ptas.

Pensión Añorga, C. Easo, 12, 1st fl. (tel. 943 46 79 45), at C. San Martín. Shares entryway with 2 other *pensiones*. Basic, but clean and breezy. Some rooms have TVs. July-

Aug. singles 3000ptas; doubles 4000ptas, with bath 6000ptas. Sept.-June singles 2000ptas; doubles 3000ptas, with bath 4000ptas.

Hostal Residencia Easo, C. San Bartolomé, 24 (tel. 943 45 39 12). Head toward the beach on C. San Martín, turn left on C. Easo, and right on C. San Bartolomé. Huge windows and TVs. July-Sept. 15 singles 5000ptas; doubles 6000ptas, with bath 8000ptas; triples 8000ptas, with bath 10,000ptas. Sept. 16-June singles 3000ptas; doubles 4000ptas, with bath 6000ptas; triples 6000ptas, with bath 8000ptas.

Camping: Camping Igueldo (tel. 943 21 45 02), 5km west of town. The 268 spots fill in the blink of an eye. Bus #16 ("Barrio de Igueldo-Camping") runs between the site and Alameda del Boulevard (every 30min., 110ptas). Keep San Sebastián's quirky weather in mind. Reception June-Aug. 8am-midnight; Sept.-May 9am-1pm and 5-9pm. *Parcela* (including tent and up to 2 people): June-Aug. and *Semana Santa* 2889ptas, extra person 425ptas; Sept.-May 1386ptas, extra person 357ptas.

🍴 FOOD

Pintxos (tapas), chased down with the fizzy regional white wine *txacoli*, are a religion here; bars in the lively old city spread an array of enticing tidbits on toothpicks or bread. *Pintxos* rarely cost more than 175ptas each, so eat up! In the harbor, many small places serve tangy sardines with the strong, slightly bitter *sidra* (cider), another regional specialty. Custom insists on pouring it with arm extended upward so the force of the stream hitting the glass releases *sidra's* bouquet of flavor. From January through April, San Sebastián's gourmands turn their attention to **sidrerías**, which are open to the public and all provide the same, standard meal (cod, beef chop, and cheese) as an accompaniment to the *sidra*.

Restaurants and bars clamor for attention on C. Fermín Calbetón, in the old quarter. In fact, the entire *parte vieja* seems to exist for no other purpose than to feed. The majority of restaurants offer their best deals on lunchtime *menús*. **Mercado de la Bretxa,** on Alameda del Boulevard at C. San Juan and **Mercado de San Martín,** on C. San Marcial between C. Loiola and C. Urbieta, sell fresh produce (both markets open M-F 7:30am-2pm and 5-7:30pm, Sa 7:30am-2pm). **Super Todo Todo** on Alameda del Boulevard, is around the corner from the tourist office (open M-Sa 8:30am-9pm, Su 10am-2pm). Buy organic munchies at **Muerdago,** San Martin, 18 (open M-F 9:30am-1:30pm and 4:30-8pm, Sa 9:30am-1:30pm).

PARTE VIEJA

PINTXOS

🔲 Bar La Cepa, C. 31 de Agosto, 7-9 (tel. 943 42 63 94). To-die-for delicacies. *Pintxos* 160-325ptas. Weekday lunch *menú* 1700ptas. Open daily 1pm-midnight. Visa, MC, AmEx, Maestro. Traveler's checks accepted.

Bar Intxa, C. Esterlines, 12 (tel. 943 42 48 33). Outdoor seating and tasty *pintxos. Bocadillos* 325-550ptas. Entrees 800ptas. Open Su-Th 10am-4pm and 6:30-11:30pm, later F-Sa. Closed May 15-June and Oct. 15-31.

Bar Juantxo, C. Embeltrán, 6 (tel. 943 42 74 05). A local favorite, famous for its *bocadillos* (285-495ptas)—they sell about 1000 a day! *Pintxos* 130-200ptas. Open daily 8:30am-midnight.

Ganbara, C. San Jerónimo, 21 (tel. 943 42 25 75). Sitting down may be out of the financial question, but the affordable *pintxos* are exquisite. Don't miss the *gambas rebozadas* (shrimp, 170ptas). Open daily 11am-3:30pm and 6pm-midnight.

RESTAURANTS

Jatetxea Morgan, C. Narrica, 7 (tel. 943 42 46 61). Pricey entrees, but *menú* (1550ptas) is a steal. Open M-Sa 1:30-3:30pm and 9-11pm, Su 1:30-3pm. Visa, MC.

Pizzeria Trattoria Capricciosa, C. Fermín Calbetón, 50 (tel. 943 43 20 48). Italian basics with a Spanish twist. Pastas 800-1100ptas, pizzas 850-1150ptas. Open M-F 1-2:30pm and 8:30pm-11pm, Sa-Su 1:30-2:30pm and 8:30-11:30pm. Visa, MC.

Santa Lucia, C. Puerto, 6 (tel. 943 42 50 19). Big meals, small prices. The "HungryMan" (#6), with lots of bacon, eggs, and toast, satiates for 500ptas. Entrees 550-900ptas. Open daily 8:30am-10pm.

PARTE NUEVA

Tenis Ondarreta (tel. 943 31 11 50 or 943 31 41 18; fax 943 46 04 39), on Po. Peine de los Vientos. Definitely worth the walk and the extra buck. Entrees 1300-1950ptas. *Menú* on Friday 1450ptas plus 7% IVA. Open M-Sa 1-4pm and 9-11pm, Su 1-4pm.

La Mamma Mia, C. San Bartolomé, 18 (tel. 943 46 52 93). Scrumptious pizza (695-975ptas) and fettucine and spaghetti (645-975ptas). *Menú* 1200ptas plus 7% IVA. Open daily 1:30-4pm and 8:30pm-12:30am. Visa, MC.

Caravanseri Café, C. San Bartolomé, 1 (tel. 943 47 54 78), east of the cathedral. Fabulous vegetarian options including tofu and veggie burgers (400ptas). Combination plates 675-1300ptas. Open M-Sa 8am-12:30am, Su 10am-midnight.

Rojo y Negro, C. San Marcial, 52 (tel. 943 42 61 46). Heavenly *pintxos* 150-175ptas. Sandwiches 400ptas. Open daily 7am-2:30am.

Cachón, C. San Marcial, 40 (tel. 943 42 75 07). A perfect stop on a marine-inspired *pintxos* tour. *Pintxos* 140-180ptas. Open daily 7:30am-11pm. Visa, MC, AmEx.

◾ SIGHTS

San Sebastián's most attractive sight is the city itself—green walks and parks, grandiose buildings, and attractive hillsides encircle a placid, fan-shaped bay and the pleasant island of Santa Clara.

◾MONTE IGUELDO. Although the views from both of San Sebastián's s mountains are spectacular, those from Monte Igueldo are superior. By day the countryside meets the ocean in a line of white and blue; by night Isla Santa Clara, lit by floodlights, seems to float on a ring of light. The sidewalk toward the mountain ends just before the base of Monte Igueldo with Eduardo Chillida's sculpture *El peine de los vientos* (Wind's Comb). The walk up is not too strenuous, but anyone with corns, blisters, or callouses will appreciate the funicular.

◾MONTE URGULL. Across the bay from Monte Igueldo, the gravel paths through the shady woods of Monte Urgull are peppered with monuments, love-struck teenagers, and stunning vistas. The overgrown **Castillo de Santa Cruz de la Mota** crowns the summit with cannons and a chapel; the castle is crowned by the statue of the Sagrado Corazón de Jesús, which blesses the city. *(Open daily June-Aug. 8am-8pm; Sept.-May 8am-6pm.)* Halfway up, the **Cementerio Británico** honors British soldiers who died defending the Spanish monarchy during the Peninsular War (1813).

MUSEO DE SAN TELMO. The Museo de San Telmo resides in a Dominican monastery. The serene, overgrown cloister is strewn with Basque funerary relics. The main museum beyond the cloister contains a fascinating array of pre-historic Basque artifacts, some El Grecos, a couple of dinosaur skeletons, and a piece of contemporary art. *(Po. Nuevo. Tel. 943 42 49 70. Open Tu-Sa 10:30am-1:30pm and 4-8pm, Su 10:30am-2pm. 350ptas, students 200ptas.)*

PALACES. As soon as Queen Isabel II started vacationing here in 1846, fancy buildings began to spring up like wildfire. **El Palacio de Miramar,** has passed through the hands of the Spanish court, Napoleon III, and Bismarck. Today anyone can stroll through the grounds. *(Between Playa de la Concha and Playa de Ondarreta. Open June-Aug. 9am-9pm; Sept.-May 10am-5pm.)* The other royal residence, **Palacio de Ayete,** is closed to the public, though the surrounding trails are not. *(Head up Cuesta de Aldapeta or take Bus #19. Grounds open June-Aug. 10am-8:30pm; Sept.-May 10am-5pm.)*

PASAJES DE SAN JUAN. Thirty minutes from the town center, between a lush hill and a dark, gray-green bay, lies the town of Pasajes de San Juan. The charming fishing village's wood-balconied houses and small bay crowded with colorful *cha-lupas* (little boats) make an enchanting time warp. *(A Herribus bus (every 20-30min., 120ptas) goes to Pasajes de San Juan from Pl. Gipúzkoa.)*

OTHER SIGHTS. An Aquarium lies on the edge of the port. *(Po. Muelle, 34. Tel. 943 44 00 99. Open July-Aug. 10am-10pm; Sept.-June 10am-1:30pm and 3:30-7:30pm. 700ptas, students 630ptas.)* Wandering through the *parte vieja* reveals **Plaza Constitución**, with the ornate portal of **Iglesia Santa María** and numbered balconies dating from the plaza's days as a bull ring.

ⓒ BEACHES AND WATER SPORTS

The gorgeous **Playa de la Concha** curves from the port to the **Pico del Loro,** the beak-shaped promontory which is home to the Palacio de Miramar. The virtually flat beach disappears during high tide, and each year erosion narrows the beaches a little more. Crowds jam onto the smaller and steeper **Playa de Ondarreta,** beyond Miramar. Across the river from Mt. Urguel, surfers crowd **Playa de la Zurrida.** Pic-nickers can head for the alluring **Isla de Santa Clara** in the center of the bay. Fre-quent motorboats leave for the island (5min., June-Sept. only, round-trip 250ptas), or rent a rowboat. Check at the portside kiosk for info on both options.

Several sports-related groups offer a variety of activities/lessons. For **windsurfing** and **kayaking,** call the Real Club Nautico, C. Igentea, 9 (tel. 943 42 35 75). For **para-chuting,** try Urruti Sport, C. José Maria Soroa, 20 (tel. 943 27 81 96). For **surfing,** check out the Pukas Surf Club, C. Mayor, 5 (tel. 943 42 72 28). For info on all sports, pick up a copy of the *UDA-Actividades deportivas* brochure at the tourist office. **Scuba Du,** Muelle, 23 (tel. 943 42 24 26), rents equipment and offers classes.

♫ NIGHTLIFE

The *parte vieja* pulls out all the stops after dark. **C. Fermín Calbetón**, three blocks in from Alameda del Boulevard, is practically sweating bars. Along the beach, the music starts thumping at midnight. Keep an eye out for discount or buy-one-get-one-free coupons on the street, as covers can be exorbitant.

Bar Tas-Tas, C. Fermín Calbetón, 35 (tel. 943 43 06 12), attracts a generous helping of international backpackers. Happy Hour M-Th. Open daily 3pm-3am.

Bars Sariketa, C. Fermín Calbetó, 23, is a dark hole behind red doors. After a few drinks you won't know what's shaking the floors. Open 5:30pm-3:30am.

Txalupa, C. Fermín Calbetó, 3. A zoo of a place. Beer 250ptas. Open 8pm-2:30am.

Bar Kai, C. Juan de Bilbao, 2. Jazz music, and one of the few places to have an intimate conversation. Open Su-Th 6pm-12:30am, F-Sa until 2am.

Akerbeltz, C. Mari near the port. Sleek, black, and cave-like. Cover 2000-3000ptas, includes 1 drink. Open until midnight.

Molly Malone, C. San Martin, 55, outside of the *parte vieja.* A classic Irish pub. Beer 400-600ptas. Open 11am-4am.

♫ FESTIVALS

The tourist office has the *Guía del Ocio* as well as a tri-monthly booklet of events. The city runs a **marathon** in November, **El Día de San Sebastián** (Jan. 19-20) brings traditional parades, a **carnival** swings forty days before *Semana Santa,* and **Festi-val Internacional de Danza** (dance festival; tel. 943 48 21 11) leaps in May.

San Sebastián's five-day **Festival de Jazz,** in mid- to late July, is one of Europe's most ambitious. Such giants as Art Blakey, Wynton Marsalis, and Dizzy Gillespie have played here. For info on the 1999 festival, contact the Oficina del Festival de Jazz (tel. 943 48 11 79; email jazzaldia_donostia@donostia.org; www.jazzaldia.com). Movie stars and directors own the streets for a week in September during the **Festival Internacional de Cine,** one of the four most important in the world (along with Venice, Cannes, and Berlin). For info about the 1999 film festival, call the Victoria Eugenia Theater (tel. 943 48 12 12; fax 943 48 12 18).

Semana Grande, the week of August 15, is ablaze with concerts, movies, and an international fireworks festival. The **Fiestas de San Juan,** on and around June 24, bring their own share of folklore performances, Basque sports competitions, and general revelry. **La Quincena Musical,** in the Teatro Victoria Eugenia, C. Reina Regente, sponsors more than two weeks of classical music concerts in late August, most of them free.

DAYTRIPS FROM SAN SEBASTIÁN

HONDARRIBIA

Less than an hour east of San Sebastián by bus, Hondarribia (pop. 14,000) is a European beach town designed the way European beach towns should be. Stretching along the Txingudi Bay, the town flaunts a silky-smooth beach and brightly painted houses with flower-filled balconies. Compared to chic San Sebastián, Hondarribia is refreshingly simple. In the peak days of summer, the beach, which lies at the far end of town past the fisherman's marina and at the end of a long seaside walk, can become ridiculously crowded with vacationers from Madrid and Barcelona. Fortunately, it's pleasantly calm through June.

⚡ PRACTICAL INFORMATION. Interurbanos buses (tel. 943 64 13 02) run from C. Zuluaga to **San Sebastián** (45min., every 15min. until 10pm, 200ptas). **AUIF** buses (tel. 943 63 31 45) go to **Irún** (10min., every 15min. until 10pm, 110ptas). The **airport** (tel. 943 66 85 00) is within walking distance of the town center. **Bidasoa Turismo,** C. Javier Ugarte, 6 (tel. 943 64 54 58), in Pl. San Cristóbal, serves as the regional **tourist office.** The English-speaking staff doles out maps and lodging lists. (Open July-Aug. daily 10am-8pm; Sept.-June M-F 9am-1:30pm and 4-6:30pm, Sa 10am-2pm). **Emergency:** tel. 091 or 092; **police** tel. 943 64 43 00. **Post office,** Pl. San Cristóbal, 1 (tel. 943 64 12 04; open M-F 8:30am-2:30pm and Sa 9:30am-1pm); **postal code:** 20280.

🏠🍴 ACCOMMODATIONS AND FOOD. Reservations are key in the summer, so call ahead. The modern **Albergue Juan Sebastián Elcano (HI)** (tel. 943 64 15 50; fax 943 64 00 28), Ctra. Faro, sits on a hillside overlooking the sea. From the bus stop, head to the beach on C. Itsasargi, bearing left at the coast and continuing straight for several long blocks. At the traffic circle turn left and follow signs uphill to the hostel. Two hundred beds and a TV room wait for travelers. (Members only; HI cards 1000-1500ptas. Breakfast included. 3-night max. stay when full. Reception daily 9am-noon and 4-7pm. Curfew midnight, but doors open at 1am and 2am. Sheets 115ptas. Dorms 1250ptas, over 30 1875ptas.) In the other direction from Pl. San Cristóbal is the darling **Hostal Txoko Goxoa,** C. Murrua, 22 (tel./fax 943 64 46 58), in the old quarter. Head up C. Javier Ugarte from the tourist office, take the second right onto C. Juan Laborda, and follow the street until the end. Walk along the old walls and go up the stairs at C. Murrua; the hostel is on the right. All rooms have big windows and bath. (Breakfast 475ptas. July-Sept. doubles 6200ptas; Oct.-June doubles 5500ptas. IVA not included. Discounts for longer stays. Visa, MC, Eurocard.) **Camping Jaizkibel** (tel. 943 64 16 79; fax 943 64 26 53) sits 2km from town, on Ctra. Guadelupe toward Monte Jaizkibel. (Reception daily 9am-11pm. 550ptas per person, per tent, and per car. Bungalows for 1-2 people 6000-9000ptas.)

Several **markets** spill onto C. San Pedro, three blocks inland from the port. **Market Goikoetxea** (tel. 943 64 10 29) includes flowers and fresh bread among its luscious outdoor offerings (open M-F 7:30am-2pm and 4:30-8pm, Sa 7am-2pm). Beach bums refuel at **Gaxen,** C. Zuloaga, 6 (tel. 943 61 14 62), six blocks from the beach and two blocks from the bay. The cafe serves full breakfasts and 36 kinds of sandwiches. (Open M-Th 9am-11pm, F-Su 9am-noon. Closes 1hr. earlier in winter.)

☎ **SIGHTS.** The gorgeous stone-and-timber *casco antiguo*, centered around Carlos V's imposing palace in Pl. Armas (now a *parador*—peek inside to catch a glimpse of the renovations), provides welcome relief from Coppertone fumes. The **Parroquia de Nuestra Señora de la Asunción,** also in Pl. Armas, is a lovely 15th century Gothic church. It was here that Louis XIV of France married, by proxy, the Spanish Habsburg Infanta María Teresa. (Officially open only for Mass and tours; check at the desk in front. 400ptas.)

⚄ **EXCURSIONS.** There are several possible excursions from Hondaribbia. Six km up Av. Monte Jaizkibel, **Monte Jaizkibel,** the highest mountain on the Costa Cantábrica, guards the **Santuario de Guadalupe.** The environs offer incredible views of the coast. On a clear day you can see as far as Bayonne, France—45km away. **Boats** (tel. 943 61 64 47) shuttle travelers 5km to Hendaye, a French town with a bigger beach. They leave from the pier at the end of C. Domingo Egia, off La Marina (every 15min, reduced service in winter, 200ptas).

IRÚN

Irún's (pop. 55,000) visitors are usually in a hurry to get somewhere else, and with good reason—the city is little more that a transportation hub with services to Paris, Madrid, San Sebastián, and the French border.

RENFE **trains** (tel. 943 61 67 08) fan out to all of Spain; connections to **San Sebastián** are frequent (25min., every 40min., 5:23am-10:23pm, 150-175ptas). The train station has **currency exchange,** a **post office,** and **luggage storage** (400ptas, ask for token at the bar; open daily 7am-11pm). The **Ayuntamiento (SAC office),** C. Juan de la Cruz, 2 (tel. 943 64 92 00), on Pl. Zabaltza off Po. Colón, dispenses maps and free pens (open M-F 8:30am-2pm and 4:30-7:30pm, Sa 9:30am-1pm). **Emergency:** tel. 112; **police** (tel. 098), in Pl. Ensanche.

Most people who stay overnight in Irún arrived too late in the day to continue on to their final destinations. Affordable *hostales* line C. Estación in front of the station. **Hostal Residencia Lizaso,** C. Aduana, 5 (tel. 943 61 16 00), has clean, simple rooms, all with TV. Follow C. Estación, bear right on Po. Colón, and take the first right. (July-Aug. singles 2300ptas; doubles 3750ptas, with shower 4750ptas, with full bath 5250-5450ptas. Sept.-June singles 2500ptas; doubles 3200ptas, with shower 3700ptas, with full bath 4300ptas. IVA not included.) **Bar Restaurant El Rincón,** C. Estación, 22 (tel. 943 61 60 30), serves a 900pta *menú* with fish and lamb (open daily 9am-1am). The **mercado** is at C. República de Argentina, 12 (open M-F 8:30am-1:30pm and 4-7:30pm, Sa 8:30am-1:30pm).

BILBAO (BILBO)

Graced with the marvelous new Guggenheim Museum, Bilbao (pop. 1,000,000) is finally overcoming its reputation as a bourgeois, business-minded industrial center. The economic engine of the Basque country, Bilbao has been making people wealthy since the 16th century, when its shipbuilding industries and coastal location made it a key trade link between Castile and Flanders. The city has bought respectability by investing heavily in the arts and its own infrastructure. Economic booms in the 19th century bestowed wide boulevards lined by grandiose buildings; 20th-century success has showered the city with a new subway system, an overhauled international airport, a new bridge, and a stylish riverwalk project, all executed by renowned international architects. However, it is the Guggenheim that has fueled Bilbao's rise to international prominence.

◱ **GETTING THERE**

Trains run to Bilbao from **Madrid** (6hr., 3 per day, 4am-11pm, 5700ptas); **Barcelona** (8½hr., 4 per day, 10am-9:50pm, 4900-5100). **Buses** run from: **San Sebastián** (1¾hr., every 30min., 6:30am-10pm, 1100ptas); **Burgos** (2-3hr., 8 per day, 6am-9pm, 1420ptas); **Santander** (3hr., 24 per day, every 30min., 925ptas).

🛈 ORIENTATION AND PRACTICAL INFORMATION

It's wise to get a map, as Bilbao's sights are all over the place. The city's main artery, **Gran Vía**, leads east from the oval Pl. Federico Moyúa to **Plaza Circular,** the axis for many important stops and stations. Past Pl. Circular, you will cross Ría de Bilbao on Puente del Arenal, which deposits you on **Plaza de Arriaga,** the entrance to the *casco viejo* to the right of the tourist office.

TRANSPORTATION

Flights: Airport (tel. 94 486 93 01), 10km from Bilbao in Sondica (Sondika). Take **Bizkai Bus** (tel. 94 448 40 70) A-3247 from C. Sendeja next to the Ayuntamiento, on the left after crossing Puente Arenal into the old town (40min., every 40min., 6am-10:30pm, 130ptas). Taxi 2500ptas. **Iberia,** C. Ercilla, 20 (tel. 94 471 12 10), C. Colón de Larreátegui. Open daily M-F 9:30am-1:30pm and 3-6pm.

Trains: Bilbao has 3 train stations.

RENFE: Estación de Abando/del Norte, Pl. Circular, 2 (tel. 94 423 86 23). Info open 7am-9pm. To: **Salamanca** (5½-6½hr., 2 per day, 9:25am and 2:05pm, 3500ptas); **Madrid** (5¾-9hr., 2 per day, 4:30pm and 11:30pm, 4200-4400ptas); **Barcelona** (9½-11hr., Su-F 2 per day, 10:05am and 10:45pm, 5100ptas).

FEVE: Estación de Santander, C. Bailén, 2 (tel. 94 423 22 66). From Pl. Circular, walk down C. Navarra toward the river and take a right before the bridge; it's the gilded building on the water. Info open M-F July-Aug. 9am-2pm and 4-7pm; Sept.-June 7-10pm. To **Santander** (2½hr., 3 per day, 9:05am-6:35pm, 920ptas).

Ferrocarriles Vascongados/Eusko Trenbideak (FV/ET): Atxuri Station, Cl. Atxuri, 6-8 (tel. 94 200 80 08). Follow river south from Pl. Arriaga. To **Guernica** (1hr., 17-20 per day, M-F 6:18am-8:18pm, Sa 8:18am-8:18pm, 300ptas).

Buses: Most bus companies are based at the **Termibús terminal,** C. Gurtubay, 1 (tel. 94 439 50 77; M: San Mamés), on the west side of town. To get to Pl. Arriaga from the station, take the Metro to Casco Viejo, exiting at Pl. Unamuno. Take a right on C. Sombrería and the first right onto C. Correo. The tourist office can help with bus info.

ANSA (GETSA, VIACAR): C. Autonomía, 17 (tel. 94 444 31 00). From Pl. Circular, go down C. Hurtado de Amézaga to Pl. Zabálburu, bearing right on C. Autonomía for 2 blocks; enter through Bar Ansa. To: **Burgos** (2hr., 4 per day, 8:30am-7pm, 1435ptas); **Madrid** (4-5hr., 9-15 per day, 7am-8pm, 3270ptas); **Barcelona** (7hr.; M-F 4 per day, 7am-11pm; Sa-Su 3 per day, 10:30am-11pm; 4900ptas); **León** (7hr., 1 per day, 8:45pm, 3200ptas).

ENATCAR: Termibús terminal (tel. 94 439 51 11). To **Salamanca** (5 hr.; M-Sa 2 per day, 8:30am and 8:45pm; Su 1 per day, 5:30pm; 3200ptas).

PESA: Termibús terminal (tel. 94 424 88 99; info tel. 902 10 12 10). To **San Sebastián** (1hr., 8-23 per day, 6:30am-10pm, 1100ptas).

La Unión: C. Henao, 29 (tel. 94 424 08 36). From Pl. Circular, walk down Gran Vía to Pl. Federico de Moyúa, turn right on Alameda de Recalde and go 2 blocks to C. Henao. To **Vitoria-Gasteiz** (1hr.; 14-22 per day; M-F 6:45am-9pm, Sa 7:30am-10pm, Su 8:30am-9:30pm; 665ptas). Leaving from Termibús (tel. 94 439 50 77) to: **Haro** (1hr., 2-5 per day, 8:30am-7:30pm, 1035ptas); **Logroño** (1¾hr., 3-5 per day, 8:30am-7:30pm, 1455ptas); **Pamplona** (2hr., 4-6 per day, 7:30am-8pm, 1560ptas).

ALSA Grupo: Termibús terminal (tel. 902 42 22 42). To: **Santander** (3½hr., 6 per day, 10am-9:45pm, 925ptas); **Zaragoza** (4hr., 4-6 per day, 6:30am-2:30pm, 2430ptas); **La Coruña** (5½hr., 4 per day, 10am-1:45pm, 5585ptas).

Public Transportation: Bilbao recently opened an attractive and user-friendly **metro** (tel. 94 425 40 25). Look for 3 interlocking red circles to find entrances. The system has 1 line with terminal points in the suburbs. Hang onto your ticket after entering—you'll need it again to exit. Travel within 1 zone 135ptas; 2 zones 160ptas; 3 zones 190ptas. 10-trip ticket within 1 zone 800ptas; 2 zones 950ptas; 3 zones 1150ptas. Trains run M-Sa 6am-2am, Su 7am-11pm. **Bilbobús** (tel. 94 475 82 00) runs 23 lines across the city (6am-11:30pm; 110ptas, 10-ride coupon 645ptas). **Bizkai Bus** (tel. 94 475 82 00) connects Bilbao to suburbs and the airport in Sondica (Sondika).

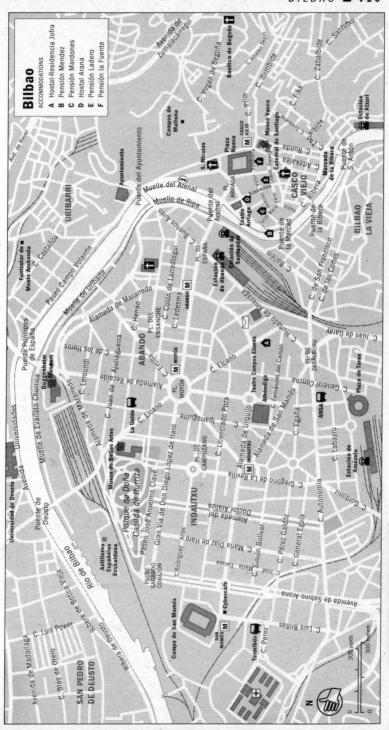

Bilbao

ACCOMMODATIONS
A Hostal-Residencia Jofra
B Pensión Mendez
C Pensión Mardones
D Hostal Arana
E Pensión Ladero
F Pensión la Fuente

NORTHEASTERN SPAIN

Taxis: Teletaxi (tel. 94 410 21 21). **Radio Taxi Bilbao** (tel. 94 444 88 88).

Car Rental: Europcar, C. Licenciado Poza, 56 (tel 94 442 22 26). Must be at least 21. 6000ptas per day. Open M-F 8am-1pm and 4-7:30pm, Sa 9am-1pm.

TOURIST AND FINANCIAL SERVICES

Tourist Office: Oficina de Turismo de Bilbao (tel. 94 479 57 60; fax 94 479 57 61; www.bilbao.net), Pl. Arenal. Gives out a good map and tri-monthly bulletin of events. English spoken. Open M-F 9am-2pm and 4-7:30pm, Sa 9am-2pm, Su 10am-2pm.

Currency Exchange: Banco Central Hispano, Pl. Circular. Open June-Aug. M-F 9am-2pm; Sept.-May M-Th 9am-5:30pm, F-Sa 9am-2pm.

American Express: Viaca, Alameda de Recalde, 68 (tel. 94 444 48 62), off C. Autonomía. Open M-F 9am-1:30pm and 4:30-7:30pm, Sa 10am-1pm.

LOCAL SERVICES

Luggage Storage: In Estación de Abando, small lockers 400ptas, large 500ptas. In Termibús, 100ptas a day. Both open daily 7:30am-11pm.

El Corte Inglés: Gran Vía, 7-9 (tel. 94 424 22 11), on the east side of Pl. España. Distributes maps. Also offers novels, guidebooks, haircuts, supermarket, cafeteria, restaurant, and currency exchange. Open M-Sa 10am-9pm.

English Bookstores: Casa del Libro, C. Urkijo, 9 (tel. 94 415 32 00). A terrific selection. Open M-Sa 9:30am-9pm. Visa, MC.

Budget Travel: TIVE, C. Iparraguirre, 3 (tel. 94 423 18 62). Open M-F 9am-2pm.

EMERGENCY AND COMMUNICATIONS

Emergency: tel. 088. **Police: Municipal,** C. Luis Briñas, 14 (tel. 94 420 50 00).

Medical Services: Hospital Civil de Basurto, Av. Montevideo, 18 (tel. 94 441 88 00 or 94 442 40 51). **Ambulance:** tel. 94 473 16 34.

Post Office: Main office, Alameda Urquijo, 19 (tel. 94 422 05 48; fax 94 443 00 24). Walk 1 block down Gran Vía from Pl. España and turn left after El Corte Inglés; it's on the corner of C. Bertendona. **Fax** and Lista de Correos (around the corner). Open M-F 8:30am-8:30pm, Sa 9:30am-2pm. **Postal Code:** 48005.

Internet Access: Cybercafé Antxi, C. Luis Briñas, 13 (tel. 94 441 04 48). Great decor. 300ptas for 30min., 575ptas per hr. Open M-F 11am-1:30pm and 4-10:30pm.

◤ ACCOMMODATIONS

At any time other than during the August festival season (when rates can be higher than those listed below), it shouldn't be hard to find a reasonably priced room if you arrive before noon; rooms tend to fill up by late afternoon from July through September. The tourist office has a list of recommended budget hostels, most of which are in the *casco viejo*. From the bridge, head down the stairs; to the right is Pl. Arriaga and to the left C. Arenal. Both offer budget accommodations galore.

Pensión Méndez, C. Santa María, 13, 4th fl. (tel. 94 416 03 64). From the bridge, turn right on C. Ribera; C. Santa María is on the left as the street turns. Insulated from the raging nightlife below. All rooms are clean, most with balconies and sinks. Singles 3000ptas, with bath 5000ptas; doubles 4000ptas, with bath 7000ptas; triples 6000ptas, with bath 9000ptas.

Pensión Ladero, C. Lotería, 1, 4th fl. (tel. 94 415 09 32). From Pl. Arriaga, take C. Bidebarrieta and turn left onto C. Lotería. Very clean rooms, all with TV and cheery blue bedspread. Singles 2500ptas; doubles 4000ptas.

Pensión de la Fuente, C. Sombrería, 2 (tel. 94 416 99 89). From C. Arenal, turn right on C. Correo, follow it 2 blocks past Pl. Nueva, then turn left. Friendly owner rents pleasant rooms with high ceilings. Heating, TV extra (500-800ptas). Singles 2000ptas; doubles 3500ptas, with bath 4500ptas.

Hostal Mardones, C. Jardines, 4, 3rd fl. (tel. 94 415 31 05). From the bridge, turn right onto C. Bidebarrieta and right again. Lovely rooms, some with balconies, all with polished wood floors and marble sinks. Call ahead in summer. Singles 4000ptas, with bath 5000ptas; doubles 4500ptas, with bath 5000ptas.

Hostal-Residencia Jofra, C. Elcano, 34, 1st fl. (tel. 94 421 29 49), in the new city. From Pl. España, walk 5 blocks down C. Hurtado de Amézaga past Estación Abando and turn right. Pleasant rooms with sinks. Singles 2400ptas; doubles 3500ptas. Closed Aug.

Hostal Gurea, C. Bidebarrieta, 14 (tel. 94 416 32 99). Decent rooms are warm in winter. Singles 2500ptas, with bath 3500ptas; doubles 3900ptas, with bath 4300ptas.

◖ FOOD

Restaurants and bars in the *casco viejo* offer a wide selection of local dishes, plus *pintxos* and *bocadillos* aplenty; the new city has more variety but less ambience. **Mercado de la Ribera,** on the bank of the river heading left from the tourist office, is the biggest indoor market in Spain. It's worth a trip even if you're not eating. (Open June 15-Sept. 15 M-Sa 8am-2pm; Sept. 16-June 14 M-F 8am-2pm and 4:30-7pm, Sa 8am-2pm.) Groceries are on the second floor of a massive **Simago,** Pl. Santos Juanes (open M-Sa 9am-9pm).

OLD CITY (CASCO VIEJO)

Restaurante Peruano Ají Colorado, C. Barrencalle, 5 (tel. 94 415 22 09). Dining area adorned with artistic masks. *Menú* 1500ptas. Entrees 550-1730ptas. Open M-Sa 1:30-3:30pm and 9-11:30pm. Visa, MC.

Aitxiar, C. María Muñoz, 8 (tel. 94 415 09 17). Ambrosial food in a lively setting. Try the *merluza a la vasca* (hake in a wine, garlic, and parsley sauce with clams; 2200ptas) and learn why it's called a special. *Tostadas* dessert is the French toast of your dreams (700ptas). Lunch *menú* 1500ptas. Open daily 1-3:30pm and 8-11pm. Visa, MC.

Restaurante Kaltzo, C. Barrencalle Barrena, 5 (tel. 94 416 66 42). A classy pick on a street lined with inexpensive options. Lunch *menú* 1000ptas. Entrees 1400-2000ptas. Open M 1-4pm, Tu-Sa 1-4pm and 8-10:30pm. Visa, MC.

Restaurante Juanak, C. Somera, 10 (tel. 94 415 99 79). Snug bar with a lively 20-something crowd, 54 *bocadillos,* and loads of vegetarian options (350-500ptas). Open F-W noon-midnight, Th 12:30pm-1am.

NEW CITY

Restaurante Bar Zuretzat, C. Iparraguirre, 7 (tel. 94 424 85 05), down the street from the Guggenheim. Don't miss the incredibly sweet pudding *a la caramel,* included in the *menú* (1500ptas) or by itself at 700ptas. Open daily 1-5pm. Visa, MC, AmEx.

Café La Granja, Pl. Circular, 3 (tel. 94 423 08 13), opposite Estación Abando. Cavernous classic cafe with decorative themes. Spanish breakfast 250ptas. *Menú* 1500ptas. Open M-Th and Su 7am-midnight, F-Sa 7am-2:30am. Visa, MC.

Resturante-Bar Al Jordan, C. Elcano, 26 (tel. 94 410 42 55), a side street near the train station. Middle Eastern food. Veg and non-veg *menús* 975ptas. Open M-Th 9am-1am, F-Sa 9am-3am. Visa, MC, AmEx.

◉ SIGHTS

◪THE GUGGENHEIM. Frank O. Gehry's Guggenheim Museum Bilbao can only be described as breathtaking. Lauded in the international press with every superlative imaginable, it has catapulted Bilbao straight into cultural stardom.

> **¡BASTA YA!** On July 10, 1997, at 4pm, Miguel Ángel Blanco, 29, the Ermua city council representative of the Basque province of Vizcaya, disappeared near his hometown. The kidnappers were members of the Basque separatist group ETA (Eskadi ta Askatasuna). ETA demanded that the government stop incarcerating ETA members in the Canary Islands rather than in their home nation. The demand was not new; the government was still adamant in refusing it. On July 12, at 5pm, the news came: Ángel Blanco had been shot in the head and died soon after in the hospital. The anger over the murder was palpable. Heads of government in the País Vasco expressed regret, outrage, and the solidarity of the Basque people against ETA. Millions took to the streets in an unprecedented display of outrage, and anti-ETA demonstrations occurred even in the País Vasco. The cry rose up across the nation: "¡Basta ya!" (Enough already!). But the killings did not stop: five Partido Popular councillors have been murdered by ETA since Blanco's death, including Manuel Zamarreño, Blanco's successor, killed by a car bomb in June of 1998. Although these subsequent incidents have failed to awaken the same unified outrage, the general consensus remains the same: violence is not the way to gain autonomy. A cease-fire was finally called in 1998, and to date the peace has been sustained.

Visitors are greeted by Jeff Koons's "Puppy," a dog composed of 60,000 plants and standing almost as tall as the actual museum. The main attraction is constructed mainly out of titanium, limestone, and glass in a series of interconnected pieces. The US$100 million building, with its undulating curves and multiple levels, resembles a scaly fish or a ship about to set sail on the river beside it. The amazingly light and airy interior features a towering atrium and a series of non-traditional exhibition spaces, including a gargantuan 130m by 30m hall. The museum currently hosts rotating exhibits drawn from the Guggenheim Foundation's collection but will gradually acquire its own international sampling of 20th-century works. Sleek black-and-red suited staff slap bracelets on the streams of visitors filing through the door—may you enjoy your stay. (*Av. Abandoibarra, 2. Tel. 94 435 90 80 or 94 435 90 59; www.guggenheim.org/bilbao.html. Open Tu-Su 10am-8pm. 800ptas, students and seniors 400ptas, under 12 free. 900ptas includes entrance to Guggenheim and Museo de Bellas Artes. Audio tour 600ptas. Free guided tours Tu-F 11:30am, 1pm (English), 4pm (English), and 6pm, Sa-Su 1pm and 4pm (English). Sign up 30min. before tour at Info Desk.*)

▨MUSEO DE BELLAS ARTES. Though often overshadowed by its popular big sister, the Museo de Bellas Artes hoards aesthetic riches behind an unassuming facade. An impressive collection ranges from the 12th to 20th century and features excellent 15th- to 17th-century Flemish paintings, works by El Greco, Zurbarán, Goya, Gauguin, Francis Bacon, Velázquez, Picasso, and Mary Cassatt, as well as numerous canvases by Basque painters. (*Pl. Museo, 2. Follow C. Elcano to Pl. Museo, or take bus #10 from Puente del Arenal. Tel. 94 439 60 60. Open Tu-Sa 10am-8:30pm, Su 10am-2pm. 400ptas, seniors and students 200ptas, under 12 free. Wednesday free.*)

MUSEO VASCO. Dip into Basque culture and history at the Museo Vasco, in the old city. Housed in a 17th-century building with a beautiful cloister, its exhibits cover a variety of topics including weaving, blacksmiths, pastoral life, and the sea. (*C. Cruz, 4. Walk past Pensión de la Fuente away from C. Correo to Pl. Miguel de Unamuno, where C. Cruz appears. Tel. 94 415 54 23. Open Tu-Sa 10am-1:30pm and 4-7pm, Su 10:30am-1:30pm. 300ptas, students 150ptas, seniors and under 12 free. Thursday free.*)

OTHER SIGHTS. The best view of Bilbao is from the *mirador* on **Monte Archanda,** north of the old town. (*Funicular to the top every 15min., 100ptas. Turn left from Pl. Arenal with your back to the new town and follow the riverside road past the Ayuntamiento. On Po. Campo de Volantin, turn right on C. Espalza and zig-zag left at its* *end.)* A short Metro ride leads to beaches north of the city at **Plencia (Plentzia)** or **Sopelana** along the way. **Getxo** lies just a little nearer to the surf; its illuminated **Puente Colgante** (suspension bridge) fords the river, leading to a spate of all-night bars.

🎵 ENTERTAINMENT

Like most Spanish cities, Bilbao has a thriving after-dark bar scene, especially (but not exclusively) on the weekends. In the *casco viejo* revelers spill out into the streets to sip their *txikitos* (small glasses of beer or wine characteristic of the region), especially on C. Barrencalle (Barrenkale). Teenagers and 20-somethings also jam on C. Licenciado Poza on the west side of town. For a mellower scene, people-watch at one of the city's elegant 19th-century cafes like **Café Boulevard,** C. Arenal, 3 (tel. 94 415 31 28), one of Miguel de Unamuno's old haunts (open daily 12:15-1:30pm and 7-11pm).

The massive blowout *fiesta* in honor of *Nuestra Señora de Begoña* takes place during **Semana Grande** (9 days, beginning the weekend after Aug. 15). Documentary filmmakers from the world over gather from October to November for the **Festival Internacional de Cine Documental de Bilbao.** During the summer, there are free **concerts** every Sunday evening at the bandstand in the Parque Arena. For current goings-on, pick up *Bilbao Guide* from the tourist office.

GUERNICA (GERNIKA)

On April 26, 1937, the Nazi "Condor Legion" released an estimated 29,000kg of explosives on Guernica. The result was the obliteration of seventy percent of the city considered the spiritual and historical center of the Basque country. Guernica's tragedy marked the first mass civilian aerial bombing attack; the nearly 2000 people who were killed are immortalized in Pablo Picasso's stark masterpiece *Guernica*, now in Madrid's Reina Sofía gallery (see **The Tragedy of Guernica,** p. 424). The eerily modern city (pop. 15,600) is in itself not much of an attraction, but for those interested in learning more about Basque history and the infamous event that occurred here, it's a rewarding daytrip.

🚩 PRACTICAL INFORMATION. Trains (tel. 94 625 11 82) journey to **Bilbao** (45min., 17-30 per day, 6:15am-9:57pm, 300ptas). **Compañía de Automóviles Vascongados (Bizkaibus)** (tel. 94 454 05 44) sends **buses** between **Bilbao's** Estación Abando and Guernica (45min., every 15-30min., 6:15am-9:50pm, 315ptas). To reach the **tourist office,** C. Artekalea, 8 (tel. 94 625 58 92; fax 94 625 32 12), from the train station, walk three blocks up C. Adolfo Urioste and turn right onto C. Artekalea. The entrance is around the corner on the right. (Open July-Sept. M-Sa 10am-7:30pm, Su 10am-2:30pm; Oct.-June M-F 10am-1pm and 4-7:30pm, Sa-Su 10:30am-1:30pm.) **Post office,** C. Iparragirre, 26 (tel. 94 625 03 87), immediately left as you exit the train station (open M-F 8:30am-2:30pm, Sa 9:30am-1pm); **postal code** 48300.

🍴 ACCOMMODATIONS AND FOOD. Although Guernica's main attractions can be seen in a daytrip, clean, comfortable rooms are available at **Pension Iratxe,** C. Industria, 6 (tel. 94 625 31 34). From the train station, go up C. Urioste and turn left on C. Pablo Picasso, which becomes C. Industria. If nobody's home, knock at Bar Frontón, down the street. (Singles 2500ptas, with bath 3000ptas; doubles 4500ptas, with bath and TV 5000ptas. Prices decrease for longer stays.) The **Merkatu** in the Pl. Alegría, the huge round building on the pedestrian street next to the tourist office, has fresh fruit, meats, and fish (open M-F 9am-1:30pm and 4:30-8:30pm, Sa 9am-1:30pm). **Supermercado Tutoricagüena** is at C. Ciudad de Berga, 2, across from the bus stop (open M-F

THE TRAGEDY OF GUERNICA

Founded on April 28, 1366, Guernica was virtually erased from the map on April 26, 1937. It was a Monday market day when the church bell rang three times to warn the small town of an aerial invasion. The German Condor Legion began to bomb the small town at 4:30pm and didn't stop until 7:45pm. Heavy bombs and hand grenades were first dropped from small planes in order to create a panic and a stampede. Next, low-flying planes machine-gunned those running on foot or hiding in the fields. These planes forced the town's people into buildings, which were then wrecked and burned by 12 bombers. The entire main city was effectively demolished. Strangely, the Casa de Juntos and the oak tree were untouched, as was Franco's war-material factory a few km down the road. Guernica was far behind the lines; the destruction was fueled solely by a desire to rob the anti-fascist Basque people of their desire to fight.

Many pictures, sketches, and paintings have attempted to capture this day. In a painting now at the Gernika Museoa, Sofía Gandarias depicted clocks stopped at 4:30, women holding dead children, and the words "*y del cielo lloría sangre*" (and the sky cried blood). But it was Pablo Picasso who brought the town's tragedy to international fame. The still-republican Spanish government had commissioned the artist to paint a mural for the Universal Exhibition in Paris in 1937, and he used the bombing for inspiration. In ten days he had 25 sketches; he finished the painting—his largest work—in only one month. When asked about the symbolism, Picasso answered, "The bull represents brutality and the horse represents the people." However, in regard to the painting as a whole, Picasso replied, "Let them interpret as they wish." Picasso was even approached by a German ambassador who asked of the painting, "Did you do this?" Picasso answered, "No, you did."

9:30am-1:30pm and 5-8:30pm). Popular family-run **Restaurante Zallo Bar**:!, C. Juan Calzada, 79 (tel. 94 625 18 00), dishes out a tasty 900pta *menú*. After exiting the train station, walk up C. Urioste and take the second left. (Open daily 8:30am-11pm; *menú* offered 1-3:30pm only. Visa, MC, AmEx.)

◎ SIGHTS. The emotional focus of Guernica is **El Arbol.** For centuries, this oak tree has marked the political center of the region, where medieval Basques gathered to debate community issues and Castilian monarchs ritually swore their respect for the autonomy of the local governments and laws. The present oak stands next to the tribune and was planted in 1860. The "Old Tree" encased in stone columns is almost 300 years old and the "sapling" (behind the present tree) is next in line and only 20 years old. The **Casa de Juntos** (tel. 94 625 11 30), next to the tree, is the meeting place of Vizkaya General Assembly (casa open daily June-Sept. 10am-2pm and 4-7pm; Oct.-May 10am-2pm and 4-6pm; free).

Eduardo Chillida's dramatic sculpture *Gure aitaren etxea* (Our Father's House), a monument of peace, was commissioned for the 50th anniversary of the city's bombing. It stands side by side with Henry Moore's 1986 voluptuous *Large Figure in a Shelter.* Both pose in the poetic **Parque de los Pueblos de Europa.** From the bus station, follow C. Adolfo Urioste as far as it goes. At the top, enter the park and cross the little wooden bridge to the right. (Open daily June-Aug. 10am-9pm; Sept.-May 10am-7pm. Free.)

Gernika Museoa, Foru Plaza, 1 (tel. 94 627 02 13), has an informative and moving exhibition chronicling the bombardment in several languages. (Open July-Aug. daily 10am-7pm; Sept.-June M-Sa 10am-2pm and 4-7pm, Su 10am-2pm. 300ptas, under 16 free.) Paintings and artifacts on display inside the **Museo de Euskal Herria,** C. Allende Salazar, 5 (tel. 94 625 54 51), fill visitors in on Basque history. (Open Tu-Sa 10am-2pm and 4-7pm, Su 10am-1:30pm. Free.) The city also has a **fiesta** on every first Saturday (June-Sept.), with crafts, music, and games. Four scenic **walking itineraries** surround the city (2.5-12km). See the tourist office for a pamphlet and map.

Vitoria-Gasteiz

ACCOMMODATIONS
A Hostal-Residencia Nuvilla
B Pensión Araba
C Casa 400

VITORIA-GASTEIZ

Vitoria-Gasteiz (pop. 282,000) is an up-and-coming city. Packed with tree-canopied avenues and leafy parks, it has the highest ratio of greenery to people in all of Spain. Magnificent churches and fresh museums speckle the city, which successfully retains its old charm, packaged into a sleek cosmopolitan center. Vitoria-Gasteiz's name game is indicative of the city's regional loyalty. In 1181, the King of Navarra changed the town's name from Gasteiz to Villa de Nueva Vitoria, promoting it to city status in a single stroke. Upon recovering regional autonomy in 1979, the Basques re-incorporated the original name, though the city is still usually referred to as Vitoria.

GETTING THERE

Trains run to Vitoria from **Pamplona** (1¼hr., 4 per day, 8:35am-7:35pm, 585ptas). **Buses** go from **Bilbao** (1hr., 14-22 per day, M-F 6:45am-9pm, Sa-Su 8am-10pm, 665ptas); **Burgos** (1½hr., 8 per day, 3:15am-10pm, 940ptas).

ORIENTATION AND PRACTICAL INFORMATION

The medieval **casco viejo** (old city) is the egg-shaped center of Vitoria-Gasteiz. At its base, **Plaza de la Virgen Blanca** marks the center of town. From the **train station,** follow C. Eduardo Dato to its end, turn left on C. Postas, and head straight to the plaza. Buses run from a glass building on C. Herrán, between C. Prudencio María Verástegui and C. Arana. To get to the center of town from the bus station, face across the street, turn left on C. Herrán, then make an immediate right onto C. Verástegui; follow it to its end and turn left on C. Francia. Follow C. Francia for four blocks as it becomes C. Paz and turn right onto C. Postas, which leads straight to Pl. Virgen Blanca.

TRANSPORTATION

Flights: Aeropuerto Vitoria-Foronda (tel. 945 16 35 11), 9km out of town. Accessible only by car or taxi (2000ptas). Info open 7:30am-10pm. **Iberia** (tel. 945 16 36 39 or 945 16 37 30). Info open 7am-11pm.

Trains: RENFE (tel. 941 23 02 02), Pl. Estación, at the end of C. Eduardo Dato, south of the old city. Info open 7:30am-10:30pm. To: **Pamplona** (1hr., 3-4 per day, 7:50am-7pm, 585-1100ptas); **Burgos** (1½hr., 4-10 per day, 7:30am-6:05pm, 1065-1500ptas); **San Sebastián** (2-2½hr., 3 per day, 9:28am-6:50pm, 1555ptas); **Zaragoza** (3hr., 3 per day, 7:50am-7pm, 2400ptas); **Madrid** (4½-7hr., 5-6 per day, 6:30am-12:56am, 4100ptas); **Barcelona** (6½hr., 1 per day, 4:16pm, 4500ptas).

Buses: C. Herrán, 50, on a traffic island east of the old city. **General info** (tel. 941 25 84 00) open M-F 8am-8pm, Sa-Su 9am-7pm. **ALSA** (tel. 902 42 22 42) to **Pamplona** (1½hr.; 3-11 per day; M-Sa 7am-8:30pm, Su 9am-9pm; 890ptas) and **Zaragoza** (3hr., 3-8 per day, 7:30am-9pm, 2020ptas). **La Unión** (tel. 941 26 46 26) to **Bilbao** (1hr.; 17-20 per day; M-F 6:45am-9pm, Sa 7:30am-10pm, Su 8:30am-9:30pm; 665ptas). **Continental Auto** (tel. 941 28 64 66) to: **Burgos** (1½hr.; 8-9 per day; M-Sa 6:45am-10:15pm, Su 10:45am-10pm; 950-1150ptas); **San Sebastián** (1½hr.; 7-10 per day, 5am-11:30pm, 935ptas); **Madrid** (4½-5hr.; 9 per day; M-Sa 6:45am-8:30pm, Su 8:45am-10pm; 2830-4390ptas). **Eurobus** (tel. 945 12 09 37) to **Barcelona** (6½-7hr.; 2-3 per day; M-Th 8am-3:30pm, F 8am-11:15pm, Sa 10:45am-midnight, Su 10:45am-11:15pm; 4500ptas).

Public Transportation: (tel. 945 16 15 70). Buses cover the metropolitan area and suburbs (90ptas, 6:30am-11pm). The tourist office has a pamphlet with routes. Bus #2 goes from the bus station to C. Florida (home of many hostels).

Taxis: Radio-Taxi (tel. 945 27 35 00 or 945 25 30 33).

Car Rental: Avis, Av. Gasteiz, 53 (tel. 945 24 46 12), just past C. Adriano VI. From 10,000ptas per day (includes mileage, insurance, and tax). Must be at least 25 and have had a license for 1 year. Open M-F 9am-1:30pm and 4-7pm, Sa 9am-1:30pm.

TOURIST AND FINANCIAL SERVICES

Tourist Office: (tel. 945 13 13 21; fax 945 13 02 93), Parque de la Florida. From the train station, follow C. Eduardo Dato (go straight exiting the station) and take the 2nd left onto C. Florida; follow it to the edge of the park. From the bus station, head towards Pl. Virgen Blanca, but follow C. Francia/Paz 2 blocks past C. Postas to C. Ortiz de Zárate on the right, which leads to C. Florida. Once in the park, follow the tree-lined path to the left; the tourist office is in a stone house. Trilingual staff gives out a great map and info on all of País Vasco. Open M-F 9am-2pm and 3-7pm, Sa-Su 9am-1pm and 3-7pm.

Currency Exchange: Banco Central Hispano, C. Eduardo Dato, 26, at the intersection with C. San Prudencio. Open M-F 8:30am-2pm; Nov.-Feb. also Sa 8:30am-1pm.

LOCAL SERVICES

Luggage storage: At the train station (400ptas). Buy token from the ticket counter 6am-1am. At the bus station (105ptas the first day, 87ptas each additional day). Open M-Sa 8am-8pm, Su 9am-7pm.

El Corte Inglés: (tel. 945 26 63 33), on the corner of C. Paz and C. Independencia, 1 block past C. Postas coming from bus station. English books, supermarket, currency exchange, and helpful staff. Open daily 10am-9:30pm.

English Bookstore: Pradello Libreria, C. Cercas Bajas, 10. Travel guides and some English texts. Open M-F 9:30am-1:30pm and 4-8pm, Sa 10am-1:30pm.

EMERGENCY AND COMMUNICATIONS

Emergency: tel. 112. **Police:** tel. 091 or 092.

Medical Services: Hospital General de Santiago (tel. 945 26 40 40 or 945 27 29 52), C. Olaguíbel. From the bus station, go left 1 block after C. Francia becomes C. Paz.

Post Office: C. Postas, 9 (tel. 945 23 05 75; fax 945 23 37 80), on the pedestrian street leading to Pl. Virgen Blanca. Open M-F 8:30am-8:30pm, Sa 9:30am-2pm. For Lista de Correos, walk around the corner to the C. Nuestra Señora del Cabello side of the building. **Postal Code:** 01008.

ACCOMMODATIONS AND CAMPING

Vitoria-Gasteiz has only a handful of cheap hostels, though slightly more deluxe hostels abound. If you plan to drop in during the *fiestas* from August 4 to 9th, make reservations at least a month in advance.

Pensión Araba (2), C. Florida, 25 (tel. 945 23 25 88). On the road to the tourist office from the bus station; from the train station, turn right onto C. Florida. Classy yet afforable. Persian-style rugs, wood floors, and beautifully tiled bathrooms. Elevator and parking garage. TVs and sound systems for all. A few singles 2800-3200ptas; doubles 3500-4000ptas, with bath 5000ptas; triples 5500ptas, with bath 6600ptas.

Hostal-Residencia Nuvilla, C. Fueros, 29, 3rd fl. (tel. 945 25 91 51). From the bus station, follow directions to Pl. Virgen Blanca (see **Orientation,** p. 425) but take the 1st left off C. Postas. Large rooms with big windows. Rare singles 2750ptas; doubles 4000ptas; triples 5400ptas.

Casa 400, C. Florida, 46, 3rd fl. (tel. 945 23 38 87), right off C. Eduardo Dato coming from the train station. Youthful atmosphere—it's a college dorm during the year. Communal bathroom. Breakfast 250ptas. Singles 2500ptas; doubles 3200ptas. *Pensión completa* (room and board) 3950ptas per person. Rooms available July 1-Sept. 30.

Camping Ibaya (tel. 945 14 76 20), 5km from town toward Madrid. Follow Portal de Castilla west from the tourist office intersection. Supermarket, cafe/restaurant, hot showers. 550ptas per person, per tent, and per car. Open Apr.-Oct.

FOOD

You can't go wrong in the *casco viejo* and the surrounding streets. From the train station, take C. Eduardo Dato, turn right on C. Postas, then turn left past the post office and uphill, where C. Cuchillería and other old town streets radiate from C. San Francisco. There are *pintxos* galore in the streets around Pl. España. Fresh produce and meat fill the two-level **Mercado de Abastos,** on Pl. Santa Bárbara off C. Paz (open M-F 9am-2pm and 5-8pm). Or buy groceries at **Simago,** C. General Alava, 10, between C. Eduardo Dato and C. San Antonio (open M-Sa 9am-9pm).

Restaurant Hirurak, C. Cuchillería, 26 (tel. 945 28 81 47), off C. San Francisco. Funky clientele bops to reggae, blues, and classics. Lunch *menú* M-F 1100ptas, Sa 1300ptas, Su 1500ptas. Entrees 950-1600ptas. Open Tu-Su 1-3:30pm and 9-11pm. Visa, MC.

Gasteiz-bi, Mateo Moraza, 23 (tel. 945 23 34 85). Hip food by day; hip bar by night. *Bocadillos* from 400ptas. Open M-Th 7:30am-11pm, F-Sa 7:30am-3am.

Café bar Otxanda, Siervas de Jesús, 27 (tel. 945 27 96 97). Follow C. Postas as it curves around the *casco viejo*. Tasty *pintxos* from 135ptas and *bocadillos* from 250ptas. Open Su-Th 8am-11:30pm, F-Sa until 1:30 or 2am.

Museo del Organo, C. Manuel Iradier, 80. Take C. Florida east from the park to Pl. Toros, then turn right. Vegetarian cuisine galore. *Menú* 1200ptas. Open M-Sa 1-4pm.

👁 SIGHTS

The tree-lined pedestrian walkways of the new city and steep narrow streets of the *casco viejo* make for pleasant wanderings. **Plaza de la Virgen Blanca** is the focal point of the *casco viejo* and site of Vitoria-Gasteiz's *fiestas*. Beside Pl. Virgen Blanca is the broad, arcaded **Plaza de España,** marking the division of the old town from the new. **Los Arquillos,** a series of arches that rise above Pl. España, were designed by architects Sefurola and Olaguíbel in 1802 to connect the *casco viejo* with the rapidly growing new town below.

PALACIOS. Many of the old quarter's Renaissance *palacios* are open to the public as museums. The gorgeous 🏛**Palacio Augustín** houses the **Museo de Bellas Artes,** with sculptures in the front garden and works by Ribera, Miró, El Greco, and Picasso inside. *(Po. Fray Francisco de Vitoria. Open Tu-F 10am-2pm and 4-6:30pm, Sa 10am-2pm, Su 11am-2pm. Free.)* The 15th-century **Casa del Cordón,** so-called because of the stone *cordón* (rope) that embellishes its central arch, is open to all. It hosts changing exhibitions, many of student art. *(C. Cuchillería, 24. Tel. 945 25 96 73. Open M-Sa 6:30-9pm, Su noon-2pm and 6:30-9pm. Free.)* The **Palacio de Bendaría,** built in 1525, houses the **Museo de Naipes.** It's main attraction is a 600-year-old deck of cards. *(C. Cuchillería. Open Tu-F 10am-2pm and 4-6:30pm, Sa 10am-2pm, Su 11am-2pm. Free.)* Over the hill, the **Casa-Torre de Doña Ochanda** invites visitors inside the home of a medieval noble that now shelters the birds, butterflies, and bones of the **Museum of Natural Science.** *(C. Siervas de Jesús, 24. Tel. 945 18 19 24. Open Tu-F 10am-2pm and 4-8pm, Sa-Su 10am-2pm and 5-8pm. Free.)*

CATHEDRALS. Construction of the Gothic **Catedral de Santa María** (also known as the Catedral Vieja, or Old Cathedral), at the top of the *casco viejo*, began in the 14th century; today it flaunts two especially expressive doors. *(Cathedral closed for restoration. Check with the tourist office for info.)* The 20th-century neo-Gothic **New Cathedral** is in the new town. Inside lies the **Diocesan Museum of Sacred Art.** *(C. Monseñor Cadena y Eleta. Cathedral open M-F 11am-2pm. Free. Museum tel. 945 15 06 31. Open Tu 4-6:30pm, W-Sa 10am-2pm and 4-6:30pm, Su 11am-2pm.)*

🎭 ENTERTAINMENT

After nightfall, the *casco viejo* is absolutely the place to be. Bars line C. Cuchillería ("La Cuchi"), C. Herrería, C. Zapatería, and Cuesta de San Francisco. Check out **Bar Carajo** and **Gasteiz-bi,** C. Mateo Moraza, 9 and 23, off Cuesta de San Francisco. Dancing types can head to **Mana,** C. Florida, 39. Music starts thumping at 1am, and it's packed with 20-somethings until 6am (cover 900ptas, includes 1 drink). **Aural,** on Po. Fray Francisco near Parque Florida, also has a 20-something crowd and two floors of dancing in the dark (open 8pm-6am; cover 1000ptas, includes 1 drink). **Sherezade,** C. Correría, 42, is a Moroccan tea room that pipes in Arabic music and puts out delicious pastries (open 11:30am-midnight).

For info on theater and special events, pick up the *Gaceta Municipal* at the tourist office or newsstands. World-class jazz grooves into Vitoria-Gasteiz in mid-July for the week-long **Festival de Jazz de Vitoria-Gasteiz.** Tickets for big name performers cost 700-3000ptas, but there are plenty of free performances on the street. On July 24-25, the "blue blouses" hold their own festival, filled with wine, music, and games. The blue (or sometimes black) shirts represent the old shepherds that used to live in Vitoria. The **Fiesta de la Virgen Blanca** (Aug. 4-9) is a big party launched by rockets in, you guessed it, Pl. Virgen Blanca.

Asturias & Cantabria

(Map labels: Ribadeo, COSTA DE CANTABRIA, Luarca, N632, Vegadeo, Gijón, Comillas, Santillana del Mar, Boal, Avilés, Villaviciosa, S. Vicente de la Barquera, Santander, Grandas de Salime, Oviedo, N634, Ribadesella, Noja, Laredo, Mieres, Cangas de Onis, Llanes, N634, A67, Castro Urdiales, ASTURIAS, A66, Covadonga, Panes, Unquera, Torrelavega, E70, Parque Nacional de los Picos de Edropa, Cuevas de Altamira, Puente Viesgo, Potes, CANTABRIA, Bilbao, N, CORDILLERA, CANTÁBRICA, Reinosa, Ponferrada, A66, León, Burgos, 0 40 miles, 0 40 kilometers)

NORTHWESTERN SPAIN

ASTURIAS AND CANTABRIA

Seething cliffs and hell-reaching ravines lend an epic scope to the tiny lands of Asturias and Cantabria, tucked away between País Vasco and Galicia. With the decline of Asturias's traditional crafts production and of the region's mining, steel, and shipping industries, the economic livelihood of Asturias and Cantabria has come to rely upon scientific research and green tourism. Now an extensive network of quaint tourist towns, cottages, and country inns in old *casas de indianos* (rambling Victorian mansions built by settlers who scored big in the Americas) provides the residents of Asturias and Cantabria a means to get rich off Spain's vacationing elite. Besides its industrial centers, the area is also known for its prosperous dairy farms and its National Parks, especially the Picos de Europa.

Agricolar Moors had little use for the region's rough terrain, enabling the Christians to make the land their northern base. The reconquest officially began in Asturias, and Cantabria was the only region never to fall to the Moors (this fact still brings Cantabrians pride to this day). Centuries later, this historical defiance translated into a legendary, blue-collar resistance to the Fascists in the Civil War.

Because of the variegated terrain and unpredictable weather, public transportation in Asturias and Cantabria can be erratic. But the roads are striking, winding through alpine forests or green valleys quilted with cornfields and pastures.

HIGHLIGHTS OF ASTURIAS AND CANTABRIA

■ Spelunking among 15,000 year-old painting s in **Cueva del Buxu** (see p. 434).
■ Bovine fraternizing beside the mesmerizing lakes of **Enol** and **Ercina** (see p. 436).
■ Viewing the west face of the mythical **Mount Naranjo** (Orange), at an hour that demonstrates the origin of its name (see p. 437).
■ A post-hike bowl of Asturian *fabada*, washed down with a tall glass of *sidra*.

> **RESURRECTING THE TOWER OF BABLE** Galicians have Gallego, Catalans have Catalán, and Asturians have...Bable? Though it's not an official language, the dialect has returned with the sweeping post-Franco reassertion of regional tradition. Although it is not spoken on the street, Bable is taught to children in school. A codification of a hodgepodge of more than 10 distinct traditional dialects originating in different corners of Asturias, Bable's grammar borrows from many but belongs to none. As a result, almost no one is fluent in the tongue, and loads of grandmothers express bewilderment at their grandchildren's *bable*-ing.

ASTURIAS

OVIEDO

Smack in the middle of Asturias's plunging green valleys sits the region's capital and transportation hub—colorful, cosmopolitan Oviedo (pop. 200,000). Named from the Latin word for city *(ovetum)*, Oviedo served as the heart of the region since 810, when it became the capital of the Kingdom of Asturias. Strategically located in the mountains, Oviedo was one of the few Spanish cities that managed to escape Moorish conquest. The city was not so lucky during Franco's regime—in 1936, the Nationalist army crushed a workers' uprising, causing widespread death and destruction. Fortunately, much of the old city, including an interesting cathedral, remained untouched. Though Oviedo may not be the prettiest city in Spain, it makes an excellent base for trips into the nearby Picos de Europa.

▐▀ GETTING THERE

Trains run to Oviedo from **León** (2½hr., 8 per day, 5am-8pm, 925-1500ptas). **Buses** go from **Santander** (4hr., 8 per day, 6:30am-7:30pm, 1710ptas) and **La Coruña** (5hr., 4 per day, 9am-5:45pm, 3060ptas).

▐ ORIENTATION AND PRACTICAL INFORMATION

The easiest way to navigate through Oviedo is to find **Calle de Uría,** which bisects the city and originates at the **RENFE station**. The **FEVE station** is located in a new building above the RENFE station. **ALSA buses** arrive in an unmarked station in the **Plaza General Primo de Rivera.** From there, take C. Fray Ceferino (on the other side of the plaza) straight to C. Uría. Walking down C. Uría with the RENFE station behind you, you'll pass the leafy Campo de San Francisco on the right; to the left is the old city, whose two main plazas are **Plaza Mayor** and **Plaza de Alfonso II**—known to locals as **Plaza de la Catedral** and to tourists as Plaza de la **Tourist Office.**

TRANSPORTATION

Flights: Aeropuerto de Ranón/ Aeropuerto Nacional de Asturias (tel. 985 12 75 00), in Avilés, northwest of Oviedo. **Prabus,** C. Marqués de Pidal, 20 (tel. 985 25 47 51), runs frequent buses from the ALSA station to the airport. **Aviaco** (tel. 985 12 76 03) and **Iberia** (tel. 985 12 76 07) flies to Madrid, Barcelona, and London.

Trains: Oviedo has two main train stations.

RENFE (tel. 985 24 33 64 or 985 25 02 02), C. Uría, at the junction with Av. Santander. Pay attention to the type of train; a slow local train through the mountains can double your travel time. Info open daily 7:45am-11:15pm. To: **Gijón** (30min., every 30min., 300-350ptas); **León** (2½hr., 8 per day, 7:30am-11pm, 925-1600ptas); **Madrid** (6½-8hr., 3 per day, 9:43am-11pm, 4500-5800ptas); **Barcelona** (13hr., 2 per day, 11am and 5:40pm, 7500-8100ptas).

FEVE (tel. 985 28 40 96), Av. Santander, above RENFE. To: **Ribadeo** (4hr., 2 per day, 7:47am and 2:47pm, 1280ptas); **Llanes** (4½hr., 3 per day, 885ptas); **Santander** (5-8hr., 2 per day, 9:08am and 3:48pm, 1685ptas); **Bilbao** (7hr., 1 per day, 8:15am, 2625ptas), via Santander; **Ferrol** (7½hr., 2 per day, 7:47am and 2:47pm, 2470ptas).

Buses: There are two major bus companies: Alsa (national) and Económicos (regional).

ALSA, Pl. General Primo de Rivera, 1 (tel. 985 28 12 00), unmarked, on the lower level of a shopping arcade. To: **León** (2hr., 8 per day, 1010ptas); **Santander** (3hr., 1 per day, 1755ptas); **Burgos** (4hr., 2 per day, 1645ptas); **La Coruña** (6hr., 5 per day, 7:30am-4:30pm, 3060ptas); **Madrid** (6hr., 15 per day, 6:30am-12:30am, 3740-6000ptas); **Santiago** (8hr., 3 per day, 7:30am, 8:30am, and 4pm, 3630ptas); **Vigo** (9hr., 2 per day, 4210ptas); **Barcelona** (12hr., 2 per day, 4850ptas).

Económicos (EASA), C. Jerónimo Ibrán, 1 (tel. 985 29 00 39). With your back to the ALSA bus station, walk up C. General Elorza, and look immediately to the right for the EASA sign. To: **Cangas de Onís** (1½hr., 10 per day, 8am-9:30pm, 670ptas); **Covadonga** (1¾hr., 4 per day, 6:45am-5:30pm, 790ptas); **Arenas de Cabrales** (2¼hr., 4 per day, 9:30am-6pm, 950ptas); **Llanes** (2½hr., 11 per day, 6:45am-11pm, 1000ptas).

Public Transportation: TUA (tel. 985 22 24 22) runs **buses** 8am-10pm (110ptas). #4 goes to bus, FEVE, and RENFE stations; #2 goes to the youth hostel and hospital; #2, 3, 5, and 7 run from the RENFE station to near the old city.

Taxis: Radio Taxi (tel. 985 25 00 00 or 985 25 25 00).

Car Rental: Avis, C. Ventura Rodríguez, 12 (tel. 985 24 13 83). From 9600ptas per day. Weekend specials. Open M-F 9am-1pm and 4-7:30pm, Sa 9am-1pm.

TOURIST, FINANCIAL, AND LOCAL SERVICES

Tourist Office: (tel. 985 21 33 85), Pl. Alfonso II. Busy staff has a handy guide to the city (maps included) and advice on Picos treks. English spoken. Open M-F 9:30am-1:30pm and 4:30-6:30pm, Sa 9am-2pm. **Municipal Tourist Office** (tel. 985 22 75 86), off C. Uría, on the corner of Parque San Francisco. Open M-F 10:30am-2pm and 4:30-7:30pm, Sa-Su 11am-2pm.

Budget Travel: TIVE, C. Calvo Sotelo, 5 (tel. 985 23 60 58), past the Campo San Francisco, up from C. Marqués de Santa Cruz. Info on nearby hiking and travel excursions. ISIC 750ptas. HI card 500ptas, over 26 1000ptas. Open M-F 8am-3pm.

Currency Exchange: Banco Central Hispano, on the corner of C. Uría and C. Argüelles. Open June-Sept. M-F 8:30am-2:30pm; Oct.-May 8:30am-4:30pm.

Luggage Storage: At the RENFE station. Lockers 300ptas. Open daily 7am-11pm. At ALSA bus station. Lockers 200-300ptas. Open daily 7am-11pm.

El Corte Inglés: C. General Alorza, opposite the ALSA station. Open M-Sa 10am-9:30pm.

EMERGENCY AND COMMUNICATIONS

Emergency: tel. 091 or 092. **Police: Policía Municipal** (tel. 985 21 80 29), C. Quintana.

Hospital: Hospital General de Asturias (tel. 985 10 80 00), C. J. Clavería.

Post Office: C. Alonso Quintanilla, 1 (tel. 985 21 41 86 or 902 19 71 97). From C. Uría, turn left onto C. Argüelles and then left again. Open for stamps and Lista de Correos M-F 8:30am-8:30pm, Sa 9:30am-2pm. **Postal Code:** 33060.

Internet Access: Laser Internet Center, C. San Francisco, 9 (tel. 985 20 00 66). 300ptas per 30min. Open daily 10am-midnight.

■ ACCOMMODATIONS

Pensiones pack the new city. They cluster on C. Uría, C. Campoamor (with the RENFE station behind you, walk 1 block to the left), C. Nueve de Mayo (2 blocks off C. Manuel Pedregal), and C. Jovellanos (near the cathedral).

Residencia Juvenil Ramón Menéndez Pidal, C. Julián Clavería, 14 (tel. 985 23 20 54), just off Pl. Toros. Walk down C. Uría from the RENFE station, take a right on Conde de Toreno, walk through 2 plazas, and turn left on C. J. Clavería (25min.). Or take bus #2 from C. Uría. TV room, library, and dining room. Reservations recommended in summer. Dorms 750ptas, over 26 1000ptas.

Pensión Pomar, C. Jovellanos, 7 (tel. 985 22 27 91). This spacious old building has super-clean, airy rooms with big windows. Singles 1500-2000ptas; doubles 3000-3500ptas; triples 4500ptas.

Pensión Martinez, C. Jovellanos, 5 (tel. 985 21 53 44). Clean rooms with sinks. Communal bathrooms. Singles 1600ptas; doubles 3000ptas; triples 3000ptas.

Pensión Riesgo, C. Nueve de Mayo, 16, 1st fl. (tel. 985 21 89 45). An Oriental rug leads to clean, simple rooms. Singles 1800ptas; doubles 3600ptas, with shower 4000ptas.

🍴 FOOD

Order *sidra* (cider) by the bottle (usually 250ptas)—it goes fast, and much of it ends up on the floor (due to the unconventional pouring method). For the best *sidra* experience, head to the wooden-beamed, ham-hung **sidrerías**, where waiters pour from above their heads. Cheap restaurants line C. Fray Ceferino, between the bus and train stations. The posh indoor **market** is on C. Fontán, off Pl. Mayor (open M-Sa 8am-8pm). For groceries, try **El Corte Inglés** (see p. 431) or C. La Lila.

🔳 **Mesón Luferca,** a.k.a. **La Casa Real del Jamón,** C. Covadonga, 20 (tel. 985 21 78 02). You may think you've seen a lot of hanging hams, but nothing can prepare you for the sheer quantity of the pig parts in this place. Feed the big bad wolf inside you; huffing and puffing optional. *Tapas* 690-3500ptas. Open M-Sa 8:30am-midnight.

Sidrería Astoria (tel. 985 21 16 09), C. Santa Clara. Careful on the *sidra*-drenched sawdust covered floor. Ham, pork, or sausage, and—of course—*sidra* (600ptas). *Menú* 1000ptas. Open daily 9am-3am.

Restaurante Pinocchio (tel. 985 22 35 21), C. Altamirana, a block up from the cathedral toward Pl. Mayor. Short-nosed waiters claim the *menú* (1100ptas) is the best in town. Open Tu-Su 1-4pm and 8pm-midnight.

👁 SIGHTS

CATHEDRAL. Built in 1388, Oviedo's cathedral has suffered much from pollution over the last 600 years. The cathedral's saving graces are its two chapels and the brilliant blue ceiling above the altar. The **Capilla del Rey Castro,** which houses the royal pantheon, was designated by Alfonso II in 802 to house the remains of Asturian monarchs and Christian relics rescued from the Moors. An intense metal relief sculpture in the unusual **Capilla de San Pedro** depicts Simon Magnus dropped from the sky by hideous demons. The cathedral complex also an 80m **tower** (that offers great views of the city's rooftops), a *cámara santa* (holy chamber), a **cloister,** and a **museum.** The museum has a fine collection of scepters, chalices, candelabras, processional crosses, and liturgical formal wear. *(Pl. Alfonso II. Tel. 985 22 10 33. Cathedral open daily 10am-1pm and 4-7pm. Free. Museum, chamber, and cloister open M-F 10am-8pm, Sa 10am-6:30pm. 400ptas, children 300ptas. Thursday free.)*

OTHER SIGHTS. The two-building, three-story **Museo de Bellas Artes** displays a wide range of Asturian art and a small collection of 16th- to 20th-century (predominately Spanish) art. *(C. Santa Ana, 1, and C. Rúa, 8, Just up C. Santa Ana from Pl. Alfonso II. Tel. 985 21 30 61 or 985 21 20 57. Open Tu-F 10:30am-1:30pm and 5-8pm, Sa-Su and holidays 11am-2pm. Free.)* For a change of pace, check out the temporary exhibits at the **Centro de Arte Moderno.** Asturian Pre-Romanesque was the first European attempt to blend architecture, sculpture (including human representations), and mural painting since the fall of the Roman Empire. The style was developed under Alfonso II (789-842) and refined under his son Ramiro I, for whom the *Ramirense* style is named. *(C. Alonso Quintanilla, 2, opposite the post office. Open M-Sa 5:30-9pm.)* Two beautiful examples of this style, **Santa María del Naranco** and **San Miguel de Lillo,** tower above Oviedo on **Monte Naranco.** *(Santa María del Naranco. Tel. 985 25 72 08. Both buildings open May-Sept. M-Sa 9:30am-1pm and 3-7pm, Su 9:30am-1pm; Oct.-Apr. M-Sa 9:30am-1pm and 3-5pm, Su 10am-1pm. 250ptas.)*

⚠ HIKING

For a good **English guidebook** to the trails and towns of the area, try Robin Walker's *Picos de Europa*. If you read *castellano*, check out the many publications of Miguel Ángel Andrados. Helpful organizations and businesses are listed below, all based in Oviedo unless otherwise noted. Most base towns in the Picos have excursion-organizers; check specific towns for listings. Oviedo is the place to buy all of your supplies—stores closer to the mountains get smaller and more expensive.

ICONA, C. Arquitecto Reguera, 13, 2nd fl. (tel. 985 24 14 12). Excursions, camping and trail info, and a video on flora and fauna. The office in **Cangas de Onís**, Av. Covadonga, 35 (tel. 985 84 91 54), is the best place to get detailed (free) info on the Picos.

Federación Asturiana de Montaña (tel. 985 25 23 62), C. de Julián Clavería, near the bull ring, a 30min. walk from the city center. Or take bus #2. If you walk, get the big map from the tourist office. Organizes excursions, has good trail maps, and provides mountain guides and info about weather conditions and the best hiking routes. Instructors for everything from paragliding to kayaking to spelunking. Open M-F 6-8:30pm.

Oxígeno (tel. 985 22 79 75), on C. Manuel Pedregal, a continuation of C. Nueve de Mayo. Pass C. Fray Ceferino and head toward the RENFE station. A hardcore mountaineer shop with 2 walls of maps, guides and hiking books. Staff of Picos veterans enthusiastically doles out advice. Open M-Sa 10am-1:30pm and 4:30-8:30pm.

Deportes Tuñón, C. Campoamor, 8. Sells camping gear on the block between C. Dr. Casal and C. Fray Ceferino. Extensive selection of camping and rock-climbing gear, long underwear, and a few maps. Open M-Sa 10am-1:30pm and 4:30-8:30pm.

🎵 ENTERTAINMENT

The streets south of the cathedral, around Pl. Riego, Pl. Fontán, and Pl. Paraguas, teem with noisy *sidrerías* and clubs. Stylish **Bar Riego**, on Pl. Riego, serves tasty *batidos* (milkshakes) on a breezy *terraza*. Wine connoisseurs follow **la ruta de los vinos,** from *bodega* to *bodega* along C. Rosal (*copas* 100-200ptas). On C. Cuna, between Alcalde García Conde and C. Jovellanos, **Danny's Jazz Café,** C. La Luna, 11 (tel. 985 21 14 83), offers jazz recordings and videos (beers 300ptas, mixed drinks 500ptas; open daily 8pm-4am). The **Teatro Filarmónica,** C. Mendizábel, 3 (tel. 98 521 27 62), hosts dramatic productions in September and musical concerts the rest of the year. Oviedo celebrates its **patronal fiesta** in honor of San Mateo on September 19 to 21.

PICOS DE EUROPA

God bless the movement of tectonic plates. Three hundred million years ago, Mother Nature's mere flapping of her limestone bedsheet erected the Picos de Europa, a mountain range of curious variation and chaotic beauty. Today, restless rivers like the Sella, the Dobra, and the Cares thread through lush valleys, both tumbling into fierce gorges and percolating into mountain-top springs. Other European mountain ranges may stretch higher than the Picos (2600m), but few are as much of a rugged playpen for mountaineers, trekkers, and nature-lovers.

The land's myriad caves and caverns, which testify to a legacy of glacial abuse, make the range a modern-day haven for spelunkers. Other popular activities include white-water rafting, kayaking, salmon and trout fishing, rock climbing, paragliding, and bungee jumping. Many hiking and mountain bike trails follow century-old mule tracks. Today the region contains some 800 species of plants and wildflowers, including 40 species of orchids. On the land, herds of wild horses, boars and *chamois* (a goat-type animal) roam free; the skies are spotted with long-eared owls, Egyptian vultures, songbirds, and eagles, which let their shadows flicker across the landscape, and the rivers are filled with enough salmon and trout to keep anglers very busy.

Most of the area has been granted environmental protection as the Picos de Europa National Park, and has become, as continental Europe's largest national park, an increasingly popular vacation destination. Despite the crowds, the best time to head for the Picos is late summer. The region is cold and often stormy through May and even June, and the autumn weather is chilly and unpredictable.

✵ ORIENTATION

Spanning a region 40km by 20km in area, the Picos de Europa are made up of three mountainous massifs: the **Occidental** (Cornión), the **Central** (Urrieles), and the **Oriental** (Ándara). The **Garganta del Cares** (Cares Gorge) marks the dramatic division between the Central and Oriental massifs, and in this area lie the park's most popular trails and most famous peaks—the life-claiming Peña Vieja and Pico Tesorero, the stark Llambrión, and the mythic **Naranjo de Bulnes**, a regional symbol.

Route **AS-114** runs along the north edge of the Picos from **Cangas de Onís** (10km north of **Covadonga**) through **Arenas de Cabrales,** and on to **Panes,** where it intersects Route **N-621.** N-621 runs 50km south and west to **Potes,** where a branch leads to **Fuente Dé.** Arenas de Cabrales is a prime base for serious hiking. Larger Potes is a more expensive take-off point. Covadonga, Onis, Cabrales, and Fuente Dé all have excellent guided day hikes (free) of varying length and difficulty. Getting to the Picos is relatively easy, since **ALSA buses** link the main towns together, and the area's highways are well maintained.

For a list of mountain **refugios** (usually cabins with bunks but not blankets) and general information on the park, contact the **Picos de Europa National Park Visitors Center** (tel. 985 84 86 14). *Refugios* can generally only be contacted by phone or short-wave radio (the Guardia Civil can often help). Other lodging options include **albergues** (ancient, non-heated buildings with bunks and cold water) and **casas** (buildings with bunks, hot water, and wood stoves). In all cases you should bring a sleeping bag. Campsites sometimes have vacancies in July and August, but they often fill up as well. Call *hostales* or *pensiones* well ahead of time to make reservations. For those in a jam, tourist offices have lists of beds in private residences.

The key to hiking in the Picos is planning ahead. Water sources and campsites are sprinkled infrequently within the range. Covadonga does not have an ATM or a supermarket, so stock up in Oviedo or Cangas de Onís. Having wheels is very helpful, and those depending on public transportation must be patient and flexible. Buses run infrequently on weekdays; service is even more limited on weekends. Throughout this section, *Let's Go* provides numerous trail suggestions. Contact the park office for details on specific trails. For more information on camping and hiking see **Camping and the Outdoors,** page 26.

CANGAS DE ONÍS

Founded after the Castilian victory over the Moors at Covadonga in 722, Cangas de Onís (pop. 6285) prides itself as the first capital of the Asturian monarchy and a launch pad for the *Reconquista*. Now known as the gateway to the Picos National Park, this picture-perfect town rests 10km away from the park's official border. Though not the most central of the Picos towns, Cangas offers its own mini-hikes as well as great eats, sleeps, and groceries between excursions.

🎑 ORIENTATION AND PRACTICAL INFORMATION. The main street in Cangas de Onís is Av. Covadonga. **ALSA** (tel. 985 84 81 33), Av. Covadonga, across from the tourist office, regularly runs **buses** to: **Arenas de Cabrales** (30min., 4 per day, 11am-7:30pm, 290ptas); **Llanes** (40min., 1 per day, 500ptas); **Oviedo** (1¼hr., 10 per day, 6:15am-8pm, 685ptas); **Madrid** (8hr., 1 per day, 10:50am, 3730ptas). The **tourist office** (tel. 985 84 80 05) is next to the Ayuntamiento, across from the bus stop behind Los Lagos Hotel. It offers maps, brochures, and a beautiful park video. (Open daily May-Sept. 10am-3pm and 4-9pm; Oct.-Apr. 10am-2pm and 4-7pm.) A couple of blocks to the left (with the tourist office behind you), the **Picos de Europa**

Picos de Europa

National Park Visitors Center, Av. Covadonga, 39 (tel./fax 985 84 91 54), in the Casa Dago, has a list of mountain *refugios*, maps, a nature exhibit, and a very helpful model of the park (open daily June-Aug. 9am-9pm; Sept.-May 9am-2pm and 4-6:30pm). **Aventura,** Av. Covadonga, s/n (tel. 985 84 92 61 or 985 84 85 76; fax 985 84 85 61), sets up various expeditions, including hiking, canyoning (4500ptas), spelunking (2500ptas), canoeing (2000ptas), horseback riding (1500ptas), 4-wheeling (3500ptas per hr.), and bungee jumping (3000ptas per jump). **Municipal police** (tel. 985 84 85 58), in the Ayuntamiento; **Red Cross** (24hr. tel. 985 94 7310), just above the **post office** (tel. 985 84 81 96). **Postal code:** 33550.

■■■ **ACCOMMODATIONS AND FOOD.** A few clean *pensiones* along Av. Covadonga will gladly accept your *pesetas*. ■**El Choffer** (tel. 98 584 83 05), C. Emilio Larea (ask in the restaurant), has clean rooms, firm beds, Oriental rugs, and hall baths. In the bar downstairs hangs a cigar-smokin' boar's head decked out in a hat and sunglasses. Winter heating. (Singles 2500ptas; doubles 4000ptas.) Or try **Hospedaje Principado,** Av. Covadonga, 16, 3rd fl. (tel. 985 84 83 50 or 985 84 83 15). Mountains, schmountains—sit on your comfy bed, close the lace curtains, and watch color TV all day. (Singles 2000ptas; doubles 4000ptas.) Campers frequent the second-class **Camping Covadonga** (tel. 98 594 00 97), on Soto de Cangas, 4km up the road toward Covadonga (5-7 buses per day). The site has a cafeteria, bar, supermarket, and showers. (550ptas per person; 425ptas per car; 475ptas per tent. Open *Semana Santa* and June-Sept. 20.) Most restaurants on Av. Covadonga serve *menús* slightly over 1000ptas; cheaper places with fewer tourists hide on side streets. **Mesón El Overtense,** C. San Pelayo, 15 (tel. 98 584 81 62), by the church off Av. Coratorga, serves a flexible 1000pta *menú* with homemade *flan*. Near the park, **Supermercados El Arbol** sells supplies for a do-it-yourself meal (open M-Sa).

■■ **SIGHTS AND EXCURSIONS.** From the **Puente Romano,** a gorgeous medieval bridge with an ornate dangling cross, walk into Cangas, turn left opposite the park, and cross a modern bridge to **Capilla de Santa Cruz.** This Romanesque chapel sits atop the town's oldest monument, a Celtic *dolmen* (monolith). The cave underneath once shielded priests from invading Moors. Also of interest is **Cueva del Buxu** (BOO-shoo), whose walls are adorned by 15,000-year-old paintings. To reach the cave, follow the main road to Arenas de Cabrales for 3km until the sign for the *cueva* directs you left. From here, it's a gradual 2km climb past pastures and chicken coops to the caves. **Buses** to Covadonga, Llanes, and Arenas run near the cave; ask to be dropped off at the *Cruce de Susierra*. (Open W-Su 10am-2pm and 4-6pm. 200ptas. Only 25 people are admitted each day, so arrive early.) Those with wheels will want to head south from Onis along Rio Sella. This route winds through Santillan, Sames, and finally to the **Desfiladero de los Beyos,** a spectacular 11km gorge filled with jagged wet rocks and blossoming beech trees.

COVADONGA

"This little mountain you see will be the salvation of Spain," prophesied Don Pelayo to his Christian army in 718, gesturing to the rocky promontory above what is now Covadonga. The mountain soon became the site of the first successful rebellion against the Moors—legend claims that the Virgin interceded on behalf of Don Pelayo's forces. Today, visitors come to Covadonga to see the cliffside basilica, the Virgin Mary cave sanctuary, and the town's incredible lakes.

ALSA buses (tel. 985 84 81 33) from Oviedo (1¾hr., 7 per day, 785ptas) and Cangas (20min., 120ptas) grace Covadonga with two stops: one at the Hospedería and one uphill at the basilica. To reach Llanes or Arenas from Covadonga, you must backtrack to Cangas and catch a bus there. Head to Covadonga's **info office** (tel. 985 84 60 35) for information on local accommodations and sights (open June-Aug. 10am-7pm; Sept.-May 11am-5pm). Those planning a serious hike should get trail info ahead of time from the visitor's center in Cangas de Onís. Though Cangas offers cheaper accommodations, it's hard to resist **Hospedería del Peregrino** (tel. 985 84 60 47), on the main highway downhill. Shutters here open onto swoon-inducing views of the mountains and basilica (4000ptas per person). The only **groceries** in town arrive twice a week (W and Sa) by truck—buy them from the driver at the Hospedería del Peregrino.

Don Pelayo prayed to the Virgin while perched atop a gushing waterfall in the **Santa Cueva (Holy Cave).** Pilgrims and tourists now crowd the quiet, candlelit sanctuary (open daily; free). The **Santuario de Covadonga,** a neo-Gothic basilica (built in 1901), towers above the town and valley (open daily). The **Museo del Tesoro,** across from the basilica, displays the *Corona de la Virgen,* a crown of gold and silver studded with 1109 diamonds and 2000 sapphires; below it lies a sparkle-encrusted crown crafted to honor Jesus (open daily; 200ptas).

■NEAR COVADONGA: LOS LAGOS DE ENOL Y ERCINA

Perhaps the most impressive site in the park, the glacial Lagos de Enol y Ercina lie among limestone slopes and open valleys. Buses run from Oviedo to Cangas and continue 12km higher, past Covadonga, en route to the lakes (July-Aug. 5 per day, Sept.-June 2 per day, 220ptas). Buses leave from the basilica at Covadonga and return on a spectacular road hemmed in by cliffs and precipitous pastures; sit on the right side of the bus on the way up for the best views. It's not worth the trip on cloudy days as you will find yourself misguided by invisible mooing cows. On Monday through Friday there are free **guided hikes** of Los Lagos (2½hr., 10:30am), leaving from the Lake Enol parking lot.

The **Refugio de Vega de Enol** (tel. 985 84 85 76; altitude 1070m) lies off the trails leading from the lakes. It has 30 spots open year-round; meals and guides provided. To get there by car, take highway C-6312 (the Cangas de Onís—Panes highway), take the *desvío hacia* (exit) for Covadongas y Lagos, go right at Lago Enol, and on to the *refugio* (400-600ptas per person, *pensión completa* 2400-2700ptas).

Two especially good hikes from the lakes take travelers east to the **Vega de Ario,** which offers a panoramic view of the Urrieles mountains (8-9hr.), or south to the **Mirador de Ordiales,** a vantage point overlooking the Pico de las Vidriosas, Río Pomperi, and a frightening gorge (6-7hr.). Alternatively, head along the westward track that runs 2km to the **Mirador de Rey** lookout point, then search for the Spanish Bambi among the beeches of the **Bosque de Pome** (4-5hr.).

ASTURIANS CUT THE CHEESE It's an odd selling point, but somehow Cabrales has become famous by emphasizing the unbridled moldy funkiness of its blue cheese. To produce the cheese, locals arduously empty cow, goat, and ewe udders into large tin bins. After allowing the mix to "mature," cheese-makers drain extra liquid, add a pinch of cow afterbirth and a twist of lamb fetus, then plop the mush in cabbage leaves, wooden bowls, or aluminum foil. The bundles then stew in mountain caves, flowering within the humid darkness. Half a year later, the holey cheese God shouts "Let there be light," and each speckled brown wheel rolls out and onto the sidestreets of every tourist attraction. Tasters rave about the pungent flavor, the creamy texture, and the "knock you to the floor and have you begging for yo' *madre*" kick.

ARENAS DE CABRALES

Some say the small-town of Arenas de Cabrales (pop. 800) sits "as close to the sky as to the ground"; they are not all that far from the truth. If tourists valued natural beauty as much as paintings and monuments, Arenas would be as packed in July as the Louvre. As it is, summer brings a fair number of outdoor enthusiasts eager to take advantage of the excellent hiking and climbing. Arenas makes an ideal base for exploring the central Picos.

⚠ PRACTICAL INFORMATION. ALSA buses go west to **Cangas de Onís** and **Oviedo** (4 per day). They run twice a day in the other direction to **Panes** (45min., 220ptas) and on to **Santander** (1½hr., 650-700ptas). **Palomera** buses leave from Panes to **Potes** (2 per day, 45min., 220ptas). **Taxis** (tel. 985 84 50 96 or 985 84 66 81) gather near the tourist kiosk. The **tourist office** (tel. 985 84 64 84) is small but helpful (open July-Sept. 20 Tu-Su 10am-2pm and 4-8pm). **Pico Urrielly** (tel. 985 85 67 70 or 670 88 34 15), outside of town toward Panes, arranges hiking expeditions (5000-30,000ptas), spelunking (3500-6500ptas), canoeing (6000-8000ptas), and horseback-riding (1500-5000ptas). For a great English-speaking guide who knows the Picos like the back of his hand, contact Emilio Fernandez Gavela (tel. 985 33 12 37). Caja de Asturias has an **ATM. Emergency: Guardia Civil,** tel. 985 84 50 04. **Post office,** up the street from the bus stop (open M-Sa 9am-1pm); **postal code: 33554.**

▐▐ ACCOMMODATIONS AND FOOD. Since many of Arenas's visitors opt for camping, the town has few reasonably priced hotels. **El Castañeu** (tel. 985 84 65 73) is near the tourist office. To get there, walk across and along the street opposite the bus stop, and look left. (Singles 1500ptas; doubles 4000ptas; triples 4500ptas.) **Pensión Casa Fermín** (tel. 985 84 65 66), around the corner from the tourist office, offers standard doubles (3500ptas, with bath 4000ptas). **Naranjo de Bulnes Camping** (tel./fax 985 84 65 78), 1km east on Crta. AS-14, has both a campsite (600ptas per person, 550ptas per car and per tent) and cabins (1-2 people 5500ptas; each additional person 1000ptas). It also has a cozy TV room, cafeteria, bar, shower facilities, and tons of info on hiking and assorted mountain sports. Spelunkers should ask about trips to **Cueva Jou de Alda,** a fascinating nearby cave. Try **Restaurante Castañeu,** under the *pensión,* for a 1000pta *menú* (Open daily 8:30-11pm). For cozy after-dinner atmosphere, **Bar La Panera,** perched on a small hill to the left of Banco Bilbao Vizcaya, has the look and the feel of an alpine lodge (*raciones* 375-1300ptas; open daily 11am-3am).

NEAR ARENAS DE CABRALES: PONCEBOS

Arenas's hiking trails actually begin 6km away from town in **Poncebos.** To get to there by car, travel along AS-114 to Las Arenas, then turn across the river to AS-264, which leads to the town (taxi 800ptas). The walk to the trailhead cruises through the roots of surrounding mountains; tight, winding roads make some corners dangerous. It's relatively easy to get a ride back to Arenas from fellow hikers. For those interested in spending the night, two hostels in Poncebos, **Hostal Ponce-**

bos (tel. 985 84 64 47) and **Hostal-Restaurante-Bar Garganta del Cares** (tel. 985 84 64 63), keep comfortable, scenic rooms. (Both: singles 3000-4000ptas, doubles 6000ptas.) Check with the tourist office about **refugio** options.

Poncebos marks the start of one of the Picos's most famous trails, the 12km **Ruta del Cares.** Blasted out of the mountains, the gorges's vertical walls drop 200m down to the Río Cares below. After a steep, rocky climb, the trail descends gradually behind small waterfalls and through tunnels, opening onto glorious views of lush cliffs and the river far below. The **Poncebos-Bulnes** route leads along the Río Tejo to Bulnes, a small village that is seemingly frozen in time. The blistering hike, which is more difficult than the Ruta del Cares, takes one-and-a-half hours out and one hour back. If Bulnes seduces you, consider tucking in at the **Albergue de Bulnes** (tel. 985 36 69 32). It has 20 beds in three rooms, a bar, library, games, showers, guides, and meals (1400ptas per person, with breakfast 2000ptas; reservations suggested). A killer 17km hike, the ⚑**Poncebos-Invernales de Cabao-Naranjo de Bulnes** route (10-12hr.), crawls first to Invernales de Cabao and then inches 9km farther to the Picos's most famous mountain, **Naranjo de Bulnes,** named for its unmistakably sunburnt orange face. From here you can see all the major *picos* in the area and the dancing blue waves of the Cantabrian Sea in the distance. Most climbers actually start the hike in Sortes and continue from there (9-10hr.).

Don't miss one of the daily free **guided tours.** If the trail is offered, definitely piggy-back beyond the **Poncebos-Camareña** path, up a rocky slope that requires use of all four limbs, and onto **Puertos de Ondón.** Padlock your lungs, because this view will take your breath away.

POTES

The cobbled streets of Potes (pop. 2000) are quiet and snow-bound in winter, while in summer they are spotted with city-fleeing hikers. Though surrounded by beautiful peaks, this way-station between excursions to the southeast and central Picos has capitalized on its charm. Typical Asturian specialty shops crowd the town center, tempting visitors with overpriced walnut honey and do-it-yourself kits for making *fabada* (a bean-based dish with chunks of sausage and ham).

🔁 PRACTICAL INFORMATION. Palomera **buses** (tel. 942 88 06 11 or 942 50 30 80) travel to and from **Fuente Dé** (45min.; 3 per day; 8:15am, 1pm, and 8pm; 185ptas) and **Santander** (3½hr.; 3 per day; 7am, 9:45am, and 10:30am; 1100ptas). Coming into town, Palomera buses stop twice—in front of Hotel Rubio and farther into town across from Pl. Jesús de Monasterio and the tourist office; they depart from the latter stop as well. The **tourist office,** C. Independencia, 30 (tel. 942 73 07 87), in the old church, has info about the region (though very little on Potes itself) and a list of suggested trails and *refugios* with contact info (open daily June-Aug. 10am-1pm and 4-7:30pm; Sept.-May 10am-2pm and 4-6pm). **Wentura** (tel. 942 73 21 61), at the end of C. Dr. Encinas toward Panes, organizes expeditions (mountain bikes 2200ptas per day; horseback-riding 4600ptas for 3hr.; ⚑paragliding 7000ptas; canyoning 5000ptas). **Bustamente,** C. Dr. Encinas, 10, sells **maps** and guidebooks. **Change money** at Caja de Madrid, Pl. Jesús de Monasterio (open M-F). **Post office** (tel. 902 19 71 97), across from Pl. Jesús de Monasterio (open M-Sa mornings).

🏠🍴 ACCOMMODATIONS AND FOOD. Several hostels line the main road. The cheapest rooms fill early in the day, so reservations are recommended. **Hostal Lombraña,** C. el Sol, 2 (tel. 942 73 05 19), through a passageway off the main road, offers spacious rooms, some overlooking the river (singles 2600ptas, with bath 3200ptas; doubles 3200ptas, with bath 3900ptas; IVA not included). **Casa Cayo,** C. Cántabra, 6 (tel. 942 73 01 50), on the right as you walk from the 2nd bus stop to town, has quaint rooms in its old wing and bright modern ones in the new wing. Enjoy in-room TVs, phones, bathrooms, and a cozy lounge with an even bigger TV. (Singles 3000ptas; doubles 6000ptas; triples 7000ptas.) Closer to Panes off C. Dr. Encinas, **Fogon de Cus** (tel. 942 73 00 60) has sunny, airy rooms (singles 2000-2500ptas; doubles 3500-4000ptas). There are also several *casas de labranza* (farm houses for rent) in the area; ask at the tourist office for details. There's no official camping in Potes proper. The closest site is first-class **Camping La Viorna** (tel. 942 73 20 21), about 2km up the road to Monasterio Santo Toribio. The site, which has a restaurant, supermarket, and pool, helps organize excursions. (475ptas per person, car, and tent. Open *Semana Santa*-Oct. 30.) The road through town brims with cafes and restaurants. Classy **Restaurante El Fogón de Cus** (tel. 942 73 00 60) is in a quiet corner below the *pensión*. The *menú* (1150ptas) will satisfy even the most famished of hikers (open daily 1:30-4 and 8:30-11pm). **Supermercado Lupa** is near the tourist office (open M-Sa).

⚄ EXCURSIONS. Luckily, there are many opportunities to get out of Potes and explore the surrounding areas. Twenty-three kilometers outside Potes, ⚄**Fuente Dé** sits humbly beneath a ferocious mountain face. Three **buses** per day traverse the 23km route from Potes to Fuente Dé. The spot includes a few restaurants, two pricey hotels, an ATM, a daily birds of prey show (1pm, 4pm, and 6:30pm; 600ptas), and a mind-blowing, cold-sweat-inducing **teleférico** that jets 800m to the mountain-top in under four minutes (Open July-Aug. 9am-8pm; Sept.-June 10am-6pm. 800ptas, round-trip 1300ptas; under 10 300ptas, round-trip 500ptas.). If cable cars aren't your thing, climb the zig-zagging trail just left of the cable (3hr.). At the top, there are many safe routes along four-wheel-drive tracks. If you're feeling ambitious, take the northern trail, past deep gullies and forgotten mines, to Sortes. Another good, less demanding Fuente Dé trek starts and ends at the cable car's lower station (11½km; 4½hr.). The **Somo Waterfall Route** swings through the Berrugas cattle sheds, the soft Bustantivo meadows, and on to the Somo waterfall.

From the top of the *teleférico*, it's a 4km walk to **Refugio de Aliva** (tel. 942 73 09 99; alt. 1670m). Don't be fooled by the name—it's a *parador* (singles 5000ptas; doubles 7500ptas). To return to road-level, retrace your steps to the *teleférico* or walk (3hr.) to **Espinama**, where **Habitaciones Sebrango** (tel. 942 73 66 15) offers respite from the Picos (singles 3800ptas; doubles 4800ptas). Behind the lower teleférico station, you can follow signs to the decent Redondo **campground**.

Urdón, 15km north of Potes on the road to Panes, is the start of a challenging 6km (4hr.) hike to **Treviso**, a tiny town where chickens out number human inhabitants. Trail details are on posters all over Potes. Another option for outings from Potes is **Peña Sagra**, about 13km east (a 2hr. walk) of the towns of **Luriezo** or **Aniezo**. From the summit, you can survey the Picos and the sea, 51km away. On your way down, visit **Iglesia de Nuestra Señora de la Luz**, where the beautifully carved patron saint of Picos lives 364 days a year. The Virgin, known affectionately as *Santuca* (tiny saint), is removed from the church and honored on May 2.

ASTURIAN COAST

Plunging eucalyptus forests to the west and rolling pastures to the east characterize the calm Asturian coast. Summer brings swarms of suntan-seeking Spaniards to the beautiful beaches. True Asturians can always be identified by their spectacular *sidra*-pouring skills—much to every tourist's appreciation.

LLANES

The secluded, monument-speckled coves of Llanes are home to some of the most popular beaches and rocky bluffs on the Asturian coast. In the summer, the entire town heads for the sand, as parties spread across its more than thirty beaches.

⚄ PRACTICAL INFORMATION. The bus and train stations are at opposite ends of town. **ALSA-Turytrans** runs **buses** to: **Cangas de Onís** (1¾hr., 1 per day, 600ptas); **Santander** (2hr., 11 per day, 845-900ptas); **Oviedo** (2hr., 6 per day, 1000ptas); **Madrid** (1 per day, 4000ptas). To reach the town center from the **bus station**, take a left down C. Cueto Bajo to the post office, then turn left; Castillo Mercaderes leads to the Ayuntamiento and tourist office. **Trains** chug from the **FEVE** station (tel. 98 540

01 24), at the end of Av. Estación, to **Santander** (2hr., 2 per day, 11:26am and 6:13pm, 810ptas) and **Oviedo** (2½hr., 5 per day, 8am-8pm, 885ptas). The busy **tourist office** (tel. 98 540 01 64) hands out maps in a 13th-century tower on C. Alfonso IX, around the corner from the yellow Ayuntamiento (open July-Aug. M-Sa 10am-2pm and 5-9pm, Su 10am-3pm; Sept.-June M-F 10am-2pm and 4-6:30pm, Sa 10am-1:30pm and 4:30-6:30pm.) **Emergency:** tel. 091 or 092; **Policía Municipal** (tel. 98 540 18 87), on C. Nemesio Sobrino. **Post office** (tel. 98 540 11 14), on C. Pidal (open M-F 8:30am-2:30pm, Sa 9:30am-1pm); **postal code** 33500.

⚑⊡ ACCOMMODATIONS AND FOOD. Rooms fill early in the day during the summer. **Casa del Río,** Av. San Pedro, 3 (tel. 98 540 11 91), is near the beach in a red house behind blue iron gates. To get there, face the Ayuntamiento and hang a left to the first real street, San Pedro. Del Río has communal bathrooms and wonderful rooms, some with *two* balconies. (Singles 2000-3000ptas; doubles 4000-6000ptas; triples 6000-7000ptas.) **Pensión La Guía,** Pl. Parres Sobrino, 1 (tel. 98 540 25 77), lies beneath a stone archway in the thick of the action (singles 2500-3500ptas; doubles 4000-7000ptas; triples 6000-9000ptas; open *Semana Santa*-Oct.). First-class camping **Las Barcenas** (tel. 98 540 15 70), with showers and currency exchange, sits 200m past the bus station, toward Santander. The view of the Picos de Europa in the distance helps you forget your neighbor is just four feet away. (Reception daily 8am-11pm. July-Aug. 475ptas per person, 450ptas per car, 550ptas per tent. June and Sept. 425ptas per person, 400ptas per car, 500ptas per tent.)

For groceries, **El Árbol** has a branch on the plaza at the intersection of C. Manuel Romano and C. Román Romano (open M-Sa). Next door, independent **Café del Árbol** bakes its own bread and serves an affordable *menú* on the *terraza* (*menú* 1100ptas; Visa, MC). For tasty regional dishes and a pleasant view, head down Castillo Mercadores (with the Ayuntamiento behind you), cross the bridge, and take an immediate right along the water. Three terraced restaurants line the dock including **El Campann** (tel. 98 540 10 21), a cider joint with filling *fabada* (1200ptas) and a 1200pta *menú* (open 11am-3am).

⊡ SIGHTS. The main attraction in Llanes is the beach. **Playa de Sablón** and **Playa Puerto Chico** host parties all summer long on their small, wavy shores. Ask at the tourist office for directions to other spots, or just wander on your own. **Paseo de San Pedro,** an elevated grassy path along a scenic bluff above Playa Sablón, is perfect for a quiet picnic or peaceful nap. For adventure activities in and around the Picos, check out **Cangas Aventura** nearby. From the bridge walking toward the

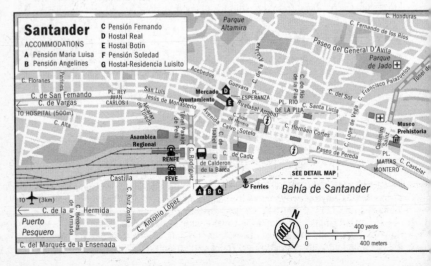

Ayuntamiento, take the last right before the Ayuntamiento, then the first left. (Horseback riding 1500ptas per hr.; canoeing 3000ptas, bungee jumping 3000ptas, caving 3500ptas, rafting 4000ptas, canyoning 5000ptas.)

CANTABRIA

Picturesque fishing villages, hopping beach towns, world-famous caves, and a crazy nightlife await visitors along the soft, sandy shores of Cantabria. Many towns along the coast make pleasant excursions from Santander, the wealthy capital and transportation hub. Claiming to have Spain's purest air, Cantabria is also known for its air sports like paragliding and bungee jumping.

SANTANDER

After an enormous fire gutted Santander (pop. 200,000) in 1941, local visionaries rebuilt this peninsular city with ambitions of high cosmopolitan standing. Today, with a slew of trendy beaches and promenades, a swanky casino, and an upscale shopping district, Santander surpasses their wildest commercial dreams. The combination of streamlined beaches and modern facilities have made Santander a favorite resort among European professionals. An active fisherman's wharf adds a touch of urban charm to the blandness of Santander's more industrialized areas, while students from the university keep things lively in the off-season.

GETTING THERE

Trains run to Santander from **Valladolid** (4¾hr., 5 per day, 7:15am-6:40pm, 2000ptas) and **Oviedo** (5-8hr., 2 per day, 9am and 3:45pm, 1685ptas). **Buses** go from **Bilbao** (3½hr., 6 per day, 10am-9:45pm, 925ptas).

ORIENTATION AND PRACTICAL INFORMATION

This slender, elongated city sits on the northwest side of a bay. The small **Plaza Porticada** is its heart. Av. Calvo Sotelo becomes Po. Pereda to the east and runs along the waterfront. Buses and trains arrive at Pl. Estaciones, six blocks west of Pl. Porticada. Beach activity centers in **El Sardinero,** a neighborhood in eastern Santander. The best way to navigate Santander's sprawling streets is to take the municipal bus; ask at the tourist office for a detailed schedule.

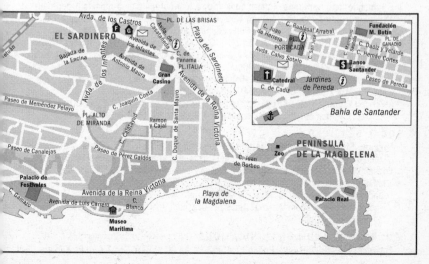

TRANSPORTATION

Flights: Aeropuerto de Santander (tel. 942 25 10 07 or 942 25 10 04), 4km away. Daily flights to Madrid and Barcelona. Accessible by taxi only (1300-1500ptas). **Iberia,** Po. Pereda, 18 (tel. 942 22 97 00). Open M-F 9am-1:30pm and 4-7pm.

Trains: Pl. Estaciones, on C. Rodríguez. **RENFE** (tel. 942 28 02 02). Info open 7:30am-11pm. To: **Palencia** (2¼hr., 8 per day, 1455-2200ptas); **Valladolid** (5hr., 5 per day, 8:35am-8:08pm, 1855-2600ptas); **Madrid** (7hr., 4 per day, 8:10am-11pm, 3575-4300ptas); **Salamanca,** via **Valladolid** (7hr., 6 per day, 8:10am-5:15pm, 3100-3900ptas). **RENFE ticket office,** Po. Pereda, 25 (tel. 942 21 23 87). Open M-F 9am-2pm and 5-7pm, Sa 9am-1:30pm. **FEVE** (tel. 942 21 16 87). Info open 9am-2pm and 4-7pm. To **Bilbao** (2½hr., 3 per day, 910ptas) and **Oviedo** (5hr., 2 per day, 1610ptas). Santander is the north terminus of one RENFE line. For service to points north, take FEVE to Bilbao and then pick up RENFE again.

Buses: (tel. 942 21 19 95), Pl. Estaciones, across C. Rodríguez from the train station. Info open M-Sa 8am-10pm, Su 9am-9pm. To: **Santillana del Mar** (45min., 4-7 per day, 10:30am-7:15pm, 300ptas); **San Vicente** (1½hr., 4-7 per day, 10:30am-7:15pm, 500ptas); **Llanes** (2hr., 10 per day, 6:30am-7:30pm, 825ptas); **Bilbao** (3hr., 24 per day, every 30min., 925ptas); **León** (3½hr., 1 per day, 2740ptas); **Oviedo** (4hr., 8 per day, 6:30am-7:30pm, 1710ptas); **Madrid** (6hr., 6 per day, 8:30am-1:30am, 3300-4550ptas); **La Coruña** (12hr., 2 per day, 11:45am, 3:30pm, 4745ptas).

Ferries: Brittany Ferries, Muelle del Ferries (tel. 942 36 06 11), near the Jardines de Pereda. To **Plymouth, England** (2 per week, 13,000-15,000ptas, plus 1400ptas for seat reservation). Get tickets at Modesto Piñeiro at the ferry station. Info open M-F 9am-3:30pm and 4:30-7:30pm. In summer reserve 2 weeks ahead. **Las Reginas** (tel. 942 21 66 19), Embarcadero, by the Jardines de Pereda, offers tours of the bay (1½hr., June-Aug. 3-6 per day, 625ptas).

Public Transportation: Municipal buses run frequently throughout the city (July-Aug. 6am-midnight, Sept.-June 6am-10:30pm, 100ptas). Buses #1, 3, 4, 5, 7, and 9 run between the city center and El Sardinero (every 15min., 110ptas).

Taxis: Radio Taxi (tel. 942 33 33 33). Gather along C. Vargas and near the Ayuntamiento.

Car Rental: Avis, C. Nicolás Salmerón, 3 (tel. 942 22 70 25). Must be at least 25 and have had license for at least one year. From 9000ptas per day. Open M-F 8am-1pm and 4-7:30pm, Sa 9am-1pm.

TOURIST AND FINANCIAL SERVICES

Tourist Office: (tel. 942 21 61 20), Jardines de Pereda. From the stations, follow C. Calderón de la Barca into the park; the office is off Po. Pereda. Maps and info on Santander and Cantabria. English spoken by a team of uniformed models. Open daily July-Sept. 9am-2pm and 4-9pm; Oct.-June 9am-1:30pm and 4:30-7:30pm. Other **offices** in the ferry station, off Pl. Porticada, and El Sardinero across from Pl. Italia.

Budget Travel: TIVE, C. Canarias, 2 (tel. 942 33 22 15), a 20min. walk northwest from the center. Or take bus #5 just off Av. General Camilo Alonso Cela. Travel discounts and flights. ISIC 700ptas. HI card 1800ptas. Open M-F 9am-2pm.

Currency Exchange: Banco Central Hispano, across from the post office. Open May-Sept. M-F 8:30am-2:30pm; Oct.-Apr. M-F 8:30am-2:30pm, Sa 8:30am-1pm.

American Express: Viajes Altair, C. Calderón de la Barca, 11 (tel. 942 31 17 00; fax 942 22 57 21). Open M-F 9:30am-1:30pm and 4:30-8pm, Sa 10am-1:30pm.

LOCAL SERVICES

Luggage Storage: At the train station, by the counter at the ticket window (400ptas). Open daily 7am-11pm. At the bus station (300ptas). Open daily 7:30am-10:30pm.

English Bookstores: Hispano Argentina, C. San Francisco, 13 (tel. 942 21 17 65). Open M-F 9:45am-1:30pm and 4:30-8pm, Sa 9:45am-1:30pm.

Laundromat: El Lavadero, C. Mies del Valle, 1 (tel. 942 23 06 07), just off C. Floranes, west of the train station. Wash 350ptas per 6kg load; dry 200ptas. Soap 50ptas. Open M-F 9:30am-1:30pm, Sa 5-8pm.

EMERGENCY AND COMMUNICATIONS

Emergency: tel. 091 or 092. **Police:** (tel. 942 33 73 00 or 942 22 07 44), Pl. Verlade.

Hospital: Hospital Valdecilla-Cantabria (tel. 942 20 25 20), off Av. Valdecilla.

Post Office: (tel. 942 21 26 73; fax 942 31 02 99), Av. Alfonso XIII, near the Jardines de Pereda. Lista de Correos and **fax.** Open M-F 8:30am-8:30pm, Sa 9:30am-2pm. **Postal Code:** 39080.

Internet Access: Libro Viejo, C. Perines, 19 (tel. 942 23 57 06). 500ptas for 1st 30min., 300ptas for each additional 30min. Open daily 6pm-2am.

ACCOMMODATIONS AND CAMPING

Santander has limited accommodation options during July and August, especially during the July festivals. The highest hotel densities are near the market, across from the train station on C. Rodríguez, and along elegant Av. Castros in El Sardinero. Call ahead to avoid getting stuck without a room.

CITY CENTER

Though not the prettiest part of Santander, the city center is very convenient to restaurants and businesses. Calle Rodríguez, near the bus and train stations, offers several good hostels. From either station, cross the street and turn right to reach this backpacker haven. *Hóspedes* on the sixth floor offer more informal (i.e., no keys) lodging at the same prices as the *pensiones* below.

Pensión Angelines, C. Rodríguez, 9, 1st fl. (tel. 942 31 25 84). High-tech motion detecting lights, strong showers, and winter heating. July-Aug. singles 2200ptas; doubles 4000ptas. Sept.-June singles 1800ptas, doubles 3000ptas. IVA not included.

Hostal Real, Pl. Esperanza, 1, 3rd fl. (tel. 942 22 57 87), in the peach building at the end of C. Isabel II. Large doubles with wood ceilings and balconies; spartan, tiny singles upstairs. Singles 1500-4000ptas; doubles 3000-6000ptas; triples 4500-7000ptas.

Fonda María Luisa, C. Rodríguez, 9, 5th fl. (tel. 942 21 08 81). Carved headboards and lively wallpaper. No heat. Singles 2000-2500ptas; doubles 3000-4500ptas.

Hostal Botín, C. Isabel II, 1, 1st fl. (tel. 942 21 00 94 or 630 49 26 06). Huge rooms with balconies overlooking the bustling market. Singles 2000-3000ptas; doubles 3400-5000ptas; triples 4600ptas; quads 7200-9600ptas.

EL SARDINERO

Both pensions are just a block from the beach. Take bus #7 to Hotel Colón (Pl. Brisas), then walk along El Sardinero's rose-colored sidewalks to the beach (3min.).

Hostal-Residencia Luisito, Av. Castros, 11 (tel. 942 27 19 71). Spacious rooms. Ask for one with a balcony overlooking the mini-orchard. Breakfast 200ptas. Baths in the hall. Singles 2400ptas; doubles 4200ptas. IVA not included. Open July-Sept.

Pensión Soledad, Av. Castros, 17 (tel. 942 27 09 36), next door to Luisito. Large, clean rooms with sinks, gaping windows, and good views. Breakfast 200ptas. Singles 2500ptas; doubles 4500ptas. IVA not included.

Camping: Two sites lie on the scenic bluff of Cabo Mayor, 3km from Playa Magdalena. Take the Cueto-Santander bus (110ptas) from Jardines de Pereda. **Camping Bellavista** (tel. 942 39 15 30). A 1st-class site on the beach. Reception daily 8am-midnight. 600ptas per person and per car, 650ptas per tent. **Camping Cabo Mayor** (tel. 942 39 15 42). Pool and tennis courts. Reception daily 8am-11pm. 500ptas per person and per car, 550ptas per tent. Open July 15-Sept. 30.

FOOD

Seafood restaurants crowd the **Puerto Pesquero** (fishing port), grilling up the day's catch on a small stretch at the end of C. Marqués de la Ensenada. From the train station, walk eight blocks down C. Castilla and turn left on C. Héroes de la Armada; cross the tracks and turn right after about 100m (20min.). Closer to the city center, reasonable *mesones* and bars line C. Hernán Cortés, C. Daóiz y Velarde, and Pl. Cañadío. The **Mercado de Plaza Esperanza,** C. Isabel II near Pl. Generalísimo, sells produce (open M-F 8am-2pm and 5-7:30pm, Sa 8am-2pm). **Supermercado BM,** C. Calderón de la Barca, 12, is one block from the train and bus stations (open M-F 9am-1:30pm and 5:15-7:45pm, Sa 9am-2pm).

■ **Bar Restaurante La Gaviota** (tel. 942 22 11 32), C. Marqués de la Ensenada, at the corner of C. Mocejón in the fishermen's neighborhood. Delicious specialties include fresh grilled sardines (12 for 600ptas). Watch your *menú* (1000ptas) being prepared in the middle of the cavernous dining room. Open daily 1-4:30pm and 7:30pm-12:15am.

La Cueva (tel. 942 22 20 87), C. Marqués de la Ensenada, next door to La Gaviota. A little cozier than its neighbors. The gigantic frying pan outside brims with steaming *paella* and lures many a hungry sailor. *Raciones* 650-1500ptas. Open daily noon-5pm and 7:30pm-midnight. Visa, MC.

Bar-Restaurante Silverio, Pl. Esperanza, 1 (tel. 942 21 31 25). Egyptian statues, of course. *Raciones* 500-700ptas. Open daily 1-4pm and 8:30pm-midnight.

Cervecería Aspy, C. Hernán Cortés, 22 (tel. 942 31 45 95), off C. Lope de Vega. Elegant dining room has it all: wine rack, busy walls, and a signed photo of golf star Seve Ballesteros. *Platos combinados* 750-900ptas. *Menú* 1100ptas. Open daily 8am-1am.

◉ SIGHTS

Santander's sights scene is small on architecture and big on seaside beauty. The many free museums are an added benefit.

■ **PENÍNSULA DE LA MAGDALENA.** Jutting into the sea between El Sardinero and Playa Magdalena, the Península de la Magdalena is crowned by a fantastic early 20th-century, neo-Gothic *palacio*. Originally Alfonso XIII's summer home, the cliff-top palace now provides classrooms and dormspace for the university. The peninsula is a **park** of beautiful lawns, hedges, and gardens overlooking the sea. *(Peninsula open daily 8am-10pm. The palacio does not have scheduled visiting hours.)*

MUSEO MARÍTIMO. The top floors of the Museo Marítimo chart regional fishing-boat evolution, while the bottom floor highlights the sea's living creatures. Form-aldehyde fishes in contorted positions peer out from glass jars. Live fish swim in a small aquarium. *(C. San Martín de Bajamar, beyond the puerto chico. Tel. 942 27 49 62. Open mid-June to mid-Sept. Tu-Sa 11am-1pm and 4-7pm, Su 11am-2pm; mid-Sept. to mid-June M-Sa 10am-1pm and 4-6pm, Su and holidays 11am-2pm. Free.)*

MUSEO DE PREHISTORIA Y ARQUEOLOGÍA. Paleolithic skulls and tools rattle at the Museo de Prehistoria y Arqueología. Artifacts from and photographs of the Cuevas de Altamira (see p. 446) are truly spectacular, especially considering the fact that they're probably as close as you'll get to the real thing. *(C. Casimiro Sáinz, 4. Tel. 942 20 71 05. Open daily June 15-Sept. 15 10am-1pm and 3-7pm, Sun 11am-2pm; Sept. 16-June 14 9am-1pm and 4-7pm, Su and holidays 11am-2pm. Free.)*

BEACHES. Santander's beaches are spectacular; **El Sardinero's** powdery sands stretch on forever. Unfortunately in July and August, every inch is covered by flu-orescent tourist sardines marinating in cocoa butter. Less crowded beaches—**Playas Puntal, Somo,** and **Loredo**—line the other side of the bay. In summer, Las Reginas **boats** (tel. 942 21 66 19) run across to the beaches of Pedreña and offer 80-minute sailing tours around the bay (see **Ferries,** p. 442).

◪ ENTERTAINMENT

As night falls, Santander goes wild as students forget their studies, tourists forget their sunburns, and everyone heads for Pl. Cañadío, C. Pedrueca, and C. Daóiz y Velarde. In El Sardinero, tourists, students, and spirits mingle all night long. Pl. Ita-lia and nearby C. Panamá are neighborhood hotspots. The **Gran Casino** on Pl. Italia brings out the card shark in everyone. Passport, proper dress (pants and shoes), and a minimum age (18 to gamble) are required. (Open daily 7pm-4am. 600ptas.)

Start the evening on C. Vargas. **Bar Gas**, C. Vargas, 31, a raw wood-and-stone joint, offers cute baby bottles of Mahou for 150ptas. Patrons often drift to the park outside between drinks (open M-F noon-1am, Sa-Su noon-3am; mixed drinks 400ptas). Later in the evening, head down toward the city on C. Vargas to Pl. Rey Juan Carlos and up to C. San Luis. Among the many back-alley bars lies **Ojoncano,** a smoky local favorite (open M-F noon-midnight, Sa-Su noon-3am; beer 175ptas, mixed drinks 425ptas). Around 2 or 3 am, crowds flood discotecas in the heart of the city. Try **Mexcal** and the **Drink Club** on Río de la Pila, trendy **Pacha** on General Mola, and **Indian** on Casimiro Sainz.

The August **Festival Internacional de Santander** brings myriad music and dance recitals, culminating in the **Concurso Internacional de Piano de Santander.** Daily classical **concerts** ring through Pl. Porticada. For more info, contact the **Oficina del Festival,** Palacio de Festivales de Cantabria (tel. 942 21 05 08 or 942 31 48 53; fax 942 31 47 67), on C. Gamazo. The *barrio pesquero* celebrates the patron of fishermen, Santiago, during the third week in July. For info about concerts, festivals, and movies, check the local paper *El Diario de las Montañas* (110ptas).

NEAR SANTANDER: CUEVAS DEL CASTILLO

In the spacious and softly lit caves of Puente Viego's Cuevas de Castillo, sculpted stairs descend into carved caverns and jagged rocks hang from the ceiling. Remind yourself that you're not in some newfangled Madrid nightclub; this is the real thing—a Neanderthal living room—and those paintings are 3 million years old. Animal depictions and red dust handprints line the walls. (Open daily 10am-12:15pm and 3-7:15pm. 225ptas, EU citizens free.) **Continental-Auto buses** stop in Puente Viego en route from Santander to Burgos (45min., 2 per day, 480ptas).

SANTILLANA DEL MAR

Known as the town of the three lies, Santillana del Mar (pop. 4000) is neither *Santa* (holy), *llana* (flat), nor *del mar* (of the sea). Despite the evocative misnomer, the town is a National Historical Monument. Opportunistic residents have converted their entryways into souvenir shops and advertise *comida típica* (typical cuisine) in the name of tourism. The winding streets, however, are thankfully quiet, save for the whistling of parrots from geranium-covered balconies.

⊓ PRACTICAL INFORMATION. Santillana is a short trip from Santander by **bus. La Cantábrica** (tel. 942 72 08 22) sends buses from Pl. Estaciones in Santander (45min., 4-6 per day, 270ptas). The **tourist office** (tel. 942 81 82 51), Pl. Mayor, supplies a bus schedule and map (open 9:30am-1:30pm and 4-8pm). To get there from the bus stop, go to Hotel Santillana on the corner and head uphill. **Medical emergencies** tel. 942 82 06 94. **Post office** (tel. 942 81 80 40), to the left of the tourist office (open M-F 8:30am-2:30pm, Sa 9:30am-1pm); **postal code** 39330.

⌂⌂ ACCOMMODATIONS, CAMPING, AND FOOD. Santillana's few budget rooms fill fast in July and August; don't worry, it's best done as a daytrip from Santander anyway. **Pensión Angélica,** C. Hornos, 3 (tel. 942 81 82 38), off Pl. Mayor next to the post office (look for the crescent *habitaciones* sign), is as beautiful inside as out (singles 2500ptas; doubles 3500-4000ptas; triples 4500-5000ptas). If *paradors* didn't have beds, they'd be **Camping Santillana,** C. Hornos, 9 (tel. 942 81 82 50, fax 942 84 01 83), 1km away, on the road to Comillas. It has a panoramic view of the town as well as a supermarket, cafeteria, pool, and tennis courts. (Reception daily 8:30am-8:30pm. 575ptas per person, 525ptas per tent and per car.) Most everyone who comes to **Casa Cossío** (tel. 942 81 83 55), Pl. Abad Francisco Navarro across from the church, orders the 1200pta *menú,* famous for its ribs. Grilled with a tasty paprika sauce in an open fire, the ribs are served near bubbly lobster tanks. (Open daily 1-4pm and 8-11pm.) The **SPAR** supermarket is at Pl. Rey, near C. Jesús de Tagle heading away from Pl. Mayor. From the bus stop, walk down the street to the left, take the first left and walk through the parking lot (open daily 9am-10pm).

⊡ SIGHTS. Above the door of virtually every house hangs a heraldic shield proclaiming the rank and honor of former noble residents. The **⊠Colegiata de Santa Juliana,** a 12th-century Romanesque church, occupies one end of C. Santo Domingo. The charming ivy-covered **claustro** has some fragmented capitals, featuring a mixture of biblical figures and fantastical beasts. The 12th-century reform of the Cistercian Order prohibited the representation of any human form on pillars— hence the odd vegetable patterns. (Open daily 9am-1pm and 4-7:30pm. 300ptas also gets you into the Museo Diocesano.) In a town that's a museum itself, the **Museo Diocesano** tries hard to pull its weight. Religious art and artifacts are spread throughout the harmonious Romanesque cloister and corridors of the Monasterio Regina Coeli. (Open Tu-Su 10am-2pm and 4-8:30pm. 100ptas.) The **Museo Regional**, in the Casa del Aguila y la Parra across from the *parador*, is Santillana's other indoor exhibition. The collection contains everything from Roman artifacts to 19th-century tools, with a few stuffed boar heads thrown in for good measure. (Open daily 10am-1:30pm and 4-7:30pm. Free.)

NEAR SANTILLANA: ⬛CUEVAS DE ALTAMIRA

Bison roam, horses graze, deer prance, and goats butt heads on the ceilings of the limestone Cuevas de Altamira, dubbed the "Sistine Chapel of Paleolithic Art." The large-scale (over 2m in length) polychrome paintings are renowned for their scrupulous attention to naturalistic detail (such as genitalia and the texture of hides) and resourceful use of the caves' natural texture; in 1985 the caves were declared a UN World Heritage site. To catch a glimpse, you must obtain written permission from the **Centro de Investigación de Altamira**, Santillana del Mar, Cantabria, Spain 39330 (tel. 942 81 80 05). **You must write at least one year in advance.** (Word on the street is that there's a 2 year waiting list.) Send a photocopy of your passport. Since the caves have been debased by excessive tourism, only 20 people per day get to take the tour (15min., Tu-Su 9:30am-2:30pm). If you don't get in, join other unlucky tourists at the **museum** of prehistory (open M-Sa 10am-1pm and 4-6pm, Su 10am-1pm; free). To walk here, follow the signs from Santillana (2km away) past the Iglesia de San Sebastián, make a detour through the streets of Herrán, and turn right into the corn field at the wooden barrier on the other side of town.

COMILLAS

Comillas (pop. 2500) is an understated resort favored by Spain's few remaining noble families, who retain their modest palaces as well as their anachronistic titles. One of the only places in northern Spain that boasts legitimate nobility, the town has a conservative nature diluted by the thousands of young people who track sand through the streets each summer. Comillas is an excellent daytrip, as it is just 18km from Santillana del Mar and 49km from Santander, but beachside camping at the first-class site is an appealing nighttime option.

🚅 ORIENTATION AND PRACTICAL INFORMATION. La Cantábrica buses (tel. 942 72 08 22) run between Santander and San Vicente de la Barquera, stopping at Comillas, and an equal number return (July-Aug. 6 per day, Sept.-June 3 per day, from Santander 145ptas, from San Vicente 105ptas). For a **taxi** call 942 72 00 34. The **tourist office** is at C. Mariá del Piélago, 2 (tel. 942 72 07 68). From the bus stop near the Palacio, continue on the main road past the turn-off for the beach, through the plaza, and then uphill one block, at which point a sign directs you left. If you got off the bus at the top of the hill, walk down 25m until the sign directs you to the right. The office stocks bus and excursion info, as well as a list of *hostales*. (Open May-Sept. M-Sa 10am-1pm and 5-9pm, Su 11am-1pm and 5-8pm.) **Police** tel. 909 44 62 01. **Post office,** C. Antonio López, 6 (tel. 942 72 00 95), on the main road uphill from the tourist office turnoff (open M-Sa mornings); **postal code:** 39520.

📷 ACCOMMODATIONS, CAMPING, AND FOOD. Comillas's budget lodgings are few and fill quickly in summer. Call ahead, especially if you're coming during the *fiestas* in July. At floral **Pensión Bolingas** (tel. 942 72 08 41), C. Gonzalo de la Torre, downhill from the tourist office, the enthusiastic owner leads you to relatively bare, clean rooms, some with gorgeous views of the hillside university (doubles 3000-3500ptas; open June 15-Sept. 15). **Camping de Comillas** (tel. 942 72 00 74) is a first choice site on the water. It has a supermarket, cafeteria, laundromat, and beautiful views. (500ptas per person, 1600ptas per *parcela*. Open June 1-Sept. 30.) While upscale restaurants dot the small streets of Comillas, less expensive bars and *cafeterías* jockey for business in Pl. Corro with 1000pta *menús*. The **Restaurante-Pizzeria Quo Vadis** (tel. 942 72 25 84), C. Marqués de Comillos, offers Italian treats (*menu* 1100ptas, pizzas 600-1300ptas; open April 1-Sept. 30, 11am-midnight). **Supermercado Greyfuss,** at the turnoff to the beach, replenishes beachgoers with fluids and fruits (open M-Sa 9am-2pm and 4:30-8pm).

⬛🎭 SIGHTS AND ENTERTAINMENT. The broad **Playa Comillas,** adjacent to the port, or the longer, quieter beach of **Oyambre,** 4km away with huge, surfer-friendly waves, are both part of a series of beaches in the **Parque Natural de Oyambre.** Many petite **palaces** and an enormous Jesuit **university** rise in Gothic splendor in Comillas, framed by sea and the Picos de Europa. The neo-Gothic **Palacio de Sobrellano,** on the outskirts of town, dominates a pretty park. Inside, the **Capilla-Pantheon** contains furniture designed by Gaudí. (Open W-Su 10am-2pm and 4-7pm. Free.) Between July 15 and 18, the **fiestas** go up in a blaze of fireworks and pole-walking, goose-chasing, and dancing in the plaza.

SAN VICENTE DE LA BARQUERA

The view from San Vicente's (pop. 5000) crescent beach scans a rapidly growing jigsaw of modern hotels and older houses, all crowned by a hillside castle with a backdrop of the Picos de Europa. It's truly gorgeous, but this might be as close as you want to get in July and August, when tourists crowd every street and ring every postcard rack with clicking cameras and humming camcorders.

🔢 PRACTICAL INFORMATION. Reaching this paradise of a zoo is not that difficult, although traffic may be horrendous on summer weekends. **ALSA-Turytrans buses** (tel. 942 21 56 50) run between **Llanes** and San Vicente (10 per day, 7:30am-8:30pm, 295ptas). **La Cantábrica** buses (tel. 942 72 08 22) travel between **Santander** and San Vicente (1½hr.; July-Aug. 6 per day, Sept.-June 3 per day; 550ptas), stopping at **Comillas** (20min., 105ptas). For ALSA-Turytrans, buy a ticket or scan a schedule at **Fotos Noly** (tel. 942 71 07 35, open 7am-2pm, 3-11pm), on C. Miramar next to the post office. For La Cantábrica buses, buy tickets on board. The **tourist office** (tel. 942 71 07 99), on Av. Generalísimo (running perpendicular to the waterfront), helps with accommodations (open *Semana Santa* and July-Sept. W-Sa 9:30am-2pm and 4-9pm). **Emergency:** tel. 091 or 092; **police** tel. 989 56 54 52.

🏕️ ACCOMMODATIONS, CAMPING, AND FOOD. There are a only a few budget accommodations in San Vicente, so make reservations weeks ahead. Along the port, awash in its own flower gardens, sprawls the best of San Vicente's lodgings, **Hostal La Barquera** (tel. 942 71 00 75), which sports enormous rooms, some with balconies. Although you might feel as if you need a lantern in this old-fashioned setting, this place has electricity and perfectly functional plumbing and overlooks San Vicente's exquisite beach. (Doubles 4000-4700ptas; reception at Hotel Miramar.) **Camping El Rosal** (tel. 942 71 01 65; fax 942 71 00 11) is near the beach. From the bus stop, cross the bridge and keep going (20min.). Stores surround the second-class site, including a lively cafeteria and bar, supermarket, laundry, and currency exchange. (Reception daily 10am-10pm. 600ptas per person and per car, 500ptas per tent. Open June 1-Sept. 30.) Most restaurants off C. Miramar and Av. Generalísimo serve 900-1000pta *menús*. Tiled **Café Bar Folia** (tel. 942 71 00 49), Av. Generalísimo, 7, serves fresh seafood *raciones* (175-800ptas), among other things (open daily 10am-11pm). **Supermercado Greyfuss,** C. El Arenal, 9, one block off Av. Generalísimo, stocks supplies (open M-Sa).

⬛ SIGHTS. Downtown, the 12th-century church-fortress **Santa María de los Angeles** shows off a handsome Romanesque portico and the Renaissance tomb of Antonio Corro, the infamous 16th-century Grand Inquisitor. Only the exterior of the 8th-century **castillo** above town can be seen. For bikinis galore, try **Merón** and **El Rosal.** From the expansive sands of Playa Merón, a 15-minute walk over the 15th-century stone **Puente de la Maza** leads to fabulous views of the Picos de Europa.

GALICIA (GALIZA)

If, as the old Galician saying goes, "rain is art," then there is no gallery more beautiful than the misty skies of northwestern Spain. Galicia looks and feels like no other region in the country. Often veiled in a silvery drizzle, it is a province of fern-laden eucalyptus woods, slate-roofed fishing villages, and seemingly endless white beaches. Rivers wind through hills and gradually widen into estuaries that empty into the Cantabrian Sea and Atlantic Ocean.

A rest stop on the Celts' journey to Ireland around 900 BC, Galicia displays enduring Celtic influences. Ancient *castros* (fortress-villages), inscriptions, and bagpipes testify to this Celtiberian past, and lingering lore of witches, fairies, and buried treasures lead to Galicia's reputation as a land of magic. Yet Galicia squirms beneath its stereotype as a rural, old-fashioned, and undeveloped region. While the rough terrain historically hampered trade, shipbuilding, auto manufacturing, and even renowned fashion labels are contributing to the region's rarely recognized modernization and development. The national and regional governments are trying to upgrade Galicia's inadequate roads, in part to perpetuate a recent surge in tourism that has permeated even to small towns. Thanks to their efforts, Santiago de Compostela, the terminus of the Camino de Santiago, continues to be one of the most popular destinations among backpackers.

Galicians speak *gallego*, a linguistic missing link of sorts between Castilian and Portuguese. While newspapers and street signs alternate between languages, most conversations are conducted in Spanish. Regional cuisine features *caldo gallego* (a vegetable broth), *vieiras* (scallops, the pilgrim's trophy), *empanadas* (turnovers stuffed with assorted fillings), and *pulpo a Gallego* (boiled, chopped octopus). Although regionalism in Galicia fails to cause the stir it does in the Basque and Catalán areas, there is occasional graffiti calling for *"liberdade."*

HIGHLIGHTS OF GALICIA (GALIZA)

■ Arriving amid mobs of pilgrims at **Santiago de Compostela's** cathedral (see below).
■ Camping on the idyllic, undeveloped **Islas Cíes** (see p. 457).
■ The enchanting Celtic **O Castro de Baroña** (see p. 462).
■ Regional **festivals**, including the crazy **Rapa das Bestas** (see p. 468).

SANTIAGO DE COMPOSTELA

Ever since the remains of the Apostle St. James were discovered here in 813, Santiago has drawn a plethora of pilgrims, many of whom have just completed the legendary Camino de Santiago. Built over the saint's alleged remains, the cathedral marks the end of the Camino, an 800 year-old, 900km pilgrimage believed to halve one's time in purgatory (see **Pilgrim's Progress,** p. 454). Today, sunburnt pilgrims, street musicians, and hordes of tourists fill the granite streets by the cathedral. In addition to the religious monuments, visitors enjoy the modern art gallery, the state-of-the-art concert hall, and an eclectic and lively nightlife. 1999 was designated *Año Santo* for Santiago. Various special activities culminated on July 24, when the Pope came to open the *puerta sacra*. In 2000, Santiago becomes the year's European cultural capital.

⌐ GETTING THERE

Trains run to Santiago from **La Coruña** (1hr., 19 per day, 6:20am-10:25pm, 505-635ptas) and **Madrid** (8hr., 2 per day, 1:20 and 10:30pm, 6000ptas). **Buses** go from **Vigo** (2hr., 27 per day, 6am-8:30pm, 900ptas).

Galicia

ATLANTIC OCEAN

Rías Altas

Cedeira • • Ortigueira
Valdoviño
El Ferrol • • Vivero
Foz
Malpica • La • Río Eume • Ribadeo
Coruña • Pontedeume • Mondoñedo • Castropol
Laxe • Corme • Miño • Betanzos
Camariñas • Carballo • NVI • Villalba
Muxía • Vimianzo • N550
Corcubión • A9 • Lugo • Fonsagrada
Santiago de
Compostela
Cabo • Muros • Noya • Río Ulla
Finisterre • Louro
O Castro • Padrón • Monterroso • Sarría
de Baroña • NV1
Villanueva de Arousa • Vilagarcía • Lalín • Monforte
La Toja • de Arousa • de Lemos
El Grove • Combados • Carballino • N
Sangenjo • Pontevedra • Río Sil • Ponferrada
Marín • Orense • La Rúa
Redondela • A52 • Ribadavia • Puebla de
Vigo • Trives
Baiona • Celanova
Túy • Bande
La Guardia • A52 • Verin

PORTUGAL

Viana do
Castelo • Braga • Bragança

0 — 20 miles
0 — 20 kilometers

🛈 ORIENTATION AND PRACTICAL INFORMATION

Street names in Santiago can be confusing since languages do not always coordinate between street signs and maps: *calle* in Castilian becomes *rúa* in Galician, *del* becomes *do*. The **cathedral** marks the center of the old city, which is located above the new city. From the **train station** in the southern end of town, three main streets lead to the cathedral: **Rúa de Franco** (C. Franco), **Rúa de Vilar** (C. Vilar), and **Rúa Nova** (C. Nueva). From the station, cross the street, bear right at the top of the stairs, and take R. Hórreo (not Av. Lugo) to Pl. Galicia, then go one more block to C. Bautizatos, where the three cathedral-bound streets originate. From the **bus station,** take bus #10 or bus C Circular to Pl. Galicia (every 15-20min., 90ptas). On foot, exit the station onto R. Angel Castro and turn left onto R. Pastoriza; continue for 20 minutes as the streets name changes. Turn right onto R. Atalia, then left after one block onto Pl. Pena. Follow this road through Pl. San Mariño to the cathedral's Pl. Immaculada.

TRANSPORTATION

Flights: Aeropuerto Lavacolla (tel. 981 54 75 00), 10km away on the road to Lugo. A bus goes to Santiago, stopping at the bus and train stations and C. General Pardiñas, 26 (8 per day, 125ptas). Schedule printed in the daily paper *El Correo Gallego* (125ptas). **Iberia,** C. General Pardiñas, 36 (tel. 981 18 72 59). Open M-F 9:30am-2pm and 4-7:15pm.

Trains: (tel. 981 52 02 02), Itòrreo. Open M-Sa 7am-9pm, Su 7am-1pm. To: **La Coruña** (1hr., 19 per day, 505ptas); **Pontevedra** (1½hr., 22 per day, 6:20am-11:38pm,

635ptas); **Vigo** (2hr., 22 per day, 6:20am-11:38pm, 775-945ptas); **León** (6½hr., 2 per day, 3500ptas); **Madrid** (8hr., 3 per day, 9:52am, 1:47pm, 10:25pm, 5700ptas). Schedule printed daily in *El Correo Gallego.*

Buses: Estación Central de Autobuses (tel. 981 58 77 00), C. San Cayetano. There's nothing central about this 30min. walk from downtown. Bus #10 and bus C Circular leave from the R. Montero Río side of Pl. Galicia for the station (every 15-20min., 90ptas). Info open daily 6am-10pm. **ALSA** (tel. 981 58 61 33). To: **San Sebastián** (6hr., 2 per day, 8am and 4:30pm, 6910ptas); **Madrid** (8-9hr., 3 per day, 8am-9:30pm, 5040ptas); **Bilbao** (9½hr., 4 per day, 8am, 9am, 4:30pm, 9:30pm, 6300ptas). **Castromil** (tel. 981 58 90 90) to: **Noya** (1hr., 15 per day, 8am-9pm, 390ptas); **La Coruña** (1½hr., every hr., 6am-9pm, 800ptas); **Pontevedra** (1½hr., 15 per day, 6:15am-9:15pm, 600ptas); **El Ferrol** (2hr., 4 per day, 7:30am-8pm, 980ptas); **Muros** (2hr., 15 per day, 8am-9pm, 765ptas); **Vigo** (2hr., 15 per day, 6:15am-9pm, 900ptas). **Finisterre** (tel. 981 56 29 24) to **Camariñas** (2hr., 3 per day, 1025ptas) and **Finisterre** (2½hr., 4 per day, 8am-6pm, 1450ptas).

Public Transportation: (tel. 981 58 18 15). Bus #6 to the train station (daily 10am-10:30pm), #9 to the campgrounds (daily 10am-8pm), #10 to the bus station. All buses stop in Pl. Galicia—check the signs to see which side. Except for bus #6 and 9, buses run daily 7am-10:30pm (90ptas).

Taxis: (tel. 981 59 84 88 or 981 58 24 50) gather in Pl. Galicia.

Car Rental: Autotur, C. General Pardiñas, 3 (tel. 981 58 64 96), 2 blocks from Pl. Galicia. Must be over 21 and have had a license at least 1 year. Small cars with unlimited mileage from 7600ptas per day. Open M-F 9am-2pm and 4-8pm.

TOURIST AND FINANCIAL SERVICES

Tourist Office: (tel. 981 58 44 00). One **branch** on R. Vilar in the old town under the arches of a colonnade. Open M-F 10am-2pm and 4-7pm, Sa 11am-2pm and 5-7pm, Su and festivals 11am-2pm. Or try the **little Modernist structure** (tel. 981 57 39 90; fax 981 58 48 55) in the center island of Pl. Galicia. Open June-Aug. M-F 10am-2pm and 5-8pm, Sa 11am-2pm; Sept.-May M-F 10am-2pm and 5-8pm.

Budget Travel: TIVE (tel. 981 57 24 26), Pl. Matadero. Turn right up R. Fonte Santo Antonio from Pl. Galiza. Train, bus, and plane tickets for international destinations. ISIC 700ptas, HI card 500ptas. Open M-F 9am-2pm.

Currency Exchange: Banco Central Hispano, R. Vilar, 30 (tel. 981 58 16 12). Open May-Sept. M-F 8:30am-2:30pm; Oct.-Apr. M-F 8:30am-2:30pm, Sa 8:30am-1pm.

American Express: Ultratur Viajes, Av. Figueroa, 6 (tel. 981 58 70 00). Open M-F 9:30am-2pm and 4:30-7pm, Sa 10am-12:30pm.

LOCAL SERVICES

Luggage Storage: At the train station, lockers 400ptas. Open 7:30am-11pm. At the bus station, 80ptas per bag. Open daily 8am-10pm.

Laundromat: Lavandería Lobato, C. Santiago de Chile, 7 (tel. 981 59 99 54), 1 block from Pl. Vigo in the new city. Self-service wash and dry 675ptas per 4kg load. Full service 800ptas per load. Open M-F 9:30am-2pm and 4-8:30pm, Sa 9am-2pm.

English Bookstore: Fallas Novas, R. Montevo Ríos, 50 (tel. 981 58 03 77; fax 981 58 01 45). Walk 5-10min. along C. Montevo Ríos (just off Pl. Galicia).

Religious Services: Mass in the cathedral M-Sa 9:30am and noon, Su 9am, 10:30am, 1pm, 5pm, and 7pm. A special **pilgrim's mass,** featuring the *botafumeiro* (an incense burner on steroids), M-F 7:30pm, Sa 6pm and 7:30pm.

EMERGENCY AND COMMUNICATIONS

Emergency: tel. 091 or 092. **Police: Guardia Civil** (tel. 981 58 16 11).

Late-Night Pharmacy: Bescansa, Pl. Toural, 11 (tel. 981 58 59 40), 1 block toward the cathedral from Pl. Galicia.

Medical Assistance: Hospital Xeral (tel. 981 54 00 00), on C. Galeras.

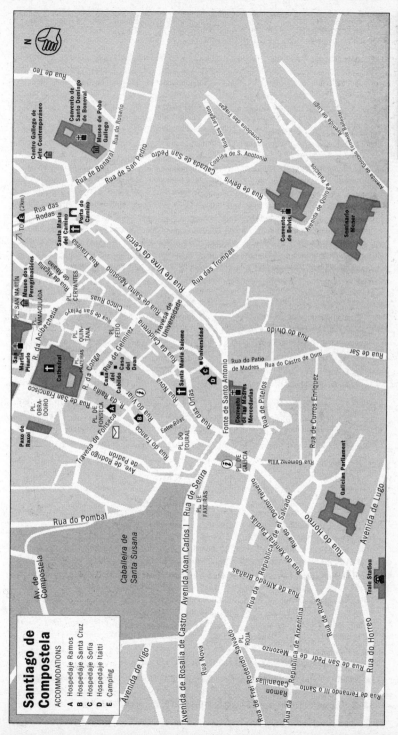

Santiago de Compostela

ACCOMMODATIONS
A Hospedaje Ramos
B Hospedaje Santa Cruz
C Hospedaje Sofía
D Hospedaje Itatti
E Camping

Post Office: (tel. 981 58 12 52; fax 981 56 32 88), Travesa de Fonseca, on the corner of R. Franco. Lista de Correos (around the corner, R. Franco, 6) and **faxes.** Open M-F 8:30am-8:30pm, Sa 9:30am-2pm. **Postal Code:** 15701.

Internet Access: Nova 50, R. Nova, 50 (tel. 981 56 01 00). 26 fast computers. 200ptas per hr. Open daily 9am-midnight. **Corredoira Virtual,** R. Doutor Teixeiro, 20, 2nd fl. (tel. 981 55 24 41). Walk past Pl. Galicia with the info booth to the left. 200ptas per hr.

ACCOMMODATIONS AND CAMPING

Santiago's rooms are not the cheapest, but they are plentiful. Hostels and *pensiones* cluster around R. Vilar and R. Raíña (between R. Vilar and R. Franco), and hand-drawn *habitaciones* signs are just about everywhere else. Call ahead in winter when university students occupy most rooms.

Hospedaje Ramos, C. Raíña, 18, 2nd fl. (tel. 981 58 18 59), above O Papa Una restaurant. Super-cozy beds and spacious, sparkling clean rooms (some with views of a cathedral tower—stick your head way out the window). Pilgrim shell decor. Winter heating. Singles 1800ptas, with bath 2000ptas; doubles 3300ptas, with bath 3600ptas.

Hospedaje Itatti, Pl. Mazarelos, 1 (tel. 981 58 06 29). From Pl. Galicia, take a right onto R. Fonte San Antonio, then the 1st left. Huge, sunny, recently renovated rooms with TVs, phones, bathrooms. Winter heating. June-Sept. singles 3000ptas, doubles 5000ptas; Oct.-May singles 2000ptas, doubles 3500ptas. Visa, MC.

Hospedaje Santa Cruz, R. Vilar, 42, 2nd fl. (tel. 981 58 28 15). Big windows in these large, simple rooms overlook the most popular street in Santiago. English spoken. Winter heating. Reserve ahead in summer. June-Sept. singles 3500ptas, doubles 4000ptas; Oct.-May singles 1500ptas, doubles 3000ptas.

Hospedaje Sofía, C. Cardenal Paya, 16 (tel. 981 58 51 50), off Pl. Mazarelos. Enter the restaurant on the ground floor, but head directly upstairs (*hospedaje* and restaurant are unrelated). Clean, spacious rooms. Practice your French with the warm owners. Communal baths. Winter heating. Singles 2500ptas; doubles 4500-5000ptas.

Camping: Camping As Cancelas, R. 25 de Xullo, 35 (tel. 981 58 02 66), 2km from the cathedral on the northern edge of town; take bus #6 or 9. Laundry, supermarket, and pool make this place the Club Med of campgrounds. Electricity 450ptas extra. 550ptas per person, per car, and per tent.

FOOD

Tapas-weary budget travelers will appreciate Santiago's selection of restaurants. Bars and cafeterias line old town streets, offering a variety of remarkably inexpensive *menús;* most restaurants are on R. Vilar, R. Franco, and R. Raíña. In the new city, try the streets radiating from Pl. Roxa. End your meal with a *tarta de Santiago,* rich almond cake emblazoned with a stylized cross. Santiago's **market,** between Pl. San Felix and Convento de San Augustín, is a sight in its own right (open M-Sa 7:30am-2pm). **Supermercado Lorenzo Froiz,** Pl. Toural, is one block into the old city from Pl. Galicia (open M-Sa 9am-3pm and 5-9pm).

O Cabaliño do Demo, R. Aller Ulloa, 7 (tel. 981 58 8146). Walk to where R. Cerca meets R. San Pedro. Chic vegetarian restaurant, serving creative, organic recipes. Specialty salad 500ptas, *menú* 1000ptas. Organic wines from 650ptas. Open daily 2-4pm and 9pm-midnight. Cafe downstairs open 8am-midnight. 5% discount with *Let's Go.*

Casa Manolo, R. Travesa, 27 (tel. 981 58 29 50). By the market and Pl. San Augustín. Come early to beat the crowd. *Menú* 750ptas. Open M-F 1-4pm and 8-11:30pm.

La Crepe (tel 981 57 76 43), Pl. Quintana. Head upstairs to this cozy *comedor* hidden above terrace cafes. Tasty crepes (600-900ptas) and entrees (900-950ptas) are made tastier by a gorgeous view of Pl. Quintana. Open 10am-1am. Visa, MC.

Entre-Rùas, Ruela de Entre-Rùas, 2 (tel. 981 58 61 08), off R. Nova. Intimate little restaurant, popular with locals. Entrees 550-900ptas. Open daily 9am-midnight.

Pizzeria Oasis, R. Nova de Abaixo, 3 (tel. 981 59 98 55). A plaque recognizes the restaurant as a Galician pizza champion. Pizzas 650-900ptas, hearty calzones 750-850ptas. Open M noon-5pm, W-Su 1-4pm and 8pm-midnight. Visa, MC.

👁 SIGHTS

⚑THE CATHEDRAL

(Pl. Obradoiro. Tel. 981 58 35 48. Open daily 7am-9pm.)

A cool, quiet sanctuary to priests, pilgrims, and tourists alike, Santiago's cathedral rises above the center of this lively old city. The nave comes gloriously to life during mass, when every candle burns and every pew buckles with pilgrims in t-shirts and shorts.

The cathedral has four facades, each a masterpiece from a different time period, with entrances opening to four different plazas: Platerías, Quintana, Obradoiro, and Azabaxería. From the southern **Plaza de Platerías** (with the spitting sea horse), enter the cathedral through the Romanesque arched double doors. Columns and assorted icons in various stages of undress cover this side of the cathedral, the oldest of the four facades. The **Torro de Reloxio** (clock tower), Pórtico Real, and Porta Santa face the **Plaza deQuintana,** to the west of the cathedral. To the north, a blend of Doric and Ionic columns grace the **Plaza de Azabaxerìa** (also called Pl. Inmaculada), combining Romanesque and Neoclassical styles. Consecrated in 1211, the cathedral later acquired Gothic chapels in the apse and transept, a 15th-century dome, a 16th-century cloister, and the 18th-century Baroque **Obradoiro facade** with two grand towers that soar above the city. This facade faces the west and **Plaza de Obradoiro,** an immense plaza scattered with camera snappers, souvenir hawkers, and *tunas* (young lute-strumming men in medieval garb).

Many consider the Maestro Mateo's **Pórtico de la Gloria,** encased in the Obradoiro facade, the crowning achievement of Spanish Romanesque sculpture. This unusual 12th-century amalgamation of angels, prophets, saints, sinners, demons, and monsters forms a compendium of Christian theology. Unlike most rigid Romanesque statues, those in the *Pórtico* smile, whisper, lean, and gab, leaving Galician author Rosalía del Castro to remark, "It looks as if their lips are moving…might they be alive?" The cathedral includes a bust of Mateo, which is unusual, as artists in the Middle Ages were rarely recognized in sculpture. Headstrong visitors knock their noggins three times against Mateo's head, hoping that some of his talent will rub off on them.

The **revered remains of St. James's** lie beneath the high altar in a silver coffer, while his bejeweled bust, polished by the embrace of thousands of pilgrims, rests above the altar. The **botafumeiro,** an enormous silver censer supposedly intended to overpower the stench of dirty pilgrims, swings from the transept during high mass and major liturgical ceremonies. Much older than the towers that house them, the **bells** of Santiago were stolen by Moorish invaders and transported to Córdoba on the backs of Christian slaves. Centuries later, when Spaniards conquered Córdoba, they took back their bells and completed their revenge by forcing some unlucky Moors to carry them.

MUSEUM AND CLOISTERS. Inside the museum are several gorgeous, intricate 16th-century tapestries and two poignant statues of the pregnant Virgin Mary. The museum also houses manuscripts from the *Códice Calixtino* and Romanesque remains from one of many archaeological excavations conducted in the cathedral. The 12th-century *Códice,* five volumes of manuscripts on the stories of the Apostles, includes traveling information for early pilgrims. *(Museum open June-Sept. M-Sa 10am-1:30pm and 4-7:30pm, Su and holidays 10am-1:30pm and 4-7pm; Oct.-May M-Sa 11am-1pm and 4-6pm, Su and holidays 10am-1:30pm and 4-7pm. Museum and cloisters 500ptas.)*

PILGRIMS' PROGRESS One night in 813, a hermit trudged through the hills on the way to his hermitage. Suddenly, miraculously, bright visions flooded his senses, revealing the long-forgotten tomb of the Apostle James ("Santiago" in Spanish). Around this *campus stellae* (field of stars) the cathedral of Santiago de Compostela was built, and around this cathedral a world-famous pilgrimage was born.

Since the 12th century, thousands of pilgrims have traveled the 900km **Camino de Santiago.** Many have made the pilgrimage in search of spiritual fulfillment, most as true believers, some to adhere to a stipulation of inheritance, a few as an alternative to prison, and at least one to find romance (the wife of Bath in Chaucer's *Canterbury Tales* sauntered to Santiago in bright red stockings to find herself a husband). Clever Benedictine monks built monasteries to host pilgrims along the *camino*, giving rise to the world's first large-scale, international tourism and helping make Santiago's cathedral the most frequented Christian shrine in the world. In the 12th century, an enterprising French monk created *Codex Calixtus*, the first known travel guide, filled with information on the quality of water at various rest stops and descriptions of villages and monuments along *La Ruta Francesa* (beginning near the French border in Roncevalles, Navarra). The scallop-edged conch shell, used for dipping water from streams along the way, became a symbol of the Camino de Santiago.

Pilgrims are easily spotted by the crook-necked walking sticks, sunburnt faces, and shells tied onto weathered backpacks. True *peregrinos* (pilgrims) must cover 100km on foot or horse or 200km on bike to receive *La Compostela*, an official certificate of the pilgrimage issued by the cathedral. A network of *refugios* (refuges) and *albergues* (shelters) offer free lodging to pilgrims on the move and stamp the requisite "pilgrims' passports" to provide evidence of completion of the full distance. For more information and free guides to the Camino de Santiago, contact the **Officinal de Acogida del Peregrino,** R. Vilar, 1 (tel. 981 56 24 19), in the Casa del Deán. At a rate of 30km per day, walking the entire *camino* takes about a month. For inspiration along the way, keep in mind that you are joining the ranks of such illustrious pilgrims as King Ferdinand and Queen Isabella, Francis of Assisi, Pope John Paul II, and Shirley MacLaine.

⊠MUSEO DAS PEREGRINACIÓNS. Those still curious about the Camino de Santiago should head to the comprehensive Museo das Peregrinacións. This three-story Gothic building is chock-full of creatively displayed historical information about the *Camino*, including exhibits on the rites and rituals of pilgrimage, the iconography of St. James, and statues of the Virgin as a baby-Jesus-toting pilgrim. *(Pl. San Miguel. Tel. 981 58 15 58. Open Tu-F 10am-8pm, Sa 10:30am-1:30pm and 5-8pm, Su 10:30am-1:30pm. 400ptas, students 200ptas.)*

HOSPITAL REAL. The 15th-century Renaissance Hospital Real, now a ritzy *parador*, upholds an ancient tradition of feeding 10 pilgrims per day. Try to catch one of three splendid art exhibitions given in the lobby; linger long enough and you may be let in to see the Hospital's four courtyards, chapel, and sculpture. *(Pl. Obradoiro. Open daily 10am-2pm and 4-7pm. Free.)*

PAZO DE RAXOI. The majestic facade of the former Pazo de Raxoi shines with gold-accented balconies and monumental Neo-classical columns. Once a royal palace, it now houses the Ayuntamiento and office of the president of the Xunta de Galicia. At night, floodlights illuminate the remarkable bas-relief of the Battle of Clavio. *(Across Pl. Obradoiro, facing the cathedral)*

MONASTERIO DE SAN MARTÍN PINARIO. Once a religious center almost as powerful as the cathedral, the monastery is a mixture of Romanesque cloisters, Plateresque facades, and Baroque sculpture. This composite style is the most outstanding architecture of its type in Santiago. *(In Pl. San Martín, across from the cathedral in Pl. Inmaculada. Open daily 10am-2pm and 5-8:30pm.)*

MUSEO DE POBO GALLEGO. Find out everything you have ever wanted to know about traditional Galician living. Documentary exhibits on shipbuilding, pottery, house construction, and bagpipe-making are the highlights, but the museum also includes several rooms dedicated to Galician painting. *(Just past the Porto de Camino, inside the Gothic Convento de Santo Domingo de Boneval. Tel. 981 58 36 20. Open M-Sa 10am-1pm and 4-7pm. Free.)*

CENTRO GALLEGO DE ARTE CONTEMPORÁNEO. The expansive galleries and rooftop *terraza* of the sparkling Centro Gallego de Arte Contemporáneo (CGAC) house bizarre, multi-media exhibitions of international modern art. *(Next door to the Museo de Pobo Gallego. Tel. 981 54 66 21. Open Tu-Sa 11am-8pm, Su 11am-4pm. Free.)*

OTHER SIGHTS. A walk in the **Caballeira de Santa Susana,** between the new and old cities, is a lovely way to stave off a holy overdose. Its manicured gardens and eucalyptus-lined walkways open onto gorgeous views of the cathedral, the university, and rolling farmland. The 15th-century **Colexiata de Santa María de Sar** has a disintegrating Romanesque cloister—it started crumbling in the 12th century and never stopped. Inside, foreboding pillars lean at frightening angles, making visitors wary. *(About 1km from the cathedral. Open M-Sa 10am-1pm and 4-7pm. Free.)*

🎵 ENTERTAINMENT

At night, crowds looking for post-pilgrimage consumption flood cellars throughout the city. To boogie with local students, hit the bars and dance joints off Pl. Roxa (take C. Montevo Ríos). Clubs open roughly from midnight-6am. **Modus Vivendi** provided a clubhouse for revolutionary Galician youths in the 1970s and now serves as headquarters for Santiago's nightlife. Combining bagpipes, Aretha Franklin, and local art, Modus's intimate setting often features concerts or debates. The local newspaper *El Correo Gallego* (125ptas) and the free monthly *Compostela Capital* list art exhibits and concert information. Consult any of three local monthlies, *Santiago Dias Guía Imprescindible, Compostelán,* or *Modus Viviendi,* for updates on the live music scene.

BARS

🎵 **Casa das Crechas,** Vía Sacra, 3 (tel. 981 56 07 51), just off Pl. Quintana. A smoky stone-and-wood pub with a witchcraft theme. Park your broom on the curb for Guinness and other magical brews. Beer 250-325ptas, mixed drinks 550ptas.

Cerveceria Dakar, R. Franco, 13 (tel. 981 57 81 92). A good late evening stop. Serves rich *batidos* (milkshakes; 300ptas) and 4 delicious liqueurs, which will draw even the most dedicated of students away from their work. Open daily 7am-midnight.

Ultramarinos Pub, Casas Reais, 34-36 (tel. 981 58 24 18), on a street that feeds into Porta de Camino. The downstairs offers drinking and dancing, while upstairs is ideal for sipping and chatting. Beers 250ptas, mixed drinks 500ptas. Open daily 11:30pm-4am.

DISCOTECAS

Casting Araguaney, C. Montevo Ríos, 25-27 (tel. 981 59 59 00, ext. 1028), a few blocks off Pl. Galicia, in Hotel Araguaney. An ultra-hip, multi-level dance club. Glass ceiling panels peer into the swimming pool above. The party begins raging after 2am. Beers 500ptas, mixed drinks 600-800ptas. Cover 500ptas. Open W-Sa 1am-6am.

Discoteca Liberti (tel. 981 59 91 81), located across from Casting Araguaney on Alfredo Branas. Salsa and "Top 40" hits. Pool table. Beers 350ptas, mixed drinks 500ptas. Cover 500ptas. Open daily midnight-6am.

Discoteca Black, C. Rosalía de Castro, 133 (tel. 981 52 18 50), a 20min. walk from the old city, in Hotel Peregrino. Revelers of all ages kiss sobriety goodbye in this popular gay club. Beers 600ptas, mixed drinks 800ptas. Open Tu-Sa midnight-6am.

RÍAS BAJAS (RÍAS BAIXAS)

According to Galician lore, the Rías Bajas (Low Estuaries) were formed by God's tremendous handprint, with each *ría* stretching like a finger through the territory. The coves and picturesque islands have lured vacationing Galicians for centuries. Foreign tourists have recently caught on, and tourism may soon eclipse fishing as the region's top industry. Public transportation between towns is often sparse, so rent a car or plan ahead with trains or buses.

VIGO

José María Alvarez once wrote that "Vigo does not end, it goes on into the sea." Vigo (pop. 300,000) is truly dependent on its coast, as the sea provides beautiful harborside views, a booming international port, and the staples of local cuisine. With ferries, buses, and trains efficiently shuttling visitors to the surrounding Ría de Vigo and nearby Río Miño, as well as a network of hotels and shops pampering tourists between excursions, Vigo promises travelers an enjoyable visit. The city's noise and pollution, however, can be a bit of a nuisance.

⚄ ORIENTATION AND PRACTICAL INFORMATION. The **Gran Vía** is Vigo's main thoroughfare, stretching south to north from Pr. América, through Pr. España, and ending at the perpendicular **Rúa Urzáiz**. A left turn (west) onto R. Urzáiz leads to Pta. do Sol and into the **casco antiguo**. As you exit the **train station** on R. Urzáiz, go right two blocks to reach the central Gran Vía-Urzáiz. The city center is a 25-minute trek from the **bus station**. Exit right uphill along busy Av. Madrid. Eventually, a right on Gran Vía at Pr. España leads to the intersection with R. Urzáiz (marked by the sculpture of a naked man). The R4 bus from the bus station also goes to R. Urzáiz (110ptas).

Aeropuerto de Vigo (tel. 986 26 82 00), on Av. Aeroporto, has daily flights to Madrid, Barcelona, Bilbao, and Valencia. The R9 bus runs regularly from R. Urzáiz near R. Colón to the airport (110ptas). **Iberia's** office is at Marqués de Valladares, 17 (tel. 986 22 70 05). **RENFE** (tel. 986 43 11 14), on Pr. Estación, downstairs from C. Lepanto, has info open daily 10am-11pm and runs trains to: **Pontevedra** (35min., 21 per day, 300ptas); **Túy** (45min., 4 per day, 325ptas); **Santiago de Compostela** (2hr., 20 per day, 6am-9:35pm, 945ptas); **La Coruña** (3hr., 17 per day, 6am-9:35pm, 1470ptas); **Madrid** (8-9hr., 3 per day, 5800ptas); **Porto, Portugal** (2½hr., 3 per day, 1845ptas). **Estación de Autobuses** (tel. 986 37 34 11) is at Av. Madrid, on the corner with R. Alcalde Gregorio Espino. **Castromil** (tel. 986 27 81 12) buses run to: **Pontevedra** (45min., 31 per day, 7am-8pm, 300ptas); **Santiago de Compostela** (2hr., 27 per day, 6am-8:30pm, 900ptas); **La Coruña** (2½hr., 9 per day, 7am-8:30pm, 1700ptas). For **ATSA buses** (tel. 986 61 02 55), buy tickets upon boarding. To: **Túy** (45min.; M-F every 30min., Sa every hr.; 5:45am-7pm; 325ptas); **Bayona** (50min., every 30min., 7am-10pm, 245ptas); **La Guardia** (1hr., every 30min., 5:45am-7pm, 605ptas). **Auto Res, S.A.** (tel. 986 37 78 78) runs to **Madrid** (9hr., 5 per day, 11:30am-11:30pm., 4255-4580ptas). **Estación Ría** (tel. 986 43 77 77), on Av. Avenidas past the nautical club, offers ferries to: **Cangas** (20min., every 30min., 225ptas); **Moaña** (30min., every hr., round-trip 400ptas); **Islas Cíes** (50min., 5 per day, round-trip 2000ptas). For car rental, head to **Atesa**, R. Urzáiz, 84 (tel. 986 42 10 33). Renters must be at least 21 and have had a license for at least one year. (Open M-F 9am-1:30pm and 4:30-7pm, Sa 10am-noon.)

There are a couple of **tourist offices** around town, the best on Av. Avenidas (tel. 986 43 05 77). Take R. Urzáiz to R. Colón, follow R. Colón to the water, turn left onto R. Montero Ríos, and walk 6 blocks. The office is in the long cement building next to the ferry station, and hands out brochures and maps. (English spoken. Open M-F 9am-2pm and 4:30-6:30pm, Sa 10am-12:30pm.) For **currency exchange**, Banco Central Hispano, R. Urzáiz, 20, charges no commission (open M-F 8:30am-2:30pm); **luggage storage** is at the train station (lockers 400ptas; open daily 7am-9:45pm) or the bus station (60ptas per bag; open M-F 9:30am-1:30pm and 3-7pm, Sa

9am-2pm). **Emergency:** tel. 091 or 092; **police:** (tel. 986 43 22 11), Pr. do Rey; **hospital: Hospital Municipal,** C. Camelias, 109 (tel. 986 41 12 44). **Post office,** Pr. Compostela, 3 (tel. 986 43 81 44 or 986 43 90 06; fax 986 37 47 26; open for stamps and Lista de Correos M-F 8:30am-8:30pm, Sa 9am-2pm; for **faxes** M-Sa 9am-9pm); **postal code:** 36200; **internet access:** CiberStation, C. Príncipe, 22 (tel. 986 44 76 10), off R. Urzáiz (300ptas per hr; open 9am-3am or until the last person leaves).

▐▐ **ACCOMMODATIONS AND FOOD.** Vigo's inexpensive rooms make the city a logical base for exploring surrounding areas. C. Alfonso XIII (to the right upon exiting the train station) is full of cheap sleeps, as are streets around the port, particularly C. Carral and C. Urzáiz. **Hostal Ría de Vigo,** C. Cervantes, 14 (tel. 986 43 72 40), left off C. Alfonso XIII, has spacious and squeaky clean rooms, some with balconies and private bathrooms (singles 2000ptas; doubles 3000ptas). **Barcia Casa de Huespedes,** C. Mexico, 2 (tel. 986 42 51 45), right off R. Urzáiz, two minutes from the train station, has comfy rooms with TVs, balconies, and huge hall bathrooms (singles 2000ptas; doubles 3200ptas). The Gran Vía and C. Venezuela are brimming with bright *cafeterías* and *terrazas*. Streets leading away from the port hide seafood paradise. **Luces de Bohemia,** C. Colón, 34 (tel. 986 43 00 20), has a bright, mirrored interior and plenty of good eats (*platos combinados* 500-1200ptas, *menú del día* 1100ptas). If fish really isn't your bag, try **Restaurante Curcuma Vegetariano,** C. Brasil, 4 (tel. 986 41 11 27), just off Gran Vía, which has red-wood paneling and a stone-block interior that could have been stolen from an Incan ruin (entrees 700-900ptas; open M-Sa 1-4pm and 8pm-midnight).

▣ ♫ **SIGHTS AND ENTERTAINMENT.** There isn't much to see or do in Vigo besides party. Starting in the late afternoon, students pack the *casco antiguo*. Cafes, bars, and discos abound just off the steep, mossy steps. **Rúa Real,** down by the water, has a few lively spots. Otherwise, check out some of the bars near the train station. In honor of its notorious past as a haven for witches (both good and evil), Vigo hosts *Expomagia*, a celebration of all things occult, in mid-June. Watch for the **Fiesta de San Juan (Xuan)** in late June, when neighborhoods light huge cauldrons of *aguardiente* (firewater) and revel in traditional song and dance. A final summer festival, **Romería Vikinga,** sails into town the first week in August, when locals reenact the Viking landing, complete with period ships and costumes.

DAYTRIPS FROM VIGO

Ría de Vigo's wide-open mouth (as if, according to one brochure, "it were about to swallow up a big piece of ocean") is home to several lively coastal towns. The Islas Cíes and Bayona are both easy daytrips from Vigo. Farther south but equally accessible, Túy and La Guardia lie along the Ría Miño, which borders Portugal.

▨ ISLAS CÍES

The Romans called them the "Islands of the Gods," and one can hardly doubt that Jupiter had at least a villa in the Islas Cíes. Guarding the mouth of the Ría de Vigo, the islands offer irresistible beaches and cliff-side hiking trails for tourist-weary travelers. Because of the islands's natural refuge status, only 2200 people are allowed in per day, ensuring wide stretches of uncrowded beach; there's not even a tourist office. **Playa de Figueiras** and **Playa de Rodas** gleam with fine sand and sheltered turquoise waters. For smaller, wavier, and more secluded spots, walk along the trail beyond Playa de Figueiras, which leads to a plethora of coves and rocky lookouts. A 4km hike to the left of the dock on the main "road" leads to a bird conservatory, a lighthouse, and breathtaking views. Watch out for territorial seagulls that dive-bomb hikers walking too close to the birds's spotted chicks.

For budget food (*bocadillos* and ice cream), head to **Restaurante Playa de Rodas** (tel. 986 68 75 11) or **Restaurante Camping** (tel. 986 68 75 04), on the other side of the Playa de Rodas. Octopus, chicken, and *calamares* come cheaply considering the restaurants' prime location. A **mini-market** is next door, as are **campsites** (tel. 986 43 83 58). Space is limited, so call in advance for reservations (595ptas per person and per tent). From June to September, five **ferries** per day make the trip to and from the island, sometimes more in nice weather. Though fairly expensive, the trip is worth every *peseta* (50min.; 2000ptas per adult, 1000ptas per child).

BAYONA (BAIONA)

Twenty-one kilometers southwest of Vigo, in its own mini-estuary, Bayona (pop. 10,000) was the first European town to receive word from the New World when Columbus returned to port in March 1493. You can visit a reconstructed version of the famous globe-trotting ship **La Carabela Pinta** in Bayona's harbor (125ptas), but the town's main attractions are its seductive **beaches** and the 16th-century **Fortress of Monte Real**, now a *parador nacional* (luxury hotel). A 2km *paseo peatonil* (foot path) loops around the grounds along the shore, passing rocks which are perfect for picnics and sunbathing. A **tourist office** (tel. 986 68 70 67) camps out in the stained wood shack just before the *parador* gates (open July-Aug. M-Sa 9am-2pm). During other months, get info in the Ayuntamiento (tel. 986 35 52 50; open M-Sa 9am-1pm). **Buses** run to and from Vigo (1hr., every 30min., 245ptas).

TÚY (TUI)

The charming border town of Túy (pop. 16,000) offers tourists the opportunity to walk into Portugal. A 1km metal walkway over the Río Miño extends to Portugal's Valença do Minho (see p. 641); some may be surprised to find that the grass is equally green in both countries. Túy also has a small but pretty **cathedral,** a mix of Gothic and Romanesque styles and home to the relics of San Telmo, patron saint of sailors. One ticket gets you into the cathedral's **museo** and the **Museo Diocesano** as well. (Both open daily July-Aug. 9:30am-2pm and 3:30-9pm; Sept.-May 9:30am-2pm. 250ptas.) An ATSA **bus** (tel. 986 61 02 55) from Vigo stops on C. Calvo Sotelo at Hostal Generosa and returns to Vigo from the other side of the street (45min., every 30min., 5:45am-9pm, 325ptas). **Trains** (tel. 986 60 08 13) run from Vigo to Túy, then on to Valença and Viana do Castelo, Portugal (3 per day, 11am-10pm, 400ptas). They stop for 15 minutes on each side for customs and passport inspections. The train stations in each town are far from the border and the center of town; taking the bus or walking across makes more sense.

LA GUARDIA (A GUARDA)

Perched between the mouth of the Río Miño and the Atlantic Ocean, La Guardia (pop. 11,000) thrives on an active fishing industry and the 500,000 tourists who annually descend on its little beach and large mountain. The bus stops at the corner of C. Domínguez Fontela and C. Concepción Arenal. To reach the majestic **Monte Santa Tecla,** take C. Domínguez Fontela to reach C. José Antonio. From C. José Antonio, bear right onto C. Rosalía de Castro, which continues to the top (6km). Alternatively, hike five minutes up the road and look for the steps off to the left that mark the start of a shorter, steeper pathway through the woods (3km). Three-quarters of the way up lie the ruins of an old Celtic village, while near the peak is a **chapel** dedicated to Santa Tecla, the patron saint of headaches and heart disease. The wax body parts inside (hearts, heads, and feet) are gifts to Santa Tecla from cured worshipers. A truly extraordinary panoramic view of the ocean and valley greets tourists at the very top, along with booths of trinkets that will delight diehard souvenir hunters but may disgust everyone else. La Guardia hosts a **lobster festival** the last Sunday in June, as well as the mysterious "Burial of the Swordfish" during *Carnaval* in March. Pilgrimages, *fútbol*, and folk festivals mark the **Feria de Monte de Santa Tecla** in the second week of August.

　　Buses run to and from La Guardia from Vigo (1hr.; M-F every 30min., Sa every hr., 5:45am-9pm; Su 6 per day, 8:30am-7pm; 605ptas). La Guardia's **tourist office** (tel. 986 61 18 50) sits on C. Rosalía de Castro during the summer (mid-June to mid-Sept. open M-Sa 11am-2pm and 5-8pm) and in the Ayuntamiento (tel. 986 61 00 00) in Pr. España the rest of the year (open M-Sa 8am-3pm).

PONTEVEDRA

According to legend, Pontevedra (pop. 74,000) was founded by the Greek archer Teucro as a place to convalesce after his Trojan War exploits. Its name comes from an old Roman bridge (Pontus Veteri), and since medieval times it has been an important stopover on the southern (Portuguese) Camino de Santiago. Centrally located in the Ría Bajas, Pontevedra is more of a transportation hub than a destination in itself. To its credit, though, this regional capital claims a wealth of beautiful parks and plazas, easy transportation to nearby villages and beaches, and the only bull ring in Galicia.

▐ GETTING THERE

Trains run to Pontevedra from **Santiago de Compostela** (1½hr., 22 per day, 6:20am-11:40pm, 635ptas). **Buses** go from **Vigo** (45min., 31 per day, 7am-8pm, 300ptas).

🛂 ORIENTATION AND PRACTICAL INFORMATION

Six streets radiate out from the center of town, **Praza Peregrina**. The main streets are C. Oliva, C. Michelena, C. Benito Corbal, and C. Peregrina. **Praza Galiza** is a five-minute walk from Pr. Peregrina (with the stations vaguely behind you, walk down C. Peregrina one block and turn right onto C. Andrés Muruais). The **train** and **bus stations,** located across from each other, are about 1km from town. To get to the city center, turn left after exiting the bus station. Continue on this street for 10-15 minutes as it changes from Av. Alféreces Provisionales to Av. de Vigo to C. Peregrina, which deposits you in Pr. Peregrina.

TRANSPORTATION

Trains: (tel. 986 85 13 13 or 986 43 11 14), Av. Alféreces Provisionales. Info open daily 7:30am-1:30pm and 3:30-9:30pm. To: **Vigo** (30min., 22 per day, 7:38am-11pm, 250ptas, express 340ptas); **Santiago** (1½hr., 22 per day, 6:29am-10:10pm., 505ptas, express 635ptas); **La Coruña** (3hr., 22 per day, 6:29am-10:10pm, 1100ptas, express 1315ptas); **Madrid** (11hr.; M-F 2 per day, 12:40pm and 9:15pm; Sa 1 per day, 8:40am; 5300ptas, express 5900ptas).

Buses: (tel. 986 85 24 08; fax 986 85 25 30), Av. Alféreces Provisionales. More frequent than rail service. Info open M-Sa 8:30am-9pm. To: **Santiago** (1hr., every hr., 7am-8:30pm, 600ptas); **Cambados** (1hr.; 12 per day, M-F 7:55am-8:35pm, Sa 11:15am-8:35pm; Su 3 per day, 12:30pm-8:35pm; 300ptas); **El Grove/La Toja** (1hr., every 30min., 7:45am-10pm, 440ptas); **La Coruña** (2½hr., 10 per day, 7:30am-9pm, 1400ptas); **Madrid** (8hr., 4 per day, 4255ptas).

Taxis: (tel. 986 85 12 85 or 986 85 12 00). 350ptas from the stations to downtown.

Car Rental: Avis, C. Peregrina, 47 (tel. 986 85 20 25). Rates vary with duration of rental. One day unlimited mileage 11,950ptas. Must be over 25 and have had a license for at least 1 year. Open M-F 9am-1pm and 4-7pm, Sa 9am-12:45pm.

TOURIST, FINANCIAL, AND LOCAL SERVICES

Tourist Office: The **main office** is at C. General Mola, 3 (tel. 986 85 08 14), one block from Pr. Peregrina, left off C. Michelena (straight ahead with the monument to your right), and offers tons of brochures and maps. English spoken. A **second office** opens in summer on Pl. de España. Both open Sa-Su 11am-2pm and 5-9pm.

Currency Exchange: Banco Central Hispano (tel. 986 85 38 12), Pl. Peregrina. No commission. Open M-F 8:30am-2:30pm.

Luggage Storage: Lockers at the train station 400ptas; at the bus station 80ptas per piece. Both open daily 8am-10pm.

EMERGENCY AND COMMUNICATIONS

Emergency: tel. 091 or 092. **Police:** C. Joaquín Costa, 19 (tel. 986 85 38 00).

Hospital: Hospital Provincial, C. Doctor Loureiro Crespo, 2 (tel. 986 85 21 15). **Medical Emergencies:** tel. 061.

Post Office: C. Oliva, 21 (tel. 986 85 54 53). Open M-F 8:30am-8:30pm, Sa 9am-2pm. **Postal Code:** 36001.

Internet: Cybercafe Gorgo, C. Javier Puig, 6 (tel. 986 85 00 21 or 986 86 62 93). Walking on C. Peregrina with the stations behind you, take a right onto C. Sagasta, then a right onto C. Benito Corbal, then a left onto C. Javier Puig. 10am-3pm 200ptas per hr.; 3-10pm 300ptas per hr. **Cyberteka** (tel. 986 86 63 25), just off Ruinas de Santo Domingo. Enter the photocopy place and go up 1 floor. 200ptas per hr.

ACCOMMODATIONS AND FOOD

C. Michelena, C. Peregrina, and Pr. Galiza are dotted with cheap accommodations.

Pensión Florida, (tel. 986 85 19 79), on C. García Camba. With the stations behind you, take a left before C. Peregrina becomes a plaza. Clean, modern rooms compensate for the long flights of stairs. Winter heating. Singles 1800ptas; doubles 2500-3500ptas.

Pensión La Cueva, C. Andrés Mellado, 7 (tel. 986 85 12 71), in Pr. Galiza. With the stations behind you, take a left onto C. Mellado from C. Peregrina. The Cave is aptly named, with large, dim rooms. It's not the Ritz, but the price is right. Communal baths. Winter heating. Singles 1000ptas; doubles 1500-2500ptas.

Hostel Madrid, C. Andrés Mellado, 11 (tel. 986 85 10 06), next door to La Cueva. The best thing is the price. Winter heating. Singles 1000ptas; doubles 3000ptas. Visa, MC.

Like many towns in Galicia, Pontevedra prides itself on seafood. In the evenings, locals crowd tiny bars on C. Figueroa and C. San Sebastián to munch on a variety of fishy *tapas*, washed down with the local Albariño wine. Follow C. Soportales out of Pl. Peregrina. For land-based goods, there's **Supermercado Froiz,** C. Benito Corbal, 28 (tel. 986 86 52 51), at the corner of C. Sagasta (open M-Sa 9am-9pm).

Bodegón Micota, C. Peregrina, 4 (tel. 986 85 59 17). This intriguing alternative to the cafe-bar scene offers pricey but delicious "cuisine," the great temptress of the budget traveler. Best if you can catch the 950pta *menú del día.* Meat dishes 600-1800ptas, salads 650ptas. Open noon-4:30pm, 8pm-1am.

O Merlos, (tel. 986 84 43 43). From Pl. Peregina, take C. Michelena with the flowered median to your left, take a right, and then a quick left before the building with large green windows. Tasty regional platters served in a unique atmosphere; tall people get lost in the thousands of key chains hanging from the ceiling. *Menú* 1000ptas, seafood entrees 400-1300ptas. Open Tu-Su 10am-2am. Visa, MC, AmEx, DC.

Mesón Pontesampaio, C. Joaquín Costa, 24 (tel. 986 86 40 77). From C. Peregrina, turn onto C. Sagasta, then take the 2nd right onto C. Joaquín Costa. Greasy seafood specialties. Lunch *menú* 700ptas, dinner *menú* 1200ptas. Open daily 7:30am-2am.

SIGHTS AND ENTERTAINMENT

MUSEO PROVINCIAL. Pontevedra proper's best sight is the extensive Museo Provincial. Exhibits in the five-building collection cover a wide range of themes, including traditional Galician cooking, sacred and contemporary art, archaeology, and glasswork. The museum also includes the Gothic **Ruinas de Santo Domingo** in Pl. de España. *(Pr. Leña. Museum open M-Sa 10am-2:15pm and 5-8:45pm, Su 11am-1pm. 200ptas, EU members free. Ruins open June 1-Sept. 30 Tu-F 10am-2pm.)*

OTHER SIGHTS. In the evening, the granite walls and arcades of Pontevedra's old town emit a luminescent glow. The 18th-century **Capilla de la Virgen Peregrina** is dedicated to Pontevedra's patron saint, a pilgrim version of the Virgin Mary, and is modeled after the scallop shell associated with Santiago. *(Open daily 9am-9pm.)* The **Basílica Menor de Santa María** features a golden Plateresque door that's illuminated by flood-lights at night. *(From Pl. España take Av. Santa María, on the left of the Ayun-*

tamiento. Open daily 10am-1pm and 5-9pm.) More off the beaten tourist track, the funky **Sala de Explosiones Teucro** holds international modern art shows in its tiny two-room gallery. *(C. Javier Puig. Open M-F 7-9:30pm, Sa noon-2pm and 7-9:30pm. Free.)*

BEACHES. If it's sunny, there's sure to be a crowd at the beaches of nearby **Marin.** A fleet of red APSA buses makes the journey from the outer corner of Pr. Galicia. (30min., every 15min., 115ptas.) You'll endure the horrid stench of a paper mill along the way, but the beaches are clean and inviting. From the bus stop in Marin, facing the water, head left on C. Angusto Miranda around the track and up the hill. To arrive at **Playa Porticelo,** turn right on C. Tiro Naval Janer, continue for 15 minutes, and bear right where the road splits. Another 10 minutes on foot brings you to the larger **Playa Mogor.** Both beaches come equipped with bar-cafes.

ENTERTAINMENT. For a glimpse of Pontevedra **nightlife,** check out the bars near the Basílica Menor de Santa María (especially along C. Isabel II). More rip-roaring bars and discotecas can be spotted along C. Cobián Roffignac. The festivals of **Santiago de Burgos** (July 25) and **La Peregrina** (2nd Sunday in August) provide more fun.

DAYTRIPS FROM PONTEVEDRA

The following towns are perfect daytrips from Pontevedra, as frequent bus service covers the area. The train from Santiago in the north swings toward the coast at Vilagarcía de Arousa, the commercial center of central Galicia.

EL GROVE (O GROVE) AND LA TOJA (A TOXA)

Every July and August, affluent Europeans come in Land Rovers and BMWs to the seaside resort of El Grove (pop. 11,000) and its island partner, La Toja. Sea-saturated El Grove, on a tranquil strait west of Pontevedra, is lined with mussel farms, colorful boats, and clam-diggers. La Toja, across the bridge, lures the wealthy (and the occasional desperate backpacker) with a casino, a decent beach, and aggressive vendors hoping to enchant with their "typical Galician dress."

All **buses** depart from the end of the waterfront. Buses run from El Grove to **Cambados** on the way to Vilagarcía (30min., 4 per day, more in July-Aug., 235ptas) and to **Pontevedra** (1hr., 19 per day, 6:30am-7:15pm, 440ptas). Schedules are posted inside and on the door of the bus office, 50m to the left. From July to mid-October the **tourist office** (tel. 986 73 14 15) in El Grove has its own little office in the square near the Ayuntamiento and the bus stop. The rest of the year, brochures are dispensed on the second floor of the Ayuntamiento. (Tel. 986 73 09 75. Open July-Oct. 15 M-Sa 10am-9pm; Oct. 16-June M-F 8am-3pm.)

LA LANZADA

Five kilometers toward Pontevedra from El Grove, La Lanzada's beach lures topless bathers with its fine white sands and irresistible waves. Home to the pagan cult of the "Ninth Wave," this area's mysterious methods of aiding romance and

SURPRISINGLY FASHIONABLE To the surprise of Spaniards everywhere, this culturally-isolated region in northwestern Spain has recently received international recognition as a hub of modern fashion, catching the eyes of top French, Italian, and American designers. Leading this Galician fashion brigade are Antonio Pernas, Roberto Verino, and Zara (once a simple neighborhood store; now it produces over $1.19 billion in annual sales). Even more impressive than such booming success is the designers' stubborn and prideful insistence on keeping their companies rooted in Galician soil. So tourists looking for a genuine Galician souvenir can toss away that cumbersome *Tetilla* cheese block and head home wearing a flashy, newfangled Antonio Pernas designer suit. Perhaps, before too long, supermodels will be storming catwalks across the globe decked in the characteristic brown cloak and scallop shells of the Pilgrims of the Camino de Santiago. Or not.

fertility will either baffle or entice you. Two hundred meters past the end of La Lanzada sits **Restaurante La Lanzada** (tel. 986 74 32 32), accessible by beach or road, a white *cabaña* with simple, spacious rooms 50m from the surf (doubles 4000ptas, with large bed and bath 5000ptas). **Camping Muiñeira** (tel. 986 73 84 04) is a short way past Restaurante La Lanzada. Sites with soft grass and wildflowers are not particularly private, but a gorgeous beach is just a street-crossing away. (500ptas per person and per tent, 400ptas per car.) To get to La Lanzada, take the **bus** from Pontevedra to El Grove/La Toja (1hr., every 30min., 7:45am-10pm, 440ptas), but tell the driver to let you off 10 minutes before the El Grove/La Toja stop.

CAMBADOS

For a glimpse of small-town life and a glass of good wine, head to harborside Cambados (pop. 14,000), 26km northwest of Pontevedra. Lack of a beach has left Cambados out of the tourist loop—its taxi drivers play cards all afternoon. On a quiet hill 15 minutes from the center, the beautiful ruins of the **Iglesia Santa María** watch over the town's cemetery. For a lovely view of the town and the *ría*, climb the steps to the left of the ruins up to the small park. The **Pazo de Fefiñanes,** an attractive 16th-century palace-turned-*bodega*, brims with gigantic, sweet-smelling barrels of wine. The lively **Praza de Fefiñanes** is filled with bar-restaurants serving the wine that is the pride of Cambados. The town throws a *fiesta* virtually every night in mid-summer, beginning with the July celebration of **Santa Mariña** and culminating the first weekend in August with an official tasting of the previous year's local Albariño, a light and fruity wine. Plus Ultra **buses** leave from the new bus station near Pr. Concello to **Pontevedra** (1hr., 9 per day, last at 7pm, 315ptas) and **Santiago** (M-F 8 per day, 7am-7pm; Sa 3 per day, 8am, 3pm and 7pm; Su 2 per day, 9am and 7pm). A new **tourist office** (near the bus station) serves Cambados (open M-Sa 10am-1:30pm and 4:30-7pm).

RÍA DE MUROS Y NOYA

Although the northern areas of the Rías Bajas don't see too many tourists, these small towns have plenty to offer visitors, with beautiful, granite old cities and popular beaches. The region's real gem is the ancient Celtic castle, **O Castro de Baroña.** Frequent buses make these towns easy daytrips from Santiago.

NOYA (NOIA)

Nicknamed "the little Compostela" for its density of monuments, Noya is distinguished by the Gothic arcades and 15th-century stone houses that surround its many small squares. The 14th-century **Igrexa de Santa María** houses a bulky collection of tomb-lids; the 16th-century **Igrexa de San Francisco** keeps the Ayuntamiento company. Well-preserved statues of curly-bearded saints compose the Gothic facade of **Igrexa de San Martín.** The Castromil **bus** (in Santiago tel. 986 58 90 90; in Noya tel. 981 82 05 19), which runs from Santiago to Muros, stops in Noya (1hr., every hr., 8am-9pm, 630ptas). Eighteen buses return from Noya to Santiago daily. The **tourist office** (tel. 981 82 41 69 or 981 82 20 76) is located in the Casa de Cultura. To get there from the bus station, walk to the top of the hill, take a right through the park, continue between BBV Bank and Cafe Avenida, take the first left on Corredoira de Luis and look to the right. (Open M-Sa 10am-2pm.)

▓O CASTRO DE BAROÑA

Nineteen kilometers south of Noya lies a little-known treasure of historical intrigue and mesmerizing natural beauty—the seaside remains of a 5th-century Celtic fortress known as O Castro de Baroña. The circular foundations dot the neck of an isthmus, ascending to a rocky promontory above the sea and then descending to a crescent **beach** (clothing very optional). Catch the sunset on one of the naturally formed cliffside rocks, then pitch a tent at the free public campsite in the forest, just 300m from the shore. **Café-Bar O Castro** (tel. 981 76 74 30), the O Castro bus stop, offers spotless rooms upstairs; there are bathrooms down the hall (singles 2000-2500ptas, doubles 3000-3500ptas). The restaurant downstairs has a *menú* for 1000ptas. **Hefsel buses** run between Noya and Riveira, stopping (but often passing—tell the driver where you are going) in front of Café-Bar O Castro (30min.; M-F 14 per day, 6:50am-9:30pm; Sa 7 per day, 8am-9pm; Su 11 per day, 8am-10pm; 250ptas). Catch the bus across the road on the way back. The nearest town, **Baroña,** 1km north, has a small supermarket, restaurant, and bus stop.

SOUTH RÍAS ALTAS

If Galicia is the forgotten corner of Spain, then the small *rías* of the Costa Muerte are the forgotten corner of Galicia. Beaches here are arguably the emptiest, cleanest, and loveliest in all of Spain. The local population still plows with oxen, and women tote homegrown produce to market in baskets balanced on their heads.

Although its appellation—"Coast of Death"—refers to the many shipwrecks along the rocky coast, it could just as well apply to tragedy bred in the name of gourmet tastes. Several fishermen die each year while attempting to extract the expensive and highly sought-after *percebes* (barnacles) from sharp rocks on the coast. The fiercest challenge for travelers, thankfully, is finding quick transportation to this remote region. Both Cabo Finisterre and Camariñas can be reached by bus from Santiago and La Coruña, but bus service to the smaller towns and isolated beaches is infrequent. The roads, tortuous and sometimes poorly paved, have vague signs, and thick mist often settles in the morning. Don't let lousy weather dissuade you, though. Like black-and-white movies and mystery novels, the Coast of Death is more enjoyable in the rain.

CABO FINISTERRE (CABO FISTERRA)

For pilgrims in the middle ages, a trip to Finisterre was almost obligatory; after completing the entire Camino de Santiago, catching a glimpse of what was then thought to be the end of the world (*finis terrae*) was a macabre pleasure. To one side of Cabo Finisterre spreads the Ría de Corcubión and its attractive beaches, Sardineiro and Langosteira; on the other side jagged mountains meet the open sea.

⊓ PRACTICAL INFORMATION. Finisterre buses make daily trips from **Santiago** to Finisterre (2½hr.; M-F 8am, 1:30pm, 4pm, and 6pm; Sa-Su 8am and 6pm; 1450ptas) and back (M-F 7am, 1:45pm, and 4pm; Sa 7am; Su 6pm). Buses often require a transfer in Vimianzo, but there is rarely a wait. Finisterre buses also travel daily to Cée, a good place for connections to all towns south. The **Casa do Concello** (tel. 981 74 07 81), C. Real, has nice stickers but only the barest minimum of **tourist information.** As you head uphill from the statue, turn left at the building with large windows. (Open M-F 9am-2pm and 7-11pm, Sa-Su 7-11pm.). **Emergency:** tel. 091, 092, or 112; **medical assistance** at Casa del Mar Clínica (tel. 981 74 02 52), next door to the tourist office.

⊓⊓ ACCOMMODATIONS AND FOOD. While Finisterre is a feasible daytrip from Santiago, **Hospedaje López**, C. Carrasqueira, 4 (tel. 981 74 04 49), has cheap, immaculate, light-filled rooms (some with ocean views) and a touch of Disney cheer. Head uphill away from the main statue at the port, turn right onto C. Carrasqueira, and walk for five minutes. (Singles 1500-2000ptas; doubles 3000-3500ptas; triples 4500ptas.) **Camping Ruta Finisterre** (tel. 981 74 63 02), Ctra. Coruña, is east of Finisterre on the Playa del Estorde in Cée (465ptas per person, per tent, and per car; open Apr.-Sept. 15). **Supermercado Froiz,** a five-minute walk left of the statue along the shore, is the big fish (open M-Sa 9am-2pm and 5-9pm). Although most restaurants along the dock are overpriced, **Restaurante O Centalo** (tel. 981 74 04 52) serves a *menú* for 1100ptas as well as tasty *raciones* (open daily 1-4:30pm and 9pm-midnight).

🕿 SIGHTS. Four kilometers from town stands the lighthouse that has beckoned ships for years, offering stunning views. Turquoise beaches here have seduced such travelers as Camilo José Cela, Spain's Nobel Prize winning novelist. The **Capilla de Santa María das Areas** contains a painting of the "Christ of the Golden Beard," thrown off a British ship and found by a local fisherman. A 12th-century **church** stands beside the road to the cape. To reach the **beach,** proceed uphill from the statue at the port past C. Carrasqueira, then turn right at the first dirt road. After 50m, turn left onto the seaward path at the white house with blue trim.

LA CORUÑA (A CORUÑA)

While the newer parts of La Coruña are gray and mundane, recent efforts have made the *ciudad vieja* (old city) and the strips along the ocean attractive to visitors. Sailboats line the north end of the port, and gardens and parks lie tucked within the old city. Many of La Coruña's 250,000 residents spend afternoons at pleasant waterfront cafes along the new Paseo Marítimo, which winds around the isthmus along marinas, rocky cliffs, and beaches. An excellent base for exploring the Rías Altas, La Coruña has stellar nightlife, a historic old town, and pleasant beaches that more than make up for the dingier parts of the city.

▣ GETTING THERE

Buses run to La Coruña from **Santiago de Compostela** (30min., every hr., 6am-9pm, 800ptas) and **Oviedo** (6hr., 5 per day, 7:30am-4:30pm, 3060ptas).

▣ ORIENTATION AND PRACTICAL INFORMATION

La Coruña's new city stretches across the mainland; the isthmus and peninsula contain the *ciudad vieja*. **Avenida de la Marina** leads past the tourist office into the old city. Surfboard havens **Praia del Orzán** and **Praia de Riazor** are 10-minute walks northwest from the tourist office, on the other side of the peninsula's neck. From the bus station, take bus #1 or 1A straight to the **tourist office** (110ptas). To get to the bus station from the train station, walk in the direction of El Corte Inglés, and take the pedestrian overpass, which leads to the bus station (5min.).

TRANSPORTATION

Flights: Aeropuerto de Alvedro (tel. 981 18 72 00), 9km south of the city. Served only by Aviaco. **Iberia/Aviaco,** C. Teresa Herrera, 1 (tel. 981 22 56 36). Open M-F 9:30am-1:30pm and 4:30-8pm, Sa 9:30am-1:30pm.

Trains: (tel 981 15 02 02), in Pr. San Cristóbal. Info open daily 7am-11pm. To: **Santiago** (1hr., 19 per day, 6:20am-10:25pm, 505-635ptas); **Pontevedra** (2½hr., 19 per day, 6:20am-10:25pm, 1100-1315ptas); **Vigo** (3hr., 19 per day, 6:20am-10:25pm, 1240-1470ptas); **Madrid** (11hr., 1-3 per day, 5500-8700ptas); **Barcelona** (16-17hr., 2 per day, 6700ptas).

Buses: (tel. 981 23 96 44), on C. Caballeros, across Av. Alcalde Molina from the train station. **ALSA-Intercar** (tel. 981 15 11 00). To: **Oviedo** (5hr., 4 per day, 9am-5:45pm, 3060ptas); **Madrid** (8½hr., 6 per day, 7:30am-10:30pm, 4890-6975ptas); **San Sebastián** (14hr., 2 per day, 9am and 5:45pm, 6330ptas). **Castromil** to **Santiago** (1½hr., 17 per day, 7am-10pm, 800ptas). **IASA** (tel. 981 23 90 01). To: **Betanzos** (45min., every 30min., 7am-10:30pm, 245ptas); **Vivero,** with stops at O Barqueiro, Ortigueiro, El Ferrol, Vicedo, and Betanzos (4hr., 3-4 per day, 1635ptas).

Public Transportation: Red buses of the **Compañía de Tranvías de la Coruña** (tel. 981 25 01 00) run frequently throughout the day (7am-11:30pm, 110ptas). Bus stops post full itineraries; buy tickets on board.

Taxis: Radio Taxi (tel. 981 24 33 33). **Tele Taxi** (tel. 981 28 77 77). With the tourist office and ocean to the right, walk along the sidewalk to the taxi stand.

La Coruña

ACCOMMODATIONS
A Hospedaje María Pita
B Pensión la Alianza

N

0 ____ 200 yards
0 ____ 200 meters

Puerto de la Coruña

Castillo de San Antón

Car Rental: Autos Brea, Av. Fernández Latorre, 110 (tel. 981 23 86 45). Must be at least 21 and have had a license for at least 1 year. From 2075ptas per day with unlimited mileage. 3-day min. rental. Open M-F 9am-1pm and 4-7pm, Sa 9am-2pm.

TOURIST, FINANCIAL, AND LOCAL SERVICES

Tourist Office: (tel. 981 22 18 22), on Dársena de la Marina, connecting the peninsula and mainland. One of Spain's finest. Tips on daytrips and an accommodations guide. English spoken. Open M-F 9am-2pm and 4:30-6:30pm, Sa 9am-2pm and 5-7pm, Su 10am-2pm and 5-7pm.

Currency exchange: Banco Central Hispano, Canton Grano, 9-12. No commission. Open M-F 8:30am-2:30pm.

American Express Travel: Viajes Amado, C. Compostela, 1 (tel. 981 22 99 72). Open M-F 9:30am-2pm and 4:30-8pm, Sa 9:45am-1:30pm.

Luggage Storage: At the train station, lockers 400ptas. Open daily 6:30am-1:30am. At the bus station, 75ptas per bag. Open daily 8am-10pm.

El Corte Inglés: C. Ramón y Cajal, 57-59 (tel. 981 29 00 11). A sharp right from the bus station exit. Currency exchange, maps, novels and guidebooks in English, haircutting, cafeteria, supermarket, restaurant, and telephones. Open M-Sa 10am-9:30pm.

Laundromat: Lavandería Glu Glu, C. Alcalde Marchesi, 4 (tel. 981 28 28 04), off Pr. Cuatro Caminos. Wash and dry self-serve 800ptas per 5kg load. Full service 950ptas per load. Open M-F 9:30am-8:30pm, Sa 9:30am-6pm.

EMERGENCY AND COMMUNICATIONS

Emergency: tel. 091 or 092. **Police: Municipal** (tel. 981 18 42 25), C. Miguel Servet.

Medical Services: Amb. San José, C. Comandante Fontanes, 8 (tel. 981 22 63 35).

Post Office: (tel. 981 22 51 75), on C. Alcalde Manuel Casas, past Teatro Colón off Av. Marina. Lista de Correos and **faxes.** Open M-F 8:30am-8:30pm, Sa 9:30am-2pm. **Postal Code:** 15070.

Internet Access: Paizon E.D., C. San Nicolas, 37 (tel. 981 20 55 24), 1 block from C. Riegode Agua. 250ptas per 30min. Open daily 9am-11pm. **La Webería,** Pedro Barrié de la Maza, 18b (tel. 981 20 91 97). 300ptas per hr. Open Su-W 10:30am-2:30pm and 4:30pm-12:30am, Th-Sa 2:30pm-3:30am.

▼ ACCOMMODATIONS

The best and most convenient area for lodging is one block back from Av. Marina, near the tourist office. C. Riego de Agua and the surrounding area (from Pr. María Pita down to Pr. San Agustín) always have available rooms. There are many *pensiones* near the stations, though miles away from the *ciudad vieja*. HI hostels are fairly inconveniently located; the cost of transportation to La Coruña proper and the burden of travel will most likely cancel out any actual benefits.

▨ **Hospedaje María Pita,** C. Riego de Agua, 38, 3rd fl. (tel. 981 22 11 87), above Hospedaje Moran (don't confuse them). White lace curtains, cheery rooms, pristine bathrooms, and a homey feel. Arrangements for singles possible. Doubles 2900-3210ptas.

Pensión la Alianza, C. Riego de Agua, 8, 1st fl. (tel. 981 22 81 14). Dark wood and home-made oil paintings decorate quiet, simple rooms. Spotless gray-tiled bathroom down the hall. Singles 1500-2100ptas; doubles 3000-3500ptas.

Marina Española (HI) (tel. 981 62 01 18), in Sada, about 20km east of La Coruña. The Empresa Calpita bus (tel. 981 23 90 72) runs to Sada (30min., 240ptas). Dorms 750ptas, over 26 1100ptas. 3-day max. stay. Call ahead, especially in summer.

◗ FOOD

Cheap eats abound on C. Estrella, C. Franja, and nearby streets. For snazzier cafes and pizzerias, head for the ocean strips and the area around C. Rubine off Playa de Raizor. Fresh fruit and vegetables are in the **market** in the oval building on Pr. San Agustín, near the old town (open M-Sa 8am-3pm). For groceries, head downstairs to **Supermercados Claudio** (open daily 9am-3pm and 5-9pm).

Mesón Trotamundos, Pr. España, 9 (tel. 981 22 16 09). Sit at wooden tables under hunks of beef and hundreds of wine bottles and watch the staff make the famous *pulpo gallego. Raciónes* 250-1100ptas. *Menú* M-Sa 800ptas. Open daily 10am-2am.

Cafetería SouSantos, C. Fransico Mariño, 10 (tel. 981 22 76 09), near Pl. Pontevedra and Pl. Riazor. During mid-afternoon, half of the city seems to crowd into this lovable spot. Entrees 350-700ptas. Open July-Aug. 8am-3am; Sept.-June F-W 8am-3am.

Gastof, Av. Marina, 6 (tel. 981 22 10 27), offers banana splits (600ptas), sandwiches (300-500ptas), and a range of entrees (600-800ptas). Open daily 11am-midnight.

SIGHTS

▨**TORRE DE HÉRCULES.** La Coruña's tourist magnet, the 2nd-century Torre de Hércules, towers over rusted ship carcasses on the west end of the peninsula. Hercules allegedly erected the tower, now the world's oldest working lighthouse, upon the remains of his defeated enemy Gerión. Enter through the lower of two entrances to creep around the original foundation, then climb a claustrophobic 237-step tunnel to the pinnacle. *(Take the seaside path from the Orzán and Riazor beaches, or bus #9 or 13 (110ptas). Open July-Sept. 10am-7pm; Oct.-June 10am-6pm. 250ptas, seniors and children free.)*

MUSEO DOMUS. Just up the esplanade connecting Playa Orzán to Playa Riazor, the brand-new Museo Domus (Museum of Man) houses three floors of interactive, high-tech exhibits on the human body. Watch "blood" spurt at 50kph from a model heart; hear "Hello, I love you" in over 30 languages (sadly, from a computer); and spend hours playing with microscopes, computers, and other fun gizmos. *(Tel. 981 22 89 47 or 981 22 89 29. Open July-Aug. Tu-Sa 11am-9pm; Sept.-June Tu-Sa 10am-7pm, Su and festivals 11am-2:30pm. 400ptas, students 100ptas. Entrance fee also gets you into the Science Museum/Planetarium in Parque de Santa Margarita.)*

REAL ACADEMIA GALLEGA. The Real Academia Gallega (Royal Galician Academy) makes its headquarters at the former family seat of 19th-century novelist Condesa Emilia Pardo Bazán; its library contains 25,000 volumes on Galician literature, history, and culture. The museum next door is dedicated to Pardo Bazán's work and a rotating exhibition of modern and 19th-century Galician art. *(C. Tabernas. Tel. 981 20 73 08. Open July-Sept. M-F 10am-1pm; Oct.-June M-F 10am-noon. Free.)*

GARDENS. Sandwiched between Av. Marina and the dock, the elegant **Jardín Méndez Núñez** has a clock snipped to botanical perfection, with arms that actually tell the correct time. Soothing **Jardín de San Carlos,** in the old city, was originally planted in 1843 on the site of the old Forte San Carlos and shelters the tomb of Sir John Moore. Local lore has it that killing this incompetent general cost Napoleon his crown, since Wellington took over Moore's command.

🎵 ENTERTAINMENT

Summer nightlife in La Coruña reflects the cheerful nature of the peninsula. Residents bar-hop around C. Franja, C. La Florida, and C. San Juan and the surrounding side streets. When bars die down at around 2am, **discos** along the two beaches start making a ruckus. Also try the discos and cafes on C. Juan Florez. **Sol. Pirámide, C.** Juan Florez, 50 (tel. 981 27 61 57), plays dance music loud enough to rouse the dead, while **Picasso** and **Lautrec,** opposite each other on C. Sol, attract the artistically inclined. Smoky **Cafe-Bar La Barra,** C. Riego de Agua, 33 (tel. 981 22 73 82), offers innocent entertainment all day long. Students and old fogies gather to play cards, dominoes, and parcheesi. (Open daily 9am-2am.)

Although it is celebrated in many parts of Europe, La Coruña greets **La Noche de San Juan** (June 23) with particular fervor since it coincides with the opening of sardine season. Locals light the traditional *aguardiente* bonfires and spend the night leaping over the flames (contrary to the image that comes to mind, the rite ensures fertility) and gorging on sardine flesh. If you drop an egg white in a glass of water on this night, it will supposedly assume the form of your future spouse's occupation; many are led to believe they'll marry a cow. The last two weeks of August bring concerts, parades, and a mock naval battle to honor **María Pita.**

NEAR LA CORUÑA: BETANZOS

A provincial capital of ancient Galicia, the modern-day city of **Betanzos** (pop. 12,000) assumes a low profile despite its position at a crucial transportation intersection. Cafes line the central **Praza García Hermanos,** home to a statue of the brothers García, the city's great benefactors. **Igrexa de San Fransisco,** located several blocks down the hill from Pr. Hamanos, features the image of San Fransisco de Betanzos resting on the backs of a huge bear and boar and surrounded by his faithful puppies. Betanzos's great **festival** involves the launching of the world's largest paper balloon (about 25m high) on August 16, the night of San Roque.

Betanzos is a good half-day trip from La Coruña, most easily reached by bus. **IASA buses** (tel. 981 23 90 01) run from La Coruña (45min., M-Sa every 30min., Su every hr., 240ptas). Two **trains** (tel. 981 77 24 02) per day stop in Betanzos on the way from La Coruña to El Ferrol (3:45pm and 9:25pm; returns 7:30am and 3:30pm; 325ptas). The train station sits across the river.

Some think **Miño,** 12km north of Betanzos, has the nicest beach in the Rías Altas. On Saturday afternoons in **Pontedeume,** 22km from Betanzos, workers at the town market cook *pulpo* (octopus) in huge copper urns and mock the citizens of Betanzos for making that ridiculously huge balloon. You can reach both towns on the bus lines heading to El Ferrol (every 30min., 280ptas).

NORTH RÍAS ALTAS

Not as isolated as their southern cousins, these urbane *rías* become calmer as they move eastward. Old lighthouses, churches, and the remains of an ancient wall or two dot the green countryside. In the misty mountains of Galicia, the weather is anything but predictable, but views are spectacular year-round. Thanks to increasing popularity among vacationing Spaniards, the north Rías Altas have accumulated enough capital to create a transportation system, rendering the unspoiled coastline easily accessible.

RÍAS DE CEDEIRA AND VIVERO

Where the average tourist seldom treads, rainforests covered with ferns give way to soft, empty beaches. Thick mists veil the valleys of these northernmost *rías*. IASA Buses and FEVE trains run inland to Vivero from El Ferrol, but the coastal bus is preferable, allowing you to hop off anytime.

CEDEIRA

When cuckolding Lancelot fled England to escape the ire of King Arthur, he allegedly landed in Cedeira (pop. 8500), founding the town and sowing his seed. Set on its own *ría* 84km northeast of La Coruña, this small town offers historical monuments, pretty beaches, and breathtaking surrounding countryside.

⚑ PRACTICAL INFORMATION. Bus service in Cedeira is fairly sparse. To get to **Vivero** take an **IASA** bus from C. Ezequiel Lopez, 28, to **Campo do Hospital** (15min., 5 per day, 120ptas), where you can change to the Campo do Hospital-Viviero IASA bus line. **RIALSA** buses run from Cedeira to **El Ferrol** (1hr., 7 per day, 490ptas), where connections can be made to La Coruña and elsewhere. Near the bus stop, the **tourist office,** C. Ezequiel Lopez, 22 (tel. 981 48 21 87), hands out brochures (open July-Aug. M-Sa 10:30am-2pm and 6-9pm, Su and holidays noon-2pm; May-June and Sept. M-Sa 10:30am-2pm and 5-8pm, Su and holidays noon-2pm). **Police** tel. 091, 092, or 981 48 07 25. **Post office,** Av. Zumalacárregui, 17 (tel. 981 48 05 52; open M-F 8:30am-2pm, Sa 9am-2pm); **postal code:** 15350.

⚑🍴 ACCOMMODATIONS AND FOOD. Hostal Chelsea, Pr. Sagrado Corazón, 9 (tel. 981 48 23 40), hosts guests in light-filled rooms around the corner from the bus stop and near the beach (doubles with shower and TV 4000-4500ptas). For a small town, Cedeira has a surprising number of culinary specialties. Open-faced *empanadas* are unique to the town, and locals love to snack on S-shaped sugar cookies *("eses")*. Commendable *bodegas* and *mesones* line both sides of the *ría*. **Taberna da Calexa,** Tras. Elrexa, 7 (tel. 981 48 20 09), up a tiny staircase off the road leading to the church, serves Galician wine (100ptas per glass) behind medieval stone walls, complemented by a variety of homemade *raciones* (400-500ptas).

📷🎭 SIGHTS AND ENTERTAINMENT. The **Santuario de San Andrés de Teixido,** a steep 12km hike from town, provides a 620m-high vista overlooking the sea. The highest coastline in Europe, the Santuario still hosts pagan cults with thriving rituals involving the worship of the *herba de enamorar* (love herb). Closer to town lies the hermitage of **San Antonio de Corbeiro,** an easy 2km walk up a gentle slope. From the tourist office, turn left and follow signs to the turnoff (50m farther on the left). Then, it's up, up, and away. The hermitage is a white structure above the *ría*, high enough to send any acrophobe into a cold sweat. The **Curro festival,** on the fourth Sunday in June, rounds up nearby wild horses.

VIVERO (VIVEIRO)

The tourist brochure's assertion that Vivero *"No es un sueño. Existe."* ("Is not a dream. It exists.") may seem a bit much, but seaside Vivero (pop. 14,000) does have a dreamy quality to it. Known throughout Spain for its beautiful, tiny old city at the forest's edge, Vivero's peaceful atmosphere, nearby beaches, and July *fiestas* draw a flotilla of Spanish tourists every summer. The nearest beach is in the resort town of **Covas,** 1km across the river from Vivero. If you tire of Covas, **Playa de Area** suns itself 4km from Vivero, and **Playa de Sacido** is not much farther away (6km). The first weekend of July is marked by the *Rapa das Bestas*, a festival celebrating the capture, enclosure, shearing, and branding of wild horses. The main *fiestas* take place the last week in July.

⚑ PRACTICAL INFORMATION. FEVE trains (tel. 982 55 07 22), down Trav. Marina past Pr. Lugo, run to: **Ribadeo,** (1hr.; M-F 4 per day; Sa-Su 2 per day, 1pm and 4:45pm; 485ptas); **El Ferrol** (2hr., 3 per day, 7:53am-7:07pm, 6750ptas); **Oviedo** (5hr., 2 per day, 10:14am and 4:44pm, 1805ptas). **Bus** companies **IASA** (tel. 981 56 01 03), on Trav. Marina, and **ERSA**, Pr. Lugo, 2 (tel. 981 56 03 90), recently merged. Together, they run to: **Ribadeo** (1½hr., 2 per day, 9:15am and 3:45pm, 625ptas); **El Ferrol** (2hr., 6 per day, 6:30am-7:30pm, 985ptas); **Lugo** (2½hr., 8 per day, 6:45am-5:45pm, 1155ptas); **La Coruña** (4hr., 5 per day, 6:30am-7:30am, 1635ptas). Rent **cars, bikes,** and **motorcycles** at **Viajes Arifran,** C. Rosalía de Castro, 54 (tel. 982 56 04 97). Motorcycles run about 9000ptas per day and bicycles 1000ptas per day. (Open July-Aug. M-F 9:30am-1pm and 4-7pm, Sa 9:30am-1:30pm.) Vivero's **tourist office** (tel. 982 56 08 79), on Av. Ramón Canosa, hands out maps and brochures and posts information about *pensiones* (open daily 11am-2pm and 5:30-8:30pm). **Emergency:** tel. 091 or 092; **police** tel. 982 56 29 22. **Post office** (tel. 982 56 09 27), just past the bus station (open M-F 8:30am-2pm, Sa 9:30am-1pm).

⌘ ACCOMMODATIONS AND FOOD. Fonda Bossanova, Av. Galicia, 11 (tel. 982 56 01 50), one block from the bus station in the direction of Covas, has small, nondescript rooms (singles 2000ptas; doubles 2500ptas). On the first floor, the owner pleases locals with a 1100pta *menú* and delicious desserts. For spacious rooms with balconies and a view of the Igrexa de Santa María, try **Fonda Nuevo Mundo** (tel. 982 56 00 25). From Pr. Maior with the ocean behind you, walk forward and to the right onto Teodoro de Quiros (singles 2000ptas; doubles 3500ptas). On the same road heading toward Vivero is **Camping Vivero** (tel. 982 56 00 04). Follow the signs to the flagged reception hut. A cafe and broad beach are just steps away from this 2nd-class campsite. (Electricity 425ptas. Reception daily 9am-11pm. 425ptas per person, per tent, and per car. Open June-Sept.)

LA RAPA DAS BESTAS

Here, we fight horses for tradition," says one rider, a sweaty, blood-speckled bandanna across his hairline. The blood, however, may not be his. For the past two hours he's straddled, head-locked, tail-pulled, herd-surfed, tackled, gotten kicked and bitten by, branded, and most importantly, sheared numerous steeds.

With the first weekend of July just around the corner, Galicia's *La Rapa Das Bestas* (The Cropping of the Beasts) kicks off in isolated Pueblo Sabucedo. Consistent with one of the central themes in Spanish culture—man versus beast—La Rapa gives a new face to the traditional noble bull-gallant Matador dynamic.

Days before the festival begins, Spanish Marlboro men comb the valleys, gathering herds of wild horses. The most exciting moment comes when the 400 unbridled horses thunder into the tight stone canal, enveloped in dust and panic. No animal can be visually separated from the rest; the arena becomes a writhing sea of horseflesh in myriad shades of brown and dirty blond.

As a pre-show teaser of sorts, local youths enter the canal first, responsible for dragging out the ponies. Proud, back-slapping "that's my boy" Dads nudge sons on. Unfortunately, a terrified pony breaks free of one child's ginger grip and lauds a KO kick across the 10 year old's face and chest. The crowd lets out a shared UMPH! and a rider swoops into the ring to cradle the motionless boy away.

Then the big boys move in—or (ahem) the big people. A fiery rugged redhead woman becomes an instant crowd-pleaser; she launches bareback atop a long-haired beauty, secured only by a handful of mares. Slapping the horse's face, she separates him from the herd. A meaty rider wraps the horse's tail around his fists and digs both boot heels into the mud. Upon securing a Sabucedan necktie, the horse drops amid teams of eager scissor-handed locals. When the dust clears, the horse has staggered to his feet, thick crops of shiny black hair beneath—to be collected later by children as souvenirs.

By the end of the three-day festival, the horses are both shaken and stirred by the unsolicited crew-cuts. But unlike the unfortunate fallen bull, these wild, wild horses will be ridden again someday.

The huge Mega-Claudio **supermarket** looms beside the bus station (open M-Sa 9:30am-9pm), and budget *mesones* are around Pr. Maior. **Mesón Xoaquín,** R. Irmans Vilarponte, 19 (tel. 982 56 27 56), up from the square, serves a *menú* for 850ptas in a stone *comedor* with stuffed boars and snazzy tablecloths (*raciones* 550-1200ptas; open daily 1-4pm and 8pm-midnight). **A Cepa,** R. Fernández Victorio, 7, dishes out cheap *tapas: chipirones* 200ptas, *patatas bravas* 110ptas, and the mysterious *bikini* 150ptas (open daily noon-3pm and 7:30pm-midnight).

RÍA DE RIBADEO

Even when inundated with summer residents, Ribadeo's (pop. 9300) stunning Galician scenery gives the town a ghostly, deserted air. Choose your mountain, *ría*, or Cantabrian Sea view, then pray for a clear day. At the water's edge, both the **Paseo Marítimo** and the **Praia Os Bloques,** just past the dock, harbor spectacular views. High above the *ría*, a 3km walk from town through farmland (follow the signs), sits the **Igrexa de Santa Cruz.** If the climb doesn't take your breath away, the view of the eucalyptus countryside and crazy-blue ocean will. Three kilometers in the other direction, at the **Praia de Rocas Blancas,** a red and white *faro* (lighthouse) towers above the water. If you're up for a 9km hike (or short bus ride), check out **Playa As Catedrals,** with incredible natural rock archways that curl into the sea.

Getting in and out of Ribadeo is easy. The **FEVE train station** (tel. 982 13 07 39) is a 15-minute walk from Pr. España straight along R. Villafranco Bierzo, which changes names four times (info open daily 6am-9pm). Trains crawl along the coastal route to: **El Ferrol** (3½hr.; 3 per day; 6:45am, 11:47am, and 3:30pm, 1145ptas); **Oviedo** (4hr., 2 per day, 11:37am and 5:58pm, 1290ptas). **IASA buses** (tel. 982 22 17 60) run to: **Vivero** (2 per day, 1250ptas); **La Coruña** (3hr., 10 per day, 1000ptas); **El Ferrol** (4 per day, 1030ptas). The **ALSA** station (tel. 982 13 10 60) off Pr. España runs buses to **Oviedo** (4hr., 4 per day, 1525ptas). Buses leave from Av. Rosalía de Castro, in front of Viajes Terra y Mar. From Pr. España, take C. San Roque (the upper left corner), head left for two blocks, turn right, and walk about 150m.

Several hostels sit on C. San Roque, on the way from the train station. On Pr. España across from the church is **Hostal Costa Verde,** 13 (tel. 982 12 86 81). Its rooms and bathrooms are pristine; some rooms have balconies. (Singles 2000-2500ptas; Doubles 4000-5000ptas.) **Camping Ribadeo** (tel. 982 13 11 67), along Av. Galicia, charges 425ptas per person, tent, and car. **Supermercado El Arbol** (tel. 982 72 58 50), on Av. Galicia, is well-stocked (open Tu-Sa 9am-2pm and 5-8:30pm, M 9:30am-2pm), and low-priced *cafeterías* dot Pr. España. **Restaurante Ros Mary,** C. San Francisco, 3, has a 1000pta *menú* of hake, steak, and *fabadas* (open daily 8am-2pm).

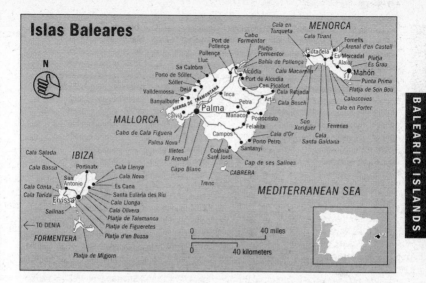

Islas Baleares

N

MENORCA

Cala en Turqueta
Cabo Formentor
Port de Pollença
Cala Tirant
Fornells
Arenal d'en Castell
Pollença
Platjo Formentor
Ciutadela
Es Mercadal
Platja Es Grau
Lluc
Bahía de Pollença
Alaior
Sa Calobra
Alcúdia
Mahón
Porto de Sóller
Port de Alcudia
Punta Prima
Sóller
Cala Macarella
Platja de Son Bou
Valldemossa
Deià
Can Picafort
Calascoves
Inca
Cala Ratjada
Cala en Porter
Banyalbufar
Petra
Artà
Cala Bosch
SIERRA DE TRAMONTANA
Palma
Manacor
Portocristo
Son
Ferreries
Càlvia
Felanitx
Xoriguer
Cala
Santa Galdana

MALLORCA

Cabo de Cala Figuera
Campos
Cala d'Or
Palma Nova
Porto Petro
Illetes
Colònia
Santanyi
El Arenal
Sant Jordi

IBIZA
Cala Salada
Cala Bassa
Portinatx
Cala Llenya
Capo Blanc
CABRERA
Cap de ses Salines
Cala Conta
San Antonio
Cala Nova
Trenc
Cala Tarida
Es Cana
Eivissa
Santa Eulària des Riu
Cala Llonga
Salinas
Cala Olivera
Platja de Talamanca

← TO DENIA
FORMENTERA
Platja de Figueretes
Platja d'en Bossa

Platja de Migjorn

MEDITERRANEAN SEA

0   40 miles
0   40 kilometers

BALEARIC ISLANDS

BALEARIC ISLANDS

Perhaps dreaming of the vast fortunes to be made in the 20th-century tourist industry, nearly every culture with boats and colonists to spare has tried to conquer the Balearic islands (which have been Spanish since the 13th century). Foreign invasion continues today as two million of the trendiest and wealthiest European tourists flood the islands' discos and beaches each year.

While all four of the islands—Mallorca, Ibiza, Formentera, and Menorca—share fame for their gorgeous beaches and alluring topography, each has its own distinguishing characteristics. **Mallorca,** home to Palma, the islands' capital, absorbs the bulk of invaders. With its museums, architecture, and nightlife, Palma competes with Eivissa (Ibiza City) as the Baleares's cultural hub. Mallorca also harbors natural beauty, albeit in the shadows of urbanization. Condominiums loom over lazy bays that scoop into the coastline, while olive and orange orchards shade its fertile interior. **Ibiza,** a counter-culture haven since the 1960s, is the entertainment and style center of the islands. Eivissa, its capital, offers what many consider the best nightlife in all of Europe. Ibiza's little sister, **Formentera,** is more peaceful, as unspoiled sands and unpaved roads abound. Wrapped in green fields and stone walls, **Menorca** leads a private life of empty white beaches, hidden coves, and mysterious Bronze Age megaliths.

Summers tend to be hot, dry, and crowded—but fun. Winters, especially on northern Mallorca and Menorca, are windy and chilly. Spring and autumn can be gorgeous, but the beaches remain a bit cool; the nightlife doesn't heat up—especially on Mallorca and Menorca—until early July. Most opening hours, schedules, and prices listed are for summer months only. Off-season prices at hotels can drop by up to 50%, and opening hours are often cut drastically.

HIGHLIGHTS OF THE BALEARIC ISLANDS

■ Need you ask? **Ibiza's** 24-hour party (see p. 493).
■ **Formentera's** sprawling expanses of untouched sands (see p. 495).
■ **Menorca,** the mysterious isle that's perfect for getting away from it all (see p. 482).

☐ GETTING THERE AND AWAY

Flying to the islands is fast and cheap—it makes a lot more sense than taking a ferry. Those under 26 can often receive discounts from **Iberia/Aviaco Airlines** (tel. 902 40 05 00 in Barcelona; www.iberia.com). **SOM** (Servicios de Ocio Marítimo; tel. 971 31 03 99; email ibizasom@ctv.es) collaborates with bus companies, ferry lines, and *discotecas* on packages to Ibiza specially designed for disco fiends with no particular use for lodging who seek transportation and an all-night party. The best way to book airline or ferry tickets is through a travel agency in Barcelona, Valencia, or on any of the islands.

BY PLANE

Scheduled flights are the easiest to book. Flights from Spain to any of the islands won't break the bank. Frequent flights soar from cities in Spain and throughout Europe (including Düsseldorf, Frankfurt, Hamburg, London, and Paris). On **Iberia** (24hr. info and reservation tel. 902 40 05 00; www.iberia.com), many daily flights connect Palma de Mallorca and Ibiza to Madrid, Barcelona, and Valencia. Service from Alicante and Bilbao exists, but is less frequent.

Iberia offers **student fares** (must be 22 of under; with an ISIC 26 or under) on round-trip flights from Barcelona (40min., 10,000-20,000ptas) and Madrid (1hr., 25,000-30,000ptas). **Air Europa** (24hr. tel. 902 24 00 42) and **Spanair** (tel. 902 13 14 15; www.spanair.com) also offer inexpensive flights to and from the islands. Schedules and prices change often, so contact a travel agent or the airlines themselves for details. Another option are **charter flights,** which can be the cheapest and quickest means of round-trip travel. Most deals entail a week's stay in a hotel, but some companies (called *mayoristas*) sell unoccupied seats on package-tour flights. The leftover spots, called "seat only" deals, can be found in newspaper ads or through travel agencies (check TIVE and other budget travel havens in any Spanish city). Prices during the summer and *Semana Santa* are often more than twice as much as much as off-season (Oct.-May) fares. Except in August, tickets are not hard to get a week or so before departure. Those planning to travel in late summer should reserve several months in advance.

BY BOAT

The only reason to take a ferry is for the ride. Ferry service is comparable in price to air service but longer in duration. On-board discos and small swimming pools on some boats help ease the longer passage. Ferries run from Barcelona and Valencia to Palma (on Mallorca) and Eivissa (on Ibiza); ferries also run from Dénia (in Alicante) to Ibiza. Though seats may be available up to an hour before departure, it's best to reserve all tickets a few days in advance. If you chose to make reservations yourself, there are several options.

Trasmediterránea (tel. 902 45 46 45; www.trasmediterranea.com), departs from Barcelona's Estació Marítima Moll and Valencia's Estació Marítima. Boats leave from both cities to Mallorca and Ibiza.

Flebasa Lines (tel. 902 16 01 80), which runs ferries out of Estació Marítima in Dénia (in the province of Alicante). The ferries make the short trip between Dénia and Ibiza (3-4½hr., 1 per day), continuing to Palma.

Pitra car ferries (Dénia tel. 971 19 10 68), which run from Denía to Formentera via Eivissa and to San Antonio de Portmany (4hr.; 2 per day; 5475ptas, children 2750ptas, cars 15,050ptas).

Buquebus (tel. 902 41 42 42 or 93 481 73 60; email reservas@buquebus.es) has a super-fast catamaran service between Barcelona and Palma (4hr., 2 per day, one-way 8150ptas, cars 18,560).

⌐ GETTING AROUND

Flying is the most efficient way to go from island to island. **Iberia** flies between Palma and Ibiza (35min., 4 per day, 8900ptas) and between Palma and Mahón, Menorca (35min., 4 per day, 8900ptas). Travel between Menorca and Ibiza requires a stopover in Palma (3 per day, prices vary). **Air Europa** (tel. 902 24 00 42) and **Span-Air** (tel. 902 13 14 15) also connect the islands at similar prices. Youth discounts are often available on round-trip flights.

A cheaper option is to take **ferries** between the islands. While they don't leave as regularly, ferries cost less than half as much as planes. Since prices and times are constantly changing, it is best to consult the tourist office or a travel agent for information. **Trasmediterránea** (tel. 902 45 46 45) ferries sail between Palma and Mahón (6½hr., 1 per week, Sunday, 3045ptas) and between Palma and Ibiza (fast 2½hr., 3 per week, 5210ptas; slow 4½hr., 3 per week, 3330ptas). There is no direct Mahón-Ibiza connection. **Trasmapi** (tel. 971 31 20 71) links Ibiza and Formentera (fast ferry, 25min., 12 per day). Formentera-based **Inserco**, C. del Carmen, Formentera (tel. 971 32 22 10 or 902 45 46 45), also runs cheap Eivissa-Formentera boats (1hr., 6 per day, 8:15am-10pm, round-trip 2000ptas). **Umafisa Lines** (tel. 971 31 45 13) runs car ferries on the same route (1hr.; M-F 6 per day, Sa 5 per day, Su 4 per day; 1350ptas, children 675ptas, cars 6000ptas).

TRANSPORT WITHIN THE ISLANDS

All three major islands have extensive **bus** systems. Mallorca has two narrow-gauge **train** systems (which unfortunately don't accept Eurailpasses). Intra-island travel is reasonably priced—bus fares between cities range from 200 to 700ptas each way. You might try renting your own wheels for greater mobility and access to remote areas. A day's rental of a tiny standard-transmission **car** costs around 4500ptas including insurance; prices are usually a little lower on Mallorca. **Moped** (2700ptas per day) and **bicycles** (1000ptas per day) are also available for rental.

MALLORCA

Mallorca, sought after since the days of the Romans, has a long history of popularity. It has continually attracted the rich and famous, whether as the site of the scandalous honeymoon of Polish pianist Fréderic Chopin and French novelist George Sand or as the vacation spot of choice for Spain's royal family. These days, ever larger numbers of European package tourists have converged on the island, in some areas virtually suffocating the coastline.

There are reasons for such Mallorca lust. To the northwest, white sand beaches, frothy water, lemon groves, and olive trees adorn the jagged Sierra de Tramontana. To the east, expansive beaches sink into calm bays, while to the southeast, a network of caves masks underground beauty. Inland, where many towns retain their unique history and culture, windmills drawing water for almond and fig trees power a thriving agricultural economy. Although the coastline has long been doomed to developers, even the most jaded of travelers sigh wistfully at the stunning expanses of sea, sand, and rock that sprawl across much of this island.

PALMA

The capital of the Balearics, Palma (pop. 323,000) does not shy from conspicuous consumption. Restaurants cater to expensive tastes and streets bustle with shoppers buying leather accessories, designer clothes, and jewelry. Even the city's namesake, the palm tree, has gone commercial: plastic palms in hotel lobbies almost outnumber the real thing. Though flooded by *pesetas* and nearly every other currency, Palma pleasantly surprises with its well-preserved old quarter, colonial architecture, and a noticeable local flavor.

BALEARIC ISLANDS

🔢 ORIENTATION AND PRACTICAL INFORMATION

To get to the town center from the airport, take bus #17 to **Plaça d'Espanya** (15min., every 20min., 295ptas). From the dock, take Pg. Marítim (a.k.a. Av. Gabriel Roca) to Av. D'Antoni Maura, which leads to **Plaça de la Reina** and Pg. Born. Pg. Born leads away from the sea to **Plaça del Rei Joan Carles I,** the bustling center of the old town. **Avinguida Rei Jaume III,** the business artery, runs to the left. To the right, Carrer de la Unió leads (after some stairs) to **Plaça Major,** the center of Palma's pedestrian shopping district.

TRANSPORTATION

Flights: Aeroport Son San Juan (tel. 971 78 90 00), 8km from downtown Palma. Bus #17 goes to and from Pl. Espanya. **Iberia** (tel. 902 40 05 00), **Air Europa** (tel. 902 24 00 42), foreign carriers, and a host of charter operators all offer service to Palma. (For more info, see **By Plane,** p. 472 or **Island Hopping,** p. 473.)

Ferries: Trasmediterránea, Estación Marítim, 2 (tel. 902 45 46 45). Ferries dock at Moll Pelaires (south of the city). Bus #1 goes through Pg. Marítim. Tickets sold M-F 9am-1pm and 5-7pm, Sa 9am-noon. Tickets and info also available at travel agencies. Or try **Flebasa** (tel. 902 16 01 80). See **By Boat,** p. 472, or **Getting Around,** p. 473.

Trains: Ferrocarril de Sóller (tel. 971 75 20 51), Pl. Espanya. To **Sóller** (5 per day, 380ptas). Avoid the 10:40am "tourist train" when prices inflate to 735ptas for a 10min. stop in Mirador del Pujol d'en Banya. **Servicios Ferroviarios de Mallorca (SFM),** Pl. Espanya, 6 (tel. 971 75 20 51), to **Inca** (35min., every hr., 240ptas).

Buses: The bus station in Palma is currently going through a "transition" period. The tourist office and the info kiosk in Pl. Espanya have a complete schedule that attempts to order the confusion, but the system is inefficient and restrictive. Though travel to and from the capital is relatively painless, travel between most other areas is indirect and will probably route you through Palma. Buy tickets aboard or in the kiosks in Pl. Espanya. **Autocares Mallorca** (tel. 971 54 56 96), in Pl. Espanya, serves **Alcúdia** (via Inca), **Sóller,** and other areas in northern Mallorca. **Autocares Aumasa** (tel. 971 75 71 78), in Pl. Espanya, provides links to the eastern seaboard, including **Manacor** and **Porto Cristo. Bus Nord Balear,** C. Arxiduc Lluís Salvador, 1 (tel. 971 49 06 80), near Pl. Espanya, connects the west coast. **Autocares Villalonga** (tel. 971 53 00 57), in Pl. Espanya, serves **Pollença** through **Inca. DarBus** (tel. 971 75 06 22 or 971 20 07 58), in Pl. Espanya, serves towns in the southeast, including **Sa Sapita, Es Trenc,** and **Colonia San Jordi. Autocares Alorda** (tel. 971 50 15 03) serves **Lluc, Consell,** and **Inca** from Pl. Espanya. **Playa-Sol** (tel. 971 29 64 17) runs to nearby resort areas **El Arenal, Magaluf, Andratx,** and **Palma Nova.** Check the write-up of individual towns for more detailed bus information.

Public Transportation: Empresa Municipal de Transportes (EMT) (tel. 971 75 22 45). Pl. Espanya is the hub. Stops around town and as far as Palma Nova and Arenal. 175ptas, 10 tickets 1500ptas. Buy tickets aboard or in the kiosks in Pl. Espanya. Buses run approximately 6am-10pm. The airport bus, #17, runs until about 2am.

Taxis: (tel. 971 75 54 40, 971 40 14 14, or 971 72 80 81). Airport fare from the center of town is about 2500ptas—agree on the price before getting in.

Car Rental: Mascaro Crespi, Av. Joan Miró, 9 (tel. 971 73 61 03). 2000-3000ptas per day with insurance. Open M-Sa 8am-1pm and 3-8pm, Su 9am-1pm and 5-8pm. **Betacar/Europcar,** Pg. Marítim, 19 (tel. 971 45 51 11) is more reliable. 4000ptas per day with insurance. Open M-Sa 9am-1pm and 4-8pm, Su 9am-noon and 6-8pm.

Scooter Rental: RTR Bike Rental, Av. Joan Miró, 340 (tel. 971 40 25 85), near Pl. Gomila. Mopeds 2150ptas per day. Open M-Sa 9am-8pm, Su 9am-1pm.

TOURIST AND FINANCIAL SERVICES

Tourist Offices: Helpful multilingual staff at the **Palma branch,** C. Sant Dominic, 11 (tel. 971 71 15 27; email turisme@palma.es), hands out bus and train schedules, a good free map of the city, and a monthly guide in Catalán. From Pl. Reina, take C. Conquista-

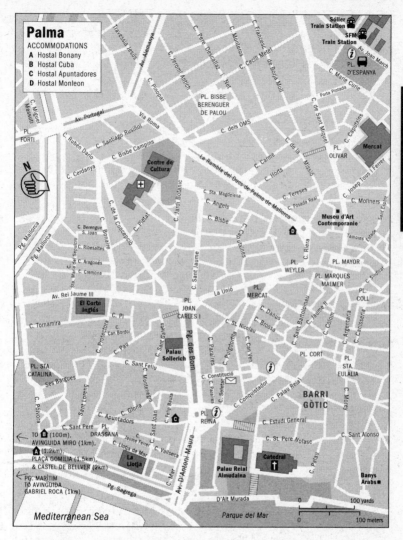

Palma

ACCOMMODATIONS

A Hostal Bonany
B Hostal Cuba
C Hostal Apuntadores
D Hostal Monleon

Mediterranean Sea

Parque del Mar

0   100 yards

0   100 meters

dor until it turns into C. Sant Dominic; the office is at the bottom of a stairway, a level below the street above. Open M-F 9am-8pm, Sa 9am-1:30pm. An **info booth** sits in Pl. Espanya (same hours). The **island tourist office,** Pl. Reina, 2 (tel. 971 71 22 16), offers info on the other islands, a good city map, bus and train schedules, hiking info, and lists of all sporting and cultural events on Mallorca. Open M-F 9am-1pm and 5-8pm, Sa 9am-1:30pm. The **branch office** (tel. 971 78 95 56) at the airport has similar info. Open M-Sa 9am-2pm and 3-8pm, Su 9am-2pm.

Budget Travel: TIVE, C. Jeróni Antich, 5 (tel. 971 71 17 85), off Pl. Bisbe Berenguer de Palou. ISIC cards, HI cards, Interrail tickets, and mainland flights. Not for inter-island travel and charters. Free internet access. Open M-F 9am-2pm and 5-7:30pm.

Currency Exchange: Seek out 24hr. **ATMs** (all around the center of town) for the best rates. **Banco Central Hispano,** Pg. Born, 17 (tel. 971 72 51 46), has good rates. Open May-Sept. M-F 8:30am-2:30pm; Oct.-Apr. M-F 8:30am-2:30pm, Sa 8:30am-1pm.

American Express: Av. Antonio Maura, 40 (tel. 971 72 23 44), downtown right next to C. Apuntadors, off Pl. Reina. Open M-F 9am-1pm and 2-8pm, Sa 10am-2pm.

LOCAL SERVICES

Luggage Storage: SFM office, Pl. Espanya. Small lockers 300ptas; big lockers 500ptas. Open M-F 7am-8pm, Sa-Su 7am-2pm.

El Corte Inglés: Av. Rei Jaume III, 15 (tel. 971 77 01 77). Fax, photocopies, phones, a free map of town, and a supermarket. Open M-Sa 10am-10pm.

English Bookstore: Book Inn, C. Horts, 20 (tel. 971 71 38 98), right off La Rambla. An impressive selection of literature. Children's books, too. Open M-F 10am-1:30pm and 5-8pm, Sa 10:30am-1:30pm. Hours change in August.

Women's Center: Centro de Derechos Mujeres, Galeria, 4 (tel. 971 72 25 51). Rape crisis assistance available. Open M-F 9am-2pm. 24hr. hotline (tel. 900 19 10 10).

Laundromat: Lavandería Fast, Joan Miró, 5 (tel. 971 45 46 14). 1300ptas for 5kg washed and dried.

EMERGENCY AND COMMUNICATIONS

Emergency: tel. 112. **Police:** (tel. 091 or 092), on Av. Sant Ferrá.

24hr. Pharmacy: See listings in local paper, *Diario de Mallorca* (125ptas).

Medical Services: Clínica Juaneda, C. Son Espanyolet, 55 (tel. 971 73 16 47), and **Femenía,** Av. Camilo José Cela, 20 (tel. 971 45 23 23). **Clínica Rotger,** Santiago Russinyol, 9 (tel. 971 71 66 00), is more centrally located. All open 24hr.

Post Office: C. Constitució, 5 (tel. 902 19 71 97), 1 block off Pl. Reina. Parcels upstairs. Lista de Correos downstairs at window #17. Fax service. Open M-F 8:30am-8:30pm, Sa 9:30am-2pm. **Postal Code:** 07080.

Internet Access: La Red, C. Concepció, 5 (tel. 971 71 35 74; www.laredcafe.com), next to the intersection with Av. San Martí. 500ptas per 30min. Drinks served. Open M-F 3pm-1am, Sa 4pm-2am, Su 4pm-11pm. **The Bureau,** C. Soletat, 4 (tel. 971 71 50 89), around the corner from the post office. 1000ptas per hr. Photocopying services as well. Open M-F 10am-8pm, Sa 10am-3pm.

◣ ACCOMMODATIONS

Accommodations vary from the bed-stuffed-in-a-closet to the mini-villa; unfortunately, there are more of the former. Call in advance for any summer stay.

Hostal Apuntadores, C. Apuntadores, 8 (tel. 971 71 34 91; email apuntadores@jet.es), smack in the middle of things, less than a block from Pl. Reina. Rooms are clean yet uninspiring, but the rooftop lounge and downstairs bar raise the quality of living (happy hour at the bar 6:30-8:30pm). Balconied rooms are cooler than the interior ones. The shared bath is better than the communal showers. Breakfast available. Singles 2400-2700ptas; doubles 3900-4200ptas, with shower 4400-4700ptas.

Hostal Cuba, C. San Magí, 1 (tel. 971 73 81 59), at C. Argentina, on the edge of the town center. From the port, go left along Av. Gabriel Roca and turn right onto C. Argentina. Look for the "Restaurant Cuba" sign. Friendly owner is always making improvements to keep ahead of the competition. Rooms are simple but clean; balconies offer views of the cathedral and the port. Singles 2000ptas; doubles with bath 4000ptas.

Hostal Bonany, C. Almirante Cervera, 5 (tel. 971 73 79 24), in a wealthy residential neighborhood, 3km from town center and 5min. from the nightlife. Take bus #3, 20, 21 or 22 from Pl. Espanya to Av. Joan Miró and walk up C. Camilio José Cela. Take the 1st right, then the 1st left. Spacious rooms with bath and balcony overlook the hostel's small pool and patio. Hearty breakfast included. Singles 3600ptas; doubles 5800ptas.

Alberg Platja de Palma (HI), C. Costa Brava, 13 (tel. 971 26 08 92), in the beach town El Arenal. Take bus #15 from Pl. Espanya (every 8 min., 175ptas), and ask to get off at Hotel Acapulco. A pristine, palatial *pensión* near the beach. Lounge with new furniture and a big-screen TV. 4-person dorms, each with shower and balcony. HI card required. Sheets 200ptas. Laundry service 1000ptas. Breakfast included. Reception daily 8am-3am. Curfew Su-Th midnight, F-Sa 3am. 1500ptas per person.

Hostal Monleon, La Rambla, 3 (tel. 971 71 53 17). An old, vaguely spooky building with tall ceilings and big windows. Dimly lit and noisy, but cheap for the area. Singles 2400ptas, with bath 3000ptas; doubles 4300ptas, with bath 5000ptas.

Camping: Platja Blava (tel. 971 53 78 63; fax 971 53 75 11), located at km8 on the highway between Alcúdia and C'an Picafort. Take Autocares Mallorca direct from Pl. Espanya (2 per day, 9am-7:30pm, 575ptas). 475-575ptas per person; 1300-1530ptas for a 6-by-6 meter plot.

🍴 FOOD

Palmas's restaurants are paradise for the *tapas*-sick. Menus come in German, French, Swedish, Hittite, English, Spanish, and *mallorquín*, but the best food is rarely as international. Mom-and-Pop operations serve tourists and locals along side streets, especially around **Passeig des Born.** Make sure to try the *ensaimadas* (pastries smothered in powdered sugar) and the *sopas mallorquinas* (stewed vegetables over brown bread). Two **markets** vie for customers. One is in Pl. Olivar off C. Padre Atanasio; the other is across town at the corner of C. Pou and C. Dameto. For **groceries,** try **Servicio y Precios** (tel. 971 72 78 11), on C. Felip Bauzà, near C. Apuntadores and Pl. Reina (open M-F 8:30am-8:30pm, Sa 9am-2pm).

Merendero Minyones, C. Minyones, 4, a teeny booth on a small street one block from C. Constitució. From Pg. Born, walk up C. Constitució, take your 1st left, and then the 1st right. As cheap as they come. Takeout only—they'll wrap up sandwiches (160-190ptas) for the beach. Open M-F 7:30am-8:30pm, Sa 8am-2:30pm.

Celler Pagès, C. Felip Bauzà, 2 (tel. 971 72 60 36), at the end of C. Pintor Guillem Mesquida, off Pl. Reina, hidden on the left. Economically delivers tasty, well presented meals to a well-off local crowd. Bowl of spiced olives with every afternoon *menú* (1100ptas). Open M-F 1-3:30pm and 8:30-11pm, Sa 1-4pm.

Bar Bosch, Pl. Rei Joan Carles I, 6, (tel. 971 72 11 31), next to McDonald's. Serving food into the wee hours, this Palma mainstay (since 1936) refreshes with tasty *tapas* (285-400ptas) and their specialty, *langostas* (a type of sandwich, 300-650ptas). Everything is cheaper at the bar. Outdoor seating. Open daily 1pm-2am.

C'an Joan de S'aigo, C. Sanç, 10 (tel. 971 71 07 59). From Pl. Major, walk through Pl. Coll down C. Canisseria; C. Sanç is the first street on the left. Red velvet curtains, a mini-garden with fountain, and marble tables deck out the city's oldest house. Enjoy the exquisite pastries and ice creams, including Mallorca's specialty *gelado de almendra* (almond ice cream, 190ptas). Open W-M 8am-9pm.

Na Bauçano, Sta. Bárbara, 4 (tel. 971 72 18 86), off C. Brossa between Pl. Mercat and Pl. Cort. All natural and all vegetarian. Try the homemade breads with curried vegetables and delicious soups. Popular with the foreign crowd. No smoking. Afternoon *menú* 1250ptas. Open Sa-Th 1-4pm, F 1-4pm and 8:30pm-midnight, closed Su.

🔲 SIGHTS

Palma's architecture is a medley of Arabic, Christian, and Modernist styles, a reflection of the island's multicultural past and present. Many of its landmarks are nestled amidst the narrow streets of the **Barri Gòtic** (medieval quarter).

🏛**CATEDRAL O LA SEA.** One of the world's largest cathedrals, this Gothic giant towers over Palma and its bay. The cathedral, dedicated to Palma's patron saint San Sebastián, was begun in the 1300s, finished in 1601, and then modified by Gaudí in modernist fashion in 1909. Now the interior and the ceiling ornamentation blend smoothly with the stately exterior. *(Off. Pl. Reina. Tel. 971 72 31 33. Cathedral and museum open M-F 10am-6pm, Sa 10am-2pm; Nov.-Mar. M-F. 10am-3pm. 500ptas.)*

⬛PALAU DEL'ALMUDAINA. Built by the Moors, this palace was later controlled by *Los Reyes Católicos*, Fernando and Isabel. Guided tours, which pass through the museum, are given in numerous languages, except when the king is here on business. *(Just off Pl. Reina. Tel. 971 72 71 45. Open M-F 10am-6:30pm, Sa 10am-2pm. 400ptas, students 225ptas, Wednesdays EU members free.)*

COLLECCIO MARCH, MUSEO D'ART ESPANYOL CONTEMPORANI. Because of its bourgeois clientele, Palma also hosts a multitude of art exhibits. This museum houses one work each of a handful of different 20th-century Spanish artists, including Picasso, Dalí, Miró, Juan Gris, and Antoni Tàpies. *(C. Sant Miquel, 11. Tel. 971 71 35 15. Open M-F 10am-6:30pm, Sa 10am-1:30pm. 300ptas.)*

CASTELL DEL BELLVER. Overlooking the city and bay and set in a circular court-yard, **Castell de Bellver** served as summer residence for 14th-century royalty. For centuries thereafter it housed Mallorca's distinguished prisoners. The castle contains a municipal **museum** with several paintings and archaeological displays. *(Bus #3, 21, or 22 from Pl. Espanya. Tel. 971 73 06 57. Castle and museum open daily Apr.-Sept. 8am-8:20pm; Oct.-Mar. 8am-7:15pm. 265ptas, students 130ptas. Su free, but museum closed.)*

POBLE ESPANYOL. This Spanish village, filled with samples of Spanish architecture, is a replica of one in Barcelona. *(C. Poble Espanyol, 39. Buses #4 and 5 pass on C. Andrea Doria. Tel. 971 73 70 75. Open daily 9am-8pm; Dec.-Mar. 9am-6pm. 800ptas.)*

OTHER MUSEUMS. Palma is filled with museums. Inaugurated in December 1992, **Fundació Pilar i Joan Miró** displays the works found in Miró's Palma studio at the time of his death. *(C. Saridakis, 29. From Pl. Espanya, take buses #3, 21, and 22 to C. Joan Miró. Tel. 971 70 14 20. Open May 16-Sept. 14 Tu-Sa 10am-7pm; Su 10am-3pm; Sept. 15-May 15 Tu-Sa 10am-6pm, Su 10am-3pm. 675ptas.).* **Fundacio "la Caixa"** hosts a permanent collection of paintings as well as other special exhibits in Domènech's modernist Gran Hotel. *(Pl. Weyler, 3. Tel. 971 72 01 11. Open T-Sa 10am-9pm, Su 10am-2pm. Free.)* The **Casal Solleric** opens modern art exhibits to the public. *(Pg. Born, 27. Open Tu-Sa 10:30am-1:45pm, Su 10am-1:45pm. Free.)* **Centre de Cultura "Sa Nostra"** features rotating contemporary exhibits and sponsors cultural events such as lectures, concerts, and movies. *(C. Concepción, 12. Tel. 971 72 52 10. Open M-F 10:30am-9pm, Sa 10am-1:30pm.)* **Museu de Mallorca** is ideal for travelers interested in archeology, medieval painting, or Moorish architecture. *(Cala Gran Christian. Open Apr.-Sept. Tu-Sa 10am-2pm and 5-8pm; Oct.-Mar. Tu-Sa 10am-1pm and 4-8pm, Su 10am-2pm.)*

BEACHES. Although better beaches speckle the island, decent ones (complete with sand and snacks) are a mere bus ride from Palma. The huge beach at **El Arenal** (Platja de Palma, bus #15), 11km to the southeast (toward the airport), is expansive and well-sanded but tends to be over-touristed. **Aquacity** (tel. 971 44 00 00), a huge water park, resides next door. **Palma Nova** (bus #21), 15km southwest, and **Illetes** (bus #3), 9km southwest, are equally crowded. The tourist office distributes a list of over 40 nearby beaches, so take your pick.

🎵 ENTERTAINMENT

The municipal tourist office keeps a comprehensive list of sporting activities, concerts, and exhibits. Every Friday, *El Día de Mundo* (125ptas) publishes an entertainment supplement with listings of bars and discos all over Mallorca. Also look for *La Calle*, a monthly review of Palma's hotspots. The streets around **Plaça Reina** and **La Llotja** flow with bar-hoppers.

The *casa-antigua*-turned-bar **ABACO**, C. Sant Joan, 1 (tel. 971 71 59 11), in the Barri Gòtic near the waterfront, may be the most perfect place on Earth for a cocktail. Sip drinks in the midst of a dreamy 19th-century courtyard, complete with elegant wicker and marble furniture, cooing doves, classical music, and a wide array of fresh fruit, flowers, and dripping candles. (Fruit shakes 1100ptas, cocktails 1900-2100ptas. Open daily 9pm-2:30am.)

You can't help but dance to the Cuban rhythms at **La Bodeguita del Medio,** C. Vallseca, 18 (tel. 971 71 49 39), featuring Hemingway's favorite: *mojito* (500ptas), a drink with seltzer water, sugar, lemon juice, rum, and *hierbabuena* (open Su-F 9pm-3:30am, Sa 9pm-4am). Follow the Aussie voices down C. Apuntadores to the popular **Bar Latitude 39,** C. Felip Bauza, 8 (tel. 971 72 02 65; beers 200ptas, mixed drinks 500ptas; "twofer nights"—two for the price of one—Tu, Th 9-10pm; open M-Sa 7pm-3am). **Barcelona,** C. Apuntadores, 5 (tel. 971 71 35 57), has live music nightly from midnight-3am (jazz M, Tu, Th, salsa W; open daily 11pm-3am). Other nightlife spots include **Blues Ville,** Má Del Moro, 3 (from Pl. Reina, take a right off C. Apunadors) and **La Longja Agua Bar,** C. Jaime Ferrer, 6 (tel. 929 63 96 32).

The rest of Palma's clubbers boogie on the beaches and in the nightclubs near **El Terreno**—a mother-load of clubs are centered on Pl. Gomilia and along C. Joan Miró. **Tito's Palace,** Pl. Gomilia, 1 (tel. 971 73 76 42), an indoor colosseum of mirrors and lights, overlooks the water (cover 1500-2000ptas; open 11am-6am). **Plato,** across the street at Pl. Gomilia, 2, keeps a lower, more local profile. **Sa Finestra,** Av. Joan Miró, 90, features live music every night after 11:30pm. **Sombrero,** on Av. Joan Miró, 26 (tel. 971 73 16 00) is a lively gay bar, and the **Baccus,** around the corner on C. Lluis Fábregas, 2, draws lesbian and gay hedonists (open until 3am). Word is that **Pachá,** Av. Gabriel Roca, will found its own island by the year 2001; for now its owners will have to make do with a large club (cover 2000-3000ptas and up, try for free tickets at bars in town; open midnight-6am).

Islanders use any and every occasion as an excuse to party. One of the more colorful bashes, **Día de Sant Joan** (June 24), brings singing, dancing, and drinking to Parc del Mar. The celebration begins with a fireworks display the night before.

WESTERN MALLORCA

The west coast of Mallorca is home to one of the most beautiful landscapes in the Mediterranean. It has attracted and inspired a range of creative minds, from Chopin and George Sand to Robert Graves and Michael Douglas. Ten minutes beyond the modern road and ever-spreading white highrises of Palma, the road enters a deep ravine (the island's first cave dwellers sheltered here) and begins to rise in tight, narrow curves. Taking the north road beyond Valldemossa, you find yourself traveling through olive groves pitching steeply toward the sea. Beyond is the northwestern cape of the island—wild, arid, volcanic, and totally uninhabited.

VALLDEMOSSA

Valldemossa's storybook colonial houses huddle against each other along cobblestone streets in the verdant slopes of the Sierra de Tramontana. Little in this tranquil village hints at the passion that shocked the townsfolk in the winter of 1838-39, when Frédéric Chopin and George Sand (her two children in tow) stayed in the picturesque and floral monastery called **Cartoixa Reial** (tel. 971 61 21 06). Chopin memorabilia includes the piano which he had to carry up the mountain in several pieces. Short piano recitals attempt to recapture the magic in the summer. (Recitals every hr. Open M-Sa 9:30am-6pm, Su 10am-1pm. 1200ptas, including visits to the Museu Municipal and the **Palau del Rei Sancho**, where folk dances take place M and Th 11-1:30pm.) **Hostal Ca'n Mario,** C. Vetam, 8 (tel. 971 61 21 22; fax 971 61 60 29), offers rooms with showers and great views of town (breakfast included; singles 3660ptas; doubles 5800ptas; Visa, MC). Several cafe-bars around the main square offer simple and cheap fare. The town goes to bed early, so don't expect much in the way of nightlife—enjoy the peace and quiet instead. **Nord Balear buses** (tel. 971 49 06 80) to Valldemosa leave from Palma at C. Arxiduc Salvador, 1 (30min., 5 per day, 200ptas).

DEIÀ

A favorite of artists and intellectuals, Deià affords sensational views of miles and miles of twisted olive trees. In the town center, picturesque houses and the occasional church line lantern-lit cobblestone squares. Local hotels cater more to international jetsetters than budget travelers, so you'd be better off staying elsewhere. If you're hungry, try the small cafe-bars in the center of town. Deià is 10km north of Valldemosa on the **Nord Balear bus** route to Sóller (45min., 5 per day, 295ptas).

SÓLLER

Thirty kilometers up the coast from Valldemossa, cobblestoned Sóller basks in a valley that widens to a golden port. Every available plot of land is lined with either citrus groves or sunburned tourists. In August, the Ajuntament hosts an international **Festival of Folk Dancing,** with dancers from all over Europe and Asia. The old-fashioned Palma-Sóller **train,** run by Ferrocarril de Sóller, C. Castanyer, 7 (tel. 971 63 03 01, Palma tel. 971 75 20 51), is a highlight in itself. Brave hearts ride between cars through olive orchards and scary tunnels (5 per day, 735ptas).

Sóller's **tourist office,** Pl. Constitució, 1 (tel. 971 63 02 00), supplies accommodation listings and maps (open M-Sa 9:30am-1:30pm; info posted in front of the church near the entrance if the office is closed). The staff can also suggest good hikes. For snacks, try the specialty *coca mallorquina,* a cold pizza-like snack (about 250ptas) in local bakeries. **Emergency:** tel. 112; **police** (tel. 971 63 02 03 or 971 63 02 00); **medical services: Clinic Balear,** Es Traves, 23 (tel. 971 63 44 11), along the water (open 24hr.).

PUERTO DE SÓLLER

From Sóller it is a pleasant half-hour walk (or a short ride on the Nord Balear bus) down the valley to Puerto de Sóller, which absorbs a large number of tourists. Trolleys also connect the two (every 30min., 115ptas). In Puerto de Sóller, a pebble-and-sand beach lines the small bay, where windsurfers zip back and forth. Numerous hotels lie on C. Marina along the water. **Hotel Miramar,** C. Marina, 12 (tel. 971 63 13 50), provides spotless rooms and full baths (singles 4900ptas; doubles 5150ptas; triples 7600ptas). Two **grocery stores** are located on C. Jaume Torrens, and numerous **restaurants** line the beach. Food tends toward the pricey, but **Restaurante Balear,** Santa Caterina d'Alexandria, 14 (tel. 971 63 15 24), a few feet off the fork with C. Marina, with its cheap *paella* (1275ptas) and *menú* (950ptas), is a godsend (open Th-Tu 12:30-3:30pm and 7:30-10pm; closed Jan.-Feb.).

Exploring the rest of the coves on the coast is easiest by **boat. Tramontana** and **Barcos Azules,** on the port near the last trolley stop, sail to **Sa Calobra,** most people's final destination (May-Oct. 15, 3-5 per day, round-trip 1900ptas), and **Cala Deià** (June-Oct. 15, round-trip 1200ptas). Nord Balear **buses** link Puerto de Sóller to **Palma** (2hr., 5 per day, 450ptas), via **Valldemossa.**

SA CALOBRA

Much like an asphalt serpent, the road to Sa Calobra drops 1000m to the sea, writhing back underneath itself over 10 nail-biting kilometers. The boat from Puerto de Sóller is easier on the nerves (see above). **Torrent de Pareis,** toward the bottom of the road, is a popular photo opportunity (look for a landing packed with camera-toting tourists). Sa Calobra itself is a smooth pebble beach, bordered by ominous cliffs and the crystalline sea. Unfortunately, despite its beauty, the cove is actually somewhat infested with tourists, restaurants, and gift shops.

MONESTIR DE LLUC

Tucked away quietly in the mountains, the Monestir de Lluc is an inland enigma. Though there is little here of interest to the secular traveler, the monastery is perpetually filled with religious tourists and pilgrims. Twenty kilometers from the coast in Escorca, Lluc is the home of the 700-year-old wood-carved *La verge de Lluc (The Virgin of Lluc).* Behind the monastery, the **Vía Crucis** winds around a hill over the valley's olive trees and jingling goats. Gaudí designed the path's Stations of the Cross. Monks, pilgrims, and a few guests stay at Lluc's **monastery** (tel. 971 51 70 25; true pilgrims stay for a donation—others pay 3850ptas for doubles with bath; quads with bath 4350ptas.) The monastery's store sells groceries, and its restaurant-bar offers pricey food and drink. To reach the monastery, take **Auto-**

cares **Alorda** direct from Palma (1hr., M-Sa 2 per day, Su 1 per day, 555ptas); it is also possible to get there from Port Pollença, Alcúdia, Inca, or Sa Calobra.

NORTHERN MALLORCA

Known for their long beaches and fine sand, the northern gulfs of Mallorca have become quite popular among the older, package-tour crowd. Though the drive can be stunning, those searching for secluded coves are best off exploring other parts of the island.

PORT POLLENÇA (PUERTO POLLENSA)

Port Pollença features a stretch of sand which is slightly whiter, finer, and less crowded than its neighbors. It is particularly popular among Brits, which explains the number of pubs and English-named establishments in town. The area hosts a **Music Festival** from July to September. A complete schedule of events and list of ticket vendors are available at the tourist office (tickets 1000-5000ptas). **Rent March,** C. Joan XXIII, 89 (tel. 971 86 47 84), rents **bikes** and **mopeds** (open April-Oct. M-Sa 9am-1pm and 3-8pm, Su 9am-1pm and 6-7:30pm; bikes 600ptas per day, mopeds 2500ptas per day). The helpful **tourist office,** C. Formentor, 31 (tel. 971 86 54 67; email fundacioboccharis@oninet.es), across from Hotel Daina, can plan excursions (open May-Oct. M-F 9am-1pm and 4-7pm, Sa 9am-1pm). Autocares Mallorca **buses** connect Alcúdia and Pollença (every 15min.).

CAP DE FORMENTOR

The end of Cap de Formentor, 15km northeast of Port Pollença, boasts views from spectacular seaside cliffs. Before the final twisting kilometer, the road drops to **Platja Formentor,** where a canopy of evergreens seems to sink into the water. These beaches are the best on the northern coast. **Autocares Villalonga,** San Isidro, 4 (tel. 971 53 00 57), sends **buses** from Palma (5 per day, 595ptas). All buses leave from the rotunda where the beach meets the pier. There's also a **boat** to **Formentor** from Port Pollença's Estación Marítima (6 per day, round-trip 825ptas to Platja Formentor, 1600ptas to Cabo Formentor).

PUERTO DE ALCÚDIA

Puerto de Alcúdia is far from undiscovered. The hard-packed beaches stretching along the bay are packed with hotels, bars, and pizzerias outnumbering the boats in the marina. If you're looking for more than just another beach, visit Alcúdia's **14th-century ramparts,** which are built around **Roman remains** dating from 2 BC (15min. walk; buses depart every 15min. from C. dels Mariners). **Museu Pollentia** (tel. 971 54 70 04) documents the archaeological discoveries on Mallorca (open Apr.-Sept. M-Sa 10am-1:30pm and 5-7pm, Su 10:30am-1pm; Oct.-Mar. M-Sa 10am-1:30pm and 4-6pm, Su 10:30-1pm; 200ptas). For mindless fun, head to **Hidropark** (tel. 971 89 16 72), a water park accessible by bus from C. Mariners (every 15min.).

For a **taxi,** call tel. 971 89 21 87. **Vanrell Bicicletas,** Av. Reina Sofía, rents **bikes.** The multilingual **tourist office** (tel. 971 89 26 15), at the intersection of Av. Pere Mas Reus and Ctra. Arta, near the waterfront, has maps (open May-Oct. M-Sa 9:30am-7pm). **Police** tel. 971 54 50 78. Autocares Mallorca **buses** (tel. 971 54 56 96) leave for Alcúdia (570ptas) and Puerto de Alcúdia (580ptas) from Pl. Espanya in Palma (1hr., M-Sa 17 per day, Su 5 per day). The bus to Port Pollença and to Cap de Formentor leaves from C. dels Mariners.

Hostal Puerto, C. Teodoro Canet, 29 (tel. 971 54 54 47), on the road that leads up to Alcúdia, offers hotel-quality rooms with private baths (doubles with shower 3800ptas, with bath 4000ptas; open May-Oct.). **Alberg Victoria (HI),** Ctra. Cap Pinar, 4 (tel. 971 54 53 95), lies 100m from an empty beach on the Bahía de Pollença. From the town center, signs lead east 4km to the hostel (1hr. walk or 1100pta taxi ride). Reserve at least six months in advance for July or August. (Members only. 1000ptas, with breakfast 2000ptas.)

SOUTHEAST MALLORCA

The signs along the highway of Mallorca's southeast coast might as well read "Welcome tourist hordes," as much of the area has been built up by big time investors. On the coast, east of **Cap de Salinas,** Mallorca's southernmost point, scalloped fringes of bays and caves are the investors's most recent discovery. To their credit, builders have aspired to some architectural integrity.

CUEVAS DRACH. The Cuevas Drach, near **Porto Cristo,** are among the most dramatic natural wonders in Mallorca's southeast. Only here can you float on an underground lake while listening to classical music. A **bus** runs from Palma to the caves. *(Bus M-Sa 4 per day, 750ptas.)*

TRENC. West of Cap de Salinas and east of Cap Blanc sprawls one of Mallorca's best beaches, Trenc. To get to Trenc, take a **Dar Bus** from Palma's Pl. Espanya to Es Trenc. In most cases, a 1-2km walk is usually enough to put plenty of sand between you and the thickest crowds.

CABRERA. Uninhabited except for a small military installation, Cabrera has a gruesome history. Eight thousand French prisoners-of-war died here during the Peninsular War in 1809 when the Spanish abandoned them without any food. A monument to the dead stands by the port. On a similar note, hundreds have died in shipwrecks as boats collided with jagged rocks poking up from the ocean floor.

MENORCA

Menorca's raw beaches, rustic landscape, and well-preserved ancient monuments draw ecologists, sun worshippers, and photographers alike. Unfortunately, although tourists are fewer on Menorca than on the other Balearics, the island's unique qualities have resulted in elevated prices that can be hard on the budget traveler. Since its incorporation into the Catalán kingdom in 1287, Menorca (pop. 69,000) has endured a succession of foreign invaders—Arab, Turkish, French, and British. After occupying the island several times during the 18th century, the Brits have returned to dominance, this time in the as tourists.

Menorca's two main cities, **Mahón** in the east and **Ciutadella** in the west, serve as gateways to the island's real attractions. In 1993, UNESCO declared the entire island a biosphere reserve. Since then, administrators have directed their efforts toward preserving its natural harbors, pristine southern beaches, rocky northern coast, and latticed network of farmlands. The act has also encouraged protection, excavation, and study of Menorca's stone burial chambers and homestead complexes, remnants of a mysterious Talayotic stone-age culture dating from 1400 BC.

MAHÓN (MAÓ)

Perched atop a steep bluff, Mahón's (pop. 23,300) white-splashed houses overlook a well-trafficked harbor. The British occupied the city for most of the 18th century, leaving Georgian doors, brass knockers, and wooden shutters in their wake. Gin distilleries, pubs, and British accents testify to a continuing British influence, as visitors here to spend money almost as old as the island. Those in search of a raging nightlife are better off on Ibiza; Mahón's residents value an early bedtime.

■ ORIENTATION AND PRACTICAL INFORMATION

It is necessary to take a taxi (1100ptas) between the **airport** and downtown Mahón. To get to the heart of the city from the **ferry station,** walk to the left (with your back to the water) about 150m, then turn right at the steps that cut through the serpentine **Costa de ses Voltes.** The steps end between Pl. Conquesta and Pl. Espanya. To reach **Plaça de s'Esplanada,** the town center, from here, take Portal de Mar to Costa de Sa, which becomes C. Hanover and then C. Ses Moreres, and continue straight ahead to the plaça. To reach **Plaça de la Miranda,** walk through Pl. Espanya and Pl. Carme; when you reach Pl. Princep, turn left, and Pl. Miranda is about 100m ahead.

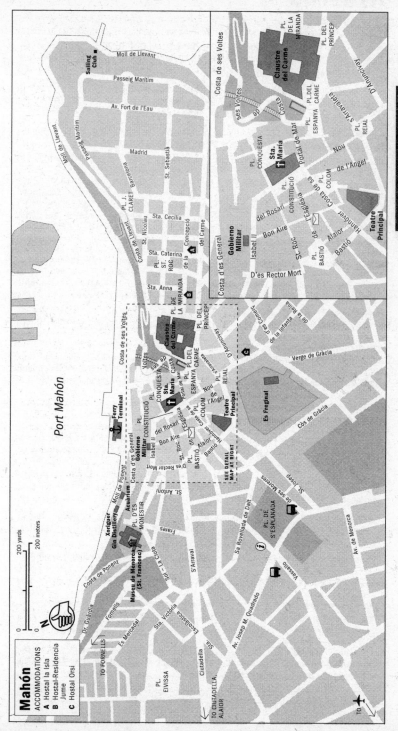

Mahón

ACCOMMODATIONS
A Hostal la Isla
B Hostal-Residencia
Jume
C Hostal Orsi

Port Mahón

Moll de Llevant
Sailing Club ■
Passeig Marítim
Av. Fort de l'Eau
Madrid

Moll de Llevant
Passeig Marítim

St. Sebastià

PL. J.
CLARET
Barcelona
St. Nicolau
Sta. Cecília
Concepció
del Carme
Sta. Caterina
PL.
ST. ROC
Sta. Anna
de la Miranda
PL. DE LA MIRANDA

Costa de ses Voltes

Ferry
Terminal

Costa de ses Voltes
ses Voltes
Claustre
del Carme
PL. DEL
PRINCEP
Sta.
Maria
PL.
CONQUESTA
PL. DEL
ESPANYA CARME
COSTA
Gobierno
Militar
Costa d'es General
Isabel II
PL. CONSTITUCIÓ
Nou
COLOM
de
l'Àngel
del Rosari
l'Església
Teatre
Principal
Bon Aire
Costa de ses
ST. ROC
Hannover
Alaior
D'es Rector Mort
PL. DE
BASTIÓ Bastió

SEE DETAIL
MAP AT RIGHT

d'es Comerç
de la Infanta
de la Reina
Verge de Gràcia
Es Freginal
Còs de Gràcia

Xoriguer
Gin Distillery
PL. D'ES
MONESTIR
Acuàrium
Moll de Ponent
Museu de Menorca
(St. Francesc)
Frares
St. Antoni
Sta.
PL. DE
S'ESPLANADA
de ses Moreres
St. Josep

Costa de Ponent
S'Arraval
Sa Rovellada de Dalt
Vassallo

Dr. Guàrdia
Es Mercadal
Fornells
Escoòssica
Sta. Victòria
Ciutadella
Av. Josep M. Quadrado
Av. de Menorca

TO FORNELLS
PL.
EIVISSA
TO CIUTADELLA,
ALAIOR

DETAIL MAP

Costa de ses Voltes
ses Voltes
Claustre
del Carme
PL.
DE LA
MIRANDA
PL. DEL
PRINCEP
PL. DEL
CARME
Sta.
Maria
PL.
CONQUESTA
PL. DEL
ESPANYA
PL.
REIAL
d'Alcantara
S'Arraval
Nou
de l'Àngel
COLOM
Portal de Mar
Teatre
Principal
PL. DE
CONSTITUCIÓ
del Rosari
l'Església
Gobierno
Militar
Isabel II
Bon Aire
Costa de ses
ST. ROC
Hannover
Alaior
Bastió
D'es Rector Mort
PL. DE
BASTIÓ

0 200 yards
0 200 meters
N

TRANSPORTATION

Airplanes: Airport (tel. 971 15 70 00), 7km out of town (see **Orientation** above). Main office open daily 7:15am-midnight. **Iberia/Aviaco** (tel. 971 36 90 15); **Air Europa** (tel. 971 24 00 42 or 971 15 70 31); **SpanAir** (tel. 971 15 70 98). In summer advance booking is essential. See **By Plane,** p. 472, or **Getting Around,** p. 473.

Ferries: Estació Marítima, on Moll Andén de Ponent. Open M-F 8am-1pm and 5-7pm, Sa 8am-noon, Su 8am-noon and 3-4:30pm. **Trasmediterránea** (tel. 971 36 29 50). For fares and routes, see **By Boat,** p. 472, or **Getting Around,** p. 473.

Buses: Check the tourist office or the newspapers *Menorca Diario Insular* (125ptas) and *Menorca* for schedules. **Transportes Menorca (TMSA),** C. Josep M. Quadrado, 7 (tel. 971 36 03 61), off Pl. s'Esplanada. To: **Es Castell** (every 30min., 125ptas); **Alaior** (6 per day, 150ptas); **Platja Punta Prima** (9 per day, 225ptas); **Son Bou** (5 per day, 250ptas); **Es Mercadal** (6 per day, 250ptas); **Ferreries** (4 per day, 300ptas); **Ciuta- della** (55min., 6 per day, 550ptas). Some depart from Pl. s'Esplanada, some from nearby C. Quadrado; check signs at the bus stop. Buy tickets at the TMSA office, except for Punta Prima and Castell, which you buy on the bus. **Autobuses Fornells Roca Triay** (tel. 971 37 66 21) has buses that depart from C. Vassallo, off Pl. s'Esplanada. To: **For- nells** (3 per day); **Arenal d'en Castell** (3 per day); **Son Parc** (3 per day); **Es Grau** (5 per day). Buy tickets on the buses.

Taxis: Main stop at Pl. s'Esplanada (tel. 971 36 12 83), or **radio taxi** from anywhere on the island (tel. 971 36 71 11). Flat rates for all routes. To: **Es Castell** (800ptas); **Air- port** (1100ptas); **Cala Mesquida** (1270ptas); **Cala'n Porter** (1865ptas).

Car Rental: English-speaking car rental at British **Jan Cars** (tel. 971 35 13 21, 24hr. tel. 971 37 71 57), Pl. s'Esplanada. 4500ptas per day; 13,000ptas for 3 days. Tourist office has list of all rental places on Menorca.

Bike and **Scooter Rental:** For a bike, try **Just Bicicletas,** C. Infanta, 19 (tel. 971 36 47 51), run out of Hostal Orsi (1 day 1000ptas plus IVA, 3 days 2500ptas). **Autos y Motos Valls,** Pl. Espanya, 13 (tel. 971 36 28 39 or 971 35 42 44), rents scooters (3000ptas per day). Open daily 9am-2pm and 5-8pm.

TOURIST AND FINANCIAL SERVICES

Tourist Office: Pl. s'Esplanada, 40 (tel. 971 36 37 90; fax 971 36 74 15; www.menorca.com), across the plaza from the taxi stand. Bus schedules and a fabu- lous free **map.** English spoken. Open M-F 8:30am-7:30pm, Sa 9am-2pm. Summer office at the **airport** (tel. 971 15 71 15) provides similar materials. Open March-Oct. daily 8:30am-10:30pm. **Free guided tours** of Mahón leave from the town hall in Pl. Constitució every Th and F at 7pm.

American Express: Viajes Iberia, C. Nou, 35 (tel. 971 36 28 48), two doors from Pl. Reial. No commission on traveler's cheques. Cardholder mail held. Open M-F 9am- 1:30pm and 4:30-7:30pm, Sa 9:30am-1pm.

Currency Exchange: Banks with 24hr. **ATMs** crowd along C. Hannover and C. Nou.

EMERGENCY AND COMMUNICATIONS

Emergency: tel. 091 or 092. **Police: Municipal** (tel. 971 36 39 61), Pl. Constitució.

Medical Assistance: Hospital Verge del Toro, C. Barcelona, 3 (tel. 971 15 77 00; emer- gency tel. 971 36 77 26), near Pg. Marítim. English spoken. **Ambulance:** dial 061.

Post Office: C. Bonaire, 11-13 (tel. 971 36 38 92), at C. Esglésias. From Pl. s'Esplanada, take C. Moreres until it turns into C. Hanover, then take the first left. Open M-F 8:30am- 8:30pm, Sa 9:30am-2pm. **Postal Code:** 07703.

Internet Access: Bar & Cafe Telegraph, C. Sant Esteve, 8 (tel. 971 36 14 00), in Hotel Capri. From Pl. s'Esplanada, take C. Josep Maria Quadrado. 100ptas for 5min.

▐ ACCOMMODATIONS

Space is a problem only in August, but call a few days in advance. The tourist office keeps a complete listing. Prices listed below are for high season.

Hostal La Isla, C. Santa Catalina, 4 (tel. 971 36 64 92). Take C. Concepció from Pl. Miranda. Family-run hostel offers clean rooms and friendly service. All rooms with private bath and powerful, hot water-pressure. The restaurant downstairs (see **Food,** below) offers a cheap and typical *menú*. Breakfast 300ptas, included with doubles. Singles 2300ptas; doubles 5000ptas. Visa.

Hostal Orsi, C. Infanta, 19 (tel. 971 36 47 51). From Pl. s'Esplanada, take C. Moreres as it becomes C. Hannover. Turn right at Pl. Constitució and follow C. Nou through Pl. Reial; Orsi is on the left. Super nice owners. Free breakfast and clean, sunlit rooms. Rooftop terrace has a great view. Discounts on bike rentals. Laundry 850ptas. Singles 2500ptas; doubles 4400ptas, with shower 5000ptas; plus 7% IVA. Visa, MC.

Hostal-Residencia Jume, C. Concepció, 6 (tel. 971 36 32 66; fax 971 36 48 78), off Pl. Miranda. TV room downstairs, lounges on each floor, restaurant, and pool table. Nondescript rooms in tip-top shape, all with full baths. Ask for a room overlooking the street rather than the steamy indoor patio. Breakfast included. 2725ptas per person.

◖ FOOD

Bar-cafes around Pl. Constitució, Reial, and s'Esplanada serve filling *platos combinados* (450-850ptas) to sidewalks full of hungry customers. The myriad restaurants on the port offer scenic views and eye-sore prices. *Mahón-esa* (mayonnaise) was invented here and local chefs won't let you forget it. Regional specialties include *sobrasada* (soft chorizo spread), *crespells* (biscuits), and *rubiols* (turnovers filled with fish or vegetables). There is a fresh fruit and vegetable **market** in the cloister of the church in Pl. Espanya (open M-Sa 9am-2pm). **Groceries** available at **Miny Prix,** C. J.A. Clavé and Av. Menorca (open M-Sa 8am-2pm and 5-8:30pm).

Restaurante La Isla, C. Santa Catalina, 4 (tel. 971 36 64 92), in the Hostal La Isla. No entrees, just a lunch or dinner *menú* (950ptas) and a host of satisfied locals. Open daily 7-10am, 1-3pm, and 8:30-10pm. Visa.

El Turronero, C. Nou, 22-26 (tel. 971 36 28 98), off Pl. Reial. This old-fashioned parlor has been serving up home-made *turrón* (Spanish nougat) and ice cream for over 100 years. Double scoops 195ptas, bigger servings 225ptas. *Bocadillos* 275-300ptas. Open M-F 9am-3pm and 4-10:30 or 11pm, Sa and Su 9am-2pm and 7-10pm.

Ristorante Pizzeria Roma, Ander de Levante, 295 (tel. 971 35 37 77), on the port. Fresh ingredients and speedy service. Surprisingly authentic Italian pizzas (660-975ptas) and *menú* 1300ptas. Open F-W 12:30pm-12:30am, Th 7pm-midnight; closed Oct.-June Th.

Mos i Glop, C. Alayor, 12 (tel. 971 36 64 57), off C. Hannover. A fabulous place to sample Menorcan dishes. *Menú* 975ptas. Open M-F 8am-midnight, Sa 8am-5pm. Visa, MC.

▐ SIGHTS

The most awe-inspiring sights in Menorca are found outside of its cities, though Mahón does offer some spectacles of its own.

MUSEO DE MENORCA. This old Franciscan monastery, closed in 1835, has excavated items and exhibits on Menorcan history dating back to Talayotic times. *(C. Dr. Guàrdia. From Pl. s'Esplanada, take Carrer des Negres to the left on C. s'Arraval, then take a right onto C. Frares and follow it to the end. The museum is on the left. Tel. 971 35 09 55. Open Tu-Sa 10am-2pm and 5-8pm, Su 10am-2pm.)*

ESGLÉSIA DE SANTA MARÍA LA MAJOR. Founded in 1287 and rebuilt in 1772, the church trembles from the 51 stops, 4 keyboards, and 3210 pipes of its disproportionately large organ, built by the Swiss Juan Kilburz in 1810. Mahón's **festival de música** in July and August showcases this immense instrument. *(Pl. Constitució. Festival concerts M-Sa 11am; seat "donation" 400ptas.)*

OTHER SIGHTS. Arc de Sant Roc, the last fragment of the medieval wall built to defend the city from marauding Catalán pirates, straddles the streets. *(Up C. Sant Roc from Pl. Constitució.)* Free liquor samples (15 brews) are available at the **Xoriguer Gin Distillery** on the port. Behind the store, visitors watch their drinks bubble and froth in large copper vats. *(Open M-F 8am-7pm, Sa 9am-1pm.)*

♫ ENTERTAINMENT

Mahón is not known for its nightlife; the curtain call is sometimes as early as midnight. A string of *bares-musicales* is down **Costa d'els Generals,** near the water. Dancing doesn't really get going until 1 or 2am on weekends, and weekdays are quiet except in August. The disputed champion is **Akelarre** (tel. 971 36 85 20), a dim and attractive two-floor bar next to the castle; a straight and gay crowd frequents the dance floors upstairs (open daily June-Oct. 7:30am-4am, Nov.-May 7pm-4am; live music W-Th 11pm-2am). Away from the port, **Discoteca Sí,** C. Virgen de Gracia, 16, turns on the strobe only after midnight, while **Nou Bar,** C. Nou, 1, 2nd fl., serves drinks, including Guinness on tap (600ptas per pint, 275ptas for other beers; open daily noon-3pm and 7:30pm-3am).

From May to September, merchants sell shoes, clothes, and souvenirs in **mercadillos** held daily in various town squares (Tu and Sa Mahón; F and Sa Ciutadella; Th Alaior; Su Mercadal; Tu and F Ferrerias; M and W Es Castell). On July 16, Mahón's **Verge del Carme** celebration floats a colorful trimmed armada into the harbor. The **Festa de Nostra Senyora de Gràcia,** the city's celebration of its patron saint, swings out September 7-8.

CIUTADELLA (CIUDADELA)

Ciutadella's blue and red townhouses sink into serpentine streets. The colorful stucco architecture above meshes with dark cobblestone below, an unlikely but successful juxtaposition. There is a seductive charm in the city's ancient streets, broad *plaças*, and winding port. Though far more tranquil than Mahón, Ciutadella (pop. 21,200) is quite expensive and out of reach for those on very tight budgets.

ⓘ ORIENTATION AND PRACTICAL INFORMATION

To get from the **bus station** to **Plaça de la Catedral** and the tourist office, head left half a block, take a left on Camí de Maó, go straight through Pl. d'Alfons III, and continue along C. de Maó as it turns into Quadrado (Ses Voltes) after crossing Pl. Nova. To get from Pl. Catedral to **Plaça de s'Esplanada** (also called Pl. Pins), exit the plaza on C. Major d'es Born with the cathedral behind you and to the right, cross P. Born on its right side, and bear diagonally across to the left. The **port,** and its accompanying street C. Marina, lie below the rest of the city and can be reached via a stone stairway just off the corner of Pl. Born.

> **Buses: Transportes Menorca** buses leave from C. Barcelona, 8 (tel. 971 38 03 93), and go to **Mahón** (6 per day, 550ptas). **Autocares Torres,** Poligona Industrial c/Sastres, 3 (tel. 971 38 64 61), offers daily service to surrounding beaches for less than 200ptas. To: **Cala Blanca** (14 per day); **Sa Caleta** and **Santandria** (14 per day); **Cala Blanes, Los Delfines,** and **Cala Forcat** (18 per day); **Cala Bosch** and **Son Xoriguer** (18 per day). Torres's ticket booth and departure point are located at Pl. s'Esplanada.

Ferries: Balear de Ferrys (tel. 902 11 91 28) has service between Ciutadella and **Alcú-dia, Mallorca** (2½hr., 2 per day, 5pm and 8:30pm, 4000ptas, students and seniors 3400ptas). **Cape Balear** (tel. 902 10 04 44) runs between Ciutadella and **Cala Rat-jada** (May-Oct. 1-2 per day).

Taxis: (tel. 971 38 28 96). Pl. s'Esplanada is a prime hailing spot.

Bike Rental: Bicicletas Tolo, C. Sant Isidor, 28-34 (tel. 971 38 15 76), across the street from Hostal Oasis. Supplies and repair services. Rental 600-800ptas per day, 3300-4600ptas per week. Open M-F 8:30am-1:30pm and 3:30-8pm, Sa 8:30am-1:30pm.

Tourist Office: Pl. Catedral, 3 (tel. 971 38 26 93; www.infotelecom.es/ciutadella). Maps, beach info, and Menorca guide. Open M-F 8am-3pm and 4:30-8pm, Sa 10am-2pm.

Banks: La Caixa, C. dés Seminari, 5, and **Central Hispano,** C. Negicle, 7.

Emergency: tel. 091 or 092. **Police: Guardia Municipal** tel. 971 38 07 87.

Medical Emergencies: Clinica Menorca (tel. 971 48 05 05), Canonge Moll. Open 24hr. **Ambulance:** call 061.

Post Office: (tel. 971 38 00 81), Pl. des Born. Lista de Correos. Open M-F 8:30am-2:30pm, Sa 9:30am-1pm. **Postal Code:** 07760.

Internet Access: Accesso Directo, Pl. s'Esplanada, 37 (tel. 971 48 40 26). 360ptas per 30min. Open M-Sa 9am-9pm.

▌ ACCOMMODATIONS

Hostels are packed (and pricey) during peak season (June 15-early Sept.). Ask about discounts in the off-season.

Hotel Geminis, C. Josepa Rossinyol, 4 (tel. 971 38 58 96; fax 971 38 36 83). Take C. Sud off Av. Capital Negrete coming from Pl. s'Esplanada; turn left onto C. Josepa Rossinyol. Quality rooms with phones, baths, fans, and TVs. Outdoor terrace has small pool. Breakfast included. Reserve early for Aug. Singles 3700ptas; doubles 7500ptas.

Hostal Residencia Oasis, C. Sant Isidre, 33 (tel. 971 38 21 97). From Pl. s'Esplanada, take Av. Capitá Negrete to Pl. d'Artrutx; C. Sant Isidre runs off the plaça. A centrally located floral paradise. Breakfast included. Doubles with bath 6000ptas.

Pensió Bar Ses Persianes, Pl. Artruitx, 2 (tel. 971 38 14 45), off Av. Jaume I. Bright white walls enclose smallish rooms. Air-conditioned bar below (also hotel reception) serves breakfast. Rooms are all doubles with shared bath. Reservations recommended in August. 2500ptas per person; 2 people 3500ptas. Closed in winter.

▌ FOOD

Cruise C. Quadrado for *platos combinados* and *tapas*. Sandwich bars have infil-trated Pl. s'Esplanada. Shop at **Supermercado Diskont,** C. Purísima, 6 (tel. 971 38 32 68; open M-Sa 8:30am-2pm and 4-9pm), or at the **market** on Pl. Llibertat.

La Guitarra, C. Dolores, 1 (tel. 971 38 13 55). Take C. Major d'es Born off Pl. Born, then turn right onto Carres del Roser, which leads to C. Dolores. Challenges patrons to "try our meals the way we do them." Take their advice. *Menú* 1000ptas, entrees 1100-6000ptas. Open June-Sept. M-Sa noon-3:30pm and 7-11pm. Visa, MC.

Hostal Ciutadella Cafeteria, S. Eloy, 10 (tel. 971 38 34 62). From Pl. s'Esplanada, take Av. Capitá Negrete and continue onto Av. Jaume el Conqueridor to Pl. d'Alfons III. Take a left onto S. Eloy; the hostel is one block down on the right. A bit off the beaten path. *Menú* 900ptas. Open daily 8-10:30am, 1-3:30pm, and 8-10:30pm.

Ca'n Magí, C. Quadrado (Ses Voltes), 24 (tel. 971 48 06 67), off Pl. Nova. Join the teem-ing mass of locals. Entrees 550-1000ptas. Open M-Su 8am-noon.

◉ 🎵 SIGHTS AND ENTERTAINMENT

An interesting complement to Menorca's beaches are the Bronze Age remnants at Menorca's archaeological sites. ◼**Naveta des Tudons,** one of the oldest structures in Europe (with some cosmetic restoration), sits 4km from the city. These ruins of community tombs are the island's best preserved. **Torretrencada** and **Torrellafuda** were rounded towers that overlooked the countryside. Both protect Stonehenge-like *taulas*, formations that have stood for over 3000 years. Buses don't come near these sights, so consider hiking (about 5km) along C. Cami Vell de Maó. The descriptive *Archeological Guide to Menorca* is available at the tourist office.

Ciutadella's community of is one of early-to-bedders. **Asere,** C. de Curniola, 23, one block off Pl. Nova, spices things up a bit with a Cuban theme and mixed frozen drinks (600ptas and under; open F-Sa 8pm-midnight). From the first week in July to the end of August, Ciutadella hosts the **Festival de Música d'Estiu,** featuring some of the world's top classical musicians. Tickets (1600-3500ptas) are sold at Foto Born, C. Seminari (C. Bisbe Vila), 14 (tel. 971 38 17 54), and at the box office (open daily 9:30am-1:30pm and 5-8pm). In late June, even veteran partiers of Palma and Ibiza join locals as they burn gallons of midnight oil during the **Festival de Sant Joan,** Menorca's biggest *fiesta*. A week before the festivities, a man clad in a sheepskin carries a decorated lamb on his shoulders through the city. The festival's main events include jousting and equestrian displays.

DAYTRIPS AROUND MENORCA

The more popular (i.e., crowded) Menorcan beaches are accessible by bus from Mahón and Ciutadella. Most bus rides take around half an hour and cost between 50 and 200ptas. Many of the best beaches require a vehicle and some legwork, but they are worth the extra hassle. Northern beaches are rocky but less crowded; finer sands are hidden under hundreds of tourists on the southern coast. Don't limit yourself to the beach scene, however—Menorca also offers a number of interesting natural and archaeological excursions.

NEAR MAHÓN

◼**CAP DE FAVÀRTIX.** Almost eerily tranquil, the edge of this grey slate coast feels like the end of the earth. *(From Mahón, take a moped or car in the direction of Es Gran/Fornells, turn off the highway at Favàrtix (9km), pass through farmlands and lush greenery, then break off to the right from the bushy-edged roadway through an open gate. Enter the black rock cove and view the lighthouse there.)*

◼**PLATGES DE SON BOU.** A gorgeous, 3km-long string of beaches on the southern shore, complete with crystal waters and a blanket of tourists covering its soft, fine sand. There is a 5th-century Paleo-Christian **basilica** in the nearby tourist settlement of Son Bou, as well as a supermarket, water slides, and more. *(Transportes Menorca buses leave from Mahón (6 per day, 8:45am-7pm) to the beaches).*

ARENAL D'EN CASTELL. This sandy, touristy ring around calm water lies on Menorca's northern shore, hidden behind a thin barrier of pine trees and coastal ravines. *(Autocares Fornells buses (6 per day, 10:30am-7pm) leave from C. Vasallo in Mahón.)*

CALAEN PORTER. Expansive and extremely touristy, Calean Porter greets thousands of visitors each summer with its gleaming whitewashed houses, orange stucco roofs, and red sidewalks. Here the **Covas d'en Xoroi,** spooky prehistoric dwellings, are inhabited by a network of bars during the day (open 11am-9pm; cover 500ptas; includes 1 soft drink). The disco inside the cave is hugely popular. *(TMSA buses (6 per day, 9:30am-7:30pm) run to Mahón.)*

CALASCOVES. The rock walls of this cove are honeycombed with prehistoric caves. Today they are inhabited by modern day hippies; expect a number of tan bodies strewn about the rocks by the aquamarine water. *(A 30min. walk to the east (left, as you face the sea) from Calaen Porter.)*

MONTE EL TORO. The island's highest peak, Monte El Toro provides fantastic views of the Menorcan landscape, including farmland gridded with stone walls, abundant greenery, and scorched red earth. *(A road from Es Mercadel connects Mt. Toro to the main Mahón-Ciutadella highway, making the peak easily accessible by car.)*

ES GRAU. The center of the biosphere, Albufera Es Grau entices visitors with lagoons, pine woods, and farmland, as well as diverse flora and fauna. Recreational activities include hiking to coves across the bay or taking a nature walk through the protected lands. **Illa d'en Colom,** a tiny island with more beaches, is just a boat ride away. *(Autocares Fornells buses (3 per day) leave from C. Vasallo in Mahón.)*

TORRALBA D'EN SALORD. This Talayotic settlement may not be the best preserved overall, but it has one of the most perfectly preserved *taulas* on the island. It is also significant because of the bronze calf found here, now in the Museum of Menorca in Mahón. *(Halfway along the road connecting Alaior and Calean Porter.)*

TORRE D'EN GAUMÉS. A sparsely-labeled but stunningly expansive Talayotic settlement dating to before 1500 BC. Includes a *taula* sanctuary, a filtration/storage system, and circular dwellings. *(Off the road from Alaior to Son Bou.)*

NEAR CIUTADELLA

◪NORTH SHORE. The stretch east of Cala Morell is home to some of the most outstanding and pristine beaches on the island. **Platges d'Algaiarens** may be the superstar of the series, which also includes Cala en Carabó, Penyal de l'Anticrist, Sa Falconera, and the beautiful Cala del Pilar Ets Alocs. *(Cars can go only up to a few kilometers from these beaches; from there you must walk.)*

CALA MACARELLA. The 600pta toll for the private road to Macarella is well worth it. No tourist developments here, only crystal clear water lapping the shores of the cove. *Naturistas* hang out on an even more secluded cove to the west. *(Access by bike, moped, or car off the country road to Sant Joan de Missa.)*

CALA BOSCH. Jagged cliffs plummet into clear pale-blue water. Crowded, but a fantastic backdrop for a refreshing dip in the Mediterranean. *(Accessible by Torres bus (18 per day, 8am-10:30pm) from Ciutadella.)*

SON XORIGUER. Located just down the road from Cala Bosch, on the same clear blue coastal water. It may be crowded, but it's only 20min. from Ciutadella. *(Accessible by Torres bus (18 per day, 8am-10:30pm) from Ciutadella.)*

FORNELLS. A small fishing village known for its lobster farms, Fornells has only recently begun to attract tourists. Windsurfers zip around Fornells' long, shallow port, while beach gurus make excursions to **Cala Tirant** and **Binimella,** both a few km west. Fornells also makes a calm base from which to explore coves and jagged cliffs by car or bike (bus service is very limited). *(Autobuses Roca Triay buses (30min., 5 per day) run to Fornells from C. Vassallo in Mahón.)*

CALA SANTA GALDANA. Though it lacks ample parking space, Galdana offers a shallow cove filled with clear waters and white cliffs. *(7 buses per day from Ciutadella, 4 from Mahón; 8am-7pm, last bus back at 4pm).*

IBIZA

Perhaps nowhere on Earth does style rule over substance more than on the island of Ibiza (pop. 84,000). Ibiza's style warriors arrive in droves to showcase themselves in the island's outrageous nightlife and to debauch in a sex- and substance-driven summertime culture. A hippie enclave since the 1960s, Ibiza's summer camp for disco fiends and high fashion evokes a sense of new-age decadence. Although a thriving gay community still lends credence to Ibiza's image as a center of tolerance, the island's high price tags preclude true diversity. As unbelievable as it may sound, there is more to Ibiza than just nightlife; the beaches and mountains are just as spectacular.

The island also has places of historical interest, including ancient castles scattered across the landscape. Since the Carthaginians retreated to Ibiza from the mainland in 656 BC, the island's list of conquerors reads like a "Who's Who of Ancient Western Civilization." Perhaps the most famous was the 1235 invasion by the Catalans, who brought Christianity and constructed the massive Renaissance walls that still fortify **Eivissa** (Ibiza City). The invasion most influential to Ibiza's modern culture was that of the hippies in the 1960s.

EIVISSA (IBIZA CITY)

Eivissa (pop. 35,000) is the world's biggest 24hr. party. When the sun rises, revelers at the city's infamous *discotecas* crawl into bed and sun-seekers scurry to nearby beaches. In the daytime, while the sun blazes, the city resembles a ghost town, as most of its visitors are tanning or sleeping off the night before. At sunset the show begins. Grab a front-row seat at one of the outdoor cafes to enjoy the action, as tourists and summer residents parade the latest fashions from the continent. Eivissa is a place to see and be seen.

▪ ORIENTATION AND PRACTICAL INFORMATION

Three distinct sections make up the city. **Sa Penya,** in front of Estació Marítima, is mobbed with vendors, bars, and boutiques. Atop the hill behind Sa Penya, high walls circle **Dalt Vila,** the old city. **Sa Marina** and the commercial district occupy the gridded streets to the far right (with your back to the water) of the Estació.

The local paper *Diario de Ibiza* (www.diariodeibiza.es; 125ptas) has an *Agenda* page that lists essential information including the bus schedule for the whole island, the ferry schedule, the schedule of all domestic flights to and from Ibiza for the day, water and weather forecasts, info on the island's 24-hour pharmacies, a list of 24-hour gas stations, and important phone numbers.

TRANSPORTATION

Flights: Airport (tel. 971 80 90 00), 7km south of the city. Buses run between the airport and Av. Isidor Macabich, 20, in town (30min., every hr., 7:30am-10:30pm, 125ptas). Info booth open for tickets and reservations 24hr. **Iberia,** Pg. Vara de Rey, 15 (tel. 902 40 05 00), at the end of the street, has flights to Palma, Barcelona, Madrid, Valencia, and Alicante. **Air Europa** and **Spanair** offer similar options. For routes and schedules, see **By Plane,** p. 472, or **Getting Around,** p. 473.

Ferries: Estació Marítima, at the end of Av. Bartolomé Roselló. To get to the city center from the waterfront, take Av. Bartolomé Roselló which becomes Av. Isidor Macabich. **Trasmediterránea** (tel. 971 31 41 73) sells tickets at Estació Marítima and sends ferries to Palma, Barcelona, and Valencia. **Flebasa Lines** (tel. 971 31 40 05) runs daily to and from Dénia, near Alicante; a connection in Eivissa continues to and from Palma. For rates, fares, and schedules, see **By Boat,** p. 472, or **Getting Around,** p.472. For transport to the island of Formentera, see **Formentera: Getting There and Away,** p. 495.

Buses: The two main bus stops are Av. Isidor Macabich, 42 and Av. Isidor Macabich, 20. For an exact schedule, check the tourist office or *El Diario.* Intercity buses are 250ptas or less and run from Av. Isidor Macabich, 42 (tel. 971 31 21 17) to **San Antonio** (M-Sa every 15min., Su every 30min.) and **Santa Eulalia** (M-F every 30min., Sa-Su every hr., 9:30am-10:30pm). Buses (tel. 971 34 03 82) to the beaches cost 125ptas and leave from Av. Isidor Macabich, 20, to: **Salinas** (every hr., on the half-hour); **Platja d'en Bossa** (every 30min.); **Cap Martinet** (M-Sa 11 per day); **Cala Tarida** (5 per day).

Taxis: tel. 971 30 70 00 or 971 30 66 02.

Car and Motorbike Rental: Casa Valentín, Av. B.V. Ramón, 19 (tel. 971 31 08 22), the street parallel to Pg. Vara de Rey. Mopeds 1500-3500ptas per day; cars 5000ptas and up per day. **Extra,** Av. Sta. Eulalia, 25 (tel. 971 19 17 17), near the Formentera ferries. Mopeds 2975ptas and up per day; cars 6900ptas per day. Open M-Sa 8am-1:30pm and 4-8:30pm, Su 8am-noon and 5:30-7:30pm.

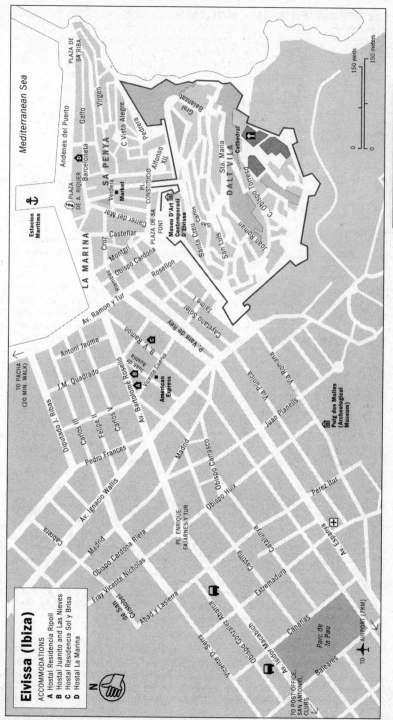

Eivissa (Ibiza)

ACCOMMODATIONS
A Hostal Residencia Ripoll
B Hostal Juanito and Las Nieves
C Hostal Residencia Sol y Brisa
D Hostal La Marina

Mediterranean Sea

Estacion Maritima

PLAZA DE SA RIBA

Andenes del Puerto

Virgen
Gallo
Barceloneta
PLAZA DE A. RIQUER
Verdera
Market
PL. CONSTITUCIO
Carrer del Mar
PLAZA DE SA FONT
Cruz
Castellar
Montgri
Obispo Cardona
Rosellon
Jaime I
Cayetano Soler
P. Vara de Rey
Av. Ramon y Tur

C Vista Alegre
Pedrera
Alfonso XII
SA PENYA
LA MARINA

Gral. Balanzat
Museu D'Art Contemporani D'Eivissa
Sta. Maria
Santa Creu
San Luis
San Carlos
Joan Roman
C. Obispo Torres
DALT VILA
Cathedral

Antoni Jaume
J.M. Quadrado
Diputado J. Ribas
Carlos III
Felipe II
Carlos V
B. V. Ramon
Av. Bartolomé Rosello
Av. Ignacio Wallis
Vicente Cuervo
Abad ap uang
American Express
Pedro Frances
Cabrera
Madrid
Obispo Cardona Riera
Fray Vicente Nicholas
de San Cristobal
Abad y Lasierra
Vicente D. Serra
Obispo González Abarca
Av. Isidor Macabich

PL. ENRIQUE FAJARNES Y TUR
Obispo Carrasco
Obispo Huix
Castilla
Cataluña
Extremadura
Cañarias
Baleares
Parc de la Pau

Via Punica
Via Romana
Juan Planells
Puig des Molins (Archeological Museum)
Perez Itur
Av. Espana

TO PACHA (20 MIN. WALK)

TO POST OFFICE, SAN ANTONIO, CLUBS

TO AIRPORT (7KM)

150 yards
150 meters
0

N

TOURIST AND FINANCIAL SERVICES

Tourist Office: C. Antoni Riquer, 2 (tel. 971 30 19 00; www.ibizaonline.com), right on the water, across from where the huge Trasmediterránea ferries come in. Good maps, especially for hiking, and a complete bus schedule. Open M-F 9:30am-1:30pm and 5-7pm, Sa 10:30am-1pm. Also a **booth** at the airport arrival terminal (tel. 971 80 91 18; fax 971 80 91 32). Open May-Oct. M-Sa 9am-2pm and 3-8pm, Su 9am-2pm.

Currency Exchange: La Caixa, Av. Isidor Macabich. Good exchange rates for cash and traveler's checks. **American Express** service at Viajes Iberia, C. Vicente Cuervo, 9 (tel. 971 31 11 11 or 971 30 43 64). Open M-F 9am-1pm and 4:30-7:45pm, Sa 9am-1pm.

EMERGENCY AND COMMUNICATIONS

Emergency: tel. 091 or 112. **Police:** (tel. 092), C. Madrid, by the post office.

Medical Assistance: Hospital (tel. 971 39 70 00), Barrio Can Misses, on the corner of Av. Espanya and C. Extremadura. **Ambulance:** tel. 971 39 32 32.

Post Office: C. Madrid, 23 (tel. 971 31 13 80). From the port, follow Av. Isidor Macabich to its end; the post office is the last building on the left. Lista de Correos. Open M-F 8:30am-8:30pm, Sa 9:30am-2pm. **Postal Code:** 07800.

Internet Access: Centro Internet Eivissa, Av. Ignacio Wallis, 39 (tel. 971 31 81 61). 400ptas for 30min., 300ptas for each additional 30min. **Eurocentro,** C. Juan de Austria, 22 (tel. 971 31 09 09; email eurocent@teleline.es). 400ptas per 30min. Open 10am-1:30pm and 5-9pm.

ACCOMMODATIONS

Decent, cheap accommodations in town are rare, especially in the summer. The letters "CH" *(casa de huespedes)* mark many doorways, but the owner can often only be reached by the phone number on the door. In July and August, prices skyrocket and you must make reservations two to three weeks in advance. Eivissa has a relatively safe and up-all-night life-style, and owners offer keys for 24-hour entry. All prices listed below are for high-season and can drop by as much as 1000ptas in the off-season.

Hostal Residencia Sol y Brisa, Av. B. V. Ramón, 15 (tel. 971 31 08 18; fax 971 30 30 32), parallel to Pg. Vara de Rey. Upstairs from Pizzeria da Franco (signs point the way to the pizzeria). Clean and cheap. Singles 3000ptas; doubles 5000ptas.

Hostal Residencia Ripoll, C. Vicente Cuervo, 14 (tel. 971 31 42 75). Guaranteed cool with huge windows in doubles and triples, fans in interior rooms. July-Sept. singles 3500ptas; doubles 5500ptas.

Hostal La Marina, Puerto de Ibiza, c/Barcelona, 8 (tel. 971 31 01 72), conveniently across from Estació Marítima. Dimly lit rooms keep the temperature low; bar next door keeps the noise level high. New owner has brought renovations and a sharp increase in prices. Singles 7000ptas; doubles 5000-12000ptas.

Hostal Juanito and **Hostal Las Nieves,** c/Juan de Austria, 17-18 (tel. 971 19 03 19). Run by the same owner, both hostels offer inexpensive housing in a central area. Singles only available for longer stays. Singles 2000ptas; doubles 4000ptas, with bath 5000ptas.

Camping: Es Cana (tel. 971 33 21 17). 500ptas per person; 600ptas per site; 450ptas extra for a tent. Bungalow 2250ptas. Open daily 9am-1pm and 4:30-9:30pm. **Cala Nova** (tel. 971 33 17 74). 500ptas per person, 475ptas per tent. Both sites are close to Santa Eulalia del Río.

FOOD

Ibiza has a limited supply of cheap eateries. Full meals rarely cost less than 1200ptas in the port and downtown areas; **Sa Penya** and **Dalt Vila** offer exquisite fare in elegant settings for no less than 1500ptas per person. For cheaper meals, try the more residential neighborhoods. Ibizan dishes worth hunting down are *sof-*

rit pagès, a deep-fried lamb and chicken dish; *flao*, a lush lemon- and mint-tinged cheesecake; and *graxonera*, cinnamon-dusted pudding made from eggs and bits of *ensaimada* (candied bread). The **market,** at C. Extremadura and C. Canarias, sells a variety of food, meat, fruits, and vegetables (open M-Sa 7am-1pm). For a supermarket, try **Comestibles Tony,** Carrer d'Enmig, 1 (open 9am-2pm and 5-8pm).

Comidas Bar San Juan, C. Montgrí, 8 (tel. 971 31 07 66). From Pg. Vara de Rey, take the 2nd right on the Puerto Moll. A tiny, popular family-run restaurant. The staff will likely keep you waiting, but they provide filling, inexpensive selections. Crowded weekend nights. Entrees 400-700ptas. Open M-Sa 1-3:15 and 8-10:15pm.

Restaurante Ca'n Costa, C. Cruz, 19 (tel. 971 31 08 65), down the street from Victoria. Rows of tables tucked away in a basement eatery. Everything cooked in a wood-burning stove. Meat dishes 575-1400ptas. Fish dishes 500-1700ptas. Afternoon *menú* 1000ptas. Open Feb.-Dec. M-Sa noon-3:30pm and 8pm-midnight.

Pizzeria da Franco e Romano, Av. B. V. Ramon, 15 (tel. 971 31 32 53), below Hostal Sol y Brisa; signs point the way. Owner promises "economy, happiness, and sympathy" at her popular pizzeria. Filling pasta and pizzas for under 1000ptas. Afternoon *menú* 1250ptas. Open daily 12:30-4pm and 7:30pm-1am. Visa, MC.

Restaurante Victoria, C. Riambau, 1 (tel. 971 31 06 22), one block up from the port along C. Montgrí. This family eatery has been an Ibiza institution for 50 years. Entrees 450-750ptas. Open M-Sa 1-4 and 8:30-11:30pm.

👁 SIGHTS

SIGHTS. Wrapped in 16th-century walls, **Dalt Vila** (High Town) hosts 20th-century urban bustle in the city's oldest buildings. Its twisting, sloping streets lead up to the 14th-century **cathedral,** which offers superb views of the city, ocean, and beyond. *(Open M-Sa 10:30am-1pm.)* Next to the cathedral stands the **Museu Arqueològic D'Eivissa.** *(Open T-Sa 10am-1pm and 5-10pm, Su 10am-2pm. 300ptas, students 150ptas.)* Amid the weathered stone walls, the small **Museu D'Art Contemporani D'Eivissa** displays a wide range of current art exhibitions. *(C. Sa Carrosa, on the left when entering through Dalt Vila's main entrance. Tel. 971 30 27 23. Open M-F 10am-1:30pm and 5-8pm, Sa 10am-1:30pm. 200ptas, students free.)* The newly renovated archaeological museum, **Puig des Molins,** is on Vía Romana, which runs off the Portal Nou at the foot of the Dalt Vila. The museum displays Punic, Roman, and Iberian art, pottery, and metals. Adjoined to Puig is the 4th-century BC Punic-Roman **necropolis.** *(Both open M-Sa 10am-2pm and 5-8pm. 150ptas.)*

BEACHES. The power of the rising sun draws thousands of solar zombies to nearby tanning grounds. **Platja Figueretes,** a thin stretch of sand in the shadow of tourists and large hotels, is a 10-minute bike rid from the port. Farther down, **Platja d'en Bossa** has one-foot waves just strong enough to bring bottle caps and other plastic goods ashore. **Platja des Duros** is tucked in across the port bay from Sa Penya and Sa Marina, just before the lighthouse. **Platja de Talamanca,** with its fine sand and plenty of snack-shops, is 20 minutes away by bike. More private sands are in the northern part of the island and are accessible by car or scooter.

🎵 NIGHTLIFE

The crowds return from the beaches by nightfall, when even the clothing stores (open until 1am) dazzle with throbbing music and flashing lights. Ibizans are full of pomp: men masquerade as women and vamps stalk the portside walkways, vying for attention and turning the sidewalks into catwalks. From sundown to sun-up, spectators gawk from cafe patios at showboating passers-by. **Calle Virgen,** the center of gay nightlife, is home to **Capricios,** C. Virgen, 42, the more familial (particularly among Germans) **Exis,** C. Virgen, 57, and the artistic **Bar Galerie,** C. Virgen, 64. People-watch on C. d'Alfons XII, off C. Virgen, where **Incognito** and **Angelo's,** catering to only gay patrons, look down on the crazy fashion scene.

The island's **■discos** (virtually all of which have a mixed gay-and-straight crowd) are world-famous and ever-changing. The best sources of information are regular disco-goers and the zillions of posters that plaster the stores and restaurants of Sa Marina and Sa Penya. There is something different going on each day of the week—for complete listings, check out *Ministry in Ibiza* or *Party Sun*, free at many hostels, bars, and restaurants. Better have some extra *pesetas* lying around—drinks at Ibiza's clubs cost about 1000ptas and covers start at 3500ptas. Look for the PR reps who distribute discount coupons (and occasionally free passes) outside the seaport cafes and bars. Generally, *discoteca*-goers pub-hop in Eivissa or San Antonio and jet off to clubs via bus or taxi (guess which is more chic) around 2am. The **Discobus** runs to and from all the major hotspots (midnight-6:30am, schedule at tourist office and hotels, 250ptas).

■ **Privilege** (tel. 971 19 81 60), on the discobus route to San Antonio or a 1500pta taxi ride from Eivissa. The wildest party ever. This minivillage/club—formerly known as KU—has everything, including double-digit bars, garden terraces, and a stage set on a pool, where bizarre rock operas are performed at night. Best known for Monday "manumission" parties that feature rather kinky live sex shows. Cover 4000ptas and up (as high as 12,000ptas), includes 1 drink. Open June-Sept. M and W-Sa midnight-7am. Visa.

■ **Amnesia,** on the road to San Antonio. Take the Discobus. Although you may not remember everything, this may be the craziest disco scene ever. Best known for cream parties on Thursdays and foam parties on Wednesdays and Sundays. Cover 4000-7000ptas. Open daily midnight-6am.

Pachá (tel. 971 31 36 12), Pg. Perimitral, 20min. from the port. The most famous club chain in Spain. A playful atmosphere with palm trees, terraces, and wax candles. On Friday nights Pachá hosts the Ministry of Sound; Wednesdays are "Renaissance nights." 5000pta cover includes one beverage. Open daily 11:15pm-7:30am.

Es Paradis (tel. 971 34 66 00; www.ibiza-online.com/EsParadis), in San Antonio, on the port across from the beach. "Clockwork Orange" theme nights on Wednesdays and water parties on Tuesdays and Saturdays. Cover 4000. Open midnight-6am.

El Divino (tel. 971 19 01 76), Puerto Ibiza Nueva, has welcomed the likes of supermodels Linda Evangelista and Karie Miller. Terraced club overlooking Eivissa has exotic dancers, strippers, and an S&M room. Caters to those with money and those looking to marry it. Have a drink at El Divino's Bar (on the port) and get a free pass for the disco shuttle boat—otherwise, it costs 150ptas one-way. Check out "Moneypenny" on Tuesdays. Cover 5000ptas. Open mid-June to mid-Sept. nightly 1-6am.

Space, Platja de Bossa (tel. 971 31 40 78 or 971 39 67 93). Cap off your night with a morning in Space, for the most happening after-parties in Ibiza. Open daily 7am-4pm, most popular Saturday through Tuesday mornings.

Bora Bora, Platja de Bossa, across from Space. The place to be if you've got any energy left after a trip through Space. With its chill beach and disco scene, this club catches the crowd around 4pm.

Discoteca Anfora, C. San Carlos, 7 (tel. 971 30 28 93), in the heart of Dalt Vila. Late-night partying for a gay crowd. Ideal for partygoers of all ages. Midnight-1am cover 500ptas, 1-6am 1500ptas.

NEAR EIVISSA: SAN ANTONIO DE PORTMANY

Every summer rowdy British hooligans storm San Antonio's huge crescent beach, harbor, and boozing 'n' bruising night scene. Most of the biggest Eivissa clubs—Privilege and Amnesia among them—are on the Eivissa-San Antonio road, actually closer to San Antonio. To get to San Antonio from Eivissa, take the bus from Av. Isador Macabich (185ptas). Those headed for the mainland can contact **Pitra car ferries** (tel. 971 19 10 88) or **Flebasa**, both of which run to Dénia, near Alicante. The Pitra office in San Antonio de Portmany is on the **Muelle Comercial** (tel. 971 34 52 99), at the end of Pg. de la Mar. The **tourist booth** (tel. 971 34

33 63) is in the stone hut at the beginning of Pg. Fonts (open M-F 9:30am-8:30pm, Sa 9am-1pm, Su 9:30am-1:30pm; Nov.-Apr. M-Sa 9:30am-1pm). **Emergency:** tel. 091 or 092; **municipal police** (tel. 971 34 08 30), on Av. Portmany; **medical assistance** (tel. 971 34 51 21), on C. Alicant.

Sand space dwindles toward noon, so many people relocate to beaches farther out. **Boats** leave from Pg. Ses Fonts (before it becomes Pg. Mar) to **Cala Bassa** (550ptas), a sandy beach on a thin strip; **Cala Conta** (600ptas), a slightly rocky beach; and the island of **Formentera** (2700ptas). **Buses,** a cheaper mode of transportation, leave from Pg. Mar (before it intersects with C. Madrid) to **Cala Gració, Port des Turrent, Santa Eulalia,** and the protected inlet of **Cala Tarida** (140ptas). If you have wheels, explore **Cueva de Ses Fontanelles,** north of Platja Cala Salada, where faint prehistoric paintings cover the walls. Or head north to **Cala Salada,** a tranquil cove that offers an escape from San Antonio's over-populated beaches. Consult the tourist office for **hiking** excursions around San Antonio. Walking routes pass by sights such as the aquarium, a small collection of fish situated inside a cave (350ptas, children 150ptas; open daily 10am-10pm).

Cala Bassa (tel. 971 44 55 99) offers **camping** on the bay, 6km west of San Antonio (500ptas per person, 475ptas per tent; tent rental 500ptas). **Cafes** fill the waterfront area, as do **bars** and tattoo parlors. For inexpensive food in a loud, thumping environment, check out **Terraza Kiwi Beach,** Av. Doctor Fleming, 2-4 (tel. 971 31 68 42), by the beach and across from Es Pardis; look for the bright orange. Live music and waterfront location creates a funky atmosphere. (Entrees 350-600ptas. Alcoholic milkshakes 750ptas, non-alcoholic 350ptas. Open daily 10am-4am.)

FORMENTERA

The tiny island of Formentera is Spain's best attempt at an island paradise. Despite recent invasions by beach-hungry Germans and Italians, the 11-mile moat separating Formentera from Eivissa has deterred complete besiegement. While Formentera is a bourgeois vacation haven, its relatively untouristed white beaches maintain a pervading sense of hypnotic calm, at least for now. Join Formentera's "save our island" spirit by hiking or renting a bike—the tourist office offers a comprehensive list of "Green Tours" for hikers and cyclists.

 GETTING THERE AND AWAY. Several ferry lines at Estación Marítima in Eivissa provide the best alternative to swimming. **Pitra car ferries** (tel. 971 19 10 88), **Trasmapi-Flebesa** (tel. 971 31 07 11), and **Umafisa car ferries** (tel. 971 31 45 13) all offer transportation to and from Formentera. For transport between Formentera and the mainland, see **By Boat,** p. 472. For transport from Evissa to Formentera, see **Getting Around,** p. 473.

 ORIENTATION AND PRACTICAL INFORMATION. Atop the northern side of the island is its main port, **La Savina.** The main artery runs from the port (km 0) to the eastern tip, **Punta D'Esfar** (km20). The island's "capital" **San Francisco,** which parts from the main artery at km3.1, has the basics but little else. **Buses** run from La Savina to **Es Pujols** (8 per day), **Playa Illete** (2 per day), **Playa Migjorn** (10 per day), and to **San Francisco** (14 per day). For a **taxi,** call tel. 971 32 80 16. **Car-scooter-bike rental booths** line the dock in La Savina (car 5000ptas per day; scooter 2500ptas; bike 500-1000ptas). Main roads have lanes where scooters can putter along freely with bicycles. The **tourist office,** Edificio Servicios La Savina (tel. 971 32 20 57; fax 971 32 28 25; www.ifsystems.es/formentera; email ifsystems@ifsystems.es.), is at the port (open M-F 10am-2pm and 5-7pm, Su 10am-2pm). **Police** (tel. 971 32 20 22, 091, or 092); **centro médico** (tel. 971 32 23 69).

 ACCOMMODATIONS AND FOOD. Cool air and the scent of pine trees mark the windy ascent through the mountainous regions of La Mola to Punta D'Esfar (which has a lighthouse at the edge of a cliff). Equally satiating are the *paella* (1300ptas) and vista from **El Mirador** (tel. 971 32 70 37), km 14.3 (open daily 12:30-4pm and 7-11pm). From the restaurant, the narrow strip of the Formentera Island looks like the stem of a champagne glass that widens out to the northern port, La Savina, and the southern tip, Cap de Barbaria. Others say it looks like a bull leering at the observer. **Hostal La Savina** (tel. 971 32 22 79), near the port on Av. Mediterránea, offers ceiling fans, brown-tiled balconies, access to a lake, and a breakfast buffet (singles 4000ptas, doubles 6500ptas). Supermarkets line all of the major roads in Formentera, as do small restaurants (*menús* about 1100ptas).

■ **BEACHES.** To bask on Formentera's best beaches, take Av. Mediterránea from the port, turn left at the sign pointing toward Es Pujols, and hop left onto the dirt road at the sign marking **Verede de Ses Salines.** Paths to the right lead to **Platja de Llevant,** a long strip of fine sand. Farther up the peninsula, roads to the left lead to **Platja de Ses Illetes,** with more popular and rocky swimming holes. While the entire peninsula provides ample privacy, walking to the end (which requires wading through two shallow pools), will assure you of absolute solitude, though you might have to nestle between rocks to catch some rays. A tourist **boat** also runs to **Ses Illetes** and **Espalmador** from La Savina (outbound from La Savina 10:45am, 11:45am, and 1:15pm; returning 4:15pm, 5:30pm, and 6:45pm, 1200ptas).

CANARY
ISLANDS

From the snowy peak of Mount Teide to the fiery volcanos of Timanfaya, the Canary Islands have enchanted humanity since the beginning of time. Homer and Herodotus often referred to their gardens of great beauty, and the lost civilization of Atlantis was said to have left behind these seven islands when it sank into the ocean. Since then, the Canaries have been known as the "Fortunate Isles"—and with good reason; they are blessed with perfect weather (a spring-like 20-24°C year-round) that attracts millions of European vacationers each year. But beyond the parties of Tenerife and Gran Canaria and the hotel-lined beaches of Fuerteventura, it is the natural beauty—the volcanic wastelands, the folding dunes, the amber mountains, and the verdant forests—that lends the Canaries their magic.

The Canary Islands were once inhabited by Guanches, light-skinned and blond-haired hunters and gatherers, descendants of Berbers who migrated to the islands from North Africa. European conquests began when the Romans heard tales of the enchanting isles from the Mauritanians. The islands were later conquered by the Portuguese, French, and Spanish; in 1479 the Treaty of Alcáçovas declared the Canaries Spanish territory. By 1496, after nearly a century of battle with the Guanches, the Spaniards wrested control of the islands, later using them as stopovers en route to their colonies in the Americas. After the conquest, the Spaniards developed a booming plantation economy, based on banana, sugar, and wine production—the islands still depend on such cash crops today.

Once a link between the Old and New Worlds, the islands have modern towns and resorts that are a confused melange of craft stalls, surf shops, fruit stands, and international restaurants. *Canarios* watch Spanish television and eat Spanish food, but their spoken Spanish resembles that of Cuba and Puerto Rico more than that of their Castilian conquerors. Remnants of Guanche culture—including *lucha canaria* (Canarian wrestling), *gofio* (a grain staple), and place names such as Tenerife, Timanfaya, and Doramas—still remain, especially in Lanzarote and the western islands. Today, a booming tourist industry of mostly northern Europeans adds to the cultural confusion.

HIGHLIGHTS OF CANARY ISLANDS

■ The rolling sand dunes of **Maspalomas** (see p. 505).
■ **El Teide National Park,** on the highest mountain in Spain (see p. 511).
■ Cesar Manrique's museums, home, and architectural impact on wonderfully under-touristed **Lanzarote** (see p. 519).
■ **Garajonay National Park,** the last living example of a laurisilva forest (see p. 521).

▐ GETTING THERE AND AWAY

Located off the western coast of Morocco, the Canaries make for a long haul by boat (2 days from Spain) but a relatively quick flight (2½-3½hr.) from the mainland. Competitive fares and quick flights make flying the best option. Many airlines fly direct from Spain, Portugal, Morocco, the U.S., and northern Europe. Flights from Madrid, which are the most frequent, are also the cheapest. European tourists, primarily Germans, flock to the islands in January and February; airfares during this time are the most expensive. As long as you plan ahead, getting to the Canary Islands does not have to be prohibitively expensive. Prices are the same whether you purchase your tickets in Spain or abroad.

Iberia/Aviaco (24hr. tel. 902 400 500; www.iberia.com) flies from Madrid and Barcelona to the islands of Gran Canaria, Tenerife, and Lanzarote. A standard round-trip ticket costs between 70,000 and 80,000ptas.

Air Europa (24hr. tel. 902 24 00 42) and **Spanair** (tel. 902 13 14 15; www.spanair.com) fly to the islands at cheaper fares (round-trip 35,000-60,000ptas).

Trasmediterránea (tel. 902 45 46 45; www.trasmediterranea.com) cruises from Cádiz, Spain to the islands of Gran Canaria, Tenerife, and La Palma (2 days; departs from Cádiz Sa, returns W; round-trip with dorm bed 58,500ptas).

▄ GETTING AROUND

Traveling between the islands by boat is the cheapest alternative. Boats come in two varieties: ferries and jetfoils. For shorter trips ferries are the best option. Jetfoils, which are faster and more comfortable, also cost almost twice as much—consider taking them on the longer voyages. Prices for both ferries and jetfoils vary with accommodation; travelers can choose between a *butaca* (a seat like those on buses) and a *camarote a compartir* (a dorm bed).

Three major lines serve the five islands. The following chart lists the prices, frequencies, and durations for several popular destinations. Departure times and prices are subject to frequent change—be sure to call ahead and confirm.

Origin	Destination	Duration	# per day	Time	Price
Las Palmas	Morro Jable	1½	1 per day	11am	5700ptas
Las Palmas	Santa Cruz, Tenerife	2hr.	9 per day	7:30am-6pm	2780-5700ptas
+Las Palmas	Santa Cruz, Tenerife	2hr.	2 per day	7am and 3pm	1900ptas
Las Palmas	Puerto Rosario	8hr.	1 every other day	midnight	3605-10,300ptas
Las Palmas	Arrecife	10hr.	2 per day	2:30pm and midnight	3605-10,300ptas
Las Palmas	Santa Cruz, La Palma	11hr.	1 per wk	6:30pm	4740ptas
Puerto Rosario	Arrecife	1½hr.	1 every other day	11am	1080-4275ptas
Puerto Rosario	Las Palmas	8hr.	1 every other day	midnight	3605-10,300ptas
Santa Cruz, La Palma	Los Cristianos	5hr.	1 every other day	2pm	2770ptas
Santa Cruz, La Palma	San Sebastián	3½hr.	1 every other day	2pm	2235ptas
San Sebastián	Los Cristianos	5hr.	4 per day	8am-6:15pm	1980ptas
San Sebastián	Santa Cruz, La Palma	3½hr.	1 every other day	10am	2235ptas
San Sebastián	Valverde	3½hr.	1 per day	10am or 7pm	2420ptas
Valle Gran Rey	Los Cristianos	1½hr.	5 per day	7:15am-5:15pm	2420ptas
Valle Gran Rey	San Sebastián	30min.	3 per day	7:15am-4pm	1030ptas
*Valverde	Los Cristianos	4hr.	1 per day	8am	5650ptas
Santa Cruz, Tenerife	Arrecife	20hr.	1 per day	6pm	4740ptas
Santa Cruz, Tenerife	Las Palmas	3½hr.	7-10 per day	7am-6pm	2780-6385ptas
*Santa Cruz, Tenerife	Las Palmas	3½hr.	4 per day	8:30am-8:30pm	4040ptas
Morro Jable	Santa Cruz, Tenerife	3hr.	1 per day	1:30pm	8100ptas
+Morro Jable	Las Palmas	1½hr.	1 per day	7:30pm	6000ptas
*Arrecife	Puerto del Rosario	3hr.	5 per day	8am-6pm	4020ptas

Unless noted, all ferries are run by Trasmediterránea. * denotes Fred Olsen jetfoils. + denotes Naviera Armas.

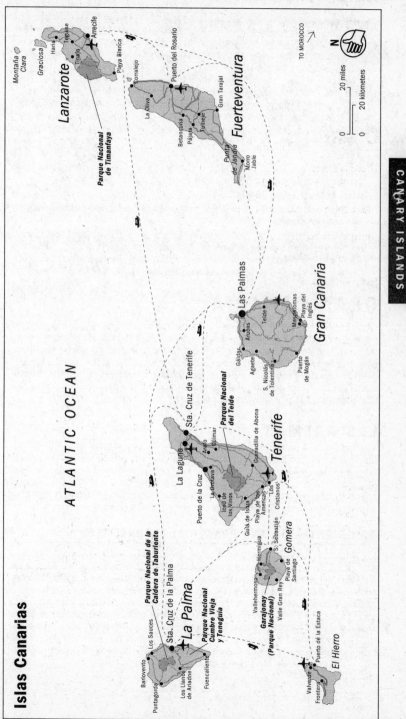

Islas Canarias

ATLANTIC OCEAN

Montaña Clara
Graciosa
Haría
Teguise
Arrecife
Tinajo
Playa Blanca
Lanzarote
Parque Nacional de Timanfaya

Corralejo
Puerto del Rosario
La Oliva
Gran Tarajal
Betancuria
Tuineje
Pájara
Fuerteventura
Punta de Jandía
Morro Jable

TO MOROCCO

N

20 miles
20 kilometers

CANARY ISLANDS

Las Palmas
Maspalomas
Playa del Inglés
Arucas
Telde
Gáldar
Agaete
S. Nicolás de Tolentino
Puerto de Mogán
Gran Canaria

Sta. Cruz de Tenerife
Parque Nacional del Teide
La Laguna
Tacoronte
Güímar
Guadilla de Abona
Puerto de la Cruz
La Orotava
Icod de los Vinos
Guía de Isora
Playa de las Américas
"Los Cristianos"
Tenerife

Parque Nacional de la Caldera de Taburiente
Sta. Cruz de la Palma
Parque Nacional Cumbre Vieja y Teneguía
Barlovento
Los Sauces
Puntagorda
Los Llanos de Aridane
Fuencaliente
La Palma

Vallehermoso
Hermigua
Garajonay (Parque Nacional)
Valle Gran Rey
S. Sebastián
Playa de Santiago
Gomera

Valverde
Puerto de la Estaca
Frontera
El Hierro

> **WHAT'S IN A NAME?** Rumored by ancient writers to be the site of divine afterlife, the Canary Islands have often been referred to as *Elysium*. The Spaniards called the islands *Islas Afortunadas* (Fortunate Islands) because of the wealth and opportunities they offered. However, there is still no definitive answer to the origin of the name "Canary Islands." Some link it to the particularly large yellow breed of *canus* special to the islands; others postulate that the islands were named after Cranus and Crana, mythical wanderers of the islands. Pliny the Elder believed that the name stemmed from the number of large *canes* (dogs) who inhabited the island. The most likely answer is that the name comes from the Guanche natives, descendants of the Moroccan Canarii tribe.

Trasmediterránea, (24hr. tel: 902 45 46 45; www.trasmediterranea.com) sends ferries between all of the islands. Ticket windows open 1hr. prior to departure. Visa, MC.

Naviera Armas (tel. 928 26 70 00).

Fred Olsen (tel. 922 62 82 31 or 928 22 81 66; email reservas@fredolsen.es) runs jet-foils between islands.

Iberia/Aviaco (tel. 902 40 05 00) has daily flights between the islands. All prices listed are one-way. **Gran Canaria** to: **Tenerife,** north and south airports (30min., 10 per day, 6000ptas); **La Palma** (30min., 1 per day, 10,000ptas); **Fuerteventura; Lanzarote.** **Spanair** (tel. 902 13 14 15) connects only Gran Canaria and Tenerife (5000ptas).

GRAN CANARIA

Often called the "miniature continent," Gran Canaria sports a wide range of climates—from the lush green forest and snow-covered Pico de las Nieves (1950m) to the rolling desert of the south—all within a circular island whose maximum diameter is 33½km. Although perhaps the least stunning of the islands, tourists (mostly German) crowd its eastern and southern beaches. While the interior towns are less touristed and perhaps more stunning, the parched mountains pale in comparison to the peaks and national parks of Tenerife and Lanzarote.

LAS PALMAS

The undisputed pleasure capital of the Canaries, Las Palmas (pop. 350,000) is inundated with bronzed and fun-loving Europeans all cruising towards one inevitable destination—the beach. The city's streets bustle with the frenzied commerce of a duty-free port where everything from cigarettes to sex is for sale. Once an important seaport linking Europe, America, and Africa, Las Palmas now serves as a transportation hub, funneling tourists to more scenic parts of the islands.

▮ ORIENTATION AND PRACTICAL INFORMATION

Las Palmas is not a compact city—to get around, you must use the bus system. The city is loosely divided into a series of districts, connected by the **Avenida del Marítima del Norte** running north to south along the east coast. **Santa Catalina,** framed by **Playa de Las Canteras** on the west and **Puerto de la Luz** on the east, is packed with accommodations, bars, discos, and sex shops—stay here for beach and bus access. Farther south through a series of residential neighborhoods lies **Triana,** a shopping district with the city's bus station, and **Vequeta,** home to most of the city's historical sights. Buses #1, 12, 13, 15, and 41 run between Parque Sta. Catalina and Vegueta. Santa Catalina's **Parque Santa Catalina** houses the tourist office; all directions in Las Palmas are given from there.

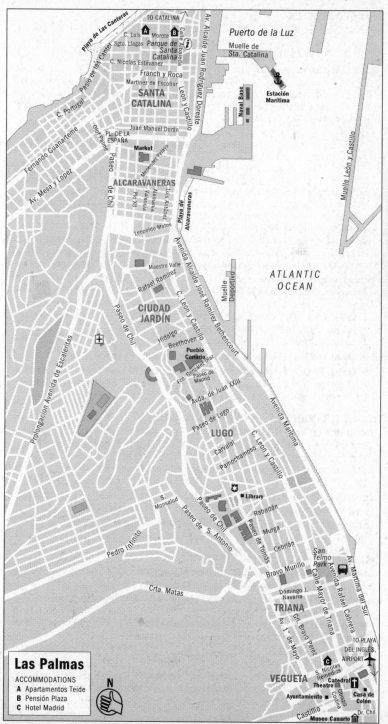

CANARY ISLANDS

Las Palmas

ACCOMMODATIONS
A Apartamentos Teide
B Pensión Plaza
C Hotel Madrid

N

TRANSPORTATION

Flights: (24hr. tel. 928 57 90 00). **Saccai buses** run between Parque Sta. Telmo and the airport (45min.; every 30min., 6:30am-9pm; every hr., 9pm-2am; 230ptas). **Iberia** (tel. 928 37 08 77). **Air Europa** (tel. 928 57 95 84). **Spanair** (tel. 928 57 94 07).

Buses: Estación de Guaguas (tel. 928 36 83 35; info tel. 928 36 86 35) in front of Parque Sta. Telmo. Office open M-F 6:30am-8:30pm. Buses are called *guaguas* here. Two companies connect Las Palmas to the rest of the island. Call for information on handicapped accessible buses. See the bus listing in the city to which you would like to travel for more info.

SALCAI (tel. 928 37 36 25; green *guaguas*) travels south. To: **Puerto Mogan** (#1; 30min., every 20min., 5:40am-7pm, 875ptas); **Maspalomas-Playa de Inglés** (#5 and 30; 30min., every 20min., 5:20am-9:20pm, 615ptas); **Puerto Rico** (#31; 4 per day, 6am-8:15pm, 755ptas). Buses also service Telde, La Garita, and Agumes.

Utinsa (tel. 928 36 01 79; orange *guaguas*) travels west. To **Arucas** (#205, 206, 209, and 210; every 30min., 5am-10:15pm, 230ptas) and **Teror** (#216 and 218; every 30min., 6:30am-10pm, 230ptas). Buses also head to El Valle, Galdar, Moya, Casablanca, Lanzarote, Valsendero, Artenera, and Santa Brigida.

Ferries: Trasmediterránea (tel. 928 47 44 39; fax 928 26 30 77), **Fred Olson** (tel. 922 62 82 31 or 928 22 81 66), and **Naviera Armas** (tel. 928 26 70 00). Ferries depart from Muelle León y Castillo. Jetfoils depart from Muelle Santa Catalina. Tickets sold at the docks or any travel agency. For destinations and times, see **Getting Around**, p. 498.

Public Transportation: Central office, C. León y Castillo, 330 (tel. 928 44 64 99), off Parque Sta. Catalina. Open M-F 8am-2pm and 4-7:30pm. Yellow **Guaguas Municipales** travel within the city. Bus #1 runs 24hr. from Puerto de la Luz-Teatro Perez Galdós, passing Parque Sta. Catalina and Parque Sta. Telmo. Complete map of routes available at *guagua* offices and tourist offices. Individual ride 125ptas; 10-ride "bono" available at *estancos* (tobacco shops) for 745ptas.

Taxi: Radio Taxi (tel. 928 46 22 12). **Taxi Radio** (tel. 928 46 56 66).

Car Rental: Hertz, at the airport (tel. 928 57 95 77). Another branch at C. Bernardo de la Torre, 94 (tel. 928 22 64 97), in the new city. Ford Fiesta 4703ptas per day, including tax, insurance, and unlimited mileage. Min age 23. Cars can be taken to other islands.

TOURIST, FINANCIAL, AND LOCAL SERVICES

Tourist Offices: Main office (tel. 928 26 46 23), in front of Parque Sta. Catalina, in a colonial-style house. Helpful city maps and bus and ferry schedules. English and German spoken. Open M-F 9am-2pm. **Branch office,** in the old Ayuntamiento, across Pl. Sta. Ana from the cathedral. Open M-F 10am-5:30pm. **Centro de Iniciaturas y Turismo** (tel. 928 24 35 93), in Pueblo Canario. Open M-F 10am-1pm and 5-8pm.

Currency Exchange: Banco Central Hispano, C. Nicolás Estévanez, 5 (tel. 902 24 24 24). No commission. Open 8:30am-2pm. **ATMs** line Parque Sta. Catalina.

Laundromat: Lavesec, C. Joaquín Costa, 46 (tel. 928 27 46 17). Wash, dry, and iron (up to 7kg) 1000ptas. Open M-F 9am-1pm and 4-8pm, Sa 9am-3pm.

EMERGENCY AND COMMUNICATIONS

Emergency: tel. 091 or 092. **Police: Policía Municipal** (tel. 928 26 05 51), in Parque Sta. Catalina. **Policía Nacional,** C. Dr. Miguel Rosa, 25 (tel. 928 26 16 71).

Hospital: Hospital Insular, Pl. Dr. Pasteur, s/n (tel. 928 44 40 00). **Ambulance:** tel. 928 24 50 23. **Interclinic,** C. Sagasta, 62 (tel. 928 27 88 26 or 928 26 90 98). From Parque Sta. Catalina, turn left on C. Luis Morote, then right on C. Sagasta. A 24hr. emergency clinic geared towards tourists. English spoken.

Post Office: Main Office, Av. Primero de Mayo, 62 (tel. 928 36 13 20). Open M-F 8:30am-8:30pm, Sa 9:30am-2:30pm. **Branch Office,** C. Nicolás Estévanez. Open M-F 8:30am-7:30pm, Sa 9:30am-1pm. **Lista de Correos,** Pl. Comandante Ramón Franco, 1 (tel. 928 26 33 72), just behind the tourist office in Parque Sta. Catalina. Open M-F 8:30am-2:30pm, Sa 9:30am-1pm. **Postal Code:** 35007.

Internet Access: InterFred, C. Pío XII, 62 (tel. 928 24 42 86). From Parque Sta. Catalina, turn left on C. Luis Morote and left on C. Tomás Miller which turns into C. Pío XII. Fast connections, but limited computers. 900ptas per hr. Open daily 9am-1pm, 4-8pm.

▌ ACCOMMODATIONS

There are more beds than residents in Las Palmas, but apparently that's not enough. It's very difficult to find a place to stay without advance notice and nearly impossible during high season (Dec.-Feb., especially during *Carnaval*). Singles are limited, and solo travelers will often end up paying for a double. Since most accommodations are unimpressive, be sure to examine a room before committing to stay. Still, Las Palmas probably has the cheapest accommodations on the island.

Hotel Madrid, Pl. Cairasco, 4 (tel. 928 36 06 64; fax 928 38 21 76), in the Triana-Vegueta district, inland from C. Mayor; enter through the cafe on the plaza. Excellent location, close to the old town and bus station, with spacious rooms and clean bathrooms. Franco stayed in room #3 the night before the Civil War began. Singles 3500ptas, with bath 4500ptas; doubles 4500ptas, with bath 5500ptas.

Apartamentos Teide, C. Luis Morote, 42 (M-Sa tel. 928 27 23 12 or 928 27 23 08), 2 blocks from the beach. Tidy and simple rooms. 1-week min. stay. For stays less than 15 days, doubles 3000ptas per night; over 15 days doubles 2500ptas per night.

Pensión Plaza, C. Luis Morote, 16 (tel. 928 26 52 12), the red building facing Parque Sta. Catalina. Spacious and simple rooms are cool even in summer. Shielded from the nightly goings-on in the Parque. Reception 24hr. Reservations recommended. Singles 2200ptas, with bath 2700ptas; doubles 3200ptas, with bath 3700ptas.

Pensión Viera, C. Pedro Castillo, 9 (tel. 928 26 96 01). From Parque Sta. Catalina, turn left on C. Luis Morote, right on C. Sagasta, and right on C. Pedro Castillo. Quiet, cheap, and 1 block from the beach. Singles with bath 2000ptas; doubles with bath 2500ptas.

Camping: Camping Guantánamo (tel. 928 56 02 07), in Mogán (a port town in the south). See **Buses** for transportation information. 3rd-class site near a eucalyptus forest and a hunting zone. A camping utopia, with snack-bar, supermarket, restaurant, and pharmacy. 350ptas per person and per car, 400ptas per large tent.

▌ FOOD

Las Palmas's cuisine is as international as its fluctuating population. A typical night might involve eating Indian *tapas* and swinging to Moroccan pop music in an Irish pub. Typical Canarian fare is itself a mixture of Guanche, Spanish, and Latin American cuisines. The *plátanos* (bananas) of the Canaries are supposedly the best in the world, and fish dishes, usually served with *mojo verde* (green sauce), are fantastic. Most restaurants cater to tourists, serving German *paella*, hamburgers, and pizza. **Cruz Mayor,** a supermarket, has a branch on C. Nicolás Estévanez, 38, in the new city, and C. Pérez Galdós, 17, in the Triana district (both open M-Sa 8:30am-8:30pm). **Mercado de Vegueta,** C. Mendizábal, a sensory parade of fruit, dairy, fish, and olives stands, is open daily.

El Herreño, C. Mendizábal, 5 (tel. 928 31 05 13), just beyond the market in Vegueta. Typical Canarian cuisine. Fresh maritime *menús* (700-1200ptas) popular with the lively clientele. Monstrous salads 600-1400ptas. Open daily until 1am.

Hipócrates, C. Colón, 4 (tel. 928 22 64 15), across from Casa-Museo Colón in Vegueta. Romantic vegetarian dining with a simple and complete *menú*. The bathroom can be a mystical experience. Open daily 1-4:30pm and 8:30pm-12:30am.

La Strada, C. Tomás Miller, 58 (tel. 928 27 33 51). From Parque St. Catalina, go left on C. Luis Morote, left on C. Tomás Miller and look for the massive sign. You might have to elbow a few tour groups out of the way to get to the desserts (1350ptas). Huge portions. Open daily noon-4pm and 6-11pm.

👁 SIGHTS

⬛MUSEO CANARIO. The Museo Canario provides a comprehensive history of Guanche society. With one of the largest collections of Cro-Magnon skulls in the world, the second floor is a morbid sea of mummified natives and reconstructed skeletons. Other exhibits include tools and ritual stamps used to decorate bodies. *(C. Dr. Chil, 33, up C. Obispo Cobina. Tel. 928 31 56 00. Open M-F 10am-5pm, Sa-Su 10am-2pm. 500ptas, students 100ptas.)*

CATEDRAL DE SANTA ANA. This 16th-century Gothic structure is an amalgam of architectural styles. José Lujan Pérez, the Canaries' favorite sculptor, designed the Neoclassical facade. The three central naves are the same height, with a majestic dome towering above the crypt. Inside is the **Museo Diocesano del Arte Sacro,** with more Lujan Pérez works. In the **Capilla de Nuestra Señora de Los Dolores** lies the "incorruptible" body of Bishop Buenaventura Codina. *(C. Espiritu Santo, 20. From the bus stop, go left up C. Cavo Sotello and left on C. Obispo Cobina. Tel. 928 31 49 89. Open M-F 9am-1:30pm and 4-6:30pm, Sa 9am-2pm. 300ptas.)*

OLD CITY. Las Palmas's historic neighborhood is an island of colonial and neoclassical architecture, a sweet respite from the commercial buildings of the new city. In the 15th century, Juan Reton and the victorious Spanish set up camp in **Vegueta,** overlooking the Guiniguada Ravine. The old city now bristles with the sharp noises and smells of open markets, pedestrian malls, flower stores, and pet shops. *(Buses #1, 12, and 13 run from Parque Sta. Catalina to Vegueta.)*

PUEBLO CANARIO. The Pueblo Canario (Canarian Village) is a whitewashed wooden wonder built specifically for tourists. Designed in 1937 by painter Néstor Martín-Fernández de la Torre, the first Canarian painter to receive international recognition, and built by his brother Miguel, the *pueblo* has practically become a historic sight. Outdoor performances with traditional Canarian music and costumes take place biweekly. At one end of the *pueblo* is the ⬛**Museo Néstor,** a stunning collection of Néstor's beautiful, pudgy figures. His *Poema del Atlántico* (Poem of the Atlantic), a series of eight paintings, is considered his most important work. *(In Dorames Park, between Parque Sta. Telmo and Parque Sta. Catalina. Take bus #1, 15, or 41. Tel. 928 24 51 25. Open M-Tu and Th-F 10am-1pm and 4-7pm, Sa 10am-noon, Su 10:30am-1:30pm. 150ptas. Performances Th 5pm, Su 11:30am and 1pm.)*

🏖 BEACHES

The 3km **Playa de Las Canteras,** one of Europe's most famous beaches, is the only reason to stay in Las Palmas. The waters are wave-free, calmed by a mammoth barrier reef 200m out; sheltered from the sea, the resulting lagoon is known as "the world's largest swimming pool." Beach-goers enjoy tanning, swimming, scuba diving, surfing, and windsurfing. **Medusa Sub,** Bernardo de La Torre, 33 (tel. 928 26 27 86), specializes in diving, instructional courses, and equipment rental and sales (open M-F 11am-2pm and 5-9pm; Sa 11am-1pm and 6-8pm).

🎵 ENTERTAINMENT

Clubs in Las Palmas are filled with tourists looking for a story-worthy night. Discos are fairly standard, with overpriced drinks (around 600ptas), flashing lights, and thumping bass. Most nightlife spots (including karaoke bars) are located around the Parque Sta. Catalina. Take advantage of year-round outdoor terraces on Pl. España and along Po. Canteras. The latter are most attractive and popular at twilight, when the beach winds are still blowing. Solo travelers should be careful late at night. Though muggings are rare, avoid the risk by bringing a friend along. Las Palmas has over 70 **festivals** each year. During **Carnaval,** the Canaries lose what little sanity they may have had.

PLAYA DEL INGLÉS

Located on the southern tip of Gran Canaria, the famed Playa del Inglés and the surrounding shores are probably the best beaches in the Canaries. Even the weather is better—the sun still shines here when clouds obscure the rest of the island. Unfortunately, the secret is out; planeloads full of European tourists crowd the beaches every year. Beyond the swathes of rolling dunes in Maspalomas, the town of Playa del Inglés is a cement wasteland, a sea of supermarkets and international restaurants catering to overnight guests. Because of exorbitant accommodations prices, budget travelers are better off exploring the beaches and dunes as a day trip from Las Palmas. Buses run to: **Las Palmas** (#4, 5, 30, 61; 1hr., every 15min., 6:30am-9:30pm, 560ptas); **Puerto Rico** (#32, 39, 61; 30min., every 20min., 7am-8:30pm, 275ptas); **Puerto Mogan** (#32, 61; 30min., every 20min., 7am-8:30pm, 415ptas); the **airport** (#4, 5, 30, 61, 90; 40min., every 30min., 6:30am-9pm, 350ptas).

The Playa del Inglés, next to the town center, is the heart of the activity. Conveniently, one of the bus stops happens to be right in front of the **tourist office** (tel. 928 77 15 50), on Av. España near C. Estados Unidos (open M-F 9am-9pm). The beach offers nearly every water-related activity conceivable: parasailing, surfing (the current world-champion lives 5min. away), jet-skiing, scuba diving, and deep-sea fishing. **Water Sport Center** (tel. 928 76 66 83), in the Kabash shopping center, rents jetskis (from 5700ptas). **Tortuga** (tel. 928 77 02 18), Edificio Habitat, offers wreck-diving trips. To explore the dunes and surrounding areas, **Happy Biking** (tel. 928 76 82 98), Jumbo Center, rents mountain bikes (1500-2600ptas per day).

To the west of Playa del Inglés lie the sand dunes, a protected area thankfully off-limits to development. Though they are miraculously desolate, the dunes also hide a few **nudist beaches** (look for posted signs or naked flesh). Farther west is another flawless beach, the less crowded **Playa de Maspalomas.** Beyond, on the western coast, lie the rockier **Playa de la Mujer** and **Playa de las Meloneras.**

THE INTERIOR

Gran Canaria is not totally overrun by Euro-tourists—just a few kilometers inland from the coast, nary a word of English or German is spoken. **Utinsa buses** #205, 206, 209, and 210 run from the bus station in Las Palmas to **Arucas** (every 30min., 5:15am-10:15pm, 230ptas) Buses #216 and 218 run to most cities in the north of the island, including **Teror** (every 30min., 6:30am-10pm, 230ptas).

Arucas, a delightful mountain town set on a dormant volcano, has a stunning neo-Gothic church and a genuine, relaxed atmosphere—for those who can tear themselves away from the beach, it makes a perfect daytrip from Las Palmas. To get to the **tourist office** (tel. 928 60 58 16) from the bus station, walk uphill to the park, and head left to Pl. Constitución (open daily). There is one (and only one) place to stay in Arucas. A little *albergue* called **La Granja Escuela Anatol,** C. Ruz de Pineda, 5 (tel./fax 928 60 55 44), provides a home for scholars—and you, too, if you reserve in advance (3000ptas per person). Overlooking a set of gardens, the **Church of San Juan Bautista** is a magnificent structure almost wholly constructed by local stonemasons and artisans, though construction began in 1909 and wasn't completed until 1977. (Open daily 9am-1pm and 4-7pm. Free.) Pl. San Juan, the square next to the church, hosts a few cafes.

The quintessential Gran Canarian town, **Teror** is tucked away in the mountains. The town's church was built on the spot where 17th-century conquistador Don Juan de Frias saw a vision of the Virgin Mary. In the plaza facing the church is a small museum, **Casa de los Patrones de la Virgen,** built to resemble a 17th-century home. **Utinsa bus** #215 connects **Arucas** and Teror (every hr., 6am-9:55pm, 130ptas).

TENERIFE

Tenerife was aptly named from the Guanche words *tener*, meaning "snow," and *ife*, meaning "high mountain." Indeed, Tenerife is home to the tallest mountain in Spain, El Teide (3718m). During Spanish conquest, the island was divided up into nine distinct *menceyatos*, and each developed its own architecture and culture. Although the island is now united, its broken landscape is indicative of its diverse rural populace; the northern half of the island is a verdant and hilly garden, while the south is an arid and endless black-sand beach. Tenerife's interior offers the Canary's greatest hiking, a welcome escape from sunburnt beaches and sauerkraut *paella*. For those who long for still more seclusion, Santa Cruz and Los Cristianos provide transportation to the westernmost islands of El Hierro, La Palma, and La Gomera, not yet sacrificed to the lesser god of Tourism.

SANTA CRUZ DE TENERIFE

Before the Spanish Civil War, the government sent troublesome officers to out-of-the-way provinces. As a result, Franco became the General-in-Chief of the Canaries, scarring the port city of Santa Cruz (pop. 250,00) with the first shots of the Civil War. Although a somber cross commemorating the war-victims shadows the Plaza de España, the city focuses on the future. With an expanding tourist industry, the port is a steel sea of ferries, jetfoils, and freighters. Though it rivals Las Palmas in commercialism, Santa Cruz is comparatively scenic and pleasant.

▼ ORIENTATION AND PRACTICAL INFORMATION

Despite an extensive bus system, Santa Cruz is easily navigable by foot. The port city expands from the **Plaza de España,** the center of tourist and local life. C. Castillo continues from the plaza into the commercial districts. Av. José Primo de Rivera and Av. Francisco la Roche (which originate in Pl. España), separate the port and the city. To get to Pl. España from the **ferry terminals,** turn left on Av. Francisco la Roche (with your back to the terminal) and follow it to the plaza (15min.). From the **bus station,** turn right on Av. Tres de Mayo, left on Av. de José Antonio Primo, and continue to the plaza (15min.).

Flights: See **Getting There and Away** and **Getting Around**, p. 497, for info on flights to, from, and around the islands. There are two airports on Tenerife. The majority of national flights head to the northern airport, **Los Rodeos,** while international flights dominate the south's larger **Reina Sofía** airport. Los Rodeos (tel. 922 25 23 50) is a few kilometers west of Santa Cruz. From Los Rodeos, buses #102, 107, and 108 run to town (20min., every 20min., 6am-midnight, 150ptas). From Reina Sofía (tel. 922 77 00 50), bus #341 heads to town (every hr., 5:30am-12:10am, 230ptas). **Iberia** (tel. 922 28 11 12). **Spanair** (tel. 922 63 58 13). **Air Europa** (tel. 922 75 92 94).

Buses: TITAS (tel. 922 21 56 99) serves all major towns from **Estación de Guaguas,** Av. Tres de Mayo, 47, down C. José Antonio Rivera from Pl. España. Some lines do not run during the summer, so call ahead for information. To **Puerto de la Cruz** (#102 and 103; 1hr., every hr., 6am-midnight, 500ptas) and **Los Cristianos/Playa de América** (#110 and 111; 1hr., every 30min., 5:30am-11pm, 600-875ptas). Those planning to explore the island by bus should consider buying the **bono ticket** (2000ptas). The amount deducted from the card per ride is less than the cost of individual tickets.

Ferries: Trasmediterránea (tel. 922 24 30 11). See **Getting Around,** p. 498.

Car Rental: Agencies are sprinkled throughout Santa Cruz, congregating around Pl. España. **Autos ADA,** C. Emilo Calzada, 10 (tel. 922 27 49 53; fax 922 24 27 56). Cheapest car 4000ptas per day, including insurance and taxes. Open M-F 8am-1pm and 4-7pm, Sa 8am-2pm and 4-6pm, Su 9am-noon. **Avis** (tel. 903 135 531 or 913 480 348), at their office at the airport. 4650ptas per day.

Tourist Office: (tel. 922 23 95 92), Pl. España. Modern and breezy interior filled with stacks of brochures. The free map, though it lacks an index, is indispensable. Open July-Sept. M-F 8am-5pm and Sa 9am-noon; Oct.-June M-F 8am-6pm, Sa 9am-1pm.

Police: Av. Tres de Mayo, 72 (tel. 922 60 60 92).

Hospital: Hospital Militar, at C. Ramón y Cajal and C. Gral. Galcerán. From Pl. España, turn left on C. Murillo, right on C. Angel Guimera, and left on C. Gral. Galcerán.

Post Office: Pl. España, 2 (tel. 922 24 20 02). Open M-F 8:30am-8:30pm, Sa 9:30am-2pm. **Postal Code:** 38002.

Internet Access: Ciber El Navegante, C. Combate, 10. A bar with a few computers in the corner. 400ptas per 30min. From Pl. España, take C. Béthencourt Alfonso and its continuations. Turn right on C. Combate; look on the right. Open M-Sa 1-10:30pm.

ACCOMMODATIONS

Unfortunately for budget travelers, hostels and *pensiones* in Santa Cruz are few and far between. What does exist fills up quickly, so reserve in advance. C. Castillo and C. Bethencourt Alfonso are scattered with one- and two-star hotels which are both luxurious and pricey. The tourist office has lists of accommodations, and their map marks hotels. Surprisingly, accommodations are even more difficult to come by elsewhere in Tenerife; to avoid further hassle consider reserving for a few days in Santa Cruz and exploring the rest of the island on daytrips.

Hotel Horizonte, C. Sta. Rosa de Lima, 11 (tel. 922 27 19 36). Simple rooms, all with bath. The cool lounge has huge wicker chairs and bright curtains. Singles 2400ptas, with double bed 3500ptas; doubles 5225ptas.

Pensión Mova, C. San Martín, 33 (tel. 922 28 32 61). From Pl. España, take C. Marina and turn right onto C. San Martín. As cheap as they come in Santa Cruz. Multiple floors of clean but charmless rooms. Singles 1700ptas; doubles 3200ptas.

Hotel Oceano, C. Castillo, 6 (tel. 922 27 08 00 or 922 27 08 04). Take C. Castillo from Pl. España. A marble extravaganza. Each room has a mini-bar, TV, and phone. Breakfast included. Singles 4500ptas; doubles 8000-9500ptas. Visa, AmEx.

Hotel Anago, C. Imeldo Serís, 19 (tel. 922 24 50 90). From the plaza, go left on C. General Gutierrez and right on C. Imeldo Serís. Spacious and spartan rooms with new TVs. Singles 3300ptas, with bath 4300ptas; doubles 5700ptas, with bath 6950ptas.

FOOD

Santa Cruz's restaurants are the unfortunate result of the city's burgeoning international tourist industry; *casas de china*, waikiki bars, and German *paella* spots line the streets. Cafes, restaurants, and bars crowd Pl. España, but Av. Francisco has better deals and chic *terrazas*. The **Mercado de Nuestra Señora de Africa,** across the river and one block inland from the Museo de la Naturaleza y el Hombre (see **Sights,** below), sells meat and produce (open most mornings).

Restaurante Da Gigi, Av. Francisco, 43. Lively *terraza* overlooking the port. Monstrous salads 600-950ptas. Scrumptious risottos 700-900ptas. Pasta dishes from 600ptas. Pizzas 750ptas. Open daily 1-5pm, 8pm-1am. Visa, MC.

Ristorante Da Orazio, C. Candaleria, 22 (tel 922 29 01 81), off Pl. Candaleria. Airy, coral interior lures a chic crowd; creative pizzas (600-1200ptas) keep them coming. Pastas 800-1100ptas. Open M-Sa 12:30-4:30pm and 7:30-11:30pm. Visa, AmEx.

Bar Restaurante La Taberna del Puerto, C. La Marina, 4 (tel. 922 27 69 95). Offers a simple and traditional *menú* with fresh fish just hauled in from the port below (700-1400ptas). Tasty and cheap *bocadillos* 200-300ptas. Open daily 8am-midnight.

🏖 SIGHTS AND BEACHES

The city's museums and sights serve as little more than distracting beach breaks for Santa Cruz's sunburnt tourists.

MUSEO DE LA NATURALEZA Y EL HOMBRE. This museum, which devotes itself to the natural sciences of the Canaries, displays Guanche mummies. It also accomplishes the impressive task of making what is essentially a big rock collection seem interesting. *(On C. San Sebastián, across from the river bed. Tel. 922 20 93 20. Open Tu-Su 10am-8pm. 400ptas, students 100ptas. Sunday free.)*

MUSEO DE BELLES ARTES. The old masters that adorn the walls contrast the museum's island canvases and sculptures. Check out the weapons collection. *(On C. Hervas Villalba, near Pl. España. Tel. 922 24 43 58. Open M-F 10am-7:30pm. 400ptas, students 100ptas.)*

OTHER SIGHTS. Santa Cruz is graced by two churches, the 16th-century **Iglesia de la Concepción** and the 17th-century **Iglesia de San Francisco.** *(Iglesia de la Concepción, 3 blocks south of Pl. España. Iglesia de San Francisco, 1 block inland on C. Hervas Villalba.)* The **Parque Garcia Sanabria** doubles as an impressive botanical garden. It houses plants from around the world and an open-air sculpture museum featuring avant-garde sculptures by Pablo Serrano, Rafael Soto, and Gustavo Torner. *(In the city's northwest corner.)*

BEACHES. As on Gran Canaria, the beaches are the island's true attraction. The black sand of **Almáciga, Benijo,** and **Las Gaviotas,** and the golden sand of **Las Teresitas,** an artificial beach, lie nearby. All beaches are accessible by frequent buses departing from the central bus station.

🎵 ENTERTAINMENT

Santa Cruz's nightlife is much calmer than that of Las Palmas. Bars and *terrazas* line C. José Antonio Rivera along the waterfront. Two discos to the north of Pl. España, **Nocturna Anaga,** Av. Anaga, 37, and **Tosca,** Av. Anaga, 41, spin vinyl for sunburned tourists until the wee hours of the morning. Santa Cruz is infamous for its celebration of **Carnaval,** the week before Lent. After a week of lavish costumed celebration, the town buries a large fake sardine.

LOS CRISTIANOS
AND PLAYA DE LAS AMÉRICAS

The man-made Playa de las Américas and the gray-sand Los Cristianos, on the southern tip of Tenerife, are the most-touristed beaches on the Canaries. Developed into full-fledged tourist resorts in the 1960s and 70s, the towns probably have more five-star hotels than residents. Although their sandy beaches are hardly the equals of Fuerteventura's, they feature better dining and nightlife than Tenerife's other tourist spots. Beyond their own more than respectable beaches, Las Américas and Los Cristianos can serve as a base for exploring other shores in the south, including **Playa del Médano,** one of Tenerife's best and a windsurfing hotspot. They also serve as the departure point for ferries to Gomera.

🗺 **ORIENTATION AND PRACTICAL INFORMATION.** Although Playa de las Américas and Los Cristianos are actually two separate towns, they are considered one by tourists and tourist offices alike. **Paseo Marítima** connects Playa de las Américas to its southern neighbor Los Cristianos. Ferries leave from the port in Los Cristianos, connecting Tenerife to the western islands. **Fred Olson** (tel. 922 79 05 56) and **Trasmediterránea** (tel. 902 45 46 45) run ferries to **San Sebastián** and **Valle Gran Rey** (on Gomera), **Valverde** (on El Hierro) and **Santa Cruz** (on La Palma). For more info, see **Getting Around,** page 498. The bus station (tel. 922 79 54 27) is on Ctra. General in Playa de las Américas. Buses run to **Santa Cruz** (every 30min.,

6:15am-11pm), **Puerto de la Cruz** (#343; 4 per day, 9am-5:45pm), and the **Reina Sofía airport** (#487; every hr., 7:20am-9:20pm, 275ptas). Buses #110 and 111 link Playa de las Américas and Los Cristianos. From the station, take C. República de Domínica and turn right on Av. Rafael Puig to get to the center of town. For car rental, try **Hertz,** C. Cial Paraison Royal, 26 (tel. 922 79 23 20), in Playa de las Américas (4494ptas per day, insurance included. Must be over 25).

   Tourist office, Av. Rafael Puig, 1 (tel. 922 75 06 33), in Playa de las Américas. **Police** (tel. 922 79 78 50), Av. Valle Menéndez, in Los Cristianos (from Av. Marítima, take C. General Franco, turn right on C. Barranquillo, and left on Av. Valle Menéndez); **medical services: Salud Medical Clinic** (tel. 922 79 12 53), C. República Dominica, in Los Cristianos (from Av. Marítima, head to Pl. Américas, turn right on Av. Litoral and right again on C. República Domínica). **Post office,** C. Sabandenos (open M-F 8:30am-2:30pm, Sa 9:30am-1pm); **postal code:** 38650

ACCOMMODATIONS AND FOOD. Pl. Américas is full of resort hotels, so unless you're planning to splurge, stick to C. General Franco in Los Cristianos. Although there are quite a few *pensiones*, they are almost always full, so be sure to call ahead. **Pensión La Playa,** C. Palmoa, 9 (tel. 922 79 07 69), off Av. Marítima, offers surprisingly quiet rooms, a welcome relief from the beach-party below. (Singles 3300ptas.) **Pensión Corisa,** C. Antigua del General Franco, 18 (tel. 922 79 07 69), connected to C. General Franco, a few blocks inland from Av. Marítima, has dark, small rooms and a boisterous restaurant below. (Singles 2000ptas.) Food in both areas caters to international taste buds and big budgets, but is marginally better in Los Cristianos. **Supermercado Carolina** (tel. 922 79 30 69), C. General Franco, is a friend to the budget traveler (open M-Sa 8am-2pm and 4-8:30pm; Visa).

BEACHES AND ENTERTAINMENT. Even if there were museums, they wouldn't distract the crowds from the infinite mini-malls and duty-free shops that surround the ultimate sight—the beach. Although Playa de las Américas appears on more postcards, the beach in Los Cristianos is less crowded. Either way, you will tan. Information kiosks fringe each beach, full of fliers for **water sports, fishing,** and **scuba diving. Naútica Eurocanaria** (tel. 922 71 26 45) offers **parasailing** (solo 4000ptas, tandem 7000ptas). **The Yellow Boat** (tel. 922 75 24 16) has three daily departures for **whale-watching** (handicapped accessible; multi-lingual tours). **Nightlife** is a collage of fluorescent lights, bikini contests, and imported beer (averaging a pricey 400ptas). Both towns have plenty of two-story discos, illuminated by their flashing neon signs. Bars, which often have theme nights, also line the main drags.

PUERTO DE LA CRUZ

Although this port town (pop. 25,000) blatantly gears itself toward international tourists, its colorful streets are surprisingly enjoyable. Draped with tropical flowers, peeling boats, and banana stands, the waterfront succeeds in combining commercialism with old-world charm, a quality that both Santa Cruz and Las Palmas lack. Once a capital of the wine trade and an important 17th-century connection to the New World, Puerto de la Cruz draws an eclectic mix of sailors and visitors: the steep streets are filled with African vendors, Spanish fishermen, tanned Europeans, and some unusually large lizards.

ORIENTATION AND PRACTICAL INFORMATION. Puerto de la Cruz wraps around a port, expanding from Playa San Telmo and the nerve-center, **Plaza del Charco.** To get to Pl. Charco from the **bus station,** turn right on C. Pozo (with your back to the station), continue as it turns into C. Dr. Ingram, and turn left on C. Blanc (10min.). **Buses,** C. Pozo, 1 (tel. 922 38 18 07) go to: **La Orotava** (#350; 30min., every hr., 6:30am-1:10am, 130ptas); **Santa Cruz** (#101, 102 and 103; 1hr., every 30 min., 6am-midnight, 500ptas); **Playa de las Américas** (#343; 1 hr., 4 per day, 9am-5:40pm, 2500 ptas); **El Teide** (#348; 1½hr., 1 per day, 9:15am, 1800ptas). Find help at the **tourist office** (tel. 922 17 60 02), in Pl. Europa. From Pl. Charco, head towards the port on C. Blanco and turn right on C. Santo Domingo; the office is on the left. (Open M-F 9am-7pm, Sa 9am-noon.) **Emergency:** tel. 091 or 092; **police,** (tel. 922 38 12 24), in Pl. Europa; **Hospital Tamaragua** (tel. 922 38 05 12 or 900 20 01 45), on the corner of C. Bethencourt and C. Valois (from Pl. Charco, go right on C. Blanco (away from the port) and left on C. Valois; open 24hr.) **Post Office,** C. Pozo, 14 (tel. 922 38 58 02), across from the bus station (open M-F 8:30am-2:30pm, Sa 9:30am-1pm); **postal code:** 38400. **Internet access: Hotel Melia** (tel. 922 34 28 85), C. Calzada de Martínez. From Pl. Charco, go right on C. Blanco (away from the port), left on C. Valois, right up C. Hoya, and follow the steep stairs to the hotel. (First min. free; 599ptas for each additional 6min. Credit card only.)

■ ■ **ACCOMMODATIONS AND FOOD.** *Pensiones* are comfortable and plush in Puerta del Cruz—reserve in advance if you don't want to pay hotel prices. An excellent option is **Pensión la Platanera,** C. Blanco, 29 (tel. 922 38 41 57), off Pl. Charco and towards the mountains. Plain rooms overlook a stunning tropical garden. (Doubles 4900ptas.) **Pensión los Geranios,** C. Lomo, 14 (tel. 922 38 28 10). From Pl. Charco, turn left on C. Felipe, right on C. Perez Zamora, and left on C. Lomo. Newly renovated rooms with sparkling bathrooms. (3500-4500ptas per person.) You can't go wrong with the cafes on C. San Telmo and in Pl. Charco. Supermarkets can be found on nearly every street hugging the port. Try **Mi Vaca y Yo,** C. Cruz Verde, 3 (tel. 922 38 52 47), off C. Lomo near the port. A jungle of floors, skylights, plants, and fish tanks. (Open daily 1-4pm and 7pm-1am. Visa, AmEx.)

■ ■ **SIGHTS AND ENTERTAIMENT.** The parade of flowers, tourists, bathing suits and palm trees makes Puerta de la Cruz a sight in itself. Although there are not many historic sights to visit, a walking tour of the city, finishing on the water, is an afternoon well spent. The pedestrian streets and port are lined with vendors, selling everything from beach towels to "authentic" Guanche artifacts. Next to Pl. Europa, fishermen display their latest catches and older women sell bunches of tropical plants. The **Museo Arqueológico** specializes in Guanche ceramics. Surprisingly interesting exhibits replicate the processes and ceremonies used by the prehistoric natives to produce pots, urns, jewelry, and decorations. (C. Lomo, 9. Tel. 922 37 14 65. Open Tu-Sa 10am-1pm and 5-8pm, Su 10am-1pm. 150ptas, students 75ptas.) Although there is a dearth of beaches, **Lago Martiánez,** a water park of pools and fountains, designed by Cesar Manrique (see **Cesar Manrique,** p. 519), fills the tanning void. Nearby **Playa Martiánez** contains Guanche caves. The wealthy resorts and sky-rise motels produce quite a virile **nightlife.** Discos, platform shoes, and exotic fruit drinks spill out onto C. Hoya, drying up around dawn. Although high-season peaks in the winter months, the **Fiestas de Julio,** 2 weeks of colorful streamers and lights, lure even more tourists in July.

NEAR PUERTO DE LA CRUZ: LA OROTAVA

Named after the lush valley that spreads out below its balconies, La Orotava warrants a daytrip from Puerto de la Cruz. Seventeenth- and eighteenth-century nobility resided here, leaving a number of elegant squares, streets, and churches renowned for their artistic balconies. If you intend to visit the sights, plan a weekday for the jaunt—most establishments are closed on weekends. Bus #350 runs from **Puerto de la Cruz** (30min., every hr., 6:30am-1:10am, 130ptas). From the bus station, follow C. Calvario and its continuations to the **tourist office,** C. Carrera del Escultor Estevanez, 2 (tel. 922 27 85 10; open M-F 10am-6pm).

The tourist office map cites over 15 houses and churches; though it would take forever to see them all, the following walking-tour should take two hours. From the tourist office, turn left down C. Tomás Zerolo to find **Iglesia de Santo Domingo,** whose chapel houses several notable paintings and a museum examining Spain's role in Latin America. (Church open during mass; free. Museo open M-F 9am-6pm, Sa 9am-2pm; 250ptas.) **Iglesia de la Concepción**, off C. Cologon, is perhaps the Canaries' most graceful Baroque building. Rebuilt in the late 18th century after earthquakes ravaged it, the church has a marble dome over the altar and its myriad works. Especially delicate is Angelo Olivari's rendition of the Conception. Check out the church's collection of jewels brought over from the Americas. (Open M-Sa 9am-1pm, 4-8pm. Free.) From the church, go uphill on C. Tomás Pérez and right on C. Carrera to see the neo-classical **Palacio Municipal** and the **Plaza del Ayuntamiento.** The cobblestones in the plaza are the result of regal egotism—Alfonso XIII ordered the streets paved before he visited. Just up C. Tomás Perez, the sensory explosion of **Hijuela del Botánico,** behind iron gates, offers celestial walkways through manicured displays of tropical flora. (Open M-F 8am-2pm. Free.)

▨EL TEIDE NATIONAL PARK

Towering 3178m over Tenerife, Spain's highest peak presides over a vast, unspoiled wilderness. El Teide itself forms the northern ridge of a much larger volcano that erupted millions of years ago; the remaining 16km-wide crater only hints at the size of the explosion. The beginnings of Tenerife's tourism can be traced to the mountain, as European doctors marveled at the serenity and the purity of the air, recommending that their patients vacation nearby. Although continuing to shift and evolve on the plates below, today El Teide and the sandy southern plateaus of **Las Canadas** shadow some of the most vibrant wildflower fields on earth (see **Wildflowers of El Teide,** below). El Teide also offers hiking trails of all levels.

The park is accessible by **bus** from Puerto de La Cruz. Bus #348 departs from the station at 9:15am and leaves El Teide at 4pm (1½hr., 1800ptas). Consider renting a **car,** as it provides more flexibility and allows exploration of the wildly different but equally beautiful views of the eastern (from Puerto de la Cruz) and western (from Los Cristianos) access roads. Bus #348 stops at the **Parador** and the nearby **visitor's center,** which offers free brochures and maps. The center has an informative video and an interesting book collection. (Open daily 9:15am-4pm).

The variety in geology, climate, and flora you will experience is almost as overwhelming as the exhausting landscapes. The Parador occupies an idyllic setting next to the emblematic **Roques de García** (2140m), rock chimneys and remnants of volcanic eruptions that face their creators, Mt. Teide and Pico Viejo.

However, for both the native Guanches and daily visitors, **El Teide** itself inspires the awe. The volcanic activity convinced the Guanches that El Teide was the home of evil spirits. But even then, the mountain was nowhere near its peak, as geologists believe it once reached over 5000m. The slow sinking has produced the park's most unique features, including the crumbling **Caldera,** a crater with a diameter of 17km. In 1798, during the last major eruption, lava seeped down the slopes of **Pico Viejo** (3102m). **Las Canadas,** comprised of collapsed craters, is another evocative product of the sinking process. Watch out for the **Lagarto Tizon,** a rather large lizard lurking in the park.

Once in the park, you'll have ample opportunity to ponder "our miserly insignificance," as the Spanish park service puts it, as you gaze across the eerie and enchanting volcanic landscape. A **cable car** climbs the final 1000m up to El Teide's peak (daily 9am-5pm; 2100ptas, children 1000ptas). Nine free guided **hikes** depart daily. Hikes vary in difficulty, although inexperienced hikers are not recommended to attempt any of the longer routes. Those who want to participate in the guided hikes must call the national park information service (tel. 922 29 01 29 or 922 29 01 83) and reserve ahead. Eight **unguided hikes** allow for independent pacing and meandering. All visitors are encouraged to follow the designated paths. Hikes to the peak require two days; walkers spend the night at **Refugio Altavista,** past the Montana Blanca. The summit is difficult to reach in the winter, especially since the refuge is only open from March to October.

Note that the 2km of earth between you and sea level exacerbate the normal strains of hiking; be sure to bring plenty of water and sunscreen. In the winter, the park is usually covered by a shimmering white coat of snow and hiking is restricted by mist and snowstorms. It's always a good idea to call ahead for conditions and bring surplus food and water.

> **WILDFLOWERS OF EL TEIDE** From the peaks of El Teide, the landscape below resembles an Impressionist painting, with splotches of decadent colors blurring the horizon. The park also doubles as a botany exhibit, filled with both flowers native to the park and those emblematic of the Canary Islands. Unique to these rocky slopes are the *Rosal del Guanche* rosebush and the *Violeta del Teide*, which grows right after the snow melts. *Viper Bugloss* is a spiky plant at almost 3m, showering the shorter *White Broom* and *Canary Mustard* with red and blue blossoms. Small green patches of coarse *Hierba Pajonera*, a species of grass, are also common.

FUERTEVENTURA

Named Fuerteventura after the "strong winds" that whip along the western coast, the island is the second largest in the archipelago. While goat farms, fallen windmills, and whitewashed villages speckle the island's interior, massive resorts dominate it's exquisite beaches. Although conqueror Jean de Béthencourt established a permanent base here in the 15th century, Fuerteventura has had a relatively quiet history, save for the occasional pirate raid. Today, its coastal resorts, towering sand dunes, and nudist beaches attract Europeans by the jumbo-jet.

PUERTO DEL ROSARIO

Until 1957, Fuerteventura's whitewashed capital was known as Puerto de Cabras (Goats' Harbor) for the abundance of, you guessed it, goats. Although goats may still outnumber citizens, Puerto del Rosario (pop. 17,000) has continued to grow as an important port and fishing center since its founding in the 18th century. Lined with cement houses, the modest neighborhoods border on bleak—visitors will want to do little more than pass through the city on their way to fairer sands.

■ ORIENTATION AND PRACTICAL INFORMATION

Everything in Puerto del Rosario is within easy walking distance. **Calle León y Castillo** is the main thoroughfare, running downhill to the port and ferry station. **Avenida Primero de Mayo,** which runs perpendicular to C. Léon y Castillo, is the town's commercial center, lined with banks, stereo stores and *panaderías*.

TRANSPORTATION
Ferries: Transmediterránea and **Naviera Armas** run frequent ferries to and from Las Palmas. See **Getting Around,** p. 498.

Buses: Tiadhe (tel. 928 85 21 66) stops at Av. Constitución and C. Léon y Castillo. To: **Morro Jable** (#2; 2 hr., 5 per day, 7am-7pm, 1055ptas); **Bentacuria** (#2; 45min., 2 per day, 10am and 2pm, 410ptas); **airport** (#2; 20min., 13 per day, 7am-8pm, 130ptas).

Taxis: (tel. 928 85 00 59 or 928 85 02 16). 800ptas from the airport to the town center.

Car Rental: Orlando has offices at the airport (tel. 928 86 90 18) and on C. Carrero Blanco in Corralejo (tel. 928 53 50 24). From 3400ptas per day, including insurance. Min. age 21.

TOURIST, LOCAL, AND FINANCIAL SERVICES
Currency Exchange: Banco Central Hispano, C. Primero de Mayo, 46 (tel. 928 85 02 48). Open M-F 8:30am-2pm.

Tourist Office: Av. Constitución, 5 (tel. 928 53 08 44), down the street from the bus station, 2 blocks from Av. Primero de Mayo. Glossy brochures of all the islands and a handy map of Fuerteventura's major towns. Open M-F 8am-2pm.

Emergency: tel. 091 or 092. **Police:** C. 23 de Mayo, 16 (tel. 928 85 05 03).

Hospital: Fuerteventura's main hospital is on Ctra. Aeropuerto.

Post Office: C. Primero de Mayo, 58 (tel. 928 85 04 12). Open M-F 8:30am-8:30pm, Sa 9:30am-1pm. **Postal Code:** 35600.

ACCOMMODATIONS AND FOOD

Unprepared budget travelers might find themselves stationed in Puerto del Rosario for a night or two until accommodations in other, more scenic towns open up. Rooms here are as cheap as they come in the Canaries. Though they have little charm, they make up for it with tons of amenities—TVs, phones, and full baths are standard. The majority of the budget accommodations reside near the port, around C. Almirante Lallermand.

Hostal Tamasite, C. Léon y Castillo, 9 (tel. 928 85 06 18). Lovely rooms right near the waterfront, complete with new TVs and phones. Bathrooms with massive tubs may even prove more alluring than the beach. Singles 3800ptas; doubles 5000ptas.

Apartamentos Rubén Tinguaro, C. Juan XXIII, 48 (tel. 928 85 10 88). From Av. Primero de Mayo, turn right on C. Léon y Castillo, following its continuation C. Almirante Laller-mand, and left on C. Juan XXIII. Although situated in a bleak, empty neighborhood, apartments are comfortable and have TVs. Singles 3000ptas; doubles 4500ptas.

Pensión Macario, C. Juan de Austria, 24 (tel. 928 85 11 97). Take C. Leon y Castillo, follow it as it becomes C. Almirante Lallermand, and turn left on C. Juan XXIII. Owner provides tidy, spartan rooms. The restaurant below is a bit noisy. Doubles 2625ptas.

Food in Puerto del Rosario is equally standard; *cafeterías* are scattered along Av. Primero de Mayo and C. Léon y Castillo.

Getaria Taberna, C. Guise, 3, on a small alley next to Hostal Tamasite. Blue walls and antique photos surround the chic patrons while they pinch at specialty *tapas* (100-800ptas) and sip regional wines (250-500ptas). Open daily 11am-4pm and 9pm-6am.

SIGHTS AND ENTERTAINMENT

Though Puerto del Rosario is an island capital and important port, it offers few diversions. Locals will even tell you that the beaches are sandboxes compared to Corralejo's. The town's only museum, **Casa Museo de Unamuno,** displays various furnishings and books used by the exiled philosopher Miguel de Unamuno. (C. Rosario 11. Open M-F 9am-1pm, Sa 10am-1:30pm. Free.) Although the town houses the barracks of the Spanish Foreign Legion, the **nightlife** is limited to little more than a beer at an average bar. For discos and dancing, head to Corralejo.

CORRALEJO

Although the main drag may look and sound like a street in Munich, Corralejo's (pop. 4400) level of tourism is tame compared to that of its neighbors. To the south, protected sand dunes unfolding into the crystal ocean remain the main attraction. Corralejo is an excellent daytrip from Puerto del Rosario, as it offers sun, water-sports, and people-watching. Daily jetfoils to Playa Blanca in Lanzarote make the town a necessary stop en route to Lanzarote.

◼ ORIENTATION AND PRACTICAL INFORMATION. All activity extends from **Avenida General Franco,** where sunburned tourists walk from the sand dunes in the south to their apartments in the north. **Fred Olsen** and **Naviera Armas** run daily **jetfoils** to **Playa Blanca, Lanzarote** (see **Getting Around,** p. 498). To get to the **port** take Av. General Franco (with the beach on the right) until it ends. Turn left, then right on C. José Segura Torres, and then right on C. Gral. García Escamez (20min.). **Tiadhe** runs **buses** from the **station** (tel 928 85 21 66), off C. Lepanto, to **Puerto del Rosario** (#6; 45min., every 30min., 7am-10pm, 360ptas). From the bus station, C. Lepanto (5min.) leads to Av. General Franco. For a **taxi,** call 928 86 61 08. Anyone who has had a license for at least 2 years can rent a **car** from **Autos Hernández,** C. Antonio Hernández Paez, 9 (tel. 928 86 70 67; 4500-8000ptas per day; Visa, MC, AmEx.). The **tourist office** is in Pl. Grande de Corralejo, at the end of Av. General Franco (open M-F 9am-1pm and 4:30-7:30pm, Sa 9am-noon). **Emergency:** tel. 062; **police** (tel. 928 86 61 07), on Po. Atlántico, near the intersection with Av. General Franco; **hospital: International Medical Center,** Av. General Franco, 13 (tel. 928 53 64 32; open M-Sa 9am-8:30pm, Su 10am-1pm). **Post office,** C. Lepanto, 19 (tel. 928 53 50 55; open M-F 8:30am-2:30pm, Sa 9:30am-1pm); **postal code:** 35660; **internet access: Internet Saloon,** C. Antonio Hernández Paez, 18 (tel. 928 53 63 97), off Av. General Franco (1000ptas per hr.; open M-Sa 9am-1pm and 5-8pm).

▓▐ ACCOMMODATIONS AND FOOD. Apartments and hotels line the beach, but budget accommodations are rare. Unless you reserve ahead, you might find yourself back in Puerto Rosario for the night. **Hostal Manhattan,** C. Gravina, 23 (tel. 928 86 66 43), a left off Av. General Franco when heading toward the port, offers plain, cool rooms, all with bath. Although the hostel is often noisy, with these prices you can afford earplugs. (Singles 2500ptas; doubles 4000ptas.) For more peaceful lodgings, try **Apartamentos Hoplaco,** Av. General Franco, 45 (tel. 928 86 60 40), which has simple rooms surrounding a quiet and flowered courtyard. Access to a small beach sets it apart from the hundred other complexes in town. (Reception open daily 10am-2pm. Studios for 1-2 people 4000ptas; apartments for 1-2 people 4800ptas; triples 5800ptas.)

Unfortunately, food in Corralejo is not much better than anywhere else on the islands. Restaurants on the waterfront are cheaper. Try **Casa Galicia** (tel. 928 53 90 88), C. Gerardo Estevez Martín, off Av. General Martín. This loud and colorful break from the touristed bistros serves large salads (1000ptas), seafood (425-1950ptas), and a typical Spanish *menú* (1000ptas). Visa and MC accepted. For picnic supplies, try **Los Corales Supermarket,** Av. General Franco, 40 (tel. 928 86 70 43; open M-Sa 9am-9:30pm, Su 2-9pm).

◢▐ BEACHES AND ENTERTAINMENT. Like nearby Morro Jable, Corrajelo offers little beyond the beach. The **Parque Natural de Corralejo y Lobos** contains 10km of protected and rugged sand dunes for walking or simply soaking up the sun's rays. Although nudists occupy the many rock structures, all are welcome regardless of attire. Adventure companies reside along Av. General Franco, catering to all athletic tastes and abilities. **Dive Centre** (tel. 928 53 59 06), C. Nuestra Señora del Pino, offers daily dive trips, lessons, and equipment rental. **Celia Cruz** (tel. 610 86 48 91) rigs daily trips on catamarans with glass bottoms for underwater viewing (1300-5000ptas per person). **Ventura Surf** (tel. 928 86 62 95), in the Apartamentos Hoplaco complex on Av. General Franco, rents windsurfing equipment (4800ptas per day) and offers a five-hour beginner's course (15,000ptas). **Nightlife** is a spectacle of tipsy tourists and leering locals. Bars tend towards the cliché, with surf or pub themes. Bar-hop along Av. General Franco and in the connecting shopping centers. Closer to the port, several live music venues spill decent tunes and a more authentic crowd into the breezy night air. The **Fiestas del Carmen** in July make for a particularly lively visit. During the festival, volleyball competitions, outdoor dances, and parades celebrate the town's patron saint.

BETANCURIA

An escape from the arid and touristed coast line, Fuerteventura's amber interior reveals rocky villages, small farms, and fallen windmills. Betancuria, self-named by the modest Jean de Béthencourt, carves itself into the side of a dormant volcano. From the bus stop it's an easy walk to the central **Iglesia de Santa Maria.** The blinding white stone edifice houses an impressive collection of relics and golden altars. The original church, dating from the 15th century, was destroyed during a pirate attack. Down the street on C. Roberto Roldán is the simple **Museo Arqueológico** (tel. 928 87 82 41). The most notable pieces of the otherwise unimpressive collection are the artifacts from the **Majos,** the islands' earliest inhabitants. (Church and museum open M-Sa 10am-5pm, Su 11am-2pm. 100ptas includes entry to the two sights.) Only two **buses** (#2; 45min., 10am and 2pm, 410ptas) run each day from Puerto del Rosario, so plan your trip wisely.

MORRO JABLE

Although rumored to be the site of buried German treasure, the only foreign gold in Morro Jable (pop. 6500) drips off the wrists of the peninsula's many tourists. The town is home to some of the Canaries' most heavenly beaches. This former fishing village, overlooking white sand and turquoise waters, shelters thousands of sun-starved Europeans every year. Unfortunately for tourist-a-phobes, Morro Jable is a necessary stop between the peninsula and northern towns.

◪ ORIENTATION AND PRACTICAL INFORMATION. Morro Jable is unique among Spanish towns for its lack of a central square. Instead, it spreads along the beach, with local life to one side and resorts to the other. **Avenida Jandia,** which becomes **Avenida del Saladar,** connects the two streets. **Centro Comercial de Jandia** and most hotels and restaurants line these two streets. Most of the town's roads inevitably lead to the beach. The **port** is located about 1km out of town. Though there is no bus station in town, **Tiadhe buses** (tel. 928 85 21 66) stop at the Centro Commercial de Jandia, on C. Gambuesas (across from the post office), and throughout town. Buses run to **Costa Calma** (#5; 1hr., 11 per day, 8:30am-9pm, 400-500ptas) and **Puerto del Rosario** (#1; 2hr., 8 per day, 6am-7pm, 1055ptas). **Taxis** (tel. 928 54 12 57) stand at the port. A ride to town costs 300ptas, to the resorts 600ptas. **Orlando** (tel. 928 54 03 09), in Apartamentos El Matorral, rents **cars** (3400-5500ptas per day; Must be at least 21; Visa, AmEx), but since most of the peninsula's rough dunes are only navigable with four-wheel-drive vehicles, consider spending those few extra *pesetas.* Though the **tourist office** (tel. 928 54 07 76), Av. Saladar, in the Centro de Comercial de Jandia, is rather unhelpful, it does stock brochures for water sports and hotels (open M-F 9am-3:30pm). **Emergency:** tel. 062; **police:** C. Hibisco, 1 (tel. 928 54 10 22); **hospital: Centro Médico Jandia** (tel. 928 54 15 43 or 928 54 74 73), Jandia Beach Center (open 24hr.; Visa, MC, AmEx). **Post office** (tel. 902 19 71 97), Av. Jandia, near C. Nuestra Señora del Carmen (open M-F 8:30am-2:30pm, Sa 9:30am-1pm); **postal code:** 35625; **internet access:** Infotex, C. Semador Velázquez Cabrera, 35 (tel. 928 54 04 10; 1500ptas per hr.; open M-F 10am-1pm and 5-9pm).

◪◪ ACCOMMODATIONS AND FOOD. Budget accommodations in Morro Jable are along C. Maxorata and C. Senador Velázquez Cabrera, a short walk away from the resorts in the western half of town. Reception desks are closed in the afternoon, so either arrive early or late or settle into a bar for a few hours. It is imperative that you call ahead for reservations; many unprepared travelers find themselves catching a bus to Puerto del Rosario for the night. **Hostal Maxorata,** C. Maxorata, 31 (tel. 928 54 10 87) has fresh and airy rooms, all with sparkling bathrooms and some with views of the beach (singles 3000ptas; doubles 4000ptas). A close and painless second choice is **Hostal Omahy,** C. Maxorata, 47 (tel. 928 54 12 54), which has plain but comfortable rooms, all with full baths and balconies (doubles 4000ptas). **Apartamentos Casa Hierro,** C. Senador Velázquez Cabrera, 16 (tel. 928 54 11 13), one street from C. Maxorata, rents small but clean apartments near the beach (doubles 5000ptas). Morro Jable's restaurants are full of international flare—the town's Italian bistros, seafood joints, and German *konfiterias* line the beach. Almost all, however, still manage to fit *bocadillos* onto the menu. For homestyle seafood, try **Jandia Restaurant,** C. Senador Velázquez Cabrera, 7 (tel. 928 87 37). The restaurant serves hearty and typical *raciones* (450-825ptas) and fresh fish (825-1550ptas).

CANARY ISLANDS

⚑🏄 BEACHES AND ENTERTAINMENT. The only physical activities indulged in by most visitors are the short walk from the beach to the bar and the occasional reapplication of sunscreen. The ⚑beaches are lined with bodies (with or without bathing suits) from early morning to late night. Blessed with some of the islands' calmest waters and lushest sea life, Morro Jable offers excellent opportunities to practice **water sports.** Innumerable **windsurfing** schools set up camp on the beach (the coast hosts the world freestyle competition in July). **Barakuda Club** (tel. 928 54 14 18), Av. Saladar, offers **scuba diving** and equipment rental (4000ptas per dive). The dunes and rock formations are playgrounds for **mountain bikers.** Rent a bike at the descriptively named **Rent a Bike** (tel. 928 54 70 62 or 928 54 70 77), in Club Ancora (1900ptas per day). Several more secluded beaches flank Morro Jable, accessible by car and bike. **Playa de Barlovento de Jandia** to the west is a less-crowded, windy sandstorm of dunes and rough waters. With neither museums nor cultural centers, the only distraction from the beach is the **Centro Comercial de Jandia,** located on Av. Saladar, which houses the town's sparse nightlife, comprised of a few raucous bars selling imported beers (450ptas).

LANZAROTE

Refusing to construct the high-rises and resorts of its western neighbors, Lanzarote preserves a landscape that has changed little over the last few decades. The Spanish called this isle the *"isla tranquila"* because of its peaceful nature, which is luckily still preserved today. Though ferry companies make it somewhat difficult to access the island, Lanzarote merits a visit.

ARRECIFE

Meaning "rocky reef," Arrecife, Lanzarote's hamlet capital (pop. 30,000), resides on the island's eastern coast, fringed with blackened lava and yellow sands. Home to the archipelago's largest fishing fleet, the harbor is packed with peeling boats. Tourism remains relatively subdued here, and although the city has little to offer beyond a modern art museum, its surplus of accommodations provide an excellent base for exploration of the rest of Lanzarote.

🛈 ORIENTATION AND PRACTICAL INFORMATION

Arrecife is easy to navigate on foot. **Av. Generalísimo Franco** and its numerous continuations spread from the western **port** to the eastern folds of Playa Reducto. The **tourist office** sits on the avenue, near its intersection with **Calle Léon y Castillo,** the main pedestrian thoroughfare. Unfortunately, both the bus station and the port are located on the fringes of Arrecife.

Flights: Guasimeta Airport serves other islands and mainland Spain. Bus #4 runs from the airport to Arrecife (20min., every 30min., 8:20am-7:20pm, 110ptas). **Iberia** (tel. 928 81 03 50).

Buses: (tel. 928 81 24 58), C. Vía Medular. To get to the center of town, turn left on C. Vía Medular and right on C. Léon y Castillo. A more accessible stop is located in front of Playa Reducto on Av. Fred Olsen, a continuation of Av. Generalísimo Franco. Info open daily 8am-10pm. To: **Costa Teguise** (#1; every 20 min., 6:40am-11:40pm, 145ptas); **Puerto del Carmen** (#2; 40min., every 20min., 6:20am-11:20pm, 200ptas); **Playa Blanca** (#6; 6 per day, 6am-8:15pm, 415ptas); **Maguez** (#7; 4 per day, 11:45am-8pm, 330ptas); **Teguise** (#7, 9, and 10; 6 per day, 7:40am-8pm, 120ptas).

Ferries: at the far edge of town. Take a taxi into central Arrecife (400ptas). **Naviera Armas** (tel. 928 82 49 30) and **Trasmediterránea** (tel. 928 81 10 19) run frequent ferries to **Puerto Rosario** (on Fuerteventura) and **Las Palmas** (on Gran Canaria). Less-frequent service to **Santa Cruz de Tenerife.** For more information, see **Getting Around,** p. 498.

Car Rental: Auto Timanfaya (tel. 928 01 30 23), C. Luis Morote. Opel Corsa 3500ptas per day. Open M-F 9am-2pm and 5-8pm, Sa 9am-1pm.

Taxi: Radio Taxi (tel. 928 80 31 04), on the corner of C. Léon y Castillo and Av. Generalísimo Franco.

Tourist Office: (tel. 928 81 18 60), Av. Generalísimo Franco, in a whitewashed building overlooking the ocean. Has the only map of Arrecife and a list of inexpensive accommodations. Open M-F 9am-1pm and 5-7pm, Sa 9am-noon.

Currency Exchange: Although there are relatively few exchange booths in Arrecife, the banks lining C. Léon y Castillo will change currency.

Emergency: tel. 091 or 092. **Police:** Av. Coll, 5 (tel. 928 81 13 17), on a continuation of Av. Generalísimo, away from the beach.

Hospital: (tel. 928 80 16 36), off the highway to San Bartólome.

Post Office: Av. Generalísimo Franco, 8 (tel. 928 80 06 73). Open M-F 8:30am-8:30pm, Sa 9:30am-1pm. **Postal Code:** 35500.

Internet Access: Redes Servicios Informática, C. Colonel Bens, 17 (tel. 928 81 22 09). 950ptas per hr., students 390ptas. Open M-F 9am-2pm and 5-8pm, Sa 9am-1pm.

ACCOMMODATIONS

While the other towns in Lanzarote often have only one *pensión*, Arrecife overflows with cheap beds. Most accommodations occupy the area around C. Léon y Castillo, and little distinguishes one from another. Most have full baths and few singles; solo travelers should phone ahead. The tourist office has a list of accommodations with phone numbers and addresses (but no prices).

Residencia Cardona, C. 18 de Julio, 11 (tel. 928 81 10 08). From the tourist office, turn left on Av. Generalísimo Franco and right on C. 18 de Julio. A pink marble delight with an impressive lounge, monstrous rooms, and gleaming bathrooms. Reservations recommended. Singles 3300ptas; doubles 4500ptas.

Hostal San Gines, C. Molina, 9 (tel. 928 81 23 51). From the tourist office, walk down C. Léon y Castillo; when it curves right, take the 1st left. Clean and ample rooms with a coral theme, all with full bath and hot water. Singles 2100ptas; doubles 3100ptas.

Pensión España, C. Gran Canaria, 4 (tel. 928 81 11 90), at the end of C. Léon y Castillo's pedestrian section, near Hostal San Gines. A group of old men occupy the benches out front from dusk to dawn; indoors is just as noisy and crowded. Small but cheap rooms. Singles 1700ptas; doubles 2500ptas.

FOOD

Unlike in the rest of the Canaries, finding an inexpensive, untouristed restaurant is not a problem. Pizzerias line the waterfront, but better eateries lie a few streets back on C. Jose Antonio de Ribera. The market, **Sabor y Gusto,** C. Canaleja, 2 (tel. 928 81 75 05) is near the water (open M-F 9am-1:30pm and 5-9pm, Sa 9am-1:30pm).

Castillo de San José Restaurante and Bar (tel. 928 81 23 21), beneath the modern art museum outside of town. Perhaps the loveliest restaurant in the Canaries, but your wallet might not think so. Wrapped in glass and overlooking the harbor, the dining room offers a view worth the price. *Tapas* 600-1900ptas. Scrumptious desserts 500-1500ptas. Open daily 1-4:45pm and 8-11:30pm; bar open 11am-1am.

Café la Unión, Pl. Constitución, 16 (tel. 928 64 23 78), behind Av. Generalisimo Franco, near the water. Tranquil and bright cafe serves creative baguettes (300-450ptas) and *bocadillos* (300-475ptas) to hungry beach goers. Open daily 10am-11pm.

📷 ♫ SIGHTS AND ENTERTAINMENT

📷**MUSEO INTERNACIONAL DE ARTE CONTEMPORÁNEO.** Arrecife is graced with the Canaries' best museum, the Museo Internacional de Arte Contemporáneo. The original building, an 18th-century fortress built by Carlos III, was intended to defend the island from pirate attacks. It was originally known as the "Fortress of Hunger," as its construction added to the famine plaguing Lanzarote. Two hundred years later, its simple stone walls epitomize **César Manrique's** revitalization of the island's history and architecture (see p. 519). Exhibits rotate frequently, but geometric, formal, and abstract works form part of the permanent collection, fitting into the grooves of the fort and hanging into the restaurant below. *(To the west of town, off Av. Naos, a continuation of Av. Generalísimo Franco. An easy 40min. walk; taxis from town cost 300ptas. Tel. 928 84 00 57. Open daily 11am-9pm. Free.)*

CASTILLO DE SAN GABRIEL. The Castillo de San Gabriel houses the **Museo Arqueológico.** Pottery pieces and a few Guanche skeletons occupy the erstwhile fort. *(Av. Generalísimo Franco, next to the tourist office. Open M-Sa 11am-6pm. 300ptas.)*

ENTERTAINMENT. C. José Antonio fills Arrecife's nightlife quota with small, rambunctious bars and restaurants. On weekends, this street is a sea of expats and young locals, flowing from one bar to the next. There's nary a nun in the packed **El Convento,** C. Jose Antonio Ribera, 76. Just down the road, the recently opened **Goa Cafe Bar** draws a crowd of beautiful people.

PUERTO DEL CARMEN

Puerto del Carmen, Lanzarote's largest tourist resort, lacks both the beaches and the character of Fuerteventura's small towns. Primarily British tourists flock to the hotels, packaged and lobster-tied by one of many tour companies. Except for the bazaars and bars lining **Avenida de las Playas,** the yellow sands of **Playa Bla.ıca** supply the only entertainment. Offshore reefs, however, offer some of the islands best **scuba diving.** For more information try the **Delfín Club,** Av. Playas, 38 (tel. 928 51 42 90), in the Centro Aquarium, which runs four dives a day. (4200ptas with equipment; 3100ptas if you have your own. Open M-Sa 9am-6pm.)

Bus #2 runs between Arrecife and Puerto del Carmen and stops along Av. Playas (40min., every 20min., 6:20am-11:20pm, 200ptas). **Fred Olsen** (tel. 922 62 82 31) and **Naviera Armas** (tel. 928 51 79 12) also run buses to Playa Blanca to meet their ferry departures. The **tourist office** (tel. 928 51 53 37) is located on Av. Playas in a white kiosk overlooking the beach and offers little more than a photocopied map (open M-F 9am-1pm and 5-7pm, Sa 9am-1pm). To explore the island to its fullest, consider renting a car—there are lots of good deals along Av. Playas. **Lanzauto,** Av. Playas, 19 (tel. 928 51 06 18), has rentals starting at 4200ptas per day with insurance and unlimited mileage (must be 21).

PARQUE NACIONAL DE TIMANFAYA

Known as **Montañas de Fuegos** (Fire Mountains), the barren landscape of Lanzarote's national park erupts with evidence of the six-year explosion that began in 1730. Resembling the surface of the moon, copper *hornitos* and blackened folds of solidified lava carve their way into the loose soil; only lichen seems to survive in the scorching ground. The only way to view the volcanic route is by tour bus. The 30-minute tour is restrictive but extremely informative. (Park open daily 9am-5:45pm. 1000ptas. Mandatory bus tour leaves from the entrance booth.)

The magic tricks of **Islote de Hilario's** geothermal heat are the tour's highlight. Legend has it that the hermit Hilario, who lived here with his lone camel, planted a fig tree whose fruit was consumed by the underground fires. Similar spectacles are performed by park employees to demonstrate the effects of the 400°C temperatures below—a piece of brush put into the earth bursts into a ball of flames, and water poured into a metal pipe turns into fountains of steam.

The █El Diablo (tel. 928 84 00 57) restaurant that now occupies the *islote* was designed by Cesar Manrique and constructed using only stone, metal, and glass (due to the high temperatures). Volcanic heat seeping from the earth powers the kitchen's grill. The panoramic view from the dining room is the best on the island, extending from the arid mountains to the azure sea. (Open daily noon-3:30pm.) Unfortunately, no buses run to the park; you'll need to rent a car.

▓TEGUISE

Brushing the side of the Guanapays mountains (452m), Teguise is hands-down Lanzarote's loveliest village. Frequent buses run daily from Arrecife to Teguise (#7, 9, 10; 6 per day, 7:40am-8pm, 120ptas), stopping in front of the Ayuntamiento. To get to the **Plaza de la Constitución,** the center of town, face the Ayuntamiento, turn right on C. Santo Domingo, right on C. Morales Lemes, then right into the plaza, the site of the **Sunday market.** Teguise is famous for its authentic Canary Islands cuisine, and food stands flood the town on market day. **Iglesia de la Virgen de Guadelupe** resides in the corner of the plaza. Decorated with understated religious icons, the church's simple stone exterior clashes with its modern interior.

Just off the plaza, Pl. San Miguel houses the **Casa Museo Palacio Spinola** (tel. 928 84 51 81), named after a wealthy local merchant. With old photos of festivals and Canarian customs, it is a worthwhile visit. (Open M-F 10am-5pm and Sa-Su 10am-4pm. 300ptas.) The 16th-century **Castillo Santa Barbara,** an uphill walk out of town, offers one of the island's best views. Built by Sancho de Herrera on the side of the Guanay volcano, the castle has changed hands several times throughout the centuries. Today it houses the **Museo del Emigrante Canario,** detailing the toils of emigration to the new world. Its collection, however, barely rivals the castle itself, with its seaward views of the whitewashed town and lava landscape. (Exit Pl. Constitución on C. Marqués Herrera, following its continuations up the mountain to the castle. Open Tu-F 10am-4pm, Sa-Su 11am-3pm. 300ptas.)

CÉSAR MANRIQUE
It is virtually impossible to spend a day on Lanzarote without hearing the name César Manrique. Born in 1919 in Arrecife, Manrique, an artist and architect, sought to construct buildings as extended natural forms. After a brief service in Franco's army, he began painting abstract canvases; by 1964, his works made their way to New York's Guggenheim Museum. When he returned to Lanzarote, Manrique dedicated himself to creating "a paradise for those who have an eye for the special." He persuaded the government to ban billboards and halt skyscraper construction, leaving the capital city an unobtrusive maze of whitewashed houses.

His individual projects, scattered throughout the island, incorporate natural surroundings and clean lines, aiming to coexist with nature, rather than against it. For the initial design of the **International Museum of Contemporary Art,** Manrique drew a small sketch on the earth with a piece of chalk. Near Guatiza and Mala resides Manrique's **Jardin de Cactus,** a decaying mill whimsically converted into a mammoth cactus garden. (Tel. 928 52 93 97. Open daily 10am-5:45pm. 500ptas.) Accessible from Arrieta on the northern coast, **Los Jameos del Agua** is another of Manriques's magical designs, a natural saltwater lagoon connected to an underground volcano tube. Within the grotto's lava formations, Manrique incorporated a concert cave, a restaurant, and a bar. (Tel. 928 84 80 20. Open daily 9:30am-6:45pm. Tu, F, Sa open for dancing 7pm-3am. Restaurant open 1-4pm and 8-11:30pm. 1000ptas., at night 1100ptas.)

In 1992, Manrique donated his home in Taro de Thiche to the citizens of Lanzarote. Now known as the **Fundación César Manrique,** it is integrated into the five volcanic bubbles below. The living room has been transformed into a gallery exhibiting his private collection of works. (Open M-Sa 10am-6pm.) Although tour companies organize buses to the sights, renting a car is the only way to see many of Manrique's creations.

GOMERA

Many believe the verdant island of Gomera, with its lush terraced hillsides, to be the most blessed of the Canaries. Luckily its relative isolation and small, stony beaches keep the droves of tourists at bay. Surrounded by bananas and avocado plantations, the island's main town, San Sebastián, is refreshingly provincial. Gomera's crown jewel, however, is the spectacular Garajonay National Park, the last refuge for a species of forest that died out elsewhere millions of years ago.

SAN SEBASTIÁN DE GOMERA

Heading off to find the mythical Middle Passage to India, Christopher Columbus dropped anchor here for a few days. He gathered water from the well and prayed at the church before continuing on his way. These days explorers skip this charming town, opting for the sandy beaches to the south. Still, as a transportation hub littered with affordable accommodations, San Sebastián makes an excellent base for discovering the rest of La Gomera.

⚡ ORIENTATION AND PRACTICAL INFORMATION

Navigating San Sebastián is a breeze. One road runs along the entire coast, intersected midway by **Calle del Medio,** the town's main drag, at Pl. Américas. To get to the plaza from the **port,** walk down the wharf and turn left on Av. Fred Olsen; the plaza is on the left (5min.). If you arrive after dark, consider taking a quick taxi into town (300ptas), as the streets aren't clearly named and are difficult to maneuver at night. Although a new **bus station** is under construction, inter-city buses also currently stop at the port. If you rent a **car,** turn right on C. Vía de Ronda and left on C. Sur to head out of town towards Valle de Gran Rey.

Buses: The main bus stop is next to the ferry station on the port. Three lines originate in the port and branch out across the island. Line 1 to **Valle Gran Rey;** Line 2 to **Playa de Santiago** and **Alajero;** Line 3 to **Hermigua, Agulo,** and **Vallehermoso.** All leave at 11am, 2pm, 5:30pm, and 9:30pm.

Ferries: Trasmediterránea (tel. 920 87 13 24 or 920 80 59 68) and **Fred Olson** run several daily ferries to **Los Cristianos.** See **Getting Around,** p. 498, for details.

Car Rental: Available in the port terminal or at Pl. Américas. **Hertz,** Av. Fred Olsen, 7 (tel. 922 87 04 39) rents cars from 4494 ptas per day. Open M-F 9am-1pm and 4-7pm, Sa 9am-1pm. Visa, MC, AmEx. **Sport Moto,** C. República de Panamá, 3 (tel. 920 87 15 31), rents **motorcycles** (5000ptas per day), **scooters** (3500ptas per day), and **mountain bikes** (2000ptas per day).

Tourist Office: C. Medio, 4 (tel. 920 14 01 47; fax 920 14 01 51), behind Pl. Américas. Photocopied maps of cities and long lists of water sports. Inside is the well Columbus used before leaving for the New World. Have a sip—maybe you'll get lucky too. Open M-Sa 9am-1:30pm and 3:30-6pm, Su 10am-1pm. For info on the park, head to **Park Service,** C. Sur, 6 (tel. 922 87 01 05). Open M-F 8am-2:30pm.

Currency Exchange: Banks line Pl. Américas. Open M-F 8:30am-2pm, Sa 8:30am-1pm.

Police: Av. Descubridores, 8 (tel. 922 87 03 20). From Pl. Américas, follow the waterfront road away from the port; the station is on the right.

Hospital: Nuestra Sra. de Guadalupe (tel. 920 14 02 02). From Pl. Américas, go away from the port, turn right on C. Vía Ronda, left across the bridge, and take the 1st right.

Post Office: C. Medio, 60 (tel. 902 19 71 97). Open M-F 8:30am-2:30pm. **Postal Code:** 38800.

Internet Access: RP-Shop, C. Medio, 48 (tel. 922 00 34 92). Only 1 computer. 750ptas per hr. Open M-F 9am-1pm and 4-7pm, Sa 9am-1pm.

ACCOMMODATIONS

San Sebastián's budget accommodations are more budget and more accommodating than those elsewhere in the Canaries. *Hostal* and *pensión* signs hang out of windows on C. Medio. Pricier hotels reside one street over on C. Rúiz de Padrón.

Pensión Victor-Leralita, C. Medio, 23 (tel. 920 60 75 17). The rooms in this 250-year-old house are spacious, clean, and high-ceilinged. Ask for the room with the terrace. Noisy restaurant downstairs provides tasty sandwiches (200ptas) and cheap beer (150ptas). Singles 2000ptas; doubles 3000ptas.

Apartamentos San Sebastián, C. Medio, 20 (tel. 920 87 13 54). Don't let the blinding pink hallways dissuade you; breezy and newly furnished rooms await. For stays under 2 weeks 4500ptas per night; over 2 weeks 4000ptas per night.

Pensión Colón, C. Medio, 59 (tel. 920 87 00 20; fax 920 87 02 35). Lace curtains and green doors frame the small, quiet rooms. Interior courtyard with swings for the young and youthful. Singles 2800ptas; doubles 3500ptas; triples 4800ptas.

FOOD

Fortunately, San Sebastián is filled with authentic Spanish restaurants and cheap *tapas* joints. Nicer options surround Pl. Constitución, and typical bars and *mesones* line C. Ruiz de Padron and C. Medio. For a meal on the run, try **Super Mercado Brito** (tel. 922 14 18 18), Pl. Constitución (open M-Sa 9am-9pm; Visa, MC).

Oasis Pizzeria, Pl. Constitución. With swaying music, shelves of red wine and a veranda inside, this pizzeria captures the *trattoria* experience. Pizzas with thin crusts and fresh toppings 500-800ptas. Open daily noon-4pm and 6pm-midnight.

Bar-Restaurant Cubano, C. Virgen de Guadalupe, 2, off Pl. Constitución. Serves seafood specialities to a local crowd. Entrees 600-1500ptas. Open daily 11am-midnight.

SIGHTS

San Sebastián sometimes seems like a Christopher Columbus theme park. On C. Medio (down the street from the Columbus Casino) is the **Iglesia de la Asunción,** where Columbus prayed before he left. The carved woodwork adorning the simple church is typical of Canarian architecture. Nearby, the **Casa de Colón** hosts a small and unimpressive exhibit on the explorer's life. Don't miss the religious icon made out of pure sugar. (C. Medio, 50. Open M-F 9am-noon and 4-8pm. Free.) The **Torre del Conde,** a small 15th-century fort, towers meekly over the beach. In 1488, the wife of the murdered governor Hernán Peraza bolted herself inside as she watched the citizens take control of the port.

No Canarian city would be complete without a **beach.** Although there is a small patch of black sand in front of Pl. Américas, the area stretching beyond the port offers more sand and calmer waters. From Pl. Américas, walk down Av. Fred Olsen toward the port and curve left (away from the wharf). The tourist office has lots of info about **diving, boating,** and **fishing** excursions from the port.

GARAJONAY NATIONAL PARK

Blanketed in thick mist and fog, the Garajonay National Park sustains the last **laurisilva forest** on earth. Once covering the Mediterranean basin, these forests died out elsewhere millions of years ago. Hikers in the 4000 hectare park wade through lush ferns, myriad streams, and dripping plants.

The park maintains numerous trails and **three self-guided paths.** Unfortunately, only a few trails are accessible via bus, so full exploration of the park requires a car. The **Alto de Garonjay** trail (1hr., medium difficulty), rising 1487m to the island's highest point, is accesible by bus #1 from San Sebastián to Valle Gran Rey. Exit at

JUST GIVE A WHISTLE No, it's not a moped alarm and probably not that sleazy guy across the street; that piercing noise you just heard is a demonstration of **El Silbo,** the Guanche whistle language. This is not just your average whistle; "speakers" make full use of both hands to manipulate the sound. The language, which has a complete alphabet, developed in order to communicate over long distances over the island's rough terrain. During the Spanish conquest, El Silbo dwindled, and today it is only used to garner a few *pesetas* from amazed tourists.

the Pajarito stop and follow the signs to the peak. The northern **Contadero** trail (3½hr., medium difficulty), which starts outside the park near Hermigua, traces the different types of forestation in the park, from heath trees to Canary wax-myrtles. Meaning "counting site," the narrow path forces walkers and animals into single file—herders once used the trail to count their sheep and cattle. In the southern part of the park, the **Las Creces** trail (1½hr., low difficulty) delves into the fayal-heath forest, moving between both virgin and regenerating trees. Most of the stops along this path feature the natural flora, including ghost trees and mushrooms. Jagged cliffs distinguish the region around the **Los Barranquillos** path (30min., low difficulty), which brushes the 200m **Lomo del Carreton.** Other sights of interest include the view of **Los Roques** and the nearby **volcanic domes** from **Mirador de El Bailadero.** On Wednesdays and Saturdays, **guided hikes** depart from **La Laguna Grande,** located about half-way into the park. The Laguna has restrooms, a small info center, and a restaurant.

Strangely, the **visitor's center** (tel. 920 80 09 93) is located in **Agulo,** 9km outside of the park (open Tu-Su 9:30am-4:30pm). To get to the visitor's center take bus #3 from San Sebastián (45min., 4 per day, 11am-9:30pm). The **Park Service,** Carretera General de Sur, 6 (tel. 920 80 09 93), in San Sebastián, provides the same info (open M-F 8am-2:30pm). Either of these offices can make the reservations required for the free guided tours.

VALLE GRAN REY

The deep gorge at the Valle Gran Rey pushes back from sandy beaches to tilted banana groves. Infamous for its stunning surroundings and peaceful atmosphere, this "Valley of the Great King" should be called "Valley of Tourism." The valley is home to three small villages: **La Calera, Vueltas,** and **La Playa,** all accessible by bus. **Bus #1** runs to La Playa from San Sebastián (2hr., 4 per day, 11am-9:30pm, 700ptas). **Trasmediterránea's** (tel. 922 80 59 68) three daily **hydrofoils** (30min., 10am-6:45pm, 1030ptas) are speedier alternatives. Sunbathing, boating, diving, and jet skiing occupy tourists by day at the **Playa de Aruga** and **Playa las Américas,** a short walk south of Vueltas. Although street signs are nonexistent, the area is easy to navigate—for help, stop at the **tourist office** in La Playa (tel. 922 80 54 58), on C. Noria (open M-Sa 9am-1:30pm and 4-6:30pm, Su 10am-1:30pm). To get to the tourist office from the La Playa stop bus, face the beach, head right down the main road, and turn left on C. Noria.

Unfortunately, Valle Gran Rey's charm and scenery come at a price—expensive **accommodations.** Most *pensiónes* only offer doubles. In La Calera, **Casa Bella Cabellos** (tel. 922 80 51 82) offers simple, balconied rooms in a typical Canarian home. From the bus stop, follow the road up the valley, take the first left, and continue until you see a dark wooden home on the left. (Doubles 2500ptas.) Although mostly littered with apartments, Vueltas has a few moderately priced *pensiónes.* **Pensión Candelaria** (tel. 920 80 54 02; doubles 4000ptas) and **Las Vueltas** (tel. 920 80 52 16; doubles 3000ptas) have spartan doubles, just north of the island's best beaches. Contact the tourist office in San Sebastián for help locating a deal.

EL HIERRO

The smallest of the Canary Islands, El Hierro was thought by Ptolemy to be the edge of the world. Even now, few venture west to its scattered villages and jagged coastline. With a horizon free of high-rise resorts and neon signs, El Hierro offers visitors an opportunity to explore traditional interior towns and small fishing ports and to do some rewarding hiking. The island's most infamous celebration, **Bajada de los Virgen de dos Reyes,** starts every four years in **La Ermita de los Reyes.**

The port town and tourist center **La Restyinga** is renowned for its scuba diving. Farther north is **El Pinar,** a series of small villages encircled by dense pine forests. To the east emerges **Malpaso** peak (1501m), El Hierro's zenith. Unfortunately, beaches are scarce and inferior to the golden stretches on Gran Canaria and Fuerteventura. On the western coast, the sun-addicted can get their fix at **Playas del Verodal** and **Arenas Blancas.** To the north-east, the capital city of **Valverde** serves as little more than a bridge to the ferry stations and airport. (See **Getting Around,** p. 498.). The main **tourist office,** C. Licenciado Bueno, 1 (tel. 922 55 03 02), is located here. The island, scattered with twisted juniper trees, is best explored by car.

El Hierro is most easily accessible by ferry from Los Cristianos de Tenerife. **Fred Olsen** (tel. 922 62 82 31) has a daily ferry to **Valverde** (1 per day, 8am, 2420ptas, students 1940ptas). A bus departs Santa Cruz's bus station at 6:30am to meet the boat. **Trasmediterránea** (tel. 902 45 46 45) has one daily departure as well from Los Cristianos to **Valverde** (1 per day, 8:30am or 7pm, 1980ptas).

LA PALMA

Painted green and lush by heavy rainfalls, it's easy to see the origins of La Palma's nickname, *"isla bonita."* It's also easy to see why Madonna used it as the subject of one of her songs. Although the island was an important transatlantic port during colonial days, today relatively few visitors sail into the capital of **Santa Cruz.** With colonial houses and carved-balconies lining the streets, the port city retains the old world-charm of its glory days.

Sharp coastlines and cliffs trace the island and dissuade sunbathers. However, hikers will discover a mountainous paradise, as La Palma is the world's steepest island. A volcanic crater almost 10km wide, **La Caldera de Taburiente,** commands the center. Thick Canarian pines cover the rest of the national park, and a world-renowned observatory caps the **Roque de los Muchachos.** Although the northern town of **Los Llanos de Aridane** has a stunning **botanical garden** in the **Pueblo Parque La Palma,** the volcanos to the south offer more opportunities for hiking. The views from **Volcán Teneguia** and **San Antonio** stretch to the neighboring eastern islands.

Ferry companies make it difficult to access La Palma, so be sure to plan ahead. **Fred Olsen** (tel. 922 41 54 33) has one ferry a day to **Santa Cruz** (5hr., 7pm, 2825ptas). **Trasmediterránea** (tel. 902 45 46 45) offers more options, with ferries from **San Sebastián** (3½hr., every other day, 10:20am, 2235ptas); **Los Cristianos** (5hr., 1 every other day, 8:35am, 2770ptas); **Santa Cruz de Tenerife** (8hr., every Th, midnight, 3605ptas); **Las Palmas** (14hr., every Th, 6:30pm, 4740ptas).

PORTUGAL

LIFE AND TIMES

During the 14th and 15th centuries, Portugal was one of the most powerful nations in the world, ruling a wealthy empire that stretched from America to Asia. Although the country's international prestige declined by 1580, Portuguese pride did not. During the following centuries, Portugal struggled to assert its national identity (and its uniqueness from Spain). Modern Portugal, with its stable democracy and fast-growing economy, has proved the strength of its national character.

HISTORY AND POLITICS

EARLY HISTORY. Several tribes inhabited the Iberian Peninsula during the first millennium BC. The first clearly identifiable inhabitants were **Celts,** who began to settle in northern Portugal and Spanish Galicia in the 9th and 8th centuries BC. These Celts established small agricultural and herding societies throughout the countryside. Around the same time, **Phoenicians** founded several fishing villages along the Algarve and ventured as far north as modern-day Lisbon. The **Greeks** and **Carthaginians** followed them, settling the southern and western coasts. After their victory over Carthage in the Second Punic War (218-201 BC) and their defeat of the Celts in 140 BC, the **Romans** gained control of central and southern Portugal, integrating the region into their Iberian province of Lusitania. Six centuries of Roman rule, which introduced the *Pax Romana* and "latinized" Portugal's language and customs, also paved the way for Christianity.

VISIGOTHS AND ARABIAN KNIGHTS (469-1139). When the Roman Empire declined in the 3rd and 4th centuries AD, the Iberian Peninsula felt the effects. By AD 469, the **Visigoths,** a tribe of migrating Germanic people, had crossed the Pyrenees, and for the next two centuries they dominated the peninsula. Under the Visigoths, who converted to Christianity by the beginning of the 7th century, the Church became the largest landholder in Europe, and monasteries and clerical schools became centers of spiritual learning. In AD 711, however, the Muslims (also known as the **Moors**) invaded Iberia, toppling the Visigoth monarchy. Although these invaders centered their new kingdom of *al-Andalus* in Córdoba, smaller Muslim communities settled along Portugal's southern coast, an area they called the *al-Gharb* (now the Algarve). While Muslim leadership tolerated both Jews and Christians, many Christians chose to convert to Islam. During the 9th and 10th centuries AD, Muslim society reached the height of its political power. After nearly four centuries of rule, the Muslims left their mark on Portugal, leaving behind many agricultural advances and architectural landmarks. As of result of the long Muslim occupation, Islamic and Arabic influences had filtered into Portuguese culture, affecting the local language and customs.

THE CHRISTIAN RECONQUEST AND THE BIRTH OF PORTUGAL (1139-1415). Though the **Reconquest** officially began in 718, it didn't pick up steam until the 11th century. When Fernando I united Castilla and León in 1035, he helped the *Reconquista* by providing a strong base from which to reclaim territory. In 1139, **Afonso Henriques** (Afonso I), a noble from the frontier territory of Portucale (a region centered around Porto), declared independence from Castilla and León. By the following decade, he had named himself the first King of Portugal, though the papacy did not officially recognize the title until 1179.

With the help of Christian military groups like the Knights Templar, the new monarchy battled Muslim forces, capturing Lisbon in 1147. By 1249, the Recon-

Portugal

N

ATLANTIC OCEAN

SPAIN

TO AZORES

TO MADEIRA

MINHO

Valença do Minho
Vila Nova de Cerveira
Caminha
Viana do Castelo
Rio Minho
Parque Nacional Peneda Gerês
Serra do Gerês
Parque Natural de Montesinho
Bragança
TRÁS-OS-MONTES
Rio Cávado
Barcelos
Braga
Guimarães
Amarante
Serra do Marão
Vila Real
COSTA VERDE
Porto
DOURO LITORAL
DOURO ALTO
Espinho
Rio Douro
Ovar
BEIRA ALTA
Aveiro
Viseu
BEIRA LITORAL
Rio Mondego
Luso
Buçaco
Serra da Estrêla
Guarda
COSTA DA PRATA
Buarcos
Figueira da Foz
Coimbra
Conimbriga
Rio Zêzere
Serra da Gardunha
BEIRA BAIXA
Leiria
Nazaré
Batalha
Fátima
Castelo Branco
São Martinho do Porto
Alcobaça
Ilhas Berlengas
Caldas da Rainha
Tomar
Cabo Carvoeiro
Óbidos
Serra de Aire
Rio Tejo
Peniche
Castelo de Vide
Marvão
ESTREMADURA
Santarém
Crato
Portalegre
Erceira
Vila Franca
RIBATEJO
Serra de São Mamede
Sintra
Mafra
Cascais
Queluz
★ Lisbon
Estoril
ALTO ALENTEJO
Estremoz
Elvas
Évora Monte
Parque Nacional de Arrábida
Setúbal
Tróia Peninsula
Évora
Cabo Espichel
Sesimbra
Serra de Ossa
COSTA AZUL
Santiago de Cacim
Beja
Rio Guadiana
Sines
BAIXO ALENTEJO
Rio Mira
COSTA DOURADA
Mértola
Serra de Monchique
Lagos
Silves
ALGARVE
Portimão
Albufeira
Tavira
Cabo São Vicente
Sagres
Faro
Olhão
Vila Real de Santo António
Golfo de Cádiz

PORTUGAL

quest defeated the last remnants of Muslim power with successful campaigns in the Alentejo and the Algarve. Along with the change in political rule came sweeping cultural reforms. The Christian kings, headlined by **Dinis I** (Dom Dinis; 1279-1325), promoted use of the Portuguese language (instead of Spanish), established Portugal's first university in 1290, and solidified its current borders 1297. With the **Treaty of Alcañices** (1297), Dinis settled border disputes with neighboring Castilla, asserting Portugal's identity as an independent nation. By the middle of the 14th century Portugal was the first unified nation-state in Europe.

THE AGE OF DISCOVERY (1415-1580). The reign of **João I** (1385-1433), the first king of the House of Aviz, ushered in unity and prosperity never before seen in Portugal. João increased the power of the crown and in so doing established a strong base for future Portuguese expansion and economic success. To further strengthen the monarchy, João also negotiated the **Treaty of Windsor** (1386), a permanent Anglo-Portuguese alliance. This alliance would influence Portugal's foreign policy well into the 19th century.

The 15th century was one of the greatest periods in the history of maritime travel and naval advances. Under the leadership of João's son, **Prince Henry the Navigator,** Portugal established itself as a world leader in maritime science and exploration. Portuguese adventurers captured the Moroccan city of Ceuta in 1415, discovered the Madeiras Islands in 1419, happened upon the uninhabited Azores in 1427, and began to exploit the African coast for slaves and riches a few years later.

Bartolomeu Dias changed the world forever when he rounded Africa's Cape of Good Hope in 1488. Dias opened the route to the East and paved the way for Portuguese entrance into the spice trade. Although the Portuguese monarchs turned down **Christopher Columbus,** they still funded a number of momentous voyages. In 1498, they supported **Vasco da Gama,** who led the first European naval expedition to India. Successive expeditions added numerous East African and Indian colonies to Portugal's empire. Two years after da Gama's voyage, **Pedro Alvares Cabral** claimed Brazil for Portugal. Although the Treaty of Tordesillas (1494) with Spain limited further Portuguese colonial expansion in the Americas, Portugal still established a far-flung empire. By the beginning of the 16th century, Portuguese traders, colonists, and missionaries, often using oppressive tactics, had secured claims all around the globe. Portugal's explorers may not have been motivated by the most admirable of ambitions, but nostalgic relics of Portugal's global muscle endure to the present day: Portuguese surnames persevere in places where lonely sailors took lovers, Catholic churches survive where missionaries passed, and political links still tie Portugal to many of its former colonies.

Portugal's monarchy reached its peak with **Manuel I The Fortunate** (1495-1521) on the throne. Known to foreigners as "the King of Gold," Manuel controlled a spectacular commercial empire. However, before the House of Aviz lost power in 1580, signs of future decline were already becoming evident, and it was not long before competition from other commercial powers took its toll.

THE HOUSES OF HABSBURG AND BRAGANÇA (1580-1807). In 1580, Habsburg King of Spain **Felipe II** forcibly affirmed his quasi-legitimate claim to the Portuguese throne, and the Iberian Peninsula was briefly ruled by one monarch. For 60 years the Habsburg family dragged Portugal into several ill-fated wars, including the Spanish-Portuguese Armada's crushing loss to England in 1588. Inattentive King Felipe did not even visit Portugal until 1619—his priorities were elsewhere. By the end of Habsburg rule, Portugal had lost much of its once vast empire.

In 1640, during a rebellion against King Felipe IV, the **House of Bragança** engineered a nationalist rebellion. After a brief struggle they assumed control, once again asserting Portuguese independence from Spain. To secure its independence, the Bragança dynasty went to great lengths to reestablish ties with England. Nearly half a century later, **João V** (1706-1750) had restored a measure of prosperity, using newly discovered Brazilian gold and diamonds to finance massive building projects, including the construction of extravagant palaces.

IF GILLIGAN HAD BEEN SO LUCKY Paradise on earth? Start with water, water, everywhere. Add some volcanic eruptions, for solidity's sake. Mix in hearty, friendly, and pleasingly relaxed inhabitants. Pepper it with astounding beauty, alluring beaches, and filter out pollution, persecution, and stress. Voilá!— you have Portugal's Atlantic islands, the Azores and Madeiras, considered by many to be the world's most beautiful and most serene. While beyond the average *Let's Go* budget, these isles are integral to Portugal.

The **Madeiras,** consisting of three islands—Madeira, Porto Santo, and Desertas—rise abruptly from the ocean off Africa's northwestern coast. Discovered uninhabited in 1419 by Portuguese seamen, the Madeiras became an essential stopover for budding explorers. Their climate, colorful fauna, tropical fruits, and luxurious hotels make them a strong contender for the ideal vacation spot.

Less commercial but no less awe-inspiring, the **Azores** lie alone in the Atlantic, thousands of miles from land. Immortalized in *Moby Dick,* the nine islands boast rolling hills, lush fauna, cavernous lakes, glimmering seas, and friendly inhabitants. Tranquil and tempting, the Azores will leave the particularly melodramatic to muse (as one brochure claims) "Is this the home of God?"

The momentous **Earthquake of 1755** devastated Lisbon and southern Portugal, killing over 15,000 people. Despite the damage, dictatorial minister **Marquês de Pombal** was able to rebuild Lisbon while instituting national economic reform.

NAPOLEON'S CONQUEST AND ITS AFTERMATH (1807-1910). Napoleon took control of France in 1801 and had grand designs on much of Europe. Napoleon's army met little resistance when it invaded Portugal in 1807. Rather than risk death, the Portuguese royal family fled to Brazil. **Dom João VI** returned to Lisbon in 1821, only to face an extremely unstable political climate. Amidst turmoil within the royal family, João's son **Pedro** declared independence for Brazil the following year, becoming the country's first ruler.

More problems developed when João's died in 1826. The **Constitution of 1822,** drawn up during the royal family's absence, had severely limited the power of the monarchy, and after 1826, the **War of the Two Brothers** (1826-1834) between constitutionalists (supporting Pedro, the new king of Brazil) and monarchists (supporting Miguel, Pedro's brother) reverberated through Portugal. Eight gory years later, with Miguel in exile, Pedro's daughter **Maria II** (1834-1854) ascended to the throne at a mere 15-years-old. The next 75 years brought continued tensions between liberals and monarchists.

FROM THE "FIRST REPUBLIC" TO SALAZAR (1910-1974). Portugal spent the first few years of the 20th century trying to recover from the political discord of the previous century. On October 5, 1910, 20-year-old King **Manuel II** fled to England. The new government, known as the **First Republic,** granted universal male suffrage and diminished the influence of the Catholic Church. Workers received the right to strike, and merit, rather than birth, became the primary qualification for civil service advancement. But the expulsion of the Jesuits and other religious orders sparked worldwide disapproval; conflict between the government and labor movements heightened tensions at home. Portugal's decision to enter World War I (even though on the side of the victorious Allies) proved economically fatal and internally divisive. The weak republic wobbled and eventually fell in a 1926 military coup. General **António Carmona** took over as leader of the provisional military government, and in the face of financial crisis, he appointed **António de Oliveira Salazar,** a prominent economics professor, his minister of finance. In 1932 Salazar became prime minister, but he soon evolved into a dictator. His *Estado Novo* (New State) granted suffrage to women, but did little else to end the country's authoritarian tradition. While Portugal's international economic standing improved, the regime laid the cost of progress squarely on the shoulders of the working class, the peasantry, and colonial subjects in Africa. A terrifying secret police (PIDE) crushed all opposition to Salazar's rule, and African rebellions were quelled in bloody battles that drained the nation's economy.

REVOLUTION AND REFORM (1974-1999). The slightly more liberal **Marcelo Caetano** dragged on the increasingly unpopular African wars after Salazar's death in 1970. By the early 70s, international disapproval of Portuguese imperialism and the army's dissatisfaction with colonial entanglements had led General António de Spinola to call for decolonization. On April 25, 1974, a left-wing military coalition calling itself the Armed Forces Movement overthrew Caetano in a quick coup. The **Revolution of the Carnations** sent Portuguese dancing into the streets; today every town in Portugal has its own Rua 25 de Abril. The Marxist-dominated armed forces established a variety of civil and political liberties and withdrew Portuguese claims on African colonies by 1975.

The socialist government nationalized several industries and appropriated large estates in the face of substantial opposition. The country's first elections in 1976 put the charismatic socialist Prime Minister **Mario Soares** into power. When a severe economic crisis exploded and foreign debt, inflation, and unemployment skyrocketed, Soares instituted "100 measures in 100 days" to shock Portugal into economic shape. Through austere reforms, he helped stimulate industrial growth. The landmark year 1986 brought Portugal into the European Community (now the European Union), ending its age-old isolation from more affluent northern Europe. Despite challenges by the newly formed Social Democratic Party (PSD), Soares won the elections in 1986, becoming the nation's first civilian president in 60 years. Forced to step down because of constitutional limitations, Soares was replaced by the Socialist former mayor of Lisbon, **Jorge Sampaio,** in 1995. During the 1990s, the Portuguese government has instituted a series of economic programs (with the help of EU funds) to prepare the country for economic integration with the rest of Europe.

CURRENT EVENTS. Portugal continues in its quest to catch up economically with the rest of Western Europe. Despite uncertainty about Portugal's future in an integrated Europe, the nation's economy reported an astounding 3.5% growth rate by the beginning of 1999. With one of the strongest economies in the EU, Portugal seemed to be thriving on the eve of its entrance into the European Monetary Union on January 1, 1999. An infusion of EU funds has not hurt the economy either. New roads, railways, hospitals, schools, port and airport facilities, and sewage and waste disposal systems have sprung up over the past several years. Although Lisbon's **Expo '98** turned out to be a disappointment, with attendance below the expected levels, preparations for the event improved Lisbon's transportation system and strengthened Portuguese national pride.

The "new" revitalized Portugal has even entered the international arena, taking on a new role in the post-colonial era. In the past few years, Portugal has worked to help negotiate peace in Angola and East Timor, two of its former colonies. On December 20, 1999, the Portuguese also ceded their last colonial holding, handing over the island of **Macau** to China after 442 years of rule. Though they lament the loss, the Portuguese are confident that their legacy in Macau will serve as a bridge between China and the European Union.

At the same time, despite Portugal's ongoing modernization, some things seem destined never to change—such as the pristine beaches along the Atlantic seaboard, the plush landscape in the north, the fine wines of Porto, and the hard-earned character and age-old traditions that have evolved over the course of Portugal's rich history.

THE ARTS

PAINTING AND SCULPTURE

The Age of Discovery (1415-1580) was an era of vast cultural exchange with Renaissance Europe and beyond. Flemish masters such as **Jan van Eyck** brought their talent to Portugal, and many Portuguese artists polished their skills in Antwerp. King Manuel's favorite, High Renaissance artist **Jorge Afonso,** created realistic portrayals of human anatomy. Afonso's best works hang at the Convento de Cristo in Tomar and Convento da Madre de Deus in Lisbon. In the late 15th century, the talented **Nuno Gonçalves** led a revival of the primitivist school.

Portuguese Baroque art featured even more diverse styles and themes. Woodcarving became extremely popular in Portugal during the Baroque period. **Joachim Machado** carved elaborate crèches in the early 1700s. On canvas, portraiture was head and shoulders above other genres. The prolific 19th-century artist **Domingos António de Sequeira** depicted historical, religious, and allegorical subjects using a technique that would later inspire French Impressionists. In another artistic tilt, Porto's **António Soares dos Reis** brought Romantic sensibility to 19th-century Portuguese sculpture.

In the 20th century, Cubism, Expressionism and Futurism trickled into Portugal despite Salazar-inspired censorship. More recently, **Maria Helena Vieira da Silva** has won international recognition for her abstract works, and the master **Carlos Botelho** has become world-renowned for his wonderful vignettes of Lisbon life.

ARCHITECTURE

Though few Moorish structures survived the Christian Reconquest, Moorish styles continued to influence Portuguese architecture. Colorfully painted ceramic tiles, known as **azulejos,** grace many walls, ceilings, and thresholds. Carved in fabulous relief by the Moors, these ornate tiles later took on flat, glazed Italian and northern European designs. Ironically enough, this Islamic concept gained its greatest fame in Catholic churches, the palaces of Christian kings, and post-17th-century Portuguese urban architecture.

Portugal's signature **Manueline** style celebrates the prosperity and imperial expansion of King Manuel I's reign (see **The Age of Discovery,** p. 526). Manueline works routinely merge Christian images and maritime motifs. Their rich and lavish ornaments reflect a hybrid of Northern Gothic, Spanish Plateresque, and Moorish influences. The Manueline style found its most elaborate expression in the church and tower at **Belém,** built to honor Vasco da Gama. Close seconds are the **Mosteiro dos Jerónimos** in Belém and the **Abadia de Santa Maria de Vitória** in Batalha.

LITERATURE

ORIGINS OF PORTUGUESE LITERATURE. Portugal's literary achievements, mostly lyric poetry and realist fiction, can be traced back to the 12th century, when the lyrical aspects of Portuguese were solidified by poet-king **Dinis I.** Dinis made Portuguese the region's official language (one of the first "official" non-Latin Romance vernaculars). **Gil Vicente** (1465-1536/7), court poet to Manuel I, is considered Portugal's equivalent to Shakespeare in style and importance. Vicente wrote dramas (tempered with comic relief) about peasants, nature, and religion. The witty realism of his *Barcas* trilogy (1517-1519) influenced contemporaries Shakespeare and Cervantes and earned him a distinguished place in both Portuguese and international literary ranks.

PORTUGUESE LITERARY RENAISSANCE. Portuguese literature blossomed during the Renaissance, most notably in the letters of **Francisco de Sá de Miranda** (1481-1558) and the lyrics of **António Ferreira** (1528-1569). During the Age of Discovery, conquest abroad inspired both historians and poets. An explorer himself, the humanist **João de Barros** (1496-1570) penned *Décadas da Ásia*, a history of Portuguese conquest in Goa. Influenced by the *Décades*, the writer **Luís de Camões** (1524-1580) celebrated Vasco de Gama's sea voyages to India in Portugal's greatest epic, *Os Lusíadas* (*The Lusiads*, 1572), modeled on the Latin classic, the *Aeneid* (see **A Camões Cameo,** p. 552).

NINETEENTH CENTURY LITERARY MOVEMENTS. Spanish hegemony, intermittent warfare, and imperial decline conspired to make the literature of the 17th and 18th centuries somewhat less triumphant than that of past eras. The 19th century, however, saw a dramatic rebirth of Portuguese literature. Poet **João Baptista de Almeida Garrett** (1799-1854) and historian **Alexandre Herculano** (1810-1877), who were both exiled because of their liberal political views, integrated Portuguese literature with the Romantic school of fiction they encountered while in exile. A lyric poet, dramatist, politician, revolutionary, frequent exile, and legendary lover, Garrett is credited with reviving drama in Portugal. His most famous play is *Frei Luís de Sousa* (*Brother Luís de Sousa*, 1843).

Portuguese literature shifted from romantic to realist when political thinkers dominated the rise of the literary intelligentsia, the **Generation of 1870.** The most visible figure to influence this shift in the late 19th century was novelist and lifelong diplomat (residing almost always outside Iberia) **José Maria Eça de Queiroz.** He conceived of a distinctly Portuguese social realism, and he documented 19th-century Portuguese society, sometimes critical of its bourgeois elements. His best works were *O Crime do Padre Amaro* (*The Sin of Father Amaro*) and *Os Maias* (*The Mayas*).

CONTEMPORARY LITERATURE. **Fernando Pessoa** (1888-1935) was Portugal's most famed and creative writer of the late 19th and early 20th centuries. Pessoa (literally, "person") wrote in English and Portuguese, developing four distinct styles under four different names: Pessoa, Alberto Caeiro, Ricardo Reis, and Alvaro de Campos. Pessoa introduced free verse to Portuguese poetry; his overall impact rivals T.S. Eliot's on English literature. His semi-autobiography, *Livro do Desassossego* (*The Book of Disgust*) is his only prose work, posthumously compiled and today seen as a modernist classic. Other influential writers of the 20th century are **Aquilino Ribeiro,** author of *O Homem que Matou o Diabo* (*The Man Who Killed the Devil*), and **José Maria Ferreira de Castro,** widely known for his realist fiction, especially his novel *A Selva* (*The Jungle*).

LOVE NOTES If the blues have a hold on your heart, then *fado* will capture your soul. The melodies and lyrics of *fado* drip with wrenching pain and passion of life and love. Although *fado* may have been rooted in African slave songs, the legendary *fadista* (*fado* singer) **Maria Severa** made *fado* quintessentially Portuguese. Although she lived a short life (1810-1836), Severa achieved mythical status because of her moving lyrics (through which she expressed her own real-life dramas). Severa's life and early death (due to excessive gastronomic consumption) were a turning point in the history of *fado*, providing the basis for the first Portuguese "talking picture" in 1931 and spawning many other poems, novels, and *fado* lyrics. Modern *fadistas*, including **Amália Rodrigues** and **Argentina Santos**, have helped spread *fado* throughout Portugal. *Fado* houses, including Adega Machado in Lisbon (p. 558), are the best places to enjoy a special *fado* moment and to celebrate the legend that Severa left behind. Coimbra is also home to many *fado* houses, though Coimbra *fado* differs significantly from the more urban, working-class-inspired Lisbon style Coimbra's has slower, more intellectual lyrics about romance and beautiful women and is often sung by male students from Coimbra's universities.

Contemporary writers, like **Miguel Torga,** have gained international fame for their wonderfully satirical novels. **José Saramago,** winner of the 1998 Nobel Prize for literature, is perhaps Portugal's most important living writer. His work, written in the realist style and laced with irony, has achieved new acclaim in the post-Salazar era. He is best known for *Baltasar and Blimunda*, the story of lovers who escape the Inquisition in a time machine, and *The Stone Raft*, a satire about Iberia's isolation from the rest of Europe.

The end of Salazar's reign brought literary liberation; repression, once the condition, is now the topic. Female writers, long discouraged or censored, have come out of the woodwork with a vengeance. In **Novas Cartas Portuguesas** *(New Portuguese Letters)*, the "Three Marias" (the authors) expose the mistreatment of women in a male-dominated society. Other acclaimed post-Salazar authors include **António Lobo Antunes** and **José Cardoso Pires.** Antunes has achieved the status of Saramago but with a dramatically different style, one known for its scattered form and psychoanalytic themes. Pires' works often comment on the repression of the Salazar regime, and his novel *Balada da Praia dos Cães (Ballad of Dog's Beach)* exposes the terror of Salazar's secret police.

MUSIC

The **fado** is said to cause the chords of the Portuguese soul to vibrate melancholically or passionately. Named after fate, *fado* is a musical tradition unique to Portugal, identified with a sense of *saudade* (yearning or longing) and characterized by tragic, romantic lyrics and mournful melodies. These solo ballads, accompanied by the acoustic *guitarra* (a flat-backed guitar, like a mandolin), appeal to the romantic side of Portuguese culture.

Apart from its folk tradition, the music of Portugal has yet to achieve international fame. Portuguese opera peaked with **António José da Silva** (1705-1739), a victim of the 1739 Inquisition. The Renaissance in Portugal led to the development of pieces geared for solo instrumentalists and vocals. Italian **Domenico Scarlatti** (1685-1757), brought to Lisbon by João V, composed brilliant keyboard pieces. His preeminent Portuguese contemporary, Coimbra's **Carlos Seixas,** thrilled 18th-century Lisbon with his genius and contributed to the development of the sonata form. **Domingos Bomtempo** (1775-1842) introduced symphonic innovations from abroad and helped establish the first Portuguese Sociedade Filarmónica, modeled after the London Philharmonic, in Lisbon in 1822.

Although the French invasion, Civil War, and decreased patronage somewhat stifled Portuguese music, folk music and dancing is still quite popular in rural areas. In the latter half of this century, Joly Braga Santo has led a modern revival of Portuguese classical music. The Calouste Gulbenkian Foundation in Lisbon has also kept Portuguese music alive, sponsoring a symphony orchestra since 1962, and hosting popular local folk singers (including Fausto and Sérgio Godinho), ballets, operas, and jazz festivals. The Teatro Nacional de São Carlos, which has its own orchestra and ballet company, has further benefitted Portuguese music. The Teatro has spawned a group of talented young composers, including Filipe Pires, A. Vitorino de Almeida, and Jorge Peixinho, all of whom have begun to make their mark in international competitions.

LANGUAGE

Thanks to the Romans who colonized Iberia in the late third century BC, practiced Latin speakers will find Portuguese an easy conquest (though pronunciation may be difficult). Although this softer sister of Spanish is closely related to the other Romance languages, modern Portuguese is an amalgam of diverse influences. A close listener will catch echoes of Italian, French, Spanish, Arabic, and even English and Slavic. Portugal's global escapades also spurred the spread of its language. Today, Portuguese (the world's fifth-most-spoken language) binds over 200 million people worldwide, most of them in Portugal, Brazil, Mozambique, and

Angola. Prospective students of the language should note the differences between Brazilian and continental Portuguese, mainly in pronunciation and usage.

Some may be heartened to know that English, Spanish, and French are widely spoken throughout Portugal, especially in tourist-oriented locales. Look to the *Let's Go* glossary in the back of this book for terms (or their Castilian cousins) that are used in this guide (see **Glossary**, p. 729).

FOOD AND DRINK

TYPICAL FARE

The Portuguese season their dishes with olive oil, garlic, herbs, and sea salt but use relatively few spices. Seafood lovers will enjoy a tantalizing selection of fish: *chocos grelhados* (grilled cuttlefish), *linguado grelhado* (grilled sole), and *peixe espada* (swordfish), to name a few. The more adventurous should try the *polvo* (boiled or grilled octopus), *mexilhões* (mussels), and *lulas grelhadas* (grilled squid). Pork, chicken, and beef appear on most menus and are often combined together as *cozida à portuguesa* (boiled beef, pork, sausage, and vegetables). True connoisseurs add a drop of *piri-piri* (mega-hot) sauce on the side. An expensive delicacy is freshly roasted *cabrito* (baby goat). No matter what you order, leave room for *batatas* (potatoes), prepared countless ways—including *batatas fritas* (french fries)—which accompany each meal.

Sopas (soups) are an inexpensive and light meal option. Common soups are *caldo de ovos* (bean soup with hard-boiled eggs), *caldo de verdura* (vegetable soup), and the tasty *caldo verde* (a potato and kale mixture with a slice of sausage and olive oil). **Sandes** (sandwiches) such as the *bifana* or *prego no pão* (meat sandwich) may be no more than a hunk of meat on a roll. Cows, goats, and ewes please the palate by providing raw material for Portugal's renowned **queijos** (cheeses). Vegetarians should accustom themselves to the cheese sandwich and Portugal's delectable bread.

Portugal's favorite **dessert** is *pudim*, or *flan*, a rich, caramel custard similar to *crême bruleé*. For the sweet tooth in all of us, the almond groves of the Algarve produce their own version of marzipan. For something different, try *pêras* (pears) drenched in sweet port wine and served with a sprinkling of raisins and hazelnuts on top. Most common are countless varieties of inexpensive, high-quality **sorvete** (ice cream)—look for vendors posting the colorful, ubiquitous "Olá" sign. *Pastelarías* (bakeries) are social centers in most towns, and tasty **pastries** make for a cheap (80-180$) breakfast.

DINING HOURS AND RESTAURANTS

Portuguese eat their hearty midday meal—*almoço* (lunch)—between noon and 2pm and *jantar* (dinner) between 9pm and midnight. Both meals entail at least three courses. There are no greasy lumberjack breakfasts to be found in Portugal—a pastry (80-180$) from a *pastelaría* (bakery) and coffee from a cafe suffices for *pequeno almoço* (breakfast). If you happen to get the munchies between 4 and 7pm, snack bars sell **sandes** (sandwiches) and sweet cinnamon-flavored cakes.

A full meal costs 1000-2000$, depending on the restaurant's location and quality. **Meia dose** (half portions) cost more than half-price but are often more than adequate—a full portion may satisfy two. The ubiquitous **prato do dia** (special of the day) and **menu** (*ementa* in Portuguese) of appetizer, bread, entree, and dessert will stifle the loudest stomach growls. The **ementa turística** (tourist menu) is usually not a good deal—restaurants with menus translated into multiple languages are more likely to charge exorbitant prices. Standard pre-meal bread, butter, cheese, and pâté may be dished without your asking, but these pre-meal munchies are not free (300-500$ per person). In restaurants (but not cafes), a service charge of 10% is usually included in the bill. When service is not included, it is customary to leave about 5% to 10% as a tip.

Outdoor food stalls are the best way to eat on the cheap. **Vegetarians** should hit the **mercado municipal** (an open-air market found in almost every town) before noon for the best produce. Produce and other groceries are also available at the **supermercado** (supermarket) or **loja de conveniência** (convenience store).

DRINKS

The quality and low cost of Portuguese *vinho* (wine) is truly astounding. The pinnacle, **vinho do porto** (port), pressed (by feet) from the red grapes of the Douro Valley and fermented with a touch of brandy, is a dessert in itself. Chilled, white port can be a snappy aperitif, while ruby or tawny port makes a classic after-dinner drink. A six-month-long heating process gives **Madeira** wines their unique "cooked" flavor. Try the dry Sercial and Verdelho before the main course, and the sweeter Bual and Malmsey after.

Sparkling *vinho verde* (green wine, referring to its youth, not its color) comes in red and white versions. The red may be a bit strong but the white is brash, delicious, and intoxicating by any standard. The Adega Cooperatives of Ponte de Lima, Monção, and Amarante produce the best (i.e., most potent) of this type. Excellent local table wines include Colares, Dão, Borba, Bairrada, Bucelas, and Periquita. If you can't decide, experiment cautiously with the **vinho de casa** (house wine); either the *tinto* (red) or the *branco* (white) is a reliable standby. Tangy **sangría** comes filled with fresh orange slices and makes even a budget meal festive at a minimal expense (usually around 500$ for a half-pitcher).

Bottled Sagres and Super Bock are excellent beers. If you don't ask for it *fresco* (cool), it may come *natural* (room temperature). A tall, slim glass of draft beer is a **fino** or an **imperial,** while a larger stein is a **caneca.** To sober up and wake up, order a **bica** (cup of black espresso), a **galão** (coffee with milk, served in a glass), or a **café com leite** (coffee with milk, served in a cup).

MEDIA

Portugal's most widely read daily newspapers are *Público* (www.publico.pt), *Diário de Notícas* (www.dn.pt), and *Jornal de Notícas.* If you haven't yet mastered Portuguese, check out *The News,* Portugal's only online English language newspaper, at www.the-news.net. Those interested in international news stories can also pick up day-old foreign papers at larger newsstands.

Portuguese TV offers four main channels: the state-run Canal 1 and TV2 and the private SIC (Sociedade Independente de Communicação) and TVI (TV Independente). Couch potatoes can also enjoy numerous cable channels, most of which air Brazilian and Portuguese soap operas and subtitled foreign sitcoms.

SPORTS

Futebol (soccer to Americans) is the sport of choice for just about everyone. The country has shown signs of making it big—at the 1996 European Championships, the national team ousted Denmark en route to the semifinals—but has fallen short at crucial moments, such as the World Cup '98 qualification matches. Games create a crazed fervor throughout Portugal. Lisbon's club, **Benfica,** possesses some of the best players in the world. Native Portuguese have also made names for themselves in long-distance running, where marathon-queen **Rosa Mota** dominated her event for a number of years. For recreation other than jogging and pick-up soccer, native Portuguese often return to the sea. **Windsurfers, body-surfers,** and **surfers** make waves along the north coast; **snorklers** and **scuba divers** set out on mini-explorations in the south and west.

FESTIVALS AND HOLIDAYS

As in Spain, festivals and form a large part of local culture. Portugal hosts plenty of lively fairs and religious celebrations, some of which span weeks or months. The list below includes major Portuguese festivals for 2000. For more information on regional events consult the local tourist office.

DATE	FESTIVAL	LOCATION
January 1	New Year's Day	National
January 6	Epiphany	National
March 2-12	Carnival	National
April 17-23	Holy Week	National
April 20	Senhor Ecce Homo (Maundy Thursday)	National
April 21	Good Friday	National
April 23	Easter	National
April 25	Liberty Day	National
May 1	Labor Day	National
early May	Queima das Fitas (Burning of the Ribbons)	Coimbra (p. 616)
June	Feira Internacional de Lisboa	Lisbon (p. 558)
first week of June	Feira Nacional de Agricultura (Feira do Ribatejo)	Santarém (p. 594)
June 12	Festa de Santo António	Lisbon (p. 558)
June 22	Corpus Christi	National
first week of July	Festas da Rainha Santa	Coimbra (p. 616)
second week of July	Feira Popular	Coimbra (p. 616)
late July	Festa do Sardinha	Peniche (p. 599)
late July to early August	Feira de Santiago	Setúbal (p. 568)
August 15	Feast of the Assumption	National
October 5	Republic Day	National
November 1	All Saints' Day	National
December 8	Feast of the Immaculate Conception	National
December 25	Christmas	National
December 31	New Year's Eve	National

RECOMMENDED READING

FICTION: PORTUGUESE AND FOREIGN. For the scoop on Portuguese classics in most every genre, check out **Literature** (p. 529). The more famous works have been translated into English; for additional options, consult your librarian.

Selected Letters and Journals, by Lord Byron. Narrates the days Byron spent in Portugal.

The Lusiads, by Luís de Camões. A Portuguese classic. Written in lyric verse, it chronicles Portuguese exploration during the Age of Discovery.

The Last Kabbalist of Lisbon, by Richard Zimler. A fantastic murder mystery by a modern American author. It explores the world of Portugal's 16th-century Jewish mystics.

Baltasar and Blimunda, The History of the Siege of Lisbon, and **The Stone Raft,** by José Saramago. See why Saramago won the 1998 Nobel Prize in Literature.

HISTORY AND CULTURE. There is no dearth of information on Portuguese history and culture for the inquisitive and intellectual traveler. Packing one of these works in your suitcase will help make the cities and towns of Portugal that much more meaningful and memorable.

A Concise History of Portugal, by David Birmingham (1991). All of Portuguese history in one handy volume.

Roads to Today's Portugal: Essays on Contemporary Portuguese Literature, Art, and Culture, by Elanea Brown (1983). This collection of essays provides an introduction to 20th-century Portuguese culture.

History of Portugal, by A.H. de Oliveira Marques (1972). Though somewhat outdated, this is among the most comprehensive Portuguese history texts available.

Europe's Best-Kept Secret: An Insider's View of Portugal, by Costa Matos (1997). Matos' witty account of Portuguese culture and history includes amusing anecdotes of peculiar Portuguese personalities.

Modern Portugal, edited by António Costa Pinto (1998). A Portuguese account that covers 20th-century Portuguese history from the rise of Salazar to the evolution of the nation's resilient democracy.

ESSENTIALS

The information in this section is mostly designed to help travelers get their bearings once they are in Portugal. For information about general **travel preparations** (including passports and permits, money, health, packing, international transportation, and more), consult the **Essentials** section at the beginning of this book (p. 7). That chapter also has important information about alternatives to tourism (**work** and **study** programs in Portugal; p. 43) and for those with specific concerns: **women travelers** (p. 39); **solo travelers** (p. 40); **older travelers** (p. 40); **bisexual, gay, and lesbian travelers** (p. 41); **travelers with disabilities** (p. 41); **minority travelers** (p. 42); **travelers with children** (p. 42); and travelers with **dietary needs** (p. 43).

GETTING THERE AND AROUND

Portugal is easily accessible by plane from the U.S. and Europe. Long-distance trains run from **Madrid** (p. 76) to Lisbon, and buses run from **Sevilla** (p. 190) to Lagos. Closer to the border, trains run from **Huelva** (easily accessible from Sevilla, p. 190) and **Cáceres** (p. 174) to Portugal. Trains and buses run from **Badajoz** (p. 183), only 6km from the border, to Elvas and elsewhere. **Ciudad Rodrigo** (p. 153) lies only 21km from the border, while buses run from **Zamora** (p. 155) to Bragança. In the north, trains run from **Vigo** (p. 456) to Porto; from **Túy** (p. 458), you can walk across the Portuguese border to Valença do Minho.

BY PLANE

Most major international airlines serve Lisbon; some serve Porto, Faro, and the Madeiras. **TAP Air Portugal** (in U.S. and Canada tel. (800) 221 7370; in U.K. tel. (171) 828 20 92; in Lisbon tel. (1) 841 69 90; www.tap.pt) is Portugal's national airline, serving all domestic locations and many major international cities. **Portugália** (www.pga.pt) is a smaller Portuguese airline that flies between Porto, Faro, Lisbon, all major Spanish cities, and other Western European destinations. Its offices include Lisbon (tel. (1) 842 55 00) and Manchester (tel. (161) 489 50 40).

BY TRAIN

Caminhos de Ferro Portugueses is Portugal's national railway, but for long-distance travel outside of the Braga-Porto-Coimbra-Lisbon line, the bus is much better. The exception is around Lisbon, where local trains and commuter rails are fast and efficient. Most trains have first- and second-class cabins, except for local and suburban routes. When you arrive in town, go to the station ticket booth to check the departure schedule; trains often run at irregular hours, and posted schedules (*horarios*) are not always accurate.

Unless you own a Eurailpass, the return on round-trip tickets must be used before 3am the following day. Anyone riding without a ticket is fined over 3500$. Children under four travel free; ages four to 11 pay half-price. **Youth discounts** are only available to Portuguese citizens. Though there is a Portugal Flexipass, it is not worth purchasing.

BY BUS

Buses are cheap, frequent, and connect just about every town in Portugal. **Rodoviária** (national info tel. (1) 354 57 75), the national bus company, has recently been privatized. Each company name corresponds to a particular region of the country, such as Rodoviária Alentejo or Minho e Douro, with notable exceptions such as EVA in the Algarve. Private regional companies also operate, among them **Cabanelas, AVIC,** and **Mafrense.** Be wary of non-express buses in small regions like Estremadura and Alentejo, which stop every few minutes. Express coach service (*expressos*) between major cities is especially good; inexpensive city buses often run to nearby villages. Schedules (*horarios*) are usually printed and posted, but double-check with the ticket vendor to make sure they are accurate.

BY CAR AND THUMB

Portugal has the highest rate of automobile accidents, per capita, in Western Europe. The new highway system (IP) is quite good, but off the main arteries, the narrow, twisting roads prove difficult to negotiate. The locals' testy reputation is well deserved. Speed limits are effectively ignored, recklessness common, and lighting and road surfaces often inadequate. Buses and trucks are safer options. Moreover, parking space in cities borders on nonexistent. **Gas** comes in super (97 octane), normal (92 octane), and unleaded. Gas prices may be high by North American standards—140-170 *escudos* (or US$0.75-0.90) per liter.

Portugal's national automobile association, the **Automóvel Clube de Portugal (ACP)**, R. Rosa Araújo, 49A (tel. (1) 711 23 60), provides **breakdown** and **towing service** (M-F 8am-11pm, Sa-Su 9am-10pm) and **first aid** (24hr.).

In Portugal, **hitchers** are rare. Beach-bound locals occasionally hitch in summer but otherwise stick to the inexpensive bus system. Rides are easiest to come by between smaller towns. Best results are reputedly at gas stations near highways and rest stops. *Let's Go* does not recommend hitchhiking.

MONEY

Official **banking hours** are Monday through Friday 8:30am to 3pm, but play it safe by giving yourself some extra time. The following exchange rates are based on published rates from August 1999. For more information on money, see p. 14.

US $1 = 190.80 ESCUDOS ($)	**100$ = US $0.52**
CDN $1 = 127.52$	**100$ = CDN $0.78**
UK £1 = 304.65$	**100$ = UK £0.33**
IR £1 = 254.56$	**100$ = IR £0.39**
AUS $1 = 121.64$	**100$ = AUS $0.82**
NZ $1 = 100.77$	**100$ = NZ $0.99**
SAR 1 = 31.33$	**100$ = SAR 3.19**
SP 1PTA = 1.20$	**100$ = SP 83.00PTAS**
MOR 1DH = 19.50$	**100$ = MOR 5.13DH**
EURO = 200.48$	**100$ = EURO 0.50**

TIPPING AND BARGAINING. Tips are customary only in fancy restaurants or hotels. Some cheaper restaurants include a 10% service charge; if they don't and you'd like to leave a tip, round up and leave the change. Taxi drivers do not expect a tip unless the trip was especially long. **Bargaining** is not customary in shops, but you can give it a shot at the local *mercado* (market) or when looking for a *quarto*.

SAFETY AND HEALTH

In Portugal, the highest rates of crime have been in the Lisbon area, especially on buses, trams, in train stations, and in airports. Exercise the most caution in the Alf-

EMERGENCY TEL.	Dial 112 for police, medical, or fire.

ama district, the Santa Apolonia and Rossio train stations, Castelo de São Jorge, and in Belém. The towns around Lisbon with the most reported crimes in recent years are Cascais, Sintra, and Fátima. Thieves sometimes try and distract people by staging loud arguments, passing a soccer ball back and forth on a crowded street, asking for directions, pretending to dance with their victim, or spilling something on their victim's clothing. Motorists should be wary of "Good Samaritans" who have been known to help ailing motorists by the side of the road and then steal their cars.

Portugal is in general a healthful country in which to travel. For general **health** information, see page 20.

ACCOMMODATIONS

YOUTH HOSTELS

Movijovem, Av. Duque de Ávila, 137, 1050 Lisbon (tel. (1) 313 88 20; fax 352 86 21), the Portuguese Hosteling International affiliate, looks over the country's HI hostels. All bookings can be made through them. A cheap bed in a *pousada da juventude* (not to be confused with plush *pousadas*) costs 1200-2900$ per night and slightly less in the off-season (breakfast and sheets included). Lunch or dinner usually costs 900$, snacks around 250$. Rates may be higher for guests 26 and older. Though often the cheapest option, hostels may lie some distance from the town center. Check-in hours are 9am to noon and 6pm to midnight. Some have lockouts 10:30am to 6pm, and early curfews might cramp club-hoppers' style. The maximum stay at one hostel is eight nights unless you get special permission.

To stay in an HI hostel an **HI card** (3000$) is usually mandatory. Although they are sold at Movijovem's Lisbon office, it is more convenient to get an HI membership before leaving home. To reserve a bed in the high season, obtain an **International Booking Voucher** from Movijovem (or your country's HI affiliate) and send it from home to the desired hostel four to eight weeks in advance. In the off-season (Oct.-Apr.), double-check to see if the hostel is open. Large groups should reserve through Movijovem at least 30 days in advance. For more info, see **Hostels,** page 25.

PENSÕES AND HOTELS

Pensões, also called **residencias,** are a budget traveler's mainstay. They're far cheaper than hotels and only slightly more expensive (and much more common) than crowded youth hostels. Like hostels, *pensões* generally provide sheets and towels and have commons rooms. All are rated on a five-star scale and are required to visibly post their category and legal price limits. (If you don't see this information, ask for it.) During the high season, many *pensões* do not take reservations, but for those that do, booking a week ahead is advisable.

Hotels in Portugal tend to be pricey. Room prices typically include showers and breakfast, and most rooms without bath or shower have a sink. However, many force you out by noon. When business is weak, try bargaining down in advance—the "official price" is just the maximum allowed.

ALTERNATIVE ACCOMMODATIONS

Quartos are rooms in private residences, similar to *casas particulares* in Spain. These rooms may be your only option in less touristed, smaller towns (particularly in the south), or the cheapest one in bigger cities. The tourist office can usually help you find a *quarto*. When all else fails, feel free to ask at bars and restaurants for names and addresses, but you should try to verify the quality of the rooms. Prices are often flexible, and can drop as much as 500-1000$ with bargaining.

Pousadas, like Spanish *paradors*, outperform standard hotel expectations (and, unfortunately, rates). They are castles, palaces, or monasteries converted into luxurious, government-run hotels. "Historical" *pousadas* play up local crafts, customs, and cuisine and may cost as much as expensive hotels. Most require reservations. Priced less extravagantly are *regional pousadas*, situated in national parks and reserves. For info, contact ENATUR, Av. Santa Joana Princesa, 10-A, 1749 Lisbon (tel. (1) 844 20 00; fax 844 20 58).

CAMPING

In Portugal, over 150 **official campgrounds** *(parques de campismo)* feature gobs of amenities and comforts. Most have a supermarket and cafes, and many are beach-accessible or near rivers or pools. Given the facilities' quality and popularity, happy campers are those who arrive early; urban and coastal parks may require reservations. Police have been cracking down on illegal camping, so don't try it—especially near official campgrounds. Tourist offices stock the free *Portugal: Camping and Caravan Sites*, a handy guide to official campgrounds. Otherwise, write the **Federação Portuguesa de Campismo e Caravanismo,** Av. 5 de Outubro, 15-3, 950 Lisbon (tel. (1) 842 84 80; open daily 9:30am-12:30pm and 1:30-6:30pm).

KEEPING IN TOUCH

Most useful communication information (including **international access codes, calling card numbers, country codes, operator** and **directory assistance,** and **emergency numbers**) is listed on the **inside back cover.**

PHONES. Portugal's national telephone company is **Telecom Portugal.** Phone offices exist in most cities, but there is little need to use them as all services are available in phone booths, located on the street and in post offices. Coin-operated phones are essentially non-existent in Portugal; you'll need phone cards. The country uses both the **Credifone** and **Telecom Portugal** systems. For both systems, the basic unit for all calls (and the price for local ones) is 18$. The Telecom phone cards, using "patch" (not strip) cards, are most common in Lisbon and Porto and increasingly elsewhere. Credifone cards, with magnetic strips, are sold at drugstores, post offices, and locations posted on phone booths, and are most useful outside these two big cities. Private calls from bars and cafes cost whatever the proprietor decides, typically 30-40$; a posted sign usually indicates the rates. Remember that the initial zero (0) in **city codes** is dialed only when dialing from another area within Portugal; from outside of Portugal the zero is omitted. Local calls do not require dialing any portion of the city code.

Calling cards probably remain the best method of making international calls (see p. 29 for more details). The numbers to access major calling card services (including AT&T, MCI, Canada Direct, BT Direct, Ireland Direct, Telstra Australia, Optus Australia, Telecom New Zealand, and Telkom South Africa) are listed on the inside back cover.

MAIL. Mail in Portugal is somewhat inefficient—**Air mail** *(via aerea)* can take from one to two weeks (or longer) to reach the U.S. or Canada. It is slightly quicker for destinations in Europe and longer for Australia, New Zealand, and South Africa. **Surface mail** *(superficie)*, for packages only, takes up to two months. **Registered** or **blue mail** takes five to eight business days (for roughly three times the price of air mail). **EMS** or **Express Mail** will probably get there in three to four days for more than double the blue mail price. **Stamps** are available at post offices *(correios)* and automatic, surprisingly efficient stamp machines outside post offices and in central locations around cities. Also at post offices, **fax** machines are available for public use at 2500$ for the first page, 1700$ per additional page.

EMAIL. Email is both faster and more reliable than the standard mail system. Cybercafes are common in cities and most smaller towns, and are listed in the Practical Information section and in the index under internet access. When in doubt, try the library; they often have at least one computer equipped for internet access. For information on how to obtain a free email account, see page 30.

EMBASSIES AND CONSULATES

Embassies and consulates are usually open Monday through Friday, mornings and evenings, with *siestas* in-between—call for specific hours.

Australian Embassy: Refer to the Australian Embassy in Paris: 4, rue Jean Rey, 15th arrondisement Paris 75724 France (tel. (01) 40 59 33 00; fax (01) 40 59 33 10).

British Embassy: R. São Bernardo, 33, 1200 **Lisbon** (tel. (1) 392 40 00; fax 392 41 86; Britembassy@mail.telepac.pt). **Consulates:** Av. Boavista, 3072, 4100 **Porto** (tel. (2) 618 47 89; fax 610 04 38); Largo Francisco A. Mauricio, 7-10, 8500 **Portimão** (tel. (8) 241 78 04; fax 241 78 06).

Canadian Embassy: Av. Liberdade, 144, 4th fl., 1250 **Lisbon** (tel. (1) 347 48 92; fax 347 64 66). **Consulate:** R. Frei Laurenço do Santa Maria, 1, 1st fl., 8000 **Faro** (tel. (89) 80 37 57; fax 88 08 88).

Irish Embassy: R. Imprensa à Estrela, 4th fl., Ste. 1, 1200 **Lisbon** (tel. (1) 392 94 40; fax 397 73 63).

New Zealand Embassy: Refer to the New Zealand Embassy in Italy at Via Zara, 28, **Rome** 00198 (tel. 06 441 71 71; fax 06 440 29 84; nzemb.rom@agora.stm.it). **Consulate:** R. S. Felix, 13-2, 1200 **Lisbon** (tel. (1) 350 96 90; fax 572 00 40).

South African Embassy: Av. Luis Bivar, 10, 1097 **Lisbon** (tel. (1) 353 50 41; fax 353 57 13; email SAfrican.Embassy@individual.EUnet.pt).

U.S. Embassy: Av. Forças Armadas, 1600 **Lisbon** (tel. (1) 727 33 00; fax 727 91 09). **Consulate:** same address and tel.; fax (1) 727 23 54.

PORTUGAL

LISBON
(LISBOA)

Over 400 years ago, Lisbon was the center of the world's richest and farthest-reaching empire. Though it was plagued by social and political problems in the last century, Lisbon has recently stepped back into the international spotlight. Today, it stands as one of Europe's grandest cities. Like Portugal itself, Lisbon has managed to preserve its traditions, continually renovating its historic monuments and meticulously maintaining its black and white mosaic sidewalks, pastel facades, and cobbled, medieval alleys.

Many ancient civilizations claim to have settled Lisbon, with one legend even crediting Odysseus as its founder. Officially, Lisbon is thought to have been inhabited over 3000 years ago by Phoenicians, Greeks, and Carthaginians in turn, until the Romans arrived in 205 BC. Under Julius Caesar's reign, Lisbon became the most important city in Lusitania; in 1255, it was made the capital of the kingdom of Portugal. City and empire reached their apex at the end of the 15th century when Portuguese navigators pioneered explorations of Asia, Africa, and South America. A huge earthquake on November 1, 1755, touched off the nation's fall from glory—close to one-fifth of the population died in the catastrophe, and two-thirds of Lisbon was reduced to a pile of smoldering rubble. Under the authoritarian leadership of Prime Minister Marquês de Pombal, the city recovered as magnificent new squares, palaces, and churches were built along the Cartesian guidelines of style and architecture in the heyday of the Enlightenment. Another wave of construction in the late 19th century extended the city to the north and west.

Lisbon has seen more than its share of changes over the course of the 20th century. During World War II, Lisbon's neutrality and Atlantic connections made the city a rendezvous for spies on both sides. In 1974, when Mozambique and Angola won independence, hundreds of thousands of refugees converged upon the Portuguese capital. Today, Portuguese of African, Asian, and European origin mix freely on the streets. In 1998 the World Expo descended upon Lisbon, providing the impetus for massive construction projects and a citywide face-lift while helping to renew Lisbon's seat at the forefront of European culture. Since then, the revival has continued, as more tourist hotspots and sites of cultural interest emerge.

HIGHLIGHTS OF LISBON AND DAYTRIPS FROM LISBON

■ The **Alfama district,** especially the view from its castle (see p. 553).
■ The extravagant monastery complex at nearby **Belém** (see p. 554).
■ Lisbon's futuristic new **Parque de Nações,** in all its glory (see p. 555).
■ The magnificent palaces and castles at **Sintra,** less than an hour away (see p. 561).

☰ GETTING THERE AND AWAY

BY PLANE

All flights land at **Aeroporto de Lisboa** (tel. 840 20 60 or 849 63 50), on the city's north edge. Walk out of the terminal, turn right, and follow the road around the curve to the bus stop. From here take bus #44 or 45 (20-40min., 160$) to Pr. Restauradores; the bus stops directly in front of the tourist office. Or take the express **AeroBus** (bus #91; 15min., every 20min., 7am-9pm, 430$) to the same location; the bus, which leaves directly from the airport exit, is a better option during rush hour. A taxi from the airport downtown costs about 1500$, plus a 300$ luggage fee.

Major airlines have offices at Pr. Marquês de Pombal and along Av. Liberdade. Call for the current rates, as prices almost always fluctuate.

TAP Air Portugal, Pr. Marquês de Pombal, 3 (tel. 841 69 90; www.tap.pt). To Faro, Funchal (Madeira), Porto, Paris, London, Madrid, and Barcelona. Open M-F 9am-6pm.

Iberia, R. Rosa Araújo, 2 (tel. 355 81 19; www.iberia.com).

Portugália Airlines, Av. Almirante Gago Coutinho, 88 (tel. 848 66 93 or 846 42 32; www.pga.pt). Airport office tel. 842 55 00. Serves major domestic destinations.

BY TRAIN

Train service in Lisbon is potentially confusing, as there are five main stations, each serving different destinations. Be aware that Portuguese trains are usually quite slow. For further info about Portugal's national railway system call **Caminhos de Ferro Portuguêses** (tel. 888 40 25).

Estação Rossio, between Pr. Restauradores and Pr. Dom Pedro IV (Rossio), services points west. M: Rossio or Restauradores. Open daily 8:30am-11:30pm. Schedules and assistance available from an info office on the ground level (open daily 10am-1pm and 2-7pm). **Luggage storage** (550$ for 48hr.; not available in any other station). English spoken. To **Sintra** (45min., every 10min., 6am-2am, 200$), via **Queluz.**

Estação Santa Apolónia, Av. Infante D. Henrique, east of the Alfama on the banks of the Rio Tejo, runs the international, northern, and eastern lines. All trains to Santa Apolónia also stop at the **Oriente Metro Station** by the Expo grounds. The international terminal, with **currency exchange** and an info desk (English spoken), is located off the right side of the main platform. To reach downtown from the station, take bus #9, 39, or 46 to Pr. Restauradores and Estação Rossio. To: **Coimbra** (2½hr., 10 per day, 6:50am-7:50pm, 1300$); **Évora** (3hr., 6 per day, 5:45am-11:10pm, 1075$); **Aveiro** (3-3½hr., 10 per day, 6:50am-7:50pm, 1650$); **Porto** (4hr., 10 per day, 6:50am-7:50pm, 2000$); **Braga** (5hr., 2 per day, 7:50am-5:50pm, 2500$); **Madrid** (10hr., 1 per day, 9:56pm, 8200$); **Paris** (23hr., 1 per day, 5:56pm, 24,000$).

Estação Cais do Sodré, just beyond the end of R. Alecrim, to the right of Pr. Comércio when walking from Baixa. M: Cais do Sodré. Take the metro or bus #1, 44, or 45 to Pr. Restauradores or bus #28 to Estação Santa Apolónia. Trains to the monastery in **Belém** (10min., every 15min., 5:30am-2:50am, 110$); the youth hostel in **Oeiras** (20min., every 15min., 150$); **Estoril** and **Cascais** (30min., every 15min., 200$). Consult the video monitors above each platform.

Estação Barreiro, across the Rio Tejo, serves southern destinations like the Costa Azul and the Algarve. Station accessible by ferries from the Terreiro do Paço dock off Pr. Comércio; be sure to distinguish the Estação from adjacent ferry docks. Ferries leave every 30min. and take 30min. to reach the other side; ferry ticket included in the price of connecting train ticket (otherwise 100$). Trains to: **Setúbal** (1½hr., every hr., 7:55am-6:50pm, 300$); **Lagos** (5½hr., every 2hr., 7:35am-11:10pm, 1700$).

BY BUS

Arco do Cego, Av. João Crisóstomo, around the block from the M: Saldanha. Exit the metro onto Av. República and walk 1 block up from the praça (toward the McDonald's), then turn right onto Av. Dunque de Ávila, and right before the McDonald's. All "Saldanha" buses (#36, 44, 45) stop in the praça (160$). This is the terminal for virtually all buses. The terminal has fast **Rede Expressos** to many destinations. To: **Caldas da Rainha** (1¼hr., 10 per day, 7am-11pm, 950$); **Peniche** (2hr., 11 per day, 7am-7:30pm, 1000$); **Coimbra** (2½hr., 16 per day, 7am-12:15am, 1450$); **Évora** (3½hr., 15 per day, 8:15am-7pm, 1450$); **Portalegre** (4hr., 4 per day, 8am-5pm, 1500$); **Porto** (4hr., 15 per day, 7am-12:15am, 2800$); **Lagos** (5hr., 10 per day, 5am-1am, 2400$); **Braga** (5hr., 6 per day, 7am-12:15am, 2300$); **Tavira** (5hr., 5 per day, 5am-1am, 2400$), via Faro; **Vila Real St. Antonio** (6hr., 6 per day, 5am-1am, 2500$).

LISBON

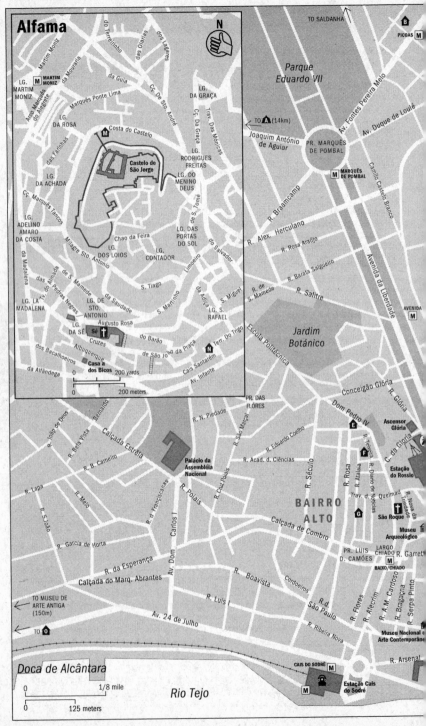

Alfama

N

TO SALDANHA

B
PICOAS **M**

LG. **M** MARTIM
MARTIM MONIZ
MONIZ

do Terreirinho

dos Lagares

das Olarias

Martim Moniz

da Guia

da Mouraria

Marquês Ponte Lima

LG. DA GRAÇA

Parque Eduardo VII

Cc. De Sto. André

Cç. Da Graça

Trav. Das Mónicas

TO ▲ (14km)

Joaquim António de Aguiar

PR. MARQUÉS DE POMBAL

Av. Fontes Pereira Melo

Av. Duque de Louié

LG. DA ROSA

das Farinhas

Costa do Castelo

M

LG. RODRIGUES FREITAS

M MARQUÉS DE POMBAL

Camilo Castelo Branco

R. Braamcamp

LG. DA ACHADA

Castelo de São Jorge

LG. DO MENINO DEUS

de S. Tomé

R. Alex. Herculano

R. Rosa Araújo

Cç. Marquês Tancos

LGi ADELINO AMARO DA COSTA

Chao da Feira

LG. DAS PORTAS DO SOL

do Salvador

R. de S. Mamede

R. Barata Salgueiro

R. Salitre

AVENIDA **M**

da Madalena

Milagre Sto. Antonio

LG. DOS LOIOS

LG. CONTADOR

Limoeiro

das Alminada

Tv. da Almada

de S. Mamede

da Saudade

S. Tiago

S. Martinho

R. da Adiça

S. Miguel

LG. S. RAFAEL

Jardim Botánico

LG. LA MADALENA

LG. DE STO. ANTONIO

Augusto Rosa

LG. S. RAFAEL

Escola Politécnica

Avenida da Liberdade

LG. DA SÉ

Sé

Cruzes

do Barão

de São José da Praça

Terr. Do Trigo

N

PR. DAS FLÔRES

Conceição Glória

Cç. Glória

dos Bacalhoeiros

Albuquerque

Casa dos Bicos

Cais Santarém

0   200 yards

da Alfândega

0   200 meters

Av. Infante

R. N. Piedade

R. São Marçal

Dom Pedro IV

Ascensor Glória

Ascensor Glória

C. da Glória

R. João de Deus

Bernardo

Calçada Estrêla

R. Bela Vista

R. B. Carneiro

R. R. N. Piedade

R. São Marçal

R. Eduardo Coelho

Palácio da Assembléia Nacional

R. Acad. d. Ciências

R. Século

R. Rosa

R. Atalia

R. Diario de Noticias

E

F

Estação do Rossio

R. Nova da Trindade

R. Lapa

R. Melo

R. d Franciscanas

R. Ciur Pojais

R. Pojais

Trav. d. Noticias

BAIRRO ALTO

São Roque

G

Queimad

R. SJoão

R. Garcia de Horta

Carlos I

Av. Dom Carlos I

Calçada de Combro

Museu Arqueológico

PR. LUIS D. CAMÓES

LARGO CHIADO

R. Garret

TO MUSEU DE ARTE ANTIGA (150m)

R. da Esperança

Calçada do Marq. Abrantes

R. Boavista

Cordoeiros

R. da São Paulo

R. Flores

R. Alecrim

R. A.M. Cardoso

R. Bragança

R. Serpa Pinto

BAIXO/CHIADO **M**

TO 🛈

Av. 24 de Julho

R. Luis I

R. Ribeira Nova

Museu Nacional e Arte Contemporâne

R. Arsenal

CAIS DO SODRÉ **M**

Doca de Alcântara

0   1/8 mile

0   125 meters

Rio Tejo

Estação Cais do Sodré

M

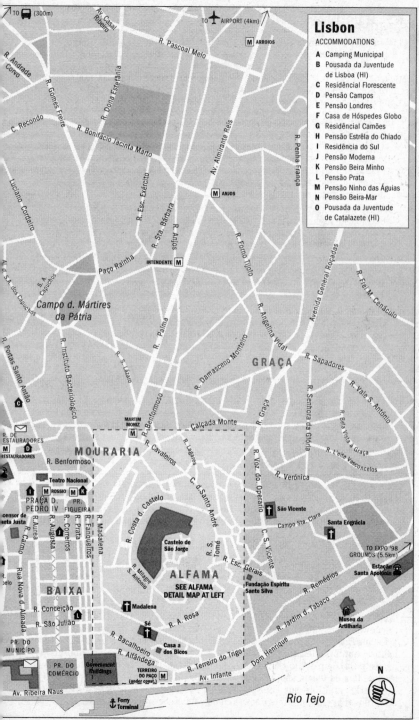

TO 🚌 (300m)

TO ✈ AIRPORT (4km)

R. Pascoal Melo

M ARROIOS

Av. Casal Ribeiro

R. Andrade Corvo

R. Gomes Freire

R. Dona Estefânia

R. Bonifácio Jacinta Marto

C. Recondo

R. Esc. Exército

R. Sta. Bárbara

R. Anjos

Av. Almirante Reis

R. Penha França

Luciano Cordeiro

Al. d.ª S.A. dos Capuchos

S. A. Capuchos

Paço Rainha

R. Forno Tijolo

M ANJOS

INTENDENTE M

R. Palma

R. S. Lázaro

Campo d. Mártires da Pátria

R. Portas Santo Antão

R. Instituto Bacteriológico

R. Damasceno Monteiro

R. Angelina Vidal

Avenida General Roçadas

R. Frei M. Cenáculo

GRAÇA

R. Sapadores

R. Vale S. António

R. Benformoso

Calçada Monte

R. Graça

R. Senhora da Glória

R. Bela Vista à Graça

R. L'eite Vasconcelos

MARTIM MONIZ M

R. Cavaleiros

R. Lagares

R. Voz do Operário

R. Verónica

R. DE ESTAURADORES

✉

M RESTAURADORES

D

MOURARIA

R. Benformoso

C. d. Santo André

São Vicente

Campo Sta. Clara

Santa Engrácia

Teatro Nacional

M ROSSIO M

PRAÇA D. PEDRO IV

PR. FIGUEIRA

R. Costa do Castelo

R. Madalena

R. Fanqueiros

R. Correeiros

R. Prata

R. Augusta

R. Áurea

R. Carmo

censor de nta Justa

Castelo de São Jorge

R. S. Tomé

R. Esc. Gerais

R. S. Vicente

C. S. Vicente

TO EXPO '98 GROUNDS (5.5km)

Estação Santa Apolónia

R. Milagre S. António

ALFAMA

SEE ALFAMA DETAIL MAP AT LEFT

Fundação Espírito Santo Silva

R. Remédios

Rua Nova d. Almada

BAIXA

R. Conceição

L

R. São Julião

Madalena

Sé

R. A. Rosa

R. Bacalhoeiro

R. Alfândega

Casa a dos Bicos

R. Jardim d. Tabaco

Museu da Artilharia

PR. DO MUNICÍPIO

✉

PR. DO COMÉRCIO

Government Buildings

TERREIRO DO PAÇO (under const.) M

R. Terreiro do Trigo

Av. Infante

Dom Henrique

Av. Ribeira Naus

⚓ Ferry Terminal

Rio Tejo

N

Lisbon
ACCOMMODATIONS

A Camping Municipal
B Pousada da Juventude de Lisboa (HI)
C Residêncial Florescente
D Pensão Campos
E Pensão Londres
F Casa de Hóspedes Globo
G Residêncial Camões
H Pensão Estrêla do Chiado
I Residência do Sul
J Pensão Moderna
K Pensão Beira Minho
L Pensão Prata
M Pensão Ninho das Águias
N Pensão Beira-Mar
O Pousada da Juventude de Catalazete (HI)

⊟ GETTING AROUND

Lisbon has an efficient system of buses, subways, trams, funiculars, and trains. Use them to full advantage—no suburb in or out of the city takes longer than 45 minutes to reach. If you don't speak Portuguese, taxi drivers and bus and train ticket booths may try to rip you off by charging an exorbitant fare or not returning all of your change. Make sure you know in advance what the fare should be, and don't hand the vendor more than 200$ for a local trip.

City Buses: CARRIS (tel. 363 93 43 or 363 20 44) runs the buses, subways, trains, and funiculars in Lisbon. Fare 160$ within the city; pay on the bus. If you plan to stay for any length of time, consider investing in a *bilhete de assinatura turístico* (tourist pass), good for unlimited travel on CARRIS transports. 1-, 4-, and 7-day passes available (430$; 1650$; 2350$). Passes sold in CARRIS booths located in most network train stations and the busier metro stations (e.g. Restauradores). Open daily 8am-8pm. You must show a passport to buy a tourist pass.

Subway: Metro (tel. 355 84 57) follows Av. Liberdade, then branches into lines covering the modern business district. A red "M" marks Metro stops (*Let's Go* indicates a metro stop by writing "M:" followed by the name of the stop). Tickets 100$. Buy them at window or from vending machines. Book of 10 tickets 800$. Trains run daily 6am-1am.

Trams: Everywhere (160$). They offer beautiful views of the harbor and older neighborhoods. Many date from before WWI. Line #28 is great for sight-seeing in the Alfama and Mouraria (stop in Pr. Comércio). Line #15 heads from Pr. Comércio or Pr. Figueira to Belém and the monastery complex.

Funiculars: They link the lower city with the hilly residential area. A common one goes up Ascensor Glória from Pr. Restauradores to Bairro Alto (160$).

Taxis: Rádio Táxis de Lisboa (tel. 815 50 61), **Autocoope** (tel. 793 27 56), and **Teletáxi** (tel. 815 20 16). Cluster along Av. Liberdade and Rossio. Flat rate of 300$ for luggage.

Car Rental: Pick up cars at the airport or in one of several locations downtown. Contact the agencies for pickup locations. **Budget,** Av. Visconte Valmar, 36BIC (tel. 796 10 28; fax 797 13 77); **Hertz,** Qto. Francelha Baixio (tel. 941 55 41; fax 941 60 68); **Avis,** Av. Praia da Vitória, 12C (tel. 346 26 76); **Mundirent,** R. Conde Redondo, 38A (tel. 313 93 60 or 352 58 25). See **By Car,** p. 36, for toll-free numbers to get rates and other info from home. If you're just planning on visiting Lisbon, a car is not necessary. You won't want to be a part of the hair-raising traffic that define's Portugal's streets.

✦ ORIENTATION

According to legend, Lisbon, like Rome, was built on seven hills, though at times it might seem like many more. Navigating the maze of Lisbon's roller-coaster streets requires patience and Stairmaster training. The three main *bairros* (neighborhoods) of the city center are the Baixa (low district, resting in the valley), the Bairro Alto (high district), and the Alfama.

The **Baixa,** Lisbon's old business center, is the center of town, sandwiched between the other two districts. Its grid of small, mostly pedestrian streets begins at the **Rossio** (also called the **Praça Dom Pedro IV**) and ends at the **Praça do Comércio,** on the **Rio Tejo** (otherwise known as the **Tagus River**). For tourists, Rossio is the center of the city. Adjacent to Rossio are two other important squares, **Praça da Figueira** and **Praça dos Restauradores,** where buses from the airport stop. Pr. Restauradores lies just above the Baixa, and from it **Avenida da Liberdade** runs uphill to the new business district centered around **Praça do Marquês de Pombal.**

Facing Baixa with your back to the river, the **Ascensor de Santa Justa**—an elegant historic outdoor elevator that marks the left-hand border of the neighborhood—heads to the Bairro Alto's upscale shopping district, the **Chiado,** traversed by fashionable **Rua do Carmo** and **Rua Garrett.** The **Bairro Alto** is a mix of narrow streets, lush parks, and Baroque churches. Young Portuguese come here to party—the level of activity on the street doesn't change much between 2pm and 2am.

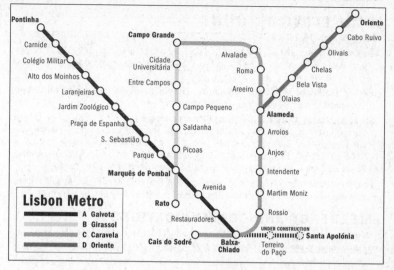

Lisbon Metro
- A Gaivota
- B Girassol
- C Caravela
- D Oriente

Pontinha
Carnide
Colégio Militar
Alto dos Moinhos
Laranjeiras
Jardim Zoológico
Praça de Espanha
S. Sebastião
Parque
Marquês de Pombal
Rato
Restauradores
Cais do Sodré

Campo Grande
Cidade Universitária
Entre Campos
Campo Pequeno
Saldanha
Picoas
Avenida

Alvalade
Roma
Areeiro
Alameda
Arroios
Anjos
Intendente
Martim Moniz
Rossio

Oriente
Cabo Ruivo
Olivais
Chelas
Bela Vista
Olaias

Balxa-Chiado
Terreiro do Paço
UNDER CONSTRUCTION ┄┄┄ Santa Apolónia

On the other side of the Baixa (to the right with your back to the river), the **Alfama,** Lisbon's famous medieval/Moorish neighborhood, is the city's oldest district, stacking tiny whitewashed houses along a labyrinth of narrow alleys and stairways beneath the **Castelo de São Jorge.** Expect to get lost. Without a detailed map expect to get twice as lost. The twisting streets either change names every three steps or include several different streets under the same name. Streets are labeled either *travessas* (side streets), *ruas* (streets), *calçadinhas* (walkways), or *escadinhas* (stairways). A street-indexed *GeoBloco* **Planta Turística de Lisboa** or the *Poseidon* **Planta de Lisboa** (with Sintra, Cascais, and Estoril on the back) are worth the money (both sold in Estação Rossio and at most newsstands for 1000$).

Stretching out along the river from the Baixa's waterfront are some of the fastest growing parts of Lisbon. The old Expo '98 grounds, now called the **Parque das Nações** (Park of Nations), welcomes tons of visitors both day and night, while the **Alcantara** and **Docas** (docks) regions show off Lisbon's most happening nightlife.

7 PRACTICAL INFORMATION

TOURIST AND FINANCIAL SERVICES

Tourist Office: Palácio da Foz (tel. 346 63 07), Pr. Restauradores. M: Restauradores. Provides bus schedules, accommodation listings, and a free map. English spoken. Open daily 9am-8pm. Another office at the **Aeroporto de Lisboa** (tel. 849 43 23 or 849 43 89), just outside the baggage claim area. English spoken. Open daily 6am-2am. Or look for kiosks with signs that read "Ask me about Lisboa" at Santa Apolónia, Rossio, Parque das Nações, and other locations around the city.

Budget Travel: Movijovem, Av. Duque d'Avila, 37 (tel. 13 88 20), will make reservations at youth hostels throughout the country.

Embassies: see **Embassies and Consulates,** p. 539.

Currency Exchange: Banks are open M-F 8:30-11:45am and 1-2:45pm. For a low commission and decent rates, try **Cota Câmbio,** R. Áurea, 283, 1 block off Pr. Dom Pedro IV in the Baixa. The main post office, most banks, and travel agencies also change money. Ask first—fees can be exorbitant (1000$ or more).

American Express: Top Tours, Av. Duque de Loulé, 108 (tel. 315 58 85). M: Marquês de Pombal. Exit the metro stop and walk up Av. Liberdade toward the Marquês de Pombal statue, then turn right. The often-crowded Top Tours office handles all AmEx functions. English spoken. Open M-F 9:30am-1pm and 2:30-6:30pm.

LOCAL SERVICES

Luggage Storage: Estação Rossio. Lockers 550$ for 48hr. Open daily 8:30am-11:30pm.

English Bookstore: Livraria Británica, R. Luis Fernandes, 14-16 (tel. 342 84 72), across from the British Institute in the Bairro Alto. Classics and best-sellers. Open M-F 9:30am-7pm. Visa, MC, AmEx.

Library: Biblioteca Municipal Central (tel. 797 38 62), Palácio Galveias. M: Campo Pequeno. Open M-Sa 9am-7pm, Su 11am-5pm.

Shopping Center: Amoreiras Shopping Center de Lisboa (tel. 69 25 58), on Av. Duarte Pacheco. Take bus #11 from Restauradores. 383 shops including a huge **Pão de Açúcar** supermarket, English bookstores, and a 10-screen **cinema. Colombo,** in front of Benefica stadium. M: Colégio Militar. Over 500 shops and a 10-screen cinema. **Centro Vasco de Gama,** Av. D. João II. M: Oriente. Has it all. Open daily 10am-midnight.

Laundromat: Lavatax, R. Francisco Sanches, 65A (tel. 812 33 92). M: Arroios. Wash, dry, and fold 1100$ per 5kg load. Open M-F 9am-1pm and 3-7pm, Sa 9am-noon.

EMERGENCY AND COMMUNICATIONS

Emergency: tel. 112. **Police:** R. Capelo, 3 (tel. 346 61 41). English spoken.

24-Hour Pharmacy: tel. 118. The address of the next night service is posted on the door of every pharmacy.

Drug Abuse Hotline: Centro das Taipas (tel. 342 85 85).

Medical Services: British Hospital, R. Saraiva de Carvalho, 49 (tel. 395 50 67; appointments tel. 397 63 29). **Cruz Vermelha Portuguesa,** R. Duarte Galvão, 54 (emergency tel. 788 60 13; **ambulance** tel. 942 11 11).

Post Office: Marked by red *Correios* signs. **Main office** (tel. 346 32 31), Pr. Comércio. **Telephone, fax,** *Posta Restante,* and international express mail (EMS). Open M-F 8:30am-6:30pm. **Second office** in Pr. Restauradores provides the same services with longer hours and a central location. Open M-F 8am-10pm, Sa-Su 9am-6pm. **Postal Code:** 1100 for central Lisbon.

Internet Access: Web Café, R. Diário de Notícias, 126 (tel. 342 11 81). 200$ for 15min., 700$ per hr. Open daily 6pm-2am. **Ciber Chiado,** Largo Picadeiro, 10 (tel. 346 67 22). 900$ per hr. Open M-F 11am-6pm and 8pm-midnight, Sa 8pm-midnight.

Telephones: Portugal Telecom, Pr. Dom Pedro IV, 68. M: Rossio. Has pay phones and booths for international calls. Pay the cashier after your call or use a phone card. Visa accepted. **Phone cards** come in 50 units (650$), 100 units (1300$), or 150 units (1900$). Buy them here or at neighborhood bookstores and stationers. Local calls consume at least 1 unit. Office open daily 8am-11pm.

TELEPHONE CODE Lisbon's phone code is (0)1.

◤ ACCOMMODATIONS AND CAMPING

A price ceiling supposedly restricts the amount hostels can charge for particular types of rooms, so if the fee seems padded request the printed price list. During low- or mid-season prices generally drop—try bargaining the price down at those times. Many establishments have rooms with only double beds and charge per person. Expect to pay from 3000 to 5000$ for a single and 5000 to 9000$ for a double, depending on amenities and location. If you're dissatisfied, ask the owner for a *livro de reclamações*—they are required to give these to the tourist bureau.

Most hotels are in the center of town on Av. Liberdade, while many convenient budget hostels are in the Baixa along the Rossio and on R. Prata, R. Correeiros, and R. Ouro. Lodgings near the Castelo de São Jorge or in the Bairro Alto are quieter and closer to the sights. If central accommodations are full, head east to the hostels along Av. Almirante Reis. At night, be careful in the Bairro Alto, the Alfama, and the Baixa; many streets are isolated and poorly lit.

YOUTH HOSTELS

Pousada da Juventude de Lisboa (HI), R. Andrade Corvo, 46 (tel. 353 26 96; fax 353 75 41). M: Picoas. Exit the metro station, turn right, and walk 1 block. This huge, ultra-clean youth haven has abandoned some of the typical HI restrictions—there is no curfew or lockout—but is typical in that it has an inconvenient location. English spoken. Breakfast included. Lockers 250$. Reception daily 8am-midnight. Check out by 10:30am. Wheelchair accessible. HI card required. June-Sept. dorms 2900$; doubles with bath 5500$. Oct.-May dorms 1900$; doubles 4700$.

Pousada da Juventude de Catalazete (HI), Estrada Marginal (tel. 443 06 38), in the coastal town of Oeiras. Take a train from Estação Cais do Sodré to Oeiras (20min., every 15min., 5:30am-2:30am, 155$). Exit through the train station underpass, cross the street, and follow signs to Lisbon and Cascais. The street curves through a residential district. At the intersection across from a bus stop (no street signs), turn left and go downhill along R. Filipa de Lencastre. At the underpass, go straight and follow HI signs to the INATEL complex. The hike will reward you with quiet rooms and beautiful ocean views from the patio. Breakfast included. Lunch and dinner each 900$. Reception daily 8am-midnight. Curfew midnight. Reservations recommended. HI card required. June-Sept. dorms 1800$; doubles with bath 4500$. Oct.-May 1500$; doubles 3700$.

BAIXA

Dozens of hostels surround the three connected praças, Pr. Restauradores, Pr. Dom Pedro IV, and Pr. Figueira, that form the heart of downtown Lisbon. Staying in this area is incredibly practical, as it makes a good base for visiting sights in and around the city. Although most hostels have fewer than 12 rooms, finding a vacancy shouldn't be difficult. For a good night's sleep, look for a hostel along the pedestrian-only street. Some *casas de hospedes* may be brothels; though occasionally located beneath hostels, they are not desirable lodgings for most tourists.

■ **Pensão Campos,** R. Jardim do Regedor, 24, 3rd fl. (tel. 346 28 64), between Pr. Restauradores and R. Portas de Santo Antão. M: Restauradores. Comfortable rooms with clean baths, overlooking a pedestrian street near the Rossio. Fun, multilingual owner. Laundry 1500$. Singles 4000$; doubles with shower 6000-7000$; triples 7000$.

Pensão Moderna, R. Correeiros, 205, 4th fl. (tel. 346 08 18), one block from Pr. Figueira, toward the water. M: Rossio. A friendly family tends to the comfortable (though somewhat noisy) apartment-style rooms. All 10 antique-filled rooms have large windows and balconies. Great location. Singles 3500$; doubles 6000$; triples 8000$.

Residencial Florescente, R. Portas de Santo Antão, 99 (tel. 342 66 09; fax 342 77 33), 1 block from Pr. Restauradores. M: Restauradores. The 72 spacious rooms, all with phone and TV, are luxurious by budget standards. Windowed rooms have incredible views of Pr. Figueira. Doubles with shower or full bath 5000-8000$; triples 7500-10,500$; large room with full bath and A/C 12,000$. Visa, AmEx, MC.

Pensão Beira Minho, Pr. Figueira, 6, 2nd fl. (tel. 346 18 46), beside the Rossio at the north end of the praça, through a flower shop. M: Rossio. Twenty-four plain, well-lit rooms with phones, some with verandas overlooking the square. Breakfast included. Singles 4500$, with bath 5500$; doubles 6000-8500$.

Residência do Sul, Pr. Dom Pedro IV, 59, 2nd fl. (tel. 342 25 11), through the souvenir shop. M: Rossio. Somewhat dark but otherwise excellent rooms, all with TV and phone. Those opposite the square are quieter. English spoken. Singles with shower 3500$, with full bath 5000$; doubles 4500-6000$; triples with shower 7000$.

Pensão Prata, R. Prata, 71, 3rd fl. (tel. 346 89 08), 2 blocks from Pr. Comércio. M: Rossio. The entrance to a busy cafe obscures the staircase. Thirteen clean, peaceful rooms with tiny baths. English-speaking owner is very knowledgeable about Lisbon's hotspots. Singles 5000$; doubles 6000-7000$.

IN AND AROUND THE BAIRRO ALTO

The quiet Bairro Alto has a communal feel that the town center lacks, but the uphill hike is inconvenient and daunting for luggage-bearers (try the Ascensor Glória from Pr. Restauradores). Blessed (and financially rewarded) are those who persevere; unto them shall be bestowed ample rooms of great value, enhanced by antiques and views of the castle. Most of Lisbon's nightlife is in Bairro Alto, but be cautious if you're out late alone.

■ **Casa de Hóspedes Globo,** R. Teixeira, 37 (tel. 346 22 79), on a small street across from the Parque São Pedro de Alcântra at the top of the funicular. From the park entrance, cross the street and turn right onto R. Teixeira. Safe and convenient. Recent renovations have refurbished spacious rooms with sturdy furniture, cheerful bedspreads, and partitioned bathrooms. English, French, Spanish, and German spoken. Reserve up to 1 week in advance. Singles 2500$, with bath 4500$; doubles 4000$.

Pensão Estrêla do Chiado, R. Garrett, 29, 4th fl. (tel. 342 61 10). From the top of the Ascensor de Santa Justa, turn left onto R. Carmo and right onto R. Garret. The 95-stair climb may be grueling, but the spotless rooms, hotter-than-hot water, and well-furnished singles reward. Some rooms have views of the castle. Recently renovated common baths. Singles 3500$, with shower 4500$; doubles 5500$, with shower 6000$.

Pensão Londres, R. Dom Pedro V, 53, 2nd fl. (tel. 346 22 03; fax 346 56 82). Take the Ascensor Glória from Pr. Restauradores to the top. Turn right and walk up R. S. Pedro to R. Dom Pedro V. The hostel is on the left near the hilltop. The elevator leads to spacious, well-lit rooms (all with phones) overlooking the old town. Breakfast included. Singles with shower 5000-8000$; doubles 7000-11,000$; triples 14,000$. Visa, MC.

Residencial Camões, Tr. Poço da Cidade, 38, 1st fl. (tel. 347 75 10; fax 346 40 48), off R. Misericórdia. From the top of Ascensor Glória, turn left onto R. S. Pedro, which becomes R. Misericórdia; Tr. Poço da Cidade is the 5th right. A pristine set of rooms in the heart of the party district. Common room with TV. English spoken. Breakfast included. Reservations (1 week ahead) essential in summer. Singles 5000$, with bath 7000-8000$; doubles 7000-8000$, with bath 8000-9000$; triples 10,000-12,000$.

ALFAMA

Staying in the Alfama grants flowering balconies and amazing views. It also means steep streets, a long walk to the hostel, and potential danger at night. Yet rooms are cheap and surprisingly comfy, and the Alfama's narrow side streets and friendly praças are well worth exploring. Reservations are highly recommended.

■ **Pensão Ninho das Águias,** R. Costa do Castelo, 74 (tel. 886 70 08), down the street from the Teatro Taborda. From Pr. Figueira take R. Madalena to Largo Adelino Costa, then head uphill to R. Costa do Castelo. Spectacular views of Lisbon are worth the long hike. Canary-filled garden looks out over the old city. Cheerful rooms with phones. Breakfast included. Singles 5000$; doubles 7000$, with bath 8000$; triples 10,000$.

Pensão Beira-Mar, Largo Terreiro do Trigo, 16, 4th fl. (tel. 886 99 33), in a small square off Av. Infante Dom Henrique (the road parallel to the Tejo) between Estação Santa Apolónia and the ferry station. Clean, spacious rooms, most with forgivably mismatched bedclothes, some with water views. Laundry 2000$ per load. Reserve ahead. Small singles 2500$; good-sized doubles 4000-6000$; triples 7500-8000$.

CAMPING

Although camping is popular in Portugal, campers are often prime targets for thieves. Info on campgrounds is available from the tourist office in the free booklet *Portugal: Camping and Caravan Sites.* There are 30 campgrounds within a 45-minute radius of the capital; listed below is the only one in Lisbon proper.

Parque de Campismo Municipal de Lisboa (tel. 760 96 20; fax 760 96 33), on the road to Benfica. Take bus #43 from the Rossio to the Parque Florestal Monsanto. Lisbon's municipal campground has a pool and supermarket. Reception daily 9am-9pm. July-Aug. 800$ per person and per tent, 500$ per car; June and Sept. 720$ per person and per tent, 450$ per car; Oct.-May 560$ per person and per tent, 350$ per car.

◘ FOOD

Lisbon has some of the least expensive restaurants and some of the best wine of any European capital. A full dinner costs about 1800-2000$ per person; the *prato do dia* (special of the day) is often a great deal—finish it off with a sinfully cheap even more sinfully delicious Portuguese pastry. The sign of a good restaurant is a clientele made up of as many locals as tourists; the odd toddler running among tables adds to the authenticity. In Lisbon, the closer to the industrial waterfront, the cheaper the restaurant. The south end of the Baixa, near the port, and the area bordering the Alfama are particularly inexpensive. If you are searching for a bargain, avoid restaurants with menus translated into a Babel of different languages. Lisbon reels with seafood specialties such as *amêjoas à bulhão pato* (steamed clams), *creme de mariscos* (seafood chowder with tomatoes), and a local classic, *bacalhau cozido com grão e batatas* (cod with chick-peas and boiled potatoes). Belém offers the world-famous, heavenly *pastéis de Belém*. ◙**Pastéis de Belém**, R. Belém 88, serves tube-fulls of the warm custard tarts.

SUPERMARKETS

◙ **Supermercado Celeiro,** R. 1 de Dezembro, 65, 2 blocks from Estação Rossio. Centrally located, this medium-sized market stocks a wide variety of fruit, meat, processed foods, fresh bread, and pastries. Open M-F 9am-8pm, Sa 9am-7pm.

Mercado Ribeira, a vast market complex inside a warehouse on Av. 24 de Julho, just outside the Estação Cais do Sodré. Accessible by bus #40. Go early for the freshest selection. Open M-Sa sunrise-2pm.

Supermercado Pão de Açucar, Amoreiras Shopping Center de Lisboa, Av. Duarte Pacheco. Take bus #11 from Pr. Restauradores or Pr. Figueira. Open M-Sa 10am-8pm, Su 10am-6pm.

BAIXA

Although the Baixa is home to Lisbon's most tourist-oriented restaurants, it also has decent food at reasonable prices. Bargain eateries line R. Correeiros (parallel to R. Prata) and neighboring streets. One block from Pr. Restauradores on R. Portas de Santo Antão, several superb seafood restaurants stack the day's catch in their windows. The small streets north of Pr. Figueira are all packed with eateries.

Restaurante Bonjardim, Tr. Santo Antão, 11 (tel. 342 43 89), off Pr. Restauradores. The self-proclaimed *rei dos frangos* (king of chicken) legitimately rules the roost with delicious roast chicken (1300$). Entrees 1000-2900$. Open daily noon-11pm. Visa, MC.

Hua Ta Li, R. Bacalhoeiros, 109-115A (tel. 887 91 70), near Pr. Comércio. Great vegetarian options. Try the noodles with vegetables (750$) or seafood salad (750$). Entrees 750-1950$. *Pratos do dia* 800-1300$. Open daily noon-3:30pm and 6:30-11pm.

Churrascaria Gáucha, R. Bacalhoeiros, 26C-D (tel. 887 06 09), 1 block from the river, near Pr. Comércio. Large, popular grill serves South American-style *churrasco* dishes like the bean-based *feijoada* (stewed with various meats, 1300$). Entrees 850-2200$. Open M-Sa 2pm-2am. Visa, MC, AmEx.

Celeiro, R. 1 de Dezembro, 65. Take the 1st right off Estação Rossio and go 2 blocks. A macrobiotic restaurant accompanied by a health food supermarket, Celeiro will please even the strictest herbivore. Entrees 200-600$. Open M-F 9am-8pm, Sa 9am-7pm.

Restaurante João do Grão, R. Correeiros, 222 (tel. 342 47 57), with a yellow sign out front. Very popular, but very touristy. Try the house special, *bacalhau com grão* (cod with chick-peas, 1600$). Entrees 990-1900$. Open daily noon-10:30pm.

LISBON

Abracadabra, Pr. Dom Pedro IV, 64 (tel. 342 62 88), next to the Portugal Telecom office on Rossio. Popular high-school hangout features magical pizza and burgers—Portuguese style, of course (285-520$). Open M-F 7am-10pm, Sa-Su 8am-10pm.

Confeitaria Nacional, Praça Figueira 18B (tel. 346 17 29). Succumb to the mirror-and-gold decor of this famous *pastelaría* (established 1829). Delicious sweets of every possible Portuguese kind (120-280$). Having trouble deciding? Try the almond-encrusted *austríaca* ($140). Open M-F 8am-8pm, Sa 8am-2pm.

Telepizza, R. Portas de Santo Antão, 41 (tel. 322 01 80). Portugal's take on New York-style pizza. Individual pizzas start at 800$; pizzas for 2-3 people start at 1200$. Also carry-out or delivery. Open Su-Th noon-11pm, F-Sa noon-midnight.

BAIRRO ALTO

Bairro is the place to be come dinner time. The neighborhood is home to a number of glamorous restaurants and an equal number of glamorous patrons. In addition, many inexpensive local haunts line Calçada do Combro, the neighborhood's main westward artery. R. Misericórdia's side streets offer cheaper restaurants for quiet dinners among an almost completely Portuguese crowd. Small culinary diamonds in the rough also pepper the area around Pr. Dom Pedro V.

Cervejaria da Trindade, R. Nova Trindade, 20C (tel. 342 35 06), 2 blocks down a side street that begins in the square in front of the Igreja do São Roque and parallels R. Misericórdia. Excellent food served in an elegant but noisy atmosphere. Popular with tourists. Entrees 790-2500$; budget finds are the *sugestões do chefe* (chef's suggestions). Open daily noon-1:30am. Visa, MC, AmEx.

Hell's Kitchen, R. Atalaia, 176 (tel. 342 28 22). From the top of C. Glória (the steep hill from Pr. Restauradores), walk a few blocks into Bairro Alto and turn right on R. Atalaia. Small, but with an extensive selection of delicious entrees (1100-1650$) and desserts (350-450$). The hummus with pita (450$) and falafel with salad (1100$) are heavenly. Open Tu-Su 8pm-12:30am.

Stravangaza, R. Grémio Lusitano, 18-26 (tel. 346 88 68), 1 block from the top of C. Glória, at R. Diário de Notícias. Quality Italian food served in a classy setting. Pastas and gourmet pizzas 900-2000$. Open W-M 12:30pm-2am.

Restaurante Tascardoso, R. Século, 244 (tel. 342 75 78), off R. Dom Pedro V. Small restaurant with thought for food. Walls inscribed with proverbs such as "He who talks much says little." Entrees 900-1050$. *Pratos do dia* 750-900$. Open daily 8am-midnight.

Café Brasil, R. São Pedro de Alcântara, 51 (tel. 346 94 76), across the street from the park of the same name. Hot, cheap food in the most local of watering holes. Meat and fish dishes 650-900$. *Prato do dia* is a bargain at 650$. Open M-Sa 7am-10pm.

ALFAMA

The winding streets of the Alfama conceal a number of tiny, unpretentious restaurants, often packed with the neighbors and friends of the owners. Lively chatter echoes through the damp, narrow alleys. Watch the clock—the labyrinthine Alfama grows dangerously dark after nightfall.

Restaurante Arco do Castelo, R. Chão de Feira, 25 (tel. 887 65 96), across from the gate to the Castelo de São Jorge. For a hearty, spicy meal, try one of their specialties from Goa, Portugal's former colony in India. Curry from 1100$. Other entrees 1080-1600$. Open M-Sa 12:30pm-midnight.

Malmequer Bemmequer, R. São Miguel, 23-25 (tel. 887 65 35). Follow Av. Infante D. Henrique to Terreiro do Trigo; take the first left and climb the stairs to R. São Miguel. The name means "He loves me not, he loves me well." The friendly owner serves delicious seafood dishes. Entrees 1000-1500$. Open daily noon-3:30pm and 7-10:30pm.

▣ SIGHTS

BAIXA

Although the Baixa features few historic sights, a lively atmosphere and the neighborhood's three main praças make it a monument in its own right.

AROUND THE ROSSIO. The best place to embark upon your tour of Lisbon's Enlightenment-era center is from its heart—the Rossio. Let your eyes traverse the city's main square, also known as the **Praça Dom Pedro IV,** before your feet do. Once a cattle market home to a public execution stage, bullfighting arena, and carnival ground, the praça is now the domain of drink-sipping tourists and heart-stopping traffic that whizzes around the central statue of Dom Pedro IV. A statue of Gil Vicente—Portugal's first great dramatist (see **Literature,** p. 529)—peers down from the top of the **Teatro Nacional de Dona Maria II** (easily recognized by its large columns) at one end of the praça. Adjoining the Rossio is the elegant **Praça Figueira,** which lies on the border of the hilly streets of the Alfama district.

AROUND PRAÇA DOS RESTAURADORES. An obelisk and a bronze sculpture of the "Spirit of Independence" in the **Praça dos Restauradores,** just past the Rossio train station when walking from the Rossio itself, commemorate Portugal's independence from Spain (1640). The tourist office, post office, and numerous shops line the praça and C. Glória—the steep hill that leads to Bairro Alto. Pr. Restauradores is also the start of **Avenida da Liberdade,** Lisbon's most imposing boulevard and one of the city's most elegant promenades. Modeled after the wide boulevards of 19th-century Paris, this shady mile-long thoroughfare ends at **Praça do Marquês do Pombal;** from there an 18th-century statue of the Marquês overlooks the city.

AROUND PRAÇA DO COMÉRCIO. The grid of pedestrian streets on the other side of the Rossio from Pr. Restauradores caters to ice-cream eaters and window shoppers. After the earthquake of 1755, the Marquês de Pombal designed the streets to serve as a conduit for goods from the ports on the Rio Tejo to the city center. Built at the height of Enlightenment urban planning, each street was designated for a specific trade; *sapateiros* (shoemakers), *correeiros* (couriers), and *bacalhoeiros* (cod merchants) each had their own avenue. Two centuries later, the streets of the Baixa retain these names and their commercial nature. Pedestrians wander the wide mosaic sidewalks, cars drag race down the stately avenues, and affluent visitors swarm upscale shops along the side streets. From the streets of the Baixa, all roads lead to **Praça do Comércio** on the banks of the Tejo. Also known as **Terreiro do Paço,** Pr. Comércio lies before the towering statue of Dom João I, cast in 1755 from 9400 pounds of bronze. The praça now serves as the headquarters of several Portuguese government ministries. Its center has been relegated to less dignified use as a fairgrounds for concerts and other events.

BAIRRO ALTO

In the *Bairro* (the hip name for Chiado), pretentious intellectuals mix with insecure teens and idealistic university students. It's the only place in Lisbon that never sleeps; here there is as much to do at night as there is to see during the day. At the center of the neighborhood is **Praça Camões,** which adjoins Largo Chiado at the top of R. Garrett, a good place to rest and help orient yourself before more sightseeing. *(To reach R. Garret and the heart of the chic Chiado neighborhood, turn left when exiting the elevator and walk one block; R. Garret is on the right.)*

AROUND THE ASCENSOR DE SANTA JUSTA. Although it's just as easy to get from the Baixa to the Bairro Alto by walking, be classy and take the **Ascensor de Santa Justa,** a historic elevator built in 1902 inside a Gothic wrought-iron tower. Tourists ride to admire the view from the upper levels, and locals use the elevator as transportation into the hilly Bairro Alto. From the upper terrace, a narrow **walkway** leads under a huge flying buttress to the 14th-century **Igreja do Carmo.** The 1755 earthquake left the church roofless but its dramatic Gothic arches remain. The ramshackle **Museu Arqueológico,** on adjacent Largo do Carmo, includes Dom Fernando I's tomb. *(Elevator runs M-F 7am-11pm, Sa-Su 9am-11pm. Walkway open 7am-6pm. 80$. The walkway periodically closes; see if it's open before buying a ticket. Museum tel. 346 04 73. Open June-Aug. M-Sa 10am-6pm; Sept.-May M-Sa 10am-1pm and 2-5pm. 300$.)*

■**MUSEU NACIONAL.** This museum hosts an interesting survey of European painting dating back as far as the 12th century and ranging from Gothic primitives to 18th-century French masterpieces. *(R. Janelas Verdes, Jardim 9 Abril. 30min down Av. Infante Santo from the Ascensor de Santa Justa. Buses #40 and 60 stop to the right of the museum exit and head back to the Baixa. Tel. 396 41 51. Open Tu 2-6pm, W-Su 10am-6pm. 500$, students 250$.)*

MUSEU DO CHIADO. An educational (and aesthetic) experience awaits in this museum, a courtesy of Portugal's most famous post-1850 artists. Though the permanent collection is somewhat small, Museu do Chiado is known for its incredible exhibits. *(R. Serpa Pinto, 4. From Pr. Camões, go through Largo Chiado and down R. Garrett, turn right onto R. Serpa Pinto, and walk two blocks downhill. Tel. 343 21 48. Open Tu 2-6pm, W-Su 10am-6pm. 400$, ages 14-25, seniors, and teachers 200$. Free Su before 2pm.)*

IGREJA DE SÃO ROQUE. This church is dedicated to the saint who is believed to have saved the Bairro Alto from the devastation of the great earthquake. Inside the church, the **Capela de São João Baptista** (4th from the left) is ablaze with precious gems and metals. The chapel caused a stir upon its installation in 1747 because it took three ships to bring it from Rome, where it was built. *(Largo Trinidade Coelho. From R. Carmo head uphill on R. Garret until R. Misericórdia. Tel. 346 03 61.)* Next door, the small but worthwhile **Museu de São Roque,** with its own share of gold and silver, features European religious art from the 16th to 18th centuries. There's also a helpful "Ask me about Lisboa" kiosk here. *(Tel. 323 50 00. Open Tu-Su 10am-5pm. 175$, students and seniors free. Sunday free.)*

PARKS. For a perfect picnic, head to the mercifully shady ■**Parque de São Pedro de Alcântara.** The Castelo de São Jorge in the Alfama stares back from the cliff opposite the park; the city of Lisbon twinkles below. A mosaic points out the landmarks included in this vista. *(On the right off R. São Pedro de Alcântara—the continuation of R. Misericórdia. It's a 5-min. walk up R. Misericórdia from Pr. Camões; the park is right next to C. Glória.)* More greenery awaits uphill along R. Dom Pedro V at the majestic **Parque Príncipe Real,** which connects to Lisbon's extensive **Jardim Botánico.** Across from the church on Largo Estrela, the wide asphalt paths of the **Jardim da Estrêla** wind through flocks of pigeons and lush flora. Park walkways are popular for Sunday strolls, and the benches fill with smoochers. Behind the park tropical plants, cypress trees, and odd gravestones mark the **Cemitério dos Inglêses (English Cemetery).** Its musty, Victorian chapel dates from 1885.

A CAMÕES CAMEO
Pr. Camões, in the heart of the Bairro Alto off R. Garrett, is marked by a monument to Luís de Camões. Camões, whose 16th-century *Os Lusíadas* chronicled his nation's discoveries in lyric verse, is considered Portugal's greatest poet. Most likely born in Lisbon in 1524 (accounts of his life vary slightly), this stud had so many affairs with ladies of the court that he fled to North Africa to escape their vengeful husbands (official sources say his politics got him banished). Camões led an adventurous life for a poet, enlisting as a common soldier in the army in 1547. His service took him all over the globe, including the Arab and Indian coasts and numerous stops in Portugal's expanding empire; all the while he was working on his verses. By the time he made his way back to Lisbon in 1570, Camões had lost an eye in battle, been jailed and injured in a sword duel, and survived a shipwreck off the coast of Cambodia (clutching his precious poetry the whole time, of course). Two years later (1572) he published *Os Lusíadas;* despite its success he died in poverty somewhere in Asia in 1580. Portugal was never able to recover his body, but Camões is remembered with an honorary tomb just outside Lisbon in Belém's **Mosteiro dos Jerónimos** and on streets and praças across the country which bear his name.

CHURCHES. For more neighborhood flavor, walk uphill through Pr. Camões and take R. Loreto, which turns into Calçada do Combro. Walk over the hill and down to where it levels out; from here turn right onto Tr. Convento de Jesús. Here flowered balconies and hanging laundry frame the **Igreja das Mercês**, a handsome, 18th-century Travertine building on a small praça. Back on Calçada do Combro, a few hundred meters ahead is Largo António Sousa de Maced and a fork in the road. Follow the right fork onto R. Poiais de São Bento, which becomes Calçada da Estrêla and leads to more churches, including the ornate ⊠**Basílica da Estrêla.** Built in 1796, the basilica's exquisitely shaped dome, poised behind a pair of tall belfries, steals the sky. Half-mad Maria I, desiring a male heir, made fervent religious vows promising God anything and everything if she were granted a son. When a baby boy was finally born, she built this church. Ask the sacristan to show you the gigantic 10th-century manger scene. *(On Pr. Estrêla. Tel. 396 09 15. Open daily 8am-12:30pm and 3-7:30pm. Free.)*

ALFAMA

The Alfama, Lisbon's medieval quarter, was the lone neighborhood to survive the famous 1755 earthquake. The neighborhood slopes in tiers from the **Castelo de São Jorge** facing the Rio Tejo. Between the Alfama and the Baixa is the quarter known as the **Mouraria** (Moorish quarter), established, ironically, after Dom Afonso Henriques and the Crusaders expelled the Moors in 1147. Here, Portuguese grandmothers gossip and elementary school boys play soccer amidst camera-toting tourists, all enjoying the enchanting ambience of Alfama's streets. Watch out for muggers, especially at night; visit by day without handbags, cameras, or snatchables. Though the constant hike that defines Alfama sightseeing is half the fun, the tired and lazy will want to hop on the scenic tram #28 (160$), which winds up through the neighborhood past most of its sights.

THE LOWER ALFAMA. While any of the small uphill streets a few blocks east of the Baixa lead to the Alfama's maze of streets, the least confusing way to see the neighborhood is by climbing up R. Madalena, which begins two blocks away from Pr. Comércio (take R. Alfandega from the praça). Hang a right when you see the **Igreja da Madalena** in the Largo Madalena on the right. Take R. Santo António da Sé and follow the tram tracks to the cleverly designed and richly ornamented **Igreja de Santo António da Sé,** built in 1812 over the saint's alleged birthplace. The construction was funded with money collected by the city's children, who fashioned miniature altars bearing images of the saint to place on doorsteps—a custom re-enacted annually on June 13, the saint's feast day and Lisbon's largest holiday. *(Tel. 886 91 45. Open daily 8am-7pm. Mass daily 11am, 5, and 7pm.)* In the square beyond the church is the stolid 12th-century **Sé** (cathedral). Although the interior of the Sé is unremarkable, its sheer antiquity and relic-filled treasury make it an intriguing visit. As a sign outside reads, "The Sé is so old that no one really knows how old it is." *(Open M-Sa 10am-5pm. Treasury open 10am-5pm.)*

⊠**CASTELO DE SÃO JORGE.** Near the top of the Alfama lies the must-see **Castelo de São Jorge,** which offers spectacular views of Lisbon and the ocean. Built in the 5th century by the Visigoths and enlarged by 9th-century Moors, this castle was a playground for the royal family between the 14th and 16th centuries. Anyone can wander around the ruins, soak in the view of the cityscape below, explore the ponds, or gawk at the exotic bird population of the castle gardens. Nooks for sitting, relaxing, and enjoying the vista as well as stands selling well-merited ice cream, drinks, and *churros* await after the long climb up the hill. *(From the cathedral, follow the yellow signs for the castle on a winding uphill walk. Castle open daily Apr.-Sept. 9am-9pm; Oct.-Mar. 9am-7pm. Free.)*

MUSEU DAS ARTES DECORATIVAS. The impressive furnishings and decorations that fill this museum's rooms convey a sense of 18th-century palatial luxury. The museum also features a tea room and bookstore with books in English on Portuguese art. *(Largo Portas do Sol, 2. To reach the museum, head up to the castle and turn right onto Largo Portas do Sol. Tel. 346 04 73. Open Tu and Th 10am-8pm, W and F-Su 10am-5pm. 500$, over 65 or under 12 250$.)*

ALONG TR. SÃO VICENTE. On the far side of the castle, follow the main tram tracks along Tr. São Tomé (which becomes R. São Vicente as it winds uphill) to Largo São Vicente and the **Igreja de São Vicente de Fora,** built between 1582 and 1629 and dedicated to Lisbon's patron saint. Ask to see the deathly still *sacristia,* with fabulous 18th-century walls inlaid with Sintra marble. *(From the bottom of R. Correeiros in the Baixa, take bus #12 or tram #28 (160$). Open Tu-Su 9am-noon and 3-5pm. Free. Chapel next door with scenic view 500$.)* At the **Feira da Ladra** (flea market) that takes place in the church's backyard, the din of a lively social scene drowns out cries of merchants hawking used goods. *(Tu and Sa 6am-5pm.)* The **Igreja de Santa Engrácia (National Pantheon)** is farther down toward the coast. This church, with its impressive dome, took almost 300 years to complete (1682-1966), giving rise to the famous Portuguese expression, "Endless like the building of Santa Engrácia." *(Walk along R. São Vicente and keep left as the road branches. Open Tu-Su 10am-5pm.)*

CONVENTO DA MADRE DE DEUS. This 16th-century convent complex houses the **Museu Nacional do Azulejo,** devoted to the classic Portuguese art of the *azulejo* tile, first introduced by the Moors (see **Architecture,** p. 529). On display are Portuguese, Spanish, and Dutch tiles from the last 500 years. The Baroque interior of the church, accessible through a fine Manueline doorway, is an explosion of oil paintings, *azulejos,* and gilded wood. The rapturous excess continues in the choir and the **Capela de Santo António,** where bright *azulejos* and paintings intoxicate the eye. *(R. Madre de Deus, 4. Follow Av. Infanta Dom Henrique, which runs parallel to the Rio Tejo. The avenue leads to the Estação Santa Apolónia; from outside the station, take bus #13. Tel. 814 77 47. Open W-Su 10am-6pm, Tu 2-6pm. 350$, students 180$.)*

SALDANHA

Though most of Saldanha is dedicated to Lisbon's business affairs, this modern district does have two excellent museums, both owned by the Fundação Gulbenkian. These museums should factor into every Lisbon visit.

▨MUSEU CALOUSTE GULBENKIAN. When oil tycoon Calouste Gubenkian died in 1955, he left his extensive art collection (some of it purchased from the Hermitage in St. Petersberg, Russia) to his beloved Portugal. Though the philanthropist was of Armenian descent and a British citizen, it was Portugal he chose to call home (the Portuguese also gave him a substantial tax break). The collection is divided into two sections, one of which is ancient art—Egyptian, Greek, Roman, Islamic, and Oriental—while the other is made up of European pieces from the 15th to 20th centuries. Highlights include the Egyptian room, Rembrants, Monets, Renoirs, and a Rodin. *(Av. Berna, 45. M: Palhavã or S. Sebastião. Bus # 16, 31, 46. Tel. 795 51 31. Open Tu-Su 10am-5pm. 500$, free Su mornings for students and seniors.)*

MUSEU DO CENTRO DE ARTE MODERNA. Though not as famous as its neighbor, this museum is home to an extensive collection of modern art. Though most of the works are by Portuguese artists, the museum also houses pieces by other notable 20th century artists. Make sure to spend some time in the gardens—the sculptures are incredible. *(R. Dr. Nicolau Bettencourt. M: Palhavã or S. Sebastião. Bus #16, 31, 46. Tel. 795 02 41. Open Tu-Su 10am-5pm. 500ptas, free Su mornings for students and seniors.)*

BELÉM

Belém is more of an outlying suburb than a neighborhood of Lisbon, but its high concentration of monuments and museums makes it a crucial stop in any comprehensive tour of the capital. Belém is imperial glory at the service of culture; here, a number of well-maintained museums and historical sites showcase the opulence and extravagance of the Portuguese empire. To visit Belém is to understand *saudade,* the "nostalgic yearning" expressed musically in *fado* (see p. 558).

To get to Belém, take tram #15 from Pr. Comércio (20min., 160$), bus #28 or 43 from Pr. Figueira (20min., 160$), or the "slow" train from Estação Cais do Sodré (10min., every 15min., 120$). From the train station, cross over the tracks, then cross the street and go left. From the bus station, follow the avenue straight ahead. All museums are free Sundays before 2pm.

▨MOSTEIRO DOS JERÓNIMOS. The Mosteiro dos Jerónimos rises from the banks of the Tejo behind a lush public garden. Granted UN World Heritage Status in the 1980s, the monastery was established by King Dom Manuel I in 1502 to give thanks for the success of Vasco da Gama's voyage to India. This monastery, the country's most refined celebration of the Age of Discovery, showcases Portugal's native Manueline style, combining Gothic forms with early Renaissance details. The main door of the church, to the right of the monastery entrance, is a sculpted anachronism; Henry the Navigator mingles with the Twelve Apostles on both sides of the central column. The symbolic tombs of Luís de Camões (see **A Camões Cameo**, p. 552) and navigator Vasco da Gama lie in two opposing transepts. Inside the monastery, the octagonal cloisters of the courtyard drip with overdone stone carvings, a contrast to the simplicity of the rose gardens in the center. *(Tel. 362 00 34. Open Tu-Su 10am-5pm. June-Sept. 400$, students 200$; Oct.-May 250$. Free Su 10am-2pm. Cloisters open Tu-Su 10am-5pm. Free.)*

▨TORRE DE BELÉM. One of two well-known towers on Belém's waterfront, the Torre de Belém rises from the north bank of the Tejo and is surrounded by the ocean on three sides. Built under Manuel I from 1515-1520 as a harbor fortress, it originally sat directly on the shoreline; today, due to the receding beach, it is only accessible by a small bridge. Nevertheless, this symbol of Portuguese grandeur and member of the UN's World Heritage list offers spectacular panoramic views of Belém, the Tejo, and the Atlantic beyond. *(A 10min. walk along the water from the monastery. Take the underpass by the gardens to cross the highway. Tel. 362 00 34. Open Tu-Su 10am-5pm. 400$; Oct.-May 250$, students 200$.)*

MONASTERY MUSEUMS. The intriguing **Museu da Marinha** proves that the Portuguese really know their ships. Globes from the mid-18th century show the assumed boundaries of the continents with incredible accuracy. *(At the far end of the monastery complex. Tel. 362 00 19. Open Tu-Su June-Aug. 10am-6pm; Sept.-May 10am-5pm. 400$, students 200$. Free Su 10am-2pm.)* In the same complex is the **Museu Nacional de Arqueologia,** which uses artifacts of various media to depict Portugal's history. *(Open Tu 2-6pm, W-Su 10am-6pm. 400$, students 200$. Free Su before 2pm.)*

CENTRO CULTURAL. Contemporary art buffs will bask in the glow of the gigantic, luminous **Centro Cultural de Belém.** With four pavilions holding regular world-class exhibitions, several art galleries, and a huge auditorium for concerts and performances, the center provides slick entertainment amid a slew of imperial landmarks. *(Tel. 361 24 00; www.ccb.pt. Open daily 11am-8pm.)*

PADRÃO DOS DESCOBRIMENTOS. Along the river is the Padrão dos Descobrimentos, built in 1960 to honor Prince Henry the Navigator. The view here is similar to that from the tower, but here an elevator (rather than stairs) transports visitors 50m up to a small terrace. Hold onto your hat; it can get windy at the top. The Padrão also hosts temporary exhibits. *(Across the highway from the monastery. Tel. 301 62 28. Open Tu-Su 9:30am-6pm. 340$, students 170$.)*

PALÁCIO NACIONAL DE AJUDA. Back toward the center of Belém is the Palácio Nacional da Ajuda, on Largo Ajuda, a short bus ride away from the hills overlooking Belém. Constructed in 1802, the 54 chambers are a rather telling display of decadence. *(Take bus #14, 32, 42, or 60 from Pr. Afonso de Albuquerque, at the corner of Calçada da Ajuda and R. Belém (160$). Alternatively, tram #18 (Ajuda) stops behind the palace. Or walk straight up Calçada da Ajuda (20min.). Tel. 363 70 95. Open Tu and Th-Su 10am-5pm. 250$, students free. Free Su 10am-2pm.)*

▨PARK OF NATIONS

The **Parque das Nações** (Park of Nations; tel. 891 93 33; www.parquedasnacoes.pt; open M-F 9:30am-1am, Sa-Su 9:30am-3am), at the former Expo '98 grounds 6km from downtown, is the newest addition to Lisbon's growing list of sights. In the mid-1990s, the area was a muddy wasteland along the banks of the Tejo; in just a few years the city transformed the land, preparing the grounds for the millennium's last World Exposition. After Expo '98, the government took a risk, pumping millions of dollars into the land and converting it into the Parque das Nações. Fortunately, the gamble has paid off. Today, the park is packed,—day and night—with people enjoying its graceful, yet futuristic setting. If the proposed construction goes according to plan, the park will soon become a small city.

The easiest way to reach the park from Lisbon is to take the metro to the end of the red line (Linha Oriente, 100$). The Oriente stop has escalators rising up to the park's main entrance at the **Centro Vasco de Gama**. Alternatively, city buses #5, 10, 19, 21, 25, 28, 44, 50, 68 and 114 all stop at the Oriente station (160$). The entrance to the park leads through the Centro Vasco de Gama **shopping mall** (tel. 893 06 00; open daily 10am-midnight) to the center of the grounds, where several information kiosks provide maps and offer free luggage storage (open 9:30am-7:30pm).

The biggest attraction is the **Pavilhão dos Oceanos,** the largest oceanarium in Europe. The enormous new aquarium has interactive sections showcasing the four major oceans (down to the sounds, smells, and climates). All of these connect to the main tank, which houses fish, sharks, and other sea creatures. (Open daily 10am-7pm. 1500$, under 18 or over 65 800$). Another solid draw is the **Museu Nacional dos Coches,** which moved here from its old home in Belém. The museum displays more than 50 carriages, ranging from late 18th-century models to the gilded Baroque coach that recently bore Queen Elizabeth II. (Open Tu-Su 10am-6pm. 450$, under 26 225$.) Other **pavilions** scattered throughout the park, including the **International Fairgrounds,** accommodate rotating exhibits during the year. The **Atlantic Pavilion** (host to many of Lisbon's big concerts) and the 145m **Torre Vasco de Gama** (the city's tallest building) grab visitors' attention with their striking, 21st-century architecture. An elevator ascends 300 ft. to the observation tower, which offers spectacular views of the city (open M-Th 10am-8pm, F-Su 10am-10pm; 500$). For those who don't want to walk between attractions, a **gondola** connects one end of the park to the other (8min.; M-F 11am-8pm, Sa-Su 10am-9pm; 500$).

🎵 ENTERTAINMENT

The *Agenda Cultural* and *Lisboa em*, free at kiosks in the Rossio, on R. Portas de Santo Antão, and at the tourist office, contain information on concerts, movies, plays, and bullfights. They also have lists of museums, gardens, and libraries.

BARS AND CLUBS

Lisbon hardly suffers from a shortage of nightlife. Bairro Alto's R. Norte, R. Diário Notícias, and R. Atalaia have many small clubs packed into three short blocks, making club-hopping as easy as crossing the street. The Rato area near the edge of Bairro Alto has a high concentration of gay and lesbian clubs. The newest hotspot is the revamped **Docas de Santo Amaro,** a strip of waterfront bars and clubs. On the way to the Docas, look for additional party places along Av. 24 de Julho. While these places along the river are all within a mile-long stretch, it's best to play it safe late at night and take a cab between clubs. A cab from Rossio (the only real choice for transportation to these locations) costs 500-1200$.

At clubs, decent clothes (pants and nicer shoes) are expected—some places have uptight fashion police at the door. Inside, beer ranges from 150-350$ and mixed drinks cost 400-1000$. Some clubs charge a cover; those that don't have higher prices at the bar. As for timing, there's no reason to show up at a club before midnight; crowds flow in around 2am.

DOCAS DE SANTO AMARO

Havana, Doca de Santo Amaro, Armazem 5 (tel. 397 98 93). Crowded and popular. Plays salsa in addition to standard pop and dance tunes. The "New Havana" feel created by palm trees and ceiling fans helps keep things cool. Beer 400$, mixed drinks 500$. Open M-Sa 11pm-5:30am.

Cosmos, Doca de Santo Amaro, Armazem 243 (tel. 397 27 47). Restaurant (open daily 11am-midnight) gives way to the disco (midnight-6am) and solid dance music. Cover 2000$, includes 4 beers or 2 mixed drinks. Beer 400$, mixed drinks 600-1000$.

Celtas & Iberos Irish Pub, Doca de Santo Amaro, Armazem 7 (tel. 397 60 37). Goes for that traditional pub feeling with its interior decorations and live music most nights (often Irish covers of pop songs). Upbeat atmosphere good for throwing back a few pints (600$). Smaller beer 300$, mixed drinks 800$. Open Tu-Su midnight-3am.

Salsa Latina, Gare Marítima de Alcântara (tel. 395 05 55), in its own building not far from the cluster at Doca de Santo Amaro. Live salsa most nights. Beer 500$, mixed drinks 1000$. Open M-Th 9pm-4am, F-Sa 9pm-6am.

Kremlin, Escandinhas da Praia, 5 (tel. 395 71 01), off Av. 24 de Julho. One of the top clubs in Lisbon with a young, fashionable crowd pulsating to house and dance music. Good-sized dance floor stays open past the time many people start work. Cover 1000-2000$ on weekends. Beer 500$, mixed drinks 1000$. Open Tu-Sa midnight-9am. Next door also are equally trendy clubs **Kapital** and **Plateau.**

Indochina, R. Cintura do Porto de Lisboa, Armazem H (tel. 395 58 75), on a crowded strip. Pop, rock, and dance music pump into the large main room. Nice outdoor section in the back where the breeze off the Tejo is a welcome relief from the dance floors inside. Open Tu-Th 11:30pm-4am, F-Sa 11:30pm-6am.

BAIRRO ALTO

Solar do Vinho do Porto, R. São Pedro de Alcântara, 45 (tel. 347 57 07). Not a club and not a bar, but close enough—enjoy port-tasting in a sedate and mature setting. Start the night in style. Port 130-2800$. Open M-F 10am-11:30pm, Sa 11am-10:30pm.

Pé Sujo, Largo Santa Martinho, 6-7 (tel. 886 56 29), in the Alfama. Live Brazilian music nightly 11:30pm-2am. Try the killer Brazilian *caipirinha* (sugarcane alcohol, 700$) or the dangerous *caipirosca* (with lime and vodka, 700$). Open Tu-Su 10pm-2am.

Memorial, R. Gustavo de Matos Sequeira, 42A (tel. 396 88 91), one block from R. Escola Politécnica in the Bairro Alto. Gay and lesbian disco-bar. The lights and Euro-pop blast from 10pm, but the fun starts after midnight. The 1000$ cover charge (except M and Th) includes 2 beers or 1 mixed drink. Open Tu-Su 11pm-4am.

Trumps, R. Imprensa Nacional, 104B (tel. 397 10 59). Lisbon's biggest gay club features several bars in addition to a massive dance floor. Mostly house and techno pump through the speakers. Open Tu-Su 11pm-6am.

CAFES

Relaxing in cafes during the day and late into the night is popular pastime in Lisbon. Look for outdoor seating, especially on summer evenings. There are several cafes in the Rossio area and on R. Augusta, the main pedestrian shopping street.

A Brasileira, R. Garrett, 120-122 (tel. 360 95 41). A famous 19th-century cafe in the Bairro Alto's stylish Chiado neighborhood. Considered by many to be "the best cafe in Portugal," it definitely has the best after-dinner scene. Look for the bust of poet Fernando Pessoa outside. Eça de Queiroz, another famous Portuguese literary figure who patronized this coffeehouse, may be long gone, but members of the new literati take his place. Gold and green woodwork and silver sconces add a little color to the scene. Coffee 80-300$. Mixed drinks about 700$. Open daily 4pm-1am.

Pastelaria Suíça (tel. 342 80 92), on the south corner of Pr. Dom Pedro IV in the Baixa. A noisy gathering place that stays packed until midnight. Coffee 150-250$. Pastries 120-180$. More substantial fare (sandwiches 300-950$) as well. Open 7am-10pm.

Restaurante Passeio D'Avenida, Av. Liberdade, just up from Pr. Restauradores. Outdoor seating for coffee (130-320$) and sandwiches (300-600$). You must be assertive to get the servers' attention. Open daily 9am-2am.

PARTY HEARTY While most nightlife in Lisbon revolves around the bars and *casas de fado*, those seeking more active revelry will definitely want to visit Lisbon in June. Open-air *feiras* (fairs)—smorgasbords of eating, drinking, live music, and dancing—fill the streets. There's a lively one called **Oreal** at Campo das Cebolas, near the waterfront in the Alfama (in June; open M-F 10pm-1am, Sa-Su 10pm-3am). Don't miss the *feira* in the Bairro Alto's **Praça Camões** (take the Elevador da Glória, or walk up R. Garrett), which lasts until 3am every night in June. After savoring *farturas* (Portuguese doughnuts, 190$) and Sagres beer (200$), pick up your feet and join in traditional Portuguese dancing. On the night of June 12, the streets become a mega-dance floor for the huge **Festa de Santo António**—banners are strung between streetlights and confetti falls like snow during a costumed parade along Av. Liberdade.

Commercial *feiras* combine shopping and cultural involvement. Bookworms burrow for three glorious weeks in the **Feira do Livro** (in the Baixa from late May to early June). The **Feira Internacional de Lisboa,** which has moved to a big new venue at the Park of Nations, occurs every few months, while in July and August the **Feira de Mar de Cascais** and the **Feira de Artesania de Estoril** take place near the casino.

Year-round *feiras* include the **Feira de Oeiras** (Antiques) on the fourth Sunday of every month, and the **Feira de Carcanelos** for clothes (Th 8am-2pm). Packrats should catch the **Feira da Ladra** (flea market), held behind the Igreja de São Vicente de Fora in the Alfama neighborhood (Tu and Sa 7am-3pm). Take bus #12 or tram #28.

FADO

Lisbon's trademark is the heart-wrenching *fado*, an expressive art that combines elements of singing and narrative poetry (see **Music**, p. 531). *Fadistas*, cloaked in black dresses and shawls, perform emotional tales of lost loves and faded glory. Their melancholy wailing is expressive of *saudade*, an emotion of nostalgia and yearning; listeners are supposed to feel the "knife turning in their hearts." On weekends, book in advance by calling the venues. The Bairro Alto has many *fado* joints off R. Misericórdia and on side streets radiating from the Museu de São Roque; it is the best place in the city for top-quality *fado*. However, many of the popular houses charge large covers or have "minimum consumption" requirements. To avoid these, try exploring nearby streets; various bars and other small venues often offer free performances.

Adega Machado, R. Norte, 91 (tel. 322 46 40). Frequented by as many locals as tourists. Dinner served (4600-6000$). Cover (with 2 drinks) 3000$. Open daily 8pm-3am.

O Faia, R. Baroca, 54 (tel. 342 19 23), between R. Atalaia and R. Diário de Notícias. Typical Portuguese food, *fado,* and folk dancing. Cover 2500$. Open M-Sa 8pm-2am.

Sr. Vinho, R. Meio à Lapa, 18 (tel. 397 26 81 or 397 74 56), in nearby Madregoa. Minimum food and drink charge 3000$, but with appetizers at 1200-2800$ this place won't entirely deplete your wallet. Open M-Sa 8:30pm-3am.

OTHER FUN THINGS TO DO

BULLFIGHTING. Portuguese bullfights (differing from the Spanish variety in that the bull is not killed) take place most Thursdays from the end of June to the end of September at **Praça de Touros de Lisboa** (tel. 793 24 42), Campo Pequeno (10pm-2am). Take bus #1, 44, 45, or 83 (160$), or get off at Metro stop "Campo Grande."

BOAT CRUISES. To refresh your sea legs, try a two-hour cruise on the Tejo. Boats leave from the Estação Fluvial Terreiro Paço (tel. 887 50 58), off Pr. Comércio. The boats run from April to October and leave at 3pm.

FUTEBOL. If sports are your thing, catch a *futebol* (soccer) match. Lisbon has two professional teams featuring some of the world's finest players: **Benfica** (tel. 726 03 21), at the Stadium of Light (M: Colégio Militar Luz), and **Sporting** (tel. 759 94 59), at Alvalade Stadium (M: Campo Grande). Check the APEB kiosk in Pr. Restauradores or the sports newspaper *A Bola*.

THEATER. The **Teatro Nacional de Dona Maria II** (tel. 347 22 26), Pr. Dom Pedro IV, stages performances of classical Portuguese and foreign plays (700-2000$, 50% student discount). At Lisbon's largest theater, the **Teatro Nacional de São Carlos,** R. Serpa Pinto, 9 (tel. 346 59 14), near the Museu do Chiado in the Bairro Alto, opera reigns from late September through mid-June (open daily 1-7pm).

MOVIES. If all else fails, try the theater (tel. 242 25 23), at the corner of Av. Liberdade and Av. Condes, directly across the square from the Pr. Restauradores tourist office. Huge 10-screen cinemas are also located in the **Oreiras** and **Colombo** shopping centers and on the top floor of the **Centro Vasco de Gama** (M: Oriente). American movies are shown with Portuguese subtitles (600$, matinees 400$).

DAYTRIPS FROM LISBON

The province of Estremadura envelops Lisbon with sun-drenched beaches, serene fields, and shady mountains, while the flat expanses of the Ribatejo cozy up to the capital city from the south. Within 30 minutes of Lisbon lie the elegant seaside resorts of Estoril and Cascais; the towns of Queluz and Mafra, both easily accessible, are also scenic and popular daytrips. Farther to the north is Sintra, with its fairy-tale castles and beautiful streets. Nearby Ericeira lures the sight-weary and fun-loving to its attractive beaches and incredible surf. South of Lisbon, beaches along the nearby Costa de Caparica attract a younger, more cosmopolitan crowd. A little farther are Sesimbra, a picturesque coastal town, and Setúbal, a busy port surrounded by some of Portugal's most beautiful rural coastline. Refreshing diversions from the city, these towns are close enough to serve as rewarding daytrips.

QUELUZ

Sitting 12km west of Lisbon and about that far south of Sintra, Queluz is remarkable for only one reason: the amazing **Palácio Nacional de Queluz.** In the mid-18th century, Dom Pedro III turned an old hunting lodge into this summer residence with the help of Portuguese architect Mateus Vicente de Oliveira and French sculptor Jean-Baptiste Robillon. The well-ordered, albeit slightly overgrown, garden makes this Rococo palace feel like a miniature Versailles. Highlights include the **Sala dos Embaixadores,** with its gilded thrones and Chinese vases, and the purely Portuguese *azulejo*-lined canal in the garden. Of historical interest is the **Quarto Don Quixote** where Dom Pedro I, the first emperor of Brazil, took his first and last breaths. (Open W-M 10am-1pm and 2-5pm; closed on major Catholic holidays. 500$, seniors, students, and children under 14 250$. Garden 100$.)

The best way to get to Queluz is by **train.** Take the Sintra line from Lisbon's Estação Rossio (M: Rossio) and get off at the Queluz-Belas (not Queluz-Massomá) stop (20min., every 15min., 150$). To get to the palace, exit the station through the ticket office and go left on Av. Antonio Ennes. Continue straight as the street becomes Av. República. Follow the signs; it's a 10-minute walk downhill.

ESTORIL

With its beautiful beaches, stately vistas, and bustling casino, Estoril's reputation is one of opulence. Luckily, visitors can savor the greatest luxuries at little to no cost, as Estoril's best assets are free. In fact, the city's beach, **Praia Estoril Tamariz,** greets tourists upon arrival, and the palm-lined **Parque do Estoril** blooms across the street. Those bored of beach scenes can walk through the park to the **Casino Estoril** (tel. 466 77 00), if not to spend money, then to marvel at the gaming palace. (Open daily 3pm-3am. No swim-wear, jeans, or shorts. Must be at least 18 for the slots and 21 for the game room. Foreigners must show passport.) Recent renovations, both inside and out, have added to the modern feel of this, Europe's largest casino. Over 25 million visitors frequent the sparkling game room, glitzy music hall, and 1000 slot machines each year. A **music festival** descends upon Estoril from mid-July to mid-August, bringing both classical and jazz performances.

▉ PRACTICAL INFORMATION. A **train** from Lisbon's Estação do Sodré (M: Cais do Sodré) runs to Estoril (30min., approximately every 20min., 180$) continuing to **Cascais** (which is also a pleasant 20-minute seaside stroll along the promenade from Estoril). Stagecoach **bus** #418 to **Sintra** departs from Av. Marginal, just down the street from the train station (40min., every hr., M-F 6:10am-11:40pm, Sa-Su and holidays 6:10am-9:50pm; 410$). At the **tourist office** (tel. 466 38 13; fax 467 22 80), on Arcada do Parque opposite the train station (take the tunnel under Av. Marginal), a multilingual staff offers detailed maps and events schedules for the entire **Costa do Estoril** (open M-Sa 9am-7pm, Su 10am-6pm).

▉▉ ACCOMMODATIONS AND FOOD. If you get lucky at the casino (or are stranded with no way back to Lisbon), cash in some chips and head over to the recently renovated **Residencial São Cristóvão,** Av. Marginal, 7079 (tel./fax 468 09 13). Facing the park, turn right off the train platform; about two block up the hill on the right are bright, airy rooms. (Continental breakfast and private parking included. July-Sept. doubles 10,000$, with bath 12,500-15,000$; Sept.-May doubles 6000-7000$.) Farther from the beach is **Residencial Smart,** R. Maestro Lacerda, 6 (tel. 468 21 64). Follow Av. Marginal uphill past the Paris Hotel to the corner of Av. Bombeiros Voluntários and turn left. Walk four blocks uphill to R. Maestro Lacerda (on your right) and follow the street three blocks until you see the *pensão* on the left. These 13 spacious doubles, all with shower, some with full bath, are definitely a smart choice. (Breakfast and parking included. July-Sept. doubles 8500-10,000$; prices lower Oct.-June.) The best options for budget meals are the cafeteria-like stands and bars along the beach. For a sit-down meal, try the restaurants in the **Arcados do Parque** lining the park. Not far from Residencial Smart is the charming **Leitanà Estoril,** Tr. Cedros, 2 (tel. 468 13 56). Head uphill on Av. Bombeiros Voluntários, turn right on R. J. dos Santos, and take a left on Tr. Cedros. Portuguese soups and desserts accompany fish and meat entrees (880-1450$).

CASCAIS

Once the summer vacation resort of the royal family, Cascais still caters to a well-to-do crowd. Four popular beaches—all just minutes from the center of town—draw throngs of locals and tourists alike, especially on weekends. More reflective of the town's days as a fishing village, Cascais's several historic sites and parks invite wandering. To reach the slightly overgrown **Parque de Gandainha,** walk away from Cascais along the coast for 10 minutes on Av. Dom Carlos, which turns into Av. Rei Humberto de Itália (open daily 8:30am-7:45pm). About 1km farther outside of Cascais (a 20 min. walk along Av. Rei Humberto de Itália) lies the **Boca do Inferno** (Mouth of Hell), a huge cleft carved in the rock by the incessant Atlantic surf. This ominous sight, which is often swamped with tourists, only gets truly crazy during storms and high tides. Still, the surrounding rocky turf, sprinkled with red sand, makes a nice perch for sitting and marveling at the powerful sea.

▉ PRACTICAL INFORMATION. Trains from **Lisbon's** Estação do Sodré heads to Cascais (30min., every 20min., 5:30am-2:30am, 200$), via Estoril. Cascais is also a pleasant 20-minute seaside stroll from Estoril. Stagecoach **buses** leave from outside the train station for **Sintra** (#417; 40min., every hr., 6:35am-7:08pm, 500$) and **Guincho** (#405 and #415; 25min., 7:15am-7:40pm, 300$). Bus #403 also goes to Sintra (700$), via **Cabo da Roca** (15-30min., every 1½hr., 9:05am-6:35pm, 200$). Those taking the bus to several destinations might opt for the dayrover ticket (1250$) good for one day's worth of unlimited use on stagecoach buses. Purchase tickets on the bus or at any stagecoach office.

If you reach Cascais by foot from Estoril, you can get to the **tourist office** by taking a right at the fork in the promenade and following the train tracks up to the station on the **Largo do Estação.** To get to the office from the front of the train station, cross the square and take a right at the McDonald's onto Av. Valbom. The tourist office, Av. Combatentes, 25 (tel. 486 82 04), has a small sign across the street from where Av. Valbom dead-ends. Look for the big "Turismo" sign outside the yellow building. The English-speaking staff can find you a budget room in a private home. (Rooms from 5000$, slightly higher in peak season. Open July-Sept. 15 M-Sa 9am-8pm, Su 10am-6pm; Sept. 16-June M-Sa 9am-7pm, Su 10am-6pm.)

ACCOMMODATIONS AND FOOD. Cascais is best done as a daytrip, but if you are too sunburned to move, your best bet is to ask at the tourist office for a reliable *quarto*. Alternatively, bed down at **Residencial Parsi,** R. Afonso Sanches, 8 (tel. 484 57 44), off the beachfront Lg. 5 do Outubro. Slightly pricey rooms all have TV and some provide stunning views of the ocean. Breakfast included. (Doubles with bath 8000-10,000$. Visa, MC, AmEx.) Camping is available in **Parque de Campismo do Guincho** (tel. 487 10 14), 5km from Cascais in the town of Areia, near the Praia do Guincho (720$ per person, 730$ per tent, 640$ per car).

If the Big Mac Super Menu meal (600$) doesn't tempt you, try the cafes along Av. dos Combatentes and R. Visconde da Luz, which offer deliciously fresh seafood. (Entrees 950-2700$.) Perhaps the least expensive and most interesting food option is to hike out to the Boca do Inferno, assemble a meal from the various food stands, and have a picnic on the rocks (sandwich, fruit, and drink for 650$).

SINTRA

In the epic poem *Childe Harold*, British Romantic poet Lord Byron described Sintra as a "glorious Eden." His adulation made Sintra (pop. 20,000) a chic destination for 19th-century European aristocrats. These days, the town is more popular among foreign tour groups eager to experience its fairy-tale castles and incredible mountain vistas. They are rewarded by Sintra's enchanting gardens and villas and its three castles, each from a different era; a walk through town presents a surreal mixture of history and fantasy.

GETTING THERE

Trains run to Sintra from **Lisbon** (45min., every 15min., 6am-2am, 200$). **Buses** go from **Estoril** (40min., every hr., M-F 6:10am-11:40pm, Sa-Su 6:10am-9:50pm, 410$) and **Cascais** (40min., every hr., 6:35am-7:08pm, 500$).

ORIENTATION AND PRACTICAL INFORMATION

Sintra is about 30km northwest of Lisbon and 10km north of Estoril. The town is split into three parts: a modern section around the train station, where most budget accommodations and banks are located, **Sintra-Vila,** where the historic sights perch on the mountainside, and Portela de Sintra, where shops and municipal offices cluster. To get to the old town from the train station (a 15min. walk), take a left out of the train station's ticket office, and turn right down the small hill at the next intersection. One block down the hill, turn left at the fountain in front of the castle-like **Câmara Municipal,** and follow the road as it curves past the **Parque da Liberdade.** From there, head up the hill to the **Praça da República;** the **Palácio Nacional** is the large white building (with two big chimneys) on the right.

Trains: Estação de Caminhos de Ferro, Av. Dr. Miguel Bombarda (tel. 923 26 05). To **Lisbon's Estação Rossio** (45min., every 15min., 6:07am-2:07am, 200$). There is no direct service to Estoril or Cascais and no luggage storage available.

Buses: Rodoviária (tel. 921 03 81), on Av. Dr. Miguel Bombarda, across the street from the train station. Open daily 7am-8pm. **Stagecoach,** on Av. Dr. Miguel Bombarda outside the train station. To: **Cascais** (#417, 40min., every hr., 7:20am-8:25pm, 500$); **Estoril** (#418, 40min., every hr., 6:19am-11pm, 410$). **Mafrense,** just down the street from the Stagecoach buses. To **Mafra** (50min., 11 per day, 6:20am-7:55pm, 380$) and

Ericeira (50min., every hr., 7:30am-8:30pm, 380$), with connections to points north. Fewer buses run on weekends and holidays.

Tourist Office: A small branch (tel. 924 16 23) is located at the train station. Grab a map as you walk through. Open June-Sept. M-Sa 9am-8pm; Oct.-May 9am-7pm. **Main office,** Sintra-Vila, Pr. República, 23 (tel. 923 11 57; fax 923 51 76). From the Pr. República, with the palace on your right, walk straight ahead 1 block; the tourist office is beyond the palace in a columned marble building. English-speaking staff provides a map and list of accommodations. They can also help you find a *quarto* (4000-10,000$). Open daily June-Sept. 9am-8pm; Oct.-May 9am-7pm.

Currency Exchange: Banco Totta e Açores, Sintra-Vila, R. Padarias, 4 (tel. 924 19 19), on a side street off the main praça. Open M-F 8:30am-noon and 1-3pm. ATMs across from the train station at **Caixa Crédito Agrícola,** Av. Miguel Bombarda, 27A/B (tel. 923 55 60). Office open M-F 8:30am-3pm. 1750$ commission.

Emergency: tel. 112. **Police:** (tel. 923 07 61), R. João de Deus, behind the end of the train tracks as you walk towards Sintra-Vila.

Medical Services: Centro de Saúde (tel. 923 34 00), Largo Dr. Gregório Almeida.

Post Office: Sintra-Vila, Pr. República, 26 (tel. 924 98 25), on the right en route to the tourist office. Small, with local **telephones,** Posta Restante (indicate Sintra-Vila). Open M-F 9am-12:30pm and 2:30-6pm. **Postal Code:** 2710.

Internet Access: At **Artes and Tastes** (see **Food,** p. 564).

TELEPHONE CODE	Sintra's phone code is (0)1.

▐ ACCOMMODATIONS AND CAMPING

While Sintra is an easy daytrip from Lisbon, it also makes an decent base for daytrips to surrounding historical sights and coastal towns. Budget accommodations—most of which cluster near the train station—fill up quickly on weekends. When in doubt, the tourist office can provide a list of *quartos* (4000-10,000$).

Piela's, R. João de Deus, 70-72 (tel. 924 16 91). Take a left out of the exit to the train station (at the end of the tracks), and then left around the bend onto the uphill street behind the station. Five rooms are large and tidy. Friendly, English-speaking owner. Cafe with pool table and game room. Doubles 5000-7500$; Oct.-June 4000-6000$.

Casa Adelaide, R. Guilherme Fernandes, 11 (tel. 923 68 73). From the train station, head downhill towards Sintra-Vila, walk past the Câmara Municipal at Largo Dr. Virg Horten and turn left down R. Guilherme Fernandes. The entrance is half a block downhill on the left. Rooms are small but cheap, with private shower or shared bath. Reception daily 9:30am-midnight. Reservations recommended. 4000$ per person.

Pousada da Juventude de Sintra (HI), Sta. Eufémia (tel./fax 924 12 10), hike a hard-core 2km uphill to São Pedro or hail a taxi (1100$ weekdays, 1500$ weekends) in front of the train station. Otherwise take the bus from the train station (180$) or the bus-stop in the old town (exit the tourist office and take a left turn in the praça; the stop is on the left across from a fountain). At São Pedro, get off the bus across from the Banco Crédito Predial Português (look for the big blue neon letters). Turn right and walk 1km (30-40min.) to the hostel (look for signs). Located amid flowering meadows, the hostel has a dining room, sitting room, TV with VCR, stereo, and winter heating. Reception daily 9am-noon and 6pm-midnight. Reservations highly recommended. Dorms 1200-1400$ per person; doubles 3200-3600$.

Pensão Nova Sintra, Largo Afonso de Albuquerque, 25 (tel./fax 923 02 20). Turn right out of the train station; the *pensão* is on the left after 1 block. A charming terrace and tidy rooms grace this recently renovated *pensão*. Breakfast included. Reservations necessary in summer. Singles 8000$; doubles 10,000-12,000$. Visa, MC, AmEx.

Camping: Parque de Campismo da Praia Grande (tel. 929 05 81), on the Atlantic coast about 12km from Sintra. Reception daily until 7pm. 520$ per person.

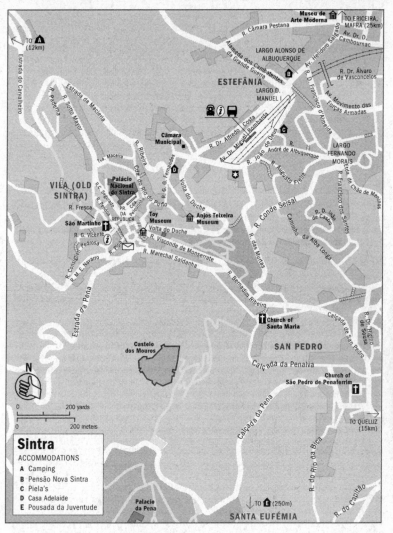

Sintra

ACCOMMODATIONS
A Camping
B Pensão Nova Sintra
C Piela's
D Casa Adelaide
E Pousada da Juventude

FOOD

Cheap places crowd the street parallel to the train station on the other side of the tracks. In the old town, narrow side streets off Pr. República, such as **Rue das Padárias** near the Palácio Nacional, host a wide range of eateries. On the second and fourth Sundays of every month, take the bus #435 from the train station to the nearby town of São Pedro (15min., 190$) for a spectacular **market.**

■ **Casa Piriquita,** R. Padarias, 1 (tel. 923 06 26), just up a small side street off Pr. República. Inspiring bakery, snack bar, and candy counter flanked by a marble-floored coffee and tea room. Sintra's tiny pastries with cheese and cinnamon or egg filling are a welcome snack (90-200$ each). Now has a **second branch** up the street at R. Padarias, 18, which serves more substantial sandwiches. Open daily 9am-10pm.

Artes & Tastes, Alemeda dos Combatentes da Grande Guerra, 12A-B (tel. 924 36 06). Exit the train station, turn right, walk 1 block, and turn left. This new cafe has as an inviting atmosphere and offers **internet access** (1000$ per hr.). Pastries and crepes 240-550$. Entrees 690-1150$. Open Tu-F 9:30am-8:30pm, Sa-Su 11am-8:30pm.

Bristol Restaurante, R. Visconce de Monserrate, 18-20 (tel. 923 34 38), directly in front of you as you come up the hill toward Pr. República. Lively atmosphere. House special-ties are its filling soups (300$) and omelettes (825$) for lunch. Sandwiches 300-550$. Fish or meat dishes 1050$ and up. Open Tu-Su 9am-10pm.

Restaurante Tulhas Bar, R. Gil Vicente, 4-6 (tel. 923 23 78). Take the street to the right of the tourist office, and walk 30m downhill; the restaurant is on the right. Cozy dining room is a great place to rest after Sintra's hikes. Meat and fish entrees 1100-1900$. Deserts 250-550$. Open daily noon-3:30pm and 7-10pm.

■ SIGHTS

Except for the modern art museum, all of the sights in Sintra (including the two must-see palaces and the castle) are accessible from the Sintra-Vila, the town's old quarter. From the train station, the road ambles and twists up the mountainside past the **Câmara Municipal** and its lush gardens before reaching the Paço Real.

■PALÁCIO NACIONAL DE SINTRA. Also known as the Paço Real or Palácio da Vila, the palace, with its complex gardens and two cone-shaped chimneys, sits prominently in Pr. República. Once the summer residence of Moorish sultans and their harems, the Paço Real and its complex gardens were built in two stages. Dur-ing the early 15th century, Dom João I built the main structure; a century later, Dom Manuel I created the best collection of *azulejos* in the world. He added vari-ous wings to create a unique mix of Moorish, Gothic, and Manueline styles. More than 20 rooms run the gamut from the *azulejo*-covered **Sala dos Árabes** (Hall of the Arabs) to the gilded **Capela** (Chapel). Don't miss the **Sala dos Cisnes** (Hall of Swans), the **Sala dos Brazões** (Coat of Arms Room), and the legendary **Sala das Pêgas** (Hall of Magpies). According to local lore, it was here that Dom João I's wife caught him kissing one of the ladies of the court. Although he claimed that it was merely a gesture of friendship, the court ladies (who the king nicknamed "mag-pies") turned it into scandalous gossip. *(Tel. 910 68 40. Open Th-Tu 10am-1pm and 2-5pm. Closed on bank holidays. Buy tickets by 4:30pm. 400$, with student ID 200$.)*

CASTELO DOS MOUROS. Perched on the boulder-studded peaks overlooking Sin-tra, this Moorish castle dates back to the 8th century. Stroll along the walls and clamber up the turrets for splendid views of the surrounding mountains and coast. The invigorating 3km ascent to the castle (and to the stunning Palácio Nacional da Pena farther up) climbs one of the highest peaks in the Sintra range. Start the steep, uphill hike (1-1½hr.) to the left of the tourist office, and follow the blue signs up the mountain. Beware the *escadinha* (stair-alley) shortcut; you might get lost. If pressed for time (or energy), it is possible to take a taxi directly from Sintra-Vila (one-way 1200-1400$). *(Bus #434 runs to the top from outside the tourist office (15min., every 30min., round-trip 500$). Open daily 10am-7pm. Free.)*

PALÁCIO NACIONAL DA PENA. Built in the 1840s by Prince Ferdinand of Bavaria, the husband of Queen Maria II, the fantastic Palácio looks like it belongs in Disney World. Nostalgic for his country, the prince rebuilt and embellished the ruined monastery with the assistance of a Prussian engineer, combining the aesthetic her-itages of both Germany and Portugal. The result is a Bavarian castle embellished with Arabic minarets, Russian onion domes, Gothic turrets, Manueline windows, and a Renaissance dome. Interior highlights—decked in *chinoiserie* and other regalia of Romantic Orientalism—include the chapel, the fully furnished kitchen, incredible views from the Queen's terrace, and Her Majesty's Toilet—crafted entirely in *azulejo*. *(One kilometer farther uphill from the Castelo dos Mouros. Open in July-Sept. Tu-Su 10am-6:30pm; Oct.-June Tu-Su 2-4:30pm. 600$, students 400$; Oct.-Apr. 200$.)*

OTHER SIGHTS. The **Sintra Museu de Arte Moderna** houses contemporary works by Andy Warhol, Morris Louis, and Gerhard Richters (among others) in a cheerful *Belle Époque* building. *(Past the train station, in modern Sintra. Open W-Su 10am-6pm, Tu 2-6pm. 600$, students 300$, children under 10 free.)* The **Anjos Teixeira Museum-House** displays sculptures by one of Portugal's most revered artists, Master Anjos Teixeira. His son, sculptor Pedro Anjos Teixeira, lives and works in the area and often greets visitors in person. *(Follow the signs into the park on the winding road between old and new Sintra. Tel. 923 61 23. Open Tu-F 9:30am-noon and 2-6pm, Sa-Su 2-6pm.)* For something very different, head to Sintra's **Toy Museum,** which showcases traditional Portuguese toys and thousands of lead soldiers, dolls, puppets, and trains. *(On R. Visconde de Monserrate, just up the block from Bristol Restaurante. Open Tu-Su 10am-6pm.)*

NEAR SINTRA: MAFRA

The sleepy, otherwise unremarkable town of Mafra (north of Sintra) is home to one of Portugal's most impressive sights and one of Europe's largest historical buildings, the ◼**Palácio Nacional de Mafra.** *(Open W-M 10am-5pm. Closed on national holidays. 400$, students 200$.)* Built by Dom João V in honor of the birth of his first child, the massive castle incorporates a cathedral-size church, monastery, library, and palace. The monstrous 2000-room building, designed by architect Johann Friedrich Ludwig, took 50,000 workers 13 years (1717-1730) to complete. This Herculean task gave rise to a style of sculpture known as the Mafra School.

The exterior of the magnificent Baroque **igreja** (tel. 81 85 00) gleams in recaptured glory after a series of restorations. Most renowned for its bell towers—two of the finest in Europe with 217 tons of bronze bells—the church also has an ornate and noteworthy dome. It was lifted from Bernini's unexecuted plan for St. Peter's in Rome. The richly decorated interior—with bas-reliefs and statues of Carrara marble—is one of Portugal's gems.

To access the building's seemingly interminable corridors and extravagant living quarters, go through the door to the right of the church exit. Although most of the original 16th-century furniture was taken by Dom João V to Brazil, the **palace** nevertheless makes a fascinating visit, if only to hear the guides' fabulous free tour. *(45min. tours in Portuguese and English. Ask at the reception desk.)* Of particular interest are the **Sala dos Trofeus** (Trophy Room), furnished with stag antlers, skins, chandeliers, and chairs, and the **biblioteca** (library), with 38,000 volumes printed in the 16th, 17th, and 18th centuries, displayed on 290 feet of Rococo shelves.

Green and white Mafrense **buses** stop in the square in front of the palace. They serve Campo Grande in **Lisbon** (1½hr., every hour, 5:30am-9pm, 500$) and **Sintra** (1hr., 8-10 per day 6:25am-7:35pm, 380$). The **train** goes to **Sintra** (1hr., 1 per hr., 370$). Do not take the train from Lisbon's Estação Sta. Apolónia unless you want to spend two hours walking to Mafra; the station is out in the countryside where cabs are few and far between. To reach the **tourist office** (tel. 81 20 23), on Av. 25 de Abril, take a right off the main steps of the palace and bear left—look for the blue Turismo sign. The office is on your right in a beige stucco building with a fountain, opposite the main bus station. (Open daily 9:30am-12:30pm and 2:30-6pm.)

ERICEIRA

The little town of Ericeira (pop. 5000) is upstaged by its beach. Known for the world-famous surfing waves to the north, Ericeira has recently become a favorite weekend hangout of young Lisbonites. With its sandy coves, fishing harbor, and white-and-blue houses, Ericeira definitely merits a visit, especially for those less disappointed by the Algarve's meager surf.

◼ **PRACTICAL INFORMATION. Buses** run from Lisbon's Campo Grande to Ericeira (1¼hr., 10 per day, 9am-7:40pm, 685$). Buses leaving Ericeira depart from the station just outside town on EN 247-2. They run to: **Mafra** (30min., every 45min., 6:30am-7:30pm, 310$), **Sintra** (50min., every hr., 6:30am-8:30pm, 385$), **Lisbon** (1¼hr., 12 per day, 6am-9pm, 685$). Check at the **tourist office,** R. Eduardo Bur-

LISBON

nay, 46 (tel. 86 31 22), for schedules. To get to the tourist office from the bus station, cross the road, turn left, and walk uphill. Turn right on Calçada do Rego, continue down R. Paroquial (to the right at the fork in the road), and turn left on R. 5 de Outubro, which runs straight to the small pedestrian Pr. República; the tourist office is just ahead. The attendant there will provide you with a map and accommodations list. (Open July.-Aug. daily 9am-midnight; Sept.-June 9am-10pm.) **Emergency** tel. 112; **police** (tel. 86 35 33), at R. 5 de Outubro; **hospital** (tel. 86 45 08), on R. Prudéncio Francisco da Trindade, inland from the praça. **Telephone code:** (0)61.

▐▐ ACCOMMODATIONS AND FOOD. If you choose to stay and party, you might have trouble finding an inexpensive room in the summer; prices decrease from October to June. **Hotel Pedro O Pescador,** R. Dr. Eduardo Burnay, 22 (tel. 86 40 32), offers pleasant rooms with TVs and private baths (singles 8500$; doubles 11,000$; prices decrease Oct.-June; Visa, MC, AmEx). A welcoming owner, two friendly cocker spaniels, and bright, clean rooms with TVs greet guests at the brand-new **Hotel Vilazul,** Calçada da Balcia, 10 (tel. 86 00 00; fax 86 29 27; breakfast included; singles 7500-9100$; doubles 10,500-13,000$; Visa, MC).

For a quick meal, try one of Ericeira's **pastry shops,** which serve regional specialties as well as sandwiches, drinks, and fruit. **Pão de Nosa Vila,** Pr. da República, 12 serves especially good cakes and biscuits (open W-M 7am-8pm). **Restaurante O Barco,** R. Capitão João Lopes (tel. 86 27 59), just down from Pr. de República and overlooking Praia Ribeira, dishes up spicy seafood. O Barco is justifiably famous for its *caldareda,* a tomato-based shellfish stew typical of Ericeira (1800$). Entrees 1250-2100$. (Open F-W noon-3pm and 7-10pm; closed Nov.)

▲ BEACHES. The town's two main beaches are **Praia do Sol** and **Praia do Norte** which crowd with happy beachgoers on summer weekends. If you are looking for something a little more secluded, take a stroll down the Largo da Feria toward Rébamar. Soon, you'll hit the unmistakable **Praia da Ribeira d'Ilhas,** with its rolling surf, dramatic tides, stunning sand dunes, and rock formations. The world surfing championships were held here in 1994, and surfers still come from around the world to test the waters. The local surf-shop **Ultimar,** R. 5 de Outubro, 25A (tel. 86 23 71) rents boards for 1200-2000$ per day.

SETÚBAL

Setúbal's factories have created a noisy commercial center, surrounded on one side by sugar cane and cork tree plantations and on the other by a bustling port. Industry doesn't attract tourists, most of whom head straight for the Algarve. But wait—don't turn the page yet. Setúbal (pop. 120,000) was once home to an important Roman settlement. Today, the city's fine castle, some of Portugal's brightest *azulejo*-covered alleys, and the waters of the largely rural Costa Azul beckon tourists. Setúbal makes an ideal base for daytrips to the beautiful beaches of Tróia and Figueirinha, the mountainous Serra da Arrábida, and the estuaries of the Rio Sado.

▐ GETTING THERE

Trains run from Estaçao Barreiro in **Lisbon** (1½hr., every hr., 7:55am-6:50pm, 300$). Buses make more sense from **Sesimbra** (45min., 9 per day, 6:20am-6:50pm, 415$).

▐ ORIENTATION AND PRACTICAL INFORMATION

Setúbal's main drag is **Avenida Luisa Todi,** a loud boulevard with a nice park and cafes down its middle, which runs parallel to the **Rio Sado.** Inland from the river and Av. Todi lies a dense pedestrian district of shops and restaurants centered around **Praça du Bocage.** Pr. Bocage leads to another major thoroughfare, **Avenida 5 de Outubro.** To the right and down Av. 5 de Outubro is the bus station. Avenida da Portela is perpendicular to Av. 5 de Outubro and runs past the train station.

Trains: Estação de Setúbal (tel. 52 68 45), in Pr. Brasil. To: **Lisbon** (1½hr., 31 per day, 350$); **Évora** (2hr., 13 per day, 880$); and **Faro** (4hr., 4 per day, 1400$).

Buses: Rodoviária do Alentejo, Av. 5 de Outubro, 44 (tel. 52 50 51). From the city tourist office, walk up to Av. 5 de Outubro and turn left. The station is about 2 blocks down on the right. To: **Lisbon** (1hr., every 30min., 7am-10pm, 580$); **Sesimbra** (1hr., 20 per day, 5:30am-11pm, 490$); **Évora** (2½hr., 5 per day, 7:30am-7pm, 870$); **Faro** (4hr., 6 per day, 7:30am-7pm, 1800$); **Porto** (6hr., 6 per day, 8am-9:30pm, 2100$).

Ferries: Transado, Doca do Comércio (tel. 52 01 52), off Av. Todi at the east end of the waterfront. Trips run back-and-forth from Setúbal to Tróia (15min.; 4am-2pm; 150$, children 80$, cars with driver 500$).

Taxis: (tel. 23 33 34 or 23 14 13), along Av. Todi and by the bus station.

Tourist Office: Posto de Turismo Municipal (tel. 53 42 22), off Pr. Quebedo. From the bus station, turn left onto Av. 5 de Outubro; take the 1st right and the office is on the left. From the train station, take the 1st left onto Av. Portela, which leads into Pr. Quebedo. Open in July-Aug. 9am-7pm; Sept.-June M-F 9am-12:30pm and 2-5:30pm.

Currency exchange: Banks line Av. Todi. For after-hours banking, visit **Agência de Câmbios Central,** Av. Todi, 226 (tel. 53 43 36). Open M-Sa 9am-7:30pm.

Emergency: tel. 112. **Police:** (tel. 53 52 31), on Av. Todi at Av. 22 de Dezembrol.

Medical Services: Hospital (tel. 52 30 24), on R. Camilo Castelo Branco.

Post office: (tel. 52 27 78), on Av. Mariano de Carvalho at Av. 22 de Dezembro. Posta Restante and **telephones.** Open M-F 8:30am-6pm. Branch office in Pr. Bocage (tel. 23 55 55). Open M-F 9am-12:30pm and 2-6pm. **Postal code:** 2900.

Internet Access: Ciber Centro, Av. Bento Gonçalves, 21A (tel. 23 48 00). Six computers. 250$ per 15min. Open M-F 9am-11pm, Sa 10am-8pm.

> **TELEPHONE CODE** Setúbal's phone code is (0)65.

LISBON

▌ ACCOMMODATIONS AND CAMPING

Finding space for the night is no problem, but summer prices can be a bit high. Many *pensãos* line Av. Todi.

Centro de Juventude de Setúbal (HI) (tel. 53 44 31), on Largo José Afonso. Take Av. Todi from the bus or train station, and hang a left on R. Trabalhadores do Mar. Take the first right, and the hostel is on the corner. Spic 'n' span rooms in a new government-sponsored youth center. Reception 8am-noon and 6pm-midnight. Reserve ahead. Dorms 1400-1700$; doubles with bath 3600-4200$.

Pensão Bom Regresso, Pr. Bocage, 48 (tel. 22 98 12). Five well-furnished rooms with TVs and views of the praça. No reservations. Doubles 5000-8000$; triples 9000$.

Camping: Get-away-from-it-all types will want to escape to Parque Natural da Arrábida or one of the smaller locations near Setúbal in Azeitão or Sesimbra. If you must stay in Setúbal, try **Toca do Pai Lopes** (tel. 52 24 75), on R. Praia da Saúde at the west end of Av. Todi on the road to Outão. On the riverbank. Reception daily June-Sept. 8am-midnight; Oct.-May 9am-9pm. June-Aug. 280$ per person and per car, 250$ per tent. Sept.-May 180$ per person and per car, 130$ per tent.

◖ FOOD

Hungry travelers will feel like they've hit the jackpot in the old town, especially off **R. A. Castelões** (turn off Pr. Bocage by the post office). **Groceries** and fresh baked goods are at **Pingo Doce,** Av. Todi, 149 (tel. 52 61 05; open daily 8am-9pm). Next door, on the corner of R. Ocidental do Mercado and Av. Todi, the **Mercado Municipal** sells groceries at open stands (open daily 7am-1pm).

Jardim de Inverno, R. Alvaro Luz, 48-50 (tel. 53 93 73), off R. A. Castelões. Green walls and a garden brighten up this dirt cheap joint. Ask about festival specials—São João in late June brings fried pork, salad, fries, and *sangriá* for 600$. Entrees 550-1200$. *Menú* 900$. Open M-F 8am-midnight, Sa-Su 8am-3pm.

Casa de Santiago, Av. Todi, 92 (tel. 22 16 88). What do all locals order when they dine at the self-proclaimed "king of *choco frito?*" You guessed it. *Choco frito* (fried cuttlefish) for 850$. Entrees 850-2100$. Open daily 9am-10pm.

📷 🎵 SIGHTS AND ENTERTAINMENT

The most impressive sight in town is not really in town—the 16th-century **Castelo de São Filipe** perches on the top of a hill, just outside the city. To reach the castle, take Av. Todi to its end (towards the beaches), turn right, continue to the cross-road, and then ascend R. Estrada do Castelo about 600m. It's about a 40-minute walk from the town center. (Castelo open daily 7am-11pm. Free.) Back in town, the **Igreja de Jesús,** begun in the 15th century, resides at Pr. Miguel Bombarda at the western end of Av. 5 de Outubro. Maritime decorations and faux-rope pillars mark the beginnings of Manueline style. (Open daily 9am-12:30pm and 2-5:30pm. Free.)

In the last week of July and first week of August, **Feira de Santiago** is an industrial and agricultural extravaganza, accompanied by a traveling amusement park, bullfighting, and folk dancing.

🔼 EXCURSIONS

The most worthwhile sights around Setúbal are the natural ones. Outside of town are the fabulous **beaches** of peninsular **Tróia,** a 15-minute ferry ride away (every 30min., 7am-8pm; every hr., 8pm-3am; 140$, children 80$, cars with driver 500$). To the west of Setúbal is a large nature preserve, the **Parque Natural da Arrábida,** which includes a variety of nature trails (tourist office has *A Walking Guide to Arrábida and Sado*) and the pristine **Praia da Figueirinha,** 9km from Setúbal. Outdoor adventurers can contact **Mil Andanças,** Av. Todi, 121 (tel. 53 29 96), for somewhat pricey mountain biking, hiking, canoeing, and other nature trips.

NEAR SETÚBAL: SESIMBRA

Nestled between unspoiled hillsides and the calm turquoise sea of *Costa Azul*, Sesimbra is a refreshingly traditional town. Still a pleasant fishing village, it has not been spoiled by recent influxes of beach-flocking tourists. Sesimbra will also appeal to the less aquatically inclined—a fairly steep hour-long hike above town to the **Moorish castle** rewards with a Kodachrome view of the ocean and surrounding mountains. To reach the castle from the beach, follow the signs and take R. Gen. Humberto Delgado to the marked path. (Castle open 7am-7pm. Free.)

Heavy traffic in the summer may lead you to take a **ferry** from Lisbon to **Cacilhas** (110$) from the Pr. Comércio station and catch a bus to Sesimbra (45min., 15 per day, 6:40am-midnight, 450$). Regular Rodoviária **buses** leave for Sesimbra from Lisbon's Pr. de Espanha (1hr., 7 per day, 7am-7:30pm, 530$). Covas e Filhos and TST (tel. 22 30 72) buses leave from the main bus station on Av. Liberdade to: **Cacilhas** (45min., 12 per day, 5:40am-11pm, 450$); **Setúbal** (45min., 9 per day, 6:20am-6:50pm, 415$); **Lisbon** (1hr., 8 per day, 8am-6:10pm, 530$). Buses for closer destinations leave from the corner of Av. 5 de Outubro and Av. Alexandro Mercularo, a block from the main bus station in Setúbal. Pick up maps, regional info, and accommodations info at the **tourist office,** Largo da Marinha, 27 (tel. 223 57 43; English spoken; open daily June-Sept. 9am-8pm; Oct.-May 9am-12:30pm and 2-5:30pm.) **Emergency** tel. 112; **police** (tel. 223 02 69), on Largo Gago Coutinino; **postal code:** 2970. **Telephone code:** (0)1.

Inexpensive rooms are difficult to find, especially in summer. The best option is to check with the tourist office for private rooms (doubles 4000$ and up). Otherwise, **Residencial Chic,** Trav. Xavier da Silva, 2-6 (tel. 223 31 10), offers four breezy, decidedly un-chic doubles with common baths. Breakfast included. (Singles 3500$; doubles 6000$). For good seafood, try **Restaurante Golfinho,** R. da República, 32 (tel. 223 35 80). Entrees 1000-2000$. (Open Th-Tu 10am-3pm and 7-10pm.)

ALGARVE

Behold the Algarve—a freak of nature, a desert on the sea, an inexhaustible vaca-tionland where happy campers from the world over bask in the sun. Nearly 3000 hours of sunshine per year have transformed this one-time fishermen's backwater into one of Europe's favorite vacation spots. In July and August, tourists mob the Algarve's resorts, packing the bars and discos from the 10pm sunset until way past the all-too-early sunrise. Still, not all is excess in the Algarve. In the off-season, the resorts become pleasantly de-populated, and the sun eases down a bit, presiding over tranquil grotto beaches at the base of rugged cliffs. The region between Olhão and the Spanish border remains understated. Salema, Burgau, and Sagres, to the west of Lagos, offer isolated beaches and steep cliffs. The west coast of the Algarve harbors a protected natural park, and Portugal's eastern border, near the town of Tavira, features floating flamingo wetlands.

The long history of the Algarve dates back almost 3000 years, to when the Phoe-nicians first landed. Then, as in most of Portugal, Romans occupied the region and left a mark unrivaled until the time of the Moors. Starting in the early 8th century and lasting for over 500 years, the Moorish occupation of southern Portugal left a cultural residue that survived even after their expulsion in the 13th century. Within 200 years, the Algarve became the most important area for Portugal's Age of Dis-covery. Prince Henry the Navigator built his famous navigational school and for-tress in Sagres; ships launched out of Lagos made it to Africa, Asia, and the New World. Today, the history and culture remains, often overshadowed by interna-tional vacationers in search of wild parties and perfect tans.

The Algarve's cuisine includes *sardinhas assadas* (grilled sardines), *caldei-rada* (seafood chowder), and dishes brought in by local fishermen. Almonds and figs are popular components of tasty regional desserts, and inexpensive wines, such as the young *vinho verde*, make for a wonderful culinary experience.

HIGHLIGHTS OF THE ALGARVE

■ **Lagos's nightlife**—it doesn't get much nuttier than this (see p. 573).
■ The amazing coast, cliffs, and history of **Sagres** (see. p. 574)
■ **Praia da Rocha,** the best beach on the Algarve (p. 575).
■ **Tavira,** a quiet town with excellent beaches and less tourists (p. 581).

LAGOS

For as long as anyone in Lagos can remember, the modestly sized town (pop. 22,000) has played host to swarms of sun-worshipping Europeans, Australians, and North Americans. Yet beneath the layers of sunblock and the plethora of bars (more than 20 clubs and watering holes stay open until the wee hours), there lies an interesting and important history. The Algarve's capital for almost 200 years, Lagos launched and received many of the ships which brought Portugal wealth, power, and fame from the 15th to the 17th century. The 1755 earthquake destroyed much of the city and with it most traces of the expeditions and naval battles fought off Lagos's coast. As the town's countless international expats will attest, Lagos is a black hole: come for two days and you'll be tempted to stay a month. Although there isn't much more than beaches and bars, no one's complaining. Whether soaking in the view from the cliffs, the sun on the beach, or the booze at the bars, you'll enjoy Lagos too.

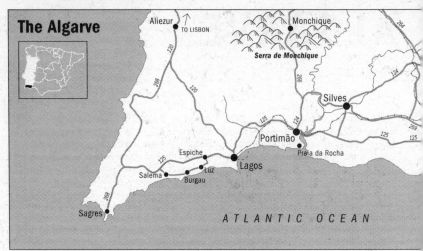

GETTING THERE

If you are trying to get to Lagos from the north, you must go through Lisbon; from the east you must transfer in Faro. **Trains** run to Lagos from **Faro** (2hr., 7 per day, 7:20am-11pm, 720$) and **Lisbon** (5½hr., every 2hr., 7:35am-11:10pm, 1700$). **Buses** also go from: **Faro** (3hr., 6 per day, 8am-5:30pm, 680$); **Lisbon** (5hr., 10 per day, 5am-1am, 2400$); **Sevilla, Spain** (1 per day, various destinations including Lagos, from 2745ptas).

ORIENTATION AND PRACTICAL INFORMATION

Running the length of the river, **Avenida dos Descobrimentos** is the main road that carries traffic in and out of Lagos. From the **train station**, exit to the left, go straight around the pinkish building, cross the river, and hang a left onto Av. Descubrimentos. Out of the **bus station**, turn right onto the main thoroughfare. Follow it to R. Portas de Portugal, which leads into **Praça Gil Eanes,** the center of the old town. Most restaurants, accommodations, and services hover about this praça (also known as the "statue square") and the adjoining R. 25 de Abril and the parallel R. Cândido dos Reis. Farther down Av. Descobrimentos, closer to the **fortaleza** and the other non-beach sights, lies **Praça República.**

TRANSPORTATION

Trains: (tel. 76 29 87). Across the river (over the metal drawbridge) from the main part of town. To: **Silves** (30min., 12 per day, 5:55am-10:17pm, 270$); **Vila Real de Santo António** (3hr., 9 per day, 5:55am-6:22pm, 1050$), via **Faro** (1¾hr., 720$); **Beja** (4hr., 2 per day, 8:50am and 5pm, 1250$), via Faro; **Évora** (6hr., 2 per day, 8:50am and 5pm, 1850$), via Faro; **Lisbon** (6½hr., 5 per day, 6:45am-10:15pm, 2175$).

Buses: The **EVA** bus station (tel. 76 29 44), off Av. Descobrimentos, is just past the train station bridge (when walking out of town). To: **Portimão** (30min., 10 per day, 7:15am-6:15pm, 345$); **Sagres** (1hr., 8 per day, 7:15am-8:30pm, 450$); **Albufeira** (1¼hr., 6 per day, 7am-6:15pm, 650$); **Faro** (2½hr., 6 per day, 7am-5:15pm, 680$); **Lisbon** (5hr., 7 per day, 7:30am-6:15pm, 2400$); **Sevilla** via **Vila Real de Santo António, Ayamonte,** and **Huelva** (6hr.; 1 per day; Tu and F-Sa 8am, W-Th and Su 2:30pm; 3000$). For more details on Lagos-Sevilla transportation, ask at the youth hostel.

Taxis: tel. 76 24 69, 76 30 48, or 76 35 87.

Car Rental: Marina Rent A Car, Av. Descobrimentos, 43 (tel. 76 47 89; fax 76 77 98). Min. age 21. June-Aug. cars start at 8700$ per day; Sept.-May 5000-6500$; tax and

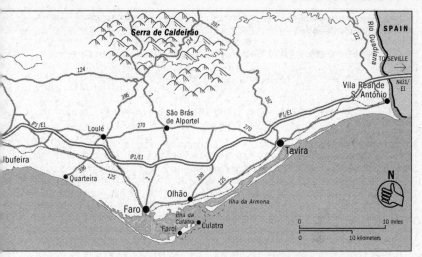

insurance included. **Motoride,** in the same office, rents bikes (1000$ per day) and scooters (4000$ per day; min. age 16; must have license). Open July 9am-7pm; Aug.-June 9am-1pm and 3-7pm. **Hertz-Portuguesa,** Rossio de S. João Ed. Panorama, 3 (tel. 76 00 08), behind the bus station. Min. age 21. Cars start at 10,000$ per day, tax and insurance included.

TOURIST, FINANCIAL, AND LOCAL SERVICES

Tourist Office: (tel. 76 30 31), R. Vasco de Gama, an inconvenient 10min. walk past the bus station going out of town on R. Descobrimentos. Go through the traffic circle and pass the gas station; the office is on the left. Brochures, maps, transport info, and a list of *quartos.* English and French spoken. Open daily 9:30am-12:30pm and 2-5:30pm.

Currency Exchange: Commission-free exchange is available at the youth hostel.

English Bookstore: Loja do Livro, R. Dr. Joaquim Telo, 3 (tel. 76 73 47). Best-sellers, pulp romances, and travel guides. Open June-Aug. M-F 10am-1pm and 3-11pm, Sa 10am-1pm; Sept.-May M-F 10am-1pm and 3-7pm.

Laundromat: Lavandaria Miele, Av. Descobrimentos, 27 (tel. 76 39 69). Wash and dry 1000$ for 5kg. Open M-F 9am-1pm and 3-7pm, Sa 9am-1pm.

Scuba Diving: Blue Ocean Diving Center (tel./fax 78 27 18), Quantro Estrados. Medical license required for difficult dives. Lessons in English, French, German, and Portuguese. Half-day 5000$; full-day 7000$.

Grotto Boat Tours: Operations offering tours of the coastal cliffs and grottoes set up shop on Av. Descobrimentos. Most tours run about 40min. and start at 3000$ for 2 people (slightly less per person with a larger group). Smaller boats are preferable, as they can maneuver into rock caves and formations.

EMERGENCY AND COMMUNICATIONS

Emergency: tel. 112. **Police:** (tel. 76 29 30), R. General Alberto Silva.

Medical Services: Hospital (tel. 76 30 34), R. Castelo dos Governadores.

Post Office: (tel. 77 02 50), R. Portas de Portugal, between Pr. Gil Eanes and the river. Open M-F 9am-6pm. For Posta Restante, label all letters "Estação Portas de Portugal" or they may arrive at the branch office. **Postal Code:** 8600.

Internet Access: The **youth hostel** has 1 computer and a wait that can be up to 2 days long. Sign up in advance or try to hop in if someone doesn't show up. 300$ per 30min. Open with hostel reception 9am-1am. **C.I.L. (Centro Informática de Lagos),** R. Dr. Francisco Sá Carneiro, 31 (tel. 78 20 33). 4 computers. 600$ for 30min., 1100$ per hr. Open M-Sa 9:30am-1pm and 2:30-7pm.

ALGARVE

TELEPHONE CODE | Lagos's phone code is (0)82.

🏠 ACCOMMODATIONS AND CAMPING

In the summertime, *pensões* (and the youth hostel) fill up quickly and cost a bundle. Reserve rooms over a week in advance. Rooms in *casas particulares*, which sometimes include kitchen access, can be the best deals in town at around 2000-3000$ per person in summer. Try haggling with owners waiting at the train and bus stations. If possible, shop before you decide, as room quality varies greatly.

🏠 **Pousada da Juventude de Lagos (HI),** R. Lançarote de Freitas, 50 (tel./fax 76 19 70). From the train and bus stations, head into town on Av. Descubrimentos, passing Pr. Gil Eanes and continuing to Pr. República (on the right). Turn right into the praça and take the small street in the back-center of the square 1 block until it becomes R. Lançarote de Freitas; the hostel is on the right in front of the big green BP sign. Friendly staff and fun lodgers who congregate in the central courtyard and TV room/bar. Fully equipped kitchen. Internet access. Free valuables storage. Breakfast included (takeout available). Laundry 340$ per kg. Reception open daily 9am-1am. Check-out noon. In summer, book through the central **Movijovem** office (tel. (0)1 313 88 20; fax (0)1 352 86 21). July-Sept. dorms 2000$; doubles with bath 5000$. Oct.-June dorms 1500$; doubles with bath 3800$. If full, the attendant will help you find a room nearby.

🏠 **Residencial Rubi Mar,** R. Barroca, 70 (tel. 76 31 65, ask for David; fax 76 77 49; rubimar01@hotmail.com), off Pr. Gil Eanes. Run by 2 friendly expats from London. Centrally located, quiet, and comfortable—a good deal if you can grab one of their 8 rooms. Breakfast included and served in the room. Reserve 2 weeks ahead in summer. Doubles 6000$, with bath 7000$; quads 10,000$.

Residencial Caravela, R. 25 de Abril, 8 (tel. 76 33 61). 16 small but well-located rooms off a courtyard. Breakfast included. Singles 4000$; doubles 5500$, with bath 6000$.

Residencial Gil Vicente, R. Gil Vicente, 26, 2nd fl. (tel./fax 76 29 82), behind the youth hostel. Business card says it's a "gay guest house," but it's open to anyone. Rooms are somewhat stuffy but have high ceilings. Showers 80$. Singles 2500$; doubles 3500$.

Camping: Camping is the way most Europeans experience the Algarve; as a result, sites are crowded and expensive. **Camping Valverde** (tel. 78 92 11), on a beach 5km outside Lagos and 1.5km west of Praia da Luz). Free showers. 700$ per person, 600-900$ per tent, 590$ per car. Jam-packed **Parque de Campismo do Imulagos** (tel. 76 00 31) is also a bit far away but linked to Lagos by a shuttle serving the train and bus stations (10min., 15 per day, 7:15am-7:10pm, except Sa and Su afternoons). Reception daily 8am-10pm. 900$ per adult, under 10 230$, 450-640$ per tent, 430$ per car. **Camping Trindade** (76 38 93), just outside of town. Follow Av. Descobrimentos toward Sagres. 400$ per person with tent, 800$ otherwise.

🍴 FOOD

Tourists can peruse multilingual menus around Pr. Gil Eanes and R. 25 de Abril, but a budget Portuguese meal is nearly impossible to find. The cheapest option is the morning **market,** on Av. Descobrimentos five minutes from the town center, or **Supermercado São Toque,** R. Portas de Portugal, opposite the post office (open July-Sept. 9am-5pm; Oct.-June M-F 9am-8pm, Sa 9am-2pm). Another nearby supermarket is **Marrachinho,** Av. Descobrimentos, 15 (open daily July-Aug. 8am-midnight; Sept.-June 8am-9pm). A convenient mini-market, **Peg Pag,** sits across from the youth hostel on R. Lançarote de Freitas (open M-Sa 9am-1pm and 3-8pm).

🍴 **Casa Rosa,** R. Ferrador, 22 (cell tel. 0936 511 10 52). A Lagos standby, for better or for worse. Enjoy cheap 600$ meal deals with backpacker hordes. Monday and Wednesday are all-you-can-eat spaghetti and garlic bread days (999$). Wide-ranging menu with many vegetarian options (600-1400$). Happy Hour 10-11pm. Late breakfast served Tu-F 11am-2:30pm. Open daily 7pm-2am.

Restaurante Piri Piri, R. Lima Leitão, 15 (tel. 76 38 03). Locals and tourists come to enjoy 91 titillating *piri piri* (hot and spicy) dishes until they get all teary teary. Good people-watching. Entrees 990-1890$. Open daily noon-11pm.

Mullen's, R. Cândido dos Reis, 86 (tel. 76 12 81). A Lagos hotspot. Attractive, international servers dance to the tables with huge portions of spicy food. Entrees 1000-2200$. After dinner, it turns into a popular bar. Restaurant open daily noon-2pm and 7-10pm; bar open until 2am.

A Vaca, R. Silva Lopes, 27 (tel. 76 44 31), a continuation of R. 25 de Abril. Once again, traditional Portuguese food is nonexistent; this restaurant serves traditional home-style Swiss dishes. Crepes 400-900$. Entrees 800-1600$. Open Su-F noon-2am.

👁🌊 SIGHTS AND BEACHES

Lagos

ACCOMMODATIONS
A Residencial Rubi Mar
B Residencial Caravela
C Residencial Gil Vicente
D Pousada da Juventude
E Campsites

SIGHTS. Although sunbathing and non-stop debauchery have long erased memories of Lagos's rugged, sea-faring past, most of the city is still surrounded by a nearly intact 16th-century wall. The **Fortaleza da Porta da Bandeira,** a 17th-century fortress holding maritime exhibitions, overlooks the Marina. *(Open Tu-Sa 10am-1pm and 2-6pm, Su 10am-1pm. 320$, students 160$.)* Also on the waterfront is the old **Mercado de Escravos** (slave market). Legend has it that in 1441 the first sale of African slaves on Portuguese ground took place here. Today the waterfront and marina offer jet-ski rentals, scuba diving lessons, sailboat trips, and motorboat tours of the coastal rocks and grottoes (see **Local Services,** p. 571).

BEACHES. Lagos's beaches are seductive any way you look at them. Flat, smooth, sunbathing sands (crowded during the summer, pristine in the off-season) line the 4km-long **Meia Praia,** across the river from town. Hop on the 30-second ferry near Pr. República (60$ each way). For beautiful cliffs that hide less-crowded beaches and caves, follow Av. Descobrimentos toward Sagres to **Praia de Pinhão** (20 min.). Five minutes farther lies **Praia Dona Ana,** with sculpted cliffs and grottoes that appear on at least half of all Algarve postcards. For other picturesque (and less populated) stretches, continue west to the **Praia do Camilo** and the grotto-speckled cliffs of **Ponta da Piedade.**

🎵 ENTERTAINMENT

You're tan, you're glam, now go find yourself a (wo)man. The streets of Lagos pick up as soon as the sun dips down, and by midnight the city's walls are shaking. The area between Pr. Gil Eanes and Pr. Luis de Camões is filled with cafes. Several areas in town are packed with bars, including R. Cândido dos Reis and the intersection of R. 25 de Abril, R. Silva Lopes, and R. Soeiro da Costa. Bars and clubs runneth over until well past 5am. Staggered happy hours make drinking easy, even on the tightest of budgets.

■ **Taverna Velha (The Old Tavern),** R. Lançarote de Freitas, 34 (tel. 76 92 31), down the street from the youth hostel. The friendliest staff around. Nightly showings of classic American movies. Happy "hour" with 2-for-1 beers or cocktails 9pm-midnight. Beer 200-400$; mixed drinks 500-700$. Open M-Sa 4pm-2am, Su 8pm-2am.

Phoenix Club, R. São Gonçalo, 29 (tel. 76 05 03), near the Old Tavern and the youth hostel. Rises from the nighttime ashes for some great after-hours dancing. Pop and dance music. Beer 500-600$. Cover 1000$, includes 2 beers or 1 mixed drink. Open nightly 1-6am, but the crowds don't arrive until 3:30.

The Lionheart, R. Castelo dos Governadores, 12 (tel. 76 22 46), off Pr. República. This bar has a small dance floor, karaoke, and an interesting assortment of patrons. 2-for-1 happy hour midnight-1am. Beer 450$; mixed drinks 450-600$. Open daily 5pm-4am.

Whyte's Bar, R. Ferrador, 7. Live, request-taking DJ keeps the place packed all night long. Opens up a basement level during the most crowded summer months. Nightly happy hours. Beer 400$; mixed drinks 500-700$. Open daily 6pm-2am.

Joe's Garage, R. 1 de Maio, 78, across from Mullen's back door. Possibly the most fun and definitely the wildest bar in town. Beer 250$. 2-for-1 beers or drinks 10pm-midnight. Open until 2am.

DAYTRIPS FROM LAGOS

SAGRES

Marooned atop a bleak, scrub-desert plateau in the barren southwestern most corner of Europe, for centuries Sagres was considered the end of the world. The windswept, rugged cape—almost as barren as the moon—leads to the Atlantic, where it plunges dramatically on three sides. Here, outward-looking Prince Henry founded his school of navigation, looking to inspire voyages to the far reaches of the globe. Sagres's dramatic, desolate location and relative lack of recreation discourages tour-groups and upscale vacationers; instead it caters to travelers interested in discovering uncharted magic.

■ **PRACTICAL INFORMATION. Rodoviária buses** (tel. 76 29 44) run from **Lagos** (1hr., 8 per day, 7:15am-8:30pm, 450$; check the schedule at the Sagres bus stop to avoid getting stranded). The friendly, English-speaking staff at the **tourist office** (tel. 62 48 73), on R. Comandante Matoso, next to the bus stop, dispenses maps and information on Sagres's illustrious history (open Tu-Sa 9:30am-12:30pm and 2-5pm, Su 9:30am-noon). Privately-run **Turinfo** (tel. 62 00 03), in Pr. República, is also a good source of info. The energetic, English-speaking staff recommends accommodations, **rents bikes** (2000$ per day, 1200$ per half-day), gives info on **jeep tours** of a nearby nature preserve (6400$, including lunch), and provides **scuba** advice. They'll even wash your clothes—seriously. (Open daily 10am-7pm.) **Emergency:** tel. 112. **Telephone code:** (0)82.

■ **ACCOMMODATIONS AND FOOD.** Finding a bed in Sagres is not a problem; windows everywhere display multilingual signs for rooms, many in boarding houses with guest kitchens. Prices range from 3000-5000$ for singles and doubles, 4000-6500$ for triples. Follow the main road toward the traffic circle and turn left after the supermarket to reach **Atalaia Apartamentos** (tel. 60 46 81). These beautiful, fully-furnished apartments and rooms above a grocery store are an exceptional value (apartments for 2 July-Oct. 8000$; Apr.-June 6000$; Nov.-Mar. 5000$). Open-air **camping** is strictly forbidden, so head to the **guarded ground** (tel. 62 43 51; fax 62 44 45), just off E.N. 268 (July-Aug. 600-700$ per person, 500-

600$ per tent, 350-400$ per car; considerably cheaper Sept.-June; open year-round). For groceries, try the **market,** on R. Mercado, which intersects R. Comandante Matoso not far from the tourist office (open M-Sa 8am-1pm), or **Supermarket Alisuper,** on the main street towards the port and Praia da Baleeira (open daily 9am-8pm). **O Dromedário Bistro** (tel. 62 41 08), on R. Comandante Matoso, whips up innovative pizzas (740-1180$) and vegetarian dishes (890-1310$). The bar is a Sagres hotspot by night. (Open daily 10am-midnight; bar open until 3am; closed Jan.-Feb.)

■■■■ **SIGHTS, BEACHES, AND ENTERTAINMENT.** Near the town lurks the **Fortaleza,** the outpost where Prince Henry stroked his beard, decided to map the world, and founded his famous **school of navigation.** The pentagonal 15th-century fortress and the surrounding area yield vertigo-inducing views of the cliffs and sea. (Fortress open June-Aug. 10am-8:30pm; Sept.-May 10am-6:30pm. 300$, students 150$.) Six kilometers farther west lies the desolate **Cabo de São Vicente,** which features the second most powerful lighthouse in Europe, a towering structure that overlooks the southwest tip of the continent and shines over 100km out to sea. Unfortunately, no buses connect the cape with Sagres. The only way to reach the cliff is by bike (see **Turinfo,** above) or on foot (1hr.) past the **Fortaleza do Beliche,** one of several fortresses perched atop the cliffs. (No fixed hours. Get permission to climb up from the gatekeeper, who is there during daylight hours but disappears noon-2pm.)

Several **beaches** fringe the peninsula, most notably **Mareta,** located at the bottom of the road from the town center. Rock formations jut into the ocean on both sides of this sandy crescent. Not as picturesque or intimate as the coves of nearby **Salema** and **Luz** (see below), Mareta is still popular for its length and isolation. West of town, the longest beach, **Praia de Martinhal,** has great **windsurfing.**

Although Sagres may seem dead on arrival, it definitely develops a pulse at sundown. At night, the young crowd the lively restaurant-bar **Rosa dos Ventos** (tel. 62 44 80), in Pr. República (open daily 10am-2am). Also check out **O Dromedário** (see **Accommodations and Food,** above). Or go all out at **The Last Chance Saloon,** which blasts English dance tunes and overlooks the beach (open daily 5pm-4am).

LUZ, BURGAU, AND SALEMA

These three towns on the way to Sagres make perfect stopovers or daytrips from Lagos. Less "discovered" than their larger neighbor and a bit more charming than windswept Sagres, they offer a quiet alternative to crowded Lagos. All three towns feature good beaches (although Salema's is less developed), and all three are accessible by the **bus** from Lagos to Sagres. To reach Luz, get off at Espiche, 1.5km away (12 per day, 7:15am-8:30pm; from Lagos to Espiche 10min., 200$; to Burgau 20min., 295$; to Salema 40min., 310$). Another way to make the trip is by scooter (see **Car Rental,** p. 570). The comfortable **Quinta dos Carrigos** (tel. (0)82 643 51) in Salema (650$ per person, 850$ per tent, 600$ per car) offers excellent **camping.** Fresh fruits, cheeses, and olives are sold by local farmers each morning at the main square in Salema, and decent bars and **restaurants** line the beachfront in all three towns.

▩PRAIA DA ROCHA

A short jaunt from Lagos, this grand beach is perhaps the very best the Algarve has to offer. With vast expanses of sand, surfable waves, rocky red cliffs, and plenty of secluded coves, the beach has a well-deserved reputation. To reach Praia da Rocha from Lagos, first take a **bus** to **Portimão** (35min., 10 per day, 7:30am-6pm, 345$), then switch at the station to the Praia da Rocha bus (10min., every 15min.). The **tourist office** (tel. 42 22 90), at the end of R. Tomás Cabreina, offers maps and lists of accommodations and restaurants (open May-Sept. 9:30am-8pm; Oct.-Apr. M-F 9:30am-12:30pm and 2-6pm, Sa-Su 9:30am-12:30pm). **Emergency:** tel. 112.

ALGARVE

ALBUFEIRA

Those who come to Albufeira (pop. 22,000), the largest seaside resort in the Algarve, are hell-bent on having a good time. Sun, surf, and *cerveja* keep the Brits, Germans, and Scandinavians satisfied; nary a Portuguese roams the cobblestone streets. The city also plays host to packaged tours, which fill the high-rise hotels with high-rolling guests. It may appear that there is little "authentic" Portuguese culture here, but a stroll through the old town or along the east edge of the beach hints at Albufeira's humble fishing origins. For those too jaded to care, the night-life jumps from dusk till dawn, and 12 beaches watch over the glassy blue surf.

⚡ PRACTICAL INFORMATION. EVA buses connect the **train station** (tel. 57 16 16), 6km inland, to the town center (every hr., 7:30am-7pm, 200$). Trains run to: **Faro** (45min., 6 per day, 5:18am-11:30pm, 300$); **Lagos** (1hr., 5 per day, 7:30am-11:30pm, 500$); **Olhão** (1½hr., 6 per day, 5:18am-11:30pm, 380$); **Tavira** (2hr., 6 per day, 5:18am-11:30pm, 580$); **Vila Real de Santo António** (2¼hr., 6 per day, 5:18am-11:30pm, 720$); **Lisbon** (4-5½hr., 5 per day, 7:49am-11:30pm, 2025-2950$). The EVA **bus station** (tel. 58 97 55), on Av. Liberdade, is more convenient to town. Buses head to: **Faro** (1hr., every hr., 7:25am-11:15pm, 600$); **Lagos** (1½hr., 7 per day, 8:35am-6pm, 870$); **Tavira** (1½hr., 5 per day, 8:45am-11:15pm, 760$); **Lisbon** (3½-4hr., 12 per day, 8:50am-2:30am, 2100-2550$).

The English-speaking staff at the **tourist office,** R. 5 de Outubro, 8 (tel. 58 52 79), offers maps, a list of rooms, and tons of brochures on water sports, including fishing and scuba diving. From the bus station, turn right and walk downhill into the main square (Largo Eng. Duarte Pacheco) then turn right out of the square and left onto R. 5 de Outubro. (Open daily 9:30am-7pm.) A booth run by **Portela** (tel. 57 11 55) hands out tourist info in front of the train station (open M-Sa 9am-7pm). Call a **taxi** at tel. 58 71 51. **Emergency:** tel. 112; **police** (tel. 51 54 20), in the *Caliços* zone, near the Mercado Municipal; **medical services: Centro de Saúde** (Health Clinic) tel. 58 75 50. **Post office** (tel. 58 08 70), next to the tourist office on R. 5 de Outubro (open M-F 9am-6pm); **postal code:** 8200. **Telephone code:** (0)89.

📷🍴 ACCOMMODATIONS AND FOOD. Many places are booked solid from late June through mid-September, and budget accommodations are scarce. Ask for *quartos* at the tourist office or any restaurant or bar. You will most likely be accosted by room renters at the bus and train stations as well. Closest to the bus station is the comfortable **Residencial Capri,** Av. Liberdade, 83 (tel. 51 26 91), where bright, spacious doubles, all with bath, overlook the avenue (singles 5000$; doubles 7000-8000$). The modern **Pensão Albufeirense,** R. Liberdade, 16 (tel. 51 20 79), a few blocks downhill from the bus station, has comfortable rooms and a TV lounge (singles 4000$; doubles 6000$; triples 7600$; open May-Sept.). Weary campers can succumb to the ritz and glitz of the highly rated **Parque de Campismo de Albufeira** (tel. 58 76 29; fax 58 76 33), a few kilometers outside town on the road to Ferreiras. It's more like a shopping mall than a campground, with four swimming pools, three restaurants, tennis courts, a supermarket, and a hefty price tag (850$ per person, per car, and per tent). Open-air camping is illegal and not tolerated.

There is no shortage of cheap and varied eats. Locals recommend **Tasca do Viegas,** R. Cais Herculano, 2 (tel. 51 40 87), near the fisherman's beach (entrees 1000-2600$; open daily noon-11pm). For something spicy, try the nearby **Minar Indian Tandoori Cuisine** (tel. 51 31 96), on R. Diogo Cão (entrees 1000-1800; open M-Sa noon-3pm and 6-11pm, Su 6-11pm).

📷🏖 SIGHTS AND BEACHES. Once the last holdout of the Moors in southern Portugal, Albufeira preserves its graceful architectural heritage in its old quarter, off R. Miguel Bombarda and Pr. Miguel Bombarda. From the main square, take Tr. 5 de Outubro across R. 5 de Outubro and walk up R. Igreja Nova toward the beach. Tiny minarets pierce the small Byzantine dome of the **Santana** chapel, an exquisite filigree doorway heralds the **São Sebastião** church (open evenings in summer;

free), an ancient Gothic portal fronts the **Misericórdia** (near Pr. República and the beach; closed to the public), and a barrel-vaulted interior receives worshippers into the **Matiz** (open M-F 2-6pm; free).

Albufeira's spectacular slate of **beaches** ranges from the popular **Galé** and **São Rafael** (4-8km toward Lagos), to the centrally located **Baleeira** and **Inatel** (the easiest to reach), to the very chic **Falésia** (10km toward Faro). Many small and relatively uncrowded beaches lie scattered among these—it pays to explore.

🎵 ENTERTAINMENT. After a day at the beach, why not go to a bar? Bars and restaurants line all the streets, and clubs blast everything from salsa to techno to *fado* as soon as the sun sets—and they continue until it rises. One prime spot is **Fastnet Bar,** R. Cândido dos Reis, 5 (tel. 58 91 16), packed with Northern Europeans (beer 500$; mixed drinks 800$; open daily 11am-4am). Down the street is **Classic Bar,** R. Cândido dos Reis, 10 (tel. 51 20 75), which covers its floor with sand every night to make the Grecian decor feel more familiar (beer 300-400$; mixed drinks 800$; open daily 10am-4am). **7½ Disco** (tel. 51 33 06), on R. São Gonçalo de Lagos, is a popular beachside dance club. Many of the hottest new clubs are just outside of Albufeira (500-1000$ by taxi). Try **Reno's Bar, IRS Disco,** or **Kiss Disco** (open daily 2am-6am). For mellower nightlife, head east along the coast to the old town. At **Café Latino,** on R. Latino Coelho, salsa tunes complement a stunning seaside view (beer 200-300$; coffee 300$; open daily 10am-2am). There's nothing strange about nearby **Bar Bizzaro,** R. Dr. Frutuoso Silva, 30, a cool, down-to-earth cafe-bar which hosts live music Tuesday at 9pm (beer 250-400$; open daily 9am-2am).

FARO

Although many northern Europeans begin their holidays in Faro (pop. 55,000), the Algarve's capital and largest city, few bother to stay long enough to absorb its charm and local color. The city is divided into two parts, each with its own personality: a modern, commercial shopping district with a slick marina, and a quiet historical neighborhood, behind the walls of the perfectly preserved old town. The calm beaches of the estuary's islands satiate those seeking the sun.

📍 GETTING THERE

Trains run to Faro from: **Lagos** (1¾hr., 9 per day, 6am-6pm, 720$); **Évora** (4hr., 4 per day, 7:45am-6:10pm, 1650$); **Beja** (5hr., 2 per day, 10am and 2pm, 1200$). **Buses** go to Faro from: **Huelva, Spain** (2½hr., 2 per day, 9am and 6pm, 700ptas) and **Beja** (3½hr., 4 per day, 10am-7:20pm, 1500$).

📋 ORIENTATION AND PRACTICAL INFORMATION

Faro's ritzy center hugs the **Doca de Recreio,** a marina lined with yachts and bordered by the Jardim Manuel Bívar. The main road into town, **Avenida da República,** runs past the train station and bus depot along the harbor, spilling into a delta of smaller streets at **Praça Dr. Francisco Gomes** (the center of town), which borders the dock and garden. **Rua Dr. Francisco Gomes** and **Rua de Santo António** are the major pedestrian thoroughfares off Pr. Gomes. The old town begins at the **Avio da Vila,** a stone arch on the far side of the garden, next to the tourist office.

TRANSPORTATION

Flights: The international **airport** (tel. 81 85 82), 5km west of the city, has a police station, bank, post office, car rental companies, and tourist info booth. Open daily 10am-midnight. Buses #14 and 16 run from the street opposite the bus station to the airport (20min., every 20min., 160$). In summer the **aerobus** runs from the big EVA Hotel on the main praça to the airport (15min., every 45min., 8am-8pm, free with plane ticket). Taxis to the airport cost 1200-1400. **TAP Air Portugal** (tel. 80 02 00), R. Dr. Francisco Gomes. Open M-F 9am-5:30pm.

Trains: (tel. 80 17 26), Largo Estação. To: **Albufeira** (45min., 14 per day, 7:20am-11pm, 300$); **Vila Real de Santo António** (1½hr., 12 per day, 6:10am-12:10am, 520$); **Lagos** (2hr., 7 per day, 7:20am-11pm, 720$); **Beja** (3hr., 2 per day, 9:05am and 5:30pm, 1250$); **Évora** (5hr., 2 per day, 9:05am and 5:30pm, 1650$); **Lisbon** (5-6hr., 6 per day, 7:20am-11pm, 2060$). Consult the schedule as departure times are often bunched together.

Buses: EVA (tel. 89 97 00), Av. República. To: **Olhão** (20min., every 30min., 7:15am-8:35pm, 190$); **Albufeira** (1hr., 14 per day, 6:30am-6:45pm, 570$); **Vila Real de Santo António** (1hr., 9 per day, 7:15am-6:20pm, 605$); **Tavira** (1hr., 11 per day, 7:15am-7:20pm, 450$); **Lagos** (3hr., 6 per day, 8am-5:30pm, 680$); **Beja** (3hr., 2 per day, 7:45am and 4pm, 1500$). **Renex** (tel. 81 29 80), across the street, provides express long-distance service. To: **Lisbon** (4½hr., 9 per day, 5:15am-1:15am, 2350$); **Porto** (8½hr., 9 per day, 5:15am-1:15am, 3400$); **Braga** (10hr., 9 per day, 5:15am-1:15am, 3500$). **Intersul** (tel. 89 97 70) runs to Sevilla (2600$), with connecting buses to France and Germany.

Taxis: Rotaxi (tel. 82 22 89). Taxis congregate near Jardim Manuel Bívar (by the tourist office) and at the bus and train stations.

TOURIST, FINANCIAL, AND LOCAL SERVICES

Tourist Office: R. Misericórdia, 8 (tel. 80 36 04), conveniently located at the entrance to the old town. From the bus or train station, turn right down Av. República along the harbor, then turn left past the garden. From the main square, go past the garden; the office is to the left of the arch with the clock and bell tower. Helps find accommodations. English spoken. Open June-Aug. 9:30am-7pm; Sept.-May 9:30am-5:30pm.

Currency Exchange: Cota Cambios, R. Dr. Francisco Gomes, 26 (tel. 82 57 35), off Pr. Gomes. 500$ commission. Open M-F 8am-8pm, Sa 10am-6pm, Su 10am-2pm.

Laundromat: Sólimpa, R. Batista Lopes, 30 (tel. 82 29 81), up R. Primeiro de Maio. to the praça. 350$ per kg. Open M-F 9am-1pm and 3-7pm, Sa 9am-1pm.

EMERGENCY AND COMMUNICATIONS

Emergency: tel. 112. **Police:** (tel. 82 20 22), R. Polícia da Segurança Pública.

Hospital: (tel. 80 34 11), R. Leão Pinedo, north of town.

Post Office: (tel. 80 30 06), Largo Carmo, across from the Igreja de Nossa Senhora do Carmo. Open M-F 8:30am-6:30pm, Sa 9am-12:30pm. **Postal Code:** 8000.

Internet Access: At the **youth hostel** and at the **Science Alive** museum (tel. 89 09 20), on R. Comandante Francisco Manuel. From Pr. Gomes, walk through the gardens and turn right, heading toward the docks. Unlimited use 500$, students 250$. Wednesday 50% off. Open July-Sept. 15 M-F 10am-5pm, Sa-Su 3-7pm.

TELEPHONE CODE	Faro's phone code is (0)89.

⌐ ACCOMMODATIONS

Rooms are always available here, even during high-season. Resort to the tourist office's top 20 list of *pensões* if necessary. Lodgings surround the bus and train stations. Most of the low-end budget *pensões* are plain but suffice. For something cheap and cheerful, try to scrape up a *quarto*.

Pensão Residencial Oceano, R. Ivens, 21, 2nd fl. (tel. 82 33 49). From the marina-side of Pr. Gomes, head up R. 1 de Maio; it's 1 block up on the right. The doubles are tidy and comfortable. Attractive *azulejos* in the halls and baths. All 22 rooms have bath and telephone, some have TV. Breakfast 250$. Singles 7000$; doubles 8000$; triples 10,000$. 500-1000$ discount in winter. Visa.

Residencial Madalena, R. Conselheiro Bívar, 109 (tel. 80 58 06; fax 80 58 07), off Pr. Gomes. Centrally located with pleasant rooms, all with full bath, telephone, fan, and heater. TV room and small bar. English spoken. Breakfast included. June-Aug. singles 7000$; doubles 10,000$. Sept.-May singles 5000$; doubles 6000$.

Pensão-Residencial Central, Largo Terreiro Do Bispo, 12 (tel. 80 72 91), near the pedestrian area. Clean, bright, comfortable rooms, all with bath, some with terraces. June-Aug. singles 5000$; doubles 7500$. Sept.-May singles 4000$; doubles 6000$.

Casa de Hóspedes Adelaide, R. Cruz das Mestras, 7-9 (tel. 80 23 83; fax 82 68 70). Twelve rough, but clean rooms. Ideal for big groups. Private bath 500$ extra. Singles 3000$; doubles 5500$; quads 8000-9000$. 500$ discount in winter.

Pousada da Juventude (tel. 82 65 21), R. Polícia de Segurança Pública, inconveniently located opposite the police station. A truly budget option. Kitchen and TV room. Reception daily 8am-noon and 6pm-midnight. Singles 1400-1700$; doubles 2700-4200$.

⍟ FOOD

Almonds and figs are native to the Algarve; local bakeries take advantage of this and transform them into delicious marzipan and fig desserts. Faro has some of the Algarve's best cafes, many along R. Conselheiro Bívar, off Pr. Gomes. At the **market,** Pr. Dr. Francisco Sá Carneiro, locals barter fresh seafood (open daily 8:30am-1pm). Live the high life on R. Santo António, a pedestrian district where costly *marisqueiras* (seafood restaurants) and credit cards reign, or shop at **Supermercado Minipreço,** Largo Terreiro do Bispo, 8-10 (tel. 80 32 92; open M-Sa 9am-8pm).

Restaurante Dois Irmãos, Largo Terreiro do Bispo, 14 (tel. 82 33 37). Go up R. 1 de Maio into the small square; the restaurant is on the right. Learn to love Portuguese top-40 music. Entrees 960-2080$. Open daily 10am-4pm and 6-11pm.

Restaurante Fim do Mundo, R. Vasco da Gama, 53 (tel. 82 62 99), down the street from Dois Irmãos. It's the end of the world, and you'll feel fine with chicken and fries (650$) or a fish omelette (850$). Open M noon-3pm, W-Su noon-3pm and 5-11pm.

Pastelaria Chantilly, R. Vasco da Gama, 63A (tel. 82 07 80), next to Fim do Mundo. Indulge in delicious marzipan sweets (110$ each) and other homemade pastries. Open June-Aug. M-Sa 8am-midnight.

⍟ SIGHTS

Faro's old town is a jewel—untouristed and traditional, it is a medley of ornate churches, museums, and shops selling local handicrafts. From Pr. Gomes, walk through the gardens to get to the entrance of the old town. Next to the tourist office, the early-19th-century **Arco da Vila** pierces the old city wall.

CAPELA DOS OSSOS. Step into **Igreja de Nossa Senhora do Carmo** to inspect the Capela dos Ossos (Chapel of Bones), a wall-to-wall macabre bonanza of crusty bones and fleshless skulls "borrowed" from the adjacent cemetery. Though not as spectacular as Évora's bone chapel, it's still worth a look. *(Largo Carmo, in the city center. Open M-F 10am-1pm and 3-5pm, Sa-Su 10am-1pm. Church free, chapel 120$.)*

MUSEU DA MARINHA. The Museu da Marinha flaunts three notable and interesting boat models. One model is of the boat that took Vasco da Gama's on his epic journey to India in 1497, another is of a boat used by a group of imperialists on their ride up the Congo River in 1482, and the third is of a boat that out-classed the Turkish navy in 1717. *(Near the marina, next to Hotel Eva. Tel. 80 36 01. Open M-F 9:30am-noon and 2:30-5pm. 100$.)*

CATHEDRAL (SÉ). A narrow road leads through an Arab portico to the Renaissance cathedral, which stands in a deserted square. The **Capela do Rosário,** decorated with 17th-century *azulejos* and a red chinoiserie organ, interrupt the cathedral's understated Renaissance interior. Under the cathedral—a site once sacred to Romans, Visigoths, and Moors—lie traces of Neolithic civilization. The striking **cloister** is an ideal spot to relax with a book from the municipal library, housed in the same building. *(Open M-F 10am-5pm. 250$.)*

OTHER SIGHTS. The city's Museu de Etnografia Regional introduces visitors to the folk life of the Algarve, with photos of the once-tranquil, pristine fishing villages of Lagos, Albufeira, and Faro. *(Pr. Liberdade, 2. Tel. 82 76 10. Open M-F 9am-12:30pm and 2-5:30pm. 300$.)* Behind the church, **Museu Arqueológico e Lapidar** flashes assorted royal memorabilia, from diamond-studded hairpins to silver spurs and swords. *(Tel. 89 74 00. Open M-F 9am-noon and 2-5pm. Free.)* Across from the old city and facing the huge and dusty Largo de São Francisco (the town fairgrounds) stands the mighty **Igreja de São Francisco,** with its hulking facade and delicate interior. *(Open M-F 10am-noon and 3-5pm.)*

⬛ ENTERTAINMENT

Sidewalk **cafes** crowd the pedestrian walkways off the garden in the center of town. Several **bars** populated by a young crowd liven R. Conselheiro Bívar and its side streets. One notable spot is **Upa Upa Café & Bar,** R. Conselheiro Bívar, 51 (tel. 80 78 32; beer 250-450$; mixed drinks 600$; coffee 150-300$; open daily 9pm-4am). Faro's rock-free **beach** hides on an islet off the coast. Take bus #16 from the stop in front of the tourist office, just across the garden from Pr. Gomes (5-10min., every hr., 8:45am-8pm, 170$).

OLHÃO

Olhão, 8km east of Faro, prefers fish to tourists. For hundreds of years, the few inhabitants of the area were fishermen. Modern locals have continued the tradition, helping to create one of Portugal's most productive fishing industries. Yet beyond this no-frills town, gorgeous beaches spread over the neighboring islands, easily accessible by ferry from Olhão's dock. Between the islands and Olhão's coast lies part of the **Parque Natural da Ria Formosa,** with its numerous species of exotic birds (including flamingos) and other water-based wildlife.

⬛ **PRACTICAL INFORMATION.** The **train station** is one block above the bus station on Av. Combatentes da Grande Guerra. Trains run to: **Faro** (30 min., 5 per day, 6:55am-10:45pm, 180$); **Tavira** (30min., 6 per day, 6:21am-12:20am, 210$); **Vila Real de Santo António** (1¼hr., 5 per day, 6:21am-12:10am, 280$). The **bus station** is on R. General Humberto Delgado, one block from Av. República (open daily 7am-7pm). Buses run to: **Faro** (20min., every 30min., 7:35am-7:50pm, 250$); **Tavira** (30min., 10 per day, 7:35am-7:50pm, 320$); **Vila Real de Santo António** (1½hr., 8 per day, 7:35am-6:40pm, 550$). To reach the **port** from Av. República, which cuts through the heart of town, turn down R. Diogo de Mendonça or R. Leonardo (heading away from the bus and train stations) for a few blocks then turn right onto R. Gil Eanes, which becomes R. Conserveira as it nears the ferry dock. Alternatively, weave down to Av. 5 de Outubro, which runs parallel to the water, and turn left.

The **tourist office** (tel. 71 39 36) is on Largo Sebastião Martins Mestre, an offshoot of R. Comércio. From the train station, head straight down R. 1 de Maio and left on R. General Humberto Delgado. Go right at the intersection with Av. República, and straight onto R. Comércio; the office is around the bend on the left. Its English-speaking staff has maps, ferry schedules, and sometimes free **luggage storage** during the day—ask nicely. (Open M-F 9am-12:30pm and 2-5:30pm, Sa-Su 9:30am-noon.) **Emergency:** tel. 112. **Post office,** Av. República, 17 (tel. 71 20 13 or 70 53 52; open daily M-F 8:30am-6pm); **postal code:** 8700. **Telephone code:** (0)89.

⬛⬛ **ACCOMMODATIONS AND FOOD. Pensão Bela Vista,** R. Teófilo Braga, 65-67 (tel. 70 25 38), off a dusty sidestreet rents cheerful, tiled rooms with baths. Exit the tourist office, turn left, take the first left and then the first right. (Singles 4000$; doubles 6000$. Sizeable discount in winter.) **Residencial Boémia,** R. Cerca, 20 (tel./fax 71 45 13), sits pretty with bright, clean rooms, all with bath and A/C. From the train or bus station, take Av. República and turn right on R. 18 de Junho. After four

A SLUG IN THE FACE Escargot? Well, not exactly. One of Portugal's favorite snack foods is the lowly *caracol* (snail). Unlike their classier French counterparts, *caracóis* are eaten in massive portions, boiled in shells with just a bit of salt and a sprig of fresh oregano. No forks here—pile a heap of the little creepies on your plate and skewer them with a toothpick. True connoisseurs use a needle-like spine carved out of palm leaves. If the dainty method doesn't suit you, crack the shell between your teeth. On a rainy day you might see folks prodding along the roadside in search of a snack; feel free to join in the fun. Alternatively, save your energy (the little fellas are surprisingly quick)—*caracóis* are served at restaurants across the country.

blocks on R. 18 de Junio, turn left again. (Breakfast included. June-Aug. singles 5000$; doubles 7000$. Sept.-May singles 3500$; doubles 5000$. Visa, MC, AmEx.) Olhão's highly recommended year-round campground is the **Parque de Campismo dos Bancários do Sul e Ilhas** (tel. 70 54 02; fax 70 54 05). It's off the highway outside of town and can be accessed by the nine buses per day which leave from in front of the gardens on R. 5 de Outubro (showers included; 620$ per person, 500$ per tent and per car). **Supermercado São Nicolau,** R. General Humberto Delgado, 62, lies up the block from the bus station (open M-Sa 9am-9pm). The **mercado,** housed in two red brick buildings, is adjacent to the city gardens along the river (open M-Sa 8am-1:30pm). Many eateries on Av. 5 de Outubro grill the day's catch. At **Casa de Pasto O Bote,** Av. 5 de Outubro, 122 (tel. 72 11 83), pick your slithery, silvery meal from the trays of fresh fish and watch it get charcoal-grilled right before your eyes (entrees 850-1500$; open M-Sa noon-3pm and 6-11pm).

▓OLHÃO'S COAST: ILHAS ARMONA, CULATRA, AND FAROL

Long expanses of uncrowded, sandy beach and deep blue sea surround **Ilhas Armona, Culatra,** and **Farol,** the three major islands off the coast of Olhão. Armona is the closest, followed by Culatra, and then Farol—all are easy daytrips from Olhão. The farther away, the quieter the beaches become (though the *praias* on all three have barely a fraction of the human traffic found in more touristed parts of the Algarve). The islands and sandbars just offshore fence off the Atlantic, creating an important wetland habitat **(Parque Nacional da Ria Formosa)** for birds, fish, and other creatures. The easiest way to get acquainted with Olhão's *ilhas* is to hop on the first ferry out to Armona. Ferries motor to **Armona** from Olhão's dock, near the intersection of R. Conserveira and R. 5 de Outubro; buy tickets from the small stand (15min; June-Aug. 12 per day, 7:30am-8pm; Sept.-May 3 per day, 8:30am-5pm; 320$; last return trip in summer 8:30pm). Another fleet of ferries service **Culatra** (30min.; June-Aug. every 2hr., 7am-7:30pm; Sept.-May 3 per day; 330$; last return trip in summer 8pm) and **Farol** (45min; June-Aug. every 2hr, 7am-7:30pm; Sept.-May 3 per day; 440$; last return trip in summer 8:20pm).

If you miss the last ride back from Armona, accommodations are available at **Orbitur's campsite** (tel. 71 41 73), on the central path, five minutes of the dock. Twenty-nine bungalows, each of which house up to four people, require a minimum stay of two nights. At 9000$ per night from June to August, it's best not to find yourself stranded here. (Reception 8:30am-11pm.) Expect to pay a little more for snacks and meals than on the mainland. Several restaurant-bars vie for attention at the dock (entrees 1000-2000$).

TAVIRA

Farmers tease police by riding their motor scooters over the Roman pedestrian bridge, and that's about as eventful as Tavira gets. But for most visitors to this small town, that's just fine. White houses and palm trees fringe the river banks, and festive Baroque churches dot the hills above. This easy-going fishing port has recently become a haven for travelers in search of relaxation on the town's peaceful beaches. But despite the influx of tourists, the town has kept its calm.

🚉 PRACTICAL INFORMATION. Trains (tel. 32 23 54) leave for **Vila Real de Santo António** (30min., 6 per day, 6:55am-12:45am, 240$) and **Faro** (1hr., 6 per day, 6:25am-10:10pm, 300$). **EVA buses** (tel. 32 25 46) leave from the station upriver from Pr. República for **Olhão** (30min., 6:50am-7:10pm, 320$); **Vila Real de Santo António** (40min., 10 per day, 7am-7:20pm, 385$); **Faro** (1hr., 10 per day, 6:50am-7:10pm, 450$). For a **taxi,** call 32 15 44. Rent **bikes and scooters** from **Loris Rent** (tel. 32 52 03 or 32 47 91), on R. Galeria. The English-speaking staff at the **tourist office,** R. Galeria, 9 (tel. 32 25 11), up some steps off Pr. República, doles out maps and lodgings info (open M-Sa 9:30am-12:30pm and 2-5:30pm, Su 9:30am-12:30pm). **Emergency:** tel. 112; **police** tel. 32 20 22; **health center:** tel. 320 10 00. The **post office,** R. Liberdade, 64, one block uphill from Pr. República, has basic services and Posta Restante (open M-F 8:30am-6pm); **postal code:** 8800. **Telephone code:** (0)81.

🏠🍴 ACCOMMODATIONS AND FOOD. No worries—Tavira has enough *pensões* and *quartos* to house an entire study-abroad program. To find riverfront **🛏Pensão Residencial Lagõas Bica,** R. Almirante Cândido dos Reis, 24 (tel. 32 22 52), from Pr. República, cross the pedestrian bridge and continue straight down R. A. Cabreira; turn right and go down one block. This *pensaõ* has well-furnished rooms, an outdoor patio and rooftop picnic area, a sitting room, washing facilities, and a fridge for guest use. The owner speaks English. (Singles 3000$; doubles 4500$, with bath 6500$. 500$ cheaper in winter.) Back on the other side of the river, expansionist **Pensão Residencial Castelo,** R. Liberdade, 4 (tel 32 39 42) is busy taking over the block with an ultra-modern, brand-new annex featuring bright, spacious rooms and beautiful apartments, all with bath. (Singles 5000-6000$; doubles 8000$; apartments 15,000$, 4-person max.) **Ilha de Tavira campground** (tel. 32 50 21), with its entourage of snack bars and restaurants, sprawls on the beach of an island 2km from Pr. República. Take the ferry from the dock at the end of Estrada das 4 Aguas, a 20-minute walk downstream along the river. (Ferry every 15min., 8:30am-midnight, 150$ round-trip. Reception 8am-midnight. Showers 100$. 430$ per person, 680$ per tent. Open May-Oct. 15.)

Cafes and restaurants line Pr. República and opposite the garden on R. José Pires Padinha. **Churrasqueira "O Manel,"** R. Almirante dos Reis, 6 (tel. 32 33 43), across the river from Pr. República, has a reasonably priced restaurant and a take-out counter. Bring your food to the park and chow down. (Entrees 700-1500$. Open W-M 11:30am-3pm and 6:30-11pm.) Also facing the square across the river is **Restaurante Ponto de Encontro,** Pr. Dr. A. Padiuha, 39 (tel. 23 730). Binge outdoors on specialties like *peixe con molho de amêndoa* (fish with almond sauce, 1400$) or the catch of the day (990$; open F-W noon-3:30pm and 6:30-11pm.)

🏖🏖 SIGHTS AND BEACHES. Most of Tavira's sights are planted along the side streets off Pr. República. Steps off the praça lead past the tourist office to the **Igreja da Misericórdia,** whose superb Renaissance doorway has faces sprouting from twisting vines (open daily 10am-1pm and 3-6:30pm; free). Just beyond, the remains of the city's **Castelo Mouro** (Moorish Castle) sit next to the church **Santa Maria do Castelo,** whose garden brims with fuchsias, chrysanthemums, and bougainvillea. (Castle open M-F 8am-5pm, Sa-Su 10am-7:30pm. Church open M-F 10am-1pm and 3-6pm, Sa 10am-1pm. Free.) The seven-arched pedestrian-only **Ponte Romana** footbridge leads to the floral Pr. 5 de Outubro. From Pr. Padinha, head up R. Alvares Botelho to the **Igreja do Carmo.** The church's elaborately decorated chancel resembles a 19th-century opera set, with false perspectives giving the illusion of windows and niches supported by columns. (Open M-F 10am-1pm. Free.)

Local **beaches,** including **Pedras do Rei,** are accessible year-round. To reach the excellent beach on **Ilha da Tavira,** an island 2km away, follow the directions to the island's campsite (see **Accommodations and Food,** above).

VILA REAL DE SANTO ANTÓNIO

Located at the east end of the Algarve and at the mouth of the Rio Guadiana, Vila Real is a transfer point for travelers going to Spain. Before the construction of the highway bridge between the two countries was completed in 1992, the town got a lot more tourist traffic, as marooned Spain-bound travelers frequently spent the night. Most tourists now bypass the quiet city.

Trains service **Faro** (2hr., 10 per day, 6am-10:15pm, 520$) and **Lagos** (4½hr., 9 per day, 6am-6:15pm, 1050$). For trains to Spain, take the **ferry** to **Ayamonte, Spain** (every 30min., 8am-8pm, 160$ per person, 430$ per car). From Ayamonte, you can take a **bus** in the main square direct to **Huelva, Spain** (2hr., every hr., 540ptas). Buses from Vila Real to the rest of the Algarve are more expensive, more reliable, and faster than trains. To: **Tavira** (40min., 9 per day, 7:05-6:30pm, 385$); **Faro** (1½hr., 9 per day, 7:05am-6:30pm, 605$); **Lagos** (4hr., 8 per day, 7:05am-6:30pm, 1150$); **Lisbon** (6hr., 5 per day, 8:15am-11:15pm, 2500$). Buses leave from the esplanade near the train station and the river. Buses to **Sevilla, Spain** (3hr., M-F 2 per day, 9:10am and 5:15pm, 1800$) eliminate the hassle of train-ferry-bus transfers.

The **Pousada da Juventude (HI),** R. D. Sousa Martins, 40 (tel./fax 54 45 65), is a white building on the fifth street from the river (2 blocks to the left of R. Teófilo Braga). Living room, bar, kitchen, and washing facilities complement decent quarters. (Breakfast included. Reception daily 8am-noon. Lockout noon-6pm, but dropoff all day. Reserve at least 3 days in advance. June-Aug. dorms 1500$; doubles 3200$. Sept.-May dorms 1200$; doubles with bath 2800$.) **Restaurante Snack-Bar El Conde** (tel. 54 19 70), in the main square on the corner of R. Teófilo Braga, cooks up excellent seafood from 700$ (open daily noon-midnight).

ALGARVE

CENTRAL PORTUGAL

ALENTEJO

The Alentejo province covers almost one-third of Portugal, but with a population barely over half a million it remains the country's least populated and least touristed region. Its arid plains stretch to the horizon, punctuated only by olive and cork-oak trees. Endless wheat fields and the vineyards covering the rolling hills of northern Alentejo make the region a vast granary, though severe droughts have restricted its agricultural capacity. Évora, Elvas, and other medieval towns preserve their relatively pristine state in the Alentejo Alto (upper), while Beja remains the only major town on the seemingly endless Alentejo Baixo (lower) plain. The Alentejo is at its best in the spring; if you come in summer, be prepared for temperatures that can soar above 40°C (100°F).

HIGHLIGHTS OF THE ALENTEJO

- The "museum city" of **Évora**, especially its fabulous **cathedral**—perhaps Portugal's finest—and its uniquely grotesque **Capela dos Ossos** (see p. 587).
- The friendly, lively little town of **Elvas** (see p. 588).
- The stunning views from enchanting **Marvão's** 13th-century **castle** (see p. 589).

ÉVORA

Designated a World Heritage site by the United Nations, Évora (pop. 54,000) is known as the "Museum City," and rightly so. Considered Portugal's foremost showpiece of medieval architecture, the picture-perfect town boasts a Roman temple, an impressive cathedral, streets that wind past Moorish arches, and a 16th-century university, not to mention several noteworthy churches. Elegant shops flash their wares in the windows, students chat on the streets, and a steady but not overwhelming stream of tourists flows in from Lisbon and the Algarve.

GETTING THERE

Trains run to Évora from **Lisbon** (3hr., 6 per day, 5:45am-11pm, 1075$) and **Lagos** (6hr., 2 per day, 9am and 5pm, 1850$). **Buses** go from **Elvas** (2hr., 4 per day, 6:40am-4:25pm, 850-1200$) and **Lisbon** (3½hr., 15 per day, 8:15am-7pm, 1450$).

ORIENTATION AND PRACTICAL INFORMATION

Évora is accessible by train from most major cities, including Lisbon, but buses are more convenient. No direct bus connects the **train station** to the center of town. To avoid hiking 20 minutes up R. Dr. Baronha from the station, hail a taxi (500$) or flag down bus #6 (100$), which halts a short way down the tracks. Near the edge of town, R. Dr. Baronha turns into R. República, which leads to **Praça do Giraldo**, the town center which is home to most of the monuments and lodgings.

Trains: (tel. 70 21 25). On the Lisbon-Faro route. To: **Beja** (2hr., 4 per day, 7:45am-6:10pm, 720$); **Lisbon** (3hr., 5 per day, 5:15am-7:32pm and 2:50am, 1075$); **Faro** (4hr., 4 per day, 7:45am-6:10pm, 1650$); **Porto** (6½hr.; M, W, F 1 per day; 6:10pm; 2750$).

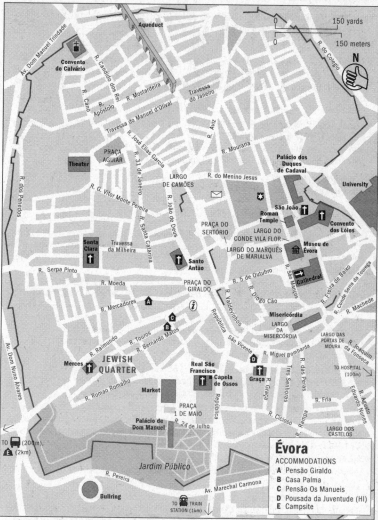

Évora
ACCOMMODATIONS
A Pensão Giraldo
B Casa Palma
C Pensão Os Manueis
D Pousada da Juventude (HI)
E Campsite

Buses: New station (tel. 76 94 10), just past the gas station on an extension of R. Raimundo, 15min. downhill from Pr. Giraldo. Much more convenient than trains. To: **Beja** (1½hr., 6-8 per day, 8:20am-8:10pm, 1100$); **Elvas** (1½hr., 2-5 per day, 8am-9:05pm, 1200$); **Portalegre** (2hr., 4 per day, 10:25am-5:40pm, 890-1250$); **Lisbon** (2½hr., 5 per day, 8:30am-5:30pm, 1450$); **Faro** (5hr., 5 per day, 8:45am-6pm, 1800$); **Vila Real de Santo António** (6hr., 2 per day, 2:15 and 6pm, 2100$); **Porto** (7hr., 6 per day, 6am-8pm, 2600$); **Braga** (8½hr., 5 per day, 6am-8pm, 2900$).

Taxis: (tel. 73 47 34 or 73 47 35). Taxis hang out 24hr. in Pr. Giraldo.

Tourist Office: Pr. Giraldo, 73 (tel. 70 26 71), to the left when facing Igreja Santa Antão. Helpful staff compensates for the illegible map. Open Apr.-Oct. M-F 9am-7pm, Sa-Su 9am-12:30pm and 2-5:30pm; Nov.-Mar. daily 9am-12:30pm and 2-5:30pm.

Currency Exchange: 24hr. machine outside the tourist office. Banks on Pr. Giraldo.

Luggage Storage: At the bus station. Open 8:30am-12:30pm and 2:30-5pm. 120$. Also available short term at the tourist office.

Laundromat: Lavandaria Ana, R. Aviz, 78 (tel. 70 73 88), up from Largo de Camões. 900$ per kg. Open daily 9am-1pm and 3-7pm.

Emergency: tel. 112. **Police:** (tel. 70 20 22), on R. Francisco Soares Lusitano.

Hospital: (tel. 70 50 01), Largo Senhor da Pobreza, near the city wall and the intersection with R. Dr. Augusto Eduardo Nunes.

Post Office: (tel. 74 98 47 or 74 59 10), R. Olivença. From Pr. Giraldo, walk up R. João de Deus, keeping right. Pass under the aqueduct and make an immediate right uphill. Posta Restante and **fax.** Open M-F 8:30am-6:30pm. **Postal Code:** 7000

Internet Access: ▓ **Oficin@,** R. Moeda, 27 (tel. 70 73 12), off Pr. Giraldo. Also a cool bar with friendly, English-speaking staff. 100$ for 10min., 500$ per hr. Open daily Sept.-June 6pm-2am; July-Aug. 8:30pm-2am. **Ciber Évora,** R. Fria, 7. 400$ for first 30min., 150$ for each additional 15min. Open M-F 11am-7pm.

TELEPHONE CODE	Évora's phone code is (0)66.

▙ ACCOMMODATIONS AND CAMPING

Most hostels cluster on side streets around Pr. Giraldo. They are crowded in summer, especially during the late June mega-fest, so reserve ahead. Prices drop 500 to 1000$ in winter. *Quartos*, from 4000 or 5000$ per double, are pleasant summer alternatives to crowded *pensões*.

▓ **Pousada da Juventude (HI),** R. Miguel Bombarda, 40 (tel. 74 48 48; fax 74 48 43). From the end of Pr. Giraldo opposite the church, walk down R. República a short distance and bear left on R. Miguel Bombarda (also called R. São Vicente). Recently converted from a hotel, this place is simply great. TV and entertainment rooms, bar, parking, and a friendly staff reward weary travelers. Reception 8am-midnight. Midnight curfew. Reservations necessary in the summer. Dorms 2500$; doubles 5500$.

▓ **Casa Palma,** R. Bernando Mato, 29-A (tel. 70 35 60). From the tourist office, walk down the street and 3 blocks to the right. Pink bedspreads in bright doubles on the bottom floor; cheaper, dimmer singles upstairs. Singles 4500$; doubles 6000$.

Pensão Giraldo, R. Mercadores, 27 (tel. 70 58 33). From the tourist office, turn left, walk 2 blocks, and turn left again. 24 rooms with windows, TVs, and either an in-room sink, shower, or full bath. Reserve 1 week in advance for rooms in the renovated annex. Singles 4000-7000$; doubles 5000-8500$. Visa, MC.

Pensão Os Manueis, R. Raimundo, 35 (tel. 70 28 61), around the corner from the tourist office. A trek up marbled stairs leads to 30 homey rooms. Singles 3500$, with bath 7000$; doubles 5000$, with bath 7500$.

Orbitur's Parque de Campismo de Évora (tel. 70 51 90; fax 70 98 30), a 3-star park on Estrada das Alcáçovas, which branches off at the bottom of R. Raimundo. A 30min. walk to town; 9 buses per day go near the site from Pr. Giraldo (7:45am-9:15pm). Washing machines and a small market. Reception 8am-10pm. Shower 50$. 620$ per person, 470$ per tent, 530$ per car. Open year-round.

▙ FOOD

Many budget restaurants are scattered near Pr. Giraldo, especially along R. Mercadores. Setting up in the square in front of Igreja de São Francisco and the public gardens, the **market** sells produce, flowers, and a wild assortment of cheese (open M-Sa 5am-1pm). For more processed food, try **Maxigrula,** R. João de Deus, 130 (open M-Sa 9am-7pm).

Restaurante A Choupana, R. Mercadores, 16-20 (tel. 70 44 27), off Pr. Giraldo, across from Pensão Giraldo. Snack bar on the left for a budget lunch, *restaurante* on the right for elegant Portuguese cuisine. Entrees 900-1600$; half-portions 800$. Open M-Sa 10am-2am. Visa, MC, AmEx.

Café-Restaurante A Gruta, Av. General Humberto Delgado, 2 (tel. 70 81 86). Exit Pr. Giraldo, follow R. República toward the train station, and turn right at the end of the park; the cafe is on the left. Lip-smacking *frango no churrasco* (barbecued chicken) buried under a heap of fries. Half-chicken 690$. Open Su-F 11am-10:30pm.

Adega do Alentejano, R. Gabriel Vitor Monte Pereira, 21-A (tel. 74 44 47). Leave Pr. Giraldo on R. Serpa Pinto, take the first right on R. Santa Catarina, then a left at the end of the street; it's on the left. Popular with locals and tourists, and with good reason. Entrees 850-1300$, hearty soups 1000$. Open T-Su noon-3pm and 7-10pm.

◉ SIGHTS

Streets brimming with architectural riches earned the "Museum City" its status as a UN World Heritage site.

CAPELLA DE OSSOS. One must-see is the truly bizarre Capella de Ossos (Chapel of Bones), attached to the pleasant **Igreja Real de São Francisco.** Above the door an irreverent sign taunts visitors: "*Nós ossos que aqui estamos, pelos vossos esperamos*" ("We bones lie here awaiting yours"). Don't let the seemingly normal exterior fool you; the interior is made entirely out of human bones. Three Franciscan monks took the remains of 5000 people (reportedly fellow monks) in order to construct this perverse chapel. Enormous femurs and baby tibias neatly panel every inch of wall, while rows of skulls and an occasional pelvis line the capitals and ceiling vaults. The three innovative founders grimace from stone sarcophagi to the right of the altar. *(Follow R. República from Pr. Giraldo; the church is on the right and the chapel is around back to the right of the main entrance. Open M-Sa 9am-1pm and 2:30-6pm, Su 10am-1pm and 2:30-6pm. Chapel closed during mass. 160$, photography permit 50$.)*

TEMPLE AND CHURCH. Évora's most famous monument is the 2nd-century **Roman temple,** which served for centuries as a slaughterhouse. Only a platform and 14 Corinthian columns remain today. Climbing up into the temple is a no-no. Immediately facing the temple is the town's best-kept secret, the **Igreja de São João Evangelista** (1485). The church is owned by the Cadaval family, who reside in their ancestors' ducal palace next door. The interior is covered with dazzling *azulejos*, but you must ask to be let into the church's hidden chambers. *(Largo do Vila Flor. Chuch open T-Su 10am-noon and 2-5pm. 250$.)*

CATHEDRAL. The 12 Apostles adorning the doorway of this colossal 12th-century cathedral are masterpieces of medieval Portuguese sculpture. The **cloister,** on the other hand, is designed in ponderous 14th-century Romanesque style, with staircases spiraling to its roof. The **Museu de Arte Sacra,** in a gallery above the nave, houses the cathedral's treasury and a 13th-century ivory *Virgem do paraíso*. *(From the center of Pr. Giraldo, head up R. 5 de Outubro. Open daily 9am-12:30pm and 2-5pm, museum closed Monday. Cloister and museum 350$, cathedral free.)*

MUSEO DE ÉVORA. Since the discovery of Roman, Visigoth, and Moorish ruins under its floor, archaeologists have sought to explore the basement of the building. Nowadays, both the museum's collection (ranging from Roman tombs to a 17th-century Virgin Mary) and the fascinating on-site digging capture the attention of visitors. *(Turn left at the top of R. 5 de Outubro when coming from Pr. Giraldo. Open Tu-Su 9:30am-12:30pm and 2-5:30pm. 250$, seniors and under 25 125$, under 14 free.)*

♫ ENTERTAINMENT

Although most of Évora turns in with the sun, **Kalmaria Discoteca,** R. Valdevinos, 21-A, the second right off R. 5 de Outubro when coming from Pr. Giraldo, opens its doors to the bar-hopping crowd (cover 1000$, includes two beers; beer 200$; open M-Sa 10pm-6am). Another popular club, **Fimdelinha,** Av. Combatentes de Grande Guerra, 56, plays a variety of music and offers live tunes on Fridays and Saturdays around 11:30pm. Take R. República outside the city walls and then follow the street parallel to and one block left of its continuation. This club, whose name means "end of the line," is bigger and more modern than Kalmaria. *(Open W-Sa 11pm-4am; closed Aug. Beer 150-300$; mixed drinks 400-600$. Cover 1000$ for men, 500$ for women.)* The liveliest Évora gets is during the **Feira de São João,** which starts the last Friday in June and lasts for seven nights. The entire town turns out for carnival rides, local dance troupes, a bullfight, and a circus.

ELVAS

Elvas is dead, you say? No, the town is just keeping a low profile. Perched on a steep hill amid arid fields 12km from the Spanish border, Elvas is the perfect place for a taste of small-town Alentejo life. Though it's often a necessary stopover to or from nearby Badajoz, Spain, Elvas merits a trip in itself. The quiet hamlet combines all things lovable in a Portuguese town: lively streets, friendly people, good food, few tourists, ruins, and great views.

◪ PRACTICAL INFORMATION. A bus connects the **train station** (tel. 62 28 16), in the town of Fontainhas, 3km north of the city, to Pr. República (M-F 6 per day, Sa 3 per day, Su 2 per day, 100$). **Trains** roll to **Badajoz, Spain** (15min., 3 per day, 12:23-4:23pm, 460$). **Buses** run from the **station** (tel. 62 28 75) on Pr. República to: **Caia,** on the border (20min., 2 per day, 6:40am and 2pm, 210$); **Évora** (2hr., 4 per day, 6:40am-4:25pm, 850-1200$); **Lisbon** (4hr., 4 per day, 1400$). *Espresso* to **Faro** (6½hr., 1 per day, 6:40am, 2200$) pass through **Évora** (1½hr., 1200$), **Beja** (3½hr., 1500$), and **Albufeira. Taxis** (tel. 62 22 87) wait in Pr. República. The **tourist office** (tel. 62 22 36), is in Pr. Rebública, next to the bus station (open daily 9am-6pm). **Emergency:** tel. 112; **police** (tel. 63 94 70), a block behind the tourist office; **hospital** tel. 62 22 25. The **post office** (tel. 62 26 96), on R. Cadeia one block behind the tourist office, has Posta Restante (open M-F 8:30am-6pm, Sa 9am-12:30pm).

▁▁ ACCOMMODATIONS AND FOOD. The few *pensões* in Elvas are boarding houses for semi-permanent residents. Renting a room in a private home may be the most practical option. Try to bargain the price of a single down to 2500$ and a double to 4000$. Be very cautious when accepting a room from those soliciting at the bus station, and confirm the price and available amenities—especially hot water—in advance. **António Mocissoe e Garcia Coelho,** R. Aires Varela, 15 (tel. 62 21 26), is no Heartbreak Hotel; its nice rooms have TVs, baths, and A/C. Take the first left below the bus station, then the first right off R. João d'Olivença. (June-Sept. singles 3000$; doubles 4500$. Oct.-May singles 2500$; doubles 4000$.) Campers may try **Camping Torre das Arcas** (tel. 62 60 30), in a secluded orchard 4km from Elvas. Any bus on the way to Évora, Lisbon, or Estremoz stops in **Varche,** a 10-minute walk from the orchard. (Hot showers. 500$ per person; 1500$ for a car, tent, two adults, and two children; 1200$ for a motorbike, tent, and two people.)

Every Monday, fresh produce is sold at a **market** immediately outside town behind the aqueduct. Many stores and restaurants line R. Cadeia and the two streets perpendicular to it, R. Carreira and R. Alcamim, just south of Pr. República. Ain't nothing but a hound dog? Sidle over to **Canal 7,** R. Sapateiros, 16 (tel. 62 35 93), on the right side of Pr. República, which has entrees from 650-1300$ (open daily 10am-2:30pm and 6-10:30pm). For Italian eats, **Rica Pizza,** R. Escorregadio, 8 (tel. 62 47 73), off R. Carreira, serves pizza (from 850$) and pasta (open M-Sa noon-10pm). Or get **groceries** at **Loja de Convêniencia,** R. Cadeia, 40, the first right downhill from the tourist office (open daily 8am-11pm).

◪ SIGHTS. Elvas's main spectacle, the ▩**Aqueduto da Amoreira,** emerges from a hill at the entrance to the city. Begun in 1529 and finished almost a century later (1622), the colossal structure is Europe's largest aqueduct (its 843 arches span almost 8000m). Don't be cruel; soak up the view from the **castelo** above Pr. República—rows of olive trees stretch to the horizon in every direction. To the

STRIP TREES Taking a bus through Alentejo? If you look closely at the short trees that dot the fields and countryside, you will notice something unique. Most of them are unabashedly stripped to the bone, flaunting their unprotected under-layers to all. These *quercus subers*, otherwise known as cork-oaks, have unusually thick bark (actually the cambium, outer layers composed of dead phloem cells) that is shaved off meticulously by hand once every nine years. On trees close to the highway you can actually see a number (0-9), painted on the bark to indicate the last time cork was taken from a particular spot—a 9 would mean 1999, revealing a newly-shorn tree. It takes 50 years to grow these trees to maturity; their splayed trunks are a result of harvesters splitting the trees early in their life in order to make them easier to harvest. Portugal's climate, especially in Alentejo, is ideal for cork growing, and the yearly harvests of more than 160,000 tons amounts to well over 60% of the world's cork output. Much of that is sent north where it is boiled, pressed, and cut into useful objects—mainly corks. If you stop for a closer look, a word of warning: don't eat the awful fruit of the cork tree—farmers reserve this for feeding the pigs, and even they seem to mind.

right of the entrance, a stairwell leads up to the castle walls. Upon request, an attendant will unlock the museum upstairs and show you around. (Castle open 9am-7pm. Free.) At Pr. República, **Igreja de Nossa Senhora da Assunção** dominates the mosaic-covered main square. Abstract *azulejos* and a beautifully ribbed ceiling give splendor to the church's interior, which was rebuilt in a Manueline style. Behind the cathedral and uphill to the right is the **Igreja de Nossa Senhora da Consolação**, also known as **Freiras.** Its octagonal interior has beautiful geometric tiles. (Both churches open daily June-Sept. 10am-1pm and 3-7pm; Oct.-May 10am-1pm and 2:30-6pm.) In the three-sided praça stands the 16th-century **pelourinho,** an octagonal pillory (originally a medieval whipping post) culminating in a pyramid.

CASTELO DE VIDE

Situated 600m above sea level on the edge of the Serra de São Mamede, the town of Castelo de Vide (pop. 4500) has maintained an age-old charm rooted in its picture-perfect whitewashed houses, cobblestone streets, and flowering fountains. The **medieval quarter** is Castelo de Vide's unique attraction. Located just below its castle, the old town consists of a series of impossibly steep and narrow cobblestone alleys overflowing with potted plants, roses and sunflowers. Up above, the **castelo,** completed in 1280, offers stunning views of surrounding mountains. (Tower open daily 9am-6pm. Free.) The town center surrounds the two 19th-century praças, evidence of Castelo's popularity as a spa resort over 100 years ago. Although today's tourists come here mainly for the old quarter and castle views, the **spa** water is said to be quite salubrious. Unfortunately, the **termas** (thermal springs) are closed indefinitely.

Buses run from behind the tourist office to **Portalegre** (30min., 5 per day, 7am-6:30pm, 160$), which offers frequent connections to larger cities. The **train station** lies 4km out of town. Express trains run to **Lisbon** (3hr., 2 per day, 6:19am and 5:55pm, 2000$) and **Madrid. Taxis** (tel. 90 12 71) to the train station cost 700$; those to Marvão cost 1500$. The **tourist office** (tel. 90 13 61), in the wide space in R. Bartolomeu, offers maps, helps find accommodations, and **stores luggage** temporarily (open daily June-Sept. 9am-7pm; Oct.-May 9am-12:30pm and 2-5:30pm). **Emergency:** tel. 112; **police** (tel. 90 13 14), Av. Anamenha. **Telephone code:** (0)45.

MARVÃO

The walled city of Marvão (pop. 185) is an unreal relic of a distant past. Lost as much in time as in the enveloping fog that descends nightly, the town perches atop a craggy mountain overlooking the **Parque Natural de São Mamede.** This national park covers over 31,000 hectares and surrounds Marvão with hillsides and flowering meadows. Almost all of the whitewashed houses of this ageless town still lie within the 17th-century walls. Marvão is as calm and deserted as they come. The virtually impenetrable 13th-century **castelo,** located at the west end of town, sits on top of the rocky ridge, guarding this town that hasn't been seized in 700 years. Prior to the castle's construction, however, Marvão passed through several different owners, among them the Romans, Visigoths, and Moors. Remnants of these early days await at the **Museo Municipal,** near the castle in the **Igreja de Santa Maria** (open daily 9am-12:30pm and 2-5:30pm; 200$, students 150$).

Buses run to **Castelo de Vide** (25min., 2 per day, 7:10am and 1:10pm, 150$) and **Portalegre** (50min., 2 per day, 7:10am and 1:10pm, 250$). Ask at the tourist office about express buses to **Lisbon** (you must buy a ticket one day in advance) and to the **train station** (9km north), where service to Lisbon and Madrid is available. **Taxis** (tel. 99 32 33) are a valid option between Marvão and **Castelo de Vide** (about 1500$ one-way). If you arrive by bus, you will be dropped off just outside the town wall. Enter through one of the gates and proceed up R. Cima until you see the pillory (ancient stone whipping-post) in Pr. Pelourinho (also a parking area). From Pr. Pelourinho, R. Espíritu Santo leads toward the castelo and the **tourist office** (tel. 99 38 86), which doles out maps and info (open daily 9am-12:30pm and 2-5:30pm). **Emergency:** tel. 112. **Telephone code:** (0)45.

BEJA

Tucked in the vast, monotonous wheat fields of the southern Alentejo, Beja (pronounced BAY-zsa) is a town of beautiful architecture and truly scorching temperatures. Though its name is similar to *beija*, Portuguese for "kiss," it is actually a corruption of the original name, Pax Julia, which the Romans gave to the town in 48 BC to commemorate peace with the Lusitanians. The similarity is highly appropriate, however, for this town is steamy in more ways than one (see **Scandals? Nun Here,** p. 591). Besides being a summertime oven, Beja is also a haven of traditional food, music, and handicrafts.

⚡ ORIENTATION AND PRACTICAL INFORMATION. Rua de **Mértola** and **Rua de Capitão João Francisco de Sousa** delineate the center of town. Other streets are unmarked and confusing; the tourist office map is quite helpful. **Trains** run from the station (tel. 32 50 56), about 1km outside of town, to: **Évora** (1hr., 6 per day, 7:50am-8:50pm and 2:30am, 720$); **Lisbon** (3hr., can be inconvenient with changes and waits in Évora, 3 per day, 5am-2:30am, 1225$); **Faro** (5hr., 2 per day, 10:05am and 2pm, 1200$). Those with heavy bags might want to take a **taxi** (tel. 224 74) to the town center (470$) rather than walk uphill (30min.). The **bus station** (tel. 32 40 44) is on R. Cidade de São Paulo, at the corner of Av. Brasil. Buses to: **Real de la Frontera, Spain** (1½hr., 1 per day, 10:50am, 1000$); **Évora** (1½hr., 5 per day, 7:30am-7:15pm, 800-1100$); **Lisbon** (3¼hr., 4 per day, 7:45am-3pm, 1450$); **Faro** (3½hr., 4 per day, 10:10am-7:20pm, 1500$); **Porto** (11hr., 3 per day, 9am-2:45pm, 3000$); **Braga** (11½hr., 3 per day, 9am-2:45pm, 3300$); and most of the Algarve. To get from the bus station to the town center, walk straight out of the terminal and through the traffic circle onto Av. Brasil. After one block, turn right on R. Afonso de Albuquerque, go past the post office on the left, and continue up the curving street. At the intersection, turn left onto R. Capitão J. F. de Sousa.

The **tourist office,** R. Capitão J. F. de Sousa, 25 (tel. 31 19 13), has an English-speaking staff that helps with accommodations (open June-Aug. M-F 9am-8pm, Sa 9am-1pm and 2-6pm; Sept.-May M-Sa 9am-1pm and 2-6pm). **Luggage storage** is in the bus station (300$ per day; open 8am-1pm and 2:30-5:30pm). The town's **swimming pool** (tel. 31 19 14), on Av. Brasil near the bus station, is excellent (pool and adjacent park 260$; open Tu-Su 9am-8pm). **Emergency:** tel. 112; **police** (tel. 32 20 22), on R. D. Nuno Álvares Pereira, one block downhill from the tourist office; **hospital,** call Dr. António Lima (tel. 32 02 00). **Post office** (tel. 32 21 12), on Largo do Correio, down the street from the beginning of R. Capitão J.F. de Sousa (open M-F 8:30am-6:30pm); **postal code:** 7800. **Telephone code:** (0)84.

☎☐ ACCOMMODATIONS AND FOOD. Most rooms and *pensões* lie within a few blocks of the tourist office and the central pedestrian street. **Residência Bejense,** R. Capitão J. F. de Sousa, 57 (tel. 32 50 01), down the street from the tourist office, features beautiful rooms with tile floors, ruffled bedspreads, TVs, phones, and pri-

SCANDALS? NUN HERE Maria Alcoforado, the daughter of a nobleman, was born in 1640; she entered the convent of Nossa Senhora da Conceição in Beja at age 11. By the age of 16 she had taken her vows and was well on her way to a life of celibacy and utter devotion to God. But in 1666, about 10 years later, French troops were stationed near Beja while helping out in the War of Restoration. The French knight Chamilly was in charge of these troops, and before long Maria and Chamilly had fallen hopelessly in love; hopeless because she could only exchange words with her boyfriend through her barred convent window (which today is on display in the Museu Rainha Dona Leonor). The scandalous affair prompted a tell-all account, *Five Love Letters of a Portugese Nun*, published in Paris in 1669 and widely considered one of masterpieces of the time. The letters were so good, in fact, that they reportedly inspired poets, novelists, and artists like Rilke and Matisse. The town of Beja was vaulted forever into the annals of sexual impropriety.

vate baths, and A/C. (Breakfast included. Singles 5500$; doubles 7000$. Visa, MC, AmEx.) **Pensão Santa Bárbara,** R. Mertola, 56 (tel. 32 20 28), around the corner from Residência Bejense, has nice rooms with bath, phone, TV, and A/C (singles 5500$; doubles 7000-8000$; breakfast included; Visa, MC, Amex). **Camping: Parque Municipal** (tel. 31 19 11), near the end of Av. Vasco da Gama, lies past the stadium on the way out of town. From the bus terminal, go straight one block and turn left. The campsite is small, shady, and clean. (340$ per person, 250$ per tent and per car. Free showers. Nearby pool 50% off for guests.) Beja is one of the best places to taste authentic (and affordable) Portuguese cuisine. The municipal **market** is one block up and one block right from the bus station (open M-Sa 6am-1:30pm). **Restaurante Alentejano,** Largo dos Duques de Beja (tel. 32 38 49), down the steps near the museum, serves unpretentious regional cuisine (entrees 900$; open Sa-Th noon-3pm and 7-10pm). Another option is the small pizzeria **Salada de Frutas,** a popular choice among locals. They serve standard lunch and dinner fare in addition to tasty pizzas (990-1300$) and pasta dishes (900-1100$). (Open M-F 8:30am-3pm and 7:15-9pm, and Sa 8:30am-3pm.)

👁 🎵 SIGHTS AND ENTERTAINMENT. The town's historical sites are scattered about, but the outstanding ▨**Museu Rainha Dona Leonor** makes an excellent starting point. (Open Tu-Su 9:30am-12:30pm and 2-5:15pm. 100$. Sunday free. Ticket also good for the Museu Visigótico.) From the major intersection of R. Capitão João Francisco de Sousa with four or five other streets, follow R. Portas de Mertola through Largo Conde de Boavista. The street then becomes R. Conde da Boavista; turn right onto Largo da Conceição and the museum is on the right. Built on the site where Sister Mariana Alcoforado had an affair with a French officer, the museum features the original grate and window (but not the actual wall or building) through which the lovers exchanged secret passionate vows. Inside, the gilded church's 18th-century *azulejos* depict the lives of Mary and St. John the Baptist. Nearby are fine *intaglio* marble altars and panels of *talha dourada* (gilded carvings). The *azulejos* and Persian-style ceiling make the house look like a mini mosque.

One block downhill from the museum is the 14th-century, adobe-like **Igreja de Santa María,** transformed into a mosque during the Moorish invasion and back into a church when the city reverted to Portuguese control. A miniature bull on its corner column symbolizes the city's spirit. (Church open daily 10am-1pm and 3-7pm. Free.) From here, R. Aresta Branco leads past handsome old houses to the city's massive **castelo,** built around 1300 on the remnants of a Roman fortress. (Open Apr.-Sept. Tu-Su 10am-1pm and 2-6pm; Oct.-Mar. 9am-noon and 1-4pm. Free.) It still flaunts an enormous crenellated marble keep, vaulted chambers, stones covered with cryptic symbols, and walls covered with ivy. The castle's **Torre de Menagem** provides an impressive view of the vast Alentejan plains (200$). Between the police station and the center of town lies the convent-turned-luxury-*pousada* on R. Dr. Nuño Alvarés Pereira. You can look around the lobby and the cloister of the Convento de São Francisco here, even if you don't have 30,000$ for a night's stay. (Visitors should check in with the reception desk between 8am-8pm and be respectful of the paying guests.)

RIBATEJO AND ESTREMADURA

Jagged cliffs and whitewashed fishing villages line Estremadura's Costa de Prata (Silver Coast), with beaches that rival even those in the Algarve. Throngs of tourists and summer residents populate seafront Nazaré and Peniche. Smaller, less touristed towns with equally fantastic beaches line the coast, and the rugged and beautiful Ilhas Berlingas lie offshore. Nearby, the fertile region of the Ribatejo ("banks of the Tejo") is perhaps the gentlest and greenest you will come across in Portugal. Known as the "Heart of Portugal," it is famous for the rich pasture that border the arid Alentejan plain and Estremaduran wetlands. Its character is closely tied to the Rio Tejo and to two of the area's renowned inhabitants: the horse and the bull. It is also home to some of the country's finest sights, from the ornate monasteries in Alcobaça and Batalha, to the mysterious Knights Templar complex above Tomar, and the medieval city of Óbidos. In this region just north of Lisbon, history and sights are packed into towns not yet overtaken by commercial tourism. Despite a few industrial blemishes, these towns remain the rule, rather than the exception.

HIGHLIGHTS OF RIBATEJO AND ESTREMADURA

■ Relaxing in peaceful **Santarém,** only an hour from Lisbon (see below).
■ **Óbidos,** a charming town with a magnificent **castle** (see p. 596).
■ The UN World Heritage sites at **Alcobaça** (see p. 602) and **Batalha** (see p. 605).

SANTARÉM

Perhaps the most charming of Ribatejo's cities, Santarém (pop. 30,000) presides from atop a rocky mound over the calm Rio Tejo and the soft green pastures. The town's name derives from the unhappy story of Santa Iria, a nun accused of a lapse of virtue and cast into the river. When she washed up in Santarém, an autopsy proved her innocence. As one of the three ruling cities of the ancient Roman province of Lusitania, Santarém enjoyed a prosperity that has persisted to the present day. Once a flourishing medieval center, the city was the capital of the Portuguese Gothic style. Still Santarém's many appealing churches boasts a mind-boggling range of architectural styles.

☐ GETTING THERE

Trains run to Santarém from **Tomar** (1hr., 12 per day, 7:15am-7pm, 500$) and **Fátima** (1½hr., 8 per day, 7am-9:40pm, 1100$). **Buses** come here from **Leiria** (1¼hr., 4 per day, 10:20am-7:05pm, 760$) and **Peniche** (1½hr., 3 per day, 7am-4:30pm, 830$).

⚡ ORIENTATION AND PRACTICAL INFORMATION

The densely packed streets between **Praça Sá da Bandeira** (the main square) and the park **Portas do Sol** (above the Tejo) form the core of Santarém. **Rua Capelo Ivêns,** which begins at the praça, houses the tourist office and many hostels.

TRANSPORTATION

Trains: Station (tel. 32 11 99), 2km outside town. Bus service to and from the bus station (10min., every 30min.-1hr., 160$). Otherwise take a taxi (500$)–the 20min. walk is steep and dangerous. To: **Tomar** (1hr., every hr., 6:20am-1:26am, 500$); **Lisbon** (1hr.; M-F 20 per day, Sa-Su 10 per day; 7:20am-12:20am; 650$); **Coimbra** (2hr., 8 per day, 7:45am-6:10pm, 1350$); **Portalegre** (3hr., 3 per day, 8:25am-4:52pm, 1050$); **Porto** (4hr., 6 per day, 8:42am-1:10am, 1650$); **Faro** (4hr., 6 per day, 6:33am-9pm, 2800$), via Lisbon.

Worldwide Calling Made Easy

The MCI WorldCom Card, designed specifically to keep you in touch with the people that matter the most to you.

www.wcom.com/worldphone

Please cut out and save this reference guide for convenient U.S. and worldwide calling with the MCI WorldCom Card.

And, it's simple to call home or to other countires.

1. Dial the WorldPhone toll-free access number of the country you're calling from (listed inside).

2. Follow the easy voice instructions or hold for a WorldPhone operator. Enter or give the operator your MCI WorldCom Card number or call collect.

3. Enter or give the WorldPhone operator your home number.

4. Share your adventures with your family!

COUNTRY		WORLDPHONE TOLL-FREE ACCESS #
St. Lucia ÷		1-800-888-8000
Sweden (CC) ◆		020-795-922
Switzerland (CC) ◆		0800-89-0222
Taiwan (CC) ◆		0080-13-4567
Thailand ★		001-999-1-2001
Turkey (CC) ◆		00-8001-1177
United Kingdom	(CC) To call using BT ■	0800-89-0222
	To call using CWC ■	0500-89-0222
United States (CC)		1-800-888-8000
U.S. Virgin Islands (CC)		1-800-888-8000
Vatican City (CC)		172-1022
Venezuela (CC) ÷ ◆		800-1114-0
Vietnam ●		1201-1022

(CC)   Country-to-country calling available to/from most international locations.
÷   Limited availability.
▼   Wait for second dial tone.
▲   When calling from public phones, use phones marked LADATEL.
■   International communications carrier.
★   Not available from public pay phones.
◆   Public phones may require deposit of coin or phone card for dial tone.
●   Local service fee in U.S. currency required to complete call.
▶   Regulation does not permit Intra-Japan calls.
✧   Available from most major cities

MCI WorldCom Worldphone Access Numbers

The MCI WorldCom Card.

The easy way to call when traveling worldwide.

The MCI WorldCom Card gives you...

- Access to the US and other countries worldwide.
- Customer Service 24 hours a day
- Operators who speak your language
- Great MCI WorldCom rates and no sign-up fees

For more information or to apply for a Card call:
1-800-955-0925

Outside the U.S., call MCI WorldCom collect (reverse charge) at:
1-712-943-6839

COUNTRY	WORLDPHONE TOLL-FREE ACCESS #
Argentina (CC)	
To call using Telefonica ■	0800-222-6249
To call using Telecom ■	0800-555-1002
Australia (CC) ◆	
To call using AAPT ■	1-800-730-014
To call using OPTUS ■	1-800-551-111
To call using TELSTRA ■	1-800-881-100
Austria (CC) ◆	0800-200-235
Bahamas	1-800-888-8000
Belgium (CC) ◆	0800-10012
Bermuda ÷	1-800-888-8000
Bolivia (CC) ◆	0-800-2222
Brazil (CC)	000-8012
British Virgin Islands ÷	1-800-888-8000
Canada (CC)	1-800-888-8000
Cayman Islands	1-800-888-8000
Chile (CC)	
To call using CTC ■	800-207-300
To call using ENTEL ■	800-360-180
China ✦	108-12
For a Mandarin-speaking Operator	108-17
Colombia (CC) ◆	980-9-16-0001
Collect Access in Spanish	980-9-16-1111
Costa Rica ✦	0800-012-2222
Czech Republic (CC) ◆	00-42-000112
Denmark (CC) ◆	8001-0022
Dominican Republic	
Collect Access	1-800-888-8000
Collect Access in Spanish	1121
Ecuador (CC) ÷	999-170
El Salvador	800-1767

COUNTRY	WORLDPHONE TOLL-FREE ACCESS #
Finland (CC) ◆	08001-102-80
France (CC) ◆	0800-99-0019
French Guiana (CC)	0-800-99-0019
Guatemala (CC) ◆	99-99-189
Germany (CC)	0-800-888-8000
Greece (CC) ◆	00-800-1211
Guam (CC)	1-800-888-8000
Haiti ÷	193
Collect Access in French/Creole	190
Honduras ÷	8000-122
Hong Kong (CC)	800-96-1121
Hungary (CC) ◆	00▼800-01411
India (CC) ÷	000-127
Collect Access	000-126
Ireland (CC)	1-800-55-1001
Israel (CC)	
BEZEQ International	1-800-940-2727
BARAK	1-800-930-2727
Italy (CC) ◆	172-1022
Jamaica ÷ Collect Access	1-800-888-8000
(From Special Hotels only)	873
(From public phones)	#2
Japan (CC) ◆ To call using KDD ■	00539-121▶
To call using IDC ■	0066-55-121
To call using JT ■	0044-11-121
Korea (CC) To call using KT ■	00729-14
To call using DACOM ■	00309-12
To call using ONSE	00369-14
Phone Booths÷	Press red button, 03, then ✱
Military Bases	550-2255
Lebanon Collect Access	600-MCI (600-624)

COUNTRY	WORLDPHONE TOLL-FREE ACCESS #
Luxembourg (CC)	0800-0112
Malaysia (CC) ◆	1-800-80-0012
To call using Time Telekom ■	1-800-18-0012
Mexico (CC) Avantel	01-800-021-8000
Telmex ▲	001-800-674-7000
Collect Access in Spanish	01-800-021-1000
Monaco (CC) ◆	800-90-019
Netherlands (CC) ◆	0800-022-9122
New Zealand (CC)	000-912
Nicaragua (CC) Collect Access in Spanish	166
(Outside of Managua, dial 02 first)	
Norway (CC) ◆	800-19912
Panama	108
Military Bases	2810-108
Philippines (CC) ◆ To call using PLDT ■	105-14
To call using PHILCOM ■	1026-14
To call using Bayantel ■	1237-14
To call using ETPI ■	1066-14
Poland (CC) ÷	00-800-111-21-22
Portugal (CC) ÷	800-800-123
Puerto Rico (CC)	1-800-888-8000
Romania (CC) ÷	01-800-1800
Russia (CC) ÷ ÷	
To call using ROSTELCOM ■	747-3322
(For Russian speaking operator)	747-3320
To call using SOVINTEL ■	960-2222
Saudi Arabia (CC) ÷	1-800-11
Singapore	8000-112-112
Slovak Republic	(CC) 00421-00112
South Africa (CC)	0800-99-0011
Spain (CC)	900-99-0014

Buses: (tel. 33 32 00; fax 33 30 54), on Rodoviária Tejo, Av. Brasil, a convenient location not far from the main praça. Luggage storage open 7am-8pm. To: **Lisbon** (*expressos:* 1hr., 10 per day, 7am-7:15pm, 900$; *regular:* 1½hr., 10 per day, 6:50am-4:45pm, 760$); **Peniche** (1¼hr., 4 per day, 7:20am-2:45pm, 810$); **Caldas da Rainha** (1½hr., 3-5 per day, 7:20am-6:20pm, 670$); **Leiria** (1½hr., 4 per day, 8:15am-6:45pm, 760$); **Nazaré** (1½hr., 3 per day, 7:30am-5:30pm, 810$); **Tomar** (1½hr., 5 per day, 9:15am-6:25pm, 750-1050$), via **Torres Novas; Coimbra** (2hr., 4 per day, 10:45am-6:45pm, 1500$); **Porto** (4hr., 4 per day, 10:45am-6:45pm, 2000$); **Braga** (5hr., 4 per day, 10:45am-6:45pm, 2200$); **Faro** (7hr., 5 per day, 10:30am-6:30pm, 2500$).

Taxis: Scaltaxis (tel. 33 29 19) has a stand across from the bus station.

TOURIST, LOCAL, AND FINANCIAL SERVICES

Tourist Office: R. Capelo Ivêns, 63 (tel. 39 15 12), down from the main praça. Maps and info on festivals, accommodations, and transportation. English spoken. Open Tu-F 9am-7pm, Sa-M 10am-12:30pm and 2:30-5:30pm.

Currency Exchange: Banco Nacional Ultramarino (tel. 33 00 07), at R. Dr. Texeira Guedes and R. Capelo Ivêns. 1000$ commission. Open M-F 8:30am-3pm.

Luggage Storage: at the bus station. 100$ per day. Open 7am-8pm.

EMERGENCY AND COMMUNICATIONS

Emergency: tel. 112. **Police:** (tel. 32 20 22), Av. Brasil, near the bus station.

Hospital: (tel. 30 02 00), Av. Bernardo Santareno. From Pr. Sá da Bandeira, walk up R. Cidade da Covilhã, which becomes R. Alexandre Herculano. English spoken.

Post Office: (tel. 32 05 77), on the corner of Largo Cândido and R. Dr. Texeira Guedes. Open M-F 8:30am-6:30pm. **Postal Code:** 2000.

TELEPHONE CODE Santarem's phone code is (0)43.

■ ACCOMMODATIONS AND CAMPING

You stay, you pay. And during the Ribatejo Fair (10 days starting the first Friday in June), prices increase 10-40%. The tourist office can help find a room in a private house (June-Aug. 3000-4000$; Sept.-May around 2500$).

Residencial Abidis, R. Guilherme de Azevedo, 4 (tel. 32 20 17 or 32 20 18), around the corner from the tourist office. Although the hallways are a bit dreary, the 27 recently renovated rooms have high ceilings and large windows; 10 have TVs. Breakfast included. Singles 4000$, with bath 5500$; doubles 4500$, with bath 7000$.

Residencial Beirante, R. Alexandre Herculano, 5 (tel. 32 25 47), on the extension of R. Cidade da Covilhã off Pr. Sá da Bandeira. Elevator to nice rooms, all with TVs, fans, and phones. Breakfast included. Singles 4500$; doubles 6000-7000$.

Residencial Muralha, R. Pedro Canavarro, 12 (tel. 32 23 99), next to the medieval wall. Basic rooms, but nothing to write home about. Singles 3500$; doubles with TV 6500$.

◨ FOOD

Eateries cluster along and between the parallel R. Capelo Ivêns and R. Serpa Pinto. The **municipal market,** in the colorful pagoda on Largo Infante Santo near the Jardim da República, supplies fresh produce and vegetables (open M-Sa 8am-2pm). The **Minipreço Supermarket,** R. Pedro Canavarro, 31, is on the street leading from the bus station to R. Capelo Ivêns (open M-Sa 9am-8pm). **Casa d'Avó,** R. Serpa Pinto, 62 (tel. 32 69 16), serves home-cooked food on petite tables surrounded by cast-iron garden chairs. Try the quiche, salad, and daily fish and meat specials. (Entrees 350-750$. Open M-Sa 9:30am-6:30pm.)

👁 SIGHTS

⬛PRAÇA VISCONDE DE SERRA PILAR. Centuries ago, Christians, Moors, and Jews gathered for social and business affairs in this wonderful praça. *(Take R. Serpa Pinto from Pr. Sá da Bandeira.)* The 12th-century **Igreja de Marvilha,** off the praça, has a 16th-century Manueline portal and a 17th-century *azulejo* interior. *(Open Tu-Su 9:30am-12:30pm and 2-5:30pm. Free.)* The early Gothic purity of nearby **Igreja da Graça** contrasts sharply with Marvilha's overflowing exuberance. Within Graça's chapel lies Pedro Alvares Cabral, the explorer who discovered Brazil and one of the few *descobrídores* to live long enough to return to his homeland. *(Church and chapel open Tu-Su 9:30am-12:30pm and 2-5:30pm. Free.)*

IGREJA DO SEMINÁRIO DOS JESUÍTAS. The austere facade of the Igreja do Seminário dos Jesuítas dominates Pr. Sá da Bandeira, Santarém's main square. Stone friezes carved like ropes separate each of its three stories, and Latin biblical mottos embellish every lintel and doorway. Left of the church, the former Colégio dos Jesuitas conceals two enormous palm trees that have outgrown their tiny **cloister.** *(Open Tu-Su 9:30am-12:30pm and 2-5:30pm. Free. If the church is closed, enter the door to the right of the main entrance and ask Sr. Domingos to unlock it.)*

TORRE DAS CABAÇAS. The medieval **Torre das Cabaças** (Tower of the Gourds) was named after the eight earthen bowls installed in the 16th century to amplify the bell's ring. Inside the tower is the **Museu de Tempo.** *(Take R. São Martinho from Pr. Visconde. Museum open Tu-Su 9:30am-12:30pm and 2-5:30pm. Free.)*

MUSEU ARQUEOLÓGICO. The **Museu Arqueológico de São João do Alporão,** in a former 13th-century church, exhibits the elaborate Gothic tomb of Dom Duarte de Meneses (see **The Tooth,** above) among other things. *(Across the street from the Torre das Cabaças. Open Tu-Su 9am-12:30pm and 2-5:30pm. 200$, students 100$.)*

GARDENS. Portas Do Sol, a paradise of flowers and fountains surrounded by old Moorish walls, is best seen on a clear day, when the walls offer a lovely view of the plains and the Tejo flowing by on its way to Lisbon. *(Take R. Serpa Pinto from Pr. Sá da Bandeira to Pr. Visconde, then continue on R. Cons. Figueire do Leal, which becomes Av. 5 de Outubro and heads straight into the Portas. Open daily 8am-11pm. Free.)*

🎵 ENTERTAINMENT

Thirsty? Head to **Cervejão,** Av. António Maria Baptista, 10 (tel. 264 33), near the bus station. The cozy place is crammed with beer (250$) and cocktails (500$). (Open M-Sa until 2am.) Or simply wait for a festival. The largest is the **Feira Nacional de Agricultura** (a.k.a. **Feira do Ribatejo**), a national agricultural exhibition. Tens of thousands of people come for the six to 10-day bullfighting and horse-racing orgy, starting the first Friday in June. Smack your lips at the **Festival e Seminário Nacional de Gastronomia** (the last half of October), when each region of Portugal has a day to prepare a typical feast complete with entertainment.

CALDAS DA RAINHA

The town takes its name, "Baths of the Queen," from Queen Leonor, who sold her jewels to finance this, the world's first thermal hospital. Victims of rheumatism, respiratory ailments, and skin afflictions still come here to be cured. Though the town may not have such a draw for healthy travelers, Caldas's beautiful park, pottery, and delicious pastries make it a short and sweet stopover en route to Óbidos.

🛈 PRACTICAL INFORMATION. The **train station** (tel. 82 36 93) is on the northwest edge of town on Largo Estação. Take Av. 1 de Maio to Pr. 25 de Abril to reach the tourist office. Trains connect to **Lisbon** (2hr., 10 per day, 4:50am-9:20pm, 900$). The **bus station** (tel. 83 10 67), on R. Heróis da Grande Guerra, services: **Óbidos** (20min., 13 per day, 8am-7:30pm, 155$); **Peniche** (45min., 11 per day, 8am-7:30pm,

THE TOOTH, THE WHOLE TOOTH, AND NOTHING BUT THE TOOTH
What's really inside the elaborate Gothic tomb in the Museu Arqueológico de São João do Alporão in Santarém? The truth: nothing. The tomb belongs to Dom Duarte de Menezes, and for many years his only remains—a single tooth—were on display in a glass case next to the tomb. Now only the stone tomb remains, and word has it that the big ol' molar was placed in a special "heritage cabinet" in Santarém's town hall. Dom Duarte, originally from a local noble family, died defending the Portuguese king in the famous 15th-century North African battle of Alcacer Ceguer. According to legend, the fight pitted the king of Portugal and only 500 Portuguese soldiers against over 10,000 Moors. Upon hearing of her husband's death, Dom Duarte's wife demanded that a special tomb be built for her husband's remains. As for the tooth? It wasn't brought all the way back from Africa (his body was never recovered), but rather had been kept by the wife after her husband had a particularly painful visit to the dentist. Had dental hygiene been better 500 years ago, there might have been no tooth and therefore no tomb.

415$); **Nazaré** (50min., 6 per day, 6:40am-7:15pm, 415$); **Leiria** (1hr., 6 per day, 8am-5:50pm, 700$); **Santarém** (1½hr., 6 per day, 8am-7:15pm, 670$); **Lisbon** (1½hr., 8 per day, 7am-9pm, 950$); **Coimbra** (2¼hr., 5 per day, 5:45am-6:45pm, 1400$); **Porto** (4½hr., 5 per day, 5:45am-6:45pm, 1800$). **Taxis:** 24hr. tel. 83 10 98 or 83 24 55. To reach the **tourist office** (tel. 83 10 03; fax 84 23 20), in Pr. 25 de Abril, exit the bus station, face Caixa Credito Agrícola, and turn left; the office is two blocks down on the right. Ask nicely for temporary **luggage storage.** (Open M-F 9am-7pm, Sa-Su 9am-1pm and 3-7pm.) **Emergency:** tel. 112; **police** (tel. 83 19 24), at Frei Jorge de São Paulo, just off Pr. República; **hospital** (tel. 83 03 00), on the first street to the right after the police station. **Telephone code:** (0)62.

■ **ACCOMMODATIONS AND FOOD. Pensão Residencial Central,** Largo Dr. José Barbosa, 22 (tel. 83 19 14; fax 84 32 82), behind Pr. República, has upscale rooms with TVs, bath, and phones. (Breakfast included. July-Aug. singles 4000$, with bath 5000$; doubles 6500$, with bath 9000$. Considerably lower in the off-season; try bargaining.) **Parque de Campismo da Foz do Arelho** (tel./fax 97 50 29) is 7km away. Take the bus to Foz do Arelho (7-8min., every hr., 160$) from the station and ask the driver to let you off at the campsite along the way. (Showers 90$; 420$ per person, 360$ per tent and per car.) Caldas is the fruit capital of Portugal, making for an especially large and colorful **Mercado da Fruta,** Pr. República, where frenzied local vendors and shoppers haggle each morning (open daily 6am-2pm). The town's sweets—including *cavacas* (frosted bowl-shaped pastries) and *trouxas de ovos* (sweetened egg yolks)—are nationally acclaimed. **Pastelarias** line R. Liberdade and Av. Duarte Pacheco; many also serve decent food (600-900$; most open 9am-10pm). **Restaurante Ó Frango,** R. Almirante Cândido dos Reis, 3 (tel. 84 47 52), off Pr. República, specializes in seafood (entrees 800-1500$, *pratos do dia* 800-1100$; open M-Sa noon-3pm and 8-10pm).

■ **SIGHTS.** Bathe at the historic **Hospital Rainha Dona Leonor** (tel. 83 03 01) which houses the **Museu do Hospital e das Caldas** (tel. 83 03 00) inside. (Follow the signs from Pr. República. Hospital open M-F 8:15-11:45am and 3:15-4:30pm, Sa 8:45-10:45am. Free. Museum open M-F 10am-noon and 2-5pm. 200$.) For non-aquatic relaxation, head to the immaculately landscaped **Parque Dom Carlos I.** The park has shady walking paths, a duck pond, and tennis courts. (Follow R. Camões on Largo Rainha Dona Leonor. Open daily 8am-11pm.) The prestige of Caldas's **pottery** is unrivaled, and art museums throughout Portugal shelve at least a few pieces from the town. **Museu de Cerâmica,** just outside the park, traces the history and manufacturing process of Caldas clay (open Tu-Su 10am-12:30pm and 2-5pm; 250$).

CENTRAL PORTUGAL

ÓBIDOS

Walking through Óbidos's formidable stone gate is like stepping into the Middle Ages. The tiny village sits atop a hill dominated by a 12th-century fortress (now a luxury inn). A recent surge of tourism seems to have reinforced, not diminished, the town's commitment to historical authenticity. Narrow streets and stunning views have made Óbidos (pop. 200, inside the walls) a romantic getaway destination since 1282, when Queen Isabel admired Óbidos's beauty so much that King Dinis gave it to her as a wedding present. For centuries Óbidos was considered the personal property of the Portuguese queen.

🚩 **PRACTICAL INFORMATION.** Óbidos is an easy **train** ride from Lisbon's Estação Rossio. Take a commuter train to Cacém, then change trains for Óbidos (3hr., 8 per day, 5am-9:30pm, 800$). Buy tickets aboard the train. Trains drop off passengers 10 minutes outside town; cross the tracks and climb the stairs to head toward the town center. Frequent **buses** connect to: **Caldas da Rainha** (20min., 10-20 per day, 7:35am-8:20pm, 155$); **Peniche** (40min.; M-F 10 per day, 8:10am-7:40pm; Sa-Su 5 per day, 8:10am-7:40pm, 375$); **Lisbon** (1½hr., 3 per day, 7am-4:10pm, 800$). Buses stop down a few stairs from the main gate, under the shelter for Caldas de Rainha. No bus schedules are posted at the stop, so ask at the tourist office for any changes. The **tourist office** (tel. 95 92 31) is on R. Direita, not to be confused with the regional bureau on the same street. From the main gate to the town, take the high road to the left and walk 200m; the office is on the left just before Pr. Santa Maria. The English-speaking staff provides maps, bus info, and **luggage storage**. (Open daily June-Aug. 9:30am-7pm; Sept.-May 9:30am-6pm.) **Emergency:** tel. 112; **police** tel. 95 91 49; **Centro de Saúde** (tel 95 91 45), just outside the city walls. The **post office** (tel. 95 91 99), Pr. Santa Maria, has **fax** and Posta Restante (open M-F 9am-12:30pm and 2:30-6pm); **postal code:** 2510. **Telephone code:** (0)62.

🍴 **ACCOMMODATIONS AND FOOD.** Óbidos is more a showpiece than a city. If you enjoy the timeless feel of Portugal's castle-towns, it only gets better with the silence, stars, and mesmerizing views of nightfall. Private rooms for rent are everywhere; look for signs. **Agostinho Pereira,** R. Direita, 40 (tel. 95 91 88), rents four homey rooms, some of which have window seats, prime for enjoying the view of the nearby church. It also has a pleasant lounge with TV and small bar. (Reserve ahead. Singles 4000$; doubles 5000-6000$; triples 6000$.) "Typical" **restaurants** (with tourist prices) and several reasonable **groceries** flesh out R. Direita. Eat light and save your *escudos* for Óbidos's signature *ginja* (wild cherry liqueur), even sweeter and more syrupy than the national norm. Stores along R. Direita sell gulp-sized bottles for 200$.

🏰 **SIGHTS.** The **castelo** on the coast, a Moorish fortress rebuilt in the 12th century, gradually lost its strategic importance as the ocean receded. Although the castle itself opens only to *pousada* guests, its walls are open to all. Head to the *pousada* and follow the signs showing stairs. The walls surround the entire town,

SCARY CHERRY Óbidos's castle has occupied its strategic position atop a steep hill since the Celts constructed it in 308 BC; in the Middle Ages, the Moors occupied the castle. From the height of the formidable walls, you'll see why Portugal's first king, Dom Afonso Henriques, was thwarted in several attempts to capture the town. But on January 11, 1148, forces at the back of the castle diverted the guards' attention, while men disguised as cherry trees tiptoed up to a small door on the other side (now known as the Door of Betrayal). Noticing the advancing trees, an astute Moorish princess asked her father if trees walked. The distracted king paid her no heed, and by the time he realized what was happening, Afonso's men had broken through the castle door. Today, January 11 is a holiday in Óbidos.

and 1.5km of them are open for walking. The only *igreja* worth a visit is the 17th-century *azulejo*-filled **Igreja de Santa Maria,** to the right of the post office in the central praça, built on the foundations of a Visigoth church and later used as a mosque. Nun Josefa de Óbidos's vivid canvases are right of the main altar. The church was the site of the 1441 wedding of 10-year-old King Afonso V to his 8-year-old cousin, Isabel. Three cheers for childhood marriages. (Open June-Sept. 9:30am-12:30pm and 2:30-7pm; Oct.-May 9:30am-12:30pm and 2:30-5pm; free.)

PENICHE

Many travelers overlook Peniche, a seaport town 22km west of Óbidos en route to the Ilhas Berlengas. What they miss is a lively port city close to good beaches and hiking. Harboring Portugal's second largest fishing fleet, this rugged peninsular city is so obsessed with seafood that it dedicated a festival to the sardine. Its fishy odor lingers throughout the streets, for better or for worse.

 GETTING THERE

Peniche is only accessible by **buses,** which run from: **Santarém** (1¼hr., 4 per day, 7:20am-2:45pm, 810$); **Nazaré** (1½hr., 6 per day, 11am-8pm, 1000$); **Lisbon** (2hr., 11 per day, 7am-7:30pm, 1000$).

ORIENTATION AND PRACTICAL INFORMATION

Most of Peniche's points of interest are situated in or around the grid of streets between **Largo Bispo Mariana** and the **fortaleza** on the coast. **Praça Jacob Rodrigues Pereira** is the center of town, near the tourist office and the start of **Avenida do Mar,** which runs along the river to the docks and fishing port.

Buses: (tel. 78 21 33), R. Estado Português da India, on an isthmus outside the town walls. To: **Caldas** (1hr., 6-10 per day, 7am-7:30pm, 375$); **Nazaré** (1½hr., 6 per day, 10am-7:30pm, 1000$); **Santarém** (1½hr., 3 per day, 7am-4:30pm, 830$); **Alcobaça** (1¾hr., 1 per day, 2:45pm, 1500$); **Leiria** (2hr., 3 per day, 7am-6pm, 1300$); **Lisbon** (2½hr., 10 per day, 6am-6:30pm, 1000$); **Porto** (5hr., 3 per day, 7am-6pm, 2000$).

Taxis: (tel. 78 24 92), in Pr. Jacob Pereira.

Tourist Office: (tel. 78 95 71), R. Alexandre Herculano. From the bus station, cross the river on Ponte Velha, turn left on R. Alexandre Herculano, and walk alongside the public garden, following signs to the office. English-speaking staff assists with accommodations and provides info on trips to the islands. Open daily June-Sept. 9am-8pm; Oct.-May 10am-1pm and 2-5pm.

Luggage Storage: In the bus station (100$ per day).

Emergency: tel. 112. **Police:** (tel. 78 95 55), R. Herois Ultramar

Hospital: (tel. 78 17 00), on R. Gen. Humberto Delgado.

Post Office: (tel. 78 00 60), R. Arquitecto Paulino Montez. From the tourist office, turn right on R. Herculano, left on Arquitecto Paulino Montez, and walk 3 blocks. Posta Restante and **fax.** Open M-F 9am-6pm. **Postal Code:** 2520.

Internet Access: The **municipal library,** R. Luís de Camões, 2E (tel. 78 01 22), offers free access to its computers. Open M-F 9:30am-12:30pm and 2-6pm.

| **TELEPHONE CODE** | Peniche's phone code is (0)62. |

CENTRAL PORTUGAL

ACCOMMODATIONS AND CAMPING

Hostels fill quickly in July and August; try to arrive early in the day. Look for signs on Av. Mar. Hostesses roam the streets advertising **beds** in their homes; insist on seeing the place and inquire about hot water and other amenities. The rooms may be good budget options. Expect to pay around 2000$ for a single and 3500$ for a double. Bargain—there are more beds than visitors.

 ▨ **Residência Mira Mar,** Av. Mar, 40-44 (tel. 78 16 66), near the beach and above a seafood restaurant of the same name. Pink shag rug, oak furniture, great views, and private
 baths. Singles 5000$; doubles with bath 7000$.

 Hospedaria Marítimo, R. António Cervantes, 14 (tel. 78 28 50), off the praça in front of
 the fortress. Newly decorated rooms with bright pine furnishings and carpets, all with TV
 and bath. Breakfast included. Singles 3500$; doubles 5000-6000$.

 Hospedaria Cristal, R. Marechal Gomes Freitas de Andrade, 14-16 (tel. 78 27 24), 3
 blocks from Pr. Jacob Pereira. Plain rooms with private baths. Singles 4000$; doubles
 6000$; triples 7000$.

 Camping: Municipal Campground (tel. 78 95 29; fax 78 96 96), 3km outside of town on
 the bus route to Caldas da Rainha. 10 buses per day speed to the campground from
 the bus station (15min., 8:10am-7pm, 150$). Otherwise, it's at least a 30min. walk
 from the station. Turn left, then left again onto Av. Porto de Pesca to reach E.N. 114;
 follow it through the traffic circle and past the waterpark. The campsite is on the left.
 520$ per person, per tent, and per car. Open year-round.

◖ FOOD

Peniche's seafood is as fresh as it gets. The real stuff sizzles in whale-sized portions on outdoor grills along Av. Mar. Peniche's *sardinhas* (sardines) are exceptional. Try the seafood *espetadas* (skewered aquatic treats served with a tub of
melted butter). The outdoor cafes on Pr. Jacob Rodrigues Pereira are lively, particularly on Sundays, when the rest of town is virtually comatose. The **market,** R.
António da Conceição Bento, has fresh produce (open Tu-Su 6am-1pm).

 Restaurante Beiramar, Av. Mar, 106-108 (tel. 78 24 09). Delectable grilled fare served
 on wood tables in a stone-walled room. The 2nd floor has some cherry balcony tables.
 Sardinhas grelhadas 950$, entrees 950-1500$. Open daily noon-11pm.

 Restaurante Mira Mar, Av. Mar, 40-44 (tel. 78 16 16). Surrounded by similar seafood
 joints, Mira Mar has remarkable *lulas* (squid; with fries 1050$). Entrees 900-1900$.
 Open May-Oct. Tu-Su noon-4pm and 6:30-10:30pm. Visa, MC, AmEx.

 Restaurante Chinês Leaõ de Ouro, Av. Mar, 30-32 (tel. 78 72 60), hidden among the
 seafood places. Chinese food provides a good change of pace. Seafood entrees 750-
 1300$; other entrees 550-950$. Open daily 11am-3pm and 6-11pm.

◖◗ SIGHTS

FORTALEZA. Salazar, Portugal's longtime dictator, chose Peniche's formidable
16th-century fortress for one of his four high-security political prisons. Its high
walls and bastions later became a camp for Angolan refugees. It now houses the
Museu de Peniche, highlighted by a fascinating anti-Fascist resistance exhibition.
Photos and text trace the dictatorship and underground resistance from the seizure of power in 1926 to the coup that toppled the regime on April 25, 1974. *(R. José
Estevão, near the dock where boats leave for the Berlengas. Open daily 8am-midnight. Free.
Museum tel. 78 18 48. Open June-Aug. 10:30am-12:30pm and 2-5:30pm; Sept.-May Tu-Su
10am-noon and 2-5pm. 130$, under 15 free.)*

BEACHES. For sun and surf, head to any of the town's three beaches. The beautiful but windy **Praia de Peniche de Cima,** along the north crescent, has the warmest
water. It merges with another beach at **Baleal,** a small fishing village popular with
tourists. The southern **Praia do Molho Leste,** known to many as "super-tubos"
because of its big surf, is a bit cooler. Beyond it is the crowded **Praia da Consolação.**
The strange humidity at this beach supposedly cures bone diseases. Unfortunately, on windless days, it also traps the stench of nearby sewers. *(Buses 7am-7pm,
155$. Check with the tourist office for changes.)*

🎵 ENTERTAINMENT

At night in Peniche, two popular bars host plenty of locals and tourists. **Adega do Becas,** R. José Estevão, 91, is a fun and sometimes crazy place. (Beer 150-250$; mixed drinks 500$. Open M-Sa 1-4pm and 9pm-2am, Su 9pm-2am.) Nearby is **Bar No. 1,** R. Dr. Francisco Seia, near the intersection with R. José Estevão, a slightly milder (but no less crowded) bar serving up lots of beer (100-300$) and mixed drinks (250-500$; open daily noon-2am). You'll need a taxi (750$) to get to the popular clubs, **Karas** and **Voila,** both several kilometers from downtown Peniche.

Don't swallow the bones at the **Festa da Sardinha,** a massive sardine-devouring, wine-chugging party at the fishing port, held for one week near the end of July. Festivities acquire a less fishy (but no more sober) tint in the first weekend of August, when boats—decked in wreaths of flags and flowers—file into the harbor in the procession that launches the two-day **Festa de Nossa Senhora da Boa Viagem,** celebrating the protector of sailors and fisherman.

🏔 EXCURSIONS

To truly enjoy the ocean air, hike around the peninsula (8km). Start at **Papôa,** just north of Peniche. From Pr. Jacob Pereira, take R. Alexandre Herculano and then Av. 25 de Abril and follow the signs along the coast. Then stroll out to the tip, where orange cliffs rise from a swirling blue sea. Nearby lie the ruins of an old fortress, **Forte da Luz. Cabo Carvoeiro,** the most popular and dramatic of Peniche's natural sights. The fortress's **farol** (lighthouse) punctuates the extreme west end of the peninsula. Nearby is a convenient snack bar where you can watch the waves crashing below as you relish *ginja* (Óbidos's cherry liqueur). The **Nau dos Corvos** (Crow's Ship), an odd rock formation and a popular bird roost, promises a seagull's-eye perspective.

NEAR PENICHE: ILHAS BERLENGAS

The rugged, terrifyingly beautiful Ilhas Berlengas (Berlenga Islands) lie in the Atlantic Ocean, 12km northwest of Peniche. One minuscule main island, numerous reefs, and isolated rocks form an archipelago that's home to thousands of screeching seagulls (attracted to the protected **Reserva Natural da Berlenga**), wild black rabbits, and a very small fishing community. Deep gorges, natural tunnels, and rocky caves ravage the main island. Although it is fringed with several protected beaches, the only one accessible by foot lies in a small cove by the landing dock. For beach-goers willing to brave the cold, dips in the calm water bring instant respite from the heat. For hikers, the tiring trek to the island's highest point yields a gorgeous view of the 17th-century **Forte de São João Batista,** now a hostel.

From Peniche's public dock, the **Viamar ferry** zips to the island (1hr.; July-Aug. 9:30am, 11:30am, and 5:30pm, returns 10:30am, 4:30pm, and 6:30pm; June and Sept. 10:30am, returns 4:30pm). In late July and August the ferry gets so crowded that people begin to line up at 7am; at other times, one hour in advance will suffice. A same-day round-trip ticket (3000$) for the 9:30am ferry means you'll return at 4:30pm; those who go at 11:30am return at 6:30pm. To stay overnight, buy a 1500$ one-way ticket for the 5:30pm boat and pay return fare on board the 10:30am boat back. Crossing can be rough—the vomit bags are all-too frequently appreciated. Alternatively, cruise around in a **motorboat. Turpesca,** with an office on the docks at Largo Ribeira, 2 (tel. 78 99 60), goes to the islands and tours underwater caves and other wonders in and around Peniche (from 2500$; 5-person min.).

The island has two budget options for an overnight stay. While the **hostel** (tel. 75 02 44) in the old fortress looks spectacular, it lacks facilities. Bring a sleeping bag and flashlight: the steep, rocky 30-minute walk from the boat landing to the hostel is lit only by periodic flashes from the lighthouse. The hostel has a kitchen, and the canteen and snack bar stock basic food. (Reception M-F 10am-noon. Tel. (0936) 87 66 05. Reservations required. Dorm beds 1500$. Open June-Oct.) There is also a small **campground** on a series of rocky terraces above the ferry landing. Be prepared to be shat upon by scores of seagulls. Make the required reservations in person at the Peniche tourist office. (7-day max. stay. 2- or 3-person tent 1500$ per night; 4-person tent 2000$. Open June-Sept. 20.)

NAZARÉ

It's hard to tell where authenticity stops and tourism starts in Nazaré. Fishermen clad in traditional garb go barefoot and women typically don seven petticoats, thick shawls, and large gold earrings. The day's catch dries in the hot sun while locals string their nets along the shoreline esplanade. This "traditional" lifestyle has, however, become the basis of Nazaré's most thriving business—tourism. In one of the most touristed beach towns in Portugal, entrepreneurial natives sell everything from seashell necklaces to fishing nets to dried fruit. But if Nazaré is part theater, at least it puts on a good show—and everyone gets front row seats on the glorious beach. Drop your anchor elsewhere at the end of July and August, when prices double and bathers jostle with each other for tiny spots on the sand.

◰ GETTING THERE

Nazaré is only accessible by **bus**. From: **Leiria** (1hr., 8 per day, 7:50am-7:10pm, 450$); **Santarém** (1½hr., 3 per day, 7:30am-5:30pm, 810$); **Tomar** (1½hr., 4 per day, 9am-6:35pm, 970$); **Peniche** (1½hr., 6 per day, 10am-7:30pm, 1000$), and Lisbon.

◪ ORIENTATION AND PRACTICAL INFORMATION

Practically all of the action in Nazaré—beach scene, nightlife, and most restaurants—is located in the **new town** along the beach. Its two main squares, **Praça Sousa Oliveira** and **Praça Dr. Manuel de Arriaga**, are near the cliffside, away from the fishing port. Either the cliffside funicular or a winding road leads up to the **Sítio,** the old town, which preserves a sense of calm and tradition less prevalent in the crowded resort below. To get to the tourist office from the bus station, go toward the beach and then right onto Av. República. The office is a five-minute walk along the beach, between the two major praças.

Buses: (tel. 55 11 72), Av. Vieira Guimarães, perpendicular to Av. República. More convenient than taking the train (6km away). To: **Alcobaça** (30min., 15 per day, 7:10am-8pm, 210$); **Batalha** (50min., 3 per day, 7:10am-5pm, 570$); **Caldas da Rainha** (1¼hr., 20 per day, 6:30am-8:15pm, 415$); **Leiria** (1¼hr., 12 per day, 6:20am-7:10pm, 450$); **Fátima** (1½hr., 6 per day, 7:10am-5pm, 450$); **Tomar** (1½hr., 3 per day, 7:10am-5pm, 810$); **Peniche** (1½hr., 6 per day, 11am-8pm, 1000$); **Lisbon** (2hr., 6 per day, 6:15am-4:40pm, 1200$); **Coimbra** (2hr., 6 per day, 6:25am-7:25pm, 1300$); **Porto** (3½hr., 4 per day, 6:25am-7:25pm, 1700$).

Taxi: tel. 55 31 25.

Car Rental: M&M Travel Agencies, Av. República, 28 (tel. 56 18 88). Renting a car is the easiest way to visit Alcobaça, Fátima, and Batalha without camping out in the bus station. Open M-F 9am-12:30pm and 2-7pm.

Tourist Office: (tel. 56 11 94), beachside on Av. República. Maps and entertainment and transportation info. English spoken. Open daily July-Aug. 10am-10pm; Sept. 10am-8pm; Oct.-March 9:30am-1pm and 2:30-6pm; Apr.-June 10am-1pm and 3-7pm.

Luggage Storage: In the bus station (100$ per bag per day).

Emergency: tel. 112. **Police:** (tel. 55 12 68), 1 block from the bus station at Av. Vieira Guimarães and R. Sub-Vila.

Hospital: Hospital da Confraria da Nossa Senhora de Nazaré (tel. 56 11 16), in the Sítio district on the cliffs above the town center. **Centro de Saúde** (tel. 55 11 82), in the new part of town.

Post Office: Av. Independência Nacional, 2 (tel. 56 16 04). From Pr. Souza Oliveira, walk up R. Mouzinho de Albuquerque, which veers to the right. It's 1 block past Pensão Central. Posta Restante. Open M-F 9:30am-12:30pm and 2:30-6pm. **Postal Code:** 2450.

Internet Access: The **municipal library,** Av. Manuel Remígio (the continuation of Av. República in the direction of the port), offers free use. Open M-F 10am-1pm and 3-7pm.

> **TELEPHONE CODE** Nazare's phone code is (0)62.

ACCOMMODATIONS

Stepping off the bus leads to swarms of room-renters; insistent old ladies await on most street corners offering rooms. Be sure to check that they are authorized by the tourist office (they should have an authorization card from the city or the tourist board). Bargain down to 3000$ for singles and 4000$ for doubles, but insist on seeing the room before settling the deal. For rooms in hostels, look above the restaurants on Pr. Dr. Manuel de Arriaga and Pr. Sousa Oliveira.

Casa Marinha de Hóspedes, R. Mouzinho de Albuquerque, 6A, 3rd fl. (tel. 55 15 41), near Pr. Sousa Oliveira. Modern, carpeted rooms with baths, close to the beach. Reservations recommended. Doubles 4500-7500$, with bath 5500-6500$. Prices vary by month, peaking in August. Open May-Oct.

Hospedaria Ideal, R. Adrião Batalha, 98 (tel. 55 13 79), between the two main praças. Plain rooms not ideal, at least the common baths are clean. Singles 3500-6000$; doubles 5000-7000$.

Camping: Vale Paraíso, Estrada Nacional, 242 (tel. 56 18 00; fax 56 19 00), 2½km out of town. Take the bus to Alcobaça or Leiria (15min., 8 per day, 7am-7pm). Swimming pools, a restaurant-bar, a supermarket, and occasional internet access. Free showers. Laundry. Pool access 300$ in summer. Reception daily 8am-10pm. 380-615$ per person, 320-700$ per tent, 320-500$ per car. Open year-round.

FOOD

For fruit and veggies, check the **market** across from the bus station (open June-Aug. daily 8am-1pm; Sept.-May Tu-Su 8am-1pm). **Supermarkets** line R. Sub-Vila, parallel to Av. República and Pr. Dr. Manuel de Arriaga (open June-Aug. 9am-10pm; Sept.-May 9am-8pm).

A Tasquinha, R. Adrião Batalha, 54 (tel. 55 19 45), 1 block left of Pr. Dr. Manuel Arriaga. Locals jostle for a seat at the family-style picnic tables. Perhaps the only restaurant in Nazaré with a Portuguese-only menu (note: this is a good thing). *Sardinhas* 700$, entrees 700-1300$. Open daily noon-3pm and 7pm-1am. Visa, MC, AmEx.

Charcutaria O Frango Assado, Pr. Dr. Manuel de Arriaga, 20 (tel. 55 18 42), facing the beach, at the far end of the square. Take-out only. Half-chicken with *piri-piri* (a tabascoesque sauce) under 500$. Open daily 9:30am-1pm and 3-8pm.

Da Vinci, Av. Nazaré, 43 (tel. 56 14 04), off Av. Manuel Remígio as it runs along the beach near the port. Good Italian food. Pizzas 650-1250$. Pastas 750-1200$. Open daily noon-midnight.

BEACHES AND ENTERTAINMENT

Why are you staring at that church? Go to the **beach.** If you've been there and done that, take the **funicular** (every 15min., 7pm-1am, 105$), which runs from R. Elevador off Av. República to the **Sítio,** a clifftop area of Nazaré that makes a perfect evening excursion. Its uneven cobbled streets and weathered buildings were there before tourism was invented. Around 7:30pm, fishing boats return to the **port** beyond the far left end (facing the ocean) of the beach; head over to

CLIFF HANGERS One-hundred twenty meters above the sea, the tiny, whitewashed **Ermida da Memória** stands in a corner of the square diagonally opposite the Sítio's church. Perched on the edge of the precipice, the chapel was built in 1182 by the lucky nobleman Dom Fuas Roupinho. Out on a hunting expedition, Dom Fuas was chasing a deer that just kept running until it fell off that cliff. Dom Fuas pulled hard on the reins and his horse stopped with two legs on *terra firme* and two over the side. In a split second, Our Lady of Nazaré appeared and pulled the horse (and Dom Fuas) to safety. Out of this event, the little chapel and the town of Nazaré were born.

watch fishermen at work and eavesdrop as local restaurateurs spiritedly bid for the most promising catches in the **fish market** (M-F 8pm-midnight).

Cafes in Pr. Souza Oliveira teem with people until 1am. For lively Brazilian and Portuguese tunes, imbibe with locals at **Ta Bar Es**, on R. Mouzinho Albuquerque (beer 200$; open daily 2pm-4am). During the summer, look out for late-night gatherings of folk music on the beach. Every Thursday and Friday at 10pm from July 15 to August 1, a local group performs *fado* and traditional dances at the **Casino**, a festival hall on R. Dr. Rui Rosa (500$). **Bullfights** are popular as well; Nazaré is on the revolving schedule that brings *corridas* to a different city in the province each summer weekend (Sa 10pm; tickets start at 2500$).

DAYTRIPS FROM NAZARÉ

ALCOBAÇA

Otherwise a sleepy town in the hills not too far from the coast, Alcobaça welcomes thousands of visitors each year for one reason: it is home to the impressive **Mosteiro de Santa Maria de Alcobaça**, the oldest church in Portugal. The town was founded in 1153, following King Afonso Henriques's expulsion of the Moors, as a grant from the king to Cistercian monks. Afonso was attempting to secure Christianity in the region, and the monks responded; construction of their new monastery began in 1178, and additions continued over the course of several centuries. Today it is the largest building of the Cistercian order in all of Europe. The massive monastery (recently granted U.N. World Heritage status) and charming town lure people from all over for an enticing daytrip from Nazaré, Leiria or Coimbra.

⚐ PRACTICAL INFORMATION. With the nearest train station 5km away in Valado dos Frades, **buses** are the clear choice for fast, easy access to Alcobaça. The **bus station** (tel. 58 22 21), on Av. Manuel da Silva Carolino, offers service to: **Nazaré** (20min., 10 per day, 7:30am-8:20pm, 210$); **Batalha** (30min., 9 per day, 7:30am-7:10 pm, 375$); **Leiria** (50 min., 7 per day, 7:30am-7:10 pm, 450$); **Coimbra** and **Porto** (2hr. and 3.5hr., 1 per day, 4:25pm, 1250 and 1600$); **Lisbon** (2hr., M-F 5 per day, Sa-Su 3 per day, 6:30am-6pm, 1250$). **Luggage storage** is next to the ticket office (120$; open 9am-12:30pm and 2:30-5pm). To get to the center of town, **Praça 25 de Abril**, from the station, turn right out of the bus station's garage and then right again onto Av. Dos Combatentes. Follow it over the small river and into Pr. Afonso Henriques, which sits to one side of the monastery. Keep walking; the town center is in front of the large building. The **tourist office** (tel. 58 23 77), in Pr. 25 de Abril, doles out maps, lists of accommodations, and regional information (open June-Aug. 10am-1pm and 3-7pm; Sept.-May 10am-1pm and 2-6pm). **Emergency:** tel. 112; **police** (tel. 58 33 88), on R. Olivença; **hospital** (59 74 16), on R. Afonso Albuquerque. **Post office** (tel. 59 71 87), on Pr. 25 de Abril, a few strides from the tourist office (open M-F 8:30am-6pm); **postal code:** 2460. **Telephone code:** (0)62.

CENTRAL PORTUGAL

▐▛▜ ACCOMMODATIONS AND FOOD. Pensão Corações Unidos, R. Frei António Brandão, 39 (tel./fax 58 21 42), off Pr. 25 de Abril, boasts 30 rooms, some with full bath and TV. (Breakfast included. Singles 2500-3500$; doubles 5000-6500$; triples 6500-8000$. Visa, MC.) Or head to the **municipal campground** (tel. 58 22 65), Av. Professor Vieira Natividade, a five- to ten-minute walk from either the bus station or Pr. 25 de Abril. (Laundry and free showers. Reception June-Aug. 8am-11pm; Sept.-May 9am-9pm. 350$ per person, 180$ per tent, and 200$ per car.) There are a number of decent places to eat along the two praças surrounding the monastery. One of the best is **Restaurante Trindade,** Pr. Afonso Henriques, 22 (tel. 58 23 97), serving delicious *frango na púcara* (chicken in a pot, 1300$; entrees 950-1800$; open daily 8am-midnight). Next door on Pr. Afonso Henriques is **Supermercado A Despensa** (open M-F 8:30am-8pm and Sa 8:30am-7pm).

▣ SIGHTS. Chances are you came to Alcobaça to see the ▣monastery. The UN liked it and you will too. In the smaller naves adjacent to the towering central one, the **tombs** of King Pedro I and his wife Inês de Castro flaunt sophisticated carvings and immortalize one of the great love stories (see **The Heart of the Matter,** p. 622). Surrounding the monastery's lovely cloisters are numerous Gothic- and Manueline-style rooms and chambers, most notably the immense **kitchen** and **refectory** (the monks could roast more than 6 oxen at a time), the **Sala dos Monges** (Monk's Hall), and the **Sala dos Reis** (Hall of Kings). (Open June-Aug. 9am-7pm; Sept.-May 9am-5pm. 400$, students 160$, 14 and under or 65 and over 200$.)

If you have some time left over after seeing the monastery, the **Museu da Vinha e do Vinho** (Museum of Wine and Winemaking; tel. 58 22 22) is 5 minutes from the bus station on R. Leiria, which branches off R. Dos Combatentes on the way out of town. The exhibition about the history and methods of Portugal's wine industry is bound to be less crowded than tourist-laden *mostiero*. (Open Tu-Su 9am-12pm and 2-5:30pm. Sept.-June Tu-F free.)

SÃO MARTINHO DO PORTO

The result of countless ages of surf smashing against, and finally through, the coastal cliffs, the bay of São Martinho is nearly enclosed on all sides. The town lies clustered at the base of the inlet, while the windless, swimmer-friendly **beach** sweeps 3km along and around the bay, forming an almost perfect circle. Hidden from the sea by the formidable cliffs and from the land by the hills behind it, São Martinho do Porto remains relatively undiscovered (except perhaps in August). With its red-roofed houses crowding down a palm-studded hillside to a small and colorful fishing harbor, São Martinho has an almost Mediterranean charm that makes the town an ideal escape from the crowded Peniche and Nazaré.

Trains connect São Martinho to **Nazaré** (20min.) and other points north and south (schedules posted in the São Martinho tourist office), but **buses** run more frequently to **Nazaré** (20min., every hr., 8am-6pm, 200$). The bus stops on the main road leading into town. The **tourist office** (tel. 98 91 10), on Largo Frederico Ulrich at the end of Av. 25 de Abril, provides a list of private rooms (open Tu-Su 10am-1pm and 3-7pm). **Emergency:** tel. 115. **Telephone code:** (0)62.

LEIRIA

Capital of the surrounding district and an important transport hub, noisy Leiria (pop. 104,000) fans out from a fertile valley, 22km from the coast. An impressive ancient castle peers over this prosperous and industrial city, gazing down upon countless shops and a shady park. While Leiria itself is not the most exciting destination in Portugal, it makes a practical base for exploring the region nearby. Buses heading away from Leiria run frequently enough to satisfy both culture-vultures aching to get to the surrounding historic towns and beach-leeches with minds and bodies firmly set on the gorgeous sands of the Costa da Prata.

GETTING THERE

Buses offer the most convenient service to Leiria. They run from: **Tomar** (1hr., 3 per day, 7:10am-5:20pm, 550$); **Nazaré** (1¼hr., 12 per day, 6:20am-7:10pm, 450$); **Santarém** (1½hr., 4 per day, 8:15am-6:45m, 760$); Lisbon.

ORIENTATION AND PRACTICAL INFORMATION

Most commerce bustles about the sight-packed path from the tourist office to the *castelo*, so don't expect to wander far.

Trains: Train station (tel. 88 20 27), 3km outside town. Buses run between the station and the tourist office (10min., every hr., 7am-7:30pm, 130$). To: **Figueira** (1¼hr., 7 per day, 6:05am-8:45pm, 500$); **Coimbra** (1½hr., 6 per day, 8:25am-7pm, 600$); **Lisbon** (3½hr., 8 per day, 7:50am-7pm, 1150$).

Buses: (tel. 81 15 07), just off Pr. Paulo VI, next to the town garden and close to the tourist office. They are the easiest way to leave Leiria. To: **Batalha** (20min., 9 per day, 7:20am-6:30pm, 190$); **Alcobaça** (50min., 5 per day, 7:20am-6:30pm, 450$); **Fátima** (1hr., 6 per day, 8am-5:15pm, 385$); **Nazaré** (1hr., 8 per day, 7:50am-7:10pm, 450$); **Coimbra** (1hr., 11 per day, 7:15am-2am, 800$); **Santarém** (1¼hr., 4 per day, 10:20am-7:05pm, 760$); **Figueira da Foz** (1½hr., 4 per day, 10:30am-8:30pm, 630$); **Tomar** (1½hr., 3 per day, 7:15am-5pm, 760$); **Lisbon** (2hr., 11 per day, 8am-8pm, 1200$); **Porto** (3½hr., 10 per day, 7:15am-2am, 1350$).

Taxis: tel. 81 59 00 or 80 17 59.

Tourist Office: (tel. 82 37 73 or 81 47 48), across the park facing the bus station. Schedules for beach-going buses and maps. English spoken. Temporary **luggage storage.** Open daily June-Aug. 10am-1pm and 3-7pm; Sept.-May 10am-1pm and 2-6pm.

Hospital: (tel. 81 70 00), on R. Olhalvas along road to Fátima.

Emergencies: tel. 112. **Police:** Largo Artilharia, 4 (tel. 81 37 99).

Post Office: (tel. 81 28 09), on Av. Combatentes da Grande Guerra 3 blocks from the youth hostel. Label Posta Restante mail "Estação Santana." Open M-F 8:45am-6:30pm, Sa 9am-12:30pm. **Main office,** Av. Herois de Angola, 99, a bit farther away. Open M-F 8:30am-6:30pm, Sa 9am-12:30pm. **Postal Code:** 2400.

Internet Access: The **library,** Largo Cândido dos Reis, a few doors down from the youth hostel, has free access. Sign up in advance. Also try **Triplex,** Av. Dom João III, 26 (tel. 82 45 18), on the bottom floor of Centro Comercial 2000. 300$ per 30min. Open Tu-F 9am-2am, Sa-Su 4pm-2am.

TELEPHONE CODE Leiria's phone code is (0)44.

ACCOMMODATIONS AND FOOD

Accommodations in Leiria will not take your breath away. Cheap rooms are hard to find and most hostels have seen better days.

Pousada da Juventude (HI), Largo Cândido dos Reis, 9 (tel. 83 18 68). From the bus station, walk to the cathedral, then exit Largo Sé (next to Largo Cónego Maia) on R. Barão de Viamonte, a narrow street lined with shops. Largo Cândido dos Reis is 6 blocks ahead. Clean and comfortable rooms. Breakfast included. Kitchen, bar/game room, shaded central courtyard. Flexible lockout noon-6pm (bag drop-off still available). Reception open daily 8am-noon and 6pm-midnight. June-Aug. dorms 1700$; doubles 4000$. Sept.-May dorms 1400$; doubles 3200$.

Residencial Dom Dinis, Tr. Tomar, 2 (tel. 81 53 42). Turn left after exiting the tourist office, cross the bridge over Rio Lis, walk 2 blocks, and turn left again. 28 cozy, modern rooms with baths, telephones, and satellite TVs. Breakfast included. Singles 4000$; doubles 6000$; triples 8500$. Visa, MC, AmEx.

Camping: Orbitur (tel. 59 91 68), 22km away in São Pedro de Muel, near the beach. Take the bus from the station (every hr., 7am-8pm, 130$). 580$ per person, 480$ per tent, and 490$ per car. Open year-round.

☕ FOOD

The **market** is in Largo Feira, on the far side of the castle from the bus station (open M-F 8am-4pm, Sa 8am-1pm). **Supermercado Ulmar,** Av. Heróis de Angola, 56, has American and Portuguese foods (open M-Sa 8am-8pm, Su 10am-1pm and 3-6pm). **Restaurante Aquário,** Mouzinho de Albuquerque, 17 (tel. 82 27 20) has tasty regional specialties at decent prices (entrees 900-1500$; open F-W 9am-10pm).

👁🎵 SIGHTS AND ENTERTAINMENT

SIGHTS. From the main square, follow the signs past the austere **sé** (cathedral) to the city's most significant monument, the **castelo.** This granite fort, built by Dom Afonso Henriques after he snatched the town from the Moors, dramatically presides atop the crest of a volcanic hill overlooking the north edge of town. Left to crumble for hundreds of years, the castle retains only the **torre de menagem** (homage tower) and the **sala dos namorados** (lovers' hall). The terrace opens onto a panoramic view of town and the river. *(Castle open Apr.-Sept. M-F 9am-6:30pm, Sa-Su 10am-6:30pm; Oct.-March M-F 9am-5:30pm, Sa-Su 10am-5:30pm. 145$, students 75$.)* Nearby sits the roofless shell of the 14th-century **Igreja da Nossa Senhora da Penha.**

BEACHES AND ENTERTAINMENT. Nearby beaches, including **Vieira, Pedrógã,** and **São Pedro de Muel,** are all easily accessible via buses from the station (every hr., 7am-8pm, 130$). **Bars** along Largo Cândido dos Reis near the youth hostel come alive after 10pm. The **Teatro José Lúcio da Silva** (tel. 82 36 00), on the corner of Av. Heróis de Angola behind the bus station, features films. (Ticket office open daily 7-10pm. The tourist office has schedules of current features.)

BATALHA

The only reason (but a good one) to visit Batalha (pop. 6000) is the gigantic **Mosteiro de Santa Maria da Vitória,** which rivals Belém's Mosteiro dos Jerónimos in monastic splendor. Built by Dom João I in 1385 to commemorate his victory over the Spanish, the complex of cloisters and chapels remains one of Portugal's greatest monuments. To get to the *mosteiro,* enter through the church.

🚩 PRACTICAL INFORMATION. The **bus** stop is a concrete structure near Pensão Vitória on Largo Misericórdia. Inquire at the tourist office for info or call the bus station in Leiria (tel. 81 15 07). Buses run to: **Leiria** (20min., 7 per day, 8am-7:40pm, 190$); **Fátima** (40min., 3 per day, 8am-6pm, 260$); **Alcobaça** (45min., 6 per day, 7:35am-6pm, 375$); **Nazaré,** change at Alcobaça (1hr., 5 per day, 9am-4pm, 490$); **Tomar** (1½hr., 4 per day, 8am-6pm, 490$); **Lisbon** (2hr., 5 per day, 7:25am-6:50pm, 2150$). The **tourist office** (tel. 76 51 80), on Pr. Mouzinho de Albuquerque along R. Nossa Senhora do Caminho, across from the unfinished chapels of the *mosteiro,* has maps and bus info (open daily May-Sept. 10am-1pm and 3-7pm; 10am-1pm and 3-6pm). **Emergency:** tel. 112; **police** tel. 76 51 34. **Post office** (tel. 76 51 11), on Largo Papa Paulo VI, near the freeway entrance (open M-F 9am-12:30pm and 2:30-6pm); **postal code:** 2440. **Telephone code:** (0)44.

🏠 ACCOMMODATIONS AND FOOD. Batalha, devoid of cheap beds or even a campground, is best as a daytrip. If you get stuck here, sleep at **Pensão Vitória** (tel. 76 56 78), on Largo Misericórdia near the bus stop. Its three simple, dim rooms are, well, monastic (3000-3500$). The **restaurant** below does wonders with *pudim* (pudding) and is a handy place to wait for the bus. Several inexpensive *churrasqueria* (barbecue houses) and **cafes** line the squares flanking the monastery.

CENTRAL PORTUGAL

THE MONASTERY. Batalha's **monastery complex** has been granted UN World Heritage status. Its flamboyant facade soars upward in a heavy Gothic and Manueline style, opulently decorated and topped off by dozens of spires. Napoleon's troops sacreligiously turned the nave into a brothel. The **Capela do Fundador,** immediately to the right of the church, shelters the elaborate sarcophagi of Dom João I, his English-born queen Philippa of Lancaster, and their son Prince Henry the Navigator. The rest of the complex is accessible via a door in the nave of the church. Enter through the broad Gothic arches of the **Claustro de Dom João I,** the delicate columns of which initiated the Manueline style. Adjacent to the cloister lies the **Tomb of the Unknown Soldier.** Through the **Claustro de Dom Afonso V,** out the door and to the right are the impressive **Capelas Imperfeitas** (Imperfect Chapels), with massive buttresses designed to support a large dome that was never actually constructed; the project was dropped when Manuel I ordered his workers to build the monastery in Belém instead. (Open daily June-Aug. 9am-6pm; Sept.-May 9am-5pm. 400$, under 25 200$. Church entrance free.)

NEAR BATALHA: **CAVES**

Nature is at its most psychedelic in a spectacular series of underground *grutas* (caves) in Estremadura's natural park between Batalha and Fátima. The vast labyrinths of rock formations are between 15 and 22km from Batalha. The **Grutas de Mira de Aire** are the deepest; though **Grutas de Santo António** and **Alvados** are a bit more difficult to reach, they are equally impressive. Most of the caves have been "enhanced" with background music and strategically placed colored spotlights. From Batalha, take a **bus** to **Torre Novas** and ask the driver to let you off at the *grutas* (20min., 2 per day, 11:30am and 2pm, last bus back to Batalha 6:30pm, 300$). Alternatively, take the **Alto do Alvados** bus from Leiria (1hr., 4 per day, 400$). The tourist offices in both Batalha and Fátima have more info on reaching the caves.

FÁTIMA

Fátima used to be a sheep pasture; now it's a religious center. Come only if you're interested in pilgrimages, and be prepared for total immersion in holy fervor. Only Lourdes rivals this site in popularity with Christian pilgrims. The miracles believed to have occurred here are modern-day phenomena, well documented and witnessed by thousands. The plaza in front of the church, larger than St. Peter's Square in the Vatican, floods with pilgrims on the 12th and 13th of each month.

GETTING THERE

Buses are the best form of transportation and run to Fátima from: **Tomar** (30min., 4 per day, 7:15am-5:20pm, 450$); **Nazaré** (1½hr., 6 per day, 7:10am-5pm, 450$).

ORIENTATION AND PRACTICAL INFORMATION

Activity in Fátima focuses in and around the basilica complex in the town center. The **Santuário de Fátima** is the huge, open praça that fills with visitors on special occasions. **Avenida Dr. José Alves Correia da Silva,** running just south of the hubbub, contains the bus station and tourist office. A right turn and ten-minute walk from the bus station leads to the tourist office at the plaza off the basilica.

Trains: (tel. 56 61 22), 20km out of town on Chão de Maças. To: **Coimbra** (1hr., 10 per day, 5:19am-1:55am, 950$); **Santarém** (1½hr., 8 per day, 7am-9:40pm, 1100$), via Entroncamento; **Lisbon** (2hr., 8 per day, 7am-9:40pm, 1200$), via Entroncamento. Buses run between train and bus stations (45min., 5 per day, 6:10am-6:35pm, 350$).

Buses: (tel. 53 16 11), Av. Dr. José Alves Correia da Silva. On bus schedules Fátima is often referred to as **Cova da Ivia.** To: **Batalha** (45min., 3 per day, 9am-6:35pm, 260$); **Leiria** (1hr., 15 per day, 7:10am-8pm, 690$); **Santarém** (1hr., 6 per day, 7:30am-4:30pm, 750$); **Tomar** (1¼hr., 4 per day, 8:30am-6:40pm, 450$); **Nazaré** (1½hr., 4 per day, 9am-6:35pm, 970$); **Lisbon** (2½hr., 8 per day, 7am-6:30pm, 1500$); **Porto** (3½hr., 7 per day, 7:55am-7:40pm, 1400$); **Coimbra** (1½hr., 7 per day, 7:55am-7:40pm, 1200$).

Taxis: tel. 53 16 31 or 53 18 84.

Tourist Office: (tel. 53 11 39), Av. Dr. José Alves Correia da Silva, to the right when exiting the bus station. Temporary **luggage storage.** Open daily 10am-1pm and 3-7pm.

Emergency: tel. 112. **Police:** (tel. 53 11 05), Av. Dr. José Alves Correia de Silva.

Hospital: tel. 53 18 36.

Post Office: (tel. 53 18 10), R. Cónego Formagião. Open M-F 8:30am-6pm. **Postal Code:** 2495.

TELEPHONE CODE Fátima's phone code is (0)49.

ACCOMMODATIONS AND FOOD

Scores of hostels inundate both sides of the basilica complex. Credit cards are almost universally accepted, and lodging prices vary little. The town fills during the grand pilgrimages on the 12th and 13th of each month; both hostel and hotel prices tend to increase 500 to 2000$ during these days. The doting owner of **Pensão Doña Maria,** R. Av. Dr. José Alves Coneia da Silva, 122 (tel. 53 12 12), between the bus station and tourist office, offers rooms with bath, some with balconies. (Breakfast included. Rooms 3500-5000$.) For the cheapest beds in town, try **Pensão A Paragem** (tel. 53 15 58), upstairs in the bus station. The *pensão* is clean, pleasant, and ideal if you miss the last bus out of town. Try to get an early start—by 7:30am, diesel fumes begin to penetrate the room. All rooms have bath; doubles have TVs. (Breakfast included. Singles 3000$; doubles 4500$; triples 5000$.)

R. Francisco Marto, R. Santa Isabela, and R. Jacinta Marto have similar, touristy restaurants. **Adega Funda,** R. Francisco Marto, 103 (tel. 53 13 72), serves hefty, traditional Portuguese dishes like *bacalhau à churrasco* (barbecued cod, 1350$) in its large wood dining room. (Entrees 850-1350$. Open daily 11am-3pm and 6-10pm.) **Snack Bar A Lovca** (tel. 53 16 21), R. Jacinta Marto in the Pope John Paul II building, is one crazy snack bar serving lighter food, including omelettes (650-900$) and *pratos do dia* (750$). (Open daily 11am-midnight.)

SIGHTS

Tall leafy trees shield the sanctuary from the commercial area, where religious memorabilia is sold for sacreligious prices.

BASÍLICA DO ROSÁRIO. At the end of the plaza rises the super-cool Basílica do Rosário (erected in 1928), featuring a crystal cruciform beacon perched atop the tower's seven-ton bronze crown. Many of the devout come to the basilica, traveling the length of the plaza on their knees. While there is no longer a dress code, do be respectful, especially to those praying on the grounds. *(Open daily 7:30am-7:30pm. 1st Mass often at 6:30am.)*

CAPELINHA DAS APARIÇÕES. Sheltered beneath a metal and glass canopy, the Capelinha das Aparições (Little Chapel of the Apparitions), built in 1919, holds masses in six languages all mornings and some evenings. The chapel is beside the same **oak tree** under which the children spoke to the Virgin (see **Mary and the Three Shepherds,** below).

MARY AND THE THREE SHEPHERDS On May 13, 1917, Mary appeared before three shepherd children—Lucía, Francisco, and Jacinta—and issued a call for the end of WWI. Our Lady of Fátima returned to speak to the children on the 13th of each month, promising a miracle for her final appearance in October. Despite the skepticism of clergy and attacks from the press, the children remained steadfast in their belief that the Virgin had spoken to them. On that morning, 70,000 believers gathered under a torrential rain storm. At noon, the sun is said to have spun around in a furious light spectacle, appearing to sink to the earth. When the light returned to normal, no evidence remained of the morning's rain. Convinced by the "fiery signature of God," the townspeople built a chapel at the site to honor Mary.

MUSEUMS. Near the basilica are various museums commemorating the miraculous vision of Mary. To the right facing the basilica, the **Museu de Arte Sacra e Etnologia** exhibits Catholic icons from various centuries. *(R. Francisco Marto, 52, 3 blocks from the basilica. Tel. 53 29 15. Open Tu-Su 9am-1pm and 2-6pm. 400$, seniors and students 200$.)* To the left of the basilica, through the park, and in the complex beneath the Hotel Fátima, the **Museu-Vivo Aparições** uses light, sound (in various languages), and special effects to re-create the apparition. *(R. Jacinta Marto. Tel. 53 28 58. Open daily May-Oct. 9am-8pm; Nov.-Apr. 9am-6pm. 450$.)*

TOMAR

For centuries the arcane Knights Templar—part monks, part warriors—plotted crusades from this small town. A celebrated convent-fortress perched high above the old town, served as the Knights' powerful and mysterious headquarters. Known as the Convento de Cristo, the complex combines architectural styles from the 12th to 17th centuries beautifully. Despite its quasi-mythical past, Tomar (pop. 22,000) now rests quietly in the shade of the eucalyptus and sycamore trees that line the banks of the Rio Nabão and the surrounding hill. Even their shade, though, is hardly enough to temper the blistering summer heat.

⌷ GETTING THERE

Trains run to Tomar from **Santarém** (1hr., every hr., 6:20am-1:26am, 500$). **Buses** head here from **Fátima** (1¼hr., 4 per day, 8:30am-6:40pm, 450$) and **Leiria** (1½hr., 3 per day, 7:15am-5pm, 760$), as well as **Lisbon.**

ⓘ ORIENTATION AND PRACTICAL INFORMATION

The **Rio Nabão** divides Tomar. Almost everything—the train and bus stations, accommodations, and sights—lies on the west bank. The lush **Parque Mouchão** straddles the two banks, while the antique (albeit fully functional) **Ponte Velha** (old bridge) connects the two. The bus and train stations lie next to each other on Av. Combatentes de Grande Guerra, near the outskirts of town. Rustic **Rua Serpa Pinto** cuts across the town from river to castle and connects the Ponte Velha to the main square, **Praça da República.**

Trains: (tel. 31 28 15), Av. Combatentes da Grande Guerra, at the southern edge of town. Tomar is the north terminus of a minor line, so most destinations require a transfer at Entroncamento; the transfer can be purchased here. To: **Santarém** (1hr., 12 per day, 7:15am-7pm, 500$); **Lisbon** (2hr., 12 per day, 7:15am-7pm, 900$); **Coimbra** (2½hr., 9 per day, 7am-6:30pm, 900$); **Porto** (4½hr., 5 per day, 7am-6:30pm, 1450$).

Buses: Rodoviaria Tejo (tel. 31 27 38), Av. Combatentes Grande Guerra, by the train station. To: **Fátima** (30min., 4 per day, 7:15am-5:20pm, 450$); **Leiria** (3 per day, 7:10am-5:20pm, 550$); **Santarém** (1hr., 5 per day, 7:30am-6pm, 750$); **Lisbon** (2hr., 5 per day., 7:30am-6pm, 1050$); **Coimbra** (2½hr., 3 per day, 7:10am-5:20pm,

1350$); **Porto** (4hr., 2 per day, 7:10am and 12:50pm, 1750$); **Lagos** (9hr.; M-Sa 2 per day; 9:15am and 10:15am; Su 1 per day, 10:15am; 2800$).

Taxis: (tel. 31 37 16 or 31 23 73), at R. Arcos.

Tourist Office: (tel. 32 24 27), Av. Dr. Cândido Madureira, facing Parque Mata Nacional. From the bus or train station, go through the small square onto Av. General Bernardo Raria. Continue 4 blocks and go left onto Av. Dr. Cândido Madureira; the office is at the end of the street on the right. Map, accommodations list, and temporary **luggage storage** (ask nicely). Open M-F 9:30am-6pm, Sa-Su 10am-6pm (until 8pm in summer).

Emergency: tel. 112. **Police:** (tel. 31 34 44), on R. Dr. Sousa.

Hospital: (tel. 32 11 00), on Av. Cândido Madureira.

Post Office: (tel. 31 04 00), on Av. Marquês de Tomar, across from Parque Mouchão. Open M-F 9am-6pm. **Postal Code:** 2300.

Internet Access: INCA, R. João do Santos Simões, 60 (tel. 32 16 06), off R. Marqués Pombal, the main road. 475$ per 30min. Open M-F 9am-1pm and 3-7pm.

TELEPHONE CODE   Tomar's phone code is (0)49.

ACCOMMODATIONS

Finding a place to stay is only a problem during the Festival dos Tabuleiros, which takes place once every four years (next in 2003). Tomar is a buyer's market—practice bargaining. Prices generally drop in the off-season.

Residencial União, R. Serpa Pinto, 94 (tel. 32 31 61; fax 32 12 99), halfway between Pr. República and the bridge. Look for the oversized *azulejos* outside. 28 bright, plush rooms upstairs; well-stocked bar on the ground floor. All rooms with full bath, telephone, and TV. Breakfast included. Reserve several days ahead in July-Aug. Singles 3500-4500; doubles 6000-7000; triples 8000$.

Residencial Luz, R. Serpa Pinto, 144 (tel. 31 23 17), down the street from União. 14 cozy, clean rooms with phones. Swanky TV room with leather couches. Singles with shower 3700$, with bath 4000$; doubles 6000$, with bath 6500$; huge 4- to 6-person rooms with bath 10,000-12,500$.

Camping: Parque Municipal de Campismo (tel. 32 26 07; fax 32 10 26), on the river, across Ponte Velha near the stadium and swimming pool. Exit off E.N. 110 on the east end of the Nabão bridge. Thickly forested campground with a pool. Showers free. Reception June-Aug. 8am-8pm; Sept.-May 8am-5pm. 420$ per person, 250$ per tent, 310$ per car.

FOOD

Tomar is a fantastic place for a **picnic.** A section of lush Parque Mouchão is set aside just for that purpose. The **market,** on the corner of Av. Norton de Matos and R. Santa Iria across the river, provides all the fixings (M-Th and Sa 8am-2pm, F 8am-5pm). Several inexpensive **mini-markets** line the side streets between the tourist office and Pr. República.

Restaurante Bela Vista, R. Fonte do Choupo, 6 (tel. 31 28 70), across the Ponte Velha on the left, has a riverside patio with a handsome view of the park. Try the diverse meat and fish entrees (750-1900$). Open M noon-3pm, W-Su noon-3pm and 7-9:30pm.

Pizzeria Bella Itaia, R. Everaro, 91 (tel. 32 29 96), near the river, between the two main bridges. Friendly family serves pastas (800-1600$) and pizzas with very Portuguese toppings. Open daily noon-3pm and 7-11pm.

CENTRAL PORTUGAL

JUDAISM IN PORTUGAL Tomar's **Museu Luso-Hebraico**, R. Dr. Joaquim Jaquinto, 73 (tel. 32 24 27), in the 15th-century Sinagoga do Arco, is Portugal's most significant reminder of its once vibrant Jewish community. Jews worshipped here for only a few decades before the convert-or-leave ultimatum of 1496. Since then the building has served as a prison, Christian chapel, hayloft, and grocery warehouse before finally becoming a national monument. In 1923, Samuel Schwartz purchased the synagogue, devoted himself to its restoration, and in 1939 donated it to the state. The government awarded Schwartz and his wife Portuguese citizenship, assuring them sanctuary during WWII. The museum keeps a collection of old tombstones, inscriptions, and donated pieces from around the world. A recent excavation of the adjacent building unearthed a sacred purification bath *(mikvah)*, used only briefly by the Jews for ritual purposes. Services are still held at the site on selected Saturdays. (Open Th-M 10am-1pm and 2-6pm, Tu-W 10-1pm and 2-5pm.)

🔍 SIGHTS

▨**CONVENTO DE CRISTO.** It's worth trekking from the far corners of the earth to explore the mysterious grounds of the Convento de Cristo. The first structure was built by the Knights Templar in 1160, but various cloisters, convents, and buildings were added in successive centuries. An ornate octagonal canopy protects the high altar of the **Templo dos Templares,** modeled after the Holy Sepulchre in Jerusalem. A 16th-century courtyard is encrusted with the rich seafaring symbolism of the Manueline style: seaweed, coral, anchors, rope, and even artichokes, which mariners use to prevent scurvy. Below stands the **Janelo do Capítula** (chapter window), an exuberant tribute to the Age of Discovery. One of Europe's masterpieces of Renaissance architecture, the **Claustro dos Felipes** honors King Felipe II of Castile, who was crowned here as Felipe I of Portugal during Iberia's unification (1580-1640). Tucked behind the Palladian main cloister and the nave is the **Claustro Santa Bárbara,** where grotesque gargoyle rain-spouts writhe in pain as they cough up a fountain. On the northeast side of the church is the Gothic **Claustro do Cemitério.** *(Walk out of the tourist office and take the 2nd right; bear left at the fork. Pedestrians can take the steeper dirt path a bit after the fork on the left or follow the cars up the paved road. From Pr. República, walk behind the praça and pick up the path. Tel. 31 34 81. Open June-Aug. 9am-6:30pm; Sept.-May 9am-5pm. 400$, seniors and students 200$.)*

OTHER SIGHTS. Pyromaniacs love the **Museu dos Fósforos** (match museum), which exhibits Europe's largest matchbox collection. *(In the Convento de São Francisco, just across from the train and bus stations. Open daily 10-11am and 3-5pm. Free.)* Nature freaks can take a hike on the trails leading away from the **Parque da Mata Nacional dos Sete Montes,** across from the tourist office.

🎵 ENTERTAINMENT

For a week near the end of June, handicrafts, folklore, *fado,* and theater storm the city during the **Feira Nacional de Artesanato.** However, the big deal around here is really the **Festa dos Tabuleiros.** Unfortunately, this massive cultural celebration, involving the laborious construction of three-foot-tall decorative hats for women using cardboard, colored paper, and bread, takes place only once every four years; the next one will occur in 2003. Children, bulls, women in hats, and horses in finery parade through town for days. If you miss the party, view some of the costumes donned by mannequins at the tourist office. Tomar also hosts three or four summer **bullfights.** Look for big posters advertising the *corridas.*

THE THREE BEIRAS

The Three Beiras region offers a sampling of the best of Portugal: the exquisite beaches of the coast, the plush greenery of the interior and the rugged peaks of the Serra de Estrela. The fertile soil in this region yields some of Portugal's best farmland, resulting in a countryside dotted with red-roofed farmhouses and seemingly endless expanses of corn, sunflower, and wheat fields. The **Beira Litoral** (Coastal region) encompasses the virtually unspoiled Costa da Prata (Silver Coast) beginning at the resort town of Figueira da Foz and passing through up-and-coming Aveiro on the way to Porto. Coimbra, a bustling university city, overlooks the region from its perch above the celebrated Rio Mondego. Unlike more progressive towns to the west, the mountainous **Beira Alta** (High Region) and the **Beira Baixa** (Low Region) have been slow to develop. The result is a group of impoverished provinces seeped in tradition.

HIGHLIGHTS OF THE THREE BEIRAS

■ The charming and popular university town of **Coimbra** (see below).
■ The enormous sandy beach of **Figueira da Foz** (see p. 617).

COIMBRA

Backpackers love Coimbra. The country's only university city from the mid-16th to the early 20th century, Coimbra is a mecca for the country's youth. The result: a slew of cheap cafes and swinging bars. The charming city, beautifully situated on the Rio Mondego, has long since blotted out Coimbra's infamous roles as center of the Portuguese Inquisition and as educator of one-time economics professor Antònio Salazar, the former dictator of Portugal. The student population keeps Coimbra on the wild side from September through May, but its vibrant energy, its diversity, and a collection of medieval buildings welcome visitors year-round.

▐ GETTING THERE

Trains run to Coimbra from **Porto** (2¼hr., 12 per day, 6am-10pm, 980$). **Buses** go from **Porto** (1½hr., 12 per day, 7:15am-12:45am, 1300$) and **Lisbon** (2½hr., 16 per day, 7am-12:15am, 1350$).

▐ ORIENTATION AND PRACTICAL INFORMATION

Coimbra's steep streets rise in tiers above the **Rio Mondego.** There are three major parts of town, all on the same side of the river. The most central is the **lower town** (site of the **tourist office** and Coimbra-A **train station**), in a triangle formed by the river, **Largo da Portagem**, and **Praça 8 de Maio.** Coimbra's ancient **university district** is atop the steep hill overlooking the lower town. On the other side of the university, **Praça da República** plays host to cafes, a shopping district, and the youth hostel. The tourist office map is very helpful in sorting it all out.

TRANSPORTATION

Trains: (tel. 82 46 32, 83 49 98, or 83 41 27). **Estação Coimbra-A (Nova)** is 2 blocks from the lower town center; **Estação Coimbra-B (Velha)** is 3km northwest of town. Buses are quicker and more reliable, but more expensive than trains. Trains to and from cities outside the region stop in Coimbra-B only. Regional trains stop first at Coimbra-B, then at Coimbra-A; they depart in the reverse order. Bus #5 connects the 2 stations (5min., every 15min., 6:25am-1:30am, 130$). To: **Aveiro** (45min., 12 per day, 8:50am-10:21pm, 500$); **Figueira da Foz** (1¼hr., 25 per day, 6:19am-12:22am, 290$); **Ovar** (1½hr., 5 per day, 11:28am-10:21pm, 700$); **Porto** (2hr., 12 per day, 8:50am-10:21pm, 980$); **Braga** (3hr., 2 per day, 9:50am and 5:58pm, 1200$); **Lisbon** (3hr., 19 per day, 7:14am-3:20am, 1350$); **Paris** (19hr., 1 per day, 8:21pm, 24,000$).

Buses: (tel. 82 70 81), Av. Fernão Magalhães, on the university side of the river about 10min. out of town, past Coimbra-A. Catch regional buses at a series of stops along the river, across the street from Largo Portagem. To: **Luso/Bussaco** (45min., 5 per day, 7:35am-7:20pm, 450$); **Porto** (1½hr., 10 per day, 8:30am-9:30pm, 1300$); **Lisbon** (2½hr., 15 per day, 7:30am-2:15am, 1450$); **Évora** (4hr., 2 per day, 9:30am and 4:15pm, 1900$); **Faro** (8hr., 4 per day, 9:30am-2:15am, 2900$). **RBL** (tel. 82 75 08), Av. Fernão Magalhães, to **Paris** (25hr., M-Sa 1 per day, 11am, 9000$). **AVIC**, R. João de Ruão, 18 (tel. 201 41 or 237 69), between R. Sofia and Av. Fernão Magalhães, next door to Viagem Mondego, serves **Condeixa** and **Conímbriga** (30min., every hr., 6:35am-10pm, 240$).

Public Transportation: Buses and street cars. 200$, book of 10 600$, 3-day tourist pass 850$. Tickets sold in kiosks at Largo Portagem and Pr. República. Main lines: #1 (Largo Portagem-University-Estádio); #2 (Pr. República-Fornos); #3 (Coimbra A-Pr. República-Santo António dos Olivais); #5 (Coimbra A-Pr. República-São José); #7 (Largo Portagem-Palácio da Justiça-Pr. República-Tovim); #29 (Coimbra A-Pr. República-Hospital); #46 (Cruz de Celas-Pr. República-Largo Portagem-Santa Clara).

Taxis: Politaxis (tel. 48 40 45). Many wait outside Coimbra-A and the bus station.

Car Rental: Avis (tel. 83 47 86; fax 80 45 95), Coimbra-A, outside the platform door. Min. age 21. Open M-F 8:30am-12:30pm and 3-7pm.

TOURIST AND FINANCIAL SERVICES

Tourist Office: (tel. 85 59 50; fax 82 55 76), off Largo Portagem, in a yellow building 2 blocks up the river from Coimbra-A. From the bus station, turn right, follow the avenue to Coimbra-A, then walk to Largo Portagem (15min.). Multilingual travel pros provide free maps and accommodation and daytrip info. Open M-F 9am-7pm, Sa-Su 10am-1pm and 2:30-5:30pm. **University branch office** (tel. 83 25 91), in Pr. Dom Dinis, up the stairs connecting the university with Pr. República. Same hours. Another **branch office** (tel. 83 32 02) in Pr. República. Open M-F 10am-1pm and 2:30-6pm.

Travel Agency: Tagus (tel. 83 49 99; fax 83 49 16), R. Padre António Vieira. Handles student and youth budget travel. Open M-F 9:30am-12:30pm and 2-6pm.

Currency Exchange: Montepio Geral (tel. 85 17 00), Largo Portagem, near the tourist office. 1000$ commission for amounts above 10,000$. Open M-F 8:30am-3pm.

LOCAL SERVICES

Luggage Storage: None in Coimbra-A or B. **Café Cristal**, Av. Fernão Magalhães, across the street and to the left of Coimbra-A. 250$ per bag. Open daily 5am-10pm.

English Bookstores: Livraria Bertrand, Largo Portagem, 9 (tel. 82 30 14), 1 block from the tourist office. Small selection of classics. Open M-F 9am-7pm, Sa 9am-1pm.

Laundromat: Lavandaria Lucira, R. Sá da Bandeira, 86 (tel. 82 57 01). Self-service wash and dry 1200$, or drop it off and wait a few days for Lucira to collect enough clothes (250$ per kg). Open M-F 8:30am-1pm and 3-7pm, Sa 8:30am-1pm.

Swimming Pool: Piscina Municipal (tel. 70 16 05), R. Dom Manuel I. Take bus #5, 7, or 10 (São José or Estádio) from Largo Portagem outside the tourist office. Trio of pools near the stadium are terrific but often packed. 160$, over 60 and under 6 free. Open July-Aug. daily 10am-1pm and 2-7pm.

EMERGENCY AND COMMUNICATIONS

Emergency: tel. 112. **Police: Special division** for foreigners (*Serviço de Estrangeiros*), R. Venâncio Rodrigues, 25 (tel. 82 40 45).

Hospital: Hospital da Universidade de Coimbra (tel. 400 400 or 400 500), Pr. Professor Mota Pinto. Near the Cruz de Celas stop on line #29, or Hospital stop on #7.

Post Office: Central office (tel. 85 07 70), in the pink powder-puff structure on Av. Fernão de Magalhães. Open M-F 9am-6pm. **Mercado office** (tel. 85 11 70), on R. Olímpio Nicolau Rui Fernandes, across from the police station, has Posta Restante, **telephones,** and **fax.** Open M-F 9am-9pm. **Branch office** (tel. 82 72 64), Pr. República, is open M-F 9am-6pm. **Postal Code: 3000** for central Coimbra.

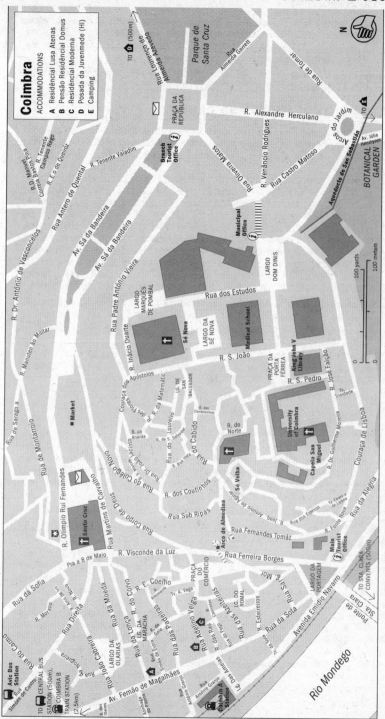

CENTRAL PORTUGAL

Internet Access: Ciber Espaço, Av. Sã Bandeira, on the top floor of the Centro Comercial Avenida. 250$ per 30min. Open daily 1pm-midnight. **Ego Mundo,** R. Antero de Ouental, 73 (tel. 84 10 25), near the youth hostel. 150$ for 15min., 500$ per hr. Open M-F 10am-midnight, Sa 2pm-midnight, Su 7pm-midnight.

TELEPHONE CODE	Coimbra's phone code is (0)39.

ACCOMMODATIONS AND CAMPING

Decent hostels, most on side streets off Av. Fernão de Magalhães, start at 3500$ for doubles; prices drop in winter. An excellent youth hostel awaits those bearing the magic HI card and willing to walk about 20 minutes uphill from the river.

Pousada da Juventude de Coimbra (HI), R. Henrique Seco, 14 (tel. 82 29 55; fax 92 17 30). From either Coimbra-A or Largo Portagem, walk 20min. uphill along R. Olímpio Nicolau Rui Fernandes to Pr. República, then up R. Lourenço Azevedo (to the left of the park). Take the 2nd right; the hostel is on the right. Alternatively, take bus #2, 7, 8, 29, or 46 to Pr. República and walk the rest of the way (5min.). This recently renovated hostel is clean, bright, and welcoming. Hot and high-pressure showers, TV room, kitchen, laundry (1000$ per machine), and parrots round out the deal. English-speaking manager. Reception daily 9-10:30am and 6pm-midnight. Lockout all other times, but bag drop-off (a godsend in hilly Coimbra) all day. Breakfast included. June-Aug. dorms 1700$; doubles 4500$, with bath 5000$. Sept.-May dorms 1500$; doubles 3700$.

Residência Moderna, R. Adelino Veiga, 49 (tel. 82 54 13). Friendly management will usher you into 17 bright, comfortable rooms in this charming hostel. All with private bath, phone, A/C, and cable TV; many with terrace. Breakfast included. Singles 4000-5000$; doubles 5500-8500$.

Pensão Residencial Domus, R. Adelino Veiga, 62 (tel. 82 85 84; fax 83 88 18). Slightly dark, but tidy rooms have private baths, phones, and cable TVs. Breakfast included. Singles 5000$; double 6000-7000$; triples 9000$. Visa, MC, AmEx.

Residência Lusa Atenas, Av. Fernão Magalhães, 68 (tel. 82 64 12; fax 82 01 33), on the main avenue between Coimbra-A and the bus station, next to Pensão Avis (look for their neon sign). Private baths, phones, A/C, and cable TVs in ritzy rooms. Breakfast included. Singles 4000-5000$; doubles 6000-7000$; triples 7000$.

Camping: Municipal Campground (tel. 70 14 97), in the recreation complex with the swimming pool and surrounded by noisy avenues. The entrance is at the arch of Pr. 25 de Abril; take the same buses as for the pool (see **Swimming Pool,** p. 612). Showers free. Reception Apr.-Sept. 9am-10pm; Oct.-Mar. 8am-6pm. 231$ per person, 153-174$ per tent, and 294$ per car.

FOOD

The best cuisine in Coimbra lies in the area around R. Direita running off Pr. 8 de Maio, on the side streets between the river and Largo Portagem, and near the university district around Pr. República. Restaurants in these areas serve up steamy portions of *arroz de lampreia* (rice cooked with lamprey meat—it does not taste like chicken). The cheapest meal around is at **UC Cantina,** the university's student cafeteria, located on the right side of R. Oliveiro Matos, about half a block downhill from the base of the steps leading to Pr. República. A mere 300$ buys an entire meal (soup, salad, dessert, and beverage). An international student ID is (theoretically) mandatory. Or grab a raw meal at the **mercado** in the huge green warehouse on the right just past the post office, uphill on R. Olímpico Nicolau Rui Fernandes (open M-Sa 8am-1pm). **Supermercado Minipreço,** R. António Granjo, 6C, is in the lower town center; turn left leaving Coimbra-A and take another left (open M-Sa 9am-8pm, Su 10am-1pm and 3:30-5:30pm).

Café Santa Cruz (tel. 83 36 17). From the tourist office, walk down R. Ferreira Borges to Pr. 8 de Maio. Formerly part of the cathedral (it still has a vaulted ceiling and stained-glass windows), it's the city's most famous cafe and a popular place to get wired on coffee (90$ and up) or grab a sandwich (around 400$). Open M-Sa 7am-2am.

Restaurante Esplendoroso, R. Sota, 29 (tel. 83 57 11), up a side-street opposite Coimbra-A. Splendid Chinese food and prompt service. The real steals are the weekday lunch *combinados,* which include an egg roll, entree, and rice for 800$. The flaming *gelado frita com rum* (fried ice cream in rum; 390$) is the house specialty. Entrees 690-920$. Open daily noon-3pm and 7-11pm. Visa, MC.

Arco Iris, Av. Fernão de Magalhães, 22 (tel. 83 33 04). The smell of freshly baked bread lures passers-by into this amazing *"boutique de pão,"* which serves fabulous bread, mini-pizzas (240-510$), countless varieties of sandwiches, and savory coffee. Open M-F 7:15am-8:30pm, Sa 7:30am-8:30pm, Su 8am-8:30pm.

📷 SIGHTS

OLD TOWN. The best way to take in Coimbra's old town sights is to climb from the river up to the university—what a climb it is. Begin the ascent at the ancient **Arco de Almedina,** a remnant of the Moorish town wall, one block uphill from Largo Portagem, next to the Banco Pinto e Sotto Mayor on R. Ferreira Borges. The gate leads to a stepped street aptly named R. Quebra-Costas (Back-Breaker Street). Up a narrow stone stairway looms the hulking 12th-century Romanesque **Sé Velha (Old Cathedral).** Take a breather in the cool, dark interior, or get there around noon to follow the guide around the principal tombs and friezes while Gregorian chants echo in the background. Don't miss the cool, peaceful cloister upstairs from the main nave. *(Open M-Sa 10am-noon and 2-6pm, Su 10am-noon. Cloisters 100$.)* Jump ahead in time a few centuries and follow the signs to nearby **Sé Nova (New Cathedral),** built for the Jesuits in the late 16th century by several different architects, each eager to leave his mark on Coimbra. The result is an unbelievably elaborate exterior. *(Open Tu-Sa 9am-noon and 2-6pm. Free.)*

THE UNIVERSITY. From the new cathedral the 16th-century University of Coimbra campus is but a few glorious blocks uphill. From Pr. República, take R. Oliveira Matos to the big staircase; this leads to the university. Although many of the buildings were built in a functional-but-ugly 1950s concrete style, the law school gets an "A" in architecture. Enter the center of the old university through the **Porta Férrea (Iron Gate),** off R. São Pedro. These buildings were Portugal's de facto royal palace when Coimbra was the capital of the kingdom. The staircase at the right leads up to the **Sala dos Capelos,** where portraits of Portugal's kings (six of whom were born in Coimbra) hang below a beautiful 17th-century ceiling. *(Open daily 9:30am-12:30pm and 2-5pm. 250$.)* The **university chapel** and mind-boggling, entirely gilded 18th-century **university library** lie past the Baroque clock tower. Press the buzzer by the library door to enter three golden halls with 300,000 works from the 12th through 19th centuries. *(Open daily 9:30am-noon and 2-5pm. 250$, teachers and students free. A package of tickets for all university sights can be purchased for 500$ from the office in the main quad.)*

ACROSS THE RIVER. Cross the bridge in front of Largo Portagem to the other side of the river to find the 14th-century **Convento de Santa Clara-a-Velha.** Far-sighted contractors built it on top of a swamp, and consequently it sinks a little more each year; today more than half of it lies underground. The convent was abandoned in 1687, but was recently renovated to reveal an ancient church founded in 1330 by Queen Isabel, wife of Dom Dinis. The Queen's Gothic tomb was moved uphill to the **Convento de Santa Clara-a-Nova** (1649-1677) when Coimbra's citizenry realized what was going down. Here, the queen's tomb and a later, solid-silver tomb rest amid panels that tell the story of her life. *(Open daily 9am-noon and 2-5pm. Free.)* Running out of time? You won't even need to see the rest of Portugal if you visit **Portugal dos Pequenitos,** between the new convent and the river bridge. It

CENTRAL PORTUGAL

features scaled-down reproductions of the country's famous castles and monuments; it's an admirable way to fit an entire country's sights into one block. *(Open July-Sept. M-Sa 9am-8pm; Sept.-Feb. M-Sa 10am-5pm; Mar.-June M-Sa 10am-7pm. 800$, under 13 and over 65 400$.)*

OTHER SIGHTS. For some green, walk downhill from the university alongside the **Aqueducto de São Sebastião** to admire the sculpture and fountains of the **Jardim Botânico.** Or descend the large staircase and pass through Pr. República into the lush **Santa Cruz Park,** home of a beautiful moss-covered fountain. Back in the lower town, the **Igreja de Santa Cruz (Church of the Holy Cross)** is a 12th-century church of somber beauty, with a splendid, barrel-vaulted **sacristía** (sacristy) and ornate **túmulos reals** (tombs) where the first two kings of Portugal rest. *(Pr. 8 de Maio, at the far end of R. Ferreira Borges. Church open M-Sa 9am-noon and 2-6pm, Su 4-6pm. Cloisters 200$.)*

🎵 ENTERTAINMENT

Nightlife gets high honors in Coimbra. After dinner, hang with the "in" crowd at outdoor cafes around Pr. República, which buzzes from midnight to 4am.

Café-Bar Cartola, Pr. República. Lots of outdoor seating for lots of rowdy patrons. Sandwiches (180-400$) appease the hungry, and beers start at 150$. Mixed drinks 400-900$. Open M-Sa 8am-2am, Su 8am-1am.

Via Latina, R. Almeida Garrett, 1 (tel. 330 34), is around the corner and uphill from Pr. República. Hot in all senses of the word. Open F-Sa midnight-8am.

Diligência Bar, R. Nova, 30 (tel. 276 67), off R. Sofia. *Fado* from 10pm to 2am.

Bar 1910, above a gymnasium on R. Simões Castro. Free-form *fado* until the wee hours of the morning. Beer about 200$. Open until 4am.

João Ratâo, Av. Afonso Henrigues, 43, Lote 4 (tel. 40 40 47). Dance and house music shake the walls until 2am.

Students rampage day and night in Coimbra's famous and distinctive week-long festival, the **Queima das Fitas (Burning of the Ribbons),** in the first or second week of May. The festivities begin when graduating students burn the narrow ribbons they received as first-years and get wide, ornamental ones in return. The carousing continues with midnight *serenatas* (groups of black-clad, serenading youth), wandering musical ensembles, parades, concerts, and folk dancing. Live choral music echoes in festooned streets during the **Festas da Rainha Santa,** held the first week of July in even-numbered years. The firework-punctuated **Feira Popular** in the second week of July offers carnival rides and games across the river, as well as traditional Portuguese dancing exhibitions in Pr. Comércio at the Camára Municipa.

NEAR COIMBRA: CONÍMBRIGA

Thirteen kilometes south of Coimbra, Conímbriga boasts the largest Roman settlement in Portugal. It was founded first by the Celts, later inhabited by the Romans, and is populated today by local children. The highlights include a 3rd-century town wall, an ancient but luxurious villa, and baths complete with sauna and furnace room. The most amazing sights are the well-preserved mosaics under the shelter of a glass canopy. (Open daily Mar. 16-Sept. 15 9am-8pm; Sept. 16-Mar. 15 9am-6pm. Buy tickets at least 30min. before closing. 350$, seniors and students 175$. Sunday free until 1pm. Price includes entrance to the Museu Monográfico de Conímbriga.) The nearby **Museu Monográfico de Conímbriga** (tel. 94 11 77) displays artifacts unearthed in the area (same schedule as the ruins, but closed Monday).

One **AVIC bus** runs from Coimbra to the ruins each morning, returning that afternoon; inquire at the Coimbra tourist office for up-to-date schedules. Buses also run from Coimbra to sleepy **Condeixa,** 2km away from Conímbriga. The tourism bureau in the Condeixa Town Hall (tel. 94 11 14) has info on the ruins. The walk up the road to Conímbriga through Condeixa and the olive groves surrounding it can seem endless (but is really only 30min.).

NEAR COIMBRA: BUÇACO FOREST AND LUSO

For centuries, Buçaco (also spelled Bussaco), home to Portugal's most revered forest, has drawn wanderers trying to escape the city. In the 6th century, Benedictine monks settled in the Buçaco Forest, established a monastery, and remained in control until the 1834 disestablishment of all religious orders. The forest owes its fame, however, to another group monks, the Carmelites, who arrived here nearly 400 years ago. Selecting the forest for their *desertos* (isolated dwellings for penitence), the Carmelites planted trees and plants brought from around the world by missionaries. Today, the fruits of their labor are inspiring, as over 700 types of vegetation flourish in and around these woods.

Dom Manuel II's exuberant **Palácio de Buçaco,** adjoining the old Carmelite **convent,** is a flamboyant display of neo-Manueline architecture. The *azulejos* adorning the outer walls depict scenes from *Os Lusíadas*, the great Portuguese epic about the Age of Discovery (see **Literature,** p. 529). The palace is now a luxury hotel with a doting staff that provides excellent maps. In the forest itself, landmarks include the **Fonte Fria (Cold Fountain),** whose water ripples down the entrance steps, the **Vale dos Fetos (Fern Valley),** and the **Porta de Reina (Queen's Gate).** Robust walkers can trek one hour along the Via Sacra to a sweeping panorama of the countryside from the **Cruz Alta** viewpoint. The little 17th-century **chapels** represent stations of the cross.

Buses from Coimbra to Buçaco continue on to Viseu (1hr., M-F 5 per day, Sa-Su 3 per day, 450$). Buses leave from Buçaco's station on Av. Fernão de Magalhães, near the palace, a 15-minute walk from downtown (last bus returns to Coimbra daily at 6:20pm). Schedules change frequently—confirm departing times at the tourist office in Coimbra.

Luso, a 3km walk downhill from Buçaco, is home to the **Fonte de São João,** the source of much of Portugal's bottled water. Be sure to get directions or a map from the hotel/palace in Buçaco before attempting the long stroll to this tiny town, made famous by a crisp, cold **spring** that spouts water for free public consumption. **Buses** back to Coimbra leave from a couple of blocks above the tourist office, across from the natural springs (M-F 5 per day, 7:58am-6:28pm; Sa-Su 3 per day, 10:38am-4:28pm; 480$). The staff at Luso's **tourist office** (tel. 93 91 33), on R. Emídio Navarro in the center of town, is a fountain of knowledge. It stacks lists of hostels, and supplies a map (open June-Sept. 9:30am-1pm and 2-7pm; Oct.-May 9:30am-12:30pm and 2:30-6pm). **Telephone code:** (0)31.

FIGUEIRA DA FOZ

Figueira da Foz's best feature is undoubtedly its giant beach, a three square km Sahara-like expanse. Even when packed, it appears to have ample room for sunbathing and swimming. Figueira is also one of the biggest party towns in Portugal, a place where pleasure-seekers who don't mind the proliferation of ugly concrete buildings come to celebrate the sun and the neon sign. At night, tanned couples and rowdy youths crowd the numerous bars and discos and press their luck at the infamous casino. For those who seek a bit more relaxation, the little fishing town of **Buarcos,** on the northern end of the beach, replaces mindless entertainment with a badly needed breath of serenity.

▐ GETTING THERE

Train runs to Figueira from **Coimbra** (1¼hr., 25 per day, 6am-12:30am, 290$). Trains from Lisbon and Porto also service Figueira.

▐ ORIENTATION AND PRACTICAL INFORMATION

Packed with hotels, beachfront **Avenida 25 de Abril** is the busy lifeline that distinguishes the town from beach; after the fortress, it turns into **Rua 5 de Outubro** and leads toward the train station. Four blocks inland and parallel to the avenue, **Rua Bernardo Lopes** harbors semi-affordable hostels and restaurants. Much of the action in Figueira revolves around the casino-cinema-disco complex on this street.

Trains: (tel. 42 83 16), Largo Estação, near the bridge. Trains are the best way to reach Coimbra and Porto. The station is an easy walk to the tourist office and beach (25min.). With the river to the left, Av. Saraiva de Carvalho becomes R. 5 de Outubro at the fountain and then curves into Av. 25 de Abril. To: **Coimbra** (1hr., 27 per day, 5:23am-12:23am, 290$); **Aveiro** (1½hr., 8 per day, 9am-10:07pm, 800$); **Leiria** (1½hr., 6 per day, 7:07am-6:12pm, 500$); **Porto** (2¼hr., 8 per day, 9am-10:07pm, 1150$); **Lisbon** (3½hr., 6 per day, 7:07am-6:12pm, 1450$).

Buses: Terminal Rodoviário (tel. 42 67 03), 15min. from the tourist office. Facing the church, turn right onto R. Dr. Santos Rocha, walk 10min. toward the waterfront, and turn right onto R. 5 de Outubro, which curves into Av. 25 de Abril. To: **Coimbra** (1½hr., 15 per day, 7:15am-8:05pm, 550$); **Leiria** (1½hr., 8 per day, 6:50am-6:15pm, 630$); **Aveiro** (1½hr., 4 per day, 11:30am-9:30pm, 680$); **Alcobaça** (1½hr., 1 per day, 8:45am, 1100$); **Fátima** (1½hr., 1 per day, 8:45am, 1100$); **Lisbon** (3hr., 4 per day, 6:50am-6:15pm, 1450$); **Faro** (12hr., 2 per day, 8:45am and 6:15pm, 2900$).

Taxis: (tel. 42 08 80, 42 04 99, or 42 35 00). At the bus or train stations.

Tourist Office: (tel. 40 28 27; fax 40 28 20), Av. 25 de Abril, next to the Aparthotel Atlântico. Useful map. English spoken. **Luggage storage** available. Open June-Sept. daily 9am-midnight; Oct.-May M-F 9am-5:30pm, Sa-Su 10am-12:30pm and 2:30-6:30pm.

Currency Exchange: Caixa Geral Depositos, Largo Luís de Camões, not far from the docks. 520$ commission on exchanges less than 10,000$; 1040$ on greater amounts.

Emergency: tel. 112. **Police:** (tel. 42 20 22), R. Joaquim Carvalho, near the bus station and the park.

Post Office: Main office, Passeio Infante Dom Henrique, 41, off R. 5 de Outubro. Posta Restante and **telephones.** Open M-F 8:30am-6:30pm, Sa 9am-12:30pm. More convenient **branch,** R. Miguel Bombarda, 76 (tel. 400 23 30). **Telephones.** Open M-F 9am-12:30pm and 2:30-6pm. **Postal Code:** 3080.

Internet Access: Café Nicola, R. Bernando Lopes, across from the casino. 500$ per hr. Open daily 9am-2am.

TELEPHONE CODE | Figueira's phone code is (0)33.

ACCOMMODATIONS AND CAMPING

Scour R. Bernardo Lopes and side streets for reasonable hostels. Proprietors may demand ridiculous prices for rooms, especially in summer. Arrive early in the day to secure a room; some pensions will not reserve rooms by phone in summer.

Pensão Central, R. Bernardo Lopes, 36 (tel. 42 23 08). Centrally located, next to Supermarket Ovo and down the street from the casino complex and all the action. High ceilings and huge rooms are comfortable and well furnished. All 25 rooms have TV and bath. Breakfast included. Singles 5000$; doubles 8000$; triples 10,000$.

Pensão Residencial Bela Figueira, R. Miguel Bombarda, 13 (tel. 42 27 28; fax 42 99 60), 2 blocks from the tourist office. All rooms have phones, some have TVs. Breakfast included. June-Aug. singles 3500-5000$; doubles 5000-7500$; triples 9000$. Sept.-May singles 2500-4500$; doubles 3000-5000$; triples 3350-5750$. Visa, MC, AmEx.

Camping: Parque Municipal de Campismo da Figueira da Foz Municipal (tel. 40 28 10), on Estrada Buarcos. With the beach on the left, walk up Av. 25 de Abril and turn right at the roundabout on R. Alexandre Herculano, then turn left at Parque Santa Catarina. Or take a taxi from the bus or train station (500$). Excellent site complete with an Olympic-size pool, tennis courts, market, and currency exchange. Reception June-Sept. 8am-8pm; Oct.-May 8am-7pm. Quiet time midnight-7am. June-Sept. each party must have a minimum of 2 people. Showers 100$. 400$ per person, under 10 free, 300$ per tent and per car. Open year-round.

◆ FOOD

Restaurants in Figueira are more expensive than average. Thankfully, hope (and good food) comes in the form of R. Bernardo Lopes. The truly lazy can frequent any of the numerous eateries right on the beach. A local **market** sets up beside the municipal garden on R. 5 de Outubro (open June-Aug. 6am-7pm; Sept.-May M-F 6am-5pm, Sa 6am-1pm). For groceries, check out **Supermercado Ovo,** on the corner of R. A. Dinis and R. B. Lopes (open M-F 9am-1pm and 3-7pm).

Restaurante Bela Figueira, R. Miguel Bombardo, 13 (tel. 42 27 28), beneath the hostel of the same name. Tasty Indian food, including vegetable curry with *roti* (1100$). *Menú* 950$, entrees 950-1500$. Open daily noon-midnight. Visa, MC, AmEx.

Restaurante Rancho, R. Miguel Bombarda, 40-44 (tel. 42 20 19), 2 blocks from the tourist office. Packed with locals. Hefty, delicious entrees 550-1100$. Open M-Sa noon-4pm and 7-10pm.

◆ ♫ SIGHTS AND ENTERTAINMENT

SIGHTS. If you tire of sunbathing, head next door to Buarcos, where remnants of a fishing village provide colorful ambiance. The **Museu Municipal do Doutor Santos Rocha,** in Parque Abadias, re-awakens the intellect with displays of ancient coins and the fashions of Portuguese nobility. *(Tel. 40 28 40. Open Tu-Su 9:30am-5:15pm. Free.)* The modest exterior of the **Palácio Sotto Mayor** belies the shameless extravagance inside. Lavish green marble columns line the main hallway, and gold leaf covers the ceiling. *(R. Joaquim Sotto Mayor. Tel. 42 21 21. Open Tu-Su 2-6pm. 150$.)*

ENTERTAINMENT. Most people do not come to Figueira for the culture. Nightlife takes off between 10pm and 2am and continues until dawn. Bars and clubs line Av. 25 de Abril, next to and above the tourist office. **Rolls Bar,** R. Poeta Acácio Antunes, 1E, is popular with just about everyone (beer 150-350$; mixed drinks 500-750$; open daily 5pm-6am). **Estudio 24,** R. Dr. Calado, beside the casino, plays host to a young, international crowd (beer 200$, mixed drinks 500$; open M-Sa 10pm-4am). Most popular of all is the **casino** complex (tel. 42 20 41), on R. Bernardo Lopes, which includes a **nightclub** (cover 1000$, includes 2 beers; beer 300$, mixed drinks 400-800$; open Oct. 5-July 1 daily 11:30-6am), **cinema** (500$), and **arcade.** Entry to the slot machines and bingo is free. You must be over 18 and show proper ID to gamble. The casino presents a nightly show, usually a flashy Las Vegas-style revue. (Casino open daily July-Aug. 4pm-4am; Sept.-June 3pm-3am.) Figueira's partying lifestyle shifts from high gear to warp speed during the **Festa de São João** (June 6-July 9), which features free public concerts every night. Around 5am, a huge rowdy procession heads for the beach at nearby Buarcos where all involved take a *banho santo* (holy bath). The **Festival de Cinema da Figueira da Foz** screens international flicks in September.

AVEIRO

The old center of Aveiro is graced with a network of charming canals, along which traditional *gonalas* (seaweed—coated fishing boats reminiscent of Venice's gondolas) drift out to sea. This storied town boasts an amalgam of historical anecdotes and houses the convent where canonized princess Santa Joana once lived (see p. 621). Even so, the maritime town is best known for its numerous beaches. Prices may seem unjustifiably high—rebel by camping at scenic São Jacinto.

◆ GETTING THERE

Trains are the most convenient means of travel to Aveiro, as the nearest bus station is 19km away in Águeda. Trains run to Aveiro from **Coimbra** (45min., 12 per day, 8:50am-10:20pm, 500$) and **Porto** (1¼hr., 30 per day, 5am-11:15pm, 330$).

CENTRAL PORTUGAL

🛈 ORIENTATION AND PRACTICAL INFORMATION

Aveiro is split by the *canal central* and a parallel street, **Avenida Dr. Lourenço Peixinho,** which runs from the train station to **Praça Humberto Delgado.** The fishermen's quarter, **Beira Mar,** lies north of the *canal central* (the side with the train station). In the south end of the city lies the residential district and all of Aveiro's historical monuments. To reach the **tourist office** from the **train station,** walk up Av. Dr. Lourenço Peixinho (the left-most street) until you reach the bridge; the office is on the right in the next block. You can also hop on a bus (every 15min., 150$) from the train station.

Trains: (tel. 42 44 85), Largo Estação, at the end of Av. Dr. Lourenço Peixinho. To: **Porto** (45min., 21 per day, 6:04am-1:04am, 350$); **Coimbra** (1hr., 21 per day, 6:12am-11:12pm, 500$); **Braga** (2hr., 2 per day, 10am and 8:40pm, 1000$); **Lisbon** (5hr., 21 per day, 6:50am-8:50pm, 1700$).

Ferries: All ferries leave from **Forte da Barra;** buses go from the train station to Forte da Barra (30min., 12 per day, 7:15am-6:40pm, 250$). Ferries run daily to the beach at **São Jacinto** (15min., 10 per day, more in July and Aug., 7:10am-7:05pm, 250$). The last ferry back from Forte da Barra is at 6:15pm, and the last bus to Aveiro is at 7pm.

Taxis: (tel. 42 29 43 or 42 37 66). Taxis surround the train station, on Av. Peixinho.

Tourist Office: R. João Mendonça, 8 (tel. 42 36 80 or 42 07 60; fax 42 83 26), in an old building off Pr. Humberto Delgado, on the street to the right of the canal when facing the ocean. Cheerful English-speaking staff doles out maps and lodging advice. If you have nothing else to do, you can watch a video about local fishermen. Free daytime **luggage storage.** Open June 15-Sept. 15 M-F 9am-8pm, Sa 9am-8pm, Su 9am-7pm; Sept. 16-June 14 M-F 9am-7pm, Sa 9am-1pm and 2:30-5:30pm.

Currency Exchange: Hotel Pomba Branca, R. Luís Gomes de Carvalho, 23 (tel. 42 25 29), the first right off Av. Dr. Lourenço Peixinho from the train station. 24hr. service.

Laundromat: Lavandaria União, Av. Dr. Lourenço Peixinho, 292 (tel. 42 35 56), near the train station. 500$ per kg. Open M-F 9am-1pm and 1:30-7pm.

Emergency: tel. 112. **Police:** (tel. 42 20 22 or 42 11 37), Pr. Marquês de Pombal.

Hospital: (tel. 37 83 00), Av. Dr. Artur Ravara, near the park across the canal.

Post Office: Estação Vera Cruz (tel. 42 71 00), Pr. Marquês de Pombal. Cross the main bridge and walk up R. Coimbra past the town hall. Posta Restante, **fax,** and **telephones.** Open M-F 8:30am-6:30pm, Sa 9am-12:30pm. A **branch office,** Av. Dr. Lourenço Peixinho, 169 (tel. 42 74 84), has similar services and is centrally located (2 blocks from the train station). Open M-F 8:30am-6:30pm. **Postal Code:** 3800.

Internet Access: Byblos.arte@net, R. Cais do Alboi, 5 (tel. 37 84 60), across the river from the tourist office and to the right, on an extension of R. Clube dos Gailitos. 40$ per 30min. Open M-F 10am-1pm and 2:30-6:45pm, Sa 10am-1pm.

> **TELEPHONE CODE** | Aveiro's phone code is (0)34.

⌂ ACCOMMODATIONS AND CAMPING

The hostels lining Av. Dr. Lourenço Peixinho and the streets around Pr. Marquês de Pombal in the old city are a little expensive, but are good backups. The tourist office has a list of other options. Most prices drop by 1000$ in winter.

Residencial Santa Joana, Av. Dr. Lourenço Peixinho, 227 (tel. 42 86 04), 1 block from the train station on the left. Five floors stack 16 spacious, no-frills, reasonably priced rooms in a transport-friendly location. Naturally cool in summer. All rooms feature phone, TV, and private bath. Singles 4000-5000$; doubles 6000-7000$.

Residencial Estrêla, R. José Estêvão, 4 (tel. 42 38 18), in an elegant building overlooking Pr. Humberto Delgado. Aristocratic rooms on the 1st floor; servant-sized quarters higher up. Friendly, English-speaking owner. All rooms with TV. Breakfast included. Singles 3000-4000$, with bath 4500$; doubles 5500$, with bath 6000$; triples 8000$.

Pensão Ferro, R. Marnotos, 30 (tel. 42 22 14). From the tourist office turn right and take the 2nd right. 35 rooms with high ceilings, common baths, pastel colors, and windows on request. Singles 3000$; doubles 4500$; triples 5500$.

Camping: Orbitur São Jacinto (tel. 83 82 84; fax 83 81 22), on the beach northwest of Aveiro. Take the bus from the Canal Central stop (across the street from the tourist office) to Forte da Barra (10min., 220$), then hop on the boat to São Jacinto (15min., 10 per day, 7:40am-7:05pm, 250$). From there, hike 5km or take a bus (150$) to the campsite. Sometimes crowded. Reception daily 8am-10pm. 570$ per person and per tent, 480$ per car. Open Jan. 16-Nov. 15.

◖ FOOD

Seafood restaurants are common, but prices will make you want to catch your own fish. Cast your nets off Av. Dr. Lourenço Peixinho and R. José Estêvão. Aveiro's specialty is a dessert pastry called *ovos moles* (sweetened egg yolks), available at most cafes in town. For normal egg yolks, patronize supermarket **Pingo Oce,** across the canal from the tourist office (open daily 9am-8pm).

Restaurante Salimar, R. Luís Cipriano, 21, (tel. 42 51 08), across the river and a block uphill from the tourist office. Ocean decor for ocean-fresh dishes. Their specialty is a bubbling, orange-red broth swimming with rice and seafood called *arroz de marisco* (1100$; 2000$ for 2). Entrees 850-1500$. Open daily 9am-10:30pm.

Sonatura Restaurante Self-Service Naturista, R. Clube dos Galitos, 6 (tel. 42 44 74), directly across the canal from the tourist office. Vegetarian-macrobiotic-dietetic-food-store-restaurant serves 2 daily menus (700$) that include soup, organic bread, and an entree. Entrees 650-900$. Open M-F 8am-7pm, Sa 9am-4:30pm.

Restaurante Zico, R. José Estêvão, 52 (tel. 296 49), off Pr. Humberto Delgado. Very popular with the locals. Pig out on *prego de porco* (pork steak with fries, 850$) or try *omelete de camarão* (shrimp omelette, 1050$). Save room for the calorie-ridden desserts (250-350$). Entrees 750-1500$. Open M-Sa 8am-2am.

◖◖ SIGHTS AND BEACHES

Aveiro is known for its beautiful *azulejo* facades and great beaches. Don't miss the former just because you are spending too much time at the latter.

OLD TOWN. Simple but strikingly blue *azulejos* make up the walls of the **Igreja da Misericórdia** in Pr. República, across the canal and a block uphill from the tourist office. *(Open daily 9am-10pm.)* In the same square, the regal **Paça do Concelho** (town hall) flaunts its French design and bell tower. The real thriller of the old town is the ◪**Museu de Aveiro.** It's on the site of a former **convent,** where King Afonso and his daughter Infanta Joana, who at 18 wished to become a nun despite her father's objections, fought it out in 1472. She won and continued to live in the convent, caring for the sick and poor of Aveiro until she died of tuberculosis at barely 30 years old. Beneath *azulejo* panels depicting the story of her life is Santa Joana's Renaissance tomb, supported by the heads of four angels; it is one of the most famous works of art in Portugal. The chapel beyond showcases elaborate decoration similar to Baroque woodcarving; its *coro alto* (high chorus) is lined with lacquered panels reminiscent of *chinoiserie.* *(R. Sta. Joana Princesa. Tel. 42 32 97. Open Tu-Su 10am–5:20pm. 250$, seniors and students 125$. Sunday before 2pm free.)*

BEACHES. Don't spend all your time *azulejo*-gawking. Neighboring beach towns and their beautiful sand dunes, like the *reserva natural* at the **Dunas de São Jacinto** (10km away), merit daytrips and are easily accessible by ferry (see **Ferries,** p. 620). Closer to Aveiro, the beaches **Barra** and **Costa Nova** can be reached by bus from the *canal central* or train station stops (15min, 12 per day, 7:10am-8:45pm, last bus back at 8:15, 250$).

EAT YOUR HEART OUT, DON JUAN There's love, and then there's *love*. Dom Pedro I was in the latter. While a prince, he fell head-over-heels for Inês de Castro, the daughter of a Spanish nobleman and lady-in-waiting to his first wife. Pedro's father, Afonso IV, objected to the romance, fearing that such an alliance would open the Portuguese throne to Spanish domination. Despite his father's opposition to the marriage, Pedro fled with Inês to Bragança, where the couple secretly wed. Soon thereafter, the disgruntled Afonso had Inês killed. Upon rising to the throne two years later, Pedro personally ripped out the hearts of the men who had slit his young wife's throat and proceeded to eat them. Henceforth, the hardy king became known as Pedro the Cruel. In a disheartening ceremony, he had Inês's body exhumed, dressed her meticulously in royal robes, set her on the throne, and officially deemed her his queen; he even, according to legend, made his court kiss her rotting hand. She was eventually reinterred in an exquisitely carved tomb in the king's favorite monastery, the Mosteiro de Santa Maria de Alcobaça. The king later joined her, in a tomb directly opposite. The inscription on their elaborately carved tombs, *"Até ao fim do mundo"* (until the end of the world), attests to Pedro's belief that the couple would finally reunite—face to face—at the moment of resurrection.

🎵 ENTERTAINMENT

At night, tap into the watering-holes along R. Canal de São Rogue, or strut your stuff with the beautiful people at neighboring **Salpoente, Estrondo Bar,** and **Urgência.** The bars around Pr. Peixe, in the old city, and those in the shopping center/entertainment complex at Av. Dr. Lourenço Peixinho, 146, are also definite possibilities. For four weeks starting in mid-July, the city shakes for the **Festa da Ria,** which celebrates Aveiro's long boating tradition. During the festivities, locals race traditional *moliceiros* (beautifully carved and decorated boats).

NEAR AVEIRO: OVAR

Ovar, a sleepy, *azulejo*-filled town hemmed in on two sides by *pinheiro* (pine forest) and on one side by an isolated beach, is a relaxing stopover on the way to Porto. The town's new youth hostel is terrific, and the nearby **Praia do Furadouro** is charming, quiet, and virtually untouristed. The tiny town, as peaceful and authentic as they come, lies along the railroad tracks about 4km from the coast.

Conveniently, **buses** to the beach and youth hostel stop right in front of the train station and just past the tourist office, to the right of the garden (June-Aug. every 15min.; Sept.-May every 45min., 6:50am-8:55pm, 120$ to the beach, 90$ to the hostel). The **train station** (tel. 57 24 78), on Largo Serpa Pinto, has service to: **Aveiro** (30min., every hr., 6:08am-12:08am, 250$); **Porto** (55min., every hr., 6:12am-12:12am, 250$); **Coimbra** (1½hr., every hr., 5:47am-10:47pm, 700$); **Lisbon** (3½hr., 10 per day, 5:47am-8:47pm, 1750$). The **tourist office** (tel. 57 22 15), on R. Elias Garcia, has maps and transportation info. From the train station, head through the traffic circle on Pr. São Cristóvão and follow Av. Bom Reitor to R. Dr. Manuel Avala, which turns into R. Elias Garcia. (Open May-Sept. M-F 9am-7pm, Sa-Su 10am-noon and 2-5:30pm; Nov.-Apr. M-Sa 10am-noon and 2-5:30pm.) The **police** (tel. 57 29 99) are on R. Dr. José Falcão. **Telephone code:** (0)56.

HI members put their feet up at the brand-new 🏠**Pousada da Juventude de Ovar (HI)** (tel./fax 59 18 32), Av. Dom Manuel I (Estrada Nacional 327). Take the bus to the beach (see above), get off at the stop just before the traffic circle 2km outside of town, turn right (follow the signs to Porto), and walk for about 10 minutes; the hostel is on the right. Pristine rooms, a bar with billiards and satellite TV, and home-cooked meals (lunch or dinner 900$) make this modern hostel a prime rest-stop. **Bike rental** and **horseback riding** are also available. (Reception daily 9am-midnight. Call ahead in high season. June-Aug. dorms 1700$; doubles with bath 4200$. Sept.-May dorms 1400$; doubles with bath 3600$.) There is **camping** on **Praia do Furadouro** (tel. 59 60 10), 4km from the city center; amenities include a restaurant, a mini-mart, and sports fields. (Reception daily 8am-10pm. 500$ per person, 330$ per tent and per car.) For food, shop at the **Mercado Municipal** (open M-Sa 8am-5pm) or the **food stalls** by the youth hostel.

NORTHERN PORTUGAL

DOURO AND MINHO

Although their landscapes and Celtic history invite comparison with the northwest of Spain, the Douro and Minho regions of northern Portugal are more populated, developed, and wealthier than Spanish Galicia. Thanks to the area's mineral richness, these regions have had a prosperous history. The evidence is everywhere from the abundance of luxurious villas to the traditional female dress (which includes layers of gold necklaces encrusted with charms). This affluence has a long legacy: the Kingdom of Portugal originated here in 1143 when Afonso Henriques defeated the Moors in Guimarães.

But neither wealth nor history impinge on the region's spectacular greenery, making Douro and Minho a haven for nature lovers. Hundreds of trellised vineyards that grow grapes for *porto* and *vinho verde* wines beckon connoisseurs, and houses tiled in brilliant *azulejos* draw visitors to its charming, quiet streets. The region's mild coastal climate is too cool to attract the beach crowd until July, and only a few ambitious travelers ever make it past Porto and the Douro Valley to the greens and blues of the Alto Minho, which hugs the border with Spain. Happily untouristed, the cities of Vila Nova de Cerveira, Braga, Viana do Castelo, and Guimarães will reward the intrepid traveler.

HIGHLIGHTS OF DOURO AND MINHO

- **Porto,** with it's dramatic **gorge** and world-famous **wine lodges** (see below).
- **Parque Nacional da Peneda-Gerês,** Portugal's finest nature reserve (see p. 636).
- **Viano do Castelo**'s marvelous **Praça da República** (see p. 639).

PORTO (OPORTO)

According to an old Portuguese proverb, "Coimbra sings, Braga prays, Lisbon shows off, and Porto works." Well, all that work has paid off—Porto is now one of Portugal's most sophisticated and modern cities. Although today it is a bustling center for all types of business, the source of its greatest fame (and its name) is its sugary-sweet port wine. Developed by English merchants in the early 18th century, the port industry is at the root of the city's successful economy. Magnificently situated on a gorge cut by the Douro River, just 6km from the sea, Portugal's second-largest city often seems more vibrant than Lisbon, and framed by an elegance reminiscent of Paris or Prague. Granite church towers pierce the skyline, closely packed orange-tiled houses huddle along the river, and three of Europe's most graceful bridges span the gorge above.

Porto's history is the stuff that nationalism is made of, dating back to the 15th century when the city gave up everything to supply native son Prince Henry the Navigator with the necessary provisions for his explorations. In 1996, much of Porto's historic district was declared a U.N. World Heritage Site. Even more recently, Porto learned it had been chosen as one of two European cities (the other is Rotterdam) to be a Cultural Capital of Europe for 2001. This honor has not only spawned a large "urban regeneration" project, but also focused new attention on the city's rich culture.

⫶ GETTING THERE

Trains run to Porto from **Coimbra** (2hr., 12 per day, 9am-10pm, 980$) and **Vigo, Spain** (2½hr., 3 per day, 1845ptas). **Buses** go from **Coimbra** (1½hr., 10 per day, 8:30am-9:30pm, 1300$) and **Bragança** (5hr., 8 per day, 12:20-11:15pm, 1400$).

THAT TOOK GUTS Porto's history is the stuff from which nationalism is made. When native son Henry the Navigator geared up to conquer Cueta (a soon-to-be Christian base in Morocco) in the early 15th century, Porto's residents slaughtered their cattle, gave all of the meat to Prince Henry's fleet, and kept only the entrails for themselves. This dramatic generosity came at a time when much of Europe was suffering in the wake the Plague and food supplies were extremely important. The tasty dish *tripàs a moda do Porto* commemorates the culinary self-sacrifice; to this day, the people of Porto are known as *tripeiros* (tripe-eaters). The sacrifice paid off. Henry's decisive victory at Ceuta made possible the spreading of the Portuguese Empire to Africa and eventually India and the Far East. If you're feeling adventurous you can try some of the tripe dishes, which locals—and few others—consider quite a delicacy.

⁊ ORIENTATION AND PRACTICAL INFORMATION

Get ready to get lost. Constant traffic and a chaotic maze of one-way streets fluster even the most well-oriented of travelers; find your location on the map as soon as possible. At the very heart of the city is hillside **Praça da Liberdade**, joined to **Praça General Humberto Delgado** by Av. Aliados. One of Porto's two train stations, **Estação São Bento**, lies in the middle of town, just off the bottom of Pr. Liberdade. The other, **Estação de Campanhã**, is 2km from the city center along the river. The **Ribeira** district's steep streets wind a few blocks downhill from the center, directly across the bridge from **Vila Nova de Gaia**, where port wine ferments in 50-odd lodges.

TRANSPORTATION

Flights: Aeroporto Francisco de Sá Carneiro (tel. 941 32 60 or 941 32 70). The city bus (#56) to the airport from Pr. Lisbon can be painfully slow. The **aerobus** leaves from Av. Aliados near Pr. Liberdade and is more efficient (45min., every 30min., 7am-6:30pm, 500$). Buy tickets on board, at an **STCP** window, or at a participating hotel. Even quicker is a **taxi** (20-30min., 2500$). **TAP Air Portugal,** Pr. Mouzinho de Albuquerque, 105 (tel. 948 22 91), flies to most major European cities.

Trains: Estação de Campanhã (tel. 519 13 00). All trains pass through Porto's main station, east of the center. Frequent connections to Estação São Bento (5min., every 20min., 5:05am-11:15pm, 130$). To: **Aveiro** (1¼hr., 30 per day, 5:05am-11:15pm, 330$); **Viana do Castelo** (2hr., 11 per day, 5:45am-12:35am, 720$); **Braga** (2hr., 20 per day, 5:45am-12:35am, 330$); **Coimbra** (2¼hr., 12 per day, 6:05am-10:05pm, 980$); **Lisbon** (4½hr., 5 per day, 7:05am-6:10pm, 2000$); **Faro** (9hr.; M, W, F 1 per day, 10:10pm; 3270$) via Santarém; **Madrid** (13-14hr., 1 per day, 6:10pm, 10,000$); **Paris** (22hr., 1 per day, 7:05pm, 22,000$). Estação de São Bento (tel. 200 27 22), centrally located 1 block off Pr. Liberdade, is the terminus for trains with mostly local and regional routes. If your train stops at Estação de Campanhã, it is usually best to take a connecting train to São Bento. Buses also run to Pr. Liberdade and beyond (every 30min., 170$). There is a handy info office at Estação São Bento, open 8:30am-8pm. Minimal English, but decent French.

Buses: There is no central bus station; over 20 different companies each operate their own garage. Some of the largest are: **Garagem Atlântico,** R. Alexandre Herculano, 366 (tel. 200 69 54). To: **Braga** (1¼hr., 12 per day, 9:55am-10:15pm, 800$); **Coimbra** (1½hr., 12 per day, 7:15am-12:45am, 1300$); **Viana do Castelo** (1¾hr.; M-F 3 per day, Sa-Su 2 per day, 10:55am-6:40pm; 1200$); **Lisbon** (4hr., 10 per day, 7:15am-12:45am, 2800$). **Rodoviaria D'entre Douro e Minho** (tel. 200 61 21), Pr. D. Filipa de Lencastre, 1 block from Av. Aliados, has buses to **Braga** (1hr., every 45min., 6:45am-

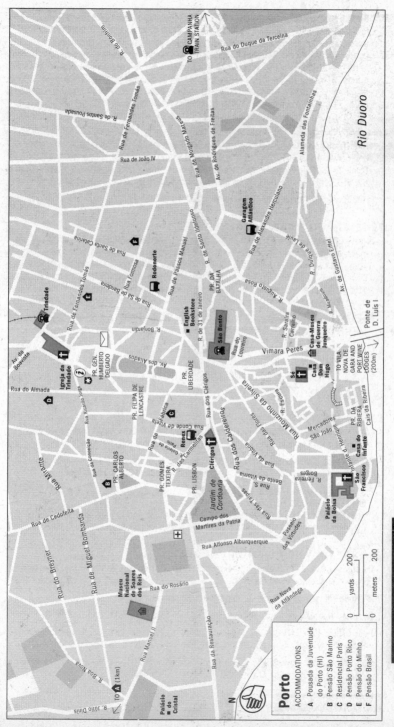

Porto

ACCOMMODATIONS

- A Pousada da Juventude do Porto (HI)
- B Pensão São Marino
- C Residencial Paris
- D Pensão Porto Rico
- E Pensão do Minho
- F Pensão Brasil

NORTHERN PORTUGAL

8pm, 650$). **Rodonorte** (tel. 200 56 37), R. Atenou Comercial do Porto, 1 block from R. Sá da Bandeira goes to **Vila Real** (2hr., 10 per day, 6:50am-9:20pm, 740-960$). **Renex,** R. Carmelitas, 34 (tel. 200 33 95), has express service to the Algarve. To: **Lagos and Vila Real San António,** (9½hr., 8 per day, 5:30am-5pm, 3400$). **Internorte,** Pr. Galiza, 96 (tel. 609 32 20 or 609 02 52) has international bus service to: **Madrid** (10½hr.; Tu, Th, Sa-Su 1 per day, 8:30am; 5230$); **Paris** (27hr., Tu-Sa 1 per day, 8am, 10,000$); **Brussels** (28hr., Tu and F 1 per day, 9:30am, 18,800$); **Geneva** (30hr.; Tu, Th, Sa 1 per day, 9:30am; 16,930$); **Berlin** (39hr., Tu and F 1 per day, 9:30am, 24,695$). Must book tickets 3 days in advance. Office open M-F 9am-12:30pm and 2-6:30pm, Sa 9am-12:30pm.

Public Transportation: *Passe Turístico* discount passes are available for Porto's trolleys and buses. 4-day pass 1600$, 7-day 2150$. Single trip ticket 170$, one-day unlimited ticket 350$. Tickets can be purchased on the bus, at small kiosks around the city, or at the **STCP** office, half a block downhill and across the street from Estação de São Bento.

Taxis: Raditáxis, R. Alegria, 1802 (tel. 502 26 93 or 502 11 32). Taxis line Av. Aliados.

TOURIST AND FINANCIAL SERVICES

Tourist Office: R. Clube dos Fenianos, 25, off Pr. Liberdade. Multilingual staff doles out maps and brochures. Open July-Sept. M-F 9am-7pm, Sa 9:30am-4:30pm, Su 10am-1pm; Oct.-June M-F 9am-5:30pm, Sa 9am-5:30pm. **ICEP (national tourism) office,** Pr. Dom João I, 25 (tel. 31 75 14), at R. Bonjardim. Open M-F 9am-7pm, Sa 9am-2pm, Su 10am-2pm. There also are 24hr. multilingual **computer info stands** in the main shopping centers and the larger squares; one sits in front of the McDonald's in Pr. Liberdade.

Youth Travel: Tagus, R. Campo Alegre, 261 (tel. 609 41 46; fax 609 41 41). English-speaking staff offers advice and student rates. Open M-F 9am-6pm, Sa 10am-1:30pm.

Currency Exchange: Most banks open M-F 8:30am-3pm.

American Express: Top Tours, R. Alferes Malheiro, 96 (tel. 208 27 85). Facing the town hall at the top of Pr. Liberdade, take the street to the left and turn left after 2 blocks. Open M-F 9am-12:30pm and 2:30-6:30pm.

LOCAL SERVICES

Luggage Storage: Free in **tourist office** during the day. At **Estação de São Bento** in lockers to the right as you enter (400-900 for 48hr.; open daily 5am-midnight).

Laundromat: Lavanderia Pinguim (tel. 609 50 32), Pr. Mouzinho do Albuquerque, in shopping center Brasília. 1500$ per 5.5kg load. Open M-Sa 10am-9:30pm.

English Bookstore: Livraria Britânico, R. José Falcão, 184 (tel. 32 39 30). Decent choice of paperbacks, hardcovers, and magazines. Open M-F 9am-7pm, Sa 9:30am-1pm. **Livraria Diário de Notícias,** R. Sá de Bandeira, 5, across from Estação São Bento. Smaller selection of books. Maps. Open M-F 9am-7pm, Sa 9am-1pm.

EMERGENCY AND COMMUNICATIONS

Emergency: tel. 112. **Police:** Multilingual **tourist station** (tel. 208 18 33), next to the main tourist office on the praça.

24-Hour Pharmacy: dial 118 for info on which pharmacy is open.

Hospital: Hospital de Santo António (tel. 200 73 54), R. Prof. Vicente José de Carvalho.

Post Office: (tel. 340 02 00), Pr. Gen. Humberto Delgado. **Fax,** telephones, and Posta Restante (65$ per item). Open M-F 8am-9pm, Sa-Su 9am-6pm. **Postal Code:** 4000.

Internet Access: Portweb, Pr. Gen. Humberto Delgado, 291. Before 2pm, 100$ per hr. After 2pm, 300$ per hr. Open M-Sa 9am-2am, Su 3pm-2am.

TELEPHONE CODE Porto's phone code is (0)2.

ACCOMMODATIONS AND CAMPING

Rates for singles are higher than the norm, and the city's only youth hostel is somewhat small. For better deals, look west of Av. Aliados, or on R. Fernandes Tomás and R. Formosa, perpendicular to Aliados Square. Most places offer discounts in the off-season. Reservations are recommended just about everywhere.

Residencial Paris, R. Fábrica, 27-9 (tel. 207 31 40; fax 207 31 49). Cross Pr. Liberdade from the train station and turn left onto R. Dr. Artur de Magalhães Basto, which turns into R. Fábrica. English-speaking manager is a wealth of information. Large rooms, common room with TV, and lush gardens. Breakfast included. Singles 2850$, with bath 4600$; doubles 4200$, with bath 6300$; triples 8200$.

Pousada da Juventude do Porto (HI), R. Paulo da Gama, 551 (tel. 617 72 47), 3km from town center. Take bus #35 from Estação Campanha or #37 from Pr. Liberdade; both stop in front of the hostel. In a somewhat sketchy neighborhood—women travelers should not walk alone at night. The vending machine makes for a lively social scene. Reception daily 9-11am and 6pm-midnight. June-Aug. dorms 2500$; doubles with bath 5500$. Sept.-May dorms 1900$; doubles with bath 4700$.

Pensão Porto Rico, R. Almada, 237, 2nd fl. (tel. 339 46 90). From Av. Aliados, go up R. Elísio de Melo; after 2 blocks turn right on R. Almada. Small but clean rooms with baths, phones, TVs, and radios. Reservations recommended. Breakfast included. Singles 4500$; doubles 7500$; triples 9000$. Visa, MC.

Pensão São Marino, Pr. Carlos Alberto, 59 (tel. 32 54 99). Facing the town hall, go up the street on the left and take the 1st left on R. Dr. Ricardo Jorge, which becomes R. Conceição; turn left on R. Oliveiras and make a quick right on Pr. Carlos Alberto. Ask the English-speaking owner for a room overlooking the praça. All 14 rooms have a bath or shower, phone, TV, and winter heat. Singles 5000$; doubles 6000$; triples 7500$.

Pensão Brasil, R. Formosa, 178 (tel. 205 05 16). From Pr. Liberdade, cross Av. Aliados to R. Formosa; it's about 3½ blocks up. Cheap, but nothing special. Doubles are nicer than singles. Singles 3500$; doubles with bath 4500$; triples 6000$.

Pensão do Minho, R. Fernandes Tomás, 926 (tel. 205 12 72). Facing the town hall, take the street to the right and then take the 1st right. Small yet functional rooms are exactly where you want them: near the train station, tourist office, and city center. Mid-sized rooms with a double bed (for 1 or 2 people) 3000$.

Camping: Prelada (tel. 831 26 16), on R. Monte dos Burgos, in Quinta da Prelada, 2km from the town center and 5km from the beach. Take bus #6 from Pr. Liberdade or #54 at night. Reception 8am-11pm. 600$ per person, 500$ per tent and per car. **Salgueiros** (tel. 781 05 00), near Praia Salgueiros in Vila Nova de Gaia, is less accessible and less equipped, but less expensive and closer to the beach. 250$ per person and per tent, 100$ per car.

FOOD

Eating out costs more in Porto than in any other Portuguese city. If you are on a tight budget, pick up fresh produce at one of the outdoor **markets** on C. Ribeira (open daily 8am-8pm), or at the **Mercado de Bolhão,** on the corner of R. Formosa and R. Sá de Bandeira (open M-F 8am-5pm, Sa 8am-1pm). Doling out a few hundred more *escudos*, however, will land you some tasty dishes. Expensive restaurants border the river in the Ribeira district, particularly on C. Ribeira, R. Reboleira, and R. Cima do Muro. Budget fare and rowdier environments prevail near Pr. Batalha on R. Cimo de Vila and R. Cativo. Even cheaper eateries lie around the Hospital de Santo António and Pr. Gomes Teixeira, a few blocks west of Pr. Liberdade. Adventurous eaters savor the city's specialty, *tripas à moda do Porto* (tripe and beans).

NORTHERN PORTUGAL

■ **Majestic Cafe,** R. Santa Catarina, 112 (tel. 200 38 87). Touts itself as "the joy of the city of Porto" and some even call it the "2nd-best cafe in Portugal." A bit pricey, but why not treat yourself with class? Tea sandwiches (500-950$), coffee (200$). Some of the fanciest (and sweetest) pastries in town (90-200$). Open daily 9am-12:30am.

Restaurante O Gancho, Largo Terreiro, 11-12, across from Boa Nova. Typical Portuguese *comida* served in a plain bar/dining room over an outdoor esplanade. Some outdoor seating. Entrees 800-1200$. Open daily noon-3pm and 7:30-10:30pm.

Restaurante Boa Nova, Muro dos Bacalhoeiros, 115 (tel. 200 60 86), in the row of houses overlooking the riverside walk, next door to the house where the inventor Gomes was born, namesake of the cod dish *à Gomes de Sá* (read the plaque yourself). *Carapaus fritos* (fried whitefish, 850$). Open M-Sa noon-3pm and 7:30-10:30pm.

Restaurante Chinês, Av. Vímara Peres, 38, just before you cross the top level of the main bridge (Ponte D. Luís I). The best Chinese food north of the Rio Douro. Entrees 650-1300$. Open M-Sa noon-3pm and 7-10pm. Visa, MC.

Churrasqueira Moura, R. Almada, 219 (tel. 200 56 36), on a street parallel to Av. Alia-dos. Dirt-cheap meals satisfy even the grumpiest of stomachs and stingiest of travelers. Half-portions 850$; full portions less than 1600$. Open M-Sa 9am-10pm.

👁 SIGHTS

Your first brush with Porto's rich stock of fine artwork may be in, of all places, the **São Bento train station,** home to a celebrated collection of *azulejos*, including iron and glass trains decorated with the beautiful tiles. Outside the station and at the top of adjacent **Praça da Liberdade,** the formidable **Prefeitura** (City Hall) is a monument to Porto's late 19th-century greatness.

■**CATHEDRAL (SÉ).** Fortified on the hilltop slightly south of the train station is Porto's pride and joy, the Romanesque sé, situated in one of the city's oldest residential districts. Built in the 12th and 13th centuries, the Gothic, *azulejo*-covered cloister was later added in the 14th century. The **Capela do Santíssimo Sacramento,** to the left of the high altar, shines with solid silver and plated gold. During the Napoleonic invasion, crafty townspeople whitewashed the altar to protect it from vandalism. Climb the staircase to the **Renaissance chapter house** for a splendid view of the old quarter. *(From Pr. Liberdade, walk past Estação São Bento and uphill on Av. Afonso Henriques; the cathedral is on the right. Open M-Sa 9am-12:30pm and 2:30-6pm, Su 2:30-6pm. Cloister 250$.)*

■**PALÁCIO DA BOLSA.** Cash acquires cachet at the Palácio da Bolsa (Stock Exchange), the epitome of 19th-century elegance. The ornate courtyard ceiling gives a hint of the opulence inside. It took a zealous artisan three years to carve the exquisite wooden table in the portrait room; the ornate **Sala Árabe** (Arabic Hall) took 18 years to decorate. Modeled after Granada's Alhambra, its gold and silver walls are covered with plaques bearing the oddly juxtaposed inscriptions "Glory to Allah" and "Glory to Queen Maria II." *(R. Ferreira Borges. From the town center, walk past Estação São Bento and downhill on R. Mouzinho da Silveira to the square; signs lead the way. Tel. 208 45 66. Open M-F 9am-6:40pm, Sa-Su 9am-12:30pm and 2-6:30pm. Multilingual tours every 30min. 750$, students 550$. Main courtyard free.)*

MUSEU DE ARTE CONTEMPORÂNEA. For modern art in a lovely setting, visit the Museu de Arte Contemporânea. The museum rotates temporary exhibits of contemporary Portuguese art and architectural design. Ask to see an English video on the artists—all descriptions in the museum are in Portuguese. The building crowns an impressive 44 acres of sculpted gardens, fountains, and old farmland, tumbling down toward the Douro River. *(Several kilometers out of town, on the way to the beach. Bus #78 leaves for the museum from Pr. Dom João I; ask the driver to stop at the museum (30min., return buses run until midnight, 170$). Museum open Tu-Su 10am-7pm. Park closes at sundown. 800$, seniors and students 400$. Thursday free.)*

FINE WINE, PORT GRATIS The thirsty budget traveler might think Porto the Garden of Eden. In the city there is an abundant supply of fine port wines available for consumption at any one of 20-odd port wine lodges. And the best part is that it's almost all completely *gratuito* (free).

As you will learn while waiting impatiently for the tours to terminate and the toasting to begin, port was discovered when some enterprising English wine dealers added a strong brandy to cheap Portuguese wine to prevent it from souring en route to England. Nowadays, wine from grapes grown in the Douro Valley, 100km west of Porto, is mixed with 170-proof brandy (unfortunately not for sale) and aged in barrels to yield port of three different varieties: white, tawny, and ruby. The lodges are all across the river in Vila Nova da Gaia—walk down to the Ribeira district and be sure to cross the lower level of the large bridge. Most lodges open to visitors operate on some variation of a 10am-6pm schedule, and only a few charge for tours and tastings. A good starter is **Sandeman,** with costumed guides and high-quality port (admission 500$, but still hugely popular). **Cálem,** next door, has a less stilted tour, and the port is almost as good. At **Ferreira,** down the road, you will learn about the illustrious *senhora* who built the Ferreira empire in the late 19th century—1996 was the 100th anniversary of her death. Last, but certainly not least, **Taylor's** wins the highly unscientific *Let's Go* poll for best port lodge in Porto. Ask for your wine on their terrace, which has a great view of the city and the River Douro.

TORRE DOS CLÉRIGOS. Up R. Clérigos from Pr. Liberade the 76m Torre dos Clérigos (Tower of Clerics) rises, adjoined to the **Igreja dos Clérigos.** Built in the mid-18th century, the granite bell tower, the city's tallest landmark, glimmers like a processional candle. Climb the 200 steps for spectacular views of Porto and the Rio Douro Valley. *(Tower open daily 10am-noon and 2-5pm. Tower 100$, church free.)*

MUSEU NACIONAL DE SOARES DOS REIS. A former royal residence, this 18th century museum houses an exhaustive collection of 19th-century Portuguese painting and sculpture, much of it by Soares dos Reis, often called Portugal's Michelangelo. *(From the town center, walk down R. Clérigos and R. Restanração, then take R. Dom Manuel II past the churches and forested park (10min.). Tel. 339 37 70. Open Tu-Su 10am-5:30pm. 350$, seniors and students 175$.)*

IGREJA DE SÃO FRANCISCO. The Gothic Igreja de São Francisco glitters with one of the most elaborately gilded wooden interiors in Portugal. Under the floor, thousands of human bones are stored in preparation for Judgment Day. *(From Pr. Liberade, follow the directions to the Palácio da Bolsa; the church is next door. Tel. 200 84 41. Open daily 9am-6pm. 500$, seniors and students 250$.)*

PARK. A beautiful park lies outside the Palácio de Cristàl (Glass Palace), near the hospital. Geese, swans, ducks, peacocks, fountains, and the best-kept garden in Portugal welcome those in search of a good reading spot. *(Exit Pr. Liberade on R. Clerigos and follow the road around the hospital (take a right on R. Alberto Gouveia) before taking a left on R. D. Manuel II. The park and palace are on the left, after passing the Museu Nacional de Soares dos Reis (10-15min.). Open daily until dark.)*

BEACH AND ESPLANADE. Porto's rocky beach, in the ritzy Foz district in the west end of the city, is a popular destination despite higher-than-normal levels of pollution. *(Bus #78 from Pr. Liberade, 160$.)* At the bottom of the hill on R. Alfândega, past a marvelous dock filled with shops and restaurants, runs the esplanade, called the **Ribeira.** *(Trolley #1 from the Igreja de São Francisco, 160$.)*

🎵 **ENTERTAINMENT**

NIGHTLIFE. The place to party on weekend nights is the tirelessly fun **Ribeira,** where bars vibrate with the rhythms of Brazilian and Latin tunes. Pr. Ribeira, M. Bacalhoeiros, and R. Alfândega harbor most of the bars and pubs. Try **Pub O Muro,**

M. Bacalhoeiros, 87-88 (tel. 38 34 26), above the riverside, near the bridge. **Discoteca Swing**, on R. Júlio Dinis near the youth hostel, has swinging action for a mixed gay-straight crowd (cover 1000$). The "beautiful people" party in the Foz beach district—try discos **Industria, Twins,** and **Dona Urraca.**

MOVIES AND THEATER. English-language movies are sometimes shown in cinemas in the town center; try **Cinema Passos Manuel,** R. Passos Manuel, 141 (tel. 200 51 96), with shows daily from 2 to 9:30pm (tickets M 400$, Tu-Su 600$). Live **concerts** and **theater** performances are held on sultry summer nights at the Claustros do Mosteiro de São Bento da Vitória (tel. 31 21 32). The historic **Teatro Nacional São João** (tel. 200 34 49), Pr. Batalha, frequently hosts international drama troupes. Consult the bulletins at the tourist office for upcoming events.

PORT. But we digress—back to your main focus of interest. You can enjoy the warm glow of port wine by embarking on a "wine connoisseurship" **cruise** down the Douro River. Grab a few pamphlets at the tourist office, or head straight for the docks. Still not tired of tasting port? For an upscale evening, try visiting the **Solar do Vinho do Porto** (tel. 609 749), R. Entre Quintas, a converted manor house that now operates as a bar/lounge. The Solar has port from 200$ a glass; take in the gorgeous river view from the terrace while sipping on the fine wine. *(Walk past the Palácio de Cristal on R. D. Manuel II (coming from Pr. Liberdade) and follow the signs (15min.). Or take a taxi (600$). Open M-F 10am-11:45pm, Sa 11am-10:45pm).*

NEAR PORTO: AMARANTE

Porto quenches thirst, but Amarante (pop. 4900) feeds the soul. Mass tourism has yet to rear its ugly head in this emerald green valley sprinkled with whitewashed houses. Amarante's two halves greet each other across the lazy Rio Tamega, both lined with shady weeping willows. For a good dose of history, cross the **Ponte de São Gonçalo,** once a Portuguese stronghold against Napoleonic troops, into **Praça da República.** The lacy facade of Amarante's gem, the Romanesque **Igreja de São Gonçalo,** hides the resting place of the town's patron saint, São Gonçalo, whose tomb is in the gilded chapel beside the altar. The **municipal library** and the **Museu Amadeo S. Cardoso** are in the same complex (open Tu-Su 10am-12:30pm and 2-5:30pm, closed holidays; 200$). The trek up R. 5 de Outubro offers a view of the ghostly remains of the **Solar dos Magalhães,** a burned-out manor which serves as a sordid but hauntingly beautiful reminder of Napoleon's pyromaniacal legacy.

Rodonorte **buses** (tel. 32 32 34) zip to: **Vila Real** (45min., 10 per day, 7:50am-10:20pm, 700$); **Guimarães** (1hr., 3 per day, 485$); **Porto** (1½hr., 6 per day, 7am-7:40pm, 700$); **Bragança** (2½hr., 5 per day, 8:30am-6pm, 1450$). To get to the **tourist office** (tel. 43 29 80), follow Av. Alexandre Herculano toward the river, then hang a left on R. 31 de Janeiro. Cross the bridge onto Pr. República; the office is in the same building as the museum entrance on Alameda Teixeira de Pascoaes. The staff hands out good maps. (Open M-F 9:30am-6pm, Sa 10am-12:30pm and 2-5pm.) **Telephone code:** (0)55. Amarante is best visited as a daytrip from Guimarães, Braga, or Porto. If you do spend the night, try three star **Pensão Restaurante Sena** (tel. 49 17 25), on S. Gens. Rooms are spacious and well lit. Demand is invariably high, so call ahead to reserve a room. (Singles 3000-4000$; doubles 4000-6000$.) After exploring the town's sights, pick a riverside terrace, drink in the sun, and gorge on Amarante's culinary specialties: sweets, sweets, and more sweets. Delicious regional *ovos moles* (egg pastries) and traditional cakes proliferate, particularly during the festival of São Gonçalo.

BRAGA

Braga (pop. 160,000), once the seat of the Archbishop of Spain, is considered by some the most extravagant, by others the most fanatic, and by all the most politically conservative city in Portugal. Not surprisingly, the 1926 coup that paved Salazar's path to power was launched from here (see **History,** p. 524). Yet in spite of Braga's austere reputation and large number of Gothic churches, hedonism—man-

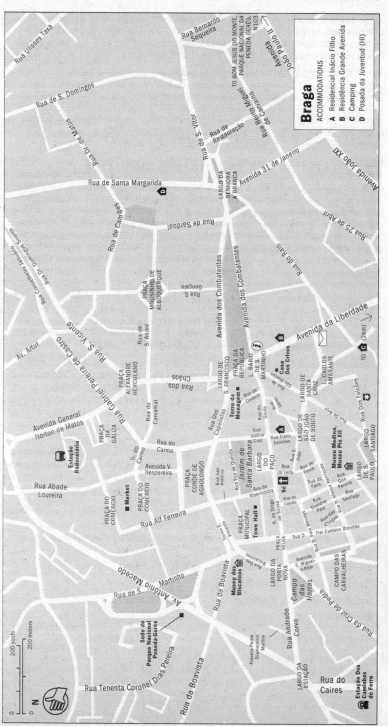

Braga

ACCOMMODATIONS
- **A** Residencial Inácio Filho
- **B** Residência Grande Avenida
- **C** Camping
- **D** Posada da Juventud (HI)

ifested in bars and discos—marches cheerfully onward. During Holy Week, a procession crosses the flower-carpeted streets; at night, somber devotion ignites into fireworks and dancing. Lively pedestrian thoroughfares and fairy-tale plazas make Braga akin to a miniature Lisbon. Braga is also a practical base for exploring the natural wonders of northern Portugal.

▀ GETTING THERE

Trains run to Braga from **Porto** (2hr., 20 per day, 5:45am-12:35am, 330$) and **Coimbra** (3hr., 2 per day, 9:50am and 6pm, 1200$). **Buses** go from **Porto** (1¼hr., 12 per day, 10am-10pm, 800$) and **Bragança** (5hr., 2 per day, 4:15pm and 1:15am, 1600$).

▊ ORIENTATION AND PRACTICAL INFORMATION

Braga's focal point is the **Praça da República,** a spirited square filled with cafes, bordered by gardens, and crowned with a fountain. Av. Liberdade stems out from the square. **Rua do Souto,** a pedestrian thoroughfare lined with shops, runs from the tourist office's corner of Pr. República. R. Souto becomes R. Dom Diogo de Sousa and then R. Andrade de Corvo, which leads straight to the **train station.** To get to Pr. República from the **bus station,** stand with your back to the entrance, take a left, and then turn right up the street. Go straight under the concrete building onto Pr. Alexandre Herculana. Follow Rúa dos Cháos (the road ahead) into the square.

Trains: (tel. 26 21 66), on Largo Estação. It is easier to get to Braga by bus. Trains to **Porto** (1½hr., 16 per day, 5:05am-2:17pm, 330$) and **Coimbra** (4hr., 2 per day, 7:50am and 6:50pm, 1150$). To get to **Viana do Castelo, Vila Nova de Cerveira,** and **Valencia, Spain,** make a connection at **Nine** (20min., 14 per day, 5:26am-2:36pm, 170$). **Inter-Cidades** runs an express to **Lisbon** via Porto (3 per day).

Buses: (tel. 61 60 80 or 053 68 31 33), Central de Camionagem, a few blocks north of the city center. **Rodoviária** runs to: **Guimarães** (1hr., every 30min., 7:15am-8:35pm, 365$); **Porto** (1½hr., every 45min., 6:45am-8pm, 650$); **Campo do Gerês** (1½hr., 8 per day, 7:15am-7:10pm, 520$); **Coimbra** (3hr., M-F 9 per day, Sa 7 per day, Su 8 per day, 6am-11:30pm, 1500$); **Lisbon** (8½hr., 6 per day, 9:30am-11:30pm, 2300$); **Faro** (12-15hr., 9 per day, 6am-11:30pm, 3200$).

Taxis: (tel. 61 40 28).

Tourist Office: Av. Central, 1 (tel. 26 25 50), on the corner of Pr. República, across from the bank. Maps and plenty of info on rustic excursions. Train schedules and bus info available. Temporary **luggage storage.** Open July-Sept. M-F 9am-7pm, Sa-Su 9am-12:30pm and 2-5pm; Oct.-June M-F 9am-7pm, Sa 9am-12:30pm and 2-5pm.

Budget Travel: Tagus Youth Travel, Pr. Município, 7 (tel. 21 51 44; fax 053 21 51 94). Student flights and other services. Open M-F 9am-6pm. Visa, MC, AmEx.

Currency Exchange: Banco Borges e Irmão, on Pr. República, across from the tourist office. Open M-F 8:30am-3pm.

English Bookstore: Liveria Central, Av. Liberdade, 726, next to Residência Avenida.

Emergency: tel. 112. **Police:** R. dos Falcões, 12 (tel. 61 32 50).

Hospital: Hospital São Marcos (tel. 60 13 00), Largo Carlos Amarante.

Post Office: (tel. 61 77 20), Av. Liberdade, 2 blocks downhill from the tourist office. For Posta Restante, indicate "Estação Avenida" in the address. Open for **telephones, fax,** and other services M-F 8:30am-6pm, Sa 9am-12:30pm. **Postal Code:** 4700.

Internet Access: Baba de Camelo/Cyberbar (tel. 25 74 90). A 25min. walk from the tourist office. Take a right out of the tourist office and follow Av. Combatentes as it curves and as its name changes. At the freeway, take a right and walk (carefully) through the rotary. Cyberbar is on your left across from the gas station. 3 reasonably fast computers. 300$ for 30min., 600$ per hr. Open 3pm-2am.

ACCOMMODATIONS

Braga resounds with *pensões*, although few are truly budget. The cheapest cluster around the **Hospital de São Marcos,** the more expensive around **Avenida Central.**

Pousada da Juventude de Braga (HI), R. Santa Margarida, 6 (tel./fax 61 61 63). From the tourist office entrance, take a right and follow Av. Combatentes. Turn left at the intersection with R. Santa Margarida. 15min. from the bus station and 35min. from the train station. A taxi from the train station costs 650$. Relaxing, but not intimate—8 beds fill each large room. Huge windows open onto a forested hill. Breakfast included. Reception daily 9am-noon and 6pm-midnight. Reservations recommended July-Aug. In June-Sept. dorms 1500$; doubles 4000$. Oct.-May dorms 1200$; doubles 3500$.

Residência Grande Avenida, Av. Liberdade, 738, 2nd fl. (tel. 60 90 20), around the corner from the tourist office. 21 rooms with elegant mirrors and plush furniture, some with TV, phone, and heat. There is even a Victorian sitting room. Breakfast included. Reserve ahead June-Aug. June-Sept. singles 3000-4000$, with bath 4500$; doubles 5000$, with bath 6000$. Oct.-May singles 3000$, with bath 4000$; doubles 4500$, with bath 5500$. Visa, MC, AmEx.

Residencial Inácio Filho, R. Francisco Sanches, 42 (tel. 26 38 49). From the praça, walk down R. Souto 1 block; it's off the first perpendicular pedestrian street to the left. Hallways cluttered with cool antiques connect 8 well-kept rooms. Curfew midnight. Winter heating. Doubles 4400$, with bath 5000$.

Camping: Parque da Ponte (tel. 27 33 55), 2km down Av. Liberdade from the center, next to the stadium and the municipal pool. Buses stop every 30min. Market and laundry facilities. 340$ per person, 260$ per tent, 280$ per car.

FOOD

Braga has many cafes and several superb restaurants, but little in between. A colorful **market** sets up in Pr. Comércio, two blocks from the bus station (open M-Sa 7am-3pm). Numerous restaurants in this praça serve the Minho's typically heavy dishes. For groceries, stop and shop at **Supermercado Mini Preço,** R. São Victor, 68-74, a long block away from the youth hostel (open M-Sa 9am-8pm). For fast food and a mall atmosphere, hit **BragaShopping,** a commercial center facing the praça.

Churrasqueira da Sé, Dom Paio Mendes, 25. This "cathedral barbecue" serves pork chops, barbecued chicken, veal, and omelettes fit for His Excellence and laymen alike. Half-portions (630-890$) could feed the whole clergy. The *prato do dia* (500$), a real bargain, is miraculous. Food served daily 11am-9pm.

Cafe Vianna, Pr. República, 87 (tel. 26 23 36), behind the fountain. A snappy, pink marble cafe with a limited menu. At night it's a popular hangout, sometimes with live music. Full breakfasts (300-750$), light lunches, and dinner (sandwiches and *pratos combinados* 375-1050$). Open daily 8am-2am.

Grupo Jolima, Av. Liberdade, 779, under the flamingo-pink archway a block from the tourist office. Serves tasty pizza (200$ per slice), breads (60$ per buttered roll), and traditional Portuguese barbecue (600$). Open daily 7am-midnight.

Restaurante Vice Versa, Av. Combatentes, 128 (tel. 21 47 64). Black and white stone setting and soft techno complemented by a stuffed fox. Standard grub for decent prices. Salads 500$. Meat dishes 650-1800$. Open daily 11am-midnight.

SIGHTS

CATHEDRAL (SÉ). Braga's sé, Portugal's oldest cathedral, has undergone a series of renovations since its construction in the 11th and 12th centuries. Guided tours (in Portuguese) of its treasury, choir, and chapels run often during visiting hours. The treasury showcases the archdiocese's most precious paintings and relics. On display is the *Cruzeiro do Brasil*, a plain iron cross from the ship Pedro Álvares Cabral commanded when he discovered Brazil on April 22, 1500. Perhaps most interesting are the cathedral's collection of *cofres cranianos* (brain boxes), one of which contains the 6th-century cortex of São Martinho Dume, Braga's first bishop. Off a Renaissance cloister lie the cathedral's two historic chapels. The more notable, **Capela dos Reis (Kings' Chapel)**, guards the 12th-century stone sarcophagi of Dom Afonso Henriques's parents as well as the mummified remains of a 14th-century archbishop. The latter has a heart-stopping effect. Also of interest is the choir—its organ has 2424 fully functional pipes. *(Cathedral and treasury open daily June-Aug. 8:30am-6:30pm; Sept.-May 8:30am-5:30pm. Cathedral free; treasury 300$.)*

IGREJA DO BOM JESÚS. Braga's most famous landmark, Igreja do Bom Jesús, is actually 5km outside of town on a hillside carpeted in greenery. Built in an effort to re-create Jerusalem in Braga, this 18th-century church was to provide Iberian Christians with a pilgrimage sight closer to home. To visit Bom Jesús, either take the 285m ride on the old funicular (100$) or take the long walk (25-30min.) up the granite-paved pathway that forks into two zig-zagging 565-step stairways. On the way up, check out the **staircase** depicting, among other things, the five senses (the "smell" fountain spouts water through a boy's nose) and the story of Christ's crucifixion. The church and some incredibly tacky cafes are at the top. *(Buses labeled "#02 Bom Jesús" depart at 10min. and 40min. past the hour from Largo Carlos Amarante in front of Hospital de São Marcos, or from Av. Liberdade in front of Farmacià Cristal. Buses drop off at the bottom of the stairway and the funicular. 185$.)*

CAPELA DE NOSSA SENHORA DA CONCEIÇÃO. The street behind the chapel leads to a square flanked by the 17th-century Capela de Nossa Senhora da Conceição. The interior is covered with *azulejos* telling the story of Adam and Eve. *(Open M-F 10am-1pm and 3-7pm. Free.)*

DAYTRIPS FROM BRAGA

■MOSTEIRO DE TIBÃES. In an unspoiled forest, this beautiful and peaceful 11th-century Benedictine monastery has suffered from centuries of neglect. Stone tombs rattle eerily underfoot in the weathered cloister. Adjoining the cloister, however, is an exceptionally preserved church. *(A city bus labeled "Sarrido" heads 6km from Braga to the monastery. Buses leave from Pr. Conde de Agroiongo, one block up R. Capelistas from Pr. República. The stop is in front of the "Arca-Lar" store, which also posts a schedule (45min., every 2hr., 230$). Open Tu-Su 9am-noon and 2-7pm. Tour free.)*

CITÂNIA DE BRITEIROS. Nine kilometers from Bom Jesús, stone house foundations and huts dot the hills in Portugal's best-preserved collection of Celtic ruins. *(Take Bus #12 to Pedraiva from the Braga tourist office (1hr., 4 per day, 370$). Get off at Lageosa and walk 2km up the road. Open Tu-Su 9am-noon and 2-5pm. 200$.)*

GUIMARÃES

Though modernization and commercialism seem to have found a place for themselves in Guimarães (pop. 170,000), the castle-dominated town center still retains a rustic air that attracts a barrage of history buffs. It was here, in 1128, that Dom Afonso Henriques defeated the troops of the King of Castilla y León to become the first King of Portugal. To honor the town he made it the jewel of his kingdom. Ever since then, Guimarães has been called the "cradle of the nation," as the huge *"Aqui nasceu Portugal"* ("Here Portugal was born") sign proclaims.

⚑ PRACTICAL INFORMATION. The **train station** (tel. 41 23 51), a 10-minute walk down Av. Afonso Henriques from the tourist office, serves **Porto** (2hr., every hr., 15 per day, 570$). The **bus station** (tel. 053 41 26 46) is located in the immense Guimarães shopping complex. To get to the bus station, follow Av. Conde Margaride downhill. **Rodoviária** dispatches buses to **Braga** (45min., every 30min., 365$) and **Porto** (1hr., 3 per day, 800$). **Rodonorte** runs to **Vila Real** via **Amarante** (1hr., 5 per day, 2:15-9:30pm, 500$).

The **tourist office** (tel. 41 24 50), on Alameda de São Dámaso, faces Pr. Toural. From the bus station, take the busy commercial road to the right, walk uphill, and turn right at the fork; the tourist office is on the corner ahead. Maps are free. An electronic sign outside displays opening hours for all sights. (Open M-Th 9:30am-12:30pm and 2-6:30pm). A **branch office,** Pr. Santiago, 37 (tel. 51 87 90), conveniently located in the old city, has the same info (open daily June-Aug. 9am-6pm; Sept.-May 9am-12:30pm and 2-5:30pm). Free **luggage storage** is available at the tourist office and the bus station. **Emergency:** tel. 112; **police station** (tel. 51 33 34), at Alameda Alfredo Pimenta; **hospital** (tel. 51 26 12), on R. dos Cutileiros, near Matadouros. **Post office** (tel. 41 65 11), on R. de Santo António (open M-F 8:30am-6:30pm, Sa 9am-12:30pm); **postal code:** 4800. **Telephone code:** (0)53.

⌨️ ACCOMMODATIONS AND FOOD. Due to the scarcity of budget accommodations, Guimarães is best visited as a daytrip from Braga or Porto. For a heavenly sleep, try the **Casa de Retiros,** R. Francisco Agra, 163 (tel. 51 15 15; fax 51 15 17), run by the Redentorista religious order. From the tourist office, head through Pr. Toural and straight up R. Santo Antônio (veering right through the plaza); follow R. Francisco Agra from the left at the traffic circle. The pristine bedrooms come complete with full bath, radio, phone, and heating. The 11:30pm curfew is non-negotiable, and unmarried couples had best introduce themselves as *Senhor* and *Senhora.* (Breakfast included. Singles 3000$; doubles 5000$.) **Camping** is located 6km outside of town at **Parque de Campismo Municipal da Penha** (tel. 51 59 12). Take the road to Fafe, following the signs to Penha, or hop on the bus to Penha (15min., from the shopping complex, 220$). The campsite has a pool, bar, supermarket, and free showers. (280$ per person, children under 10 250$; 250$ per tent and per car. Reception open daily 8am-7pm. Open April 15-Nov. 15.) **Groceries** are sold at **Hipermercado Guimarães** (tel. 41 22 00), in the air-conditioned shopping center. Restaurants in the old city are generally very expensive. For something cheaper, try **Restaurante Mumadona,** Rúa Serpa Pinto, 260 (tel. 41 61 11), just down the hill from the castle. The food's nothing to write home about, but with soup for 150$ and meat dishes for 650-1250$, the credit card company won't be writing you either. (Open M-F 9am-midnight. Visa, MC, AmEx.)

☀️ SIGHTS. Guimarães is old, very old. In fact, it predates Portugal itself by a few centuries. The Galician countess Mumadona founded a Benedictine monastery here in the 10th century, and the founding of the city came a few years later. Though Mumadona's monastery no longer stands, her influence over the city is still evident in the **castelo,** which she also sponsored. Though it was nearly stripped to pave the city's roads, the castle, a grand granite structure perched on a hill near the town center, is one of Portugal's foremost national symbols. (Open daily July-Aug. 9:30am-7pm; Sept.-June 9:30am-5pm. Tower access 100$.)

Though the *castelo* protected its inhabitants from the Normans and the Moors, the Dukes of Bragança considered it too stuffy a place to live. So in the 15th century they built the versatile, spacious **Ducal Palace** next door, modeling it after the manor houses of northern Europe. A museum inside includes furniture, silverware, crockery, tapestries, and weapons once used at the palace. In the banquet hall, tables that once seated 15th-century nobles now serve presidents of Portugal at their powwows. At dinnertime, at least a quarter of the 39 fireplaces burn in an attempt to heat the building. (Open July-Aug. 9:30am-7pm; Sept.-June 9:30am-5pm. 400$, seniors and students 200$, Sunday morning free.)

The **Museu de Alberto Sampaio,** in the Renaissance cloister of the **Igreja Colegiada de Nossa Senhora da Oliveira,** is just to the left off Av. Alberto Sampaio (when walking towards the castle). The church entrance faces an arched medieval square and an outdoor temple. The museum, on Largo da Oliveira, displays late Gothic and Renaissance art. The 15th-century Gothic **Capela de São Brax** holds the granite tomb of Dona Constança de Noronha, the first duchess of Bragrança. The *oliveira* (olive tree) in the courtyard symbolizes the patron saint of Guimarães. (Church open daily 9am-noon and 3-6pm. Free. Museum open Tu-Su 10am-12:30pm and 2-5:30pm. 200$, seniors and students 100$, Sunday morning free.)

CALDAS DE GERÊS

Elegant Caldas de Gerês, though characterized by its spa and geriatric inhabitants, provides a logical base for accessing Parque Nacional da Peneda-Gerês. Caldas sits comfortably within a fiercely green valley, surrounded by private homes on the slopes of the neighboring mountains. While the town certainly accommodates visiting hikers, the real pastimes in Caldas are crossword puzzles and knitting. The quiet atmosphere makes Caldas an ideal base for explorations of the park.

🛈 ORIENTATION AND PRACTICAL INFORMATION. Caldas's spa dominates the center of town, about 50m above where the buses stop. Restaurants, cafes, *pensãos*, and the tourist office lie along Av. Manuel Francisco da Costa, just up and around the corner from the bus stop. **Buses** leave from **Empresa Hoteleira Do Gerês** (tel. 61 58 96) to **Braga** (1½hr., M-F 11 per day, Sa 10 per day, Su 7 per day, 6:30am-9pm, 550$). **Tourist Office:** (tel. 39 11 33; fax 39 12 82). From the bus stop, walk uphill along Av. Manuel Francisco da Costa until you see the office surrounded by a semicircle of shops. (English spoken. Open M-Sa 9am-noon and 2-6pm, Su 9am-noon.) The **Park Info Office** (tel. 39 01 10; fax 39 11 496) is located to the right of the tourist office (with the entrance behind you) and uphill. (English spoken. Maps available.) **Police** (tel. 39 11 37), one block from the tourist office, just off Av. Manuel Francisco da Costa. **Post office** (tel. 39 11 11 or 39 00 10; fax 39 00 16), off the rotary that leads uphill into the town's center (open M-F 9am-12:30pm and 2-5:30pm). **Telephone code:** (0)53.

🍴 ACCOMMODATIONS AND FOOD. There are so many *pensãos* in Caldas that the traveler has the upper hand. Weekdays and off-season prices are rarely fixed—try bargaining. A great option is **🏠Hospedaria Dormidas** (tel. 39 11 46). From the bus stop, walk downhill outside the town's border until you see the sign on the right (5-10min.). The owners, an eccentric and fun couple, offer apartment-style rooms, complete with porch, bathroom, and fireplace. Prices vary based on the time of year and the length of the stay. Another option is **Casa de Ponte,** Gerês, 4845 (tel. 39 11 25). From the bus stop, head downhill until you see the hostel on the left corner where the road splits. Spacious rooms with lots of light, elevated TVs, and low beds. Most have porches that peer out into the garden. Owner speaks English. (Curfew midnight. Singles 3000-4500$; doubles 6500-7000$. Credit cards accepted.) The pleasant **Camping Vidoeiro** (tel. 39 12 89; fax 45 24 50; aderepg@mail.telepac.pt; www.adere.pg.pt), is by the river, 1km outside of town. Facing the tourist office, take the uphill road to the left. Meals in Gerês are available at the *pensãos* throughout the town (as always, be aware that you must pay extra for bread, butter, or olives). **Pensão Adelaide** garners a crowd at one of the town's highest perches (soup 200ptas, meat dishes 1250-1600ptas; open noon-2:30 and 7-9:30pm). For some fast food places, walk down Av. Manuel Francisco da Costa, away from the center of town. The **Supermarket** there is the best bet for those not interested in spending many *escudos* (open 8am-12:30pm and 2:30-7pm).

⚐ EXCURSIONS. Though Caldas itself offers few attractions, one option is to explore the private, spa-owned **Parques de Témas.** The entrance is by the tourist office (170$, children under 12 80$; access to the pool 700$, under 12 400$). Don't feel like walking? The Vidoeiro Campsite rents **horses** for 1400$ per hr.

PARQUE NACIONAL DA PENEDA-GERÊS

Parque Nacional da Peneda-Gerês has been called Portugal's finest natural reserve. Each year it attracts swarms of local and foreign nature lovers, all looking to escape city smog for an invigorating breadth of flora, fauna, and landscape. The second-largest protected area in the country (after Parque Natural da Serra de Estrela), the crescent-shaped park is sandwiched along the Spanish border. Some might say that park officials at Peneda-Gerês have taken the reserve's "untouched" status too far—ambitious hikers must often brave unmarked trails (and unpleas-

WHO'S AFRAID OF THE BIG BAD WOLF?

Centuries ago the proverbial Big Bad Wolf was a burdensome and frightening reality for many villagers in the mountains of Peneda-Soajo, Amarela, and Gerês. Cattle, sheep, and goats that grazed in the hills above the villages lived at the mercy of the wolves that occupied the woodlands. During times of agricultural desperation, the wolves were even known to attack humans for food. As a result, villages began to hunt wolves to preserve their way of life. Successful hunters received special privileges and honors for their skills. The first hunt of the season occurred on the first Friday of Lent, and each home was expected to contribute a hunter. Anyone opting out of the hunt had to pay 12 liters of wine. During the hunts, the hunters used cleverly-fashioned *fojos* (traps); one of the traps they made involved a circular stone construction around a sacrificial lamb. The trap was inclined at such an angle that once the wolf entered, he could not get back out, and his days of huffing and puffing ended.

ant weeds and thorn bushes) to see the megalithic graves, Roman ruins, medieval churches, and small villages located inside the park.

Parque Nacional da Peneda-Gerês became Portugal's first protected area in 1971. The 72,000 hectares can be divided into the southern Serra do Gerês and the northern Serra da Peneda. The more casual hikers stay south while hard-core mountaineers head to the uncharted north. Travelers visiting Peneda-Gerês are best off heading to the southern section of the park, where the few roads provide scenic and manageable journeys. Bilingual officials in the Caldas de Gerês office can point you to some fun short hikes. Always bring one of the info office maps (530$) and a compass; long pants aren't such a bad idea either. While train service is non-existent, buses from Braga make daily runs to both Caldas de Gerês and Campo de Gerês (but not between the two sites).

NEAR CALDAS DO GERÊS: CAMPO DO GERÊS

Those interested in a less touristy, more youthful base will prefer Campo do Gerês over its older neighbor. **Rodaviaria** runs daily **buses** to **Braga** (M-F 7 per day, 6:50am-5:35pm; Sa 4 per day, Su 3 per day, 7:20am-5:35pm; 520$). There are not many housing options in Campo, but a **youth hostel** (tel. 053 35 13 39), once a dormitory for construction workers, offers rooms for 1500-1800$. For camping, try the **Parque de Campismo de Cerdeira** (tel. 35 10 05; fax 35 70 65), a lovely site north of the town's center.

VIANA DO CASTELO

Viana do Castelo (pop. 20,000) is an elegant and immaculate beach town. Rampant commercialism has yet to rear its ugly head in this beautiful stop-over between Porto and Galicia, Spain. Viana boasts some intriguing architecture, including a pleasant main plaza and a bridge designed by Gustave Eiffel, as well as a superb beach just a ferry ride away. Even when the beach fills in July and August, empty and enticing expanses of sand can still be found north of town.

◤ GETTING THERE

Trains run to Viana from **Porto** (2hr., 11 per day, 5:45am-12:35am, 720$) and **Tuy, Spain** (1¾hr., 3 per day, 11am-10pm, 400ptas).

▸ ORIENTATION AND PRACTICAL INFORMATION

Avenida dos Combatentes da Grande Guerra, the main drag along the Rio Lima, glitters from the **train station** south to the **port**. Most accommodations and restaurants are located on or just off the Avenida. The **old town** stretches east of the Avenida, while the fortress and sea lie to the west.

Trains: (tel. 82 22 96 or 82 12 15), at the north end of Av. Combatentes, under Santa Luzia hill. From the bus station, go left on Av. 28 de Setembro through a pedestrian underpass (15min.), or take the bus (110$). To: **Caminha** (30min., 7 per day, 8:06am-8:18pm, 240$); **Vila Nova de Cerveira** (1hr., 7 per day, 8:06am-8:18pm, 300$); **Porto** (2½hr., 12 per day, 6am-10:37pm, 720$); **Vigo, Spain** (2½hr., 3 per day, 9:18am, 2:41 and 8:19pm, 1440$).

Buses: Rodoviária sends local buses from **Central de Camionagem,** on the east edge of town. To **Braga** (1½hr., 8 per day, 7am-7:05pm, 570$). Express agencies **AVIC** (tel. 058 82 97 05) and **Auto-Viação do Minho** (tel. 82 88 34) run from Av. Combatentes. To **Porto** (1½hr., 5 per day, 8am-7pm, 750$, express 900$) and **Lisbon** (6hr., 5 per day, 8am-7pm, 2300$).

Taxi: Táxis de Viana (tel. 82 23 22 or 82 20 61). Or try Av. Combatentes.

Tourist Office: (tel. 82 26 20 or 82 49 71; fax 82 78 73), Pr. Erva, one block east of Av. Combatentes. From the train station, take the 4th left at the sharp corner, then a quick right. Maps and lists of lodgings. English spoken. Open M-Sa 9am-12:30pm and 2:30-6pm, Su 9:30am-12:30pm. A handy **info desk** at the train station has similar info. Open M-Sa 9am-12:30pm and 2-5:30pm, Su 2-5:30pm.

Currency Exchange: Montepio Geral, Av. Combatentes, 332 (tel. 82 88 97), near the train station. Open M-F 8:30am-3pm. Also has a 24hr. **ATM.**

Emergency: tel. 112. **Police:** (tel. 82 20 22), on R. Aveiro.

Hospital: Hospital de Santa Luzia, Av. Abril, 25 (tel. 82 90 81).

Post Office: (tel. 82 27 11), Av. Combatentes across from the train station. Open M-F 8:30am-6:30pm, Sa 9am-12:30pm. **Postal Code:** 4900.

Internet Access: Public library (tel. 82 85 80), R. Cândido Dos Reis. **Instituto de Juventude** (tel. 82 88 82), off Pr. Erva on R. Poço.

▌ ACCOMMODATIONS AND CAMPING

Except in mid-August, accommodations in Viana are easy to find, though not particularly cheap. *Quartos* (private rooms) are the best option. Small, informal *pensões* (usually above family restaurants) are slightly cheaper but lower in quality. Check the tourist office's list of accommodations or hunt on side streets off Av. Combatentes. Listed prices can drop by as much as 500$ in the off season.

Pensão Guerreiro, R. Grande, 14 (tel. 82 20 99), at the corner of Av. Combatentes. Bright rooms with high ceilings and big windows. Ask for a view of the port. Reservations recommended. Singles 2000$; doubles 4000$; triples 5000$. Visa, MC, AmEx.

Residencial Viana Mar, Av. Combatentes, 215 (tel./fax 82 89 62), off Pr. República. Large, luxurious rooms, all with phones. Breakfast included. Singles 2500$, with bath and TV 4000$; doubles 3500$, with bath and TV 6500$; triples with bath and TV 7500$. Visa, MC, AmEx.

Residencial Magalhães, R. Manuel Espregueira, 62 (tel. 82 32 93). From the tourist office, turn left onto Pr. República, then left again, and cross Av. Combatentes onto R. Manuel Espregueira. A homey, traditional establishment. Breakfast included. Singles 4000-6500$; doubles 5000-7500$; triples 6000-9500$. Visa, MC, AmEx.

Camping: Two campsites are found near the Praia do Cabedelo, Viana's ocean beach. Hop a "Cabedelo" bus (100$) from the bus station or from behind the train station (near the funicular stop). Or take the ferry, located at the end of Av. Combatentes (100$), and hike 1km from the 1st stop; signs point the way. **INATEL** (tel. 32 20 42), off Av. Trabalhadores. Tents for rent. Showers 100$. 500$ per person. Open Jan. 16-Dec. 15. **Orbitur** (tel. 32 21 67) is closer to the beach and better equipped. Showers included. 600$ per person, per tent, and per car. Open Jan. 16-Nov. 15.

☐ FOOD

The bloodthirsty will drool over the local specialty *arroz de sarabulho*, rice cooked in blood and served with sausages and potatoes. Most budget restaurants lie on the small streets off Av. Combatentes. The large municipal **market** (tel. 058 82 26 57) is in Pr. Dona Maria II, several blocks from Av. Combatentes (open M-Sa 8am-3pm). Hit **Brito's Auto Serviço**, R. Manjovos, 31, for groceries (open daily 8:30am-12:30pm and 2:30-8pm).

Maria de Perre, R. de Viana, 118 (tel. 82 24 10), the last side street on the left off Av. Combatentes heading toward the water. Delicious meals (especially the regional dishes) are complemented by an good selection of Portuguese wines and occasionally by live music. Leave the t-shirt and flip-flops at home. Soup 300$, entrees 950-1900$.

Restaurante O Vasco, R. Grande, 21 (tel. 82 46 65), on the side street across from Pensão Guerreiro. A clinically white interior with cheap, tasty specialties. Entrees 750-1500$. Open daily 11:30am-11pm. Visa, MC, AmEx.

Restaurante Dolce Vita, R. Poço, 44 (tel. 82 48 60), across the square from the tourist office. Wonderful Italian cuisine. Pizza 730-950$. Portuguese dishes 1150-1900$. Open daily noon-3pm and 7:30-10:30pm. Visa, MC, AmEx.

Restaurante Arcada, R. Grande, 34 (tel. 82 36 43). Relatively untouristed and popular with local families. Entrees 800-1000$. Open M-F 9am-10pm.

☐ SIGHTS

Contrary to popular belief, there is more to Viana than just sand. Though the beaches may be the town's main draw, architecture buffs will appreciate the buildings which make up Viana's center.

☐PRAÇA DA REPÚBLICA. Even in a country famed for its impressive squares, Viana's Praça da República is remarkable. Its centerpiece is a 16th-century fountain encrusted with sculpture and crowned with a sphere bearing a cross of the Order of Christ. The small **Paço do Concelho** (1502), formerly the town hall, seals the square to the east. Diagonally across the plaza, granite columns support the playful and flowery facade of the **Igreja da Misericórdia** (1598, rebuilt in 1714). An intriguing *azulejo* interior lies within.

CASTELO DE SÃO TIAGO DA BARRA. For great views of the harbor and ocean, visit Castelo de São Tiago da Barra, built in 1589 by Felipe I of Spain. *(From the train station, take the 2nd right off Av. Combatentes (R. Gen. Luis do Rego) and walk 5 blocks.)*

COLINA DE SANTA LUZIA. The cliff-like **Colina de Santa Luzia,** north of the city, is crowned by magnificent Celtic ruins and an early 20th-century neo-Byzantine church. To reach the hilltop, head 200m behind the train station and take the long stairway. Otherwise take the **funicular.** *(Daily, every hr. in the morning, every 30min. in the afternoon, 9am-7pm, 120$.)*

BEACHES. Anyone who loves the beach will love Viana. The recently renovated beach on **Rio Lima,** a short ferry ride across the harbor, offers beautiful gardens and play areas for children. You can also head directly for the **Praia do Cabedelo beach** via the **ferry** behind the parking lot at the end of Av. Combatentes. *(Daily every 30min.; July-Sept. 8:45am-midnight; May-June and Oct.-Dec. 8:45am-10pm; Jan.-Apr. 8:45am-5pm. 120$, 30$ per piece of luggage.)* Those in search of a pristine beach experience abandon Viana and head north to some of the cleanest and least crowded beaches in Portugal. **Vila Praia de Âncora,** 16km north of Viana, is the largest and most popular. **Moledo** and **Caminha,** farther north, are equally gorgeous. But Viana is still the best place to spend the night—plan your return trip ahead of time.

ALTO MINHO

The Alto Minho, set apart from Spain only by the crystal clear Rio Minho, could have inspired Henry David Thoreau to pen a second *Walden*. Rocky mountains rise between unspoiled small towns and wildflowers spring from riverbanks, broken only by cottage gardens. Intrepid travelers jump the train at stops between towns and camp in the farmers' fields (with permission, of course).

CAMINHA

One day Jesus and Peter were passing through these parts...
St. Peter: My Lord, what should this place be called?
Jesus: Caminha, Caminha (keep walking) we're in a hurry.
　　　　　　　　　　　　　　　　　　—an age-old Caminha legend.

While everyone else keeps on going, slip off the train into Caminha (pop. 20,000) and enjoy the hypnotically green hills, wide beaches, and peaceful medieval square. The village is slightly larger than its cousin five stops down the line, Vila Nova de Cerveira. The latter may have a youth hostel, but Caminha has a **beach.** Put on your bathing suit, turn left on the riverside road, and keep going along the river about 1.5km to bask under the sun or get whipped by the wind (on breezy days). The zealous will hop on the bus (10min.) or trek 3km to the wide, pristine **Praia de Moledo,** where the Rio Minho rushes into the Atlantic.

Caminha makes a good daytrip from Viana do Castelo or Vila Nova de Cerveira, as accommodations are generally expensive and difficult to come by. The **train station** (tel. 92 29 25), on Av. Saraira de Carvalho, has trains to: **Vila Nova de Cerveira** (10min., 8 per day, 8:50am-8:39pm, 130$); **Viana do Castelo** (30min., 9 per day, 6:07am-9:29pm, 240$); **Porto** (2-3hr., 8 per day, 8:48am-9:29pm, 900$). **AVIC buses** leave from the shopping center by the riverside road and head to **Porto** (2hr., 820$) and **Lisbon** (6hr., 3 per day, 2100$). The **tourist office** (tel. 92 19 52) is on R. Ricardo Joaquim Sousa. From the train station, walk straight ahead on Av. Manuel Xavier to the traffic circle, go down Tr. São João (diagonally to the right), and take the second left. (Open M-Sa 9:30am-12:30pm and 2:30-6pm.) For a cheap bite, check out **A Petisqueira** (tel. 058 72 14 78). With the tourist office entrance at your back, walk a couple blocks on Joaquin de Souzaan. This inconspicuous local hangout offers sizeable portions of fresh meat and fish. (Entrees 850-1500$.)

VILA NOVA DE CERVEIRA

Just 100m from Spain (close enough to hear Galicians partying at night), Vila Nova de Cerveira (pop. 11,000) is a sleepy town with lush mountain scenery, a historic town center, and most importantly, a great youth hostel. The only thing to see in the town itself is the 14th-century **castle,** now the luxurious **Pousada Dom Dinis—** walks atop its walls offer great views of the countryside. Hardy travelers can hike up the winding road, through heath and rocky outcrops, to the **Veado** (deer) statue (4km). From the main road just past town to the east, turn right and begin climbing at the sign reading *Lovelhe (Igreja)*.

🛈 **PRACTICAL INFORMATION.** The **train station** (tel. 051 79 62 65), off the highway half a kilometer east of town, has service to: **Valença do Minho** (25min., 8 per day, 9:10am-8:48pm, 170$); **Viana do Castelo** (1hr., 9 per day, 5:54am-9:17pm, 300$); **Porto** (2½hr., 7 per day, 8:25am-9:05pm, 900$). Three **bus** companies take the same route as the train—upstream to Valença and down the coast to Porto. **AVIC** and **A.V. Minho** depart from Cafe A Forja, R. 25 de Abril, 63 (tel. 051 79 53 11), between the hostel and the town center, to: **Valença do Minho** (15min., 10 per day, 8:10am-6:15pm, 205$); **Porto** (2¼hr., 5 per day, 1050$); **Lisbon** (6hr., 5 per day, 2400$). Vila Nova's **tourist office** (tel. 051 70 80 23), on R. Antônio Douro in Pr. Muntápio, is diagonally across from Igreja de São Roque. From the train station, turn left and the office is the first yellow building on the right. It offers **luggage storage.** (Open M-Sa 9:30am-12:30pm and 2-6pm.) **Emergency:** tel. 112; **police** (tel. 051 79 51 13), at

NORTHERN PORTUGAL

R. do Forte. **Post office** (tel. 051 79 51 11), on Por. Alto Minho next to the bank (open M-F 9am-12:30pm and 2-5:30pm); **postal code:** 4920.

⊓⌐⌐ ACCOMMODATIONS AND FOOD. To find the ⊠**Pousada da Juventude de Vila Nova (HI),** Largo 16 de Fevreiro, 21 (tel./fax 051 79 61 13), head to the left from the train station, then right at the fork, and then left at the Fonseca Porto mini-market (15min., signs lead the way). Guests enjoy large rooms, a grassy patio with a great view, TV with VCR, and a kitchen. Although there's usually plenty of space, the hostel hosts a summer camp and often fills to the brim with Portuguese youngsters. (Breakfast included. English spoken. Reception 8am-noon and 6pm-midnight. Call ahead. June-Aug. dorms 1500$; doubles 3200$, with bath 3700$. Sept.-May dorms 1200$; doubles 2700$, with bath 3200$.) The nearest **campground** (tel. 051 72 74 72) is 4km southwest in **Vilar de Mouros** (550$ per person, 500$ per tent, 450$ per car). Restaurants can be expensive, as there are only seven of them. At **Cafe-Restaurante A Forja,** however, upstairs at R. 25 de Abril, 63 (tel. 051 79 53 11), you can feast on *arroz de mariscos* (huge half portions 600$) and cheap local specialties. (Soups 150$. Meat dishes 500-800$. Open Tu-Su 8am-midnight.)

VALENÇA DO MINHO

Within easy reach of Vila Nova, Valença do Minho salutes Spanish Túy (Tui) from the entrance to northern Portugal. A 17th-century **fortaleza** (fortress) protects the town's historic section. Valença's stone arches and cannon portals frame stunning views of rolling hills and the Rio Minho. Some of the most historically rich aspects of Valença have sadly fallen victim to commercial tackiness. If you're the type that likes to shut your eyes and imagine that you're back in the 17th century, the traffic lights in the fortress courtyard and the numerous campers couched in the moat will no doubt spoil the illusion. Fortunately, the impressive stone walls still yield spectacular views of both Spain and Portugal. A road winds 4km up to the breathtaking summit of **Monte do Faro,** overlooking the coastline, the Vale do Minho, and the Galician mountains.

Valença is a stop on the Porto-Vigo **train** line with connections to: **Vila Nova de Cerveira** (15min., 9 per day, 5:40am-9:05pm, 160$); **Viana** (1 hr., 9 per day, 5:40am-9:05pm, 420$); **Vigo, Spain** (1hr., 2 per day, 1465$); **Porto** (4hr., 5 per day, 8:25am-9:05pm, 980$). From **Redondela, Spain** (1 stop before Vigo; 1260$), you can connect to Spanish RENFE trains serving points north. The **tourist office** (tel. 051 233 74) is on Av. Espanha in a log cabin-like building; exiting the train station, walk through the rotary and turn right on the main drag (open daily 9am-12:30pm and 2:30-6pm). **Pensão Rio Minho** (tel. 051 223 31) has spacious, tidy rooms next to the train station (singles 4000$; doubles 5500$; prices drop in off-season; Visa, MC, AmEx). The cheapest restaurants are in the old town. **Restaurante Cristina,** in the *centro comercial* next to the Lara Hotel (the pink and white striped building on the road leading to the castle) serves a hearty *prato do dia* for 750$. (Soups 250ptas. Meat dishes 800-1750ptas. Open daily 8am-midnight.)

AN ARMY OF DEER Vila Nova de Cerveira gets its name from the old Portuguese-Galician word for deer, an animal that turned out to be the town's unlikely war hero. Back in the days before Spain and Portugal were EU buddies, the Rio Minho frontier hosted countless skirmishes. At one point when the Spanish invaded the town, fleet-footed locals ran into the hills surrounding Vila Nova and tied torches to the horns of all the deer they could catch. When the Spaniards saw the hills filled with the torches of what they presumed to be a massive army, they gave up and fled. To this day, Vila de Cerveira rests quietly under the gaze of a huge metal deer sculpture, visible on the summit of the mountain behind town.

TRÁS-OS-MONTES

The country's roughest, rainiest, and most isolated region, Trás-Os-Montes ("behind the mountains") is light years off the beaten path. Though almost twice the size of its neighbor Minho, it has only a fraction of the population. Getting there epitomizes the Trás-Os-Montes experience. Train service (where it exists at all) is slow and rickety, and roads tend to be torturous and treacherous. But the landscapes of Trás-Os-Montes—considered the last untouched region of Western Europe—are some of the most incredible in all of Iberia. Hikers will delight in the isolation of unspoiled natural reserves in the Parque Natural de Alvão (accessible from Vila Real) and the Serra de Montesinho (north of Bragança).

Trás-Os-Montes has long been home to Portugal's political and religious exiles. Dom Sancho I practically had to beg people to settle here after he incorporated it into Portugal in the 11th century. And it was here that the Jews chose to hide during the Inquisition. Today, it is the region's isolation, combined with its beauty and tranquility, that is its biggest draw.

Trás-Os-Montes is quite distinct from the rest of the country. With its conical stacks of hand-cut hay and its old stone houses, it is one of the last outposts of traditional Portugal. The gastronomic specialities devoured in the houses hint at the region's rusticity: *cozido à Portuguesa* is made from sausages, other pig parts, carrots, and turnips. Visitors to the region can consume lots of bread and *feijoada à Transmontana* (bean stew) and then burn it off with some serious hikes.

HIGHLIGHTS OF TRAS OS MONTES

■ **Parque Natural de Montesinho,** utterly wild and wonderfully timeless (see p. 644).

BRAGANÇA

Built on rough ground, Bragança (pop. 40,000), the capital of Trás-Os-Montes, is a proud and steadfast wilderness outpost. While most visitors come for the clean air and blue skies, Bragança's impeccably preserved medieval old town draws its share of admirers as well. Because of the city's massive 13th-century castle, Bragança's frontier days live on in the imaginations of visitors. From its foothold on a terraced hilltop covered in hay and olives, Bragança is an excellent base for exploring the starkly beautiful terrain of the **Parque Natural de Montesinho,** which extends north into Spain.

▐ GETTING THERE

Buses run to Bragança from **Porto** (5hr., 8 per day, 12:20-11:15pm, 1400$) and **Braga** (5hr., 2 per day, 4pm and 1:15am, 1600$).

▐ ORIENTATION AND PRACTICAL INFORMATION

Buses let you out on the modern square fronted by the cafe-lined **Avenida João da Cruz** (to your right when standing with your back to the bus station's front entrance). Downward-sloping R. Almirante Reis leads to budget *pensões* and the **Praça da Sé** at the heart of the old town. To reach the **fortress,** situated on a hill west of Pr. Sé, take **Rua Combatentes da Grande Guerra** from Pr. Sé, walk uphill, and enter through the opening in the stone walls.

Trains: No train service. The Portuguese rail system does, however, organize a somewhat awkward combination bus-train route between Porto and Bragança (4 connections required). Eurail passes can be used to pay for this combo. You can pick up a train in **Mirandela,** the nearest station (accessible by bus).

Buses: Three competing agencies offer expresses to Porto and Lisbon. **Rodonorte** (tel. 073 30 01 83) buses leave from Av. João da Cruz to **Porto** via **Mirandela** and **Vila Real** (5hr., 4-6 per day, 6am-5pm, 1440$) and **Lisbon** (8hr., 3 per day, 6-11am, 2680$). **Rede Expressos** (tel. 01 310 31 11; www.rede-expressos.pt) buses leave from the same stop. Office open erratically, though always pre-departure. To: **Vila Real** (2hr., M-F 6 per day, Sa-Su 4 per day, 10:30am-9:45pm, 1250$); **Amarante and Guimarães** (2½hr., 13 per day, 1400$); **Porto** (5hr., M-F 8 per day, Sa-Su 6 per day, 12:20-11:15pm, 1400$); **Coimbra** (6hr., M-F 6 per day, Sa 5 per day, 7:40pm-2:10am, 1700$); **Lisbon** (8hr., M-F 8 per day, Sa-Su 6 per day, 8am-9pm, 2400$). **Internorte** runs to **Zamora, Spain** (2½hr., 1 per day, M-Sa 2pm, Su 5:45pm, 2050$) and **Braga** (5hr., 2 per day, 4:15pm and 1:15am, 1600$).

Taxis: (tel. 073 32 21 38 or 073 32 37 13). Cabs congregate across from the post office and old train station.

Tourist Office: (tel. 073 38 12 73; fax 073 33 19 13), Av. Cidade de Zamora. With your back to the bus station front entrance, cross the street, take a right, and walk 1 block (with the strip of grass to your right). Take the 1st left up the street. Continue to the top of the hill, keeping the small cement house with a cross to the right, and walk down the hill (with multicolored garages on the left and a cemetery on the right). The office is at the bottom of the hill on the right. Maps, free daytime **luggage storage,** and help finding accommodations. English spoken. Open M-F 9am-2pm and 2:30-7pm, Sa 10am-2pm and 2:30-6pm, Su 10am-1pm.

Currency Exchange: Banco Nacional Ultramarino, Av. João da Cruz, 2-6 (tel. 073 33 16 45), next to the post office, has **ATMs.** Open M-F 8:30am-3pm.

English Bookstore: Livraria Liz, R. Combatentes de G. Guerra, 178 (tel. 073 32 25 49), a few doors from Restaurante Pocas. Classic and trashy novels in English.

Emergency: tel. 112. **Police:** (tel. 073 33 12 67 or 073 33 12 51), behind the town hall.

Hospital: Hospital Distrital de Bragança (tel. 073 33 12 33), Av. Abade de Baçal, before the stadium on the road to Chaves.

Post Office: (tel. 073 30 03 50), at the end of Av. João da Cruz. Posta Restante, **fax,** and **telephones.** Open M-F 9am-5pm. **Postal Code:** 5300.

▟ ACCOMMODATIONS

Plenty of cheap *pensões* cluster about Pr. Sé and up R. Almirante Reis.

Pensão Poças, R. Combatentes da Grande Guerra, 206 (tel. 073 33 12 16). With your back to the bus station entrance, cross the street, take a right, and walk until the major intersection. Pass the gray building that says "Correio" on the right. Continue through the plaza with the tall cross and veer right down the street. The hostel will be on the left. Large and airy yet spartan and unattractive rooms are kept clean by the family that monopolizes the block; they own Restaurant Poças next door and the Charcutaria Poças across the street. Beds are firm but creaky and there's no heat in winter, but the price is right. Singles 2000$, with bath 2500$; doubles with bath 4000$.

Pensão Rucha, R. Almirante Reis, 42 (tel. 073 33 16 72), on the street connecting Pr. Sé to Av. João da Cruz. Follow the directions to Poças; Rucha is on the right just past the "Correio" building. The sign is *inside* the doors. Clean, decorated lodgings with communal baths. Large common room with TV. No heat. Singles 2500$; doubles 4500$.

Camping: Parque de Campismo Municipal do Sabor (tel. 268 20), 6km from town on the edge of the Montesinho park. From the **Caixa Geral de Depósitos** on the corner of Av. João da Cruz, yellow-and-blue #7 STUB buses head to the campground (10min., M-F 3 per day, 120$). If you choose to hike, be careful—the roads are narrow and the corners sharp. Open May-Sept. Electricity 100$. 200$ per person and per car, 150$ per tent. **Parque de Campismo Cêpo Verde** (tel. 993 71), on the road to Vinhais, 8km from town. Swimming pool. Open year-round. 500$ per person, 350$ per tent and per car.

🍴 FOOD

Bragança's few restaurants are pricey but the portions are hefty. Try hunting around Pr. Sé and Av. João da Cruz. The region is celebrated for *presunto* (cured ham) and *salsichão* (sausages), both available at **Supermercado Bem Servir,** R. Abílio Beça, 120, below Pr. Sé (open M-Sa 9am-1pm and 2-7pm). **Restaurante Poças,** R. Combatantes da Grande Guerra, 200 (tel. 073 33 14 28), off Pr. Sé, next to the *pensão* of the same name, serves large portions of regional specialties in a no-frills setting. The house specialty is *costeleta de vitela grelhada* (grilled steak; 1000$). (Entrees 900-1500$. Open daily 8am-midnight.) An easy place to grab a meal is **Dom Fernando Restaurante,** within the castle yard. (Entrees 900-1400$, salads 400-800$, *menú* 1500$. Open daily 8am-11pm.)

👁 🎵 SIGHTS AND ENTERTAINMENT

Uphill from the main part of Bragança sits the historic old town, with the brooding **castelo** as its centerpiece. The castle's **Museu Militar** has a wide range of military paraphernalia, from medieval swords to a World War I machine gun to African art collected by Portuguese soldiers. (Tel. 223 78. Open daily 9-11:45am and 2-4:45pm. 200$, free Sunday morning.) The venerable **pelourinho** (pillory) in the square in back of the castle bears the coat of arms of the House of Bragança. At the base of the whipping post is a prehistoric granite pig, where sinners and criminals were bound during the Iron Age. The **Domus Municipalis,** behind the church on the other side of the square from the castle, had cisterns in the 13th century and later became the municipal meeting house. If closed, the *senhora* across the street at #46 has the key (but will expect a tip). On the 3rd, 12th, and 21st of each month, **feiras** (fairs) take place near the hospital, 2km out of town. If you are in town at the time, they are definitely worth a visit. Take a taxi from the town center for 400$.

NEAR BRAGANÇA: PARQUE NATURAL DE MONTESINHO

One of the largest protected areas in Portugal, the 290 sq. mile Parque Natural de Montesinho is proof that parts of Western Europe are still untouched by tourism. Some 9000 inhabitants, divided among 92 villages, continue to live much as they have since the land was first settled in the 8th century. Rich with tradition, these villages preserve age-old communal customs and enact ancient rituals—such as the December 25th "Youth Men's Rite," when young men, adorned with shaggy suits and painted masks, skip throughout their villages in a tribute to Saturn.

Trekking on the old mountain paths linking the villages affords ample opportunity to mingle with the park's flora (oak, chestnut, pine, and cherry trees) and less frequently sighted fauna (the endangered Iberian wolf, royal eagle, and black stork, among others). The **information office** in Bragança, Bo. Salvador Nunes Teixeira, lote 5 (tel. 073 38 14 44; fax 073 38 11 79), is a necessary first stop. Walk downhill from the tourist office, take the first left on a *paved* street and the first left again. The staff provides tons of useful maps, brochures, and advice. Though trails are unmarked, the office provides military maps and can help plan hikes. (Open M-W and F-Sa 9am-12:30pm and 2-5:30pm.) There is no **camping** allowed in the park, but the information office rents **Casas Abrigos** (traditional houses) for reasonable prices (doubles 5000-7500$; quads 10,000$; 23-person rooms 50,000$).

VILA REAL

Vila Real (pop. 10,000) teeters over the edge of the gorges of the Corgo and Cabril Rivers in the foothills of the Serra do Marão. The charming and untouristed old town center is surrounded by new neighborhoods reaching into the hills, a main street swooning with the scent of rosebuds, and a few hopping cafes. As the principal commercial center for the southern farms and villages of Trás-Os-Montes, Vila Real is a good point of departure for excursions into the fertile fields and rocky slopes of the Serra do Alvão and Serra do Marão.

⌨ GETTING THERE

Buses run to Vila Real from **Porto** (2hr., 10 per day, 7am-9:20pm, 740-960$) and **Bragança** (5hr., 4-6 per day, 6am-5pm, 1440$).

🔢 ORIENTATION AND PRACTICAL INFORMATION

Vila Real's old neighborhood is centered around **Avenida Carvalho Araújo,** a broad tree-lined avenue that streams downhill from the bus station to the Câmara Municipal. All the action—cafes, shops, and hostels—is in this area. The bus lets you off at Rodonorte Station on **Rua Don Pedro de Castro;** head right after exiting the station to hit the main drag.

Trains: (tel. 32 21 93), Av. 5 de Outubro. To Vila Real's center, walk up Av. 5 de Outubro over the iron bridge onto R. Miguel Bombarda and turn left on R. Roque da Silveira. Continue to bear left until Av. Primeiro de Maio. Trains take longer than buses and require transfers at Régua. To **Porto** (4½hr., 6 per day, 7:31am-7:45pm, 990$).

Buses: Rodonorte (tel. 32 32 34), R. D. Pedro de Castro, on the square directly uphill from the tourist office. To: **Porto** (2hr., 6 per day, 6:25am-8:20pm, 960$); **Guimarães** via **Amarante** (3hr., 2-5 per day, 10am-5:20pm, 960$); **Bragança** (4hr., 4 per day, 8:45am-11pm, 1250$); **Lisbon** (7½hr., 4 per day, 8am-7:20pm, 2400$). **Rodoviária do Norte,** R. Gonçalo Cristóvão, 16 (tel. 37 12 34), uphill from Rodonorte. To: **Viseu** (2½hr., 2 per day, 1180$); **Bragança** (4hr., 3 per day, 1250$); Braga (4½hr., 5 per day, 1000$); **Coimbra** (4½hr., 2 per day, 1350$); **Lisbon** (7½hr., 2 per day, 2100$).

Taxis: 24hr. tel. 32 12 96. They cluster along Av. Carvalho Araújo.

Tourist Office: Av. Carvalho Araújo, 94 (tel. 32 28 19; fax 32 17 12), to the right and downhill from the bus stations. Info on Parque Natural do Alvão and other excursions. Some transportation schedules. Temporary free **luggage storage.** Some English spoken. Open June-Sept. M-F 9:30am-7pm, Sa 10:30am-12:30pm and 2-5pm; Oct.-May M-F 9:30am-12:30pm and 2-5pm.

Currency Exchange: Realvitur, Largo Pioledo, 2 (tel. 32 18 00), 4 blocks uphill from the tourist office and to the right. Open M-F 9am-7pm, Sa 9am-1pm. **ATM,** Av. Carvalho Araújo, 84, at Banco Pinto and Sotto Mayor, next to the tourist office.

Emergency: tel. 112. **Police:** (tel. 33 02 45), Largo Condes de Amarante.

Hospital: Distrital de Vila Real (tel. 34 10 41 or 300 500), in Lordelo, north of town.

Post Office: (tel. 32 28 19), Av. Carvalho Araújo, up from the tourist office. Posta Restante, telephones, and **fax**. Open M-F 9am-6:30pm. **Postal Code:** 5000.

TELEPHONE CODE	Vila Real's phone code is (0)59.

⌂ ACCOMMODATIONS

Accommodations cluster in the town center. Several cafes along Av. Carvalho Araújo advertise rooms upstairs.

Residencial da Sé, Trav. São Domingos, 19-23 (tel. 32 45 75). As you descend Av. Carvalho Araújo, it's down a sleepy side street to the right next to the cathedral. Clean, bright rooms, all with bath and TV. Request one with windows. Breakfast included. Singles 3500-5000$; doubles 6000-7000$. Visa, MC, AmEx.

Pensão Mondego and **Residencial São Domingos,** Trav. São Domingos, 33 (tel./fax 32 30 97 or 32 30 39), down from Residencial da Sé. Bright, carpeted rooms, all with TV, phone, and bath. Singles 2500-3000$; doubles 4000-6000$. No winter heating.

Camping: Parque de Campismo Municipal de Vila Real (tel. 32 47 24), R. Dr. Manuel Cardona, just outside of town. Get on Av. Marginal and follow the signs (10min.). 500$ per person, under 10 230$, 320$ per tent and per car. Free showers. Free swimming in the pool. Reception daily June-Aug. 8am-11pm; Sept.-May 8am-12:30pm and 2-6pm.

◘ FOOD

Restaurants and cafes around Av. António de Azevedo and Av. Primeiro de Maio cook affordable meals. For **groceries,** hit **Mercado da Praça,** R. D. Maria das Chaves, 75 (open M-F 9am-1pm and 3-7pm, Sa 9am-1pm). **Restaurante Nova Pompeia,** R. Carvalho Araújo, 82 (tel. 33 80 80), on the main drag, next to the tourist office above a popular cafe of the same name has low prices, high A/C. (*Prato do dia* 790$. Excellent, filling entrees 600-1100$. Open M-Sa 8am-midnight.) **Restaurante Museu dos Presuntos,** Av. Cidade de Orense, 43 (tel. 32 60 17), at R. D. Afonso III and R. Morgado de Mateus, serves numerous *presunto* (ham) combinations. Walk uphill from the tourist office, take the right fork, and turn left on R. Morgado de Mateus. (Entrees 950-1500$. Open M-Sa noon-3pm and 7-10pm.)

◙ ◘ SIGHTS AND ENTERTAINMENT

Most of Vila Real's sights lie outside of the city proper, but camera-toters still dote on three churches in town. The stodgy 15th-century **sé,** its simple interior divided by thick, arched columns, looms at the lower end of Av. Carvalho Araújo. Two blocks east of the cathedral, **Capela Nova** (New Chapel) blushes behind a floral facade. At the end of R. Combatentes da Grande Guerra, **Igreja de São Pedro** resounds with 17th-century *azulejos*. At night, locals rendezvous at the ensemble of cafes on Largo do Proledo. **Copos e Rezas, Billiards Bar,** and **Ritmin** are lively draws within steps of each other.

NEAR VILA REAL: MATEUS AND MOUNTAINS

While transportation for backpackers without wheels can be a pain, only a scarce few will regret a visit to the village of Mateus, 3km east of Vila Real, world-renowned for its rosé wine. The **Sogrape Winery,** on the main road from Vila Real, 200m from the turn-off for the Palácio Mateus, has a terrific free tour of the wine-processing center, which includes complementary and unlimited tasting. (Open daily June-Sept. 9am-noon and 2-4pm; Oct.-May 9am-noon and 2-5pm.)

Up the road from the Sogrape Winery glitters the Baroque **Palácio de Mateus,** featured on the label of every bottle of rosé wine. The palace boasts a beautiful garden and features an original 1817 edition of Luís de Camões's *Os Lusíadas*, Portugal's famous epic. (Tel. 059 32 31 21. Open daily June-Aug. 9am-1pm and 2-7:30pm; Sept.-May 9am-12:30pm and 2-6pm. Gardens 650$; with mansion 1000$.)

To get to Mateus, take the **Rodonorte bus** (see **Buses,** p. 645) from Vila Real to the nearby town of Abambres (10min., 7 per day, 7:30am-7pm, 170$). Ask the driver to let you off at Mateus; walk from Mateus to Abambres to catch the return bus to Vila Real. Many people **walk** from Vila Real to Mateus (30min.); the road loops, so follow signs south from Vila Real's train station. A **taxi** costs around 850$.

Using Vila Real as a base, hardy souls explore the **Parque Natural do Alvão,** a protected area reaching to the heights of the mountainous Serra country to the north. Visit the park's **information office,** Pr. Tronco, 17 (tel. 059 759 37), in Vila Real. From the tourist office, head uphill and take the right fork on R. Dr. Margarida Chaves. Keep straight past Pr. Diogo Cão and then curve left on Cruz das Almas. The office is on the corner with R. Stuart Carvalhais. (Open M-F 9am-noon and 2-6pm.)

MOROCCO المغرب

LIFE AND TIMES

Morocco has carved its identity out of a host of different influences. At the crossroads of Africa, Europe, and the Near East, Morocco is also the Far West of the Arab world. It is referred to as part of the Maghreb (meaning "that which is found to the west"), the area of North Africa bordering the Mediterranean Sea. The country is linked in both history and landscape to the rest of North Africa. It is both an ancient civilization descended from nomadic tribes and a modern nation that has struggled against imperial powers for its sovereignty.

HISTORY

PRE-ISLAMIC

Archaeological evidence along Morocco's Atlantic coast suggests that regions of the country have been settled for anywhere from 100,000 to 1,000,000 years. The **Berber** people arrived between 4000 and 2000 BC; evidence of the use of early Berber tools can still be found in rock carvings scattered throughout the High Atlas Mountains. Though the **Phoenicians** began to explore the area in the 12th century BC and developed small colonies along the coast, they exerted little control or influence over the area. The **Romans**, on the other hand, made their presence known. The sack of Carthage, near modern Tunis in Tunisia, in 146 BC brought about a major change in the history of Morocco. Rome became dependent on North Africa's agricultural supply and as a result, the Romans created the province of Mauritania Tingitana, in what is now Morocco. It was a client-state with a somewhat independent status. But when the *Pax Romana* deteriorated Morocco was not immune. The Romans abandoned Morocco in the 4th century AD. By 420 it was ruled by the Vandals, followed by a period of brief **Byzantine** rule. The problem that each of these civilizations faced was that it seemed nearly impossible to exert any control over the land as a result of the absence of any reliable overland route. As a result, the majority of the country remained unexplored for centuries.

THE RISE AND FALL OF ISLAM (669-1554 AD)

Morocco achieved stability in the in the late 7th and early 8th century when Muslim armies invaded the **Maghreb.** In 669 AD, **Uqba bin Nafi al-Fihri** spread the religion of the prophet Mohammed to Morocco. The Berbers could not hold off the Islamic troops, so instead of fighting they made peace with the leader Musa bin Nusayr and many converted to Islam. This set the stage for the Arab invasion of Spain.

Arab rule was short lived in Morocco, ending in 740 AD. Although Arabs remained in the Maghreb, they would not regain power until the 20th-century. Instead, a series of local Islamic dynasties rose up to take control of the area, though most rulers, including the current king, claim descent from the prophet Mohammed to legitimize their rule. **Idris Ibn 'Abdullah,** after fleeing Arabia, founded the first truly Moroccan state in 789 AD. When Idris was poisoned in 791 AD, his son moved the capital to Fez, but his kingdom did not last. Over the next few hundred years, Morocco was conquered by one minor dynasty after another, the most important of which was the **Almoravid Dynasty** from the Western Sahara, who founded Marrakesh in 1062, and the **Almohad Dynasty,** who conquered it in 1160.

A golden age during **Marinid** (a Berber dynasty that ruled from the 13-15th century) and then **Wattasid** rule (1244-1554) promoted a cultural and intellec-

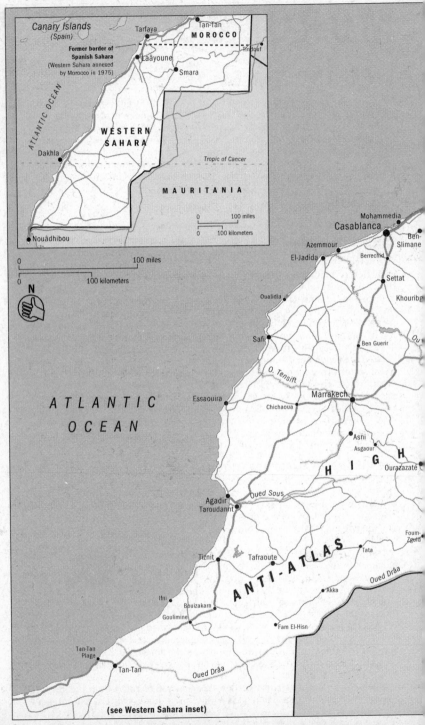

Canary Islands
(Spain)

Tarfaya

Tan-Tan

MOROCCO

**Former border of
Spanish Sahara**
(Western Sahara annexed
by Morocco in 1975)

Laâyoune

Tindouf

Smara

ATLANTIC OCEAN

WESTERN
SAHARA

Dakhla

Tropic of Cancer

MAURITANIA

Nouâdhibou

0   100 miles
0   100 kilometers

0   100 miles
0   100 kilometers

N

ATLANTIC
OCEAN

Mohammedia

Casablanca

Ben-
Slimane

Azemmour

Berrechid

El-Jadida

Settat

Khouribg

Oualidia

Ou

Safi

Ben Guerir

O. Tensift

Essaouira

Marrakech

Chichaoua

Ashi

Asgaour

HIGH

Ouarzazate

Agadir
Taroudannt

Oued Sous

Foum-
Zguid

Tiznit

Tafraoute

Tata

ANTI-ATLAS

Oued Drâa

Ifni

Akka

Bouizakarn

Goulimine

Fam El-Hisn

Tan-Tan
Plage

Tan-Tan

Oued Drâa

(see Western Sahara inset)

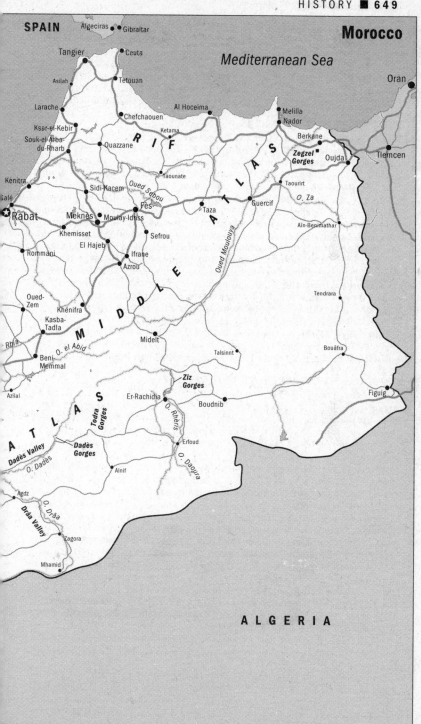

tual boom and tied Morocco to Spain. As Muslim influence in Christian Iberia waned, however, the Spanish turned aggressive. A second wave of Jewish immigrants from Spain fled to Morocco in 1492, when Queen Isabel and King Fernando forced them to choose between conversion or death. The Wattasids formed an army of refugees and converted or mercenary Christians to battle the conquering Spanish and Portuguese, but by the early 1500s, the Iberians had established control over Moroccan ports and a number of inland territories.

THE EUROPEAN CONTENDERS (1415-1912)

The **Sa'adis** drove out the foreign influences and reunited Morocco. Under **Ahmed el Mansour**—a.k.a. Ahmed the Gilded—Morocco expanded its trade in slaves and gold in Timbuktu and parts of the Sudan. When the **Alawite dynasty** overthrew the Saadis in 1659, they took over Marrakesh and the area around Fez. The Alawite dynasty that rules to this day.

Morocco was one of the first African countries to be colonized by European armies. In 1415, Portugal seized Sebta (Ceuta) and began erecting forts along the Moroccan coast. Spain took possession of Melilla in 1497; it is still a Spanish enclave today. The Saadians were able to push the Iberians back for several centuries, ruling the rest of the country from Marrakesh and remaining in power until the 17th century. England took possession of Tangier in 1662 and Spain began controlling the northern coast. France unsuccessfully began to invade North Africa after winning the battle of Isly in 1844; their major stroke of luck did not come until the death of Sultan Hassan of Rabat in 1893 and the ascension of his thirteen-year-old son Abdul Aziz to the throne.

In the end colonialism prevailed; there was dissension over which country should control Morocco—the last independent state in North Africa. Under the Treaty of Fez (March 30th, 1912) Morocco became a protectorate of France. The north fell to the Spanish, while Tangier was governed by a European council.

STRUGGLE FOR INDEPENDENCE (1921-1977)

In 1921, **Abd el Krim,** now considered the founder of modern Morocco, began to organize a rebel army against the Spanish in the Rif Country. Beginning in 1925, Spain took part in a war with the Rifian tribes over who was to control the area. In the same year these Rifian tribes actually managed to get as far as Fez before a combined French and Spanish army drove them out, restoring peace in 1927.

Morocco's nationalist movement begun in 1944 with the founding of the Independence Party, Istiqlal; by 1947 it had gained the support of the Moroccan Sultan, Moulay Muhammad V. The French deported nationalist leaders and exiled Mohammed without so much as a suitcase in 1953. The ensuing popular unrest combined with the revolt in Algeria forced the French to abandon their hard line. Mohammed was returned to the throne on November 18, 1955, and signed a treaty of independence for French Morocco on March 2, 1956. The independence of most of Spanish Morocco followed one month later.

Mohammed V's successor, King Hassan II, came to the throne in 1961 and introduced a constitution favoring pro-monarchists. This was heavily protested by the opposition party UNFP; in 1963, ten of UNFP's leaders, including **Ben Barka,** were implicated in a plot to overthrow the monarchy and sentenced to death. In 1965, King Hassan declared a national **state of emergency,** snagging direct control of executive and legislative powers. Hassan's 1970 constitution ended the emergency and restored limited parliamentary government, but two military coups and governmental divisions delayed democratic parliamentary elections until 1977.

Perhaps the most significant of King Hassan's political triumphs was the **Green March** in 1975. The Spanish, who had long since controlled the Spanish Sahara were confronted with a Saharan rebel group—the **Polisario Front**—at the same time as General Franco (see p. 53) lay dying. Hassan capitalized on

Spanish weakness, marching his troops into the Sahara. The Polisario Front was disorganized, the Spanish preoccupied, and Hassan was successful. Unfortunately, peace did not come easily or immediately. The Polisario Front gained support from the Algerians; they were at war in the Sahara until the UN declared a cease-fire in 1989.

MODERN MOROCCO (1977-1999)

Today Morocco is nominally a **constitutional monarchy:** though assisted by a parliament and a Chamber of Representatives, the king can dissolve parliament and easily manipulate the country's political parties. Hassan pledged to "improve the balance between legislative and executive powers," but Morocco's human rights abuses, alleviated only in part by a 1991 initiative, have failed to foster political freedom. Censorship rules out opposition from such groups as trade union activists and university radicals. A drought further sapped monarchist support, but after sluggish industrial growth, riots, and the drain of war in Western Sahara, Morocco began recovery in the 90s. Islamist movements throughout North Africa have kept Morocco on paranoid, though King Hassan's regime was stable in comparison to those in neighboring countries. Morocco's relations with neighbors are strained, particularly with Algeria, where illegal arms shuttling resulted in the closing of the Morocco-Algeria border in 1994. Southern Europe, also aligned against Islamist infiltration, has been taking a greater interest in Morocco, and has advocated tighter border controls.

CURRENT EVENTS

This past year was an eventful one for Morocco. Hilary and Chelsea Clinton brought attention to the country with their visit in the winter of 1999 as did Morocco's bid to host the 2006 World Cup. The issue of censorship in Morocco came to a head when two of Morocco's weekly newspapers, *Le Journal* and *Assahifa*, were suspended by the printer on the heels of failed government attempts to ban the titles, due to their advocation of freedom of the press.

The most pressing issue currently facing Morocco is what to do with the **Western Sahara.** In the summer of 1999 the UN finally named a special representative to oversee the referendum on independence for Western Sahara, which was annexed by Morocco in 1975 (see above). The date of the referendum has been set as July 31, 2000. At this point, the UN will determine if Western Sahara should be a part of Morocco or if the Polisario Front will be granted an independent state. The referendum has been delayed so long because of disagreements over who should be able to vote on both sides. The decisions have become a contentious and byzantine process of genealogical research—each potential voter is being vetted by having tribal elders quiz them on their family tree. To complicate matters, hundreds of thousands of Moroccans have recently been lured to the Western Sahara through tax breaks, subsidies, and public works projects. Sorting out these jumbled masses and deciding the status of the omitted has proven exceedingly difficult.

In June 1999, President Mubarak of Egypt and King Hassan II met and established a trade agreement between Morocco and Egypt. They signed nine accords, one of which established the Egyptian-Moroccan Company for International Trade. The leaders also discussed other issues relating to the Middle East. Both countries agreed that it is essential that Israel carry out all agreements it has made towards the peace process, and noted that the United States and Europe need to continue to contribute as well. Morocco remains in opposition to Israeli occupation of Jerusalem and what they consider to be Palestine.

Tragedy hit Morocco on July 23, 1999, when King Hassan II passed away. The seventy-year-old monarch had ruled the country since 1968. Postmortem, he was lauded by politicians from around the world for his contributions to the Arab-Israeli peace efforts. During his lifetime, Hassan survived two deadly assassination attempts, established the country's first constitution, built one of the largest mosques in the world (see **The Hassan Mosque**, p. 699) and united Moroccans over the Western Sahara issue. He is succeeded by his son, Sidi Mohammed, a technology buff, who is respected both by his people, and the international community.

LANGUAGE

Morocco is a paradise for polyglots. Though Classical Arabic (*al-Fusha*) is the official language of the country, it is rarely spoken and has become almost exclusively a written language. Most people speak a modern Moroccan dialect called *Darija;* almost everyone you meet will speak at least some French and will expect you to as well. In certain northern towns, Spanish is also common. Many Moroccans also speak English, but while they can bargain with you, their conversational ability is sometimes limited.

> In this book, **city names** appear first in English, then in Arabic. Therefore Fez is not written as Fés, the French spelling, or Faas, the Arabic spelling. Also, a massive shift from European street names is underway, so some of the streets mentioned in this book may go by a different title (here they are listed in both French and Arabic when necessary). *Rues* and *calles* (streets and roads) may revolt and become *zanqats, derbs,* or *sharías.*

RELIGION

The religion of Islam was founded by the Arab prophet Mohammed in 622 AD. Informed of his prophetic calling by the angel Gabriel, Mohammed is believed by Muslims to be the "seal of the prophets" and the end of a long chain of visionaries that included Abraham, Moses, Elijah, and Jesus. Mohammed led the polity until his death in 632, during which time his words and deeds were recorded in *hadiths* (sayings) that comprise the *Sunna*, or exemplary practice of Mohammed. His death provoked a "who rules?" crisis, spurring the Sunni and Shia division; the former believed his successor should be chosen among a community of men, the latter insisted that only pure spiritual leaders, who are blood relatives of Mohammed (*Imams*) should succeed.

At the heart of the Islamic faith is the Arabic word *islam*, meaning submission. The believer, or *Muslim*, accepts complete submission to the will of *Allah* (God) as embodied in the sacred scriptures of Islam and the Koran (book of recitation). This Arabic text is considered by Muslims to be a miracle—perfect, immutable, and untranslatable; it replaces all earlier revealed books and is the final definitive form of God's word. Unlike the Christian conception of Jesus, the Islamic view considers Mohammed a human messenger of God. All practicing Muslims must adhere to the five pillars of Islam. These are: the formal profession of faith, prayer towards Mecca five times daily, alms-giving, fasting during the month of Ramadan, and, if possible, a pilgrimage to Mecca.

What Morocco may lack in cultural cohesion, it makes up for in religious uniformity. More than 99% of all Moroccans are Sunnī Muslim, though Morocco also has a small Jewish minority and an even smaller Christian one. Islam is the official state religion. The king is often referred to as "Amiir al-Mu'miniin," or "Commander of the Faithful," the traditional title of a Caliph (religious leader).

Moroccan Islam is somewhat unique. While there is the inevitable difference between popular and orthodox Islam in Morocco, there is less of a gap between the intellectuals and populace than in other Arab countries. There is religious diversity to the extent of whether or not someone is Sufi. Sufism is linked to mysticism, and is based on the belief that Muslims will find the truth of God's love and knowledge through a personal experience with God. Sufis

UNDERSTANDING RAMADAN It is believed that Mohammed received the Koran during the month of **Ramadan.** Fasting during this holy month is the fourth pillar of Islam. Between dawn and sunset, Muslims are not permitted to smoke, have sexual intercourse, or let any food or water pass their lips; exceptions are made for women who are pregnant or menstruating, people who are sick, and people who are traveling (though all must make up the fast at a later date). Fasting is meant to teach Muslims to resist temptation and thereby control all their unchaste urges. In addition, by experiencing hunger they are meant to better understand the plight of the poor and to be more thankful for the food which Allah has provided them. Finally, Ramadan inspires a sense of community. Ideally, Muslims read the Koran during the daylight hours. As soon as the sun sets, they break the fast and begin a night of feasting, visits to friends and relatives, and revelry, only to begin fasting again at dawn. It is insensitive to eat in public during Ramadan.

were once quite politically influential; they are still a large presence, but their influence in politics has faded. Morocco has had its share of Islamic fundamentalist movements, but they have been substantially weaker than those in other North African countries, due to the popular belief in that the king is a religious as well as political leader.

THE ARTS

ART AND ARCHITECTURE

Diverse architectural forms define Moroccan landscapes and cityscapes. An intense climate, combined with Berber austerity and Islamic privacy give **Berber architecture** an enclosed and stark nature. Kasbah, the monumental houses of the Berbers, feature central courtyards, dark and narrow passageways, animal shelters, simple high slope-walled towers, thick walls, and plain facades. *Qsour* (plural of *qsar*; or fortified Berber villages) house densely packed "apartments." Both are made with *pisé* (packed earth), but are unfortunately gradually turning to ruins, unable to withstand wind and sand storms.

In the 10th century, Fez residents built the first Moroccan **mosques** (sometimes called *djemmas* or *masajid*), al-Andalus and the Kairaouine. The *qibla* (wall) contains the prayer niche *(mihrab)* and indicates the direction of Mecca. There are two basic designs for mosques: Arab style, based on Mohammed's house with a pillared cloister around a courtyard, and Persian style with a vaulted arch on each side. Attached to most mosques, Koranic schools (**madrasas**) have classrooms, libraries, and a prayer hall around a central courtyard and fountain.

Because of a desire to avoid idolatry, Muslim artists are forbidden from portraying figures of people, animals, or even plants. The result is a style of incredibly ingenious geometric and calligraphic decorations. Colorful patterns swirl across tiles, woodwork, stone, and ceramic. In less doctrinaire times, Almoravid artists slipped in designs that vaguely resemble leaves and flowers. **Calligraphy,** particularly elegant renderings and illuminations of the Qur'an, became another outlet for creativity as well as religious devotion.

Sultans reserved their most dazzling designs for **imperial palaces,** with long, symmetrical reception and dwelling rooms studded with decorative gates, hidden gardens, and tiny pools and fountains. The diversity of styles is truly incredible.

! Non-Muslims may not enter Moroccan mosques, but tourists can gawk at the splendor through doorways. Out of respect, visitors should stay away during services (five times daily; Fridays at midday).

CRAFTS

Of Moroccan handicrafts, **carpets** are the most popular with tourists. There are two types of carpets: rugs and *killims*. The difference is that rugs have a shag ruffle and *killims* do not. Price is based on age, the intricacy of design, the type of dye, and materials used. The most expensive carpets will be old, with very detailed embroidery, with vegetable dyes instead of chemical dyes, and made of wool or linen, not cotton. Carpets from the Rif or Middle and High Atlas mountains are filled with a wide variety of colorful markings. Those from Rabat and other coastal cities are modeled on the famed Turkish carpets.

Fez has been the center of a renowned **leather** industry since the 15th century. High-quality Moroccan leather can be purchased in Morocco for a fraction of its international price. Fez is also the center for Moroccan **pottery** and is famous for its classic blue and white designs. Saharan and Berber **terracotta** ware and roof tiles are also common. The South is known for distinctive and chunky **silver jewelry**, often inlaid with colorful stones or plastic. Moroccan woodwork is amazing; craftsmen seem to effortlessly turn blocks of cedar wood into intricate boxes, chess pieces, and desk sets.

All these handicrafts are sold in **souqs** (markets). *Souq*s target tourists for the sale of craftwork. Bargaining is key in buying anything. In general, the final price should be about 50% of the seller's starting price. When you walk in, act uninterested—even the slightest sign of interest gives merchants something to work with. To avoid getting hassled, declare that you've done your shopping already or claim student status. If you're interested in something but can't get the right price, try walking out the door and down the block: the owner is likely to chase after you with a better price; even if he doesn't, you'll find the same thing two stores down.

FOOD AND DRINK

Moroccan chefs lavish aromatic and colorful spices on their dishes—pepper, ginger, cumin, saffron, honey, and sugar are culinary staples. No matter how delicious everything may seem, be prepared to get sick at least once. Even those who take every precaution may still end up running to the bathroom on an hourly basis. Bottled mineral water is always recommended. A policy of peeling all fruit and cooked vegetables. The truly cautious should avoid salads and raw vegetables, or at least request that the restaurant wash them in purified water. *Kefta*, or any meat dish sold on the street, can be delicious but often dangerous. The meat grinders used to clean the meat are rarely cleaned, providing an ideal breeding ground for *E coli* and other bacteria. In general, beware of anything sold by street vendors.

TYPICAL FARE

Cuisine in Morocco consists mainly of couscous, tajine, and soups. **Tajine** is a stew that is steamed in a hot oven within a cone-shaped clay dish. It usually consists of some kind of meat, chicken, lamb, or pigeon along with an assortment of vegetables, olives, and prunes. Vegetarian forms of tajine are common as well. **Couscous** is a seminola-grain pasta about the size of sesame seeds, and also served with meat or vegetables. The most popular of the Moroccan soups is **harira**, a salty chick-pea soup, sometimes consuming meat (it is served every day during Ramadan). **Brochettes** and **honey-soaked pastries** are everywhere, as are delicious Moroccan breads.

Other common dishes include **poulet** (chicken), which can be prepared either *rôti* (roasted on a spit with olives) or *limon* (with lemon). Pricier and harder-to-find specialties include **mechoui**, whole lamb spitted over an open fire, or **pastilla**, a combination of pigeon or chicken, onions, almonds, eggs, butter, cinnamon, and sugar under a pastry shell. For a lighter treat, slurp sweet natural yogurt with mounds of peaches, nectarines, or strawberries, or try an oily Moroccan salad with finely chopped tomatoes, cucumbers, and onions. Snackers munch briny olives (about 1dh per scoop), roasted almonds, dried chick-peas, and cactus buds (1dh bud). Oranges are the cheapest, sweetest, safest fruit in the country.

EATING

The restaurant scene in Morocco consists mainly of tourist-oriented restaurants Small, and often undiscovered local restaurants can be found in the medina. A complete meal includes a choice of entree (*tajine*, couscous, or perhaps a third option), salad or *harira*, a side of vegetables, and yogurt or an orange for dessert. Almost every Moroccan main course includes meat; *couscous aux legumes* (couscous with vegetables) probably has the least meat. For vegetarians, the best bet is to cook with produce from the market, or request an omelette at restaurants. Less expensive *tajine* is made with *kefta* (a ground beef cooked in an array of herbs and spices) and often served on a baguette, as is *Merguez (*a spicy beef or lamb sausage).

Lunchtime spans from noon to 2pm, dinner between 7 and 9pm. Still, many restaurants will serve food at any time. If a service charge isn't automatically included, a 10% **tip** will suffice.

DRINKING

Drink only **purified water** by **Sidi Ali** and **Sidi Harazem.** If you get a bottle that isn't completely sealed, return it—chances are the bottled has been filled with tap water. Orange Juice and other fruit drinks are popular, but make sure that they are diluted with purified water and not tap water.

Despite Islam's prohibition of alcohol, Morocco is a wine-lover's paradise. The local wines are excellent and have won international recognition. While the two best local wines are the Cabernet Medallion and Beauvillion (about 80dh a piece), the less expensive Vabernet du President, Amazir, and Guerraine Rouge are also quite good (all about 35dh). Moroccan, French, and Spanish **wines** are available in most supermarkets and some restaurants (but not in the medina). Watery local **beer,** usually Stork or Flag Speciale, is cheap but not particularly good. Moroccan **bars** are entirely male and focus on heavy drinking rather than socializing; otherwise, they are pricey and tourist-oriented. They also tend to attract sleazy types. Instead, hang out in the many Moroccan coffee houses where you can get inexpensive Moroccan **coffee** and **tea.** Tea, the national drink, was introduced by the English in the 18th century. Green tea with fresh mint leaves and lots of sugar seems to be almost a staple of the Moroccan diet.

SPORTS

Moroccans are deeply passionate about soccer, and there are intense rivalries between competing clubs. Their national team was undefeated in qualifying matches for the 1998 World Cup; once in the cup, they were on the verge of advancing to the second round before they were edged out by Norway. Basketball runs a distant second to soccer, but it is still quite popular. Participatory sports abound. Skiing is possible in Ifrane and Ourika Valley (late Dec.-early March), hiking everywhere, water sports on the Atlantic coast, and biking nationwide.

CULT FICTION Paul Bowles has become somewhat of a cult figure in Morocco and is considered one of America's best expatriate writers. He initially gained fame through his involvement in radical politics, but Bowles turned from politics to travel after marrying Jane Auer in 1938, and he ultimately settled in Morocco on the advice of Gertrude Stein. It was there that he began to use Moroccan drugs to enhance his creativity (don't get any ideas) and started writing fiction. His first and most famous novel, *The Sheltering Sky* (1949) details the lives of an American couple and their struggle with the Moroccan culture and themselves. Many reviewers likened the novel to the works of Poe (who happened to be Bowles' childhood idol) and Hemingway. From that point on, most of Bowles's fiction was set in Morocco, though his only other piece to gain much fame was *The Spiders House* (1955). When Jane died in 1973, Bowles' work showed signs of a loss of hope. His career, however, received a boost in the early 1990s when Bernardo Berotolucci made the movie of *The Sheltering Sky*, starring Deborah Winger. He continues to live in Tangier today.

FESTIVALS AND HOLIDAYS

Moroccans celebrate several secular and Islamic holidays. The dates of all Muslim holidays, which begin at sundown before the day listed, are based on the lunar calendar and are valid for 2000 only. Be aware that many establishments are closed during most holidays, particularly the religious ones.

DATE	FESTIVAL	LOCATION
December 9, 1999 to January 8, 2000	Ramadan	National
January 1	New Year's Day	National
January 11	Independence Manifesto	National
March 3	Throne Day	National
March 6	*Ras as-Sana*	National
May 1	Labor Day	National
May 14	*Ashoora*	National
May 23	National Day	National
June 14	*Mawlid an-Nabi*	National
July 9	Young People's Day	National
August 14	Allegiance of Wadi-Eddahab	National
August 20	Anniversary of the King's and People's Revolution	National
November 6	Anniversary of the Green March	National
November 18	Independence Day	National
Nov. 27 to Dec. 27	Ramadan	National

RECOMMENDED READING

LITERATURE ABOUT MOROCCO

In Morocco, by Edith Wharton. A collection of episodic descriptions of Rabat, Salé, Fez, and Meknes.

Morocco That Was, by Walter Harris. A turn-of-the-century journalist's diary, featuring a wry account of a Brit's kidnapping by the international bandit Raissouli.

The Voices of Marrakech, by Bulgarian Nobel Prize recipient Elias Canetti. Eloquently records a European Jew's encounter with Moroccan Jews.

The House of Si Abd Allah, edited by noted scholar Henry Munson. An oral history of a Moroccan family which provides insight into the country's social history.

The Sheltering Sky, The Spider's House, Days: Tangier Journal, by Paul Bowles. Numbingly gorgeous introductions to the country and to Bowles (see **Cult Fiction,** above).

MOROCCAN LITERATURE TRANSLATED INTO ENGLISH

Love With a Few Hairs, The Lemon, and **M'hashis,** by Muhammad Mrabet. Bits of contemporary Moroccan life, translated by Paul Bowles.

The Battle of Three Kings, by Youssef Necrouf. An entertaining account of medieval violence and intrigue under the Saadian dynasty.

Dreams of Trespass (Tales of a Moroccan Girlhood), by Fatima Mernissa. The author's story of growing up in Fez in the 1950s.

ESSENTIALS

The information in this section is mostly designed to help travelers get their bearings once they are in Morocco. For information about general **travel preparations** (including passports and permits, money, health, packing, international transportation, and more), consult the **Essentials** section at the beginning of this book. Essentials also has important information for those with specific concerns: **women travelers** (p. 39); **solo travelers** (p. 40); **older travelers** (p. 40); **bisexual, gay, and lesbian travelers** (p. 41); **travelers with disabilities** (p. 41); **minority travelers** (p. 42); **travelers with children** (p. 42); and travelers with **dietary needs** (p. 43).

GETTING THERE AND AROUND

The transportation network between southern Spain and northern Morocco is frequent and reliable enough to allow one to "do" Ceuta or Tangier as a daytrip. The easiest way to reach Morocco is through Algeciras (see p. 231), which is well connected to the rest of Spain by train and bus. From Algeciras, ferries depart all day long to both Ceuta (see p. 670) and Tangier (see p. 663). Tangier is also accessible from Gibraltar (see p. 233) and Tarifa (see p. 255), though ferry service is much more infrequent.

Once in Morocco, navigating the winding streets can be difficult. A little hint: the chief intersection of every Moroccan city's *ville nouvelle* (new city) is that of rue Hassan II and rue Mohammed V.

BY PLANE

Royal Air Maroc (in Casablanca tel. (2) 31 41 41; in U.S. tel. (800) 344-6726; in U.K. tel. (0171) 439 43 61), Morocco's national airline, flies to most major cities in Europe, including Madrid and Lisbon. Domestically, a network of flights radiates from the Mohammed V Airport outside Casablanca. Planes fly daily to Marrakesh, Agadir, Tangier, and Fez; flights occasionally go to Ouarzazate as well.

If you hope to see a lot of Morocco in a short time, flying can be both a convenient and affordable option; you don't have to commit to a flight until the day before and the price of the ticket always remains the same, whether you buy it 3 months, 3 weeks, or 3 days beforehand. Royal Air Maroc (RAM) and its competitor, Regional Airlines, fly to all major domestic cities. RAM offers the best deals for students and the under-26 crowd, though Regional airlines often flies more frequently within the county.

BY TRAIN

Where possible, trains are the best way to travel. They are faster than buses, more comfortable, and fairly reliable and prompt. Second-class tickets on trains are slightly more expensive than corresponding CTM bus fares; first-class tickets cost around 20% more than second-class ones.

The main line runs from Tangier via Rabat and Casablanca to Marrakesh. A spur connects Fez, Meknes, and points east with the main line at Sidi Kasem, near Meknes. There is one nightly *couchette* train between Fez and Marrakesh.

Air-conditioning and "non-smoking" cars are usually available. Tickets bought on board cost at least 10% more and may cause you all kinds of trouble with the conductor. No student fares are available. Be wary of old schedules that show times for the Atlantic coast, south of Casa—this route has been out of service for a few years now. InterRail (see p. 34) *is* valid in Morocco, but Eurail is not. Fares are so low, however, that InterRail is not worth using in Morocco.

BY BUS

In Morocco, wherever and whenever you want to go, there is a bus waiting to take you. They're not all that fast, and they're not very comfortable, but they're extremely cheap and travel to nearly every corner of the country. **CTM (Compagnie de Transports du Maroc),** the state-owned line, has the fastest, most luxurious, most reliable, and generally most expensive buses (though "expensive" here means just a few more dirhams). In many cities, CTM has a station separate from other lines; reservations are usually not necessary. *Let's Go* lists CTM stations in each city. Several dozen other private companies operate as well. Though they may offer more frequent departures, the comfort level is so low, you'll probably wish you had waited for the next CTM. Other private companies, called **cars publiques** (a.k.a. souq buses), have far more departures and are generally slower, less comfortable, and cheaper. In the bus stations, each bus company has its own info window; window-hop for information on destinations and schedules.

The **baggage check** at CTM bus depots is usually safe. Your bags, however, may not be accepted for storage if you don't have padlocks on the zippers. Private bus companies also have baggage checkrooms; they're generally trustworthy and accept any kind of bag.

BY TAXI

Two separate hordes of taxis prowl Moroccan streets: intra-urban *petit taxis* and inter-urban *grand taxis*, both dirt cheap by European standards. *Petit taxis*, small Renaults or Fiats that can each hold a strict maximum of three passengers, are all painted in one color depending on the municipality (red in Fez, blue in Meknes, etc.) and can't leave the city or take you to the airport. Make sure the driver turns the meter on; they are required to do so by law. If the driver won't turn it on, take another cab; at the very least, agree on the price before you go (around 50% of what the driver asks is fair). There is a 50% surcharge after 8pm. Don't be surprised if the driver stops for other passengers or picks you up with other passengers in the car, but if you are picked up after the meter has been started, note the initial price.

Grand taxis, typically beige or dark blue Mercedes sedans, are the most expensive way to travel, but do go just about everywhere. Unlike their *petit* cousins, they don't usually cruise for passengers, instead congregating at a central area in town. They hold up to six passengers (four in the back, two in the front), but if you plan on taking a long ride, you might buy two spaces to allow for extra room. A taxi won't go until it is filled with passengers going in the same direction. Ask other passengers what they are paying to avoid being ripped off.

BY CAR AND BY THUMB

There are two reasons to rent a car in Morocco: large group travel, or travel to areas not reached by Morocco's public transportation system. Otherwise, car rental is unnecessary. Moroccan roads can be very dangerous; reckless passing maneuvers, excessive speed, shoddy maintenance, and poorly equipped vehicles are all par for the course.

Hertz, Avis, and **Europcar** all rent cars; expect to pay about 400dh per day for an economy car, including taxes and insurance. Large local firms such as **Afric Car, Moroloc,** and **Locoto** offer cars for considerably less money but are also less reliable. Both international and local firms are easy to find in all major cities.

Once in your car, you face a myriad of complications, the most serious being police **security checks.** Virtually any trip you take will bring you to at least one checkpoint. Expect to be pulled over and asked to produce your passport and proof of rental. One tactic if pulled over is to immediately ask for directions, either in French or Arabic. You also may be stopped for **traffic violations,** real or not. The fine is payable on the spot in dirhams and may be negotiable; asking for a receipt could be construed as provocative. Whatever you do, do not travel with drugs (which are illegal) in your car.

Routes goudronées (principal roads), marked "P," are paved and connect most cities. **Pistes** (secondary roads), designated "S," are less smooth. If travelling in the **desert,** be sure to bring at least 10 liters of bottled water for each person and for the radiator. Move rapidly over sand; if you start to bog down, put the car in low gear and step on the gas. If you come to a stop in soft sand, push rather than sink. **Gas** cost about 10dh per liter.

Driving in Morocco without the **Michelin map** of Morocco all but ensures that you will get lost. Fortunately it is available both abroad and in Morocco. Even with the map, you still should inquire about specific road conditions. One place to make such inquiries is the automobile association, **Touring Club du Maroc,** 3 av. F.A.R., Casablanca (tel. (2) 20 30 64).

Almost no one in Morocco **hitches,** although flagging down buses and trains may sometimes feel like hitchhiking. Transportation is dirt cheap by European and North American standards. If Moroccans do pick up a foreigner, they will most likely expect payment for the ride. Hitching is more frequent in the south and in the mountains, where transportation is irregular.

MONEY

Budget travelers, once over the shock at the expense of arriving here, especially appreciate Moroccan prices. You may not be able to do Morocco on $5 per day, but you'd have a hard time spending $10. Do be warned that any Western-looking person is a target for the omnipresent hustlers (called faux guides in local lingo) and some are amazingly persistent, aggressive, and even insulting.

In Morocco, **banking hours** are Monday through Friday 8:30 to 11:30am and 2:30 to 4:30pm, during Ramadan from 9:30am to 2pm. In the summer, certain banks close at 1pm and do not re-open in the afternoon. Do not try the **black market** for currency exchange—you'll probably be swindled. The following exchange rates are from August 1999. For more information on money, see p. 14.

US$1 = 9.80 DIRHAMS (DH)	1DH = US $0.10
CDN$1 = 6.55DH	1DH = CDN $0.15
UK£1 = 15.65DH	1DH = UK £0.06
IR£1 = 13.09DH	1DH = IR£0.08
AUS$1 = 6.25DH	1DH = AUS $0.16
NZ$1 = 5.17DH	1DH = NZ $0.19
SAR1 = 1.61DH	1DH = SA R0.62
SP 1PTAS = 0.06DH	1DH = SP 16.16PTAS
POR 1$ = 0.05DH	1DH = POR 19.47$
EURO 1= 10.30DH	1DH = EURO .10

MOROCCO

SAFETY AND SECURITY

EMERGENCY TEL. **Police:** 19. **Highway services:** 177.

Unfortunately, Morocco has received a bad rap among European travelers. While the **crime rate** is higher than in Spain or Portugal, there is more to Morocco than just hustlers, prostitutes, and drugs. However, visitors should be suspicious of people offering free food, drinks, or cigarettes, as they have been known to be drugged. Large cities like Tangier and Fez are filled with fake guides (see below) offering a tour of the city for a small price; they should be avoided, as there is a reason these people aren't employed by hotels and tour agencies.

Debates between the Moroccan government and the Algerian-based Polisario Front over possession of the Western Sahara resulted in a guerrilla war until the late 1980s. The UN called a ceasefire in 1991, but there are still a number of unexploded landmines in the area. Travel to Western Sahara is difficult and not recommended. Those interested in traveling there can obtain clearance information from the Moroccan Embassy.

In Morocco, foreigners with **drugs** have regularly been arrested and faced severe punishments. Keep in mind that although drugs may seem more prevalent in Morocco, the Moroccan government enforces drug laws more strictly than most governments and frequently uses road-blocks and other measures to search for drug peddlers and users.

Women travelers will probably have extra difficulties traveling through Morocco without a male companion At the very least, women should never travel alone. Everyone, but especially women, should dress conservatively, both to avoid potential problems and as a sign of respect for Moroccan culture. For more info, see page 39.

> **HUSTLERS AND FAUX GUIDES.** Moroccans are generally extremely hospitable and friendly toward travelers. Unfortunately, it is often hard to distinguish between genuine hospitality and the friendly traps of an exploiter. Hustlers are responsible for Morocco's extraordinarily low tourist return rate (between 10 and 20 percent). Faux guides, loitering around attractions and city gates, usually have two motives: getting a cut of whatever you buy from local merchants (which is added to the cost of your purchase) or extorting money out of you to leave you alone. You may at times feel under siege—subtle threats are part of many hustlers' rhetoric—but rest assured that they pose almost no physical danger if you just keep your cool and repeat either "Non, merci" or "La shukran" enough times. Hustling is illegal and cops will help if you ask. On the flip side, these are simply unemployed Moroccans trying to make a little money from foreigners that, to them, are quite wealthy. These hustlers do not reflect the overall culture of Morocco, though they are often people's main association with the country. If you want a certified guide (especially in the High Atlas Mountains, Fez, or Marrakesh), go to the tourist office and hire an official guide there for 120dh for a ½-day, 150dh per full day. They generally know more historical information than faux guides and are great for keeping other hustlers away.

HEALTH

All travelers in Morocco face a different set of health issues than in Iberia. It is not generally advisable to drink tap water (or drinks with ice in them), and street vendors may sell aged or otherwise bad food. No vaccinations are required to enter Morocco, but the CDC (see p. 21) recommends **hepatitis A** or immune globulin (IG). Travelers who will be spending longer amounts of time in Morocco or visiting more rural areas might consider getting a **typhoid fever** vaccination, a **hepatitis B** vaccination, or taking **malaria** pills. For general health information, see page 20.

ACCOMMODATIONS

YOUTH HOSTELS

The **Federation Royale des Auberges de Jeunesse (FRMAJ)** is the Moroccan Hosteling International (HI) affiliate. Beds cost 20-40dh per night, and there is a surcharge for non-members everywhere but in Casablanca. Some hostels sell HI memberships on the spot. Call ahead for reservations as beds can be popular. To reserve beds in high season, get an International Booking Voucher from FRMAJ (or your nearby HI affiliate) and send it to the hostel four to eight weeks in advance. You'll probably need to bring your own sleepsack and towel, and there are usually curfew and lock-out times. For hostel addresses, write to FRMAJ, Parc de la Ligue Arabe, B.P. 15998, Casa-Principale, Casablanca 21000 (tel. (2) 47 09 52; fax 47 20 24). For info on your national youth hostel association and other general info, see **Accommodations,** page 25.

HOTELS

Although there is an official star system for rating hotels in Morocco, the number of stars reflects little more than price. Hotels that are not part of the system are not necessarily worse—their standards vary greatly—but are usually cheaper. Rooms can vary widely even within a particular hotel, so ask to see another room if you don't like the first. Or find another hotel, often next door. Cheap hotels in Morocco are really cheap—as little as 40dh per night. Listings are generally divided between medina and *ville nouvelle* establishments. Medina hotels are usually cheaper than their *ville nouvelle* counterparts, but less comfortable and with fewer amenities. Hot showers, when available, may cost extra (usually less than 10dh). Cold showers are usually free. Many hotels do offer laundry service.

CAMPING

Camping is popular and cheap (about 10dh per person), especially in the desert, mountains, and beaches. Like hotels, conditions vary widely. You can usually expect to find restrooms, but electricity is not as readily available. Use caution if camping unofficially, especially on the beaches, as theft is a problem.

KEEPING IN TOUCH

Most useful communication information (including **international access codes, calling card numbers, country codes, operator** and **directory assistance,** and **emergency numbers**) is listed on the **inside back cover.**

PHONES. Morocco has recently invested hundreds of millions of dollars into modernizing its telephone system, resulting in markedly improved services. Pay phones accept either coins (2dh will cover most local calls) or Moroccan phone cards. The rates for the two types of phones are the same. Available at post offices, phone cards are usually in denominations too large to be practical. Entrepreneurial Moroccans hang around phone banks (found near all post offices) and let you use their phone cards. You pay them only for the units used—typically 2dh per unit, a rate not much worse than doing it yourself. To use the card, insert and dial 00. Once the dial tone turns into a catchy tune, dial the number.

Phone offices *(teleboutiques)* are located in most cities. If you can't find one, head to the post office—they always have at least one phone for international calls. To make a collect call, ask the desk attendant at the local telephone office to place a call *en P.C.V.* ("ahn PAY-SAY-VAY"). Write down your name and the country, state, city, and telephone number you want to call. Collect calls can also be made from payphones; simply dial 12 and ask to call *en P.C.V.* Remember that the initial zero (0) in **city codes** is dialed only when calling from another area within Morocco; from outside of Morocco the number is omitted. Local calls do not require dialing any portion of the city code.

The best way to make international calls is with a **calling card;** see page 29 for more details. Numbers for major international calling cards (AT&T, MCI, Canada Direct, BT Direct, Ireland Direct) are listed on the inside back cover. If they are not listed it means that there is no international direct dial code for that country.

MAIL. Sending something **Air mail** *(par avion)* can take a week to a month to reach the U.S. or Canada (about 10dh for a slim letter, postcards 4-7dh). Less reliable **surface mail** *(par terre)* takes up to two months. **Express mail** *(recommande* or *exprès postaux)*, slightly faster than regular air mail, is also more reliable. Post offices, shops, and some *tabacs* sell postcards and **stamps.** For very fast service (2 days to the U.S.), your best bet is DHL (www.dhl.com), which has drop-off locations in most major cities.

EMAIL. Yes, email has reached Morocco. Cyber-cafes aren't everywhere, but they can be found at least in most major cities, as well as in the more touristed towns. *Let's Go* lists internet access and rates whenever applicable.

EMBASSIES AND CONSULATES

In Morocco, most embassies and consulates are open Monday through Friday from around 8am to noon; some reopen after lunch until 6pm.

Algerian Embassy: 46-48 rue Tarek Ibr Ziad, B.P. 448, **Rabat** (tel. (7) 76 55 91; fax 76 22 37).

British Embassy: 17 bd. Tour Hassan, B.P. 45, **Rabat** (tel. (7) 72 09 05 or 72 09 06; fax 70 45 31). **Consulates:** 43 bd. d'Anfa, B.P. 13, #762, **Casablanca** 01 (tel. (2) 22 17 41 or 29 58 96; fax 26 57 79); 41 bd. Mohammed V, B.P. 2122, **Tangiers** (tel. (9) 94 15 57; fax 94 22 84).

Canadian Embassy: 13 Bis, Jaafar Assadik, B.P. 709, Agdal, **Rabat** (tel. (7) 67 28 80; fax 67 21 78).

Irish Embassy: Refer to the Irish Embassy in Lisbon (above). In case of emergency, contact any Commonwealth embassy.

Australian Embassy: Refer to the Canadian Embassy in Rabat (above). In case of emergency, contact any Commonwealth embassy.

New Zealand Embassy: Refer to the New Zealand Embassy in Spain (above). In case of emergency, contact any Commonwealth embassy.

South African Embassy: Rabat (tel. (7) 70 67 60; fax 70 67 56).

Tunisian Embassy: 6 av. Fés, **Rabat** (tel. (7) 73 06 36; fax 73 06 37).

U.S. Embassy: 2 av. Marrakesh, **Rabat** (tel. (7) 76 22 65; 24hr tel. 76 96 39; fax 76 56 61). **Consulate:** 8 bd. Moulay Youssef, **Casablanca** (tel. (2) 26 45 50; fax 20 41 27).

EXPLORING MOROCCO

Morocco offers an enticing medley of sights, sounds, and smells. Despite its proximity to Europe, Morocco is no more "European" than is any other Arab country and provides an excellent introduction to the Arab World. Morocco is blessed with a huge variety of climates and cultures in a relatively compact area (though short distances do not necessarily imply ease of travel). Many visitors who are limited to visiting, say, the four imperial cities (Fez, Meknes, Rabat, and Marrakesh), can hardly believe that they haven't crossed any international borders during their trip, so contrasting are the local atmospheres.

HIGHLIGHTS OF MOROCCO

- **Fez,** with its 9000-street **medina** and exquisite **Bou Inania Madrassa** (see p. 679).
- A solitary walk through the Roman ruins of **Lixus** (see p. 690).
- **Rabat's** eerily incomplete **Hassan Tower** and **Mohammad V Mosque** (see p. 690).
- Castles in the sand at Jimi Hendrix's old hangout, **Essaouira** (see p. 702).
- **Marrakesh,** especially its otherworldly bazaar, **Djemâa el-Fna** (see p. 707).

THE MEDITERRANEAN COAST

Northern Morocco comprises Mediterranean ports and beaches and the jagged Rif Mountains. As the region most accessible from Spain, the Mediterranean coast is a likely point of entry into the country. Because of its proximity to Europe and the prevalence of European influence throughout its history, the coast is not always considered "real Morocco." Still, a visit to the Mediterranean cities provides a taste of the country (but may not leave visitors with the most favorable impression). Those interested in observing true Moroccan culture should keep pushing south.

TANGIER طَنجَة

For travelers venturing out of Europe for the first time, disembarking in Tangier (pop. 554,000) can be a distressing experience (see warning below). Even so, Tangier attracts visitors with its peculiar, captivating charm, a result of its complex history. For centuries the region bounced from one imperial power to the next (Phoenicians, Romans, Portuguese, British, and Spaniards, to name a few), culminating in 1923 with the declaration of Tangier as an "international zone," in which the city was loosely governed by the U.S. and eight European powers. During this period, the ruling regime cared more about Tangier's image than about law enforcement. As a result, the city began to attract rich heiresses, drug users, spies, and Beat Generation poets. When Morocco declared its independence in 1956, the new government attempted to change Tangier's image, closing down most of the brothels and increasing police presence. But Tangier's days as an international zone have left behind a continued legacy. The Café de Paris—*the* cafe of WWII secret agents—churns out lattes, the Anglican church conducts mass, and a gay community remains visible; at the same time, goods still trade on the black mar-

> **!** Upon entering Tangier you will be harassed by people offering their services as guides. Do not trust any of them; most are hustlers, unemployed Moroccans hoping to make money off confused tourists. The best way to deal with the situation is to say *"la shokran"* (No thank you) when they approach you and keep walking. Pick a hostel or hotel before you arrive and either take a *petit taxi* or find your own way. Do not pay attention to their warnings that the hostels listed in *Let's Go* are bad, difficult to find, or closed down. (See **Hustlers and Faux Guides,** p. 660, and **Orientation and Practical Information,** below.)

MOROCCO

ket, hashish still flows from the Rif, and hotels still rent by the hour. Despite this legacy, Tangier is looking toward the future, inaugurating plans to improve the port facilities. While the maze-like medina (old town) overlooks the Mediterranean and European continent beyond, the *ville nouvelle* (new town) and its businesses are helping to move Tangier away from its past and into the 21st century.

GETTING THERE

The best way to get to Tangier is by ferry through Algeciras, not from Gibraltar. **Ferries** sail from **Tarifa** (1hr., 1 per day, Sa-Th 9:30am, F 9am, 2800ptas), **Algeciras** (2½hr., every hr., 7am-7pm, 3200ptas) and Gibraltar (M and W 8:15am, F 6:30pm). **Trains** run from **Rabat** (5½hr., 4 per day, 8am-1am, 87dh). **Buses** go from **Chefchaouen** (1 per day, 3pm, 33dh) and **Rabat** (5hr., 5 per day, 7:30am-1am, 80dh).

ORIENTATION

Compared to other Moroccan cities, Tangier is quite navigable. From the ferry terminal, you can take a blue *petit taxi* or walk to the center of town. If you take a **taxi**—which is advisable—either agree on the fare in advance (about 5dh to the center of town) or make sure the driver uses the meter. If you **walk,** leave the ferry terminal along the main road running through the port compound; it will lead you through the large double arches onto the **avenue d'Espagne.** On the right is a **CTM bus station;** the **train station** is 6km down the same road.

The sprawling **ville nouvelle** (new town) surrounds the port in all directions and houses most of the city's businesses. The town's central road is the **boulevard Pasteur.** To find this road, follow av. d'Espagne running parallel to the beach and take a right on the narrow rue Ibn Zohr after the Hotel Marco Polo. Follow this street up as it bends to the right and changes into rue Marco Polo (straight through an intersection). After one more block, you will run into the intersection of bd. Pasteur to your right and bd. Mohammed V to your left. Turn right onto bd. Pasteur toward **place de France,** the heart of Tangier's *ville nouvelle.* A right turn at pl. France onto rue de la Liberté and a short walk down a winding hill leads to the **Grand Socco,** which is Tangier's largest square and sits outside the west wall of the **medina.** The **Petit Socco** can be reached by crossing the Grand Socco and entering the medina on rue as-Siaghin, which runs through the medina. For an alternate route to the medina and the Petit Socco from the port, take a sharp right and climb the steep road to the medina entrance. The Petit Socco is a short walk up av. Mokhtar Ahardan. When you get to the sign that reads "Hotel Continental 100m" pointing to the right, turn left and walk for two blocks.

PRACTICAL INFORMATION

TRANSPORTATION

Airplanes: Royal Air Maroc (tel. 93 55 01), pl. France. To Marrakesh, Casablanca, Gibraltar, Barcelona, Madrid, and London. **British Airways** (tel. 93 52 11 or 93 58 77; fax 93 11 12), 1 block down rue de la Liberté off of pl. France. To **London** (W and Sa 9:55am). A taxi to the **airport,** 16km from Tangier, costs 70dh for up to 6 people.

Trains: Trains leave from **Mghagha Station** (tel. 21 09 98), 6km from the port (not the old station on av. d'Espagne). A *petit taxi* to the train station will cost around 15dh. 2nd-class to: **Asilah** (1hr., 1 per day, 13dh); **Meknes** (5hr., 3 per day, 7am-10:15pm, 77dh); **Rabat** (5½hr., 3 per day, 7am-10:15pm, 87dh); **Fez** (5½hr., 3 per day, 7am-10:15pm, 93dh); **Casablanca** (6hr., 3 per day, 7am-10:15pm, 114dh).

Buses: Non-CTM buses leave from av. Yacoub el-Mansour at pl. Jamia al Arabia, 2km from the port entrance. Ask blue-coated personnel or check the boards for ticket info. The standard price for luggage is 5dh. To: **Ceuta** (40min., 7 per day, 6:15am-2:45pm, 10dh); **Tetouan** (1hr., 10 per day, 7am-10pm, 14dh); **Rabat** (5hr., 15 per day, 5am-11:15pm, 57dh); **Casablanca** (6hr., 15 per day, 5am-11:15pm, 69dh); **Fez** (6hr., 10

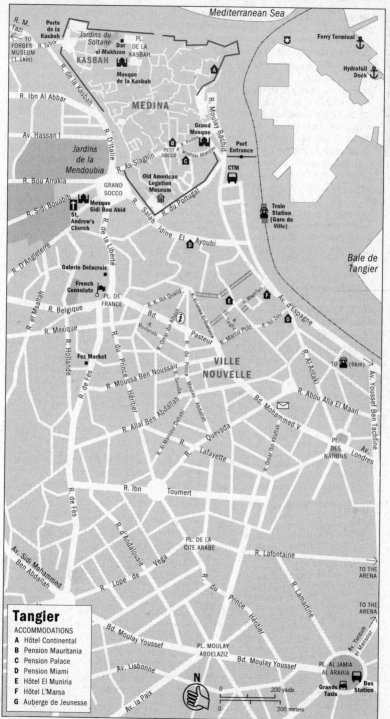

MOROCCO

Mediterranean Sea

Ferry Terminal

Hydrofoil Dock

R. M. Tazi

TO FORBES MUSEUM (1.1km)

Porte de la Kasbah

R. Tabor

Jardins du Soltane

Dar el-Makhzen

PL. DE LA KASBAH

KASBAH

A

R. de la Kasbah

Mosque de la Kasbah

R. Ibn Al Abbar

MEDINA

R. Moulay Rachid

Av. Hassan I

R. D'Italie

Grand Mosque

Port Entrance

Jardins de la Mendoubia

R. As-Siaghin

B
PETIT SOCCO
R. Post
Mokhtar Ahardan

C

CTM

R. Bou Arrakia

GRAND SOCCO

Old American Legation Museum

R. Sidi Bouabih

Mosque Sidi Bou Abid

St. Andrew's Church

R. du Portugal

R. Salah Idine El Ayoubi

Train Station (Gare de Ville)

R. D'Angleterre

R. de la Liberté

D

Galerie Delacroix

Baie de Tangier

R. el Msallah

French Consulate

PL. DE FRANCE

R. Belgique

Bd.

R. K. Ibn Qualid

R. Chakib Es-Ourssane

Magellan

E

F

Av. d'Espagne

G

R. Mexique

R. Moutanabi

R. du Omar Ibn Aliba

i

Pasteur

R. Tangib

R. Marco Polo

R. Ibn Zohr

R. Hollande

Fez Market

R. de Fès

R. du Prince Moulay Abdallah

R. Moussa Ben Noussair

Héritier

VILLE NOUVELLE

R. Al Antaki

TO (6km)

Av. Youssef Ben Tachfine

R. Allal Ben Abdallah

R. Al Mansour Dahabi

R. Seralia

R. Prince Moulay Abdallah

Bd. Mohammed V

R. Abou Alla El Maari

Quevada

R. Omar Ibn Khattab

PL. DES NATIONS

Av. Londres

R. Lafayette

R. de Fès

R. Ibn Toumert

PL. DE LA CITE ARABE

R. Lafontaine

TO THE ARENA

R. Lope de Vega

R. d'Andalousie

R. du Prince Héritier

R. Lamartine

Av. Sidi Mohammed Ben Abdallah

TO THE ARENA

Av. Yacoub el Mansour

Bd. Moulay Youssef

PL. MOULAY ABDELAZIZ

Bd. Moulay Youssef

PL. AL JAMIA AL ARABIA

Av. Lisbonne

Av. la Paix

N

PL. MOULAY ABDELAZIZ

Grands Taxis

Bus Station

Tangier

ACCOMMODATIONS

A Hôtel Continental
B Pension Mauritania
C Pension Palace
D Pension Miami
E Hôtel El Muniria
F Hôtel L'Marsa
G Auberge de Jeunesse

0   200 yards
0   200 meters

per day, 8:40am-9:30pm, 63dh); **Meknes** (5hr., 10 per day, 6am-2:15pm); **Marrakesh** (10hr., 5 per day, 6:45am-8:30pm, 115 dh). The **CTM Station** (tel. 93 24 15 or 93 11 72) near the port entrance offers pricier and more posh bus service. A *petit taxi* from the port to the terminal costs 12dh.

Ferries: Try **Voyages Hispamaroc** (tel. 93 31 13; fax 94 40 31) on bd. Pasteur, below Hôtel Rembrandt. Open daily 8am-12:30pm and 3-7pm. To reach the ferry companies directly, call **Trasmediterránea**, 31 av. de la Résistance (tel. 93 48 83); **Limadet Ferry** (tel. 93 39 14), av. Prince Moulay Abdallah; **Comanau,** 43 rue Abou Ala El Maari (tel. 93 26 49); or **Transtour,** 4 rue El Jabha Ouatania (tel. 93 40 04). The cheapest option is to buy a ticket at the port. You'll need a boarding pass (available at any ticket desk) and a customs form (ask uniformed agents). Near the terminal, pushy men with ID cards will try to arrange your ticket and obtain (and fill out) your customs card for 10dh. Just do it yourself. To: **Tarifa** (2hr., 1 per day, Sa-Th 3pm, F 7pm, 210dh); **Algeciras** (2½hr., 8 per day, 7am-9pm, Class B 2960ptas or 210dh); **Gibraltar** (2½hr., 3 per week, Tu, F, and Su 4pm, 250dh).

Grand Taxis: Quick transport to nearby locations (Tetouan, Ceuta, Asilah). Prices subject to bargaining, but a fair price is 20dh when taxis are full (6 passengers). They can be found everywhere, but they congregate by the main bus stop, the Grand Socco, and the intersection of bd. Pasteur and bd. Mohammed V.

Car Rental: Avis, 54 bd. Pasteur (open 8am-noon and 2-7pm). **Hertz,** 36 av. Mohammed V (tel. 32 21 65; fax 32 22 10; open M-Sa 8:30am-noon and 2-6:30pm, Su 9am-noon). Both charge 250dh per day, plus 2.50dh per km and a 20% tax. Minimum age is 21 for small cars, 25 for four-wheel-drive vehicles.

TOURIST, FINANCIAL, AND LOCAL SERVICES

Tourist Office: 29 bd. Pasteur (tel. 94 80 50). Friendly staff. Some English, French, and Spanish spoken. Free tourist brochures, and a nice road map of Morocco available on request. Open M-F 8:30am-noon and 2:30-6:30pm.

Currency Exchange: There is a branch of **BMCE** on most ferries and one in the port complex, although these only change cash. BMCE's main office in Tangier is located at 21 bd. Pasteur (tel. 93 11 25). No commission here or at other Moroccan banks. Open M-F 9am-12:45pm and 3-6:45pm. There is an **ATM** on bd. Pasteur. Travel agencies near the port are required to change money at official rates. Major banks line bd. Pasteur and bd. Mohammed V. Say *non* to hustlers offering exchange service.

Luggage Storage: At the **train station** (5dh per bag). Open 24hr. Also at the **bus station** (4dh per bag). Open daily 5:30am-12:30am.

English Bookstore: Librairie des Colonnes, 54 bd. Pasteur (tel. 93 69 55), near pl. France. Novels, books, and magazines on Moroccan culture, English classics, and popular French and Spanish fiction. Open M-F 9:30am-1pm and 4-7pm, Sa 9:30am-1pm.

EMERGENCY AND COMMUNICATIONS

Police: (tel. 19), located at the port and main train station.

Late-Night Pharmacy: 22 rue de Fez (tel. 94 21 85), two blocks from bd. Pasteur at pl. France across from Cinema Le Paris. They dispense medicine through tiny windows in the green wall on the left side of the entrance. Open M-Th 9am-1pm and 4-8pm, F 9am-12:30pm and 4-8:30pm, Sa 9am-1pm, Su 9am-8pm. Call if you have an emergency.

Medical Services: Red Cross, 6 rue el-Monoui Dahbi (tel. 94 25 17), runs a 24hr. English-speaking medical service. **Ambulance:** (tel. 93 33 00).

Post Office: 33 bd. Mohammed V (tel. 93 25 18 or 93 21 25), the downhill continuation of bd. Pasteur. Poste Restante and telephones. Open M-Th 8:30am-6:30pm, Sa 8:30am-12:15pm.

Internet Access: Halfway down bd. Pasteur. 15dh per hr. Open 9am-midnight.

Telephones: 33 bd. Mohammed V, to the right and around the corner from the post office. Open 24hr. There are dozens of teleboutiques around town as well.

TELEPHONE CODE Tangier's phone code is (0)9.

ACCOMMODATIONS

If you're unfazed by the frenzy that is Tangier, pick from a number of hostels in the medina; if you're a little overwhelmed by it all, stay in the *ville nouvelle*. Expect to pay around 50-60dh for a single and 80-90dh for a double, though rates may decrease by as much as 10dh in the winter.

MEDINA

The most convenient hostels cluster near **rue Mokhtar Ahardan** (formerly rue des Postes), off the Petit Socco. From the Grand Socco (see **Orientation,** above), take the first right down rue as-Siaghin to the Petit Socco. Rue Mokhtar Ahardan begins at the end of the Petit Socco closest to the port. At night the smaller streets off the medina can be unsafe.

Pension Mauritania (tel. 93 46 77), rue des Halmouahades at the Petit Socco. Follow directions to the Petit Socco (see above). Enter directly off the Socco. A backpacker's mecca. Shared toilets, free cold showers, and clean rooms. Great views of the medina and port from some rooms. Singles from 60dh; doubles 120dh; triples 150dh.

Hôtel Continental, 36 Dar Baroud (tel. 93 10 24; fax 93 11 43). From the Petit Socco, follow the signs; take rue Jemaa el Kebir (ex-rue de la Marine) downhill toward the port, until you hit Continental's blue gate. Veer left at the raised overlook. A truly grand hotel. The piano and bird cage in the lobby have aged better than the mattresses, but the Art Deco rooms ooze character. Showers are hot only in the mornings. Reservations recommended. Singles 257dh; doubles 326dh; triples 424dh. Breakfast included.

Pension Palace, 2 rue Mokhtar Ahardan (tel. 93 61 28). Downhill, on the alley exiting the Petit Socco to the right. Sanitary, if teeny-tiny, rooms. Clean communal bathrooms. The courtyard was featured in Bertolucci's film adaptation of *The Sheltering Sky.* Singles 40-50dh; doubles 80-90dh, with bath 120dh; triples 120-140dh, with bath 160-170dh; quads 160-180dh, with bath 200-220dh.

VILLE NOUVELLE

Hotels line av. d'Espagne as it heads away from the port. The best values lie a few blocks uphill toward bd. Pasteur and bd. Mohammed V.

Auberge de Jeunesse (HI), 8 rue el-Antaki (tel. 94 61 27), down av. d'Espagne away from the port and half a block up the road to the right, after Hôtel Marco Polo. A backpacker hotspot. The common room is the perfect place to find new traveling companions. New, firm dormitory beds. HI members 25dh; non-members 30dh. Showers 5dh. Office open M-Sa 8-10am, noon-3pm, and 6-10:30pm, Su 8-10am and 6pm-midnight; closes at 10:30pm in winter, though there is some flexibility.

Hôtel El Muniria (Tanger Inn) (tel. 93 53 37), rue Magellan. Take the 1st right after Hôtel Biarritz on av. d'Espagne, walking away from the medina, and follow as it winds uphill. No matter what the hustlers say, the hotel is open; just knock. William Burroughs wrote *Naked Lunch* in room #9 (unfortunately now the owner's room). Ask for room #4, where Jack Kerouac and Allen Ginsberg stayed. A great deal for Tangier, offering spacious rooms, hot showers, and towels. Even if you don't stay here, be sure to hit the relaxed, expat-frequented Tanger Inn Bar next door. Singles 100dh; doubles 120dh.

Pension Miami, 126 rue Salah Idine el-Ayoubi (tel. 93 29 00), off av. d'Espagne. 45 frayed turquoise and magenta rooms, handsomely carved high ceilings, and a balcony cluster on each floor. Basic communal bathroom. Singles 50dh; doubles 80dh; triples 120dh; quads 160dh. Hot showers 10dh.

Hôtel L'Marsa, 92 av. d'Espagne (tel. 93 23 39), away from the port on the main drag; you can't miss its restaurant (see **Food,** below), which juts out onto the sidewalk. Clean rooms with closets and mirrors. A good deal for the location. Hot showers 7dh. Laundry 5dh per piece. Singles 80dh; doubles 120dh; quads 200dh. Visa, MC.

MOROCCO

📷 FOOD

MEDINA

The medina dining experience begins at the **Grand Socco,** where you can stall-hop while feasting upon Moroccan treats (including some delicacies usually only available during Ramadan). On the corner near the pl. France sprawls a huge vegetable and meat **market.** Head from the Grand Socco in the direction of the Petit Socco and you will find a slew of inexpensive local eateries.

Restaurant Hammadi, 2 rue de la Kasbah (tel. 93 45 14), the continuation of rue d'Italie just outside the medina walls. The only Moroccans here are the waiters and serenading musicians. Despite the touristy veneer, the food is excellent. Avoid lunchtime, when tour groups fill every seat. Specialties are *tajine* (40dh) and couscous (45dh). Entrees 25-60dh. A 20% tax is added to each meal. Beer and wine served. Visa, MC, Eurocard. Open 11am-3pm and 7pm-midnight.

VILLE NOUVELLE

International cuisine is available throughout the *ville nouvelle*—more a product of enterprising Moroccans than a vestige of Tangier's international past. The restaurants along av. d'Espagne tout unspectacular and overpriced *menus touristiques* for 50dh and up. Beachfront restaurants run by the high-end hotels are just what you'd expect—expensive and boring. You're better off starting at pl. France and scouting from there. For hot sandwiches, try the storefronts off bd. Pasteur.

Restaurant Africa, 83 rue Salah Eddine el-Ayoubi (tel. 93 54 36), just off av. d'Espagne near Pension Miami, opposite Hôtel Valencia. The name seems to indicate a sure-fire tourist trap, but the food and prices prove otherwise. Big 4-course *menu du jour* 50dh. Entrees 25-80dh. Beer served. Open daily 9am-12:30am.

L'Marsa, 92 av. d'Espagne (tel. 93 19 28). This popular restaurant and cafe has outdoor dining and a mixed Italian and Moroccan menu. Praiseworthy pizzas (30-35dh) and 10 flavors of Italian ice cream (12-25dh). Entrees 25-70dh. Open daily 5am-3am, Sept.-May closes at midnight.

Marco Polo (tel. 32 24 51 or 94 11 24), on the corner of av. d'Espagne and rue el-Antaki. Pleasant restaurant and bar where German and smoke are everywhere. Entrees 30-80dh. Visa, MC. Open noon-midnight; bar open until 3am.

Restaurant Miramar (tel. 94 40 33), on av. d'Espagne near the big hotels. A surprisingly cheap beach spot. Entrees 30-60dh. Open 10am-11pm; bar open until 3am.

👁 SIGHTS

IN AND NEAR THE MEDINA

📷DAR EL-MAKHZEN. An opulent palace with handwoven tapestries, inlaid ceilings, and foliated archways, the Dar el-Makhzen was once home to the ruling pasha of Tangier and is now a **Museum of Moroccan Art.** The collection includes intriguing exhibits of ceramics, carpets, silver jewelry, weapons, and musical instruments, with plaques in French and English. *(Near the Mosque de la Kasbah. Tel. 93 20 97. Open W-M 9am-12:30pm and 3-5:30pm. 10dh.)*

MARKETS. The medina's commercial center is the **Grand Socco.** This busy square and traffic circle is cluttered with fruit vendors, parsley stands, and kebab and fish stalls. In the colorful **Fez Market,** local merchants cater to Tangier's European community. *(Uphill on rue de la Liberté, across pl. France, and two blocks down rue de Fez on the right.)* Berbers from the Rif come to the **Dradeb district** (west of the Grand Socco along rue Bou Arrakia and northwest on rue de la Montagne) to vend pottery, olives, mint, and fresh fruit. *(Thursdays and Sundays.)*

OLD AMERICAN LEGATION. If you're looking for something different, try the Old American Legation. In 1820 this former home of the U.S. ambassador became the first foreign property acquired by the United States. The museum contains many documents relating to Tangier's international past, including correspondence between George Washington and his "great and magnanimous friend," Sultan Moulay ben Abdallah. The ever-changing selection of art ranges from 16th-century maps to photographs of the 1943 Casablanca conference. The friendly curators will give excellent tours on request, although restoration efforts may limit accessibility. *(8 rue d'America. In the far corner of the medina, at the farthest point from the water. Tel. 93 53 17. Look for the yellow archway emblazoned with the U.S. seal. Open M-F 10am-1pm and 3-5pm. Free, but donations are appreciated.)*

OTHER SIGHTS. 17th- and 18th-century bronze cannons hide in the **Jardins de la Mendoubia,** a peaceful park that seems far away from the excitement of the Soccos. *(Opposite rue de la Liberté, where rue Bou Arrakia joins the Grand Socco through the big white gate marked #50.)* Rue Riad Sultan runs alongside the **Jardins du Soltane,** where artisans weave carpets, and continues to **place de la Kasbah,** a sunny courtyard and adjacent promontory offering a view of Spain and the Atlantic Ocean. With your back to the water, walk straight ahead toward the far right corner of the plaza, where just around the corner to the right the sharp **Mosque de la Kasbah** rears its octagonal minaret.

VILLE NOUVELLE

ST. ANDREW'S CHURCH. British expats congregate in and around St. Andrew's Church, designed by the British to look like a mosque; even the Lord's Prayer is carved in decorative Arabic. Surrounding gardens and benches offer respite from the medina. Mustafa, the caretaker of 32 years, leads informal tours. *(Rue Amengnedu Sud. Take a left as you enter the Grand Socco from rue de la Liberté and then a quick left onto rue Amengnedu Sud. Tours daily 9:30am-12:30pm and 2:30-6pm. A tip of a few dh is appreciated. Sunday communion 8:30am, morning service 11am.)*

OTHER SIGHTS. Though run by the French Cultural Center, the **Galerie Delacroix** also displays works by Moroccan and foreign artists. All works either depict Tangier or were painted in the city. The museum closed for repairs as of June 1999. *(Rue de la Liberté, heading toward the medina. Open Tu-Su 11am-1pm and 4-8pm. Free.)* The city's most recent monumental construction is the towering **New Mosque,** an ochre-and-white structure on pl. el-Koweit. *(Southwest of the Grand Socco along rue Sidi Bouabib. Visits by non-Muslims are prohibited.)*

♫ ENTERTAINMENT

Pl. France has hosted Tangier's social activity since the city's heyday. The most popular evening activity is sipping mint tea and people-watching from a cafe on bd. Pasteur. The **Café de Paris,** more elegant than its neighbors, hosted countless *rendezvous* between secret agents during WWII (on the left coming from the Grand Socco; tea and coffee 5-6dh; open daily 5:30am-11pm). Another pleasant option is **Café Central,** a favorite of William S. Burroughs (off the Petit Socco; same hours and prices). Cafes tend to attract a male crowd, but female tourists should not be afraid to grab a table and a mint tea—it's perfectly acceptable.

The best place for a quiet drink with little hassle is the pub-like **Tanger Inn.** Those in search of a quiet drink can try the relaxed **Negresco,** 20 rue Mexique (tel. 93 80 97), off the pl. France. The city's longest-running bar, Negresco regularly attracts resident expats and backpackers. (Beer 15-18dh, mixed drinks 30-35dh. Open daily 10am-1am.) Boisterous and seedy affairs run their shady course at many of the discos along rue el-Moutanabi, parallel to bd. Pasteur near pl. France. Try **Morocco Palace,** 11 av. Moulay Abdallah, or **Borsalino,** 30 av. Moulay Abdallah. Bear in mind that Moroccan discos are not safe for solo travelers but can be fun for groups.

CEUTA سبتة

Those interested in avoiding the craze of Tangier may opt to enter Morocco through Ceuta, a Spanish sovereign enclave (over half of which is owned by the military). Ceuta, however, is less convenient for train travel to the Atlantic coast or Marrakesh. Most visitors don't stay long, opting instead to go on to Tetouan or Chefchaouen for their first night.

Public **buses** and **taxis** ply the route between downtown Ceuta, a couple of blocks from the port, and the border crossing into Morocco, 3km away. Bus #47 runs from pl. Constitución and costs 100ptas. Taxis are 400ptas. Once at the Moroccan border, you must cross on foot and find a **grand taxi**, in the big parking lot, to Tetouan. They won't leave until full; don't pay more than 15dh. There are eight **ferry** departures daily heading both to and from Spain (1½hr., 6:30am-10pm, 1801ptas), with more during the high season. There are also eight **fast-ferry** departures (35min., 6:30am-10pm, 2945ptas). It is always safer to buy your tickets at the port itself. There is a small **tourist office** on the way out of the port as well as a larger one in town that can help with lodging or transportation details.

NEAR CEUTA: TETOUAN ططوان

Odds are that most travelers in Tetouan either just crossed into Morocco via Ceuta or are about to leave from there. For new arrivals, Tetouan can be very intimidating (see **Hustlers and Guides**, p. 660). Don't let them prevent your enjoyment of the whitewashed medina—one of Morocco's best—and the engaging Hispanic architecture in this former capital of the Spanish protectorate. As long as you stick to the popular areas, Tetouan is an enjoyable experience.

◪ ORIENTATION AND PRACTICAL INFORMATION. The *ville nouvelle* centers around **place Moulay el-Mehdi**, with the medina and the spacious pl. Hassan II to the east, a few blocks down av. Mohammed V. The **bus station** is two blocks downhill from pl. Moulay el-Mehdi. Take the street to the left of the bank BCME. **CTM buses** run to: **Tangier** (1½hr., 2 per day, 5:30am and 4:15pm, 15dh); **Chefchaouen** (1½hr., 4 per day, 5am-8pm, 25dh); **Rabat** (3 per day, 6:30am-11pm, 100dh); **Casablanca** (3 per day, 6:30am-11pm, 120dh); **Fez** (5hr., 2 per day, 11:30am and 1:45pm, 60dh). **Grand taxis** (15dh) to Ceuta leave from the bus station. Taxis to Chefchaouen (25dh) run from a stand several blocks away; walk from pl. Moulay el-Mehdi away from the bus station along rue Achra Mai and bear left onto rue al-Jazeer. The **tourist office** is a half block down av. Mohammed V toward the medina. The friendly officials offer a map and info on guides. (Open M-F 8:30am-noon and 2:30-6:30pm). The **post office**, **telephone** office, and banks with ATMs and currency exchange are in pl. Moulay el-Mehdi. **Police** tel. 19.

▛▛ ACCOMMODATIONS AND FOOD. The best option in town is ◪**Pension Iberia** (tel. 96 20 93), pl. Moulay el-Mehd, above BMCE, 3rd. fl. Clean and breezy rooms make up for the long walk upstairs. (Hot showers 5dh; singles 40dh; doubles 70dh; triples 105dh.) Another option is **Hôtel Trébol**, 3 bd. Yacoub el-Mancoun al Mouahidi (tel. 96 20 93). Exit the bus station from the lower level and walk a few meters uphill to the right; it's the first left. The rooms have balconies and are close to the bus station. (Singles 30dh, with shower 40dh; doubles 50dh, with showers 60dh.) Restaurants are cheaper and more authentic in the medina, more western in the *ville nouvelle*. **Restaurant La Union**, 1 av. Mohammed Torres (tel. 96 63 34), just off pl. al-Jula, one block from pl. Hassan II away from the medina, has been a local mainstay for 40 years. (Entrees 22-40dh. Open 24hr.)

CHEFCHAOUEN (CHAOUEN) شَفْشاون

A whitewashed town high in the Rif Mountains, Chefchaouen is no longer the complete escape from hustlers it once was, but its relaxed atmosphere and cool mountain air still refresh even the weariest of travelers. Tourists are attracted by both its manageable, Mediterranean medina and the proximity to *kif* (hashish) farms, which have dominated the hills for centuries. This mellow town is a good place to spend your first few days in Morocco or your last night before departing.

GETTING THERE

Buses run from **Tetouan** (1½hr., 4 per day, 5am-8pm, 25dh) and Tangier.

ORIENTATION AND PRACTICAL INFORMATION

From the **bus station,** head up the steep hill and turn right after several blocks onto the large road, which leads to the tree-filled, circular pl. Mohammed V; it's about a 20-minute walk to the center of town (or a few dirhams for a cab). Cross the plaza and continue east on **avenue Hassan II,** the *ville nouvelle's* main road. Av. Hassan II terminates at the small but busy **Bab al-Ain,** the main gate into the medina. From Bab al-Ain, the main, twisting street uphill leads to **place Uta el-Hammam,** the large plaza at the heart of the medina.

Buses: The bus station is downhill from town. Buses heading south fill up, so get tickets early. **CTM** goes to: **Tetouan** (4 per day, all in the afternoon, 16-18dh); **Ouazzene,** the best bet for connections (3 per day; 7am, 1:15pm, and 3:30pm; 18dh); **Tangier** (1 per day, 3pm, 33dh); **Fez** (2 per day, 1:15 and 3pm, 52dh). Private companies also have daily buses to Ceuta, Tangier, Fez, and Meknes.

Grand Taxis: Probably the easiest way to get to **Tetouan** (24dh), although they often take a while to fill. They leave a block downhill from pl. Mohammed V. Also to **Ceuta** (35dh).

Tourist Office: There isn't one. Come on, you didn't come for the sightseeing anyway.

Currency Exchange: BMCE, av. Hassan II. Open M-F 8:15am-2:15pm.

Police and Emergency: tel. 19.

Medical Services: Hospital Mohammed V, a block west from pl. Mohammed V.

Post Office: av. Hassan II. Telephones. Open M-F 8:30am-12:15pm and 2:30-6:30pm.

Internet Access: Internet a Chefchaouen, 44 Ghazouat badr (tel. 98 89 30) in front of the Mobile station, 1 block from pl. Mohammed V away from the medina. 30dh per hr. Open daily 8:30am-1pm and 3-10pm.

ACCOMMODATIONS AND FOOD

Chefchaouen has a slew of colorful budget hotels. In the medina, head up from Bab el-Ain; hotels are clustered all along this street and around pl. Uta el-Hammam. Outside, follow av. Hassan II toward Hotel Rif and beyond.

▓**Pension la Castellana,** 4 Sidi Ahmad Bouhali (tel. 98 62 95), at the end of pl Uta el-Hammam, near Credit Agricola. Tucked in the corner of whitewashed walls and next to a *hammam,* this friendly place caters almost exclusively to backpackers and encourages long stays. Communal kitchen and common room with stereo. Free hot showers. Singles 30dh; doubles 60dh; triples 90dh; quads 120dh; terrace 15dh.

▓**Hotel Andalus,** 1 rue Sidi Salem (tel. 98 60 34), directly behind Credit Agricola on pl. Uta el-Hammam. Super-cheap rooms and a super-friendly staff make for a super-good value. Possibly the cheapest rooms in all of Morocco. Cold showers free, hot showers 5dh. Singles 25dh; doubles 50dh; triples 75dh; quads 100dh; lovely terrace 15dh.

Hotel Rif (tel. 98 69 82), just outside the medina walls. Follow av. Hassan II to the right around the medina; it's on the left after a few blocks. This classy hotel has clean, comfy rooms, great views, a common room with satellite TV, and terraces decorated in a combination 16th-century Moroccan and 1970s Americana motif. Singles 50dh, with shower 90dh; doubles 80dh, with shower 120dh; triples 120dh, with shower 160dh.

Restaurants and cafes are ubiquitous—even inescapable. Outdoor seating is available in pl. Uta el-Hammam; classier joints are along av. Hassan II.

Chez Aziz, just outside Bab el-Ain. Tasty sandwiches at low prices. Shrimp 15dh. *Kefta* (a Moroccan hamburger) 10dh. Sandwiches 10-15dh. Open daily noon-midnight.

Cafe Restaurant Sindibad (tel. 98 97 42), pl. Uta el-Hammam, across from the kasbah. Although menu is limited, the couscous and tajine are great values and the ambience is perfect. Entrees 17-25dh. Open daily 7am-midnight.

👁 SIGHTS

SIGHTS. Chefchaouen's steep ◪**medina** is one of Morocco's best. Enter through Bab al-Ain and walk uphill toward pl. Uta el-Hammam, the center of the medina. There stands the 15th-century **Tower of Homage,** inside the kasbah built in the 17th century by the famous Moroccan rogue Moulay Ismail. Inside is a small **crafts museum,** a pleasant garden, and a scholarly institute. *(Open daily 9am-1pm and 3-6:30pm. 10dh.)* Chefchaouen's **souq** operates Mondays and Thursdays in the square beside the Hotel Magou. Berbers come from all over the Rif to sell fresh veggies and not-so-fresh clothes. *(Down the stairs from av. Hassan II.)* The octagonal minaret, visible from the square, soars above the 16th-century **Grand Mosque.**

HIKING. Also appealing are hiking possibilities in the region. Follow the **Ouad Laou River** upstream into the hills for just a few kilometers for spectacular results. Another good hike begins above the medina behind the Hotel Asmaq (follow signs for the *ville nouvelle*), winds up the peak to the left, and then runs down into the valley. You might try reaching the "Spanish mosque," about halfway up the peak to the right of the medina. Ask at your hotel about more organized hikes and guides.

THE MIDDLE ATLAS الأطلَس المُتَوَسِّط

The cities and towns that lie among the peaks of the Middle Atlas mountains form Morocco's heartland. Home to the imperial cities of Fez and Meknes, the nation's agricultural bread basket, the Roman ruins of Volubilis, and the spiritual center of Moulay Idriss, this region embodies the true spirit of Morocco.

MEKNES مَكْناس

Meknes lies amid a gray-green agricultural checkerboard, an hour west of Fez and three hours east of Rabat. Named for the Berber tribe Meknassa, this provincial town has the largest Berber population in Morocco. Because Meknes is less arresting than Morocco's other imperial cities, its atmosphere is less touristy and its souqs are a bit tamer. Nevertheless, the monuments left by Sultan Moulay Ismail, the famous Moroccan rogue, remain impressive. Ismail chose Meknes as his seat of power in 1672 and used notoriously brutal tactics to try and turn this relative backwater into a capital to rival Versailles. The city peaked during Ismail's reign and has never regained its former glory. Still, with the world-renowned ruins of Volubilis nearby, Meknes is worth a visit.

▟ GETTING THERE

Trains run to Meknes from **Rabat** (3hr., 8 per day, 7:15am-11:45pm, 53dh) and **Marrakesh** (7hr., 6 per day, 6:30am-7pm, 150dh). **Buses** go from: **Fez** (1hr., 9 per day, 6am-1am, 18dh); **Rabat** (2½hr., 8 per day, 8am-9:30pm, 40dh); **Tangier** (5hr., 10 per day, 6am-2:15am); **Marrakesh** (8-9hr., 5 per day, 6:30am-9pm, 115dh).

MOROCCO

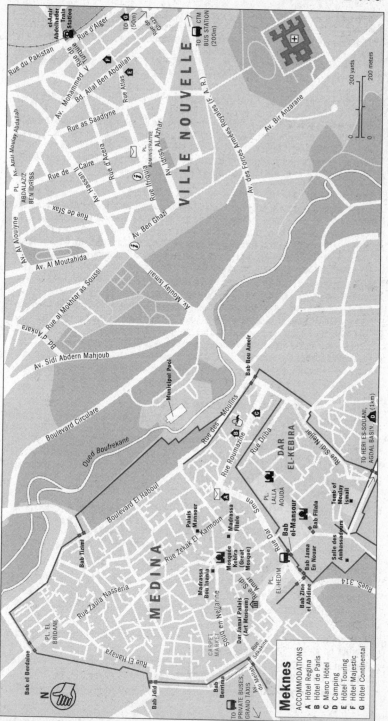

To el-Amir Abdelhader Train Station

Rue du Pakistan

Rue d'Alger

To Gare (50m)

To CTM BUS STATION (200m)

Av. Mohammed Rhenie

Rue de Turkie

Av. Amir Moulay Abdallah

Bd. Allal Ben Abdallah

Rue Atlas

Rue as Saadiyne

PL. ABDALAZIZ BEN IDRISS

Av. Al Alouiyne

Rue de IL Caire

Rue d'Aceïa

Av. Hassani

Rue de Sfax

Av. Idriss Al Azhar

PL. ADMINISTRATIVE

Rue Ifriquia

VILLE NOUVELLE

Av. Ben Ghazi

Av. des Forces Armées Royales (F.A.R.)

Av. Al Moutahida

Av. Bir Anzarane

Rue al Mokhtar as Soussi

Bd. d'Ankara

Av. Moulay Ismail

Av. Sidi Abdern Mahjoub

Bab Bou Ameir

Municipal Pool

Boulevard Circulare

Oued Boufrekane

Rue des Moulins

Rue Roumazine

Rue Driba

DAR EL-KEBIRA

Boulevard El Haboul

Bab Tizimi

Palais Mansour

Rue Zekak El Karmoun

Madrassa Filale

Smen

PL. LALLA AOUDA

To HERI ES-SOUANI, AGDAL BASIN (1km)

Rue Sidi Nejjar

MEDINA

Madrassa Bou Inania

Mosquée Kebira (Great Mosque)

Rue Dar

Bab el-Mansour

Bab Filala

Tomb of Moulay Ismail

Rue Sidi Amar

PL. EL-HEDIM

Bab Jama En Nouar

Salle des Ambassadeurs

Bab el Berdaine

PL. EL BRIDANE

Rue Zaula Nasseria

Dar Jamal Palais (Art Museum)

Bab Zine el Abidine

RTES. 314

Rue El Hanya

CARPET MARKET

Souq en Nejjarine

Rue Sekakine

Au Mellah

Bab Berrina

Bab Idid

To PRIVATE BUSES, GRAND TAXIS

N

0   200 yards
0   200 meters

Meknes

ACCOMMODATIONS
A Hôtel Regina
B Hôtel de Paris
C Maroc Hôtel
D Camping
E Hôtel Touring
F Hôtel Majestic
G Hôtel Continental

ⓘ ORIENTATION AND PRACTICAL INFORMATION

The river **Oued Boufrekane** divides Meknes into three "boroughs": the **medina** and the **imperial city** to the west and the modern **ville nouvelle** to the east. The train and CTM buses deposit passengers in the *ville nouvelle*. Tree-lined **avenue Mohammed V**, the new city's main drag, intersects with av. Hassan II north of the large square, pl. Administrative, west of both the train (straight from the exit) and CTM (to the left upon exiting) stations. From the intersection, follow av. Hassan II, which turns into av. Moulay Ismail, to approach the medina via Bab Bou-Amir. To reach the colossal **Bab el-Mansour** (the entrance to the imperial complex) and **plaza el Hedim** (the medina's main square), head up the hill from Bab Bou-Amir, take a right on rue Roumazine and then a left on rue Dar Smen. Local buses #5, 7, and 9 shuttle between the CTM bus station in the *ville nouvelle* and Bab el-Mansour (a 20min. walk); a *petit taxi* should cost no more than 10dh.

TRANSPORTATION

Trains: Meknes has 2 stations. Use the **Meknes el-Amir Abdelkader Station,** on rue d'Alger, 2 blocks from av. Mohammed V. The misnamed **Meknes Main Station** is far from the center of town. Both have identical service. To: **Fez** (50min., 10 per day, 9:57am-2:05am, 15dh); **Rabat** (2½hr., 8 per day, 8:04am-3:35am, 45dh); **Casablanca** (3¾hr., 8 per day, 8:04am-3:35am, 70dh); and **Tangier** (5hr., 10 per day, 9:57am-2:05am, 60dh). For more information, go to www.oncf.org.ma.

Buses: CTM (tel. 51 47 59), on av. des F.A.R., a brand-new station about 5 blocks from av. Mohammed V (a left when exiting the station). To: **Fez** (1½hr., 8 per day, 11am-11pm, 18dh); **Rabat** (3hr., 8 per day, 5am-2am, 38dh); **Casablanca** (4hr., 8 per day, 5am-2am, 63dh); **Tangier** (5hr., 3 per day, 1pm-2:30am, 70dh); **Er-Rachidia** (6hr., 1 per day, 10pm, 80dh), via Fez; and **Marrakesh** (8hr., 1 per day, 7pm, 132dh). **Private companies** depart from a station on av. Mellah just outside Bab el-Khemis, outside the medina opposite the *ville nouvelle*. Prices and departures vary.

Taxis: *Grand taxis* cluster next to the private bus station and outside the el-Amir Abdelkader train station. To **Fez** (17dh) and **Rabat** (40dh).

TOURIST, FINANCIAL, AND LOCAL SERVICES

Tourist Office: 27 pl. Administrative (tel. 52 44 26). From the Abdelkader train station, go straight 2 blocks, turn left on av. Mohammed V, and make an immediate right. Cross rue Allal ben Abdallah, continue toward the Hôtel de Ville, and veer right. The tourist office is on the right just after the post office. Friendly staff. Limited English. Official but unnecessary guides: half-day 120dh, full-day 150dh. Open M-F 8:30am-noon and 2:30-6:30pm. **Syndicat d'Initiative** (tel. 52 01 91), on Esplanade de la Foire, off av. Moulay Ismail and inside the yellow gate. Open M-F 8:30am-noon and 2:30-6:30pm.

Currency Exchange: BMCE, 98 av. des F.A.R. (tel. 52 03 52). Exchange window open daily 10am-2pm and 4-8pm. **ATM** accepts Visa and MC. **Hôtel Rif,** on Zenkat Accra, around the corner from the tourist office, cashes traveler's checks.

Hammam: on rue Roumazine. 5dh.

EMERGENCY AND COMMUNICATIONS

Late-Night Pharmacy: Red Cross Emergency Pharmacy (tel. 52 33 75), in pl. Administrative. Open daily 8:30am-8:30pm.

Hospitals: Hôpital Moulay Ismail, (tel. 52 28 05 or 52 28 06) on av. des F.A.R., near av. Moulay Youssef.

Post Office: pl. Administrative. Open M-Sa 8:30am-12:15pm and 2:30-6:45pm. **Branch office** on rue Dar Smen, near the medina.

Internet Access: La LM (tel. 55 80 40), near the BMCE on rue Roumazine. 20dh per hr., but not very reliable. A cybercafe is slated to open in the *ville nouvelle* by fall 1999.

Telephones: Available at the post office daily 8:30am-9pm. Use the side entrance if the post office is closed.

TELEPHONE CODE Meknes's phone code is (0)5.

ACCOMMODATIONS AND CAMPING

MEDINA

R. Roumazine and R. Dar Smen house most of the medina's budget hotels.

Maroc Hôtel, 7 av. Roumazine Derb Ben Brahim (tel. 53 07 05), off rue Roumazine. Mellow owner presides over a collection of clean, small rooms arranged around a leafy courtyard. Cold showers and squat toilets. Breakfast 20dh. 60dh per person.

Hôtel de Paris, 58 rue Roumazine, opposite a dentist's office. Look for the sign that says "Hôtel." Basic and clean. Singles 35dh; doubles and triples 70dh; sleeping on the terrace 20dh.

Hôtel Regina, 19 rue Dar Smen (tel. 53 02 80). Another adequate medina hotel, although this one has been recently renovated. Hot showers 5dh. Singles 60dh; doubles 90dh; triples 120dh; quads 150dh.

Camping: Municipal Camping Agdal (tel. 55 53 96), on the ramparts of the medina. Follow the signs from either Bab Mansour or Bab Bou Amir. Outdoes any option in the hotel scene. Crowds gather in the beautiful, wooded park with amenities including hot showers (7dh) and kitchen. Restaurant's 3-course *menu* 45dh. Reception daily 8am-1pm and 4-8pm. 17dh per adult, 12dh per child, 10dh per tent, 17dh per car.

VILLE NOUVELLE

The *ville nouvelle* offers greater comfort, higher prices, and easy access to banks, CTM buses, and trains. Most of the cheapest hotels lie around av. Mohammed V and bd. Allal ben Abdallah.

Auberge de Jeunesse (HI) (tel. 52 46 98), on av. Okba Ben Nafii, near the stadium. Head toward the medina on av. Hassan II; follow the arrows toward Hôtel Trans Atlantique. A 20min. walk or 5dh taxi ride from Abdelkader station. Clean mattresses, TV room, and a pleasant courtyard. In high season members only. Cold showers free, hot showers 5dh (7-8pm only). Reception summer 8-9am, noon-4pm and 7pm-midnight; in winter 8-10am, noon-3pm, and 6-10pm. Closed Su 10am-6pm. Dorms 27dh.

Hôtel Majestic, 19 av. Mohammed V (tel. 52 20 35), close to the train station. Wins the prize for the most portraits of King Hassan II per square inch. Newly refurbished rooms, modern restrooms, and hot showers. Singles 112-189dh; doubles 150-225dh; triples 217-292dh; prices depend on bathroom options. 15% *Let's Go* discount.

Hôtel Continental (tel. 52 54 71), on av. des F.A.R., opposite the Hôtel Volubilis. Coming from the train station, head down av. Mohammed V to the left and take a left at the junction with av. des F.A.R. Comfortable, new, and cleaner than clean. Singles 105dh; with shower 133dh; doubles 133dh, with shower 154dh.

Hôtel Touring, 34 av. Allal ben Abdallah (tel. 52 23 51), one block from av. Mohammed V when heading away from the train and CTM stations. One of the cheapest places in the *ville nouvelle,* this hotel is dark and without character, but clean and spacious. Singles 70dh, with shower 106dh; doubles 95dh, with shower 134dh.

FOOD

MEDINA

Vendors in **place el-Hedim** hawk *mergouz* sandwiches, freshly made potato chips, and corn on the cob roasted over open coals. Other inexpensive fare sizzles in the one-man *brochetteries* on **rue Dar Smen.** Few places have menus, let alone ones in English or French—most have their options on display. The daily **vegetable market** sprouts beside Bab Mansour.

> **Restaurant Moulay Bab,** 101 rue Roumanzine (tel. 55 77 28), next to the Maroc Hôtel. The best deal in town, with tasty *brochettes* (2dh each), *kefta* (2dh each), and salads (3dh.), Most options under 10dh. Open daily 7am-10pm.

> **Restaurant Economique,** 123 rue Dar Smen. Friendly manager serves staples at reasonable prices. Couscous or *tajine* 25dh. 4-course *menu* 40dh. Open daily 7am-10pm.

VILLE NOUVELLE

> **Restaurant Marhaba,** 23 av. Mohammed V (tel. 52 16 32). Head away from the train station and pass Hôtel Majestic. Locals flock here for the spicy *harira*. Tourists come, lured by a plaque of recommendation from a French travel guide. *Brochettes* 18dh. *Tajine* 30dh. Salads 6dh. Omelettes 6dh. Entrees 18-30dh.

> **Restaurant Pizza Fongue,** 8 rue Accra (tel. 51 32 76). Walk 1 block past the post office and take a right. Wide variety, from 10 kinds of pizza to *tajines*. Entrees 25-30dh. Open daily 11am-11pm.

> **Rotisserie Karam,** 2 Zankat Ghana (tel. 52 24 75), just off av. Hassan II. 20 years of experience have resulted in high-quality fare. So Americanized that they even serve "sheese-burger *garni*" (22dh). Entrees 22-35dh. Open daily 11am-11pm.

> **Pizzeria le Four,** av. Zenkat Atlas (tel. 52 08 57), off av. Mohammed V near the train station. Tasty Italian cuisine. Even tacky decor doesn't keep lots of tourists and hip locals from enjoying the food. Entrees 20-70dh. Open daily noon-3pm and 7pm-midnight.

> **Restaurant Lorraine,** 32 rue Moulay Abdelkader (tel. 52 17 10). From el-Amir Abdelkader Station, head 2 blocks to the left. This family-run restaurant serves simple, well-prepared dishes. Entrees 20-30dh. Open daily 11am-4pm and 6-10pm.

◉ SIGHTS

Meknes's best sights cluster around the magnificent **Bab el-Mansour,** which has become a national symbol. Through the gate lie the remainders of Meknes's imperial past, and around it thrives the present-day medina and the lively pl. el-Hedim.

IMPERIAL MEKNES

Weakened by war, weather, and the Great Earthquake of 1755, the ramparts of the **Dar el-Kebira** (Imperial City) testify to Meknes's former glory. Sultan Moulay Ismail personally supervised the building of over 25km of protective **walls** for his city within a city. Strolling about the site with a pick-ax and whip in hand, the sultan criticized and occasionally decapitated workers who displeased him. Plundering materials from sights all over Morocco, including Roman marble from the ruins at Volubilis, Moulay Ismail created a radiant city. Ismail razed part of the medina to create **place el-Hedim** (place of destruction), an approach to **Bab el-Mansour,** Morocco's finest gate. Today, only the walls and several large monuments remain.

SALLE DES AMBASSADEURS. Standing by itself in an open court is the green-tiled roof of the recently restored Salle des Ambassadeurs, where Ismail conducted affairs of state. Ask the guard to unlock the doors to the so-called **"Christian Dungeon,"** a six-square-kilometer underground storehouse and granary for the Sultan, his entourage, and their horses. This storehouse is said to have once housed some 50 to 100,000 Christian prisoners. Since the "dungeon" remains a cool 15°C even in summer, it is the perfect place to avoid the midday sun. *(From pl. el-Hedim, pass through Bab el-Mansour or one of the nearby smaller gates, walk straight, and follow the wall around the bend. Open June-Aug. Sa-Th 9am-noon and 3-6:30pm; Sept.-May Sa-Th 9am-noon and 3-6pm. 10dh.)*

TOMB OF MOULAY ISMAIL. The tomb, along with its accompanying **mosque,** is one of only two Moroccan religious buildings open to non-Muslims. Part of the building remains off-limits, but anyone may peer in. Walk through the bright yellow rooms to reach the tomb, flanked by two functioning grandfather clocks. These clocks are a consolation prize from Louis XIV, who sent them after refusing

Moulay Ismail's proposal to his daughter. *(Through the two blue arches, on the left. Open daily 9am-noon and 3-6pm. Free. Conservative dress appropriate.)*

OTHER SIGHTS. A short trek from Moulay Ismail's tomb is the **Heri es-Souani** (storehouse), a cool granary with immense cisterns designed to withstand prolonged sieges. Trees and birds have invaded, giving it a jungle-like feel. *(Open daily 9am-noon and 3-6pm. 10dh.)* Nearby, the **Agdal Basin** was once Moulay Ismail's private country club and his reservoir in case of siege. His wives (more than 300 of them) and their 800 kids were said to swim there to escape the stifling summer heat. *(To get to the Heri es-Souani and Agdal Basin from Bab el-Mansour, follow the signs for camping and continue straight past the campsite for 30min. Free.)*

MEDINA

Meknes's **medina** is more pleasant, tranquil, and compact than those of the other imperial cities. Facing the Dar Jamaï Museum of Moroccan Art, take the alley to the left of the entrance. Push straight ahead to **Souq en Nejjarine,** a major street. Heading left here brings you first to the **textile souq,** the **carpenters' souq,** and the **carpet market.** The rest of the medina is best explored like any other: wander until you get lost, then try to find your way out.

GREAT MOSQUE AND ■MADRASSA BOU INANIA. While everything except the green-glazed minaret of the Great Mosque *(al-masjid al-kebira)* is off-limits to non-Muslims, the breathtaking 14th-century Madrassa Bou Inania, across from it, is not. A college of theology and Muslim law, this *madrassa* typifies traditional Merenid architecture—the courtyard combines cedar, stucco, and mosaics with characteristic flair. Upstairs are a number of cells, each of which snugly hosted at least two students. The roof offers a splendid view of the minaret of the Great Mosque and the rooftops of Meknes. *(Face Dar Jamaï in pl. el-Hedim, turn right onto rue Sidi Amar, and enter the medina. Follow the alley as it turns left. Then fork right. Madrassa open Sa-Th 8:30am-12:30pm and 2:30-6pm, F 8:30-11:30am and 2:30-6pm. 10dh.)*

DAR JAMAI PALACE. Built in the 19th century by one of Sultan Moulay Hassan I's powerful government ministers, the Dar Jamaï Palace now houses a **Museum of Moroccan Art** which flaunts one of Morocco's best craft collections. Most pieces are contextualized in restored versions of the rooms where they were originally displayed. Check out the carpets and the master bedroom, stuffed with embroidered divans and topped by a magnificent cupola. *(At the far end of pl. el-Hedim. Tel. 53 08 63. Open W-M 9am-noon and 3-6pm. 10dh.)*

DAYTRIPS FROM MEKNES

VOLUBILIS وَليلي

Thirty-three kilometers from Meknes lie the ruins of Volubilis, the best-preserved Roman site in Morocco and perhaps all of North Africa. An extensive collection of **Roman mosaics** has earned these ruins must-see status on any traveler's itinerary. Once a major center for the olive oil trade, the city flourished under Roman rule, reaching its zenith in the 2nd and 3rd centuries AD when it became the capital of the kingdom of Mauritania. The Romans, who viewed their North African possessions as a bread-basket for their European citizens, ordered the deforestation of the area to make room for grain crops—as the surrounding treeless plain can attest, they did a super job. When the Romans withdrew from North Africa, an isolated colony of Jews and Christianized Berbers continued to inhabit the city, which by that time had declined in power and importance. The city declined further in the 18th century, when Moulay Idriss siphoned the population off to Fez and Meknes and recycled much of Volubilis's pillars and stones for his palace in Meknes. The so-called Lisbon Earthquake of 1755, which wreaked devastation all along the Atlantic seaboard, finally sealed the city's fate.

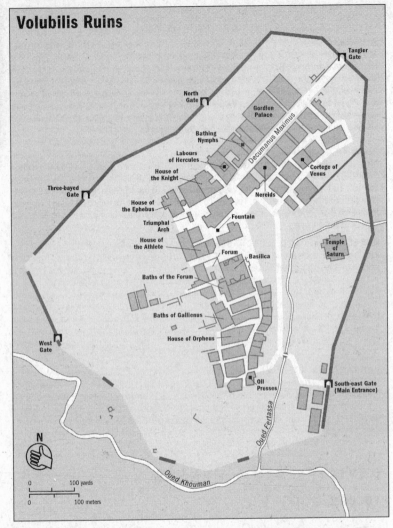

Volubilis Ruins

Tangier Gate

North Gate

Gordien Palace

Decumanus Maximus

Bathing Nymphs

Labours of Hercules

Cortege of Venus

House of the Knight

Nereids

Three-bayed Gate

House of the Ephebus

Fountain

Triumphal Arch

House of the Athlete

Temple of Saturn

Forum

Basilica

Baths of the Forum

Baths of Gallienus

House of Orpheus

West Gate

Oil Presses

South-east Gate (Main Entrance)

Oued Fertassa

N

Oued Khouman

0   100 yards

0   100 meters

▶ **PRACTICAL INFORMATION.** The ruins are open daily sunrise to sunset. They are more peaceful and scenic in the early morning or late afternoon (admission 20dh). Unfortunately, there are no tourist booklets, maps, or signs on-site. **Buses** going from Meknes to **Ouezzare** (every hr., 7am-7pm, 10dh) will drop you off near the ruins. You can also hire a **grand taxi** near the private bus station in Meknes. Since *grand taxis* require six passengers, arranging transportation to Volubilis may be difficult. Consider taking a *grand taxi* to **Moulay Idriss** (10dh) and walking the rest of the way (about 3km, follow signs straight from the junction).

▲ **WALKING TOUR.** When U.S. General George C. Patton visited the ruins, he declined an offer of a guided tour—he believed he had been stationed here as a Roman centurion in his previous life and thus knew his way around. If you've been equally lucky, stop reading here. Otherwise, head past the ticket office and over a bridge, take a left and work your way up the hill, where among the ruins of a housing and industrial area are several **olive presses**. Walk down the main path to the

House of Orpheus to view its **dolphin mosaic.** Continue through the ruins of **public baths** to the **Forum,** with the columned **capitol** and **basilica** on the right. The basilica, despite its name, served as the courthouse during Roman times. Follow the path to the **House of the Athlete** on the left, named for its mosaic depicting the victor of a *desultor* race (which involved mounting a moving horse).

In the middle of town looms the **Triumphal Arch,** built in 217 AD to celebrate Emperor Caracalla and his scheming mother Julia Domna. Julia assured her son's power by helping him murder his rival Gota in 212 AD. The gate marks the beginning of the town's main street, **Decumanus Maximus.** The houses along the street, including the **House of the Ephebus** and the **House of the Knight,** have impressive mosaics of Dionysus, Hercules, Orpheus, and other mythical figures. From the top of the hill is an amazing panoramic view of Volubilis. The **Tangier Gate,** with the **Gordien Palace** just before it, is atop the hill. Walk down the hill and head toward the only tree in front. Under it is the **Cortege of Venus,** which holds several mosaics including *Chariot Race, Bacchus Surrounded by the Four Seasons, Diana Bathing,* and the *Abduction of Hylas by Nymphs,* all dating as far back as the late 2nd or early 3rd century AD. Cross the stream back to the ticket gate to see the ruins of a **Temple** dedicated to Jupiter, Juno, and Minerva.

MOULAY IDRISS مولاي إدريس

Five kilometers before Volubilis, the road from Meknes passes through Moulay Idriss, a pilgrimage site named after the man who spread Islam through Morocco. A third-generation descendant of Muhammad, Idriss united the Berber tribes and founded the country's first dynasty. Non-Muslims cannot spend the night or visit the mosques or shrines; even so, Moulay Idriss is an easy enough stop on the way to Volubilis. A youth will guide you or point out a magnificent view of the sacred **Mausoleum of Moulay Idriss** and the only **cylindrical minaret** in Morocco. Take a **bus** (30min., every hr., 7am-7pm, 10dh; same schedule back to Meknes) or **grand taxi** (10dh) from the private bus station in Meknes.

FEZ فاس

The medina in Fez is why you came to Morocco. Artisans bang out sheets of brass, donkeys strain under crates of Coca-Cola, prayer callers wail, and children balance trays of dough on their heads. Along narrow streets, the scent of *brochettes* on open grills combine with whiffs of hash, the sweet aroma of cedar shavings, and the stench of the open sewer. Since UNESCO designated Fez a World Heritage Site, the city's walls have been largely restored, and fresh plaster and cobblestones make the medina even more fantastic. Founded in the 8th century by Moulay Idriss I, Fez rose to prominence with the construction of the Qaraouine, a university-mosque complex, which was one of the world's first universities. With such a wealth of resources, Fez emerged as the most prominent city in the Maghreb, nurturing (or destroying) political dynasties and handing down legal rulings to the rest of the region. Today, post-independence Fez has been somewhat eclipsed by Rabat (the political capital), Casablanca (the economic capital), and Marrakesh (the tourist capital). All the same, the city remains at the intellectual and spiritual helm of the nation, and central to many Moroccans' senses of national pride.

⊏ GETTING THERE

Trains run to Fez from **Meknes** (50min., 10 per day, 10am-2am, 15dh). **Buses** go from: **Chefchaouen** (2 per day, 1:15 and 3pm, 52dh); **Rabat** (3½hr., 8 per day, 8am-midnight, 57dh); **Tangier** (6hr., 10 per day, 8:40am-9:30pm, 63dh).

⁊ ORIENTATION AND PRACTICAL INFORMATION

Fez is three cities in one: the French-built **ville nouvelle** and the Arab **Fez el-Jdid** ("New Fez") and **Fez el-Bali** ("Old Fez"). The *ville nouvelle's* two central streets are, predictably, the divided **Avenue Hassan II** and **Boulevard Mohammed V,** which intersect at **Plaza Florence,** the center of activity. Walking down av. Moulay Youssef from the *ville nouvelle* brings you to pl. Alouites in Fez el-Jdid, directly in front of the king's palace, **Dar-el-Makhzen.** After passing through Bab Sommarin on the left, rue Fez el-Jdid takes you the length of the palace. At the end, a right through Bab Dakakene leads to Fez el-Bali and its main gate **Bab Boujeloud,** where several cheap hotels cluster. The two main streets of Fez el-Bali, the **Talâa Kebina** and **Talâa Seghira,** are where most of the excitement lies, although they are barely wide enough for its shops, a donkey and your backpack. For more info on getting around Fez el-Bali, see **Sights,** page 684. For navigating between different parts of the city, see **Public Transportation,** below.

TRANSPORTATION

Flights: Aérodrome de Fès-Saïs (tel. 62 47 12), 12km out of town on the road to Immouzzèr. Bus #16 leaves from pl. Mohammed V (3dh). *Grand taxis* (120dh) also run there. **Royal Air Maroc** (tel. 62 04 56), av. Hassan II, flies daily to Casablanca. Also services Tangier, Marrakesh, Marseilles, and Paris.

Trains: (tel. 62 50 01), av. Almohades, at rue Chenguit. 2nd-class trains are comfier than buses, and only cost a few dirhams more. To: **Meknes** (1hr., 9 per day, 7:15am-2:40am, 22dh); **Rabat** (3½hr., 8 per day, 7:15am-2:40am, 50dh); **Casablanca** (5hr., 8 per day, 7:15am-2:40am, 70dh); **Tangier** (5½hr., 4 per day, 7:15am-2:40am, 72dh); **Marrakesh** (9hr., 6 per day, 7:15am-2:40am, 130dh).

Buses: CTM (tel. 73 29 84) stops near pl. d'Atlas, at the far end of the *ville nouvelle.* From pl. Florence, walk down bd. Mohammed V and turn left onto av. Youssef Ben Tachfine. At pl. d'Atlas, take the 1st right. To: **Meknes** (1hr., 9 per day, 6am-1am, 18dh); **Rabat** (3hr., 4 per day, 6am-1am, 55dh); **Chefchaouen** (4hr., 3 per day, 8am-11:45pm, 40dh); **Casablanca** (5hr., 9 per day, 6am-1am, 80dh); **Tangier** (6hr., 5 per day, 11am-1:30am, 85dh); **Marrakesh** (8hr., 3 per day, 6am-1am, 130dh).

Public Transportation: Pl. Mohammed V and pl. Résistance are the major hubs for city buses. Important routes include: bus #9 and 11 from the Syndicat d'Initiative to Bab Boujeloud and Dav Batha; #3 from the train station and pl. Mohammed V to Bab Ftouh; #4 from pl. Résistance to Bab Smarine in Fez al-Jdid. 2.2dh; fares increase 20% July-Sept. 15 after 8:30pm, Sept. 16-June after 8pm.

Taxis: Stands at the post office, Syndicat d'Initiative, Bab Boujeloud, and Bab Guissa. Fares increase 50% July-Sept. 15 after 8:30pm, Sept. 16-June after 8pm. Staff at the Syndicat d'Initiative will help you onto the correct *grand taxi.*

Car Rental: Avis, 50 bd. Chefchaouni (tel. 62 67 46). **Hertz,** 1 Kissauiat de la Foire (tel. 62 28 12). Fiat Unos 25dh per day, plus 2.4dh per km.

TOURIST, FINANCIAL, AND LOCAL SERVICES

Tourist Office: Syndicat d'Initiative (tel. 62 47 69), pl. Mohammed V, on the way to the CTM bus station from av. Hassan II. Helpful Fassi (citizens of Fez) answer almost any question. Same meager maps as the Moroccan National Tourism Office. Hire ◼ official guides here for 120dh for half-day or 150dh for full-day. Open M-F 8:30am-noon and 2:30-6:30pm, Sa 8:30am-noon.

Currency Exchange: BMCE, pl. Mohammed V, opposite the Syndicat d'Initiative, to the right of the main bank entrance. Handles Visa/MC transactions and traveler's checks, and has **ATMs.** Open M-F 8:15-11:30am and 2:15-4pm. **Sheraton Fez Hôtel,** at the end of av. Hassan II 4 blocks from the post office, has after-hours exchange.

Luggage Storage: At the train station. 2.5dh per bag per day. Open 24hr.

EMERGENCY AND COMMUNICATIONS

Police: tel. 19.

Late-Night Pharmacy: Municipalité de Fès (tel. 62 33 80), bd. Moulay Youssef off Pl. Résistance, 5min. uphill from the royal palace. Open daily 8pm-8am.

Hospital: Ghastani, at the end of av. Hassan II away from the medina.

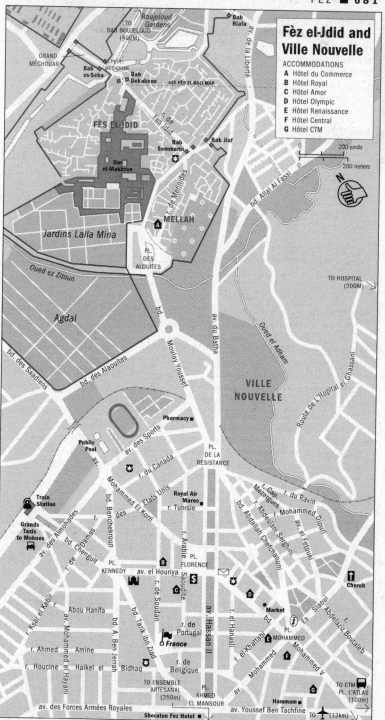

Fèz el-Jdid and Ville Nouvelle

ACCOMMODATIONS
A Hôtel du Commerce
B Hôtel Royal
C Hôtel Amor
D Hôtel Olympic
E Hôtel Renaissance
F Hôtel Central
G Hôtel CTM

0   200 yards
0   200 meters

Bab Riafa

Boujeloud Gardens
TO BAB BOUJELOUD (400M)

GRAND MÉCHOUAR

Bab es-Seba
PETIT MÉCHOUAR
Bab Dekakene

SEE FÈS EL-BALI MAP

FÈS EL-JDID

r. de Fès Jdid

av. de la Liberté

Bab Semmarin
Bab Jiaf

Dar el-Makhzen

r. de Mernides

bd. Allal Al Fassi

MELLAH

Jardins Lalla Mina

PL. DES ALOUITES

Oued ez Zitoun

Oued el Adham

TO HOSPITAL (200M)

Agdal

bd. des Saadiens

bd. des Alaouites

Moulay Youssef

av. du Batha

VILLE NOUVELLE

Route de L'Hopital El Ghassani

Pharmacy

Public Pool

av. des Sports

r. du Canada

PL. DE LA RÉSISTANCE

av.

r. Cap. Mézergues

r. du Ravin

Train Station

Mohammed El Korri

bd. Benchekroun

Royal Air Maroc
r. Tunisie

r. Mohammed Diouri

r. Abdeslam Serghini

bd. Abdallah Chetchaouni

av. el Fetouki

Grands Taxis to Meknes

av. des Almohades

des

r.

r. de Chenguit

r. Arabie

PL. KENNEDY

B
av. el Houriya

C
Saoudite

PL. FLORENCE

r. Ksar el Kebir

av. de Mohammed el Hayani

Abou Hanifa

bd. Tarik Ibn Ziad

D
Market

r. Slaoui Abdelaziz Boutaleb

Church

r. Ahmed

Amine

r. de Soudan

r. de Portugal

r. el Hanasli

i

PL. MOHAMMED

E

F

Mohammed V

r. Houcine

Haikel el Bidhaq

France

r. de Beligique

av. Hassan II

r. el-Khattabi

Mohammed

TO ENSEMBLE ARTESANAL (250m)

PL. AHMED EL MANSOUR

Hammam

G

TO CTM PL. L'ATLAS (100m)

av. des Forces Armées Royales

av. Youssef Ben Tachfine

TO ✈ (12km)

Sheraton Fez Hotel

Post Office: At the corner of av. Hassan II and bd. Mohammed V in the *ville nouvelle*. **Branch offices** at pl. d'Atlas and in the medina at pl. Batha. All open July-Sept. 15 M-F 8am-3pm; Sept. 16-June M-F 8:30am-6:45pm.

Internet Access: Casanet (tel. 93 29 27), av. Hassan II, 2nd fl. of the Im al-Watanya Insurance building next to Waffa Bank. 20dh per hr.

Telephones: In the **main post office.** Enter from bd. Mohammed V, to the right of the main entrance. Open daily 8:30am-9pm. The **branch office** in the medina also has international phones. Open daily 8:30am-9pm.

TELEPHONE CODE	Fez's phone code is (0)5.

■ ACCOMMODATIONS AND CAMPING

VILLE NOUVELLE

Rooms here are hustler-free and more comfortable than those in the medina. The cheapest lodgings clump on or just off bd. Mohammed V, between av. Mohammed es-Slaoui near the bus station and av. Hassan II near the post office.

Hôtel Renaissance, 29 rue Abdelkarim El Khattabi (tel. 62 21 93), 1 block toward the medina from pl. Mohammed V. The cheapest of the *ville nouvelle* hotels, it combines the amenities of the new city with the prices of the medina. Don't be deterred by the gloomy entrance—the rooms are bright and cheery. Hot showers 5dh. Singles 40dh; doubles 70dh; triples 90dh; quads 120dh.

Hôtel Central, 50 rue Brahim Roudant (tel. 62 23 33), 1 block away from the medina and to the left of pl. Mohammed V. Springy beds and surplus chairs in plain but spotless rooms. Hot water in room sinks. Singles 59dh, with shower 87dh; doubles 83dh, with shower 114dh; triples 129dh, with shower 159dh.

Hôtel Amor, 31 rue Arabie Saoudite (tel. 62 27 24). From the post office, cross the street toward Bauk al-Maghrib and turn left (look for the sign). Almoravid decor is a bit disturbing, but comfortable. All rooms with private bath. Singles 128dh; doubles 160dh.

Hôtel Royal, 36 rue de Soudan (tel. 62 46 56). From the post office, walk past Bauk el-Maghrib and turn right. A bit out of the way, but near the train station. All rooms with shower. Singles 84dh, with toilet 109dh; doubles 111dh, with toilet 129dh.

Hôtel CTM (tel. 62 28 11), rue Ksarelkbir, next to the old CTM station, 2 blocks away from the medina on bd. Mohammed V. This place has seen better days—like when the bus station still functioned. Singles 53dh, with shower 76dh; doubles 73dh, with shower 96dh; triples 118dh, with shower 141dh.

FEZ EL-JDID

Fez el-Jdid has only one hotel of note, but the location is perfect—close to the medina without the annoyance of hustlers.

■**Hotel du Commerce** (tel. 62 22 31), pl. Alaouites. That this place is always packed is a testament to the friendly owners, comfortable rooms, and affordable prices. Cold showers. Singles 40dh; doubles 60dh; triples 90dh.

FEZ EL-BALI

Step right up to Bab Boujeloud for budget rooms—they're less pleasant than those in the *ville nouvelle*, and hustlers may seem to have tourist-radar. Still, they're economical and perfect for that 24-hour medina experience.

■**Hôtel Cascade,** 26 Serrajine Boujeloud (tel. 63 84 42), just inside Bab Boujeloud and to the right. A popular place with backpackers and families. Sanitary and spacious rooms. The terrace and some rooms have a bird's-eye view of the medina. Squat toilets. Hot showers 5dh, but there's a 6dh *hammam* next door. Singles 60dh; doubles 80dh; triples 120dh; quads 160dh; terrace 15dh.

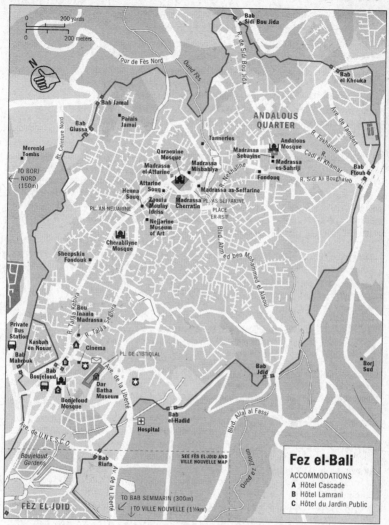

Fez el-Bali

ACCOMMODATIONS
A Hôtel Cascade
B Hôtel Lamrani
C Hôtel du Jardin Public

Hôtel Lamrani (tel. 63 44 11), Talâa Seghira. Enter Bab Boujeloud; take the 1st right, then a left and through the arch. Unusually clean, with in-room sinks. Benevolent manager says showers will be added when there is enough money. Nearby *hammam*. Singles 40-50dh; doubles 80-100dh; triples 120-150dh.

Hôtel du Jardin Public, 153 Kasbah Boujeloud (tel. 63 30 86), a small alley across from the Bab Boujeloud parking area. Relatively clean rooms; some with views, all with pretty saggy beds. Communal cold showers (hot in winter, 5dh) and toilets. Singles 40dh; doubles 60dh; triples 75dh; quads 100dh.

◨ FOOD

VILLE NOUVELLE

Cheap food huts line the streets on either side of bd. Mohammed V. Poke through stalls of fresh food at the **central market** on bd. Mohammed V, two blocks up from pl. Mohammed V (open daily 7am-1pm).

La Mamia, 43 lmh Urbain (tel. 62 31 64), pl. Florence. Popular joint sells delectable pizzas and decent burgers. Entrees 12-40dh. Open daily noon-midnight.

Restaurant Alaela (tel. 64 44 55), pl. d'Atlas. Doubles as a butcher shop so the meat is as fresh as can be. Entrees 13-25dh. Open daily 11am-midnight.

Sandwich Florence (tel. 93 21 29), av. Hassan II, next to the lmh al-Watanya building. Menu attempts to include all parts of the animal. Standard *tajines, brochettes,* and fried fish (25-30dh). Open daily 11am-midnight.

Chez Vittoria, 21 rue Brahim Rouda (tel. 62 47 30), across from Hôtel Central. Head 2 blocks down from pl. Mohammed V and 1 block to the right. Serves pastas, salads, and other European dishes (25-100dh). Wine 90-160dh. Beer 20-30dh.

FEZ EL-BALI

Food stalls line Talâa Kebira and Talâa Seghira, near the Bab Boujeloud entrance to Fez el-Bali. A vegetarian feast of *harira*, roasted peppers and eggplant, potato fritters, and bread will only set you back 10dh at the stalls inside, while a good *kefta* (ground meat) sandwich goes for 15dh. Go left from Talâa Kebira at Madrassa al-Atarrine (see p. 686), and head deeper in the medina toward pl. Achabine for some of the cheapest eateries in Morocco.

Restaurant des Jeunes, 16 rue Serrajine (tel. 63 49 75), on the right as you enter the *bab*. Friendly staff serves regional favorites. Entrees 20-30dh. Open daily 6am-midnight.

Restaurant Bouayad, 26 rue Serrajine (tel. 63 62 78). Locals eat around satellite TV. *Menu* 40dh—don't pay the tourist rate (60dh). Open 24hr.

👁 SIGHTS

FEZ EL-BALI

With over 9000 streets, Fez's medina is possibly the most difficult to navigate in all Morocco. There are three ways to approach it. The first is simple and expensive: hire a guide. **Official guides** are available at the Syndicat d'Initiative. (Ask for a local guide; they know Fez better and are cheaper. Prices for local guides are 120dh for a half-day or 150dh per day.) Ali Lamrani (tourist guide #1335, tel. 63 70 12) is particularly recommended for his mastery of English and his knowledge of Fez. Though **unofficial guides** are much cheaper, they are not recommended. They are illegal, they often lack historical knowledge, and they take travelers to shops for which they get a 25% commission. If you do hire one, nail down an itinerary beforehand and establish your aversion to shopping. A second option is to follow the route below, which hits the major "sights." The final option is simply to get lost in the magnificent atmosphere that is Fez's medina. When it's time to tear yourself away, ask merchants or women how to get to Talâa Kebira and follow it back uphill to Bab Boujeloud. Just remember: walking downhill will take you farther into the medina, while trekking uphill will lead you out (to Bab Boujeloud).

To see the medina at its liveliest, avoid the hours between noon and 3pm, when most shops and sights close, and Friday, the Muslim day of prayer. Although faux guides will probably follow you for a while, ignoring them or repeating *"Non, merci"* or *"La shukran"* should keep them at bay (see **Hustlers and Guides,** p. 660). The best way to see the main monuments in the medina is to head to Bab Boujeloud and then wander down Talâa Kebira from there.

A WALKING TOUR OF FEZ EL-BALI

TALÂA KEBIRA. Virtually all of the sights in Fez's medina lie along the Talâa Kebira (a.k.a. the Grand Talâa), old Fez's main street and an essential reference point for anyone attempting to navigate the medina. The Talâa Kebira heads downhill from Bab Boujeloud to the Qaraouine Mosque area. The Bab Boujeloud is the main entrance to the medina; you know it, and the faux guides know it too. Once you pass the gate, however, they will more or less leave you alone. Built in 1912 by

SEEING RED Throughout the country, the hands, feet and hair of Moroccan women are decorated with the original temporary tattoo, *henna*. Stemming from the Arabic words meaning "tenderness" and "good luck," henna is made from the leaf of the *tafilat* plant, ground into a powder and mixed with warm water to make a paste. It has three main uses: as a medicine; for pregnant women in their 7th month; and for ceremonies of marriage and the "Festival of the Girls" on the 27th day of Ramadan. In a culture where little of a woman is supposed to be seen, it brings a touch of red beauty—and cover—to the only visible skin.

the Frenchman Marichal Lauyote to gain the confidence of the locals, the *bab* is tiled in blue on one side (the color of Fez) and green on the other (the favorite color of Mohammed and consequently the color most identified with Islam). The square just inside the *bab* is where the Moroccan revolution against the French occupation began. Down to the right is the **Talâa Seghira,** Fez's other main street, lined mostly by shops catering to locals (i.e., the famed underwear *souq*).

█BOU INANIA MADRASSA. To the right after a food *souq* is the spectacular Bou Inania Madrassa and mosque, a school for teaching the Koran and other Islamic sciences, built in 1326. The intricacy of the cedar and stucco work make this arguably the best *madrassa* in Morocco, and perhaps the world—not bad for a college dorm. Classes were held in the courtyard and the adjacent salons, and the students lived three or four to a two-by-two meter cell on the upper floor. It's no surprise that this building came at a ridiculous cost. When the Merinid Sultan Abou Inan was presented with the totals for the construction, he simply threw them into the canal separating the mosque from the *madrassa*, exclaiming that no price tag could be placed on beauty. *(Open Sa-Th 9am-7pm. 10dh.)*

FONDOUQS. Plunging ahead down a little jog in the road, you'll notice a series of *fondouqs* (old inns now used as factories) on the left side. First is the drum *fondouq*, where skins are stretched and thinned to produce that perfect tone. Next is the *fondouq* for honey, olive oil, and butter, which was formerly a mental hospital. Lastly, you'll sniff the (almost) cured products of the **sheepskin fondouq,** just after the entrance to a parking lot on the left. Beware the cries of "*Batica!*" (watch out) from the drivers of heavily laden donkeys.

NEJJARINE MUSEUM OF ART. To get to the **Place Nejjarine,** with its tiled fountain, step off the Talâa Kebira and turn right onto the only main street in the leather *souq;* go down the ramp, turn left again, and continue about 25m. The Nejjarine Museum of Art displays the standard tools, musical instruments, and decorated doors, but in a particularly pleasant fashion. A luxury inn until the end of the 18th century, it was later used by the French as a police station. Today, its rooftop **cafe** offers a tranquil escape from the rushing traffic of peddlers and tourists.

SPICE SOUQ TO ZAOUIA MOULAY IDRISS II. Back on the Talâa Kebira, the **Attarine ("Spice") Souq,** perhaps the most exotic market, awaits about 200m down. When spices were a more prestigious commodity, its vendors got the privileged spot near the mosque. Off to the right at the beginning of the spice *souq* is the **Henna Souq,** which sells the plant used to temporarily tattoo women at weddings (see **Seeing Red,** above). At the far end is the **Maristan Sidi Frej,** which was built in 1286 and was the model for psychiatric hospitals in the West. Toward the end of the Attarine Souq are several turn-offs into a **cloth market,** selling slippers and *jelabas* (robes), and a **dried fruit market.** The fruit market in turn leads to **Zaouia Moulay Idriss II,** the resting place of the Islamic saint credited with founding Fez. Pilgrims touch the tomb through a slot in a brass star. Wooden barriers on the streets leading to the tomb delineate a sacred zone and were built to prevent donkeys from entering holy ground. As always, non-Muslims are not allowed to enter.

MADRASSA AL-ATTARINE. The Talâa Kebira ends at Madrassa al-Attarine, dating from 1324. Though much overlooked by visitors, this could be the most peaceful place in the old city. Built by Abou Siad, a Merenid, it is one of the smallest *madrassas* in Morocco, but is notable for its details and mosaics. The intricacies of the carvings are spectacular—they rival the Bou Inania's in beauty and style. *(Open daily June-Aug. 9am-6pm, Sept.-May 9am-5pm. 10dh.)*

QARAOUINE MOSQUE. Exiting the *madrassa*, turn left, and then left again; a few meters down is a little opening into the Qaraouine mosque. Founded in 857 by Fatima el-Fihria, a woman, the mosque is one of the oldest universities in the world. It trained students in logic, math, rhetoric, and the Koran while Europe stumbled through the Dark Ages. You can thank (or curse) the mosque for educating Pope Sylvester II, who introduced algebra and the modern number system. Non-Muslims can take pictures through the portals but may not enter. Its library, off-limits to tourists, holds what some think is the first manuscript of the Koran.

Keeping the mosque on the right, you'll eventually come to pl. Seffarine, known for its **metal souq,** which deafens travelers with incessant cauldron-pounding. There are several potential routes from here. To reach the **tanneries,** turn sharply left and continue to bear left (follow the worn, six-sided cobblestones). Once the smell becomes intense, head right down a microscopic alley (a tannery *"guardien"* has probably grabbed you by now; 10dh is the basic fee). From a balcony above, you may view skins being soaked in green liquid, rinsed in a washing machine/cement-mixer hybrid, dunked in diluted pigeon excrement or waterlogged wheat husks (for suppleness), and saturated in dye.

To exit the medina or reach Bab ar-Rcif, a major bus and cab hub, follow the street heading away from the mosque to its end, turn left, and then right.

OTHER SIGHTS IN FEZ EL-BALI

■**THE DAR BATHA MUSEUM.** The Dar Batha Museum, with its well-kept garden, makes an excellent diversion for those tired of the endless, winding medina streets. The building, a 19th-century palace, may be the highlight of this beautiful and well-kept museum. The spacious Andalucian mansion headquartered Sultan Hassan I and his playboy son, Moulay Abd el-Aziz, during the final years of decadence before the French occupation. The museum, host to Moroccan music concerts in September, chronicles Fez's artistic and intellectual history. The keynote is the display of ceramics with the signature "Fez blue," derived from cobalt, standing out on a white enamel background. *(Start at Bab Boujeloud, head straight down the Talâa Seghira, take the 1st right past the movie theater, then turn right again at pl. l'Istiqlal, home to the museum. Open W-M 8:30am-noon and 2:30–6pm. 10dh.)*

ANDALOUS QUARTER. The Andalous Quarter and its less-crowded streets are across the Oued Fez (river) from the heart of Fez el-Bali. Many of the Moors who fled from Muslim Spain to Morocco during the 15th-century Reconquest settled around the grand Almohad house of worship in Fez, the **Andalous Mosque.** Its main attraction is the grandiose 13th-century doorway. *(To find the mosque, cross pl. Rcif, go through a small arched gate, turn right, and follow the wall on the right. From Fez el-Bali, cross the river at Port Bein el-Moudoun near the tanneries and head straight down rue Seffrah.)*

A WALKING TOUR OF FEZ EL-JDID

Hit Fez el-Jdid after you've had enough of Fez el-Bali; the latter is more interesting. Christians, Jews, and Muslims once co-existed in Fez el-Jdid, built by the Merinids in the 13th century. King Mohammed VI's sprawling modern palace, the **Dar el-Makhzen** (off-limits to everyone not royal), borders pl. Alaouites. Diagonally off the plaza, grande rue des Merinides runs up to Bab Semmarin and its seven bronze gates installed by King Hassan II in 1968. Just before the beginning of the main street is a peaceful, 17th-century **Jewish cemetery,** which provides the resting place for over 12,000 people (open daily dawn-dusk; 10dh). Off this boulevard, the meter-wide streets open into miniature underground tailors' shops, half-timbered houses, and covert alleyways. The **jewelers' souq** glitters at the top of grande rue des Merinides. Cackling chickens, salty fish, and dried okra vie for attention in the **covered market,** inside Bab Semmarin at the entrance to Fez el-Jdid proper.

Bear left at the end of rue des Fez el-Jdid into the **Petit Méchouar;** on the left is **Bab Dekaken,** the back entrance to the Dar el-Makhzen. **Bab es-Seba,** an imperial gate, opens onto the **Grand Méchouar,** a roomy plaza lined with street lamps. From here it's an easy walk to Bab Boujeloud—turn through the opening to the right of Bab es-Seba, continue straight for 250m, veer to the right, and pass through a large arch at the end of road. The entrance to the refreshing **Boujeloud Gardens,** a refuge from the midday sun, is on the right (open Tu-Su; free), while Bab Boujaloud is another 300m down the same road.

OUTSIDE THE MEDINA

In addition to the medina, a set of tombs and an odd museum are of interest. To reach the tombs and museum, exit the medina through a small gate to the right on pl. Baghdadi when walking from Bab Boujeloud toward Fez el-Jdid. Turn right on the main road, walk past the bus station 200m, then take a small path that winds its way up the hillside; the tombs are to the right and the museum to the left.

MERENID TOMBS. To the north of the old city lie the Merenid Tombs. The Palais des Merenides, a five-star hotel, overlooks the ever-decaying tombs and occupies one of the most picturesque hillsides in the Maghreb. From here, the medina unfolds with the same poetry that inspired Paul Bowles and countless other Orientalist writers. The panorama is most impressive in the half-light of dawn or dusk. During calls to prayer, when over a hundred *muezzin* simultaneously summon the faithful, the experience is almost mystical.

BORJ NORD MUSEUM. A few hundred paces west of the tombs is the Borj Nord Museum, a collection of Moroccan arms and other military apparati stored in an old lookout tower. *(Open daily 9am-noon and 3-6pm. 10dh.)*

THE ATLANTIC COAST

The towns along Morocco's Atlantic coast, connected by the country's only extensive railway line, are undoubtedly more liberal, laid-back, and open than their conservative cousins in the interior. Men and women alike go to the beach regularly to sunbathe, swim, surf, and windsurf, often among European tourists. The west coast contains Morocco's industrial boom towns—Casablanca, the country's commercial center, and Rabat, its most westernized city—which are best avoided by those with limited time in Morocco. If you're headed to the coast, your best bets are the peaceful and tranquil smaller cities.

ASILAH أَصِيلَة

Just a short trip from Tangier, Asilah's sandy shores, quiet streets, and brilliant white medina offer respite from the usual tensions of Moroccan tourism. Over the last 1000 years, every European power from the Vikings to the French have sent flotillas, armies, and even a crusade to wrench tiny Asilah from Moroccan hands. Rarely did Europeans last more than a generation or two before being sent packing from this fabled port city. Except for a few weeks in August when a large art and horse festival is held, Asilah remains a peaceful spot for kicking back and soaking up the sun on Atlantic beaches.

🛐 ORIENTATION AND PRACTICAL INFORMATION. The main street heading into town is bd. Mohammed V, which ends at the town's center, **place Mohammed V** (a traffic circle). The **train station** (tel. 41 73 27) is a 20min. walk from town on the Asilah-Tangier highway, near a strip of campgrounds. To get to town, follow the road by the beach, keeping the sea to the right. A taxi to or from town costs about

10dh. A minibus connects the station to town; it leaves from the front of the station just after the train arrives (10dh; you may have to bargain). Buses run to: **Tangier** (1hr., 4 per day, 5am-11pm, 15dh); **Rabat** (5hr., 3 per day, 7:45am-11pm, 75 dh); **Casablanca** (6hr., 3 per day, 7:45am-11pm, 95dh); **Marrakesh** (9 hr., 1 per day, 11pm, 130dh). **CTM** and **private bus companies** vend tickets together in the same stall off av. Prince Heritier Sidi Mohammed. Take the first right leaving pl. Mohammed V away from the medina; the station is in the lot on the left. To: **Tangier** (every 30min., 7:45am-5:15pm, 13dh); **Larache** (45min., 14 per day, 11:45am-5:15pm, 10dh); **Fez** (3½hr., 4 per day, 9:45am-11pm, 55dh); **Rabat** (4hr., 14 per day, 5:45am-11:15pm, 50dh); **Meknes** (4hr., 8 per day, 10am-11pm, 50dh); **Casablanca** (4½-5½hr., 14 per day, 5:45am-10:15pm, 60dh); **Marrakesh** (9hr., 1 per day, 5:15pm, 80dh). Many buses arrive full, so get to the station early, especially during the summer. *Grand taxis* cluster in pl. Mohammed V, by the bus station, and head to Tangier (12dh). To get to the **post office** (tel. 41 72 00) from pl. Mohammed V, take bd. Mohammed V and turn right onto pl. Nations Unis, keeping the park on the right. The post office is 20m up on the left. (Open M-F 8am-noon and 2:30-6:30pm.) **Telephone code:** (0)9.

▓▔▏ ACCOMMODATIONS AND FOOD. Most hotels cluster around pl. Mohammed V and the end of av. Hassan II away from pl. Mohammed V. **Hôtel Marhaba,** 9 rue Zallakah (tel. 41 71 44), on the right as you approach the medina from pl. Mohammed V. This popular hotel fills up quickly in the summer. Prime location, low rates, nice rooms, free hot showers, and a great view of the town from the roof. (Singles 80dh; doubles 100dh; 10dh less during the winter.) **Hôtel Sahara,** 9 rue Tarfaya (tel. 41 71 85), a block inland from av. Mohammed V and two blocks before pl. Mohammed V, is similar to the Marhaba in facilities and quality, but without the prime location. To its credit, the place is spotless. (Hot showers 5dh. Singles 98dh; doubles 126dh; triples 186dh; quads 252dh.) **Hôtel Belle Vue** (tel./fax 41 77 47), rue Hassan Ben Tabit. From the top of av. Hassan II, take a left on av. Imam Asili and then the next right; there is a sign on av. Hassan II. Friendly management offers pleasant rooms with hot showers. The terrace view is an added bonus. (July-Aug. singles 100dh; doubles 200dh; triples 300dh; quads 400dh. Sept.-June singles 50dh; doubles 120dh; triples 180dh; quads 250dh. Visa, MC.) **Camping Echrigui** (tel. 41 71 82), 700m from the train station in the direction of town, where the new port finally ends, has a lounge with billiards and a restaurant. Bug repellent will come in handy here. (Hot showers 5dh. 10dh per person, per tent, and per car. Straw roofed bungalows that can fit 3 people 80dh; a large one for 3-4 with showers and a kitchen 150dh.)

The restaurants facing the ramparts along av. Hassan II specialize in seafood and serve good meals for around 35dh. The town **market** is also along av. Hassan II. **La Al Kasabah** (tel. 41 70 12), rue Zallakah, toward the ocean and past Hôtel Marhaba, is definitely the best restaurant in town. Patrons dine on seafood and pasta from a terrace overlooking the street and port. (Entrees 25-70dh. Open daily 9am-2am, closes earlier in winter. Visa, MC.) **Restaurant Marhaba,** 33 av. Hassan II (tel. 41 83 98), offers outdoor dining under towering ramparts. Try the house specialties of swordfish and calamari (each 30dh; entrees 20-40dh; open daily noon-1am).

▓ SIGHTS. The most popular beaches are those toward the train station and farthest from the medina. The best of Asilah's beaches is the enclosed **Paradise Beach,** an hour's walk from the medina. Those with extra cash can take a horse-drawn wagon for around 200dh round-trip. On the beach, some men might jeer at the sight of foreign women swimming; if you feel uncomfortable, just walk to a less-crowded area. Asilah's stunning ▓medina is bounded by heavily fortified 15th-century Portuguese walls. The Bab Kasaba, the gate off rue Zallakah, leads past the **Grand Mosque.** Right across from the mosque is the **Centre Hassan II des Rencontres Internationales** (tel. 41 70 65), a new building which houses a collection of art created during the great International Festival (open 9am-12:30pm and 3-7pm; free). During the festival (held in August) artists from all over the Arab and African worlds flock to Asilah. The city also glows with artistic flair throughout the rest of the year: walls are covered with murals, music is everywhere, and the locals seem to be perpetually dancing on the beaches.

LARACHE الأعرايش

In the summer, when tourists and faux guides descend on nearby Asilah, Larache compensates with quiet relief. This relaxing town along the Atlantic coast has no touristy veneer. A former colony of Spain (with the Spanish-style architecture to prove it), Larache is all about inexpensive accommodations and fresh seafood. Its whitewashed medina is more manageable than those in most Moroccan cities. Larache also makes a good base for exploring the Roman ruins at Lixus.

⁊ ORIENTATION AND PRACTICAL INFORMATION. Buses to Larache drop passengers off five blocks from **place de la Libération**, the center of activity. From the station, exit from where the buses enter, turn right, and head down **av. Mohammed ben Abdallah**, which runs into pl. Libération (about 8min.). Branching off pl. Libération to the right is the main artery, **bd. Mohammed V.** Also off pl. Libération, **Bab al-Hemis** (also called Bab Medina) leads to the **medina** and the **Zoko de la Alcaiceria** (a.k.a. Zoko Chico). Larache's **beach,** beyond the medina and across the Loukkos estuary, and is accessible by bus (2.50dh) or boat (2dh over, 4dh back).

To reach the **bus station** from pl. Libération, turn right onto av. Mohammed ben Abdallah and continue past Pension Salama; take the first left and go straight. **CTM** service to: **Asilah** (50min., 4 per day, 11:15am-10:45pm, 13dh); **Tangier** (2hr., 4 per day, 11:15am-10:45pm, 29dh); **Rabat** (4hr., 3 per day, 8:15am-6pm, 56dh); **Casablanca** (5hr., 3 per day, 8:15am-6pm, 82dh); **Meknes** (5hr., 3 per day, 4:30pm-10:15pm, 46dh); **Fez** (6½hr., 3 per day, 4:30pm-10:15pm, 61dh); **Marrakesh** (8hr., 1 per day, 6pm, 143dh). **Private buses** leave from the same station and send packed buses to the same locations at cheaper prices. **Taxis** park outside the bus station. **Local buses** (2.5dh) depart Kasbah de la Cigone off av. Mohammed V, traveling to Lixus (buses #4 and 5) and the beaches (bus #4). **Banks,** across from the post office on bd. Mohammed V heading away from pl. Libération, exchange money and have **ATMs. Police** tel. 19; international **telephones** are located in and around the **post office** (open M-F 8:30am-noon and 2:30-6:30pm; phones inside available M-Sa 8:30am-noon and 2:30-6:30pm). **Telephone code:** (0)9.

⁊ ACCOMMODATIONS AND FOOD. While there are extremely basic hotels on the medina, many nicer budget options can be found on av. Mohammed ben Abdallah and off pl. Libération. The best bargain is **Pension Amal**, 10 av. Abdallah ben Yassine (tel. 91 27 88). Head up av. Mohammed ben Abdallah for five blocks and then turn left; follow the sign (hot showers 6dh; cold showers 2dh; singles 40dh; doubles 70-80dh; triples 90dh; quads 115dh). **Hôtel España** (tel. 91 31 95), pl. Libération, is part of the family of once-grand hotels that are worth the extra cash (singles 100dh, with bath 170dh; doubles 150dh, with bath 200dh; triples 200dh, with bath 250dh; quads with bath and TV 320dh). Cheap **restaurants** line pl. Libération and the Zoko. Larache's Spanish roots are apparent in the seafood dishes that appear on each menu. **Restaurant Eskala** (tel. 91 40 80), on the Zoko Chico, through the Bab Medina and to the left, is always a safe bet (entrees 20-40dh). **Restaurant Commerciale** (tel. 91 02 60), on pl. Libération away from the ocean, serves some of the cheapest fresh seafood, chicken, and *paella* around (entrees 15-25dh).

◉ SIGHTS. Though most tourists come to Larache to visit the Roman ruins of Lixus, Larache itself makes for pleasant wandering. From pl. Libération head into the Moorish area (Bab al-Khemis) and turn right into **Zoco de la Alcaiceria**, a Spanish-built, 17th-century courtyard, now a bustling souq. The Zoco leads to **Kasbah de la Cigogne** (the Stork's Kasbah), located near the tall minaret of the mosque. Built by Felipe III, it is Larache's only intact 17th-century fortification. Unfortunately it's not open to visitors. Around the corner, next to the citadel, sits the little **archaeological museum** (tel. 91 20 91), containing a small assortment of Roman and Phoenician artifacts. (Open M-Sa 9am-noon and 3-6pm. 10dh.) The old city walls and ruined **kasbah** built by the Portuguese in the 16th century are visible from the walkway just off pl. Libération. You can climb among the fallen turrets, but beware of loose footholds. Continue downhill on the walkway, where couples and families stroll at sunset, for the **beach** across the **Loukkos estuary.** Entrepreneurial boatmen ferry passengers over for 2dh (4dh back) from dawn to dusk.

NEAR LARACHE: LIXUS

The Roman ruins of Lixus are located 5km north of Larache on the highway to Tangier. Though it may not be as impressive as Volubilis (see p. 677), Lixus is one of the most interesting sights that the Atlantic coast has to offer. Lixus figured prominently in Greco-Roman mythology as the site where Hercules completed his 11th labor: collecting the golden apples from Mount Atlas. Originally settled by an ancient sun-worshipping cult, Lixus became a highly successful **Phoenician settlement** around 1000 BC. As did all things Phoenician, the area fell to the Romans around 140 BC. Within a few years it had become a rich trading city occupying an important place in the Roman Empire. Unfortunately, the city lost prominence with the Empire's fall, and by the 5th century it was totally abandoned.

Visitors to the unrestored, unguarded, unmarked, and often entirely empty ruins may feel as though they are discovering them for the first time. From the main road between Larache and Asilah, follow the path that leads past the port silo and **factory** where *garum*, Lixus's famous fish-intestine paste, was made and stored for shipment. Farther along lie the ruins of a Greco-Roman **theater** containing an orchestra pit, one of the largest of the ancient world. It was later converted to an **amphitheater** and, during Spanish occupation, a bullring. Located near the theater are the relatively famous **Mosaic of the Sea God** and the **Roman baths**. Follow the fork uphill and to the left to temples, villas, churches, and a view of the entire site.

To get to Lixus, hop on **bus** #4 or 5 from the stop near Kasbah de la Cigogne in Larache (2.5dh) and tell the ticket collector you want to go to Lixus. Unfortunately buses going toward Larache don't stop here. To get back, walk along the highway (45 min.) or flag down one of the rare taxis. *Let's Go* does not recommend hitchhiking, although tired travelers have reported it as a useful option.

RABAT الرّباط

For most Moroccans, Rabat means business. During the 17th century, Rabat was indeed the pirates' cove that many authors (like Daniel Defoe in *Robinson Crusoe*) have made it out to be. The Mediterranean and Atlantic were the pirates' oysters until the Alaouites subdued them around 1700. Not until 1912 did Rabat return to prominence, when the French selected it as the seat of government.

Despite its colorful past, Rabat is now one of the few Moroccan cities not plagued by hustlers and other travel annoyances. King Mohammed VI resides here and his personal guards have kept hustlers off the main streets. The king, moreover, nurtures a healthy local economy not chiefly reliant upon tourism for revenue. As a political and business capital, Rabat has a fleet of public employees, a swelling upper-middle class, and a flourishing Mercedes-Benz trade. Admittedly, today's Rabat lacks the tradition of Fez, the color of Marrakesh, and the money of Casablanca, but don't be tempted to skip out. Not only can its moderation be a treat in and of itself, but calm and order, Western facilities, and several important sights all weigh heavily in this capital city's favor. Rabat is also the Moroccan city where Western women tend to feel most comfortable.

▐ GETTING THERE

Trains run to Rabat from **Casablanca** (1hr., 17 per day, 6:45am-8:45pm, 27dh) and **Fez** (3½hr., 8 per day, 7:15am-2:40am, 50dh). **Buses** go from **Casablanca** (1½hr., 18 per day, 6am-11:30pm, 30dh); **Meknes** (3hr., 8 per day, 5am-2am, 38dh); **Marrakesh** (5hr., 10 per day, 5am-9pm, 55dh); **Tangier** (5hr., 15 per day, 5am-11:15pm, 57dh).

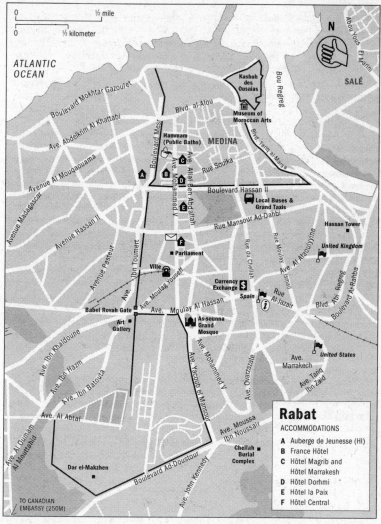

Rabat

ACCOMMODATIONS

A Auberge de Jeunesse (HI)
B France Hôtel
C Hôtel Magrib and
   Hôtel Marrakesh
D Hôtel Dorhmi
E Hôtel la Paix
F Hôtel Central

▼ ORIENTATION AND PRACTICAL INFORMATION

Rabat could not be easier to navigate. Av. Mohammed V parades north to south from the **medina**, past the post office and train station, to the **Great Mosque (As-Sounna)**. Exiting the train station (the Rabat Ville stop), turn left up av. Mohammed V to reach most budget hotels and bd. Hassan II, which runs perpendicular to av. Mohammed V along the medina's walls; the center of town is at this junction. When facing the medina, you will see Rabat's sister city **Salé** over the river to the right; the bus station on rte. de Casablanca is a good distance to the left.

TRANSPORTATION

Flights: Rabat is served by the airport in Casablanca. **Royal Air Maroc** (tel. 70 90 66), on av. Mohammed V across from the Rabat Ville train station. Open M-Sa 8:30am-12:15pm and 2:30-7pm. **Air France,** 281 av. Mohammed V (tel. 70 70 66). Open M-Th 8:30am-12:15pm and 2:30-6:30pm, F 8:30am-12:15pm and 3:30-6:30pm, Sa 9am-12:15pm.

Trains: Rabat Ville Station, (tel. 70 14 69) av. Mohammed V, at av. Moulay Youssef. To: **Casablanca Port** (1hr., 19 per day, 6:15am-9:30pm, 27dh); **Casablanca Voyageurs** (1 hr., 17 per day, 4am-11:30pm, 25dh); **Meknes** (3hr., 8 per day, 7:15am-11:45pm, 53dh); **Fez** (4hr., 8 per day, 7:15am-11:45pm, 69dh); **Marrakesh** (5hr., 7 per day, 4am-11:30pm, 99dh); **Tangier** (5½hr., 4 per day, 8am-1am, 87dh).

Buses: All companies operate from an enormous station (tel. 28 02 62) on the road to Casablanca, at pl. Mohammed Zerktouni. It's several kilometers from the town center, so take a *petit taxi* (12dh) or bus #30 from av. Hassan, near rue Mohammed V (2.50dh). **CTM** tickets at windows #14 and 15; other windows are private companies. CTM to: **Casablanca** (1hr., 6 per day, 3:20am-10:30pm, 27dh); **Meknés** (2½hr., 8 per day, 8am-9:30pm, 40dh); **Fez** (3½hr., 8 per day, 8am-midnight, 57dh); **Tangier** (5hr., 5 per day, 7:30am-1am, 80dh); **Chefchaouen** (6hr., 1 per day, 10am, 65dh).

Taxis: Stands can be found at the train station, in front of the bus station along av. Hassan II, and at the entrance to the medina by the corner of av. Hassan II and av. Mohammed V. Expect to pay about 18dh from the bus station to the center of town and about 6dh from the train station (plus a surcharge of 5dh at night).

Car Rental: Hertz, 467 av. Mohammed V (tel. 62 92 27). **Budget** (tel. 70 57 89), headquartered in the train station. Both rent the fabulous Fiat Uno starting at 415dh per day, plus 2.4dh per km. Both open M-Sa 8am-noon and 2-7pm, Su 8:30am-6:30pm. Minimum age is 21 for most cars.

TOURIST, FINANCIAL, AND LOCAL SERVICES

Tourist Office: Municipal, 22 rue al-Jazair (tel. 73 05 62). Way out there. Turn right out of the train station, walk up av. Mohammed V to the Grand As-Sounna Mosque, turn left on av. Moulay Hassan, and after four blocks bear right onto rue al-Jazair. Not-so-fabulous maps of Rabat and other large cities. Some English and Spanish spoken. Open June 16 to mid-Sept. M-F 8am-2pm; mid-Sept. to June 15 M-F 8am-noon and 12:30-5:30pm; during Ramadan M-F 9am-3pm.

Currency Exchange: Banks and **ATMs** are located on av. Mohammed V and av. Allal ben Abdallah. **BMCE** is located at 260 av. Mohammed V and at the train station. Open M-F 8am-noon and 3-6pm, Sa-Su 10am-2pm and 4-8pm.

Luggage Storage: At the train station (2.50dh per bag, must be locked, locks for sale in station: coincidence?). At the bus station (3dh per day). Both open daily 4am-midnight.

English Bookstores: English Bookstore, 7 rue al-Yamama (tel. 70 65 93). From the train station, take a hard right and cut diagonally through the parking lot to rue al-Yamama. Kerouac, Foucault, Dostoevsky, and *Let's Go.* Open M-Sa 9am-12:30pm and 3-7pm. **American Bookstore,** 4 Zankat Tanja (tel. 76 87 17). Take av. Mohammed V past the Grand Mosque and turn left 3 blocks later. Great paperback selection. Open M-F 9:30am-12:30pm and 2:30-7:30pm, Sa 10am-12:30pm and 1:30-5:30pm.

Laundromat: Hotels are the best option—expect to pay 20-30dh per load.

EMERGENCY AND COMMUNICATIONS

Police: (tel. 19), rue Soekarno, 2 blocks from the post office off av. Mohammed V.

Late-Night Pharmacy: Pharmacie de Préfecture (tel. 70 70 72), av. Moulay Slimane. From the post office, cross av. Mohammed V and veer to the right onto rue el-Qahira (as if going to the Syndicat d'Initiative). On your right a few blocks down and across from Theatre Mohammed V. Open nightly 8:30pm-8am.

Medical Assistance: Hôpital Avicenne (tel. 77 44 11), av. Ibn Sina, at the end of bd. d'Argonne away from the medina. Free emergency medical care. U.S. citizens can also go to the **U.S. Embassy** (see p. 662) for medical assistance.

Post Office: (tel. 72 07 31) av. Mohammed V at rue Soekarno, to the left when leaving the train station. Open M-Th 8:30am-12:15pm and 2:30-6:45pm, F 11:30am-3pm.

Internet: I.N.T. Plus, 379 av. Mohammed V (tel. 20 43 88), half a block towards the train station from the medina. Up 3 flights of stairs. 15dh per hr. Open daily 9am-10pm.

Telephones: Rue Soekarno, facing the post office. International phones and collect calls. Open 24hr. **Poste Restante** is also located in this building (2dh per piece).

| TELEPHONE CODE | Rabat's phone code is (0)7. |

ACCOMMODATIONS AND CAMPING

As usual, medina hotels are cheaper (and often less appealing) than those in the *ville nouvelle*. Cushier hotels line **av. Mohammed V, av. Allal ben Abdallah,** and environs. From the train station, turn left onto av. Mohammed V and walk toward the medina; av. Allal ben Abdallah runs parallel, one block to the right.

VILLE NOUVELLE

Auberge de Jeunesse (HI), 43 rue Marassa (tel. 72 57 69), 2 blocks along the medina walls on the road perpendicular to av. Hassan II. In an old mansion with a beautiful courtyard. Separate dorms for men and women, complete with cold showers and European-style toilets. The friendly manager even speaks English. Breakfast 8dh. Reception open 8-10am, noon-3pm, and 6:30-10:30pm. Dorms 31dh, members 27dh.

Hôtel Central, 2 rue al-Basra (tel. 70 73 56). From the train station, cross av. Mohammed V, walk 2 blocks toward the medina, and turn right; it's on the corner of rue al-Basra and rue Dimachh. Big, clean rooms with high ceilings, sinks, and firm beds. Hot showers 10dh. Singles 80dh, with shower 100dh; doubles 110dh, with shower 136dh; triples 140dh, with shower 172dh; quads 170dh, with shower 208dh.

Hôtel de la Paix, 2 rue Ghazza (tel. 73 20 31 or 72 29 26), on the corner of av. Allal ben Abdallah and rue Ghazza, about 10min. from the train station and 2 blocks before the medina. Super-friendly management offers spotless, airy rooms with full baths, some with tables, chairs, and telephones. Ask for a balcony. Singles 160dh; doubles 200dh.

Camping de la Plage (tel. 78 23 68), far away on the beach in Salé. Take a *grand taxi* to the site (10dh), or grab a bus from the av. Hassan II station (see map); if you take the bus, ask to be dropped off at Bab Mrisa, and follow the river towards the ocean. Running water, toilets, and a store/restaurant. Facilities are primitive and a bit shabby, but the price is right. Electricity included. Reception 24hr. Cold showers 2dh. 5dh per person, per tent, and per car; slightly more for vans or larger vehicles.

MEDINA

Hôtel Dohrmi, 313 av. Mohammed V (tel. 72 38 98), 1½ blocks inside the medina walls, on the right. A real find. Female management makes women feel at home. Rooms surround a pleasant courtyard. European-style toilets in some rooms. Get here early in summer, as the place fills up quickly. Hot showers 7dh. Singles 80dh; doubles 100dh; triples 150dh; quads 200dh.

Hôtel Maghrib El-Jadid, 2 rue Sebbahi (tel. 73 22 07), at av. Mohammed V, a few blocks past Hôtel Dohrmi on the right. Spotless rooms and rather small beds. Rooftop terrace a nice place to relax or dry clothes. English spoken. Singles 50dh; doubles 80dh; triples 120dh; quads 150dh. Cold showers 2dh; hot showers 5dh. If full, try its sister **Hôtel Marrakesh,** 10 rue Sebbahi (tel. 72 77 03), down the block. Same prices.

France Hôtel, 46 rue Sout Sewara (tel. 72 34 57), off av. Mohammed V. Cheaper than cheap, offering only the most basic rooms. No showers, but a *hammam* (5-10dh) nearby; ask at the desk. Singles 30-35dh; doubles 50dh; triples 60dh.

FOOD

Rabat is filled with mediocre international food options. The homesick might enjoy **Hong Kong,** a Chinese/Vietnamese restaurant on av. Mohammed V one block towards the train station from av. Hassan II, **McDonald's,** across from the train station, or **Taki Fried Chicken,** Rabat's original fast food, in a small arcade across from the Parliament. A **food market** guards the entrance to the **medina** at av. Mohammed V, and *brochetteries* and sandwich shops are located within the medina walls.

MOROCCO

Cafe Restaurant Taghazout (tel. 72 40 61), across from Hotêl Maghrib El-Jadid. Generally considered one of the best restaurants in the medina. The Moroccan entrees (20-23dh) are some of the cheapest around. Open 7:30am-11pm.

Restaurant El-Bahia (tel. 73 45 04), av. Hassan II, to the right as you head toward the medina on av. Mohammed V. Includes an interior courtyard and fountain. The lunch crowd devours appetizing dishes, sometimes leaving a small selection for dinner patrons. Tasty vegetarian options. Entrees 22-55dh. Open daily 10am-11pm.

Cafe-Restaurant La Clef (tel. 70 19 72). Exiting the train station, make a hard right onto av. Moulay Youssef, then skip down the first alley on the left. A bit pricier than the other restaurants, but worth it. Good *tajine pigeon* (55dh). Entrees 45-85dh. One of the few places in town to get gin or whiskey (38dh). Open daily noon-3pm and 7-11pm.

Snack Bar Balima, under the Balima Hotel a block north of the train station on av. Mohammed V. Serves Western-style fast food. Entrees 20-40dh.

◉ SIGHTS

◪**AS-SOUNNA MOSQUE AND ARCHAEOLOGICAL MUSEUM.** Rabat's principal place of worship, the splendid As-Sounna Mosque towers above the *ville nouvelle*. Although non-Muslims cannot enter, they may peek in. Near the mosque, the archaeological museum, often considered the best of Morocco's less-than-stellar museums, has an impressive collection of Hellenistic bronze works, all cast before 25 BC. *(Walk down av. Mohammed V away from the medina and turn left onto Abd Al Aziz at the Grand Mosque; the museum is on the next street off Abd Al Aziz to the right, near the Hôtel Chellah. Open W-M 9-11:30am and 2:30-5:30pm. 10dh.)*

◪**THE HASSAN TOWER.** Across town along av. Abi Regreg (near the Moulay Hassan bridge to Salé) towers the famous minaret of the **Hassan Mosque,** a testament to the ambition of Sultan Yacoub al-Mansour. The huge courtyard was once the prayer hall of what was to be the largest mosque in the Muslim world, begun in 1195 to commemorate a victory in Spain but abandoned shortly thereafter upon the sultan's death. All that remains are the 44m minaret (meant to reach a staggering 60m) and the stubby reconstructions of the support pillars (which were originally destroyed by an 18th-century earthquake). The mosque was to be al-Mansour's greatest achievement, to be built in the same style as the Giralda of Sevilla and the Koutoubia of Marrakesh—historians conjecture that he had Caliphal ambition. *(Follow bd. Hassan II to the right when facing the medina; after a 15min. walk, the tower will be on the right. Open daily, sunrise to sunset. Free.)*

BAB EL-ROUAH AND ART GALLERY. The salmon-pink Bab El-Rouah (Gate of Winds) is a massive four-arched gate, one of the most decorated and impressive gates in all of Morocco. The nearby art gallery houses an often-changing collection of paintings and sculpture. *(Facing the Grand Mosque with the train station at your back, follow av. Moulay Hassan to the right for 10min. Open daily 8:30am-12pm and 2:30-8pm. Free.)*

THE CHELLAH. Beyond the city walls at the end of av. Yacoub el-Mansour loom the decrepit but impressive ruins of the Chellah, a former Roman city. In the 14th century the ruling Merenids encircled the city with walls and converted it into a royal necropolis. Because of its tranquil aura and spectacular views, the Chellah is often called one of the most romantic sites in Morocco. From the gate, descend through the overgrown gardens to reach the necropolis and its ruined mosque. Step inside to see the 13th-century tombs of Sultan Abu Yacoub Youssef and the adjacent stork-filled minaret. On the way back, a path to the right circles the Roman ruins once the sight of a military camp and the first occupied territory in the region. Nowadays it's a favorite local picnic spot. *(Follow av. Mohammed V to the As-Sounna Mosque (see below) and keep going, with the wall on the right. At the end, the Chellah is diagonally across the square to the left. Open daily, sunrise to sunset. 10dh.)*

MOHAMMED V MAUSOLEUM. In the structure to the left when facing the Hassan Mosque is the Mausoleum of King Mohammed V, a tribute to the king who led Morocco's independence movement and lent his name to seemingly every third street in the country. Non-Muslims can enter the lower room of the spectacular, traditional-style building, where spectacularly clad guards keep company with Mohammed V himself in his marble sarcophagus. *(Open daily, sunrise to sunset. Free.)*

DAR EL-MAKHZEN. Begun in the 18th century, most construction on this palace was finished after the end of the French occupation. Visitors who get too close will be chased away by soldiers. Photography is only permitted from afar. *(Follow the same road to the Bab el-Rouah but turn left when you see a long straight street.)*

OTHER SIGHTS. There is little of interest in the medina for the traveler who has visited Fez or Marrakesh. The **Kasbah des Oudaias,** however, just outside the medina, is impressive. It used to be a pirate stronghold until Moulay Idriss sent Saharan mercenaries to oversee the buccaneers' tributes of gold and slaves. Exiting the kasbah through Bab Oudaia and heading through the keyhole-shaped gate down the stairs leads to the sublime **Andalusian gardens,** of medieval Islamic-Spanish design and French construction. *(On your right after you enter the bab.)* The **Museum of Moroccan Arts,** next to the gardens, was the 17th-century hideaway of the infamous Moulay Ismail. The excellent ethnographic collection shows off the sultan's private apartment, signature Rabat-style carpets, traditional local costumes, and musical instruments. A charming cafe lies on the opposite side of the garden. *(Follow av. Mohammed V. through the medina and take a right on bd. al-Alou to its end, a 15min. walk. The kasbah is just to the left and gardens and museum just to the right. Museum and gardens open 8am-noon and 2-7:30pm. Museum entrance 10dh.)*

🎵 ENTERTAINMENT

Visitors to Rabat have a rare opportunity to sample **Moroccan and Arab cinema** at the movie house on av. Allal ben Abdallah, a few blocks off the medina (Sa 10:30am; 20dh; in French or with French subtitles). The rest of the week the movie house screens recycled foreign flicks. The prosperous youth of Rabat scope one another out at cinemas and pricey, pseudo-European discos such as **Amnesia,** on rue Monastir near the Cinema Royale (weekends and Wednesdays are crowded). **Café Balima** (see **Food,** p. 693) has a disco downstairs, sometimes with live music (open 10pm-3am; cover and a drink Su-Th 70dh, F-Sa 100dh). Those looking for something more sophisticated might call the palatial **Tour Hassan Hôtel,** 22 av. Chellah (tel. 72 14 91), to sit in on a performance or concert.

NEAR RABAT: SALÉ سلا

Across the Bou Regreg from Rabat sits Salé, an ancient trading city that has recently become more a suburb of the ever-expanding Rabat. This virtually tourist-free "White City" makes for an intriguing half-day trip from Rabat. The medina in Salé has three main attractions: the **souqs** along the **rue Grande Mosquée,** those along **rue Kechachine,** and the Grand Mosque and accompanying 14th century *madrassa* (college of theology, literature, and law). The best way to see these sights is by walking along the walls perpendicular to the river and entering the medina through the towering **Bab Mrisa** (just on the right if walking or where the taxis/buses will drop you off). Follow the inside wall on the left until you get to a square. Since there are few tourists, the souqs in Salé are more traditional, lacking the high-tech goods often found in the medinas of Fez or Marrakesh.

The two main streets from the Bab Mrisa lead to the **Grand Mosque,** which dates from the Almohad era. You'll know you're close when the path and walls suddenly become shiny white and clean. As usual, the mosque is closed to non-Muslims. The nearby **Madrassa,** however, invites visitors to gaze at its architectural riches. Completed in 1333, this school once instructed students in the Qur'an and Islamic sciences. Today Moroccan architects consider the building the model to which all universities should conform. Paved with an intricate mosaic and decorated with elegant cedar carvings, the courtyard invites meticulous study. Up a little flight of stairs, students' rooms are open for viewing. The rooftop affords a splendid panorama of Salé and Rabat. (Entrance to the *madrassa* 10dh.)

The easiest way to get to Salé is via a **grand taxi** (2dh) or by **bus** #6 or #12 (2.5dh). Both leave from bd. Hassan II in Rabat and drop passengers off at Bab Mrisa, at the corner of the city. If you decide to take the bus, make sure to let the driver know where you want to get off. If you choose to walk from Rabat, head east on av. Hassan II and cross the bridge to Salé (30min. from av. Mohammed V).

CASABLANCA الدّارالبَيضاء

As time goes by, Casablanca (known as "Casa") continues to bloat under the Maghreb sun. Already the largest city in Morocco, with nearly 4 million inhabitants (up from a mere 20,000 in 1900), Casablanca continues to attract rural Moroccans seeking urban prosperity. In this, the country's financial capital and Africa's largest port, Western dress predominates, and women participate actively and visibly in city life. With the construction of the gargantuan **Hassan II Mosque,** Casablanca established itself as a major religious center as well. Although the mosque is indeed spectacular, foreign backpackers generally view Casa as little more than a transport hub—and not without reason. Unfortunately there is no Rick's Café Américain in the kasbah; no getaway plane at the airport; and no one looking at you, kid, except the hustlers who prowl the port and medina. Those dying to experience the legendary Rick's Cafe will have to settle for a martini served by a trench-coated Moroccan at the local Hyatt; the movie *Casablanca* was based more on Tangier anyway.

▐ GETTING THERE

Trains run to Casablanca from **Rabat** (1hr., 19 per day, 6:15am-9:30pm, 27dh). **Buses** go from: **Marrakesh** (4hr., 10 per day, 4am-8pm, 40dh); **Essaouira** (5hr., 26 per day, 5am-12:30am, 75dh); **Tangier** (6hr., 15 per day, 5am-11:15pm, 69dh).

🛈 ORIENTATION AND PRACTICAL INFORMATION

Casa is Morocco's transit hub for planes, trains, and buses. The **Casa Port train station** is near the youth hostel and the city center; the **Casa Voyageurs train station** is near nothing, a 50-minute walk from Casa Port or a 30dh *petit taxi* ride. To get from Casa Port to the **CTM bus station,** conveniently located downtown, cross the street, follow bd. Felix Houphëit-Boigny to pl. Nations Unies, turn left on av. Armée Royale, and watch for Hôtel Safir on the right; the station is behind and to the right of the hotel. The city has two main squares, **place Nations Unies,** below the landmark clock tower, and **place Mohammed V.** Pl. Nations Unies spreads out in front of the Hyatt Regency at the intersection of bd. Mohammed V, av. Hassan II, and av. Forces Armées Royales (F.A.R.). Pl. Mohammed V lies six blocks away from the port along av. Hassan II.

TRANSPORTATION

Flights: Aéroport Mohammed V (tel. 33 90 40) handles international and domestic flights. Trains run between the airport terminal and the Casa Port train station (55min., every hr., 24dh), some stopping at Casa Voyageurs en route; some trains head to Rabat. **Royal Air Maroc** (tel. 31 11 22 or 31 41 41; fax 44 24 09), at the airport and 44 av. des Forces Armées Royales, sells tickets for international and domestic (Agadir, Marrakesh) flights. For more information see **Getting Around,** p. 657.

Trains: Casa Port (tel. 27 18 37), Port de Casablanca. Mainly northbound service. To: **Rabat** (1hr., 17 per day, 6:45am-8:45pm, 27dh); **Fez** (4½hr., 2 per day, 8am and 8:45pm, 100dh); **Tangier** (6hr., 2 per day, 6:45am and 5:50pm, 120dh); **Marrakesh** (3½hr., 1 per day, 7:15am, 50dh). **Casa Voyageurs** (tel. 24 58 01), bd. Ba Hammed,

MOROCCO

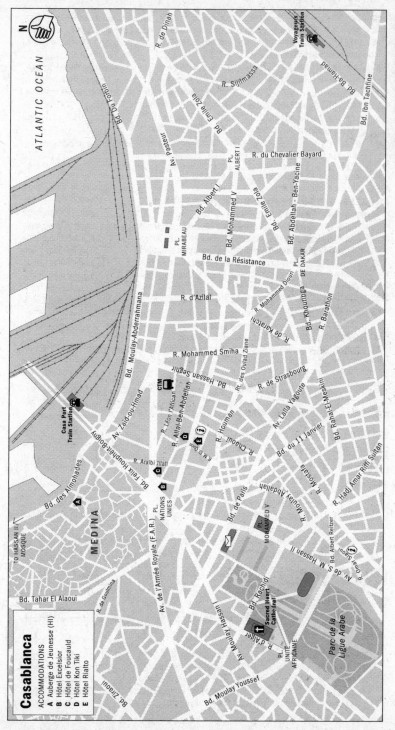

N

ATLANTIC OCEAN

R. de Dinah

Voyageurs
Train Station

R. Sijilmassa

Bd. Ba-Hamad

Bd. Ibn Tachfine

Av. Pasteur

Bd. Emile Zola

PL.
ALBERT I

R. du Chevalier Bayard

Bd. Albert I

Bd. Mohammed V

Bd. Emile Zola

Bd. Abdellah - Ben-Yacine

PL.
MIRABEAU

Bd. de la Résistance

PL.
DE DAKAR

R. d'Azilal

R. Mohammed Diouri

Bd. Khouribga

R. Barathon

R. de Karatchi

Bd. Moulay-Abderrahmana

R. Mohammed Smiha

Rt. des Oulad Ziane

R. de Strasbourg

Casa Port
Train Station

CTM

Bd. Hassan Seghir

Av. Lalla Yagoute

Av. Zaid-ou-Hmad

R. Léon l'African

R. Allal-Ben-Abdellah

R. Chaoui

R. Houman

Bd. du 11 Janvier

R. Araibi Jilati

D

E i

R. El Qued

R. Rahal-El-Meskini

Bd. des Almohades

Bd. Félix Houphet-Boigny

A

B

C

PL.
NATIONS
UNIES

Bd. de Paris

Bd. Mohammed V

R. Moulay Abdallah

R. Mostafa

R. Hadj Amar Riffi Sultan

TO HASSAN II/
MOSQUE

MEDINA

Av. de l'Armée Royale (F.A.R.)

PL.
MOHAMMED V

Bd. Albert Retzer

R. Oms Sgoul

Z

Bd. Tahar El Alaoui

R. de Goulmima

Av. de S.M. Hassan II

Bd. Rachidi

Sacred Heart
Cathedral

Parc de la
Ligue Arabe

Av. Moulay Hassan I

R. d'Alger

PL.
UNITÉ
AFRICAINE

Bd. Zrioui

Bd. Moulay Youssef

Casablanca

ACCOMMODATIONS
A Auberge de Jeunesse (HI)
B Hôtel Excelsior
C Hôtel de Foucauld
D Hôtel Kon Tiki
E Hôtel Rialto

698 ■ THE ATLANTIC COAST

away from the city center. Mainly southbound service but more extensive connections. To: **Marrakesh** (3½hr., 8 per day, 70dh); **Meknes** (4½hr., 7 per day, 90dh.) and on to **Fez** (5¼hr., 7 per day, 110dh); **Tangier** (6hr., 3 per day, 120dh; you may have to change trains at Sidi Kacem).

Buses: CTM, 23 rue Léon L'Africain (tel. 44 81 27), off rue Chaouia. To: **Rabat** (1½hr., 18 per day, 6am-11:30pm, 30dh); **El-Jadida** (1½hr., 6 per day, 5:30am-3pm, 25dh); **Marrakesh** (4hr., 6 per day, 7:30am-11:30pm, 65dh); **Meknes** (5hr., 9 per day, 6:30am-11:30pm, 63dh); **Essaouira** (5½hr., 3 per day, 5:30am-5pm, 100dh); **Fez** (6hr., 8 per day, 6:30am-11:30pm, 80dh); **Tangier** (6½hr., 6 per day, 6am-11:30pm, 100dh); **Agadir** (10hr., 6 per day, 5:30am-5pm, 140dh).

Car Rental: Casa has dozens of companies. For rates and more detailed info about renting a car in Morocco, see **By Car,** p. 658. **Europcar,** 44 av. des F.A.R. (tel. 31 37 37); **Avis,** 19 av. de l'Armée (tel. 31 24 24); and **Budget** (tel. 31 31 24), av. des F.A.R., have similar rates. Minimum age 21 for small car rental.

TOURIST, FINANCIAL, AND LOCAL SERVICES

Tourist Office: Syndicat d'Initiative et de Tourisme, 98 bd. Mohammed V (tel. 22 15 24 or 27 05 38), at rue Chaoui, about four blocks down from pl. Nations Unies. Glossy brochures and maps. English spoken. Open M-Sa 8:30am-noon and 2:30-6:30pm, Su 9am-noon. The **Office de Tourisme,** 55 rue Omar Slaoui (tel. 27 95 33 or 27 11 77; fax 20 59 29), has similar services. From pl. Mohammed V, take av. Hassan II, turn left on rue Reitzer, and then right on rue Omar Slaoui. Open M-F 8:30am-noon and 2:30-6:30pm, Su 9am-noon.

Currency Exchange: When the **banks** in the city are closed, try the airport and larger hotels, which change money at Morocco's official, uniform rates. The Hyatt Regency, Hôtel Suisse, and Hôtel Safir near the bus station and the other big hotels near pl. Nations Unies are all safe bets. **ATMs** are everywhere.

American Express: Voyages Schwartz, 112 av. du Prince Moulay Abdallah (tel. 22 29 47; fax 27 31 30). They offer standard services but won't receive wired money. Open M-F 8:30am-noon and 2:30-6:30pm, Sa 8:30am-noon.

English Bookstore: American Language Center Bookstore (tel. 27 95 59), bd. Moulay Youssef at pl. Unité Africaine. Vast array of novels and reference books. Open M-F 9:30am-12:30pm and 3:30-6:30pm, Sa 9:30am-noon.

EMERGENCY AND COMMUNICATIONS

Emergency: Police (tel. 19), bd. Brahim Roudani.

Late-Night Pharmacy: Pharmacie de Nuit (tel. 26 94 91), pl. Nations Unies. Open nightly 8pm-8am. Other pharmacies are found on almost any city block.

Medical Assistance: Croix-Rouge Marocain, 19 bd. Al Massira Al Khadra (tel. 25 25 21). **S.O.S. Medicins,** 81 av. F.A.R. (tel. 44 44 44).

Post Office: Bd. Paris, at av. Hassan II. Poste Restante and telephones. M-Th 8:30am-12:15pm and 2:30-6:30pm, F 8:30-11:30am and 3-6:30pm.

Internet Access: Casa Net, 2nd fl. of the Sheraton Hotel. 50dh per hr. Open M-F 10am-10pm, Sa 1pm-midnight. Many others rumored to be opening soon at cheaper rates.

TELEPHONE CODE	Casablanca's phone code is (0)2.

◤ ACCOMMODATIONS

For budget deals look along **rue Chaouia,** as well as **av. des Forces Armées Royales** (F.A.R.) and side streets. Avoid the overpriced medina.

Auberge de Jeunesse (HI), 6 pl. Amiral Philibert (tel. 22 05 51). From Casa Port, head right along bd. Almohades, walk along the medina walls, and go left up a small ramplike street. Blue signs point the way. The biggest hostel in Morocco, with a pleasant courtyard and communal kitchen. Breakfast included. Reception open daily 8-10am and noon-11pm. HI card required. Dorms 45dh; doubles 120dh.

Hôtel Rialto (tel. 27 51 22), av. Mohammed el-Qorri. From pl. Nations Unies, take bd. Mohammed V, then the 3rd right off it, and then the first left. These clean, airy rooms are about as quiet as Casa gets. All rooms have showers (hot in the mornings). Singles 84dh; doubles 112dh.

Hôtel Kon-Tiki, 88 rue Allal ben Abdallah (tel. 31 49 27). Despite the exotic name, it's pretty ordinary. Still, rooms are extremely clean—all with sinks, some with terraces. Hot showers 5dh. Singles 62dh; doubles 76dh; triples 110dh.

Hôtel de Foucauld, 52 rue Araibi Jilali (tel. 22 26 66). From bd. Felix Houphëit-Boigny, take a left on av. des F.A.R., then the 1st right; it's adjacent to Hôtel Perigord. Whether or not you can fill the Foucauld's huge wardrobes, you're bound to appreciate its cozy, tidy, but dimly lit rooms. Singles 75dh, with bath 120dh; doubles 120dh, with bath 150dh; triples with bath 180dh.

Hôtel Excelsior, 2 rue el-Amraoui Brahim (tel. 20 02 63 or 20 00 48). Just opposite the clock tower and across pl. des Nations Unies. A great way to escape the city, these luxurious rooms, complete with couches, curtains, and full baths, might be worth a splurge. Old but functioning elevator. Singles 246dh; doubles 316dh; triples 423dh.

◯ FOOD

While it's true that cosmopolitan Casablanca offers everything from French *haute cuisine* to Korean food to McDonald's (on bd. Mohammed V at pl. Nations Unies), most restaurants are geared towards the city's wealthy business clientele. Kabab eateries line **rue Chaouia** in the *ville nouvelle*. Good value meals are also available near pl. Nations Unies and in the medina, though prices there are a bit higher. For fresh meats and produce, try haggling at the **central market,** 7 rue Chaouia (open daily approximately 8am-1pm).

Snackbar Bouli de Nega, 72 rue Arabi Jilai. One block away from the port, on the same street as Hôtel Focault. A cheap, quality Moroccan diner-style joint. Entrees 20-30dh. Open 10am-midnight.

Le Buffet, 99 bd. Mohammed V (tel. 31 23 44), 3 blocks on the left past pl. Nations Unies. A vast array of options (pizza, pasta, *tajines*) and a 75dh *menu*. Entrees 30-80dh. Open 6am-1am. Visa, MC.

Taverne au Dauphin, 75 bd. Felix Houphëit-Boigny (tel. 22 12 00), up the road from the port. Tuxedoed waiters serve sizzling seafood to Casablancan professionals. House specialties include *Crevettes grillées* (grilled shrimp, 55dh) and *filet de lotte* (filet o' fish, 70dh). Entrees 45-100dh. Beer 15dh. Open M-Sa noon-4pm and 7-11pm. Visa, MC.

▧ SIGHTS

▨**HASSAN II MOSQUE.** The biggest sight in Casa, literally, is the fabulous new Hassan II Mosque, the third-largest mosque in existence. It's very easy to find: from anywhere in Casa, look toward the sea and spot the shiny minaret (200m high, the tallest minaret in the world). Begun in 1980 and inaugurated in 1994, this massive structure carried a price tag of over one billion U.S. dollars (much of it was collected from the Moroccan people through "universal voluntary conscription"). Though designed by a Frenchman the mosque was constructed by 3300 Moroccan craftsmen. The prayer hall, much larger than St. Peter's in Rome, combines glass, marble, and precious wood in a space that holds over 25,000 worshippers. The courtyard accommodates another 80,000. Here, technology galvanizes religious devotion: the floor is heated for bare feet, the hall boasts a huge retractable roof, and a 20-mile-long laser beam shoots from the minaret toward Mecca. Morocco is so proud of this functioning mosque that non-believers are actually allowed inside. *(Walk past the medina along the coastal road (about 15min.), or take a petit taxi (no more than 10dh). Mandatory tours given Sa-Th 9, 10, 11am, and 2pm. Tours in English, French, and Arabic. 100dh, students 50dh. Elevator up the side of the minaret 10dh.)*

OTHER SIGHTS AND ENTERTAINMENT. The Hassan II Mosque aside, Casa is too preoccupied with commerce to maintain a romantic veneer. A decaying **medina** disappoints veterans of Fez and Marrakesh, and the portside **Centre 2000,** meant to be a tourist draw, is just a collection of unexciting western cafes and restaurants. Government buildings, relics of French occupation, surround the green **place Mohammed V.** Two blocks further south along av. Hassan II sprawls the **Parc de la Ligue Arabe,** the grandest of Casa's parks. In the northwest corner you can enjoy a nice **picnic** in the shadows of the old **Sacred Heart Cathedral,** built in 1930. Since the local bars often attract a raucous and sketchy clientele, the best bet for nighttime activities are the big hotel bars, like that in **Hôtel Safir** on av. des F.A.R.

EL-JADIDA الجَديدَة

El-Jadida, a two-hour bus ride from Casablanca, is one of Morocco's largest Atlantic beach towns. With a quiet medina, historic Portuguese battlements, palmy boulevards, and some of the country's most pleasant beaches, it's a welcome relief from the hustle and bustle of Casa and Marrakesh. The city's European air comes courtesy of the Portuguese, as El-Jadida (formerly known as Mazagan) was their first Moroccan foothold and last Moroccan stronghold. Once Morocco won independence, the city was renamed El-Jadida ("The New One") and became a retreat for Marrakesh's affluent families. Today a prime destination for foreign and domestic tourists alike, El-Jadida attracts crowds in July and August.

☐ GETTING THERE

Buses run to El-Jadida from **Casablanca** (1½hr., 6 per day, 5:30am-3pm, 25dh) and **Essaouira** (3hr., 5 per day, 8:30am-12:30am, 54dh).

☑ ORIENTATION AND PRACTICAL INFORMATION

Situated on a well-protected harbor, the northeast side of El-Jadida faces the Atlantic. From the **bus station,** exit left on bd. Mohammed V and continue up toward the city center (10min.). First you'll pass **place Mohammed V,** the center of town, which joins bd. Mohammed V at the post office, then **place el-Hansali** (a pleasant pedestrian square), and finally **place Mohammed ben Abdallah,** which connects bd. Suez to the old Portuguese **medina.**

Buses: Bd. Mohammed V. CTM buses go to: **Casablanca** (2hr., 3 per day, 24dh); **Essaouira** (3hr., 2 per day, 7am and 4:30pm, 45dh). Buses to Essaouira begin in Casablanca and often have few seats left by the time they arrive in El-Jadida; get a ticket in advance. For connections to Rabat, Fez, and other major cities, transfer in Casablanca.

Tourist Office: In pl. Mohammed V, next to Bata Shoes. Some English spoken. Open mid-June to mid-Sept. M-F 8:30am-noon and 2:30-6:30pm; mid-Sept. to mid-June M-F 8:30am-noon.

Currency Exchange: BMCE, located 1 block from pl. Mohammed V along av. Mohammed Errafil, changes money and has an ATM. Open M-F 8:15am-2:15pm. **The Bank of Morocco,** pl. Mohammed V on the side toward the bus station, exchanges traveler's checks. Hôtel de Provence also changes money.

Police: (tel. 19). Located at the bus station, at the beach, and on av. Al Jamia al Arabi.

Late-Night Pharmacy: Av. Ligue Arabe off pl. Mohammed V. Look for the plaque next door to the Croissant Rouge Marocain (Red Cross). Open nightly 9pm-8am.

Medical Assistance: Hospital: (tel. 34 20 04 or 34 20 05), rue Roux, near rue Boucharette in the south of town. **Ambulance:** tel. 34 37 30.

Post Office: Pl. Mohammed V. Poste Restante and **telephones.** Open M-F 8:30am-noon and 2:30-6:30pm.

TELEPHONE CODE   El Jadida's phone code is (0)3.

ACCOMMODATIONS AND CAMPING

For a resort town, Jadida has a surprisingly large number of budget hotels. Most cluster around **place Mohammed V,** a few blocks from the sea. Ask to see a room before you commit because rooms range in quality even within a hotel. Reservations are wise in July and August, when prices rise considerably.

Hôtel Maghreb/Hôtel de France, 16 rue Lescould (tel. 34 21 81), just off pl. el-Hansali. The best budget deal between Casablanca and Mauritania. Spacious rooms with high ceilings, most with sinks and bidets, and some with excellent views of the water. Hot showers 5dh. Singles 41dh; doubles 57dh. Extra bed 21dh.

Hôtel Bourdeaux, 47 rue Moulay Ahmed Tahiri (tel. 37 39 21). A few narrow streets away from pl. el-Hansali; follow signs at the end of the pl. el-Hansali toward the medina (about 100m). Carpeted, bright modern rooms at low prices. Hot shower 5dh. Singles 41dh; doubles 57dh; triples 78dh.

Hôtel de Provence, 42 rue Fquih Mohammed Errafi (tel. 34 23 47; fax 35 21 15). Coming from the bus station, turn left off av. Mohammed V (away from the beach) at the post office. The "in" hotel for English speakers. All the amenities (toilet paper, towels, nice sheets, and currency exchange). Continental breakfast (22dh) at the excellent French/Moroccan restaurant. Singles 134dh, with shower 166dh; doubles 161dh, with shower 198dh; triples 246dh, with shower 283dh; quads with shower 368dh. Visa.

Camping: Camping Caravaning International (tel. 34 27 55), av. Al Oman al Mouttahida. From the post office at pl. Mohammed V, head toward the beach and take a right on av. el-Jamia el-Arabi. Take the 6th right (20min.). A large site with electricity, showers, and aging bungalows (160dh). 12dh per adult, 6.5dh per car, 10dh per tent. Add 4dh *emplacement* and 14% TVA.

FOOD

Cheap eateries serve *brochettes* along **place Mohammed V.** Most restaurants cluster in and around **place el-Hansali,** and numerous cafes dot the waterfront. On Sundays, a weekly **souq** that sells everything from fruits to cow lungs is held by the lighthouse around rue Zerktouni.

Restaurant Tchikito, 7 rue Moulan Ahmed Tahiri (tel. 37 18 19), a few meters off pl. el-Hansali on the street to Hôtel Bordeaux. Obviously *the* place to be, Tchikito draws crowds of locals with its huge plates of fried fresh fish. Knife and fork are optional. Fish 25-30dh per plate. Open daily noon-10pm.

Restaurant la Broche, 46 pl. el-Hansali (tel. 34 22 99), next to the Paris Cinema. Intimate dining rooms complemented by an extensive menu and speedy service. *Tajine* 25-30dh. Fish dishes 30-40dh. Entrees 20-50dh. Open daily 7am-11pm, but actual hours depend upon the owner's whim.

Restaurant Chahrazad, 38 pl. el-Hansali. The menu is impressive, but unfortunately not everything is available. What they do have is tasty and filling. Couscous and 14 varieties of *tajine* 20-25dh. Entrees 20-25dh. Open 10am-11pm.

SIGHTS

El-Jadida's main attractions are its **Cité Portugaise,** at the end of av. Mohammed V, and its **beaches,** on the east side of town, to the right when walking toward the Cité Portugaise.

CITÉ PORTUGAISE. The heart of Jadida is its lovely ramparted **Cité Portugaise,** completed in 1502 by Portuguese traders. In 1769, Moroccan forces finally sent them packing, but not before the retreating Portuguese blasted the old town walls to bits. After a sultan renovated the ramparts in the 19th century, the city was rebuilt as a Jewish settlement *(mellah)* mostly populated by merchants. Enter this atypical medina through the first fortified gate off pl. Mohammed ben Abdallah at the top of bd. Suez.

Up rue Mohammed Hachemi Bahbai on the left, a yellow plaque marks the entrance to the famed **Portuguese Cistern,** a Gothic structure lucky enough to have survived the Portuguese bombardment. It was designed in 1514 as an arsenal and later converted into a cistern. The water, illuminated by a shaft of light from the roof, reflects the cistern's columns and arches. The riot scene in Orson Welles's *Othello* was filmed here. *(Open daily 9am-1pm and 3-7pm. 10dh.)*

To join the locals promenading along the city's **ramparts,** either continue along and up a ramp or head back to the southwest corner of the medina (down the street to the right as you enter the medina), where there's a rickety staircase. Guards let you in and out for a tip of a few dirhams. Along the port side, the walls plunge inward at the **Porto do Mara,** where the Portuguese used to unload their ships. Continuing along the walls leads to the **Bastion of St. Sebastian,** beneath which sits a crumbling synagogue, once the Portuguese tribunal. At the **Bastion of St. Antoine,** in the northwest corner of the medina, there's another exit. If the guard isn't there to meet you, make some noise and he will appear.

BEACHES. The town beach is popular among football-playing and sun-bathing locals and is ideal for walking as it extends a good distance to the south. For more peaceful beaches, head north of town beyond the Cité Portugaise. **Sidi Bouzid,** a beach 5km to the south, is sprawling and chic. Take a *grand taxi* (5dh per person) or the orange #2 bus (2.5dh) from near the Cité Portugaise.

ESSAOUIRA الصَّوِيرة

Essaouira is one of Morocco's most enchanting communities. Piracy boosted this port in the 18th century, when Sultan Muhammad bin Abdallah leveled the Portuguese city of Mogador and constructed the town fortifications to protect his band of pirates. In the late 1960s, the arrival of Jimi Hendrix and Cat Stevens triggered a mass hippie migration. Over the next decade Essaouira achieved international fame as an expat enclave. Though most of the hash smoke has cleared, Essaouira remains Morocco's most laid-back city. The miles of beautiful beaches are often too windy for sunbathing, but the tranquil fortified medina and splendid scenery provide ample diversion. Visitors to Essaouira often stay an extra day, sometimes an extra week, and occasionally a lifetime.

▐ GETTING THERE

Buses run to Essaouira from: **Marrakesh** (3hr., 8 per day, 6am-5pm, 30dh); **Agadir** (3hr., 2 per day, 7:30am and 7pm, 45dh); **El-Jadida** (3hr., 2 per day, 7am and 4:30pm, 45dh); **Casablanca** (5½hr., 3 per day, 5:30am-5pm, 100dh).

▐ ORIENTATION AND PRACTICAL INFORMATION

Buses arrive at the **bus station,** about 1km northeast of the medina along bd. Industrie. Exit the rear of the station (where the buses park) and walk to the right, passing two souqs (or deserted wastelands, depending on the hour), to reach the medina gate, **Bab Doukkala** (10min.). The gate opens onto **avenue Mohammed Zerktouni,** one of two main arteries; the other is the parallel street of **rue Mohammed bin Abdallah.** To reach the city center from Bab Doukkala, continue on av. Mohammed Zerktouni as it becomes av. l'Istiqlal (at an intersection surrounded by souqs and a mosque). Walk until you see a clock tower on the right. Go through the gate underneath the tower, pass through the square, and follow the road as it zig-zags to **place Moulay Hassan,** the heart of Essaouira.

Buses: Buses leave across the square from Bab Marrakesh, at **Agence Supratours** (tel. 47 53 17), where tickets are sold. To: **Agadir** (2½hr., 33 per day, 5:30am-3:30pm,

37dh); **Marrakesh** (2½hr., 10 per day, 4am-5pm, 40dh); **El Jadida** (3hr., 5 per day, 8:30am-12:30am, 54dh); **Casablanca** (5hr., 26 per day, 5am-12:30am, 75dh; midnight express 100dh). The fastest and most luxurious bus to **Marrakesh** (2½hr., 1 per day, 5pm, 40dh) is run by a train company, **ONCF.**

Currency Exchange: Banks cluster around pl. Moulay Hassan. **Bank Credit du Maroc** (tel. 47 58 19), in pl. Moulay Hassan, cashes traveler's checks and has an **ATM.** Open M-F 8-11:30am and 2:15-3:30pm. Higher rates at **Hôtel Beau Rivage.** Open 24hr.

Tourist Office: Syndicat d'Initiative du Tourism, on rue de Caine. From the top of pl. Hassan (away from the port), take a right and follow the road as it zig-zags out a gate (under a clock tower). Continue one more block. Though they have few maps, the helpful and smiling staff provides a bevy of great information and tips. Definitely worth a visit. Open M-F 8:30am-noon and 2:30-6:30pm.

Luggage Storage: available 24hr. at the bus station (5dh per bag).

Police: (tel. 19), in the *ville nouvelle* near the tourist office.

Hospital: (tel. 47 27 16), on av. el-Moquamah next to the post office.

Post Office: av. el-Moquamah at Lalla Aicha, the first left after Hôtel les Isles when walking away from the medina by the shore. Near the radio tower. Poste Restante and telephones. Open June-Sept. M-F 8am-3pm; Oct.-May 8:30am-noon and 2:30-6:30pm.

Internet Access: at the **teleboutique** next to the tourist office. 30dh per hr.

TELEPHONE CODE — Essaouira's phone code is (0)4.

ACCOMMODATIONS AND CAMPING

Though once Morocco's best kept secret, Essaouira has lost its anonymity. Reservations may be necessary in the summer. Despite its popularity, Essaouira still offers a number of nice, fairly cheap hotels.

Hôtel Smara, 26 rue Skala (tel. 47 56 55). From the top of pl. Moulay Hassan, head toward the port and take a right. Follow this street as it follows the ramparts (3min.). The beds are a bit worn, but rooms are clean and many have great views. Relax on the terrace. Arrive early—this is the most popular hotel among backpackers. Laundry for a fair price (around 20dh). Breakfast 10dh. Hot shower 2dh. No reservations. Singles 60dh; doubles 80dh, with ocean view 100dh; triples 120dh; quads 150dh.

Hôtel Majestic, 40 rue Derb Laâlouj (tel. 47 49 09). From pl. Moulay Hassan, head away from the port down the street to the right; take a quick left and then another. Clean, newly renovated rooms maintained by a friendly owner. The terrace—and a few toilets—have an ocean view. Hot showers 5dh. Singles 50dh; doubles 90dh.

Hôtel Tafraout, 7 rue Marrakesh (tel. 47 62 76). From the top of pl. Hassan, take a right and then a quick left onto the busy rue Sidi Mohammed Ben Abdallah. Look for the sign a few blocks up. Newly renovated rooms and courtyard shine. Hot showers 6dh. Singles 70dh, with shower 100dh; doubles 100dh, with shower 150dh. Extra bed 45dh.

Hôtel Beau Rivage (tel./fax 47 29 25), pl. Moulay Hassan. Large, old hotel located above the main square's cafes. Bright, clean rooms, many with balconies, and a pleasant terrace. Singles 60dh; doubles 90dh, with shower 180dh; triples 150dh, with shower 220dh; quads with shower 240dh.

FOOD

Informal dining, mostly geared toward tourists, is common near the port and **place Moulay Hassan.** At the **port fish grilles,** fried sardines (with fish, bread, and tomatoes, 20dh) and grilled shrimp (25dh) are sure bets. The so-called **Berber cafes,** near Porte Portugaise and off av. de l'Istiqlal, have low tables, straw mats, and fresh fish *tajine* and couscous (20dh). Establish prices before biting in.

■ **Restaurant Laayoure** (tel. 47 46 43). From the top of pl. Hassan (away from the port), take a right and continue past rue Sidi Ben Mohammed Abdul. Follow the road as it turns right and then left; the restaurant is up ahead on the left. The best Moroccan food in town served in a beautiful, well-decorated setting. Reasonable prices. Banana and chocolate crepes 12dh. Entrees 38-50 dh. Open 10am-midnight, later in summer.

Café Restaurant Essalem (tel. 47 55 48), pl. Moulay Hassan. Popular hangout for visitors since the 60s. The waiter will gladly point out the table where Cat Stevens sat studying Islam. The clientele is touristy, but the food good and cheap. Standard range of *tajines* and couscous *menus* 33-40dh. Breakfast for 10dh. Open daily 8am-3pm and 6-11:30pm. Visa, MC.

Chez Sam (tel. 47 65 13), at the end of the harbor. Shazam! Warped ceilings and walls plastered with Hollywood movie stars. Pricey and touristy, but it's got a nice ocean view and the town's only liquor license. Steaming heap of mussels 25dh. Fish dishes 40-70dh. *Menu* 70dh. Open daily noon-3pm and 7:30-10:30pm. Visa, MC, AmEx.

Dar Baba Restaurant, 2 rue de Marrakesh, near the Hôtel Tafraout. Home of the city's only Italian cuisine, including their famous lasagna (38dh.) Entrees 28-38dh. Open noon-2:30pm and 6:30-10pm. Visa, MC.

■ SIGHTS

While many come to Essaouira to do nothing at all, the ramparts, port, medina shops and museums, and of course the beaches can distract for hours on end.

RAMPARTS AND PORT. The view of the medina from the coastal walls provides the backdrop for one of the nicest walks in Morocco. Two *skalas* (forts) scowl atop the fortifications. Dotted by formidable ramparts, dramatic, sea-sprayed **Skala de la Ville,** up the street from Hôtel Smara, is the nicer of the two (it's also free). Visitors can go up the large turret and artillery-lined wall to where the cannons, gifts to the sultan from European merchants, face the sea and the medina. The other fort, **Skala de Port,** is near the port and less interesting (10dh).

MEDINA SHOPS AND MUSEUMS. Follow the sound of pounding hammers and the scent of *thuya* wood to the **carpenters' district,** comprised of cell-like niches set in the **Skala Stata de la Ville.** The craftsmen here inlay cedar and *thuya* wood with lemonwood and ebony to create some of the best woodwork in Morocco. On sale are some unique masks and statuary, as well as the more typical boxes, chess sets, dice, and desk tools. For a quality overview of Essaouira's goods and prices, go to **Afalkai Art** (pl. Moulay Hassan) and browse the many shops lining **rue Abdul Aziz el-Fechtaly** (off rue Sidi ben Abdallah). At the carpenters' workshops themselves, prices are the cheapest and the marketing the least aggressive. The local **museum** (tel. 47 23 00), near the Hôtel Majestic, is located in the former residence of a *pasha.* It features antique woodwork and important manuscripts, including a 13th-century Qur'an. (Open W-M 9am-noon and 3-6:30pm. 10dh.) Numerous galleries dot the medina—the best one, **Galerie d'Art Exposition,** near the clock tower, displays modern art crafted by local artists. (Open 10am-1pm and 3-7pm. Free.)

PURPLE ISLES HAZE While certain stimulants are still available (especially for foreigners), Essaouira's heyday of "good times" was in the early 1970s when Jimi Hendrix and fellow hippies took over the isles. The fort **Bordj El Berad** at the far end of the beach and the ruins farther inland supposedly served as an inspiration to Hendrix's song *Castles Made of Sand.* When he tried to buy the nearby Berber village-turned-hippie-colony of **Diabat,** the Moroccan government decided that it had had enough of Hendrix and his expat friends. A sudden police sweep of the area sent most non-Moroccans packing. Today, the village residents have almost forgotten their raucous past; the Purple (Isles) Haze has burned away.

BEACHES. To get to the beach, face the port and take a left. Essaouira's beaches fill with soccer matches in between high tides. High winds can be painful for sunbathers—go in the morning when the winds are less fierce. Windsurfing clubs farther down rent boards by the hour. Try **Fanatic Fun Center** (tel. 34 70 13; fax 47 28 18) for good deals on rentals. (Windsurfing boards (with harness and wet-suit) 100dh per hr. or 300dh for 5hr.; body boards 20dh per hr. or 100dh per day; jet-skis 60dh per 15min.) **Sidi Kaoki** (below) is *the* place for true windsurfing enthusiasts, but the wind might be a little much for beginners.

DAYTRIPS FROM ESSAOUIRA

PURPLE ISLES. At the famed Purple Isles, just off-shore from Essaouira, the rare Eleanora's falcons hang out and breed. A Berber king from Mauritania, Juba II, set up dye factories on the islands around 100 BC, producing the purple dye used to color Julius Caesar's cape, among other things. In 1506, the Portuguese, under King Manuel, contributed a fortress and Moulay Hassan added a prison. Recently, the islands, including **Isle of Mogador,** have become a nature reserve. Though you can't visit the islands, you may be able to see the reserve's birds from the beach.

SIDI KAOUKI. Many Europeans consider **Sidi Kaouki,** located 25km south of Essaouira, to be the best **windsurfing** beach in the world. A blue sign on the main road points the way to the beach, where "Wind City" bumper stickers crowd the parking lot. A constant wind blows spurts of stinging sand down a shore filled only with windsurfers. Unfortunately, there are no lifeguards, and you must BYOB (bring your own board). Take bus #5 (6dh), which departs from the southwest corner of the medina (outside the gates).

AGADIR أَگَادِير

Backpackers who come to Agadir may feel somewhat betrayed. At the juncture of the routes to the western Sahara, Agadir stands in stark contrast to the rugged High Atlas and Anti-Atlas mountains that surround it. Devastated by an earthquake in 1960, the town was redesigned as a European-style beach resort, and serves that purpose ably: broad, clean beaches and a multitude of hotels, discos, and cafes lure Northern European tourists, driving prices up considerably. All the same, Agadir can be affordably managed by the budget traveler who needs respite from traditional Morocco or wants to spend some time on the Atlantic coast.

◼ ORIENTATION AND PRACTICAL INFORMATION. Buses arrive and depart along bd. Mohammed Cheikh Saadi, where most budget hotels and eateries cluster. Going downhill toward the beach, you'll cross av. Prince Moulay Abdallah, av. Hassan II, and bd. Mohammed V, finally coming to the esplanade.

Flights leave from **Airport El-Massira** (tel. 83 91 22), 25km out of town. The **Royal Air Morocco** office (tel. 84 07 93) is on av. du General Kettani (open M-F 8:30am-12:15pm and 4:30-7pm, Sa 8:30am-noon and 3-6pm). **Bus stations** are scattered along bd. Mohammed Cheikh Saadi. **CTM** (tel. 82 20 77) runs buses to: **Taroudannt** (2hr., 1 per day, 5:30am, 35dh); **Essaouira** (3hr., 2 per day, 7:30am and 7pm, 45dh); **Marrakesh** (4hr., 2 per day, 3 and 6pm, 75dh); **Ouarzazate** (5hr., 1 per day, 9:30am, 60dh); **Rabat** (1 per day, 10:15pm). There are many options for **car rental** on bd. Mohammed V, including Hertz, Budget, and Eurocar. Many offer reduced "low season" rates, though the definition of "low season" seems to vary.

One **tourist office** can be found on pl. L'Esperance. From the CTM station, take a left when facing the beach onto av. du 29 Feurier, walk for 6 blocks, then take a right on av. Prince Moulay Abdullah and a left on av. Prince Sidi Mohammed. There is also the **Syndicat d'Initiative et Tourisme** (tel. 84 06 95), av. Mohammed V. Free map and bus schedule available; some English spoken. (Both open M-Sa 8:30am-noon and 2:30-6:30pm.) **Luggage storage** is available at the CTM station. **Police,** rue 18 Novembre (emergency tel. 19), at Hôtel de Police; **Hospital Hassan II** (tel. 84 14 77) on Route de Marrakech. **Post office,** on

MOROCCO

av. Sidi Mohammed, near the tourist office on the corner of av. Prince Moulay Abdallah (open M-Th 8:30am-12:15pm and 2:30-6:30pm, F 8:30-11am and 3-6:30pm); **internet access: Agadia Net,** 33-34 av. Hassan II, 4th fl. (tel. 82 11 80); **telephones** next to the post office (open daily 8:30am-noon and 2-6pm). **Telephone code:** (0)8.

⚑⌂ ACCOMMODATIONS AND FOOD. Budget hotels congregate around the bus stations. **Hôtel Paris** (tel. 82 26 94), av. President Kennedy, is nicer than its competitors and the prices reflect it. Rooms are arranged around a central courtyard. (Breakfast 20dh. Singles 90dh, with shower 140dh; doubles 130dh, with shower 170dh.) **Hotel el Bahia** (tel. 82 39 54 or 82 45 15; fax 82 45 15), rue el Mehdi Ibn Toumert, a block toward the beach from the CTM station, is the cheapest of the upscale hotels, with pleasant rooms with full baths (singles 188dh; doubles 223dh; triples 280dh). There is a **campground** (tel. 84 66 83) on bd. Mohammed V on the western edge of town (2dh for water, 7.5dh for showers; 10dh per person, 15dh per tent; 14% tax not included).

Like budget hotels, affordable eateries cluster around the bus stations. Boardwalk cafes offer more expensive, non-Moroccan cuisine. Four comparable restaurants behind the CTM station all have similar menus and outdoor tables (*menus* 35dh; open daily 8am-11pm). For something different, try the upscale Chinese restaurant **La Tonkinoise** (tel. 84 25 27), on av. du Prince Sidi Mohammed between the beach and the post office. (Entrees 20-85dh. Open 10am-noon and 6pm-midnight.)

◉ SIGHTS. For the budget traveler not willing to shell out the dirhams for excursions to harbor villages, kasbahs, and "natural spectacles" offered by large hotels, the **beach** is the main attraction in Agadir. Take the 15-minute walk down and enjoy one of the cleanest beaches in Morocco, with good swimming and surfing. Later on compare sunburns with thousands of pink Northern Europeans. There are a few other diversions in Agadir. Perched atop a hill overlooking the port is the partially restored **kasbah.** Up to 1000 troops—alternately Portuguese, French, and Moroccan—have been garrisoned here at various points in history. (*Petit taxi* 50dh.) The **Musee Municipal** (tel. 84 07 84), bd. Mohammed V, shows a decent collection of South Moroccan folk art, although with few explanations in any language. (Open M-Sa 9am-1pm and 2:30-6pm. 10dh.) As for **nightlife,** head toward the beach and any one of a number of resort-type bars. For dancing, try **Club Almoggarb** on bd. Mohammed V near the campsite. There is even a casino, **Shem's,** also on bd. Mohammed V, which has blackjack, slot machines, and roulette.

THE HIGH ATLAS الأطلَس الأعلى

Hollywood has anointed Southern Morocco one of the most beautiful regions in the world, as evidenced by the numerous movies which have been filmed here over the last fifty years. Most visitors to the region would agree. Dunes, valleys, and mountains do eventually give way to sizable cities like Marrakesh, but not without much protest and occasional sandstorms. With its unique architecture and exotic bazaar, Marrakesh vies with the natural scenery for a traveler's attention.

Falling southeast from the Atlas ranges and stretching through Ouarzazate to the sand-dune seas of the Sahara is Morocco's desert. Mountainous and desolate, its deep reds and oranges are softened only by the rare green veins of oases that creep through the valley floors. Set into this landscape are fantastic Berber towns and kasbahs, where *piste* (mud and straw) castles tower over the road. Even though excursions are possible by local transportation, a rental car is useful for exploring this southeasternmost part of Morocco.

MARRAKESH مُرّاكُش

An oasis at the foot of the High Atlas mountains, Marrakesh is both a remote desert enclave and Morocco's most important imperial city. The Almoravid dynasty founded the city in 1062, elevating an infamous highwaymen's outpost to the status of cultural capital and infusing it with Andalusian influences from their empire in southern Spain. As it has for centuries, Marrakesh exerts an unshakable grip on the traveler. Tourists are still a minority at the Djemâa el-Fna, the medina's main square, where lively crowds of snake charmers, musicians, boxers, acrobats, mystics, dentists (you'll just have to see it for yourself), scribes, and storytellers practice their crafts. The old city is huge, labyrinthine, and definitely worth a visit; the invasive hustlers and faux guides are part of the experience. In addition to its own fantastic merits, Marrakesh also serves as a base for expeditions into the surrounding Atlas Mountains or the Sahara to the south.

▐ GETTING THERE

Trains run to Marrakesh from: **Casablanca** (3½hr., 8 per day, 70dh); **Rabat** (5hr., 7 per day, 4am-11:30pm, 99dh); **Fez** (9hr., 6 per day, 7am-2am, 130dh). **Buses** go from: **Essaouira** (2½hr., 10 per day, 4am-5pm, 40dh); **Meknes** (8hr., 1 per day, 7pm, 132dh).

▐ ORIENTATION AND PRACTICAL INFORMATION

Most of the excitement, as well as budget food and accommodations, centers on the **Djemâa el-Fna** and surround the **medina**. The **bus** and **train stations,** administrative buildings, and luxury hotels are in the **Guéliz** *(ville nouvelle)* down av. Mohammed V; from the Djemâa el-Fna, walk to the towering Koutoubia Minaret and turn right. Also in the Guéliz are most of the car rentals, newsstands, banks, and travel agencies. Bus #1 runs between the minaret and the heart of the Guéliz (1.5dh). Or take one of the many *petits taxis* (despite the driver's demands, you shouldn't pay more than 10dh) or horse-drawn carriages.

TRANSPORTATION

Flights: Aéroport de Marrakesh Menara (tel. 44 78 65), 5km south of town. Taxi from town 50dh. Bus #11 from the Koutoubia Mosque to the airport (about 7am-10pm). Domestic and international flights on Royal Air Maroc.

Trains: (tel. 44 77 68 or 44 77 63), av. Hassan II. Going away from the medina on av. Mohammed V, turn left on av. Hassan II and walk 5min. To: **Casablanca** (4hr., 8 per day, 6:30am-8:30pm, 73dh); **Rabat** (5hr., 7 per day, 6:30am-8:30pm, 95dh); **Meknes** (7hr., 6 per day, 6:30am-7pm, 150dh); **Tangier** (8hr., 5 per day, 6:30am-8:30pm, 140dh); **Fez** (8hr., 2 per day, 6:30am-7pm, 169dh).

Buses: (tel. 43 39 33), outside the medina walls by Bab Doukkala. To get there, walk out of the medina on av. Mohammed V, pass through Bab Larissa, and then turn right, continuing along the walls to Bab Doukkala. The station is to the left. Arrive early (30min.-1hr.) as seats fill quickly. **CTM** is window #10. To: **Essaouira** (3hr., 8 per day, 6am-5pm, 30dh); **Agadir** (4hr., 6 per day, 4:45am-6:30pm, 61dh); **Casablanca** (4hr., 10 per day, 4am-8pm, 40dh); **Ouarzazate** (4½hr., 12 per day, 5am-5:15pm, 65dh); **Zagora** (4-5hr., 4 per day, 10am-10pm, 79dh); **Rabat** (5hr., 10 per day, 5am-9pm, 55dh); **Taroudannt** via Agadir (6hr., 2 per day, 4:30 and 6pm, 83dh); **Meknes** (8-9hr., 5 per day, 6:30am-9pm, 115dh); **Fez** (10hr., 5 per day, 6:30am-9pm, 130dh). Private buses leave from Bab er-Rob, just south of Djemâa el-Fna, to locations in the High Atlas including **Asni** (every 30min., 10dh) and **Setti Fatma** (every 30min., 13dh).

Grand Taxis: It's best to start from Bab er-Rob, where you can share a taxi to Asni or Setti-Fatma. 15dh per person for 6 passengers; slightly more for smaller groups.

Car Rental: Avis, 137 bd. Mohammed V (tel. 43 37 27), and **Hertz,** 154 bd. Mohammed V (tel. 43 99 84). Both rent Fiat Unos for 250dh per day plus 2.5dh per km or around 500dh per day for unlimited mileage. Minimum age 21 for small cars, 25 for all others. Many hotels (like Hôtel Ali) will arrange rentals for a discount.

MOROCCO

TOURIST AND FINANCIAL SERVICES

Tourist Office: Office National Marocain du Tourisme (ONMT) (tel. 43 62 39), av. Mohammed V, at pl. Abdel Moumen ben Ali, about a 35min. walk from Djemâa el-Fna. The office offers a mediocre map and access to **official guides** (half-day 120dh, full day 150dh). Office open daily 8:30am-noon and 2:30-6:30pm; Ramadan daily 9am-3pm.

Currency Exchange: Banks line av. Mohammed V and av. Hassan II in the Guéliz, and cluster in the medina around the post office. Most touristy hotels will change money 24hr.—try Hôtel Ali or Hôtel Essaouira.

American Express: Voyages Schwartz, rue Mauritania, 2nd fl. (tel. 43 33 21 or 43 06 44), off av. Mohammed V, 2nd left after post office. Open daily 6am-11pm.

EMERGENCY AND COMMUNICATIONS

Police: (tel. 19), south of the Djemâa el-Fna.

Late-Night Pharmacy: Off the Djemâa el-Fna, on the way to av. Mohammed V, on the right. Open Tu-Su 9pm-6am.

Medical Emergency: Doctor on call until 10pm at the late-night pharmacy. It's best to avoid the government-run *polyclinique;* ask your consulate to recommend a private physician. See **Embassies and Consulates,** p. 662.

Post Office: pl. 16 Novembre, off av. Mohammed V. Unreliable Poste Restante; it's a madhouse. Open M-F 8am-noon and 4-7pm, Sa 8:30-11:30am. **Branch office** in the Djemâa el-Fna. Open M-F 8:30am-noon and 2:30-6:45pm.

Internet Access: Reliably at the **Hôtel Ali** for 30dh per hr. The **Internet Cafe,** 2 blocks from Djemâa el-Fna on the walking street (rue Bab Agnaou) on the left, charges less (25dh per hr.) and has A/C, but sometimes has trouble with the network.

TELEPHONE CODE   Marrakesh's phone code is (0)4.

◤ ACCOMMODATIONS

All of Marrakesh's cheap accommodations are within a stone's throw of the Djemâa el-Fna. Many places allow you to sleep on the roof for about 20dh.

▨ **Hôtel Ali** (tel. 44 49 79; fax 44 05 22), on rue Moulay Ismael past the post office in the Djemâa el-Fna. Draws tourists with its reputation as *the* budget hotel. Good suites with soap, towels, usually A/C, and toilet paper (stock up!). English spoken. Also has a complete restaurant (see **Food,** below) and organizes good expeditions into the High Atlas for around 300dh per day (food, lodging, guide, and transport included). If it's full, don't agree to go to Hôtel Farouk—it is far from the Djemâa and is no better than other budget hotels near Hôtel Ali. Singles with fan and shower 70dh; doubles with A/C and shower 90dh; triples 125dh, with A/C 170dh; quads with A/C 160dh. Dorm bed 25dh. Say you don't want breakfast or they'll add 15dh to your bill.

▨ **Hôtel Essaouira,** 3 Derb Sidi Bouloukat (tel. 44 38 05). From Djemâa el-Fna, facing the post office, head down the road in the left corner, through an archway. Take the first right after the Hôtel de France and look for the signs. The best terrace in town, with a cafe and laundry basins. Luggage storage 5dh per day. Hot showers 5dh. 40dh per person, but there are few singles; don't pay more than 60dh for a bed in a double room.

Hôtel Medina, 1 Derb Sidi Bouloukat (tel. 44 29 97), beside the Hôtel Essaouira (and run by its manager's cousin). Great terrace and clean rooms. Laundry basins and cafe. Breakfast 9dh. Hot showers 5dh. 40dh per person.

Hôtel Afriquia, 45 Sidi Boulouliate (tel. 44 24 03). Set apart by its cool courtyard filled with slender orange trees. Clean rooms and bathrooms. Hot showers 5dh. Singles 40dh; doubles 70dh; triples 110dh, with shower 120dh; quads 160dh.

Hôtel Chellah, 14 riad Zitoun Kédim (tel. 44 29 77). From Djemâa el-Fna, walk down the same street as to Essaouira and Medina, but take the next right. Pleasant rooms surrounding a great courtyard. Hot showers 10dh, cold showers 2.5dh. 40dh per person.

MOROCCO

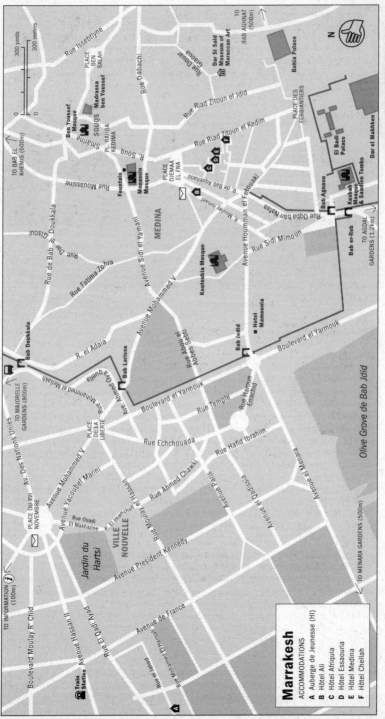

Marrakesh

ACCOMMODATIONS
A Auberge de Jeunesse (HI)
B Hôtel Ali
C Hôtel Afriquia
D Hôtel Essaouria
E Hôtel Medina
F Hôtel Chellah

Auberge de Jeunesse (HI) (tel. 44 77 13), on rue el-Jahed. 5min. from the train station in a dreamy part of the *ville nouvelle,* but a 30min. walk from the Djemâa el-Fna. Exit the train station and turn left on av. Hassan II. Take the 1st right at the traffic circle onto av. France. Take the 2nd right, continue for 2 blocks, then take a left and the 1st right. The hostel is at the end of the street. Cold showers. BYOTP (Bring Your Own Toilet Paper). Reception daily 8-9am, noon-2pm, and 6-10pm. Some rules—such as lockout, 10pm curfew, and membership requirement—*may* be flexible. Dorms 25dh.

🍴 FOOD

Two **markets** peddle fresh produce along the fortifications surrounding the city, far from pl. Djemâa el-Fna. A closer daily fruit and vegetable market lies just outside Bab Aghmat. Bab el-Kemis hosts a lively Thursday market. For delicious bargains, head for the **food stalls** in pl. Djemâa El-Fna. Food vendors contribute to the square's madness—dozens of stalls deal from late afternoon until after midnight. Follow the crowds to the best *harira* (2dh) and *kebab* (2dh).

Chez Chegrouni, 4-6 pl. Djemâa el-Fna, just to the right of Café Montréal. Unassuming but rewarding. Look for the brown-and-gold awning to find 3dh *soupe marocaine,* a meal in itself. Excellent *couscous* (25dh). Entrees 25-27dh. Open 5am-midnight.

Café-Patisserie Toubkal, pl. Djemâa el-Fna, near the archway that leads to Hôtel Essaouira. Relax on the shady outdoor patio. Scrumptious *shish kebab* with fried onions and peppers (20dh). Entrees 20dh. Open 7am-2pm and 4pm-midnight.

Hôtel Ali (see **Accommodations,** above). Popular with tourists. Check out the all-you-can-eat Moroccan buffet dinner (50dh for guests of the Hôtel; 60dh for all others).

Restaurant Argana (tel. 44 53 50), pl. Djemâa el-Fna. Typical *menu* (75-90dh) and a pleasant terrace overlooking the square. Entrees 50-70dh. Open daily 6am-1am.

👁 SIGHTS

🗺DJEMÂA EL-FNA. Welcome to the Djemâa el-Fna (Assembly of the Dead), one of the world's most frantically exotic squares, where sultans once beheaded criminals and displayed the remains (hence the name). Crowds of thousands participate in the bizarre bazaar that picks up in the afternoon and peters out after midnight. While snake-charmers and water-sellers pose to entice tourists, the vast majority of the audience are townspeople and Berbers from outlying villages. Solitary figures consult with potion dealers and fortune tellers; crowds congregate around the preachers, storytellers, and musicians; women have their children blessed by mystics; promoters encourage bets on boxing matches between young boys (and girls). People come back night after night for the wonderful food and the chance to watch something spectacular. Djemâa el-Fna induces absolute sensory overload, and is one of Morocco's most enthralling attractions.

KOUTOUBIA MOSQUE. Almost every tour of Marrakesh begins at the 12th-century Koutoubia Mosque, whose magnificent 🗺**minaret** presides over the Djemâa el-Fna. Crowned by a lantern of three golden spheres and shrouded by scaffolding as it undergoes restoration, the minaret is the oldest (and best) surviving example of the art of the Almohads, who made Marrakesh their capital (1130-1213) and at their peak ruled the region from Spain to present-day Tunisia. In 1157, Abd el-Mumin acquired one of four editions of the Qur'an authorized by the caliph Uthman, and used it as inspiration for the design of the 2nd Koutoubia Mosque. Possession of this holy book turned Marrakesh into a center of religious study. In fact, the name Koutoubia comes from the Arabic *kutubiyyin* ("of the books"). Art historians revere the minaret, which has influenced eight centuries of Islamic architecture. *(As with most Moroccan mosques, entrance is forbidden to non-Muslims.)*

THE MEDINA AND SOUQS

A worthwhile survey of the medina (prime time 5-8pm) begins at the souqs. Although dazzling and intimidating, the maze of streets doesn't necessitate a guide. If you do get lost, ask a merchant for directions, or a child will lead you out for a few dirhams.

From the Djemâa el-Fna, enter the medina on the pathway directly across from the Café-Restaurant-Hôtel de France. This path runs through the medina's main thoroughfare, turns past the enormous **souq smarine,** and takes a turn at the **pottery souq.** Berber blankets and cards of yarn pile the alleyways of the **fabric souq.** Head through the first major orange gateway and make a quick right to the Zahba Kedima, a small plaza containing the **spice souq,** complete with massive sacks of saffron, cumin, ginger, and orange flower, as well as the apothecaries' more unusual wares—goat hoof for hair treatment, ground-up ferrets for depression, and live chameleons for sexual frustration. Nearby is **La Criée Berbère** (the Berber Auction), once a slave-trading center. Nowadays it hosts aggressive carpet merchants. Farther on are the bubbling vats of the **dye souq.** Fragrant whiffs of cedar signal the nearby **carpentry souq,** where workers carve chess pieces with astounding speed. Go left through these stalls to see the 16th-century **Mouassin Fountain** bathe its colorful carvings, which are covered by an outer layer of grime. On the road going right where **souq attarine** (perfume) forks, an endless selection of colorful leather footwear glows at the **babouche souq** (untinted yellow is traditional for men; women wear the fancier models). The right fork at the end of the street leads to the **cherratine souq,** which connects the *babouche souq* to the **souq el-Kubir,** the leather souq. Those with strong stomachs can visit the **tanneries.** Continue through the souqs and take a right after the Madrassa ben Youssef.

MADRASSA BEN YOUSSEF. In 1565, Sultan Moulay Abdallah el-Ghalib raised the Madrassa ben Youssef in the center of the medina. It reigned as the largest Koranic school in the Maghreb until closing in 1956. The Andalusian style includes the requisite calligraphy and intricate floral designs. Visitors can roam the students' cells and appreciate the size of their hostel room. *(Walk down the main souq street (rue Souq Smarine) and bear right onto rue Souq el-Kubir; follow it to its end. Open June-Aug. Tu-Su 8am-noon and 3-7pm; Sept.-May Tu-Su 8am-noon and 2-6pm. 10dh.)*

KOUBBA EL-BA'ADIYN MONUMENT. Beside the Madrassa juts the unpainted cupola of 12th-century Koubba el-Ba'adiyn, the oldest monument in town and the only relic of the Almoravid dynasty. It was the original that all other Moroccan buildings borrowed their style from. Excavated around the middle of the 20th century, much remains hidden either underground or by other structures. If you've had enough of keyhole arches, pinecone and palm motifs, and intricate dome carvings, ask the guard to open an ancient wooden door to the subterranean cisterns. *(Walk down the main souq street (rue Souq Smarine), bear right onto rue Souq el-Kabir, and turn left at the Madrassa. Open daily 8:30am-noon and 2:30-6pm. Bang on the door if it's closed. 10dh, plus tip for the custodian-guide.)*

PALACES AND MUSEUMS

EL BAHIA. The ruthless late-19th-century vizier Si Ahmad Ibn Musa, also known as Ba Ahmed, constructed this palace, naming it El Bahia (The Brilliance). Serving as the de facto seat of government for the man who ruled in the sultan's stead, El Bahia was built in an effort to assert Morocco's historical and cultural significance and thus stave off European domination. Today it is beautifully preserved and makes for a wonderful stroll, although little artwork or furniture adorns its halls. It is, however, a sometime gallery for modern art exhibits. *(From the Djemâa el-Fna, walk down rue Riad Zitoun el-Kédim to its end at pl. Ferbiantiers, then turn left; on the right, a red archway opens onto a long, tree-lined avenue that leads to the palace door. Open Sa-Th 8:30-11:45am and 2:30-5:45pm, F 8:30-11:30am and 3-5:45pm. 10dh.)*

SAADIEN TOMBS. Modeled after the interior of the Alhambra in Granada, the Saadien Tombs are Morocco's most lavish mausoleum. The tombs served as the royal Saadien necropolis during the 16th and 17th centuries, until Moulay Ismail walled them off in an effort to efface the memory of his predecessors. In 1912 the burial complex was rediscovered during a French aerial survey. One **mausoleum,** the tomb of Sultan Yacoub al-Mansur (the Victorious), brims opulently with illuminated *zellij* (mosaic tilework). A second was built for his mother. Both date from the late 16th century. In the neighboring **Hall of the Twelve Columns,** trapezoidal tombs rise from a pool of polished marble. The sultan's four wives, 23 concubines, and the most favored of his hundreds of children are buried nearby; the unmarked tombs belong to the women. The turquoise minaret of the Mosque of the Kasbah, el-Mansour's own personal mosque, towers above the complex. *(From Djemâa el-Fna, walk away from the souqs to the walkway left of Banque de Maghreb and walk for 5min. to Bab er-Rob. Take a left through Bab Agnaou and follow the signs. Multilingual tours. Open daily 8:30am-noon and 2:30-6pm. 10dh.)*

DAR SI SAID. Dar Si Said, a 19th-century palace built by Si Said, brother of Grand Vizier Ba Ahmed and chamberlain of Sultan Moulay el-Hassan, houses a **Museum of Moroccan Art.** The collection features splendid Berber carpets, pottery, jewelry, Essaouiran ebony, and Saadien woodcarving. One of the best classical Moroccan art museums in the country, it is well worth a visit (although the plaques are in French only). *(Go toward El Bahia, and continue on rue Zitoun el-Jadid, taking the 2nd right heading toward the Djemâa el-Fna. Open W-Th and Sa-M 9-11:45am and 2:30-5:45pm, F 9-11:30am and 3-5:45pm. 10dh.)*

GARDENS

JARDIN AGDAL. The midday sun in Marrakesh can be cruel; since the 12th century, rulers have dealt with it by constructing massive irrigated gardens. The largest of these is the Agdal, a 3km enclosure accessible via a roofed portal overlooking the Grand Méchouar. While olive trees predominate, the garden contains all manner of fruit-bearing trees that shade the avenues and large pools. *(From Bab er-Rob, walk left along the medina walls until you reach Bab Ahmar. Walk down rue Bab Ahmar for 5min.; the garden is on the right. Free. Closed only when the king is in residence.)*

MENARA GARDENS. A vast enclave of olive groves around an enormous pond, the Menara Gardens are best visited at sunset, when mauve and tangerine light reflects off the water. The cold green reservoir (800m by 1200m) dates from the Almohad era. To the left lies the expansive olive grove of Bab el-Jedid, a continuation of the gardens. *(Head through Bab el-Jedid and straight down av. Menara, the wide boulevard that resembles an airport runway. Free.)*

MAJORELLE GARDENS. Menara and Agdal date back centuries, yet are almost overshadowed by the 1920s upstart Majorelle Gardens. Designed by French painter Jacques Majorelle, its exquisitely engineered explosions of colorful flowers contrast strongly with the stately greens of the Agdal and Menara. The garden is owned and maintained by fashion designer Yves Saint-Laurent (who occasionally zips around the Djemâa el-Fna on his moped), and its fanciful colors rival his wildest collections. *(From Djemâa el-Fna, walk toward Koutoubia Mosque and take a right on av. Mohammed V. After exiting the medina, take a right and follow the walls to the bus station. Bear left onto bd. Safi and turn right onto av. Yacoub el-Mansour; the gardens are on the left. Open daily June-Aug. 8am-noon and 3-7pm; Sept.-May 8am-noon and 2-5pm. 15dh.)*

GATES

The imperial city had considerable military importance (many sultans' campaigns to quell the tribes of the Atlas were launched from here), as evidenced by 2km of pink-tinged fortifications. The walls are punctuated by numerous gates. The **Bab Agnaou,** three blocks from the Koutoubia mosque away from Djemâa el-Fna, was formerly a portal to the Kasbah of Yacoub el-Mansour and is the most dazzling

THE GREAT GLAOUI The Glaoui Kasbahs, located outside Marrakesh and throughout the region, are some of the most extravagant sights in Morocco. By the turn of the century, the Glaoui family had become the dominant political and financial force in the region. When France took over in 1912, the Glaouis were granted almost uncontested power over the entire south. El Glaoui, Pasha of Marrakesh during France's rule and a buddy of Winston Churchill, relished a good party as much as anyone. It certainly didn't hurt that he was fabulously rich—gold, diamonds, and most anything else imaginable adorned his palaces. He regularly threw extravagant events at which, according to Gavin Maxwell in *Lords of the Atlas*, "nothing was impossible." It is said that El Glaoui doled out hash, opium, gold, and even little boys and girls to his Western guests. But the fate of his palaces was quite Ozymandian: abandoned in 1956, today most of the kasbahs remain unoccupied and in ruins.

gate. Built in the 12th century, it often displayed trophies of war—mutilated corpses and heads of slain enemies. **Bab er-Rob,** next to Bab Agnaou, was once the southern doorway to the city. The Saadien tombs are just inside; *grand taxis* and buses wait outside. **Bab el-Khemis,** the site of a lively Thursday market, sits in the corner of Marrakesh, beyond the souqs if coming from Djemâa el-Fna. The bastion was reputedly designed and built by Andalusian architects and artisans. (Head around the corner of the Madrassa ben Youssef and take the first major left.)

🎵 ENTERTAINMENT

Most travelers hang around the Djemâa el-Fna or in one of the terrace cafes that overlooks it for most of the night. If you do want to take part in the more international pastime of beer sipping, try the **bars** at the **Tazi** and **Foucauld** hotels. Here locals and tourists mix, with the help of 15dh Flag *spéciales*. To find the Tazi, head away from the Djemâa el-Fna 200m down the street to the left of the Banque du Maroc. For the Foucauld, turn right by the Tazi onto the road that becomes av. Mohammed V and walk two blocks. For a change of scene, try the **Diamant Noir,** a nightclub on Mohammed V in Guéliz.

NEAR MARRAKESH: CASCADES D'OUZOOD

Quite simply, the Cascades d'Ouzood (167km northeast of Marrakesh) are not to be missed. The Moroccan tourist board agrees—posters of the falls crashing into the pool below appear all over Morocco. Descend the 300 or so steps to the pools, admiring the velocity of the falling water all the way. For a Kodak moment, climb up to a cliff directly facing the falls.

With a car, it's an easy daytrip from Marrakesh. It is still easy to get there without one, although it might be necessary to spend the night, a pleasant enough option, especially for those planning on camping. To get there, take a bus (window #18) from the main bus station in Marrakesh (2 per day, 8:30am-2pm, 40dh) and ask to be dropped off at the Cascades. From there, you'll have to get a spot in a *grand taxi* the rest of the way (10dh). Coming back is trickier: find a group willing to share a taxi back to Marrakesh (total 400dh) or catch one of the buses back (2 per day, 8:30am-2pm, 40dh), or you may have to spend the night. Most cafes along the trail will let you camp for a nominal fee (5-10dh), while the **Hotel Restaurant Cafe Camping Daressalena** (tel. 45 96 57) charges 60dh per room.

THE OURIKA VALLEY

Just south of Marrakesh is the Ourika Valley, offering a break from the bustle of Marrakesh and a hint of what the High Atlas has to offer. It is extremely popular with locals, with the southernmost destination of **Setti Fatma** and its seven waterfalls the focus of most of the attention. The country's best skiing can be found here too, at **Oukaimeden,** just an hour or so from Marrakesh.

SETTI FATMA

Two hours south of Marrakesh by bus is a collection of small waterfalls and cool pools which make a pleasant daytrip. Crowd-lovers will want to go during the **mousem** (festival) in mid-August, when much of the region descends on the tiny town. Getting to the falls from the town requires a fair amount of hiking. Start by crossing the river near the farthest cluster of hotels and cafes and clamber up to the first, most popular cascade. Climbing farther up will yield a much more isolated and tranquil waterfall and pool, great for a lounging afternoon. To get to Setti Fatma, hop on a bus from Marrakesh's Bab el-Rob station (6am-noon); the same ones run back (4-7pm). *Grand taxis* also make frequent runs. If you want to stay, try the **Cafe-Restaurant Asgaour** near the bridge (singles 50dh; doubles 70dh; triples 100dh) or the **Auberge Tafoulet,** a bit farther from the center of town (singles or doubles 100dh). Both places serve food (entrees 30-80dh).

OUKAIMEDEN

Between November and April, the ski resort of Oukaimeden is open. From Marrakesh, take a *grand taxi* (1hr., 60-70dh per person). Once the highest ski lift in the world, it remains Africa's highest at 3273m. Lift passes cost about 250dh for a whole day (group discounts available), and rentals can be found at any of the numerous outfitters (100-200dh per day, depending on quality). February is said to be the best month, but slopes are usually snow-covered until late April. The best place to stay is the classy ■**Club Alpine Français (CAF)** (tel. 31 90 36), on the main road. Make sure to call for reservations during the peak months. (Dorm beds with CAF card 24dh; with other ski club cards 36dh; nonmembers 48dh. Bring your own sleeping bag.) Campsites are available directly across from the slopes (hot showers 13dh; 11dh per person, 12dh per tent, 9dh per car).

HIGH ATLAS MOUNTAINS الأطلس الأعلى

Trekking in the Atlas Mountains can be a wonderful addition to your stories-to-tell-your-grandchildren repertoire. Unlike its European counterparts, the range's trails have yet to be fitted for tourists, and the valleys below remain green, unspoiled, and very accessible. Even travelers with limited funds, time, and skills can huff to the summit of **Djebal Toubkal,** North Africa's highest peak (4167m). Ascending Toubkal takes only two days; however, treks of up to two weeks are plausible. For Toubkal, little more than a sleeping bag, food, water, and sturdy shoes are necessary. For anything longer, though, unless one is skilled and equipped with a full outfit of backpacking equipment (i.e., a stove, tent, water purification system, compass, maps, etc.), the services of a guide and/or mule and muleteer are basically essential, as there are many trails, most of which are unmarked. **Official guides** (ask to see their papers) and **mules** can be hired in **Imlil** for 160dh per day and 75dh per day respectively (not including tip). Alternatively, treks can be organized in Marrakesh at **Hôtel Ali** (see p. 710), where the owner knows several experienced guides. From Hôtel Ali, prices are about 250dh per day per person, with everything from food-and-shelter deals to guide-and-mule setups. All this only applies during the summer, since during the **winter** snow covers Toubkal and the upper valleys. In winter, full alpine gear and an experienced guide are completely necessary. Also, no matter what time of year, **altitude sickness** must be taken into consideration, as the altitude change from Marrakesh is drastic.

The ascent of **Toubkal,** through the towns of **Asni** and **Imlil,** is outlined here; for longer treks, such as a three-day trek from Asni to Setti Fatma or an eight-day trek of the whole area, refer to books (*The Atlas Mountains, Morocco* by Robin G. Collomb is a renowned source), guides, and other trekkers.

ASNI

The first step up the mountain is a trip to the village of Asni, 1150m up the mountain. Try not to organize a trek here, as there is a greater chance of getting scammed. Most people move on to Imlil for the first night, but if you get stuck, there is a pleasant **youth hostel** at the far end of town (turn left before the abandoned Hôtel du Toubkal) which has free showers and cooking facilities (20dh per bed; camping 20dh). To get to Asni from Marrakesh, take one of the **buses** that leave often (dawn to dusk; 10dh) or a shared *grand taxi* (about 15dh).

IMLIL

The tiny village of Imlil is the ideal base for trekking Toubkal. There are plenty of places to stay, eat, and stock up on supplies, and the crisp mountain air and constant sound of running water soothe tired climbers and invigorate future ones. Martin Scorcese used this village as the setting for his film *Kundun,* which told the story of the Dalai Lama, substituting the Atlas Mountains for the Himalayas and the village mosque for a Buddhist temple. In the center of town, next to the CAF refuge, is the **official bureau of guides.** Ask questions and pick a personal guide from the photos on the wall. If you're aiming to top Toubkal, however, no guide is necessary (see **The Toubkal Trek,** p. 715). To get to Imlil from Asni, hop on the first truck up, crowding in with the produce and poultry (10-15dh). The ride is an experience in itself; stand in the back and don't let anyone try to charge you more or take you to any shops.

There are a bunch of high-quality hotels that will provide meals (with a few hours notice) and store luggage as you trek. **Hôtel El'Aine,** at the start of town on the right, boasts a lovely courtyard, garden, terrace, and even a library of old French mountain books. The owners are extremely helpful with any trekking info you might need (90dh per person, hot showers included). The **Cafe Soleil** (tel./fax 48 56 22) has clean rooms but cold showers (35dh per person), and is the most reliable place in town for a meal (entrees 25-30dh). You can also rent hiking gear here (crampons 30dh, axes 15dh, boots 30dh). The **Shopping Centre** across the street also rents boots (20dh per day) and skis (100dh per day). The **Club Alpine Français (CAF)** refuge is worth it for members (cooking gas 6dh per hr.; dorm beds 26dh with CAF membership; 39dh with another ski club membership; 52dh without; camping outside 10dh per tent, 5dh per person).

THE TOUBKAL TREK

The trickiest part of the trek is finding the trailhead, which is about an hour's walk from Imlil. Walk uphill on the village's only road, taking a sharp right when you see a large boulder. Then veer onto a smaller path to the left (look for the sign for the Toubkal Kasbah on a building). Follow this path up past the kasbah for about 15 minutes until it joins a dirt road, weaving to the left. After five or 10 minutes you'll see the village of **Armoumd** on the opposite bank of the river. Continue on until you descend into a broad valley; the trailhead is on the opposite side (through a small village—look for the sign).

This path is very clear the entire way up the mountain. At about the 2-2½ hour mark you'll reach the tiny outpost of **Sidi Chamarouch,** home to a fiercely guarded **marabout** shrine and expensive beverages. A room here costs 50dh and *tajine* is 100dh (talk about a cornered market). The village marks the spring snow line, so be prepared for icy conditions through late April. Another three hours gets you to the **Toubkal** (or **Neltner**) **Refuge** (32dh with CAF card; 48dh with other club cards; 64dh without). After complaints of overcrowding, the refuge is expanding and will be done by the end of the summer of 2000. It gets mighty cold during all parts of the year at this altitude, so most hikers prefer to spend the night here and then ascend to the summit (3-4hr.) early the next morning. This strategy also allows for the best view, as it clouds over in the afternoon. Ask for the best route at the refuge. After reaching the summit, most people descend on the same day.

⬛TIZI-N-TEST

The direct route between Marrakesh and Taroudannt, the Tizi-n-Test is one of the most entertaining drives in the country. Built by the French in the 1920s and 30s, the road is still deemed so laborious and time-consuming that most buses prefer to take a longer, roundabout path. There is sometimes a bus that runs from Marrakesh to Taroudannt (6am), but the return trip is even less frequent. Tizi-n-Test is best explored with a car. Along the way, **Ijoukak** acts as a good base for trekking, although it is not as established as other parts of the High Atlas. Several kasbahs established by the Goundafi family can be explored (or at least spotted from a zooming bus). The **Tin Mal Mosque,** an excellently preserved specimen of 12th-century Almohad architecture, offers a rare chance for non-Muslims to peek at a part of life kept secret from visitors. It is unique, as its minaret is on the eastern side and the *mihvab* does not point toward Mecca.

TAROUDANNT تارودانت

The long, winding descent of the Tizi-n-Test through the High Atlas ends at Taroudannt's red earth walls. The northern gateway to the Anti-Atlas mountains, its bastions have controlled traffic through the mountains for centuries. An enormous rectangle of fortifications encloses the town, making Taroudannt one of Morocco's best-preserved walled cities, free of any *villes nouvelles*. Taroudannt has great souqs and comparatively few tourists (with only the occasional tour bus); it serves primarily as a quiet stop for those waiting to cross into the mountains or head down to the coast.

🚩 **ORIENTATION AND PRACTICAL INFORMATION.** Most buses drop passengers off outside the city walls at **Bab Zorgane.** To get to the center of town, go through the gate, turn left when the road terminates, and follow this road as it weaves through the town, past a mosque, then through pl. an-Nasr, and finally to **place al-Alaouyine,** where banks and several budget hotels are located. **Buses** are infrequent, inconvenient, and confusing. It's best to ask around at different companies, as routes change frequently. **SATAS** and **CTM** offices are found in pl. al-Alaouyine, while most private buses have their offices in pl. an-Nasr. SATAS buses go to **Agadir** (2hr., 1 per day, 3:30pm, 15dh) and **Ouarzazate** (5hr., 1 per day, 12:30pm, 50dh). CTM runs to **Ouarzazate** (5hr., 1 per day, 60dh) and **Marrakesh** via Agadir (6hr., 1 per day, 6am, 91dh). Once in a while, a bus runs to Marrakesh via Tizi-n-Test from Pl. an-Nasr (55dh), but there is no set schedule. **Banks** that change traveler's checks are in pl. al-Alaouyine; after hours, Hôtel Palais Salam, set in the eastern wall of the kasbah, changes small amounts of traveler's checks or cash (around $50). **Police** (tel. 19), outside Bab El Kasbah in the basement of the Public Works building, along the city walls to the right of the bus station (10min); **hospital: Hôpital Mokhtar Soussi** (tel. 85 30 80), inside the town walls through the Bab El Kasbah. **Post office,** in Bab El Kasbah, just beyond the police station and in front of the mosque (open M-F 8:30am-12:15pm and 2:30-6:30pm, Sa 8-11am).

📷 **ACCOMMODATIONS AND FOOD.** Both of the following hotels are in pl. al-Alaouyine. **Hôtel Taroudannt** (tel. 85 24 16) spices up its clean rooms with a pleasant bar, a courtyard jungle, and a rooftop terrace (singles 55dh, with shower 80dh; doubles 70dh, with shower 100dh; triples with shower 140dh). Its **restaurant,** complete with white tablecloths, serves excellent French dishes and wine (*menu* 60-75ptas; open daily noon-2:30pm and 7-10pm). **Hôtel Roudani** (tel. 85 22 19) is the best of the budget hotels (small rooms for 1 or 2 people 40dh; larger rooms 70dh; showers included). Its **restaurant** serves Moroccan specialties at tables on the square (open daily 8am-10pm). **Suak Al Baraka,** 70 bd. Prince Sidi Mohammed (tel. 85 03 31), is between the two main squares and serves tasty and cheap chicken, *brochettes,* and *kefta* (20-25dh; open daily 10am-3pm and 6-10pm).

🕐 **SIGHTS.** Taroudannt's monumental **fortified walls** and **kasbah** have been knocked down and reconstructed numerous times. The oldest ramparts date from the 16th century, when the town was an important military center; much of what stands today is left over from the 18th century. To fully enjoy the grandeur of the walls as you circumnavigate the town, walk or rent a bike (try a small shop next to a dentist's office across from the Hotel Taroudannt; 5dh per hr.). The **souqs** around the two squares are also worth a brief stop. Although their wares pale in comparison with the souqs of Fez or Marrakesh, Taroudannt is one of Morocco's silver-working centers. (Note that real silver bears a government stamp on the back—don't believe merchants who will try to convince you otherwise.) From pl. al-Alaouyine facing pl. an-Nasr, the **Arabic souq** is on your left, while the **Berber souq** is to your right, just below pl. an-Nasr. Continuing past the two main squares on av. Mohammed V and out Bab Targhount are Taroudannt's **tanneries.**

TIZI-N-TICHKA

The route from Marrakesh to Ouarzazate, known as the Tizi-n-Tichka, will entertain passengers and drivers alike. While not as breathtaking as its western cousin Tizi-n-Test, the diverse landscape is eye-catching. As you wind south from Marrakesh, the land becomes more and more arid; geology lovers will delight in the numerous folded and tilted outcroppings. **Buses** run quite often (see the Marrakesh and Ouarzazate sections), as do *grand taxis*. However, renting a car from Marrakesh with a drop-off later in Ouarzazate might be worth the expense.

About two hours south of Marrakesh by car is the town of **Telouet,** 21km from the main road (P31) and home to a **Glaoui Kasbah** (see **The Great Glaoui,** p. 713). Inhabited by the powerful Glaoui family up until the middle of this century, its red sandstone walls continue to crumble. Ask the caretaker to let you in (tip about 10dh) and he'll explain (in French) how the one well-preserved part of the kasbah was used for parties and feasts. Of particular note are the skylights and extensive mosaics. Transport to Telouet is difficult and expensive, even with a car, so it's more of a short excursion rather than a daytrip or destination.

THE SOUTHERN DESERTS

OUARZAZATE ورزازات

After the scenic Tizi-n-Tichka, Ouarzazate is somewhat anticlimactic. Although once envisioned by the Moroccan government as a tourist mecca (they built a four-lane highway and erected four- and five-star hotels), this French-built administrative center never lived up to expectations. The town, however, does make a convenient spot to rent a car for exploring nearby towns, deserts, and valleys.

🔖 **PRACTICAL INFORMATION.** The **CTM station** is located in the center of town, one block from the main street, **avenue Mohammed V,** also home to most administrative buildings, budget hotels, and restaurants. Buses go to: **Marrakesh** (4½hr., 5 per day, 8am-9:45pm, 50dh); **Er-Rachidia,** via Skoura, Boumalne du Dadès, and Tinerhir (1 per day, 10:30am); **Agadir** (6hr., 1 per day, noon, 60dh); **M'Hamid,** via Agdz and Zagora (6½hr., 1 per day, 12:30pm, 55dh); **Casablanca** (3 per day, 10am-9:45pm, 125dh). **Grand taxis** line up by the bus station and run fairly often to nearby destinations such as **Skoura** (45min., 10dh), **Zagora** (3hr., 45dh), and **Marrakesh** (4hr., 80dh). If the taxis are not full (fewer than 6 people crammed in), be prepared to pay extra. There are several **rental car** agencies in Ouarzazate, including Hertz, Avis, Eurocar, and Budget, all on av. Mohammed V. Larger companies charge about 500dh per day for a Fiat Uno (unlimited mileage); local companies offer fewer services, but charge half that. Check out your car before making any payments. Hôtel Royal rents **mopeds**

(150dh per half-day, 250dh per day; haggling acceptable). One of Morocco's more helpful **tourist offices** (tel. 88 24 85) is on av. Mohammed V, where the road forks to follow the Oued Drâa and the Oued Dadès. It offers bus info and a directory of hotels in the Drâa and Dadès Valleys. (Open M-F 8:30am-noon and 2:30-6:30pm.) **Currency exchange** is at the banks on av. Mohammed V; four- and five-star hotels will only exchange cash. **Post office** and **telephones,** on av. Mohammed V by the tourist office (open July-Aug. M-Sa 8am-noon and 2:30-6:45pm; Sept.-June M-Sa 8am-noon and 2:30-6pm). **Telephone code:** (0)4.

ACCOMMODATIONS AND FOOD. For inexpensive lodging, try av. Mohammed V or parallel streets. **Hôtel Royal,** 24 av. Mohammed V (tel. 88 22 58), next to Chez Dimitri, is a good bet (warm showers 10dh; singles 36dh, with shower 80dh; doubles 72dh, with shower 93dh; triples with shower 93dh; quads with shower 134dh). The **Hôtel Bab Es Sahara** (tel. 88 47 22 or 88 44 65), on the corner of pl. Mouhadine where buses arrive, has large cheap rooms. It also has a restaurant and currency exchange, and accepts credit cards. (Singles 50dh, with bath 70dh; doubles 80dh, with bath 120dh; triples 120dh, with shower 150dh.) The **supermarket,** on av. Mohammed V across the street from Hôtel Royal, has an unrivaled selection of cured meats, canned goods, chocolate, wine, cold beer, and European goods. The best restaurant value in town is the **Cafe-Restaurant Essalem** (tel. 88 23 76), on av. Prince Hertier Sidi Mohammed, just off av. Mohammed V. The tajine or couscous *menu* is 55dh, while big parties can order a pigeon *pastilla* for a negotiable rate of about 200dh. (Open daily 7am-11pm.) **Restaurante-Café Royal** (tel. 88 24 75), av. Mohammed V, is a great spot for chess matches and chicken *tajine* (35dh)—the only dish they serve regularly, despite an extensive menu. (Entrees 35-40dh, full *menu* 42dh. Open daily 7am-11pm.)

SIGHTS. The nearest example of desert architecture is the **Taourirt Kasbah,** once a Glaoui stronghold (see **The Great Glaoui,** p. 713). The kasbah, 1½km east of town, was built in the mid-18th century and occupied until 1956. Recently restored, its interior is an entertaining maze of winding streets, stairways, and balconies. Tall visitors beware: low ceilings can make exploration painful. Its massive Krupp cannon, given by Moulay Hassan, could easily level any neighboring village (quite a way to establish authority). To get there, walk down av. Mohammed V, bear left at the tourist office, and head toward Club Med. To enter, step onto the bamboo floors that are through the doorway just to the left of the kasbah as you face it from the street. (Open daily 8:30-6:30pm. 10dh.)

NEAR OUARZAZATE

The area to the north of Ouarzazate is a hot and dusty palette of desert browns and greens, periodically interrupted by small Berber **kasbahs.** Perhaps the most spectacular of these is in the village **Aït Benhaddou,** 30km on the road toward Marrakesh. Built in the 17th century and last inhabited by the Glaoui family (see **The Great Glaoui,** p. 713) in 1955, the kasbah today is home to a Berber family and several nests of storks. A member of the family will show you around for a 10dh tip. Some rooms still have intricate stone carvings and vegetable-dyed cedar wood ceilings. The terrace has a great view of the surrounding mountains. Movie buffs may recognize the forest of tapered turrets and backdrop—they're the region's film stars, featured in *Lawrence of Arabia* and *Jesus of Nazareth.* UNESCO has designated the village a world heritage sight. The best way to get there is to take a *grand taxi* from Ouarzazate (about 250dh round-trip; the driver will wait, but don't pay him until the journey is complete). It's also a beautiful ride on a rented moped, as long as the gas tank is filled. From Marrakesh, take the second signed road (the paved one) to Aït Benhaddou and drive until the kasbah is on the left.

THE DRÂA VALLEY وادي‌دراع

South of Ouarzazate, passing through Agdz and Zagora and ending in M'Hamid, is the narrow Drâa Valley, along which stretches a continuous grove of palm trees strewn with kasbahs and *ksours* (fortified strongholds). The route is best toured in a leisurely manner by rental car, although people also hop from village to village by bus, taxi, or thumb (hitchhiking is common in the south). Expeditions by camel or 4x4 are best taken from M'Hamid. Temperatures can reach 67°C here during July and August, but are tolerable the rest of the year and always cool off at night.

NORTHERN DRÂA TO ZAGORA

The route south from Ouarzazate (P31) is unexciting for the first 15km, although the lunar landscape continues in all directions. Volcanic rock soon gives way to an oasis of sorts; a small road to the left leads to the **El Mansour Eddahbi reservoir,** formed by heavy rains in 1989. **Ait Saour** is the first *ksour* along the way and marks the beginning of a steep ascent over the **Tizi-n-Tinifift,** which ultimately reaches an altitude of 1660m.

On the way back down, the road passes by several kilometers of layered rock until the start of the Drâa's main oases. The first city to take advantage of the waters is **Agdz,** 67km south of Ouarzazate. Set below **Jbel Kissane,** an imposing peak of the Jbel Sharo to the east, the town mainly functions as a resting point before continuing south; buses stop for 30 minutes to allow passengers to grab a cold drink. If you have time and your own transport, there is a palmery to the left when approaching from Ouarzazate, with a few small kasbahs tucked within.

Just a few kilometers south of Agdz, the real *ksours* begin. The road intersects the Drâa River, at which point it seems to become one long town, conforming itself to the snake-like river. The layout of the seemingly unending villages is remarkable: each community is divided into several clusters surrounding an oasis, with smaller homes adjoining central, fortified kasbahs. Many of the *ksours* are quite similar; the most notable is the first, **Tamnougalt,** 6km south of Agdz. Each building seems to exhibit its own towers, a tribute to its history as the area's capital. The next *ksour* is **Timiderte,** which boasts another Glaoui Kasbah (see **The Great Glaoui,** p. 713), worth investigating only if you have not yet seen one. Blending in next is **Tangihlit** and its explosion of palm trees; its neighbor **Tamezmoute** has another large kasbah. Just 37km north of Zagora is the somewhat larger **Tinezouline,** which has a kasbah and a lively Monday souq. The **Azlag Pass** just before Zagora opens the valley to a vast ocean of palms.

> **! HUSTLERS AND HITCHERS.** Many hustlers pose as hitchhikers or victims of auto breakdowns along the Ouarzazate to Zagora road. They invite anyone who picks them up back to their place in "gratitude" for the ride, and once there, try to get the driver to take a camel trek, buy jewelry, etc. A good way to avoid this is to pile your bags on the seats and say there is no space. Better yet, don't stop at all; just smile and wave as you go by.

ZAGORA الزّاكورة

Stiflingly hot, tourist-trodden, and hustler-ridden, Zagora is the traditional jumping-off point for treks and excursions into the valley or desert. Built by the French as an administrative town, Zagora is not a very appealing place. For those who wish to take a camel trek, M'Hamid offers a more authentic experience. The only time it is worth staying in Zagora is during the Mouloud, when the **Moussem of Moulay Abdelkader Jilali** makes the city a fun place to be.

MOROCCO

◪ PRACTICAL INFORMATION. All **buses** stop on av. Mohammed V, the road that the highway turns into, although **CTM** (tel. 84 73 27) stops on the far side of town while other private companies stop on the near side, along with *grand taxis*. CTM buses run to: **Ouarzazate** (2hr., 2 per day, 7am and 7pm, 36-45dh); **M'Hamid** (2hr., 1 per day, 4pm, 18dh); **Marrakesh** (6hr., 2 per day, 7am and 7pm, 82-110dh); **Casablanca** (1 per day, 9pm, 170dh). The best way to get to M'Hamid is by *grand taxi* (25dh). Every sort of tourist and financial service is along av. Mohammed V, including **banks,** the **post office,** the **souq,** and most hotels and restaurants. **Telephone code:** (0)4.

▐▊▐ ACCOMMODATIONS AND FOOD. The best value accommodation is the **Hôtel des Amis** (tel. 84 79 24), in the middle of av. Mohammed V, with slightly dingy but decent rooms (singles with shower 30dh; doubles 50dh, with shower 60dh; triples with shower 75dh). Signs indicate the way to **Camping Sindibad** (tel. 84 75 53), on av. Hassan II, just off av. Mohammed V. Spots are shaded and covered with grass; there is also a pool at no extra charge. (10dh per person, 5dh per car, 10dh per caravan.) Both accommodations have restaurants; another option is the **Cafe-Restaurant Tombouktou** (tel. 84 71 27), on av. Mohammed V. The *menu* (48dh) and the entrees (15-23dh) are both good bargains.

◪ TREKS. The main attraction of Zagora is indicated by its famous half-serious sign at the lower end of town: "To Tombouktou 52 *jours*—by camel." Numerous trek agencies line av. Mohammed V, with the best and cheapest deals at the hotels or campgrounds (Hôtel des Amis and Camping Sindibad are good bets). Expect to pay around 200-250dh per person per day for trips around Zagora and 300-400dh per person per day to trek near M'Hamid (transportation included). The more people trekking, the cheaper the price per person.

SOUTHERN DRÂA

To cross the Drâa at the southern edge of Zagora, travel out of town (away from Ouarzazate) for 3km and watch for a dirt road on the left (at the sign for Camping de la Montagne de Zagora). This rough track trundles its way to **Jbel Zagora**, a lone volcanic outcrop overlooking the fertile Drâa. The best time to visit the mountain is at sunset, when the peaks shimmer in the dying light. Just south of Tamegroute (see below), the **Dunes of Tinfou** rise from the valley floor in smooth golden mounds. They are rare because they can be easily reached by foot or any kind of car from the main road. Just watch for a well-marked dirt turn-off on the left as you come from Zagora. The dunes are visible from the road.

TAMEGROUTE

Just off the main highway is the town of Tamegroute, an oasis of date palms and *ksours*. Here, in what seems to be the middle of nowhere, is Morocco's best historical resource, Tamegroute's **library,** containing 4000 Moroccan manuscripts dating from the 11th to the 18th centuries. The collection includes a history of Fez, a copy of Bukhari's *Hadish*, poetry of al-Andalusi, countless astronomical algebraic charts, Mohammed's family tree, and a history of Egypt. The library's most treasured document is a history of Islam written on gazelle skin in 1063 by the great legal authority Iman Malik. To get to the library, ignore the painted *biblioteque* signs (a scam) and turn left (coming from Zagora) down the one paved road in Tamegroute. Just after the pavement ends, walk straight for a block and look for a large brown gate on the right; this leads to the library courtyard. (Open daily 9am-noon and 3-6pm. Free, but tip the multilingual caretaker.)

> **ROCK THE KASBAH** A simple guide to understanding the names of **kasbahs** and **ksours:** A kasbah is fortress-like structure for one family and has four towers, while a ksour is a fortified village and has more than four towers. Either of these (or a section of a city) may be referred to as a **mellah,** which means it was/is inhabited by Jews. They are almost all built with **pizid,** a mixture of straw and mud that needs to be reapplied each year; that is why there are so many ruined kasbahs only 40 or 50 years old. The first floor of each is generally used for animals, the second for dining and the kitchen, and the third for living and sleeping. The prefixes **Ben** and **Ait** modify the family name: Ben means "son of" while Ait refers to the entire family.

M'HAMID

M'Hamid is literally the end of the road. Forty-five kilometers from the Algerian border and 97km from Zagora, it stands as a lone outpost at the edge of the great deserts. M'Hamid lacks all but the most basic facilities; electricity made its debut a few years back. This is the best place for guided **camel treks** into the Sahara, which range from 250-350dh per person per day, with meals included. **Four-by-four trips,** and even trips with your own car, are arranged as well. The best centers are in the center of town: **Hôtel-Restaurant Sahara** (tel. 84 80 09; talk to Habi or M'Barek Naamani), which is a bit cheaper and better than **L'Hôtel Iriqui** (tel. 84 80 23). If you start here instead of in Zagora, you can reach endless seas of sand dunes and isolated oases with a five- or six-day voyage, and very impressive landscapes on only a one- or two-day trip. The best times to go are November or December, when temperatures are not as extreme. One CTM **bus** leaves each day for **Marrakesh** via Ouarzazate and Zagora (11hr., 5am, 18dh), as well as one private-owned bus (11hr., 7am or 2pm, 18dh). **Taxis** and trucks are more frequent. There are no banks and only a tiny **post office. Telephone code:** (0)4. In town, head for **Hôtel-Restaurant Sahara** (tel. 84 80 09), with free hot showers (singles 25dh; doubles 45dh; triples 75dh; sleeping in a Berber tent 10dh). They also serve food (entrees 15-45dh).

THE DADÈS VALLEY وادي‌دانس

Broader, drier, and more scenic than the Drâa Valley, the Dadès Valley stretches eastward from Ouarzazate. Other than the kasbahs and palmeries along the way, the valley's main attractions are the **Dadès Gorge** and the **Todra Gorge,** extending north into the dry escarpment of the High Atlas, although the oasis of **Skoura** is an interesting stop as well. It is possible to get from one valley to the other across the **Jbel Sharo,** but a four-wheel-drive vehicle is required. This area is best explored through a guide or expedition company. The **telephone code** for the valley is (0)4.

SKOURA

Forty-two kilometers east of Ouarzazate is the kasbah-filled oasis of Skoura, surrounded by fields of grain and roses. Turn left off the highway to reach the first kasbah, **Ben Moro.** Although it's only used as storage now by the 5th generation of Moros, the original Moro built it in the 17th century. The hill and horse decorations above the doorways indicate that the Moro family was formerly a nomadic Berber tribe. From the roof you can see the **Amridil Ksar** in the palms. An old Glaoui home (see **The Great Glaoui,** p. 713), it gained fame with its appearance on the 50-dirham bill. Now inhabited by the Nassar family, it is only accessible when they are away (knock to find out). Nearby is the **mellah** Kasbah Ait Sidi Maocti, with its intricate exterior carvings. The owner of the Ben Moro Kasbah, Mohammed Sibir, is happy to show anyone around (tip 10-20dh). The town has little to offer, so plan to move on once you've seen the kasbahs. **Buses** may stop on the Ouarzazate to Er-Rachidia route, but a *grand taxi* from Ouarzazate should cost no more than 20dh.

BOUMALNE DU DADÈS

At a key junction between the Dadès Gorge and the Jbel Sharo, Boumalne du Dadès has succeeded where its neighbors have failed. An tourist-friendly town and attractive town, it is perched on a steep cliff overlooking the Dadès River valley below. Watching the sunset over the town is a popular pastime for both visitors and locals.

🛈 PRACTICAL INFORMATION. The highway turns into the main road (P32) and goes through town and up the cliff to reach the plateau above. **Buses** arrive on the lower part of this street. The **CTM** office is farther downtown. Buses run to **Er-Rachidia** (1 per day, 12:30pm, 42dh) and **Marrakesh** via Ouarzazate (1 per day, 9am, 70dh). Non-CTM buses go to **Agadir** (1 per day, 8:30pm) and **Rabat** (1 per day, 7:30pm). *Grand taxis* leave from near the bus station for Ouarzazate and Tinerhir, while minibuses and lorries (pickup trucks) will carry you up the Dadès Gorge for around 15-20dh. **Post office** with several **telebotiques**, on top of the hill (a left at the Shell gas station; a 20min. walk). **Telephone code:** (0)4.

🛈🍴 ACCOMMODATIONS AND FOOD. The best place to stay is the **Hôtel Al Manadar** (tel. 83 01 72), five minutes up the hill from the main square. The terrace has a stunning view of the valley, and for a bit more so will your room (singles 40dh, with view 60dh; doubles 80dh, with view 120dh; triples 120dh, with view 180dh; quads 160dh, with view 240dh). Its **restaurant** serves good food with a minimal wait (*menu* 60dh, entrees 35dh). If you get into town late or don't like to walk, the **Hôtel Adrar** (tel. 83 03 05), near the main square, is convenient, if a bit shabby (hot showers 10dh; singles 40dh; doubles 60dh; triples 90dh; quads 120dh). Its **restaurant** serves adequate food (entrees 30-35dh).

DADÈS GORGE

The winding ride up the Dadès Gorge rivals the Tizi-n-Test as the best in Morocco. The wild, stunning scenery attests to the power of nature, as the earth serves to have been literally ripped away. Towering kasbahs rise up on the slopes and dissolve into the surrounding land. At about the 27km mark, the road narrows and several hotels mark the beginning of a foot path through the gorge (directly across from the **Kasbah de la Ville,** to the left of the camping driveway). The path crosses a stream and winds its way up the gorge, where the walls are closer and closer together. An hour walk yields great scenery, though the physically fit will want to tackle the entire circuit (5hr.). To get here, take a right once you cross the river coming from Boumalne. Lorries run quite frequently to and from the gorge. There are several places to stay and eat, the best being the ◨**Restaurant Hôtel Lagazelle du Dadès** (tel. 83 17 53), with lodge-like atmosphere at great rates (doubles 30dh, with shower 60dh; triples 80dh; quads 100dh; sleeping on the terrace 10dh, in the *salon* 20dh; camping 5dh per person, shower included). It is possible to get a guide here (200dh per day), arrange rafting expeditions when the water is high (Jan.-Apr.; 200dh per person per day), and rent bikes (60dh per day). Its restaurant serves filling meals (3-course *menu* 45dh).

TINERHIR (TINGHIR)

Like Boumalne du Dadès, Tinerhir acts mainly as a base for exploring the nearby Todra gorge. For those with time, however, the eastern part of town (on the right when coming from Ouarzazate) contains an old medina and *mallah* worthy of an hour or two of exploration. As you wind through the dark passages, look for the "cross of the south" above the windows, signifying the existence of an ancient trading route between central Africa and the Jews of Tinerhir.

🛈 PRACTICAL INFORMATION. The highway turns into av. Mohammed V as it reaches the town. **Buses** arrive just off it, in pl. Principale. Parallel to av. Moham-med V is av. Hassan II, where most of the cheaper hotels and restaurants are located. Buses go to **Marrakesh** via Ouarzazate (CTM 1 per day, 8am, 83dh; private lines 8am-6pm, prices vary) and **Er-Rachidia** (CTM 1 per day, 1:30pm, 31dh; private lines 7:30am-6pm, 28dh). *Grand taxis* running east and west and lorries going up the gorge (15-20dh) leave on the other side of the garden in between the two main roads. **Banks** line av. Mohammed V. **Post office,** near the *grand taxi* stand on av. Hassan II. **Telephone code:** (0)4.

█ █ ACCOMMODATIONS AND FOOD. Next to the CTM office is the **Résidence El Fath,** 56 av. Hassan II (tel. 83 48 06), which is pleasant enough and has showers in every room (singles 35dh; doubles 70dh; triples 85dh). Its real draw is its **restaurant,** which serves on its rooftop terrace (entrees 30-45dh). Just down the road is the **Hôtel Al Qods,** 8 av. Hassan II (tel. 83 46 05), a bit cheaper and with equally clean rooms (singles 30dh; doubles 60dh; triples 90dh). Its **restaurant** follows the hotel's standards and offers decent fare (entrees 20-25dh). Just outside of town toward Ouarzazate is **Camping Ourti** (tel. 83 32 05), av. Mohammed V, which has bungalow-type rooms (35dh per person) and a swimming pool (free for occupants, 10dh otherwise; camping 12dh per person, 10dh per tent, 8dh per car). Camping Ourti will also arrange outings up the gorge and to palmeries.

TODRA GORGE

The road out of Tinerhir snakes up the **Todra River Valley** for 14km before reaching the mouth of the **gorge** (5dh entrance fee per car). From here, hike up between the towering walls. Todra is more developed than the Dadès; while more extensive facilities are available, privacy and a sense of wilderness are lost. Still, the hike is spectacular. Almost a thousand feet high, the sienna walls frame a blue strip of sky above and fall to a rocky riverbed below. A half-day hike is enough to appreciate the magnificence of the gorge, but a few days, or even a week, will allow you to climb well into the High Atlas. Rock climbing is popular, but there are no agencies to equip or guide. Along the way to the gorge are a trio of beautiful campgrounds. **Auberge de l'Atlas** (tel. 83 42 09) is slightly better than the other two facilities and offers free hot showers (camping 10dh per person, 15dh per tent, 6dh per car; doubles 90dh, triples 140dh; Berber tent 20dh). Its restaurant serves standard fare (*menu* 50dh). **Cafe-Restaurant Auberge Etoile des Gorges** (tel. 83 51 58) has six rooms, or you can sleep on the roof below the walls of the gorge (singles 25dh; doubles 50dh; roof 5dh). It also serves entrees (35-40dh) and a *menu* (50-60dh). At the end of the road is the pricey **Hôtel Les Roches** (tel. 83 48 14; fax 83 36 11), which is frequented by tour groups. The rooms are decent, but for a more enchanting night's rest, sleep on the rooftop terrace under the high rock walls. (Singles 100dh; doubles 150dh; triples 180dh. Visa, MC, AmEx). The **restaurant** serves some of the finest food in the region at some of the highest prices (entrees 50dh for hotel guests, 70dh otherwise).

THE ZIZ VALLEY

ER RACHIDIA

Although named after the first Alawite sultan, Moulay ar-Rashid, Er Rachidia was founded by the French as an administrative capital and military outpost. Today, Er Rachidia's university and successful businesses have brought the town an air of prosperity and friendliness. Although it offers little to do or see, the town makes a pleasant stop for travelers heading into the southern deserts and gorges.

█ ORIENTATION AND PRACTICAL INFORMATION. All **buses** arrive in town at the main bus station at pl. Principale, just off the town's main street, av. Moulay Ali Cherif. Buses go to **Erfoud** and **Rissani** (1hr.; CTM 1 per day, 5am; private companies 5 per day, 7:30am-7:30pm; 15-20dh); **Meknes** (7 hr.; CTM 1 per day, 10pm; private companies 4 per day, 6am-10pm; 80dh); **Fez** (8hr., private companies 10 per day, 7am-11:15pm); **Marrakesh** (11hr.; CTM 1 per day, 5:45am; private companies 2 per day, 8:30am and 7pm; 115dh); **Agadir** (12hr.; CTM 1 per day, 7am; private companies 5 per day, 10am-7pm; 168dh) via **Ouarzazate; Casablanca** (16hr.; CTM 1 per day, 8pm; private companies 5 per day, 5:30-10pm; 133-160dh) via **Rabat.** To find *grand taxis*, walk down av. Moulay Ali Cherif toward the center of town, turn right after Restaurant Imilchil, and ask around. Taxis to **Erfoud** (16dh); **Rissani** (20dh) and **Tinerhir** (about 50dh). There are several **banks** in town, although none have ATMs. **Police,** (tel. 19), at the bus station; **Red Cross,** on av. Moulay Ali Cherif next to Restaurant Imilchil. **Post office,** on av. Mohammed V, a left off av. Moulay Ali Cherif when coming from the bus station (open daily in summer 7am-2:30pm; in winter 7am-9pm). **Telephone code:** (0)5.

⌘ ACCOMMODATIONS AND FOOD. Most budget hotels are, thankfully, near the bus station. **Hotel El Ansar,** 34 rue Ibn Batouta (tel. 57 39 19), behind the bus station and to the left, has the best value, offering sparkling rooms, complete with free hot showers (singles 40dh; doubles 60dh; triples 80dh). Another good value is older and more established **Hotel Renaissance,** 19 rue Moulay Youseff (tel. 57 26 33), directly across pl. Principale from the bus station. Rooms are standard and many have showers (singles 30dh; with shower 46dh; doubles with shower 70dh; triples with shower 90dh). Most restaurants and **markets** cluster on av. Moulay Ali Cherif. For fresh produce, try the **supermarket,** across from Hotel M'Daghra. **Cafe-Restaurant Echajara,** 38 av. Moulay Ali Cherif (tel. 57 15 10), serves a complete *menu* (30dh), including the regional specialty *qualia* (minced beef, tomato, onion, and 15 spices cooked in a *tajine* dish). Here you can also find Larbi Lamhamdi, who will arrange sunrise and sunset tours to the Merzouga dunes (250dh). **Restaurant Imilchild** (tel. 57 21 23), on av. Mohammed V, is slightly pricier, with standard entrees for 25-30dh.

ERFOUD

One of the last places to fall to the French (in 1932) Erfoud today has little of the spark of revolution left. Although famous for its marble fossils and its annual date festival (in October), and convenient as a base for exploring the Dunes of Merzuga, Erfoud has little to entertain visitors. In winter, when temperatures stay below 50° C, the town is a pleasant place to relax—stop here before heading to the dunes or imperial cities.

CTM **buses** depart from av. Mohammed V, Erfoud's main street, and go to **Rissani** (1 per day, 6am, 6dh), **Er Rachidia** (1 per day, 8:30am, 15dh), and **Meknes** (1 per day, 8:30pm, 95dh). All other destinations require transit through Er Rachidia. More frequent private buses leave from pl. des F.A.R., at the far end of av. Mohammed V. *grand taxis* go to **Rissani** (6dh) and **Er Rachidia** (16dh), departing from the intersection of av. Mohammed V and av. Moulay Ismail. **Banks,** a **hospital,** and a **post office** lie there as well. **Telephone code:** (0)5.

Erfoud's hotels are all on the expensive side. ⌘**Hôtel Merzouga,** 114 av. Mohammed V (tel. 57 65 32), outshines the rest, offering spotless and cheery rooms, all with showers (singles 60dh; doubles 80dh; triples 120dh; terrace 25dh). The hotel's **restaurant** serves Moroccan cuisine (3-course *menu* 40dh). Another option is the **Hôtel Lahmada** (tel. 57 69 80), down av. Moulay Ismail and to the left (when facing the post office). With carpeting, imitation kasbah tiling, and private bathrooms stocked with towels, toilet paper, and soap, amenities nearly outweigh the price (singles 121dh; doubles 140dh; triples 187dh). Its **restaurant** is a bit pricier as well (entrees 35-40dh; *menu* 60dh). Those running low on funds can stay at the newly renovated **campground,** not far from the center of town. Follow the signs from av. Moulay Ismail (10min.). The numerous sink, toilet, and shower facilities make up for the heat and lack of shade. (10dh per person and per tent; 15dh for electricity).

NEAR ERFOUD: ◪THE DUNES OF MERZOUGA

About 50km south of Erfoud is one of Morocco's most enduring images: the monstrous **Er Chebbi** dunes of Merzouga. The largest in the world—some claim they are up to 125m tall—they are definitely worth a visit. They are most enchanting at sunrise and sunset, when golden light and cooler air make for a more captivating experience. But legend has it that the dunes have more than just aesthetic value— it is said that burying the body in the sweltering sand will cure heart disease and rheumatism.

Arrange excursions from Erfoud—hire a 4x4 *grand taxi* (5-6hr., 300-400dh per taxi) in pl. des F.A.R. or join the air-conditioned package tour (600dh per car) leaving from Hôtel Merzouga. Those with their own vehicles should consider enlisting a guide to help navigate through the sand-blown roads. **Auberges Yasmina, Cafe du Sud,** and **Er Chebbi,** along the road to the dunes, offer ideal spots for meals or overnight stays (3-course *menu* 50dh; singles and doubles 60dh; "Berber" tent on the terrace 20dh). These hostels can organize **camel trips.**

APPENDIX

TIME ZONES

Spain is one hour later than Greenwhich Mean Time (GMT) and six hours later than U.S. EST. **Portugal** and **Morocco** are on GMT and 5 hours later than EST. Thus, when it is 3pm in New York, it is 8pm in Portugal and Morocco and 9pm in Spain. Spain and Portugal, together with the rest of Europe, switch to and from Daylight Savings time about one week before the U.S. Morocco does not switch, and is thus four hours later than U.S. EST and two hours earlier than Spain in the summer.

MEASUREMENTS

The following is a list of U.S. units and their metric equivalents:

MEASUREMENT CONVERSIONS

1 inch (in.) = 25.4 millimeters (mm)	1 millimeter (mm) = 0.039 in.
1 foot (ft.) = 0.30 m	1 meter (m) = 3.28 ft.
1 yard (yd.) = 0.914m	1 meter (m) = 1.09 yd.
1 mile = 1.61km	1 kilometer (km) = 0.62 mi.
1 ounce (oz.) = 28.35g	1 gram (g) = 0.035 oz.
1 pound (lb.) = 0.454kg	1 kilogram (kg) = 2.202 lb.
1 fluid ounce (fl. oz.) = 29.57ml	1 milliliter (ml) = 0.034 fl. oz.
1 gallon (gal.) = 3.785L	1 liter (L) = 0.264 gal.
1 acre (ac.) = 0.405ha	1 hectare (ha) = 2.47 ac.
1 square mile (sq. mi.) = 2.59km^2	1 square kilometer (km^2) = 0.386 sq. mi.

ADDRESSES

Spain & Portugal: "Av.", "C.", "R.", and "Trav." are abbreviations for street, "Po." and "Pg." for promenade, "Pl." for square, and "Ctra." for highway. A building's number follows the street name. The letters "s/n" stand for the Spanish *sin numero*, which means that the building has no number. **Morocco:** "av.", "bd.", "rue", and "calle" mean street; "pl." is a plaza. The building number comes before the street name. When hunting for an address, note that many streets are being renamed in Arabic; "rue" and "calle" may be replaced by "zankat," "derb," or "sharia."

LANGUAGE

A basic vocabulary in the local tongue will go a long way toward making your trip easier and more enjoyable. Any attempts at the local language are appreciated and encouraged. Learn the vocabulary of courtesy as well; you'll be treated more kindly if you are polite to those around you.

SPANISH

Spanish pronunciation is very regular. Vowels are always pronounced the same way: *a* ("ah" in father); *e* ("eh" in escapade); *i* ("ee" in eat); *o* ("oh" in oat); *u* ("oo" in boot); *y*, by itself, is pronounced like *ee*. Most consonants are the same as English. Important exceptions are: *j* ("h" in "hello"); *ll* ("y" in "yes"); *ñ* ("gn" in "cognac"); *rr* (trilled "r"); *h* is always silent; *x* retains its English sound. The stress in Spanish words falls on the last syllable, unless the word ends in a vowel, an "s", or a "n". All exceptions require a written accent on the stressed syllable. For Portuguese and Moroccan Arabic, this phrasebook provides pronunciation tips.

ENGLISH	SPANISH	ENGLISH	SPANISH
	The Bare Minimum		
Yes/No	Sí/No	Do you speak English?	¿Habla (usted) inglés?
Hello	Hola (Sí on the phone)	I don't understand	No entiendo
Good morning!	¡Buenos días!	I don't speak Spanish	No hablo español
Good afternoon!	¡Buenas tardes!	What/When	¿Qué?/¿Cuándo?
Good evening/night!	¡Buenas noches!	Where/How	¿Dónde?/¿Cómo?
Goodbye	Adiós/Hasta luego	Who/Why	¿Quién?/¿Por qué?
Please/Thank you	Por favor/Gracias	How are you?	¿Cómo está (usted)?
Excuse me	Perdón/Perdóname	Good/Bad/So-so	Bién/Mal/Así así
Help	¡Socorro!	What time is it?	¿Qué hora es?
No smoking/Gotta lighter (cigarette)?	No fumar/¿Tiene fuego (un cigarillo)?	How much does this cost?	¿Cuánto cuesta?
Here/There/Left/Right/Straight	Aquí/Allí/Izquierda/Derecha/Recto	Where is the bathroom?	¿Dónde está el baño?
Open/Closed	Abierto/Cerrado	My name is...	Me llamo...
Hot/Cold	Caliente/Frío	What is your name?	¿Cómo se llama?
	Accomodation and Transportation		
I want/I would like	Quiero/Quisiera	How do I reach...?	¿Cómo llego a...?
I would like a room	Quisiera un cuarto	One ticket to...	Un billete para...
Do you have any rooms?	¿Tiene cuartos libres?	Bus (Train) station/Airport	Estación de Tren (Autobús)/Aeropuerto
bath/shower/water	baño/ducha/agua	train/plane/bus	tren/avión/autobús
key/sheets	llave/sábanas	round-trip	ida y vuelta
air conditioning	aire acondicionado	How long is the trip?	¿Cuánto dura el viaje?
Hotel/Hostel/Campgrounds/Inn	Hotel/Hostal or Albergue/Camping/Posada	At what time does it leave/arrive?	¿A qué hora sale/llega?
	Food and Dining (also See Glossary)		
breakfast	desayuno	the check, please	la cuenta, por favor
lunch	almuerzo	drink	bebida
dinner	cena	dessert	postre
	Days		
Sunday	domingo	Today	hoy
Monday	lunes	Tomorrow	mañana
Tuesday	martes	Day after tomorrow	pasado mañana
Wednesday	miércoles	Yesterday	ayer
Thursday	jueves	Day before yesterday	antes de ayer/anteayer
Friday	viernes	Week	semana
Saturday	sábado	Weekend	fin de semana
	Numbers		
0	cero	30	treinta
1	uno	40	cuarenta
2	dos	50	cincuenta
3	tres	60	sesenta
4	cuatro	70	setenta
5	cinco	80	ochenta
6	seis	90	noventa
7	siete	100	cien
8	ocho	101	ciento uno
9	nueve	142	ciento cuarenta y dos
10	diez	200	doscientos (dos-cientos)
20	veinte	1000	mil
21	veintiuno (viente y uno)	1 million	un millón

PORTUGUESE PHRASEBOOK

ENGLISH	PORTUGUESE	PRONOUNCIATION
Yes/No	Sim/Não	seeng/now
Hello	Olá	oh-LAH
Good day, afternoon/night	Bom dia, Boa tarde/noite	bom DEEer, BOAer tard/noyt
Goodbye	Adeus	ah-DAY-oosh
Please	Por favor	pur fah-VOR
Thank you	Obrigad(o)/(a) (to male/female)	oh-bree-GAH-doo/dah
Sorry	Desculpe	dish-KOOL-peh
Excuse me, please	Desculpe	dish-KOOLP
Do you speak English?	Fala inglês?	FAH-lah een-GLAYSH?
I don't understand	Não compreendo	now kohm-pree-AYN-doo
Where is ...?	Onde é que é ...?	OHN-deh eh keh eh...?
Hotel/Bathroom	Hotel/Casa de banho	ot-TEL/KA-zer der BA-nyoo
How much does this cost	Quanto custa?	KWAHN-too KOOSH-tah?
Do you have a single/double room?	Tem um quarto individual /duple?	tem om KWAR-toe een-DE-vee-DU-ahl/DOO-play?
Help!	Socorro!	so-ko-RO!

MOROCCO PHRASEBOOK

ENGLISH	MOROCCAN ARABIC	FRENCH
Hello (polite)	assa-LAH-mu-'a-LEY-kum / 'a-LEY-kum as-sa-LAM (response)	Bonjour (day) / Bonsoir (night)
Hello/How are you (informal)	la-BAS?	Ca va?
Fine thanks	la-bas, al-HAM-du-li-lah	Tres bien, merci
Yes/No	NA'uhm/LA	Oui/Non
Please	meenFAD-lik/'AF-fak/ al-LAH-i-khaleek	S'il vous plaît
Thank you	shokron	Merci
I want (I would like)...	b-GHEET...	Je voudrais...
Where is...?	feen...?	Où est...? / Où se trouve ...?
When is...?	fo-QASH...?	A quelle heure est...? C'est quand...?
Bus/Taxi/Train	ut-tu-BEES/TAK-see/al-MA-shina	Bus/Taxi/Train
Hotel/Bathroom	u-TEEL/mar-HAD	Hôtel/Toilette
Is there a room?	wash kayn shee beet?	Est-ce qu'il y a une chambre libre?
I don't speak Arabic (French)	ma-kan-ntkal-LAMCH al-'A-rabiya (al-Fransaweeya)	Je ne parle pas arabe (français)
Do you speak English?	wash-kat-TKAL-lim- in-gi-LEE-zee?	Parlez vous anglais?
How much does it cost?	ch-HAL ta-MAN?	Combien ça coute?
Let's work on a better price.	DIR-I-na shee taman mezyan / wa-TSOW-wab m'ana (very colloquial)	Faites-moi un bon prix.
A lot/A little bit	bez-ZAF/sh-WEEY-ya	Beaucoup/Un peu
Cheap/Expensive	ri-KHEES/GHEH-lee	Pas cher/cher
I'm not interested/Leave me alone	ma bagh-EESH/khal-LEE-nee f-teesa'	Je ne suis pas interessé
Excuse me	SMEH-li	Pardon
Help!	an-NAJ-da! an-qee-DOO-nee!	Au secours!

ARABIC NUMERALS										
0	1	2	3	4	5	6	7	8	9	10
٠	١	٢	٣	٤	٥	٦	٧	٨	٩	١٠
sifir	waahid	ithnayn	thalaatha	arba'a	khamsa	sitta	sab'a	tha-maniya	tis'a	'ashara

GLOSSARY

In the following glossary of common terms, **S** denotes Spain, **P** stands for Portugal, and **M** means Morocco. When a Spanish word is in a language other than Castillian Spanish (such as Catalán, Basque, or Gallego), the language is specified.

TERM	ENGLISH	TERM	ENGLISH
	General		
abadía (S)	abbey	kiosco (S)	newsstand
acueducto (S)	aqueduct	masjid (M)	mosque
ajuntament (Catalán)	city hall	medina (M)	Arab bit of modern city
albergue (S)	youth hostel	mellah (M)	Jewish quarter
alcazaba (S)	Muslim citadel	mercado (S, P)	market
alcázar (S)	Muslim fortress-palace	mercado municipal (S, P)	local farmers' market
aqueduto (P)	aqueduct	mercat (Catalán)	market
arco (P)	arch	mesquita (P)	mosque
avenida (S, P)	avenue	mezquita (S)	mosque
avinguda (Catalán)	avenue	monestir (Catalán)	monastery
ayuntamiento (S)	city hall	monte (S)	mountain
azulejo (P)	glazed ceramic tile	mosteiro (Gallego, P)	monastery
bab (M)	gate	Mozárabe (S)	Christian style of art
bahía (S)	bay	Mudéjar (S)	Muslim architectural style
barrio viejo (S)	old city	museo (S)	museum
baños (S)	baths	museu (Catalán, P)	museum
biblioteca municipal (P)	public library	muralla (S)	wall
borj (M)	fort or tower	palacio (S)	palace
cabo (P)	cape	palau (Catalán)	palace
calle (S)	street	parador nacional (S)	state-run hotel in an old fortress or palace
capela (P)	chapel	parc (Catalán)	park
capilla mayor (S)	chapel with high altar	parque (S and P)	park
carrer (Catalán)	street	paseo, Po. (S)	promenade
carrera (S)	road	passeig, Pg. (Catalán)	promenade
carretera (S)	highway	plaça, Pl. (Catalán)	square
casa particular (S, P)	lodging in private home	plage (M)	beach
casco antiguo (S)	old city	plaia (Gallego)	beach
castell (Catalán)	castle	platja (Catalán)	beach
castelo (P)	castle	playa (S)	beach
castillo (S)	castle	playa nudista, playa natural (S)	nude beach
catedral (S)	cathedral	plaza, Pl. (S)	square
(el) centro (S)	city center	polideportivo (S)	sports center
ciudad nueva (S)	new city	ponta (P)	bridge
ciudad vieja (S)	old city	porta (P)	gate
ciutat vella (Catalán)	old city	pousada (P)	a state-run hotel

APPENDIX

TERM	ENGLISH	TERM	ENGLISH
claustro (S, P)	cloister	pousada juventude (P)	youth hostel
colegiata (S)	collegiate church	praça, Pr. (P)	square
colegio (S)	school	praia (P)	beach
convento (P)	convent	praza, Pr. (Gallego)	square
coro (S, P)	choir in a church	puente (S)	bridge
coro alto (P)	upper choir	quarto (P)	lodging in private house
corrida (S)	bullfight	real (S)	royal
cripta (S)	crypt	reina/rey (S)	queen/king
encierro (S)	running of the bulls	ría (Gallego)	mouth of river; estuary
ermida (Catalán)	hermitage	río (S)	river
ermita (S)	hermitage	rio (P)	river
església (Catalán)	church	riu (Catalán)	river
estacão (P)	station (train or bus)	retablo (S)	altarpiece, retable
estación (S)	station (train or bus)	rossio (P)	rotary
estanco (S)	tobacco shop	rua, R. (P)	street
estanque (S)	pond	rúa, R. (S, G.)	street
estany (Catalán)	lake	rue, r. (M)	street
fachada (S)	façade	sala (S)	room or hall
feira (P)	outdoor market or fair	Semana Santa (S)	week before Easter Sun.
feria (S)	outdoor market or fair	serra (Catalán)	mountain range
ferrocarriles (S)	trains	seu (Catalán)	cathedral
floresta (P)	forest	sevillanas (S)	type of flamenco dance
fonte (P)	fountain	sierra (S)	mountain range
fortaleza (S, P)	fortress	sillería (S)	choir stalls
fuente (S)	fountain	s/n (sin número; S)	unnumbered address
glorieta (S)	rotary	souk (M)	market
grutas (P)	caves	tesoro (S)	treasury
hammam (M)	Turkish-style bathhouse	tesouro (P)	treasury
iglesia (S)	church	torre (S, P)	tower
igreja (P)	church	torre de menagem (P)	castle keep
igreja do seminário (P)	seminary church	universidad (S)	university
igrexa (Gallego)	church	universidade (P)	university
jardim botanico (P)	botanical garden	valle (S)	valley
jardim público (P)	public garden	ville nouvelle (M)	new city
jardín público (S)	public garden	zarzuela (S)	Spanish operetta
kasbah (M)	fort or citadel	zelij (M)	decorative ceramic tiles
Dining			
menú (S, Catalán)	meal with bread, drink, and side dish	plato del día (S)	special of the day
mercado (S, P)	market	platos combinados (S)	entree and side order
mercat (Catalán)	market	taberna (S)	tapas bar
para llevar (S)	to go (take-away)	terraza (S)	patio seating
Food			
aceitunas (S)	olives	lomo (S)	pork loin
albóndigas (S)	meatballs	lulas (Gallego, P)	squid
anchoas (S)	anchovies	mantequilla (S)	butter
al ajillo (S)	cooked in garlic	manzana (S)	apple
a la parilla (P)	roasted	marisco (S)	shellfish
arroz (S, P)	rice	mejillones (S)	mussels
asado/a (S)	grilled	melocotón (S)	peach

TERM	ENGLISH	TERM	ENGLISH
atún (S)	tuna	menestra de verduras (S)	mixed vegetables
bocadillo (S)	sandwich on a baguette	merluza (S)	hake (fresh white fish)
boquerones (S)	smelts	paella (S)	saffron rice with shell-fish and vegetables
brochette (M)	kebab	pan (S)	bread
cabrito (P)	kid goat	pão (P)	bread
camaroes (P)	shrimp	patatas bravas (S)	spicy fried potatoes
caracois (P)	snails	peixe (P)	fish
caracoles (S)	snails	pescado (S)	fish
cebolla (S)	onion	pimientos (S)	peppers
champiñones (S)	mushrooms	pincho (S)	tapa on a toothpick
chocos (S)	squid	pisto (S)	vegetable stew
chorizo (S)	sausage	plancha (S)	grilled
churrasco (S)	barbecued meat	pollo (S)	chicken
churros (S)	lightly fried fritters	queso (S)	cheese
cocido (S)	stew with chickpeas	ración, raciones (S)	a large tapa
comida (S)	madday meal; food	salsichas (P)	sausages
empanada (S)	meat or vegetable turn-over	sande (P)	sandwich
ensalada (S)	salad	sardinhas assadas (P)	grilled sardines
fabada (S)	bean stew	serrano (S)	smoked or cured
feijoada (P)	bean stew with meat	sopa (S, P)	soup
frango no churrasco (P)	barbecued chicken	tajine (M)	stew, usually with meat
fresa (S)	strawberry	tapa, tapas (S)	see p. 60
gambas (S)	shrimp	tortilla española (S)	potato omelette
gazpacho (S)	cold tomato-based veg-etable soup	tortilla francesa (S)	plain omelette
jamón (S)	mountain-cured ham	verduras (S)	vegetables
judías (S)	beans	zarzuela (S, Catalán)	seafood and tomato bouillabaisse

Drinks and Drinking			
agaurdiente (S)	firewater	manzanilla (S)	dry, sherry-like wine
bica (S)	a mixed drink	medronho (P)	firewater
bodega (S)	winery	resolí (S)	coffee, sugar, eau-de-vie
calimocho (S)	red wine and coke	sidra (S)	alcoholic cider
caña (S)	normal-sized beer	suco (P)	juice
cava (Catalán)	champagne variation	tubo (S)	large-sized beer
cerveja (Port.)	beer	txacoli (Basque)	a type of Basque wine
cerveza (S)	beer (general term)	vino blanco (S)	white wine
chato (S)	a little drink	vinho blanco (P)	white wine
chupito (S)	a shot	vino rosado (S)	rosé wine
copa (S)	a cocktail	vino tinto (S)	red wine
horchata (S)	a sweet almond drink	vinho verde (P)	young wine
jarra (S)	pitcher or mug	xampanyería (Catalán)	champagne factory
jerez (S)	sherry	zumo (S)	juice

AVERAGE TRAVEL TIMES IN SPAIN AND PORTUGAL

	Algeciras	Badajoz	Barcelona	Bilbao	Córdoba	Granada	León	Málaga	Madrid	Pamplona	Salamanca	San Sebastián	Santiago	Sevilla	Toledo	Valencia	Zaragoza
Algeciras																	
Badajoz	10hr.																
Barcelona	19½hr.	13½hr.															
Bilbao	11-13hr.	10-11½hr.	8-11hr.														
Córdoba	5-6hr.	6hr.	11hr.	9-11hr.													
Granada	5-7hr.	7½-9½hr.	12-13hr.	10-12hr.	3hr.												
León	11hr.	8½hr.	11½hr.	7hr.	7-9hr.	10hr.											
Málaga	5½hr.	7-8hr.	13hr.	11-13hr.	2½-3hr.	2hr.	9-11½hr.										
Madrid	6hr.	4½hr.	7hr.	5-7hr.	2-6hr.	5hr.	4½-5½hr.	4-6hr.									
Pamplona	11hr.	9½hr.	6-8hr.	2hr.	9hr.	10hr.	4hr.	9-11hr.	5hr.								
Salamanca	9hr.	5½hr	11½hr.	5½-6½hr.	6-8hr.	8hr.	3hr.	7-9hr.	3hr.	6-7hr.							
San Sebastián	12-14hr.	10-12hr.	7-10hr.	11hr.	10-12hr.	11-13hr.	5¼hr.	12-14hr.	6-8hr.	1-2hr.	5½-6½hr.						
Santiago de Campostela	14hr.	12-13hr.	15hr.	11hr.	11-13hr.	13hr.	5½hr.	12-14hr.	7½-8hr.	12hr.	7-8hr.	12hr.					
Sevilla	4-5hr.	4½hr.	13-16hr.	8-11hr.	1½hr.	3-5hr.	7-9hr.	2½-3hr.	2½-3½hr.	8hr.	8hr.	9-11hr.	11hr.				
Toledo	6hr.	5hr.	7hr.	6-8hr.	3-5hr.	14hr.	6hr.	5-6hr.	1½hr.	9hr.	4hr.	7-9hr.	12hr.	3hr.			
Valencia	13-15hr.	10hr.	4-6hr.	12hr.	7hr.	8hr.	10-13hr.	11hr.	5-7½hr.	10hr.	8-10½hr.	10hr.	11hr.	9hr.	5-7½hr.		
Zaragoza	9hr.	8hr.	4hr.	4hr.	6-8hr.	8hr.	5½-6hr.	7-9hr.	3hr.	2hr.	7hr.	4hr.	11-12hr.	8½hr.	4hr.	6hr.	

	Braga	Coimbra	Évora	Faro	Fátima	Lisbon	Porto
Braga		4hr.	9-10hr.	12-15hr.	5½hr.	8½hr.	2hr.
Coimbra			6hr.	12hr.	1½hr.	3hr.	3hr.
Évora				6hr.	5½hr.	3hr.	7hr.
Faro					7½hr.	5hr.	8½hr.
Fátima						2½hr.	3½hr.
Lisbon							6hr.
Porto							

INDEX

A

ABC 61
Abd el Krim, founder of
 modern Morocco 650
Abd el-Mumin 710
Abderramán III 48, 214
abortion 23
Abul Hassan 255, 262,
 263
accommodations 25–26
 in Morocco 661
 in Portugal 537
 in Spain 67
The Aeneid 530
Afonso, Jorge 529
Agadir 705
Age of Discovery 526
 art 529
Agrippa 181
Águilas 294
Aigüestortes 359
Aínsa (L'Ainsa) 383
Air Europa 64
airplane travel 31–33
 in Morocco 657
 in Portugal 535
 in Spain 64
airports
 Agadir 705
 Alicante 285
 Arrecife 516
 Badajoz 183
 Barcelona 296
 Bilbao 418
 Casablanca 696
 Córdoba 207
 Faro 577
 Fez 680
 Granada 255
 Jerez de la Frontera 215
 La Coruña 464
 Las Palmas 502
 Lisbon 540

 Madrid 71
 Mahón 484
 Málaga 237
 Marrakesh 707
 Murcia 293
 Oviedo 430
 Pamplona 391
 Porto 624
 Rabat 691
 San Sebastián 410
 Santa Cruz de Tenerife
  506
 Santander 442
 Santiago de Compostela
  449
 Sevilla 190
 Tangier 664
 Valencia 274
 Valladolid 161
 Vigo 456
 Vitoria-Gasteiz 426
 Zaragoza 370
Aït Benhaddou 718
Al Mansur 48, 650, 694,
 712
Alawite dynasty 650
Alba de Tormes 154
Albarracín 378
Albergue de Juventud
 Kabul (not **Kubal**) 306
Albufeira 576
Alcalá de Henares 114
Alcobaça 602
Alcúdia 481
Alemán, Rodrigo 154
Alentejo 584–591
Alfonso el Sabio 294
Alfonso II 432
Alfonso VI 390
Alfonso VIII 168
Alfonso X 140
Alfonso XI 178, 213
Alfonso XIII 52, 101, 444
Algarve 569–583
Algeciras 231–233

Alhambra 56
Alicante 285–289
 daytrips 289
Almagro 129
Almería 247
Almodovar, Pedro 58
Almohads 710
Almoravid dynasty 711
Almuñécar 245
Altamira 54, 446
 artifacts from 444
Altea 290
Alto Minho 640–641
Amarante 630
American Express
 as phone card 69
 traveler's checks 15
amusement parks
 Parque de Atracciones,
  Madrid 99
 Port Aventura 337
Âncora 639
Andalucía 186–223
Andersen, Hans Christian
 237
Andorra 362–366
Andorra la Vella 363–365
Aniezo 439
Ansi 715
Ansó 381
Antequera 249–254
Anti-terrorist Liberation
 Groups (GAL) 53
aqueducts
 Segovia 56, 140
Aragón 367–384
Aragonese Pyrenees
 378–384
Aranjuez 120
architecture
 Baroque 56
 Churrigueresque 56
 Gothic 56
 Modernista 57, 314
 Moorish 56

Morocco 653
Mozarabic 56
Mudéjar 56
Plateresque 56
Portugal 529
Renaissance 56
Spain 56
Spanish Gothic 56
Arcos de la Frontera
221–223
Arenas de Cabrales 437
Argamasilla de Alba 128
Arguedas 400
Arrecife 516–518
art
Morocco 653
Portugal 529
Spain 54
Arucas 505
Astorga 160
Asturian Coast 439
Asturias 430–433
Asturias and Cantabria
429–447
Atalanta 101
Atlantic Coast, Morocco
687–706
ATMs 17
au pair 45
Auritz-Burguete 404
Aveiro 619–622
Aviaco 64
Ávila 142–146
Azores 527
azulejos 529
Aveiro 621
Beja 591
El Escorial 117
Vila Real 646

B

backpacks 24
Badajoz 183–185
Baeza 269
Balearic Islands 471–
496
Formentera 495
getting around 473
getting there and away
472
Ibiza 489
Mallorca 473
Menorca 482
Banderas, Antonio 58,

244
banking hours, see money
Baquiera-Beret, see skiing
The Barber of Seville 186
Barceló, Miguel 56
Barcelona 296–328
accommodations and
camping 306–310
entertainment 323–328
food 310–314
getting around 302–303
getting there and away
302
museums 320–322
orientation 303
practical information
304–306
Ruta del Modernisme
314
sights 314–320
Bardenas Reales 400
bargaining
in Portugal 536
in Spain 67
Barka, Ben 650
Baroña 463
Baroque architecture 56
Basque
language 54
Basque Country, see País
Vasco
Batalha
only reason to visit 605
Batalla del Vino 390
Battle of San Quintín 117
Bayona 458
Baywatch 61
Beavis and Butthead 279
Bécquer, Gustavo Adolfo
199
beer
Cruzcampo 195, 200
in Portugal 533
in Spain 61
Beira Alta 611
Beira Baixa 611
Beira Litoral 611
Beja 590
Belle Epoque 59
Ben, meaning of 721
Benaoján 252
Benasque 384
Benidorm 289
Benjamin, Walter 354
Berber 647
architecture 653

Berruguete, Pedro 55
best
attempt at an island
paradise 495
bananas in the world
503
cafe in Portugal 557
ocean view, Costa del
Sol 244
windsurfing beach in the
world 705
Betancuria 514
Betanzos 467
bicycles 37
biggest
24hr. party in the world
490
indoor market in Spain
421
biking
Arguedas 400
Cazorla 272
Morro Jable 516
Puigcerdà 359
Bilbao 417–423
bisexual travelers 41
Black Paintings 55
Blanco, Miguel Ángel 422
Boabdil 255, 262, 263
bodegas
B. Domecq 218
González Byass 218
Haro 389
Jerez de la Frontera 217
Puerto de Santa María
228
Williams and Humbert,
Ltd. 218
Bofill, Ricardo 57
Bomtempo, Domingos
531
Bosch, Hieronymous 106
Madrid 117
Boumalne du Dadés 722
Bourbon monarchy 97
Bowles, Paul 656, 687
Braga 630–634
daytrips 634
Bragança 642–644
Braque, Georges 55
Brazil 527
Breughel, Jan 199
Buarcos 619
Bubión 267
Buçaco Forest 617
bullboards 181

bullfighters
  Fulton, John 198
bullfighting
  Barcelona 327
  history 59
  Lisbon 558
  Madrid 112
  Plaza de Ventas 112
  Sevilla 203
  Spanish 59
Buñuel, Luis 58, 133
Burgau 575
Burgo de Osma 172
Burgos 165–169
The Burial of Count Orgaz 55
Burroughs, William S. 667, 669
bus travel 36
  in Morocco 658
  in Portugal 536
  in Spain 65
Busot 289
Byron, Lord
  Childe Harold 561

C

cabalistas 345
Cabo de Gata 248
Cabo Finisterre 463
Cabral, Pedro Alvares 526, 594
Cáceres 174–176
Cadaqués 353
Cádiz 223–227
Caesar, Augustus 179, 368
Caesar, Julius 186, 204, 251, 705
  and Lisbon 540
Caetano, Marcelo 528
Café de Paris 663
Café Gijón 94
Caldas da Rainha 594
Caldas de Gerês 636
Callela 340, 342
calling cards 30
Calpe (Calp) 290
Cambados 462
Camerón de la Isla 58
Caminha 640
Camino de Hemingway 405
Camino de Santiago 55

Burgos 165
Carrión 164
Casa de las Conchas, Salamanca 150
  end of 448
  Jaca 378
  La Rioja 386
  Logroño 386
  Navarrese Pyrenees 402
  Roncesvalles, first stop 404
  Sangüesa 402
  Santo Domingo de la Calzada 390
Camões, Luís de 530, 552, 646
  tomb 555
camping 26
  in Morocco 661
  in Portugal 538
  in Spain 68
Campo do Gerês 637
Canary Islands 497–523
  El Hierro 523
  Fuerteventura 512
  getting around 498
  getting there and away 497
  Gomera 520
  Gran Canaria 500
  La Palma 523
  Lanzarote 516
  Tenerife 506
Cangas de Onís 434
Canillo 365
Cantabria 441–447
Cap de Formentor 481
Capileira 267
car travel 36
  in Morocco 658
  in Portugal 536
  in Spain 66
caracóis, Portugal's favorite food 581
Carlist Wars 52
Carlos I 49, 102
Carlos II 49
Carlos III 49, 71, 96, 97, 100, 121, 197, 252, 518
  court life 398
Carlos IV 55, 121
Carlos V 122, 130, 140, 212, 262, 263, 417
Carmen 186, 201
Carmona 205
Carmona, António 527

Carnaval (Cádiz) 223
Carreras, José 58, 315
Carrión de los Condes 164
Carthaginians 524
Casablanca 696–700
Casals, Pablo 58
casas colgadas 133
Cascades d'Ouzood 713
Cascais 560
cash cards 17
casinos
  Agadir 706
  Estoril 559
  La Toja 461
  Murcia 293
  Puerto de Santa María 227
  San Sebastián de Gomera 521
  Sant Feliu 343
  Santander 444
Castelo de Vide 589
Castilla La Mancha 122–135
Castilla y León 136–172
Castillo de Javier 403
Castillo de Loarre 380
Cat Stevens 702
Catalán 54
  language issues 333
Catalán Pyrenees 355–361
Catalina de Palacios 128
Cataluña 333–361
cathedrals
  Ávila 145
  Baeza 270
  Braga 633
  Burgos 168
  Cádiz 226
  Girona (Gerona) 349
  Granada 263
  Haro 390
  León 159
  Oviedo 432
  Palencia 164
  Palma 477
  Porto 628
  Salamanca 152
  Santa María 176
  Santiago de Compostela 453
  Segovia 140
  Sevilla 196
  Teruel 377
  Toledo 126

Valencia 279
Valladolid 163
Zamora 156
caves
Altamira 54, 444, 446
Alto de Alvados 606
Antequera 254
Buxu 435
Castillo 445
Dólmenes 254
Mira de Aire 606
Nerja 245
Pileta 252
Santo António 606
Cazorla 271
Cedeira 468
Cela, Camilo José 464
Celts 524
in Galicia 448
Centers for Disease Control (CDC) 21
Centro de Arte Reina Sofia 55
Cercedilla 118
Cervantes, Miguel de 57, 114, 115, 122, 130, 163, 197, 198, 199
house 128
Cesar Manrique 518, 519
Ceuta 670
Chagall, Marc 337
Chapel of Bones
Évora 587
Faro 579
Charlemagne 362
charter flights 32
cheese
Asturia 437
Burgos 167
Chefchaouen 671–672
children and travel 42
Chillida, Eduardo 199
sculpture in Guernica 424
Chipiona 220
Chopin, Fréderic 473, 479
Christian dogs 185
Churriguera, Alberto 146, 150, 152
Churrigueresque architecture 56
Cibeles 101
Citânia de Briteiros 634
Citicorp 15
Ciudad Rodrigo 153
Ciutadella 486–488

climate 7
Coimbra 611–616
collect calls, see keeping in touch
colonialism
in Morocco 650
Portuguese 526
Spanish 49
Columbus, Christopher 48, 152, 178, 197, 213, 262, 303, 526
as monk 152
his tomb 197
in Burgos 169
letters to Fernando and Isabel 197
second voyage 228
sword 106
Comillas 446
communications, see keeping in touch
Comunidad de Madrid 114–121
Condeixa 616
Conil de la Frontera 229
Conímbriga 616
Connery, Sean 242
conquistadors
Cabral, Pedro Alvares 526, 594
Cortés, Hernán 173
Orellana, Francisco de 177
Pizarro, Francisco 130, 173, 177, 178
Constitución de Cádiz 52, 223
Constitution of 1822 527
Consuegra 129
consulates, see embassies and consulates
contact lenses 25
contraceptives 23
conversions
metric 726
time 726
Córdoba 207–214
Corpus Christi (Toledo) 128
Corralejo 513
Cortés, Hernán 173
Costa Blanca 289–295
Costa Brava 337–340
Costa del Sol 236–248
Costa Dorada 334–337
courier flights 32

Covadonga 436
Covas de Canalobre 289
crafts
Morocco 654
credit cards 17
Los Cristianos 508
cross-country skiing
Ochagavía 405
Val D'Aran 360
Valle de Roncal 406
Cruzcampo beer 195, 200
Cubism 55
Cuenca 130–134
Cueva de Nerja 245
Cuevas de Altamira 446
Cuevas de Dólmenes 254
Cuevas del Castillo 445
Cullera 281
currency exchange, see money
current events
Morocco 651
Portugal 528
Spain 53
customs 13

D

Dadés Gorge 721, 722
Dadés Valley 721
Dalai Lama 267
Dalí, Salvador 55, 333, 337, 350
film works 58
his home 354
in a hostel! 286
The Persistence of Memory 56
Premonition of the Civil War 56
Teatre-Museu Dalí 56
understanding his paintings 351
Dama de Elche, Madrid 106
Daroca 374
Defoe, Daniel 690
dehydration 22
Deià 479
Dénia 291
DHL 29
Diana, Princess 244
diarrhea 22
Dias, Bartolomeu 526
Díaz de Vivar, Rodrigo, see

El Cid
dietary concerns 43
Dinis I 526, 529
Diocles 181
disabled travelers 41
The Disasters of War 55
disease, see health
Disney, Walt
  birthplace? 249
Djemâa el-Fna 710
Domènech i Montaner,
  Luis 57, 314
Domingo, Plácido 58
Don Giovanni 186
Don Juan
  model for 199
  tomb 146
Don Quijote 57, 97, 152,
214
  El Toboso 128
  in La Mancha 122
El Dos de mayo 55
Douglas, Michael 479
Douro and Minho 623–
641
Drâa Valley 719
Drake, Sir Francis 49
drinks
  Morocco 654
  Portugal 533
  Spain 61
driving permits 36
drugs 20
Dulcinea 128
dunes
  Merzouga 725
  São Jacinto 621
  Tinfou 720

E

Earthquake of 1755 527,
540, 676, 677
  and Lagos 569
Echo, see Hecho
Eiffel, Gustave 637
Eivissa 490–494
El Cid 164, 168
  Burgos 165, 168
  chronicles of 57
  found dead 168
  in Valencia 274
El Escorial 49, 55, 56,
115, 116
El Greco 55, 104, 106,

127, 164, 178, 199
  El Escorial 117
  El Espolio 127
  in Toledo 127
El Grove 461
El Hierro 523
El Mundo 61
El País 61
El Palmar 229
El Puerto de Santa María
227
El Rastro 113
El Silbo 522
El Teide National Park 511
El Toboso 128
Elche (Elx) 291
elderly travelers 40
electric current 24, 25
electronic banking 17
El-Jadida 700–702
Elvas 588
Elvis jokes 588
email 30
embassies and consulates
  at home 8
  in Morocco 662
  in Portugal 539
  in Spain 69
emergency medical
  assistance 21
emergency numbers
  in Morocco 660
  in Portugal 537
  in Spain 67
Empúries 344
Encamp 366
end of the world, once
  463, 574
entrance requirements 8
Er Rachidia 723
Erfoud 724
Ericeira 565
Ermita de San Saturio 172
escargot 581
Espinama 439
Espot 360
Esquivias 128
Essaouira 702–705
  daytrips 705
Estany de Sant Maurici
360
Estella 400
Estibaliz 410
Estoril 559
ETA 53, 408, 422
EU

Portugal's entry 528
  Spain's entry 53
Eurail 33
euro 14
European Monetary Union
  Portugal 528
  Spain 54
euskera 410
Évora 584–588
exchange, see money
Expo '98 528
  grounds 555
Extremadura 173–185
Extremaduran Samson
178

F

fado 531
  Lisbon 558
Fahd, King 244
families and travel 42
Faro 577–580
fashion designers
  Galicia 461
Fátima 606–608
Federal Express 29
Felipe el Hermoso 49,
169, 263
Felipe I 610
Felipe II 49, 55, 71, 95,
96, 121, 197, 368, 395,
526
  celebrates victory 117
  gift to God 116
  Jaca citadel 380
  sister 106
Felipe III 49, 95, 689
Felipe IV 49, 55, 97, 100
Felipe V 49, 97, 142, 316,
317, 333
Felipe VI 121
Felipe, Prince 361
Ferdinand, see Fernando
  and Isabel
Feria de Abril (Sevilla) 203
Fernando and Isabel 71,
161, 197, 213, 255,
262, 263, 478
  Burgos 169
  daughter of 49
  Granada 262
  marriage 48
  Morocco 650
  summer home 146

Fernando II 154
Fernando III 168, 197, 198
Fernando VI 97, 99
Fernando VII 52
Ferreira de Castro, José Maria 530
festivals
  Barcelona 328
  Batalla del Vino, Haro 390
  Betanzos, launching of world's largest paper balloon 467
  Carnaval, Cádiz 223
  Feira de Santiago 568
  Feira Nacional de Agricultura (Feria do Ribatejo), Santarém 594
  Festa da Sardinha, Peniche 599
  Festival Internacional de la Porta Ferrada, Sant Feliu 343
  Festival Internacional de Teatro Clásico de Almagro 130
  Granada 265
  International Festival, Asilah 688
  Las Fallas, Valencia 280
  Lisbon 558
  Madrid 112
  Nuestra Señora de Begoña, Bilbao 423
  Queima das Fitas, Coimbra 616
  Sanlucar 220
  Sevilla 203
  see also music festivals
  see also theater festivals
Fez 679–687
Figueira da Foz 617–619
Figueres 350–353
film
  Spain 58
film (for cameras) 25
financial matters, see money
first
  property acquired overseas by the U.S. 669
  sale of African slaves in Portugal? 573

Spanish film 58, 86
  thermal hospital 594
Five Love Letters of a Portuguese Nun 591
flamenco
  Córdoba 214
  Granada 264
  history of 58
  Jerez de la Frontera 218
  Madrid 111
  national contest 214
  Sevilla 202
Flemish tapestries 164
  world's finest 142
flights, see airplane travel
foam parties 494
Fontainhas 588
food
  dietary concerns 43
  Morocco 654
  Portugal 532
  Spain 59
food and water safety 22
Formentera 495–496
Fortaleza 575
Foz de Arbayún 403
Foz de Lumbier (Lumbier Gorge) 403
Franco, Francisco 176, 223, 385
  as muse 56
  coup 52
  his tomb 118
Freudian nightmare longest sausage 357
Fuengirola 241
Fuente Dé 439
Fuentevaqueros 265
Fuerteventura 512–516
Fuggers 130
Fulton, John 198
Fundació Joan Miró 321
fútbol
  Atlético de Madrid 112
  Barcelona 327
  Betis 202
  F.C. Barcelona 62, 327
  in Portugal 533
  in Spain 62
  Lisbon 558
  Madrid 112
  Real Madrid 62
  Real Valladolid 163
  Sevilla 202

G

GAL (Anti-terrorist Liberation Groups) 53
Galicia (Galiza) 448–470
gallego 448
Gallego brothers, Francisco and Fernando 151
Gallego, Fernando 152
Gama, Vasco da 526
Game of the Goose 61
Gardner, Ava 337
Gargallo, Pablo 373
Garganta del Chorro 241
Garrett, Almeida 530
Gaudí, Antoni 57, 159, 314, 315, 318, 333
  Casa Milà 318
  commissions 296
  Palacio Episcopal, Astorga 160
  Parc Güell 319
  Sagrada Familia 317
gay and lesbian services
  Barcelona 305
  Madrid 82
  Salamanca 149
  Sevilla 192
gay travelers 41
Generation of '98 57, 151
Generation of 1870 530
Generation of 1927 57
get lost 624
getting there and around 30–39
  by bicycles 37
  by bus 36
  by car 36
  by mopeds and motorcycles 38
  by thumb 38
  by train 33
  in Morocco 657
  in Portugal 535
  in Spain 64
giardia 23
Gibraltar 233–236
Ginsberg, Allen 667
Girona 345–350
Glaoui Kasbah 713
Globe Theatre, replica 130
glossary 729
GO25 card 13
Golden Age (Siglo de Oro)

57, 130
  painting 55
  precursors 198
  Sevilla 199
Golfín, Don 176
Gomera 520–522
Gonçalves, Nuno 529
Góngora, Luís de 207
González, Felipe 53
The Good, the Bad, and the Ugly 248
Gothic architecture 56
Goya, Francisco 55, 71, 103, 105, 197, 373
  brother-in-law 105
  burial site 99
  El Escorial 117
Gran Canaria 500–505
Granada 255–265
Grand Socco 668
Grande Mosquée Hassan II 699
Graves, Robert 479
grayboxes
  ¡Basta Ya! 422
  A Camões Cameo 552
  A Feathery Reminder 390
  A Rose By Any Other Name 263
  A Slug in the Face 581
  A Whole Lot of Bull 251
  An Army of Deer 641
  Asturians Cut the Cheese 437
  Buddhism in Bubión 267
  Bullboards 181
  César Manrique 519
  Cliff Hangers 602
  Cult Fiction 656
  Eat Your Heart Out, Don Juan 622
  El Cid Campeador 168
  El Greco's Three Mistakes 127
  El Sexenni 281
  Far Trek 383
  Fine Wine, Port Gratis 629
  Flamenco Frills and Drills 58
  If Gilligan Had Been So Lucky 527
  Is It a Small World After All? 249
  Is That a Melting Candle in Your Pocket, or Are You Just a Rotting Donkey? 351
  Isn't It Romanesque? 356
  Jews in Spain 52
  Judaism in Portugal 610
  Just Give a Whistle 522
  La Movida 106
  La Mujer Muerta 141
  La Rapa das Bestas 469
  Living on the Edge 133
  Love Notes 530
  Marvelous Modernisme 314
  Mary and the Three Shepherds 608
  Mother Nature and Family 219
  Our Virgin of Fertility Drugs 358
  Pagan Lovin' 101
  Party Hearty 558
  Pilgrims' Progress 454
  Purple Isles Haze 704
  Pyromaniac's Paradise 279
  Read This 79
  Rebuilding Sepharad 349
  Remembering Sepharad 128
  Resurrecting a Tower of Bable 430
  Ribbit For Her Pleasure 151
  Rock the Kasbah 721
  Running Scared (San Fermines #2) 397
  Ruta de los Pueblos Blancos 222
  Scandals? Nun Here 590
  Scary Cherry 596
  Seeing Red 685
  Sevillanas 203
  Star-Crossed Lovers 377
  Strawberries and Steam 120
  Strip Trees 589
  Surprisingly Fashionable 461
  SWM Seeking... 361
  Tapas 93
  That Took Guts 624
  That's a Whole Lot of Eggs 389
  The Dead King's Club 117
  The Fifth Bomb 246
  The Great Glaoui 713
  The Last Days of Benjamin 354
  The Tooth, the Whole Tooth, and Nothing but the Tooth 595
  The Tragedy of Guernica 424
  Traditions of Navarra (Without Horns) 405
  Understanding Ramadan 653
  What the Devil Are They Txpeaking? 410
  What's in a Name? 500
  Who's Afraid of the Big Bad Wolf? 637
  Wildflowers of El Teide 512
Great Earthquake of 1755, see Earthquake of 1755
Greeks 524
Greenwhich Mean Time 726
Gregorian chants 169
Guadalupe 178
Guernica 423
Guernica 55, 104, 423
Guggenheim Museum, Bilbao 54, 417, 421
Guimarães 634

H

Hadrian 204
Halevi, Yehuda 128
handicapped travelers 41
Haro 388
Hassan I 686
Hassan II
  death 651
  Grande Mosquée 699
  state of emergency 650
health 20–23
  emergency medical assistance 21
  food and water 22
  general tips 21
  immunizations 21
  in Morocco 660
  in Portugal 536

in Spain 67
medical conditions 21
women 23
heat exhaustion 22
Hecho 381
Hemingway, Ernest
and Pamplona 391
Death in the Afternoon
59
The Sun Also Rises 59
Hendrix, Jimi 663, 702,
704
Henriques, Afonso 524,
553, 596, 602, 605,
623, 634
Hercules 466, 690
Herrera, Juan de 56, 105,
121, 182
cathedral, Valladolid
163
Madrid's Plaza Mayor 95
**High Atlas and Deserts,
Morocco** 706–725
highest
mountains in Spain 266
peak in North Africa 714
hiking
Andorra 366
Capileira 267
Cazorla 272
Chefchaouen 672
Cuenca 133
Fuente Dé 439
Gran Recomido (Great
Hike) trails 383
High Atlas Mountains
714
Oviedo 433
Parque Nacional de
Ordesa 383
Picos de Europa 438
Puerto de Navacerrada
119
Sierra Nevada 266
Toubkal Trek 715
Trevélez 268
Valle de Benasque 384
Valle de Salazar 405
hiking equipment 26
history
Morocco 647
Portugal 524
Spain 48
hitchhiking 38
Holy Grail 380
Holy Roman Emperor

last official 49
Hondarribia 416
Hostelling International
(HI) 25
hostels 25
in Morocco 661
in Portugal 537
in Spain 67
Huelva 206
Hugo, Victor 279
Hugonell, legend of 390

I

Iberia (airline) 64
Ibiza 489–495
identification 12
Idris Ibn 'Abdullah 647
Iglesias, Julio 58
Ilhas Berlengas 599
Iman Malik 720
Imlil 715
immunizations 21
Indalo Man 249
Indurain, Miguel 62
Inquisition 48, 146, 213,
611
insects 22
insurance 23
International Identity Cards
(ISIC, ITIC) 13
Internet 30, 47
InterRail 35
Invincible Armada 49
Irún 417
Irving, Washington 262
Isaba 406
Isabel de Castilla 52, 197,
264
see also Fernando and
Isabel
coronation 141
marriage 48
Isabel II 408
ISIC card 13
Isla Santa Clara 414
Isla Tabarca 289
Islam
in Morocco 647
Islas Baleares, see
Balearic Islands
Islas Canarias, see Canary
Islands
Islas Cíes 457
Isle of Mogador 705

Iso 403
ITIC card 13

J

Jaca 378
Jaén 268
Jamón Jamón 59
Játiva (Xàtiva) 282
Jávea (Xàbia) 292
Javier 403
Jbel Zagora 720
jerez (sherry) 61
Jerez de la Frontera 215–
219
Jerez de los Caballeros
182
Jesus of Nazareth 718
Jewish history
Girona 348
Morocco 650
Portugal 642
Spain 52
Toledo 122
Tomar 610
Jewish travelers 43
João I 526, 564, 605
statue in Lisbon 551
João V 526, 565
João VI 527
John Paul II 372, 454
Joplin, Janis 230
Juan Carlos I 53, 473
Juan II
celebrates a victory 117
Juana la Loca 49, 169,
263
driven mad 169
Juba II 705
judaism in Spain 52

K

Kabbalah 345, 349
studies of 348
kasbahs 721
kayaking
San Sebastián 415
Tossa del Mar 340
keeping in touch 28
from Morocco 661
from Portugal 538
from Spain 68
Kerouac, Jack 667

kings
Afonso I 524
Alfonso II 432
Alfonso VI 390
Alfonso VIII 168
Alfonso X 140
Alfonso XI 178, 213
Alfonso XIII 52, 101, 444
Arthur 468
Carlos I 49, 102
Carlos II 49
Carlos III 49, 71, 96, 97, 100, 121, 197, 252, 398, 518
Carlos IV 55, 121
Carlos V 122, 130, 140, 212, 262, 263, 417
Dinis I 526
Felipe I 610
Felipe II 49, 55, 71, 95, 96, 106, 116, 117, 121, 197, 368, 380, 395, 526
Felipe III 95, 689
Felipe IIII 49
Felipe IV 49, 55, 97, 100
Felipe V 49, 97, 142, 316, 317, 333
Felipe VI 121
Fernando and Isabel 71, 161, 197, 255, 262, 263, 478, 650
Fernando II 154
Fernando III 168, 197, 198
Fernando VI 97, 99
Fernando VII 52
Hassan I 686
Hassan II 650, 651, 699
Henriques, Afonso 553, 602, 605, 623, 634
João I 526, 551, 564, 605
João V 526, 565
João VI 527
Juan Carlos I 53, 473
Juba II 705
Manuel I 526, 555, 564, 606
Manuel II 527, 617
Pedro I 559, 622
Pedro the Cruel 200, 205, 603, 622
Knights Templar 122, 182, 524, 592, 608
Koran 652

kosher 43
kosher food 81
Koutoubia Mosque 710

L

L'Ainsa, see Aínsa
L'Albufera 281
L'Escala 344
La Alberca 155
La Alpujarra 266–268
La Cartuja 265
La Coruña 464–467
La Giralda 197
La Granja de San Ildefonso 142
La Guardia (A Guarda) 458
La Herradura 247
La Lanzada 461
La Manga del Mar Menor 294
La Mezquita 212
La Orotava 510
La Palma 523
La Rioja and Navarra 385–406
La Seu d'Urgell 362
La Toja 461
Lagos 569–574
Los Lagos de Enol y Ercina 436
Lancelot 468
language
Bable 430
Basque 54, 410
Catalán 54
Morocco 652
Portugal 531
Spain 54
language schools 44
Lanjarón 267
Lanzarote 516–519
Larache 689
largest
aqueduct in Europe 588
horse parade in the world 219
matchbox collection in Europe 610
national park in continental Europe 434
paper balloon 467
Rococo stairway in Europe 349

swimming pool 504
Las Meninas 55
Las Palmas de Gran Canaria 500–504
laser, 20-mile-long 699
Lawrence of Arabia 718
Lazarillo de Tormes 57, 152
Leiria 603–605
León 156–160
León, Fray Luis de 151
Lerma, Duque de 49, 161
lesbian travelers 41
life and times
Morocco 647
Portugal 524
Spain 48
Lincoln, Abraham 352
Lisbon 540–559
accommodations and camping 546–549
daytrips 559
entertainment 556–559
food 549–550
getting around 544
getting there and away 540–541
orientation 544
practical information 545–546
sights 551–555
literature
Morocco 657
Portugal 529
Spain 57
Lixus 690
Lizarra Declaration 53
Llafranc 340, 342
Llanes 439
Llerena 182
Lluc 480
Logroño 386–388
longest
sausage in the world 357
López García, Antonio 56
Lorca 294
Lorca, Federico García 57
birthplace 265
Los Cotos 119
Louis XIV 417
grandson 49
Lucía, Paco de 58
luggage 24
Luisa, Queen María 55
Luna, Bigas 59
Luriezo 439

Lusitania 179
Luso 617
Luz 575

M

M'Hamid 721
Macarena, not the dance
  200
Macau 528
Machado, Antonio 171,
  269, 270
MacLaine, Shirley 454
Madeiras 527
Madinat Al-Zahra 214
Madrid 71–113
  accommodations and
    camping 83–88
  entertainment 111–113
  food 88–94
  getting around 77–79
  getting there and away
    71–77
  Museo del Prado 103
  Museo Nacional Centro
    de Arte Reina Sofía 104
  museums 103–106
  nightlife 107–110
  orientation 79
  Parque del Buen Retiro
    100
  practical information
    80–83
  Read This 79
  shopping 113
  sights 94–103
  tapas 93
Madrid, Comunidad de,
  see Comunidad de
  Madrid
Mafra 565
Maghreb 647
Mahón 482–486
mail
  from home 28
  from Morocco 661
  from Portugal 538
  from Spain 68
Maimonides 207
Majorelle, Jacques 712
Málaga 237–241
Mallorca 473–482
  Northern 481
  Southeast 482
  Western Coast 479

Manises 281
mannequin, talking 236
Manuel I 526, 555, 564,
  606
Manuel II 527, 617
Manueline art 529
Marbella 242–244
Margarita, Queen of
  Austria 150
María Aznar, José 53
Maria II 527
Marin 461
Marinid 647
Maro 245
Marquês de Pombal 527
Marrakesh 707–713
Marvão 589
MasterCard
  traveler's checks 15
Mateus 646
Matisse, Henri 591
Mauritania 705
McGee, Bobby 230
measurements 726
media
  Portugal 533
  Spain 61
medinas
  Asilah 688
  Chefchaouen 672
  Fez 684
  Marrakesh 711
  Meknes 677
  Tangier 668
**Mediterranean Coast,
  Morocco** 663–672
Meknes 672–677
Menorca 482–489
  daytrips 488
menú 60
Mergouza 725
Mérida 179–182
metric conversions 726
Mezquita 56
Middle Atlas, Morocco
  672–687
miniature version of
  Portugal 615
Miño 467
minority travelers 42
Miró, Joan 55, 201, 333,
  478
  Fundacío Joan Miró,
    Barcelona 321
  pavement mosaic 315
Moby Dick 527

Moctezuma, Isabel 176
Modernista architecture
  57
Modernista movement 52
Mohammed 652
Mohammed V 262
  mausoleum 695
Mojácar 248
monasteries
  Encarnación, Ávila 146
  Jerónimos, Belém 555
  Leyre 403
  Lluc 480
  Piedra 374
  San Juan de Duero, Soria
    172
  San Juan de la Peña 380
  San Lorenzo del Escorial
    116
  Santa Maria da Vitória,
    Batalha 605
  Santa Maria, Ripoll 356
  Tibães 634
  Veruela 376
Moneo, Rafael 57
money 14–18
  cash cards 17
  credit cards 17
  currency and exchange
    15
  getting money from
    home 17
  Morocco 659
  Portugal 536
  Spain 66
  traveler's checks 15
Montajaque 252
Monte Igueldo 414
Monte Santa Tecla 458
Montserrat 328
Moore, Henry
  sculpture in Guernica
    424
Moors
  architecture 56
  captured banner 169
  in Portugal 524
  in Spain 48
mopeds 38
Mora de Rubielos 378
Moraira 290
Morella 282
Morocco 647–725
  accommodations 661
  arts 653
  Atlantic Coast 687

crafts 654
food and drink 654
getting there and around 657
High Atlas and Deserts 706
history 647
hustlers and faux guides 660
independence 650
keeping in touch 661
language 652
Mediterranean Coast 663
Middle Atlas 672
recommended reading 656
religion 652
sports 655
Morro Jable 515
Mosaic of the Sea God 690
mosques
　Asilah 688
　Chefcaouen 672
　Córdoba 212
　Hassan II, Casablanca 699
　Jerez de la Frontera 218
　Koutoubia, Marrakesh 710
　Meknes 677
　Mezquita 212
　Morocco 653
mosquitoes 22
most
　beautiful cathedral 159
　enchanting public park, world's 319
　important film festivals 416
　impressive archaeological finds 214
motorcycles 38
Moulay Idriss 679
Moulay Ismail 672
Mouth of Hell 560
Mozarabs 186
Mudéjar 48
　architecture 56, 376
Mudéjares (peoples) 186
Muhammed bin Abdallah 702
Mulhacén 268
Murcia 293

Murcia, province of 292–295
Murillo, Bartolomé Estebán 55, 197, 199
　house 198
museums
　Gernika Museoa 424
　Guggenheim, Bilbao 421
　Museo Canario, Las Palmas 504
　Museo del Prado 55, 103
　Museo Extremeño e Iberoamericano de Arte Contemporáneo, Badajoz 184
　Museo Internacional de Arte Contemporaneo, Arrecife 518
　Museo Nacional Centro de Arte Reina Sofía 104
　Museo Nacional de Arte Romano, Mérida 181
　Museo Nacional de Escultura, Valladolid 163
　Museo Provincial de Bellas Artes, Sevilla 199
　Museu Luso-Hebraico, Tomar 610
　Museu Picasso 321
　Teatre-Museu Dalí 352
music
　Portugal 531
　Spain 58
music festivals
　Estoril 559
　Festas da Rainha Santa, Coimbra 616
　Festival Cueva de Nerja 245
　Festival de Jazz de la Costa Brava 342
　Festival de Jazz, San Sebastián 415
　Festival de Música d'Estiu, Ciutadella 488
　International Guitar Festival, Córdoba 214
　International Jazz Festival, Sitges 331
　International Organ Festival, León 160
　International Program for Ancient Music, Daroca 375

N

Naked Lunch 667
Napoleon 52, 223, 395, 527
Napoleonic invasion 52, 55
national parks
　Aigüestortes 359
　Alvão 646
　Arrábida 568
　Cabo de Gata-Níjar 248
　Comillas 447
　Corralejo y Lobos 514
　Coto de Doñana 219
　El Teide 511
　Empúries 345
　Garajonay 521
　Montesinho 644
　Ordesa 368, 378, 382
　Peneda-Gerês 636
　Ria Formosa 580
　Sierra Espuña 294
　Sierras de Cazorla, Segura, y las Villas 271
　Timanfaya 518
NATO 246
　and Spain 53
Navarra, see La Rioja and Navarra
Navarra's flag 404
Navarrese Pyrenees 402–406
Nazaré 600–602
Nebrija, Antonio de 146
Necrouf, Youssef 657
Neoclassicism
　Fascist 100
Nerja 244
Neruda, Pablo 99
Néstor, Martín-Fernández de la Torre 504
New World
　museum 197
Nobel Prize in Literature
　Portuguese winners 531
　Spanish winners 57
nonexistent fairy tale, **Olivia's** 282
North Rías Altas 467–470
Noya 462
nude sunbathing

El Grove 461
La Herradura 247
Morro Jable 516
Playa del Ingés 505
Numancia 172
Núria 357

O

O Castro de Baroña 462
Óbidos 596
Ochagavía 405
Odysseus 540
Olazabal, José-María 62
older travelers 40
oldest
  bar in Tangier 669
  cathedral in Portugal
    633
  caves in Europe 254
Olhão 580
Olite 398
Olivares, Conde Duque de
  49
Olivenza 182
Olympic Games
  1992 296
ONCE (national lottery)
  186
opera
  Carmen 186, 201
  Don Giovanni 186
  in Barcelona 326
  in Madrid 111
  The Barber of Seville 186
Orbaitzeta 405
Order of Christ 639
Ordino 365
Orellana, Francisco de 177
Ortega y Gasset, Josè 57
Os Lusíadas 552, 617,
  646
Osuna 204
Ouarzazate 717
Oukaimeden 714
Ourika Valley 713
outdoors 26
Ovar 622
Oviedo 430–433

P

packing 24
paella 59, 274

País Vasco 407–428
Pal 366
palaces
  Alcázar, Sevilla 197
  El Pardo, Madrid 102
  El Escorial 55, 56
  Mateus 646
  Palácio da Bolsa, Porto
    628
  Palácio de Buçaco 617
  Palacio de la Aljafería,
    Zaragoza 373
  Palacio de los Duques de
    San Carlos, Trujillo 177
  Palacio de Miramar, San
    Sebastián 414
  Palacio Episcopal,
    Astorga 160
  Palácio Nacional da
    Pena 564
  Palácio Nacional de
    Mafra 565
  Palácio Nacional de
    Queluz 559
  Palácio Nacional de
    Sintra 564
  Palacio Real, Aranjuez
    121
  Palacio Real, Madrid 97
  Palacio Real, Olite 398
  Palau de la Música
    Catalana, Barcelona
    316
  Palau del'Almudaina,
    Palma 478
Palafrugell 340–342
Palencia 163
Palma 473–479
Pampaneira 267
Pamplona 391–398
  San Fermines (running of
    the bulls) 396
Panes 439
Panteón Real (tomb of
  kings) 117
parasites 23
Parc Güell 319
Parc Nacional
  d'Aigüestortes 359–360
Partido Popular (PP) 53
Pas de la Casa 362, 366
Pasajes de San Juan 415
passports 11
Peace Corps 46
Pedro I 622
  born and died here 559

Pedro the Cruel 52, 200,
  205, 603
  source of his name 622
pelota (jai alai)
  game of death 169
Peña de Francia 155
Peña Ezkaurre 406
Peña Sagra 439
Peniche 597–599
The Persistence of Memory
  56
Personal Identification
  Number (PIN) 17
Peru 177
Pessoa, Fernando 530
Phoenicians 223, 524
phrasebook
  Morocco 728
  Portuguese 728
  Spanish 726
Pic Alt de la Coma Pedrosa
  366
Picasso, Pablo 55, 333,
  423
  and the Nazis 424
  birthplace 240
  eating habits 312
  Guernica 55, 104, 424
  Museo de Montserrat
    329
  Museu Picasso,
    Barcelona 321
  on himself 320
  party at 467
pickpockets 19
Picos de Europa 433–
  439
PIN numbers 17
pintxos 413
Pizarro, Francisco 122,
  173, 177, 178
planes, see airplane travel
Plateresque architecture
  56
Platja de Piles 284
Playa de las Américas 508
Playa del Inglés 505
Poncebos 437
Pontedeume 467
Pontevedra 459–461
  daytrips 461
Pope John Paul II 372,
  454
Popular Front 53
Poqueira Gorge 267
Port Aventura 337

Portbou 354
Porto 623–630
Portugal 524–646
  accommodations 537
  arts 529
  food and drink 532
  getting there and around 535
  history and politics 524
  keeping in touch 538
  language 531
  life and times 524
  media 533
  recommended reading 534
  sports 533
  tipping and bargaining 536
Potes 438
pousadas 538
Prado, see museums
  Museo del Prado
Praia da Rocha 575
precipitation, see climate
Premonition of the Civil War 56
Prince Henry the Navigator 526, 555, 569, 574, 575, 606, 623, 624
PSOE 53
pueblos blancos 182, 222
Puerto Banús 244
Puerto de la Cruz 509
Puerto de Navacerrada 119
Puerto de Pollença 481
Puerto de Sóller 480
Puerto del Carmen 518
Puerto del Rosario 512–513
Puig i Caldafach, José 57, 314
Puigcerdà 357
Punta Abizondo 406
Purple Isles 705

Q

Qu'ran, see Koran
Queluz 559
Quevedo, Francisco de 57, 114

R

Rabat 690–695
railpasses 34
Ramadan 7, 653
recommended reading
  Morocco 656
  Portugal 534
  Spain 63
Reconquest 48, 524, 686
religion
  Morocco 652
Renaissance architecture 56
Revolution of the Carnations 528
Ría de Muros y Noya 462
Ría de Ribadeo 470
Ría en un Cafe, Spain's first film 58
Rías Altas, see North or South Rías Altas
Rías Bajas 456–463
Rías de Cedeira and Vivero 468
Rías de la Costa de la Muerte 463
Ribatejo and Estremadura 592–610
Ribeiro, Aquilino 530
Ribera, José de 55, 105, 197, 200
  home 282
Rilke, Rainer Maria 250, 591
Río Duero 171
Rio Minho 640
Rioja wines 385
Rioja, see La Rioja and Navarra
Ripoll 355
Rivera, General Primo de 52, 151
Rocío 204
Roland 404
Roman ruins
  Carmona 205
  Empúries 344
  Évora 587
  in Spain 56
  Itálica 204
  Lixus 690
  Mérida 181
  Necrópolis Romana 205
  Numancia 172

Salamanca 152
Segovia 136, 140
Tarragona 334, 336
Tossa del Mar 339
Volubilis 677
Romanesque architecture 356
Romans
  in Morocco 647
  in Portugal 524
  in Spain 48
Romero, Julio 213
Roncal 406
Roncesvalles and Auritz-Burguete 404
Ronda 249–252
Rubens
  El Escorial 117
  Madrid 106, 117
Rubielos de Mora 378
Rueda, Lope de 198
running of the bulls (Pamplona) 396
Ruta del Dinosaurio 386
Ruta del Modernisme, see Barcelona

S

Sa Calobra 480
Saadien Tombs 712
Saadis 650
Sabatini, Francisco 96
Sachetti, Giovanni 97
safety 18–20
  drugs 20
  general tips 19
  getting around 19
  in Morocco 660
  in Portugal 536
  in Spain 67
  self defense 20
  wilderness 28
Sagrada Familia 317
Sagres 574
Sagunto 280
Sahara
  expeditions into 707
Saint James 448
  remains 453
Saint Ursula 106
Salamanca 146–153
Salazar, António de Oliveira 527, 598, 611, 630

Salé 695
Salema 575
Sampaio, Jorge 528
San Antonio de Portmany 494
San Fermín 391
San José 248
San Juan de la Cruz 142, 154
San Martín de Montalbán 128
San Miguel de Cabo de Gata 248
San Sebastián 408–416
San Sebastián de Gomera 520–521
San Vicente de La Barquera 447
Sancho El Fuerte 404
Sancho Ramírez 380
Sand, George 473, 479
sandwich, metaphorical 223
Sangüesa 402
Sant Feliu de Guíxols 342
Sant Joan de les Abadesses 356
Santa Cruz de Tenerife 506–508
Santa Cruz del Valle de los Caídos 118
Santa Teresa 52, 57, 142, 186, 198
  a conversation 146
  a metaphor 145
  festivals 146
  remains 154
Santander 441–445
Santarém 592–594
Santiago de Compostela 448–455
Santillana del Mar 445
Santiponce 204
Santo Domingo de la Calzada 390
Santo Domingo de Silos 169
São Martinho do Porto 603
Saramago, José 531
sardana 326, 350
Scipio Africanus 172
Scorsese, Martin
  Kundun 715
scuba diving
  Callela 342

Corrajelo 514
Lagos 571
Las Palmas de Gran Canaria 504
Los Cristianos 509
Morro Jable 516
Near Alicante 289
Playa del Inglés 505
Puerto del Carmen 518
San Sebastián 415
Tossa del Mar 340
Second Republic 52
security, see safety
Segovia 136–142
Segovia, Andrés 58
Seinfeld 61
self-defense 20
Semana Santa
  in Sevilla 203
Semana Santa 7
Seneca 207
senior travelers 40
Serra da Arrábida 566
Sert, Joseph María 57
Sesimbra 568
Setenil de las Bodegas 233
Setti Fatma 714
Setúbal 566–568
Severa, Maria 530
Sevilla 186–204
  accommodations and camping 193–195
  Alcázar 197
  entertainment 201–204
  food 195–196
  getting around 191
  getting there and away 190–191
  orientation 192
  practical information 192–193
  sights 196–201
sevillana 58, 203
Sexi 245
The Sheltering Sky 656, 667
sherry 217
  sherry triangle 219, 227
Sicilia, José María 56
sidra 61, 432
Sierra de Guadarrama 118
Sierra de Torcal 254
Sierra de Tramontana 473
Sierra Morena 214
Sigüenza 134

Sinatra, Frank 337
Sintra 561–565
Siresa 381
Sitges 330
skiing
  Andorra 366
  Aragón 368
  Aragonese Pyrenees 378
  Baquiera-Beret 360
  Isaba and Environs 406
  Puerto de Navacerrada 119
  Puigcerdà 359
  Sierra Nevada 266
  Val D'Aran 360
Skoura 721
Soares, Mario 528
soccer, see fútbol
Solano, Susana 56
Soldeu-El Tarter 366
Solis family 176
Sóller 480
solo travel 40
Soria 170–172
South Rías Altas 463–467
Southern Deserts 717
Southern Drâa 720
Spain
  architecture 56
  art 54
  bullfighting 59
  drinks 61
  film 58
  food 59
  fútbol 62
  history 48
  language 54
  life and times 48
  literature 57
  media 61
  music 58
  Roman occupation 48
  Roman ruins 56
  sports 62
  wines 61
Spanair 64
Spanish Civil War 52, 71
  Navarra 385
Spanish Gothic architecture 56
The Spanish Sistine Chapel 178
Spanish-American War 52, 57
sports

Morocco 655
Portugal 533
Spain 62
St. Lawrence
fresco of 117
Stalin, Joseph 53
strawberries
Aranjuez 120
studying abroad 43
sunburn 22
surfing
Playa del Inglés 505
Surrealism 55
Susona 198
Sylvester II 686
synagogues
Toledo 127

T

tajine 654
Tamariu 340
Tamegroute 720
Tangier 663–669
Tápies, Antonio 56
Tarazona 375
Tarifa 255
Taroudannt 716
Tarragona 334–337
Tavira 581
taxes
in Spain 67
Teatre-Museu Dalí 56, 352
Teguise 519
telephones
calling cards 30
calling from home 29
television
Spain 61
temperature, see climate
Tenerife 506–511
tennis stars, Spanish 62
Teror 505
terrorism
ETA 408
Teruel 376
Tetouan 670
theater festivals
Almagro 129
Barcelona 326
Granada 265
Mérida 179
Sitges 331
theft 19
Thirty Years' War 49

Thomas Cook
traveler's checks 15
The Three Beiras 611–622
Three Marias 531
ticks 22
Timanfaya 518
time zones 726
Tinerhir 722
Tintoretto 117
tipping
in Portugal 536
in Spain 67
Titian 104, 105, 117
Tizi-n-Test 716
Tizi-n-Tichka 717
Todra Gorges 723
Toledo 122–128
daytrips 128
Tomar 608–610
Torre de Hércules 466
Torremolinos 241
Tossa de Mar 337–340
Toubkal 714
train travel 33
in Morocco 657
in Portugal 535
in Spain 65
Trajan 204
transportation, see getting there and around
Trás-Os-Montes 642–646
Trastámara, Enrique de 52
travel agencies 31
traveler's checks 15
lost or stolen 15
traveling alone 40
Treaty of Alcañices 526
Treaty of Utrecht 49, 233
Treaty of Windsor 526
El Tres de mayo 55
Trevélez 268
Treviso 439
Trujillo 177
Tudela 399
tunas 153
turtles, fossilized
second most important collection in the world 151
Túy 458

U

U.S. State Department 21

Úbeda 270
Ujué 398
UN World Heritage sites
Aït Benhaddou 718
Batalha 606
Cuevas de Altamira 446
Évora 584
Fez 679
monastery at Alcobaça 603
Mosteiro dos Jerónimos, Lisbon 555
Porto 623
Torre de Belém, Lisbon 555
Unamuno, Miguel de 57, 146, 151, 513
UNESCO 482
universities
Coimbra 615
Salamanca 151
Uqba bin Nafi al-Fihri 647
Urdón 439
Uthman 710

V

vaccinations 21
Val d'Aran 360–361
Valença do Minho 641
Valencia 274–280
daytrips 280
Valencia, province of 273–292
Vall de Boí 359
Valladolid 161–163
Valldemosa 479
Valle de Ansó 381
Valle de Benasque 384
Valle de Hecho 380
Valle de los Caídos 118
Valle de Roncal 406
Valle de Salazar 405
Valle Gran Rey 522
Vega, Lope de 49, 57, 114, 130, 199
house 98
vegetarians 43
Vejer de la Frontera 228
Velázquez, Diego 49, 55, 103, 154
Ciudad Rodrigo 154
El Escorial 117
El Prado (Madrid) 103
San Fernando (Madrid)

105

Veleta 266

Ventas, Plaza de (Madrid) 112

Verdi

Il Trovatore 283, 373

Versailles

and its rivals 672

of Spain 142

Viana do Castelo 637–639

Vicente, Gil 551

Portuguese Shakespeare 529

Vielha 361

Vigo 456

daytrips 457

Vila Nova de Cerveira 640

Vila Real 644–646

Vila Real de Santo António 583

Vilanova i la Geltrù 332

Vinci, Leonardo de 106, 212

vinho do Porto 623, 629

Virgin Mary 328, 368

and the devil 136

and three children 608

Visa

traveler's checks 17

visas 12

Viseu 617

Visigoths

in Portugal 524

in Spain 48

Vitoria-Gasteiz 425–428

Vivero (Viveiro) 468

Volubilis 677

volunteering abroad 46

W

War of Spanish Succession 97, 233

War of the Two Brothers 527

Waterloo 52

Wattasid 647

weather, see climate

Welles, Orson 250

Othello 702

Western Sahara 651

Western Union 17

whale watching

Los Cristianos 509

widest

Gothic nave in the world 349

wilderness safety 28

Wind City 705

windsurfing

Corrajelo 514

Las Palmas de Gran Canaria 504

Manga del Mar Menor 294

Morro Jable 516

Playa de las Américas 508

Sagres 575

San Sebastián 415

Sidi Kaouki 705

Tarifa 230

Tossa del Mar 340

wines

Madeira 533

Portugal 533

sangría 61

Spain 61

Winston Churchill

his buddies 713

women travelers 39

health 23

work permits 12

working abroad 45

world surfing championships

Prais da Ribeira d'Ilhas 566

world wide web 47

world's only albino gorilla 317

world-renowned

Julián Gayarre 406

WWII secret agents

and the cafes they frequent 663

X

Xàbia, see Jávea

Xàtiva, see Játiva

Y

Yesa 403

Yusuf I 262

Yves Saint Laurent 712

Z

Zafra 182

Zagora 719

Zamora 155

Zaragoza 368–374

daytrips 374

Zugarramundi 404

Zurbarán, Francisco de 55, 197, 199

Zuriza 382, 406

ABOUT LET'S GO

FORTY YEARS OF WISDOM

As a new millennium arrives, *Let's Go: Europe*, now in its 40th edition and translated into seven languages, reigns as the world's bestselling international travel guide. For four decades, travelers criss-crossing the Continent have relied on *Let's Go* for inside information on the hippest backstreet cafes, the most pristine secluded beaches, and the best routes from border to border. In the last 20 years, our rugged researchers have stretched the frontiers of backpacking and expanded our coverage into Asia, Africa, Australia, and the Americas. We're celebrating our 40th birthday with the release of *Let's Go: China*, blazing the traveler's trail from the Forbidden City to the Tibetan frontier; *Let's Go: Perú & Ecuador*, spanning the lands of the ancient Inca Empire; *Let's Go: Middle East*, with coverage from Istanbul to the Persian Gulf; and the maiden edition of *Let's Go: Israel*.

It all started in 1960 when a handful of well-traveled students at Harvard University handed out a 20-page mimeographed pamphlet offering a collection of their tips on budget travel to passengers on student charter flights to Europe. The following year, in response to the instant popularity of the first volume, students traveling to Europe researched the first full-fledged edition of *Let's Go: Europe*, a pocket-sized book featuring honest, practical advice, witty writing, and a decidedly youthful slant on the world. Throughout the 60s and 70s, our guides reflected the times. In 1969 we taught travelers how to get from Paris to Prague on "no dollars a day" by singing in the street. In the 80s and 90s, we looked beyond Europe and North America and set off to all corners of the earth. Meanwhile, we focused in on the world's most exciting urban areas to produce in-depth, fold-out map guides. Our new guides bring the total number of titles to 48, each infused with the spirit of adventure and voice of opinion that travelers around the world have come to count on. But some things never change: our guides are still researched, written, and produced entirely by students who know first-hand how to see the world on the cheap.

HOW WE DO IT

Each guide is completely revised and thoroughly updated every year by a well-traveled set of over 250 students. Every spring, we recruit over 180 researchers and 70 editors to overhaul every book. After several months of training, researcher-writers hit the road for seven weeks of exploration, from Anchorage to Adelaide, Estonia to El Salvador, Iceland to Indonesia. Hired for their rare combination of budget travel sense, writing ability, stamina, and courage, these adventurous travelers know that train strikes, stolen luggage, food poisoning, and marriage proposals are all part of a day's work. Back at our offices, editors work from spring to fall, massaging copy written on Himalayan bus rides into witty, informative prose. A student staff of typesetters, cartographers, publicists, and managers keeps our lively team together. In September, the collected efforts of the summer are delivered to our printer, which turns them into books in record time, so that you have the most up-to-date information available for your vacation. Even as you read this, work on next year's editions is well underway.

WHY WE DO IT

We don't think of budget travel as the last recourse of the destitute; we believe that it's the only way to travel. Living cheaply and simply brings you closer to the people and places you've been saving up to visit. Our books will ease your anxieties and answer your questions about the basics—so you can get off the beaten track and explore. Once you learn the ropes, we encourage you to put *Let's Go* down now and then to strike out on your own. You know as well as we that the best discoveries are often those you make yourself. When you find something worth sharing, please drop us a line. We're Let's Go Publications, 67 Mount Auburn St., Cambridge, MA 02138, USA (email: feedback@letsgo.com). For more info, visit our website, http://www.letsgo.com.

Next time, make your *own* hotel arrangements.

Yahoo! Travel

READER QUESTIONNAIRE

Name: _____

Address: _____

City: _____ State: _____ Country: _____

ZIP/Postal Code:_____ E-mail: _____ How old are you?____

And you're...?   in high school   in college   in graduate school

           employed   retired   between jobs

Which book(s) have you used? _____

Where have you gone with Let's Go? _____

Have you traveled extensively before?   yes   no

Had you used Let's Go before?   yes   no   **Would you use it again?**   yes   no

How did you hear about Let's Go? friend   store clerk   television

                              review   bookstore display

                              ad/promotion   internet   other: _____

Why did you choose Let's Go?   reputation   budget focus   annual updating

                            wit & incision   price   other: _____

Which guides have you used?   Fodor's   Footprint Handbooks   Frommer's $-a-day

                           Lonely Planet   Moon Guides   Rick Steve's

                           Rough Guides   UpClose   other: _____

Which guide do you prefer? Why? _____

Please rank the following in your Let's Go guide: (1=needs improvement, 5=perfect)

packaging/cover 1 2 3 4 5	food 1 2 3 4 5	maps 1 2 3 4 5
cultural introduction 1 2 3 4 5	sights 1 2 3 4 5	directions 1 2 3 4 5
"Essentials" 1 2 3 4 5	entertainment 1 2 3 4 5	writing style 1 2 3 4 5
practical info 1 2 3 4 5	gay/lesbian info 1 2 3 4 5	budget resources 1 2 3 4 5
accommodations 1 2 3 4 5	up-to-date info 1 2 3 4 5	other: _____ 1 2 3 4 5

How long was your trip?   one week   two wks.   three wks.   a month   2+ months

Why did you go?   sightseeing   adventure travel   study abroad   other: _____

What was your average daily budget, not including flights? _____

Do you buy a separate map when you visit a foreign city?   yes   no

Have you used a Let's Go Map Guide?   yes   no   **If you have, which one?** _____

Would you recommend them to others?   yes   no

Have you visited Let's Go's website?   yes   no

What would you like to see included on Let's Go's website? _____

What percentage of your trip planning did you do on the web? _____

What kind of Let's Go guide would you like to see? recreation (e.g., skiing)   phrasebook

           spring break   adventure/trekking   first-time travel info   Europe altas

Which of the following destinations would you like to see Let's Go cover?

      Argentina   Brazil   Canada   Caribbean   Chile   Costa Rica   Cuba

      Morocco   Nepal   Russia   Scandinavia   Southwest USA   other: _____

Where did you buy your guidebook?   independent bookstore   college bookstore

      travel store   Internet   chain bookstore   gift   other: _____

Please fill this out and return it to **Let's Go, St. Martin's Press,** 175 Fifth Ave., New York, NY 10010-7848. All respondents will receive a free subscription to *The Yellow-jacket*, the Let's Go Newsletter. You can find a more extensive version of this survey on the web at http://www.letsgo.com.

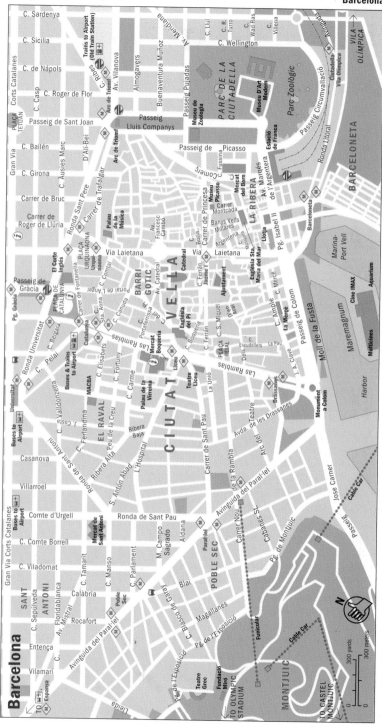

Madrid Metro